ENCYCLOPEDIA OF

Violence, Peace, & Conflict

VOLUME 1 A–E

ENCYCLOPEDIA OF

VOLUME 1 A–E

ACADEMIC PRESS

SAN DIEGO LONDON BOSTON NEW YORK SYDNEY TOKYO TORONTO

This book is printed on acid-free paper. 

Academic Press
A Harcourt Science and Technology Company
525 B Street, Suite 1900, San Diego, California 92101-4495, USA
http://www.apnet.com

Academic Press
24-28 Oval Road, London NW1 7DX, UK
http://www.hbuk.co.uk/ap/

Library of Congress Catalog Card Number: 99-60408

International Standard Book Number: 0-12-227010-X (set)
International Standard Book Number: 0-12-227011-8 (Volume 1)
International Standard Book Number: 0-12-227012-6 (Volume 2)
International Standard Book Number: 0-12-227013-4 (Volume 3)

PRINTED IN THE UNITED STATES OF AMERICA
99 00 01 02 03 04 MM 9 8 7 6 5 4 3 2 1

Contents

Contents of Other Volumes

CONTENTS OF VOLUME 2

CONTENTS OF VOLUME 3

Contents by Subject Area

Cultural Studies

Economic Studies

Ethical Studies

Historical Studies

International Relations

Peace and Conflict Studies

Political Studies

Psychological Studies

Public Policy Studies

Sociological Studies

Warfare and Military Studies

Contributors

Mimi Ajzenstadt
Women, Violence Against
Hebrew University
Jerusalem, Israel

Peter Almquist
Economic Conversion
US Arms Control and Disarmament Agency
Washington, DC, USA

Randall Amster
Power and Deviance
Arizona State University
Tempe, Arizona, USA

Kristin L. Anderson
Child Abuse
Drew University
Madison, New Jersey, USA

Kauko Aromaa
Victimology
National Research Institute of Legal Policy
Helsinki, Finland

Sidney Axinn
Moral Judgments and Values
Temple University
Philadelphia, Pennsylvania, USA

Kerri Lynn Bates
Urban and Community Studies
University of British Columbia
Vancouver, British Columbia, Canada

Hugo Adam Bedau
Death Penalty
Tufts University
Medford, Massachusetts, USA

Nancy Bell
Power, Alternative Theories of
University of Texas
Austin, Texas, USA

Robert D. Benford
Peace Movements
University of Nebraska
Lincoln, Nebraska, USA

Chawki Benkelfat
Biochemical Factors
McGill University
Montreal, Quebec, Canada

Nachman Ben-Yehuda
Assassinations, Political
Hebrew University
Jerusalem, Israel

Jacob Bercovitch
Mediation and Negotiation Techniques
University of Canterbury
Christchurch, New Zealand

Leonard Berkowitz
Aggression, Psychology of
University of Wisconsin
Madison, Wisconsin, USA

Irwin S. Bernstein
Animal Behavior Studies, Primates
University of Georgia
Athens, Georgia, USA

Mike Berry
Communication Studies, Overview
University of California, Santa Barbara
Santa Barbara, California

Vincent Boudreau
Political Theories
City University of New York
New York, NY, USA

Elise Boulding
Peace Culture
Dartmouth College (emerita)
Hanover, New Hampshire, USA

Janet Welsh Brown
Environmental Issues and Politics
Nongovernmental Actors in International Politics
Trade and the Environment
World Resources Institute
Washington, DC, USA

Lisa Brown
Ethnicity and Identity Politics
University of Florida
Gainesville, Florida, USA

Arden Bucholz
Militarism
State University of New York
Brockport, New York, USA

James Burk
Military Culture
Texas A&M University
College Station, Texas, USA

Gabriella Cagliesi
Trade Wars (Disputes)
Rutgers University
Newark, New Jersey, USA

Deborah Cai
Interpersonal Conflict, History of
University of Maryland
College Park, Maryland, USA

James Calleja
Aged Population, Violence and Nonviolence toward
International Institute on Aging
United Nations, Malta

Jesus Casquette
Draft, Resistance and Evasion of
Universidad del Pais Vasco
Leioa, Spain

Victor D. Cha
Collective Security Systems
Georgetown University
Washington, DC, USA

Paul Chevigny
Police Brutality
New York University Law School
New York, NY, USA

Stephen J. Cimbala
Nuclear Weapons Policies
Pennsylvania State University, Delaware County
Media, Pennsylvania, USA

Murray Code
Reason and Violence
University of Guelph
Toronto, Ontario, Canada

Irwin Cohen
Torture (State)
Simon Fraser University
Burnaby, British Columbia, Canada

Noé Cornago-Prieto
Diplomacy
University of the Basque Country
Bilbao, Spain

Raymond R. Corrado
Torture (State)
Simon Fraser University
Burnaby, British Columbia, Canada

Alex E. Crosby
Public Health Models of Violence and Violence Prevention
Centers for Disease Control
Atlanta, Georgia, USA

S. Cumner
Peacekeeping
Pearson Peacekeeping Centre
Clementsport, Nova Scotia, Canada

G. David Curry
Gangs
Law and Violence
University of Missouri, St. Louis
St. Louis, Missouri, USA

Thomas C. Daffern
Peacemaking and Peacebuilding
International Institute of Peace Studies
London, UK

Linda L. Dahlberg
Public Health Models of Violence and Violence Prevention
Centers for Disease Control
Atlanta, Georgia, USA

James C. Davies
Human Nature, Views of
University of Oregon (Emeritus)
Eugene, Oregon, USA

Angela Davis
Crime and Punishment, Changing Attitudes toward
University of California, Santa Cruz
Santa Cruz, California, USA

Scott H. Decker
Gangs
University of Missouri, St. Louis
St. Louis, Missouri, USA

Paul F. Diehl
Territorial Disputes
University of Illinois
Urbana, Illinois, USA

Edward Donnerstein
Mass Media, General View
University of California, Santa Barbara
Santa Barbara, California, USA

William Donohue
Interpersonal Conflict, History of
Michigan State University
East Lansing, Michigan, USA

Steven Dubin
Peace and the Arts
State University of New York
Purchase, New York, USA

Antulio J. Echevarria
Warfare, Modern
U.S. Army Training and Doctrine Command
Fort Monroe, Virginia, USA

Riane Eisler
Family Structure and Family Violence and Nonviolence
Carmel, California, USA

Robert Elias
Violence as Solution, Culture of
University of San Francisco
San Francisco, California, USA

Leonard D. Eron
Television Programming and Violence, U.S.
University of Michigan
Ann Arbor, Michigan, USA

Paul Lawrence Farber
Evolutionary Theory
Oregon State University
Corvallis, Oregon, USA

David N. Farnsworth
International Relations, Overview
Wichita State University
Wichita, Kansas, USA

Gordon Fellman
Enemy, Concept and Identity of
Brandeis University
Waltham, Massachusetts, USA

Juanita M. Firestone
Warfare and Military Studies, Overview
University of Texas
San Antonio, Texas, USA

Dietrich Fischer
Economics of War and Peace, Overview
Pace University
Pleasantville, New York, USA

Virginia Floresca-Cawages
Institutionalization of Nonviolence
University of Alberta
Edmonton, Alberta, Canada

Linda Rennie Forcey
Feminist and Peace Perspectives on Women
Binghamton University
Binghamton, New York, USA

Nicholas G. Fotion
Warfare, Trends in
Emory University
Atlanta, Georgia, USA

Karen Franklin
Homosexuals, Violence toward
University of Washington
Seattle, Washington, USA

Marvin D. Free
Minorities as Perpetrators and Victims of Crime
University of Wisconsin
Madison, Wisconsin, USA

David Noel Freedman
Religious Traditions, Violence and Nonviolence
University of California, San Diego
San Diego, California, USA

William C. French
Ecoethics
Loyola University
Chicago, Illinois, USA

Gregory Fried
Critiques of Violence
Boston University
Boston, Massachusetts, USA

Robert Friedmann
Policing and Society
Georgia State University
Atlanta, Georgia, USA

Douglas P. Fry
Aggression and Altruism
Peaceful Societies
University of Abo
Helsinki, Finland

Theodore Gabriel
Ethical and Religious Traditions, Eastern
Cheltenham and Gloucester College
Gloucester, UK

James Garbarino
Long-Term Effects of War on Children
Cornell University
Ithaca, New York, USA

William Gay
Language of War and Peace, The
University of North Carolina
Charlotte, North Carolina, USA

George Gerbner
Mass Media and Dissent
Temple University
Philadelphia, Pennsylvania, USA

Douglas M. Gibler
Alliance Systems
Stanford University
Stanford, California, USA

Howard Giles
Communication Studies, Overview
University of California, Santa Barbara
Santa Barbara, California, USA

William Gissy
Political Economy of Violence and Nonviolence
Morehouse College
Atlanta, Georgia, USA

Nils-Petter Gleditsch
Peace and Democracy
International Peace Research Institute
Oslo, Norway

Mark Gold
Drugs and Violence
University of Florida College of Medicine
Gainesville, Florida, USA

Ralph M. Goldman
Political Systems and Conflict Management
San Francisco State University
San Francisco, California, USA

Janine Goldman-Pach
Sexual Assault
University of Arizona
Tucson, Arizona, USA

Jeff Goodwin
Revolutions
New York University
New York, NY, USA

Deborah Gorman-Smith
Urban Violence, Youth
University of Illinois
Chicago, Illinois, USA

F. Lincoln Grahlfs
Veterans in the Political Culture
National Association of Radiation Survivors
St. Louis, Missouri, USA

Adam Green
Revolutions
New York University
New York, NY, USA

Allen D. Grimshaw
Genocide and Democide
Indiana University
Bloomington, Indiana, USA

Linda Groff
Religion and Peace, Inner-Outer Dimensions of
California State University
Dominguez Hills, California, USA

David Grossman
Behavioral Psychology
Psychological Effects of Combat
Weaponry, Evolution of
Arkansas State University
Jonesboro, Arkansas, USA

Barrie Gunter
Television Programming and Violence, International
University of Sheffield
Sheffield, UK

Brien Hallett
Just-War Criteria
University of Hawaii
Honolulu, Hawaii, USA

Fen Osler Hampson
Peace Agreements
Carleton University
Ottawa, Ontario, Canada

Michael Hanagan
Industrial vs. Preindustrial Forms of Violence
New School for Social Research
New York, NY, USA

Ian M. Harris
Peace Education: Colleges and Universities
University of Wisconsin, Milwaukee
Milwaukee, Wisconsin, USA

John Hartman
Psychoanalysis
University of Michigan
Ann Arbor, Michigan, USA

Akira Hattori
Economics of War and Peace, Overview
Fukuoka University
Fukuoka, Japan

Mark Haugaard
Power, Social and Political Theories of
University College, Galway
Galway City, Ireland

Ira Heilveil
Violence Prediction
Ojai, California
USA

Errol A. Henderson
Civil Wars
Ethnic Conflicts and Cooperation
University of Florida
Gainesville, Florida, USA

Gregory Herek
Homosexuals, Violence toward
University of California, Davis
Davis, California, USA

Marjorie Hogan
Popular Music
Hennepin County Medical Center
Minneapolis, Minnesota, USA

Gregory Hooks
Military-Industrial Complex, Organization and History
Washington State University
Pullman, Washington, USA

Brenda Horrigan
Security Studies
Vineyard Haven, Massachusetts, USA

Michael W. Hovey
Conscientious Objection, Ethics of
Iona College
New Rochelle, New York, USA

L. Rowell Huesmann
Television Programming and Violence, U.S.
Institute for Social Research, University of Michigan
Ann Arbor, Michigan, USA

Paul K. Huth
Military Deterrence and Statecraft
University of Michigan
Ann Arbor, Michigan, USA

Larry W. Isaac
Class Conflict
Florida State University
Tallahassee, Florida, USA

James M. Jasper
Animals, Violence toward
New York University
New York, NY, USA

Ho-Won Jeong
Conflict Management and Resolution
Theories of Conflict
George Mason University
Fairfax, Virginia, USA

Hans Joas
Social Theorizing about War and Peace
Free University of Berlin
Berlin, Germany

Anthony James Joes
Guerrilla Warfare
St. Joseph's University
Philadelphia, Pennsylvania, USA

Hubert C. Johnson
Warfare, Strategies and Tactics of
University of Saskatchewan
Saskatoon, Saskatchewan, Canada

Theodore Karasik
Security Studies
University of California, Los Angeles
Los Angeles, California, USA

Robert W. Kentridge
Behavioral Psychology
University of Durham
Durham, UK

James R. Kerin, Jr.
Combat
United States Military Academy
West Point, New York, USA

Wolfgang Knöbl
Social Control and Violence
Free University of Berlin
Berlin, Germany

Edward Kolodziej
Arms Control
University of Illinois
Urbana, Illinois, USA

Fiona M. Kay
Urban and Community Studies
University of British Columbia
Vancouver, British Columbia, Canada

Mary Koss
Sexual Assault
Arizona Prevention Center
Tucson, Arizona, USA

Rajini Kothari
Institutionalization of Violence
Center for the Study of Developing Societies
Delhi, India

Louis Kriesberg
Conflict Transformation
Syracuse University
Syracuse, New York, USA

Mitsuru Kurosawa
Arms Control and Disarmament Treaties
Osaka School of International Public Policy
Osaka, Japan

John Kydd
Violence to Children, Definition and Prevention of
Child VIP—Child Violence Identification and Prevention Project
Seattle, Washington, USA

Christos N. Kyrou
Cultural Anthropology Studies of Conflict
Syracuse, New York, USA
Syracuse University

Linda Lantieri
Peace Education: Youth
Educators for Social Responsibility
New York, NY, USA

Pat Lauderdale
Power and Deviance
Arizona State University
Tempe, Arizona, USA

Colin Wayne Leach
Ethnicity and Identity Politics
Swarthmore College
Swarthmore, Pennsylvania, USA

David LeMarquand
Biochemical Factors
McGill University
Montreal, Quebec, Canada

David Lester
Suicide and Other Violence toward the Self
Center for the Study of Suicide
Blackwood, New Jersey, USA

Amy Leventhal
Urban Violence, Youth
University of Illinois
Chicago, Illinois, USA

Howard S. Levie
Chemical and Biological Warfare
War Crimes
U.S. Naval War College
Newport, Rhode Island, USA

Jack Levin
Hate Crimes
Northeastern University
Boston, Massachusetts, USA

Sheldon G. Levy
Conformity and Obedience
Cooperation, Competition, and Conflict
Mass Conflict and the Participants, Attitudes toward
Wayne State University
Detroit, Michigan, USA

Elliott Leyton
Serial and Mass Murderers
Memorial University of Newfoundland
St. John's, Newfoundland, Canada

Daniel G. Linz
Mass Media, General View
University of California
Santa Barbara, California, USA

David Loye
Evil, Concept of
Center for Partnership Studies
Carmel, California, USA

Derek F. Lynch
Balance of Power Relationships
University of Huddersfield
Queensgate, Yorkshire, UK

Graeme MacQueen
Spirituality and Peacemaking
McMaster University
Hamilton, Ontario, Canada

Esther Madriz
Criminology, Overview
University of San Francisco
San Francisco, California, USA

Sanja Magdalenic
Folklore
Stockholm University
Stockholm, Sweden

Kevin Magill
Justification for Violence
University of Wolverhampton
Dudley, UK

Neil Malamuth
Pornography
University of California, Los Angeles
Los Angeles, California, USA

Brian Martin
Technology, Violence, and Peace
University of Wollongong
Wollongong, Australia

Peter B. Mayer
Militarism and Development in Underdeveloped Societies
University of Adelaide
Adelaide, Australia

Alfred McAlister
International Variation in Attitudes toward Violence
University of Texas
Austin, Texas, USA

Laura Ann McCloskey
Family Structure and Family Violence and Nonviolence
University of Arizona
Tucson, Arizona, USA

Michael J. McClymond
Religious Traditions, Violence and Nonviolence
University of California, San Diego
San Diego, California, USA

Jack McDevitt
Hate Crimes
Northeastern University
Boston, Massachusetts, USA

Gregory McLauchlan
Military-Industrial Complex, Contemporary Significance
University of Oregon
Eugene, Oregon, USA

Eduardo Mendieta
Ethical Studies, Overview
University of San Francisco
San Francisco, California, USA

James A. Mercy
Public Health Models of Violence and Violence Prevention
Centers for Disease Control
Atlanta, Georgia, USA

Thomas Mieczkowski
Drug Control Policies
University of South Florida
St. Petersburg, Florida, USA

Dinshaw Mistry
Arms Control
University of Illinois
Urbana, Illinois, USA

Alex Morrison
Peacekeeping
Pearson Peacekeeping Centre
Clementsport, Nova Scotia, Canada

C. David Mortensen
Linguistic Constructions of Violence, Peace, and Conflict
University of Wisconsin
Madison, Wisconsin, USA

Kenneth R. Murray
Behavioral Psychology
Armiger Police Training Institute
Ottawa, Ontario, Canada

Hanna Newcombe
World Government
Peace Research Institute
Dundas, Ontario, Canada

Roderick Ogley
Conflict Theory
University of Sussex
Brighton, UK

Tamayo Okamoto
Means and Ends
Hiroshima Prefectural College of Health and Welfare
Hiroshima, Japan

Marie Olson
Arms Trade, Economics of
Center for Peace and Conflict Studies
Wayne State University
Detroit, Michigan, USA

Keith F. Otterbein
Clan and Tribal Conflict
State University of New York
Buffalo, New York, USA

Jan Pakulski
Social Equality and Inequality
University of Tasmania
Hobart, Tasmania, Australia

Edward L. Palmer
Children, Impact of Television on
Davidson College
Davidson, North Carolina, USA

Martin Palous
Totalitarianism and Authoritarianism
Charles University
Prague, Czech Republic

Hanbin Park
Peacekeeping
Pearson Peacekeeping Centre
Clementsport, Nova Scotia, Canada

Janet Patti
Peace Education: Youth
Hunter College of the City of New York
New York, NY, USA

Frederic S. Pearson
Arms Trade, Economics of
Center for Peace and Conflict Studies, Wayne State University
Detroit, Michigan, USA

Jordan B. Peterson
Neuropsychology and Mythology of Motivation for Group Aggression
Harvard University
Cambridge, Massachusetts, USA

Robert O. Pihl
Biochemical Factors
McGill University
Montreal, Quebec, Canada

Solomon W. Polachek
Trade, Conflict, and Cooperation among Nations
State University of New York
Binghamton, New York, USA

Kenneth Powell
Public Health Models of Violence and Violence Prevention
Centers for Disease Control
Atlanta, Georgia, USA

Jason Pribilsky
Cultural Anthropology Studies of Conflict
Syracuse, New York, USA
Syracuse University

Anatol Rapoport
Decision Theory and Game Theory
Peace, Definitions and Concepts of
University of Toronto
Toronto, Ontario, Canada

David C. Rapoport
Terrorism
University of California, Los Angeles
Los Angeles, California, USA

Alison Dundes Renteln
Human Rights
University of Southern California
Los Angeles, California, USA

Claire Renzetti
Criminal Behavior, Theories of
St. Joseph's University
Philadelphia, Pennsylvania, USA

Patricia Richards
Effects of War and Political Violence on Health Services
Health Consequences of War and Political Violence
London School of Hygiene and Tropical Medicine
London, UK

Marc Riedel
Homicide
Southern Illinois University
Carbondale, Illinois, USA

John Robst
Trade, Conflict, and Cooperation among Nations
State University of New York
Binghamton, New York, USA

Robert A. Rubinstein
Cultural Anthropology Studies of Conflict
Syracuse University
Syracuse, New York, USA

Gordon W. Russell
Sports
University of Lethbridge
Lethbridge, Alberta, Canada

Andrew Sanders
Warriors, Anthropology of
University of Ulster
Coleraine, Northern Ireland, UK

Joanna Santa Barbara
Childrearing, Violent and Nonviolent
McMaster University
Hamilton, Ontario, Canada

Robert K. Schaeffer
Secession and Separatism
San Jose State University
San Jose, California, USA

Thomas J. Scheff
Collective Emotions in Warfare
University of California, Santa Barbara
Santa Barbara, California, USA

Christian P. Scherrer
Structural Prevention and Conflict Management, Imperatives of
Copenhagen Peace Research Institute
Copenhagen, Denmark

Brigitte H. Schulz
Cold War
Trinity College
Hartford, Connecticut, USA

John Paul Scott
Animal Behavior Studies, Nonprimates
Bowling Green University
Bowling Green, Ohio, USA

Leslie Sebba
Punishment of Criminals
Hebrew Institute of Jerusalem
Jerusalem, Israel

Daniel M. Segesser
World War I
Universiy of Berne
Berne, Switzerland

Carlos Seiglie
Economic Costs and Consequences of War
Rutgers University
Newark, New Jersey, USA

Gene Sharp
Nonviolent Action
Albert Einstein Institution
Cambridge, Massachusetts, USA

Martin Shaw
Civil Society
University of Sussex
Brighton, UK

James F. Short, Jr.
Youth Violence
Washington State University
Pullman, Washington, USA

Bruce K. Siddle
Psychological Effects of Combat
Executive Director, PPCT Management
Millstadt, Illinois, USA

Thomas R. Simon
Public Health Models of Violence and Violence Prevention
Centers for Disease Control
Atlanta, Georgia, USA

J. David Singer
Correlates of War
University of Michigan
Ann Arbor, Michigan, USA

Simon I. Singer
Juvenile Crime
State University of New York
Buffalo, New York, USA

John Sislin
Arms Trade, Economics of
Center for International Studies, University of Missouri
St. Louis, Missouri, USA

Elisabeth Skons
Arms Production, Economics of
Stockholm International Peace Research Institute
Stockholm, Sweden

Jackie Smith
Transnational Organizations
State University of New York at Stony Brook
Stony Brook, NY, USA

Philip Smith
Cultural Studies, Overview
Ritual and Symbolic Behavior
University of Queensland
Queensland, Australia

Paul Smoker
Religion and Peace, Inner-Outer Dimensions of
Antioch College
Yellow Springs, Ohio, USA

H. F. (Rika) Snyman
Organized Crime
Technikon SA
Florida, South Africa

Metta Spencer
Sociological Studies, Overview
University of Toronto
Toronto, Ontario, Canada

Carolyn M. Stephenson
Peace Studies, Overview
University of Hawaii at Manoa
Honolulu, Hawaii, USA

Pamela J. Stewart
Anthropology of Violence and Conflict, Overview
University of Pittsburgh
Pittsburgh, Pennsylvania, USA

Victor C. Strasburger
Popular Music
University of New Mexico School of Medicine
Albuquerque, New Mexico

Andrew Strathern
Anthropology of Violence and Conflict, Overview
University of Pittsburgh
Pittsburgh, Pennsylvania, USA

Mira Sucharov
Collective Security
Georgetown University
Washington, DC, USA

Keith Suter
Peace Organizations, Nongovernmental
United Nations Association of Australia and Wesley Mission
Sydney, Australia

Jukka-Pekka Takala
Evolutionary Factors
Victimology
National Research Institute of Legal Policy
Helsinki, Finland

Kenneth Tardiff
Mental Illness
Cornell University Medical School, New York Hospital
New York, NY, USA

Frank O. Taylor IV
Peace Movements
Dana College
Blair, Nebraska, USA

Bryan Teixeira
Nonviolence Theory and Practice
Camosun College
Victoria, British Columbia, Canada

Charles Thomas
World War II
U.S. Naval War College
Newport, Rhode Island, USA

David Tindall
Urban and Community Studies
University of British Columbia
Vancouver, British Columbia, Canada

Swee-Hin Toh
Institutionalization of Nonviolence
University of Alberta
Edmonton, Alberta, Canada

Patrick Tolan
Urban Violence, Youth
University of Illinois
Chicago, Illinois, USA

Jennifer Turpin
Women and War
University of San Francisco
San Francisco, California, USA

Bernard Udis
Economic Conversion
University of Colorado
Boulder, Colorado, USA

Antonio Ugalde
Effects of War and Political Violence on Health Services
Health Consequences of War and Political Violence
University of Texas
Austin, Texas, USA

Debra Umberson
Child Abuse
University of Texas
Austin, Texas, USA

Sheldon Ungar
Total War, Social Impact of
University of Toronto
Toronto, Ontario, Canada

Alonzo Valentine
Ethical and Religious Traditions, Western
Earlham College and School of Religion
Richmond, Indiana, USA

Peter van den Dungen
Peace Education: Peace Museums
Peace Prizes
University of Bradford
West Yorkshire, UK

Paul Viotti
Professional versus Citizen Soldiery
University of Denver
Denver, Colorado, USA

Joseph Vorrasi
Long-Term Effects of War on Children
Cornell University
Ithaca, New York, USA

Dierk Walter
Colonialism and Imperialism
University of Berne
Berne, Switzerland

Kathleen Maas Weigert
Structural Violence
University of Notre Dame
Notre Dame, Indiana, USA

Reinhilde Weidacher
Arms Production, Economics of
Stockholm International Peace Research Institute
Stockholm, Sweden

Peter Weiss
Legal Theories and Remedies
Center for Constitutional Rights
New York, NY, USA

Michael G. Wessells
Psychology, General View
Randolph-Macon College
Ashland, Virginia, USA

Dean A. Wilkening
Nuclear Warfare
Center for International Security and Cooperation
Stanford University
Stanford, California, USA

Angie Williams
Communication Studies, Overview
Cardiff University
Cardiff, Wales, UK

Franke Wilmer
Indigenous Peoples' Responses to Conquest
Montana State University
Bozeman, Montana, USA

Jon D. Wisman
Economic Causes of War and Peace
American University
Washington, DC, USA

Lynne Woehrle
Gender Studies
Wilson College
Chambersburg, Pennsylvania, USA

Gordon C. Zahn
Conscientious Objection, Ethics of
University of Wisconsin
Milwaukee, Wisconsin, USA

Kristeva A. Zoë
Peacekeeping
Pearson Peacekeeping Centre
Clementsport, Nova Scotia, Canada

Anthony Zwi
Effects of War and Political Violence on Health Services
Health Consequences of War and Political Violence
London School of Hygiene and Tropical Medicine
London, UK

Guide to the Encyclopedia

The *Encyclopedia of Violence, Peace, and Conflict* is a complete source of information within the covers of a single unified work. It is the first reference book to address a full range of topics in the field of violence, peace, and conflict studies, with coverage of issues as disparate as peace education, trends in warfare, mental illness, and violence toward animals. It also includes many topics of concern to contemporary society, such as ethnic conflict, hate crimes, drug control policies, and child abuse.

The Encyclopedia consists of three volumes and includes 196 separate full-length articles, all prepared especially for this publication. It includes not only entries on the leading theories and concepts of violence, peace, and conflict, but also a vast selection of entries on applied topics in areas such as criminology, politics, economics, communications, and biomedicine. Each article provides a detailed overview of the selected topic to inform a broad spectrum of readers, from research professionals to students to the interested general public.

In order that you, the reader, will derive maximum benefit from your use of the Encyclopedia, we have provided this Guide. It explains how the work is organized and how the information within it can be located.

ORGANIZATION

The *Encyclopedia of Violence, Peace, and Conflict* is organized to provide the maximum ease of use for its readers. All of the articles are arranged in a single alphabetical sequence by title. So that they can be easily located, article titles generally begin with the key word or phrase indicating the topic, with any descriptive terms following. For example, "Criminal Behavior, Theories of" is the article title rather than "Theories of Criminal Behavior" because the specific phrase *criminal behavior* is the key term rather than the more general term *theories*. Similarly, "Criminology, Overview" is the article title rather than "Overview of Criminology" and "Warfare, Trends in" is the title rather than "Trends in Warfare."

TABLE OF CONTENTS

A complete alphabetical table of contents for the Encyclopedia appears at the front of each volume of the set, beginning on page v of the Introduction. This list includes not only the articles that appear in that particular volume but also those in the other two volumes.

The list of article titles represents topics that have been carefully selected by the Editor-in-Chief, Prof. Lester Kurtz of the University of Texas, Austin, in collaboration with the members of the Editorial Board.

In addition to the alphabetical table of contents, the Encyclopedia also provides a second table of contents at the front of each volume, listing all the articles according to their subject area. The Encyclopedia provides coverage of 15 specific subject areas within the overall field of violence, peace, and conflict, as indicated below:

- **Anthropological Studies**
- **Biomedical Studies**
- **Communications**
- **Criminology**
- **Cultural Studies**
- **Economic Studies**
- **Ethical Studies**
- **Historical Studies**
- **International Relations**
- **Peace and Conflict Studies**
- **Political Studies**
- **Psychological Studies**
- **Public Policy Studies**
- **Sociological Studies**
- **Warfare and Military Studies**

OUTLINE

Each article in the Encyclopedia begins with an Outline that indicates the general content of the article. This outline serves two functions. First, it provides a brief preview of the article, so that the reader can get a sense of what is contained there without having to leaf through the pages. Second, it highlights important subtopics that are discussed within the article. For example, the article "Youth Violence" includes among its subtopics "The Age/Crime Connection" and "Understanding and Controlling Youth Violence."

The Outline is intended as an overview and thus it lists only the major headings of the article. In addition, extensive second-level and third-level headings will be found within the article.

GLOSSARY

The Glossary contains terms that are important to an understanding of the article and that may be unfamiliar to the reader, or that may need clarification as to their specific use in the article. Each term is defined in the context of the particular article in which it is used. Thus the same term may appear as a Glossary entry in two or more articles, with the details of the definition varying slightly from one article to another. The Encyclopedia includes more than 1,000 glossary entries.

The following example is a glossary entry that appears with the article "Aged Population."

> **Dementia** An acquired, ongoing impairment of general intellectual abilities to such a degree as to seriously interfere with social and occupational functioning, including memory loss and failures of abstract thinking and judgment, as well as personality changes; an age-related condition and especially associated with Alzheimer's disease.

DEFINING STATEMENT

The text of each article in the Encyclopedia begins with a single introductory paragraph that defines the topic under discussion and summarizes the content of the article. For example, the article "Ecoethics" begins with the following statement:

> *ECOETHICS* is an emerging discipline that in recent decades has been prompted by alarm about increasing environmental degradation and its impact on human and nonhuman life.

CROSS-REFERENCES

Virtually all of the articles in the Encyclopedia have cross-references to other articles. These cross-references appear at the end of the article, following the conclusion of the text. They indicate related articles that can be consulted for further information on the same topic, or for other information on a related topic. For example, the article "Guerrilla Warfare" contains cross references to the articles "Civil Wars," "Colonialism and Imperialism," "Revolutions," "Terrorism," "Warfare, Modern," and "Warfare, Strategies and Tactics of." The Encyclopedia contains about 1,150 cross-references in all.

BIBLIOGRAPHY

The Bibliography appears as the last element in an article. It lists recent secondary sources to aid the reader in locating more detailed or technical information. Review articles and research papers that are important to an understanding of the topic are also listed.

The bibliographies in this Encyclopedia are for the benefit of the reader, to provide references for further reading or research on the given topic. Thus they typically consist of a limited number of entries. They are not intended to represent a complete listing of all the materials consulted by the author in preparing the article.

INDEX

The Subject Index in Volume 3 contains more than 10,000 entries. The entries indicate the volume and page number where information on this topic will be found. The Index serves, along with the alphabetical Table of Contents, as the starting point for information on a subject of interest.

INTERNET RESOURCES

The *Encyclopedia of Violence, Peace, and Conflict* maintains its own editorial Web Page on the Internet at:

http://www.apnet.com/violence/

This site gives information about the Encyclopedia project. It also features a link to the Academic Press Reference Works home page, which has information about related titles, such as the *Encyclopedia of Applied Ethics* and the *Encyclopedia of Human Behavior*.

Preface

The problem of violence poses such a monumental challenge at the end of the 20th century that it is surprising we have addressed it so inadequately. We have not made much progress in learning how to cooperate with one another more effectively or how to conduct our conflicts more peacefully. Instead, we have increased the lethality of our combat through revolutions in weapons technology and military training. The *Encyclopedia of Violence, Peace, and Conflict* is designed to help us to take stock of our knowledge concerning these crucial phenomena.

Most people have a profound ambivalence about violence, a simultaneous abhorrence of and reliance upon it; consequently we engage what policy makers use to guide their discourse and decisions. The relationship between knowledge and practice is complex, of course; many Moderns seem to have something like an addiction to violent solutions that is much like any dependency and escapes rational analysis. Knowledge of dire consequences does not automatically promote constructive action or deter destructive behavior; like the smoker who wants to quit but cannot, we sometimes move ahead consciously along a destructive path. Many of the articles in this encyclopedia, while remaining rooted in academic research, attempt to explore the policy implications of those investigations.

The study of violence—especially war—is as ancient as our religious texts, from the reflective insights of the Mahabharata and Sun Tzu in the East to the Torah and Thucydides in the West, and has an overwhelming advantage over the study of peace when it comes to research funding. The conduct of war is so significant to those in power that its study has a privileged place in the production of knowledge. A large proportion of public expenditures on all research in both the natural and social sciences is, in fact, controlled by military establishments. In the United States, for example, the Army Research Bureau's annual budget exceeds the total combined funding for every other federally funded social science research program including such agencies as the National Science Foundation, the National Institutes of Health, and the National Institute for Mental Health.

As a consequence of massive data-gathering we have, in recent decades, learned a great deal about a wide range of violent behaviors from war to patterns of crime. In these volumes readers can find summaries of those findings; e.g., David Singer's "Correlates of War" project, criminological investigations and cross-cultural anthropological studies of violence, psychological studies of combat and aggressive behavior, case studies of urban and youth violence, UN investigations of the causes of war, and so forth. We have gained a great deal of insight into specific types of violence and have some reasonable theories about what causes people to engage in them. We are still uncertain, however, about how to construct social institutions that provide secure neighborhoods and nations or how to nurture peaceful cultures.

The academic study of peace—a poor cousin to the science of war—is a relatively recent development. This encyclopedia encompasses both enterprises, along with an array of academic disciplines in neither camp that can deepen our understanding of violence. Most of the Enlightenment philosophers—in the same intellectual movement that gave birth to the modern encyclopedia—incorrectly speculated that war would gradually disappear as human society became more rational and civilized. It was not until the 20th century—in response to the horrors of modern warfare—that empirical research and systematic study oriented toward the construction of peace became a part of the academy. Indeed, the field called "peace studies" remains marginal to the academy despite its remarkable growth worldwide since the 1960s with formal programs in hundreds of universities and professional associations such as the International Peace Research Association, the Peace Studies Association, and the Consortium on Peace Research, Education, and Development (COPRED), as well as organized groups of conflict resolution professionals and sections devoted to peace studies in disciplinary societies.

The purpose of this encyclopedia is to bring together in one place a broad range of information and perspectives on violence, peace, and conflict in order to enhance our understanding of these crucial phenomena and to stimulate new research, insights, and better public policies. The encyclopedia's most significant contribution is its addressing the problem of intellectual compartmentalization by including scholarship from diverse disciplines from around the world, from military and peace sciences, to the social and biological sciences, as well as the humanities.

What Do We Know?

It is impossible to summarize briefly the information contained in these three volumes; I would, however, like to highlight some of the themes that emerge. First of all, it is salient that we do not even have a consensus on how to define these three concepts. Rather than impose one on the authors, we include a variety of approaches and a discussion of the debates. Some perceive conflict as a broader phenomenon that encompasses the other two: one can engage in either violent or peaceful conflict. Others perceive peace as something that reflects the absence of conflict. These conflicting definitions reflect salient domain assumptions and produce different theories and policies regarding how to manage the conflicts that seem to be an inevitable part of social life.

Similarly, violence is defined in several markedly different ways. Whereas some contend that the term should refer only to the deliberate infliction of physical harm, others insist that psychological harm must be included as well. Still others claim that we must include the injury caused by inequality (what Johan Galtung calls "structural violence") if the definition is to be sufficiently inclusive. Indeed, the holocaust-like deaths caused by contemporary malnutrition can scarcely be seen as anything but violent, especially by its victims, although usually not inflicted deliberately. UNICEF estimates that six million children under the age of five die annually from malnutrition—as many each year as were murdered in all the German death camps. How violence is defined is an issue with profound policy implications, as demonstrated in the elaborate taxonomy provided in the article "Violence to Children, Definition and Prevention of."

An adequate definition of peace seems almost as elusive as peace itself. The most basic concept, of course, is the absence of war, or more broadly the mitigation of violence. Some would insist, however, that one cannot have peace without justice. Whereas some, following Thomas Hobbes, view peace as something that must be imposed from the top, others claim that it will result only from the grassroots mobilization of common people demanding policy changes from the elites. Some contend that it is something that one must first find within oneself; for others, inner peace comes from living within a peaceful culture. As Linda Groff and Paul Smoker note, peace has many dimensions and understandings of it vary over time and across cultures.

Differing perceptions of peace within the academy reflect the participation of different groups involved in its study. Whereas scholars in the military sciences tend to see peace as primarily the absence of war, for example, many Third World students of peace will emphasize justice as a crucial component of peace; those in religious and cultural studies, as well as many psychologists, may include inner peace as a necessary condition for peace. We have included a range of these positions in this collection.

A second central theme that emerges in these volumes is that conflict has always been part of the human experience, but that the way in which it is carried out varies substantially across time and space, in different eras and cultures. Radical changes in our technologies and strategies of conflict in the 20th century, moreover, distinguish our conflicts from those of past eras. Because they are more destructive in their scale and scope, some age-old wisdom may become inappropriate, whereas other elements of our shared ethical and cultural heritage may be revived.

Conflict can be carried out in a variety of ways from war and violence on one end of the spectrum to nonviolent struggle on the other. In recent decades the means of violent conflict have changed so radically as to transform the very character of violence; dual revolutions in weapons technology and military training have made violence increasingly deadly in both interpersonal and large-scale conflicts. Warfare has been relatively limited until quite recently in scale and scope. Despite widespread destruction bordering on genocide reported in ancient scriptures, premodern combat was relatively inefficient compared to contemporary warfare, and it occurred infrequently. David Grossman observes that a significant majority of soldiers in World War II combat were reportedly not firing directly at the enemy. Modern training thus incorporates operant conditioning to help recruits to the military and police overcome what appears to be a natural resistance to killing.

A growing body of evidence suggests that violent television programs, movies, and interactive video games are providing the sort of psychological conditioning for violence previously reserved for the military and police, whose behavior is usually bounded by strict rules of discipline that are missing from the lay version of the process. Consequently, although it is too early to tell what the larger impact of video games might be on various cultures, the evidence suggests strongly that homicide rates and aggressive behavior—at least among males—increase with the introduction of violent entertainment media into a culture. What is less clear is the nature of human nature with regard to propensities to violence.

A final theme of this compilation is that our understanding of peace and of nonviolent conflict has undergone a revolution that (not accidentally) parallels the transformation of violent conflict in the 20th century. Whereas the change in combat is symbolized by the atomic bomb, the revolution in nonviolence is symbolized by Mahatma Gandhi, Martin Luther King, Jr., and the mobilization of nonviolent social movements. As with warfare, the basic strategies and tactics of nonviolent struggle have been used throughout human history but were transformed in scale and scope in the 20th century. People in many cultures have employed methods of nonviolent direct action and conflict resolution over the millennia, but their development and elaboration in recent decades is unprecedented. Nonviolent struggles are not always successful (nor are violent ones) but they have been remarkably effective in country after country, especially in toppling unpopular dictatorships through mass mobilization and nonviolent tactics of resistance from the people-power movements that toppled U.S.-backed dictatorships in the Philippines and Chile to the Velvet Revolution in Czechoslovakia and the Solidarity movement in Poland that overthrew Soviet-backed regimes.

Scholarly studies of both nonviolence and military combat converge in a surprising possibility, something perhaps never fully verifiable empirically but certainly suggested by the evidence: that human beings—like other species—have not only a capacity for aggression but also a natural resistance to killing their own kind. They may also inherit an inclination toward nonviolent behaviors such as cooperation, affection, and so forth. How else could one explain the remarkable successes of nonviolent social movements in recent decades and the resistance to killing in combat addressed by modern military training? Human genetics seem to provide relatively broad parameters for potential behavioral choices, allowing for a strong influence by culture. The question of the inherent aggressiveness or tendency toward violence in human nature remains a key unanswered question at the turn of the century, one that has profound policy implications and poses complicated methodological dilemmas for students of violence.

Nature versus Nurture

Are humans inherently violent and condemned to periodic and increasingly destructive warfare? A review of our knowledge may produce more questions than answers. We do know that violent behavior is not universal among animal species (see J. P. Scott's article "Animal Behavior Studies, Nonprimates"). We also know that humans exhibit a wide range of behaviors and that their language and tool-making abilities set them somewhat apart from other species in their use of violence and the extent to which their lives are limited by biological parameters. Certainly some individuals and cultures engage in more violence than others; is that because of biological or cultural differences, or is the variation a result of some complex interaction between the two? Most of the violence caused by humans is carried out by the males of the species; is that a direct result of genetic differences or does it come from gender socialization that promotes the use of force by males in solving problems while females are taught to create less violent solutions?

Is war inevitable, given our biological makeup? This question was addressed recently at a conference organized by the Spanish office of the United Nations Educational, Social, and Cultural Organization (UNESCO). An interdisciplinary group of scientists participating from around the world endorsed "The Seville Statement of Violence" that calls into question much popular wisdom about the inherently violent nature of humanity. In their evaluation of the available scientific literature on violence they concluded that it is scientifically incorrect to say that:

- we have inherited a tendency to make war from our animal ancestors;
- war or any other violent behavior is genetically programmed into our human nature;
- in the course of human evolution there has been selection for aggressive behavior more than for other kinds of behavior;
- humans have a "violent brain";
- war is caused by "instinct" or any single motivation.

They conclude that "biology does not condemn humanity to war, and that humanity can be freed from the bondage of biological pessimism" that prevents it from seeking peace. "The same species that invented war," they contend, "is capable of inventing peace." Although the nature–nurture debate will probably not be solved, at least in the near future, one interesting development is recent attention—especially by UNESCO—to cultures of peace in human social organization.

Cultures vary dramatically in the extent to which they promote violent behavior; indeed, many societies can be characterized as having cultures of peace. An ongoing UNESCO project initiated in 1995 analyzes the elements of peaceful cultures in hopes that they might be incorporated elsewhere, such as in war-torn societies attempting to rebuild their civil societies. A pioneer in this field of peace culture, Elise Boulding, outlines some of those characteristics in her article "Peace Culture," noting that humans have a natural tendency to respond to other humans. They are capable of conducting their conflicts peacefully and developing cultures that nurture cooperation, democratic decision making, and nonviolent conflict. Comparative studies of conflict resolution demonstrate that human cultures can organize social life on a peaceful basis. In many communities, children are socialized to conduct their conflicts nonviolently, to cooperate with and respect others, and to create social environments that are not free of conflict but have relatively little coercion or violence.

If humans may not be genetically programmed for violence and war, but are capable of developing cultures of peace, why then is there so much carnage in human life? Although the evidence is far from conclusive, and there is clearly a biological component—especially in extreme sociopathic cases—current studies of violence seem to suggest that it is a consequence primarily of the way in which we instruct our youth, construct our values and beliefs about violence, and structure our options for carrying out conflict. In short, levels of violence probably have more to do with cultural values and social institutions than with the biological parameters within which we operate.

Violence, Culture, and Society

Many of the articles in this encyclopedia outline aspects of the way in which societies are organized within what Robert Elias calls a "culture of violent solutions." The underlying assumption in such a culture is that violence must be used to solve serious problems, including the problem of violence itself. Consequently, we often declare war upon those who commit acts of violence, using "legitimate" violence to put an end to their "illegitimate" use of force. A great deal of time, energy, and money in modern societies and governments is invested in a sort of war over impression management, a struggle to gain the upper hand in how one's use of violence is defined so that ours is viewed as legitimate and necessary, whereas our adversary's is illegitimate and despicable.

This framing process often involves an effort to obtain hegemony in public discourse about violence, as states, social movements, and various interest groups all struggle to have the situation defined in their favor. The ruling ideas about violence in any given social context are, of course, profoundly influenced by the ideas of those who have the most power in that context. In cultures that emphasize the use of violence in their conflicts, the narratives used to differentiate between legitimate and illegitimate violence usually reflect the social structure: violence by the state and elites is considered legitimate. The poor and marginalized are scapegoated and blamed for the violence in their society even if they actually perpetrate a small proportion of it.

Even in societies where there is relatively free public discourse, a limited range of options for defining violence and its use are enforced, setting up boundaries around what is considered viable. This aspect of framing varies dramatically from culture to culture. In some societies the use of violence is so soundly condemned that it is seldom considered as a serious option for conflict management. In other contexts, the failure to use violence is condemned as weak and ineffective. Control over the narrative process defining these norms thus becomes crucial in determining whose violence is accepted and whose is rejected, which modes of conflict are considered useful and which ineffective. St. Augustine understood this when he laid the groundwork for Just War theory in the fourth century, just as did Clausewitz when he founded modern military science centuries later. The nature of those narratives and who controls them has varied widely over time and across cultures.

In most preagricultural and even preindustiral societies, religious elites and institutions tend to control the defining narratives. The legends and stories of oral traditions and sacred scriptures provide the standards by which particular acts of violence or modes of conflict are evaluated. From the Hebrew Torah to the Bhagavad Gita and the Qur'an, stories told around the campfire by village storytellers and recited in places of worship, people learn which styles of conflict are considered ethical with regard to the use of force. The violence of nature, as well as that of foreign peoples, is often explained as an "act of God," and remedies that can be applied to problematic situations are provided in the narratives.

In modern cultures, authoritative storytelling—like many other social functions—is wrested from religious institutions and given to the state in an effort to democratize political authority. Giving the state authority does offer some remedies to earlier abuses, but modern political elites claim a monopoly of violence for the state and use force so widely to back up their claims that state violence has caused an unprecedented number of deaths by war, genocide, and democide in the 20th century, as Alan Grimshaw observes.

Now a new force is moving to center stage, the commercialization of storytelling, so that the narratives that have the most impact on popular culture are written by professionals, told in the media of the age—television, movies, and interactive video games, etc.—and sponsored by multinational corporations.

These new myths and legends regarding the appropriate use of force continue to reflect the interests of those in power and have three major themes. First, we find the age-old maxim that force is often necessary for serious problem solving. This idea is presented repeatedly in narrative form in the popular media and recounted by people who discuss the latest television shows and movies: a crime is committed and the police track down the criminals and drag them off to jail. They are brought to trial, convicted, and justice prevails. In the international arena parallel narratives unfold as criminal heads of state and marginal groups lacking states are apprehended and brought to justice. Terrorists operating on behalf of a dictator or religious fanatic are hunted down and punished, and so on. We all know the stories and their various reincarnations—how security is threatened by criminals and then reestablished by proper authorities using necessary force within a framework of laws.

Embedded within these entertaining narratives are lessons to be drawn about how people are to solve their problems and to recognize the necessity for legitimate authorities to use violence, thus raising the second theme, i.e., that some violence is legitimate and other force is not. As with the first theme, a social problem emerges, a struggle ensues, and sooner or later the problem is solved by force. Erich Fromm once observed that when individuals behave like nations do, we put them in an institution, either a prison or a mental hospital. When states kill, maim, or appropriate property, we hear stories about the honor of such acts. When the same acts are committed by individuals or groups not sanctioned by the state, or by enemy states, they are condemned as horrific.

The difference between the two kinds of violence is determined, of course, by the power of those who use it. The mechanism by which the violence employed by those in power is defined as legitimate is the cultural process embedded in the narratives of the culture. The monopoly of legitimacy still lies with the state even in postmodern culture, but it is not taken for granted; even well-established and popular regimes must now hire professional storytellers to frame their use of violence as legitimate and to counter the critics of their war-fighting, crime-fighting policies.

These for-profit stories about the necessity of fighting bad violence with good are not the only frame provided by modern culture. The major alternative to the good-versus-bad-violence frame is the innovative idea of the industrial age that consumerism can be used to solve problems as well, as told explicitly in advertisements and more subtly in the story lines of other genres. The paradigm here appears in fast food advertisements: within a 60-second story an entire drama unfolds. A problem disrupts the routine of social life but is quickly and efficiently solved by having everyone buy fast food. Everyone sits around smiling and eating; conflicts are resolved and order is restored.

This example seems to have taken us far afield from the initial problem of violence. It is, however, extremely salient: the consumer alternative to brute force seems less violent, certainly, than the use of guns, and many claim that a peaceful future will result from world trade, the free market, and the creation of an affluent lifestyle for everyone. This vision, others argue, is only superficially benign. Hidden behind the smiling consumer faces, they claim, is a very elaborate story of structural violence and destruction. The apparently positive search for happiness through material consumption is globally seductive, the critics argue. It promises more than it delivers because the satisfaction it brings is elusive and temporary, and the process creates a global social system with the hidden violence of mass poverty held in place by a system of overt violence in the form of a military–industrial complex that protects the interests of the rich and powerful. This sort of violence is the object of more recent research, and we know little about its mechansims because it is subtle, complex, and global, and its investigation often marginalized or politicized.

A final set of narratives in the postmodern era is also examined in this encyclopedia: those of nonviolent resistance from Gandhi and the Indian Freedom Movement to Martin Luther King, Jr. and the U.S. civil rights movement, as well as the prodemocracy and other nonviolent movements for social change that they inspired. These stories challenge much conventional wisdom but have their roots in ancient cultures and have taken their place in the dominant culture of the late 20th century, legitimating what Czech president Vaclav Havel calls the power of the powerless. From this perspective, violence accentuates and forces hierarchy and embellishes inequality, whereas nonviolence facilitates equality and empowers democratic movements.

We know much less about how to mobilize Gandhi-style nonviolent struggles than we do about training and employing military forces. After all, we have not been doing it very long. The strategies and tactics of nonviolent action have been examined historically and explicitly only in the 20th century and are summarized here by the most prominent student of modern nonviolent action, Gene Sharp, as well as in Bryan Teixeira's broader discussion of nonviolence in theory and practice. We know even less about how individuals, families, and nations might be organized nonviolently, but that too is a subject of analysis that will persist into the next century. The future of nonviolence remains problematic, of course, especially given the domain assumptions of prevailing realpolitik theories of conflict and current structures for militarizing international conflict, but some remarkable changes have occurred in recent decades that are explored in this encyclopedia. These volumes attempt to bring into clearer focus the options before us and the consequences of our collective choices, as we evaluate these debates and study our policies.

Our hope is that this work will provide us with a more comprehensive picture of our current state of knowledge about violence, peace, and conflict. This collection is broader in its coverage than any other currently available resource, but we cannot claim to raise all of the right questions, let alone provide the necessary answers to them. It is not as comprehensive as one might hope, however, and some caveats are in order.

First, despite our best efforts to broaden the authorship of the encyclopedia, the majority of the contributors are Western, notably North American. Although this does in some sense reflect the current state of scholarship (because of Western dominance and resources), it does not necessarily reveal our best knowledge.

Second, the very genre of the Encyclopedia—with its nonadversarial standpoint and objective tone—may ironically exclude some of our best insights into the subject matter. Indeed, articles by two people, each knowing more about violence and peace (in my opinion) than some entire university faculties put together, were not included because their articles were inappropriate for the genre because they were too argumentative. Another piece was edited substantially but in the end was deemed too pejorative in tone. One prominent Latin American scholar declined our invitation up front, suggesting that if we wanted an objective article on the topic we had asked the wrong person.

Finally, the publication of this sort of resource—which we hope will be relevant for some time—can give the misleading notion that knowledge about a topic is fixed and definitive. On the contrary, the truth about any topic—and especially our understanding of the truth—changes dramatically over time so that it can be misleading to interpret the contents of these volumes in a reified manner. Although this work reviews our current state of knowledge about violence, peace, and conflict, it is a snapshot of a rapidly changing area of inquiry into a constantly shifting set of phenomena.

Thank you for joining us in this ongoing investigation. I would be happy to hear from you if you have comments, criticisms, or information about ongoing research or perspectives that are not adequately represented here.

Lester R. Kurtz
University of Texas at Austin

Aged Population, Violence and Nonviolence toward

James Calleja
International Institute on Ageing (UN-MALTA)

GLOSSARY

Active Aging The fact of maintaining a participant role in society after the traditional retirement age, through continued employment, social interaction, financial and physical independence, and so on.

Aged In this context, describing a person over 60 years of age.

Dementia An acquired, ongoing impairment of general intellectual abilities to such a degree as to seriously interfere with social and occupational functioning, including memory loss and failures of abstract thinking and judgment, as well as personality changes; an age-related condition and especially associated with Alzheimer's disease.

Marginalize To treat an identifiable social group, e.g., the elderly, as if that group is not part of the central or core society, thus identifying them as less significant members of the society than others.

Subjectivity The fact of interacting socially with another person, or interacting professionally in the case of a care giver, according to the unique characteristics and behaviors of that individual and of the setting in which the individual lives.

IT IS AN UNDENIABLE FACT THAT THE WORLD POPULATION IS AGING. It has been growing for ages. What is new is that today there is a rapid pace of aging. The latest figures from the U.S. Bureau of the Census show that in most developed countries, more than 20% of the population is over 60 years of age. This phenomenon is also hitting less-developed nations as a whole with the difference that these countries are aging even faster than their more developed counterparts. The world's 60 and older population increased by more than 12 million persons in 1995; nearly 80% of this increase occurred in developing countries.

This changing global age structure is the result of various factors: low fertility rates, a decline in infant and childhood mortality, advances in medical science and therefore control over infectious and parasitic diseases, basic education for the widest possible population, and public old age security, which safeguards the quality of life in the postretirement period. Of course these scenarios change from one socioeconomic and political context to another. But the trend is clear in that many more older persons around the world are living better, healthier, and longer.

Certainly, living longer does not mean living better

and happier unless the healthy conditions of an individual allow the person to be an independent old person. Dependency as a result of illness in old age or loneliness may lead to neglect, abuse, and often violence, especially when a person, due to a number of circumstances, is deprived of a close family circle. Creating structures to deter these conditions will be one of the major areas of concern for peace research as we turn our attention to the second millennium. More and more elderly people are asking for counseling and services to counteract these threats toward the end of their lifetime.

I. VIOLENCE: ABUSER AND ABUSED

Violence is as old as humanity. The human being (like all other animals) is inclined to possess, secure, and defend given territorial boundaries whether physical, psychological, or emotional. In many cases an abuser/abused dichotomy is created when the solution to conflicts or disputes is provoked by violence: direct, structural, or cultural. In cases in which this violence is applied to older persons, then such violence may easily lead to death since old-aged people are vulnerable compared to other age groups. The elderly are abused when others *in relationship to them* use them to their advantage. Similarly, old people abuse others, when in their relationship, they exploit them to their advantage. Therefore, in an abused/abuser relationship it is important to keep in mind the diversity in role playing in the complex dynamics of interrelationships. The emphasis on the relational context of abuse is very important.

In the first place the abuser/abused relationship is characterized by three conditions: cause and effect, contiguity, and a necessary connection. Whether it is the younger or the old person who is abused or is abusing, the condition has a cause that will lead to effect or effects upon the abused or the abuser. If, for example, an old person is bathed in cold water when this should be warm, then the abuser is certainly the nursing aid or the caretaker; the abused is the old person. But if an old person calls a nursing aid at regular intervals for trivial purposes or simply to attract attention then it is precisely the opposite. Abuser/abused relationships need to be contextualized in order to define preventive or remedial measures.

The act and its actors must necessarily be related to advantages or/and disadvantages. It is from such acts that old people might take the advantage of being cared for more often by, for example, pestering the carer; a caregiver might use marginalization or neglect of an old person as a means to obtain favors from the elderly themselves such as money or other valuable objects. Continuity is a relationship that associates acts and actors with advantages and disadvantages. It is in this relationship that violence is often called for to sort out the end results in the least possible time. In such a situation the impact on the actors can be devastating. Bearing in mind the vulnerability of dependent older persons, the impact can also be fatal.

Now cause/effect and contiguity must be necessarily connected, otherwise the violence exercised by the abuser on the abused will not yield the damage any violence causes whether physical, emotional, and/or psychological. This necessary connection is the result of a process of structural violence in which the abuser plans and executes the acts of violence while the abused tries to deter such violence by protecting his/her own rights and personality from the aggressor. In many cases aggression can be hidden or manifest depending on the short- or long-term strategies the abuser uses in the process. The juxtaposition or proximity between the acts, and the contexts and the actors play an important role in the level of violence used and the results it is expected to achieve. Violence in old age by young or old people themselves will be on the increase as we move into the 21st century with an aged population on the increase, with increasing demands on the resources, and with new expectations that will ensure a good standard and quality of life even after retirement.

In the second place violence can take place *anywhere*. In the case of older persons, violence through abuse, neglect, and other means occurs in institutional settings as well as in their own homes. It is therefore advisable to look into violence in these two different settings and to assess to what extent and for what reasons such violence takes place, by whom, and by what means. Research shows that there are strong links between the abuse of older persons or by older persons, the quality of residential care, and the level of education of carers whether professional or family based. It is in this connection that violence and aged populations requires a more detailed investigation so that when the demographic projections for the next 20 years become a reality, the aged will be more protected and they themselves will be empowered to live a constructive, productive, and creative way of life, relying less on a service-society and participating more in development.

In a society in which older persons will play a more active role in its development, policy is expected to define the framework within which older persons are protected against all sorts of violence and they themselves are bound to respect the extent of services and care available to them. The welfare state as originally conceived in the second part of the 20th century is gradually giving way to an undefined welfare society in which age is not necessarily exclusive of participation in development. Although statistics show that there are more people who want to retire than those who wish to continue with their working life (or new occupation), the quality of life in most highly technological societies will make it easier for some people to continue working after the traditional retiring age of 61 or 65 or later and therefore extending *independence* or mobility (depending on health) toward the late 70s. Active aging is one out of many measures that deters violence toward or by older persons. However, like the welfare society active aging requires a conceptual and operational framework so that when old people look out for opportunities to give concrete contributions toward their society, they find the right structures and legislation that will ensure social and financial sustainability for as long as possible. In this way the satisfaction of basic needs, here defined as survival, well-being, freedom, and identity will be satisfied. Violence will be prevented as early as possible.

II. PHYSICAL VIOLENCE

In discussing relations of older persons with other members of the family or with institutions, physical violence is one common expression of abuse of the elderly or by the elderly themselves. The majority of abusers are spouses and adult children in homes, and carers and fellow elderly persons in residential homes. In a large number of studies, alcohol abuse, a history of mental illness, and ongoing physical or emotional problems appear as the main causes of physical abuse. There are various reasons why the elderly are physically abused by younger generations. One of these is that the elderly are a vulnerable group of persons who are at risk in comparison with other younger groups. They are physically weak but at the same time they may have accumulated enough material resources to become prey to perpetrators. In fact the most common physical violence registered is that related to theft of elderly who may live on their own or who happen to be on their own at home at a particular time of the day. The assailants are normally young unemployed persons, often drug addicts, who desperately need money or objects to sell in order to obtain a new dosage. This is an increasing problem, especially in big towns and cities in developed as well as in developing countries.

Old people are therefore subject to physical violence. But they themselves can use physical violence to attract attention or as a form of protest against younger generations or carers. In institutionalized homes this kind of behavior is very frequent, especially in institutions with amateurish organizational management. The elderly, like other vulnerable groups, want constant attention. Of course in institutionalized homes this is not always possible, especially when the ratio of carers to clients is very low. In developing countries this can be as far as one carer to 30 or 40 clients. In such situations and considering that dependent elderly need constant care and help, physical violence can be a natural reaction to unintentional neglect. In various cases caregivers have had traumatic experiences of elderly assault with unpleasant consequences. Patients suffering from dementia tend to be more aggressive since their memory span is very limited and therefore they cannot appreciate the care and love of those around them.

Physical violence varies from independent to dependent clients. Independent elderly in their own home are more relaxed than those in residential homes for the elderly. The reason is obvious. When an elderly person is forced to leave his or her own environment and take up residence in a home outside his or her community, the first trauma is that associated with space—from a particular physical space that one has become accustomed to throughout a person's lifetime to a limited space shared and confined with others. Many elderly persons living in such a new environment and having to share a room with others become introverts, and this effects their physical health; consequently, they become aggressive and die in a short time. In cases when families neglect the elderly, their behavior becomes even more aggressive and consequently carers and nursing aids find it difficult to cope with such behaviors. On their own part the elderly resort to such behavior out of their need for socialization. Physical aggression may crop in if the elderly person is devoid of attention, although this varies from one person to another.

When dependency becomes an irreversible condition, physical violence by the elderly becomes rare, but that of carers and social workers may eventually increase. This is due to the fact that the demands on the carer increase as the elderly person requires more services at regular intervals. In such cases, unless the ratio between carers and clients is reduced, physical violence is likely to increase to the extent that either the old person is partially marginalized or the carer is under heavy stress and often leaves the job for a more relaxed caregiving environment. In families dependent elderly can really become a burden especially if the caregivers are not prepared to take care of the old person or they do not know how to. The situation can become worse if there are the following conditions within a household:

- Poverty and overcrowding
- The presence of several children
- Unemployment
- Continual family arguments
- One person bearing the burden of caring for an elderly relative without assistance
- Husbands and wives *torn into two* trying to please both family and parent
- A very demanding elderly person
- Social isolation of both parent and carer
- A very dependent old person who may be paralyzed, incontinent, or suffering from dementia.

In such situations the place of the elderly within the family becomes unbearable and therefore admittance in a residential home is inevitable although not always possible. Alternatively, what is often witnessed in such situations is an increase in physical violence on the elderly and by the elderly themselves when ill health makes living very difficult for the elderly and for their carers. Dependency is very much prone to physical violence if the right professional and caring facilities are not available. It is very difficult to expect families to provide this service no matter what financial support they are given. These cases can only be resolved if professional care is sought as early as possible.

Physical violence on the elderly can be of various forms. From surveys and interviews with older persons themselves it transpires that the most frequent examples of physical abuse and violence are the following:

- Hitting
- Throwing something hard
- Tipping
- Burning or scalding
- Bathing in cold water
- Pushing and shoving
- Rough handling
- Unwanted sexual acts
- Spitting
- Tying to furniture
- Locking in a room
- Forcing a senior to remain in bed

Why is it that carers resort to physical violence of the type mentioned forehand? There are two main reasons; namely, that while elderly persons, dependent or independent, require constant attention, carers or family members cannot *afford the time* for regular individual attention; secondly, we live in a complex society in which the time for care is very limited; hence we neglect even those who require our attention. If abuse is to exploit, to one's own advantage another person's weakness or insecurity, neglect is to abandon, to one's own world, another person's need for socialization. Now physical violence is often used by carers under stress as a means of neglect. In fact if any of the acts mentioned before is used on an elderly person what follows is a break in communication between the carer (who could be a family member) and the older person. It is the communicative aspect of physical violence that needs to be studied in the relationship between the carer and the older person. With independent elderly this is less of a problem, especially among elderly citizens who remain active within their social circles. But, with dependent elderly, in particular those who are bedridden, physical violence serves as a means to control the increasing needs of the client. It is natural that after physical violence the old person is unlikely to disturb the carer for a period of time.

In discussing physical violence and the elderly mention has also to be made about the structures in which violence occurs. Overcrowding, poverty, lack of education, and mismanagement of resources are four basic contexts that provoke physical violence.

Whether it is within the family or within a residential home, overcrowding is one of the major problems leading to physical violence. Experience has shown that one of the basic needs of elderly persons is privacy. In residential homes in which older persons are expected to share a confined physical space, determined company, and given carers, it is not easy to adjust to this new reality. The change in the environmental aspects of their new home often leaves the elderly disarmed from those defense mechanisms they normally use to keep their status intact. The physical environment has changed; so does the cultural and social environment. The old person is now subject to new furniture surroundings, new rules and regulations, new sounds, new eating habits, new "comforts," and an environment devoid of the freedom to do what one likes and at any time. As a result, both the elderly and the carers may resort to physical violence if the *rapport* between the elders themselves and the carers is difficult to establish on a short- or long-term basis. The impact with the new environment is extremely important and one has to make an effort to create an environment conducive to the old person's original surroundings.

Poverty is a second basic context that provokes physical violence. In a world in which the rich are becoming richer and the poor poorer, it is imperative that basic needs are met through income-generating activities. With the increase in the number of older persons and the decrease in fertility rates, the burden on the taxpayer will be larger compared to that in the so-called "welfare state." Hence, the question of retirement should be readdressed in order to avoid the clash between the haves and the have-nots! Older persons, who are among the most vulnerable groups in society, are easy prey to economic recessions, a high cost of living, and a more demanding free-market economy. To avoid poverty in old age is therefore a prerequisite to development and a deterrence to the use of physical violence as a means to *silence* old people's demands or old people's protests.

The issue of education is paramount to well-being in old age and to the avoidance of physical violence. The more a person reaches a higher level of education the less likely it will become for him/her to resort to physical violence. Investment in education has always been regarded by many governments as a priority in their development plans. However in a society in which, in a few year's time, one-fourth of the population will be over the age of 60, lifelong education should become compulsory in order to keep the older population as educated and trained in life skills as possible. The failure to educate people means that rights and obligations will be sought through *might* and not *right*.

Finally, resource management is a necessary tool to ensure that as many people as possible share the benefits of economic growth and social opportunities. The lack of resource management may lead to the misuse of resources and therefore to a bitter struggle between the users [old people] and the providers (family members or carers) or between the users themselves. It is obvious that in cases where physical violence is used on the elderly or by the elderly themselves because of the misuse of human or financial resources it will be very difficult to reinstate a sense of partnership. The battle for resources is felt among older persons, especially those who either lack a regular pension or whose pension is inadequate to cope with the rising cost of living. In this connection work after the traditional retirement age may well become a measure to avoid a lowering of the standards of living of older persons and a way how to avoid direct clashes between the users of finite resources.

III. PSYCHOLOGICAL VIOLENCE

A common definition of psychological abuse among researchers is chronic verbal aggression. Verbal chronic abuse may lead to physical violence, especially if users and providers of services for older persons base their personal or professional relationship with one another on tolerance rather than mutual respect. Psychological violence is intimately related to a person's inability to tolerate another when circumstances make communication difficult. Within families or residential homes for the elderly it is even more difficult to maintain such a relationship because the demands on the young are often disproportionate to their capacity of satisfying such needs. Verbal aggression is a way of reacting to such incapacitates that may be due to lack of personnel or funds or resources. In such cases the aggressor (carer) plays the role of an executive power ready to decide whether an older person in given circumstances should be rewarded or punished for his/her behavior.

The roots of psychological abuse are varied but there are at least five causes that are intimately related to the aged, whether in family care or in residential home care. These are:

- Subjectivity
- Undue pressure
- Humiliating behavior
- Health problems
- Exploitation.

The subjective context determines any relationship. Many say that they either like or dislike a person; others tolerate diversity of opinion and style; while others can respect another person notwithstanding the fact that they might not like the individual. Every person is different and has a specific way in which he or she perceives the other. Enemy images are built that way. So are friendships and professional relationships. In analyzing psychological violence the subjective context has to be constantly kept in mind. Old people in particular are sensitive to the way people communicate with them or relate to them. Within families you may find the quiet husband and the vociferous wife or the other way round! Similarly, within institutions such as residential homes, every carer and client is different and behaviors change according to one's character, mood, or circumstances.

It is extremely important that to avoid psychological violence in institutional care measures are taken to ensure that the right carers are employed and that regular training and in-house informal social activities are organized on a regular basis. An institution for older persons must be seen as a family in which every member is respected (and not tolerated) for what he or she stands for. Second, social activities such as birthday parties, anniversaries, special occasions, outings, discussions, and religious services serve to bring old people and their carer closer to one another in a spirit of partnership rather than mere professional collaboration. It is through this environment that the subjective aspects of relationships are established in which each individual becomes familiar with the character, style, and role of the other person and a spirit of symbiosis is established between the partners concerned.

Subjectivity also varies among the elderly between dependent and independent older persons. Those who are generally bedridden will find it more difficult to relate to others and in certain cases to their carers because of their physical deterioration. Hence the carers must be more sensitive to their needs and less demanding on their expectations. With independent elderly the situation can be very different, although experience shows that even when the elderly can fend for themselves they can still be very demanding on their family members and carers. It all boils down to the fact that in the care of older persons psychological violence is a variable conditioned by the individual's disposition to accept or reject the attention from and the *rapport* with the other, whether the person happens to be from his/her own generation or younger. In this respect it is important to consider to what extent intergenerational relations are determined according to the psychological perspectives of the young vis-à-vis the old and vice versa. In fact most of the intergenerational conflicts that occur are normally characterized by psychological violence rather than physical violence—a fight of wits rather than fists!

Psychological violence can be avoided if efforts are made to understand the individual as a *subject* in specific contexts, which include the physical environment, health, social, or/and professional status, family ties, peer relations and the rapport between the old person and the carer.

Psychological violence is also the result of undue pressure that family members in particular, but also professional carers, exercise on older persons. The most frequent examples of undue pressures on the elderly are the following:

- To sign legal documents or those poorly understood
- To prevent access to legal help
- To move from or relinquish ownership of the home
- To buy alcohol or other drugs
- To engage in paid work to bring in extra money
- To avoid help for abuse of alcohol and drugs
- To make or change a will
- To change or not to change marital status
- To give money to relatives or other caregivers
- To do things the senior does not want to do
- To be places to which the older person does not want to go

Undue pressure is often the result of selfish behavior against the elderly who, due to their vulnerable state, succumb to the will of those exercising such pressure. In surveys conducted among the elderly it transpires that very often the elderly are placed in situations in which they are given no options. Within families, younger relatives may use pressure on the elderly to sign legal documents to their own advantage. It is only after such acts that the elderly may realize the mistake they have made when it might be too late. Cases have also been registered in which older persons ask for legal help that they are denied on the basis that such advice is not required. Younger persons often abuse the trust that older generations place in them. As a result of this, old people often find themselves torn between members of the same family they and end up dividing their loyalty between one member and another and are unable to create a consensual atmosphere for the whole family. This is one of the most painful situations that many elderly persons have to face toward the end of their lives.

There are other situations in which old people are asked to pay extra money for services rendered and this psychological pressure can be detrimental not only to their health but also to their financial situation which, already at old age is undermined by limited income from productive work.

Psychological violence is also used when old people decide to change their marital or social status. An old man or women is not expected to remarry or to live with another partner, especially if she or he had children from a previous partner. Many old people find it hard to establish a new relationship because in many societies, traditionally and culturally, it is not the norm to indulge into a new emotional partnership. Some old persons are also ridiculed for taking such a step in their later part of their life.

Humiliating behavior can be physical, verbal, or psychological. There are at least five humiliating behaviors of the physical type associated with older person:

- Forcing a senior to eat unappetizing/unwanted food
- Treating a senior like a servant
- Treating a senior like a child
- Withholding information of importance
- Failure to check allegations of elder abuse.

In discussing humiliating behavior and the elderly it is imperative that mention should be made of the fact that many family members and carers consciously and unconsciously treat old people like servants or slaves or like children. Old people do not like being ordered around or asked to do things they do not wish to do. Neither do they want other people to talk to and treat them like children. But this often happens. A visit to a residential home for the aged will quickly unfold this reality, especially during bathing and lunch time or during social activities. The difference between children and the aged is enormous as an older person once remarked. Old people have treated children like children so they know exactly when such behavior is being imposed on them. Of course the main question here is Why do adults treat old people like children or talk to them like children? The answer lies in the fact that sometimes old people *behave* like children. They are emotionally weak; they are possessive; they enjoy play; they are reluctant to accept reality; they take life easy; they are mischievous by mature adult standards; they are easily irritated; they do what they like and not what they are supposed to be doing; they want to be alone for some time; they want to be sheltered; they tend to forget very easily; they argue a lot, and among other things repetitive story telling is a routine.

On the other hand children, relatives, and carers tend to naturally become very protective of their own parents or clients and therefore they feel that they should dictate the behavior of older generations. So they adopt the same language used to protect and safeguard the interests of children. The difference is that old people can observe this kind of language while young children find it natural to be addressed in such a way; they themselves use the same style with their peers, while older persons talk to each other in a different way than when addressed by relatives, children, and carers.

The similar characteristics between children and old people and the overwhelming care of children, relatives, and carers do not justify the fact that old people should be treated like children or that they can be ordered around. Younger generations must make an extra effort to treat old people as mature persons or to train themselves to disregard the characteristics mentioned before and to respect the old persons for what they stand for rather than for what they appear to be.

This attitude can be aggravated when verbal humiliation is used to confront old persons. This may take the form of:

- Excessive criticism
- Lying
- Swearing
- Insulting
- Calling names
- Unreasonably ordering around
- Telling a senior he/she is too much trouble
- Talking unkindly about death
- Statements that convey false beliefs about illness.

In summing up these points one has to bear in mind that no one has a right to use unwarranted comments toward another person, let alone toward a generation that we are expected to respect for their valid contribution toward society in general and where applicable to our personal and social upbringing. Any of the abovementioned items are offensive toward any human being but unfortunately many old persons whether they live within their own family or in an institution claim that they are often exposed to such treatment. Eliminating this abuse through sensitive behavior is one important step toward deterring psychological violence against the elderly.

Health problems can also provoke psychological violence. In cases in which it is the carer or the relative who is suffering from ill health the old person has to put up with a very difficult situation. But in most cases psychological violence puts health at risk in the following circumstances:

- When leaving an incapacitated or bedridden senior alone too long
- Withholding food or other necessities as a form of punishment
- Unnecessary or traumatic personal medical information
- Incorrect administration of prescribed medicine due to misinformation
- Overprescribing medications to keep the patient in bed
- Inadequate medical attention or information
- Exposing an old person to undue risk and danger
- Talking about alcohol when a senior often gets drunk
- Threats of admission to a "mental hospital."

Health is at risk for the elderly not just because one fails to administer the right treatment or takes too long to do so but also when the wrong information is transmitted to the old person or when there is unnecessary talk about the state of health of the individual. The same holds for threats of admission to a mental hospital, which is seen by many elderly as one of the most frequent forms of psychological violence that is used with patients who suffer from dementia. Coupled with the circumstances mentioned before are those instances in which carers:

- Intimidate
- Manipulate information
- Threaten to withhold specific support
- Talk about abandonment
- Talk about threats of assault
- Frighten the elderly through aggressive talk or behavior
- Send messages of planned assault

While the first group are examples of psychological violence used on the elderly that put health at risk, the second group is characterized by threats and therefore is a form of structural violence that is meant to make the old person as miserable as possible and hence subservient to the will of the carer. Threatening to assault an elderly person can be as traumatic as actually assaulting them. The same holds for using fear as a tool of communication or sending messages that can confuse the old person and put him/her in a more vulnerable position vis-à-vis the carer.

Health is a priority for an old person. Putting health at risk through psychological violence is one way of telling an old individual that their life is in your hands and that they either accept your conditions or they are doomed to suffer the consequences. In such situations, the elderly are left with no other option but to resign to the carer's commands. If health is at risk then any condition is acceptable to the old person. The use of psychological violence will therefore serve to reach the objective of creating an environment conducive to constant risks and a relationship based on fear.

One of the common examples of psychological violence is verbal exploitation, which can lead to taking advantage of an old person or a situation. Verbal exploitation of old persons at home or in residential homes can take various forms, in particular if one fails to:

- Respect older persons' opinion
- Consider older persons' requests
- Provide adequate personal care
- Treat residents or relatives of different financial status equally
- Facilitate through information access to medical care
- Enable access to aids or assisting devices
- Take a senior to necessary appointments
- Remain with a senior who needs reasonable company
- Provide necessary information about basic necessities
- Provide safe and comfortable social conditions.

Failure to give care in words or in deeds or putting the elderly in unwanted situations too often is a form of psychological violence that is meant to eliminate (psychologically first, then physically) the old person as quickly as possible. The objective is to marginalize elderly individuals and in making them believe that they are a burden upon the carers whether they are paid or unpaid caregivers or nursing aids. All the examples mentioned indicate that often the idea of the old person is that attached to an individual who is more of a number than a human being who needs privacy, attention, fair treatment, medical care, respect, and comfort. Stress and carelessness often lead to the type of psychological violence that hurts older persons, especially if they are aware of the fact that they themselves, because of their health situation, are somehow a *burden* on the carer. In fact many older persons consider themselves as an extra responsibility for younger generations, whether relatives or professional carers. Their needs, partly due to their loss of independence because of frailty, are seen as a continuous demand on their carers and therefore they feel obliged towards their caregivers irrespective of how they are being treated or whether they approve of the treatment.

Psychological violence is often used as a means to create a gap between the strong and the weak partner in any relationship. In the case of older persons, the gap is already there due to age and experience. With the deterioration in physical health a new gap opens up that is unfortunately often bridged through psychological violence as a form of control by carers of older persons. In institutional homes, especially in those where human resources are limited to the barest minimum, such control is felt necessary in order to cope with all the requests for services. However, such violence can be deterred if older persons and carers (including family members) are brought together on a regular basis and asked to air their complaints in an atmosphere of friendship and solidarity. Keeping the two sectors apart or, even worse, organizing and training one sector while neglecting the other, can only aggravate the situation. Psychological violence can be eliminated if clients and carers are given the opportunity to understand each others' point of view in a structured way so that resources are utilized in a more constructive and in agreement with both parties concerned.

In interrelationships such as those between older and younger generations, a structural dialogue that breeds mutual respect is one of the most important aspects to stress if psychological violence is to be avoided at all costs.

IV. FINANCIAL VIOLENCE

Many studies use *financial abuse* rather than *financial violence*. There is a hairline difference in the epistemological significance of the two terms that is important to highlight for the purpose of this study. Financial abuse conveys the idea of an abuser who makes *his* what is of *others* without taking into account the consequences thereof. On the other hand financial violence is an act in which the abuser is fully conscious of his/her acts, designs a plan of action, and does it specifically to hurt the person concerned.

In a Canadian survey, financial abuse was the commonly reported type of abuse, constituting five times as many cases as physical abuse. The definition covered a wide range of behaviors, and interviewees were asked if, at any time since they turned 65, anyone they knew had taken any one of the following actions:

- Tried to persuade you to give them money
- Tried to cheat or trick you into giving them money
- Tried to persuade you to relinquish control over finances
- Tried to influence you to change your will
- Tried to make you give up something of value
- Tried to persuade you to sign over your house to them

It was interesting to note from the research findings that those who were financially abused were more likely to live on their own, to be socially isolated and to have health problems. The Canadian survey found no difference between victims of abuse and the rest of the respondents with respect to sex, education, income, or unemployment status, but victims were good deal more unhappy in a number of ways. Another interesting finding was that the perpetrators of financial abuse tend not to be close relatives; that abusers had financial problems or that they have recently experienced financial or employment problems, and that alcohol consumption was a relevant factor.

Financial violence as defined earlier is somehow a different matter although there are similarities such as:

- There is an abuser and an abused;
- The perpetrator might have financial problems or is inclined to steal;
- The victim is a vulnerable person who may (a) live on his/her own; (b) is considered to be a person who possesses wealth; and (c) is unprotected;
- The abuser is knowledgeable enough to select the victims.

However there are also basic differences between perpetrators of abuse and those who perform acts of violence namely:

- The perpetrator is normally inclined to be violent and is prepared to physically hurt the victim if there is resistance;
- The perpetrator normally has a record of acts of violence of different types such as taking part in riots, car thefts, etc.;
- The perpetrators plan their acts of violence in such a way that it is very unlikely to fail;
- The perpetrators often have accomplices with them in case something goes wrong and they need help;
- Their victims are all vulnerable groups who possess money or valuables;
- The elderly are easy prey for perpetrators of financial violence since many of them possess both money and valuables that they can exchange for hard currency or other possessions;
- The elderly, especially those living on their own in cities or in above-average houses in small towns, villages, or the countryside, are the prime targets.

In defining the whole conceptual framework for financial violence one also needs to include other types of financial exploitation such as:

- Selling property without the permission of the elderly person;
- Controlling money without the permission of the old person;
- Charging excessively for goods and services;
- Failing to repay borrowed money especially when asked to do so;
- Sharing a senior's home without paying fairly for expenses if asked.

Of course it is sometimes very hard to tell whether a perpetrator is doing acts of violence or abuse. But if the victim is physically hurt or socially excluded to the detriment of his/her health, then abuse becomes an act of direct or indirect violence. The victim is eliminated to the advantage of the perpetrator. The perpetrator is normally rewarded financially.

There are three main aspects of financial violence:

- Open financial violence
- Organic financial violence
- Cultural financial violence.

A. Open Financial Violence

Most common forms of violence against older persons are those in which the perpetrator uses physical violence to steal or to take valuables. These are the stories that normally hit the headlines, especially when the old person is severely injured or killed. It is *open* because the perpetrator must face the victim whether this happens at the victim's residence or in the street or at any other place that the perpetrator chooses to perform his violent act. In this way the perpetrator makes sure that all the variables mounting to his/her execution are under control and that it is very likely that he or she or they can get away with it. The perpetrator would have done his or her preparations well.

The perpetrator would have first identified the victim; then they make the necessary preparations to decide when to attack, how and what means to use to ensure that the exercise is brought to fruition. The next step is to seek allies if necessary, namely a person who would provide assistance during the act of violence and an accomplice to provide the necessary information in order to reach the victim—it could be the porter of a block of apartments or *friends* of the victim or even neighbors. Much of the information that a perpetrator asks for is normally given unintentionally.

This act is characterized by direct violence. The victim is normally assaulted, beaten, or thrown on the floor, or tied to furniture or immovable objects. Then the old person is asked where the money or other valuables are and beaten if he/she fails to collaborate. The perpetrator always threatens to hurt the old victim if he/she is not satisfied with the response to the demands. In some cases old people have reported that they are humiliated by being stripped and raped if the perpetrator does not find what he/she aims for. In extreme cases the victims are killed, especially if they resist or threaten to report the incident to the police and are capable of describing the aggressor.

With the increase in unemployment and drug abuse physical violence on the elderly is on the increase. So are the preventive measures in the form of frequent patrols by the police, special telephone lines for help such as the telecare system and specialised schemes such as the *Neighbourhood Watch Schemes* in which someone is keeping an eye on particular households in order to protect others. The elderly themselves could become the main providers of these schemes by setting up *Neighbourhood Watch Schemes* run by the elderly for the elderly in close collaboration with the local government.

B. Organic Financial Violence

This type of violence is characterized by three main techniques: persuasion, cheating, and undue influence. Mention was made earlier that financial violence is caused by perpetrators who persuade old persons to give them money. This often happens in residential homes in exchange for services but also within families where old people take up residence with their sons or daughters. Many elderly persons complain that in residential homes they are systematically asked for money in order to obtain services to which they are entitled in any case. In most of these cases, the elderly observe that the perpetrators are always the same two or three persons who unscrupulously abuse their official position to obtain extra money. These perpetrators are normally nursing aides, medical doctors who often encourage patients to been seen privately, and medical assistants as well as carers and support staff. Taking advantage of an old person's situation and exploiting this advantage by making money out of it leads many old people to refuse services that they would normally take if they are not asked for extra money. The incidence in government-run homes is much higher than in private or religious homes. This of course is due to the fact that the bigger the home the larger the incidence of abuse and violence.

Organic financial violence is therefore planned violence. It is systematic and the aggressor will do it on a give-and-take basis. It is done discreetly and normally very politely. The elderly are generally given the impression that extra money means a more caring and personalized service. Hence the use of persuasion to obtain favors that under normal circumstances they should not be given.

A second technique used as a form of financial violence is cheating. Old people, for example, often complain that the prices they are charged for certain goods others buy for them rise unexpectedly or that they are cheated in being given products that they have not asked for. Cheating is a problem that the elderly can do very little about unless they are protected by law or by specific regulations, especially in residential homes or in social activities.

A third technique concerns undue influence that perpetrators exercise on the elderly to obtain money as a result of a change in personal decision making or the acquisition of objects that can be eventually transferred on to a will later on. Specifically, such influence is normally used to:

- Change a will
- Donate a valuable object to a relative
- Buy an object for the house
- Sell the house and live in a smaller apartment
- Spend less money on leisure activities and necessities
- Avoid private medical care.

In all these cases there is an organic plan of action that puts the elderly in a disadvantaged position vis-à-vis the perpetrator since they cannot afford to be marginalized or socially excluded.

C. Cultural Financial Violence

In peace research Johan Galtung defines cultural violence as those aspects of culture, the symbolic sphere of our existence—exemplified by religion and ideology, language and art, empirical science and formal science (logic and mathematics)—that can be used to justify or legitimize direct or structural violence. Cultural financial violence is an attempt by perpetrators to create an environment that financially excludes the elderly on the basis of status, creed, sex, and health. Many private residential homes for the elderly adopt this philosophy on the pretext that not everybody can afford the money needed for such services. Even within the care services in private residential homes, class and status are encouraged. What determines this is the amount of money one is prepared to or can afford to pay. Certainly no private home for the elderly can be run unless it can make a profit. Alternatively, the services must be subsidized by local or central government or the church, or other charitable or nongovernmental organizations.

What is gradually being maintained is that status and class, which are intimately related to culture, are creating a divide between the haves and the have-nots irrespective of the principles of equality and justice that many democracies around the world advocate. Private entrepreneurs and some governments rightly argue that in a free market economy every person should be given the choice and the opportunity to live and eventually to die wherever the person likes and under the conditions he or she chooses. Although this is a very valid argument, one has to be extremely careful not to encourage a culture of extreme consumerism in which added burdens are placed on workers to invest heavily in private pension schemes in order to sustain the retiring years (which may be 15 to 20 years on average) or hospitalization in old age if they require such service. Such policy very often places the role of governments in service provision for the elderly at a disadvantage. It is wrong to invest in services for the few at the detriment of those for the many. Several studies show a new poverty coming as a result of a consumerist mentality in which there will be a great divide between those who supply and those who consume.

Financial violence of the cultural type is therefore any new mentality that will undermine the dignity of the human being at an age when it is more likely that such prestige is lost because of the deterioration of the physical abilities. This means efforts have to be invested in policies that would uplift those elderly persons in need of services and provide them with a safety and comfortable physical, medical, and human environment that is conducive to peace of mind. In this same breath and if the resources of a given territory permit, choice should be allowed in the provision of services to all other older persons so that freedom and well-being, two of the basic needs of any human being, will be respected.

V. NEGLECT

Homer and Gilleard found that neglect, like verbal violence or abuse, was related to a long-standing poor relationship between the old person and the caregiver or relative. Those who are neglected are often a source of stress and are socially isolated. To neglect an older person must be therefore seen as a form of violence in that the caregiver is leaving the elder in a state of risk and therefore easy prey for physical, psychological, and verbal violence.

Neglect carries a number of meanings. It means to disregard, ignore, fail to give proper attention to or take proper care of a person; it also means to fail to do or perform through carelessness or oversight one's own business. In the care of older persons, neglect is related to the following meanings:

1. Carelessness
2. Indifference
3. Negligence
4. Inattention
5. Failure.

A. Carelessness

Neglect through carelessness is an act of violence against an elderly person. An old person is in need of proper service, especially if the individual is entirely dependent on the carer. Many bedridden elderly persons complain about the lack of tact used by caregivers and nursing aids in bathing them, in helping them to move around, or in giving the right attention at the right time. In residential homes where the number of elderly persons in relation to the nursing aids determines the level of care, many old people spend considerable time waiting to be attended. Neglecting an old person who has bedsores for a long time is considered by many as an act of physical violence in that the old person is suffering pain as a result. Of course, no one can blame nursing aids if the demand is greater than what is humanly possible to supply. Many residential homes, especially those run by governments, cannot afford individual attention due to the lack of personnel or specialized nurses ready to provide the care old people need. Carelessness is therefore seen from at least two main perspectives vis-à-vis violence:

- Carelessness as a deliberate act
- Carelessness as an act imposed by circumstances.

A deliberate act is when the resources are available but they are misused or abused; an act imposed by circumstances is when neither the resources nor the availability of the resources are possible. In both cases, it is the old person who suffers the consequences. Defining such acts as violent underpins the commitment that the so-called care services should stress in order to avoid further discomfort that, bearing in mind the vulnerable state of many elderly persons in residential homes, may lead to precocious death.

B. Indifference

Sensitivity is one of the major qualities that carers and nursing aids should have in their relationship with older persons. To be sensitive to one's needs, especially if these are related to pain, is an important part of the care that is normally given to old people. Not every carer is sensitive enough to pain whether this is physical or psychological. Old people are more likely to suffer physical pain than any other group. They are becoming more and more prone to disease and hence they are subject to continuous stress due to the change in their body functioning. Indifference to such pain can be due to various reasons. The first is that many old people fail to open up their hearts with their carers. They are afraid that they bother them too often and therefore they try to hide their pain, especially if they had been ridiculed before. Second, many old people find it hard or do not wish to disclose their state of health with a carer whom they find "cool" in the way he/she considers their particular situations. One finds many old persons saying that disclosing the state of their health does not help them improve it at all. Third, many elderly look upon their physical and mental deterioration as a natural state of their health and therefore find it useless to try to make an issue out of a situation that is natural at this particular stage in one's lifetime. Fourth, many older persons, especially those living in residential homes, prefer to remain silent than to bother their carers about their particular health. Some have said that even if they do ask for special attention they are hardly given any attention or if attention is forthcoming it is not to their satisfaction.

Indifference as a form of neglect can be seen through these different facets and can bring about additional pain that can be avoided in the first place if a person is sensitive enough. It is of course very difficult to train people to be sensitive. Sensitivity is considered by many as a natural rather than a learned attribute in a carer's character. Therefore, carers are distinguished between those who care and those who are indifferent or, worse, who "train" their own clients (that is, older persons) to avoid asking for help when this is related to old age deterioration! Such indifference and insensitivity is one of the most common features in the care of dependent elderly persons. With independent elderly and those who can still contribute toward social development, indifference to their requests, needs, and expectations can also be considered as acts of what Johan Galtung terms structural violence, in which the old person is marginalized on the basis of age rather than individual capacity.

C. Negligence

Threats in one's life are very often related to negligence on the part of the carer or the relative of an old person. H.B. Danesh makes a very interesting distinction between three categories of threats that I consider to be the result of negligence. The first are those related to self-integrity, such as life-threatening disease, the loss of a partner, physical harm, or loss of purpose and meaning in life. Many neglected older persons suffer from such syndromes. They feel that notwithstanding the fact that they have given a valid contribution in life, in old age they have been neglected and this marginalization that is often due to negligence is interpreted by the old person as a loss of self-integrity. Common examples are those related to invitations for social functions. An old person welcomes these invitations. Forgetting through negligence to invite an old person to a social function can be very distressful.

The second category relates to those threats that affect the self-identity of the individual, such as humiliation, domination, manipulation, failure, and frustration. These threats cause the old person to become less self-assured and less capable of relating to others at a mature and equal level. If through negligence in service provision, for example, old people are subject to such treatment then one should consider such behavior as violent vis-à-vis the old client. Of particular significance is the act of domination between the carer and the old person, whether this happens among relatives or professional caregivers. To dominate in this case is to enslave and render the old person subject to one's own wishes and moods of the day. Negligence in role-playing can be detrimental to old people. Just because an old person, like a child, is often vulnerable and defenseless does not in any way allow the caregiver to exploit the situation and render the client an object of manipulation.

Finally, there are threats of injustice, poverty, tyranny, and prejudice that negligence on the part of the caregiver can induce insanity and suicide in an old person. Fairness in treatment, comfort in the provision of services, gentleness in the way one addresses older persons, and respect for old age are all part and parcel of the care for the elderly. Old age is a period in one's lifetime when the demands on the carer increase radically, especially with dependent old persons. Yet it is also a time when much can be gained through a proper understanding of the relationship between the old person and the caregiver if both parties accept and respect one another. Eradicating negligence in this relationship is one important step forward.

D. Inattention

In the care and welfare of older persons, threats can also be actual or assumed. They can originate from the external environment and assume the form of physical and social threats, or they can rise like mist from within, in the shape of psychological and spiritual crisis. Having older persons under the constant care of another person may lead to an attitude of taking old persons for granted and therefore elements of inattention to particular needs are neglected. Birthdays, anniversaries, special occasions, annual social gatherings, and other personalized events mean a lot to everyone, especially to an old person. In an overcrowded environment in which old people are considered as numbers on a list, these events are completely neglected. Yet the individual person cannot forget personal events in his/her lifetime. Inattention to such sensitive dates is painful, especially if the old person has no relatives or friends, or if they are not aware of these special dates. Of course, it is quite taxing for caregivers, especially in huge institutions, to note such particular events; yet, with the help of the elderly themselves one can reach this objective very easily. Some residential homes have designated elderly persons to look into these occasions and bring them to the attention of those concerned. Empowering the elderly in little but significant aspects such as these is one step toward creating an environment in which everyone is important because each has a history that is brought to the attention of those concerned.

E. Failure

Neglect can also take the form of failure. Failure is related to unsuccessful results or to the inability to perform one's duty according to set rules and regulations. Failing to give proper and timely attention to the elderly can be a serious threat to their well-being and in some cases to their lives. When can we detect failure as a form of neglect, and to what extent is failure an act of violence? Failure is seen from results. Surveys show whether persons are happy in a given context. Interviews also reveal the quality of the service being given. Talking directly to the elderly can be a very worthwhile exercise in trying to improve the care for the elderly. By using tact and professional techniques failure can be easily detected and improved on through retraining or a change of responsibilities. But to neglect the existence of such failures in the home or in institutional care can lead to serious flaws and damaging consequences. In many cases the elderly are fully aware of a situation in which there is something going wrong. If, for example, an old person is given cold baths or cold food then the fault lies in the sensitivity of the caregiver and in the management of the food supply. By ignoring or neglecting complaints one is only encouraging a situation in which old people suffer—physically, psychologically, and emotionally. Failure as a result of negligence is a show of indifference and inhuman treatment. It is also a form of violence in that the end result is characterized by pain. An environment that breeds openness in the rapport between the client and the old person avoids situations in which there is:

- Fear of retaliation or of making the situation worse because failure has been brought to the attention of the carer (especially if the elderly person is dependent on the perpetrator for basic survival needs)
- Assumption of blame for the perpetrator's behavior

- Fear of the elderly of being removed from one place and therefore the loss of established peer groups and friendships
- Guilt and stigma at having reported the failure or at being the failure
- Concern about jeopardizing the status quo of the home or the institution.

Failure as a form of neglect and violence toward the elderly is still to be looked into through proper research. One augers that the elderly themselves will be given the opportunity to air, in confidence, their views on the subject so that standards in the care and welfare of older persons will be improved and signs of neglect eliminated as much as possible. Of great importance is not only the fact that the elderly themselves need to be empowered to advocate for the quality of their lives but that they themselves must learn how to defend their interests and earn a respectful place in society whether they are dependent or independent elderly persons.

VI. NONVIOLENCE AND TRAINING

Training workers in the field of aging against violence and abuse of elderly people is likely to become one of the most important areas in the study of aging in the future. According to various specialists this is due to the following reasons: the first is the growing body of research highlighting both the different types of violence and its impact on the community of elderly persons; the second, the emergence of guidelines advising workers how to handle problems related to abuse, neglect, and violence on older persons; third, the publication of training manuals with a direct focus on the issue of mistreatment of elderly people; fourth, the setting of working groups among the elderly themselves to design strategies against violence in homes and institutions of care; fifth, the organization in various countries of Neighbourhood Watch Schemes, some of which are run by the elderly.

The need for training on elderly abuse and violence has already been established by a number of institutions in Britain, the United States, and within the United Nations system. In developing training E. Podnieks identifies five main recipients, namely:

- The professionals
- The caregivers
- Older adults
- The public
- The children.

The education and training of **professionals** about all aspects of violence against the elderly is an important step in the prevention of such violence. Training should take place on an ad hoc basis through seminars or in-service courses, or within the context of higher education, in particular in courses in gerontology or/and social studies or peace studies. Furthermore, the training of counselors, policemen, lawyers, legislators, and the clergy, among others, should be a major component in any educational undertaking to fight abuse and violence. Such training courses must be designed by experts in the field and tailor-made to the specific profession of the recipients.

Carers are the closest group of persons to the elderly. They provide care and ensure that the old person lives in comfort and away from physical and psychological hazards. Training carers in detecting and alleviating violence and abuse must be considered as a fundamental component in their training or in-service training courses. These courses should also be offered to a wide range of caregivers such as church groups, medical faculties, telemedicine, senior organizations, family service agencies, community colleges, and social services agencies. All of these support groups help in raising awareness of the significant issues related to violence against the elderly and improve the mechanisms to prevent abuse and violence in the first instance.

The importance of educating **older persons** in preventing violence and abuse cannot be overstated. Every training course should be elderly oriented, and the elderly should play a leading role in the course itself. It would be very helpful if old persons who have been victims of violence are asked to exchange experience and to design strategies that they themselves can implement together with the police, social workers, and others involved in their welfare. Such courses can be held in senior organizations and in particular in Universities of the Third Age (where these exist) so that further research and investigations by the elderly are encouraged. Action groups should also be encouraged from these courses so that the elderly, especially those independent old persons who are prepared to provide help and assistance, set up task forces in the local communities in order to reach more cases.

The media can play a leading role in **public** education in preventing violence and abuse against the elderly. Often the media highlights the sensational aspects of violence on the elderly. But carefully planned campaigns through television and radio can make a difference if they are geared toward abused seniors and those who can and are in a position to recognize elder violence such as family members, neighbors, friends, public service providers, the clergy, postal workers, bank tellers, meter readers, and so on, thus creating a web of protection within the community that would deter any abuse or signs of violence against the elderly themselves. Ad hoc courses, talks, or seminars in the various communities on elder abuse and violence can also help to create awareness. Furthermore, it would also be very useful if specific training is conducted for journalists so that reporters become better informed on the issues and responsible reporting rather than the customary sensational approaches to violence on the elderly as referred to earlier on.

Finally, **children** need to understand that the elderly, like themselves, are a vulnerable group in society that deserves respect and above all protection from violence. Since attitudes and stereotypes are formed earlier in life and influence behavior throughout one's lifetime, it is important that within school programs children are exposed to the reality of violence against the elderly and on how they themselves can deter such violence. Education with an intergenerational perspective and with a positive influence on children's attitudes toward the elderly cannot be overstated. This education helps young people to bridge the cultural gaps between the ages and to find ways and means to offer help to older generations whose life or well-being is at peril because of violent attitudes or deeds in the home, in the community, and in other institutions. Projects within the school that involve the elderly themselves will help a great deal. Also, the presence of older persons in educational institutions can create greater awareness of the problems that violence and abuse entail.

In designing such training courses Biggs and Phillipson set out some guiding principles and themes:

- Aims and objectives of training
- Anti-agist perspectives
- Theoretical perspectives
- Empowering older people.

In this context it is important that a target group is carefully identified and that the training takes place within given socioeconomic and cultural contexts so that learning becomes relevant and applicable in the day-to-day running of institutions or care for the elderly.

The need for sensitization to the issue of violence against the elderly is an important leading component in social policy. A great deal is being conducted in a number of countries, especially in the developed world. However, a lot more needs to be done in order to ensure that the elderly live safely in their homes, in the community, and in institutions. What training and other means of communication can do to prevent violence cannot be divorced from the role that elderly themselves can play in this process. It is therefore important that every caregiver and professional person engaged in the care and welfare of older persons seeks proper training in this field of concern. On the other hand every institution concerned with research on violence and care must make it a point to set up proper courses designed to reach the roots of the problem and to create proper tools and mechanisms to deter, prevent, challenge, and severely punish the perpetrators of violence on the elderly.

Also See the Following Articles

FAMILY STRUCTURE AND FAMILY VIOLENCE AND NONVIOLENCE • VIOLENCE TO CHILDREN, DEFINITION AND PREVENTION OF

Bibliography

Cassell, E. J. (1989). *Abuse of the elderly: Misuse of power. New York State Journal of Medicine.* March , p. 160.

Eastman, M. (1984). *Old age abuse*, p. 85. Portsmouth: Age Concern.

Eastman M. (Ed.). (1994). *Old age abuse, age concern*, pp. 15, 16, 215, 216. London: Chapman and Hall.

Galtung, J. (1996). *Peace by peaceful means*, p. 196. London: PRIO and Sage Publications.

Danesh, H. B. (1995). *The violence-free family—Building block of peaceful civilization*, pp. 47, 48. Ottawa: Baha'I Studies Publications.

MacLean, J. M. (1995) *Abuse and neglect of older Canadians: Strategies for change*, p. 80. Toronto: Canadian Association on Gerontology and Thompson Educational Publishing, Inc.

Aggression and Altruism

Douglas P. Fry
Åbo Akademi University and University of Arizona

GLOSSARY

Aggression Acts that inflict physical, psychological, and/or social harm (pain/injury) on an individual or individuals.

Altruism (A) Evolutionary definition: Any act that increases the fitness of others while simultaneously decreasing the fitness of the actor. (B) Nonevolutionary definition: An act involving some self-sacrifice from the actor that benefits another or others.

Emics Interpretations of behavior and cultural meanings as expressed by the members of a culture themselves (*see also* Etics).

Enculturation The processes through which culture is transmitted to new generations.

Etics Observer-based interpretations of behavior and meanings, usually offered by a cultural outsider (*see also* Emics).

Fitness (or Genetic Fitness) The average number of offspring contributed to the next generation of a population by individuals with a particular genetic constitution, or genotype, relative to the contributions of individuals with other genotypes (*see also* Inclusive Fitness).

Inclusive Fitness The fitness of an individual when the degree of genetic relationship with other individuals is also taken into consideration (*see also* Fitness and Kin Selection).

Indirect (Covert) Aggression When an individual uses social networks, third parties, elements of the social organization, and/or other covert means to inflict harm on another individual or individuals.

Kin Selection Groups of relatives form the evolutionary units of selection that are acted upon by natural selection (*see also* Fitness and Inclusive Fitness).

Reciprocal Altruism "The trading of altruistic acts in which benefit is larger than cost so that over a period of time both enjoy a net gain" (Trivers, 1985, 361).

Reciprocity Transactions wherein goods and services (here defined not only in economic terms, but rather in the broadest possible sense) are exchanged. Hence, reciprocity includes phenomena such as dinner invitations, exchange of favors, gifts, and so on. Marshall Sahlins discusses three subtypes of reciprocity. (A) *Generalized*: The type of exchange wherein the value of the gift is not calculated, nor are the conditions of repayment specified. A typical example noted across cultural settings is the giving of food to one's family members and relatives. (B) *Balanced*: A type of equal, "balanced," exchange wherein the nature and value of the transaction are specified, such as when individuals engage in trading. (C) *Negative*: A type of exchange wherein one party receives a clear benefit at the expense of the other party, as occurs, for example, during swindling, cheating, or theft.

AGGRESSION AND ALTRUISM can be seen as resting on the opposite poles of a social-interaction continuum; aggressive acts cause *harm* to others, whereas altruistic acts *benefit* others. Neither aggression nor altruism are without definitional complexities. One definitional issue, for example, involves assessing emic (actor-conceptualized) and etic (observer-operationalized) considerations when defining aggression. Clearly, aggression and altruism are greatly affected by cultural processes. Cross-cultural examples and comparisons illustrate the range of possible aggressive and altruistic behaviors engaged in by humans. For instance, some cultures have extremely low levels of physical aggression, while others have very high levels of physical aggression. Levels and manifestations of altruism also vary among cultures as well as among individuals within a culture. The impact of socialization and psychocultural processes on altruism and aggression is illustrated as peaceful Semai culture and violent Waorani culture are compared (in section II) and also as a peaceful Zapotec community is compared with a more aggressive Zapotec community (in section IV). Among the cultural variation, underlying patterns also can be detected: The greatest degrees of altruism, helping, sharing, and caring tend to occur among close relatives, and these behaviors decrease in intensity as social distance between individuals increases. Also, with greater social distance, restraints against aggression seem to decrease. These general tendencies are not without exceptions, of course, but the patterns are detectable across numerous social circumstances. Sex differences in aggression also show cross-cultural regularity. While women do engage in physical aggression in many cultures, the cross-cultural pattern is that men are more frequently and more severely physically aggressive than women. However, it should be held in mind that in some cultures, both women and men are nonaggressive. Additionally, in some societies, women appear to use more indirect aggression than men, where indirect aggression entails use of social networks, third parties, and/or elements of the social organization to inflict harm covertly on another individual. In the concluding section of this article, the flexibility of human behavior and cultural systems is considered. Culture change wherein aggressive practices are supplanted by more peaceful alternatives does occur. Conflicts may be part and parcel of social life, but physical aggression is not. Cultural alternatives to violence exist.

I. DEFINITIONAL COMPLEXITIES

A. Multiple Meanings of Aggression

In general usage, the word aggression is employed in a multitude of ways. The same term is used, for example, to describe a schoolyard fight, serial murder, warfare, or the "pushiness" of over-the-telephone solicitors. Furthermore, the concept at times is used to refer to *behavior* (e.g., killings) and at other times to personality or cultural *attributes* of persons or groups (e.g., "an aggressive culture"). Sometimes aggression implies physical contact (which might range in severity from a slap to a stabbing), sometimes verbal behavior (again with great variation of expression), and sometimes social actions (such as ostracism). A distinction also can be made between direct aggression, wherein the identity of the actor typically is known, and indirect or covert aggression, wherein the identity of the perpetrator of the aggressive deed (and sometimes occurrence of the deed itself) may never be known by the recipient (e.g., malicious gossip). Another manifestation of the multifaceted usage of the term aggression involves the range of social levels across which it is applied, from individuals, sports teams, cultures, countries, and so on.

B. Emic and Etic Definitions of Aggression

Another definitional issue particularly relevant in anthropological investigations involves whether to favor emic (actor-conceptualized) or etic (observer-operationalized) approaches to defining aggression. Paul Heelas stresses emics and notes the role of culture in determining the meaning of particular actions. Heelas points out that actions that may be considered aggression in one culture may not be considered aggression in others, and he stresses that human aggression always occurs within a cultural context. Heelas sees no value in etic, observer-based definitions of aggression: "we must resist asserting that Ilongot youths are aggressive simply because they lop off heads; that Samoan fathers are aggressive simply because they beat their children; or, for that matter, that the British were aggressive when they lined up to exterminate the indigenous people of Tasmania" (1989, 240). To illustrate his argument, Heelas cites Napoleon Chagnon's work among the Yanomamö of South America and suggests that Yanomamö wife-beating should *not* be considered aggression because inflicting physical injuries is how a husband shows that he "cares" for his wife. James Silverberg and Patrick Gray find Heelas' interpretation unconvincing and see value in both emic and etic perspectives: "Just because beatings may signify 'caring' to some Yanomamö women (how many is unclear) does not negate the etic reality of the beatings as violent acts" (1992, 12). Chagnon's ethnographic observations indicate that the wives attempt to avoid beatings by their husbands, in other words, that they are not eager recipients of this type of husbandly "care," a point that Silverberg and Gray note in their critique of Heelas' interpretation. The cultural context of Yanomamö wife beating also suggests that this so-called "caring" occurs when a husband is angry at his wife, and that much of it results from a husband's sexual jealousy. Chagnon (1992, 124–125) writes, for instance: "Some men are given to punishing their wives by holding the glowing end of a piece of firewood against them, producing painful and serious burns.... It is not uncommon for a man to injure his sexually errant wife seriously and some men have even killed wives for infidelity by shooting them with arrows."

An assessment of this emic-etic issue suggests there is utility in both perspectives, and that it is futile to argue the "correctness" of one approach to the exclusion of the other. When the research goals are culturally comparative, then an etic perspective on aggression is critical, but when the goals are culturally interpretive, oriented toward understanding the belief system within a particular culture, focusing on emic "participant understandings" obviously is of central importance. It can also be noted that these approaches need not be polarized to the point of mutual exclusivity. Choice of an emic, etic, or combined perspective for defining aggression relates in part to whether the research goals are culturally, comparative or ethnographically focused.

C. A Tentative Consensus for Defining Aggression

In the social and biological sciences, various definitions of aggression have been proposed, but in the recent literature some consensus can be noted that aggression generally refers to acts that inflict physical, psychological, and/or social harm (pain/injury) on an individual or individuals. This definition is considerably more narrow than the range of conceptions about aggression in society generally, yet it is still broad enough to include physical and verbal, and direct and indirect, actions. It also is broad enough to encompass diverse forms of "harm" to the recipient, including various social harms. The definition also focuses on behavior and its consequences, rather than on attributes of the actor(s), whether they be long term (e.g., personality, cultural) or short term (e.g., intentions, emotions). Also, this conceptual definition of aggression can branch in both emic and etic directions. On the one hand, this definition can provide a *general* point of departure for subsequent emic specification. That is, a researcher can pursue an emic understanding of what types of acts cause physical, psychological, and/or social harm within a particular cultural belief system. Or heading in an etic direction, this same conceptual definition of aggression also can be operationalized in specific ways for either culturally internal or culturally comparative purposes. As discussed above, the gathering of emic information on aggression does not preclude the undertaking of culturally comparative etic analyses also, and vice versa.

D. Difficulties in Defining Altruism

While the idea of acting for the social good or for the benefit of others is a concept that has been considered for centuries, Charles Batson notes that Auguste Comte (1798–1857) coined the term *altruism* only about 150 years ago to refer to an unselfish desire to live for others, a term he juxtaposed to *egoism*, or, the desire for self-gratification and self-benefit. More recently, *Webster's Third New International Dictionary* defines Comte's term as "uncalculated consideration of, regard for, or devotion to others' interests sometimes in accordance with an ethical principle."

In recent decades, the concept of altruism has taken two definitional directions, with the development of a relatively standard evolutionary definition, on the one hand, and a more diverse set of ethical and motivational definitions, on the other. In evolutionary terms, altruism can be defined as any act that increases the fitness of others while simultaneously decreasing the fitness of the actor. For example, a noted biological theorist, Robert Trivers (1971, 35), proposes that "altruistic behavior can be defined as behavior that benefits another organism, not closely related, while being apparently detrimental to the organism performing the behavior, benefit and detriment being defined in terms of contribution to inclusive fitness."

The reason that evolutionists have paid a great deal of attention to altruism in recent decades is because behaviors that are *genuinely* altruistic in an evolutionary sense pose a problem for the neo-Darwinian theory of natural selection. Namely, if altruistic behaviors are detrimental to the fitness of the individual engaging in them, while simultaneously increasing the fitness of others, then how could such behaviors have evolved? True altruism should be selected against by natural selection, since by definition, it lowers the fitness of the individual performing the act. Jeffery Kurland, Robert Trivers, and others have independently noted that upon careful examination, many behaviors that at first seemed to be altruistic in nature, actually may benefit the individuals engaging in the behaviors. For example, the helping behavior of older offspring towards their parents in rearing younger siblings, the giving of warning calls when a predator approaches, or the sharing of food—actions previously suspected or assumed to be examples of evolutionary altruism—have been shown also to accrue certain fitness benefits to the performers of the behaviors. Two primary mechanisms (1) kin selection/inclusive fitness and (2) reciprocal altruism have been used to reinterpret many actions once assumed to be strictly altruistic and will be discussed further in section III.

Generally, definitions of altruism used in the social sciences and humanities tend to focus on ethics and/or motivations, not evolutionary fitness. For example, Charles Batson (1991, 6) proposes that altruism be defined as "a motivational state with the ultimate goal of increasing another's welfare." Paul Miller, Jane Bernzweig, Nancy Eisenberg, and Richard Fabes (1991, 54) also focus on motivations: "altruistic behaviors are defined as those prosocial behaviors that are motivated by other-oriented concern (e.g., sympathy) and internalized values. Additionally, altruistic behaviors are defined as *not* being motivated primarily by the desires to obtain concrete or social rewards or to reduce aversive internal states (e.g., anxiety, guilt) due to being exposed to another's distress or knowing that one has not behaved appropriately." Finally, Walter Swap (1991, 156) offers a definition of altruism as "behavior intended to, and resulting in, benefit to a needy recipient unrelated to the actor; that does not intentionally benefit the actor or, especially, that involves some sacrifice by the actor; and which occurs outside a normal helping role, or despite a help inhibiting role."

The variation in the nonevolutionary definitions of altruism is an indication that multiple theoretical and conceptual questions are involved, some of which are discussed by Batson, Kurland, Miller and his coauthors, Swap, and others. A mere sampling of the questions that have been considered include: How can a person's true motivations be determined? If motivation involves a mixture of altruistic and self-interested considerations, should the behavior be considered altruism? Does true altruism, untainted by some self-interest, really exist? What about cases when actions do *not* appear to be based on conscious motivations or conscious calculations (such as spur of the moment rescue attempts)? Is it necessary to consider motivations at all in defining altruism or can altruism be assessed based on a consideration of the effects of behaviors? What are the "currencies" of altruism (evolutionary fitness, money, resources, risks, etc.)? Should behavior directed toward relatives be included or excluded from a definition of altruism? Why or why not?

Several observations can be offered. First, given the number of unresolved issues pertaining to the definition of altruism, perhaps it is not surprising that the only feature that all of the above quoted evolutionary and nonevolutionary definitions of altruism have in common is that *an actor is benefiting other(s)*. Evolutionary definitions (for example, that of Trivers) specify that fitness is the currency relevant for assessing the costs and benefits of behaviors both to the actor and recipient(s), while other definitions more vaguely and more diversely refer to satisfying "needs" of the recipient (as in Swap's definition), the "welfare" of another or the group (as in Batson's definition), and so on. Because evolutionary definitions of altruism share a focus on fitness, it is not surprising that they are fairly uniform, differing more in terms of phrasing and style than regarding the central concept itself. A second feature—which almost all of the definitions include—is the idea that altruism involves self-sacrifice, or "costs" to the actor. For evolutionary definitions, "costs," like "benefits," are assessed in terms of fitness. In other definitions, self-sacrifice implies various "currencies" such as giving up or sharing resources, spending time helping, or taking risks for the recipient. Only one of the definitions, Batson's, does *not* include the condition of self-sacrifice. Third, most of the definitions (such as Miller's *et al.*, Swap's, and *Webster's*) hold that the actor is "uncalculating," or not consciously motivated by potential self-gains or self-interest. Finally, at least when viewed from the point of view of the recipient, altruism and aggression have opposite effects: aggression inflicts harm while altruism bestows benefits on others.

II. CULTURAL VARIATION IN AGGRESSION AND ALTRUISM

A. Introduction

The main purpose of this section is to illustrate the tremendous cultural variation that exists regarding how aggression and altruism are manifested. Cultural examples will be presented, including a comparison of aggression and altruism among the peaceful Semai and the violent Waorani. Additionally, several analytical points emerge from a consideration of cultural variation. First, aggression is merely one of many ways that people deal with conflict. Second, culture provides a set of "rules" regarding appropriate expressions of aggression and altruism. Third, a continuum exists ranging from peaceful cultures to violent ones; not all human cultures are violent. Fourth, aggression and altruism are expressed in a multitude of ways, and therefore, different manifestations of each concept may not intercorrelate exactly.

B. Cultural Variation in Conflict Strategies

Since divergent interests among individuals and groups of individuals occur in any society, conflict can be considered a natural aspect of social life. Conflict, however, does not always find expression in aggression, but rather can be dealt with in a variety of ways, for example, by denying its very existence, negotiating a mutually acceptable solution to a problem, appealing to a third party such as a judge, avoiding another person, and so on. In their book, Jeffrey Rubin, Dean Pruitt, and Sung Hee Kim propose that conflict—which they define as perceived divergence of interests—can be viewed in terms of three coping strategies (each with various more specific tactics) and a couple of avoidance strategies. The strategies vary both in terms of outcomes and the perceived feasibility for the parties involved in the conflict. The three coping strategies include contending (high concern for one's own outcomes and low concern for other's outcomes), problem solving (high concern for both one's own and other's outcomes), and yielding (low concern for one's own outcomes and high concern for other's outcomes). The two avoidance strategies—inaction and withdrawal—entail low concern for both one's own and other's outcomes.

Cross-cultural examples illustrate these conflict strategies (as well as culturally specific tactics). In the Middle East, two Bedouins disputing the ownership of a particular camel have the culturally available option of taking their case to an arbitrator within their tribe, and in this system, their own kinfolk guarantee the disputants will follow the ruling of the arbitrator. This is an example of the contending strategy, in this case without tactics involving physical aggression. Instead, a set of tactics based on Bedouin cultural values, social institutions, and kinship organization involve relying on an arbitrating third party and the Bedouin kinship system. Other examples of the contending strategy abound among the Yanomamö people of Amazonia, although recent findings suggest that not all Yanomamö are as violent as those described by Napoleon Chagnon. Culturally specific Yanomamö contending tactics that involve aggression include verbal and physical threatening, exchange of insults, shifting alliance formation for defense and offense, ambushing and raiding, abduction of women, chest-pounding duels, club fights, ax fights, and spear fights.

Among native Hawaiian families and among Semai Senoi bands of Malaysia, conflict-resolving events called *ho'oponopono* and *becharaa'*, respectively, provide examples of the problem-solving strategy for dealing with conflict. The Hawaiian *ho'oponopono* involves discussion, prayer, apology, and forgiveness with the goal of restoring harmonious relations among family members. The Semai *becharaa'* is a formal dispute-resolving assembly. Clayton Robarchek's 1997 chapter describes how the disputants, their kin, and any other interested parties convene at the headman's house. The headman serves as a mediator-arbitrator in the dispute. The headman and others repeatedly emphasizes the interdependence of the band and may recall specific incidences of assistance given and received, in order to remind the disputants of the need to maintain harmony within the band. The *becharaa'* may continue for several hours, or more typically, for several days and nights, continuously, until the conflict is resolved. "All the events leading up to the conflict are examined and re-examined from every conceivable perspective in a kind of marathon encounter group. Every possible explanation is offered, every imaginable motive introduced, every conceivable mitigating circumstance examined," observes Robarchek (1997, 55). The overall emphasis is not to determine which disputant is "right" and which is "wrong," but rather to restore harmonious relations within the band. In the process, an emotional catharsis, or abreaction, seems to take place. Additionally, the value of social harmony and the mutual interdependence of the band are reiterated and reinforced.

Examples of avoidance and yielding strategies are also apparent in a variety of ethnographic contexts. For instance, the avoidance strategy is widely employed among Finns, when faced with conflict, and also is described for the Toraja of Indonesia, the Fore of New Guinea, the !Kung of southern Africa, the Zapotec of southern Mexico, the Buid of the Philippines, and the Chewong of Malaysia, among others (readers are referred to edited volumes by Douglas Fry and Kaj Björkqvist, Ashley Montagu, and Leslie Sponsel and Thomas Gregor for more information). An interesting example of the yielding strategy is provided in Colin Turnbull's book, *The Forest People*, when he describes "the crime of Cephu," an African Mbuti hunter who ignored group obligations, reciprocal exchanges, and attempted to "cheat" others during a cooperative hunt. The band members first responded to these serious social transgressions by employing a series of nonviolent contending tactics: They ridiculed, insulted, criticized, lectured, and laughed at Cephu before finally suggesting that he and his family could leave the band, an outcome that would have been disastrous for Cephu and his kin, since a small group cannot hunt effectively. When faced with group ridicule and the threat of ostracism, Cephu yielded by apologizing profusely and giving up to the rest of the band all of his ill-acquired meat. He was then allowed to remain a member of the band.

C. Cultures with Low Levels of Aggression

While there are numerous cross-cultural examples of aggression—the wife beating of the Yanomamö, the scalp-taking and horse-raiding exploits of the North American Plains cultures such as the Blackfoot, the killing and head-shrinking practices of the Jívaro of South America—anthropologists such as Montagu and Sponsel and Gregor have compiled descriptions of cultures with very low levels of physical aggression, for example, the Buid of the Philippines, the Chewong of Malaysia, the Copper Eskimo of Canada, the Hutterites of Canada and the United States, the Mbuti of central Africa, the Piaroa of Amazonia, the Semai of Malaysia, the Siriono of Bolivia, the Tikopia of the western Pacific, the Toraja of Indonesia, the Veddahs of Sri Lanka, the Yames of Orchid Island near Taiwan, and certain Zapotec communities of Mexico, among others. Physical aggression is just one of a number of ways in which conflict can be dealt with, and every culture has a set of rules regarding to what degree, if any, physical aggression in acceptable, under what circumstances it might be appropriate, and in what manner it can be used. A cross-cultural perspective shows that besides physical aggression, nonphysical contending tactics (e.g., use of arbitrators, judges, or persuasive arguments) as well as numerous yielding, avoiding, and problem-solving tactics are also employed. The selection of particular conflict strategies and tactics is in large part culturally influenced.

The following examples, from Zapotec and Toraja cultures, illustrate how physical aggression can be kept at low levels. Various mechanisms reduce aggression in a Mexican Zapotec community that Douglas Fry refers to as La Paz. First, the members of this tranquil community share—and regularly express—an image of themselves and others in their village as peaceful, respectful, cooperative, and nonjealous. People from La Paz express nonviolent sentiments such as "we are all one family," "we are peaceful," and "we don't fight." It is noteworthy that values and beliefs which discourage aggression also have been reported in other peaceful cultures such as the Buid, Chewong, Mbuti, Semai, and Toraja. Second, children socialized within the La Paz cultural environment learn that acting aggressively is unacceptable. In section IV of this article, socialization practices will be contrasted between La Paz and a neighboring Zapotec village that is markedly more aggressive. Third, members of this peaceful community act in accordance with their internalized attitudes that favor conflict avoidance, denial of anger, and the prevention of dispute escalation. La Paz Zapotec are likely to respond to another's anger or potential aggression by withdrawing. Such community attitudes also are reflected in the opinion of one La Paz citizen that it is better to drop a grievance against another person than to "prolong a dispute and make someone angry at you for a long time" (Fry, 1994, 141). While the village mayor and other local authorities are available to mediate and adjudicate disputes in the formal setting of the municipal building—a fourth peace-maintaining mechanism—many, if not most, conflicts in fact never make it to the "courtroom" due to the self-restraint and the peace-ensuring beliefs held by the citizens of the community. As can be seen in Table I, which summarizes some of the psychocultural factors that minimize aggression in La Paz, many mechanisms that inhibit physical aggression are internalized, or intra-individual processes.

The Toraja of Indonesia also devalue anger and aggression, and their maintenance of a peaceful life-style is discussed by Douglas Hollan in a book edited by Fry and Björkqvist. The Toraja place a high value on cooperation and community interdependence. They manage to avoid and defuse many conflicts, keeping them from ever becoming aggressive. Part of the Toraja's success at maintaining social tranquility is due to mutually reinforcing psychocultural checks on conflict and aggression. For instance, when someone has a conflict with another person, avoidance of that individual is a typical response. The Toraja also believe that feeling anger can be harmful to one's health, so for this and other reasons, they avoid discussing distressing events—including conflict situations—that might evoke or prolong feelings of distress, anger, or envy in themselves or others. If a person feels wronged in some way by another, the cultural belief that supernatural forces eventually give each person what he or she deserves can have a calming, peace-maintaining effect by helping to remove any thoughts of pressing a grievance

TABLE I

Zapotec Psycho-Cultural Conflict Management Mechanisms

Level 1: Internal (intra-individual)	Level 2: External-informal	Level 3: External-formal
Denial of anger. Denial that a conflict exits. Avoidance of conflict situations and/or disputants. Internalization of values incompatible with the expression of aggression (e.g., respect, equality). Positive image of others in the community. Fear of witchcraft. Beliefs that anger, hostility, and/or aggression are associated with illness. Fear of gossip.	Gossip. Witchcraft. Intervention by nonauthoritarian other(s), such as a family member. Ostracism.	Local authority structure for mediation and adjudication of disputes; allows for the airing of grievances, apologies, reconciliation, and punishments, such as fines and overnight jailtime. District and state authorities; hearings, legal fees, fines, prison sentences.

Note: Level 1 is largely self-imposed, although culturally constructed. Levels 2 and 3 are both largely imposed by others.
Source: Adapted from Fry (1994).

or seeking some form of personal revenge. In conclusion, among the La Paz Zapotec and the Toraja, as well as among various other peaceful cultures, belief systems, attitudes, and norms that discourage aggression while promoting alternative, nonaggressive responses to conflict, coupled with redundant, mutually reinforcing psychocultural mechanisms—including both formal and informal means of dealing with conflict—appear to contribute significantly to the maintenance of a peaceful social life.

D. Variation in Altruism

Interestingly, explicit use of the term altruism is rare within cultural anthropology. This is reflected in the observation that probably the most widely used introductory text in anthropology (now in its 8th edition) has no index or glossary entries for altruism; additionally, a library computer search for altruism in the anthropology data-base produced only 36 sources (most of them related to the evolutionary considerations of altruism), while a comparable search of the psychology data base produced 959 entries. Perhaps this difference in part can be accounted for by the greater usage within anthropology of terms such as cooperation, mutual assistance, helping, care giving, sharing, exchange, and the like, to refer to behavior that sometimes would meet the definition of altruism. For instance, although Douglas Oliver does not use the term altruism, he writes pertaining to a Solomon Island culture that, "although the Siuai have separate terms for 'generosity,' 'cooperativeness,' 'morality' (that is, rule abiding), and 'geniality,' I believe that they consider all these to be closely interrelated aspects of the same attribute of goodness" (in Sahlins, 1965, 153).

Paralleling the cross-cultural variation in conflict and aggression, altruistic and helping behaviors also show cultural influence and cross-cultural diversity. At one extreme, the Ik, an African culture under extreme ecological and social stress, illustrates the egotistic, nonaltruistic capacities of human beings. The prime focus of the Ik is on maintaining a selfish personal autonomy. Providing another example of a culture with minimal sharing, Marshall Sahlins explains how the Dobu, who are extremely suspicious of others, share food only with a small circle of relatives and no one else.

On the other end of the continuum, behaviors such as sharing, generosity, and helping—that is, approximate anthropological synonyms for altruism—are valued in cultures such as the Yukaghir, who voice the belief that a person "who possesses provisions must share them with those who do not possess them," and among the Nuer of Africa, "it is the scarcity and not sufficiency that makes people generous, since everybody is thereby ensured against hunger. He who is in need today receives help from him who may be in like need tomorrow" (Jochelson and Evans-Pritchard, quoted in Sahlins, 1995, 165).

A clear example of self-sacrifice can be drawn from the cultural ideology and behavior of Sikh separatists in India who are fighting for the establishment of their own independent state. Mahmood (1996, 26) discusses the beliefs and actions that sometimes lead to the loss of one's life: "A Sikh on the path of Guru has what is called *charhdi kala*, the ever-rising spirits associated with total liberation from the restrictions of ego. . . . The Sikh denial of fear in the face of danger, which some take as a kind of military bravado, has its roots in the theology of selflessness in which ego's attachment to its own life has been extinguished in favor of identification with a greater spirit." Another example of supreme self-sacrifice engaged in for the benefit of the larger social group, occurred in 1981 when Bobby Sands and 9 other IRA prisoners in Northern Ireland engaged in a hunger strike to the death. The striking men volunteered from a group of 60 IRA prisoners, and they thought that their sacrifice would benefit the other prisoners and their cause in general. The majority of the strikers died as a result of their actions.

Thus a range of behavior extending from the ultimate altruistic sacrifice of one's own life for the good of one's companions, at one end, to the selfish disregard for others, at the other, can be found among humans. Additional examples of these contrasting sides of humanity are apparent as the Semai and Waorani cultures are now compared.

E. Case Study: The Peaceful Semai and the Aggressive Waorani

Anthropologists Clayton and Carole Robarchek have conducted comparative fieldwork among the Semai of Malaysia, who they describe as one of "the world's most peaceful people," and the Waorani of Ecuador, a culture that until recently was "the most violent society known" (1996, 64; 1992, 189, 192). Among the peaceful Semai, "husbands and wives do not assault one another, parents do not physically punish their children, neighbors do not fight with one another, and homicide is so rare as to be virtually nonexistent" (1996, 64). Among the Waorani, at the other extreme, 60% of the deaths over the last five or six generations have been homicides, largely resulting from raiding and feuding. And the Waorani traditionally killed all foreigners on sight.

The Semai and the Waorani are remarkably similar in many ways, including their ecological adaptions and many facets of social organization. Both groups, for example, live at similar altitudes in equatorial rainforests and are swidden gardeners, hunters, and foragers. Their technologies are almost identical. Both the Semai and Waorani are band-level societies. The bands are generally fewer than 100 persons and are autonomous and acephalous. The basic economic unit is the household.

Robarchek and Robarchek account for the extreme differences in aggressiveness between the Semai and the Waorani in terms of differing cultural-social-psychological complexes. Important differences exist between the otherwise similar Semai and Waorani cultures regarding "their assumptions about human beings and the worlds they inhabit, in the cultural values that come to constitute central components of their constructions of self, and in their differing conceptions of the relationships of the individual to a wider community" (1996, 66).

During socialization and enculturation, each Semai acquires a group-dependent self-conception and an image of a dangerous and hostile world external to the band, with security and nurturance only stemming from kin and other band members. In marked contrast, Waorani socialization results in both women and men who see themselves as independent from others and self-reliant. Waorani culture values and emphasizes individualism and autonomy; Semai culture stresses the interdependence of the band members and promotes sharing, generosity, and helping behavior. Robarchek and Robarchek (1992, 203) quote the commonly reiterated Semai ideal pertaining to all the relationships within the band: "We are all siblings here and we take care of one another." Among the Waorani, values of autonomy, independence, and self-reliance are reflected in the examples of women giving birth alone, men regularly hunting alone for days at a time, the elderly being neglected by their families when they become a burden or at times being speared to death by their relatives, snakebite victims being left in the rainforest to recover or perish on their own, and in the event of a raid, individuals generally running for their lives without assisting others, even their close family members, to escape (1992, 202; 1996, 69–70). In short, among the Waorani, "some assistance can be expected from close kin, but a person's survival and well-being are primarily his or her own responsibility," while among the Semai, by contrast, "any person in need has a legitimate claim on the resources of anyone else in the community" (1996, 67–68). Occasional altruism and helping behavior can be found among close relatives in Waorani society, while by contrast sharing and generosity are common occurrences within the entire Semai band: "They inform a self-image that has generosity and nonviolence as its central components. Since most people do, in fact, approximate this ideal, the image is actualized in day-to-day behavior" (1996, 69).

In essence, the central cultural values, worldviews, and conceptions of self differ dramatically between these two cultures. Regarding both aggression and altruism, it is hard to image two cultures that are more different. The Semai stress generosity, sharing, cooperation, unity, and dependence, while the Waorani emphasize individual independence, autonomy, and self-reliance. The Semai see the peace and harmony of the band as paramount and conceptualize themselves as critically dependent on others in the band; the Waorani lack a sense of community and disputes are primarily the concern of the actual participants. The Semai value nonviolence, while this obviously is not true of the Waorani. As discussed earlier in this section, the Semai have a special conflict resolution mechanism, the *becharaa'*, which serves primarily to restore harmony and reinforce Semai values following a dispute. In terms of daily life, dominant cultural values, self-conceptualizations, the virtual absence of homicides, and other indicators, the Semai are one of the most peaceful cultures known. Until recent cultural changes (which will be discussed in section VI of this article), the Waorani were the polar opposite of the Semai in this regard, for example, with probably the highest homicide rates of any human culture. "Among the Waorani, neither a commitment to peacefulness in the abstract nor a concern with the group well-being prevailed. Absent a sense of community, conflict is primarily the concern of the individuals involved and their immediate kin. No formal mechanisms exist for dispute settlement, and when serious conflicts arise, the only options are to surrender, retreat, threaten, or attack" (Robarchek and Robarchek 1996, 71–72).

The cross-cultural variation in aggression and altruism, of which the Semai and Waorani represent contrasting extremes (see Table II), shows that humans are not always or inevitably aggressive. Human beings

TABLE II

Comparison of Semai and Waorani Cultures

Semai (peaceful)	Waorani (aggressive)
Location: Malaysia.	Location: Ecuador.
Live in equatorial rainforests.	Live in equatorial rainforests.
Swidden gardeners; also hunt and gather.	Swidden gardeners; also hunt and gather.
Main crops: Manioc, bananas, plantains.	Main crops: Manioc, bananas, plantains.
Technologies: axes, machetes, blowpipes, spears, etc.	Technologies: axes, machetes, blowpipes, spears, etc.
Social organization: Band level.	Social organization: Band level.
Highly egalitarian.	Highly egalitarian.
Bilateral decent.	Bilateral decent.
Socialization: Indulgent and nonpunitive.	Socialization: Indulgent and nonpunitive.
Resolve disputes through the *Becharaa'*.	No formal mechanism for resolving disputes.
Homicide is virtually nonexistent.	Over the last 5 or 6 generations, 60% of deaths due to homicide.
View the world as a dangerous, hostile place with numerous malevolent supernatural beings and forces.	View the world as nonthreatening and nondangerous except for dangers posed by human violence.
Believe that human beings are helpless and dependent.	Believe that human beings are capable, autonomous, and self-reliant.
The world is beyond human control	The world exists for human purposes and humans can control it.
Impulsive action, emotions, and affect are dangerous and must be controlled.	Humans are emotional and act impulsively; anger is a common explanation for aggression
Kin and other band members provide security and nurturance; outsiders are dangerous.	Social obligations are limited to the closest kin; all other Waorani are potential enemies; non-Waorani traditionally were killed on sight.
Religious rituals are focused toward gaining assistance of protective spirits to cure and prevent the illness caused by malevolent spirits.	There are few taboos, no protective spirits, and little use of magic.
Living in a dangerous world, humans are dependent on their kin and other band members for security, nurturance, and support.	Human skills and knowledge are seen as adequat for satisfying human needs; each individual is largely self-reliant.
Sharing, helping, cooperating are common, on a bandwide basis.	Sharing, helping, cooperating are uncommon and limited to close kin.

Note: Information in this table is compiled from Robarchek and Robarchek (1996).

have capacities that range between the extremes of Semai peacefulness and cooperativeness to Waorani violence and autonomy. Thus the human species exhibits a great deal of flexibility regarding selfishness and helping behaviors, aggression and peacefulness, and the manifestation of these behaviors depends on interacting psychocultural processes. Consequently violence is not an inevitable human characteristic seen in all cultures.

III. AGGRESSION AND ALTRUISM IN RELATION TO SOCIAL DISTANCE

A. Evolutionary and Cultural Considerations of Kin Selection and Reciprocal Altruism

In 1964, theoretical biologist William Hamilton suggested that the degree of biological relatedness between socially interacting individuals affects the manner in which they interact with each other. The more closely individuals are related, the more examples of helping, sharing, and caring should be expected, while harmful behaviors such as aggression, should be minimized in accordance with the closeness of the genetic relationship. Hamilton reasoned that since relatives share a certain percentage of genes in common, helping relatives is an indirect way to enhance one's own genetic fitness. Hamilton (1964, 19) called this idea inclusive fitness, reasoning that "the social behaviour of a species evolves in such a way that in each behaviour-evoking situation the individual will seem to value his neighbours' fitness against his own according to the coefficients of relationship appropriate to that situation." Hamilton was *not* suggesting that individuals *consciously* calculate the degree to which they are related to others before behaving either altruistically or selfishly, but rather that natural selection performs this fitness "cost-benefit" analysis on individuals over many generations.

The concept of inclusive fitness, also sometimes called kin selection, provides one answer to the evolutionary problem, mentioned in section I, regarding how altruism could have evolved if it is detrimental to the fitness of the actor. That is, Hamilton's concept of inclusive fitness extends the evaluation of an individual's fitness beyond the individual to include also the individual's relatives, those who carry some of the same genes. For example, when an individual protects and cares for close relatives, thereby increasing the relatives' chance of survival and their fitness, the actor is simultaneously enhancing his or her own inclusive fitness. When this is the case, such sacrifices cannot truly be called altruism in an evolutionary meaning.

Over the last decades, as discussed separately by Jeffery Kurland and Robert Trivers, biologists investigating animal behavior in relation to the inclusive fitness, kin selection concept have found a great deal of evidence to support the model. For example, alarm calls previously assumed to be altruistic have been determined to be given by mothers and directed at their own offspring and other relatives, and helping behavior of older siblings in avian species have been found to be beneficial to the helper's own fitness, and hence not an example of altruism at all.

Turning to humans, helping relatives is thought to be such normal and natural human behavior that it is at least partially taken for granted. In 1965, social-cultural anthropologist Marshall Sahlins reviewed the cross-cultural patterns of exchange relationships in what has become a classic paper. Sahlins reminds the reader of 19th century anthropologist Edward Tyler's dictum that one of the primary principles of social life is that kindness goes with kindred, a point reflected in the common derivation of these two English words. Sahlins employs three terms to classify reciprocity in social relationships: generalized, balanced, and negative. Sahlins sees these types of reciprocity as forming a continuum from "assistance freely given" in generalized reciprocity to "self-interested seizure, appropriation by chicanery or force" in negative reciprocity (1965, 144). Sahlins uses copious cross-cultural examples to illustrate how these forms of reciprocity correlate with kinship distance: "Reciprocity is inclined toward the generalized pole by close kinship, toward the negative extreme in proportion to kinship distance" (1965, 149). Generalized reciprocity "refers to transactions that are putatively altruistic, transactions on the line of assistance given and, if possible and necessary, assistance returned.... 'sharing,' 'hospitality,' 'free gift,' 'help,' and 'generosity'" (1965, 147). Sahlins notes that generalized reciprocity—for example the suckling of an infant by its mother or the sharing of food among close relatives—lacks any expectation of direct repayment. Lorna Marshall's (1961, 231) observation pertaining to the !Kung also corresponds with this assessment: "Altruism, kindness, sympathy, or genuine generosity were not qualities which I observed often in their behaviour. However, these qualities were not entirely lacking, especially between parents and offspring, between siblings and between spouses."

Balanced reciprocity involves a direct and equal exchange, as seen in trade or gift exchange, while negative reciprocity is an attempt to get something for nothing through haggling, theft, seizure, and so on. Negative reciprocity can involve aggression, and again, the cross-cultural data indicate that negative reciprocity tends to occur at the greatest social distances. Sahlins' (1965, 149) comment that, "it is a long way from suckling a child to a Plains Indians' horse-raid," reflects the arrangement of altruistic-to-aggressive behaviors along the social distance continuum.

The cross-cultural pattern of reciprocity type and social distance is directly in accordance with Hamilton's (1964) inclusive fitness concept. This cross-cultural pattern suggests that relatives generally are less likely to behave so as to harm one another, while to the contrary, relatives are most likely to engage in altruistic acts for one another. Pertaining to both aggression and prosocial behavior, R. Dunbar, Amanda Clark, and Nicola Hurst provide additional evidence that behavioral decisions do in fact relate to inclusive fitness, kin-selection considerations. These researchers analyze historical data on Viking populations and find that kinship is involved in decisions regarding both alliance formation and revenge murder. Viking alliances were more likely to be made among relatives than among unrelated families, and the kin-based alliances also proved to be longer in duration and involved less preconditions than alliances among nonrelatives. Dunbar, Clark, and Hurst also conclude that decisions related to homicides reflect both inclusive fitness theory and cost-benefit ratios. Nonrelatives were murdered at times for no economic gain—such as during drunken brawls—whereas relatives were infrequently killed to begin with, but when a relative was killed, there always existed some substantial benefit for the killer. Much evidence presented by Martin Daly and Margo Wilson on homicides in different settings also are in accordance with inclusive fitness theory. For instance, they demonstrate that when murders occur within a household, biological relatives are much less likely to be the victims than are nonbiological relatives.

The concept of reciprocal altruism, like inclusive fitness, is relevant for re-interpreting behaviors that sometimes were assumed to be examples of genuine altruism. Reciprocal altruism can be seen as an example of what Sahlins calls balanced reciprocity, or equal exchange. The originator of the reciprocal altruism concept, Robert Trivers (1985, 361), explains the concept as "the trading of altruistic acts in which benefit is larger than cost so that over a period of time both enjoy a net gain."

The balanced exchange of goods and obligations is nearly ubiquitous across cultures. Lorna Marshall (1961, 239), for example, notes that a meat sharing rule among the !Kung is that "the person who receives a gift of meat must give a reciprocal gift some time in the future." This rule closely reflects the reciprocal altruism concept.

Divergent theoretical perspectives within anthropology have proposed different interpretations of reciprocal exchange. On the one hand, exchange has been interpreted by functionalists and economic substantivists as representing altruistic and integrative behaviors serving the social group overall. This perspective speaks of the integrative value of reciprocity and the community intent of protecting social group solidarity. On the other hand, formal economic anthropologists and others view reciprocal exchanges as permitting the participants to be better off than they would have been had they not conducted the exchange transaction. For example, John Bennett analyzes exchange among Saskatchewan farmers and ranchers from this perspective. Bennett reports that nearly all ranchers and farmers lend and borrow agricultural machinery on a regular basis, cooperatively assist each other in rounding-up and branding their livestock, and engage in dyadic partnerships and/or labor exchange networks. Bennett notes that while the participants in exchanges represent their activities as spontaneous and altruistic, in actuality, the exchanges are very important economically and each party benefits.

While inclusive fitness can account for some types of human altruism, humans often aid nonrelatives. As Trivers (1971, 39) suggests, the concept of reciprocal altruism accounts for such actions, because he explains, reciprocal altruism is a kind of symbiosis, "each partner helping the other while he helps himself. The symbiosis has a time lag; one partner helps the other and must wait a period of time before he is helped in turn." This type of arrangement is exactly what Bennett documents for Saskatchewan farmers and ranchers, and also matches Lorna Marshall's (1961, 236) description of meat sharing among the !Kung, wherein "the person one shares with will share in turn when he gets meat and people are sustained by a web of mutual obligation."

Trivers also notes that inclusive fitness and reciprocal altruism are compatible concepts. Both mechanisms can operate simultaneously within an exchange relationship, and each can also operate simultaneously in different exchange relationships. Data from a recent study on information exchange among lobster fishermen not only support both these evolutionary concepts, but also suggest that information sharing may result in the participating individuals maintaining advantageous membership within a web of community social relationships.

C. Beyond Nature Versus Nurture

The study of aggression and altruism is multidisciplinary, and even within anthropology, there are various perspectives on altruism and aggression. For example, psychological anthropologists in approaching altruism and selfishness, aggression or peacefulness, may highlight socialization, enculturation, and/or other social-psychological-cultural processes such as conceptions of self or internalization of values, while evolutionary anthropologists are apt to focus on altruism and aggression using inclusive fitness, sexual selection, reciprocal altruism, and other evolutionary concepts. As mentioned above, the diverse interpretations of reciprocal exchange offered by functionalist, formal economic, and other anthropologists also illustrate the diversity of theoretical interpretations within anthropology.

An anthropological rendition of the nature–nurture fallacy entails juxtaposing evolutionary and more proximate cultural analysis as mutually exclusive perspectives. However, such polarization of explanations is unfortunate, because aggression, altruism, and other multifaceted behaviors are too complex to be accounted for exclusively through any single perspective. Both biological and cultural perspectives can contribute to an understanding of aggression and altruism, and to acknowledge a contribution from biology does not automatically imply "determinism" or "reductionism," nor does it diminish the obviously important influences of culture and learning. Furthermore, evolutionary and proximate interpretations are at times quite complementary.

A model developed by psychologist Kevin MacDonald illustrates an integrated biocultural model of human altruism. MacDonald emphasizes the behavioral flexibility of human beings, and suggests that cognitive, affective, and perceptual processes are based on fundamental biologically based predispositions to respond during individual development to certain social inputs, especially from parents, related to the social learning of altruistic behavior. MacDonald (1984, 103) clearly attempts to integrate evolutionary and a variety of more proximate psychocultural mechanism in his discussion of altruism: "The proposal here is that by understanding altruism as a behavioral system involving a variety of cognitive and affective subsystems and genetic predispositions we will be better able to account for these cross-cultural data." Furthermore, MacDonald's perspective is in accordance with the wide cultural variation from altruistic to egoistic cultural systems, represented in extreme form, for example, through the comparison of the interdependent Semai and the self-reliant Waorani.

IV. SOCIALIZATION AND ENCULTURATION INFLUENCES

A. Introductory Considerations

Socialization and social learning processes are crucial in shaping behaviors, including aggression and altruism. Through socialization within a particular culture, individuals acquire views as to what the world is like and the nature of "human nature," adopt particular attitudes and values, and gain an understanding of the cultural meaning of events and behaviors. In any culture, socialization involves modeling and imitation, reinforcement and punishment, cognition and reflection, and such processes have direct influences on the development of aggressive, peaceful, altruistic, and egocentric attitudes and behaviors. Psychologists note that conditions which have been shown to be particularly relevant to the learning and continuance of aggressive behavior patterns, for example, are those in which aggression is reinforced, there are many opportunities to witness aggression in others, there are few opportunities for developing affective social ties with others, and the individual personally is a recipient of aggression. Longitudinal psychological studies show that both aggressive and prosocial behaviors tend to persist into adulthood once they are learned in childhood; in one study, individuals who behaved aggressively when they were 8-years-old also tended to behave aggressively when they were 30-years-old. The same intra-individual consistency also was found for prosocial behaviors such as sharing.

B. An Example: The Learning of Peacefulness or Aggressiveness among Zapotec Children

A comparison of two Zapotec communities illustrates the impact of socialization and enculturation influences on the development of conflict styles. San Andrés and La Paz are pseudonyms for two endogamous Zapotec communities, studied by Douglas Fry, that are similar in many respects and lie about 6 kilometers apart in the Valley of Oaxaca in southern Mexico.

La Paz is considerably more peaceful than San Andrés. The murder and physical assault rates are higher in San Andrés, fistfights and wife beatings are more common in San Andrés, and children are struck more often. Additionally, the community images and ideologies related to conflict differ in the two communities. The people of La Paz hold a consistent image of themselves as peaceful and respectful people, while the citizens of San Andrés perceive that at least some persons from their community are aggressive and disrespectful. In other words, these communities present the growing child with different social and ideological learning environments, conducive to learning and adopting differing modes of interaction with other persons. Youngsters in La Paz see adults avoiding physical aggression and overt expressions of conflict, while simultaneously cooperating and treating others with respect. These children from La Paz hardly ever witness physical aggression, nor are they likely to be the objects of aggression themselves, because adults in this community consider words to be appropriate for effective child rearing. Parents emphasize the importance of teaching, explaining, and showing their children appropriate behaviors; one La Paz father expressed a typical sentiment, that "One must explain to the child with love, with patience, so that little by little the child understands you." By contrast, in San Andrés, a homicide occurs every 3-to-5 years, and the growing children of the community hear the details of such murders repeatedly recounted by the adults. The youngsters of San Andrés also have many opportunities to observe fistfights, wife beatings, and child beatings with their own eyes, and they learn in this cultural environment that the use of physical aggression is sometimes acceptable.

Systematic behavior observations which Fry conducted on samples of 3-to-8 year-old children in La Paz and San Andrés revealed that La Paz children participated in significantly less aggression and play aggression than San Andrés children. The nature and content of the children's aggression also differed between the two communities. The less frequent aggressive episodes in La Paz were also less severe, consisting of proportionately more noncontact threatening and less actual physical aggression compared with the aggressive episodes engaged in by the San Andrés children. Additionally, while over the 3-to-8 year age range play aggression significantly increased in San Andrés, the same was *not* the case in La Paz. There also is some indication that nonplay, or serious, aggression increased over this age range in San Andrés and decreased with age in La Paz, this latter trend being extremely close to statistical significance.

Considered together, the behavioral findings suggest that a reluctance to engage in aggression and play aggression already has developed in the 3-to-8 year age range among La Paz children relative to the San Andrés children. These differences in children's behavior correspond with the interpretation that different beliefs and values regarding the expression of aggression and prosocial behaviors such as respect are internalized beginning at an early age in these two communities. Prevalent attitudes regarding what constitutes acceptable behavior, shared expectations about the nature of the citizenry, and overall images of the community's aggressiveness and peacefulness are all elements of a child's learning environment. Through socialization, even by the 3-to-8 year age range, La Paz children have begun to develop internal controls against engaging in both aggression and play aggression. While the total picture as to why La Paz and San Andrés differ regarding conflict and aggression involves various interacting factors, the findings on differences in children's behavior clearly indicate that the differing socialization environments are contributing to the perpetuation of community differences in peacefulness and aggressiveness.

V. SEX AND GENDER

A. Sex Differences

Cross-culturally, men are more *physically* aggressive than women. For example, cross-culturally, with very few exceptions, it is men who fight in wars. Men also tend to commit more homicides than women, as demonstrated, for instance, by Martin Daly and Margo Wilson in their book *Homicide*. After reviewing the psychological literature, Eleanor Maccoby and Carol Jacklin (1974, 368) conclude that "the greater aggressiveness of the male is one of the best established, and most pervasive, of all psychological sex differences." However, Kaj Björkqvist and Pirkko Niemelä have suggested that much of the Western psychological literature on gender differences in aggression focuses primarily on physical aggression and also reflect other methodological limitations. Nonetheless, psychological, anthropological, and criminological sources suggest that physical aggression is both more frequent and more severe among males than females, and this species-typical pattern (which also is typical of mammals generally) is understandable through evolutionary models advanced by Martin Daly and Margo Wilson, and Robert Trivers in his 1985 book, among others, that consider differential male-female parental investment and sexual selection.

Based on the findings of a cross-cultural survey of societies, Victoria Burbank emphasizes that simply because males are physically more aggressive than females does not mean that women are always nonaggressive.

Burbank reports that women do engage in physical aggression in 61% of 137 cultures she examined. To consider a specific ethnographic example, Kimberley Cook reports that out of 18 instances of physical aggression she observed on Margarita Island off the coast of Venezuela, eight (44%) involved women being physically aggressive. Cook (1993, 63) writes, "In San Fernando, the use of verbal and physical aggression by women is a frequent and expected occurrence.... Upon several occasions I observed women engaged in ferocious verbal fight among themselves which were accompanied by fist waving, insults, and the hurling of pebbles at the feet of their opponents." Victoria Burbank, Kimberley Cook, and Nicole Hines and Douglas Fry, among other researchers, have described physical and verbal aggression among women in cultures ranging from the Argentines and Australian Aborigines to the Zambians and Zapotecs. "Women in Argentina do engage in physical aggression. They may push and shove each other in lines or hit their husbands or boyfriends. But women's physical aggression is perceived as less frequent, less severe, and relatively harmless compared to men's aggression" (Hines and Fry 1994, 232). Hence, women in some cultural settings do engage in physical aggression, although they are generally less physically aggressive than men.

Women may well express aggression differently than men. As discussed in section I, aggression can be verbal as well as physical, and indirect as well as direct. In Argentina, both sexes are verbally aggressive, and this finding corresponds with several reviews, such as Burbank's, that suggest that both men and women use verbal aggression. However, the subtleties of how men and women employ verbal aggression within various cultural settings have yet to be studied.

B. Indirect Aggression

Indirect or covert aggression involves use of social networks, third parties, elements of the social organization, and/or other covert means to inflict harm on another individual. By using indirect aggression, the attacker can inflict physical, psychological, and/or social harm on a victim, perhaps without ever being detected. Indirect aggression, as expressed within the social context of a given cultural meaning system, might entail, for example, the spreading of malicious gossip about someone, arranging for the social exclusion of a rival from group activities, blocking social benefits that an individual would otherwise accrue, arranging for a third party to attack the victim, either verbally or physically, practicing witchcraft or sorcery directed at harming the victim, and so on. Research on conflict behavior in Finland conducted by Douglas Fry provides examples of indirect aggression wherein persons maliciously provide government agencies with "tips" about supposed wrongdoings committed by other persons that range, for instance, from alleged zoning infractions to tax avoidance. The reported persons then suffer various degrees of embarrassment, aggravation, and lost time and resources, necessitated by having to respond to investigations launched by authorities. Research indicates that at least in several cultural contexts, females may make greater use of indirect aggression than males, although members of both sexes have been found to employ indirect tactics. Examples of women employing indirect aggression, perhaps in greater frequency than men, have been noted for Finland, Argentina, and Mexican Zapotec. For instance, among Argentines of Buenos Aires "women, more than men, favor indirect aggression ... respondents tend to agree that women, more than men, judge others, gossip, lie about others, exclude persons from social events, and interrupt conversations" (Hines and Fry 1994, 231).

In conclusion, cross-culturally men tend to engage in more physical aggression, and more severe physical aggression, such as homicides, than women. However, women also are reported to engage in physical aggression in many cultures, although incidences may be rare. And, as discussed in previous sections, some cultures have very low levels of physical aggression overall, among *both* sexes. Cultural patterns are clearly very influential regarding the expression of both male and female aggression, as shown, for instance, by Cook's work in Margaritaño society. And as shown by Burbank, there are numerous cases of both men and women acting verbally aggressive cross-culturally. Finally, there is tentative evidence from several cultural settings that women may make greater use of indirect aggression than men.

VI. CONCLUSIONS: HUMAN FLEXIBILITY AND VIOLENCE REDUCTION

A. Human Flexibility and Social Change

History and anthropology provide numerous instances of major social change, including examples of cultures supplanting violent practices or institutions with less violent ones, sometimes on their own and at other times when influenced by outside forces. James Greenberg recounts how a Chatino community in the southern highlands of Mexico, which was once fraught with violent murders and maimings, instituted an agrarian reform and, in a movement initiated by the women and later supported by the majority of villagers, banned alcohol consumption—a major social change—which drastically reduced the bloodshed. Greenberg (1989, 231) recounts that "sick of seeing their men killed in blood feuds, the women of the village had organized and had managed to pass an ordinance prohibiting the sale and consumption of alcohol and the carrying of knives or guns. These measures were effective and put an end to the blood feuding and factionalism in the village." This ban on alcohol was strictly enforced, for the good of the community, and even when someone from the village was seen drinking in a neighboring town, they were jailed and fined upon their return to the village, even if sober at that time.

Another example of social change leading away from violence is the abolition of the army in Costa Rica in 1948, an action that created the world's first totally disarmed country. Oscar Arias (1997, 148) expresses that the spirit of peace lives on "in a country that has proven the seemingly utopian hypothesis that a small, poor, demilitarized country can survive amidst mighty and wealthy neighbors. Costa Rica serves as an example of peace and democracy in a region of war and dictatorship."

In section II of this article, the Waorani of Ecuador are described as an example of an extremely violent society. Besides demonstrating a cultural extreme regarding aggressiveness and self-reliance, the Waorani also dramatically illustrate the human capacity to enact cultural change, to bring about peace. While not becoming an inherently nonviolent society, the Waorani have managed to reduce their homicide rate by *more than 90%* in a matter of a few years. Clayton and Carole Robarchek (1996, 76) explain: "The killers are still there—many were our friends and neighbors—but with relatively rare exceptions, they have stopped killing. They were not conquered or incarcerated, nor were they incorporated as equals into the socioeconomic system of Ecuadorian society. Rather, new leaders emerged who possessed new information and offered a new set of alternatives."

The catalyst for the astounding reduction in violence among the Waorani, as among the Chatino studied by James Greenberg, involved women. Two Waorani women, who had fled the territory to escape being killed in vendettas, returned in the accompaniment of two Protestant missionary women. The two returnees presented the other members of their culture with a new vision of the world, one where all outsiders did not have to be killed upon contact and one where feuding could cease. The two women missionaries provided the means through airplane gift-drops and radio-technology to make initial contacts with a widening circle of hostile Waorani groups. Robarchek and Robarchek (1996, 72) describe how newly contacted hostile groups also were presented with the possibility of a new reality, a reality based on peace, "without constant fear of violent death. As bands became convinced that the feuding could stop, peace became a goal in its own right, even superseding the desire for revenge." The cultural change was not brought about simply through a Christianization process. The decision, though, to end the vendettas and pursue a new, more peaceful reality was "reinforced among some, but by no means all, individuals and groups by the acceptance of some of the other Christian values and beliefs stressed by the missionaries. The result was that new cultural knowledge—new information and new perceptions of reality—allowed people to visualize new options and new goals" (Robarchek and Robarchek 1996, 72). In essence, the Waorani themselves decided that they wanted to stop the violence and adopt a new manner of existence.

B. Conclusions

Aggression and altruism can be seen as opposites: aggressive acts cause *harm* to others, while altruistic acts *benefit* others. Clearly, both aggression and altruism are greatly affected by cultural processes. Cross-cultural comparisons show the range of possible aggressive and altruistic behaviors engaged in by humans. Some cultures have extremely low levels of physical aggression, while others have very high levels of physical aggression. Levels and manifestations of altruism also vary across cultures. However, among the cultural variation, underlying patterns also can be detected. The greatest degrees of altruism, helping, sharing, and caring tend to occur among close relatives, and these behaviors decrease in intensity as social distance between individuals increases. Furthermore, with greater social distance, restraints against aggression seem to decrease. These general tendencies are not without exceptions, of course, but the patterns are detectable across numerous social circumstances. Sex differences in aggression also show a cross-cultural pattern. While women engage in physical aggression in many cultures, the cross-cultural pattern is that men are more frequently and more severely physically aggressive than women. However, it should be held in mind that in some cultures, both women and men are nonaggressive.

The bold political decision of Costa Rican leaders to abolish their armed forces and the violence-reduction successes of the Chatino and Waorani peoples clearly show the tremendous potential for human cultural change. These examples considered in conjunction with the other evidence reviewed in this article—such as the comparisons between the peaceful Semai and violent Waorani and between the peaceful Zapotec community of La Paz and more aggressive San Andrés—demonstrate the extent of human flexibility regarding aggression and altruism. The great cultural variation in human aggression and altruism is possible because of human behavioral flexibility. Behavioral flexibility also makes possible cultural transitions away from violence, cultural transformations that the Chatino, Costa Rican, and Waorani examples demonstrate can be as dramatic in their magnitude as they are rapid in their realization. The evidence considered in this article shows that while conflicts may be part and parcel of social life, physical aggression need not be. Many alternatives to violence exist, and it is possible for societies to become less violent.

Also See the Following Articles

AGGRESSION, PSYCHOLOGY OF • CLAN AND TRIBAL CONFLICT • CULTURAL ANTHROPOLOGY STUDIES • EVOLUTIONARY FACTORS • EVOLUTIONARY THEORY • GENDER STUDIES • NEUROPSYCHOLOGY OF MOTIVATON FOR GROUP AGGRESSION • PEACEFUL SOCIETIES

Acknowledgments

The author is grateful to scholars C. Brooks Fry and Heikki Sarmaja for engaging in stimulating discussions on the subject matter and also for providing bibliographic sources.

Bibliography on Altruism

Batson, C. D. (1991). *The altruism question: Toward a social-psychological answer.* Hillsdale, NJ: Lawrence Erlbaum Associates.

Bennett, J. W. (1968). Reciprocal economic exchanges among North American agricultural operators. *Southwestern Journal of Anthropology,* 24, 276–309.

Dunbar, R. I. M., Clark, A., & Hurst, N. L. (1995). Conflict and cooperation among the Vikings: Contingent behavioral decisions. *Ethology and Sociobiology,* 16, 233–246.

Hamilton, W. D. (1964). The genetical evolution of social behaviour. II. *Journal of Theoretical Biology,* 7, 17–52.

Kurland, J. A. (1996). Altruism. In D. Levinson & M. Ember (Eds.), *Encyclopedia of cultural anthropology* (Volume 1, pp. 50–52). New York, NY: Henry Holt & Co.

MacDonald, K. (1984). An ethological-social learning theory of the development of altruism: Implications for human sociobiology. *Ethology and Sociobiology,* 5, 97–109.

Mahmood, C. K. (1996). Why Sikhs fight. In A. W. Wolfe & H. Yang (Eds.), *Anthropological contributions to conflict resolution* (pp. 11–30). Athens, GA: University of Georgia Press.

Marshall, L. (1961). Sharing, talking, and giving: Relief of social tensions among !Kung bushmen. *Africa,* 31, 231–249.

Miller, P. A., Bernzweig, J., Eisenberg, N., & Fabes, R. A. (1991). The development and socialization of prosocial behavior. In R. A. Hinde & J. Groebel (Eds.), *Cooperation and prosocial behaviour* (pp. 54–77). Cambridge, UK: Cambridge University Press.

Robarcheck, C. A., & Robarchek, C. J. (1992). Cultures of war and peace: A comparative study of Waorani and Semai. In J. Silverberg and J. P. Gray (Eds.), *Aggression and peacefulness in humans and other primates* (pp. 189–213). New York, NY: Oxford University Press.

Sahlins, M. D. (1965). On the sociology of primitive exchange. In M. Banton (Ed.), *The relevance of models for social anthropology* (pp. 139–236). New York, NY: Tavistock.

Swap, W. C. (1991). Perceiving the causes of altruism. In R. A. Hinde & J. Groebel (Eds.), *Cooperation and prosocial behaviour* (pp. 147–158). Cambridge, UK: Cambridge University Press.

Trivers, R. L. (1971). The evolution of reciprocal altruism. *Quarterly Review of Biology,* 46, 35–57.

Trivers, R. L. (1985). *Social evolution.* Menlo Park, CA: Benjamin/Cummings.

Bibliography on Aggression

Arias, O. (1997). Esquipulas II: The management of a regional crisis. In D. P. Fry & K. Björkqvist (Eds.), *Cultural variation in conflict resolution: Alternatives to violence* (pp. 147–158). Mahwah, NJ: Erlbaum.

Björkqvist, K, & Niemelä, P. (1992). New trends in the study of female aggression. In K. Björkqvist & P. Niemelä (Eds.), *Of mice and women: Aspects of female aggression* (pp. 3–16). San Diego, CA: Academic Press.

Burbank, V. K. (1987). Female aggression in cross-cultural perspective. *Behavior Science Research,* 21, 70–100.

Chagnon, N. A. (1992). Yanomamö (4th ed.). Fort Worth, TX: Harcourt, Brace Jovanovich.

Cook, H. B. K. (1993). *Small town, big hell: An ethnographic study of aggression in a Margariteño community.* Caracas, Venezuela: Instituto Caribe de Antropología y Sociologia, Fundación La Salle de Ciencias Naturales.

Daly, M., & Wilson, M. (1988). *Homicide.* New York, NY: Aldine de Gruyter.

Fry, D. P. (1994). Maintaining social tranquility: Internal and external loci of aggression control. In L. E. Sponsel & T. Gregor (Eds.), *The anthropology of peace and nonviolence* (pp. 133–154). Boulder, CO: Lynne Rienner.

Fry, D. P., & Björkqvist, K. (Eds.). (1997). *Cultural variation in conflict resolution: Alternatives to violence.* Mahwah, NJ: Erlbaum.

Greenberg, J. B. (1989). *Blood ties: Life and violence in rural Mexico.* Tucson, AZ: University of Arizona Press.

Heelas, P. (1989). Identifying peaceful societies. In S. Howell & R. Willis (Eds.), *Societies at peace: Anthropological perspectives* (pp. 225–243). New York, NY: Routledge.

Hines, N. J., & Fry, D. P. (1994). Indirect modes of aggression among women of Buenos Aires, Argentina. *Sex Roles,* 30, 213–236.

Maccoby, E., & Jacklin, C. (1974). *The psychology of sex differences.* Stanford, CA: Stanford University Press.

Montagu, A. (Ed.). (1978). *Learning non-aggression: The experience of non-literate societies.* New York, NY: Oxford University Press.

Rubin, J. Z., Pruitt, D. G., & Kim, S. H. (1994). *Social conflict: Escalation, stalemate, and settlement* (2nd ed.). New York, NY: McGraw-Hill.

Robarchek, C. A. (1997). A community of interests: Semai conflict resolution. In D. P. Fry & K. Björkqvist (Eds.), *Cultural variation in conflict resolution: Alternatives to violence* (pp. 51–58). Mahwah, NJ: Erlbaum.

Robarchek, C. A., & Robarchek, C. J. (1996). Waging peace: The psychological and sociocultural dynamics of positive peace. In A. W. Wolfe & H. Yang (Eds.), *Anthropological contributions to conflict resolution* (pp. 64–80). Athens, GA: University of Georgia Press.

Silverberg, J., & Gray, J. P. (1992). Violence and peacefulness as behavioral potentialities of primates. In J. Silverberg & J. P. Gray (Eds.), *Aggression and peacefulness in humans and other primates* (pp. 1–36). New York, NY: Oxford University Press.

Sponsel, L. E., & Gregor, T. (Eds.). (1994). *The anthropology of peace and nonviolence.* Boulder, CO: Lynne Rienner.

Aggression, Psychology of

Leonard Berkowitz
University of Wisconsin-Madison

GLOSSARY

Affective or Expressive Describing violence or aggression that is characterized as having the injury of the target as its primary goal; contrasted with instrumental violence.

Association In this context, the principle that aggression in response to a negative event will be directed toward a target that is psychologically associated with the origin of that negative event, even though this target may not be the actual cause of the event.

Aversion The principle or theory that painful or highly unpleasant physical conditions will tend to generate anger and aggression, even in the absence of a perceived cause of those conditions.

Instrumental Describing violence or aggression that is characterized as having some goal other than simply the injury of the target; e.g., to acquire money or social approval.

Priming (Effect) The principle or theory that certain ideas, having been activated by some aspect of the surrounding situation, will then tend to "prime" other semantically related ideas so that they come more readily to mind.

THIS ARTICLE will focus on the theorizing and research of many of the leading social-psychological investigators of human aggression. Relatively little attention will be given to psychodynamic and psychoanalytic conceptions since these ideas have little part in guiding the empirically oriented, largely laboratory-based research to be covered here. And moreover, because of the necessary space limitations, I will concentrate on the sources of aggressive conduct and will not deal with such vitally important matters as the consequences of an aggressor's assault and how aggressive tendencies can be controlled.

I. CONCEPTIONS OF AGGRESSION

A. Should Intentions Be Inferred?

Psychologists have not been entirely agreed as to how to define aggression in the past 6 decades and more. Before the widespread adoption of the cognitive perspective in contemporary psychology, some investigators inclined to orthodox behaviorism were unwilling to make inferences about people's intentions, and generally thought of aggression only as an action that delivers noxious stimuli to other persons. Many other writers have gone somewhat farther along these lines by insisting that the main defining criterion has to do with whether the behavior is socially disapproved or not. In their view, most people say an action is aggressive in nature only when they believe the actor had a socially unjustified motive.

This emphasis on the public's moral evaluation obviously has a major difficulty. Social standards vary from group to group and can shift over time. Revolutionaries and their supporters often believe that their cause can at times justify the killing of innocent bystanders whereas such an action is condemned as brutal violence by others. The moral evaluation perspective does not allow us to say unequivocally whether the blowing up of, say, a city bus by a dissident guerrilla group is an act of aggression or not. Similarly, in earlier years society permitted fathers to beat disobedient children but the same punishment is today apt to be viewed as violent child abuse. Is it possible to achieve a truly scientific analysis of this behavior if violence exists only in the eyes of the beholder?

Because of problems such as this, most of the present-day psychological discussions of aggression have been willing to make assumptions about the actors' aims, although they often differ as to specifically what objective the actors were pursuing. Psychologists nowadays rarely link their analyses of this behavior to the formulation employed by Dollard, Doob, Miller, Mowrer, and Sears in their 1939 monograph on the frustration-aggression hypothesis, and few of them share these earlier authors' behavioristic terminology. Nevertheless, many contemporary theorists essentially hold, with the Dollard team, that aggression is "behavior whose goal-response in the inflicting of injury on some object or person." Put more simply, the action is presumably carried out in an attempt to injure the target either psychologically or physically.

B. What Are the Goals of Aggression?

Although aggression is usually regarded as purposive, at least in large degree, analyses of this behavior differ considerably in their specification of what goals are being sought. For some writers aggression is an aversive act aimed primarily at the control of others. Taking this position on the basis of their observations of the interactions among family members, Patterson and his colleagues at the Oregon Research Institute concluded that many hyperaggressive children perform a variety of unpleasant behaviors in an attempt to coerce their parents and/or siblings. These children are then reinforced, so that their conduct is apt to be repeated, if the aggression is successful and the victim acquiesces.

A variation on this theme holds that aggressive behavior is often aimed at preserving or enhancing the attackers' power and dominance. Aggressors may want to get their own way when they assault their victims but, it is sometimes claimed, they want their own way in order to assert their dominant position over those they attacked. This kind of interpretation is often employed in the literature on family violence. Writers in this area frequently contend that the most powerful members of the family—those who have the greatest physical strength or who possess the highest status—are all too likely to assault other family members with less power, especially when the powerful persons believe their dominant position is challenged. In the national survey of domestic violence conducted by Straus, Gelles, and Steinmetz, as a case in point, it was found that battered wives were especially likely to be relatively powerless in their households; quite a few of them lacked paid jobs, had little education, and had little role in household decision making. Noting observations such as this, some authorities suggest that powerless women are easily abused by their psychologically and sociologically more powerful men when there is a dispute.

Perhaps more commonly, especially in psychiatry, sociology, and clinical psychology, aggression is interpreted as a self-preservation or self-enhancement tactic. As an example, several exponents of this conception contend that when people see themselves as threatened or challenged, they think they have been devalued. They may then attack someone in an effort to nullify "the imputed negative identity by showing [their] strength, competence, and courage." In striking at their victim, they seek to show that they are "someone whose self must be respected" (Felson, 1978). The "culture of violence" analyses of the high rates of violence committed by members of particular ethnic groups or in certain geographic areas generally follow this approach. Thus, in Marvin Wolfgang's well-known discussion of group differences in rates of violent crimes, persons who grow up in a violence-prone culture are said to be easily angered because they are quick to define altercations or other interpersonal difficulties as provocations. Presumably, they then believe that they must react aggressively if they are to maintain their standing with the others around them.

Without questioning the validity of all of these interpretations, the most active social-psychological investigators of aggression today usually take a less psychodynamic view of assaultive behavior. In their laboratory experiments they typically view the participants' reactions as an attempt to injure the target, whatever ancillary motives might also be operating. The aggressors presumably want to hurt their victim for the sake of doing harm. This desire to hurt can be seen in the experimental studies of the effects of "pain cues" conducted by Baron and others. As the subjects in one of Baron's experiments administered electric shocks to a peer, supposedly as punishment for that person's mistakes on an assigned task, some of them received information that the shocks were fairly painful to their victim. This pain information actually served to intensify the severity of the shocks given by those subjects who had previously been angered by their target, but reduced the severity of the punishment delivered by the nonangered participants. It is as if the pain information had implicitly told the angry subjects they were close to fulfilling their desire to hurt and "get even" with the one who had provoked them, thereby whetting their "aggressive appetite" still further.

C. Different Goals and Different Types of Aggression

Most social psychological theorists now reconcile the different conceptions just summarized by following the distinction between two types of aggression first proposed by Feshbach in 1964. Although all aggression seeks to hurt the target, they say, in some cases the attack is instrumental to the attainment of other, non-injury-related goals such as money, social approval, an enhanced self-concept, or even the elimination of a source of displeasure. This is the kind of aggression sociological and psychodynamic analysts have in mind when they refer to the defensive and/or self-enhancement purposes served by violence. In other instances, though, the aggression is primarily hostile in nature in that the target's injury is the main objective. This latter type of aggression often arises when people are angered or otherwise emotionally aroused, and thus, is frequently thought of as affective or emotional aggression. Zillmann divided aggressive behavior into similar categories in his 1979 text: incentive-motivated and annoyance-motivated aggression. The first type has to do with aggression controlled by external incentives, and clearly is instrumental in nature. The second category is evoked by aversive stimulation, and thus is relatively emotional. I will argue later, however, that there may well be a third kind of aggression, one that is basically hostile in nature but that is not necessarily the result of an unpleasant experience. For the present, though, the discussion will focus on the two, more widely recognized kinds of aggression.

Outside of psychology, a number of criminologists, such as Zimring and Block, have also drawn this distinction in their crime analyses. Differentiating between instrumental and more expressive violent crimes, they noted that most robberies are instrumental offenses in that the perpetrator is mainly concerned with monetary gain even though he threatens his victim with a gun. By contrast, the man who shoots a neighbor following a quarrel and the husband who beats his wife in an outburst of rage are engaged in affective (or expressive) violence. Of course, an instrumentally oriented offender might assault or even kill his victim if he believes it is to his benefit to do so. But even so, this instrumental aggression is usually different from affective aggression in important respects. As just one example, crime statistics, such as those published by Williams and Flewelling in 1988, suggest that the victims of instrumental crimes are apt to be strangers, whereas the victims of the affective aggression stemming from conflict situations are much more likely to be known to the perpetrators.

It is important to recognize that these two categories of aggression—and other typologies have also been advanced—do not mean that the factors governing one form of aggression have no effect whatsoever on the other kind. Learning, for one thing, can contribute to both. The extrinsic rewards that heighten the likelihood of instrumental aggression can also increase the chances of an aggressive reaction to an aversive situation. Experiments by Walters and Brown in 1963 and by Geen in 1968 have demonstrated this experimentally. And so, in the former study, after schoolchildren had been frustrated (because they could not see a promised movie), those whose make-believe aggression had previously been appropriately rewarded later exhibited more realistic aggression in their game-playing with a peer than did other children who had not received the earlier rewards.

II. DETERMINANTS OF AGGRESSION

A. Biological Influences

1. The Classic Instinct Doctrine

The classic notion of an instinct to aggression espoused by such theorists as Sigmund Freud and Konrad Lorenz is now in disrepute, and few research-oriented zoologists and psychologists subscribe to this idea today. One reason has to do with the instinct doctrine's conception of a unitary drive impelling not only assaults but also the strivings for mastery and for assertiveness; those holding this position, including Freud and Lorenz, generally assumed that all aggression is alike and that all kinds of aggression arise from one common source. As we have seen, this view is not tenable. Perhaps more important, the traditional notion posits a spontaneously generated drive that continually spurs the individual to attack others. Here, too, there is no empirical basis for such a contention. The idea of a reservoir of "aggressive energy" always building up inside the person that somehow must be "drained" has not held up under close, careful examination. Scott's well-known 1958 observation is still a good summary of the evidence:

> There is no physiological evidence of any spontaneous stimulation for fighting arising within the body. This means that there is no need for fighting . . . apart from what happens in the external environment (p. 62).

2. Neurochemical and Hormonal Influences

All this is not to say there are no biological influences on aggression. Neurochemical research indicates that a number of neuroregulators, including norepinephrine and serotonin, have some part in this behavior. Interestingly, just what role these neuroregulators play seems to depend on the type of aggression. Increased norepinephrine is associated with affective aggression but appears to inhibit instrumental (predatory) aggression by animals. There may also be hormonal influences. In a number of species, including monkeys, the prenatal injection of testosterone into females leads to heightened aggressiveness. Research has demonstrated that male hormones can also have an influence at the human level. According to Erhardt and Baker, adolescent females who had been exposed to high levels of androgens in utero tended to engage in more rough and tumble play and initiate more fighting than did their nonandrogenized sisters. And similarly, Reinisch found that when children were asked to say how they would respond to conflict situations, both boys and girls who had been exposed to a masculinizing hormone as fetuses were more likely to prefer physically aggressive reactions than their siblings who had not been exposed to the hormone. The male hormones seem to have these aggression-facilitating effects not by spurring the affected individuals to fight but by so organizing their developing brains, before and soon after birth, in such a manner that they are more inclined to react aggressively to provocations. The Dabbs and Morris investigation of the records of some 4500 U.S. military veterans is also suggestive. In this study, it was only those men with below average income and education whose high testosterone levels were associated with high rates of antisocial behavior. The researchers hypothesized that all of the high-testosterone individuals might have had antisocial predispositions but that those with better income and education had learned to restrain these inclinations, thereby weakening the hormonal influence. In sum, rather than creating an urge to aggression, neurochemicals and hormones apparently facilitate the processes through which aversive events give rise to aggression.

3. Gender Differences in Aggression

The research regarding the influence of male hormones on aggression is obviously highly pertinent to the question of gender differences in aggressiveness. There is now considerable evidence that in most species investigated, from mice to humans, males tend to display more open violence than do their female counterparts. Females in many species do become assaultive at times, of course, especially when fighting off a dangerous intruder, and they occasionally can do as much deliberate harm to others as males do. Nevertheless, in line with what was said above about hormonal influences, over a great variety of situations males are more likely than females to exhibit physical aggression. These differences can be seen in the surveys of the relevant psychological research reported by Maccoby and Jacklin in 1974 and by Eagly and Steffen in 1986, although the latter survey indicated that the differences were greatest in the case of physical aggression. Crime statistics are consistent with these findings. In many different countries around the world, violent criminal offenses are much more apt to be committed by men than by women. Furthermore, although there has been an increase over the past generation in the rate at which women have been arrested for property crimes, there does not seem to have been a corresponding jump in women's commission of violent crimes.

The real dispute in the controversy regarding this gender difference in aggressiveness has to do with why it exists. A good many social scientists, including Eagly and Steffen, believe that women tend to be less assaultive than their masculine counterparts primarily because of how they have been traditionally socialized. Children are generally taught that fighting is more appropriate for males than for females. And not surprisingly, probably because their aggression has been more frequently rewarded as they were growing up, more men than women approve of the use of force and aggression in various areas of life including interpersonal relationships. Maccoby and Jacklin have questioned whether cultural learning sufficiently explains all that is known about gender differences in aggressiveness.

In their view, the following four points strongly indicate that these differences are due to biology as well as culture:

1. Males are more aggressive than females in all human societies for which evidence is available.
2. The sex differences are found early in life, at a time when there is no evidence that differential socialization pressures have been brought to bear by adults to "shape" aggression differently in the two sexes . . .
3. Similar sex differences are found in man [sic] and subhuman primates.
4. Aggression is related to levels of sex hormones.

B. Persistent Antisocial Conduct

1. Consistency in Aggressive Behavior

Even though there is little evidence of built-in biological forces driving people to attack others, there can be little doubt that some persons have a particularly strong predisposition to aggression. In a great many studies, those people who exhibited a relatively high level of aggression on one or more occasions—whether in a personality test or a laboratory experiment or in a "real-world" interpersonal encounter—had a better than chance likelihood of being highly aggressive in other situations as well, especially if the antecedent measure and/or the outcome to be predicted is/are based on an aggregation of a number of situations. Furthermore, this relationship existed in several investigations even when the situations were fairly dissimilar or even quite far apart in time.

2. Longitudinal Studies

Olweus was one of the first psychologists to document the impressive stability in aggressive patterns of conduct over time. In his survey of U.S., English, and Swedish studies of male subjects ranging from 2 to 18 years of age, published in 1979, he reported that initial measures of aggressiveness successfully predicted later aggressiveness in each of the 16 different samples he examined. This relationship was moderately high (average correlation = .7) when the follow-up was a year or less after the first assessment, and then declined regularly to about .4 when there was a 21-year gap between the first and later measurements.

Other psychologists have also seen this consistency over time in their own investigations. The best known of these longitudinal studies probably are those conducted by Farrington and his associates at Cambridge University, based on a sample of working-class boys in London, and by Eron and his colleagues, employing male and female schoolchildren from a rural county in upstate New York. (There are now a number of other such longitudinal investigations as well.) In both cases the participants were first studied when they were about 8 years of age and then were reassessed periodically as they grew older and entered adulthood. Other people's reports of the participants' behavior were the primary measures of aggressiveness but self-reports were also employed and these were supplemented by official records.

The findings of both investigations were remarkably similar. Although a good number of the youngsters changed their conduct with the passage of the years, a sizable fraction of participants tended to maintain their general level of aggressiveness. More particularly, there was a significant likelihood that those who were highly aggressive before puberty would also be among the most aggressive members of their respective samples as teenagers and as young adults. This was true for the females as well as the males in the New York State study. Other research conducted in other Western countries has obtained comparable findings: Early aggressiveness is a risk factor predicting the chances of adult violence.

3. Aggression and Antisocial Behavior

Going beyond these demonstrations of consistency in aggressiveness, both the London and New York State investigations, and other similar studies as well, also found that a persistent high level of aggressiveness is part of a general pattern of social deviation. Thus, seeing that many of his youthful English troublemakers had engaged in many different kinds of socially disapproved behavior, Farrington concluded that they had a general tendency to antisocial conduct. In Eron's sample, as another illustration, those persons, males and females, who had been regarded by their peers as the most aggressive members of their school classes at age 8 tended to have the greatest number of criminal convictions by the time they were 30 years old.

From a mental health perspective it appears that quite a few of the extremely aggressive people uncovered in these investigations can be characterized as having what the American Psychiatric Association's *Diagnostic and Statistical Manual-III* termed an "aggressive conduct disorder." According to *DSM-III*, this disorder refers to:

> . . . a repetitive and persistent pattern of aggressive conduct in which the rights of others are violated, by either physical violence against persons, or

thefts outside the home involving confrontation with a victim. The physical violence may take the form of rape, mugging, assault, or, in rare cases, homicide. . . .

C. Different Types of Aggressive Personalities

This reference to the psychiatric *DSM-III* type "aggressive character disorder" does not mean that all highly aggressive individuals should be placed in this category. There undoubtedly are different kinds of aggressive personalities and a variety of traits can contribute to high levels of assaultiveness. One interesting typology, proposed by Dodge and Coie in 1987 is worth mentioning because it fits into the distinction between instrumental and affective aggression that is emphasized here.

Studying first- and third-grade schoolboys, Dodge and Coie classified the youngsters in terms of how they processed information regarding their interpersonal interactions (according to their teachers' descriptions of the children). Some were said to be highly reactive aggressors in that they were easily threatened and, when threatened, would quickly become very angry. These individuals can be viewed as prone to affective aggression. The other boys can be termed instrumentally oriented aggressors who used their aggression as a means of controlling and dominating their peers. (Other boys were mixtures of these two types, but I will here discuss only the two "pure" categories.) When the youngsters watched a videotaped series of interactions between two school-age boys, the two groups of youngsters were equally accurate in recognizing clearly intentional hostility, but in ambiguous situations the emotionally reactive (i.e., affective) aggressors were especially apt to attribute hostility to the actors. And when the participants were asked what they would do in a similar situation, these boys were more likely than their instrumentally oriented peers to say they would respond with some form of aggression.

1. Emotionally Reactive (Affective) Aggressors

On the basis of the Dodge and Coie results and the findings from studies of consistent individual differences in the tendency to become angry, it seems reasonable to say that many of those persons who are easily angered and prone to aggressive outbursts tend to have an underlying hostile attitude toward the surrounding world. This attitude predisposes them to interpret other people's ambiguous actions as being hostile in nature. Unless situational demands stifle their emotional arousal right away, these individuals can become very angry very quickly. Then, having only relatively weak personal restraints against aggression, they might lash out in an impulsive attack on those they believe have offended them.

Research published by Bushman also indicates that it is possible to think of affective aggressors in stimulus-response-association terms. In one of his studies he found that the minds of many persons with strong aggressive traits typically link different kinds of aggressive ideas together in a broad network of aggressive associations. One consequence of such an extensive associative network is that these persons can be readily aroused by a range of external stimuli having aggressive connotations. And so, in a 1995 experiment Bushman demonstrated that the mere sight of others acting violently tended to evoke aggression-facilitating reactions in people scoring high on a measure of aggressive traits so that they were more punitive to a peer than were their low-scoring counterparts.

2. Instrumentally Oriented Aggressors

Instrumentally oriented aggressors are generally much more controlled. These are the persons who employ aggression, often unemotionally, in a calculated attempt to further their aims. School-age bullies are a good example. According to research by Olweus (1993) in Scandinavia, and the results from similar studies carried out elsewhere, bullies (like their more emotionally reactive counterparts) tend to regard aggression positively. But possessing considerable self-confidence, proud of their toughness, and lacking sympathy for their victims, they are often assaultive in an unemotional effort to dominate and coerce others, to get the benefits they desire. According to Olweus, these qualities can be part of a generally antisocial pattern of conduct that inclines them to break many of society's rules. In his follow-up studies, 60% of the boys who were identified as teenage bullies had at least one conviction by their mid-twenties.

D. Learning to Be Aggressive

Although a good number of conditions—hereditary, familial, social, and situational—can contribute to the development of persistent antisocial dispositions, Patterson's (1986) social learning analysis is a helpful summary of how many of these influences might operate.

Contending that many children are basically trained to become aggressive through their interactions with other family members, Patterson and his colleagues maintain that the parents of hyperaggressive youngsters are typically bad "managers" who (a) do not monitor their offsprings' activities, in and outside the home, effectively; (b) fail to discipline antisocial conduct adequately; (c) do not reward socially desirable behavior sufficiently; and (d) are not good "problem-solvers." As a consequence, these inept parents often allow the family members (siblings as well as the mother and father) to interact in ways that reinforce their children's aggressiveness. But besides being ineffective in controlling their offspring, the parents of antisocial youngsters also tend to provoke their children relatively often by being frequently harsh, punitive, and inconsistent. A result of this unfortunate upbringing is that the children are not only disposed to be assaultive but also are unlikely to have acquired adequate social skills. Not infrequently, they then tend to be rejected by their better socialized peers and may even do poorly in school.

This formulation does not really minimize the importance of low self-esteem, hostile attributions, and/or the role of peer influences in producing hyperaggressiveness. What it does, instead, is propose how particular family experiences can help give rise to these aggression-disposing factors.

III. AFFECTIVE AGGRESSION

Since the notion of instrumental aggression is readily understood and well accepted, I will devote much more attention to research having to do with affective aggression. We will first consider the effects of frustrations and then will look at other kinds of decidedly unpleasant situations.

A. Frustration

Observers of human behavior have long noted the way humans occasionally become aggressive when they are unable to reach a desired goal, and social scientists have posited a connection between frustration and aggression at least since the early years of the 20th century. This notion continues to appear today in many different forms. As just one example, the strain theory of crime causation, initially advanced by Merton and then adapted by other sociological theorists such as Cloward and Ohlin, essentially traces antisocial deviancy to socially produced frustrations. However, the best known formulation of a relationship between frustration and aggression was offered by Dollard, Doob, Miller, Mowrer, and Sears, at Yale University in 1939.

These writers defined a frustration not as an emotional reaction but, more objectively, as an external impediment to expected goal attainment. In the behavioristic terminology of the period, it was "an interference with an occurrence of an instigated goal-response at its proper time in the behavior sequence" (p. 7). If we follow this conception strictly, Dollard and his colleagues would not have regarded poverty-stricken persons as frustrated unless these individuals had anticipated getting some of the good things money can buy and then, unexpectedly, failed to have their wishes fulfilled. Such a state of affairs was presumably related to aggression in two ways. First, according to the Yale group, all aggressive behavior could be traced back to some prior thwarting. And second, they said that every frustration creates an instigation to aggression. Berkowitz has questioned the first of these propositions, pointing out that a good many aggressive actions are instrumental in nature; people are at times assaultive because they have learned that aggression can pay off. However, the second proposition is worth examining more closely.

Critics of the "frustration-aggression hypothesis" have generally argued that frustrations give rise to aggression only when (a) they regard the thwarting as improper, and (b) they had previously learned to react aggressively to barriers to their goal attainment. Although there can be no doubt that these two conditions heighten the likelihood of aggressive reactions to thwartings, research has shown that unexpected failures to obtain desired rewards can indeed produce aggressive responses even when the impediments are legitimate. And moreover, there is now suggestive evidence from experiments with human infants that the frustration-aggression relationship holds even when there was little opportunity for prior learning. In one of these investigations, reported by Lewis and his colleagues in 1990, 2-month-old babies first learned that one of their movements brought an image of a smiling face, and then suddenly found that this instrumental activity no longer had the expected result. Coding of the infants' facial expressions indicated that they felt anger at this unanticipated frustration.

All this is not to say that every failure to obtain a desired and expected goal will lead to open aggression. Prior learning can heighten (or reduce) the chances of a nonaggressive reaction to a thwarting—although the probability of an aggressive response increases if the nonaggressive actions prove to be unsuccessful and the frustration persists. And of course, inhibitions activated by the threat of punishment and/or prior learning can suppress the aggressive reaction. Perhaps most important of all, the thwarting might not be sufficiently unpleasant. In a major revision of the original frustration-aggression hypothesis, Berkowitz has proposed that an interference with goal attainment will produce aggressive inclinations only to the degree that this interference is aversive. This reformulation basically holds that it is the experienced decidedly negative feeling generated by the frustration rather than the frustration itself that creates the instigation to aggression.

B. Aversive Conditions as Instigators to Aggression

The interpretation of the frustration-aggression relationship just offered rests on a rapidly growing body of evidence. As Berkowitz has noted, a good number of studies have now demonstrated that a truly impressive variety of decidedly unpleasant conditions—physically painful events as well as cigarette smoke, foul odors, high room temperatures, and repugnant scenes—can generate anger and aggression. In regard to the first of these factors, animal research, especially the experiments by Azrin, Ulrich, and their associates, and also investigations with humans, have shown that painful occurrences frequently produce anger displays and aggressive inclinations. Izard has recognized this effect in his 1991 text on emotions, remarking that:

> . . . pain is a direct and immediate cause of anger. Even in very young infants, we see anger expression to inoculation long before they can appraise or understand what has happened to them (p. 237).

Anderson's systematic investigations of the aggression-stimulating consequences of uncomfortable heat provide other good examples of this effect. Going beyond his earlier experimental and naturalistic studies (demonstrating, for example, that many of the urban riots of the 1960s burst out in unusually hot weather), one of his most recent papers in this area (Anderson & Anderson, 1996) showed that there was a significant association between how hot U.S. cities were and their rate of violent crime even when many alternative explanations of this relationship were ruled out statistically. Indices of the "southern culture of violence" also forecast the violent crime rate in the Anderson's study but were generally not as good predictors as the temperature measure.

Berkowitz's cognitive-neoassociationist model attempts to account for these aggressive affects by positing a multistage process. According to this formulation, in the initial stage decidedly unpleasant feelings automatically activate at least two different emotional networks (or syndromes), one associated with aggressive inclinations and the other linked to escape/avoidance tendencies. Genetic, learning, and situational influences determine the relative strengths of the two opposing syndromes. Then, later, as the person thinks about the aversive occurrence, appraisals and attributions presumably come into play so that the initial, fairly primitive emotional reactions can be differentiated, intensified, or suppressed. Anderson's (1989) analysis of heat effects is somewhat similar except that he believes the afflicted person decides whether or not to attack an available target, whereas in Berkowitz's model the intense negative affect theoretically activates an aggression-related motor program, automatically producing impulses to aggression which then may or may not be inhibited.

Whatever the specifics of the theoretical analysis, we can extend the findings just mentioned and propose that a broad spectrum of social stresses can spur aggressive inclinations and antisocial tendencies. Among the results showing this, the women in a laboratory experiment who were afflicted by a relatively high level of task stress tended to be most punitive to young children who were nearby, and similarly, in the 1975 survey of a representative sample of U.S. families, conducted by Straus and his associates, those respondents reporting the greatest number of life stresses (from a list of 18) were especially likely to have assaulted their spouses that year. Adding to these observations, Landau has noted that the level of stress in Israel, as indexed by objective measures of unemployment and hyperinflation as well as by more subjective reports of worry about political, economic, and national security conditions, was significantly related to violent crime indicators. It is possible to continue with the evidence, but I will here suggest only that sociological strain theories of criminality basically rest on these stress effects.

C. Appraisals and Attributions

Many (if not most) psychological analyses of affective experiences would fault the theoretical argument just spelled out for omitting consideration of people's appraisals of the emotional event. Holding that the meaning of the experience is all important, these analyses maintain that this meaning is entirely dependent upon the appraisals made of the occurrence—appraisals of the incident's personal significance and, especially, of its cause. In the terminology of contemporary social psychology, the cause to which the emotion arousal is attributed determines the specific nature of the resulting feelings and what actions are undertaken. Thus, as was noted earlier, the proponents of this view contend that frustrations and other decidedly unpleasant incidents do not give rise to anger and aggression unless they are regarded as having been deliberately and unjustifiably produced by someone. For Averill and other appraisal theorists, anger is an accusation of blame.

Contrary to such a view, as I pointed out before, mounting evidence now indicates that decidedly aversive occurrences can produce aggressive inclinations independently of these appraisals, at least if the person does not think much about what had happened. Nevertheless, appraisals of an event's significance and cause undoubtedly can affect the strength of the resulting emotional reactions and even their duration. Interpreting an unpleasant incident as an unintended accident might lessen its aversiveness over time and also erect inhibitions against assaulting the perceived source of the event. And on the other side, thinking of the negative occurrence as a deliberate and illegitimate affront heightens its unpleasantness and also lessens restraints against attacking the perceived perpetrator. Moreover, frequent recollection of the unhappy incident can maintain the ill effects by keeping the afflicted person stirred up.

IV. EFFECTS OF EXTERNAL STIMULI

When people think of a negative event they might become angry because they essentially have exposed themselves to an internal, mental representation of the aversive stimulus. External stimuli that have an unpleasant or aggressive meaning can similarly also activate aggressive inclinations in a fairly automatic manner. Here we have a third type of phenomenon affecting the likelihood of aggression, one that is conceptually different from the influences reviewed up to this point. It does not involve the external incentives that govern instrumental aggression or the strong negative feelings that produce affective aggression, but rather, has to do with a generally quick and relatively involuntary responses to some salient detail in the immediate situation.

A. Associations with Aversive Source and Displaced Aggression

Applying the associationistic behavior theory of the period, Neal Miller showed in 1948 how displaced aggression could be explained in terms of a possible target's association with the perceived source of an aversive experience. In general, Miller's argument went, even though some person or group had actually not caused the unpleasant occurrence, the more closely this person or group was psychologically associated with the supposed origin of the negative event, the stronger would be the aggressive inclinations that would be elicited by the person/group. The aversively generated urge to attack a possible target generalizes to others in proportion to their degree of association with the perceived cause of the displeasure. However, if it is dangerous to assault the aversive source for some reason, inhibitions against aggression would also generalize from the perceived cause to the other possible targets. The provoked person would then refrain from attacking the perceived perpetrator and the other possible targets close to him/her on the psychological association dimension. Still, Miller postulated, since the strength of the inhibitory tendency often declines more rapidly than the strength of the aggressive urge as one moves away from the perceived aversive source on the degree-of-association dimension, at some intermediate position on this dimension the aggressive urge would be stronger than the inhibitory tendencies. People having a moderate degree of connection with the cause of the aversive experience are then apt to be the victims of displaced aggression.

B. Priming Effects

Psychologists these days rarely speak of involuntary or impulsive acts in terms of stimulus-response generalization. Instead, when they do discuss how someone can be the victim of unwarranted hostility, they are likely to base their account on priming effects. Cognitive psychologists have repeatedly shown that thoughts activated by some aspect of the surrounding situation, such as a particular word that one reads, tend to "prime" other, semantically related ideas so that these ideas then become more accessible and easily come to mind. A well-known experiment illustrates this priming by showing that the participants' impression of a stranger was greatly affected by a list of words they had read just before in a supposedly unrelated task. If many of the words in the list had hostile connotations, hostile ideas evidently became highly accessible and these colored the participants' impressions of the stranger in a hostile manner.

Although this kind of influence is quite reliable under particular circumstances, later research indicates it is most likely to arise when people are not especially motivated to be accurate in their judgments and do not realize their thinking might be affected by the priming experience. Furthermore, in accord with the cognitive-neoassociationistic model summarized earlier, research and theory suggests that the people most likely to be primed by a given experience are those whose minds possess a highly developed network of associations that can be linked to that experience. Finally, it should also be noted that there is some debate among psychologists as to whether the priming has only cognitive effects or can also activate motor tendencies. A series of experiments by Bargh and his colleagues supports the latter possibility.

1. Presence of Weapons

Priming undoubtedly operates at times to affect aggressive behavior. One notable example is the so-called weapons effect first identified by Berkowitz and LePage in 1967. As they showed, the mere sight of weapons can induce people to be more aggressive than they otherwise would have been. The weapons' presence apparently brings hostile ideas to mind and may even activate aggression-related motor impulses. Although there have been some published failures to replicate the original findings, a good many studies carried out in the United States and in other countries indicate that this is a fairly general phenomenon. As the priming conception implies, though, this kind of influence is dependent on the meaning that the weapons have for the people seeing them. The guns and/or knives will promote hostile ideas and aggressive inclinations only to the extent that they are regarded as *aggressive* objects, instruments used to hurt or kill people. They presumably will not have an aggression-facilitating effect if they are associated only with sport and recreation or if they strongly activate ideas and feelings of danger and anxiety.

2. Movie and Television Violence

Some of the adverse effects of movie and television violence can also be understood in priming terms. It is now widely recognized that children can learn lessons from what they see on movie and TV screens and that susceptible youngsters are at risk of developing long-lasting aggressive patterns of conduct if they are repeatedly exposed to heavy doses of violent programming in the mass media. Although this is less widely known, a considerable number of experiments, in natural settings as well as in laboratories, have shown that violent scenes can also promote relatively short-lived hostile ideas and overt aggression in susceptible adults as well as in youthful members of the audience.

This relatively transient priming effect is most apparent under particular conditions: For one thing, as was mentioned before, the violent scene is particularly apt to activate aggressive inclinations in viewers with strong aggressive dispositions. Then too, according to several experiments, the priming experience (the sight of violence) is most likely to lead to aggressive behavior in a later situation if, on this later occasion, (a) they encounter a cue associated with the observed violence, and/or (b) the available target is somehow associated with the victim in the previously witnessed violent scene. Inhibitions against aggression obviously are also important. The observed violence might give many people hostile ideas, but they are unlikely to display an openly aggressive action afterwards if their inhibitions against aggression are strong at that time. These restraints could be activated by a threat of punishment or even by cues that bring the viewers' aggression-opposing moral standards to mind. It is interesting to note in this connection that the depicted violence itself could influence what moral standards operate. Findings from a series of studies by Berkowitz and his collaborators, and replicated by other investigators, indicate how this can happen. When people see what they regard as morally justified aggression (as when a "good guy" beats up a "bad" person), for a short time afterwards they are apt to become more willing to attack the "bad" people in their own lives. It is as if the supposedly proper action on the screen had temporarily shaped their conception of how they might properly behave.

V. CONCLUSION

There is more than one kind of aggression even though all of them are basically deliberate attempts to hurt or destroy some target. Most analyses of this behavior in the social sciences emphasize instrumental aggression in which the assault is intended to achieve some purpose besides the target's injury or destruction. Perhaps because they believe that most human actions are fundamentally rational (from the actor's viewpoint) as well as purposive, many theorists have focused on one or more of the nonaggressive goals that can be served by instrumental aggression, such as the reduction or elimination of a disturbing object or stimulation, the restoration of a wounded self-concept, the winning of a desired social approval, and the attainment of a position of power and dominance over others. However, aggressive acts can also be largely involuntary responses produced by decidedly unpleasant events and even by the operation of features in the surrounding situation that have an aggressive meaning.

Besides highlighting the different kinds of aggression and the many different influences that can determine whether someone will attack others, this article has argued that a good many aggressive acts are essentially reactions to external events rather than being impelled by internal forces. It is true, as the article also pointed out, that some persons have a relatively persistent disposition to aggression. But their dispositions are only a *readiness* to be assaultive rather than a constantly operative urge to violence. By and large, humans have a *capacity* for violence, with this capacity being a function of biological, learning, and situationally-induced processes. However, theoretically at least, this potential need not be fulfilled. Humans will not suffer inevitable physiological or psychological damage if they refrain from attacking others around them.

Also See the Following Articles

AGGRESSION AND ALTRUISM • BIOCHEMICAL FACTORS • EVOLUTIONARY FACTORS • GENDER STUDIES • NEUROPSYCHOLOGY OF MOTIVATION FOR GROUP AGGRESSION • WOMEN, VIOLENCE AGAINST

Bibliography

Anderson, C., Deuser, W., & DeNeve, K. (1995). Hot temperatures, hostile affect, hostile cognition, and arousal: Tests of a general model of affective aggression. *Personality and Social Psychology Bulletin, 21,* 434–448.

Anderson, C., & Anderson, K. (1996). Violent crime rate studies in philosophical context: A destructive testing approach to heat and southern culture of violence effects. *Journal of Personality and Social Psychology, 70,* 740–756.

Baron, R. A., & Richardson, D. R. (1994). *Human aggression* (2nd ed.). New York/London: Plenum.

Berkowitz, L. (1984). Some effects of thoughts on anti- and prosocial influences of media events: A cognitive-neoassociation analysis. *Psychological Bulletin, 95,* 410–427.

Berkowitz, L. (1989). The frustration-aggression hypothesis: An examination and reformulation. *Psychological Bulletin, 106,* 59–73.

Berkowitz, L. (1993). *Aggression: Its causes, consequences, and control.* New York: McGraw-Hill.

Bushman, B. (1995). Moderating role of trait aggressiveness in the effect of violent media on aggression. *Journal of Personality and Social Psychology, 69,* 950–960.

Dodge, K., & Coie, J. (1987). Social-information-processing factors in reactive and proactive aggression in children's peer groups. *Journal of Personality and Social Psychology, 53,* 1146–1158.

Dollard, J., Doob, L., Miller, N., Mowrer, O., & Sears, R. (1939). *Frustration and aggression.* New Haven: Yale University Press.

Felson, R. B. (1978). Aggression as impression management. *Social Psychology, 41,* 205–213.

Geen, R. G. (1990). *Human aggression.* Milton Keynes, UK: Open University Press.

Huesmann, L., Eron, L., Lefkowitz, M., & Walder, L. (1984). The stability of aggression over time and generations. *Developmental Psychology, 20,* 1120–1134.

Izard, C. (1991). *The psychology of emotions.* New York/London: Plenum.

Maccoby, E. & Jacklin, C. (1980). Sex differences in aggression: A rejoinder and reprise. *Child Development, 51,* 964–980.

Scott, J. P. (1958). *Aggression.* Chicago: University of Chicago Press.

Alliance Systems

Douglas M. Gibler
Stanford University

GLOSSARY

Balance of Power A theory, derived from realism, that asserts that states in the international system tend to balance power against their enemies.

Polarization The separation of the international state system, usually through the formation of alliances, into competing and hostile blocs.

Realism A paradigm that sees international relations as a struggle for power between states. Within this paradigm, alliances are a means to aggregate power for states.

Typology A theoretical tool that organizes observations into discrete (mutually exclusive and logically exhaustive) categories based on theoretically important variables.

IN ITS BAREST FORM an alliance is a formal commitment by two or more states to some future military action. The action involved could entail almost anything—detailed military planning, consultation during a crisis, or a promise by one state to abstain from an upcoming war. Once reached, the agreement is usually in written form and is made public to other states in the system at the discretion of the states making the alliance. Although less important today, secret alliances and commitments have affected the outcomes of many crises, battles, and wars. For example, the Hitler-Stalin Pact (1939), with its many secret accords, immediately sealed the fate of the much weaker Poland.

Alliances have been widely discussed by students of international relations because, even though hundreds or perhaps thousands of interactions take place between states in any given year, few interactions leave the sort of "trace" that alliance formation does. This trace makes alliance behavior, unlike most other forms of international actions, quite open to systematic investigation. However, despite the ease of tracing these actions researchers have often disagreed as to what constitutes an alliance commitment. Issues of trade and legal reciprocity are often ignored even though these may constitute a large portion of an alliance relationship, and alliances never formalized by treaty are omitted from most alliance data sets.

Although conceptual problems persist, empirical studies have developed a consensus that operationalization of the alliance variable depends upon two factors. First, alliance members have to be independent nation-members of the international system (for example, "alliances" between international terrorist organizations do not qualify), and second, a treaty text has to exist that identifies a *military* commitment that is either defensive, a neutrality arrangement, or an entente or "understanding." Lists of the alliances that meet these criteria have been printed in various forms, and a current listing is available from the Correlates of War project or from the Inter-University Consortium for Political and Social Research (ICPSR), Ann Arbor, Michigan.

I. ALLIANCES IN THEORY

Alliances and alliance theory originally developed as an extension of balance of power theory. Stated simply, balance of power theory predicts that, when the relative capabilities are more or less equally distributed, peace will ensue. As large disparities become apparent in these distributions of power, the probability of war among the major powers increases dramatically. The mechanism that maintains the balance of power is the quickly formed, or ad hoc, alliance. When confronted with the prospect of a possible threat, each nation has the choice to either arm itself or to pursue a policy of alliances. If a nation chooses to arm, it risks an endless spiral of increasing armaments that could result in an arms race. According to balance of power theory, choosing alliances allows states to respond more quickly and with more precision to increased threats from other states. Diplomats and statesmen are able to use alliance networks to properly balance the capabilities of opposing nations that would maintain peace in the international system. Alliances in this framework function only to serve the balance of power.

Alliances traditionally have been conceptualized as a method of avoiding war or of winning a war once it starts. A state involved in a crisis may seek alliance partners in order to warn potentially hostile states that winning a war against it would be difficult. The alliance commitments reduce the level of uncertainty in the system and minimize the likelihood of war that may result due to misperception and miscalculation. These commitments can also reduce the chances of catastrophic shifts in the systemic balance of power.

Some balance of power theorists claim that alliances are also necessary to avoid the most dangerous wars. A belligerent world power, seeking domination of the system, would likely restrain itself when confronted with an alliance system poised against it. Alliances, then, are an indispensable means of maintaining equilibrium in the system. Morgenthau argues that the "balancer" in the system has the charge of maintaining stability between two counterweights (1967: 209–212). As the system evolves into coalitions matched against each other, the balancer's interest becomes that of opposing "the strongest, most aggressive, most dominating Power" (Winston Churchill quoted in Morgenthau, 1967: 212). The balancer, as part of the balance of power system, uses its weight to counter the aggressive policies of each coalition. "The holder of the balance has no permanent friends, it has no permanent enemies either; it has only the permanent interest of maintaining the balance of power itself" (1967: 209).

Alliances are also thought to preserve peace in other ways. Major states may use alliances to constrain revisionist alliance partners, or an alliance can preserve peace by enhancing the prestige of a failing power whose collapse could be destabilizing to the international system. Many neorealists argue that these alliances become meaningless in periods of bipolarity since the major state has enough capabilities to ignore the belligerent policies of its weaker allies. Waltz's observation that the major state must have enough power to ignore the policies of its allies was a response to anecdotal evidence that weaker allies tended to bring major state allies into expanded wars.

That minor states bring major states into war is only one hypothesis linking alliances to war in the traditional literature, however. A state seeking alliances to show resolve could be interpreted by another state as attempting a strategy of encirclement. The targeted state would naturally respond by seeking counter-alliances. Although such alliance partners may have been hard to find prior to the signing of the initial alliance, the developing cleavages could make other states more likely to become involved.

The polarized system or region could also simply clarify the situation and make it easier for the aggressor to determine its odds of winning. As Bueno de Mesquita notes, "The reduction of uncertainty brought about by such information may be all that is needed to facilitate an aggressor's desire to attack another state" (1981: 151).

Balance of power theory can also support the existence of large, systemwide wars against potential dominance caused by alliance formation. In the example given above, the revisionist state is seeking dominance of the system but is confronted with an alliance against it. Instead of being rebuffed by this alliance, the revisionist state continues its policies and fights the war. As Levy (1989: 230) notes, a number of general wars over the past 5 centuries appear to fit this proposition. These include the "wars against Philip of Spain in the late sixteenth century, against Louis XIV in the late seventeenth century, against revolutionary and Napoleonic France a century later, and against Germany twice in this century" (1989: 230–231).

As is obvious from these debates, no clear understanding of the relationship between alliance formation and war has ever been developed. Based mostly upon logic and historical anecdote and often mired in post hoc balance of power explanations, the traditional literature is divided as to whether alliances promote peace or war, and each "camp" has plausible arguments to support its deductive positions.

Not until the investigatory process turned systematically empirical did researchers begin to start a process of cumulation that provided some answers to the alliance/war puzzle. However, before turning to the empirical literature on alliances, it should be noted that the traditional literature on alliances never really died. Still conceiving of alliance formation as a method of balancing power, the (mostly) neorealist literature has attempted to profitably amend the early realist predictions on the alliance/war relationship. For example, in one of the few direct tests of balancing theory by a neorealist, Walt (1987) was unable to confirm the traditional expectations that states move to balance power. Instead, Walt argued that realists had missed the fact that states were actually trying to balance threat. Of course, this emendation did not go unaltered for very long either. Noting further problems with Waltz's original theory as well as Walt's new conceptualization, Christensen and Snyder (1990) attempted to differentiate between different alliance "pathologies" of "chain-ganging" and "buck-passing" in Waltz's theory. ("Chain-ganging" and "buck-passing" refers to the distribution of alliances and allies under conditions of multipolarity. "Chain-ganging" occurs when alliances form to greatly increase the capability of one coalition rather than to balance two or more coalitions. "Buck-passing" occurs when states neglect to form alliance to balance two or more coalitions.) Unfortunately, however, even with the changes that have been made to the original realist theories, little progress has been made in explaining the effects of alliance formation. Instead, all of the changes to the original theory have led some to argue that realism is, in effect, a degenerating paradigm since *post hoc* explanations are being used to account for the empirical anomalies of the original theory.

II. ALLIANCES IN PRACTICE

A. Alliance Data

The Correlates of War data set on formal alliances lists 234 alliances formed between 1815 and 1980. Major states formed 49 alliances and had minor state partners in 75 alliances. Minor states formed 66 alliances. Defense pacts formed the bulk of these alliances (96), but each of the Singer and Small types were well represented (53 neutrality and nonaggression pacts, 43 ententes). The Correlates of War formal alliance data set has recently been augmented to include alliance data from 1648 to 1815. This alliance data set uses the original coding rules developed by Singer and Small (1966) to produce 160 more years of cases. Table I adds this data to the Correlates of War data set and gives aggregate

TABLE I
The Correlates of War Formal Alliance Data Set (1815–1980) and an Extended Formal Alliance Data Set (1648–1815)

	17th century*					18th century					Expanded data set	
	Type I	Type II	Type III	Total	% of Total	Type I	Type II	Type III	Total	% of Total	by Status	% of Total
Status of Signatories												
Majors with Majors	5	1	1	7	23.33%	9	3	0	12	23.08%	19	23.17%
Majors with Minors	10	5	4	19	63.33%	17	16	5	38	73.08%	57	69.51%
Minors with Minors	3	1	0	4	13.33%	2	0	0	2	3.85%	6	7.32%
Totals	18	7	5	30		28	19	5	52		82	
	19th century					20th century*					COW data set	
	Type I	Type II	Type III	Total	% of Total	Type I	Type II	Type III	Total	% of Total	by Status	% of Total
Status of Signatories												
Majors with Majors	10	5	8	23	52.27%	7	6	13	26	16.99%	49	24.87%
Majors with Minors	12	4	1	17	38.64%	25	28	12	65	42.48%	82	41.62%
Minors with Minors	4	0	0	4	9.09%	39	14	9	62	40.52%	66	33.50%
Totals	26	9	9	44		71	48	34	153		197	

* 17th century data are from 1648 to 1699; 20th century data are from 1900 to 1980.

results by membership status and by the Singer and Small (1966) alliance type.

Additional data is almost always useful, but these data may be particularly useful in light of the fact that researchers have discovered that the 19th century may differ dramatically from the 20th century with regard to alliance formation and war. A major question puzzling alliance researchers has been the relative peacefulness of the 19th-century alliances. This inter-century difference is a major anomaly in the empirical research that has generally found alliances to be associated with war in four of the last five centuries.

B. Onset of War

One of the first empirical tests of the alliance/war relationship was Singer and Small's (1966) examination of the behavior of major states. They found that states ranking high on alliance activity also rank high on war engagement, initiation, and battle deaths. This study provided the first systematic evidence that alliances were associated with war, which contradicted the traditional, realist balance of power literature. Following this work, Wallace (1973) and Bueno de Mesquita (1975 and 1978) examined the effects polarization has had on war onset. Wallace found that very high or very low levels of polarity in the system produced war. Refining the indicators of polarity, Bueno de Mesquita showed that the "tightness" of an alliance system is not necessarily related to war onset. However, he found that increases in the tightness of alliances are correlated with war. Discrete alliances, on the other hand, are not associated with war.

Levy (1981) reformulated the questions about alliance formation and war and, with a limited extension of the Correlates of War data, found that, with the exception of the 19th century, most alliances are followed by war. More significantly, a relationship between power and alliance formation was found, since all "Great Power" alliances in the 16th, 17th, and 20th centuries were followed by war within 5 years.

Alliances between major states may also be linked to increased probabilities of war in a second and less obvious way according to Vasquez (1993: 163–164). Schroeder (1976) has discussed how major, "predatory" states may sign nonaggression pacts in order to remove potential adversaries before attacking smaller states. Moul (1988: 34–35) shows that there is an increased likelihood for unequals to go to war in the presence of a nonaggression pact with another state. These "pacts of restraint," or *pacta de contrahendo*, limit the expansion of war but promote hostilities between unequals.

The finding that alliances are often associated with war has been tempered, however, by the inability to explain a large number of "anomalous," peaceful alliances. Levy (1981) has clearly shown that a large minority of alliances are not followed by war, and the variegated effects of the alliances he examined led Levy to speculate that "further conceptualization of the alliance variable is necessary" (1981: 610) and to argue that ignored differences among the alliances may be obscuring some important alliance/war relationships.

The problem with the early empirical investigations, as Levy seems to point out, was that researchers concentrated their early "brush clearing" exercises on alliances in the aggregate rather than differentiating between the types of alliances being formed. Without a clear understanding of alliances as a multifaceted behavior, early research often found weak or inconsistent intercentury results. Trusting balance of power theory to explain alliance formation often led researchers to miss large groups of alliances that were not responses to either power or threat. In order to produce consistent findings linking alliances with either war or peace (or both), alliance research would have to reexamine the concept of alliance and what states were actually doing when they agreed to form one.

C. Friends as Foes

Although alliances may be more likely to be followed by war than by peace, it is also interesting to note that alliances may have some unanticipated effects on the sides states choose to fight on in a coming war. A small literature exists on the probability of "friends" becoming "foes." Expected utility theory notes that it is sometimes rational for allied states to end up in war with each other rather than against a common foe. Most arguments start between friends or acquaintances, and it follows that alliances may increase the probability of war between states. Ray (1990), however, has noted that this probability is quite small and is dependent on both the definition of war and the definition of alliance (in both cases, dyadic or multilateral). Bremer (1992) has seemingly ended this controversy by controlling for the proximity of the allies. Noting that allies are likely to fight each other rather than unallied states, Bremer also finds that the addition of contiguity into a multivariate analysis eliminates the relationship between alliance ties and war. Although the logic of opportunity is consistent with Bueno de Mesquita's argument, Bremer's findings suggest that allies are becoming "foes" not because of their alliances but because they are neighbors. Allies that are not neighbors are not likely to go to war with each other.

Despite these results, the dangers of alliance formation should be noted. Research has shown that alliances increase rather than decrease the chances of war against nonallied states, and even Bremer's research has shown that alliances can increase the chances of war even against allies in certain situations. Both of these findings run counter to realist prescriptions advocating the quickly formed alliance, and both underscore the dangerous potential that alliances may have for naive policymakers.

D. A Typology of Alliances

As was mentioned earlier, Levy (1981) called for a reexamination of the alliance concept, but this plea for more theoretical research only echoed earlier reviews of the alliance literature. For example, a monograph by Ward (1982) argued that confusion among definitions, causal processes, and alliance dynamics had hampered a necessary cumulation of knowledge. Although never directly arguing for a typology of alliances, per se, he did find that previous scientific studies had led to inconclusive, often contradictory results because not enough attention had been paid to the theoretical linkages between alliance dynamics and war.

In a similar effort Singer and Bueno de Mesquita (1973: 272–273) also elaborated the need for further conceptualization: "The labels and definitions are not merely elusive and slippery; they are, all too often, logically inconsistent and semantically misleading." As they argued it, the only way for the alliance literature to develop consistent findings was to embark upon a wholesale restructuring of alliances as a concept.

Much has been written and learned about alliances in the 25 years since these early reviews were written. However, very little effort has been made to examine how different types of alliances affect the dependent variable of war. There are exceptions: Sabrosky (1980) found that nonaggression pacts and neutrality agreements (Singer and Small Type II alliances) were likely to promote wars among the signatories; Moul (1988) and Schroeder (1978), as described earlier, showed that certain alliance types "permitted" the instigation of smaller wars; and Kegley and Raymond (1982) described how certain commitment norms affected the systemic incidences of violence throughout the years. Nevertheless, although much has been learned there still exists no clear understanding of the complex relationship between alliances and war.

The lack of consensus on the theoretical linkages between alliances and war (or peace) has even led some to argue for a reexamination of the methods used to investigate the alliance/war process, substituting choice-theoretic models for correlation-based hypothesis testing. However, despite these recent assertions, it is not at all clear that the methods currently used are to blame for the theoretical confusion. As Vasquez (1993) describes in a recent review of the Correlates of War findings, alliances have been found to generally be associated with war and do indeed comprise a large part in the "steps to war" between rival states.

Vasquez argues that, as an extension of power politics behavior, states respond to security issues and follow the realist prescriptions of security by forming alliances, thinking that the increase in capabilities will make potentially hostile states more cautious. The problem with this action, though, is that the formation of an alliance constitutes a part of a process, or path, that will increase the likelihood of war rather than peace. The state responds to insecurity and threat by forming the alliance, but then this response breeds increased insecurity and uncertainty among other actors and forces these states to turn toward the other means of augmenting their capabilities—counteralliances and/or military buildups (Vasquez 1993: 169).

It is very significant that Vasquez distinguishes between alliances that attempt to form winning coalitions and those that attempt to avoid war, since this simple but central distinction outlines a large gap in the extant literature on alliances. Vasquez's "steps to war" model assumes that a certain type of alliance will increase the hostilities between rivals, but Vasquez also argues elsewhere that other types of alliances may have pacifying effects both on the signatories and the system as a whole either through the resolution of territorial disputes or through the creation of norms of behavior within the system (1993: 123–152, 263–291).

The distinctions made by Vasquez form the basis of a recently developed typology of alliances. This typology separates alliances into two basic types: the territorial settlement treaty and the capability-aggregation alliance. First, a significant minority of alliances attempts to avoid war by removing contentious issues from the system. Instead of trying to establish peace through realist prescriptions of balancing, these "territorial settlement treaties" resolve disputes by removing the contentious issue of territory from the agendas of states. The territorial settlement treaty is an alliance that also contains provisions for the maintenance of the status quo by states in a given region, or it contains an agreement to exchange territories between the alliance partners. The alliance signed after the territorial settlement formalizes the states' commitments to the agreement.

Alliances that resolve territorial issues between states are intrinsically different than other commitment types and are least likely to be followed by war. These tools of conflict management are seen as such and are not viewed as provocative acts by other states. In the case of the territorial settlement treaties, the type of commitment is much more important than the types of states forming it. However, for all other alliances the war-proneness of the alliance is most likely best determined by the characteristics of the states involved in that alliance.

It is widely assumed that when states form an alliance, a signal is sent to other states in the system. Gibler (1997) argues that, for most alliances, the type of signal sent depends upon the states involved in the alliance rather than the type of commitment made. Gibler shows that major states, successful in their previous war, and dissatisfied with the status quo, are most likely to form the dangerous alliances. Their alliances are dangerous both because they increase the hostilities and insecurities of other states and because they are most likely to be used as tools to win an upcoming war. Major states have been inculcated into a value system that sees alliance diplomacy as a tool of war. Similarly, successful states are more likely to appeal to war to win policy objectives since these policies have worked in the past. Lastly, dissatisfied states approach alliance making as a necessary step to change the status quo to their liking; a coalition is necessary to force change on the states protecting the status quo. The perception of an alliance as threatening, and the likelihood that an alliance was formed as an attempt to win a war, decrease as the number of major, successful, and dissatisfied states in an alliance decrease.

Table II illustrates the different effects that alliances may have. The territorial settlement treaty is expected to be associated with peace. The territorial settlement treaty decreases hostility levels between states, which, in turn, tends to decrease armament expenditures, counteralliances, and other power politics measures. Once again, this type of commitment is clearly not an attempt to either avoid or make war, it is an attempt at conflict resolution and is probably viewed as such by other states. Gibler (1997: Table 5.8) showed that only one alliance out of 27 was followed by war involving an ally within 5 years of the formation of the alliance. The percentage rate of 3.7% is dramatically less than the percentage rate for all alliances (26.8%), a difference that is statistically significant (-2.99, $p < 0.01$).

Table II also presents the likely relationship between the capability aggregation alliances and war. This relationship is much more variegated. Alliances made by major states, successful in their previous war, and dissatisfied with the status quo are the alliances most likely to trigger increased military expenditures and counter-alliances in target states. These attempts to build war-winning coalitions are also the alliances that are most likely to be followed by war. On the other hand, as the states in alliance decrease in the three important variables of status, success, and satisfaction, the likelihood of war following these alliances decreases. The alliances made by satisfied minor states, unsuccessful in their previous war, are the alliances least likely to provoke bellicose responses from other states.

In order to measure the impact of the different capability aggregation alliances, Gibler (1997) devised a "bellicosity rating" from the product of the status, satisfaction, and success in war measures. Each of the three

TABLE II

The Overall Relationship Between Alliances and War (Predicted and Actual)

Type of alliance	Anticipated reaction	Predicted result	Actual result		
			Wars	*N*	Rate
Territorial settlement treaty	Decreased armament levels Decreased involvement in crises Decreased involvement in alliances	Peace	1	27	0.0370
Capability-aggregation alliances					
Low-bellicosity alliances (At least two factors absent)	None	No effect/peace	6	40	0.1500
Mixed-bellicosity alliances	Uncertain	Situation dependent	31	92	0.3370
High-bellicosity alliances (At least two factors present)	Increased armament levels Increased involvement in crises Increased involvement in alliances	War	19	35	0.5429

measures has three categories—absent, mixed, or present—so the bellicosity rating was also made to be a three-part measure: low, mixed, or high. Low-bellicosity alliances ranked lowest (absent) on at least two of three measures. High-bellicosity alliances ranked highest (present) on at least two of three measures. Mixed-bellicosity alliances had rankings that ranged between these two extremes. For example, if an alliance contained satisfied (dissatisfaction absent), unsuccessful (success absent), minor states (major status absent), then it was given a low-bellicosity rating. An alliance made by dissatisfied, successful, major states produces a high-bellicosity rating.

The results for the low-bellicosity alliances are given first. These alliances are expected to have little impact upon the perceptions of other states because the states forming these alliances have neither the capability nor the willingness to change the status quo. Although peace is predicted to follow these alliance types, it is a different form of peace than the one that follows the territorial settlement treaties. The territorial settlement treaties are attempts at conflict resolution and, if successful, are likely to result in decreased hostility levels between states. The peaceful capability aggregation alliances are not attempts at conflict resolution, but they are not provocative attempts to change the status quo either. Therefore, the predicted result of these alliances is better described as "no effect." The results in Table II tend to confirm these expectations. Out of 40 alliances, only 6 were followed by war within 5 years after alliances formation. Only 15% of these alliances are followed by war compared to a likelihood of close to 30% for all alliances ($p < 0.01$).

The mixed-bellicosity alliances were formed by different types of states and for different reasons. A satisfied state may seek an alliance with a dissatisfied state in order to pacify it, or a major state may seek control over a minor state. The predicted reaction to these alliances by other states is uncertain and is dependent upon contextual situations, such as the presence of rivalry, repeated crises, or continuing arms races. If the alliances are formed during times of hostility, then the chances of war obviously increase. Conversely, during times of low hostility levels, the alliances are likely to produce an increased sensitivity in other states, but are unlikely to generate the processes that would lead to war. Out of 92 alliances, more than one-third (31) are followed by war within 5 years. The 4% increase in the likelihood of war for these alliances compared to alliances in aggregate is significant ($p < 0.05$).

The high-bellicosity alliances are highly provocative attempts to influence and eventually change the status quo. They are likely to promote increased armament levels, crises, and an increase in counteralliances. Their predicted result is war. Of 35 high-bellicosity alliances formed between 1815 and 1980, more than half were followed by war within 5 years. These alliances are almost twice as likely to generate war as a result than alliances in general ($p < 0.01$) and are probably attempts to build war-winning coalitions.

The results in Table II show why reconceptualization of the alliance variable was necessary. After the disaggregation of alliances into various smaller groups, theories can be constructed that assess the impacts of the various alliance types. Peaceful alliances can be separated from other alliances in order to examine their ability to manage conflict. War-prone alliances can be isolated from the larger set of general alliances so as to assess the processes that led their alliance members to war. Finally, the remaining group of mixed-bellicosity alliances can be studied in further detail to delineate the types of situations in which these alliances are likely to generate war.

E. Alliances and the Expansion of War

The onset of war and its expansion beyond the original participants are often regarded as distinct events (see Bremer, 1992, for example), and while the relationship between alliances and the onset of war is variegated, the relationship between alliances and war expansion is much simpler. Alliances cause wars to spread.

Some of the best evidence linking alliances with the expansion of war was provided by Siverson and King (1979). Siverson and King (1979: 45) found that, between 1815 and 1965, there were 112 instances in which actors fought wars in coalitions. In the remaining 76 instances, the actors fought alone. Of the 112 instances of coalition, 76 had prewar alliances and 36 did not; of the 76 instances of participants fighting alone, 52 had no prewar alliances and 24 did.

It could be inferred from these findings that alliances may be a necessary condition for wars to spread, and indeed, Siverson and King (1979: 48) show that this may be the case. Over the same time period, 1815 to 1965, 19 wars were fought without war participants having pre-war alliance bonds. Of these 19 wars, only 3 expanded beyond the original two war participants.

Although alliances are perhaps a necessary condition for the spread of war, they are not a sufficient condition. In a follow-up study, Siverson and King (1980) showed that only about one-quarter of alliance bonds serve to bring nonbelligerents into a war once the war has begun. The characteristics of alliances that make them more likely to spread war include major-minor state partnerships, defense pacts, and new alliances. Alliances may also act as a contagion mechanism for states involved in many alliances but with few actual alliance partners or for wars in which other alliance members have already intervened.

The findings of Siverson and King are generally consistent with a large literature that shows that alliances may contribute to the expansion of war. However, it should be emphasized that, although alliance formation contributes greatly to the expansion of conflict once it begins, it is not the only source of contagion. As Siverson and King (1979: 46–47) point out, World War I, World War II, and the Korean War each had war participants that were not involved in prewar alliance bonds.

III. PATHS FOR FUTURE RESEARCH

Research has shown that alliances are associated with war and that alliances may cause wars to spread once they begin. These findings suggest a reconsideration of traditional alliance theory, which asserts that alliances, especially when used to balance power or threat, are associated with peace. For future research to continue this progress linking alliances with war, several relationships will have to be uncovered.

First, the peaceful alliances, especially the territorial settlement treaties, will have to be studied in greater depth to understand the processes that lead them to peace. It is possible that a useful new tool of conflict resolution has been discovered, but because this is a relatively new insight, it will take much more research to substantiate this conclusion. As for the other peaceful alliances, the nonthreatening, capability-aggregation alliances, future researchers may want to concentrate their efforts on collecting primary data on the events immediately prior to and after the formation of these alliances. There is often a tendency in historical accounts to shed light on the events that promote war and to neglect the rest, and this is definitely the case for these alliances. Of the more than 200 alliances in the Correlates of War data set on alliances, the historical record is most sketchy on these alliances.

The second avenue of possible research would travel down a well-trodden path. Investigating the alliances that promote war, that is, those ranking high on the bellicosity ratings provided earlier, has been a longstanding project for both historians and political scientists alike. However, despite these efforts, no general theories exist that link the processes that lead these alliances to be perceived as threatening and the processes that produce behaviors like counter-alliances and increased military expenditures.

The final possible area for research on the linkages between alliances and war will probably provide the best area for important original research. As was noted in Table II and the text surrounding it, the likelihood that a mixed-bellicosity alliance will be followed by war is dependent upon the situation during which it was formed. Further investigation of the types of situations that lead these alliances to war is greatly needed. Are rivalries or repeated conflicts necessary for these alliances to be followed by war? Under what circumstances will these alliances cause counteralliances and increased arms expenditures in their targets? These and a myriad of other questions will have to be answered by future research.

Also See the Following Articles

BALANCE OF POWER RELATIONSHIPS • COLLECTIVE SECURITY SYSTEMS • INTERNATIONAL RELATIONS, OVERVIEW • POWER, SOCIAL AND POLITICAL THEORIES OF • WARFARE, TRENDS IN

Bibliography

Altfeld, M., & B. Bueno de Mesquita (1979). Choosing sides in wars. *International Studies Quarterly* 27:225–231.

Bremer, Stuart (1992). Dangerous dyads: Conditions affecting the likelihood of interstate war, 1816–1965. *Journal of Conflict Resolution* 36 (June): 309–41.

Bueno de Mesquita, B. (1975). Measuring systemic polarity. *Journal of Conflict Resolution* 19: 77–96.

Bueno de Mesquita, B. (1978). "Systemic Polarization and the Occurrence and Duration of War." *Journal of Conflict Resolution* 22 (June): 241–67.

Bueno de Mesquita, B. (1981). *The war trap*. New Haven: Yale University Press.

Bueno de Mesquita, B., & Singer, J. D. (1973). Alliances, capabilities, and war: A review and synthesis. *Political Science Annual* 237–281.

Christensen, T., & Snyder, J. (1990). Chain gangs and passed bucks: Predicting alliance patterns in multipolarity. *International Organization* 44 (Spring): 137–168.

Gibler, D. M. (1996) "Alliances that Never Balance: The Territorial Settlement Treaty." *Conflict Management and Peace Science* 15 (1).

Gibler, D. M. (1997). *Reconceptualizing the alliance variable: An empirical typology of alliances*. Vanderbilt University, Doctoral Thesis.

Gibler, D. M. (forthcoming). An extension of the correlates of war formal alliance data set, 1648–1815. *International Interactions*.

Gulick, E. V. (1955). *Europe's classical balance of power*. New York: Norton.

Kaplan, M. (1957). *System and process in international politics*. New York: Wiley.

Kegley, C. W., & Raymond, G. (1982). Alliance norms and war: A new piece in an old puzzle. *International Studies Quarterly* 26 (December): 572–595.

Levy, J. (1981). Alliance formation and war behavior: An analysis of the great powers, 1495–1975. *Journal of Conflict Resolution* 25 (December): 581–613.

Levy, J. (1989). The causes of war: A review of theories and evidence. In P. E. Tetlock *et al.* (Eds.), *Behavior, society, and nuclear war*, vol. I, New York: Oxford University Press, pp. 209–333.

Liska, G. (1962) *Nations in alliance*. Baltimore: Johns Hopkins University Press.

McGowan, P. J., & Rood, R. (1975). Alliance behavior in balance of power systems: Applying a Poisson model to nineteenth century Europe. *American Political Science Review* 69 (September) 859–870.

Midlarsky, M. (1986). A hierarchical equilibrium theory of systemic war." *International Studies Quarterly* 30 (March): 77–105.

Morgan, T. C., & Palmer, G. (1996). Alliance formation and foreign-policy portfolios: To protect and serve. Paper presented at the Annual Meeting of the American Political Science Association, San Francisco.

Morgenthau, H. (1967). *Politics among nations: The struggle for power and peace*. 3rd ed. New York: Knopf.

Morrow, J. (1991) Alliances and asymmetry: An alternative to the capability aggregation model of alliances. *American Journal of Political Science* 35: 904–933.

Most, B., & Siverson, R. (1987). Substituting arms and alliances, 1870–1914: An exploration in comparative foreign policy. In Herman, Kegley, and Rosenau (Eds.), *New directions in the study of foreign policy*, Boston: Allen and Unwin, 131–57.

Moul, W. (1988). Great power nondefense alliances and the escalation to war of conflicts between unequals, 1815–1939. *International Interactions* 15 (1): 25–43.

Organski, A. F. K., & Kugler, J. (1980). *The war ledger*. Chicago: University of Chicago Press.

Osgood, R. E. (1967). The expansion of force. In R. E. Osgood and R. W. Tucker (eds.), *Force, order, and justice*. Baltimore: Johns Hopkins University Press.

Ray, J. L. (1990). Friends as foes: International conflict and wars between formal allies. In C. Gochman and Sabrosky, A. (Eds.), *Prisoners of war*. Lexington, Mass.: Lexington Books: 73–91.

Ray, J. L. (1995). *Democracy and international conflict: An evaluation of the democratic peace proposition*. Columbia: University of South Carolina Press.

Sabrosky, A. N. (1980) "Interstate Alliances: Their Reliability and the Expansion of War," in J. David Singer (ed.) *The Correlates of War II: Testing Some Realpolitik Models*. New York: Free Press: 161–198.

Sabrosky, A. N. (1985). Alliance aggregation, capability distribution, and the expansion of interstate war. In A. Sabrosky (ed.), *Polarity and war*, Boulder: Westview, pp. 145–89.

Schroeder, P. (1976). Alliances, 1815–1945: Weapons of power and tools of management. In Knorr (ed.) *Historical dimensions of national security problems*. Lawrence: University Press of Kansas: 227–262.

Singer, J. D., Bremer, S., & Stuckey, J. (1972). "Capability Distribution, Uncertainty, and Major Power War, 1820–1965," in B. Russett (ed.) *Peace, War, and Numbers*. Beverly Hills: Sage: 19–48.

Singer, J. D., & Small, M. (1966). Formal alliances, 1815–1939: A quantitative description. *Journal of Peace Research* 3: 1–32.

Singer, J. D., & Small, M. (1968). Alliance aggregation and the onset of war, 1815–1945. In J. D. Singer (ed.) *Quantitative international politics: Insights and evidence*. New York: Free Press: 247–286.

Singer, J. D., & Small, M. (1972). *The wages of war, 1816–1965: A statistical handbook*. New York: Wiley & Sons

Siverson, R., & King, J. (1979). Alliances and the expansion of war. In J. D. Singer and M. Wallace (Eds.), *To augur well*. Beverly Hills: Sage, 37–49.

Siverson, R., & King, J. (1980) Attributes of national alliance membership and war participation, 1815–1965. *American Journal of Political Science* 24 (February): 1–15.

Small, M., & Singer, J. D. (1982) *Resort to arms: International and civil wars, 1816–1980*. Beverly Hills, CA: Sage.

Smith, A. (1995). Alliance formation and war. *International Studies Quarterly* 39 (4): 405–426.

Smith, A. (1996). To intervene or not to intervene: A biased decision. *Journal of Conflict Resolution* 40 (1) March: 16–40.

Vasquez, J. (1997). The realist paradigm as a degenerating research program: An appraisal of neotraditional research on Waltz's balancing proposition. *American Political Science Review* 91 (3).

Vasquez, J. (1993). *The war puzzle*. Cambridge: Cambridge University Press.

Wallace, M. D. (1973). Alliance polarization, cross-cutting, and international war, 1815–1964. *Journal of Conflict Resolution* 17 (December): 575–604.

Walt, S. (1987). *The origins of alliances*. Ithaca: Cornell University Press.

Waltz, K. (1979). *Theory of international politics*. Reading, MA: Addison-Wesley.

Ward, M. D. (1982). *Research gaps in alliance dynamics*. University of Denver Monograph Series in World Affairs, Vol. XIX, Book 1.

Wayman, F. (1984). "Bipolarity and war: The role of capability concentration and alliance patterns among major powers, 1816–1965. *Journal of Peace Research* 21 (No. 1): 61–78.

Wright, Q. (1965). *A study of war* (2nd Ed.). Chicago: University of Chicago Press.

Yamamoto, Y., & Bremer, S. A. (1980). Wider wars and restless nights: Major power intervention in ongoing war." In J. D. Singer (Ed.), *The correlates of war*, vol. II. New York: Free Press, pp. 85–119.

Animal Behavior Studies, Nonprimates

John Paul Scott
Bowling Green State University

GLOSSARY

Agonistic Behavior A kind of social behavior involving struggle.

Amphibia A group of cold blooded vertebrate animals whose life history involves existence both in water and on land (e.g., frogs and salamanders).

Annelida A phylum including segmented worms (e.g., earth worms).

Anthropleura Elegantissima A species of sea anemone.

Arthropoda The phylum of jointed legged animals with external skeletons (e.g., crustaceans, spiders, and insects).

Army Ants A group of predatory tropical ants that have no fixed nesting places.

Cephlalopoda The group of marine animals that includes octopuses, squids, and nautiluses.

Chitons A group of marine mollusks that are bilaterally symmetrical.

Coelenterata A plylum of water living animals that have only two cell layers (e.g., jelly fishes and corals).

Crustacea A major division of the arthropods having a hard external skeleton (e.g., lobsters and crayfish).

Dominance, social A variety of social organization based on struggle that usually produces pairs of dominant and subordinate individuals.

Echinodermata The phylum that includes the spiny skinned invertebrates such as starfish and sea urchins.

Estrus The period of sexual receptivity in a female mammal.

Hymenoptera The order of insects that includes the ants, bees, and wasps.

Mammalia A group of warm blooded vertebrates in which adult females secrete milk for young. (Humans are placed in this group.)

Mollusca One of the major animal phyla in terms of numbers of individuals and numbers of species. Most have an external skeleton consisting of a shell or shells.

Phylum A major division of either plants or animals. Humans belong to the subphylum vertebrata.

Porifera This animal phylum consists of the sponges that have no powers of locomotion as adults.

Reptilia A group of cold blooded air breathing vertebrates that have 3-chambered hearts (e.g., turtles, snakes, and lizards).

Sociobiology A science based on the study of the biological basis of behavior and organization.

Territoriality Social organization based on the possession of a particular piece of land.

I. INTRODUCTION

The concept that has dominated research on animal behavior in the last half century is that of *sociobiology*. I wished to develop a new science concerning the social behavior of animals, and at first thought of the term "biosociology," but finally selected *sociobiology* (Scott, 1946) because the more basic science was emphasized. I then developed a classification of systems of social behavior (Scott, 1958, 1972) that could be used for descriptive and comparative studies. This consisted of ten categories, the most directly relevant to the content of this book being *agonistic behavior*, defined as fighting or struggling between members of the same species.

It is obvious that social organization is a fundamental general concept, and I have chosen it as a basis for summarizing the known information on violence, peace, and conflict in the animal kingdom, excluding the primates. Since a complete summary of these facts would require an encyclopedia in itself, I have selected some of the most highly developed cases of social organization in each major section of the animal kingdom and summarized the occurrence and function of violent behavior in each. At the end, I summarize the relationship of these facts and theories to human behavior.

Violent behavior is not universal in the animal kingdom. Very little if any occurs among one-celled animals, and none can occur in the *Porifera*, or sponges, which grow like plants on the sea bottom and never move. Nor does it occur among the more lowly organized phyla of multicellular animals. For example, round worms are covered with a rubbery skeleton that has little sensation and that prevents motor activity. Nor do the soft-bodied flatworms attack each other. External armor inhibits fighting. The starfish and other animals belonging to the *Echinodermata* are covered with a horny armor. Likewise the mollusks, one of the major phyla in the animal kingdom, are protected by shells that prevent any injurious sensations.

According to basic evolutionary theory, violence should occur where it promotes the long-range survival of the species. It follows that destructive violence is aberrant and should not survive. This article will survey the major cases of animal violence and point out how these may have relevance of any kind to human affairs.

II. VIOLENCE AMONG THE LOWER INVERTEBRATES

I have seen only one report of serious fighting in the Phylum *Coelenterata*. These creatures, which include such animals as the hydra, jellyfish, and sea anemones, are armed with stinging cells that inflict fatal wounds on their prey, and can be equally fatal to their own kind. One species of sea anemones, *Anthropleura elegantissima,* lives in colonies on the sea bottom and reproduces by fission. The two halves live together without violence and eventually form a large colony. But if two members of adjacent colonies that are not genetically identical come into contact they attack each other with special organs carrying numerous stinging cells and may inflict fatal or serious injuries. The result is to keep the colonies apart.

The segmented worms (Phylum *Annelida*) have free-living forms with jaw-like organs that can be used to attack prey. In at least one case, the tube worm, *Neanthes caudata*, these are used to attack species mates. The males of this species build U-shaped tubes on the sea bottom and draw water through them. In the breeding season, a female may enter a tube, mate, and deposit her fertilized eggs, which are guarded by the male until they hatch. All other worms, male or female are attacked and ejected. This is a case of *territoriality*, or defense of a particular space, a phenomenon that is common among more highly organized animals such as the vertebrates.

III. VIOLENCE AMONG THE HIGHLY ORGANIZED INVERTEBRATES

These animals include the *Cephalopods,* which at one time were very numerous marine animals, but are now reduced to the various species of octopuses and squids. Octopuses are usually solitary animals, but females can fight to defend a nest. Squids live in schools like fishes and are not known to fight.

The mollusks, most of which live in shells, are still one of the most successful groups of animals. They live in both fresh and salt water, and are so well-protected by shells that fighting is impossible. One of the few cases of conflict that I have been able to find occurs in a species of chiton *Acanthropleura gemmata*. These are bilaterally symmetrical and covered with flexible segmented shells. They are reported to live on soft rocks on the sea shore, in which they excavate resting places. Two chitons sometimes engage in pushing contests over the possession of a shelter. One may be ejected, or both may settle for joint possession. This is another case of territoriality. No injuries are inflicted.

The major cases of invertebrate violent behavior occur among the arthropoda, the phylum that includes the crustaceans, spiders, and insects. As biologists have pointed out, insects are man's chief competitors, and their behavior is particularly interesting from that viewpoint.

A. Arachnida

Spiders are almost entirely terrestrial in their habitats, and make their living as predators, especially on insects. A spider web is a trap for catching flying insects and is occupied by a single female who defends her web against all other spiders. The fighting is therefore territorial in function, with the result that each female is solitary except briefly during mating.

There is one notable exception. The Afghan spiders, *Stegodyphus sarasinorum,* build communal webs several feet in diameter, each occupied by dozens of individuals. Any prey that are caught are shared without conflict. Often there are several adjacent webs along a hedgerow. Although spiders usually stay in their home webs, a spider that wanders into another web is not attacked. Females lay eggs and hatch young in special parts of the web, and feed the young until they mature. Since the mother herself does not eat, she eventually dies and is "sucked out" (the spider method of eating a prey animal) by her offspring. This is a unique case of completely peaceable organization in an invertebrate animal society, almost like the "Peaceable Kingdom" of Christian mythology.

B. Crustacea

Crustacea are the largest in size of the phylum Arthropoda, or jointed footed animals, and are largely aquatic in habitat. Most of the scientific work on them has been done with freshwater crayfish. These animals dig holes along the banks of streams and defend them against strangers. Fighting is thus territorial in nature and inflicts little damage because of the hard shells.

Marine crustacea include the fiddler crabs. These are small shore-dwelling animals that live in burrows on the intertidal zone. The males have one very large claw, hence the name "fiddler". Each burrow is held by a single male who will forcibly eject any stranger that enters. The fight is therefore territorial in nature. Because of the external skeleton very few injuries are inflicted.

C. Insects

Insects are the most successful of the Arthropods, with thousands of different species divided into 20 different orders. The most highly sociable species belong to the order *Hymenoptera,* which includes the ants, bees, and wasps. Both wild and domesticated bees collect nectar from flowers, which they incidentally cross-fertilize. They live in colonies, each inhabited by a single fertile female that lays thousands of eggs, most of which develop into workers as the result of a low-protein diet. There is no fighting within a hive, except at the time of the replacement of the fertile female or queen, when the number of possible successors is reduced to one by the workers. Workers will attack any strange bee that attempts to enter the hive, and also larger animals that attempt to steal the honey. Thus a bee hive is really a single family. Any fighting between such families is territorial in nature.

An ant colony is organized in much the same way as a bee colony, except that the reproductive caste consists of a mated pair rather than a single female.

D. Violence in and among Ant Colonies

Unlike bees and wasps, which are flying insects, ants are terrestrial, spending their lives on the ground or beneath it. They fly at only one time in their life cycle, usually in the spring while reproducing. At this time an ant colony may produce hundreds of winged ants, small males and larger females. As they fly, they mate in pairs, then drop to the ground and shed their wings. Each pair digs an underground burrow in which it lays eggs that hatch as larvae that eventually mature as worker ants. These are sterile females that take over the care and feeding of the female's offspring, which become a larger and larger colony. Some ant species continually excavate pebbles, sand grains, and small twigs that they pile into an ant "hill." Others simply pile grains around the opening of the burrow in a shallow ring. The ants may close the opening of such a hill during a rain. Ants that forage near their burrows lay down scent trails that enable them to find their way about. There is no violence among members of the colony, but the workers will attack any worker from another colony that attempts to enter the hill. Workers from different species that live in adjacent hills have been observed fighting, apparently a case of territorial fighting.

"Army" ants are tropical species of ants that have no fixed burrows or other abodes. They have been called "army" ants because when moving from one location ("bivouac") to another they travel in lines following scent trails. These are not armies in the human sense, as they do not involve armed conflicts between organized groups of the same species. The behavior is not warfare but group hunting, consisting of attacks on prey animals.

IV. VIOLENCE, PEACE, AND CONFLICT IN NONHUMAN VERTEBRATE SOCIETIES

As we have seen, fighting among invertebrate animal societies is limited and largely confined to one function, territoriality. Such is not the case among vertebrates and is probably largely due to the excellent vision provided by the vertebrate eye, making possible recognition of individuals at a distance. There is only one invertebrate group that has such an eye, the cephalopod mollusks. But octopuses and squids nevertheless do not develop an elaborate social organization, perhaps limited by their simple molluskan bodily organization, consisting of a few motor organs and the equally simple nervous system that activates them. Nor do they exhibit much fighting.

A. Conflict among Fishes

These are aquatic animals and evolutionarily the oldest of the group. An example is the Jack Dempsey aquarium fish, in which the males battle for small breeding territories. These fish also show social dominance, a widespread phenomenon in vertebrate societies. This dominance-subordination relationship means that when two neighoring males meet, one attacks and the other one retreats, with a consequent reduction in violence. This leads to a general principle, that social organization results in peace, or at least a reduction of violence. This results in a converse principle, that a major cause of destructive violence is social disorganization.

B. Peaceable Fishes

Many species of fish live in schools, large groups whose behavior is regulated by mutual imitation. The individuals maintain constant distances from each other without fighting.

C. Cold-Blooded Terrestrial Vertebrates

These belong to two groups, the amphibians and the reptiles. Amphibians represent the transition of backboned animals from water to land, and most of them still lay eggs in water. There are some cases of terrestrial aggression, but little damage is done. Modern reptiles are a remnant of what were once the dominant vertebrate animals living on land, and they still lay their eggs there. Amphibians are covered with moist, soft skins and show relatively little violent behavior. Most modern reptiles, on the other hand, are either covered by hard shells as in the turtles, or tough and horny skins such as alligators and their relatives, and show relatively little fighting, although the female crocodiles defend a nest in which they have laid their eggs. Neither group shows any novel or unusual functions of aggression.

D. Birds

Birds are the dominant warm-blooded vertebrates in the air and show interesting and complicated forms of social interaction involving dominance and territoriality. *Social dominance* based on fighting was first described by Schjelderup-Ebbe (1922) in flocks of domestic chickens and has since been extensively studied. When a strange hen enters a flock it is attacked in succession by all the resident hens, and the result of the fight in each pair determines which hen is dominant and has prior access to food. The dominance order so established may take the form of a straight line, but not necessarily so. Hens can recognize their dominance relationships in flocks at least as large as 100.

Chickens—domesticated from the wild Indian jungle fowl—are normally polygamous and when allowed to go wild into flocks each is headed by a single male whose crow is a territorial call. Each adult female then has a subflock of her offspring in a subterritory. Under such conditions little conflict goes on. But it is magnified when domestic chickens are forced to live together in close contact. As in other animal societies violence is magnified by social disorganization.

Elliot Howard's (1920) book, *Territory in Bird Life,* was the first scientific description of this phenomenon, but it is well illustrated by the life history of the red-winged blackbird, a common wild resident in central North America. In February flocks of males that have wintered in the South come and settle in favorable nesting areas. Each bird occupies a territory on which he sings and from which he attacks and ejects all other males.

Female flocks arrive later, and each one builds a nest in a male's territory, later laying eggs and raising young. Males that are unable to get territories live in separate flocks and do not reproduce. The result of this territorial organization is to limit population growth, but the size of populations may nevertheless be quite large. At the end of the summer the birds abandon their territories and gather into peaceful autumn flocks, which often feed in fields where grain has been harvested, and eventually fly south to spend the winter in a warm climate where food is available through the winter.

Once the breeding territories are organized there is relatively little conflict and no severe injuries. Violence is renewed only if a resident bird is killed by a predator or dies for some other reason. This again demonstrates the principle that fighting is reduced by social organization and increased by social disorganization.

E. Violent and Peaceful Behavior among Mammals

These warm-blooded and milk-producing animals, the group to which humans themselves belong, are a numerous and successful group. Because of their excellent sense organs, including vision, they can readily recognize individuals. Probably because of this, there are numerous examples of socially organized violent behavior, most of which is not destructive in well-organized social systems.

Prairie Dogs are large rodents that are classified as ground squirrels. They formerly lived in large colonies on the dry western plains of the United States. These animals construct burrows and form the earth into mounds. Each burrow is occupied by an adult male, and two or three females with their young. A male will sit on his mound and give a territorial cry, or a danger call if the colony is approached by a predator such as a coyote or hawk, and dive into his burrow if approached. The burrows are strung out in a line so that each burrow has other burrows on two sides, and is adjacent to grass, which is the chief food of the animals, on the other two sides. The line between the two territories is defended, but ordinarily no serious violence occurs. Each male approaches the line, reverses and holding its tail in the air backs up to the other male, who displays in a similar fashion, without overt violence. Like many other social animals, young prairie dogs can be easily tamed and can become pets. Such pets do not exhibit violence toward their owners.

However, prairie dogs are not entirely peaceable, and some fighting occurs elsewhere. Each male occupies a territory for two seasons, then leaves it to his offspring, and goes off to the unoccupied end of the line where he competes with other males for a new territory. Fighting occurs here, but ordinarily without serious injury. The end result is a linear colony that may be as long as a mile in extent. This again illustrates the principle that violence results from social disorganization. Also Hoogland found that underground the females sometimes killed the young, and young males fight to establish new territories above ground.

F. Peace and Violence among Carnivores

This group of mammals is adapted physiologically and behaviorally for the pursuit and killing of prey animals, usually herbivores. The same anatomical equipment can obviously be used for attacking members of the same species.

Among social carnivores, one of the best studied species is the wolf, *Canis lupus*, the ancestor of the domestic dog. Wolves are a species that evolved and are adapted to life in the North Temperate and Arctic regions. In a wooded area, a wolf pack may set up a territory as much as 50 miles in diameter. When the pack approaches the boundary it will scent mark the line, leaving urine or feces on conspicuous spots such as trees or large stones. Such scent marking is also common in domestic dogs, which usually set up a boundary around the place where they live with the owner.

Among themselves, the members of a wolf pack set up a dominance order through fighting. Male and female dominance orders are separate, and the most dominant animal is commonly a male, but in some packs it may be a female. In either case the dominant female will mate, usually with the most dominant male, but will not allow subordinate females to mate. The most usual result is a single litter in the pack, which is fed by regurgitation of food from all pack members; the result is an efficient reproductive system that controls population numbers. Surplus food is buried, to be dug up later. Thus the dominance order controls both food consumption and reproduction.

G. Peace and Violence in Domestic Dogs and Cats

1. Violence in Dogs

In its domestication from the wolf, the domestic dog has inherited many of its behavior patterns, but these have become enormously modified and variegated.

In our experiments a fresh bone given to two puppies from the same litter at approximately 5 weeks of age will stimulate fighting, including growling and attempts to bite. Puppies of this age have their baby teeth, sharp, pin-pointed, but quite small. Each pair in a litter was given a fresh bone, beginning at 5 weeks, and continued every 2 weeks through 15 weeks. At an early age, two male litter mates will attack each other, each attempting to seize the other by the scruff of the neck, an area with long hair and tough skin. Each tries to force the other to the ground, and if one succeeds he becomes dominant over the other in succeeding contests. The greatest injury is likely to be a drop of blood.

If it is a male–female pair, the male attacks first and usually wins. Two females will settle the contest by threats and vocalizations. In male pairs or male–female pairs, the larger pup is usually the winner, so that males dominate females. The outcome of the contest is that the larger animal gets the bone and chews on it undisturbed.

The peaceable behavior of the females carries over into adult life. Mothers never attack their offspring, and at the time of weaning, usually about 7 weeks of age, the mother may rush at a puppy trying to nurse, using vocal threats and growls. But a normal female never bites a puppy.

In reproduction, both dogs and wolves show the sexual tie. The female wolf will not allow the male to enter her until she becomes receptive. The male then mounts, inserts his penis, gives several rapid strokes and then at the moment of ejaculation enlarges his prostate gland at the base of the penis, so that it cannot be withdrawn. There follows a slow dribbling ejaculation of sperm. In a well-organized pack, the females form a dominance order.

The various dog breeds have been selected for the expression or nonexpression of violent behavior (Scott & Fuller, 1965). Thus dachshunds and terriers, which have been selected for attacking cornered prey animals, tend to be much more aggressive toward each other than do the beagles, a dog that has been selected to hunt in packs without being aggressive toward each other. Also, the terriers are very resistant to pain, and it is difficult to control them by physical punishment.

One of the most aggressive breeds is that of the pit bull terriers. Most breeds will retreat when physically hurt or punished, but these will continue to bite even when severely hurt. They can be quite dangerous, especially to small children, who are sometimes fatally wounded by them. Most other breeds will allow small children to play with them, even when they get rough, treating them as if they were puppies.

2. Violence in Cats

Unlike the dog, which is descended from pack-hunting wolves, the domestic cat was derived from the European wild cat, a solitary hunter. Each cat defends a home area and wanders over a larger hunting area, threatening any strange cat that it meets. Like the dog, cats have a critical period for primary social attachment, during which a kitten becomes attached to a home area that is defended.

During the season of estrus, a female becomes attractive to males. An interesting peculiarity is that the male's erect penis is covered with small barbs that make sexual behavior painful. Ovulation occurs only in response to pain. Actual fighting consists mostly of vocal threats, but biting and clawing may also occur.

H. Destructive Violence in Carnivore Species

1. Lions

Lions are the only members of the cat family that develop an elaborate social organization. They are also the largest of the carnivores, and therefore require a large amount of food. Adult males are much larger than females. Most lions live in the South African plains and live off the abundant species of food there. Most of the hunting is done by the females in prides, but the large males take their share.

When a young male becomes an adult, it may attack another pride and attempt to take it over. If successful, it will kill the resident male and attack the females, establishing dominance over them and killing their offspring, so that all subsequent offspring are fathered by the new male. Such violent behavior has the result of keeping the total number of lions, as well as the number of prides, relatively constant. In this way, the destructive violent behavior in this species maintains a limited population number. Violence thus functions to control population size.

2. Hyenas

Hyena behavior also results in limitation of a predator population. These carnivores are classified in a separate family, the Hyenidae. Their social organization is also unusual in that females are larger than males, and a dominant female rules the entire pack. Hyenas are also unique in another way. The adult female develops a pseudo-penis that is capable of erections and can be inserted in a male, although the sperm is contributed by the male and internal development takes place in the female in the usual mammalian fashion.

Severe and often fatal fighting takes place between young hyenas in a litter, providing another case of limitation on population growth. If this did not take place these efficient hunters might easily outrun their food supply of grazing animals.

I. Male–Female Differences

Male-female differences are widely distributed among mammals, the males usually being larger, stronger, and more overtly aggressive. One exception is the hamster, where the females are larger and stronger than the males. But most small rodents such as mice show the usual physical superiority of males.

J. Fighting Behavior in House Mice

Wild house mice are a species of small rodent that lives chiefly on seeds and grains. They readily adapt to human habitations and eat stored human food. The tame varieties are strains that have been held captive and selected for various color mutations and other oddities that attract their human owners. Most of the genetic strains of mice are derived from such varieties.

In the wild, each male will set up a territory, which he defends. Females are allowed to enter a male's territory, where they mate with him and raise young. Wild mice construct burrows and build nests in them. Fighting between males functions to establish territories, but these do not have as definite boundaries as those of dogs and wolves.

In the usual laboratory experiment on fighting a mature male is placed in a fresh cage. He explores this unfamiliar territory thoroughly with nose and whiskers. After a day or so, he becomes attached to the area, and thereafter will attack any strange male that is placed in the cage. The pattern of fighting is to rush at the stranger and attempt to bite. The stranger can either run or fight back. In the usual pattern of behavior, two males will each attempt to bite the other on the rump, a spot that is not easily injured. But one male may bite the other so severely that it attempts to run away, the resident in pursuit. In the usual cage situation there is no escape. If cornered, the beaten male will stand upright, facing its attacker with front paws outstretched. Thus a vulnerable part of the body is exposed, but the attacker tries to get behind it and bite the rump. This defensive posture has the effect of inhibiting fighting.

K. Genetic Differences in the Expression of Fighting Behavior in House Mice

These small rodents can fight fiercely among themselves, but there are differences in the expression of fighting behavior between different inbred strains, so that these animals have been widely used to study the effects of genic variation on fighting. Among the laboratory strains, fighting between females is rarely seen, but wild females fight readily and fiercely.

In my own studies of aggressive behavior in mice I started with three inbred strains, C57 blacks, C3H agoutis, and Bagg albinos, comparing the fighting behavior of young adults. The C3H strain tended to be aggressive, but was seldom successful in winning a fight. It turned out that the C3Hs were congenitally blind, and hence handicapped in fighting. The Bagg albinos, which have pink eyes and have some defects of vision, were not as severely handicapped. The C57 blacks had normal vision, but nevertheless varied in fighting ability.

L. Fighting in Horned Ruminants

The Rocky Mountain sheep is a wild species that formerly lived in high mountains in summer and migrated to lower altitudes in winter, but is now confined to the high altitudes the year around. It escapes from predators such as wolves by climbing on rocky cliffs.

Males and females live in separate flocks except during the autumn mating season, at which time males fight for mating privileges. Males have large, heavy horns that grow continuously, so that the older a male, the larger its horns, which gives it an advantage over younger males. In these contests, two males will back up, rear up, and rush together so that the horns clash. Attacks are never directed toward the vulnerable soft body parts. After a few clashes, the beaten male retires and the winner is free to mate with any female in estrus. This illustrates a phenomenon of *ritualized* violence, in which fighting is exhibited in a formal way, almost as if governed by rules.

The evolutionary result of this system is to select in favor of size and age, particularly in males. The age-related dominance order is related only to mating and has no effect on territory or feeding. Fatalities or serious injuries from fighting are quite rare. Except during the mating season the males live peacefully together. During cud-chewing, the most dominant male in a group takes the highest position, presumably the safest from any predator.

Females have short horns and use these to drive off stray lambs that might attempt to nurse. Otherwise there is no fighting in females. Sheep also exhibit playful fighting among the lambs. These small animals are well fed on milk, do not have to graze like their elders, and have time for play. The lambs ofter run and jump together, and sometimes play a game that could be called "king of the hill". One lamb gets on top of a high point, perhaps a rock, and butts all others who attempt to join him.

The fighting between male bighorns could be called ritualized fighting, defined here as following certain patterns of behavior that do not produce certain injury. Both fighting games and ritualized fighting are often seen in human societies, although we come from a different biological ancestry than the sheep.

Fighting is found universally among other ruminants, most of which have permanent hollow horns. Examples are the bison and domestic cattle. Spectacular fights between males also occur among members of the deer family. In these animals males grow branching antlers that are shed each year. The deer with the largest antlers has the advantage. Since larger antlers are grown each year the older deer tend to win, resulting in selection for older animals.

Fighting is quite common among mammals, but there are also instances of peaceful behavior, as among the baleen whales, which live by straining the small organisms out of sea water, and whose mouths—the only possible organ of offense—are not adapted for inflicting injury on large animals like themselves.

V. THE EVOLUTION OF SOCIAL SYSTEMS

Violent behavior may result in social organization which also regulates it. *Sociobiology* is defined as the biological study of social organization. This has attracted the attention of many evolutionary theorists, who attempt to analyze changes in social organization. Evolutionary theory must include *mutation*, defined as changes in the genes, the primary units of hereditary variation. Genes occur in pairs on chromosomes, and during the process of reproduction, these pairs are separated and recombined in a random fashion. Thus, *sexual reproduction* plus *mutation* are the primary producers of *genetic variation*, an essential part of evolutionary theory. These in turn are subjected to the process of *differential survival*, originally called *natural selection* by Darwin. There is one other way in which genetic change in a population may occur, and this is *inbreeding*, which limits the number of gene combinations that can occur. Unlike natural selection, inbreeding has no relationship to adaptation.

In evaluating any evolutionary explanation of violent and peaceful behavior, one must always check to be sure that all of the above change processes are included. The situation is complicated even more by the fact that genes often interact, sometimes in a nonadditive fashion.

Predatory violence is always affected by ecological factors such as the relative frequency of the predator and prey species, as with the wolf-moose population on Isle Royale in Lake Superior. Then there was the case of the deer population in the Kaibab Forest, where there were no predators. The deer eventually ate most of the vegetation and then began to starve to death.

VI. SUMMARY

This brief survey of the outstanding cases of violence indicates that violence is by no means universal among members of the animal kingdom. Peaceful coexistence is common. Also, there are two major kinds of violent behavior. One is *predatory violence* between different species, producing organization on the ecological level. The other is violence between members of the same species, which is usually a part of social organization. In order to have a specific term for social violence, I devised the term *agonistic* behavior, defined as fighting or violence between two or more members of the same species. This is the foundation of social organization based on violence, the basic unit of which is a dominance-subordination relationship. This is widespread among members of the vertebrate phylum, particularly fishes, birds, and mammals, and examples are given above.

In this survey of fighting and violence several points are obvious. One is that among nonprimate animals *territoriality* in the most common foundation of agonistic behavior. Fighting serves to divide up the available living space for a given species. A second is that while fighting is widespread, it is not universal. There are a great many species, especially among the more lowly organized invertebrates, in which agonistic behavior never occurs. Third, there are a few scattered species in which fighting results in death and so limits the size of populations. Two of these are group-hunting carnivorous mammals, lions and hyenas. Fourth, the most elaborate functions of agonistic behavior have evolved in two groups of vertebrates, the birds and mammals. A very important aspect of agonistic behavior among vertebrates is the dominance–subordination relationship that is almost universal among birds and mammals, but also occurs among species of fish.

Finally, models of human behavior are easy to find among other mammals. Ritualized fighting proceeds almost as if the animals were playing games with formal rules that limit the amount of damage done. Then, there is the playful fighting that occurs in the young of mammals. The only unique characteristic of the human species is the ability to communicate through language. In analyzing the behavior of other species we should always remember that they lack the communicative and analytic functions of language. Comparisons are therefore legitimate only with respect to behavior that is not based on language.

Also See the Following Articles

AGGRESSION AND ALTRUISM • ANIMAL BEHAVIOR STUDIES, PRIMATES • EVOLUTIONARY FACTORS

Bibliography

Allen, A. A. (1911–1913). The red-winged blackbird: A study in the ecology of a cat-tail marsh. *Abstract Proceedings of the Linnean Society of New York* (43–128).

Bovbjerg, R. V. (1956). Factors affecting aggressive behavior in the crayfish, *Procambarus alleni* (Faxon). *Physiological Zoology, 29,* 127–136.

Brain, P. F., Mainardi, D., and Parmagiani, S. (1987). *House mouse aggression: A model for understanding the evolution of social behavior.* London: Harwood.

Chelazzi, G., Focardi, S., Denenbourg, J. L., and Innocenti, R. (1983). Competition for the home and aggressive behavior in the chiton, *Acanthropleura gemmata* (Blainville) (Mollusca). *Behavioral Ecology and Sociobiology, 14,* 15–20.

Clifford, D. H., Green, K. A., and Scott, J. P. (1993). *Do's and don'ts concerning vicious dogs.* Chicago: AVMA Professional Liability Insurance Trust.

Collias, N. E., Collias, E. C., Hunsaker, D., and Minning, L. (1966). Locality fixation, mobility and social organization within an unconfined population of red jungle fowl. *Animal Behavior, 14,* 550–559.

Crane, J. (1975). *Fiddler crabs of the world: Ocypoidea, genus Uca.* Princeton, N.J.: Princeton University Press.

Ebert, P. D. (1983). Selection for aggression in a natural population. In E. C. Simmel, M. E. Hahn, and J. K. Wallers (Eds.), *Aggressive behavior: Genetic and neural approaches,* pp. 103–127. Hillsdale, N.J.: Erlbaum.

Francis, L. (1973a). Clone specific segregation in the sea anemone, *Acanthropleura elegantissima. Biological Bulletin, 144,* 64–72.

Francis, L. (1973b). Intraspecific aggression and its effect on the distribution of *Acanthropleura elegantissima* and some related sea anemones. *Biological Bulletin, 144,* 73–92.

Geist, V. (1971). *Mountain sheep.* Chicago: University of Chicago Press.

Ginsburg, B. E.. (1987). The wolf pack as a socio-genetic unit. In H. Frank (Ed.), *Man and wolf,* pp. 401–413. The Hague: Dr. W. Junk, Publisher.

Gottier, R. F. (1968). The effects of social disorganization in *Cichlasoma biocellatum.* Unpublished Ph.D. dissertation. Bowling Green State University, Bowling Green, Ohio.

Hoogland, J. L. (1995). *The black-tailed prairie dog: Social life of a burrowing mammal.* Chicago: University of Chicago Press.

Howard, E. (1920). *Territory in bird life.* London: John Murray Publisher.

Huxley, J. S. (1923). Courtship activities of the red-throated diver (*Colymbus stellatus* Pontopp) together with a discussion of courtship behavior in grebes. *Journal of the Linnean Society, 35,* 253–293.

King, J. A. (1955). Social behavior, social organization,and population dynamics in a black-tailed prairie dog town in the Black Hills of South Dakota. Contribution, Laboratory Vertebrate Biology, No. 67. Ann Arbor, MI: University of Michigan Press.

Kruuk, H. (1972). *The spotted hyena: A study of predation and social behavior.*Chicago: University of Chicago Press.

Kullman, E., Nawabi, S., and Zimmerman, W. (1971–1972). Neue Ergebnisse zur Brutbiologie cribillaten Spinnen auf Afganistan und der Serengeti. *Zeitschrift des Kollner Zoo, 14,* 87–108.

Leyhausen, P. (1979). *Cat behavior: The predatory and social behavior of domestic and wild cats* (B. A. Tonkin, translator). New York: Garland STPM Press.

Mech, L. D. (1966). *The wolves of Isle Royale.* Fauna of the National Parks of the United States, Fauna Series 7. Washington, D.C.: U. S. Government Printing Office.

Mech, L. D. (1988). *The Arctic wolf: Living with the pack.* Stillwater, MN: Voyageur Press.

Reish, D. J. (1957). The life history of the polychaeta annelid *Neanthes caudata* (della Chiaji) including a summary of development in the family Nereidae. *Pacific Science, 11,* 216–228.

Schjelderup-Ebbe, T. (1922). Beitrage zur soziale Psychologie des Haushuhns. *Zeitschrift Psychologie, 88,* 225–252.

Scott, J. P. (1946). Minutes of the conference on genetics and social behavior, R. B. Jackson Laboratory, Bar Harbor, ME; also see *Oxford english dictionary* (2nd ed.). Oxford: Clarendon Press.

Scott, J. P. (1958). *Animal behavior.* Chicago: University of Chicago Press. (Revised, 1972)

Scott, J. P. (1968). Evolution and domestication of the dog. In Th. Dobzhansky (Ed.), *Evolutionary biology,* Vol. 2 (pp. 243–275). New York: Appleton, Century & Crofts.

Scott, J. P. (1975). *Aggression* (2nd ed.). Chicago: University of Chicago Press.

Scott, J. P. (1989). *The evolution of social systems.* New York: Gordon and Breach.

Scott, J. P., and Fredericson, E. (1951). The causes of fighting in mice and rats. *Physiological Zoology, 24,* 273–309.

Scott, J. P., and Fuller, J. L. (1965). *Genetics and the social behavior of the dog.* Chicago: University of Chicago Press.

Vila, C., Savolainen, P., Maldonado, J. E., Amorim, I. R., Rice, J. E., Honeycutt, R. L., Crandall, K. A., Lundeberg, J., and Wayne, R. K. (1997). Multiple and ancient origins of the domestic dog. *Science, 276,* 1687–1289.

Wilson, E. O. (1971). *The insect societies.* Cambridge MA: Belknap-Harvard University Press.

Wilson, E. O. (1975). *Sociobiology: The new synthesis.* Cambridge. MA: Belknap-Harvard University Press.

Animal Behavior Studies, Primates

Irwin S. Bernstein
University of Georgia

GLOSSARY

Aggression Behavior that increases the probability of injury to the recipient.

Agonistic Aggression and typical responses to aggression, including submission.

Dominance A learned relationship between individuals that influences the directionality of agonistic signals.

Reconciliation Behavior that restores relationships following agonistic encounters.

Submission Behavior indicating that aggression will not be initiated, but aggression may be provoked by attacks.

Territoriality A learned relationship between individuals, specific to a geographic location.

I. DEFINITIONS

When we try to define aggression we often do so in terms of the motivations and intentions of the actor, and sometimes the recipient as well. We may define aggression as behavior that is intended to harm another, or behavior that deprives others of their rights, or freedom, against their will. Such a definition implies that we know that the motivation of the actor was selfish or spiteful, that the actor intended harm to the victim, and that the victim would rather have avoided the consequences imposed. Of course we may find that after we have classified an act as "aggression," the victim denies that s/he was forced to do anything against his/her will and/or, that the perpetrator denies any ill intent, insisting that s/he had no intention of actually harming the victim, that his/her behavior was for the victim's own good, and that the victim was a willing participant (s/he had "asked for it") or deserved the treatment received. The very existence of such arguments implies that the definition is subjective and judgmental rather than an objective description of observable behavior.

If we can have disagreements about whether human behavior meets such a definition of aggression think of how much more difficult it is to classify nonhuman behavior as "aggressive." How would we know if an oyster or lobster were motivated to harm another or deprive it of its freedom or rights? Are these animals even aware that others have rights, or even that others exist? One can readily decide that an individual has been harmed, or deprived of a necessary resource, but this is not, in itself, evidence that the victim suffered as the target of another's aggression. To invoke the concept of aggression we require that the "aggressor" be at least aware of the existence of its victim and that the aggressor engages in the injurious behavior with some knowledge that the victim is motivated to avoid such treatment. This is particularly difficult for us to ascertain when dealing with invertebrates, but is it any easier to determine for nonhuman primates, even if these are the animals most like ourselves? We do not have the ability to ask them their motivations nor do they have the ability to reply and explain the state of their cognitive awareness. Believing that they must act and feel as we do, and that they share the same motivations as we do, is anthropomorphism. We are less tempted to engage in anthropomorphism when we deal with spiders but readily succumb to this temptation when monkeys and apes are viewed as "furry" people.

If we wish to study and understand aggression in nonhuman subjects and to learn about the fundamental principles of aggression, we must define aggression in terms of observable behavior so that we can all, at least, agree what it is that we are trying to understand. Niko Tinbergen, in 1951, stated that we should begin by describing what we can see, hear, feel, taste, and smell; the structure of behavior. Such a description is much like what a video camera or other recording device would store. It is devoid of interpretation and, perhaps, relatively dry and uninteresting. It only becomes more interesting when we ask why it happened. Tinbergen said that there were four answers to that question.

The first answer can be obtained by identifying the situation in the environment that acted as the trigger for, or the stimulus that elicited, the behavior. This event, which releases or elicits the behavior of interest, is called the proximal cause. Proximal causes are observable events that can be described just as we can describe the behavior of interest, but proximal causes become more interesting to us when we think of them as being responsible for the occurrence of the behavior that follows. An extremely high correlation between the occurrence of a putative proximal cause and the behavior of interest (which follows in a brief temporal period) leads us to accept an hypothesis of causation.

Of course, we know that individuals do not respond to the same situations in the same ways all through their lives. To understand why their behavior changes requires us to examine ontogenetic causes of behavior. Here we may explain the change in response to a stimulus over time as being due to maturational processes, physical alteration of the individual due to environmental events (injuries, amputations, the effects of exercise, etc.), and behavioral changes that result from learning.

We may also note that different individuals (or species) respond differently to the same stimulus even when we control for ontogenetic events. In these cases we invoke the concepts of genetics to explain the differences in response to the same stimuli (or the different stimuli that produce the same responses), in different individuals or populations. The evolutionary cause of these differences relates to different evolutionary histories and the differences in selective pressures that operated on the ancestors of the subjects thereby accounting for differences in the genetic material with which each began life. Of course, it is often very difficult to experimentally verify the effects of purported differences in selective pressures in the past and, as a consequence, research is often directed to animals with short generation times, such as fruit flies, so that evolution can be observed within the lifetime of the scientist.

Finally, the "why" question may be addressed to the functional consequences of the behavior. The consequences can be conceived of as the objectively described events that follow the behavior of interest, or they may be perceived of as the long-term effects of the behavior on the genetic fitness of the actor, the adaptive significance of the behavior. Whereas the immediate consequent can be directly described, the question "What good did it do?" requires a longer view of consequence and casts everything in terms of evolutionary theory.

The two views of function lend themselves to a ready confusion of function with proximal cause. If the immediate consequence of the behavior is taken as equivalent to the motivation or intent of the subject just prior to or at the time of the response, then we are making a teleological error. Most of us are all too well aware of the differences between our intentions and the realities or results of our behavior. Why then are we so quick to gloss over this difference and to ascribe to an animal the intention to achieve the consequent observed? The second view of function leads to an even more egregious error when we assume that the animal was trying to improve its genetic fitness, as we later determined resulted as a consequence of its behavior. Of course, no one ever really assumes that animals understand evolutionary theory, nor that they are consciously attempting to improve their genetic fitness, but when we argue that the reason that the animal behaved in that manner was because evolution acted to select for individuals that behaved in a manner that maximized their genetic fitness, what are we implying? How could the individual have chosen among available alternative behavioral responses? What we are doing is hopelessly confusing proximal cause, evolutionary cause and function.

In dealing with aggression our task is made even more difficult by the fact that aggression is not a structure that can be objectively described. It is, instead, a class of behavioral responses linked to one another by some common consequent or function (as opposed to adaptive significance). We define broad categories such as feeding, reproduction, infant care, aggression, and locomotion based on the contribution of each element in the category to a particular function. Alternatively, we can postulate a common drive state, such as hunger, a maternal instinct, anger or such as the common cause of the behavior in a category, but with animals it is easier to observe what happens at the time of a behavior and what follows immediately from that behavior. How an animal felt (angry or not) and whether it intended to produce harm (meanness) are only subjects of conjecture. We can, however, note whether an injury occurred or whether the target individual was deprived of something as a consequence of the behavior of the actor. Losing something to another may occur as a result of several forms of competition and, in scramble competition, the competitors may even be totally unaware of each other's existence. Being deprived of a resource due to the actions of another who is not even aware of your existence does not meet our subjective feel for what aggression is. On the other hand, an injury is believed to be a likely result of aggression, even if not all aggression results in injuries and not all injuries are a result of aggression.

If an action is usually embedded in sequences where its presence increases the probability that the recipient is likely to suffer a physical injury due to the activities of the actor, then we are inclined to see that action as aggressive. This is a probabilistic definition in that we say that the behavior increases the likelihood of an injury following, rather than that it always produces an injury. Verification requires sufficient data to determine what the usual consequent of such sequences are when the act of interest is, and is not, present. It does not require us to know what the intentions or emotions of the parties involved were at the time of the activity, nor does it ask if the long-term effects reduced or contributed to the genetic fitness of the participants. These latter become empirical questions and we can now independently ask what functions aggression serves in terms of long-term consequences. If aggression in some cases harms the recipient but benefits the actor it will be selfish; if it harms both the actor and the recipient it will be spiteful; if it benefits the actor and recipient it will be mutualistic, and if it benefits the recipient at some expense to the actor it can even be altruistic. At first it may seem contradictory to ask if aggression can ever be altruistic. On reflection, however, we readily perceive that aggression can modify the behavior of the recipient; such behavioral modification may be brief or relatively long term (a learned response); and if this behavioral modification functions as a positive socialization experience, then it can modify the behavior of the recipient in such a manner as to enhance survival and reproduction. When we find that short-term injurious consequences can produce long-term benefits we tend to search for new words like "punishment" or "avoidance training" rather than aggression to describe the very same motor acts with the very same immediate functional outcomes.

II. FUNCTIONS OF AGGRESSION

Nonhuman primates, lacking language skills, use relatively little positive reinforcement in the socialization of their young. They cannot explain that a reward was for not doing "bad" behavior, or even for having done a particular good deed. Of course, they have no greater skill explaining punishment, but behavior that immediately elicits behavior in others with injurious consequences to yourself immediately receives your attention. The behavior of others that produces injuries to yourself, or the behavior of others associated with imminent escalation to behavior that produces injuries to yourself can powerfully alter behavior. Learning to avoid future injurious attacks is the basic element of avoidance learning. When an individual can respond to the threat of injury in such a manner as to avoid the injury, that individual has gained some measure of control over the behavior of the threatening individual. By providing a response that terminates sequences that otherwise escalate into exchanges that would be injurious to itself, an individual has controlled the behavior of another. This is avoidance learning as opposed to punishment or negative reinforcement where a response is required to terminate a noxious or injurious sequence already in progress.

Of course there are many cases where aggression modifies the behavior of the recipient in ways that only benefit the actor. Although the target may avoid the aggressive consequences of the actor, the target must modify its behavior in some fashion such that it gives up a resource or engages in a behavioral pattern that it was not otherwise motivated to engage in. In contest competition aggression is used as an instrumental act to gain preferential or exclusive access to a resource.

The loser is deprived of the resource but one may question if the winner was "trying" to harm the victim or only attempting to further its own selfish goals in obtaining the resource. In nonhuman primates "grudges" and personal animosities generated during such competitions may occur, but they are not invariable consequents and must be independently measured and verified. They can be recognized when we note that a pair immediately resumes a fight on their next encounter even when there is nothing to provoke a new fight and nothing to compete for. This is essentially a continuation of the previous fight, regardless of what the original cause of fighting was, and the relationship between the two parties may not be resolved until there is a clear winner and a clear loser. Even in such a case, where a fight might be described as occurring to determine who the winner or loser will be, one might not know if either combatant was motivated to harm the other rather than that each was just trying to elicit nonthreatening or submissive behavior from its opponent.

III. CONFLICT, COMPETITION, AND AGGRESSION

In nonhuman primates we can identify situations where individuals come into conflict (initiate different incompatible behavioral sequences), are in competition (both attempt to use the same limited resource at the expense of the other), or are engaged in aggression (one or both engages in behavior that is, or is likely to be, physically injurious to the other). Bill Mason has clearly differentiated conflict, competition and aggression, and there is no reason to equate the three terms. Each can occur in the absence of the other two. For example, a conflict occurs when two individuals, who both want to remain together, each want to travel in a different direction. Competition may involve "scramble contests" where whoever gets there first wins the resource even if the "winner" and "loser" are unaware of each other's existence. Aggression can occur when an individual attacks an uninvolved third party when attacked by another. Such "redirection" is based on availability and proximity rather than any interaction with or behavior of the third party. Likewise, an individual may attack a party to an ongoing fight with another. Aiding another in a fight does not require any prior conflict or competition with the individual against whom aid is directed.

Aggression, then, is not an invariable outcome of competition or conflict, nor is it limited to contexts involving competition and/or conflict. This has promoted some to talk of different "kinds" of aggression with each kind defined by the situation in which it occurs or the specific functional outcome. Thus we get "predatory aggression" when an animal attacks a victim that it will feed on; "instrumental aggression" when the behavior is seen as directed toward achieving some specific goal; "infanticidal aggression" when an infant is killed as a consequence of the aggression; "pain-induced aggression" when no clear function is apparent but pain is ascribed to the actor prior to the aggressive response; and, perhaps, aggression due to just plain "meanness," a hypothesized temperament variable. Each possible outcome and each possible cause then becomes a separate type of aggression. Such a plethora of terminology only confuses matters as all are called "aggression" and the common feature in each is that the recipient is likely to be injured, either immediately or in further escalated responses in the same sequence. Such sequences, in some cases, can be terminated or altered by specific changes in the behavior of the recipient, and then we sometimes assume that the change in the recipient's behavior was what the aggressor was trying to achieve.

IV. AGGRESSION IN A SOCIAL CONTEXT

Most nonhuman primates are social animals, and in many species most individuals spend all of their lives as members of a social unit. Individuals may transfer between units and/or spend some time as solitaries in transit between units. In some species individuals may travel or forage independently but nonetheless have frequent contact with certain specified individuals with whom they preferentially interact. Whatever the level of sociality, social units are collections of individuals that may come into conflict, or that may compete for the same resources. Some of these conflicts and competitions may be resolved by resorting to aggressive techniques. Social relationships between individuals may be described on a dimension of affiliative to antagonistic based on the ratio of agonistic to affiliative exchanges.

If aggression increases the probability of injury to at least the recipient, then life in a social unit will require the development of means to prevent and control aggressive solutions to problems engendered by conflict and competition in socially living individuals. If aggression is elicited, then it must be limited, controlled, and regulated such that it terminates with minimal risk of injuries. The expression and control of aggression must be regulated in any social unit lest the costs of aggression outweigh the benefits of sociality.

On the other hand, all aggression is not antisocial. Aggression can serve as a social means of protecting a group against external sources of disruption. It can also be used to modify the behavior of group members in ways that benefit the individual whose behavior is being modified as well as other group members. Aggression can be used to socialize individuals into a group and it can be used to promote the interests of members of one group over members of another group. Uncontrolled aggression within a group, however, can destroy the group.

Aggression in nonhuman primate groups has a multitude of expressions. These may vary from intense stares and various body postures and facial expressions to locomotor displays, such as charging, lunging, and rhythmic leaping, to interactions involving physical contact with the potential for bodily injury, such as slapping, kicking, pulling, biting, and slashing. Many nonhuman primates, and especially males, possess formidable canine teeth with the potential to inflict lethal injury. Some, such as drills and mandrills, literally have canines as large as those of any of the great cats, although they are only a fraction of the body size of a great cat and largely vegetarian or at most omnivorous in their diet. Despite this formidable armament, relatively few agonistic encounters between or within primate groups result in severe injuries or deaths, although some dramatic outcomes do result and excite all of our imaginations. It would also be a mistake to equate the potential for producing injury with aggressivity. Even if formidable canines do result in obvious severe injuries, whereas less impressive physical equipment fails to do so, it would be a mistake to count injuries inflicted as a measure of aggression. Despite the sexually dimorphic nature of most nonhuman primates and the fact that males do often inflict most of the injuries in or by a group, females may engage in very comparable levels of aggressive behavior. The question, of whether sex differences in aggression exist, is an empirical question and incompletely answered by evidence of injuries inflicted by members of the two sexes.

Given this extensive potential for mayhem, the question then becomes "Why does life in a social group not result in a continuous set of injuries and wounds resulting from daily conflicts and the inevitable competition evoked when similar individuals, all with similar needs, seek the same limited resources?" There is no single answer to this question but, thankfully, we find that there are multiple mechanisms that come into play. These include: ritualization of aggressive expression, such that the most damaging forms of expression are rare within the group; development of nonaggressive means of resolving conflicts and competitions; and development of mechanisms that regulate aggressive expression within a group, including social means of terminating ongoing agonistic encounters.

V. THE CONTROL OF AGGRESSIVE SEQUENCES

Although there are multiple causes of aggression, few aggressive encounters begin with an all-out fight. The potential costs of fighting are such that natural selection has favored individuals that avoid taking risks when the cost to themselves is likely to exceed the benefits of anything obtained by engaging in that interaction. When a situation develops where aggression is one possible way to achieve a desired outcome, the individual involved should first attempt to determine the likelihood of resistance and, second, the likely magnitude of that resistance. In other words, is the target signaling readiness to resist or counter attack? (Is it threatening?), and, if it is threatening, then what will be the likely strength of its resistance and/or attack in terms of the costs that will be imposed? Animals often use body size, indicators of strength and physical vigor, and a variety of bodily postures, facial expressions, and vocalizations as indicators of the potential costs that an opponent can inflict and the willingness of that opponent to inflict such costs.

If insufficient information is available to decide whether to precede or to break off an encounter, based on available visual, auditory, chemical, or other signal modalities, then physical contact may follow. Physical contacts may gradually escalate such that initial contacts convey information about strength and ability without either participant running the risk of extensive injury. If such initial probing attacks do not provide sufficient information for one participant to break off the encounter, then further escalation to more damaging forms of aggression may follow. Finally, when one of the opponents has obtained sufficient information to convince it that the costs of further aggression will be unacceptable, that opponent may retreat, or use a ritualized signal of submission, to end the encounter. The victor now has unrestrained access to whatever resource was being contested, or can now obtain whatever goal it had been seeking, and further attacks on the part of the victor would only serve as "spite," since the victor risks further injury in resuming aggression against a retreating opponent. There is no further benefit to be gained and inflicting additional injury on a defeated rival at some risk to one's self meets the definition of spite.

Contest competition can thus be seen as being extraordinarily dangerous if the two opponents are nearly equal in ability and motivation so that neither perceives the other as a likely winner and both continue to escalate the encounter to obtain more and more information about the abilities of their rival. Alternatively, contest competitions can prove to be extremely dangerous to one or both participants even when there is a great disparity in abilities if one or more of the opponents is incapable of recognizing that disparity. Monkeys reared in social isolation seem to lack the social skills required to assess: the willingness of a rival to engage in escalated aggression, the ability of the rival to inflict aggressive costs, and even the meaning of signals that a rival uses when conceding access to a contested resource. In these situations contests escalate rapidly and monkeys reared in social isolation may launch suicidal attacks against opponents that are clearly physically superior to themselves or, alternatively, they may mount murderous attacks on opponents that are signaling submission and attempting to withdraw from the site of a contest. We might describe such monkeys as "sociopaths" or "psychopaths."

Every aggressive episode concludes when the parties involved cease further aggressive behavior. The individual that stops first may withdraw or otherwise show behavior incompatible with further aggression, and this individual is labeled the "loser." The aggressive behavior of most winners ends when the goal is achieved, be that goal the attainment of a particular prize or the particular behavior demanded of the opponent (such as retreat).

VI. LOSING, DOMINANCE, AND TERRITORIALITY

A winner and a loser emerge from a fight as a consequence of the sequence of events in that interaction. No further information is required to explain why one party retreated or ceased further aggression other than the events that transpired during the encounter. If every successive encounter followed exactly the same course as the initial encounter then our explanation for the change in behavior observed in all encounters would be identical and limited to the exchanges that occurred during that encounter. The observer, on the other hand, may quickly recognize the similarities in the series of encounters and may soon learn to predict, with great accuracy, the outcome of each new encounter. This does not mean that the two opponents have established any special relationship or that either of them has learned anything, not if both go through exactly the same sequence on each new encounter. In this case only the observer has learned anything.

If, on the other hand, there is a directionality in the change of behavior between the two opponents at the start of a new encounter, then we might believe that one or both were now more willing to attack or retreat and that this was due to the history of exchanges in prior encounters, that is, something had been learned.

In most cases this learning means that one party immediately displays the behavior that it used to terminate the previous encounters. This is then the "loser" and it is the loser that has learned something. The question now is what exactly was learned.

If the learned component is so general that an individual that has lost previous encounters now immediately retreats or signals submission at the start of any future encounter, then we say that we have a "trained loser." Such an individual is expected to break off any encounter whenever its opponent shows aggression. It has "learned" because in the absence of such learning we should expect every encounter to proceed much as had the first. When there is no change in behavior, no learning can be invoked in our explanations of behavior.

If the loser has learned not to fight a particular opponent, but does not generalize to all opponents, then it will immediately yield to the aggressive signals of that particular opponent while continuing to respond aggressively to other opponents that it has previously defeated, and/or new opponents. What has been learned is specific to a particular individual and we can say that the subject has learned to be subordinate to that opponent, that is, that a dominance relationship has been established. In future agonistic encounters the subject will use the identity of its opponent in making its decision to submit or resist when faced with an aggressive challenge.

Submission is in response to a perceived aggressive signal rather than a general response to the partner; dominant and subordinate partners can interact in nonagonistic forms of interaction. They may even come into conflict, or compete with one another, without aggression. When aggression is expressed, however, the subordinate will submit. Dominant animals can lose in competitions where scramble is involved and may yield resources whenever they are not willing to use aggressive means to claim them.

In territoriality the relationship between the antagonists is complicated one step further. The individual that shows submission and the individual that shows aggression in a particular dyad will be determined by the geographical location of the encounter. When neither is on its territory, neither may show aggression, or both may do so, or some other mechanism will determine which of the two will be aggressive and which submissive. When a territorial individual is on its territory, however, we expect that the territorial holder will show aggression toward any member of a specified class of intruders. The key here is geography and not proximity. Whereas a territorial holder will cross any intervening distance to challenge a detected intrusion, many animals display flight and fight distances, or defense of personal space unrelated to geography. When another unexpectedly appears within a critical distance then the individual withdraws, but if the intrusion is within a smaller critical distance aggressive responses may be provoked. This should not be equated with territoriality as a "moving territory." The physical laws of nature preclude two physical objects from occupying the same space at the same time but this would mean that all objects possessed territories if we followed this logic to *reductum ad absurdum*.

Territoriality and dominance both regulate the expression of aggression between individuals, but slightly but significantly different mechanisms are involved. Territoriality may be seen as the more complex of the two in that, in addition to the past history of interactions between the individuals, the location of the encounter determines which of the two will exhibit aggressive behavior and which of the two will retreat. Dominance relationships also influence which individual will show aggressive behavior and which will retreat, but this influence is independent of geographical location. In dominance, as a function of a past history of interaction between the individuals there is a learned relationship specific to the two partners that is independent of geographic location.

In territoriality, dominance, and encounters involving trained losers, the aggressive encounters are curtailed by learned elements so that only one or neither of the dyad displays aggressive behavior. Since the intruder or the subordinate or the trained loser leaves or submits immediately upon receiving an aggressive signal, escalation is rare and injuries are avoided. Assessments of opponents are based on membership in a class (trained losers) or individual identity (dominance) or individual identity and location (territoriality) rather than on displays and contests testing another's abilities and resolve.

Injuries often occur in aggressive encounters as part of the assessment process. In an aggressive encounter one or both participants uses aggressive techniques to modify the behavior of the other. Since the use of aggressive behavioral elements entails some risk of retaliation, the opponents must assess the value of the goal they seek and the likely costs to be incurred in attaining that goal. If an individual can anticipate costs greater than it is willing to bear to attain the goal, then retreat would be the better part of valor. Aggressive encounters thus may be seen as periods during which constant assessments are being made.

For example, if two individuals are using aggression to compete for a particular resource, neither should be willing to sustain a cost greater than the value of that resource to themself. The value of the resource may not be equal to both and the costs that each can impose on the other may also be unequal. The antagonists therefore begin by assessing the value of the resource to themselves, and then the likely costs to be imposed by the antagonist based on indications of the antagonist's aggressive potential and resolve. If sufficient information is available on the amount of cost that the antagonist can impose based on past interactions, and the resolve of the antagonist to impose such costs based on geographic location, then territoriality applies. If only the identity of the opponent is sufficient to assess the likely costs of aggressive resistance, then dominance applies. If all aggressive signals from any opponent are equally effective in eliciting retreat then we have a trained loser. Of course, the application of these principles requires signals from the antagonist indicating that it is prepared to impose an aggressive cost—"threat" behavior. Lacking such signals, a subordinate, or an intruder, or a trained loser should readily collect a valuable resource even if all the while monitoring the potential antagonist for any sign that an aggressive cost was about to be imposed.

VII. POLYADIC SOCIAL AGGRESSION

Aggressive episodes in nonhuman primates are not limited to dyadic encounters. Primates are social creatures and use social techniques to meet environmental (physical and social) challenges. Antagonists in aggressive encounters are often rapidly joined by others that take sides in the dispute. Assessment in these cases is not simply restricted to the opponents' size, strength, and willingness to escalate, but also on the size and strength of the opponents' allies and their availability and willingness to join in the encounter. When monkeys and apes become involved in agonistic encounters the episodes are usually noisy, with each vocalizing its presence (and identity) and scanning the vicinity for potential allies and adversaries. Monkeys and apes often resolve fights based on the willingness of others to join on one side or another. In this way size and strength become much less important than the size and reliability of social alliances in resolving fights between individuals. It is no longer the largest and most powerful that will be the victor, but now perhaps the most socially adept.

The cohesion shown by all of the members of a group when faced by an extragroup source of threat or disturbance results in mobbing of predators and joint attacks on rival groups. This same cohesion by subunits of a social group in resolving fights within a group results in cliques and alliances. Unresolved struggles between such cliques and alliances can cause fissioning or fragmentation of groups. To remain cohesive, groups must develop means of resolving conflicts between subunits within the group.

VIII. RESTORING PEACE

Having developed methods to assess rivals and to regulate and avoid fights, it should not be surprising to find that nonhuman primates have also developed techniques to restore peace and harmony in their all-important social units once fighting and/or conflict has occurred. Whereas fight interference, the joining in of uninvolved parties in an ongoing aggressive encounter, excited initial attention, more recently attention has been focused on the behavior that follows after an agonistic episode. Monkeys and apes have been noted to seek out former opponents in the minutes immediately following a fight, not to further the agonistic exchange, but to engage in positive affiliative contact. Such positive social behavior immediately following a fight exceeds the rate that would have been predicted based on positive social exchanges when no fight occurs and this has, therefore, been described as reconciliation. Either of the two former combatants, the winner or the loser, may be the first to initiate affiliative social interactions, although the loser is somewhat more likely to do so. If this is functionally "reconciliation" then the occurrence of positive affiliative behavior immediately following an agonistic encounter should mean that the former opponents can now interact or engage in behavior in proximity to one another without resumption of hostilities. Indeed, Marina Cords found that former combatants that were allowed to reconcile did indeed share resources and cooperate in matters where they had formerly done so, whereas in the absence of such reconciliations tension continued and the animals were reluctant to come into close proximity. The functional definition of "reconciliation" therefore seems to be firmly established.

Following what was said about the polyadic nature of agonistic encounters it should be no surprise to discover that many monkeys and apes reconcile polyadically. Following an agonistic encounter the aggressor, and/or the victim, may initiate positive social interactions with the close associates (generally kin and close allies) of its opponent in the minutes immediately following a fight. Alternatively, an animal's usual allies may initiate the positive interactions with its opponent. These indirect reconciliations may thus restore the relationships between alliances as well as between the individual combatants.

On the other hand, whereas consolation may be considered related to reconciliation, but instead of the allies of a combatant showing positive behavior to the combatant's opponent, positive behavior is directed to the combatant, nonetheless, evidence for consolation among monkeys is sparse indeed. Although some evidence is available to support its presence in apes, this evidence is not nearly as convincing as is the evidence for reconciliation. It has been speculated that reconciliation serves the immediate interests of the reconciling parties whereas consolation requires empathic ability on the part of the consoling agent that, itself, receives no direct benefit.

Empathic abilities may be poorly developed in monkeys that do not readily take the perspective of another, and only rudimentary in apes where such cognitive skills seem at the upper limits of ape abilities. Research in these areas is still ongoing, new, and hardly conclusive.

IX. CONCLUSION

Aggression, then, is not disorganized antisocial behavior. It is not base and basic animal behavior. Aggression is of sufficient consequence to individuals that all of an individual's skills can be expected to be called into play in aggressive encounters. In nonhuman primates, with extensive social and cognitive skills, these skills will be employed in aggressive conflicts. Extensive cognitive skills will be employed in the difficult assessments of opponents' abilities and resolve. Well-developed social skills will be employed to establish alliances and to detect the existence of opposing alliances. Social mechanisms within a group developed in order to maintain social units so that group members would each receive the benefits of social living. These social mechanisms include mechanisms that use aggression to preserve the social unit, but they must also include mechanisms to ensure that aggression between members of the unit does not destroy the unit.

Aggression occurs within a social environment in nonhuman primates and that environment shapes the expression of aggression and modifies the sequences of behavior in aggressive encounters. Social mechanisms have developed to restore social relationships threatened by disruption due to aggressive episodes, and both direct reconciliation and social reconciliation involving third parties can be demonstrated. Restoring the peace may be one of the more demanding social skills; elimination of aggression is virtually impossible. Aggression socializes newcomers into the group, protects the group from external threats, modifies the behavior of disruptive group members and is used as an instrument to further the goals of a group in competition with rival groups. On the other hand aggression between members of a social unit threatens the integrity of the group. Social and individual mechanisms exist to limit the expression of aggression within a group and to counteract disruptive consequences. Social relationships among individuals must be restored, for these are the very fabric that constitutes the social group, and the social group provides extensive advantages to nonhuman primates. All of a group's highest capabilities will be expressed in dealing with problems associated with aggression and its consequences, not so much to eliminate what in some form is essential, but to control the consequences so as to reap the maximum benefits with the least risk.

Also See the Following Articles

AGGRESSION AND ALTRUISM • ANIMAL BEHAVIOR STUDIES, NONPRIMATES • BEHAVIORAL PSYCHOLOGY • EVOLUTIONARY FACTORS • NEUROPSYCHOLOGY OF MOTIVATION FOR GROUP AGGRESSION

Bibliography

Aureli, F., Veenama, H. C., van Pathaleon van Eck, C. J., van Hooff, J. A. R. A. M. (1993). Reconciliation, consolation, and redirection in Japanese macaques (*Macaca fuscata*). *Behaviour,* 124, 1–21.

Bernstein, I. S. (1981). Dominance: The baby and the bathwater. *Behavioral and Brain Sciences,* 4, 419–457.

Bernstein, I., Ehardt, C. L. (1985). Agonistic aiding: Kinship, rank age, and sex influences. *American Journal of Primatology,* 8, 37–52.

Cords, M. (1994). Experimental approaches to the study of primate conflict resolution. In J. J. Roeder, B. Thierry, J. R. Anderson, & N. Herrenschmidt (Eds.), *Current Primatology,* VOL. II. *Social Development, Learning Behaviour,* 127–136. Strasbourg: Univ. Louis Pasteur.

Cords, M., & Aureli, F. (1993). Patterns of reconciliation among juvenile long-tailed macaques. In M. E. Pereira & L. A. Fairbanks (Eds.), *Juvenile primates: Life history, development, and behavior,* New York: Oxford University Press, 271–284.

Cords, M., & Thurnheer, S. (1993). Reconciling with valuable partners by long-tailed macaques. *Ethology,* 93, 315–325.

de Waal, F. (1989). *Peacemaking among primates.* Cambridge, MA: Harvard University Press.

de Waal, F. B., & Aureli, F. (1996). Consolation, reconciliation, and possible cognitive difference between macaques and chimpanzees. In A. E. Russon, K. A. Bard, & S. T. Parker, (Eds.), *Reaching into thought: The minds of the great apes,* 80–110. Cambridge: New York, Cambridge University Press.

Gust, D. A., & Gordon, T. P. (1993). Conflict resolution in sooty mangabeys. *Animal Behaviour,* 46, 685–694.

Mason, W. A., & Mendoza, S. P. (1993). *Primate social conflict.* Albany: State University of New York Press.

Tinbergen, N. (1951). *The study of instinct.* Oxford: Clarendon Press of Oxford University Press.

Animals, Violence toward

James M. Jasper
New York City

GLOSSARY

Animal Rights The claim, popularized in the 1980s, that nonhuman species have absolute rights of various kinds, including protection from unnecessary suffering and the opportunity to live an existence "natural" or appropriate to the species.

Animal Baiting A form of entertainment, once quite popular, in which one animal is attacked or tormented by others, especially a large species like a bull or bear attacked by dogs.

Anthropomorphism The perception or projection of human traits onto nonhuman creatures or objects, which has helped many humans to see considerable similarities between themselves and other species.

Factory Farming A term for modern agricultural techniques involving the mass processing of vast numbers of anonymous animals in controlled environments.

Habitat The local environment that sustains the life of a species or individual.

Vegetarianism The refusal to eat any form of meat; in its extreme form (called veganism), the additional refusal to eat products derived from animals, such as eggs, cheese, and milk.

Vivisection Literally, the cutting up of live subjects in scientific research; more broadly, the use of animals in research.

IN ONLY A TINY PORTION of the human societies that have ever existed would the concept of violence toward animals make sense, since the pejorative tone of the word "violence" implies unjust, unnatural, or unexpected aggression. For most humans through history, inflicting pain, suffering, and death on nonhuman species was a natural and expected part of life, and violence toward animals made no more sense than the idea of violence against timber, iron ore, or corn. Only in the last several hundred years, the tiniest blip out of the 2 million years of human existence, have significant numbers of people felt and argued that violence was even a possibility in the treatment of animals. To them, violence against animals occurs when humans intentionally inflict or tolerate suffering in other species, perhaps even when they prevent those species from living "natural" lives.

Whatever anachronistic labels we apply, all human societies have relied on animals in one way, or many ways, so much so that over many generations humans and other species have made considerable adjustments to each other. One use of animals, as pets, is unique in the concern for the life and comfort of the animals, in contrast to virtually all other uses in which the nonhuman species either dies or suffers considerably for human benefit. It is no accident that it is primarily citizens of industrial societies, who encounter living animals almost exclusively as pets rather than as prey, predator, or economic resource, who have begun to see other human uses of animals as questionable or even violent. By today's most refined standards, the history of humans and animals is almost identical with the history of human violence toward animals.

Most societies have treated nonhuman species with the same respect, indifference, or even cruelty with which people treated each other. Hunter-gatherer bands face considerable pain and suffering themselves, and have few compunctions about inflicting it on other species. In the no-nonsense worldview of most settled agrarian societies, animals are treated more kindly—as long as this does not interfere with their use as economic resources, which is paramount. But then, children in these societies are also treated as simultaneously a source of pleasure and an economic investment. In the industrial world, with decreasing direct contact with animals in the wild or as resources, the treasured pet has become the paradigm, at the same time that the rights of individuals and the cherishing of children has expanded. From this perspective, in which individual humans and animals are recognized as having inherent value and rights, it is possible to reframe many uses of animals as violence against them.

There are different ways in which animals suffer because of the actions of humans. Deliberate cruelty is the most likely to be recognized as violent. Neglect, in contrast, is a sin of omission, often through ignorance of an animal's needs or a human's inadequate resources for proper care. But animals also frequently suffer through their "normal" use by humans, which often involves coercion and force. Finally, animals may suffer quite inadvertently when human development threatens their necessary habitats. In the right perspective, any of these may be framed as violence against other species.

I. HUNTING IN PRE-AGRICULTURAL SOCIETIES

Hunting is the oldest use of animals, predating the steady supply that comes from domestication. For more than 99% of the time that *Homo sapiens* have existed, they were hunter-gatherers, and hundreds of such groups survive today. In the absence of technology, however, humans are not especially adept as hunters, so that our earliest ancestors' hunting had a kind of equality to it. They were able to capture small mammals, birds, and fish, and to pick over the remains left by larger, more efficient, hunting species. But if they encountered one of the latter—leopards, lions, even hyenas—our ancestors were more likely to be prey than predator. Despite several generations of anthropologists who saw hunting as a defining characteristic of humans, it is now thought that most hunter-gatherer societies have relied primarily on gathered fruits and vegetables, with meat as only an occasional treat.

The efficiency of hunting depends on the tools available, and hunter-gatherers use rather primitive ones. Bows and arrows and spears require patience and tenacity on the part of those who use them, who must track and stalk animals in order to get close enough to wound or kill them. Depending on how sharp and hard the spear or arrow, and how good the hit, the animal may only be wounded, requiring further tracking until it dies. Snares and nets work on many animals. They require less strength or stamina from humans, although there is often a live and frantic animal to be dispatched.

Societies in which one must kill one's own meat often encourage children to be indifferent to animal suffering. When a litter of puppies is born among the Inuit, for instance, children are encouraged to adopt the strongest as pets, to cuddle them, speak lovingly to them, and treat them—before they are put to work—as pets. At the same time they enthusiastically kill the weaker litter mates by smashing their skulls against rocks, throwing them off cliffs, or into the sea. Animals are distinguished by their utility to humans, not their ability to feel pain. Those who live in industrial societies tend to see these attitudes and behaviors as cruel or contradictory, but they are appropriate to the context. Life is harsh for many hunter-gatherers, and survival may depend on the ability to kill another creature quickly and thoughtlessly, or to be fearlessly aggressive in the face of large animals. One cannot be squeamish about blood or violence. For humans too, there is plenty of blood, suffering, and death to be more or less stoically faced.

The lack of concern for animals' pain often coexists with spiritual reverence. In a society of hunters, the grace and stamina of other species are naturally a thing of awe and inspiration. But only rarely does this respect interfere with human's utilitarian use of the animals. They may ask the animal's soul to forgive them for killing it, but kill it they do. Similarly, many animals are sacrificed to various gods, but eaten by the human celebrants.

II. DOMESTICATION AND TRADITIONAL AGRICULTURE

Around 10,000 years ago, independently in several parts of the world, many hunter-gatherers settled down and started to raise their own plants and animals, drastically changing the ways they used animals. Dogs seem to have been the first species tamed, possibly even before settled agriculture developed, and they have remained one of the most useful animals in hunting and agriculture ever since.

Agriculturalists have almost unanimously held dual attitudes toward animals: fondness and concern for some, especially those that help get the farming done, but a harshly realistic view of animals as economic resources. Some animals have value through sustained service: the dogs that help herd sheep, the horses or mules used for transportation and plowing, the cows used for dairy and breeding, and so on. Others have value primarily as meat, and their lives last no longer than it takes to fatten them sufficiently. Even these might be valued when young, as the young lambs so often kept in the huts of their owners for the first year of their lives, treated as pets, especially by children. But when their time for slaughter comes, their status shifts abruptly from pet to resource.

Like hunting, agriculture has grown more sophisticated over time, with an increasing division of labor in the uses to which animals are put. Especially among wealthy farmers, and peaking with aristocratic estates, dogs have been bred to accentuate valuable traits. Some became expert sheepherders, others tenacious watchdogs. Of the many breeds kept for hunting, some grew adept at pointing or flushing game, others at following a scent, some at retrieving downed birds, others at restraining large exhausted prey. Horses too have been bred to pull heavy weight, or to move swiftly with a single rider. These animals are, in many ways, lucky, performing valuable labor. Unlike the animals they help to hunt or herd, they will not usually be cooked and eaten as soon as they are mature (although they might be eaten or rendered later, when no longer productive).

Cats have few uses on farms beyond rodent control, at which they excel when partly feral. So even as dogs gained status in early modern Europe, most cats remained outside the charmed circle of pets. As late as the 18th century they were valued more because of the noise they made when tortured than from familial affections. Throughout the 19th century dogs remained by far the favorite, seen as loyal and loving, with the noted independence of cats prized mostly by intellectuals and artists. Cats' fortunes improved in the 20th century, and in the United States they have now surpassed dogs as the most popular pet.

Traditional agriculture is a good example of what philosopher Mary Midgley calls a "mixed community" in which humans and other species live together in a kind of symbiotic division of labor. There is a clear distinction between those animals that "work" alongside the humans and shorter-term residents whose ultimate utility will be as food. It is easier to label the treatment of the latter as violence.

III. HUNTING FOR PLEASURE

In the agricultural and industrial worlds hunting continues, more as a sport than a serious source of food. Aristocrats were probably the first to pursue game primarily for the social and ceremonial pleasures of hunting, although in late medieval Europe hunting was also defended (not very plausibly) as a way for warriors to maintain their skills between campaigns. Before the modern era, hunting did require a certain strength, even bravery. The chase, through thick woods and underbrush, on either foot or horse, demanded stamina, and the kill, when still accomplished with spear or dagger, a certain degree of strength. In the 16th and 17th centuries, however, servants flushed out the prey, increasing numbers of dogs were used to pursue and corner it, and nets would often be used to hold the exhausted animals for final slaughter. In England there were no wild boars left to pursue, so less-than-ferocious deer became the favorite prey. Queen Elizabeth I was said to enjoy slicing the animal's throat herself, although firearms were used more and more often to do the job. Other forms of hunting—letting teams of whippets or greyhounds chase hares or using hawks and falcons to kill other birds—were even less warriorly.

Hunting became more of a pageant for displaying the wealth, power, and leisure of landowners. Deer parks were carefully fenced, hedged, or ditched in, and the "hunters" would be accompanied by an enormous retinue of servants and guests, including ladies, who often had the privilege of finally dispatching a terrified and exhausted deer. No one loved the sight of blood more than Henry VIII, but his increasing weight and ill health shifted his—and consequently England's—style of hunting toward the more sedentary. At the extreme, the deer from a park would be rounded up in advance, the king would pick the one he wished to hunt, and a pack of dogs would herd it past a platform from which the king and his guests would shoot at it.

Technological innovations as well as wealth made hunting the rather one-sided affair it remains today. Men would sneak up on their prey hidden behind "stalking horses." They would hide in trees and shoot at deer with powerful crossbows. Or deer would be driven into water, where men in boats would slice their throats. Most of all, long guns with multiple shot were invented and deployed. Patience replaced valor as the virtue taught by modern hunting.

In Britain, at least, hunting retained a link to warfare only in its legal restrictions and political battles around these. The Normans claimed one-quarter of England as the King's own forests, and over time further regulations were designed to restrict deer hunting to the wealthiest landowners. For many, then, poaching became a political act. Sometimes it was done in order to defy new regulations or enclosures, at other times to test the power of a local aristocrat. Bands of as many as 50 men (often led by gentry, but mixing gentry and commoners) would invade a deer park, leading to physical battles with gamekeepers. In the most political forms of poaching the bodies would not even be carried off for food, but left as an insult. Only after the Black Act of 1723, which made it a capital felony to hunt in disguise, did poaching decline.

There is probably nothing that British aristocrats have done that American upper classes have not mimicked, but hunting, horses, and dogs are foremost. In the United States sport hunting became popular with the upper classes in the late 19th century, as part of a more general nostalgia for nature on the part of an increasingly urbanized elite. As these wealthy classes built estates on the fringes of the emerging cities, they populated them with horses and dogs, and they took up hunting as a pastime. Here was a way to spend time outside, to ride a horse, as well as to examine and show off one's property. They applied new and peculiar rules to hunting to transform it from an occupation into a sport. They were sure to allow a bird to take wing before firing at it, and only aimed at one bird at a time. Through etiquette books on hunting and field sports, they sustained an elaborate jargon, with different names for different numbers of different species: a flock of partridge were a "covey," of ducks, a "badelynge." A pair of partridge were a "brace," but two grouse were a "leash." Most of all, they insisted that true sportsmen did not eat their prey. As a result they favored smaller, less edible birds. They also successfully promoted state laws aimed at banning professional hunters who sold wild birds in local markets. "Pot shot" became a pejorative term for birds destined for the table.

Hunting was a symbolically important facet of Europe's colonization of much of the rest of the world, especially in Africa and in India, where the British often adopted existing aristocratic traditions such as hunting from atop elephants. Hunting parties, not so different in size or arms from war parties, no doubt impressed locals with their firepower. The wanton slaughter of large numbers of animals, without any practical intent such as food, was probably meant as a humiliation of the natives as well as a warning.

Proponents of hunting universally speak of the pleasures of male camaraderie, and solitary hunting is rare. In hunting-gathering societies, the men often leave the women behind when they hunt, sometimes for days or weeks at a time, and hunting has regularly been a rite of passage from boyhood to manhood. The poaching fraternities of early modern Britain were secret and stable, often lasting 5 or 10 years, with a typical size of 8 or 10 men. Even former President Jimmy Carter has written nostalgically about his boyhood hunting in Georgia. His father would take him in the pre-dawn dark to rendezvous with friends, and they would stand around a pot-bellied stove or hearth fire. They would indulge in—and these seem to be the heart of the pleasure of hunting—ribald stories and alcohol. Only then would they divide into pairs to enter, along with their dogs, the woods.

In the contemporary United States, around 7% of adults hunt. This is a considerably higher proportion than in other developed countries. Ninety percent of these hunters are men, and they devote an average of 17 days to hunting each year. Most of them hunt large game, especially deer, although they manage to kill far greater numbers of birds. In the United States hunters kill a total of more than 200 million animals a year, spending an average of $900 a year doing so. From the point of view of both time and money, hunting is an inefficient way to procure meat, even with modern firearms. Most hunters have motives like Jimmy Carter's: hunting connects them to their fathers, to other men, and to what they perceive as a broader male subculture. After increasing through most of the 20th century, despite urbanization, hunting in the United States has declined in the last 30 years.

Not all animals are killed with firearms; trapping remains popular in certain areas of the United States, where it appears to be primarily the activity of adolescent boys. These are not necessarily rural areas, and a significant number of pets are among the 15 million animals caught in American traps each year. Most industrial countries, and many of the individual American states, have banned traditional steel-jaw traps. Animals suffer considerably in these traps, which frequently break an animal's leg without killing the creature. Animals have been known to break their own teeth and gnaw off their own legs in efforts to escape. Even among indigenous peoples, few make a living at trapping, in part because the majority of animals used in the fur industry are raised on ranches. The average American trapper makes only a few hundred dollars a year at the activity.

The treatment of wild animals raises different issues from that of domesticated ones, for humans control the lives of the latter more directly. In nature, animals suffer. They are stalked, attacked, and eaten by other animals. They suffer accidents, illnesses, and diseases that either kill them slowly or make them more vulnerable to predators. They starve when populations of species get out of balance. During the 20th century we have become keenly aware of the effects of ecological balance among species, including humans' unfortunate contributions to imbalances. Hunters claim that they help keep populations in balance, especially the deer who have proliferated in suburban America since the destruction of their natural predators. They argue that a sudden shotgun blast is preferable to most forms of death wild animals face, a claim that applies only to clean, fatal wounds rather than those that fester and debilitate an animal.

IV. SUFFERING AS ENTERTAINMENT

In ways that many people today find hard to understand, humans throughout history have been keenly amused by the suffering of other creatures. Organized public activities include bull- and bear-baiting, the once extremely popular practice of setting a pack of dogs loose to torment these large animals. Bulldogs have the shape they do because the English bred them specifically so that they would be low to the ground, avoiding the bull's horns, but with powerful jaws so that they could hang on when they bit into a bull's nose or mouth. Singly and in groups, animals have been pitted against each other for the amusement (and, often, betting opportunities) of humans. Cockfights, for which animals are specifically bred and raised to be vicious, apparently originated in Asia 3000 years ago. In other cases, such as bullfighting, humans themselves inflict the pain. Until they grew more popular in the late 19th century, cats were a favorite target, in part because of the terrible noise—caterwauling—they make when tormented. A favorite use was to stuff them into burlap sacks making up the "body" of political figures being burned in effigy. We can only imagine the full range of treatments practiced locally, but they include various kinds of mutilation, decapitation, and the pursuit of terrified animals. The fear and squirming of smaller creatures seems to have retained its special delight for children, especially boys, somewhat longer than it did for most adults—one reason that humane societies in the 19th century concentrated their efforts on the humane education of children.

Although it is comforting to believe that such cruelty—the most blatant, inexcusable form of violence against animals—is a thing of the past, this is hardly the case. Bullfights continue in many parts of the Spanish-speaking world. A 1995 raid in New York City led to the arrest of 300 spectators at a cockfighting tournament, which are said to persist in many other parts of the United States despite laws against them. Live bird shoots also continue, legally. They have some similarities to hunting: except the predictable release of the birds (usually pigeons), the vast numbers killed, and the crowds of spectators. At one annual shoot in eastern Pennsylvania, young boys are employed to capture the victims, many of them still flopping around, which the boys despatch by breaking their necks.

Animals also entertain humans in circuses and zoos, and many of today's animal protectionists claim that these animals are being abused in various ways ranging from beatings and deprivation during training to their being prevented from living "natural" lives. A few activists go so far as to claim that pets exist only for the satisfaction of their owners, not for the benefit of the pets.

Although most animal suffering arises from neglect or as a byproduct of other uses to which humans put animals, the pain of animals has been directly amusing to large numbers of humans through history. Both the direct infliction of cruelty and the accompanying lack of sympathy or empathy with these animals may parallel attitudes toward fellow humans. Humane societies once centered their arguments on the idea that cruelty to animals taught children cruelty to other humans, and some research—despite difficulties in testing the hypothesis—supports that link. In addition to direct causal links, actions toward those who cannot fight back are thought to be especially telling signs of human character. On this dimension of violence toward animals, there seems to have been considerable improvement with the rise of modernity.

V. MODERN AGRICULTURE

Although domestication, breeding, and agriculture always require systematic efforts, the Enlightenment seems to have brought new attention to farm techniques. Systematic experimentation helped to increase yields in Britain in the 18th century, and prepared the way for the application of scientific discoveries to agriculture. Because agriculture was more respectable than commerce or industry, enterprising gentry applied their talents to raising animals. Although beef had been raised in England since prehistory, it was only in the 1700s that it overtook venison as the most popular meat. Landowners began to commission paintings of their favorite bulls, hold competitions and exhibitions of their prize animals, and organize meetings for the dissemination of breeding tips. They enclosed new lands for cattle and sheep grazing, began feeding their animals turnips and other foods to fatten them even in the winter, and selectively bred ever-larger animals. The elite who could afford these experiments, far from an interest in profits, congratulated themselves on their patriotism and public service.

Today's prize-winning farm animals are still treated more like pets than resources, but the highly efficient, rationalized lives of all other farm animals are seen as nothing but a source of profit. The term "factory farming" has been applied to contemporary agriculture because so many animals are kept indoors in crowded conditions, remaining alive just long enough to be fattened to a profitable point. Veal calves, as many critics have pointed out, are not even allowed to walk, for this would darken their flesh. Food, water, and ventilation have been automated to save on labor costs. The dogs and horses that once assisted farmers have now disappeared. Laying hens rest in wire cages so that their droppings fall out and can be swept up without disturbing the animals. A regimen of hormones and other drugs prevents disease and stimulates rapid growth. The size of these operations is staggering: the number of laying hens in an average building increased from 20,000 to 80,000 in the two decades (1955 to 1975) that much of the new mechanization took place.

The number of animals eaten by humans dwarfs all other uses. Worldwide, around a billion animals are killed each year for food—not even including poultry. In the United States alone, roughly 7 billion chickens and turkeys are sold as food each year, as well as 100 million pigs, 35 million cattle, 5 million sheep and lambs, and a million calves, in addition to the 300 million hens that are kept busy laying eggs.

Assembly-line farming is efficient, to be sure. A hen, for example, lays up to 10 times as many eggs as its ancestors did. But it lives only about a year and a half rather than 10 to 15 years, before being used as food itself. In the United States alone, 200 million male chicks, unnecessary for egg production, are destroyed each year. According to critics many of them are still, despite prohibitions, sealed in large garbage bags to suffocate. It should not be concluded, however, that farm animals were treated well in the past. In fact their transportation and slaughter were the subject of laws passed in the United States and Britain in the 19th and early 20th centuries. Most of the American states passed protective legislation, but federal laws of the period only covered interstate transportation of animals.

Under pressure from environmentalists and animal protectionists, recent decades have seen a spate of new laws regulating farm animals, most of them in the nations of Europe. Britain has passed a series of laws banning tiny crates and anemic diets for veal, the keeping of breeding sows in tight stalls, the hot branding of cattle, and most tail docking of pigs and cattle. Germany and Switzerland have restricted the use of batteries of cages for laying hens, insisting that the natural movements and behaviors of the animals be possible. The European Community is inching toward similar measures. Sweden passed the most sweeping regulations in 1988, aimed at allowing animals to perform natural behaviors, protecting them from illness, restricting the use of drugs except to protect the animals' health, and controlling genetic manipulation. Such efforts to encourage "humane" farming, however, are balanced by the situation in the United States. There, much protective legislation, at both the state and federal levels, exempts farm animals. In 1992 federal legislation, intended to discourage animal protectionists, increased penalties for vandalism and other crimes against agricultural business. In contrast to Europe, humane products such as free-range chickens and eggs depend entirely upon consumer demand in the United States.

VI. BIOMEDICAL SCIENCE

Although much in the news in the last two decades, the number of animals used in scientific research has always been modest compared to those used as food. The ancient Greeks and Romans had performed some demonstrations with animals, but vivisection gained prominence with the beginnings of modern medicine in the seventeenth century. For example, William Harvey published *De Motu Cordis* in 1628, arguing that blood circulated through the bodies of humans and animals, pumped by the heart. Both backers and opponents cut into live animals in the ensuing debates, as direct experiments became more credible as sources of evidence. Such activities expanded again in the 19th century with the development of modern research laboratories and universities. Experimental physiology, hitherto a rather disreputable hobby of a few physicians, became a respected academic pursuit in France and Germany after 1850, in England after 1870, and in the United States after 1880 (at which time they were joined by bacteriologists, who also used live animals). Because anesthetics and analgesics were only developed in the 19th century (ranging from morphine in 1806 to aspirin in 1899), vivisection in this period entailed rather horrible pain during procedures and considerable suffering afterward. The most that can be said in defense of those who inflicted this pain is that they performed surgery on humans in much the same way. There was wide opposition to vivisection, based largely on religious resistance to the perceived "soullessness" of modern science.

The 20th century saw an enormous expansion of animals in laboratories. In the 1890s the biomedical profession managed to fuse the interests of scientists and physicians, establishing their credibility and market power on the basis of scientific advances. With the rise of chemical and pharmaceutical industries, the use of animals, especially for substance testing, grew exponentially from the 1890s until the 1970s. Although good data are rarely collected, the worldwide number of animals used in testing and research each year for the past two decades is probably in the vicinity of 100 million, most of them mice and rats. In countries with strong animal protection movements, the numbers have actually fallen in the last 20 years. In Britain and the Netherlands, which collect the best data, they have been cut almost in half. Many new methods of testing toxicity in new products and substances have been developed, including the use of eggs, computer models, and various cell cultures. The notorious Draize test, in which substances are put into the eyes of white rabbits to see how badly irritated they become, has been severely curtailed. Private corporations, especially cosmetics companies, have been eager to switch to the alternatives, which are usually less expensive than older animal tests (see Fig. 1).

FIGURE 1 Rabbits lined up for the Draize test of toxicity. Substances are put in their eyes so that researchers can observe the degree of redness, swelling, and pus formation. Albinos are used so that these effects can be judged more accurately. Once the animal protection movement began attacking the test in the 1980s, many scientists questioned its utility, and the number of Draize tests used each year has fallen dramatically. (Courtesy of AFAAR.)

Most advanced industrial nations now regulate the use of animals in research. In the Netherlands, all investigators must take a course on ethics before they conduct research. Denmark, Germany, and Britain also have detailed rules, and in 1986 the European Community adopted guidelines. The United States passed an Animal Welfare Act in 1966, since amended several times, but this law excluded rodents (which comprise 90% of lab animals) and was directed at the care of the animals more than the uses to which they are put in experiments. In 1985, amendments to this act required laboratories with federal funding to establish Institutional Animal Care and Use Committees, which review the protocols of experiments in an effort to reduce pain and stress. There is some agreement that researchers today have grown more sensitive to the suffering of their animal subjects because of regulations such as these.

Illegal break-ins at animal laboratories handed effective recruitment materials to animal protectionists in the United States and Britain. In 1984 the Animal Liberation Front removed videotapes of experiments using baboons at the University of Pennsylvania, which People for the Ethical Treatment of Animals edited into a short film. Graduate student researchers were seen making fun of severely injured animals. In Britain the following year, a raid at the Royal College of Surgeons uncovered rather dubious treatment of experimental monkeys, one of which had the word "crap" tattooed on its forehead. Memorable cases such as these helped spark the rapid growth of the animal rights movement of the 1980s.

VII. EXTINCTION AND ENDANGERMENT

Wherever they have traveled, now the entire planet, humans have destroyed native species, especially the large mammals and birds that were good eating. Ten thousand years ago, as humans spread southward through the Americas, they caused the extinction of roughly 75% of the large mammals then existing in North America, 80% in South America—species such as sabertooth cats, mammoths, camels, long-horned bison, ground sloths, even a form of horse only distantly related to the Spanish species later introduced. Similar catastrophes occurred after the arrival of humans in Hawaii, Australia, and New Zealand. Native species were not accustomed to these predators, and disappeared before any kind of balance was achieved. Direct slaughter was not the only mechanism for destruction: the introduction of new, non-native species brought not only competitors but new diseases. And as many large mammals disappeared, they took with them other species that depended on them, usually species of vulture or condor.

In recent centuries, humans have threatened species primarily by destroying the habitats necessary for their survival—a process that has been accelerating throughout the 20th century. In addition to the disappearance of many habitats, chemical pollution has rendered others unsuitable for the sustained reproduction of certain species. Rachel Carson's 1962 exposé, *Silent Spring*, helped inspire the modern environmental movement by documenting the devastating effects of DDT and other pesticides on the environment. Some species are especially vulnerable because their habitats are extremely limited—often to a single forest, pond, or field.

Changes in habitat also affect the destinies of animals in ways that fall short of extinction or endangerment. Some even flourish because predators have been eliminated. Deer are perhaps the preeminent example: in suburban parts of the United States their numbers fluctuate according to local laws governing their hunting and other policies concerning wildlife "management." Active intervention is one reason so many of the deer's predators have disappeared. At various times in American history, for example, there have been bounties placed on wolves, coyotes, rattlesnakes, bobcats, mountain lions, groundhogs, blue jays, crows, and woodpeckers, in many cases decimating these populations.

The destruction of habitats often leads directly to animal suffering. More often, species lose their ability to reproduce themselves over time. Although the latter appears less violent, the endpoint of endangerment or extinction is the same.

VIII. ANIMAL PROTECTION EFFORTS

Before the 18th century, concern for animals, in the rare cases when it developed, usually grew out of religious visions. Hinduism and its offspring, perhaps because followers believe in reincarnation, and the possibility of reincarnation as other species, have been especially concerned with how practitioners treated animals. To build up good karma for the next life, it is desirable to practice ahimsa, or respect and noninjury to all living things. This concern is most developed in Jainism, whose followers (numbering four million today) pursue ahimsa through an extreme asceticism, even striving to avoid killing tiny insects by stepping on them or breathing them in. Jainist monks, who normally wander freely, move into temples during the rainy season to avoid crushing the invisible creatures living in the mud.

Most vegetarians have adopted their practices because of theories, some accurate and others not, concerning human health, but the result has always been fewer animals consumed. In the sixth century B.C.E., Pythagoras argued that humans were poised between the divine and the bestial, and that killing other creatures for food drew people toward the latter. In the late 17th century an Englishman named Thomas Tryon popularized these ideas in *The Way to Health,* adding a Christian interpretation of the divine in humans. Tryon also showed some concern for the suffering of the slaughtered animals, an issue that reappeared in a cluster of works around 1800 also espousing vegetarianism. With both Tryon and his successors, however, abstention from meat was primarily seen as good for human health. In the West, vegetarianism became more common in the early 19th century, and the English word, coined in the 1840s, seems to have been popularized by the founding of the Vegetarian Society in Britain in 1847. The most famous vegetarians, such as Percy Bysshe Shelley and Sylvester Graham, continued to see vegetarianism as a way to preserve one's health in an industrial, urbanizing environment.

In early modern Europe, isolated individuals began to appear who were concerned about violence toward animals for secular reasons that had nothing to do with human health. These were often philosophers, clergy, or aristocratic ladies of letters. Their appeals were generally ridiculed, although the 18th century did see some increase in benevolent concern for other humans as well as other species.

It was the rapid industrialization in much of 19th-century Europe and North America that seems to have spurred, not only vegetarianism, but the first organized movements for animal protection. Reasons may include decreased contact with animals as economic resources, the sentimentalization of nature, an increase in pet owning, and a broader climate of altruistic, often religiously based, benevolent movements for reform. Scientific discoveries, culminating in Darwin's arguments about natural selection, made the differences between humans and other species appear considerably smaller and less significant than they once had seemed. Anthropomorphism, the perception of human traits in things other than humans, has helped greatly, and certain kinds of animals easily anthropomorphized (those with faces, large eyes, or fur, for instance) have been the main beneficiaries of the recent increase in sympathy.

An organized movement to help nonhuman species dates from England in the early nineteenth century. From 1800 to 1822, when an act finally passed, several Parliamentary bills were introduced to ban bull baiting. Two years later an organization called the Society for the Prevention of Cruelty to Animals was formed, later adding Royal to its name when Queen Victoria adopted the cause in 1840. It was a favorite charity of the upper classes, who saw it as a way to civilize the working classes who abused cart and carriage horses in congested city streets. In the 1860s similar organizations began to appear in the United States, eventually spreading to all the major American cities outside the South. These groups addressed the suffering of animals in a wide range of practices: the beating or starvation of pets by owners, the use of carriage horses in extreme heat, the beating of such horses, cockfights, the inadequate anesthetization of animals in scientific experiments, and the conditions and transportation of animals raised for food (see Fig. 2). They persuaded many states to pass protective legislation. After 1900, under the counterattack of scientists and with horses being replaced by motors, most of these humane societies came to focus on the treatment of pets. From then until the 1980s they would be known primarily for their work in reducing pet overpopulation and strays.

Antivivisection appeared alongside other issues on the agendas of the early humane societies, but it met a different fate. Much antivivisectionist sentiment was based on distrust of the medical profession, which had done little over the centuries to win popular confidence. The status of both physicians and scientists changed rapidly in the 1880s and 1890s, however. One reason was the series of medical breakthroughs, especially in immunology, that began to save lives in the fights against rabies, diphtheria, and typhoid. But medicine's status was rising even before these triumphs, due to

FIGURE 2 A collapsed carriage horse. The mistreatment of carriage horses was one of the earliest issues addressed by the humane societies of the 19th century, as middle- and upper-class patrons were horrified by the language and abuse used by drivers, often immigrants, in carrying out their work. This was one of the last utilitarian contacts with live animals most people had in the emerging industrial city. (Credit: PETA)

efforts at institutionalization and legitimation on the part of practitioners: state licensing, more rigorous training in medical schools, and other ventures by the profession to police itself. Such efforts were largely a response to antivivisectionists, who soon found themselves on the defensive. Even humane societies began to back away from their antivivisectionist stances in the 1890s, and antivivisectionism became a marginal concern until it rejoined animal protectionism in the 1980s.

Some of the 19th-century groups, such as the American Society for the Protection of Animals created in 1866, became large and wealthy. Others, such as Henry Salt's Humanitarian League of the 1890s, remained essentially the work of one person. Most older groups—especially those that have lasted—were driven by compassion for creatures seen as helpless victims, emphasizing animals' feelings more than their cognitive capacities. Although many groups represented only the idiosyncratic concerns of their founders, they usually appeared in waves that reflected widespread changes in public sentiment. A cluster of groups were founded in the United States in the late 1950s and early 1960s, concerned in part that stray pets were ending up in unpleasant laboratory experiments. The most recent surge began in the 1970s in Britain and the 1980s in the United States.

In the 1960s and 1970s a wave of protest movements had questioned basic aspects of modern societies, including large bureaucracies, corporate profits, the uses to which science and technology were put, unrestrained economic growth, and various ways that individuals oppressed each other. There appeared a general sense that industrial societies hurt the powerless in many ways. In particular, the environmental movement demonstrated the social, economic, and esthetic costs of ecological imbalance and pollution, and large numbers of people began to worry about the disappearance of many species of wild animals. With the women's movement, many women began to recognize both large and small ways that they were disadvantaged, and to develop a language for criticizing the major institutions of advanced industrial societies.

These movements eventually affected how people thought about animals. In the late 1960s and early 1970s new groups were formed to aid wild animals, including baby seals that were hunted for their white fur, dolphins that were being killed in nets meant for tuna, and the wolf, which had been almost completely eliminated from the continental United States (see Fig. 3). Through generations of television specials, magazine articles, and books, Americans had come to appreciate the complex mental capacities and deep emotional loyalties of other species. Gorillas and chimpanzees can communicate with humans by learning more than a hundred keyboard symbols; they even play jokes on their keepers. Many people began to feel uneasy over the destruction of these animals' natural habitats, but also over how other mammals were treated every day in modern societies. The humane societies of 100 years ago saw animal cruelty as aberrant and unusual; those trained in the movements of the 1960s saw the same practices as systemic and widespread. Key institutions of contemporary society depended deeply on what increasing numbers of activists now saw as violence against animals.

FIGURE 3 Canadian seal about to be clubbed. Among the most effective photographs for the environmental movement in the early 1970s were those of seals being killed for their fur. With their large eyes, cute faces, and unthreatening behavior, these animals are easily perceived as similar to humans in many ways. Sympathies like these helped form the animal rights movement 10 years later.

Unlike many men and women with the same sentiments who were content to volunteer at local animal shelters, this small constellation of interested citizens was dissatisfied with traditional activities. They saw existing humane societies as timid in their protective efforts, more concerned with maintaining the support of wealthy patrons than with extending their activities on behalf of animals. For these would-be activists, the works of several philosophers provided a language and ideology that seemed to crystallize their new concerns over the treatment of animals. Most influential was Peter Singer's *Animal Liberation,* which denounced "speciesism" as a bias parallel to racism and sexism, arguing that, because the pains and pleasures of nonhumans were as intense as those of humans, they should not be ignored or discounted. The book also contained considerable evidence of animal suffering in scientific research and modern farming-two core institutional arenas ignored by most animal welfare organizations.

In the United States these initial activists founded a new generation of groups in the early 1980s, perceiving violence in a wide range of animal treatments, including the issues raised by the first generation of humane societies, but also questioning practices in which the animals did not suffer obvious physical harm, such as the keeping of animals in zoos, the use of fully anesthetized animals in research, the performances of animals in circuses, and the shearing of sheep for their wool. Violence against animals could be mental as well as simply physical. Many of the new activists attacked every domestication of animals as an infringement on these beings' deserved autonomy, including the keeping of pets (or "companion animals," in the phrase of activists more sympathetic to the practice). Thus a more radical "animal rights" movement developed alongside existing humane societies and animal "welfare" organizations: even the language implied that animals were active subjects rather than passive recipients of charity or of good and bad treatment.

Different groups used different tactics. The Animal Liberation Front (ALF) began in Britain in the 1960s and favored property destruction and threats. When it was imported to the United States at the end of the 1970s, it favored sabotage and laboratory break-ins-which not only "liberated" animals but also yielded notorious videotapes showing experimenters in an unfavorable light. Even activists within the movement debated whether such tactics helped or hurt the movement's public image, especially after the FBI labeled the group "terrorist." People for the Ethical Treatment of Animals (PETA), the United States' largest animal rights group with several hundred thousand paying members, deployed many tactics, especially those involving media attention that would enhance its direct-mail fundraising. For example, it sponsored a "barf-in' at the headquarters of cosmetics giant l'Oréal; protestors pretended to vomit into a large papier-maché toilet to show that animal testing "makes us sick." Older organizations, like the Humane Society of the United States, founded in 1954, also grew more radical under the influence of new groups and ideas, although they continued their traditional practices of lobbying and education. During the 1980s as many as one million Americans joined or contributed to the radical new groups.

Especially in the Christian world, there have been fundamental shifts in humans' views of animals, so that today it is possible to conceive of violence against them. Wherever an individual or public policymakers draw the line between acceptable and unacceptable treatments, they must confront questions that once could not be seriously entertained. Although the animal rights movement of the 1980s faded somewhat, notably in media visibility, during the 1990s, it created a controversy that seems likely to endure.

IX. PARALLELS AND NON-PARALLELS WITH VIOLENCE AGAINST HUMANS

Moral judgments about how humans treat animals—whether a given case is violence or something more mundane and innocuous—usually depends on the similarities we see between animals and humans. Today, throughout the world, there are standards for human treatment, even when they are broken, that recognize an ideal of an individual as autonomous, capable of making decisions, free from bodily constraints or torture, and having some say in one's government. There is no such universally accepted standard for nonhuman species. Those who emphasize that many animals, especially mammals, have nervous systems close to those of humans easily empathize with the suffering of those animals under conditions that would hurt humans. As do those who believe that, like humans, animals make choices or plans that affect their lives. In contrast, those who reject any such similarities between humans and other species seem less likely to worry about the suffering or death of these animals. Even within the same society, there are widely different moral intuitions about the suffering and rights of animals.

The evidence seems clearest concerning physical suffering. Closest to humans are chimpanzees, which share over 98% of our genes, making it extremely likely that they feel pain much as we do. Other mammals also seem close and thus comprehensible; nonmammals and especially invertebrates are more opaque. It is hard for humans to imagine what it is like for a frog or insect to feel pain, and our science has not been able to give us much direction. Physical pain, in the eyes of those who have benefited from industrialization and modern medicine, is a rare and undesirable experience, which should be prevented not only in humans but in other animals that can feel it.

Assessing and empathizing with physical pain is easy compared to what we might anthropomorphically call psychological suffering. There is, however, considerable evidence that individual animals feel some sort of bond to other individuals, for example mating for life. In some cases, such as dogs or elephants, we easily believe that these animals suffer when a parent or companion dies. But there are considerable cultural differences in this empathy.

The life of an animal is a different issue from its suffering. Protectionist claims that it is wrong to take the life of an animal, even if this could be done painlessly, assume that its life has meaning and positive value to an animal. This seems most acutely true for humans, who plan and think about what their lives will be like decades in the future, who have certain expectations about when or how they might die, who usually maintain affectionate contact with children, grandchildren, and beyond. Humans have a cultural image of a "natural" or expected life span, and cutting this short seems wrong or tragic. Few other animals, if any, have such an elaborate vision of the future, and the positive value of its life, if it has any, must lie more in the present. Pampered pets, provided good health care, presumably enjoy their lives, so that taking their lives from them is a deprivation. It is harder to fathom how a crated veal calf feels about its life, or a laboratory rat about its.

Large gaps persist in our knowledge about animals, especially about their subjective consciousness. We fall back on our own intuitions about how they think and feel, intuitions that differ greatly even within the same society. Whether accurate or not, the tendency in modern societies has been more and more to see other species as like us, capable of suffering, of controlling their lives, of having intentions and preferences, and thus capable of being treated violently. This historical trend directly parallels that toward greater recognition of human rights.

Also See the Following Articles

AGGRESSION, PSYCHOLOGY OF • EVOLUTIONARY FACTORS • INTERNATIONAL VARIATIONS IN CULTURAL NORMS AND ATTITUDES TOWARD VIOLENCE

Bibliography

Blum, D. (1994). *The monkey wars.* New York: Oxford University Press.

Carter, J. (1994). *An outdoor journal.* Fayetteville: University of Arkansas Press.

Cartmill, M. (1993). *A view to a death in the morning: Hunting and nature though history.* Cambridge: Harvard University Press.

Dizard, J. E. (1994). *Going wild: Hunting, animal rights, and the contested meaning of nature.* Amherst: University of Massachusetts Press.

Dunlap, T. R. (1988). *Saving America's wildlife: Ecology and the American mind, 1850–1990.* Princeton: Princeton University Press.

Garner, R. (1993). *Animals, politics and morality.* Manchester: Manchester University Press.

Jasper, J. M., & Nelkin, D. (1992). *The animal rights crusade: The growth of a moral protest.* New York: The Free Press.

Kellert, S. R., & Edward O. Wilson E. O. (Eds.). (1993). *The Biophilia hypothesis.* Washington, DC: Island Press.

Midgley, M. (1983). *Animals and why they matter.* Athens, GA: University of Georgia Press.

Norton, B. G. (1987). *Why preserve natural variety?* Princeton: Princeton University Press.

Ortega y Gasset, J. (1972). *Meditations on hunting.* New York: Scribner's.

Ritvo, H. (1987). *The animal estate: The English and other creatures in the Victorian age.* Cambridge: Harvard University Press.

Rowan, A. N. (1984). *Of mice, models, and men.* Albany: State University of New York Press.

Serpell, J. A. (1986). *In the company of animals.* New York: Basil Blackwell.

Singer, P. (1990). *Animal liberation* (2nd ed.). New York: New York Review of Books.

Turner, J. (1980). *Reckoning with the beast: Animals, pain, and humanity in the Victorian mind.* Baltimore: Johns Hopkins University Press.

Wilson, E. O. (1992). *The diversity of life.* New York: W. W. Norton.

Anthropology of Violence and Conflict

Andrew J. Strathern and Pamela J. Stewart
University of Pittsburgh

GLOSSARY

Cultural Materialism An anthropological theory in which it is argued that material factors are the primary causes of the development of cultural patterns.

Divination A ritual act by which the causes of an event or the guilt or innocence of accused persons is determined.

Egalitarian Society A society based on the idea of relative equality between groups and persons within it.

Ethology The study of fixed motor patterns in animals and the way in which these contribute to social relationships.

Genital Mutilation The act of surgically removing parts of human genitalia, for example, in rituals marking a transition from childhood to sexual maturity.

Ritualization The process whereby a dispute or conflict is handled peacefully by transforming an aggressive signal into a peaceful one.

Segmentary System A social system in which the groups are arranged in such a way that smaller, closely related groups combine in opposition to similar more distantly related ones.

Sociobiology A branch of biology in which it is argued that the maximization of individual reproductive success is an important determinant of behavior.

Violence An act or a threat of physical force between persons, the legitimacy of which may be contested.

CONFLICT involves disputing over issues and interests that may lead to violence or the use of force whose legitimacy may be contested. Anthropologists have made their greatest contribution in discussing these topics as they relate to small-scale, stateless societies in which a balance of power obtains between the different groups. This article discusses this contribution and it also considers a range of related themes on both states and stateless societies in contemporary circumstances.

I. OVERVIEW

Conflict and violence are long-standing aspects of human behavior and social relationships. As with many other such phenomena, explanations for this fact have appealed either to biological/genetic patterns or to cultural/historical ones, or to a combination of both. General explanations may certainly implicate biological characteristics, but specific ones require that we at least take into account cultural factors as they have developed historically in particular formations. Such an approach may also lead to further levels of sociological generalization.

Given the prevalence of conflict and violence in historical experience, our scope in this survey needs to be delimited. We have chosen a range of topics that have been recognized widely as anthropological, along with their extensions into contemporary arenas of conflict linked to ethnicity, nationalism, and globalization. Hallmarks of the anthropological approach, as we see it, are (1) an emphasis on first-hand observation and fieldwork, augmented by the use of other sources; (2) a concern with the small-scale as well as with larger scales of events and processes; (3) an interest in the interpretation of meanings and the expression of intentionality, agency, and the capacity for action, including sensitivity to language use; and (4) an understanding generally of the role of symbols and ritual in sociopolitical history.

A concern with meanings obliges us also at the outset to consider the meaning of the term "violence" (conflict is taken to be less problematic here, referring to any situation in which the participants see themselves as at odds over an issue or set of issues and engage practically in attempts to settle the issue by negotiation, force, or other means). D. Riches has examined the definitional question in a collection of studies on the topic and points out that the choice lies between adopting a new definition of a general kind or building on what he calls Anglo-Saxon meanings. Opting for the latter, and stressing the intentional agency of social actors, he pinpoints a crucial feature: violent behavior is behavior that is subject to contested legitimacy, and this is inherent to it. Violence is thus not simply physical force, although it stereotypically involves the use of force. Rather it is the use of force in contexts where one or more parties may consider it to be legitimate (and the definition of what is legitimate may also be subject to varying interpretations). Riches also speaks of the triangle of performer, victim, and witness, in which the witness is often the agent who evaluates the question of the legitimacy of a violent action. Riches's viewpoint enables us to understand how a state agency may undertake a violent action in order to curb violent offenders, since violence in a sense is in the eye of the beholder/actor. In particular, a performer of violence may consider it a justifiable or legitimate use of force while the victim disagrees and witnesses are divided in opinion. For our purposes here, without claiming this as a generally valid definition for all purposes, we shall adopt Riches's viewpoint, focusing attention on violence as an action characterized by force (physical or otherwise) that is subject to contested interpretations of legitimacy.

Finally, the placement of violence in a typology of forms of disputing and dispute settlement needs to be specified. Such a typology may have to do with: (1) social contexts of disputing, in terms of scale and the degree of closeness or distance between the parties: an act that is heinous between siblings (e.g., incest, fratricide) may be acceptable or even expected between major enemies; (2) the matters at issue: serious matters may elicit violent responses whereas trivial ones may, or should, not.

In terms of non-violent disputing processes, Philip Gulliver made a clear distinction between settlement by adjudication, mediation, and negotiation. Adjudication occurs in a context where laws exist and decisions can be imposed in terms of them; mediation where a third party attempts to act as go-between or broker between disputants and is given power to do so; negotiation typically occurs between the disputants themselves and their support groups, who may take on in part roles of mediators or adjudicators. In the context of negotiation, Gulliver further noted an alternation between coordination and antagonism, leading ideally to a coordination that in some way is ritually confirmed, beginning with the search to define an arena of dispute, through an attempt to narrow differences, and then on to the final bargaining. The model presumes settlement, but in reality negotiations often break down. Since breakdown is marked by antagonism, it is here that violence may come into play, either as a way of settling matters or as a way of postponing and complicating a settlement. Socially defined emotions become involved also, and enter into political definitions of what is done.

II. CLASSIC ETHNOGRAPHIC STUDIES

B. Malinowski, in *Crime and Custom in Savage Society*, was concerned to introduce questions of individual motivation and emotion into the study of primitive law and to overturn the notion of the savage who was supposed to follow blindly the dictates of custom and tradition within the group. His extensive case history account of a youth who committed suicide as a result of shame sparked off a long tradition of looking at the significance of self-regulated sanctions in behavior. His major stress, however, was on the positive incentives and ideals that keep people in conformity with expectations and remove a need for violence or for imposed punishments in situations of conflict. Certain elements of adjudication were, of course, present in the Trobriands case history he was describing, since chiefs could impose certain decisions and were also feared for the sorcery and magical powers they commanded (see section III). This overall Malinowskian approach, via the study of emotions, has returned in contemporary anthropology after having been displaced for a while by the functionalism of Radcliffe-Brown and the structurally oriented work of Evans-Pritchard and Fortes.

Evans-Pritchard, in *The Nuer,* discusses politics, law, social control, and violence in a tribal social system based on a balancing of forces between territorial segments and a principle of the merging of segments in widening scales of opposition or conflict. Evans-Pritchard developed his model to account for (1) order in a society without government (the ordered anarchy concept) and (2) the place of physical force in such a society. The Nuer people were warlike and had been expanding at the cost of neighboring peoples such as the Dinka, who were captured and assimilated into Nuer local groups. Evans-Pritchard pointed out that bloodwealth or compensation for killings was likely to be paid only within the tribe, the largest political group. He also noted the important role of the leopard-skin chief or man of the earth in giving ritual protection to killers and mediating in discussions over bloodwealth. A combination of structural rules and ritual role-playing kept violence to certain limits within the tribe. The threat of forceful action, however, was equally important in ensuring the territorial spacing of people and their access to resources. Such an ordered anarchy requires a certain level of consciousness of violence to maintain itself.

Both Malinowski and Evans-Pritchard were, from different angles, tackling the question of whether all societies have, in some sense, law. The same matter was explicitly at issue between P. Bohannan and M. Gluckman. Gluckman, in his study of the court system of the Lozi or Barotse people in Rhodesia (Zambia), argued that definite rules could be derived from the study of court cases heard by magistrates and that the principles of law involved could be compared with English-law concepts such as that of the reasonable man. Bohannan, on the other hand, stressed the local cultural contexts in which the Tiv people of Central Nigeria pursued disputes through moots, general meetings, rather than in introduced courts. Bohannan's account therefore implied difficulties of comparison between societies, based on the problem of cultural difference. The debate between Bohannan and Gluckman has often been taken as an example of the conflict between the particularizing and generalizing moments in anthropology. More specifically the difference of viewpoint they exhibited can be derived from (1) the differences between Tiv and Lozi society, (relatively egalitarian versus relatively hierarchical) and (2) Bohannan's stress on indigenous processes, Gluckman's on a court system influenced by British colonial ideas.

Comaroff and Roberts, in their survey of legal anthropology, settled the issue of rules versus processes by pointing out that even the most complex rules are formulated and brought to bear only in elaborate negotiated processes, whose outcomes are therefore unpredictable and multiplex. They demonstrated this argument with reference to Tswana (South Africa) succession patterns and marriage disputes. The debate between Gluckman and Bohannan was thus in a sense finally laid to rest.

None of these studies was particularly concerned with violence, or the intersection between law and politics. Bohannan's study, however, was of interest here because of his chapter on the moot at home, in which he discusses the concept of *tsav*. Leadership, and in fact ability generally, was thought by Tiv to depend on a substance called *tsav*. Men with *tsav* were said to repair the *tar,* or local community, through sitting in moots by day and settling disputes. But the same men also acted by night to protect the *tar* mystically against attacks by outsiders and were said periodically to require a human to be sacrificed as a victim for their work of mystical protection. *Tsav* in this context was a kind of witchcraft power. In other words, political power, seen as a form of witchcraft, depended also on notions of mystical violence. In times of political upheaval, Bohannan notes, the men with *tsav* were thought to kill for personal gain and the love of consuming human flesh.

III. STUDIES IN RELIGION, WITCHCRAFT, AND SORCERY

The use of sorcery and witchcraft as a means of controlling the acts of others is a common anthropological theme. It is often considered an illegitimate form of social control but examples also demonstrate its accepted and legitimate uses.

Types of sorcery that are used include: food sorcery (poison), leavings sorcery (taking something that has a part of the persons "soul" in it and imprisoning it or subjecting it to torture to make the person ill or die), and assault sorcery (violently attacking someone from another community and causing their death). All these forms of sorcery are greatly feared and attacks of these sorts are repelled through proper actions and/or the assistance of healers who possess magical spells or means of divining who the sorcerers or witch is and thereby confronting the individual.

In Melanesia among the Melpa, Pangia, and Duna peoples sorcery and witchcraft are greatly feared and not generally considered to be a legitimate form of social interaction. Those who are witches are viewed as greedy persons who are attempting to take the health or life of another to satisfy their own desires. The fear of witches (*kum koimb*, in Melpa) who eat human flesh—stealing children and waylaying adults—has increased in conjunction with changing sociopolitical and religious circumstances. This description is paralleled in the African ethnographic records in which sorcery and witchcraft are socially condemned practices. In Africa, sorcerers use medicines to harm those toward whom they have an ill will, while witches are able to do extraordinary things beyond the capabilities of ordinary human beings in order to harm other people. In both the African and Melanesian contexts sorcery and witchcraft accusations have often been read as indices of conflict and tension. Sorcery accusations directed at enemy groups may increase ingroup solidarity and increase the likelihood that a war will be initiated against the accused group. In addition, among the Kuma of the Western Highlands of Papua New Guinea war sorcerers were highly respected and legitimately used their powers to enlist the spirits of the dead and the ancestors to aid in battle against the enemy. Among the Wola of the Southern Highlands of Papua New Guinea sorcery is also used to attack the enemy in war in addition to appealing to the clan spirits and ancestors of the enemy side to ask that a long-standing dispute be resolved through a divination process in which the physical substance from the decomposing body of a sorcery victim is allowed to pass onto a pig that is to be eaten to determine who is guilty of the sorcery killing. The victim's essence is thought to act as a poison that will kill those who are lying and their relatives. Just before eating the potentially lethal piece of pork the accused swears an oath declaring the truth of his assertions of innocence. After the eating of pork the feuding ceases, and further revenge deaths will be caused, it is thought, by the ancestors if they judge that they are warranted.

Ideas regarding sorcery and witchcraft are appropriate to consider here, since they both reflect and constitute modes of hostility between categories of people, and are experienced as forms of violent action. This is particularly true of notions of assault sorcery that effectively depict images of assassination and murder by a mixture of physical and mystical means. As the example of the Wola indicates, the same forms of cultural logic that inform fears of sorcery can be brought into play in the service of divination and oath-taking (on the latter see also section IV).

IV. MODES OF SETTLING CONFLICTS, INCLUDING RITUAL

Within the category of settlement by negotiation we can distinguish between settlements that lead to an ending of the specific dispute, or at least a phase of it (partial settlement) and settlements that lead to a reconciliation or to the establishment of new positive relations between the parties. A number of writers have cautioned against too easy an assumption that settlement means good feelings. Moore (in Caplan, 1995) cites Gluckman's description of "the case of the headman's fishdams" and how it was cleverly settled at the time but how Gluckman later found that one of the parties involved had subsequently killed the other. Similarly, Elizabeth Colson in the same volume sums up materials on the Gwembe Valley Tonga of Zambia by arguing that moots and courts can settle individual claims but "have much less success in convincing contenders that they are in the wrong, and they do little or nothing to heal ruptured relationships or abate anger and contempt." A dispute occasion may be a part of a longer term and more deep-seated conflict involving persons other than the immediate parties. It has been argued for Melanesia that ongoing dispute is a part of a normal mode of social interaction and as with debt the aim is not to end but to continue it. While this may be overstated as a generalization there is certainly some truth in it. Nevertheless, in the Mount Hagen area, at any rate, there is an idea that a proper settlement should lead to an admission or confession of wrong-doing followed by a compensation payment to enable the offended party to recover good feelings. For Hagen, and for many parts of the Pacific and Indonesia, there is a special equation of wealth with human life itself, so that killings can also be compensated for by bloodwealth payments that may in turn lead to ongoing exchanges of wealth goods (pigs, shells, money) between the parties and their groupmates. If negotiations about the size of such a compensation payment break down, however, direct reprisals by way of retaliatory killings, destruction of property, or the confiscation of wealth goods may cut in. In contemporary disputes, settlements leading to productive exchanges have become harder to arrange and the possibility of violence has come much closer again, because of the increase in scale of social relations, a process that began with pacification in the 1930s and was evident already by the early 1970s. If disputes are "both theater and real contests," in Colson's formulation, we might expect them to become a locus of the major tensions caused by the complicated overlapping and layering of institutions and processes in a postcolonial context, such as we find among both the Gwembe Tonga and in Hagen.

Colson also has some sharp words to say about the potential of ritual for bringing about the healing of social relations. Compensation in Hagen would fall into the definition of ritual here, but it is important to note that where the ritual consists of the handing over of large amounts of wealth this carries its own potential for efficacy. It was Victor Turner, in his work on the Ndembu people of Zambia, who most powerfully expressed the role of ritual in these terms, but we should note the specific context into which much of his material was set, that is, rituals of healing for sickness in the bodies of particular persons. Turner was arguing that such healing rituals were constructed in terms of a specific cultural idea, that deep-seated disharmony of feelings can cause sickness, and therefore sickness can be healed only by the (re)establishment of harmony. The idea of dispute as sickness is found also in Papua New Guinea. In Hagen, for example, there is a strong idea that frustration (*popokl*) can cause sickness and such sickness will again be healed only by overtly venting (confessing) the cause of one's anger, leading at least to an attempt to put matters to rights. Ndembu and Hagen logic are at one within this fundamental, or cosmological, level, then. Turner's approach therefore does not imply that harmony is always achieved, only that it is seen as a prerequisite for healing certain sickness conditions. Sickness prompts people to bring up matters of dispute that have not been settled and to make a fresh attempt at dealing with them. Disputes where sickness is not (yet) implicated may nevertheless refer to the potentiality of both sickness and violence as their outcome if talk cannot solve them.

Gulliver, in his book on disputes among the Arusha of Tanganyika (Tanzania), spends the bulk of his time explaining the modes of discussion that lead to settlements, mostly through the influence of agemates. At the end of the book, however, he turns to the topic of additional means of coercion. The coercion he has been discussing is, as he says, "of a non-violent kind," and it may have to be followed up with further modes of persuasion after an agreement is reached in order to make sure that a promised payment, for example, is made. Occasionally, physical seizure is resorted to, but ritual curses and oaths may be employed also. Both curse and oath appeal to an authority or power beyond the immediate context and they bridge the gap of doubt or mistrust that can arise between disputants. Arusha say that oaths are resorted to only when a dispute cannot otherwise be settled agreeably. The ritual mechanisms "all operate by producing illness or death in an offender" (p. 287), and a diviner is employed post mortem to verify that the ritual has worked in this way. Effects can be warded off, however, by confession. The Arusha know several categories of oaths appropriate to different circumstances, for example, *olmoma,* to bring peace to two related men, involving the consumption of sacrificial meat as an embodied act: the meat is accepted by one party and offered by the other. This is a striking instance of the importance of the consumption of substances as a marker of truth on the body. These Arusha mechanisms are closely paralleled again by ideas from the Pacific. In Mt. Hagen consumption or burning of the sacred *mi* plant that is a group's emblem brings with it the putative sanction of death if one lies. Such mechanisms, going beyond words and into the bodies of the disputants, but invoking the deepest levels of cosmological notions, are perhaps important as backstops to Arusha discourse.

V. THE PLACE OF LANGUAGE FORMS AND DISCOURSE IN DISPUTING

The idea of disputing brings primarily to mind words: images of words spoken in contest, and therefore of the stylistic and rhetorical resources people bring to bear on an issue. Also brought to mind is the question of how people view words and truth-telling. In Hagen, for example, it is assumed that people readily lie, but the group divination substance, the *mi* (or nowadays the Bible) can equally readily find them out. A refusal to swear on the *mi* is tantamount, therefore, to admitting guilt. The aim of an investigation is to "dig out the roots of the talk," which are buried, entangled, and hard to bring to light but are at the bottom of the problem.

Brenneis, in a survey article on this theme, makes a number of significant points. He refers to Mather and Yngvesson's model of dispute transformation dealing with how and when/why issues are broadened or narrowed and points out that analysis of the verbal ways in which transitions are made from one phase to another would be productive. Brenneis also notes Maurice Bloch's argument linking formalization of style to authority in the rhetoric of the Merina, a hierarchical society in Madagascar, noting that the argument works less well in egalitarian communities. In Bloch's original edited volume, A. J. Strathern remarked on a variant of the Merina pattern found among the Melpa of Mt. Hagen, in which stylized oratory called "arrow talk" (*el ik*) stands for a ritualized statement of the outcome of an event as if it were authoritative, marking a stage of consensual agreement between competitive groups.

Brenneis goes on to note that forms of expression may play different roles at different phases of a dispute. Insults, for example, may function as preludes to physical violence or as an understood way of expressing and discharging hostility, depending on the stage of a dispute or the relationship between the parties. Silence as an avoidance of talk may also be highly significant and in effect communicate meanings. In the Papua New Guinea Highlands the winners of contemporary parliamentary elections are often advised not to say anything about their win, not out of any false modesty but simply to avoid antagonizing the supporters of the jealous losers and provoking violence. The winner of the regional election in the Western Highlands in July 1997, a Catholic priest, mediated this problem by announcing that he would celebrate his victory by drawing all the other elected members of his Province together and "giving all the praise and thanks to God."

Brenneis outlines two different approaches to the relationship between language and social process in disputes. In one (called ethnomethodology) social organization is seen as produced through language interaction. The other is the ethnography of speaking, which takes speakers' intentions, strategies, and extralinguistic power differentials more into account. While the second approach provides a valuable expansion of the first, Brenneis also notes that language does not just reflect relations, it also often brings them into being and gives them form. In this regard, it is worthwhile to add that he does not greatly take into account here the question of emotions in disputing nor does he discuss the markers of transition from verbal to nonverbal expression that occur when talking stops and physical violence begins. A. J. Strathern has discussed how in Hagen verbal behaviors may copy patterns of dominance and appeasement that can also be expressed nonverbally. When such verbal rituals break down, violence may result, and peacemaking is thereby made harder.

VI. VIOLENCE, PEACEMAKING, AND ETHOLOGY

The mention of dominance and appeasement reminds us of the question of peacemaking generally, and the distinction between peace founded on mutual agreement and peace imposed by winners on losers. It reminds us also of the general debate on aggression, territoriality, and ritualization stemming from the work of Konrad Lorenz and I. Eibl-Eibesfeldt. We are not concerned here with the aspect of debates stemming from Lorenz's work that deals with the possible innate or genetic basis for aggressive behavior in humans and other animals. We are rather interested in the question of ritualization. In certain animals gestures of appeasement in conflict situations are made by motor actions that correspond to fixed dispositions. In human social interactions standardized rituals are developed that function in a similar way, within a shared cultural milieu, to move from confrontation to conciliation. The mechanisms involved may be verbal, but often are nonverbal. Human ethology can thus provide interesting pointers for the analysis of rituals of both aggression and peacemaking, whether or not we consider these have an innate basis.

Sociobiological theory provides a more focused, and more disputed, approach to conflict, arguing that the maximization of reproductive success is at stake, as argued by Napoleon Chagnon for the Yanomamo people. Chagnon presents the male war-leaders among these people as motivated in their violence not by protein scarcity but by polygyny, suggesting a correlation between killings and wives. Other scholars have taken a different view (see below).

Eibl-Eibesfeldt has collected together several examples of appeasement behavior that are interesting: for example, the waving of plant fronds and flowers to indicate a wish for peace, and the inclusion of women and children in parades as an indication of a desire for a resumption of friendly relation. In Hagen, this is directly expressed in a verbal mode also, when men say they are coming "like women" to a meeting, not to fight but to settle.

VII. THE ANTHROPOLOGY OF WAR, AND WARFARE IN "TRIBAL" CONTEXTS

R. Brian Ferguson has described war as "organized, purposeful group action, directed against another group . . . involving the actual or potential application of lethal force." The anthropology of war is complex and can involve conflict over a myriad of diverse factors (e.g., political stakes, an expression of witchcraft beliefs, revenge, wealth, etc.). Ferguson has pointed out the importance of conflict over material resources, such as land, food, and trade goods, suggesting that an analytical research strategy on the anthropology of war must not overlook cultural materialism. Robarchek (In Haas, 1990: 62–64) notes that commonly the explanations of conflict in preindustrial societies are materialistic. He suggests that a focus on the capacity of humans to decide to become involved in conflict at the individual level by examining motivations (defined as all the forces, factors, options, and constraints, both intrinsic and extrinsic that influence the choices people make) for participation is crucial and that in all conflicts and disputes multiple levels of causality and contexts of tension coexist. He goes on to state that "warfare or nonviolence, like other behaviors, occur when they are perceived and selected from among a field of possible alternatives as viable means of achieving specific, largely culturally defined, goals" (p. 75). Robarchek does not deny the importance of biology or the environment in shaping the forces that lead to warfare but he points out that cultural constraints and individual and collective behavior determine if war will ensue.

As noted already, many different views have been taken of the causes of warfare and also of its prevalence in various kinds of social contexts. Materialist theories generally argue that warfare has to do with competition over resources and therefore with population growth and territorial expansion. These theories hold in many contexts, but not all. Some kinds of warfare take the form more of tournaments, becoming themselves an arena for the pursuit of prestige, such as the Great Wars among the Enga of Papua New Guinea. Some are connected with religious imperatives, such as headhunting, although from within the people's own life-worlds this may have to do with the aim of increasing fertility and population. The Marind-Anim of New Guinea undertook raids not only for heads but to obtain children in order to increase their population.

Aside from the general debates, interesting discussions have been entered into with regard to the place of warfare in interactions between state and nonstate societies. Ferguson and Whitehead have argued strongly that warfare in nonstate (tribal) societies has been greatly influenced by interactions with state societies, and that consolidated tribal formations themselves are sometimes the historical product of such interactions, especially in contexts of encounters with expanding states. The same argument applies to colonial contexts, as for example among the Nuer of the Anglo-Egyptian Sudan. Ferguson and Whitehead's argument is applied broadly to cases from Roman North Africa, early Sri Lanka, the Aztecs and the Spanish, the West African slave coast, the Iroquois, Eastern Peru, and Papua New Guinea, as well as to their own work in South America. Whitehead argues it both ways: tribes make states and states make tribes.

Ferguson uses a sophisticated version of cultural materialism to argue that Yanomami aggressiveness was greatly influenced by the historical impingement of Europeans bringing disease, different settlement patterns, and new wants, and thereby increasing the shortage of game and levels of tensions in social groups. The Yanomami emerge as much the victims of colonization as the warlike tribesmen projected in the work of Chagnon. Ferguson concludes: "The 'fierce people' represent Yanomami culture in an extreme conflict mode, a mode that is clearly attributable to the exogenous factors of Western contact." This conclusion does not absolutely refute Chagnon's view, but it does contextualize it considerably and provides another way of viewing the situation. That warfare has been a pervasive feature of human life is not in doubt, but the specifics of its historical development need also to be examined carefully, as we have repeatedly noted.

A different argument concerns the place of revenge practices and feuding in cultural practice. Revenge and intergroup hostilities are closely connected in Melanesian histories of war. Otterbein has argued that these practices tend to be most marked where hostilities are based on fraternal interest groups. Feud, he argues, with its limited reciprocities of retaliatory killings, is a way of avoiding larger-scale warfare between such groups. One can comment here that if so it nevertheless can escalate into war, and the more effective way to halt escalation is to pay compensation, as has happened in the historical development of New Guinea Highland societies. Feud without compensation could interestingly be compared with feud with compensation in this regard, a comparative study that waits to be done in detail.

The social and historical construction of tribes feeds in topical terms into consideration of the construction of ethnicity and the relationship between ethnicity and violence in the contemporary world.

VIII. VIOLENCE, ETHNICITY, AND NATIONALISM

The end of the 20th century has seen a series of world historical changes that have forced a new alignment between the interests of historians, political scientists, and anthropologists. Nation-states have broken up, violent and lethal conflicts based on ethnic ideologies have arisen, and new claims to national status have been made with bewildering rapidity and complexity around the world. In general these events can be attributed to the recent collapse of the Soviet Union and to the longer term results of colonial and postcolonial history in Africa. Anthropologists have been forced to expand their scope of reference, while political scientists have had to contract theirs and attempt seriously to understand the intertwining of kinship and politics. Descriptive/analytical categories such as "warlords," applied to political leaders in Somalia, have emerged in this new context.

Here we use a selection of anthropological ideas to comment briefly on this situation. The first is that of the "segmentary system" and the scale of politics. The "segmentary principle" means that different ranges of persons may come into conflict depending on the social distance involved. This idea gives us a calculus for the rapid expansions and contractions of arenas of conflict that can be seen in contexts of ethnicity. It does not, however, account for the fluidity and partiality of such arenas that are sometimes found. The same idea, however, also implies that a tribe may become an ethnic group tomorrow and a nation the next day, depending on the historical trajectory of conflict it may become involved with. The nation may thus draw on a naturalized symbolic repertoire of notions based on blood and kinship, thus creating itself as markedly different from others, a process that Eibl-Eibesfeldt calls "pseudo-speciation."

The phenomenon of physical violence tends to outrun the explanatory theories we apply to it. Allan Feldman has combined versions of anthropological and psychological theory to considerable effect in exploring ideas about violence in Northern Ireland; and E. Valentine Daniel, among others, has given a moving account of how the experience of lethal violence is mediated in Sri Lanka. Both of these authors manage to convey a sense of the construction of meaning even in an arena of mass killing, that may lead us to reflect further on events in other parts of the world, such as Cambodia and Rwanda. Most scholars agree that we cannot simply ascribe violence to an aggressive human nature, yet neither can we argue that violence is simply a manifestation of culture. Rather, we need detailed studies of its social construction and the use of grounded generalizations such as the fact that in a cross-ethnic dispute both sides may feel that they are victimized minorities, depending on what majority is chosen for comparison. Processes of learned misunderstanding and extreme othering are also involved here. A combination of approaches from social psychology and anthropology could help greatly in rendering comprehensible the human capacity to kill. Where anthropology also needs to come into its own is in the study of the means, largely ritual and by no means always effective, whereby a measure of peace and healing can be constructed out of the destructiveness of warfare. New Guinea Highlanders, with their conversion of warfare via killings into compensation payments, and these into productive exchanges between groups, have in this regard been at the forefront of human political development. Their subsequent interactions with state systems and the new development of forms of violence and criminality within them, along with their own attempts to develop new compensatory rituals, have further shown how such a development can itself be overtaken by history.

IX. VIOLENCE, INDIVIDUAL ACTION, AND THE STATE

In a number of ways, the actions of authorities in society and of dominant or deviant persons in the community, may be seen as violent, and may produce violent responses, including that of self-punishment by suicide. In this final section we look at a range of actions that belong under this heading, from capital punishment to domestic violence.

A. Capital Punishment

Capital punishment may be considered the supreme act of governmental violence in state contexts, and jurists point out that to distinguish it from mere execution or lynching elements such as judicial interpretation and the stay of execution have to be brought into play. Recently, Austin Sarat has pointed out that the practice of allowing the kin of victims to make statements at the sentencing of persons convicted of violence has reintroduced elements of revenge found in retaliatory killings in nonstate societies.

B. Homicide and Suicide

Homicide may in certain instances take on some of the characteristics of capital punishment, in societies without state institutions of control, as when suspected sorcerers or witches are killed for their alleged offenses. Community opinion, however, may be divided over such killings and they may represent the interests of a particular faction rather than a whole community. Bruce Knauft, in his study of homicide among a Papua New Guinean people, the Gebusi, found a surprisingly high rate of homicide among them to be related to male competition over marriageable women. There was a tendency for sorcery accusations and killings of sorcerers to be focused on those who had failed to reciprocate in marriage exchanges. Outbreaks of homicidal actions punctuated long periods in which harmony was stressed and the expression of anger or aggression discouraged. The Gebusi are unusual in terms of their very high putative homicide rate but not in terms of a cultural emphasis on male violence, which is found elsewhere in the world, for example, in other New Guinea societies and in Amazonia, and is connected with warfare.

Suicide may also sometimes be forced on persons in a manner reminiscent of capital punishment, as among the Duna people of the Papua New Guinea highlands in the precolonial past when female witches were, according to accounts, forced to hang themselves if found guilty. The element of shame is powerfully involved here, as in other cases where persons found guilty of transgressing norms voluntarily choose suicide. The motivation of shame may be compounded further by a desire to protest against a situation and to bring shame on those held to have caused it. Classically, a woman forced into a marriage or treated badly within it may in male-dominated societies make a protest in this way, either by drowning or hanging herself (examples also from New Guinea). The sociologist Émile Durkheim in 1897 classified suicide into three types: egoistic, altruistic, and anomic. In the first, the individual is seen as insufficiently integrated in the group, in the second the individual is overidentified and may commit suicide out of shame or as an act of sacrifice, while in the third the cause of suicide is a social crisis in which individuals are unable to realize their aims. The first and third types are commonly found in contexts of rapid familial and social change such as have been commented on since the early 1970s for many parts of Micronesia in the Pacific. Rates of suicide in Micronesia are by far the highest for young males, indicating their problems of adjustment to society, their inability to find monetary employment, their use of alcohol and drugs, and the breakdown of kin structures such as lineage ownership of land that provided orderly patterns of resource control in the past. Conflicts of interest are always involved in all three types of suicide: quarrels over marriage and sexual activity, over the disposition or availability of resources, and the resulting feelings of shame and frustration, may all be involved. Suicide as protest is quite marked in Pacific contexts where the idea is that the suicide's ghost may continue to bring trouble to the living. It also may be on the increase in contexts where other social sanctions on behavior have broken down or altered.

C. Assault and Robbery

Similar patterns of disintegration of social ties of control equally lead to an increase in violence on the part of young males who form into gangs and prey on social groups in urban contexts away from their home places. In Papua New Guinea such gangs concentrate their activities of robbery on the major towns and on the highways that connect them, holding up travelers, killing them if necessary, and sometimes compounding their actions by rape and torture. Narratives of their activities circulate as cautionary tales and tales of horror among the rest of the community. We may call this, following Durkheim, a category of egoistic violence, prompted also by contexts where youths cannot easily meet their economic aspirations. Some of these gang members or "rascals" in Papua New Guinea have voluntarily given up their ways when they have received grants to start small businesses or have been converted to Christianity.

D. Torture

Torture itself has most often been used as a means of domination to extract confessions of information about activities from enemies or from persons suspected of witchcraft (internal enemies) or from dissidents. State authority may legitimize such forms of violence, as it does capital punishment and imprisonment. Torture need not be compounded by killing the victim, although it may do so, making a demonstration of the humiliation of the body as in case of the "Shankill butchers" in Northern Ireland, who were said to torture or kill both Catholics and, by mistake, Protestants in gruesome ways. Paramilitaries themselves in Northern Ireland could expect that they would be arrested by the authorities and interrogated violently with a view to breaking down their resistance and the extracting information. As Feldman points out, torture is concentrated on the captive's body and creates its sense of power out of that concentration, as well as by the terror of threatened or simulated execution. Pointing the gun or the knife here is the same gesture as that exercised by the robber or gang member, but with the force of the state behind it. Further action, such as rape, is also often enforced by means of a threat of other violence. One of the ways in which domination over others is exercised is through forms of torture and forced work, such as in the coercive contexts of slavery and forced child labor.

E. Rape

Rape is a form of violence directly mainly at females, although males may also be violently and forcefully sodomized, especially in prison conditions. During wartime rape is often used as a form of terror and revenge-taking against enemy groups. A recent example is the Bosnian war where women were frequently raped in attempts to subjugate enemy groups. In contemporary Papua New Guinea violence sometimes erupts in the Highlands during and after local and national elections. At these times women who belong to groups targeted for violence are sometimes raped while males are beaten or threatened and property is destroyed. The form of rape on these occasions may involve a group of males attacking one female in what is known as gang rape. The same action may be undertaken as a form of humiliating "discipline" exercised against a wife who has been defined as errant. Control of this sort is also sometimes cited in other contexts as a reason for what has been described as female genital mutilation.

F. Female Genital Mutilation

Female genital mutilation can be discussed here under violence although this category, like suicide, falls into the grey zone of actions that are undertaken freely in some instances. Some outside (i.e., Western) observers have placed this practice under the rubric of child abuse since the female are generally very young when the operations are performed on them. The phrase genital mutilation may be seen as placing a culturally accepted practice into an unacceptable category by relabeling it. Female circumcision has also been called a "maladaptive cultural pattern" by those who would like to see the practice halted. One consideration here is that these practices are also followed when families move to the United States or elsewhere in the world where female circumcision is not an accepted practice. Thus, issues of religious and ideological freedom arise.

There is some evidence that lowered fertility may occur in some individuals as a result of scar tissue, which may inhibit sexual activity, and from chronic infections that result in higher rates of miscarriages. Janice Boddy has pointed out that these same problems have entered into the social construction of female cults of possession in the Sudan, in which women take control of their bodies and express themselves in ways that modify male control over them and express also their own view of themselves in the wider patterns of life. In this context, they do not oppose, but support, the practices of female circumcision and infibulation.

G. Domestic Violence

Domestic violence is a common problem in many parts of the world and much of it is directed at women and children. According to a United Nations study on this subject, it appears that to one degree or another violence against women in the home is a problem that can be found across all cultures and in all countries. The issues that bring on domestic violence often center on establishing authority and control in the household over the sexual activity of the partner as well as availability and use of resources such as animals (pigs and cows) and garden spaces, or property (e.g., house and vehicle). At other times domestic violence arises because of over consumption of alcohol and/or drugs, or as a means of releasing anger/frustration that has arisen from some event outside of the domestic sphere but triggers violence in the home solely as a "coping" mechanism in which anger is released against an innocent third party who is in some sense an easier target.

Frequently reported forms of domestic violence include: (1) punishment/discipline, when a person is beaten because they are to be "taught a particular lesson," that is, forced into one or another action or behavior pattern; (2) preventive, when a household member is beaten in order to remind them who is in control of the relationship and the materials goods that are associated with it; and (3) defensive, when one household member hits back after being hit or threatened.

Of course, domestic violence often involves forms of verbal abuse in addition to physical violence which can be equally devastating and destructive to the individuals involved. Both forms of domestic violence are disturbing to children and may produce life-long psychological problems in addition to physical scars.

Also See the Following Articles

CLAN AND TRIBAL CONFLICT • CULTURAL ANTHROPOLOGY STUDIES • ETHNIC CONFLICTS AND COOPERATION • LANGUAGE OF WAR AND PEACE, THE • PEACEFUL SOCIETIES • RITUAL AND SYMBOLIC BEHAVIOR • WARRIORS, ANTHROPOLOGY OF

Bibliography

Bloch, M. (Ed.). (1975). *Political language and oratory in traditional societies.* New York: Academic Press.

Bohannan, P. (1957). *Justice and Judgement among the Tiv.* London: Oxford University Press, for the International African Institute.

Brenneis, D. (1988). Language and disputing. *Annual Review of Anthropology,* 17, 224–237.

Caplan, P. (Ed.). (1995). *Understanding disputes: The politics of argument.* Oxford: Berg.

Chagnon, N. (1990). Reproductive and somatic conflicts of interest in the genesis of violence and warfare among tribesmen. In J. Haas (Ed.), *The anthropology of War,* pp. 77–104. Cambridge: Cambridge University Press.

Colson, E. (1995). The contentiousness of disputes. In P. Caplan (Ed.), *Understanding disputes: The politics of argument*, pp. 65–82. Oxford: Berg.

Comaroff, J., & Roberts, S. (1981). *Rules and processes. The cultural logic of dispute in an African context*. Chicago: University of Chicago Press.

Daniel, V. V. (1996). *Charred lullabies: Chapters in an anthropograph of violence*. Princeton: Princeton University Press.

Eibl-Eibesfeldt, I. (1979). *The biology of peace and war: Men, animals and aggression*. New York: Viking Press.

Evans-Pritchard, E. E. (1940). *The Nuer*. Oxford: Clarendon Press.

Feldman, A. (1991). *Formations of violence: The narrative of the body and political terror in Northern Ireland*. Chicago: University of Chicago Press.

Ferguson, R. B. (1990). Explaining War. In J. Haas (Ed.). *The anthropology of war*, pp. 26–55. Cambridge: Cambridge University Press.

Ferguson, R. B., & Whitehead, N. (Eds.). (1992). *War in the tribal zone. Expanding states and indigenous warfare*. Santa Fe: School of American Research.

Gluckman, M. (1955). *The judicial process among the Barotse*. Manchester: Manchester University Press.

Gulliver, P. (1963). *Social control in an African society*. London: Routledge and Kegan Paul.

Gulliver, P. (1979). *Disputes and negotiation: A cross-cultural perspective*. New York and London: Academic Press.

Haas, J. (Ed.). (1990). *The anthropology of war*. Cambridge: Cambridge University Press.

Hutchinson, S. E. (1996). *Nuer dilemmas. Coping with money, war, and the state*. Berkeley: University of California Press.

Knauft, B. M. (1985). *Good company and violence*, Berkeley: University of California Press.

Malinowski, B. (1926). *Crime and custom in savage society*. London: Routledge and Kegan Paul.

Moore, S. F. (1995). Imperfect communications. In P. Caplan (Ed.), *Understanding disputes: The politics of argument*, pp. 11–38. Oxford: Berg.

Otterbein, K. (1994). *Feuding and warfare. Selected works of Keith Otterbein*. New York: Gordon & Breach Science Publishers.

Riches, D. (Ed.). (1988). *The anthropology of violence*. Oxford: Basil Blackwell.

Stewart, P. J., & Strathern, A. J. (1997). *Sorcery and sickness. Spatial and temporal movements in Papua New Guinea and Australia*. Townsville, James Cook University, Centre for Pacific Studies, Discussion Papers Series No. 1.

Strathern, A. J., & Stewart, P. J. (1997). The Problems of Peacemakers in Papua New Guinea: Modalities of Negotiation and Settlement. *Cornell International Law Journal 30*, 3, 681–699.

Strathern, A. J. (1971). *The rope of Moka. Big-men and ceremonial exchange in Mount Hagen*. Cambridge: Cambridge University Press.

Strathern, A. (1992). Let the bow go down. In R. B. Ferguson and N. Whitehead (Eds.), *War in the tribal zone*, pp. 229–250. Santa Fe: School of American Research.

Strathern, A. (1993a). *Voices of Conflict*. Pittsburgh: Ethnology Monographs no. 14.

Strathern, A. (1993b). Violence and political change in Papua New Guinea. *Pacific Studies, 16*, 4, 41–60.

Turner, V. (1957). *Schism and continuity in an African society*. New York: Humanities Press, Inc.

Arms Control

Dinshaw Mistry and Edward A. Kolodziej
University of Illinois at Urbana-Champaign

GLOSSARY

Arms Control A form of collaboration on military issues between generally antagonistic states, involving the limitation of the development, production, deployment, or use of arms.

BWC Biological Weapons Convention. An international treaty signed in 1972 requiring states to renounce the development and possession of biological weapons; the treaty contains no verification mechanism.

CBMs Confidence-Building Measures. Initiatives such as the advance notification and monitoring of military exercises intended to promote transparency and foster trust between states; also known as operational arms control.

CFE Conventional Armed Forces in Europe Treaty. A treaty signed in 1990 by former Warsaw Pact and NATO states limiting their conventional armed force sizes.

CSCE Conference on Security and Cooperation in Europe. A forum for dialogue on European security issues, renamed OSCE—the Organization for Security and Cooperation in Europe—in 1995.

CWC Chemical Weapons Convention. An international treaty signed in 1993 requiring states to renounce the development and possession of chemical weapons: contains an extensive international verification system.

Nonproliferation Measures to prevent states from acquiring nuclear, chemical, or biological weapons.

NPT Nuclear Nonproliferation Treaty. An international treaty signed in 1968 under which states undertake to not develop or acquire nuclear weapons, in exchange for which they are permitted the peaceful use of nuclear energy, and the declared nuclear states undertake to eventually eliminate their nuclear forces.

NWS Nuclear Weapon States. The U.S., Russia, the UK, France, and China; states that acquired nuclear weapons before 1968 and are legally permitted to keep them under the NPT with the understanding of eventually eliminating them.

OPCW Organization for Prohibition of Chemical Weapons. Monitoring Agency for the Chemical Weapons Convention.

SALT Strategic Arms Limitation Talks. Arms control understanding between the U.S. and former Soviet Union. SALT I restricted the U.S. to 1054 ICBMs and 710 SLBMs and the Soviet Union to 1618 ICBMs and 710 SLBMs. SALT II limited the total number of delivery systems—both missiles and bombers—to 2400 for each superpower.

START Strategic Arms Reduction Treaty. Arms control agreements between the U.S. and Russia to reduce their nuclear arsenals to 1600 delivery systems and 6000 warheads (START I), followed by deeper cuts down to 3000–3500 strategic nuclear warheads (START II), and aiming for reductions to 2000–2500 strategic nuclear warheads under START III.

Supply-Side Regimes Informal agreements among approximately 30 supplier states to restrict their export of sensitive dual-use industrial technologies and materials that may be used to build WMDs or ballistic missiles.

WMDs Weapons of Mass Destruction. Nuclear, chemical, and biological weapons.

ARMS CONTROL is a very complex notion. It can be understood in several ways: (a) as a tool of military strategy and diplomacy between competing states, (b) as a set of formal and informal agreements between states to regulate their security relations, (c) as a process of strategic and political bargaining, (d) as a mechanism for strengthening regional and global security, and (e) as an ideological slogan used by arms control supporters and opponents to advance their political agendas.

I. ARMS CONTROL: DEFINITIONS, THEORY, AND AIMS

An arms control accord may be defined as an agreement between states to define the military environment within which they act and to adjust their specific strategic relations in mutually desirable ways. Some arms control endeavors seek to incorporate all states in the international system—for example, the Nuclear Nonproliferation Treaty that aims to control nuclear nonproliferation. Other arms control agreements, such as regional nuclear free zone treaties, seek the inclusion of states in a region or continent. Still other types of arms control arrangements do not desire universality but rather only seek the participation of selected key states associated with a specific arms control problem; for example, the Missile Technology Control Regime seeks the membership of states producing and capable of exporting missile technology. Arms control accords may also involve just two states when the issue is of purely bilateral concern; for example, United States–Russian nuclear arms control treaties or Argentina–Brazil confidence-building agreements.

Arms control between rivals rests on the seemingly paradoxical assumption that armed opponents, each seeking to use or threaten force to get its rival to behave in preferred ways, will mutually agree to limits on its military capabilities, their deployment, development, and use. The incentives for rivals to enter into arms control accords generally arise under conditions in which neither opponent is able to impose its will on the other through force or threats without running unacceptable risks of reciprocal damage to valued material assets and life. When adversaries perceive that they have reached this stage, or seek to avoid a costly and damaging arms race, they have reason to enter into bargaining and negotiations to reach mutually satisfactory arms control accords that lower levels of risk and cost for all concerned parties. This point became particularly relevant in superpower nuclear arms control during the Cold War because the introduction of nuclear weapons produced a *qualitative* change in the security environment, requiring new types of agreements *even among adversaries*. The massive destructiveness of nuclear weapons, their capacity for destroying a nation's economic infrastructure and living environment and for killing millions of its civilian population, meant that wars fought with such weapons would negate any possible gains even in the case of a victory.

The feasibility of arms control accords also depends on the prevailing security environment. When states are involved in war or intractable conflicts, arms control may be impossible; when states are engaged in a cooperative pluralistic security community, arms control may be unnecessary. It is between these two extremes of inter-state relations that arms control becomes relevant and feasible.

Arms control fulfills broadly overlapping political, economic, and social objectives. On social and economic grounds, arms control may result in reduced military expenditures, thereby releasing resources that contribute to national social and economic development. In addition, arms control has humanitarian objectives, seeking to reduce damage if war occurs and aiming to eliminate mass destruction and inhumane weapons. On political grounds, arms control aims to diminish the likelihood of war by (a) limiting the overall level of world armaments, (b) preventing the spread of arms to specific regions, and (c) creating transparency between rivals and reconfiguring military force structures and balances to preserve crisis stability and maintain deterrence stability. The several interrelated goals of arms control are elaborated upon below.

First, arms control aims to prevent the outbreak of hostilities between rivals as a consequence of accident, miscalculation, misperception, or inadvertence. A border skirmish or an armed clash between units of each side—provoked, say, by mismanaged military exercises or by random firing of weapons—could prompt a major confrontation that neither opponent sought. Such unanticipated incidents might also arise during periods of political tensions in which the movement of troops or weapons might be misperceived as an imminent attack. Of particular concern to states is the possibility of being subject to surprise attack, with the threat appearing more ominous in situations where weapons of mass destruction might be used. Such threat perceptions may lead one side to initiate a war by launching a preemptive attack. These varied concerns to both rivals prompt the search for arms control accords to preclude such unsought outcomes and to prevent unexpected incidents that either side might perceive as hostile from escalating into crisis and possible war.

Second, and following on the first objective, arms control agreements seek to stabilize the military balance and environment of the rivals. Of specific significance to both sides is the preservation of mutual deterrence between them. If either can gain a strategic advantage by striking first or by developing a greater quantity or superior quality of arms, deterrence may be undermined to the potential disadvantage of the contending parties. Under the condition of rapid technological change, each side has an interest in checking the other's incentives to defect by cooperating in sustaining a deterrence regime. To maintain stable deterrence, both sides may under some circumstances actually have to increase their arsenals, develop new weapons, and deploy forces to ensure that they cannot be disarmed by a surprise attack. Opponents may also have to assist each other to achieve this level of mutual deterrence through improved command, control, and communications mechanisms as well as through the exchange of strategic intelligence about the state of readiness and whereabouts of their forces.

The above examples underline the point that arms control should not be confused with disarmament. Arms control is a more varied and potentially supple strategic and diplomatic tool than disarmament, and it places more demanding limits on rivals and allies in managing their real or potential conflicts. Arms control requires the continuous maintenance of transparency and communication between rivals and possibly even a mutually acceptable increase in forces in the search for deterrence stability. In contrast, disarmament aims solely at force reductions eventually leading to elimination of entire categories of arms, a process which may not automatically provide for stability and security. Under certain circumstances, for example when the pace of reductions is unequal, leaving one side with a military advantage at any particular stage of the arms reduction process, disarmament initiatives can actually create incentives for opponents to attack or to use their perceived advantage to coerce their rival because the contending states failed to negotiate a stable and reassuring military balance.

A third goal of arms control is to limit damage to life and material assets if deterrence fails and war erupts. Such arms control may take the form of international treaties banning inhumane weapons or chemical and biological agents. Another aspect of damage-limitation involves setting in place checks on the escalation of armed conflict beyond the interests of each party. This implies that open communications be maintained between adversaries during periods of hostilities. Measures to contain their conflict might include the limitation on military exchanges to areas outside their territories or zones of primary concern or the use of surrogates and satellites to conduct military operations. These limits have in varying degrees been observed by states, most notably by the United States, the Soviet Union, and Communist China during the Korean War.

Fourth, rivals also have incentive to bring hostilities to a swift close, but not at the expense of their respective vital strategic and political interests. Mechanisms for third-party intervention, including that of international organizations like the United Nations, might have to be in place before hostilities erupt. Provisions for ceasefires and moratoriums on bombing or military operations might have to be defined beforehand. Secure and confident communications of intent might also have to be devised since armed clashes cloud perceptions of an enemy's intentions and weaken adherence to limits on the scope of an armed confrontation and the weapons and forces employed in battle.

Fifth, arms control agreements can also foster regional and global security by lowering tensions between rivals, reducing overall expenditures on arms and the level and sophistication of national arsenals, and increasing transparency and mutual confidence among states. The historical sketch below of arms control treaties, conventions, protocols, and understandings testifies to this growing collective concern on the part of the states of the world that they have a shared interest in addressing threats to regional and international security. While these agreements—ranging from accords to banning inhumane means of killing, such as using dumdum bullets, to checking the spread of chemical, biological, and nuclear arms—have not always met with universal adherence, efforts to universalize such controls are now permanent parts of international arms control negotiations and their global promotion is enshrined in the United Nations Charter.

Sixth, arms control agreements may be undertaken for, or may nevertheless result in, economic benefits. By placing limits on the size of armed forces or on the development of particular weapons, arms control agreements prevent excessive military expenditures that would arise from an unchecked arms race. Reducing defense spending holds the theoretical promise of providing a peace dividend, releasing resources that may be utilized for social and economic development.

Arms control accords, whatever their specific aim or composition, also have two additional characteristics worth mentioning. The first concerns verification. A common feature of most arms control agreements is their verification provisions, whether, for example, through on-site inspections, monitoring stations, or aerial or satellite reconnaissance. Verification increases the confidence of parties in an arms control agreement by assuring states that violations are not occurring and that other parties are complying with the agreement. Verification provides states with warning of a possible breakdown of an arms control agreement and allows for countermeasures to be undertaken in a timely manner. These countermeasures may involve sanctions to penalize transgressors and to deter future violations, steps to seek political and strategic compensations, or rearming to provide an adequate defense against an adversary's military attack.

Moreover, arms control accords and their accompanying verification provisions may be viewed as a stepping-stone to confidence-building measures (CBMs) between states, most notably adversaries. These may include the right to observe military exercises of the opponent or timely notification of troop movements. They may lead to the exchange of military officers and attendance at their respective military colleges and schools. In turn, these CBMs may also set the stage for structural arms control accords involving force reductions or adjustments to create a stable military balance. Both CBMs and structural arms control may be keyed to a diplomacy of détente to create a political atmosphere disposed to the relaxation or resolution of political differences.

Finally, it should be noted that some scholars and policymakers eschew the very notion of arms control. For some the notion is incompatible with military strategy and diplomacy. If adversaries are assumed to be engaged in attempting to impose their interests and values on their opponent, arms controls are viewed then as a snare to induce one of the parties to let its guard down. Conversely, there are many so opposed to the solution of differences by force or threats that they insist on disarmament as the only justifiable objective of a nation's strategy and foreign policy. Arms control appears, then, to weaken the incentives and drive for disarmament. Worse, it is seen by some as justifying arms and arms races. An intermediate position between these polarized schools of thought regards arms control as an important mechanism, in conjunction with other forms of diplomacy, to avoid not only self-defeating arms races but also to advance wider strategic and political accords between adversaries on the way to surmounting their military competition and rivalry. What cannot be stressed enough is the point that arms control accords and the process of arms control negotiations have application and importance for the security interests of all states, not just the big powers.

II. A HISTORICAL REVIEW OF ARMS CONTROL

A. Arms Control Before World War II

Attempts to practice arms control date back many centuries. Almost every advance in weaponry—from the crossbow to firearms and from the bomber to nuclear weapons—has been accompanied by calls for its abolition. In the modern era, important pre-World War II arms control agreements concerning regional issues included the Rush–Bagot Treaty, arms control in Central America, and the Versailles Treaty. Other arms control endeavors—naval arms control, the Hague conferences, and attempts to regulate the arms trade—involved a limited number of states but dealt with issues having wider global implications.

The Rush–Bagot Treaty was signed in 1817 following naval warfare between the U.S. and Great Britain on the Great Lakes in 1812. This treaty called for and attained the removal of U.S. and British (later Canadian) naval vessels from the Great Lakes. Arms control in Central America sought to preserve regional peace following the outbreak of armed clashes in the region in the early 1920s. A U.S.-backed conference of Central American states adopted the Central American Arms Limitation Treaty in 1923, which restricted armed force sizes for Guatemala, El Salvador, Honduras, Nicaragua, and Costa Rica and served to prevent further outbreaks of hostilities between these states.

The Hague Conferences of 1899 and 1907 codified the laws of war and addressed the arms control objective of reducing the scope of violence. These conferences barred the use of arms such as fragmenting or dum-dum bullets and poisonous weapons that caused unnecessary suffering. They also prohibited the killing or wounding of prisoners. In subsequent decades, as a response to the use of chemical weapons—primarily gases such as chlorine and phosgene—in World War I, the Geneva Protocol of 1925 banned the use (but not the development or acquisition) of chemical and bacteriological weapons. Although the majority of participants at the Hague and Geneva conferences were European states, the laws and norms adopted at these conferences were concerned with wars on all continents.

Post-World War I attempts to incorporate government regulations on the commercial arms trade included the 1919 St. Germain Convention, which aimed at prohibiting the transfer of surplus World War I equipment to Africa and Asia; the 1925 Geneva Convention on Arms Trade; and a draft conventional arms convention in 1929. These initiatives were implemented, with varying degrees of success, by national governments through legislation that regulated and licensed the arms trade.

The 1919 Treaty of Versailles sought to prevent future war in Europe by disarming Germany and by limiting its future military build-up. The treaty restricted the German army to 100,000 men and prohibited Germany from maintaining submarines (U-boats) and an air force. Germany violated the Versailles Treaty by maintaining hundreds of thousands of paramilitary forces and by secretly conducting submarine and aviation research and construction through firms based in other European states. The Versailles Treaty failed to attain its long-term peace and security objectives since Germany's violations, through continuing military research and development, permitted the rapid expansion of German armed forces once Germany renounced the treaty and undertook rearmament. The 1932 World Disarmament Conference was the long-delayed fulfillment of a key section of the Versailles settlement that projected German disarmament as the first step toward general disarmament. This conference unsuccessfully attempted to limit the military force sizes of all European states. The conference failed after Germany insisted on military parity with France, while France sought to retain military superiority for security against any future German attack.

Naval arms control in the 1920s and 1930s had its origins in an initiative by President Warren Harding to restrict economically burdensome defense expenditures by averting a naval arms race among the major naval powers. The reduction in the aggregate level of naval forces was also intended to reduce the probability of armed clashes between the major powers. The 1922 Washington Treaty restricted total capital ship tonnage to 500,000 tons for the U.S. and Great Britain; 300,000 tons for Japan; and 175,000 tons for France and Italy. The 1930 London Treaty stipulated tonnage restrictions for cruisers, destroyers, and submarines. In 1934, Japan abrogated its adherence to the Washington Treaty. While naval arms control involved only a handful of major naval powers, these arms control accords had wider global security implications because naval forces allowed states to project their power across continents.

B. Post-World War II Arms Control

The belief that the first World War had been caused by an arms race fostered a climate for arms control following that war. The UN Charter emphasized the pacific settlement of disputes and the pursuit of disarmament. In practice, however, the first half-decade after the end of World War II presents a confused picture with respect to arms control. On the one hand, the United States, militarily the most powerful Western state, undertook a vast program of demobilization and disarmament. Further, the disarmament of the defeated states—Germany and Japan—was vigorously pursued. On the other hand, the Soviet Union, Britain, and France, while cutting their forces to below World War II levels, did not dismantle them. The Soviet Union extended its military control over eastern Europe and half of Germany, while Britain and France found themselves deeply engaged in hostilities around the globe to preserve their failing empires. Meanwhile, China was divided by civil war, and colonial wars were erupting around the globe as people in the developing world fought for their independence.

In this setting, the victorious powers had agreed that a newly created United Nations, to replace the defunct League of Nations, would be invested with enhanced collective security powers. These were lodged in the Security Council, whose five permanent members—the United States, Soviet Union, China, Britain, and France—were expected to cooperate in keeping the peace. That expectation was shattered with the onset of the Cold War in Europe, the victory of the Communist Chinese in 1949, the eruption of the Korean War in June, 1950, and the creation of the NATO and Warsaw pacts. In this context, arms control gave way to rearmament in the Western states, including West Germany. The Cold War essentially framed arms control negotiations for the next 40 years. The East–West struggle, paradoxically, limited the scope of the agreements and proposals that could be realistically advanced and yet prompted arms control efforts by rivals, principally the superpowers, to prevent the Cold War from spiraling into a world conflagration.

III. THE GLOBAL NONPROLIFERATION REGIME AGAINST WEAPONS OF MASS DESTRUCTION

A. The Baruch Plan and Nuclear Arms Control

The U.S.-initiated Báruch Plan of 1946 represented the first, but failed, attempt to achieve global nuclear disarmament. This plan called for an international authority to be entrusted with worldwide control and ownership of atomic energy. Once a global nuclear control regime was in place, the U.S. would eliminate its atomic stockpile. The Soviet Union rejected this plan and proposed instead that the U.S. first relinquish its atomic monopoly, after which an international control system would be implemented. The onset of the Cold War and heightened U.S.–Soviet tensions contributed to the eventual collapse of the Baruch plan and alternative global nuclear disarmament proposals. Thereafter, the goals of disarmament gave way to more pragmatic but nevertheless important nuclear arms control objectives. These involved limiting the nuclear forces of the declared nuclear states (vertical nonproliferation, which forms the first step toward nuclear disarmament) and preventing additional states from acquiring nuclear weapons (horizontal nonproliferation, often referred to simply as nonproliferation). It should be noted that the term "declared nuclear states" refers to the five states that acquired and tested nuclear weapons before the NPT was signed in 1968: the U.S., the then-Soviet Union (now Russia), Great Britain, France, and China; three other states that retain nuclear arsenals acquired after 1968 are India, Israel, and Pakistan and have been termed threshold nuclear states. All other states have signed the NPT and are nonnuclear states. The Limited Test Ban Treaty, the Nuclear Nonproliferation Treaty (NPT), regional nuclear free zones, and supplier controls addressed the vertical and horizontal nonproliferation objectives, discussed above.

B. Nuclear Test Ban Treaties

Following a U.S. thermonuclear test in 1954, during which the crew of a Japanese trawler was exposed to radiation, calls by international leaders and organizations arose to end nuclear testing. World public opinion for a nuclear test ban was driven by concerns about the health hazards of radioactivity released from nuclear testing in the atmosphere. Under these circumstances, the then-nuclear states (the U.S., United Kingdom (UK), and the Soviet Union) commenced negotiations in 1958 and came close to agreeing upon a comprehensive test ban treaty. The negotiations failed mainly because of disagreement over the number of on-site inspections necessary for the treaty's verification. In lieu of a total test ban, a Limited Test Ban Treaty (LTBT), also called the Partial Test Ban Treaty (PTBT), which did not require inspections for verification, was attained in 1963. This treaty banned testing in the atmosphere and underwater and restricted nuclear tests to underground sites.

The LTBT achieved in 1963 symbolized cooperation among two antagonistic superpowers that were on the brink of nuclear confrontation barely a year earlier during the 1962 Cuban Missile Crisis. The LTBT thus contributed to confidence building among the superpowers. The nonproliferation goals of a test ban were not achieved. France and China did not sign the LTBT for more than a decade and continued to conduct atmospheric nuclear tests until 1974 and 1980, respectively. The LTBT also did not constrain nuclear weapons development by the U.S., the UK, and the Soviet Union, who continued nuclear testing underground and developed new generations of nuclear weapons.

Some 3 decades after the LTBT was signed, and following the end of the Cold War, efforts to attain a comprehensive test ban treaty (CTBT) intensified. The then-Soviet Union, the UK, and the U.S. ended nuclear testing in 1990, 1991, and 1992, respectively. International negotiations on a test ban began in January, 1994 at the Conference on Disarmament (CD) in Geneva. The 1995 NPT Extension Conference specifically called for the CTBT to be complete by 1996. The CTBT was significant as a vertical nonproliferation measure in the NPT context because by prohibiting the declared nuclear states from testing, the test ban served to halt their nuclear arms build-up and prevented them from developing a new generation of nuclear weapons. The CTBT thereby assumed significance, both substantially as well as symbolically, as a first step toward and a partial fulfillment of the declared nuclear states' NPT commitment to undertake nuclear restraint in the run up to disarmament. The test ban also acquired significance because of its role in stemming horizontal proliferation. It was intended to constrain threshold and nonnuclear states from advancing their nuclear programs in two ways. First, in the absence of testing, the threshold states would not have confidence in miniaturizing their first-generation Hiroshima-type nuclear capability for deployment on missiles; second, the inability to conduct nuclear tests would also prevent threshold or nuclear-seeking states from developing more advanced second-generation thermonuclear weapons.

The CTBT was finally adopted by the UN General Assembly in September, 1996. The CTBT was comprehensive to the maximum extent verifiable. It banned nuclear explosions but did not prohibit subcritical and laboratory tests (compliance with which cannot be verified). Proponents of subcritical and laboratory tests note that these permit the nuclear states to check the reliability and safety of their nuclear arsenals, while critics note that such tests may also permit nuclear force modernization. Further, one key state—India—strongly opposed the CTBT because the treaty was not placed within a disarmament context.

India's disarmament-related objections to the treaty were overshadowed when India and Pakistan broke the global moratorium on nuclear testing and conducted a short series of nuclear tests in May, 1998. On the one hand, these tests provided India and Pakistan with data for maintaining their nuclear programs through computer simulations, with the result that both India and Pakistan now have less to lose by signing (and therefore could join) the test ban treaty; it should be noted that France and China had also conducted a short series of tests in 1995 and 1996 before signing the CTBT. On the other hand, India's and Pakistan's nuclear tests illustrate some limitations of the test ban. Neither state had signed the treaty when they conducted nuclear tests, and their signing the treaty after testing is less meaningful. Thus because India and Pakistan gained technical data and tested at least some nuclear weapons designs, the CTBT did not serve its horizontal nonproliferation goals of restraining these states from advancing their nuclear programs. However, the CTBT still remains significant in freezing all states at their present nuclear capability. Thus while both India and Pakistan may have tested missile-deliverable first-generation Hiroshima-type weapons, Pakistan cannot reliably develop a thermonuclear second-generation weapon without testing, and India's second-generation thermonuclear device, although tested and aircraft-deliverable, still requires additional testing and refinement for deployment on missiles. Further, because only some but not all of India's and Pakistan's claimed nuclear tests were detected by seismic stations, this raised concerns about whether the treaty could be verified. These limitations decrease the possibility that the US Senate may ratify the treaty. In this case, Russia and China may also then refrain from ratifying the treaty, resulting in the treaty never entering into force. Thus while in the short term the CTBT may yet reinforce a moratorium on nuclear testing, some but not all of its significance has been diminished and its future status remains uncertain. If the CTBT is eventually ratified by all the required states and then enters into force, it would contribute to horizontal and vertical nonproliferation objectives and thereby strengthen the nuclear nonproliferation regime.

C. The Nuclear Nonproliferation Treaty

The Nuclear Nonproliferation Treaty signed in 1968 provides the institutional foundations for the global nuclear nonproliferation regime. Under the NPT, nonnuclear states undertake not to develop or acquire nuclear weapons. In exchange, Article IV of the NPT permits the peaceful use of nuclear energy by nonnuclear states, while Article VI of the NPT calls upon the declared nuclear states to eventually pursue nuclear disarmament. The NPT addresses nuclear security concerns of nonnuclear states by operating through the logic of collective action. If all states in a region signed the treaty and renounced their nuclear option, then each state would not face a nuclear threat from its neighbors, thereby enhancing the security of all parties in the region. The International Atomic Energy Agency (IAEA) provides a verification mechanism for the NPT to support collective action in practice and to ensure that parties do not renege on their NPT commitments.

One major criticism of the NPT has been that the treaty is discriminatory because it does not impose equal obligations on all states. The NPT permits the five declared states, which acquired and tested nuclear weapons before 1968, to retain their nuclear arsenals, while all other states have to renounce their nuclear weapon options. Disapproval of this inequality in the NPT is reflected in an Argentine statement made in 1978 at the UN, which noted that "from the very beginning we [Argentina] rejected the Nonproliferation Treaty because of its discriminatory character, since, for the first time in history, it legitimized a division of the world into two categories: countries which can do anything as regards nuclear affairs and countries which have their rights curtailed." On account of similar objections, a few key states—including nuclear states France and China, as well as Argentina, Brazil, and India—opposed and stayed out of the treaty until the early 1990s, although France went on record to abide unilaterally with the NPT's provisions. Argentina, Brazil, and India, as well as Pakistan and Israel, also had national security reasons for remaining outside the treaty.

A second criticism of the NPT was that the nuclear

states did not seriously pursue their NPT commitments to undertake steps toward disarmament, for which they have been condemned by nonnuclear states, especially the nonaligned states, at NPT Review Conferences of 1975, 1980, 1985, and 1990.

By the mid-1990s, ideological criticism of the NPT's discriminatory nature has substantially diminished and has been replaced by recognition of the treaty's nonproliferation benefits. In 1992, France and China joined the treaty, Argentina entered the treaty in 1995, and in 1998 Brazil joined the treaty. A number of other states that previously maintained nuclear programs have also acceded the NPT. South Africa built seven nuclear devices in the period from 1979 to 1989, then dismantled them in 1990–1991, and signed the NPT in July, 1991. Three former Soviet republics that inherited nuclear weapons from the Soviet nuclear arsenal have returned these weapons to the Russian Federation under whose control they remain. These states subsequently joined the NPT: Belarus ratified its accession to the NPT in February, 1993; Kazakhstan in December, 1993; and Ukraine in November, 1994. The accessions of the above states represent important gains for the NPT.

Two cases—those of North Korea and Iraq—which highlight past drawbacks of the NPT, should also be noted. North Korea announced its intention to withdraw from the NPT in 1993; if North Korea had left the treaty, it could have legally pursued a nuclear weapons program unconstrained by international monitoring. A combination of international pressure through the threat of sanctions, as well as incentives under a U.S.–North Korea agreement, persuaded North Korea to remain in the NPT. The October, 1994 U.S.–North Korea agreement places limitations and strict monitoring on North Korea's nuclear facilities, which are required to be eventually dismantled. In exchange, North Korea will be supplied with oil and provided with light water reactors to meet its energy requirements.

Iraq violated the NPT in the 1980s and early 1990s by pursuing a covert nuclear weapons program that escaped IAEA detection. Previously, in 1981, Israel sought to halt Iraq's nuclear program by bombing Baghdad's Osiris nuclear reactor. Iraq subsequently rebuilt its nuclear facilities and, following the end of the Iran–Iraq war in 1988, accelerated the pursuit of a clandestine nuclear weapons development program. The extent of Iraq's covert nuclear program only became known in 1992 following the Gulf War, after which the Iraqi program had been placed under stricter international monitoring.

The NPT was indefinitely extended at the May, 1995 Extension and Review Conference. Despite its limitations noted above, nonnuclear states recognized the treaty's significance in stemming proliferation and agreed to its indefinite extension. In exchange, nuclear states were called upon to undertake stronger steps to fulfill their Article VI obligations of curbing their nuclear programs. These steps included the cessation of nuclear testing and attaining a comprehensive test ban treaty no later than 1996 (a goal that was fulfilled although the treaty's entry into force remains uncertain for reasons discussed above), to be followed by a legal undertaking to halt the production of nuclear materials under a Fissile Material Cut-off Treaty (FMCT), and measures to provide legally binding positive and negative security guarantees banning the threat or use of nuclear weapons against nonnuclear states.

To summarize, the NPT has been moderately successful in its goals of minimizing horizontal proliferation, but its future success remains uncertain. On the positive side, it should be noted that besides the five declared nuclear states, only the three nuclear threshold states—India, Israel, and Pakistan—have acquired nuclear weapons and remain outside the NPT. Thus as of 1998, only eight states—five declared nuclear states and three threshold states—have nuclear weapons. While the number of nuclear states has been minimized, the positive trend in nonproliferation in the early and mid-1990s has been broken with India's and Pakistan's nuclear tests of May, 1998. These tests jolted the nonproliferation regime by signaling the emergence of two additional nuclear powers, which in turn could reverse the regime's gains in the middle term. Thus Iran may cite a security threat from a nuclear Pakistan or Israel as grounds to leave the NPT and pursue a nuclear weapons program; an Iranian nuclear program would cause Iraq to revive its nuclear ambitions. In the middle term, if a few states revive their nuclear programs, additional states may also begin challenging the nonproliferation regime with the result that the regime may gradually break down or lose its significance.

D. U.S.–Soviet (Russian) Strategic Nuclear Weapons Arms Control

Bilateral U.S.–Soviet arms control agreements were intended to maintain deterrence stability by regulating the number and composition of strategic nuclear forces—intercontinental ballistic missiles (ICBMs), submarine launched ballistic missiles (SLBMs), and long-range bombers—upon which each side based its nuclear deterrent. By bringing the two superpowers to the negotiating table, arms control also aimed at fostering dialogue and decreasing tensions between the two

Cold War adversaries. In addition, nuclear arms control was an obligation undertaken by the superpowers under Article VI of the NPT. It should be noted that although strategic nuclear arms control involved only the two nuclear superpowers, it dealt with issues that were global in scope. If deterrence failed and a nuclear war erupted, the effects of a nuclear exchange would not be confined to the territories of the United States and the Soviet Union, but rather would rapidly spread globally.

The Strategic Arms Limitation Talks (SALT) began in 1969 and produced two agreements in 1972—the Anti-Ballistic Missile (ABM) treaty and SALT I. The ABM treaty limited both sides to 100 defensive interceptor missiles at two sites; these provisions were later amended to restrict ABMs to only a single site. In general, defensive systems undermine deterrence, and by limiting the number of defensive interceptors, the ABM treaty intended to preserve deterrence stability. The ABM treaty has been adhered to for over 2 decades. It imposed obstacles on the Reagan administration's Strategic Defense Initiative (SDI) program, and it has curbed the scope of subsequent U.S. National Missile Defense (NMD) initiatives. The ABM treaty permits Theater Missile Defense (TMD) interceptors, such as the Patriot, to defend against short-range ballistic missiles.

It should be noted that the TMD demarcation line has been an issue of controversy. Some sections of the U.S. military and Congress have sought to remove all ABM-related constraints on the development of TMD systems. On the other hand, the Russian Duma desired stricter controls on TMD development so that the more advanced TMD systems would not have the potential to intercept ICBMs. This controversy has been resolved under a 1997 U.S.–Russia understanding that permits TMD systems that have velocities under 3 km/s and are not tested against ballistic missiles with ranges greater than 3500 km; U.S. systems such as the Patriot PAC-3, THAAD, and Navy Wide-Area TMD would be allowed under this framework. This agreement increases the transparency of TMD activities and reassures both sides that TMD systems are not being developed for national missile defense purposes and therefore are compliant with the ABM treaty.

The SALT I Interim Agreement of 1972 limited the U.S. and Soviet Union to their then-existing strategic nuclear missile forces. The U.S. was permitted 1054 ICBMs and 710 SLBMs, while the Soviet Union was allowed 1618 ICBMs and 710 SLBMs. SALT I did not place restrictions on an emerging technology, Multiple Independently-targetable Reentry Vehicles (MIRVs), which allowed each missile to carry several warheads capable of hitting up to an equal number of targets. MIRVs raised the total number of nuclear warheads on each side to over 10,000 and thereby negated any significant gains in terms of nuclear force reductions.

SALT II was signed in 1979. It reaffirmed the previously reached Vladivostok agreement of 1974 restricting both superpowers to 2400 nuclear delivery systems (to be reduced to 2250 by 1981), of which no more than 1320 could be MIRVed missiles. It also counted long-range bombers, which had been excluded from the SALT I understanding. While placing no overall total limit on warheads, SALT II restricted the number of warheads to no more than 10 on each new ICBM and 14 on each SLBM.

The next significant U.S.–Soviet nuclear arms control agreement was the Intermediate Nuclear Force (INF) treaty signed in 1987. This treaty was not directed at strategic nuclear forces, but rather was aimed at eliminating short- and intermediate-range nuclear forces whose deployment had resulted in a quantitative and qualitative change in the European security situation. The INF treaty called for the destruction of the newly deployed and particularly destabilizing MIRVed SS-20 as well as older SS-4 and SS-5 missiles on the Soviet side and the elimination of Pershing II and cruise missiles on the U.S. side. An additional outcome of the INF agreement was that it brought about the elimination of an entire category of nuclear delivery systems on a global basis—all U.S. and Russian missiles (not just those in Europe) having ranges between 500 and 5000 km were destroyed under this treaty.

The Strategic Arms Reduction Talks (START), initiated in 1982, took 9 years to result in the first START treaty in July, 1991. START emphasized *reductions,* in contrast to the focus on *limitations* in SALT. START I restricts the U.S. and Russia to 1600 strategic nuclear delivery vehicles (SNDVs)—missiles and bombers—and 6000 accountable warheads each, with these limits to be attained by December, 2001. START II, signed in January, 1993, called for the U.S. and Russia to reduce their nuclear forces to 3000–3500 strategic nuclear warheads by the year 2003; this date was later extended to 2007. START II is also important because it calls for the elimination of all MIRVed ICBMs, systems which are considered to be particularly destabilizing. A START III framework reducing U.S. and Russian arsenals to 2000–2500 deployed strategic nuclear warheads has been informally agreed upon. An additional feature of START III is that while START I and START II primarily require the elimination of delivery systems, but allow nuclear warheads to be retained in storage, START III will include provisions for the destruction of strategic nuclear warheads. Table I summarizes START limits.

TABLE I
START Treaty Aggregate Limits on Strategic Nuclear Arms

	START I	START II	START III
Date signed	July, 1991	January, 1993	—
Deployed SNDVs (ICBMs, SLBMs, bombers)	1600		
Deployed warheads on all SNDVs	6000	3000–3500	2000–2500
Deployed ICBM and SLBM warheads	4900	1700–1750 on SLBMs	
Date for attaining limits	December, 2001	December, 2007 (originally 2003)	December, 2007
Prominent features		Eliminates MIRVed ICBMs	Destruction of warheads

As of July, 1997, Russia had reduced its nuclear arsenal to 1,500 deployed SNDVs carrying 6,700 strategic nuclear warheads, while the U.S. had 1,500 deployed SNDVs and 7,900 strategic warheads in its nuclear arsenal. Besides warheads on SNDVs, however, the nuclear states also maintain a larger number of nuclear warheads in their arsenals—some 12,000 with the U.S. and 22,000 with Russia. A 1998 Natural Resource Defense Council report noted that the five declared nuclear states together had approximately 36,000 nuclear weapons in their arsenals; this figure represented a 50% decrease from the mid-1980s, when the five nuclear states together maintained some 70,000 nuclear weapons.

The overall significance of SALT and START stems not merely from the extent to which they imposed limitations or reductions on nuclear forces, but also from their facilitating continuing superpower dialogue during the Cold War and seeking to preserve a deterrence-stable military balance. The pace of negotiation, ratification, and implementation of the SALT and START agreements was considerably influenced by prevailing political events. SALT I and START II were negotiated within a short period of a few years, while SALT II and START I took several years longer. The Soviet invasion of Afghanistan in 1979 and the subsequent deterioration in U.S.–Soviet relations caused SALT II ratification to be put on hold. While the treaty was never ratified by the U.S. Senate, the Reagan administration abided by its limits until 1986. Mikhail Gorbachev's coming to power in the Soviet Union in 1985 and his willingness to reduce nuclear forces and accept unequal cuts gave impetus to the INF and START initiatives. The Reagan administration's insistence either on deep cuts in long-range nuclear capabilities, particularly warheads, or, absent such an accord, the pursuit of a nuclear warfighting capability, including SDI as a component, considerably delayed a final agreement on START I. START II was ratified by the U.S. Senate in January, 1996, but has not entered into force because the treaty has not been ratified by the Russian Duma. The Duma has held back ratification of START II citing security concerns over NATO expansion. This in turn has affected START III; while START III limits have been informally agreed upon, formal START III negotiations have not commenced because START II has not entered into force.

E. Chemical and Biological Weapons Arms Control

Two international treaties—the Biological Weapons Convention (BWC) of 1972 and the Chemical Weapons Convention (CWC) signed in 1993 and entering into force in 1997—aim to control chemical and biological weapons proliferation in a manner similar to which the NPT controls nuclear proliferation. One important difference between these treaties is that the CWC and BWC impose equal obligations on all parties—they do not permit *any* signatory to retain chemical and biological weapons—while the NPT allows five states to keep nuclear weapons. Under the BWC, states pledge not to develop or acquire biological agents and toxins. The BWC contains no verification provisions, although negotiations have been undertaken, through an ad hoc group of states that was established in 1994, to invest the treaty with verification and compliance measures. The CWC prohibits states from developing and acquiring chemical weapons; these undertakings are subject to verification by an international agency, the Organization for Prohibition of Chemical Weapons (OPCW).

Chemical and biological weapons, along with nuclear weapons, are regarded as weapons of mass destruction (WMDs). The CWC and BWC, like the NPT, are international treaties which states voluntarily sign. As of 1998, a number of states have not signed or ratified the CWC, notably Egypt, Libya, Iraq, Syria, and North Korea. Further, especially for the BWC, states may sign but nevertheless violate this treaty without much difficulty since the treaty has no verification agency. Nonstate actors, such as separatist or terrorist groups, may also resort to chemical and biological warfare, although it should be noted that such incidents have been rare. Only one major incident of terrorist-related chemical warfare has taken place—a sarin gas attack in a Tokyo subway in 1995.

F. Supply-Side Regimes

In an effort to address limitations of the NPT, CWC, and BWC, supply-side regimes attempt to create additional barriers against WMD proliferation. Supply-side regimes are agreements among a group of 30–35 primarily industrialized states aimed at restricting and regulating their exports of nuclear, chemical, and biological technologies which may be used in building WMDs. The Nuclear Suppliers Group (NSG) that restricts nuclear transfers was formed in 1975 in response to the 1974 Indian nuclear test. The Australia Group (AG), restricting the export of certain chemicals, was established in 1984, following the use of chemical weapons in the Iran–Iraq war. The Missile Technology Control Regime (MTCR) was formally established in 1987, aiming to halt ballistic missile proliferation; ballistic missiles are systems of concern because of their WMD delivery capability. The MTCR prohibits the sale of ballistic missiles and restricts the transfer of missile-related industrial technology such as engines, guidance systems, and manufacturing and testing equipment.

Another supplier group, formed in 1995, is the Wassenaar Arrangement on Export Controls for Conventional Arms and Dual-Use Goods and Technologies. This arrangement is more concerned with conventional arms trade control rather than WMD proliferation. The Wassenaar arrangement seeks to prevent the acquisition of armaments and sensitive dual-use items having military end-uses by states of concern to the group's participants, states that are sometimes termed as "rogue" states. While not formally directed against any particular state, in practice the Wassenaar framework targets Iran, Iraq, Libya, Syria, and North Korea, states that are also subject to U.S. trade restrictions or sanctions. Wassenaar is the successor to a U.S.-initiated Cold War export control regime, Cocom (the Coordinating Committee), which curbed Western technology transfers to the former East bloc. The above supply-side regimes complement national domestic legislation such as U.S. export control laws that restrict the transfer of weapons-related technology and munitions.

Supplier groups are not international treaties and do not seek universal membership. The Australia Group, the Nuclear Suppliers Group, the MTCR, and Wassenaar consist of some 30 member states. Initially these groups comprised the Western bloc—the U.S., Canada, the west European states, Japan, and Australia—and subsequently expanded to include all European Union states, Russia, some Central and East European states, and Argentina, Brazil, South Africa, and South Korea. Table II lists supply-side regime members.

In terms of their nature and obligations, supplier groups are somewhat discriminatory because while they permit trade in specified dual-use industrial goods

TABLE II

Membership in Supply-Side Regimes[a]

	Nuclear Suppliers Group	Australia Group	MTCR	Wassenaar
Argentina	x	x	x	x
Australia	x	x	x	x
Austria	x	x	x	x
Belgium	x	x	x	x
Brazil	x		x	
Bulgaria	x			x
Canada	x	x	x	x
Czech Republic	x	x		x
Denmark	x	x	x	x
Finland	x	x	x	x
France	x	x	x	x
Germany	x	x	x	x
Greece	x	x	x	x
Hungary	x	x	x	x
Iceland		x	x	
Ireland	x	x	x	x
Italy	x	x	x	x
Japan	x	x	x	x
S. Korea	x	x		x
Luxembourg	x	x	x	x
Netherlands	x	x	x	x
New Zealand	x	x	x	x
Norway	x	x	x	x
Poland	x	x	x	x
Portugal	x	x		x
Romania	x	x		x
Russia	x	x	x	x
Slovakia	x	x		x
S. Africa	x		x	x
Spain	x	x	x	x
Sweden	x	x	x	x
Switzerland	x	x	x	x
Turkey			x	x
Ukraine		x		x
UK	x	x	x	x
U.S.	x	x	x	x

[a] Membership as of December, 1998. States that are not members but are formal adherents with some of the above regimes include China and Israel. Latvia is an NSG member.

among group members, they restrict the transfer of these technologies to certain nonmembers. Yet supplier groups are also a barrier to proliferation and thus advance broader nonproliferation objectives. Export control regimes have been criticized by some developing countries of the South for hindering their economic development by restricting their acquisition of high-technology items. Export controls are also opposed by economic, trade, and business interests within the supplier countries. These groups note that restrictions on technology transfer result in lowering the overall volume of exports, which consequently reduces employment in export-oriented technology sectors, lowers corporate revenues, and, at a macroeconomic level, impacts negatively on trade balances and the overall national economy. The long-term viability of maintaining export controls will depend on whether their economic costs and shortcomings mentioned above are outweighed by their nonproliferation and security benefits.

G. Future Proliferation Concerns

International treaties and supplier controls both have their limitations. International treaties are not binding on nonsignatory states. States that sign a treaty may nevertheless violate their treaty commitments and pursue a clandestine WMD program. Supplier controls are often inadequate barriers to proliferation. While nuclear weapons and ballistic missiles are hard to indigenously develop, a large number of states have the industrial capability to build chemical and biological weapons and cruise missiles. Thus neither international treaties nor supplier controls can halt a state that is determined to develop WMDs and their means of delivery.

One additional issue of proliferation concern is the control of weapons-grade uranium and plutonium from the former Soviet nuclear arsenal. The U.S. government's Cooperative Threat Reduction (CTR) program has attempted to address this issue. CTR facilitated the return to Russia of 1000 nuclear warheads from Belarus, Kazakhstan, and Ukraine and the removal of secure storage of over 2000 warheads from missile and bomber bases. CTR also allowed some 5000 former Soviet weapon scientists and engineers to be employed on civilian research projects, thus reducing the possibility of the transfer of their expertise to potential WMD-seeking states.

In summary, the NPT regime as well as other WMD regimes, comprising international treaties and supplier control groups as shown in Table III, have been moderately successful. If norms against WMD acquisition are strengthened, then proliferation can be halted or slowed in the future. Yet a determined proliferator may nonetheless overcome obstacles posed by the nonproliferation regime and acquire WMDs. The further pursuit of bilateral U.S.–Russian nuclear force reductions, and the eventual inclusion of all declared nuclear states in nuclear force reduction talks, has important implications for proliferation. Positive actions involving nuclear force reductions by the nuclear states could further increase the confidence of nonnuclear states in the present nuclear nonproliferation regime. This in turn diminishes the nuclear weapons aspirations of states, thus reducing the dangers of proliferation. On the other hand, nuclear force reductions by the nuclear states, especially the U.S. may also jeopardize the extended deterrence provided by the U.S. nuclear umbrella to states such as Germany, Japan, and South Korea. If these states are confronted with future security threats, say from Russia or China, and have less confidence in security guarantees and the U.S. nuclear umbrella, then they (like Great Britain, France, and Israel before them) may seek to acquire independent nuclear weapons programs, thus increasing the risks of further proliferation as additional states would then follow the nuclear path.

IV. CONVENTIONAL ARMS AND REGIONAL ARMS CONTROL

A. The UN Conventional Arms Register

The conventional arms trade has been largely unaffected by arms control regimes. Conventional arms are viewed as a legitimate means to national security. The arms industry is also an important source of employment and revenue for the national economies of many states. Global arms transfers were valued at approximately $60 billion in 1984 and have averaged $30 billion each year in the period from 1990 to 1997. In the period from 1985 to 1990, the U.S. and former Soviet Union accounted for 25–30% and 30–35% of global arms exports, respectively. In the period from 1991 to 1995, U.S. arms exports averaged $12 to 15 billion per year, accounting for 40–50% of the global share. Russian arms exports fell drastically before reviving; they were valued at $5 billion in 1995, or 10% of world arms exports. The U.S., Russia, UK, France, Germany, and China together account for 80% of global arms exports. The Middle East (30–40%), East Asia (15%), and Western Europe (15%) together accounted for 60–70% of world arms imports in the 1980s and 1990s.

Two global initiatives on conventional arms control

TABLE III

Weapons of Mass Destruction: Treaties and States Involved

	Nuclear[a]	Biological	Chemical[b]	Ballistic missiles[c,d]
International treaties Banning Possession or Development	NPT (1968)	BWC (1972)	CWC (1993)	—
International Verification Agency for treaty	IAEA	None	OPCW	—
States permitted weapon possession by treaty	P-5 (US, Russia, UK, France, China)	None	None	—
States not signing and ratifying treaty as of 1997	T-3 (India, Israel, Pakistan), Cuba	Some	Egypt, Iraq, Libya, N. Korea, Syria, others	—
States declared or presumed to have weapons	P-5, T-3	Some	Some	P-5: long-range; 20 others: short-range
States building systems as of 1997	Fissile material production: China, T-3 (presumed).	Some	Some	ICBMs: China, Russia; Short-range: T-3, N. Korea, Iran
States eliminating or renouncing weapons programs in the 1990s	S. Africa, Ukraine, Kazakhstan, Belarus			Argentina, Brazil, S. Africa, Hungary
Other treaties and regimes				
Supply-side regime restricting sale of weapons or production technology	Nuclear Suppliers Group (1974)	Australia Group (1984)	Australia Group (1984)	Missile Technology Control Regime (1987)
Regional treaties prohibiting WMDs	Antarctica, Latin America, S. Pacific, Africa, SE Asia		Mendoza Accord (1991) for Latin America	
Bilateral U.S.–Russian Treaty restricting systems	START II: 3000–3500 strategic warheads by 2007		1990 Destruction Agreement: stockpile of 5000 tons by 2002	START I: 1600 delivery systems. INF: bans 500- to 5000-km-range missiles

[a] P-5: Permanent members of the UN Security Council, declared nuclear states; T-3: Threshold or de facto Nuclear States.

[b] Chemical weapons: In 1997, the U.S. government suspected Ethiopia, Iran, Syria, Israel, Egypt, Libya Pakistan, Myanmar, Vietnam, China, and North and South Korea to have chemical weapons.

[c] Ballistic missiles: Afghanistan, Algeria, Belarus, Bulgaria, the Czech Republic, Egypt, Iran, Iraq, Libya, Poland, Romania, Slovakia, Syria, Ukraine, and Yemen have Soviet-suplied 300 to 500-km-range Scuds, 120-km-range SS-21s, or 70-km-range Frog-7 missiles. North Korean-built Scuds have been exported to Iran and Syria. China has transferred missiles to Iran (150-km-range M-7s), Pakistan (300-km-range M-11s), and Saudi Arabia (2,500-km-range CSS-2s). U.S.-supplied 130-km-range Lance missiles in NATO states are being retired and placed in storage. U.S.-built 100 to 200-km-range ATACM missiles are to be exported to U.S. allies and clients. The declared nuclear states have 5,000- to 12,000-km-range ICBMs and SLBMs.

[d] Missile development: Egypt and Syria may be undertaking Scud-type missile development. Israel has built and deployed 500-km-range Jericho I and 1500-km-range Jericho II missiles, N. Korea has flight-tested the 1000-km-range Nodong and 1300-km-range Taepodong missiles; Iran is developing a 1000-km-range Nodong-derived Shahbab-3 missile. India is building 150 to 250-km-range Prithvi missiles and has flight-tested the 1500-km-range Agni; Pakistan may be building the 600 to 800-km-range Half-3 and has also flight-tested the 1000-km-range Nodong-derived Ghauri missile. The United States is upgrading its Minuteman-3 ICBMs, Russia is building a new ICBM (called Topol) and the D-31 SLBM, and China is also building a small number of new-generation ICBMs and SLBMs. The P-5 states, Japan, the European Space Agency, and India have or are developing satellite launch vehicles (SLVs) with capabilities similar to ICBMs; Brazil is building shorter-range SLVs.

have been undertaken in the 1990s. First, the UN Conventional Arms Register was created in 1992. Following the Gulf War, the five permanent members of the UN Security Council undertook talks in 1991–1992 on limiting their conventional arms sales; these talks were not successful. Nevertheless, the Iraqi invasion of Kuwait had generated an international consensus that the accumulation of advanced conventional weapons can result in the outbreak of armed conflict. Consequently, the UN Register was created to expand transparency with respect to conventional arms. The Register requires states to voluntarily provide data on their arms exports and imports, thereby facilitating the identification of potentially destabilizing arms transfers. Approximately 80 states have participated in the Register each year. The Register lacks an international verification agency, although informal verification occurs by comparing Register entries with public data, and cross-checking export and import entries within the Register. A second drawback of the Register is that by including only arms transfers but not indigenous arms production or military inventories, the Register does not allow for an accurate assessment of military balances between states.

Despite its shortcomings, the Register has important implications for regional security. If it is eventually strengthened by addressing the above-mentioned limitations, it would promote greater transparency on military balances thus facilitating regional confidence building. It would also allow for the identification of destabilizing military build-ups which, if unchecked, would exacerbate local conflicts. The Register is thus an international arms control initiative that addresses regional security issues. The UN arms embargoes on regions of conflict—for example, Iraq and the former Yugoslavia—are other internationally mandated forms of arms control intended to reduce the scale of regional conflict.

B. The Inhumane Weapons Convention and the Land Mine Convention

A second global conventional arms control initiative in the 1990s is the Convention on the Prohibition of the Use, Stockpiling, Production and Transfer of Anti-Personnel Mines and on Their Destruction, also known as the Ottawa treaty. Negotiations for the treaty were initiated in Ottawa in October, 1996; the treaty was completed in September, 1997 in Oslo, Norway and opened for signature in Ottawa on December 2–4, 1997. The Ottawa treaty process represented a departure from traditional inter-state arms control negotiations. Its impetus came not from national governments but rather from a group of nongovernmental organizations and the International Red Cross, which mobilized international public opinion against antipersonnel land mines (APLs) and pressured governments into negotiating the treaty. Further, negotiations were undertaken outside traditional fora, such as the UN and the Conference on Disarmament, and pursued under the leadership of states such as Canada and Norway without the involvement of the major powers.

The land mine treaty is concerned with humanitarian objectives rather than with conflict prevention through arms trade control. Its goals are similar to those of the pre-World War I Hague Conventions and the 1980 Convention on Prohibitions and Restrictions on the Use of Certain Conventional Weapons Which May be Deemed to be Excessively Injurious or to Have Indiscriminate Effects (the CCW Convention, also called the Inhumane Weapons Convention). These conventions are based on the principle that the right of the parties in an armed conflict to choose methods or means of warfare is not unlimited. The CCW convention prohibits the employment of weapons and methods of warfare which cause superfluous injury or unnecessary suffering. Its protocols cover undetectable fragmenting munitions, booby traps, incendiary devices, and blinding laser weapons.

The campaign to ban APLs actually gained momentum following the 1995 CCW review conference, which highlighted the extent of the land mine problem. An estimated 2 million new APLs are deployed each year, largely for use in civil wars, resulting in the accumulation of 100 million APLs in 60 countries. These land mines kill or maim approximately 26,000 people each year; 90% of the casualties are civilian and occur in the years after conflicts have ended. While the Ottawa treaty has been signed by over 120 states, it had (at the end of 1997) not been signed by several major states such as the U.S., China, Russia, and several states in South Asia and the Middle East. Many of these nonsignatory states have, however, pledged support for international demining efforts that are part of the treaty. Therefore, the land mine treaty and related demining efforts promise to reduce civilian casualties caused by antipersonnel land mines.

C. Regional Nuclear Free Zones

Nuclear weapon free zones (NWFZs) have been successfully established in five geographic regions—Latin America, the South Pacific, Southeast Asia, Africa, and Antarctica—encompassing an estimated population of 1.7 billion. NWFZs prohibit the deployment, transport, manufacture, or testing of nuclear weapons in the area covered by the zone and thus go beyond the NPT's nonproliferation agreements which permit some of the above activities. While regional nuclear free zones serve to strengthen and reinforce the global nonproliferation regime, they assume greater significance as a nuclear confidence and security-building measure among states in a region. They also symbolize regional solidarity and are aimed at keeping external nuclear forces outside the region. The declared nuclear states were initially reluctant to participate in regional nuclear free zones because they preferred to maintain unrestricted rights of passage for their naval vessels and to retain the option of nuclear testing, especially in the South Pacific. Since the end of the Cold War, the declared nuclear states have generally agreed to respect regional nuclear free zones, although they have also noted difficulties in formally adhering to all provisions of the Southeast Asian zone. In this respect, the nuclear weapon states have sought to exclude oceanic regions such as national exclusive economic zones (EEZs) and continental shelves that are contained in the definition of the Southeast Asian zone.

The 1959 Antarctic Treaty, originally signed by 12 states, prohibited the establishment of military bases and nuclear activities in the region. This treaty, besides establishing a regional nuclear free zone, is more important for averting inter-state discord over territorial claims in Antarctica. The 1967 Treaty of Tlatelolco, negotiated among Latin American states, establishes a nuclear free zone in Latin America. The treaty was greatly strengthened following bilateral Argentina–Brazil nuclear confidence-building measures that included the establishment of the Argentina–Brazil Agency for Accounting and Control of Nuclear Materials in 1991; these Argentina–Brazil CBMs have ensured that nuclear facilities in both states are placed under inspection and therefore not of proliferation concern, thus strengthening the regional nuclear free zone. The South Pacific Nuclear Free Zone, established in 1985 in response to French nuclear testing in the South Pacific, was enhanced with the end of nuclear testing and the accession of France, the U.S., and the UK to the zone in 1996. Nuclear free zones have also been established in South East Asia (1995) and Africa (1996), and Mongolia declared itself to be a single-state nuclear free zone in 1992. Table IV identifies current nuclear free zones.

D. Confidence Building and Conventional Arms Control in Europe

European arms control has involved two parallel processes—a confidence-building aspect involving the Conference on Security and Cooperation in Europe (CSCE), renamed the Organization on Security and Cooperation in Europe (OSCE) in 1995, and structural conventional arms control negotiations concerned with military balances. CSCE talks between NATO, the Warsaw Pact, and neutral European states began in 1972 in the wake of improved East–West relations. These led to politically binding agreements on military confidence-building measures, which are incorporated in the Helsinki Final Act of 1975; the 1986 Stockholm Declarations; and the 1990, 1992, and 1994 Vienna Documents. These CBMs include advance notification of and size restrictions on military exercises. These require a 21-day notification for exercises involving over 25,000 troops in the Helsinki Final Act, lengthened to a 42-day notification for smaller exercises involving 9,000 troops or 250 tanks in the 1992 Vienna Document, and a 2-year advance notice for exercises involving over

TABLE IV

Nuclear Free Zones

	Latin America	South Pacific	Southeast Asia	Africa
Treaty	Treaty of Tlatelolco	Treaty of Rarotonga	Treaty of Bangkok	Treaty of Pelindaba
Date signed	February 14, 1967	August 6, 1985	December 15, 1995	April 11, 1996
Place signed	Distrito Federal, Mexico	Rarotonga, Cook Islands	Bangkok, Thailand	Cairo, Egypt
Entry into force (EIF)	April 22, 1968	December 11, 1986	March 27, 1997	49 signatures, 3 ratifications by January 1998; EIF upon 28 ratifications
Geographic coverage	Latin America and the Caribbean	Australia, Cook Islands, Fiji, Kiribati, Nauru, New Zealand, Niue, Papua New Guinea, Samoa, Solomon Islands, Tuvalu	Brunei, Indonesia, Malaysia, Philippines, Singapore, Thailand, Vietnam, Cambodia, Laos, Myanmar	Continent of Africa and offshore islands

40,000 troops. Another significant CBM among European states is the 1992 "Open Skies" treaty permitting mutually agreed-upon aerial reconnaissance to ensure transparency on military deployments and movements.

Structural arms control in Europe was attempted through talks between NATO and the Warsaw Pact on Mutual and Balanced Force Reductions (MBFR), held at Vienna from 1973–1989. MBFR failed to result in agreement because NATO favored parity between the two blocs, under which the Warsaw Pact would have had to make larger force reductions, while the Warsaw Pact favored equal percentage reductions on both sides, which would have preserved Warsaw Pact superiority during almost all phases of the reductions. In 1989, MBFR talks were replaced by CFE negotiations. Despite its lack of results, MBFR produced a few positive spin-offs. The shared working experience between delegations and expertise acquired on arms control issues in many countries facilitated the rapid conclusion of the CFE negotiations that began in 1989; Soviet leader Mikhail Gorbachev's willingness to accept unequal reductions also facilitated progress at the CFE talks.

Twenty-two European states (NATO and former Warsaw Pact states) signed the Conventional Armed Forces in Europe (CFE) Treaty in November, 1990. The treaty called for parity in conventional forces between NATO and the then Warsaw Pact, with each side's total conventional forces limited to 20,000 tanks; 30,000 armored combat vehicles (ACVs); 20,000 artillery pieces; 6,800 combat aircraft; and 2,000 helicopters. Sublimits were applied on the concentration of forces in designated geographic zones, and no more than two-thirds of the total forces permitted to each bloc could be employed in a single country. Within each bloc, states negotiated national force size ceilings that would facilitate the bloc's compliance with aggregate CFE limits; these national limits were announced at the time of the CFE's signing.

A follow-up to the CFE treaty, a politically binding CFE-1A agreement, was signed in July, 1992 by 29 states. It set troops and personnel limits on all participating states, including 250,000 for U.S. forces in Europe; 1,450,000 for the Russian Federation; 345,000 for Germany; 450,000 for Ukraine; 530,000 for Turkey; 325,000 for France; and 260,000 for the UK. Virtually all these ceilings were larger than actual deployments in 1992. CFE and CFE-IA limits are shown in Table V.

Arms control accords eventually have to adapt to changed political circumstances. The provisions of the CFE treaty have been modified in the years after its signing to reflect the disappearance of the Warsaw Pact and the breakup of the Soviet Union. In 1992, the former republics of the Soviet Union agreed to join CFE without modifying its terms. They also decided among themselves the apportionment of the forces allocated under CFE to the former Soviet Union.

A more important issue concerned the deployment of Russian forces to comply with CFE zone limits. This arose in the southern flank zone, which was previously a rear peripheral area in Soviet defense planning, but which subsequently became a forward line of defense in the post-Soviet era. Russia was placed in a situation where it could keep only 20% of its forces in the Leningrad and Caucasus districts, which accounted for half its European territory. Russian forces, withdrawn from Eastern Europe and the Baltic states, were also concentrated in the Kaliningrad enclave of the Leningrad region, exceeding CFE zone limits.

The above issues were resolved under the 1996 CFE Flank accords, where the boundaries for the Leningrad military district and the North Caucasus region were redrawn. Russian and Ukrainian forces in these regions are now counted under two or more zones and thereby do not violate treaty sublimits for any single zone. Another outcome of the Flank accord is that it permits Russia to maintain high force concentrations in the trans-Caucasus, which is an area of security concern for Russia and where the Russian military was engaged in the Chechnyan conflict.

An important future issue on the CFE agenda is NATO expansion, which will result in former Warsaw Treaty states joining NATO, beginning with Poland, the Czech Republic, and Hungary. NATO expansion changes the balance of forces between NATO and Russia. This issue will have to be addressed through a CFE-II treaty. CFE parties have agreed that CFE-II would emphasize force size limits for each country rather than bloc limits and would cover all OSCE states.

Overall, the CFE treaty has introduced an element of stability in European security. It also brought about the destruction of some 50,000 items of military equipment in Europe, mostly in the former Soviet Union. The successful and rapid completion of CFE reflected the reduction of tensions in Europe and the dissolution of the Soviet Union and the collapse of the Warsaw Pact. Reciprocally, the reduced offensive forces as well as transparency and notification procedures of CFE and CSCE made a surprise attack on Western Europe almost impossible and facilitated further CBMs under CFE-1A and the 1992 and 1994 Vienna CSCE initiatives.

E. Regional Arms Control outside Europe

Lessons from European arms control have important implications for regions where arms control successes remain unattained. The East–West conflict in Europe

TABLE V

CFE Limits, National Ceilings, and CFE-IA Troop Limits

	CFE					CFE-IA
	Tanks	ACVs	Artillery	Aircraft	Helicopters	Troops
Bloc limits	20,000	30,000	20,000	6,800	2,000	—
NATO states						
Belgium	334	1,099	320	232	46	70,000
Britain	1,015	3,176	636	900	384	260,000
Canada	77	277	38	90	13	10,660
Denmark	353	316	553	106	12	39,000
France	1,306	3,820	1,292	800	352	325,000
Germany	4,166	3,466	2,705	900	306	345,000
Greece	1,735	2,534	1,878	650	18	158,620
Iceland	0	0	0	0	0	0
Italy	1,348	3,339	1,955	650	142	315,000
Luxembourg	0	0	0	0	0	900
Netherlands	743	1,080	607	230	69	80,000
Norway	170	225	527	100	0	32,000
Portugal	300	430	450	160	26	75,000
Spain	794	1,588	1,310	310	71	300,000
Turkey	2,795	3,120	3,523	750	43	530,000
U.S.	4,006	5,372	2,492	784	518	250,000
Former Warsaw Pact states						
Bulgaria	1,475	2,000	1,750	235	67	104,000
Czechoslovakia	1,435	2,050	1,150	345	75	140,000
Hungary	835	1,700	840	180	108	100,000
Poland	1,730	2,150	1,610	460	130	234,000
Romania	1,375	2,100	1,475	430	120	230,000
Soviet Union	13,150	20,000	13,175	5,150	1,500	—
Azerbaijan	220	220	285	100	50	70,000
Armenia	220	220	285	100	50	60,000
Belarus	1,800	2,600	1,615	260	80	100,000
Georgia	220	220	285	100	50	40,000
Kazakhstan	0	0	0	0	0	0
Moldova	210	210	250	50	50	20,000
Russia	6,400	11,480	6,415	3,450	890	1,450,000
Ukraine	4,080	5,050	4,040	1,090	330	450,000

CFE treaty limits are indicated in bold. Ceilings for individual countries are not contained in the CFE treaty but were negotiated within each bloc and announced at the time of the treaty's signing in November, 1990. Ceilings mutually agreed between ex-Soviet states were announced in May, 1992. Kazakhstan may retain no treaty limited equipment in the part of its territory covered by the treaty. The Czechoslovak total was subsequently apportioned on a 2:1 basis between the Czech and Slovak republics. CFE-IA is not a treaty but a politically binding agreement specifying troop limits, announced in July, 1992.

allowed a simple yardstick of military force size to define the relative power of states in the region. Based on this measure, it was possible to devise structural arms control agreements creating stable and nonthreatening military balances. Yet because many different conflicts—ethnic, religious, territorial—exist in the Middle East, Africa, and South Asia, CFE-like arms control, which regulates military force sizes, may not be best suited for these regions. Arms control eventually has to be tailored to the needs of each region to be successful.

It should also be noted that many arms control successes concerning East-West issues—INF (1987), CFE (1990), START I (1991), and START II (1993)—were attained toward, or after, the end of the Cold War, at a time of greater trust and reduced tension between the two sides. In contrast, arms control negotiations during the Cold War—MBFR (1973–1989), SALT II (1972–1979), and START I (1982–1991)—were prolonged due to unfavorable political circumstances and often resulted in no final treaty (MBFR) or an unratified treaty (SALT II). Similar trends should be expected in regional arms control—when tensions are high, arms control may not be easily attained; when tensions are low, arms control successes are likely to follow.

While the implementation of CBMs has been slow in the Middle East and South Asia, significant CBMs are being undertaken in Latin America. CFE, OSCE, and the UN Conventional Arms Register provide a model for these regional initiatives. The Organization of American States (OAS) adopted a resolution in 1997 seeking a legally binding regional agreement on the advance notification of major arms acquisitions covered by the UN Register. A prior OAS-sponsored meeting led to the Declaration of Santiago in 1995; this declaration called upon states to undertake OSCE-like measures requiring advance notification of military exercises and the exchange of information on defense policies. Latin American CBMs seek to strengthen regional security and allow Latin American governments to maintain and modernize defense forces without triggering suspicions from their neighbors or leading to arms races.

Arms control has achieved limited success on WMD issues in areas where tensions remain high (i.e., the Middle East, South Asia, and the Korean peninsula); CBMs involving conventional armed forces have been attempted in these regions with mixed success. Arms Control and Regional Security (ACRS) talks on conventional arms are included in the Middle East Peace Process. While these talks have resulted in limited CBMs such as cooperation in maritime search and rescue operations, the slowdown of the Middle East Peace Process has prevented further CBMs from being attained. Moreover, Egypt has sought to include issues concerning Israel's nuclear status, further complicating ACRS talks. As a result, CBM initiatives are likely to follow rather than precede advances in the Middle East Peace Process.

In South Asia, the main WMD CBMs between India and Pakistan are a 1988 agreement not to attack each other's nuclear facilities and a 1992 agreement requiring both states to sign the CWC. India and Pakistan have also undertaken conventional force CBMs, such as a 1991 agreement for advance notice on military exercises and the prevention of air space violations. Despite these CBMs, cross-border firing between Indian and Pakistani armed forces has continued, resulting in dozens of casualties each year. Further, CBMs did not prevent India and Pakistan from conducting nuclear tests in May, 1998. At this time, Pakistan expressed fears of an Indian strike on its nuclear facilities and noted that such a strike by India would be countered with a "devastating" response by Pakistan. Even if Pakistan's concerns were exaggerated, they demonstrated that neither state placed great faith in the 1988 CBMs that specifically prohibited such a strike on nuclear sites. Thus during this crisis, CBMs did not serve their purpose of reassuring both parties against a military attack. India and Pakistan have abided by a 1960 agreement on sharing river waters in the Indus River Basin; yet this significant act of cooperation on river waters has not spilled over into gains concerning military CBMs.

India and China have signed important CBMs since 1993. The 1993 China–India Treaty on Peace and Tranquillity notes that pending an ultimate solution on their disputed boundary, both states will respect and observe the line of actual control. A follow-up treaty in 1996 reaffirms that both countries would not use or threaten to use force against the other or seek unilateral military superiority. It also contains military CBMs such as the advance notification of military exercises and force reductions in border areas. The utility of Sino–Indian CBMs eventually depends on broader developments in Sino–India relations; CBMs did contribute to a strengthening of Sino–Indian ties in the early and mid-1990s, but eventually CBM-induced cooperation may become marginalized under changing political circumstances. Thus India's nuclear tests of May, 1998 resulted in the partial deterioration of Sino–Indian relations thereafter with both sides exchanging a war of words on nuclear issues; the 1993 and 1996 CBMs did not prevent this deterioration in Sino–Indian relations.

The Korean peninsula, while currently a nuclear free zone, remains an area of proliferation concern. The October, 1994 U.S.–North Korea agreement (discussed in the NPT section of this essay), if adhered to and completed, will adequately address security threats from the North Korean nuclear program. It should be noted that North Korea has not signed the Chemical Weapons Convention and also continues the development of ballistic missiles which can strike Japan—the 1000-km-range Nodong and 1300-km range Taepodong—and therefore remains a proliferation concern.

F. Unilateral Arms Control

Unilateral arms control initiatives, such as conventional force reductions announced by Soviet leader Mikhail Gorbachev (1988) and Russian President Boris Yeltsin (1991–1992) and the removal of U.S. tactical nuclear weapons from naval vessels and overseas bases, announced by President Bush in 1991 and completed in 1992, are made outside the framework of negotiated international treaties. Unilateral initiatives often have ulterior motives; they may involve the retiring of obsolete or economically burdensome weapons, and they are widely publicized as unilateral arms control for propaganda purposes. Yet unilateral proposals also reflect a desire for reciprocity, and when reciprocated, they contribute to confidence building and further arms control progress. For example, a moratorium on nuclear testing by the former Soviet Union in 1990 was reciprocated by the UK in 1991 and the U.S. in 1992. No further nuclear tests were conducted by these states, a situation which fostered a conducive and positive negotiating environment during the test ban treaty discussions (1994–1996) and eventually resulted in a comprehensive test ban treaty in 1996.

G. Limitations of Arms Control

The historical review of arms control undertaken in the previous pages suggests that arms control has had limited success outside Europe. Progress on nonnuclear issues has been particularly difficult. The limitations and critiques of arms control should also be noted.

Arms control does not always lead to positive, security enhancing outcomes. Arms control involving deep cuts may upset a stable arms balance. Large force reductions or reduced defense spending leave states unable to rearm in time to defend themselves when faced with a breakdown of an arms control accord and a rapid military build-up by adversaries. For example, in the period before World War II, France delayed rearming in response to the German build-up until it was too late. Arms control often fails to control modernization or the development of new technologies that may leave one side at a disadvantage. Arms control is counterproductive when it leads to the development of new technologies that are more destabilizing than the technologies that are restricted under existing arms control agreements. In this regard, naval arms control of the 1920s limited battleships but eventually resulted in the escalating construction of aircraft carriers which are offensive and destabilizing systems. Aircraft carriers enabled the attack on Pearl Harbor and facilitated Japanese expansion in the Pacific. SALT I limited nuclear delivery systems but caused an arms race in MIRVs, which led to concerns that the United States would face a "window of vulnerability" when confronted with a larger number of Soviet nuclear forces.

Critics of arms control have noted that arms control is flawed because it reflects the incorrect notion that military, technical, and legal solutions can fix international security problems. The political aspirations of the owners of arms, and not the military-technical condition of military balances, stimulates conflict. Arms control as a tool of diplomacy aiming to create a more secure international order should be viewed in its proper perspective: while arms control regulates military force structures and may thus preserve the peace by preventing surprise military attack, only some of the potential causes of inter-state conflict are militarily related and addressed by arms control. Nonmilitary sources of conflict are not influenced by arms control.

The conditions under which arms control occurs is also important when analyzing a strategic issue. Deep cuts applied to initially large forces leave enough remaining forces to provide for national defense in case of the breakdown of arms control. Large cuts on small forces leave states with even smaller militaries that are unable to provide for national security in the event of a breakdown of arms control agreements and rapid rearmament or the development of new technologies by adversaries. Verification mechanisms providing timely warning of a breakout allow states to adequately counter the adverse consequences resulting from a breakdown of arms control.

Another criticism of arms control is that while attempts to freeze the world level of armaments and prevent the transfer of arms to specific regions may have (or result in) humanitarian goals, such arms control may also freeze an unequal status quo and thus facilitate conquest or control by imperial powers. Such a critique notes some similarities between 19th and early 20th century efforts to prevent the transfer of "advanced" weapons such as firearms to Africa, Asia, or to Native Americans and late 20th century attempts at controlling the proliferation of WMDs to "rogue" states in Africa and Asia through supply-side regimes.

V. CONCLUSIONS: ASSESSING ARMS CONTROL

Arms control has had varying degrees of success in different regions. The issues and actors involved in arms control have somewhat changed over time, but the theoretical basis of arms control remains largely intact. Long-range systems with an inherently global reach—naval forces in the interwar period and strategic nuclear forces in the post-World War II period—have been particularly important issues for arms control during the 20th century. In the post-Cold War era, the proliferation of weapons of mass destruction has emerged as the leading issue of international security concern. In contrast to naval and strategic nuclear arms control, proliferation involves not just a small group of great powers, but a large number of countries, some quite small like Israel. As a result, arms control is becoming increasingly globalized in its scope.

Arms control treaties are useful because they have legal standing in international law and, consequently, are more difficult to violate or overturn. Verification mechanisms accompanying arms control agreements provide transparency, deter violations, and eventually reduce misperception between states, allowing for confidence building that leads to further arms control. Arms control accords themselves offer a framework for follow-up talks and deeper cuts. In the future, as the value of military power declines, unilateral force reductions, a slowdown in force modernization and procurement, and the enlargement of confidence-building transparency measures may acquire greater significance than traditional structural arms control.

Judging arms control as a process rather than as an outcome provides the best understanding of the issue. Arms control serves to maintain an active diplomatic relationship between states during periods of tension and provides a forum for dialogue on military issues. While arms control successes often follow a thaw in political relations between antagonistic states, these arms control successes in turn foster a strengthening of political relations between states, which allows for greater CBMs and deeper arms control that helps consolidate and institutionalize political cooperation.

Strongly institutionalized arms control endeavors, such as the NPT regime, the CSCE process, and CFE treaty, have proved to be invaluable tools in addressing the issues of nonproliferation and European security, respectively. In the absence of the NPT, an even larger number of states might have acquired nuclear weapons, making prospects for nonproliferation much harder, although this optimistic assessment may have to be revised in light of the decisions of the Indian–Pakistani governments to develop nuclear weapons and long-range strike capabilities. The CSCE process and the CFE treaty have paved the way for an orderly transition from the Cold War to a more cooperative post-Cold War security regime in Europe. These cases illustrate that despite its limitations, arms control has attained some notable successes. Arms control, while not the only or even the most important means for maintaining national and international security, can under favorable political circumstances be successfully applied toward these objectives.

Also See the Following Articles

ARMS PRODUCTION, ECONOMICS OF • ARMS TRADE, ECONOMICS OF • BALANCE OF POWER RELATIONSHIPS • CHEMICAL AND BIOLOGICAL WARFARE • COLD WAR • COLLECTIVE SECURITY SYSTEMS • MILITARY DETERRENCE AND STATECRAFT • NUCLEAR WEAPONS POLICIES • PEACE AGREEMENTS

Bibliography

Adler, E. (Ed.) (1992). *The international practice of arms control.* Baltimore/London: Johns Hopkins University Press.

Barton, J. & Weiler, L. (Ed.) (1987). *International arms control: Issues and agreements.* Stanford, CA: Stanford University Press.

Burns, R. D. (Ed.) (1993). *Encyclopedia of arms control and disarmament.* New York: Scribner's.

Daalder, I. & Terriff, T. (Ed.) (1993). *Rethinking the unthinkable: New directions for nuclear arms control.* London: Frank Cass.

Goldblat, J. (1982). *Agreements for arms control: A critical survey.* London: Taylor and Francis/Stockholm: Stockholm International Peace Research Institute.

Goldblat, J. (1994). *Arms control: A guide to negotiations and agreements.* London: Sage/Oslo: International Peace Research Institute.

Gray, C. (1992). *House of cards: Why arms control must fail.* Ithaca, NY: Cornell University Press.

Schelling, T. & Halperin, M. (1985). *Strategy and arms control.* Washington: Pergamon-Brassey's.

Sullivan, J. (1998). The comprehensive test ban treaty. *Physics Today* March, 24–29.

Stockholm International Peace Research Institute (1997 and previous years). *SIPRI yearbook 1997: Armaments, disarmament and international security.* Stockholm: SIPRI.

U.S. Arms Control and Disarmament Agency (1997 and previous years). *World military expenditures and arms transfers.*

U.S. Arms Control and Disarmament Agency (1996). *Arms control and disarmament agreements: Texts and histories of the negotiations.* Washington, DC: U.S. Arms Control and Disarmament Agency.

Journals and Periodicals

Arms Control Today; The Arms Control Reporter; Contemporary Security Policy; Daedalus; International Security; The Nonproliferation Review; Orbis; Security Dialogue; Security Studies; Survival; The Washington Quarterly.

Internet Sites

Arms Control and Disarmament Agency (ACDA), http://www.acda.gov

Acronym Institute, http://www.gn.apc.org/acronym

Center for Nonproliferation Studies (CNS) at the Monterey Institute of International Studies, http://cns.miis.edu

Defense and Arms Control Resources (DFAX), http://csf.colorado.edu/dfax/index.htm

British American Security Information Council (BASIC), http://www.basicint.org

Federation of American Scientists (FAS), http://www.fas.org

Henry L. Stimson Center, http://www.stimson.org

Program in Arms Control, Disarmament and International Security (ACDIS) at the University of Illinois, http://acdisweb.acdis.uiuc.edu

Stockholm Institute for Peace Research (SIPRI), http://www.sipri.se

United Nations Peace and Security Homepage, http://www.un.org/peace

Arms Control and Disarmament Treaties

Mitsuru Kurosawa
Osaka University

GLOSSARY

Ballistic Missile A self-propelled weapon delivery vehicle that follows a parabolic trajectory when thrust is terminated.

Biological Weapon A device containing living organisms, or infective material derived from them, intended for use in warfare to cause disease or death in humans, animals or plants.

Chemical Weapon A device containing one or more chemical substances, whether gaseous, liquid, or solid, intended for use in warfare to cause direct toxic effects on humans, animals or plants.

Conventional Weapon A device intended to cause destruction in warfare, but lacking mass destruction effects.

Cruise Missile A guided weapon delivery vehicle that sustains flight at subsonic or supersonic speeds through aerodynamic lift.

Fissile Material Material composed of atoms capable of being split when irradiated by either fast or slow neutrons. Uranium-235 and plutonium-239 are the most common fissile materials.

Intercontinental Ballistic Missile (ICBM) Ground-launched ballistic missile with a range greater than 5500 kilometers.

Nuclear Weapon A device that is capable of releasing nuclear energy in an uncontrolled manner, causing damage by blast, heat, and radioactivity.

Short-Range Nuclear Forces Nuclear weapons, including artillery, mines, missiles, and so on, with ranges of up to 500 kilometers.

Strategic Nuclear Weapons ICBMs and SLBMs, usually with a range of more than 5500 kilometers, as well as bombs and missiles carried on aircraft of intercontinental range.

Submarine-Launched Ballistic Missile (SLBM) A ballistic missile launched from a submarine, usually with a range in excess of 5500 kilometers.

Theater Nuclear Forces Nuclear weapons with a range of 500 to 5500 kilometers. Nuclear missiles with a range of 1000 to 5500 kilometers are called intermediate range and missiles with a range of 500 to 1000 kilometers are called shorter range or medium range nuclear forces.

Warhead That part of a weapon that contains the explosives or other material intended to inflict damage.

Weapon of Mass Destruction Nuclear weapons, chemical weapons, and biological weapons, and any other weapons which may produce comparable effects.

ARMS CONTROL AND DISARMAMENT TREATIES are international agreements in legally binding form, which provide for the limitation, reduction, or elimination of certain types of weapons, or the prohibition of their development, manufacture, production, testing, possession, stockpile, transfer, receipt, or deployment. Coverage includes nuclear, chemical, biological, and conventional weapons, as well as their delivery systems. The purpose of this article is to provide a concise description of the international legal environment that has evolved regarding arms control and disarmament, with a particular focus on nuclear weapons and other weapons of mass destruction. Table I shows a chronological chart of bilateral treaties between the United States and the Soviet Union (Russia), and multilateral treaties.

I. ARMS CONTROL NEGOTIATIONS: A HISTORICAL OVERVIEW

Disarmament has been advocated from early modern years, but it was not until the end of the last century when disarmament was discussed among states. The

TABLE I

Chronological Chart of the Treaties

Bilateral Treaties Between the U.S. and the Soviet Union (Russia)

Treaty	Signature	Ratification
ABM Treaty	May 26, 1972	October 3, 1972
SALT I Interim Agreement	May 26, 1972	October 3, 1972
Protocol to ABM Treaty	July 3, 1974	May 24, 1976
Threshold Test Ban Treaty	July 3, 1974	December 10, 1990
Peaceful Nuclear Explosion Treaty	May 28, 1976	December 10, 1990
SALT II Treaty	June 18, 1979	
INF Treaty	December 8, 1987	June 1, 1988
Chemical Weapon Agreement	June 1, 1990	
START I Treaty	July 31, 1991	December 5, 1994
Protocol to START I Treaty	May 23, 1992	December 5, 1994
START II Treaty	January 3, 1993	

Multilateral Treaties

Treaty	Signature	Ratification	Parties
Antarctic Treaty	December 1, 1959	June 23, 1961	43
Partial Test Ban Treaty	August 5, 1963	October 10, 1963	124
Outer Space Treaty	January 27, 1967	October 10, 1967	94
Tlatelolco Treaty	February 14, 1967	April 22, 1968	32
Non-Proliferation Treaty	July 1, 1968	March 5, 1970	186
Seabed Treaty	February 11, 1971	May 18, 1972	93
Biological Weapon Treaty	April 10, 1972	March 26, 1975	140
Rarotonga Treaty	August 6, 1985	December 11, 1986	12
CFE Treaty	November 19, 1990	November 9, 1992	30
Chemical Weapon Convention	January 13, 1993	April 29, 1997	91
Southeast Asia NWFZ Treaty	December 15, 1995	March 27, 1997	8
Pelindaba Treaty	April 11, 1996		
Comprehensive Nuclear Test Ban Treaty	September 24, 1996		

As of July 31, 1997.

first Hague Peace Conference of 1899 included disarmament issues among its agenda. The League of Nations emphasized the importance of disarmament for international peace as shown in Article 8 of the Covenant of the League of Nations, its constitutional document, but it did not succeed in producing disarmament treaties. Among major powers, the limitation of naval armament was agreed in the 1922 Washington Treaty between the United States, the United Kingdom, Japan, Italy, and France, and the 1930 London Treaty between the United States, the United Kingdom, and Japan. Disarmament negotiations after the Second World War began within the United Nations and then gradually moved to Geneva.

A. The United Nations and Disarmament

The Charter of the United Nations entered into force on October 24, 1945, shortly after the end of World War II. As the founding treaty of the United Nations, a worldwide organization of states, it did not emphasize disarmament as the Covenant did, because collective security was thought to need armaments, and nuclear weapons did not exist when the Charter was adopted. However, the first resolution of its General Assembly in 1946 established the Atomic Energy Commission to deal with nuclear weapons, although the difference of positions of the United States, which argued for international control first, and the Soviet Union, which argued for elimination of nuclear weapons first, produced no agreement. The United Nations Security Council established a Commission for Conventional Weapons in 1947. In 1952, this commission was merged with the Atomic Energy Commission to form the Disarmament Commission, which was composed of the members of the Security Council and Canada, and negotiated comprehensive measures of disarmament. In the late 1950s, the Soviet Union became dissatisfied with the membership and the Commission stopped its work. After active negotiations in the early days of the United Nations, the Commission has played a role in deliberation rather than negotiation on disarmament, following its revival in 1978. The UN General Assembly has held three special sessions devoted to disarmament in 1978, 1982, and 1988. The UN General Assembly also adopts many resolutions on disarmament each year.

B. The Geneva Forum

Outside of the United Nations, the Ten-Nation Disarmament Committee consisting of five Western states and five Eastern states began its work in 1960 in Geneva, and the Committee evolved into the Eighteen-Nation Committee on Disarmament by adding eight nonaligned nations as members in 1962. The Committee again changed its name into the Conference of the Committee on Disarmament with 26 members in 1969 and 31 members in 1975. This Geneva Forum was a main negotiating mechanism in 1960s and 1970s, producing the Nuclear Non-Proliferation Treaty, the Seabed Treaty, and the Biological Weapons Convention. At the first special session of the UN General Assembly devoted to disarmament, the Conference was again enlarged to 40, including France and China, and renamed the Committee on Disarmament. It changed its name in 1984 to the Conference on Disarmament and enlarged its members to 61 in 1996. This is the only multilateral negotiating body and it negotiated chemical weapons and a nuclear test ban into treaties.

C. Bilateral Negotiations

Bilateral negotiations between the United States and the Soviet Union began at the end of the 1960s when a rough parity in strategic nuclear power was established between the two superpowers. Negotiations in the 1970s and 1980s aimed at ensuring strategic stability by limiting the nuclear delivery systems of each side, and in particular, their strategic defensive capability. Since the end of the Cold War, however, the main focus has shifted to the reduction of nuclear warheads between the United States and the Russian Federation and both sides have agreed to substantial cuts.

D. Regional Negotiations

Disarmament measures can be taken region by region depending on the particular circumstances of the area. In Europe, negotiations on conventional weapons have been conducted since the 1970s and parties succeeded in making a treaty after the end of the Cold War. The creation of a nuclear-weapon-free zone is also a regional measure of this nature and negotiations have taken place in various areas including Latin America, the South Pacific, Africa, Southeast Asia, and elsewhere.

II. BILATERAL NUCLEAR ARMS CONTROL AND DISARMAMENT

Four years after the first U.S. nuclear test in 1945, the Soviet Union joined the nuclear club. With the serious confrontation of the Cold War, the two countries continued the nuclear arms race quantitatively and qualitatively until the end of the 1980s when they entered the post-Cold War era. The maximum number of nuclear weapons possessed by the United States and the Soviet Union were 32,500 and 45,000, respectively, and the maximum number of their strategic nuclear weapons were 13,000 and 11,000. Table II represents the number of nuclear weapons held by the five nuclear weapon states. The arms control negotiations that began at the end of the 1960s purported not to reduce nuclear weapons but to stabilize their strategic relations, especially in crisis, by limiting their delivery systems. During the 1970s and early 1980s, the two superpowers were competing militarily, politically, and ideologically, although they agreed on some arms control measures. In the late 1980s and early 1990s the world experienced radical change with the dissolution of the Soviet Union in 1991 and the dismantlement of the Warsaw Treaty Organization in 1993, resulting in the disappearance of the confrontation between East and West. Nuclear reduction finally became a reality in the nuclear disarmament negotiations between the United States and the Soviet Union, now the Russian Federation. As a result of these negotiations, it is expected that the number of strategic nuclear warheads is going to be reduced by two-thirds.

A. SALT I

SALT (Strategic Arms Limitation Talks), whose initiation was agreed by the United States and the Soviet Union in July 1968, was the first attempt to limit the strategic nuclear forces of the two superpowers. The main reason for the initiation of this series of negotiations was the emergence of a rough parity of strategic forces and détente between the two nations. In addition, the conclusion of the NPT (Nuclear Non-Proliferation Treaty) requested the United States and Soviet Union to negotiate nuclear disarmament, and the development of satellites made it possible to verify compliance. On May 26, 1972, they signed the ABM Treaty (Treaty Between the United States of America and the Union of Soviet Socialist Republics on the Limitation of Anti-Ballistic Missile Systems) and the SALT I Interim Agreement (Interim Agreement Between the United States of America and the Union of Soviet Socialist Republics on Certain Measures With Respect to the Limitation of Strategic Offensive Arms). Under the ABM Treaty, which is of unlimited duration, each party undertakes not to deploy ABM systems for the defense of the territory of its country and to limit their deployment to two areas only: one, for the protection of its national capital, and the other, for ICBM bases. The SALT I Interim Agreement, which was valid for only 5 years,

TABLE II

Global Nuclear Stockpiles, 1945–1995
Quantities for the Five Declared Nuclear Powers, Year by Year

End year	USA	SU/R	UK	FR	CH	Total
1945	2	—	—	—	—	2
1946	9	—	—	—	—	9
1947	13	—	—	—	—	13
1948	50	—	—	—	—	50
1949	170	1	—	—	—	171
1950	299	2	—	—	—	301
1951	438	5	—	—	—	443
1952	841	10	—	—	—	851
1953	1,169	120	1	—	—	1,290
1954	1,703	150	5	—	—	1,858
1955	2,422	200	10	—	—	2,632
1956	3,692	400	15	—	—	4,107
1957	5,543	650	20	—	—	6,213
1958	7,345	900	22	—	—	8,267
1959	12,298	1,050	25	—	—	13,373
1960	18,638	1,700	30	—	—	20,368
1961	22,229	2,450	50	—	—	24,729
1962	26,317	3,100	205	—	—	29,622
1963	29,300	4,000	280	—	—	33,580
1964	30,817	5,100	310	4	1	36,232
1965	32,400	6,300	310	32	5	39,047
1966	32,472	7,550	270	36	20	40,348
1967	32,516	8,850	270	36	25	41,697
1968	30,858	10,000	280	36	35	41,209
1969	28,497	11,000	308	36	50	39,891
1970	26,780	12,700	280	36	75	39,871
1971	26,506	14,500	220	45	100	41,371
1972	27,000	16,600	220	70	130	44,020
1973	28,250	18,800	275	116	150	47,591
1974	28,950	21,100	325	145	170	50,690
1975	27,950	23,500	350	188	185	52,173
1976	26,552	25,800	350	212	190	53,104
1977	25,775	28,400	350	228	200	54,953
1978	24,677	31,400	350	235	220	56,882
1979	24,300	34,000	350	235	235	59,120
1980	24,472	36,300	350	250	280	61,652
1981	23,882	38,700	350	275	330	63,537
1982	23,684	40,800	335	275	360	65,454
1983	23,513	42,600	320	280	380	67,093
1984	24,062	43,300	270	280	415	68,327
1985	24,209	44,000	300	360	425	69,294
1986	24,218	45,000	300	355	425	70,298
1987	24,187	44,000	300	420	415	69,322
1988	24,329	42,500	300	415	430	67,974
1989	24,015	40,000	300	415	435	65,165
1990	23,206	37,500	300	505	435	61,946
1991	21,611	35,000	300	540	435	57,886
1992	19,755	32,500	200	540	435	53,430
1993	18,199	29,000	200	525	435	48,359
1994	16,830	26,500	250	485	435	44,500
1995	15,430	24,000	300	485	425	40,640

USA: United States of America; SU/R: Soviet Union/Russia; UK: United Kingdom; FR: France; CH: China.
Source: Natural Resources Defense Council.

purported to freeze at the existing levels the number of ICBMs, SLBMs and modern ballistic missile submarines.

B. SALT II

The second phase of SALT began in November 1972, and the parties agreed to the Protocol to the ABM Treaty, which reduced the ABM deployment areas from two to one, to either the national capital or ICBM bases, at the selection of each party. Regarding offensive weapons, after a long negotiation, the SALT II Treaty (Treaty Between the United States of America and the Union of Soviet Socialist Republics on the Limitation of Strategic Offensive Arms) was signed on June 18, 1979. The Treaty limited the aggregate number of ICBM launchers, SLBM launchers, and heavy bombers to 2400, which was about the existing level, and set subceilings for ICBMs with MIRVs (multiple independently targettable reentry vehicles) at 820, for MIRVed ICBMs and MIRVed SLBMs at 1200, and for MIRVed ICBMs and SLBMs and heavy bombers with cruise missiles at 1320. These subceilings were much higher than the existing levels, permitting certain improvement of strategic force capability. The SALT II Treaty has not taken effect because the United States could not ratify it when it met with strong opposition due to perceived disadvantages and the occurrence of the Soviet invasion of Afghanistan. Despite this, the contents of the Treaty were abided by until the mid-1980s. The SDI (Strategic Defense Initiative), which was launched by President Ronald Reagan in 1983 to make nuclear weapons obsolete with a defense that used exotic technologies, elicited strong arguments in connection with its incompatibility with the terms of the ABM Treaty because the Treaty specifically prohibits the development of a space-based system.

C. INF

The INF Treaty (Treaty Between the United States of America and the Union of Soviet Socialist Republics on the Elimination of their Intermediate-Range and Shorter-Range Missiles) was signed on December 8, 1987, and became effective on June 1, 1988. Negotiations began in 1981, but were interrupted in 1983 until the emergence of Mikhail Gorbachev and the accompanying political change in the Soviet Union, which made it possible to reach an agreement. The Treaty provided for the total elimination, within 3 years, of intermediate-range missiles such as the SS-20 and Pershing II, and shorter range missiles. This is the first treaty that asked for the total elimination of a category of weapons and it had a strict verification system, including six types of on-site inspections. This total elimination was successfully accomplished within the 3-year period; however, it covered only land-based missiles and it ordered the elimination of just the missile delivery vehicles themselves, not the nuclear warheads. Despite these limitations, the complete implementation of the Treaty was one of the catalysts for the end of the Cold War.

D. START I

START (Strategic Arms Reduction Talks), which began in 1982, but were interrupted between 1983 and 1985, produced the START I Treaty (Treaty Between the United States of America and the Union of Soviet Socialist Republics on the Reduction and Limitation of Strategic Offensive Arms) on July 31, 1991. Agreement had been reached in 1986 on the fundamental content, that strategic nuclear warheads would be reduced by half to 6000 each, but it took 4 years to resolve the numerous remaining issues, including the SDI supported by the Reagan administration. The START I Treaty provides for the reduction of the aggregate number of delivery systems of ICBMs, SLBMs, and bombers to 1600, and for the aggregate number of warheads to 6000. It limits the aggregate number of warheads of ICBMs and SLBMs to 4900, and reduces the number of heavy ICBMs by half. The verification system includes 12 kinds of on-site inspections. Due to the dissolution of the Soviet Union at the end of 1991, before the Treaty took effect, as Ukraine, Beralus, and Khazakhstan acquired independence, the nuclear weapons deployed on their territories had to be taken into account. In May 1992, the five states signed the Protocol to the START I Treaty to apply the Treaty to Ukraine, Beralus, and Khazakhstan, and these three states agreed to join the NPT (Treaty on the Non-Proliferation of Nuclear Weapons) as non-nuclear-weapon states. The START I Treaty took effect on December 5, 1994.

E. START II

After the signature of the START I Treaty, in September and October 1992, the United States and Russia announced their intention to unilaterally withdraw most tactical nuclear weapons deployed in foreign countries and at sea. Regarding strategic arms, on January 3, 1993, they reached agreement on the START II Treaty (Treaty Between the United States of America and the Russian Federation on Further Reduction and Limitation of Strategic Offensive Arms) for further reductions. Under the START II Treaty, they each agreed to reduce the

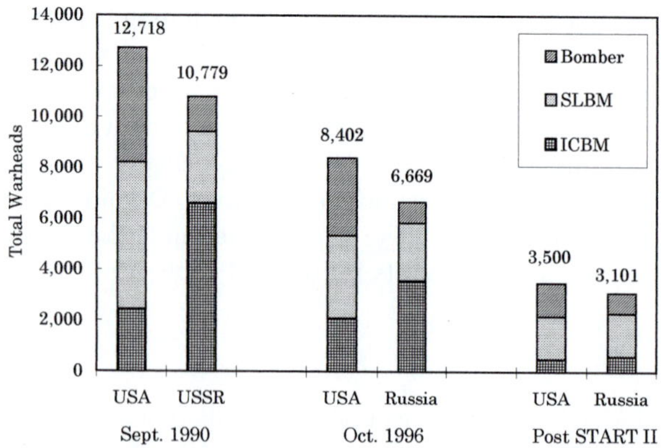

FIGURE 1 U.S. and Soviet/Russian Strategic Nuclear Forces: Past, Present and Projected

Source: Arms Control Association.

aggregate number of the warheads attributed to ICBMs, SLBMs, and bombers to between 3000 and 3500 by January 1, 2003. In addition, they agreed to eliminate MIRVed ICBMs and heavy ICBMs, and to reduce the number of warheads on SLBMs to between 1700 and 1750. This amounts to the reduction of the existing level of nuclear weapons by two-thirds. Figure 1 shows the aggregate number and structure of the U.S. and Soviet/Russia strategic nuclear forces.

III. NONPROLIFERATION OF NUCLEAR WEAPONS

Following the United States and the Soviet Union, the United Kingdom conducted its first nuclear test in 1952, becoming the third nuclear-weapon state (NWS). In the late 1950s, the increase of states possessing nuclear weapons was a concern of many governments because the knowledge of the means of using atomic energy had expanded and the United States had begun deploying nuclear weapons in West Germany. In 1958, Ireland submitted the concern of nuclear proliferation to the UN General Assembly, stating that the increase of states possessing nuclear weapons would increase the possibility of the use of nuclear weapons. Table III shows the current nuclear status of states.

A. The Development of the NPT

France and China conducted their first nuclear tests in 1960 and 1964, respectively, and the United States and the Soviet Union realized that they shared a common interest in preventing other states from possessing nuclear weapons. The NPT (Treaty on the Non-Proliferation of Nuclear Weapons) was signed on July 1, 1968, after 3 years of negotiation at the Geneva Eighteen-Nation Committee on Disarmament. The Treaty, as a basic structure, distinguishes NWSs, which include the United States, Russia, the United Kingdom, France, and China, from non-nuclear-weapon states (NNWSs) which include all other nations. Under the Treaty, the NWSs undertake not to transfer nuclear weapons, and the NNWSs undertake not to receive, manufacture or otherwise acquire nuclear weapons. In addition, the NNWSs have to accept safeguards by the IAEA (International Atomic Energy Agency) to verify that nuclear energy is not diverted from peaceful uses to nuclear weapons. The concept of nuclear nonproliferation deals with only horizontal proliferation, that is, the increase of new NWSs, not with vertical proliferation, that is, the increase of nuclear weapon capability of the existing NWSs. Many NNWSs criticized this concept of nonproliferation as discriminatory, and asked the NWSs to proceed to nuclear disarmament. In order to create a balance of the obligations between the NWSs and the NNWSs, the right to use nuclear energy for peaceful purposes is reconfirmed, and the obligation to pursue negotiations on nuclear disarmament is provided for in the Treaty. More than 180 states have since become parties to the NPT, and the concept of nonproliferation is accepted as a necessary first step toward nuclear disarmament. States not party to the NPT, however, include India, Israel, and Pakistan.

B. New Developments Since the End of the Cold War

With the end of the Cold War, the bipolar system of the world dissolved and the two superpowers began withdrawing their nuclear weapons and military personnel from abroad. China and France acceded to the

TABLE III

Nuclear Status of States
(Current as of April, 1997)

Nuclear Status	States
Declared nuclear-weapon states	China, France, Russia, United Kingdom, United States of America.
Undeclared nuclear-weapon states (Threshold states)	India, Israel, Pakistan.
Non-nuclear-weapon states that violated NPT provisions	Iraq, North Korea.

NPT, and South Africa, which had once possessed six nuclear weapons, became a party to the NPT. Argentina and Brazil, once thought to be competing for nuclear weapon development, accepted full-scope IAEA safeguards. Ukraine, Belarus, and Khazakhstan also became parties to the NPT as NNWSs. On the other hand, after the Gulf War in 1991 it was found that Iraq, which is a party to the NPT, had been conducting nuclear weapon development clandestinely. North Korea, which is also a party to the Treaty, aroused suspicions about its nuclear activities by refusing the request of a special inspection by the IAEA in 1993. In addition, with the dismantlement of the Soviet Union, the control over nuclear weapons and fissile material has become a worry from the viewpoint of proliferation, with fears of possible smuggling or theft by terrorist groups. The initial response to these concerns has been to tighten export control over nuclear-related materials, and to strengthen the IAEA safeguards to cover undeclared nuclear activities.

C. The 1995 NPT Review and Extension Conference

Under the terms of the NPT, a conference to review the operation of the Treaty is required to be held every 5 years, and a special conference was required to be held 25 years after the Treaty's entry into force to decide on a possible extension of the Treaty and the terms for any extension. These two conferences were held simultaneously in April and May 1995. As a result of this conference, the parties decided to extend the Treaty indefinitely and agreed on two other decisions. "Principles and Objectives on Nuclear Non-Proliferation and Disarmament" listed substantive measures to be taken toward the control and reduction of nuclear weapons, and "Strengthening the Review Process for the Treaty" gave more frequent opportunities for review. The decision on "Principles and Objectives on Nuclear Non-Proliferation and Disarmament" includes recommended concrete measures for universality, nonproliferation, nuclear disarmament, nuclear-weapon-free zones, security assurances, safeguards, and peaceful uses of nuclear energy. As nuclear disarmament measures, it listed: (i) the completion of the negotiation on a Comprehensive Nuclear-Test-Ban Treaty no later than 1996; (ii) the immediate commencement and early conclusion of negotiation of a convention banning the production of fissile material for nuclear weapons; and (iii) the determined pursuit by the NWSs of systematic and progressive efforts to reduce nuclear weapons globally, with the ultimate goal of eliminating those weapons.

IV. NUCLEAR TEST BAN

Nuclear tests are indispensable for nuclear development, especially for development of new types of nuclear warheads. During the Cold War era, the NWSs conducted many nuclear tests for qualitatively improving their nuclear systems while continuing the nuclear arms race. Nuclear tests are said to be necessary to ensure the reliability and safety of nuclear weapons. The United States conducted more than 1000 tests and the Soviet Union more than 700. All together, the five NWSs have conducted more than 2000 tests. In early years, tests were usually conducted in the atmosphere or under water, but due to concerns over the environment, and as a result of technical progress, the NWSs were able to shift tests underground. The U.S. thermonuclear test at Bikini Atoll in 1954 caused a Japanese death and motivated world opinion to campaign for the banning of nuclear tests. Since then, a nuclear test ban has been given top priority in the disarmament campaign, because it has been a symbol of nuclear development. It was not until the end of the Cold War that international society succeeded in adopting a comprehensive test ban treaty. Table IV represents the number of nuclear tests conducted by the five Nuclear Weapon States each year from 1945.

A. The Partial Test Ban Treaty

The Partial Test Ban Treaty (Treaty Banning Nuclear Tests in the Atmosphere, in Outer Space and Under Water) was signed on August 5, 1963, and became effective on October 10, 1963, originally among the United States, the United Kingdom, and the Soviet Union, and later acceded to by many NNWSs. After many tests had been conducted in the atmosphere, it was agreed to shift tests underground, mainly for environmental reasons. Another reason for the Treaty is that tests in these circumstances could be detected without on-site inspections, which was one of the stumbling blocks during the negotiation. The Treaty did not prevent nuclear weapon development, because the United States, the United Kingdom, and the Soviet Union could continue their nuclear weapon development through underground tests. France and China did not join the Treaty because their technology had not developed enough to restrict the tests only to underground. The Treaty also helped to prevent proliferation.

B. The Threshold Test Ban Treaty

In the process toward limiting underground tests, the United States and the Soviet Union signed the Thresh-

TABLE IV

Nuclear Testing Since 1945

Number of Tests for the Five Declared Nuclear Powers, Year by Year

End year	USA	SU/R	UK	FR	CH	Total
1945	1	—	—	—	—	1
1946	2	—	—	—	—	2
1947	0	—	—	—	—	0
1948	3	—	—	—	—	3
1949	0	1	—	—	—	1
1950	0	0	—	—	—	0
1951	16	2	—	—	—	18
1952	10	0	1	—	—	11
1953	11	5	2	—	—	18
1954	6	10	0	—	—	16
1955	18	6	0	—	—	24
1956	18	9	6	—	—	33
1957	32	16	7	—	—	55
1958	77	34	5	—	—	116
1959	0	0	0	—	—	0
1960	0	0	0	3	—	3
1961	10	59	0	2	—	71
1962	96	79	2	1	—	178
1963	47	0	0	3	—	50
1964	45	9	2	3	1	60
1965	38	14	1	4	1	58
1966	48	18	0	7	3	76
1967	42	17	0	3	2	64
1968	56	17	0	5	1	79
1969	46	19	0	0	2	67
1970	39	16	0	8	1	64
1971	24	23	0	5	1	53
1972	27	24	0	4	2	57
1973	24	17	0	6	1	48
1974	22	21	1	9	1	54
1975	22	19	0	2	1	44
1976	20	21	1	5	4	51
1977	20	24	0	9	1	54
1978	19	31	2	11	3	66
1979	15	31	1	10	1	58
1980	14	24	3	12	1	54
1981	16	21	1	12	0	50
1982	18	19	1	10	1	49
1983	18	25	1	9	2	55
1984	18	27	2	8	2	57
1985	17	10	1	8	0	36
1986	14	0	1	8	0	23
1987	14	23	1	8	1	47
1988	15	16	0	8	1	40
1989	11	7	1	9	0	28
1990	0	1	1	6	2	18
1991	7	0	1	6	0	14
1992	6	0	0	0	2	8
1993	0	0	0	0	1	1
1994	0	0	0	0	2	2
1995	0	0	0	5	2	7
1996	0	0	0	1	2	3
TOTAL	1,030	715	45	210	45	2,046*

USA: United States of America; SU/R: Soviety Union/Russia; UK: United Kingdom; FR: France; CH: China.

* The total number of tests includes one test by India, which exploded a nuclear device in 1974.

Sources: Arms Control Association, Department of Energy, National Resources Defense Council.

old Test Ban Treaty (Treaty Between the United States of America and the Union of Soviet Socialist Republics on the Limitation of Underground Nuclear Weapon Tests) on July 3, 1974, and the Peaceful Nuclear Explosion Treaty (Treaty Between the United States of America and the Union of the Soviet Socialist Republics on Underground Nuclear Explosions for Peaceful Purposes) on May 28, 1976. Under these Treaties, the parties have undertaken the prohibition of military and peaceful underground nuclear tests having a yield exceeding 150 kilotons. Following a long delay in implementation, after 3 years of further negotiations and agreement on new verification protocols to these Treaties, they took effect on December 11, 1990.

C. The Comprehensive Nuclear Test Ban Treaty

With the end of the Cold War, the United States and Russia had declared a moratorium on testing together with France and the United Kingdom. Negotiations for a comprehensive nuclear test ban began at the Geneva Conference on Disarmament in January 1994, and the parties at 1995 NPT Conference asked for the completion of the negotiation on a treaty to ban all nuclear tests no later than 1996. The Geneva Conference concluded its work in August 1996, but India strongly opposed the draft treaty, primarily because it failed to include provisions for the eventual nuclear disarmament of the NWSs and because it desired to keep open its nuclear option. Due to the necessity of achieving consensus for the Conference to adopt the Treaty, India's refusal to support the Treaty effectively prevented the Treaty's adoption at the Geneva Conference. It was finally adopted at the United Nations General Assembly on September 10 and opened for signature on September 24, 1996. The CTBT (Comprehensive Nuclear Test-Ban Treaty), prohibits any nuclear weapon test explosion or any other nuclear explosion, including tests underground. The Treaty establishes the Comprehensive Nuclear Test Ban Treaty Organization in Vienna to implement its provisions and a verification regime to be established under the Treaty includes an international monitoring system and on-site inspections. The international monitoring system comprised facilities for seismological monitoring, radionuclid monitoring, hydroacoustic monitoring, and infrasound monitoring. Due to strong arguments by China, Pakistan, Russia, and the United Kingdom the condition for entry into force of the Treaty is very stringent, requiring all of the 44 designated states, including India, which was opposed to the adoption of the Treaty at the Conference on Disarmament, to ratify it. The fact that the five NWSs have already stopped testing and signed the Treaty is a great success for nuclear disarmament, but it will take long for the Treaty to enter into force.

V. NUCLEAR-WEAPON-FREE ZONES

A Nuclear-Weapon-Free Zone (NWFZ) is defined as an area where a total absence of nuclear weapons is maintained by an agreement among two or more states. It is not only supplementary to nonproliferation, but also ensures the nondeployment of nuclear weapons, and asks NWSs not to use nuclear weapons against the zonal states. The first proposal on a NWFZ came from a Polish Foreign Minister regarding Central Europe in the late 1950s. A NWFZ was proposed in other areas including Nordic states, Balkan states, Latin America, Africa, South Asia, the Middle East, the South Pacific, Southeast Asia, and Eastern Europe. In particular, proposals for NWFZs in the Middle East and South Asia, where threshold countries such as Israel, India, and Pakistan are included, have been on the agenda at the UN General Assembly since the middle 1970s, but it will be very hard to accomplish these goals without progress in the peace processes of each area. Only the four territories described below have succeeded in establishing NWFZs.

A. The Tlatelolco Treaty

The Tlatelolco Treaty (Treaty for the Prohibition of Nuclear Weapons in Latin America and the Caribbean), was signed on February 14, 1967, and became effective on April 22, 1968. This was the first treaty establishing a NWFZ, achieved in large part due to the effect of the Cuban missile crisis of 1962. The Treaty prohibits any activity connected with nuclear weapons, including their deployment. In order to ensure compliance of the Treaty, OPANAL (Agency for the Prohibition of Nuclear Weapons in Latin America) was established. After the end of the Cold War, the Treaty became almost complete as Argentina, Brazil, and Chile acceded to the Treaty. The Additional Protocol I to the Treaty obligates those states that have territories within the Zone, such as the British Virgin Islands, to apply this statute of denuclearization, and four eligible states ratified it by 1992. The Additional Protocol II, under which NWSs agree not to use or threaten to use nuclear weapons against the Contracting Parties of the Treaty, was ratified by all five NWSs by 1979. This undertaking of negative security assurances is one of the eminent characteristics of a NWFZ, distinguished from the concept of nonproliferation.

B. The Rarotonga Treaty

The Rarotonga Treaty (South Pacific Nuclear Free Zone Treaty) established the second NWFZ. It was adopted by the South Pacific Forum and signed on August 6, 1985, and entered into force on December 11, 1986. The main motivation of the states in the region for establishing a NWFZ was to make France stop testing. France had been conducting nuclear tests in this region since 1966, and Australia and New Zealand had asked the International Court of Justice to proclaim the illegality of the nuclear tests in 1983. Shortly thereafter, France shifted to underground testing. The Treaty prohibits any nuclear-weapon related activities and also includes the dumping of nuclear waste. Under Protocol 1, France, the United Kingdom, and the United States apply the obligations of the NWFZ to their territories situated within the Zone. Under Protocol 2, the NWSs agree not to use or threaten to use nuclear weapons against the treaty parties. Under Protocol 3, the NWSs agree not to test. France had conducted nuclear tests until January 1996, several months before the CTBT was adopted. In March 1996, France, the United Kingdom, and the United States signed the three Protocols. Russia (in 1988) and China (in 1989) had already ratified Protocols 2 and 3.

C. The Pelindaba Treaty

The Pelindaba Treaty (Treaty on an African Nuclear-Weapon-Free Zone), which was adopted by the OAU (Organization of African Unity) in June 1995 and signed in Cairo on April 11, 1996, was the outcome of more than 30 years of effort by African states. In 1960, France conducted its first nuclear test in the Sahara desert in Africa, and the OAU adopted the Declaration on the Denuclearization of Africa in 1964. After South Africa acceded to the NPT as a non-nuclear-weapon state in 1991, and announced that it had once had six nuclear bombs and destroyed them, the Group of Experts designated by the United Nations and the OAU began drafting a treaty. The Treaty prohibits any activity connected with nuclear weapons, and, in addition, provides for the declaration, dismantlement, destruction, or conversion of nuclear explosive devices. It established the African Commission on Nuclear Energy to ensure compliance with the undertakings of the Treaty. Like the Rarotonga Treaty, the Pelindaba Treaty has three Protocols, on extraterritorial states, on negative security assurances, and on nuclear testing. All five NWSs have already signed these Protocols.

D. The Southeast Asia NWFZ Treaty

The Treaty on the Southeast Asia Nuclear Weapon-Free Zone was signed by 10 Southeast Asian Nations at the summit meeting of the ASEAN (Association of Southeast Asian Nations) on December 15, 1995. In November 1971, the Declaration on the Zone of Peace, Freedom and Neutrality (ZOPFAN) was signed, and in July 1993, the Program of Action on ZOPFAN was adopted. The establishment of the NWFZ is an essential component of the ZOPFAN. With the end of the Cold War, nuclear weapons deployed by the United States and the Soviet Union were withdrawn. The Treaty prohibits any activity relating to nuclear weapons and establishes the Commission for the Southeast Asia NWFZ to oversee the implementation of the Treaty and ensure compliance with its provisions. In a major difference from other NWFZs, the Treaty is applied not only to the territories but also to the continental shelves and exclusive economic zones of the states party to the Treaty, which is opposed by the United States, China, and other NWSs.

VI. CHEMICAL WEAPONS

The Chemical Weapons Convention (Convention on the Prohibition of the Development, Production, Stockpiling and Use of Chemical Weapons and on Their Destruction) was negotiated at and adopted by the Geneva Conference on Disarmament in 1992, signed in Paris on January 13, 1993, and entered into force on April 29, 1997. Chemical weapons had been used during the First World War, and the Geneva Gas Protocol (Protocol for the Prohibition of the Use in War of Asphyxiating, Poisonous or Other Gases, and Bacteriological Methods of Warfare) was signed in June 1925. It prohibited only their use. Chemical weapons have been on the agenda for disarmament negotiations since the 1960s but real negotiations did not begin until the 1990s; chemical weapons were used during Iran-Iraq War in the 1980s. On June 1, 1990, the United States and the Soviet Union signed the bilateral Chemical Weapons Agreement (Agreement Between the United States of America and the Union of Soviet Socialist Republics on Destruction and Non-Production of Chemical Weapons and on Measures to Facilitate the Multilateral Convention on Banning Chemical Weapons), under which they agreed to start the destruction of their chemical weapons. It was thought to be a catalyst for a multilateral convention. The multilateral Chemical Weapons Convention not only prohibits the development, production, stockpiling, and use of chemical weapons, but also provides for their complete destruction within 10 years. This Convention thus provides for the real and complete disarmament of chemical weapons. In order to achieve the object and purpose of the Convention and to ensure the implementation of its provisions, the Convention established the Organization for the Prohibition of Chemical Weapons at the Hague. Chemical weapons and their related facilities are subject to systematic verification through on-site inspection and monitoring. In addition, each signatory has the right to request an on-site challenge inspection to clarify possible non-compliance of other states. However, there are nonsignatories, including North Korea and most Arab states, and signatories that have not ratified, including Israel and Russia. Many of these states are suspected of having chemical weapons.

VII. BIOLOGICAL WEAPONS

The Biological Weapons Convention (Convention on the Prohibition of the Development, Production and Stockpiling of Bacteriological (Biological) and Toxin Weapons and on Their Destruction) was signed on April 10, 1972 and became effective on March 26, 1975. The use of biological weapons was prohibited by the Geneva Gas Protocol of 1925. In 1969, negotiations on chemical and biological weapons were separated and negotiation on biological weapons was given priority. Biological weapons were thought to be militarily inefficient and ineffective because of their uncontrollability and unpredictability, and easier to negotiate through a convention. Under the Convention, each signatory agrees not only to never develop, produce, nor stockpile microbial or other biological organs or toxins, but also to destroy them within 9 months. The Convention currently has no international verification system because of the perceived military ineffectiveness of biological weapons; however, with the development of biotechnology, their possible military usefulness has necessitated an international system for stricter verification, which is now under consideration by the Parties.

VIII. CONVENTIONAL WEAPONS

Although conventional weapons were included in the negotiations of comprehensive disarmament in the 1950s, the priority has been given to nuclear weapons first, and then to other weapons of mass destruction, that is, chemical and biological weapons. Until the end of the Cold War, there was no agreement on conventional weapons. In Europe, under the CSCE (Conference on Security and Co-operation in Europe), the reduction of conventional weapons was agreed as described below. The UN General Assembly in 1991 established the UN Register of Conventional Arms, which asks the members to report, voluntarily and on an annual basis, their arms transfer in seven categories. This is thought to be a confidence-building measure because it increases transparency. Recently, the regulation and the prohibition of antipersonnel landmines is the focus of discussion.

The CFE Treaty (Treaty on Conventional Arms Forces in Europe) was signed in Paris on November 19, 1990, and took effect on November 9, 1992. The Treaty was the result of negotiation between the 16 member states of NATO (North Atlantic Treaty Organization) and the 6 member states of WTO (Warsaw Treaty Organization), held in Vienna beginning in March 1989 as a part of the CSCE process. During the Cold War era, conventional forces in Europe had been the subject of negotiations under MBFR (Mutual and Balanced Force Reduction) talks, but an agreement could not be reached. The CFE Treaty sets ceilings on five categories of weapons in the ATTU (Atlantic-to-the Urals) zone, resulting in the same level between the aggregate numbers of each weapon between NATO and the WTO. The main purposes of the Treaty are to eliminate the capacity for launching surprise attacks and for initiating large-scale offensive action, and to eliminate disparities between the two blocs. For the purpose of ensuring verification of compliance with the provisions of the Treaty, each signatory has the right to conduct inspections. The force reduction stipulated in the Treaty had almost been completed by 1996; however, the dissolution of the Soviet Union and new security situations in Europe made it necessary to amend some parts of the Treaty. As a follow-on, the CFE-1A Agreement (The Concluding Act of the Negotiation on Personnel Strength of Conventional Armed Forces in Europe) was signed in Helsinki on July 10, 1992, and became effective on July 17, 1992. The Agreement sets limits on the number of military personnel permitted in the ATTU zone.

IX. ARMS CONTROL IN INTERNATIONAL SPHERES

Antarctica, outer space, and the seabed are international spheres that are not under the sovereignty or control of any state, and as a result of technological developments, the potential exists for an arms race in these locations if there is no international regulation. Arms control has been necessary in these international spheres and the treaties detailed below have been created for that purpose. Regulation by the international community in international spheres is easier than in national territories because these regions are open to every nation and international public interest can be pursued.

A. The Antarctic Treaty

The Antarctic Treaty was signed by 12 original parties in Washington on December 1, 1959, as the first arms control treaty after the Second World War, and it became effective on June 23, 1961. Although some states had claimed sovereignty over areas of Antarctica, they agreed to use Antarctica for peaceful uses only under the Treaty, following the scientific cooperation under the International Geophysical Year of 1957–1958. Any measures of a military nature, such as the establishment of military bases and fortifications, the carrying out of military maneuvers, as well as the testing of any types of weapons are completely prohibited. The Treaty provides for the complete demilitarization of Antarctica. Any nuclear explosions there or the disposal of radioactive waste material is prohibited, even if it is for peaceful purposes. In order to ensure the observance of the Treaty's provisions, each observer designated by the signatory has complete freedom of access at any time to any or all areas of Antarctica, as Antarctica is recognized as an area that is open to every state, and all claims of sovereignty are frozen.

B. The Outer Space Treaty

The Outer Space Treaty (Treaty on Principles Governing the Activities of States in the Exploration and Use of Outer Space, Including the Moon and Other Celestial Bodies) was open for signature on January 27, 1967, after the negotiation under the United Nations Committee on Peaceful Uses of Outer Space, and took effect on October 10, 1967. The success of the Soviet Union in launching the first satellite, Sputnik, in 1957 motivated the early negotiation. The Treaty has two faces: the Charter of Outer Space, stipulating the fundamental principles of activities there, and the Arms Control Treaty, providing for its denuclearization. Each signatory agrees not to place in orbit around the Earth any objects carrying nuclear weapons or any other kind of weapons of mass destruction, to install such weapons on celestial bodies, or to station such weapons in outer space in any manner. The moon and other celestial bodies shall be used exclusively for peaceful purposes. All stations, installations, equipment, and space vehicles on the moon and other celestial bodies shall be open to representatives of other signatories on the basis of reciprocity. However, the use of military satellites is not prohibited, as some of these are used as a national technical means for verifying the obligation of disarmament.

C. The Seabed Treaty

The Seabed Treaty (Treaty on the Prohibition of the Emplacement of Nuclear Weapons and Other Weapons of Mass Destruction on the Seabed and the Ocean Floor and in the Subsoil Thereof) was signed on February 11, 1971, and took effect on May 18, 1972. With advances in technology and increased interest in natural resources, the ocean floor became the cause for concern for potential conflicts and arms races. In 1967, the United Nations established the Committee on Peaceful Uses of the Seabed, and seabed-related military and arms control issues were referred to the Geneva Eighteen-Nation Committee on Disarmament as an urgent part of the agenda. The Treaty prohibits the implantation or emplacement on the seabed and ocean floor and in the subsoil thereof of any nuclear weapons or any other types of weapons of mass destruction as well as facilities for them. In order to ensure compliance, each state has the right to verify through observation the activities of other signatories.

X. CONCLUSION

With the end of the Cold War, the two superpowers began to reduce their nuclear weapons, nuclear testing was prohibited, and new nuclear-weapon-free zones were established. Accordingly, the military and political value of nuclear weapons has depreciated. However, a lot of effort and time is necessary to reach the ultimate goal of nuclear elimination. Recently, governmental and nongovernmental institutes have presented several programs for achieving the goal of a nuclear-free world, and the International Court of Justice gave an advisory opinion in favor of nuclear disarmament. In order to realize a nuclear-free world, the substantial restructuring of international society will be necessary, including a stronger international organization to prevent violations of international standards of conduct from occurring. In the case of chemical and biological weapons, the treaties that provide for their complete prohibition and elimination need to be universally applied. Conventional weapons are now at the initial stage for regulation and reduction and further efforts are necessary for international peace and security.

Also See the Following Articles

ARMS CONTROL • ARMS PRODUCTION, ECONOMICS OF • MILITARY DETERRENCE AND STATECRAFT • NUCLEAR WEAPONS POLICIES • PEACE AGREEMENTS

Bibliography

Arnett, E. (Ed.). (1996). *Nuclear weapons after the comprehensive test ban: Implications for modernization and proliferation.* New York: Oxford University Press.

Bardonnet, D. (Ed.). (1996). *The convention of the prohibition and elimination of chemical weapons.* Dordrecht: Nijhoff.

Brown, J. (Ed.). (1995). *Old issues and new strategies in arms control and verification.* Amsterdam: Free University.

Clark, W., & Imai, R. (Ed.). (1996). *Next steps in arms control and non-proliferation,* Washington, DC: Carnegie Endowment for International Peace.

Goldblat, J. (1994). *Arms control: A guide to negotiations and agreements.* London: Sage.

Larson, J., & Rattray, G. (1996). *Arms control: Toward the 21st century.* Boulder, CO: Lynne Rienner Publishers.

Leeuwen, M. (1995). *The future of the international nuclear non-proliferation regime.* Dordrecht: Martinus Nijhoff.

Mueller, H., & Fischer, D. (1994). *Nuclear non-proliferation and global order.* Oxford: Oxford University Press.

Stockholm International Peace Research Institute. (1996). *SIPRI Yearbook 1996.* Oxford: Oxford University Press.

Sur, S. (1994). *Disarmament and arms limitation obligations: Problems of compliance and enforcement.* Aldershort, UK: Darthmouth Publishing Co.

United Nations. (1996). *United Nations disarmament yearbook 1995.* New York: United Nations.

Arms Production, Economics of

Elisabeth Sköns and Reinhilde Weidacher
Stockholm International Peace Research Institute, SIPRI

GLOSSARY

Arms Industry The set of arms-producing companies, which is not a defined sector in industrial statistics but cuts across several of these.

Arms Procurement Government purchases of military equipment.

Arms Production The production of military equipment.

Arms Producing Company A company which produces military equipment, often in addition to civil production.

Conversion The reuse of resources, which previously were tied to arms production, to the production of civilian goods.

Diversification Increasing the variety of manufactured products; civilian diversification involves an increase in the civilian share of total production, either through the reallocation of available resources (conversion), or through an expansion of total production.

Downsizing Reduction of production capacity.

Lay-offs Employment cuts by the discarding of staff.

Internationalization Cross border operations, including (in the context of arms production) arms trade, sub-contracting, company takeovers, mergers, production in foreign subsidiary companies, joint ventures, and other forms of armaments collaboration.

Military Industrial Complex (MIC) Coalitions of vested interests within the state and industry, including the armed services, government politicians and officials, and representatives of the arms industry.

Offsets Compensations by the export country to the import country, in non-monetary forms, including counter-trade, sub-contracting, capital investment, and technology transfers.

Rationalization Reorganization according to principles which will lead to greater efficiency.

ARMS PRODUCTION is a general term for the production of military equipment. It is not a defined industrial sector but cuts across many other sectors in the manufacturing industry, such as aerospace, electronics, vehicles and shipbuilding. Arms production most often takes place within companies which have both military and civilian production. Still, it has some unique characteristics, which distinguishes it from other types of production. Firstly, it produces the means of violence, which has led to a higher degree of state control and regulation than for other types of production. Secondly, although to some extent it operates under the same economic conditions as any industrial sector which it is part of, the fact that the state is the sole or main purchaser of many products results in monopsonist market features and associated exceptional economic conditions for the production of military equipment. The economics of arms production include topics, such as: the size and geographic distribution of world-wide arms production, the trends in its output and employment, the economic conditions under which the arms industry operates, and its economic importance. This is the subject of this article.

I. INTRODUCTION

The production of armaments has a number of unique features that make the arms industry operate in a different way than the rest of industry. This is in spite of the fact that arms production to a large extent takes place within companies that are privately owned and that also produce civilian goods for nongovernment commercial markets. The primary reason for this difference is the monopsonistic position of the buyer of its products. The demand side for military equipment consists primarily of a single customer, the national government. The export customers normally represent a rather small share of the total demand for most categories of military equipment. Thus, the domestic government has—through its procurement decisions—a significant influence over the volume of orders, the type of equipment to be produced, and the technology to be developed. In addition, through its legislative power, the government can also control competition and military exports. On the other hand, the government depends on the defense industrial base for its supplies of military equipment, and therefore tends to protect the arms industry and guarantee it a certain amount of economic viability. Furthermore, the increasing concentration in national arms industries is leading toward oligopolistic and even monopolistic positions of suppliers in certain product areas, which are protected from foreign competition. Thus, there exists no real competitive "market" for weapon systems, since this "market" by tradition is monopsonistic, and is gradually moving toward increasing interdependence between government and industry. This does not mean that there is no competition between companies. On the contrary, companies make great efforts to win the small number of very large contracts awarded by their own or foreign governments.

Arms production is an area that has not been much explored, especially not in the context of war and peace. However, research into issues of arms production was elevated in the late 1980s, when a dramatic worldwide restructuring of the arms industry began. In 1987 the previous trend of a long-term increase in global military expenditure was interrupted. During the 10-year period from 1987 through 1996 there was a profound reduction in defense budgets, due to the end of the Cold War and the general economic recession in large parts of the industrial world. Expenditures on arms procurement generally declined by at least as much as total military expenditures. This led to a crisis in the arms industry. It became clear to companies and governments all over the world that it would not be possible to maintain the existing military-industrial capacities and facilities. A radical downsizing of the worldwide arms industry was necessary. This led to a fundamental restructuring of the industry, including production cuts, rationalization, diversification, concentration and internationalization, and fierce competition between companies for domestic and world markets.

The purpose of this article is to summarize the available knowledge about arms production and the arms industry. This includes a description of the size and geographical distribution of arms production, a survey of the profound changes in the arms industry since the late 1980s, a discussion about the unique characteristics of military production, and finally a rough assessment of the economic impact of arms production. The article begins with an explanation of the basic terms used and the status of data in this field.

II. TERMS AND DATA

A. Explanation of Terms

There exists no generally agreed on definition of arms production, and it is difficult to formulate a definition that it is possible to operationalize. In a very general sense, arms production can be defined as the production of military equipment, while military equipment is usually defined to denote not only weapon systems but also all other products that have been developed and produced specifically for military use. This definition excludes items such as food, electricity, ordinary computers, and construction activities. The production of services is also a problematic item. Activities such as research and development, testing, and evaluation (RDT&E) of weapons systems, and the maintenance, servicing, and repairs of such systems assume an increasing importance and are often carried out by private companies. These types of services ideally should be included in the definition of arms production, but in practice this is often not the case.

One important reason for the difficulty in defining the "arms industry" is that there are many tiers in the process of producing a weapon system. These include the raw material, the parts, the components, the subsystems, the final assembly, and the integration of all subsystems into the final weapon system. These are preceded by a design stage and an RDT&E stage. Most often the term "arms production" is used to mean only the output of final weapon systems.

An arms-producing company is a company that is engaged in arms production, regardless of the proportion of military sales in the total sales of the company. Few companies produce exclusively for the military market any longer. Most companies have a mixed military and civil production, although single divisions or units within large diversified companies are often highly dependent on military production.

The arms industry is a vague concept. It is sometimes used to refer to the sum of arms-producing companies, and sometimes refers only to the arms-producing parts of these companies. The difference can be great, since arms production can take up a small part of a company's total sales and employment.

The defense industrial base (DIB) or the defense technology and industrial base (DTIB) is a broader concept than the arms industry. It encompasses the entire national resources required for providing and maintaining the national requirements of military equipment. There are many different definitions of the defense industrial base. A general definition is as follows: "The defence technology and industrial base is defined as the combination of people, institutions, technological know-how, and facilities used to design, develop, manufacture, and maintain the weapons and supporting defence equipment needed to meet national security objectives. It consists of three broad elements—R&D, production and maintenance" (Office of Technology Assessment, 1992).

In general, it should be noted that all these terms are used in a rather fluid way, especially in empirical studies, because of the difficulties of applying any of those definitions properly in the real world and finding the appropriate data.

B. Data on Arms Production

Data on arms production are not shown separately in the official industrial statistics, since arms production is not an industrial sector of its own but cuts across several industrial sectors, such as aerospace, motor vehicles, chemical products, and so on. Therefore, the available data are produced in special projects for this purpose and are based on different types of surveys of arms-producing companies. Such projects are carried out by some governments (defense ministries), defense industry associations, or research institutes. There are few governments, however, that systematically collect and publish aggregate data on arms production. It is more common for national defense industrial associations to collect data, but it is still a rather small number of associations that compile such data from their member companies.

The most comprehensive data related to arms production are provided by research organizations. Data on arms production in OECD and developing countries are collected by the Stockholm International Peace Research Institute (SIPRI) and published in the SIPRI yearbooks. These data are based primarily on company annual reports and company responses to questionnaires and also on information in official documents, military journals, and newspapers. The Bonn International Conversion Centre (BICC) collects data on global arms industry employment that are published in the BICC conversion surveys.

Company practices of releasing data on their defense production vary widely. Some companies provide rather detailed information in their company reports, while others do not compile separate statistics for military production or keep such data secret. It is often difficult even for the companies themselves to identify separate revenues, profits, and employment in the military business segment of the company because of the fact that most arms-producing companies also produce for the civil market and resources flow between their civil and military production processes.

Data on the total arms production or arms industry employment of a country are usually rough approximations and are calculated in different ways in different countries. Some data refer exclusively to the production of final weapon systems, while other data also include the production of parts and maintenance and repairs of military equipment, and some countries include all types of equipment procured by the armed services. Some estimates include also the production by subcontractors and suppliers of parts and raw material to the prime contractors. Therefore, data related to arms production are difficult to interpret and must be treated by caution.

III. THE GLOBAL ARMS INDUSTRY: SIZE AND DISTRIBUTION

A. Global Arms Production

The global arms industry is characterized by a high rate of concentration, mainly in a few industrial countries.

Thus, the capability to produce weapons is spread very unevenly across the world, much more unevenly than industrial production in general. Few countries have a significant defense industrial base. Most depend on imports for their arms purchases. Twenty major arms-producing countries account for more than 90% of worldwide production of armaments.

Table I provides available data on the arms production in the 20 countries that are believed to be the main arms-producing countries in the world, apart from several countries for which even rough estimates are unavailable, such as Belarus, Iran, Iraq, and Kazakhstan. Table I estimates on national arms sales, employment in arms production, and arms exports of these 20 countries provide a general impression of the structure of the global arms industry.

TABLE I

The Global Arms Industry in 1995

Arms production intervals (in billions) $	Country	Arms production[a] (in billions)	Employment in arms production[b] (in thousands)	Arms exports (in millions)
>75	USA	$90	2200	$15,200
50–75				
25–50				
15–25	UK	18	290	3275
	France	18	250	2185
10–15				
5–10	Germany	9	120	1385
	Japan	9	100	0
	Russia	7–9	1800	3100
2.5–5	Italy[c]	4	40	755
	Canada	4	35	325
	South Korea	3–5	60	75
	Israel[c]	3	50	1240
	China	n.a.	3500	n.a.
1–2.5	Poland	2	90	n.a.
	Sweden	2	30	465
	Netherlands	1–2	15	641
	Spain	1.5	30	665
	India	1.5	250	21
	Switzerland	1–1.5	22	162
	Australia[c]	1–1.5	10	21
	South Africa	1	75	285
	Ukraine	n.a.	1000	183
	Total	**180–186**	**10,000**	**31–32,000**

Notes: Countries are ranked by the value of their arms production.

[a] Arms production data are from official statistics, either on arms production or on domestic procurement and arms exports, unless otherwise stated.

[b] Data on employment include indirect employment (employees in the production of materials and parts).

[c] Arms production data is an estimate based on the sum of military sales of the major arms-producing companies.

Sources: Data on production and exports: SIPRI Arms Industry Files; data on employment: *BICC Conversion Survey 1997*.

There exists no exact figure for the total value of global arms production. A rough estimate can be made, based on the knowledge that the 20 countries in Table I account for slightly more than 90% of global military industrial output. The aggregate value of arms production in these 20 countries amounted to between $180 and $186 billion in the mid-1990s, which leads to a global total of about $200 billion in the mid-1990s. This represents a small share of world output: 0.7% of global gross domestic product (GDP) in 1995. Global employment in arms production is estimated by BICC to be 10.9 million people in 1995, including indirect employment. This represented 0.2% of the world's population in 1995 and 0.4% of the global labor force.

The only two countries that have long been self-sufficient in weapon systems are the United States and Russia, although the defense industrial base of Russia by 1995 had shrunk to one-tenth that of the Soviet Union in 1991. The United States is now by far the largest arms-producing country, accounting for almost 50% of total global arms production in 1995. Of the next two groups of countries, those five (including Russia) that had national arms sales in between $5 and $20 billion in 1995 accounted for another 30% of global output of military equipment.

From Table I it can also be seen that there is no strong correlation between output and employment in arms production. In spite of their similar size in arms industry employment, China, Russia, and the United States account for widely different shares in global military industrial output and arms exports. Some of the divergence can be accounted for by differences in definitions and reporting of data. However, the main explanation for this divergence in shares is the major differences in national economic environment and industrial organization. This was clearly seen during the period of downsizing in the 1990s. While downsizing of arms production was associated with massive layoffs in the U.S. arms industry, the dramatic decline in Russian arms production took place without any significant employment cuts because social considerations made it impossible to lay off large numbers of people in Russia. A similar situation of hidden unemployment exists in the Chinese military industry, although its extent is unknown.

TABLE II

Regional/National Shares of Arms Sales[a] for the Top 100 Arms-Producing Companies in the OECD and in Developing Countries, 1995 Compared to 1994[b]

Number of companies, 1995	Region/country	Percentage of total arms sales 1994	Percentage of total arms sales 1995	Arms sales 1995 (in billions)
40	USA	58.8	57.0	$87.7
40	West European OECD	32.9	34.4	53.0
12	France	12.5	13.2	20.4
12	UK	10.5	11.5	17.7
8	Germany	5.2	5.1	7.8
2	Italy	1.8	2.1	3.3
3	Sweden	1.2	1.2	1.9
2	Switzerland	1.0	0.9	1.3
1	Spain	0.7	0.4	0.7
12	Other OECD	5.5	5.9	9.1
10	Japan[c]	5.1	5.5	8.4
1	Turkey	0.2	0.2	0.4
1	Canada	0.2	0.2	0.3
8	Non-OECD countries	2.8	2.7	4.2
5	Israel	1.7	1.6	2.5
2	India	0.6	0.6	1.0
1	South Africa	0.4	0.4	0.7
100		**100.0**	**100.0**	**$154.0**

[a] Arms sales include both arms sales for domestic procurement and arms exports.

[b] China and South Korea are not included because of the lack of comparable company data. Four companies in South Korea would be among the top 100 if data were available for 1995.

[c] For Japanese companies data in the arms sales column represent new military contracts rather than arms sales.

Source: SIPRI Yearbook 1997, Table 8.1, in Skōns, E., and Cooper, J., "Arms Production," Chapter 8.

B. The Top 100 Arms-Producing Companies

More precise data are available for individual companies. SIPRI provides data on the top 100 arms-producing companies in the OECD and developing countries (excluding China and South Korea because of the lack of comparable data). The top 100 companies in 1995 included companies located in 14 different countries with combined arms sales of $154 billion (see Table II). This represented about three-quarters of total global arms production, which again illustrates the strong geographical and also the corporate concentration in the worldwide arms industry.

The top 100 also shows the strong dominance of U.S. companies. Among the top 100 companies in 1995, there were 40 U.S. companies, accounting for 57% of their combined arms sales, 40 West European companies (34%), 12 companies in other OECD countries (around 6%), and 8 companies in the developing world, accounting for 2.7% of the combined arms sales of the top 100 companies.

IV. THE ECONOMIC CONTEXT OF ARMS PRODUCTION

The production of military equipment has a number of distinguishing characteristics from those applying to most other types of industrial production. This is due primarily to the monopsonistic nature of military sales. There is one sole or dominant customer of the products of the arms industry—the national armed forces through their national government. Through its scale of arms procurement, choice of equipment types, and its legislative authority, the government has a significant influence over the volume, type, and characteristics of arms production. The only potential competitors are governments in other countries, but in most countries military exports constitute a small share of total national arms production, and, furthermore, the national government also has considerable influence over military exports.

The main distinguishing characteristics of arms production are the following (Dunne, 1995):

1. An emphasis on performance of high-technology weaponry rather than on cost.
2. Large armaments R&D programs, financed or guaranteed by the government.
3. Government regulations on contracts, competition, and exports. Market mechanisms are replaced by a contracting system, in which the government specifies requirements and selects the contractor for R&D and production contracts, either by direct negotiation with the preferred supplier or by competition.
4. Close relations between industry, government, and military.

These characteristics have led to a number of tendencies in arms production:

1. A tendency toward concentration and monopolies or oligopolies. The emphasis on performance and the large scale of R&D programs are associated with a trend of rising costs of research and development (R&D), which in turn has made it increasingly difficult for single companies or even single countries to develop new advanced weapon systems. This has created a pressure in the arms industry toward concentration into fewer and larger companies, and toward international collaboration in arms production.

2. A tendency towards low efficiency and high profitability. The granting of large R&D contracts with risk borne by government together with specific types of production contracts with guaranteed cost coverage has created a tendency toward high profitability in spite of low efficiency in production.

3. A tendency towards a military industrial complex (MIC). There are several types of theories and concepts regarding the existence of an MIC, most often used to designate the interrelation between groups with a vested interest in arms production irrespective of rational considerations of national security. They all originate in the warning by U.S. President Eisenhower in 1961 against the potential misplacement of power due to the "conjunction of an immense military establishment and a large arms industry," which at the time was a new phenomenon.

V. TRENDS AND DEVELOPMENTS IN ARMS PRODUCTION

Since the end of the 1980s, global arms production has undergone profound changes in most parts of the world (see Table III). These changes were driven primarily by three factors: (1) declining demand for military equipment worldwide; (2) rapid development in military technology, which pushes up the R&D content in advanced weapons systems and makes these increasingly difficult for national governments to finance; and (3) reversal in the relationship between military and civil technology, so that civil technology is becoming increasingly important for the production of military equipment instead of vice versa.

There has been a significant decline in the market for military equipment since 1987, which was the peak year of global military expenditures. Again, there are no hard data on the size of this decline but a rough estimate can be made. The global demand for weapons is to a great extent concentrated in the industrial countries. Around three-quarters of world military expenditure is spent by the industrial countries, and in arms procurement the concentration to the industrial world is even stronger. Therefore, arms procurement expenditure in the industrial world provides a good indication of the trend in the global demand for weapons. Available data for NATO countries show that their combined expenditures on military equipment declined by one-third in the period between 1988 and 1997, while the arms procurement budget of Russia in 1997 was two-thirds lower than that of the Soviet Union in 1988. In the developing world the best indicator for the demand

TABLE III

Developments in Arms Production since the Late 1980s

Driving forces	Declining markets
	Increasing R&D content in advanced weapon systems
	Changing relations between civil and military production
Trends	Downsizing
	Rationalization
	Diversification and conversion
	Concentration
	Internationalization
	Increased export competition

for weapons is arms imports, since these countries depend on imports for most of their arms procurement. Imports of major conventional weapons by developing countries dropped by around one-third between 1987 and 1997. Thus, it can be estimated that the reductions in the global demand for military equipment amounted to between one-third and one-half between 1987 and 1997. Towards the end of this period, however, there were indications of a return to growth in arms procurement expenditures in several of the major arms-producing countries.

The rapid decline in the demand for weapons has caused a minor revolution in the arms industry. Companies had to downsize and many companies sold off their military business, while other companies—most often companies that were already leaders in a product area—acquired other companies or divisions engaged in military production. Companies responded to the sharp cuts in the demand for weapons in several ways. In addition to production cuts and plant closures, these responses include rationalization, diversification, concentration of production, internationalization, and increased export efforts.

A. Production Cuts and Plant Closures

The most notable trend in arms production in the first half of the 1990s was the reduction in output. An overwhelming share of this decrease has taken place in the countries that used to belong to the two major defense alliances, the North Atlantic Treaty Organisation (NATO), which is still in existence, and the Warsaw Treaty Organization (WTO), which was dissolved in 1991. Arms production was concentrated in these countries. A few third-tier arms-producing countries have also experienced a sharp decline in military industrial output since the late 1980s. This is the case in two countries that used to have the largest arms industries among the developing countries: South Africa, which centered upon a course of disarmament in 1989, and Brazil, which lost its major arms export market, Iraq, with the termination of the Gulf War.

In the industrial countries the decline in production follows rather closely the decline in domestic arms procurement. In Russia the military output of the defense complex has dropped dramatically to one-tenth of what it was in 1991, according to official statistics. Arms production in the Central and East European (CEE) countries was seriously affected by the disintegration of the former WTO and with it the integrated system of military production among these countries. Therefore, arms production in the CEE countries was in disarray in the years immediately after the dissolution of the WTO and the output of military equipment dropped significantly, although it is difficult to say by exactly how much.

B. Rationalization

Parallel with downsizing was a trend of rationalization. Companies were streamlined and staff was laid off. This resulted in very significant employment cuts in arms production in most countries. Between the years 1987 and 1995, according to BICC global arms industry employment declined by more than one-third: from 17.5 million people in 1987 to 10.9 million people in 1995 (BICC, 1997).

C. Diversification and Conversion

Diversification from military to civil production takes place in three major ways: through expansion of already existing civil business; through the development of new products and thus production lines; or through the acquisition of other companies or company units. Conversion can be seen as one form of diversification in which there is a transfer of production resources from military to civil production. Such resources include production facilities, machinery, labor, or technology.

There are many interesting issues involved in assessing the success of diversification and conversion. Two of the more important ones are (1) to what extent the reduction in arms sales takes place through diversification into civil production, and (2) to what extent companies are able to compensate for lost military production with new commercial production. These are interrelated, since the more successful individual companies are in compensating themselves for lost arms production, the more feasible is this method of cutting arms production.

Among the big companies, the reduction in arms sales between 1990 and 1995 has not taken place primarily through diversification; only 18 companies among the top 100 arms-producing companies in 1995 reduced the military share in their total sales by 10% or more. Most of these were in the electronics sector. However, when looking separately at only those 50 companies that lost arms sales during this period, more than half of these (27 companies) were able to compensate fully for this through increases in civil sales, and another 10 companies were able to compensate for part of their losses with civil sales (SIPRI, 1997).

Few studies are available on the experiences of small defense firms. However, from a survey of small U.S.

defense firms in the early 1990s Feldman found that these companies were able to reduce their dependence on arms sales considerably, increasing their sales of civilian products and, more so, their employment in civilian production. Their expansion in nonmilitary government sales provided the key to successful diversification (Feldman, 1997).

D. Concentration

Another very marked feature of the changes in the arms industry during the 1990s was the restructuring of ownership, through mergers and acquisitions, which resulted in a heavy concentration of production in the industry.

The concentration process was particularly rapid in the United States, where it also was reinforced through government financial support with the purpose of achieving savings in weapons costs. The extraordinarily high pace of concentration in the U.S. arms industry can be illustrated by the fact that Lockheed Martin, which was the leading company in 1995, over the past decade has acquired 18 other arms-producing companies. The mergers in the U.S. arms industry have resulted in giant arms-producing firms. During 1997 two new giant U.S. defense conglomerates were created through the merger of the two aircraft manufacturers Boeing and McDonnell Douglas, and the take over of Hughes Electronics' military business units by Raytheon. The new companies will have annual arms sales of about $19 billion and $13 billion, respectively. The volume of the arms sales of each of these individual companies can be compared with the combined annual arms procurement expenditures of all European NATO countries, which amounted to $40 billion in 1997 (at 1995 prices and exchange rates). Such companies will of course have a very strong market dominance. Governments try to maintain a more or less artificial competition, but in many respects these companies will have a monopoly position in their markets.

E. Internationalization

There are many different forms of internationalization, ranging from foreign trade (arms exports in this case) to the development of transnational corporations. The most notable development in recent years is the internationalization in company ownership and, to some extent, of the production process itself. This is a marked change compared to the situation before 1990. Until then the production of armaments was a sector characterized by strict national protection. The long-term efforts of armaments cooperation within NATO resulted in some collaboration, but much less than was the policy goal, due to national protection.

This has gradually changed with the end of the Cold War and as a result of the budgetary and economic difficulties in most of the major arms-producing countries. In Europe, the economic and industrial pressures toward concentration of ownership have been inhibited by the fragmentation of the market. The small size of each national procurement budget has prevented achievement of economies of scale through long production runs. In most countries the national concentration process has resulted in one or two major players, but these are very small compared to their U.S. counterparts. Further concentration would have to cross borders, but this was prevented by the lack of harmonization in weapon requirements, the absence of a common arms market, and government reluctance regarding foreign ownership in the arms industry. Therefore, forms of concentration other than acquisitions were dominant in Europe, such as international joint ventures, often for the purposes of a specific weapon system program, or other forms of international armaments collaboration.

F. Increased Export Efforts

The decline of the global arms market has resulted in intense competition in arms exports. Companies are striving to capture a larger slice of a rapidly declining export market. In the competition for export markets, companies turn increasingly to their governments for support, and most governments have also increased their involvement in the international arms trade. This has led to some long-term changes in the global arms export market. The more significant changes include the following: (1) a strong increase in what are called "offset" terms in international arms contracts; (2) political involvement at the ministerial level in support of major arms export contracts; (3) government support for international arms exhibitions; and (4) strong pressures to deregulate the international arms trade.

Offset terms are now "standard element" in military contracts. An offset is an agreement between a supplier and a buyer that imposes obligations on the seller to compensate the buyer for the costs of the purchase. They can be either direct or indirect. Direct offsets involve the goods and services in the sales agreement while indirect offsets involve any other goods and services. The most common types of offsets are subcontracting, licensed production or co-production in the importing country, technology transfers to and capital investment in the importing country, and countertrade. Arms trade offsets normally amounts to more than 100% of the arms deal. This means that the value of the compensation exceeds the full value of the arms sales contract, which is possible because of the strong position of the importers in the current international arms market.

VI. THE ECONOMIC IMPACT OF ARMS PRODUCTION

Although the relative importance of arms production in national economies is rather small, it is often argued that its economic and industrial impact is significant, or even of vital importance. This argument is focused on the technological dimension and thus on military R&D and production of the most advanced weapon systems. The relative economic importance of arms production is shown in Table IV for the 20 major arms-producing countries in the world. In most of these countries arms production accounts for around 1% or less of gross domestic product, national employment, and total exports.

TABLE IV

The Economic Importance of Arms Production in 1995

Country	Share of GDP	Share of total employment	Share of total exports
USA	1.3%	1.8%	2.0%
UK	1.3	1.1	1.4
France	1.2	1.1	0.8
Germany	0.4	0.3	0.3
Japan	0.2	0.2	—
Russia	1.1–1.4	n.a.	3.8
Italy	0.4	0.2	0.3
Canada	0.7	0.3	0.2
South Korea	0.8	0.3	0.7
Israel	3.5	2.5	6.5
China	n.a.	0.6	n.a.
Poland	1.7	1.0	n.a.
Sweden	0.9	0.8	0.6
Netherlands	0.4	0.2	0.3
Spain	0.3	0.3	0.7
India	0.4	n.a.	0.1
Switzerland	0.4	0.6	0.2
Australia	0.4	0.1	0.04
South Africa	0.7	1.4	0.9
Ukraine	n.a.	n.a.	1.6

Note: Countries are listed by the value of their arms production (see Table I).

Sources: SIPRI Arms Industry Files; *BICC Conversion Survey 1997.*

The debate on the economic impact of military production is strongly related to the more general debate on the economic impact of military expenditure. The economic costs and benefits of defense spending are difficult to assess on a purely empirical level. Furthermore, theoretical models and methodological approaches inform the findings of studies on the economic impact of military expenditure to a very high degree. Studies have been made based on supply, demand, or combined demand/supply-side theoretical models. In neoclassical supplyside models economic growth is derived from the aggregate production function, that is, the input of labor, capital, and technology. In Keynesian demand-side models economic growth is derived from the aggregate demand function, that is, the output of consumption, investment, military expenditure, and balance of trade. In a review of the findings of a large number of empirical studies in both developing and developed countries, the results have been summarized as follows: demand-side models reveal the negative effect of defense expenditure on growth due to the competition for resources with civil investment, while supply-side models uncover a small positive impact of defense spending on growth due to the multiplier effect of defense spending. Combined, demand/supply-side models, finally, find that the negative demand-side impact outweighs the slightly positive supply-side effect (Sandler and Hartley).

Quantitative studies on the macroeconomic impact of military production have been challenged by qualitative or descriptive approaches, as well as by meso- and microeconomic models that focus on structural changes in single arms-producing enterprises or industrial and geographic units on a disaggregated level.

The beneficial impact of arms production on economic growth within an analytical approach is generally related to the transfer of technological innovation from the military sector to the civil one, or technological *spin-off*. It has been argued that the high level of technology in military production stimulates the modernization of the overall industrial complex in developing countries. This traditional spin-off paradigm, that is, the one-way relation between the military and the civil sector of the productive structure, has in recent years been increasingly challenged. Due to the rapid development in commercial technologies, especially in electronics, it is argued, the direction of technology benefits is being reversed into one of *spin-on* from civil to military technology.

To sum up, arms production may have a positive economic side impact on the aggregate economy by its income and employment multiplier effects, as well as through military technological innovation. Yet it is also true that civil production and technological progress would benefit more from direct investment in civil production than from any side-effect deriving from military production.

Also See the Following Articles

ARMS CONTROL • ECONOMIC CONVERSION • MILITARY–INDUSTRIAL COMPLEX, CONTEMPORARY SIGNIFICANCE • MILITARY–INDUSTRIAL COMPLEX, ORGANIZATION AND HISTORY • WEAPONRY, EVOLUTION OF

Bibliography

Alic, J. A., Branscomb, L. M., Brooks, H., Carter, A. B., & Epstein, G. L. (1992). *Beyond spin-off: Military and commercial technologies in a changing world.* Boston: Harvard Business School Press.

Ball, N., & Leitenberg, M. (1983). *The structure of the defense industry.* London & Canberra: Croom Helm.

Batchelor, P., & Willett, S. (1998). *Disarmament and defence industrial adjustment in South Africa.* SIPRI. Oxford: Oxford University Press.

Bonn International Centre for Conversion, BICC. (Annual). *Conversion survey.* Oxford: Oxford University Press.

Brömmelhörster, J., & Frankenstein, J. (Eds.) (1997). *Mixed motives, uncertain outcomes: Defence Conversion in China.* Boulder: Lynne Rienner.

Brzoska, M., & Lock, P. (1992). *The restructuring of arms production in Western Europe.* SIPRI. Oxford: Oxford University Press.

Brzoska, M., & Olsson, T. (1986). *Arms production in the Third World.* SIPRI. London: Taylor & Francis.

Cooper, J. (1993). *The conversion of the former Soviet defence industry.* London: Royal Institute of International Affairs.

Dunne, P. (1995), The defense industrial base. In Sandler, T. and Hartley, K. (eds.) *Handbook of defense economics,* Volume 1. Amsterdam: Elsevier.

Feldman, J. F. (1997). *Diversification after the Cold War: Results of the national defense economy survey.* Working Paper No. 112, Center for Urban Policy Research, Rutgers, The State University of New Jersey, Revised Version.

Gansler, J. S. (1980). *The defense industry,* 2nd ed. Cambridge, MA: MIT Press.

Gummett, P., & Reppy, J. (Eds.). (1988). *The relations between defence and military technologies.* Dordrecht: Kluwer Academic Publishers.

Kaldor, M. (1981). *The baroque arsenal.* New York: Hill & Wang.

Kaldor, M. (1998). *The European rupture: The defence sector in transition.* Cheltenham and Lyme: Edward Elgar and United Nations University Press.

Kapstein, E. (Ed.) (1992). *Global arms production: Policy dilemmas for the 1990s.* Center for International Affairs. Lanham: Harvard University Press.

Krause, K. (1992). *Arms and the state: Patterns of military production and trade.* Cambridge: Cambridge University Press.

Kiss, J., (1997). *The defence industry in East-Central Europe: Restructuring and conversion.* SIPRI. Oxford: Oxford Univ. Press.

Markusen, A., & Yudken, J. (1992). *Dismantling the Cold War economy.* New York: Basic Books.

Martin, S. (Ed.). (1996). *The Economics of offsets: Defence procurement and countertrade.* Amsterdam: Harwood Academis Publishers.

Melman, S. (1970). *Pentagon capitalism. The political economy of war.* New York: McGraw-Hill.

Molas-Gallart, J. (1992). The economic aspect of defence: The theory. pp. 7–39. *Military production and innovation in Spain,* pp. 7–39. Chur: Harwood Academic Publishers.

Office of Technology Assessment. (1992). US Congress. *Building future security: Strategies for restructuring the defense technology and industrial base.* Washington, DC: OTA, US GPO.

Peck, M. J., & Scherer, F. M.(1992). *The weapons acquisition process: An economic analysis.* Boston: Harvard University Press.

Sandler, T., & Hartley, K. (1995a). *The economics of defense.* Cambridge Surveys of Economic Literature. Cambridge: Cambridge University Press.

Stockholm International Peace Research Institute, SIPRI. (Annual). *SIPRI yearbook.* Oxford: Oxford University Press.

Wulf, H. (Ed.). (1993). *Arms industry limited.* SIPRI. Oxford: Oxford University Press.

Arms Trade, Economics of

Frederic S. Pearson
Wayne State University

John Sislin
Bowling Green State University

Marie Olson
Wayne State University

GLOSSARY

Arms Race An action and reaction pattern whereby adversaries arm against each other competitively.

Black Market The covert sale of weapons by smugglers and dealers.

Commercial Sale The sale of arms by a private dealer or manufacturer.

Concessional Sale An arms sale subsidized by credit arrangements below prevailing bank interest rates.

Coproduction An intergovernmental or interindustry agreement to produce a weapon or share production technology jointly in more than one country.

Countertrade Agreements to purchase products from an arms customer to help relieve the costs of the weapon purchase.

Foreign Military Sales Program The system of U.S. governmental sponsorship and review of major commercial weapon sales, in which the government helps identify and service customers, negotiates the terms of sale, arranges with the company for production, and collects the funds.

Government Sale The sale of arms by or through a government; can include sales from government stocks or government purchases from arms manufacturers, which are then sold to foreign buyers.

Gray Market Governmentally approved arms sales that skirt the letter of the law, such as covert sales to groups or to circumvent embargoes.

Offsets Agreements to help arms purchasers relieve the cost of the weapons by arranging for such measures as partial production in the customer state and other technological sharing.

Retrofitting The process of mounting equipment and weapons components from various sources on a weapon platform such as a plane or ship.

Third Tier Arms-producing states that entered the weapons trade later than the major powers and tended to specialize in certain types of weapons for specific fighting conditions or types of customers.

Transparency Procedures to track and publicly report agreements to transfer weapons and weapon deliveries.

THE ECONOMICS OF THE EMERGING WORLDWIDE ARMS DISTRIBUTION SYSTEM can be understood by focusing on the supply and demand for both major and smaller conventional arms. Arms transfers refer to the supply of weapons, spare parts, ammunition, and technical/logistical items or training associated with these systems, by gift, sale, or subsidy. Major conventional arms traditionally include such categories as tanks, heavy artillery, aircraft, and naval vessels, while smaller or "light" weapons include more easily portable arms such as rifles, grenades, mines, light artillery (e.g., mortars), and shoulder-mounted missiles. "Dual use" items, with civilian and military applications, such as trucks, computers, transport aircraft, small vessels, machetes, and other potentially lethal items pose a definitional problem for those accounting for arms sales. Excluded from this discussion of "conventional arms" are weapons of "mass destruction," which include nuclear, chemical, and biological arms (though obviously delivery systems for these weapons—aircraft, ships, tanks, artillery, and missiles—generally are classified as conventional arms).

The overall network of arms supply, including used or second-hand weapons, is difficult to track down, although the search for "transparency" in the distribution of arms has increased significantly in the past decade. Transfers can go from government to government, from government to foreign faction or group, from faction/group in one country to those in another, from arms companies to governments, or from company to private interests or groups in a recipient state. By "arms trade" is meant the sale, export/import, of arms and related equipment as distinct from other types of military shipments such as aid and gifts. The history by which the arms transfer system has developed, today's export and import patterns and interests, the technological and policy changes anticipated for the new century, and the prospects for managing or controlling the arms trade in relation to conflict resolution will be discussed below.

I. ECONOMIC AND SECURITY CONSIDERATIONS

During the Cold war, American-Soviet competition led to worldwide arms sales driven primarily by security concerns, but also having an economic incentive in some cases. Other arms suppliers, such as Britain, France, West Germany, Sweden, Switzerland, and Italy, took advantage of an insecure world to export arms primarily for economic gain. Since the end of the Cold War, however, the security competition fueling arms sales has diminished, leaving Washington and Moscow themselves more focused on economic interests. Economic incentives have come to the fore with the decline of superpower competition, but security concerns remain important especially in contemplating control of arms transfers.

One of the pressing security questions of the post-Cold War period concerns the effects of arms shipments in either escalating or deescalating conflict situations. While arms shipments have always had this potential effect, the prominence of certain ethno-political conflicts since 1990 has reminded arms-supplying states of the pitfalls and dangers of unrestrained supply. Crises in Bosnia and Rwanda have highlighted the importance of arms in spurring ethnic fighting and even genocidal attacks. Additionally, arms shipments seem to complicate the mediation and peacekeeping missions of the UN, NATO, and regional organizations, as weapons fall into hands of hostile governmental, militia, or rebel forces.

Yet it is also argued that groups and nations have an inherent right of self-defense against attacks, and that by establishing balances of power through armament, fighting can be ended or averted. Therefore, the premium for peacekeeping or peace enforcement is on controlling armament, even disarming the warring sides if possible, while the premium for security planners and arms dealers often is on maintaining the supply of weapons. The growing economic incentives in arms sales conflict with these inclinations toward arms control. From each perspective there are ambiguities and policy dilemmas.

Arms suppliers' and recipients' security interests generally are found in producing "stabilizing" military balances or overwhelming power for conquest; the aim can be deterrence, defense, the promotion of peace negotiations, or conquest. Thus, the stabilizing or destabilizing impact of arms supplies depends upon the situation and the viewer's perspective. Studies of the effect of armament on ongoing international wars have shown that precise arms balances are extremely difficult to achieve, that embargoes can be either ineffective or pacifying depending upon the degree of client dependence on suppliers, and that arms resupply during wars can lead to stalemates and cease-fire negotiations, or to prolonged fighting. One of the key determining factors appears to be the degree of major power pressure for an end to fighting which accompanies arms diplomacy.

Cross-border fighting has diminished since the last years of the Cold War, and violence within countries has become more visible, if not necessarily more frequent than before. The precise effects of armament in spurring these domestic conflicts is little known as yet. It appears extremely difficult to clamp down completely on the flow of smaller arms that are most relevant to many civil wars. Indeed, while some heavy weapons were employed in Rwanda, much of the carnage was carried out with primitive machetes; the sophistication of armament appears to matter less in domestic than in international fighting. As the combatants establish control over greater swaths of territory and move closer to political sovereignty, though, they appear to seek heavier weapons—as in the case of the contestants in Bosnia.

Since arms supplies can exacerbate severe conflict situations, it would be theoretically desirable to reach conventional arms control agreements, just as it has been desirable to move toward nuclear nonproliferation, yet other factors play a role in deterring control agreements. Aside from the "sovereign right to arm," such control is complicated by the dual nature of the arms trade, that is, the fact that both security and commercial interests are at stake. Both these interests are further complicated by concerns over technological development, since arms are a reflection of technology and technology signals both security and commercial capabilities. For example, when aspiring Latin American powers such as Argentina, Brazil, and Chile geared up their domestic arms industries and began exporting weapons in the 1970s, it was easy to conclude that they were mainly after commercial profits; in fact, aside from a low-level local rivalry and Argentina's 1982 Falklands/Malvinas war with Britain, the three states had no discernible pressing security threats. However, keeping up with the latest advanced technologies, many of which are reflected in weaponry, had itself become a security concern, particularly for military rulers. For these Latin states, and for ambitious military producers in other regions, the threatening environment perceived in both the international and regional political system was enough to generate concern about being left behind in weapons potential. Indeed, one finds that those developing states that have undertaken significant industrial arms development—states such as India, Pakistan, China, Israel, South Africa, Brazil, Argentina—generally also had at least experimented with nuclear and other forms of advanced technology. Of course, there is also money to be made in such pursuits, so it becomes difficult to sort out completely the effects of security, commercial, and technological motives; all three are interwoven in the arms production and export business.

Global powers such as the United States and Russia, which together have supplied between 50 and 70% of global arms shipments, traditionally have been the most likely to emphasize security interests, often imposing formal restrictions or distinctions about where, to whom, and in what form various types of arms or related supplies could be transferred or retransferred (i.e., shipped by the recipient to third parties). Other major powers, such as Britain, France, and Germany, have tended to be somewhat less oriented to a security calculus, and interested more in bolstering trade revenues, though they too have imposed bans or conditions if the recipients seemed likely to cause regional instability or harm to vital regional interests.

One of the key economic factors in the arms supply equation is the need to keep domestic arms production facilities operating, for example, to generate enough revenue to reinvest in research and development. For big powers with ambitious military establishments, the domestic arms market can be sufficiently large to absorb enough new weapons to provide a strong basis for continued production and technological updates; for smaller powers, however, enlarging sales to wider export markets becomes a necessity to maintain such capabilities. All arms producers are tempted to export for profit; the smaller ones are driven by harsh economic realities either to merge production in collaboration with other countries or to export competitively in order to survive as military producers.

Even as Washington and Moscow experienced less security concern about each other during the 1990s—for example, about arms technologies falling into the enemy's hands through export—they retained their economic and military interests in producing arms. The expected "peace dividend" of drastically reduced defense production and military spending hardly materialized. Military expenditures continued to decline in nearly all major arms producing states, but in the United States this trend was tempered in tradeoffs between cutting personnel and bases versus cutting weapons programs. In the mid-1990s, congressional pressure maintained certain new weapons systems even in the face of Pentagon opposition. In Russia as well as other former East bloc states such as the Czech Republic, Poland, and Ukraine, defense still represented one of the few viable indigenous industries capable of employing relatively large numbers of workers.

The global arms trade peaked at over $60 billion in 1984, and began a consistent gradual decline thereafter due to the easing of the Cold War competition in Europe and the settlement of several long-running local wars in the Third World. The market stabilized at over $20 billion in major weapons and a total of approximately $40 billion annually in total sales of all types of arms during the 1990s. Thus, diminished though still considerable market demand affected the incentives, patterns, and forms of arms transfers and policies, generally boosting competition and driving less competitive arms companies and arms-producing states either out of the arms business or toward drastic new strategies. Among such strategies were consolidations, mergers, joint ventures, and the production of "dual use" equipment for both civilian and military purposes. Turkey and Indonesia, for example, have worked towards an agreement that would upgrade the F-16 aircraft for the Indonesian Air Force.

In the United States, the Pentagon contracted for a single new jet fighter in 1996, instead of several as in the past; the new plane would have to satisfy the needs of the army, navy, marines, and air force. In addition to creating design complications, this stiffened competition among industrial firms; indeed by denying McDonnell-Douglas' bid to compete for this contract, the Pentagon in effect encouraged the merger of McDonnell-Douglas with Boeing—creating the world's largest aerospace firm—since Boeing itself needed McDonnell's fighter jet design experience. Mergers, consolidations, and restructuring of industrial arms producers, sometimes with companies abandoning the market and selling out, became the order of the day in North America and Europe. Governments were more willing to risk the loss of certain production lines as long as basic capabilities could be maintained. Even these cost reduction and government budget balancing efforts, however, increased rather than obviated the pursuit of arms export markets. Any revenues derived overseas presumably would be that much less required of domestic taxpayers or corporate investors.

As noted, the end of the Cold War did not spell the end of security interests in propelling the arms trade. American political leaders cited fears of regional security threats, concerns fed by events such as the 1990–1991 Gulf War and various terrorist acts. "Rogue" leaders such as Saddam Hussein, Iranian, Afghani, and Sudanese militants, North Koreans, and Libya's Col. Gadhafi symbolized anti-Western threats thought to justify continued arms development and export. Whether one could reasonably argue that they justified the most advanced forms of weapons technology, previously confined to competition with the Soviet Union, was not much considered. Clearly, bureaucratic interests among military services and local Congressional "pork barrel" in military contracts also played into such procurement planning, but it is far more compelling in congressional deliberations to point to a "still dangerous world" and cite the potential for threats to oil supplies, shipping, friends and allies, commerce, and tourism. The preference for "deterrence" strategies, such as the dual deterrence of Iran and Iraq, made reliance on increased military preparedness more acceptable. Deterrence potential would be extended to key regional clients, such as Saudi Arabia and the Gulf oil kingdoms through arms sales. In addition, new peacekeeping responsibilities for NATO as well as UN forces have made it necessary to refine weapons, even if they do not exactly call for new heights of military technology.

Thus, we are left with a complicated and vague arms control environment. Arms suppliers generally recognize risks and potential untoward consequences of indiscriminate foreign supply of arms. They are nervous about the potential for "black" and "gray" markets in which private dealers, merchants, and crime or terrorist syndicates acquire and distribute potent weapons—even simple ones such as bombs, rockets, and shoulder fired missiles. Surplus arms flow from one violent conflict to another, as in the aftermath of the Iran–Iraq and Afghan wars of the 1980s. Public interest groups have campaigned against aspects of the weapons trade, citing the lingering threats to civilians from such leftover war legacies as land mines. However, while the threats of excesses are understood, the temptation to continue the supply continues, mainly for economic gain, sometimes for ethnic solidarity as groups in one country supply those in a neighboring state, but also because the force of arms is easier to comprehend politically than the potential of diplomacy.

II. HISTORICAL EVOLUTION

Since the Second World War the international arms transfer system has evolved from grant shipments of mainly outdated surplus equipment to the sale and strategic supply of relatively sophisticated weapon systems. Indeed during the 1960s, increasing emphasis was put on lucrative military sales first by the U.S. Defense Department (in part to recover research and development costs) and then by European defense ministries. The superpowers geared up for indirect competition in the Third World through supplies to favored strategic allies and clients. At the same time, for reasons of prestige and competition, these clients also came to demand and expect "top of the line equipment" similar to that used by the major powers. The latest arms generally were supplied only to the closest allies in NATO and the Warsaw Pact, but exceptions were made for key regional clients such as Iran under the Shah, Israel, Egypt, Syria, and Vietnam. Lesser equipment was sometimes upgraded, or advanced systems slightly modified or downgraded for export in order to satisfy consumer demand while guarding the latest technological secrets. Weapons downgrades also proved useful in reassuring the recipient's enemy about upsetting the balance of power—for example, reassuring Israel about Saudi arms or China concerning Taiwan's latest U.S. acquisitions.

Occasionally arms shipments were banned to certain states in conflict, as in the "tripartite," U.S.–U.K.–French, restrictions on arms supplied to the Arabs and Israel beginning in 1950, similar U.S.-U.K. restrictions on arms to India and Pakistan in the 1960s, and a long-term UN imposed embargo of South Africa. Informally Washington also has had a recurring policy of refusing to introduce advanced highly sophisticated weapons into the Americas, though Europeans have from time to time done so and the United States increasingly has been tempted. Because of their past wartime practices, Germany and Japan also had constitutional provisions limiting the extent of their arms distribution to war-prone regions. With ready alternate suppliers, such as those in the Soviet bloc and France, however, the effects of sanctions and restrictions were diluted. Embargoed states also tended quickly to mount their own arms production efforts and to seek a more diverse set of suppliers in order to avert sanctions, as in the case of India and Israel in the 1960s, South Africa and Chile (after the embargo of the Pinochet government) in the 1970s.

Booming oil income during the 1970s, particularly in the Middle East, spurred vast competitive arms sales efforts. Aside from commercial gain, the superpowers saw their arms competition as a surrogate for direct military confrontation. Arms supposedly provided both protection for favored regimes and potential control over arms recipients, through these regimes' dependence on spare parts and training. Hence the nearly unlimited American conventional military transfer deals with the Shah of Iran were rationalized as a way to preclude his interest in developing nuclear weapons. Relatively little attention was paid to recipients' use of arms against domestic opponents, an issue that would come back to haunt Americans in Iran. At one point in the 1973 Arab–Israeli fighting, then U.S. Secretary of State Henry Kissinger was quoted as saying that Washington would resupply Israel (there had been some calculated delay) because the United States could not afford to see American arms defeated by Soviet arms. The reputation for arms superiority had begun to rival arms suppliers' interests in the arms clients themselves, a trend that continued with the seemingly stunning successes of advanced American equipment in the 1990–1991 confrontation with Iraq.

Declining oil income, national budgetary difficulties, diminished Cold War tensions and completed arms acquisition cycles during the 1980s undercut the arms market. Indeed there was a steep decline in the volume of arms transfers (measured by value of major weapons) from 1987 through 1990, with volume remaining relatively stable and slightly recovering through the mid-1990s, only to dip again with global economic crises in the late 1990s. This is illustrated in Fig. 1, which shows the top five exporters of arms to developing countries from 1988 to 1995. The settlement of a series of regional wars that had lasted from the late 1970s through the 1980s—in Angola, Ethiopia–Somalia, Iran–Iraq, Afghanistan—contributed to the diminished demand for arms. Yet clandestine trade continued, and certain countries, such as Israel, Japan, and those in the Persian Gulf region, continued to import advanced equipment through governmental channels for reasons of threat perception and military technology. Indeed for 8 consecutive years dating back from 1996, the Pentagon underestimated the volume of actual U.S. arms deliveries through the government's Foreign Military Sales (FMS) program; in 1995 alone, according to Defense Department and Congressional Research Service figures, FMS weapon sales went to 112 countries, and while France and Russia gained on Washington in new sales agreements (which can take years to fulfill), the United States remained far and away the world leader in actual arms deliveries.

Although Russia continues to be an important player in the international arms trade, in the years immediately following the end of the Cold War, the United States

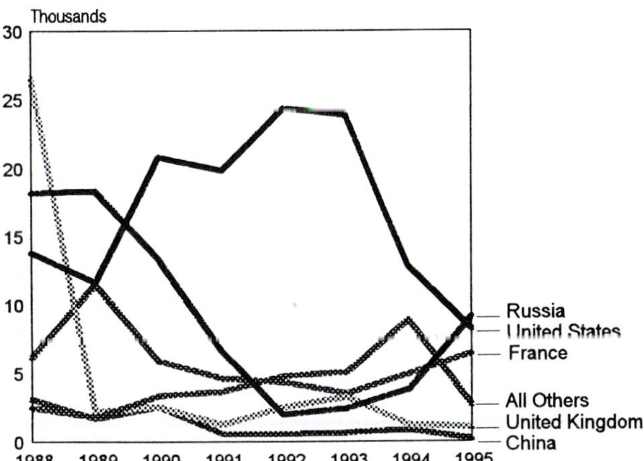

FIGURE 1 Conventional arms transfer agreements to developing nations. Data from Congressional Research Service via *Arms Trade News*, August/September 1996.

led the arms market in total sales. According to the data presented in Fig. 1, the United States was clearly dominant in arms transfer agreements from 1990 through 1994. The Bush administration began the post-Cold War era with a new policy that would allow for arms transfers to an increased number of customers, especially in the developing world. The Gulf War had provided a stage for the promotion of American arms, and as a result, they were in heavy demand. There would be significant political repercussions to some of these sales, such as the shipment of advanced aircraft to Taiwan and new arms to South Korea; in particular, the former policy would raise Chinese objections and further stimulate a significant increase of Chinese sales of even nuclear-capable equipment to customers such as Iran and Pakistan. While China's arms sales appear to be driven mainly by needs for hard currency, Beijing's participation in the five-power arms supplier agreement and in stabilizing the effects of arms shipments were undermined by such disputes.

The growing array of arms exporters, which in the 1980s included developing countries, could not be sustained given the diminished global demand. These "third tier" suppliers tended to export weapons for a certain "niche" in the market, for example, Brazil's specialty weapons such as desert fighting vehicles—built on the experience of auto assembly plants—and small aircraft. Once Iraq became engaged in conflict with the United States in 1990, it was unable to pay for contracted equipment purchases from suppliers such as Brazil. Such market disruptions are painful for major arms suppliers such as Britain or Germany, but can totally undermine less established third tier producers.

As the East bloc disintegrated at the end of the 1980s, former East bloc arms manufacturing states (e.g., the Czech Republic, Slovakia, Ukraine) entered the global market with hopes of bolstering their exports. Initial Czech promises to convert from military to consumer goods production quickly evaporated in the face of economic crisis. As Russia and its former allies sought arms transfer business, Washington alternated between attempts to gain international arms transfer control agreements and coordination on the one hand and competing in sales promotions to retain market dominance on the other.

In the wake of the Gulf War the Bush administration explored a supplier consultation agreement among the five major arms-producing states, the "P-5" talks involving the United States, Russia, China, Britain, and France. However, actual coordination and mutual restraint remained elusive in specific cases. UN-authorized arms embargoes meant to dampen the Bosnian fighting proved relatively leaky, as certain factions had the advantage of local supplies and others received help through nearby countries such as Romania and more distant interested powers such as Iran.

The Clinton administration followed its predecessor's lead with an explicitly "Economics First" arms trade policy, aimed at active commercial sales promotions designed to bolster trade balances and assist the arms industry's survival and transformation. By arguing that increased sales of conventional arms to developing countries were not a pressing strategic issue, since no coalition of states armed with conventional weapons could overwhelm the West, the U.S. government began an active promotional program to facilitate international sales while at the same time cutting governmental defense expenditures. In its "Blueprint for Change," the administration sought simultaneously to enhance U.S. industrial (export) competitiveness and national security by integrating the "Defense Industrial Base" into the commercial economy, increasing Defense Department (DOD) reliance on commercial business practices, technologies, and facilities. This was an attempt to circumvent the separate Pentagon-based specifications and standards prevailing previously, and make the entire system more commercially exploitable. Arms transfers would be promoted both in the form of finished products (entire weapon systems), but more particularly as shared technological agreements with foreign and especially allied states and firms so that U.S. designs could be "coproduced" overseas.

III. CHANGE AND CONTINUITY IN THE ECONOMICS OF ARMS TRANSFERS

As a result of the ideological transformation in the international system during the 1980s and 1990s, while the pattern of dominant exporters generally has been maintained, the nature of the arms trade has been at least partially transformed. By the late 1990s, with the market still relatively shrunken but beginning to recover, the United States and Russia had regained the position of joint leaders in arms transfers, with the United States considerably ahead, especially in terms of arms deliveries. South and East Asia came to rival the Middle East as the main venue for governmental arms shipments, as is evident in Fig. 2. With the decline in major power tensions, developing states grew to account for 78% of all arms imports ($522 billion out of a total of $669 billion) over the last decade of the Cold

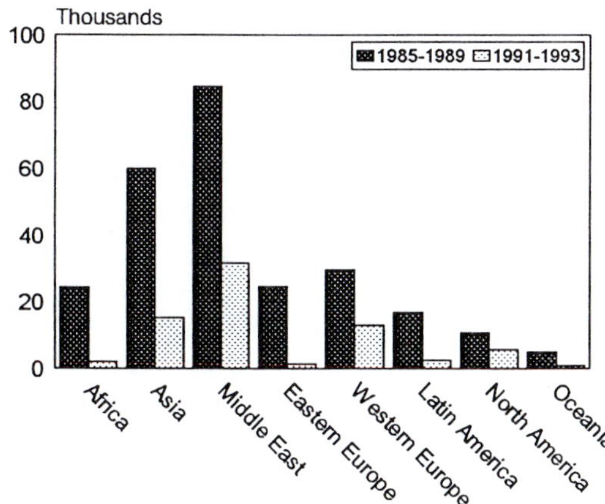

FIGURE 2 World arms imports by region (millions of current dollars). Data from US Arms Control and Disarmament Agency, *World Military Expenditures and Arms Transfers* 1990 and 1993–1994 via Neuman (1995).

War. Indeed, the stage was set for the Gulf War of 1990–1991 in the massive supplies Saddam Hussein's Iraq had received throughout the 1980s as it fought Iran (which indeed likewise received considerable Western armament). By contrast to the prominence of LDCs as arms recipients, however, on the supply side developed states exported about 90% of weapons as calculated by the U.S. Arms Control and Disarmament Agency. Thus, during and after the Cold War the international arms economy differed sharply from the rest of the international economy, which centered mostly on trade among developed states themselves.

The leading importers of arms vary year to year. Figure 3 illustrates the top ten arms importers from the year 1994. The information was compiled by the SIPRI data base utilizing the categories of items provided by the United Nations.

Market and political trends also have affected arms buyers. On the one hand, weapons are more plentifully available worldwide. States that previously purchased from the Soviet Union, particularly prime clients with security problems, such as India, now face the necessity of purchasing from various suppliers. Many such states still purchase from the former East bloc states because of low prices and weapon familiarity. Although potential dependency and restrictions on spare parts and ammunition remain, buyers with the financial ability to shop among sellers have found that they often no longer have to provide assurances about the use of the weapons. If customers are willing to settle for somewhat less advanced technologies and greater uncertainties about spare parts and technical support, they can gain quite an arsenal.

On the other hand, these arms, while plentiful, are more difficult for many to afford despite cheaper prices from some suppliers. Previous concessional terms for sales all but disappeared with the end of strategic arms transfers in the Cold War bipolar system. Suppliers are more likely to demand either cash payment or commercial credit rates. States no longer can depend on their strategic importance as a motivation for a superpower to provide arms at discounted rates, although China may still do so in response to other powers' policies. Without subsidies, many less developed states' budgets are insufficient to support major weapons purchases even at cut rate prices. States unable to afford to purchase arms outright are finding themselves with fewer diplomatic and strategic options, though they may enter the "gray markets" of covert or used equipment supplies.

China is a pivotal state in this arms trade equation, since it is at once a lower cost source of reliable military equipment and at the same time a primary importer of relatively high technology equipment, especially from its former political nemesis—Russia. Indeed, Russian sales to China in the mid-1990s, along with those to Iran, were largely responsible for Moscow's reemergence as a leading weapons dealer. China had been waiting since the days of its difficult battles with Vietnam in the 1970s to modernize its antiquated arsenal with compatible equipment. At the same time, the leadership of the Chinese People's Liberation Army evidently obtained significant subsidies to support the costs of this modernization through arms exports to the Middle East and South Asia.

Meanwhile, in line with the increased interdependence of the international economy and in an attempt

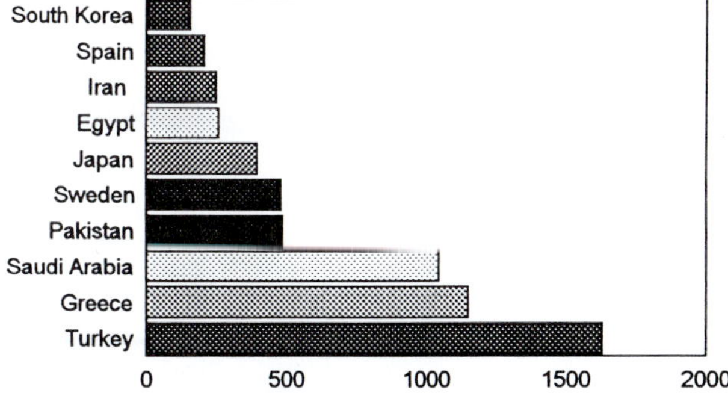

FIGURE 3 1994 arms deliveries: top 10 importers of number of items received (arms imports and licensed production). Data from Sislin and Wezeman (1995).

to reach the market more effectively, Western arms industries have increased their transnational collaboration. Figure 4 shows the dramatic increase in the number of joint ventures, strategic alliances, and mergers and acquisitions. While Western Europe has become a major source of international collaboration, other arms-producing nations are following suit, including those of the developing world. Although the arms industry, especially in the United States, remains somewhat more nationalistic than other economic sectors due in part to the perceived strategic value of arms production, the primacy of technological competitiveness in a post-Cold War setting has meant more cross-national collaboration and fewer restrictions on the sharing of technology or the transfer of weapons to various regions. This has been particularly pronounced with the establishment of joint ventures, production, and distribution schemes within Europe and across the Atlantic. The kinds of complications this presents for customers is illustrated in the complex Saudi Arabian acquisition of armored vehicles, begun in 1991 and continuing through 1995, originating in a contract with a Swiss firm, subcontracted for production to a U.S. General Motors subsidiary in Canada, and related to a separate version produced in Britain—thus involving the priorities and specifications of two different Saudi customers (National Guard and Land Forces) and four different supplier governments.

Higher weapon costs, a burden to arms purchasers, and stagnant demand also represent a lingering problem for arms manufacturing states and firms, especially in Europe. Since the 1980s it has been clear that no single European state can maintain production over the full range of advanced military technology in land, sea, and air equipment. Indeed, Clinton administration officials argued that even the United States could be forced into a cut-rate price battle with Europe and Russia to sell off excess defense goods, and that a national export policy alone is not sufficient to save industries. To reach efficient economies of scale, international joint ventures in production became commonplace, with the principle of *juste retour* (fair return) utilized to allocate shares of work and proceeds from sales, usually in proportion to the financial commitment made by the participating industrial partners and governments. The effect has been to perpetuate what many see as excess production capabilities, even though total global arms production has been falling.

Even in the face of global overcapacity in many parts of the arms industry, because of government contracting and research costs, price cutting has remained rare and largely confined to the former East bloc. Collaborative production also has been shown to increase the overall costs of research and production in particular projects, thus prompting price inflation. Among other factors affecting arms prices at any given time are the effects of wars, embargoes, and boycotts, budgetary stringency, acquisition cycles (military forces must be able to "digest" or prepare to use the equipment), and governmental changes. All of these factors introduce uncertainty in the minds of suppliers and recipients concerning the availability and "terms of trade" for arms, related equipment, supplies, and technical assistance.

Such costs and uncertainties are likely to affect the future competition among arms suppliers. It remains to be seen, for example, whether Europe and Russia will choose to compete full force against U.S. advances in expensive stealth, optical, computer, and electronic weapons technologies. Indeed, some analysts predict a near U.S. monopoly of advanced weapons production

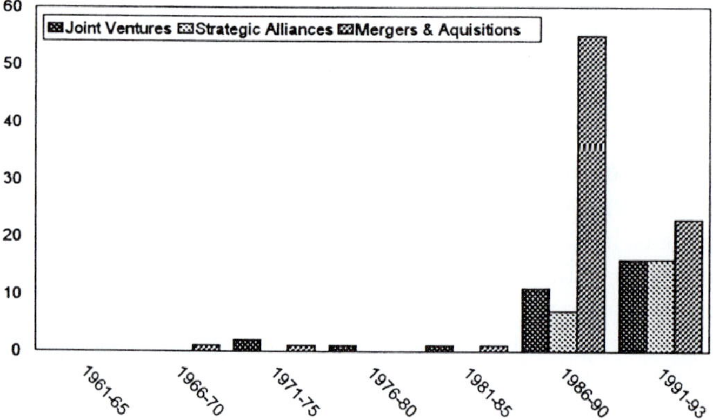

FIGURE 4 The globalization of the defense industry, 1961–1993. Data from DBP Globalization Database via Bitzinger (1994).

by the early 21st century. If Europe does compete, the pressure will increase to do so on a unified European Union (EU) basis. However, the infrastructure for a European defense industry—a common currency, common monetary and fiscal policy, common defense policy and procurement—are not yet in place. It is also likely, especially with NATO's expansion, that U.S. firms will be encouraged to develop these new technologies jointly with European partners in order to forestall full scale competition among arms producers.

Clearly, the trend in international weapons production and sales has been toward cross-national collaboration engineered mainly by the companies themselves, and less frequently as time has gone on, by governments. Since Russian and Chinese firms are late entering this mix, they will be hard pressed to attract Western partners willing to share high technology approaches and invest significant capital. Conceivably, Russia and China could find common arms production ground for joint ventures of their own in the lower cost end of the market. In a variety of ways, from the sale of government weapons factories and establishments, to corporate-led mergers, acquisitions, and coproduction agreements, the international arms business has become both more privatized and more concentrated in fewer centers of production, even as governments retain their interest in fostering technology, production capacity, defense procurement, and weapon planning. As noted, nongovernmental arms transfers, those from companies and groups, also appear to be gaining precedence and visibility.

Alongside the shift from government sales to greater company involvement, the arms being transferred are undergoing change in the post-Cold War marketplace. Increasingly, arms transfers consist not simply of finished equipment, but of components available for assembly abroad and of licenses to continue production in the recipient country or countries. Customers want greater flexibility to mount various components on weapon "platforms" such as tanks, planes, or ships. They also want the employment and economic benefits of manufacturing the weapons they purchase, or of guaranteed "counter-trade," that is, commitments that weapons-supplying states will purchase their exports in return. Only in this way can expensive foreign weapons purchases be justified to edgy domestic political constituents.

As arms manufacturing firms have come to greater prominence in structuring the arms transfer system, the United States and other major power governments have encouraged them and offered incentives to develop dual use products, as in advanced radar and computers, for example. Such products, of course, are more difficult to keep track of and restrict in their potential availability to foreign states and groups, a trend that worries some arms control advocates and defense planners. Theoretically, militarily useful technology can be identified and restricted as to distribution, but there is a greater probability of items proliferating through lack of oversight, as they fall into more hands, and as more advanced civilian technology becomes incorporated into military products in a process known as "spin-on" (a reversal of earlier disappointments with "spin off," i.e., the expectation that military developments would become commercially useful in consumer products).

Given the costs and risks associated with developing expensive new major military products, it also has been suggested that computer models of products will be developed, along with a few prototypes for testing, but that actual mass production and deployment of major weapon systems might be delayed until actual battlefield needs develop. If so, this would put greater premium on updates of existing systems and designs, along with technology and licenses for export purposes, since the most advanced concepts would not exist in finished form.

Thus, the sale of various forms of military technology, rather than fixed weapon systems themselves, appears to be a high priority for the future. Less developed states demand greater know-how in acquiring and producing (usually assembling, sometimes redesigning and "retrofitting") arms. It will remain difficult for minor powers to afford the technology to produce complete major weapons such as jet aircraft and tanks, since so many different forms of technology—materials design, electronics, munitions, engines, and so on—go into such systems. Yet they will at least want to be able to make use of these technologies, and push for "spin-ons" of their own.

Technology transfers, increasingly in private business deals outside official governmental channels, will continue to attract government interest and control attempts. The United States has expressed hopes of confining commercially useful advanced technology sharing to a relatively small "circle of friends" (presumably in Europe, the Middle East, and Asia) who would agree not to release it more widely. However, it remains unclear how effective such a transfer regime might be in restricting technology on offer to less developed states, or acquired by rival powers such as China or Russia, and in maintaining the basic hierarchy and dominance of developed states. Some have argued that the trend toward international corporate collaboration will inevitably erode these hierarchies.

IV. CONFLICT, WAR, AND THE ECONOMICS OF ARMS TRANSFERS

While arms can be collected for prestige and deterrent purposes, the "payoff" of arms acquisition is basically use in war. Only in this way do weapons become a "consumable" product. Yet the bulk of major equipment obtained by governments may never be used in battle, indeed may be too sophisticated and costly to risk in battle. Saddam Hussein dispatched many of his advanced jet fighters for safekeeping in rival Iran when he was attacked by U.S.-led coalition forces in 1991.

The relationship of armament and warfare is complicated and something of a two-way street; it is difficult to predict whether arms acquisitions and buildups precede or follow war outbreaks. Despite the "conventional wisdom" that armament leads to warfare, acquisition of newer and more advanced arms may have little to do with the probability of war initiation, either domestic or foreign. Arms are sought for a variety of domestic and foreign security reasons, as well as for technology, prestige, and bargaining influence. Advanced weapon systems may be desired mainly for reputation and to satisfy military/bureaucratic interests, while simpler arms are more exclusively relevant to battlefield needs. Nevertheless, arms acquisitions can be a catalyst for war-making by emboldening already aggressive leaders or frightening their opponents. As noted earlier, arms acquired over a long period by Iraq allowed for its subsequent attack on Kuwait, and went little noticed by the international community. Historically, it has been shown that arms races between rivals tend to precede wars, but that not all such races end in war.

In given wars, the pattern of arms acquisition tends to show peaks and valleys. Often the fighting is preceded by gradual arms buildups on one or both sides over a period of years, but these buildups seldom coincide with the exact outbreak of fighting itself. If fighting is prolonged, one or more supply replenishments may be needed, and the arrival of new arms shipments often follows major offensives, as depleted supplies are replaced. These replenishments generally appear to prolong and intensify the combat. Especially in civil wars, as much as 40% of a force's armaments may be acquired through capture, raids, and battlefield pickup.

Major ongoing wars have attracted huge weapon influxes, as in the case of the Iran–Iraq and the Afghanistan fighting of the 1980s. Supplies of both major and light weapons are stepped up; in fact, the sources of light arms are far more numerous than the relatively few producers of heavy equipment, so supplies may come from inside a country or through foreign connections. As these wars play themselves out, arms tend to be sold off and redistributed to the next war theater; in the case of Afghanistan, for example, much equipment found its way subsequently into the erupting civil conflicts of South Asia—India–Pakistan skirmishing, Pakistan's Sind province upheavals, Kashmir uprisings, northern Indian states and ethnic fighting, Sri Lanka, and so on. Thus, we find that arms cascade from war to war, as local groups gain incentive to sell them off for profit or to provide aid to friends abroad.

In the context of civil conflict, now the most frequent type of fighting reported internationally, arms have come both from foreign governments, from private or clandestine sources, and from raids on armories and battlefield capture. The conventional wisdom has maintained that governments provide arms mainly to other governments in order to maintain "stability" in key states, which often translates to maintaining the status-quo regime in power (for example for more than three decades in a state such as Zaire). One of the clear failures of such policy, in addition to that in Zaire, was the downfall of the Shah's government in Iran, then one of the best-armed Third World states. Sometimes the security threat is not well defined, so that when arms are sold to Indonesia, for example, they may be designed for external threats but end up being used in domestic campaigns, as against East Timorese rebels, thus creating human rights controversies and confronting the arms supplier with the dilemma of whether to cut them off and risk overall relations with the recipient regime.

Occasionally, as well, a government will provide arms to foreign insurgents in order to help overthrow an existing government, as the United States did during the 1980s to "contra" forces in Nicaragua (including the embarrassing Iran-Contra deal), to UNITA forces in Angola, and to Islamic militants in Afghanistan. Such supplies were driven by Cold War strategic and ideological competition, and therefore may be less frequent in the post-Cold War period. Yet for a government such as Russia's, confronted with break-away republics and complex multiparty ethnic disputes along its borders, arms supplies to various governmental and nongovernmental factions can be seen as a mechanism of influence and control. Nongovernmental arms transfers, of course, also can fuel the flames of war, and can be decisive in outcomes but generally may be less volatile because the scope of the transfers and the interests and activities involved may be far narrower than in government supplies. Government arms transfers can raise the probability of direct military intervention by the supplying state to make sure its arms investments do not go down the drain if the recipients themselves cannot win.

V. PROSPECTS FOR CONVENTIONAL ARMS CONTROL

Given the continued and increased push for arms exports, and the multifaceted nature of arms supplies—from governmental and nongovernmental sources—the possibility of controlling conventional arms proliferation appears to be diminishing even as governments talk of coordination. Indeed the arms supply system has been described as one whose rhetoric speaks of control and whose reality is chaos. Arms cascade through regions, and it is very difficult to predict or control in whose hands they end up. While optimists point to the relatively small number of major arms customers and the rise of democracies in many parts of the world (with their supposed potential for precluding violence and peacefully resolving disputes among themselves), much of the arms transfers in recent years has gone to less than fully democratic regimes. Indeed one estimate claimed that, depending upon how one counts "democracies," 84% of U.S. government-to-government weapon sales agreements during the first half of the 1990s went to undemocratic regimes. Furthermore, the widespread availability of weapons among various societal groups and nations, can foster insecurities and militaristic policies, and skew budgets away from social programs, all of which can undermine the principles of democratic rule as well as peace. Thus, the need for conventional arms control remains strong in the post-Cold War era.

Ironically, even as weapons remain plentiful, arms recipients' ability to ensure autonomy through arms imports is reduced by changes in the international arms market. Recipients have maneuvered to maintain their options and avoid overdependence on specific foreign arms suppliers. However, the end of the Cold War has diminished their options to play major powers off against each other. The number of suppliers per recipient seemed to peak during the late 1980s, and has diminished somewhat during the 1990s, indicating a recurrent rise of dependency on fewer suppliers. Thus, while arms may reverberate through the system for years, finding their way from war to war, the supply of new high technology equipment at the top of the pyramid can still be restrictive. This provides an avenue for potential arms control agreements.

However, arms transfer controls can only work if major suppliers agree on the provisions and work seriously toward their implementation, and if recipients are included in the negotiations. Given the erosion of strategic restraint on arms agreements, the commercialization and privatization of the arms supply system, and continuing production overcapacities, the prospects for such coordination are not bright. Restrictions would have to apply to two characteristics of arms transfers: "vertical proliferation," that is, the transfer of specific and often new and advanced arms technologies to regions that do not now have them; and "horizontal proliferation," that is, the spread of weapons to specific states. Little progress has been made so far in either of these areas.

Very few existing agreements have been implemented to restrict technology transfers, though there has been an attempt to carry over old Western Cold War "COCOM" rules against strategic exports in to the post-Cold War setting. Exporters have consulted especially on limiting the availability of missiles above certain ranges (the Missile Technology Control Regime) or particularly harmful forms of weaponry, such as expanding bullets and land mines. Despite such efforts, the American Director of Central Intelligence reported in 1996 that "the industrialized states in Europe and South America" along with others in the Third World and among private dealers, "supply ballistic missile technology—and in some cases entire missile systems—to developing countries around the world." America's own sales of advanced jet fighters, able to deliver weapons of mass destruction, tend to undermine Washington's credibility in objecting to missile transfers by other states.

Major power "P-5" consultations bore slight additional fruit when they were renewed in 1996, under the designation the "Wassenaar Arrangement" (after the Netherlands town where discussions began); the agenda included an international system for regular data exchanges on trade in conventional weapons and dual use equipment. Russia at first balked at requirements for early disclosure of export licenses, especially for goods denied licenses by other states. Moscow dropped these objections following the 1996 Russian elections, but the future of Russian-Western collaboration in conventional arms control depends both on the state of the Russian economy (desperation for exports) and on the state of competition with Western arms dealers (a matter of nationalist resentment in Moscow). The ongoing rivalry in arms sales between the United States, Europe, China, and Russia, with the latter feeling especially disadvantaged, constitutes a particular impediment to coordination. Washington, in turn, is reluctant to implement a formal secretariat for the Wassenaar group to monitor and report sales data until Russia complies. In general, it is difficult to specify a list of "enemies" and a definitive list of dangerous technologies, especially with so many economic incentives working against such restrictions.

With the collapse of the former Soviet Union, U.S. officials became especially worried not only about the proliferation of nuclear technology, but about the control of advanced conventional weapon technologies as well. It was feared that such products would go up for sale in the highly stressed Russian economy. U.S. intelligence officials warned that past reluctance to sell the most advanced equipment abroad had now been worn away by economic temptation and necessity, and states and individuals were more willing to create offset arrangements, barter and bribery deals to make such sales. One conceivable negative consequence of the planned eastward expansion of NATO would be to create the image of a new set of arms customers, if not arms production partners for the West to the disadvantage of their former patrons in Moscow, an image which could further impede Russian cooperation in an arms control regime. In 1996 Washington quietly dropped arms sales restrictions on several former Soviet central Asian republics, some of which have considerable oil resources and most of which have ongoing ethnic hostilities of concern to Russia.

At the same time, worries about technological proliferation are sometimes sufficient enough to produce at least unilateral arms trade restrictions. In 1996 the U.S. Congress effectively blocked several potentially lucrative U.S. sales out of concern about the introduction of advanced weapon technologies into a nearby region traditionally less subject to arms races than some others. For example, the reported sale of 15 Harpoon antiship cruise missiles to Brazil, a deal worth approximately $36 million, was canceled after key congressional leaders questioned the introduction of higher technology. The administration had been ready to proceed with the sale on the premise that Argentina already had the technology and that democracies in the region were more trustworthy than the former authoritarian regimes. The State Department also had tended to question the latter premise, which the Defense Department defended. Thus intragovernmental battles between economic interests and security and diplomatic concerns sometimes can lead to arms sale cancellations.

Unless arms purchasers also agree on the necessity for restraint, supplier controls will be controversial and probably less than fully effective. Such controls can appear to customers as thinly veiled attempts by the well armed to impose hegemony on the weak, especially if the advanced states do not themselves pledge to renounce and abandon certain advanced weapon technologies or make available those that can be most commercially rewarding in the civilian sector. While it is difficult to play major powers off against each other, customers generally can find at least one arms supplier willing to sell, although they might have to settle for a somewhat lower level of technology. Thus, in one sense a supplier imposed restrictive system is subject to being undermined, while in another sense the proliferation of technologies can be somewhat slowed. Again, though, economic desperation on the part of key suppliers can loosen the rein on technology transfers.

One lower level but very lethal technology category on which many suppliers and recipients generally have come to agree involves land mines. Significant progress was made during the 1990s in raising consciousness and harmonizing viewpoints on the long-term dangers of dispersed mines in killing and maiming innocent civilians. Military leaders in some major powers, and particularly the U.S., remained opposed to a complete ban on the availability of such antipersonnel weapons. The U.S. argued that potential battlefields such as those in Korea, could only be defended with the use of mines. Seeking a moderate position in Canadian-led international negotiations, the Clinton Administration supported the notion of some sort of ban on development and deployment of the least detectable mines and substitution with self-disarming types along with mine clearance assistance and victim assistance. Still, the U.S. failed to sign the international convention against the manufacture and use of land mines in 1997.

Going beyond land mines themselves, the general category of small and light arms drew increased international attention as their effect in civil and ethno-political wars became increasingly evident in the post-Cold War period. Although some see them as a hedge against government tyranny, the widespread availability of such weapons tends to increase the number of actors and degree of factional fighting in domestic conflicts, tends to facilitate acts of terrorism, increases casualties and vendettas, complicates peacemaking and peacekeeping efforts, and generally impedes the rule of law. These concerns culminated in the first meeting of the United Nations Panel of Governmental Experts on Small Arms in 1996. The difficulties of finding common ground in managing the flow of rifles, mortars, grenades, rocket launchers, and miniature missiles became evident in these initial efforts, which themselves were kept extraordinarily secret. The panel's charge included three issues: (1) studying types of small arms and light weapons being used in conflicts in which the UN is playing a role; (2) factors in the "excessive and destabilizing transfer" of such weapons, including illicit production and trade; (3) ways and means of preventing or reducing such destabilizing transfers and accumulations of arms, in particular in relation to conflict management. Disagreements emerged, however, as to the exact definitions of "small" and "light"—for example whether to include pistols and explosives; "destabilizing transfers" also appeared difficult to define. Some on the panel opposed looking deeply into supposed "causes" of violent conflicts, and appropriate arms control measures promised to be controversial. Experts from certain countries pressed only for exposing the problem rather than campaigning right away for solutions, while hard-pressed Latin and Asian countries, concerned about such phenomena as "narco-terrorism," tended to favor immediate emphasis on the illicit and clandestine arms trade. As arms control filters down to ever smaller arms, a process dubbed by some "micro-disarmament," more nongovernmental organizations campaign to be allowed into the discussions—groups as diverse as the American National Rifle Association and human rights organizations.

Those who looked for feasible options to carry on with the control of smaller arms have offered the following suggestions: (1) improved policing, designed to get arms off the streets of larger cities and out of the countryside of states throughout the world, allowing people to go about their daily lives with less disruption; (2) production, export, and import controls, which would pose legislative barriers to the manufacture and possession of certain types of arms—a tactic quite successful in some countries; (3) incentives to turn in weapons—having been tried in U.S. cities, Haiti, Panama, and Nicaragua with some limited success; (4) fact-finding and capacity-building assistance, through the UN or regional organizations, to states struggling against arms proliferation; (5) extending the UN Register system (see Table I) to smaller arms, which some fear would undermine the already less than universal participation in that system; (6) embargoes (see below); (7) forced disarmament of factions and fighters, particularly in peacekeeping missions—which some see as a contradiction in terms and training; (8) bans on certain types of weapons, for example, mines and blinding lasers—the arguments for which gain power as the brutal nature of the armament becomes more apparent; (9) "conditionalities" which tie the payment of foreign aid to progress in arms control or disarmament—a variant of this is a "peace tax" on weapons sales and manufacture—neither of which seems feasible very soon given policy dilemmas on the foreign assistance question; and (10) multilateral consultative mechanisms such as the Panel of Experts meetings and renewed conventional arms transfer (CAT) talks among major weapon governmental suppliers—an approach that seems to gain urgency after particular wars or crises.

Among the proposals to help control the horizontal proliferation of conventional arms has been a series of measures to promote greater "transparency," that is, to allow for public disclosure of weapon deals and thereby to foster the ability of governments and the public to track where weapons are going—at least in initial formal sales. Reminiscent of past attempts during the League of Nations to register the arms trade, the annual United Nations Arms Trade Register was inaugurated in 1993 with a surprising degree of participation by approximately 90 supplier and recipient states. The Register deals with seven categories of major weapons, but does not include all such weapons or issues of transparency in the trade of small and light arms. While many African states remained hesitant—or unable—to give precise accounts of their defense acquisitions, the majority of states in other regions have reported (with some states reporting no imports or exports for the prior year). Table I provides an example of the UN Register of Conventional Arms for 1995. It is followed with an illustration in Fig. 5 of the percentage of sales by each country within each conventional arm category.

One key goal of the Register process is to prevent, or at least expose, the "excessive and destabilizing" accumulation of arms, a task that, as seen previously, is subject to definitional and practical problems. Clearly, no enforcement or restriction mechanisms are built into the registration process, as the emphasis was laid on encouraging universality of reporting. This allows some calculus of arms preparations and replenishments, and can spark diplomatic questioning among governments as to hostile intent or threat perception, or about the whereabouts of weapons or implication of deals known through other sources to have taken place. In essence the Register is an aid in arms control verification, such as that undertaken by inspectors in Iraq (mainly looking for mass destructive weapons and encountering significant Iraqi resistance), but there is a natural reluctance to label states as arms race offenders.

The use of arms embargoes also gained prominence during the early 1990s, but with rather indifferent results in stifling violent conflict. Seldom used during the Cold War, embargoes of various types were declared in the 1990s in situations of cross-border threats (Iraq), internal wars (Somalia, Liberia, Rwanda, Sudan, and the former Yugoslavia), human rights violations (Haiti), and noncompliance with antiterrorism norms (Libya).

TABLE I

British American Security Information Council Basic Reports
28 October 1996. Number 54. ISSN 0966-9175
Summary of Supplier Submissions to the UN Register of Conventional Arms for 1995

	Battle tanks	Armored combat vehicles	Large calibre artillery systems	Combat aircraft	Attack helicopters	Warships	Missiles and missle launchers
Argentina	0	0	18	0	0	0	0
Belgium	0	118	0	1	0	0	0
Canada	0	294	0	0	0	0	0
China	51	20	0	1	0	0	18
Czech Rep.	0	62	70	21	0	0	0
Finland	0	31	0	0	0	0	0
France	25	0	0	3	6	0	11
Germany	0	335	15	0	20	6	0
Israel	0	0	0	3	0	0	20
Italy	0	0	18	0	0	0	0
Kazakhstan	0	0	0	6	0	0	0
Netherlands	0	0	0	0	0	1	0
Poland	72	0	0	0	0	0	0
Rep. of Korea	0	47	0	3	0	0	0
Romania	0	81	1	0	0	0	0
Russian Fed.	0	451	210	46	0	1	0
Slovakia	6	57	6	0	0	0	0
South Africa	0	43	0	0	0	0	0
Switzerland	0	10	0	0	0	0	0
Ukraine	64	8	0	4	0	0	159
United Kingdom	12	137	55	12	1	1	0
United States	416	1089	152	128	25	0	3033
TOTAL	646	2783	545	228	52	9	3241

The United States also sought international bans against Iran, but compliance was confined mainly to NATO allies, with Russia, for economic and geopolitical reasons, constituting a major defector. In general, the targets of embargoes did not abandon objectionable policies; arms deliveries may have been delayed or detoured but were not precluded, and the pacifying effects of the arms bans were sporadic at best. Nevertheless, some encouraging signs emerged, as in progress by the EU in creating a standardized list of items that should fall under embargoes of varying degrees of comprehensiveness and intensity.

It is very difficult to isolate or "quarantine" a given internal dispute, particularly as factions may have friends across nearby borders. A state such as Croatia, for example, was able to play a key role, probably with the knowledge if not the blessing of Washington, in routing weapons to the Bosnian government despite an official UN embargo. Many onlookers became sympathetic to the notion that the Muslim-dominated Bosnian government should be allowed to catch up to the better armed Bosnian Serbs (also an interest of Croatia's), but not that it should be so emboldened as to go on a binge of "ethnic cleansing" of its own. Such precise balances are indeed difficult to achieve, and put arms suppliers among "strange bedfellows"; in Bosnia's case many became alarmed at the growing role of Iran in the arms pipeline, and NATO itself felt compelled to send in troops.

Recognizing that the arms trade will continue at least in some forms as long as economic incentives allow, many arms control advocates, including a number in the U.S. Congress, have begun to suggest a code of conduct for that trade. Public disclosure of arms deals, through the UN Register, the Wassenaar Arrangements, and other forums, tends to breed such demands. Early in 1996, for example, Britain's Labour Party, recalling U.K. sales to Iraq during the 1980s, called for the EU to adopt a code restricting conventional arms sales, specifically to bar sales to regimes that "would use them for repressive purposes or to threaten to invade neighboring countries." By April 1997, the EU was attempting to combat illegal weapons exports through a common policy focused on the difficulty in tracking the movements of conventional arms. Other advocates, including Costa Rica's Nobel Laureate Oscar Arias, have proposed corresponding codes of conduct for arms purchasing nations. Sometimes stemming from political debates inside major power capitals, and sometimes from the pressure of citizen groups, the emphasis here is on potential use of arms in warfare and human rights abuses. However, the questions of legitimate self-defense, of gaining common definitions of human rights (economic versus political versus social rights), and of commercial sales interests are imported into these debates as well. If adopted, such codes would lack enforcement mechanisms, and might or might not gain the status of international law; they are bound to have escape clauses that would be put into contention in specific cases. Nevertheless, the development of accepted norms and standards leading to greater legal standing and authority is as imperative in this field of international commerce as in any other, if not more so.

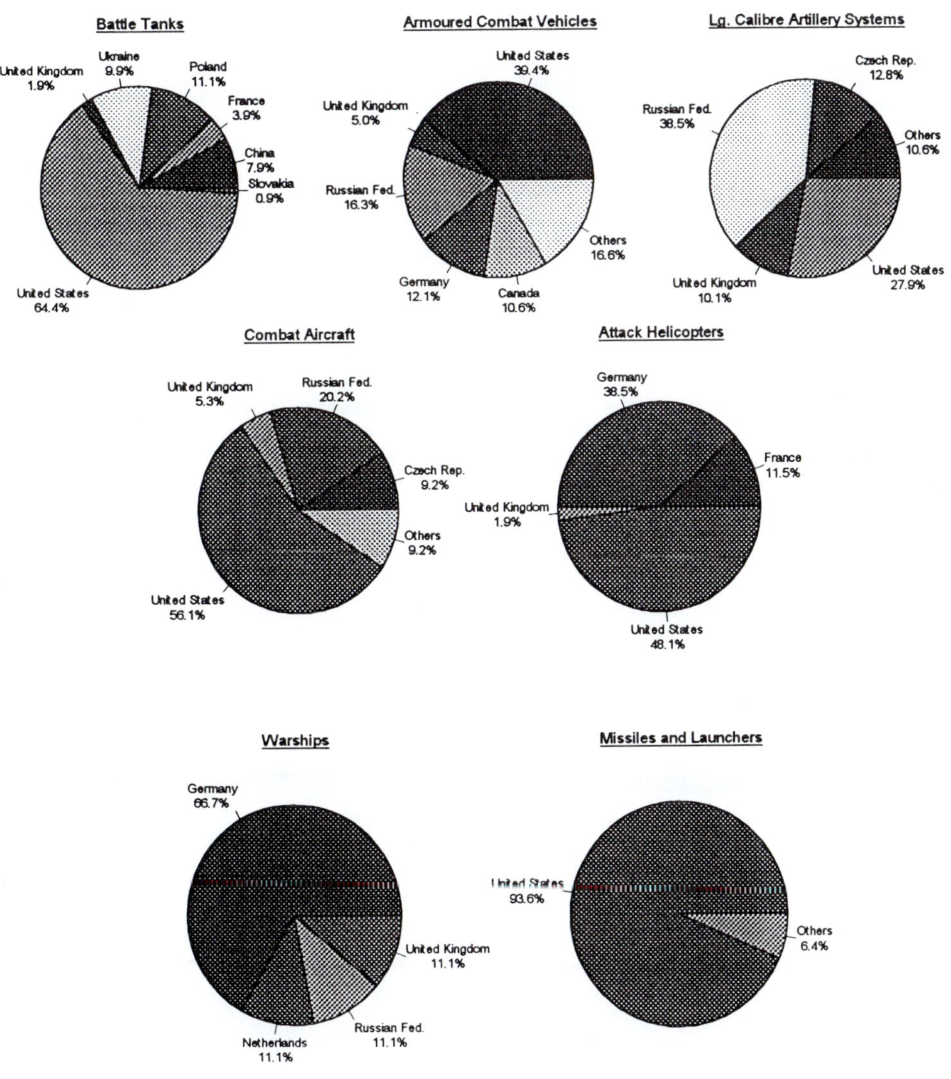

FIGURE 5 Weapons categories for UN Register, 1995.

Also See the Following Articles

ARMS CONTROL • COLD WAR • MILITARY–INDUSTRIAL COMPLEX, CONTEMPORARY SIGNIFICANCE • MILITARY–INDUSTRIAL COMPLEX, ORGANIZATION AND HISTORY

Bibliography

Arms Trade News. (*passim*, 1996). Washington, DC: Council for a Livable World Education Fund.

Brzoska, M., & Pearson, F. (1995). *Arms and warfare: Escalation, deescalation, negotiation*. Columbia, SC: University of South Carolina Press.

Brzoska, M., & Pearson, F. (1994, September). "Developments in the global supply of arms: Opportunity and motivation. *Annals, American Association of Political and Social Sciences*, 58–72.

Catrina, C. (1988). *Arms transfers and dependence*. New York: Taylor and Francis/UNIDIR.

Cupitt, R. T. (1993, March). The political economy of arms exports in post-communist societies: The cases of Poland and the CSFR. *Communist and Post-Communist Studies*, *26*, 87–103.

Defense News. (*passim*). Springfield, VA: Army Times Publishing Co.

Dyer, S. L. (1996). UN register data compilation. *Basic Reports*. Washington, DC: British American Security Information Council, October.

Fact Sheet. (1996). Washington, DC: Peace Action Education Fund, November.

Goldring, N. J. (1996, October). UN Experts' panel on small arms faces obstacles. *Basic Reports*. Washington, DC: British American Security Information Council.

Hull, A., & Markov, D. (1996, March). *The changing nature of the international arms market*. Alexandria, VA: Institute for Defense Analysis.

Kapstein, E. B. (1994, May/June). America's arms-trade monopoly: Lagging sales will starve lesser suppliers. *Foreign Affairs*, *73*, 13–19.

Keller, W. W. (1995). *Arm in arm: The political economy of the global arms trade*. New York: Basic Books.

Kolodziej, E., & Pearson, F. (1989, April). The political economy of making and marketing arms: A test for the systemic imperatives of order and welfare. *Occasional Papers* 8904. St Louis: Center for International Studies, University of Missouri-St. Louis.

Krause, K. (1992). *Arms and the state: Patterns of military production and trade*. New York: Cambridge.

Laurance, E., & Meek, S. (1996, September). The new field of micro-disarmament: Addressing the proliferation and buildup of small arms and light weapons. Brief 7, Bonn International Center for Conversion.

Mandel, R. (1996). *Exploding myths about global arms transfers*. Unpublished paper.

Neuman, S. G. (1995, September). The arms trade, military assistance, and recent wars: Change and continuity. *The Annals of the American Academy*, *541*, 47–73.

Neuman. (1984, Winter). International stratification and Third World military industries. *International Organization*, *38*, 167–197.

Pearson, F. S. (1995). *The global spread of arms: Political economy of international security*. Boulder, CO: Westview.

Pearson, F. S. (1989). The correlates of arms importation. *Journal of Peace Research*, *26*(2), 153–163.

Pearson, F. S. (1986, Summer). "Necessary evil': Perspectives on West German arms transfer policies. *Armed Forces and Society*, *12*, 531–533.

Pearson, F. S. (1983, Spring). The question of control in British defence sales policy. *International Affairs*, 59, 223–228.

Pearson, F. S. (1981, May). U.S. arms transfer policy: The feasibility of restraint." *Arms Control*, 2, 24–65.

SIPRI Yearbook. (*passim*). Oxford: Oxford University Press/Stockholm International Peace Research Institute.

Sislin, J., & Pearson, F. (1996, Winter). Arms and mediation in ethno-political disputes. *Peace Reviews* 8.

Smaldone, J. P. (1995, November). *Military burden, conflict, and arms control in sub-Saharan Africa: Puzzles, paradoxes and prescriptions*. Paper presented at the 38th Annual Meeting of the African Studies Association, Orlando, FL.

The Defense Monitor. (*passim*). Washington, DC: Center for Defense Information.

Volman, D. (1996, April). *The light weapons trade in Africa*. Paper presented at the International Studies Association Annual Meeting, San Diego, CA, April.

Assassinations, Political

Nachman Ben-Yehuda
Hebrew University

GLOSSARY

Assassinations Killings of individuals for political reasons by individuals and/or illicit or illegal groups.

Executions Killings of individuals by the state.

Terror Indiscriminate killings of individuals or groups by the state.

Constructionism A theory that examines how we construct meanings.

THE NATURE AND PATTERNS OF POLITICAL ASSASSINATIONS constitute one of the most interesting, challenging, yet frustrating enigmatic riddles for social science research. Unfortunately, the area of political assassinations has lacked clear definitions and systematic research. Typical works in this area can be divided into four categories. Those that: (1) discuss a large number of cases, an encyclopedic type of work; (2) focus in depth on one particular case (e.g., Lincoln, Aldo Moro, Kennedy); (3) focus on a few selected cases in depth; (4) concentrate on patterns of assassinations in specific cultures. The purpose of this entry is to develop a *conceptual* and analytical understanding of the very nature of political assassinations.

I. ASSASSINATIONS AND ASSASSINS

The word "assassin" has an Arabic origin, and refers to a particular pattern of killing that was practiced by an Islamic religion cult that called itself the Ismaili. As Rapoport points out, the goal of the early Ismaili was to help purify Islam by terror, and by killing major officials who the Ismaili saw as corrupt and wrongdoers. The Ismailis, however, had no exclusive rights on this form of killing. Rapoport delineates other ancient movements that used assassination as part of their struggle. Well-known groups are the Thugs, who killed for Kali, or the Sicariis. Both Ford and Rapoport reveal accounts about the practice of political assassinations which can be found in Biblical times, during the Greco-Roman period, in medieval Europe, and in other times, cultures, and places. Nonetheless, and as Ford, Lewis, and

Rapoport detail, the order of Assassins is probably the most famous of them all.

Following the death of the Islamic prophet, Mohammed, in 632 the Caliphate, which institutionalized his charisma, was created. Abu Bakr became the Khalifa. There were those, though, who disagreed, and felt that Ali—the cousin and son-in-law of the Prophet, had a better and stronger claim than did Abu Bakr. This particular dissenting group became known as the *Shiatu Ali* (Ali's party), and later as *Shia.* That early conflict gave birth to a most important cleavage in Islam.

Around the year 760 a particular group broke away from Shiism. They called themselves Ismailis, after Ismail, son of Jafar al-Sadiq, great-grandson of Ali and Fatima. At the end of the eleventh century, a secret society of the Ismailite sect was founded in Persia by Hassan-i Sabbah. Hassan-i Sabbah was born, at an unknown date, in the Persian city of Qum, and died in 1124. Hassan traveled extensively in the Middle East, North Africa, and Egypt, winning converts. His goal was to disseminate heterodox doctrine and battle the Seljuq Empire.

Hassan and his followers conquered (1090–1091) the fortress of Alamut in the Elburz mountains (northern Persia). It became the headquarters of Hassan's sect and Hassan himself became known as the Old Man of the Mountain, or the Grand Master. Hassan apparently felt that Islam could, and should, be purified by assassinating in a systematic way, all of its major officials, defined by him as corrupt. He and his sect have thus developed the "art of assassination."

They were quite successful in spreading what Rapoport referred to as "fear and trembling." He chose young, intelligent, and able people, full of enthusiasm and faith. They were trained and taught the principles of Hassan's interpretation of the faith and then sent on their deadly missions.

The groups of these young men were called *Fidais.* There are uncorroborated reports (traced to Marco Polo) that Hassan's young assassins, at Alamut, were led into a so-called "garden of paradise" where they consumed hashish. The purpose of this supposed ritual was to persuade the converts that paradise awaits them, even if they get caught and executed after carrying out their assassination plots. Hence the name Hashishin became synonymous with Hassan's sect. As Ford, Lewis, and Rapoport point out, there are indeed some good reasons to suspect the validity and truthfulness of the story about the hashish consumption.

The Assassins, as they became known to the West by the Crusaders, were quite successful, and gained almost full control of Syria. Furthermore, in the Muslim context the basis of power was personal. When a Sultan, or an Amir, were assassinated (or died), the base of power risked disintegration (Rapoport, 1984). Assassinations within this cultural context were a powerful weapon.

In the 12th century the Assassins were led by the last Grand Master—Rukh-al-Din Khurshah. The end of Rukh, and of the Assassins, came under the double assault of the Mongols and of the Mamluk Sultan of Egypt, Baybars. As the fortress of Alamut fell (1256) and later other Assassins' strongholds too, thousands of Assassins where killed. That was the end of that ruthless organization. The tales about the Assassins were brought to Europe by the Crusaders.

The assassins developed an organized attempt, and policy, that exhibited one of the most important features characterizing political assassinations: a painstakingly and nonrandom selection of a target, coupled with a carefully planned and executed assassination plot. As Rapoport notes, what made this pattern of assassination so very interesting and unique is the fact that the assassins killed unprovoked, in a particularly vile manner, and after they had befriended their victim.

The word "assassination" in English, following the Ismaili practice, was focused not on the person attacked so much as in the *manner* of attack. It was conceptualized to be a premeditated form of killing, committed by stealth or by lying in wait—the opposite of a duel. The victim was not always a prominent person, and the assassin was often hired. There generally was not a personal relationship between assassin and victim. Rapoport conceptualized the Ismaili assassins' main "crime," in this context, as one of betraying trust and ignoring natural sentiments created by an intimate relationship. It must be the combination of planning the assassination *and* the intimate relationship that must have been so bizarre. After all, most typical homicides take place between people who know each other fairly intimately.

It is not too difficult to realize that a dazzling variety of phenomena may exist under the names political assassination, assassination, political murder, individual terror, and the like. In fact, one may even claim that the interpretations of the phenomena we refer to as "political assassinations" are so diverse and culturally dependent that we may be in a better analytical position if we do not attempt to define it altogether. Indeed, Kirkham, Levy, and Crotty chose exactly this approach. Unfortunately, without a definition no real or precise empirical and analytical progress can be accomplished.

II. THEORETICAL BACKGROUND FOR UNDERSTANDING POLITICAL ASSASSINATIONS

Rapoport delineates the three justifications that developed in the West for assassinations. The *first* was a purely instrumental one, developed by the Greeks and Romans, stipulating that the moral value of an assassination depends entirely on the end(s) achieved. The *second*, developed by Christian philosophers, stipulates that political assassination is evil in itself, but nonetheless can be justified on the grounds that it can prevent a greater evil. The *third* was developed solely to justify an assassination that was part of a terrorist campaign. Participation in an assassination was seen as a good thing in itself regardless of the particular results achieved.

Some scholars such as Kirkham, Levy, and Crotty associated political assassinations with terrorism and political instability in particular. The value of this approach is that it does *not* attribute assassinations primarily to "crazy" and "irrational" individuals. It negates, for the most part, what Clarke (1982:5) labeled as the "pathological theory of assassination," namely theorizing that "assassins are acutely disturbed persons who suffer from such a diminished sense of self that their lives become increasingly isolated, bitter and unbearable." This approach received much support from a few studies that suggested that most of those "who have assassinated, or attempted to assassinate Presidents of the United States ... have been mentally disturbed persons who did not kill to advance any rational political plan" (Kirkham, Levy, and Crotty, 1970:78). However, this position can be easily challenged, both on the grounds of questionable diagnoses and as not accurately characterizing assassins who were sent by groups.

Some prominent research of assassinations such as that of Kirkham, Levy, and Crotty, Crotty, and Clarke views assassinations as a systemic property of specific cultures at particular times. The conditions under which political assassinations flourish hence becomes an important issue for these researchers.

It may well be that destabilization and chaos result from many political assassinations, but the reverse is conceivable too.

Havens, Leiden, and Schmitt point out that the level of societal institutionalization of the political system is a crucial variable. Stable societies experience fewer political assassinations, and the systemic impact of such events—if they happen—is minimal. Rapoport offers a dissenting position noting that the extraordinarily high number of assassinations of U.S. presidents compared to that of Latin America suggests that the centralization of administrative *and* symbolic authority in the hands of one person may be a more important condition.

III. DEFINITIONS OF ASSASSINATIONS IN THE LITERATURE

The relevant literature does not provide a crystallized consensus regarding this issue. A major reason for this confusion may be that it is not at all clear whether different researchers were defining the same phenomenon. For example, political assassinations were discussed in the contexts of terror, mass murder, political executions, and the like. And, yet, the issue of defining the phenomenon of political assassinations has kept a small army of scholars busy. It is vitally important to examine and understand the deliberations here because different definitional approaches make different assumptions and create altogether different databases, and consequently give rise to incongruous conclusions. By examining critically the different important definitions of assassinations we stand to gain much better insights and understandings about the complex analytical nature of this phenomenon.

As we shall see below, the different definitional approaches to political assassinations focus on a range that spans from specific to collective targets, from prominent to any target, from state-sponsored to individual and group killings, and from actual to attempted assassinations. This theoretical mixture provides, no doubt, a good prescription for a decent analytical chaos. Following our critical examination of the different definitions, we will be in a better position to suggest a comprehensive new definition.

One frequently quoted definition was suggested by Lerner (1930:27): "Assassination refers to those killings or murders, usually directed against individuals in public life, motivated by political rather than by personal relationships ... Assassination is the deliberate, extralegal killing of an individual for political purposes...." Kirkham, Levy, and Crotty (1970), writing some 40 years after Lerner, stated that "we do not undertake to define precisely what is meant by an 'assassination,' nor do we limit consideration ... to a particular consistent definition of 'assassination'. There are at least three separate elements woven into the concept of "assassination" which identify it as a particular kind of murder: (1) a target that is a prominent political figure (2) a political motive for the killing (3) the potential political impact of the death or escape from death, as the case may be ..." (p. 1).

Padover (1943:680) defined assassinations as: "the trucidation ... of a political figure without due process of law." Havens, Leiden, and Schmitt (1970:4) suggest that assassination refers to "the deliberate, extralegal killing of an individual for political purposes." Hurwood (1970, 1) chose a broader approach, stating that "what generally distinguished assassination from ordinary homicide ... was an assumption that the assassin acted on behalf of others, or out of fanatical devotion to some cause or faith." Crotty (1971, 8) broadened this approach even further by defining political assassination as "the murder of an individual, whether of public prominence or not, in an effort to achieve political gains."

Lester avoided the problem of the definition by stating that: "Assassins fall into three categories: murders by a hired killer who has no personal involvement with the victim, conspiracies for political change, and killings based on personal animosities" (1986:216). Obviously, the emphasis on a "hired assassin" and on categorization evades the core question—what *is* a political assassination?

The broadest definition (and thus less useful) is Ford's (1985): "Assassination is the intentional killing of a specified victim, or group of victims, perpetrated for reasons related to his (her, their) public prominence and undertaken with a political purpose in view" (p. 2).

Ivianski prefers the term "individual terror." Although he never defines the opposite ("collective terror"?), the definition he provides is: "a system of modern revolutionary violence aimed at leading personalities in the government or the Establishment (or any other human targets). The motivation is not necessarily personal but rather ideological or strategic" (1977, 50). In 1981 he stated that "individual terror" was different from political assassination in that the former aimed to hit the state or the regime that was represented by the target, and not the target per se (p. 409). However, already on the first page of his 1977 paper he falls into what may be an unavoidable trap when stating that: "One act of 'individual terror' [is] the assassination of Archduke Francis Ferdinand at Sarajevo. ..." Thus, although Ivianski may give the impression that he discusses a theory which is aimed to explain late 19th-century terror (especially Russian and the infamous *Narodnaya Volya*), he is in fact discussing political assassinations proper as well (also in his later work). If we confine his definition only to 19th-century terrorism (which is doubtful), than obviously fewer generalizations can be made. If we do not, then his definition is too broad and lacks specificity.

Political assassination is not just "violence," it is the use of deadly force. Also, it does not have to be defined as "revolutionary" (e.g., James Earl Ray's assassination of Martin Luther King on April 4, 1968; Sirhan Sirhan's June 5, 1968, assassination of Robert F. Kennedy; the killing of fleet admiral Isoruku Yamamoto, planner of the December 7, 1941, Japanese preemptive strike on Pearl Harbor, by a squadron of U.S. P-38 Lightning fighters on April 18, 1943; Yigael Amir's assassination of Yitzhak Rabin on November 4, 1995). Furthermore, Ivianski fails to take notice of the fact that governments may in fact commit acts of political assassinations (e.g., the assassination of Leon Trotsky on August 20, 1940, outside Mexico City), not to mention individual terror and terrorism in general and genocide and mass murder (for more on this see Ben-Yehuda's discussions).

Although Turk is quick to point out that motivation is extremely difficult to establish, he nevertheless defines assassination as: "a politically motivated killing in which victims are selected because of the expected political impact of their dying" (1983, 83). Turk's definition is particularly useful because it emphasizes the *selection* of the victim.

Rapoport suggested an elaborate and thoughtful definition of an assassin that: "means murderer but more than that, it means an unprovoked murderer who kills in a particularly vile manner. In the common law assassination is murder committed without warning by stealth, surprise, or lying in wait. The assailant has been hired for the occasion, or he undertakes it for political purposes. In any case the victim, usually though not necessarily a prominent person, has not provoked the assault by offering the assassin a personal offense" (1971, 4).

An attempt to develop a social perspective of assassinations, based on Smelser's theory of collective behavior, is provided by Wilkinson. This theory, however, is complex and difficult to operationalize and consequently has not become widely used.

It is thus evident that defining/characterizing the concept of political assassination has become an Herculean and Sisyphian task. Different definitions focus on a range that goes from a specific target to a collective target, and from a "prominent" political target to any target. Such an analytical mix is not very useful.

IV. TOWARD A CONSTRUCTIONIST DEFINITION OF POLITICAL ASSASSINATIONS

Attempting to solve the inherent and essential problematics involved in conceptualizing political assassinations, Ben-Yehuda developed a social constructionism perspective. Using this particular approach enables the researcher to bypass almost all the problems mentioned above and make the important distinction between the act of assassinating and its cultural interpretation. First and foremost, it views political assassinations as a form of violent and aggressive human behavior focused on taking somebody else's life against the wish of that person. Akin to other, and perhaps similar, forms of behavior such as murder, killing, blood-revenge, executions and the like.

A. Taking Somebody Else's Life

The biblical injunction "Thou Shall Not Murder" could be interpreted to mean that taking another human being's life is a universal crime. It is not. As Nettler and Lester point out, such an act is defined differently in different times and/or cultures. It is also defined differently in the same culture. Hence different types of accounts and rhetorical devices are used to make such an act culturally meaningful, that is, "explainable" or "justifiable." These, in turn, depend on the interpretation of the circumstances. Thus, while the act of taking somebody's life against his or her wish may appear to the lay person as universally forbidden, the interpretation of such acts is culturally dependent and hence, very relative. Consequently, taking somebody's life is not universally forbidden. Killing other people, in short, is not always interpreted as a negative and stigmatized act—it can certainly be interpreted as positive as in wars.

The type of rhetorical device that will be used to describe the death of any particular actor will, first of all, depend on whether we view that death as natural. A natural death would usually mean that the actor has finished what we may consider his/her natural life span and dies, without any intentional (e.g., suicidal, criminal), or unintentional (e.g., accidental), help from himself or herself or another person. The rhetorical devices "deceased," "passed away," "died in an accident," or simply "died," would typically be employed in this case.

When death is not defined as "natural," other rhetorical devices are invoked. One very basic distinction in this case is whether the potential victim agreed, or even willed and wished, to die. If the answer to this question is positive, then a small pool of rhetorical devices becomes available. For example, "suicide" and its variations (e.g., Japanese culture had at least three different forms of suicide: Hara-kiri, Kamikaze, Kaiten), euthanasia (with consent) and the like. This category, however, is not very relevant to political assassinations.

The other possibility is that the potential victim does not agree, or wish, to die. The act of taking the victim's life against his or her wish thus becomes a typically forceful and violent act. In such a case, another cultural pool of rhetorical devices becomes available to make culturally meaningful interpretation of the act.

When a situation is defined using the rhetoric device of war, then taking other humans' life is not only excusable, it is mandatory for so-called "combat soldiers." It is even rewarded by powerful symbols and can, perhaps, be defined as "positive deviance." Hence, under normal combat circumstances, we do not say that a soldier murdered his enemy, or vice versa. Wars, however, do have some rules, and some acts of taking other peoples' lives—even in a war situation—may in fact be regarded as murder. Killing prisoners of war is indeed considered a war crime, as, for example, the massacre of 86 American prisoners of war near Malmedy on December 17, 1944, by Nazi soldiers from SS *Standartenfuhrer* [colonel] Joachim Peiper's special battle group during the Nazi Ardennes campaign. Peiper himself probably perished when his house in Traves (France) was set ablaze by anonymous people on July 14, 1976.

Such rhetorical devices as "infanticide," "child homicide," "self-defense," or "blood revenge" in some societies, as well as "genocide" and "lynching" may also be used to justify and/or explain acts of taking other peoples' lives, as well as such other ritualistic situations defined as vendettas, human sacrifices, and duels.

The famous rhetorical device homicide may itself be classified into criminal and noncriminal. Each of these devices can be further divided into such finer distinctions as murder, voluntary manslaughter, involuntary manslaughter or criminally negligent homicide. Furthermore, some view abortion as homicide. Hence, cultures provide a variety of rhetorical devices, vocabularies of motives and accounts (some of which are institutionalized in the law) aimed at defining differentially acts of taking other peoples' lives.

There are two sets of variables that may be of help to get us out of the problematics of the definition. First, the term "assassination" is focused on the specificity of the act. Unlike the impersonal and indiscriminate acts of terrorism, political assassination is selective, discriminate, and has a very specific target.

Second, the term assassination implies something very different from criminal homicide. The rhetorical device "assassination" is used primarily in noncriminal contexts and is closely affiliated to power, politics, and morality in an explicit way. Hence, while a "typical murder" (as a specific subcategory of criminal homicide) refers to something that is most frequently unplanned and tends to occur between intimates, not strangers, a "political assassination" refers to something that is diametrically opposed: it is planned and typically takes place between strangers. Thus one important element in the characterization of "assassination" is what assassination is not—it is *not* a "typical" murder.

"Political assassination" is a name given to a particular form of taking somebody else's life against his or her wish. Therefore, we have first to delineate the theoretical parameters that are needed to understand those characteristics that constitute this distinct form of killing.

B. Political Assassination Events and Their Interpretation

We should distinguish between the *act* of assassinating, and its *interpretation.*

Kirkham, Levy, and Crotty suggest the use of an important and useful term: assassination events. The term event is useful for two reasons. First, it helps to demarcate the *act* from its *cultural interpretation.* Second, it helps reveal the important distinction between executions and assassinations. The concept refers to:

> ... an act that consists of a plotted, attempted or actual, murder of a prominent political figure (elite) by an individual (assassin) who performs this act in other than a governmental role. This definition draws a distinction between political execution and assassination. An execution may be regarded as a political killing, but it is initiated by the organs of the state, while an assassination can always be characterized as an illegal act ... (1970, Appendix A).

A *political assassination event* thus refers to the act of taking someone's life against the wish of that person. The next question obviously is what makes this form of killing unique? How is such an event interpreted culturally in a way that makes sense to members of that culture? The working definition regarding the nature of political assassinations and executions which emerges from the analytical discussion so far (and used empirically in Ben-Yehuda's 1993 study) is as follows:

> The characterization of a homicidal event as a political assassination or execution is a social construction. It is a rhetorical device which is used to socially construct and interpret (that is, to make a culturally meaningful account of) the discriminate, deliberate, intentionally planned, and serious attempt(s), whether successful or not, to kill a specific social actor for political reasons having something to do with the political position (or role) of the victim, his symbolic-moral universe, and with the symbolic-moral universe out of which the assassin/s act(s). This universe generates the legitimacy and justifications required for the act, which are usually presented in quasi-legal terms. However, decisions to assassinate are typically *not* the result of a fair legal procedure, based on a "due process."

Let us look closely at this definition. First, political assassination is a name (or term) that we use to interpret (and, for some, to justify) a particular act of killing. This name helps us to make sense of what otherwise is a terrible situation, and to construct a culturally meaningful account. The point is that there is no "real" or "objective" meaning to the term precisely because meaning is negotiable and culturally dependent. The term is socially constructed and interpreted. It means that the interpretation of a political assassination event is not objectively given but culturally constructed. What for one person (or group) is a bona fide political assassination may be interpreted as a simple murder for another person (or group). For example, the assassination of Baron Walter Edward Guinness Moyne, British minister resident in the Middle East, on November 6, 1944, in Cairo by two members of Lehi (a prestate Jewish Israeli underground group) was defined by the British as an act of simple murder. However, the very same act was defined by Lehi as a legitimized and justified act of "individual terror." Using the term "rhetorical device" in the definition enables us to keep some distance from the event itself and yet give room for a real and indigenous cultural interpretation. This term also helps us transcend the many different and divergent definitions of political assassinations and suggest a more unified approach.

Second, political assassinations are *not* "crimes of passion." They constitute attempts to kill that are very carefully planned. This is why the definition emphasizes the deliberate and the intentional. Third, political assassinations are target specific. It is the *specificity* of the target that distinguishes political assassinations from other acts of indiscriminate terrorism. Fourth, the definition emphasizes that the attempt to assassinate must be serious. It is not important whether the attempt was successful or not (that is, whether the specific target died or not). The "seriousness" of the attempt can be translated into four distinct types (more on this later): preplanned, planned, unsuccessful and successful. Fifth, the "reasons" for which the potential victim is targeted are political, and associated with the political role, or position, of the victim. For example, the assassinations of both Egyptian President Anwar Sadat (October 6, 1981) and Israeli Prime Minister Yitzhak Rabin

(November 4, 1995) for their leading roles in the Israeli–Arab peace process. This definition does not assume that the victim must be a prominent target. The elements of power and morality enter this definition through the front door because this part of the definition emphasizes that political assassinations events are the expression of power in the form of lethal force, whose use is justified on the basis of political–moral reasoning.

Sixth, the symbolic–moral universe out of which the assassin acts, and of which the victim is part, is a crucial element in the interpretation. The elements of power and morality place assassination events squarely within the area of politics and deviance. Seventh, while the justifications for political assassinations tend to be presented by the assassins in quasi-legal rhetorical devices, decisions to assassinate are typically *not* the result of a procedure that is based on a "due process." The victim typically does not stand a fair chance to defend him or herself properly. This definition does not make a distinction whether the assassin was hired or not, and it does not stipulate the existence of specified technical methods (or procedures) of killing (e.g., whether the assassin befriends his future victim). Finally, the definition neither makes assumptions about the relationships between assassin and victim; nor that the assassination be (or not) the result of a situational provocation.

It is often (but not always) in the interest of the assassin to publicize, explain and justify the act because in this way the function of demarcating the boundaries of symbolic–moral universes is accomplished.

C. The Issue of Legitimacy

"Assassination, no matter how narrowly or broadly defined, belong among a larger class of politically aggressive and violent behavior" (Kirkham, Levy, and Crotty, 1970, 164). It involves the use of power and its legitimation. This legitimation is either anchored in a different symbolic-moral universe than that of a state or a country, usually opposing or disagreeing with it in a most fundamental way (e.g., the assassinations of Lincoln, Gandhi, Sadat, Rabin); or in a secret process activated by specific organizations (or individuals) of a state (e.g., a secret intelligence service, e.g., the executions of Trotsky, Yamamoto) or its equivalent (in terms of legitimizing the act). Thus, Hurwood points out that only the king had the authority to give the legitimacy (and the order) for a political execution. Hence, when the Israeli secret service set out to execute members of "Black September" (following the massacre of Israeli athletes at the 1972 Munich Olympics), the authorization for those acts came from the Prime Minister. According to the *Los Angeles Times* (April 12, 1989) it also appears that in the United States decisions to commit political executions involve the highest echelons of the military and political elites.

A country, a state, sometimes even a society, has—or generates—the legitimacy to use power. A country may legitimize the use of deadly force in war, death penalty or define other situations where taking actor/s' life is considered legitimate, even mandatory. Such legitimacy, however, can be generated also by much smaller and integrated ideological groups.

The existence, or nonexistence, of legitimacy (and who grants it) refers to a few related questions:

a. Whether a state or a country, through its official organs, approves a particular act of killing.
b. How is the decision arrived at; secretly or through an open public and fair due process (e.g., where a proper defense is presented and the potential victim has a chance of presenting his/her case in a persuasive way).
c. Whether the potential assassin accepts the right of that state, or country, to give such a legitimacy.

Relating the variables of the specificity of the target to the legitimation to use deadly force enables us to draw a classificatory scheme: as shown in Table I.

Table I cross-tabulates two distinct analytical levels: a state and an individual. No need for an intervening level variable is called for because the two levels are sufficient to explain the different possible outcomes.

On the left side of the table two questions are answered: (a) Whether the country/state approves, or does not approve, the assassination/killing; (b) Whether the potential assassin/killer accepts, or does not accept, the legitimacy of the country/state to grant such authorization.

The differences between terrorism and political assassinations are evident. Terrorism usually aims at a general and collective target. Political assassination is highly discriminative. It seeks the death of a particular actor, and does not aim at the collective, or at an indiscriminate target. The table indicates that political assassinations and political executions are similar. The major difference between the two is the issue of who legitimizes and authorizes assassination and why.

D. State-Sponsored Killings

A distinction is made in the table between terror and state-sponsored terror. Both are directed against a nonspecific target. However, while terror is typically directed from the periphery, state-sponsored terrorism is

TABLE I
Specificity of Target and Legitimation to Use Deadly Force

Legitimation to use deadly force	Target: Specific	Target: General
State approves secretly, potential killer accepts.	Political execution.	State-sponsored terror; genocide.
State approves openly, potential killer accepts.	Death penalty.	War.
State approves, potential killer does not accept.	(No case.)	(No case.)
State does not approve, potential killer accepts.	Regular homicide (criminal and noncriminal).	Multiple murders Mass murders Serial murders.
State does not approve, potential killer does not accept.	Political assassination.	Terror.

directed from the state's center. There are many differences in justifications, scope and pervasiveness between such groups as late 19th-century Russian revolutionaries—*Narodnaya Volya* (and its tactics of terror), and Stalin's mass terror, or the mass terror (including the use of "death squads") aimed by the Guatemalan government against the Ixil. Likewise, *Amnesty International Report* for 1978 points out that in the 1970s, at least 15,000 "disappeared" in Argentina, and death/assassination squads operated in El Salvador. The August 1, 1988, issue of *Time* magazine and the 1983 Amnesty International *Political Killings by Governments* point out more such killings. The Iranian government, following the Islamic revolution there in 1979, executed tens of thousands it viewed as its opponents. Saddam Hussein's Iraq also executed large numbers of such people. The Syrian massacre of Muslems in Hama is another illustration. Much worse and horrendous state-sponsored terror and genocide campaigns were carried out by Nazi Germany against Jews, Gypsies, and others, by Pol Pot's regime in Cambodia (Kampuchea) against millions of Cambodians, and more recently in Bosnia and Serbia, as well as in Africa.

In a similar fashion, the column under "specific" target makes a distinction between a political execution, which is a political assassination sponsored by a state (e.g., Stalin's ordered assassination of Trotsky in 1940, or his "assassination squad," which was active during the late 1930s in Europe), and a political assassination, which is not. Both are not dissimilar, but there are some important analytical and methodological differences between the two. First, a major difference is the fact that states (totalitarian or democracies) have a very different basis of legitimacy than individuals, or groups. The amount, and type, of power that they can generate and use is very different too. Second, while political assassinations are typically directed from the periphery, political executions are directed from the center. There are some substantial methodological differences too. The process of decision making in each case is very different; the methods of killing vary; and it is relatively easier to identify and validate cases of political assassinations than cases of political executions. States are typically very secret and evasive about their involvement in cases of political executions.

E. Explanations for Murder and Assassinations

Are explanations invoked for the micro, individual level, of murder (e.g., why murderers kill) applicable to political assassinations and executions? In principle, such comparisons are not—prima facie—useful. There are, however, some cases where this comparison is suggestive. A revengeful political assassination may, in some general philosophical aspect, remind us of blood revenge. In both cases there is a planned act of killing. However, while political assassination events are target specific, blood revenge is specific only on the family level, that is, the choice of a specific target is less important than hitting the specific collective.

One other comparison may be with "hired killers" (for nonpolitical reasons), or with organized crime sponsored murders. The cold-blood planning of the killing of a specific target must remind us of political assassination. Indeed, some may even identify similar "political" aspects in both cases. However, the similarities end here. Political assassination events are initiated by—and from—an ideological point of view. The conflict there is between opposing symbolic–moral universes struggling to change something meaningful and of significance in society. Hired killers for criminal purposes have no political ideology. The act is done for a fee, and typically there is no group that may give legitimacy to the act. Even if such a "group" exists (e.g., organized crime), its goal is not to achieve any kind of political-ideological social change. On the contrary, hired killers are typically employed to "solve" local problems (e.g., of area) that are usually focused on such down-to-earth problems as monetary interests, intimidation of opponents, or gaining control over a territory.

F. Assassinations and Repeated Murders

While the above working definition/characterization of political assassination events seems exclusive and capable of providing generalizable and distinct guidelines, there are two categories of taking other people's life that may appear, prima facie, close. These are mass murders, compulsive killers and serial murderers. While these types of killing may, sometimes, share some common characteristics with political assassinations (e.g., the fact that a few groups committed a number of political assassinations), there are some significant differences between them. Mass, compulsive, and serial murderers do not typically select their victims on a basis characterized by a strong political "reasoning." The murders are usually hidden, and the personal pathology of the murderers is also typically present and emphasized. The dynamics of making a decision to assassinate, the "reason" given, the specific choice of targets—all render the comparison as not valid.

G. Assassinations and Boundaries

Assassinations form the moral and political boundaries between the legitimate and illegitimate, the powerful and the powerless. In a pluralistic society political assassinations and executions may become not only important boundary markers, but may be used as a conflict resolution technique. It is not uncommon for individual assassins, and their sponsoring groups, to view themselves as moral crusaders, in a moral crusade. Typical are Princip's (assassin of the archduke Ferdinand) last account before he was executed, in which he stated that he was innocent, and expressing his belief that his death was required by Serbia. He must have obviously felt like a very righteous moral crusader. Individual assassins, and sponsoring groups, typically reject the prevailing hierarchy of morality and credibility, and project an alternative hierarchy. Therefore, it is not surprising that bitter arguments are waged around the social construction and interpretation of the meaning of political assassinations. In a sense, the debate is focused on turning a particular form of killing into political statements. Consequently, political assassinations, and political executions, involve—in the deepest sense—arguments about power, and social and political justice. In some instances, political assassinations may involve political trials and political prisoners—if the assassin is caught and brought to trial, which is not very common.

V. IMPACT AND RESULTS OF ASSASSINATIONS

Most scholars working in this area were interested in the question of the impact, or usefulness, of assassinations. Some even confused the question of the *impact* with the question of the *morality* of assassination.

Havens, Leiden, and Schmitt indeed point out that assessing the impact of assassinations is difficult. They distinguish between (a) the immediate impact of the act and the significance that history ultimately assigns to it, and (b) the personal impact versus the systemic impact. They (1970:37–39) suggest six possible types of systemic impacts of political assassinations:

1. No discernible changes are produced.
2. Personal changes occur that would not have taken place otherwise (e.g., the succession of Lyndon Johnson after Kennedy's assassination).
3. Some change induced in particular policies (e.g., the assassination of Israeli Prime Minister Rabin in November 1995).
4. Inducing profound alteration in the political system [e.g., the assassination of Rafael Trujillo Molina in the Dominican Republic, (May 30, 1961), Patrice Lumumba in the Congo, (January 1961), Julius Caesar].
5. Inducing an actual social revolution (e.g., the assassination of Alvaro Obregon in Mexico in 1928).
6. Helping a whole political system to collapse and disappear (e.g., the assassination of Engelbert Dollfus, Austria's Chancellor in 1934; that of Archduke Franz Ferdinand and his wife on June 28, 1914, by Gavrilo Princip in Sarajevo).

It is more useful to discuss the *results* of political assassinations and not so much the "impact." As most authors point out, "impact" refers to "usefulness" hence, some moral judgment may be involved in assessing "impact" in terms of a "good" or "bad" impact, and from whose point of view. The term "result" (or, "outcome" if one wishes) avoids that implicit moral problem by examining the results of the assassinations, regardless of their "usefulness" as judged by this or that criteria. To illustrate this distinction, let us examine one of Ford's main conclusions.

Summarizing his wide-lens work, Ford (1985, 387) asks "Is assassination ever justified?" (that is, is it "useful"?); "Does assassination work?" and "Has assassination proved that it can solve problems, not only in the short but also in the long run?" Ford unequivocally answers that "the history of countless assassinations, examined with an eye to comparing apparent motives with actual outcomes, contains almost none that produced results consonant with the aim of the doer, assuming those aims to have extended at all beyond the miserable taking of a life." Put, perhaps, in different terms one could rephrase and dramatize Ford by stating that "political assassination is morally wrong and pragmatically useless." Judging by his impressive work, one must cope with this strong generalization.

Being opposed, in principle, to murder, one can not object to the moral part of the statement, based on universalistic principles, that political assassination is morally wrong. However, the other question is whether political assassinations can be justified, and if so, on what grounds. There can hardly be a question that there are indeed quite a few moral justifications for assassinations. From this "pragmatic" aspect Ford's position is much more difficult to accept and defend. Obviously, numerous political assassinations and executions had results—both on the personal and on the system level. Even Hassan's Assassins achieved, for a while, some rather impressive results. We certainly may not always like those results, but we cannot simply deny their existence.

Assassinations that were aimed as revenge, as an alternative justice system, as propaganda by deed or for elite substitution, were certainly pragmatic in the sense that more than once, they achieved clear results. Furthermore, the fact that political assassinations achieved results more than once is well documented.

It is beneficial, at this point, also to remind ourselves of one of Rapoport's wise observations: "The lone assassin can set furious political forces in motion, but only conspirators have a reasonable chance of controlling them, and the best way to exploit the opportunity provided by an assassination is to usurp the powers of government . . ." (1971:22). One must also be reminded that assassinating for revenge, for propaganda and tyrannicide may all achieve their explicit goals, and significant results, even without following it up with an immediate and integral (to the assassination) political process.

Leiden (in Kirkham, Levi, and Crotty 1970, 9–10) argued that: "An assassination can have a high impact when (a) the system is highly centralized, (b) the political support of the victim is highly personal, (c) the "replaceability" of the victim is low, (d) the system is in crisis and/or in a period of rapid political and social change, and (e) if the death of the victim involves the system in confrontation with other powers." It is not entirely clear whether all these conditions must co-exist simultaneously for an impact effect to exist, or whether only part of the conditions must be present, and if so what part. For example, it is not obvious whether condition (b) was valid for the fateful June 28, 1914, assassination of Archduke Franz Ferdinand in Sarajevo. Likewise, it is not obvious that condition (d) was valid for the July 20, 1944, attempt to assassinate Hitler. Both events did have severe impacts. Once we switch from thinking in terms of "impacts" into thinking in terms of "results," the question of "under what conditions are results achieved?" takes on very different meaning. One indeed can and should be interested to answer questions about "results" for the short and long run, as well as for the different social actors who were involved in the assassination. While such "impact" as "revenge" is meaningless, as a "result" it is meaningful.

VI. TERROR AND ASSASSINATION

A major and typical problem has been the analytic tendency to associate and blur between the concept of political assassination with that of terrorism. The most important variable, which distinguishes political assassination from terrorism, is the specificity of the target. Assassination always involves a particular target. It is the death of actor *X* the assassin desires, and not the explosion of, say, an airplane per se.

Snitch identified five basic goals for terrorism and, in his approach, for political assassinations as well. These goals are to:

1. Receive popular recognition for a cause/group.
2. Receive official recognition for a cause/group.
3. Gain recruits.
4. Undermine the morale and prestige of the government.
5. Provoke the government to use such harsh and desperate measures as martial law, curfews, massive arrests, so that popular discontent would take place and help throw the government.

Rapoport distinguishes between discrete assassinations and those that are part of a terrorist campaign.

The former are viewed as a legitimate, useful means in power struggles. Thus, the word "assassination" can be used legitimately to describe an act of a terrorist. Indeed, Rapoport and Ivianski argue that the theory of modern terror developed from the concept of tyrannicide, which was, after all, a theory of assassination. Likewise, it is not difficult to conceptualize the Islamic Ismaili ("Assassins") as terrorists. Ivianski's concept of "individual terror" perhaps illustrates this possible confusion in the sharpest sense. An added confusing element is that assassination as "propaganda by deed" was a strategy which was used in the 19th century (it was also used by the Sicarii in the A.D. 60s Jewish revolt against the Roman empire) and it is typically associated today with terrorism.

While I do not deny the validity, legitimacy, and usefulness of viewing political assassinations within the context of terror, it is well worth our while to examine political assassinations as a separate analytical and empirical entity, as one more specific form of lethal violence. In this way, a magnified (and more sensitive) perspective of this particular phenomenon emerges.

David C. Rapoport has tried to develop one of the most interesting, thoughtful, and intriguing distinctions between terrorism and assassination (1971, 37–38, and continued in 1988): "In his mind, the assassin destroys men who are corrupting a system while the terrorist destroys a system which has already corrupted everyone it touches ... Assassination is an incident, a passing deed, an event; terrorism is a process, a way of life, a dedication. At most assassination involves a conspiracy, but terrorism requires a movement." However, this approach presents several obstacles. First, Rapoport seems to hover between two separate analytical levels without making an explicit distinction between them. On the one hand, he talks of the assassin and the terrorist, and what may happen in their mind, that is, his focus is on subjective meanings. This is a difficult intellectual exercise, bordering on psychological reductionism, and apparently unsatisfactory. On the other hand, Rapoport resorts to the acts (incident vs. process) themselves: those of terrorism and assassinations. Hence, we have here two distinct categories: the mind and the act itself. The discussion does not clarify the connection between these categories. Second, Rapoport's general approach tends to support the direction of including assassinations within terrorism, and consequently views such groups as the Sicarii, Ismaili, and others primarily as terrorist movements (indeed, a tendency shared by many modern researchers of terrorism). The major drawback of such an approach is that it may lead to less than sensitive findings and to cruder generalizations. This tendency may blur the differences between terrorism and assassinations. Third, making a distinction only on the basis of the meaning of the action on the microlevel may become problematic. If we interpret "meaning" as the one imputed to the act by the assassin, than we may end up with a classification which will have non-mutually exclusive types (e.g., see next section).

Furthermore, it would be very difficult, if not impossible, to distinguish terrorism from assassination only on the basis of subjective meanings. Even Rapoport must have been aware of this problem and he suggests another nonsubjective distinction—one between an "incident" (assassination) and a "process" (terrorism). One of the prestate underground Jewish Israeli groups—Lehi—had an explicit ideology in favor of, and practiced, political assassinations. One can argue that the 19th-century Russian *Narodnaya Volya* had some of this as well. It is no mere coincidence that Ivianski, who feels so uncomfortable with "political assassinations" but very comfortable with "individual terror," was a former member in Lehi. The interpretative term "political assassination" is more threatening and derogatory than "individual terror." The latter terms "allows" Ivianski to connect Lehi's assassinations to the 19th-century Russian revolutionaries.

VII. CLASSIFICATION AND CATEGORIES OF POLITICAL ASSASSINATION EVENTS

There are two prevalent typologies of political assassinations. As Rapoport points out, the first typology is close to a much older typology developed originally by Machiavelli, and focuses on the modus operandi. He suggested that assassinations have two stages: preparation and execution. Each of these stages is characterized by a specific set of problems. For example, the danger of informers in the preparation stage is magnified when a group conspires to assassinate someone. The advantage of this classificatory scheme is heuristic. We can use it to develop a four category classificatory scheme.

The first is "preplanning." In this category we have cases of serious deliberations and discussions whether or not to assassinate a specific social actor. However, this is where things stop.

The second category is "planning," that is, when the assassination plot passed the preplanning stage and a decision and commitment to assassinate is made. However, planning means that for some reason, sometimes technical and sometimes substantial, the plan was not executed.

The third category is "unsuccessful." In this category we have cases that passed the first two stages but that no assassination, or even serious physical injury to the victim, was made. The usual reason is technical—a mine that did not explode, a gun that malfunctioned at the critical moment, an explosive envelope that did not reach its destination (or, reached the wrong target).

The fourth category is "successful." In this category are those cases that passed the first two stages and culminated in an action that was either fully successful (victim died) or partially successful (victim wounded in a serious way).

It is well worth noting that the above categorization is very different from legal categorizations about forms of killing and wounding. For example, the above categorization does not use the concept of a conspiracy, or the fact that "successful" includes both killing and serious wounding. The major rational for the above categorization is the question of How far?, or To what extent? did the assassination event proceed. Viewed in this way, the classification is empirically helpful.

The above classification is based on a description of the event itself, regardless of the motivation of the assassin. However, the works by Kirkham, Levy, and Crotty, Crotty, and others seem to share a particular form of a classification of political assassination events, which is based on the motivation for the act. This classification has five types:

1. *Elite substitution:* The assassination of a political leader in order to replace him or her. Usually, without aiming to create any substantial systemic or ideological change. This type of assassinations typically refers to a power struggle when a particular leader is assassinated in order to replace him/her or those he/she represent in power with an opposing group at the same level.

2. *Tyrannicide:* The assassination of a despot in order to replace him with a better, usually less repressive, oppressive, and more rational ruler. This is one of the oldest forms of assassination as well as the one that has many moral and philosophical justifications.

3. *Terroristic assassination:* Assassination on a mass and indiscriminate basis in order to demonstrate the government's inability to rule, or to let a minority govern a majority.

4. *Anomic assassination:* Assassination of a political figure for private reasons. This type usually refers to the "crazy" lonely assassin who may use a political rhetoric to justify the act, but appears to demonstrate a psychiatric disorder.

5. *Propaganda by deed:* Assassination that is carefully planned for a particular political figure and that aims to draw and direct attention to a specific problem.

The above classification has at least two problems. First, the different types are not mutually exclusive. Second, the third type obviously attempts to combine—on one analytical level—assassination and terror.

Ben-Yehuda developed an additional category based on motivation:

Revengeful assassination: Aimed at some form of revenge. Included in this act is the fact that this type of assassination may serve as a warning sign to others. There is something of a "propaganda by deed" here.

VIII. ASSASSINATIONS AND POLITICAL JUSTICE

Beyond the different approaches, definitions, and classifications, and using Ocam's razor type of logic, how can one conceptualize in a culturally meaningful way, this peculiar and violent behavior focused on political assassinations and executions? Ben-Yehuda suggested that the most appropriate conceptualization is one focused on political justice.

When we examine the sets of accounts provided by assassins to justify their acts, we find there frequently references to the victims as "traitors," "squealers," "spies," "collaborators," and the like. Moreover, political assassinations tend to involve killers and victims from the same cultural group. Thus, the conceptualization of political assassinations as violent acts and cultural devices that are invoked to explain and justify acts that the assassins want to project as political "justice" receive much empirical support. These acts tend to occur in situations where the assassins feel (rightly or wrongly) that they cannot receive justice because the opportunities for justice are felt to be blocked. It is as if an alternative, informal, and popular system of "justice" is put into operation. This system operates on principles of political justice, and social control. Such systems arise typically during struggles for national independence and formation of national identities.

The type of justice that operates here is based on some information, sometimes on "confessions," and on command/administrative decisions. In such a system, the potential victim does not stand much of a chance to

TABLE II

Famous Assassinations

Date	Victim	Date	Victim
Dec. 25, 1170	Thomas Becket, Archbishop of Canterbury	Nov. 22, 1963	John F. Kennedy, U.S. president
April 14, 1865	Abraham Lincoln, U.S. president	Feb. 21, 1965	Malcolm X, American Black activist
August 6, 1875	Gabriel Garcia Moreno, president of Ecuador	Oct. (?) 1965	Mehdi Ben Barka, Moroccan opposition political activist
March 1, 1881	Alexander II, Russian emperor	Jan. 15, 1966	Alahaji Si Abubaker Tefawa Balewa, Nigeria's prime minister
April 8, 1895	Queen Min, Korean queen	April 4, 1968	Rev. Dr. Martin Luther King, Jr., American Black activist and intellectual
May 1, 1896	Nasir Ad-Din, Persian shah	June 5, 1968	Robert F. Kennedy, American politician
June 28, 1914	Archduke Francis Ferdinand and Countess Sophie Chotek	Nov. 28, 1971	Wasfi Al-tal, Jordanian prime minister
Dec. 31, 1916	Grigori Rasputin, Russian clergyman and adviser	March 25, 1975	Faisal Ibn Abd Al Aziz, Saudi Arabian king
Jan. 15, 1919	Rosa Luxemburg and Karl Liebknecht, German political activists and intellectuals	April 13, 1975	N'Garte Tombalbaye, Chad's first president
June 24, 1922	Walther Rathenau, German activist	April 15, 1975	Mujibur Rahman, Bangladeshi president
May 25, 1926	Simon Petelyura, Ukrainian nationalist	July 12, 1977	Osmin Aguirre Salinas, El Salvador's former president
July 17, 1928	Alvaro Obregon, Mexican president	Sept. 5, 1977	Hans-Martin Schleyer, German industrialist and activist
July 25, 1934	Engelbert Dollfuss, Austrian chancellor	May 9, 1978	Aldo Moro, Italy's former prime minister
August 12, 1935	Tetsuzan Nagata, Japanese military officer (Maj. Gen.)	Nov. 27, 1978	George Moscone, Mayor of San Francisco
Sept. 8, 1935	Huey P. Long, U.S. senator	Jan. 22, 1979	Ali Hassan Salameh, Palestinian activist and guerrilla member
August 20, 1940	Leon Trotsky, Russian politician	Aug. 27, 1979	Louis Mountbatten, British political and military leader
May 27, 1942	Reinhard Heydrich, S.S. official	Oct. 26, 1979	Chung Hee Park, South Korean president
Dec. 24, 1942	Jean Francois Darlan, Admiral, head of French military under Vichy's government	July 21, 1980	Salah Ad-Din Bitar, Syria's former prime minister
April 18, 1943	Isoruku Yamamoto, Admiral, commander-in-chief Japanese navy	Sept. 17, 1980	Anastasio Somoza Debayle, Nicaragua's former president
Nov. 16, 1944	Walter Guinness Moyne, British resident minister, Middle East	Dec. 8, 1980	John Lennon, British musician and former member of the Beatles
Jan. 30, 1948	Mohandas K. Gandhi, Indian Hindu political nationalist and intellectual	Sept. 4, 1981	Louis Delamare, French ambassador to Lebanon
March 10, 1948	Jan Masaryk, Czechoslovakian politician	Oct. 6, 1981	Anwar Sadat, Egyptian president
Sept. 17, 1948	Count Folke Bernadotte, Swedish mediator for the Middle East	Sept. 14, 1982	Bashir Gemayel, Lebanese president-elect
July 20, 1951	King Abdullah Ibn Hussein, King of Jordan	Aug. 21, 1983	Benigno Simeon Aquino, Philippines' opposition political activist
Jan. 2, 1955	Jose Antonio Remon, president of Panama	Oct. 31, 1984	Indira Gandhi, Indian prime minister
Sept. 25, 1959	Solomon W. R. D. Bandaranaike, Ceylon prime minister	Oct. 1984	Rev. Jerzy Popieluszko, Polish clergyman
Jan. 17, 1961	Patrice Lumumba, Congo Republic's first prime minister	July 29, 1985	Fausto Escrigas Estrada, Spanish vice admiral
May 30, 1961	Rafael Leonidas Trujillo y Molina, president, Dominican Republic	April 16, 1988	Khalil El Wazir, Palestinian political and guerrilla activist
Oct. 13, 1961	Prince Louis Rwagasore, Burundi prime minister	March 22, 1990	Gerald Bull, world expert on long-range cannons
Nov. 2, 1963	Ngo Dinh Diem, South Vietnam's first president	Nov. 4, 1995	Yitzhak Rabin, Israeli prime minister

"prove his/her innocence." This is a system of political justice which is based on negotiated claims, hearsay, partial information and on social constructions of "guilt"; "collaboration"; "treason" and "vengeance". In almost all important aspects, political executions can be placed within this framework as well.

In reality, the way this system works is by selecting a target and then expose this target to a process of strangerization whereby a specific human being is socially constructed as a "dangerous alien" who must be eliminated. The linguistic devices which are used in this process are usually embedded within specific ideologies, and this whole complex of ideology and linguistic justifications is used to propel the potential killers into suspending their recoil from killing and then into both committing the act and feeling justified in doing so.

IX. SOME CROSS-CULTURAL ILLUSTRATIONS FOR POLITICAL ASSASSINATION EVENTS

There are many different cases of political assassinations (e.g., see Ford, 1985), and it is not too difficult to conceptualize an encyclopedia focused just on this topic (e.g., see Lentz, 1988). Much of the information we have, as well as the analytical formulations we create in this area, are based on Western experience. More information is derived from West Asia, on the boundaries between West and East. This, obviously, does not mean that assassinations cannot be found in, nor that they are not a significant feature of, South and East Asian and African cultures. Since we lack accessible, thorough studies for these regions, and since we can assume that conditions of the human existence, interests, ideologies, and economic and political competitions are probably similar there, we can perhaps risk stating that (a) we can, and should, assume that similar patterns may exist there too, and (b) there is a very strong need for conducting studies on assassinations in those regions.

It may be beneficial, from an illustrative point of view, to remind ourselves about some of the more famous cases we are aware of. There are, of course, the famous Biblical cases (e.g., see Ford, 1985, 7–24), and some cases in ancient Greece (e.g., see Ford, 1985, 25–46). The most famous of cases during the period of the Roman empire is probably that of the assassination of Julius Caesar on March 15 in 44 B.C. There are quite a few recorded cases during the middle ages, and there are some fairly well-known cases in the modern era as listed in Table II (based on the works by Ford and Lentz):

Also See the Following Articles

REVOLUTIONS • TERRORISM • VIOLENCE AS SOLUTION, CULTURE OF

Acknowledgments

This article is based partly on my 1990 paper and 1993 book. I am grateful to Frank Cass and to SUNY Press for allowing use of materials from my previous works. The research on assassinations was funded by the Israeli Foundations Trustees, contract no. 86–01-007.

Bibliography

Ben-Yehuda, N. (1990). Political assassinations as rhetorical devices: Events and interpretations. *The Journal of Terrorism and Political Violence,* 2 (3), 324–350.

Ben-Yehuda, N. (1993). *Political assassinations by Jews. A rhetorical device for justice.* Albany: State University of New York Press.

Clarke, J. W. (1982). *American assassins: The darker side of politics.* Princeton, NJ: Princeton University Press.

Crotty, W. J. (Ed.). (1971). *Assassinations and the political order.* New York: Harper and Row Publications.

Ford, F. L. (1985). *Political Murder from Tyrannicide to Terrorism.* Cambridge, MA: Harvard University Press.

Havens, M. C., Leiden, C., & Schmitt, K. M. (1970). *The Politics of Assassination.* Englewood Cliffs, NJ: Prentice Hall, Inc.

Hurwood, B. J. (1970). *Society and the Assassin.* New York: Parents' Magazine Press.

Ivianski, Z. (1977). Individual terror: Concept and typology. *Journal of Contemporary History, 12:*43–63.

Kirkham, J. F., Levy, S. G., & Crotty, W. J. (ed.). (1970). *Assassination and Political Violence.* New York: Praeger Publishers.

Lentz, H. M. III. (1988). *Assassinations and executions. An encyclopedia of political violence, 1865–1986.* Jefferson, NC, and London: McFarland & Company, Inc.

Lerner, M. (1930). Assassination. In Edwin Seligman (ed.), *Encyclopedia of the Social Sciences,* Vol. II. New York: The MacMillan Company.

Lewis, B. (1967). *The Assassins: A radical sect in Islam.* London: Weidenfeld and Nicolson. (A 1985 edition published in London by Al Saqi Books.)

Nettler, G. (1982). *Killing One Another: Criminal Careers* (Vol. 2). Cincinnati, OH: Anderson Publishing Company.

Padover, S. K. (1943). Patterns of assassination in occupied territory. *Public Opinion Quarterly, 7,* 680–693.

Rapoport, D. C. (1971). *Assassination and terrorism.* Toronto: Canadian Publishing Corporation.

Rapoport, D. C. (1982). Introduction. In D. C. Rapoport & Y. Alexander (Eds.), *The rationalization of terrorism* (pp. 1–7). Frederic, MD: Altheia Books, University Publications of America.

Rapoport, D. C. (1984). Fear and trembling: Terrorism in three religious traditions. *The American Political Science Review, 78*(30), 658–677.

Rapoport, D. C. (1988). Messianic sanctions for terror. *Comparative Politics, 20*(2), 195–213.

Snitch, T. H. (1982, September). Terrorism and political assassinations: A transnational assessment, 1968–1980. *The Annals of the American Academy of Political and Social Science, 463,* 54–68.

Turk, A. (1983). Assassination. In S. H. Kadish (Ed.), *Encyclopedia of Crime and Justice* (pp. 82–88). New York: The Free Press.

Wilkinson, D. Y. (Ed.). (1976). *Social structure and assassination behavior.* Cambridge, MA: Schenkman Publishing Company.

Balance of Power Relationships

Derek F. Lynch
University of Huddersfield

GLOSSARY

Anarchic System A political system in which there is no overarching power, no world government to turn to for protection.

Balancer A state or an actor whose foreign policy is directed at the preservation of a balance of power between competing forces, usually by intervening on the side of the weaker party.

Concert of Europe A system for the collective management and coordination of Great Power relations in Europe after 1815; also, the name given to the leading participants in that system.

Deterrence A policy designed to counter the aggressive intentions of one actor by the use or threatened use of greater or equal force deployed against it.

Equilibrium Balance A balance of power in which two or more forces of equivalent strength are ranged against one another so that no one actor can exercise hegemony over the others.

International Regimes Sets of rules, norms and decision-making procedures governing specific issue-areas in international relations.

Mutually Assured Destruction (MAD) The assumption behind mutual deterrence and the balance of terror in the Cold War, namely, that a conflict between two heavily armed nuclear-weapons states would result in the utter destruction of both countries. This was believed to deter either one from seriously threatening the status quo or from launching an all-out military attack on the other.

Realism A paradigm or theoretical approach to international relations that stresses that state behavior is based on the pursuit of interests defined in terms of power. Adherents, such as E. H. Carr, Henry Morgenthau, and Henry Kissinger, stressed the need to explain the world as it is rather than as it ought to be. Neorealism, a later variant associated with Kenneth Waltz, Robert Gilpin, and Stephen Krasner, explains foreign policy and international economic relations in terms of a state's location in the global military and economic power structure

Realpolitik An approach to the conduct of foreign policy that suggests that the ends justify the means in the pursuit of the national interest.

System A set of interacting parts.

Utrecht, Treaty of (1713) This ended the War of Spanish Succession. To preserve the then-existing balance of power in Europe, it stipulated that France and Spain should never be united.

Westphalia, Treaty of (1648) This ended the Thirty Years War. The Westphalian settlement confirmed and institutionalized the principles of state sovereignty and non-interference in the domestic affairs of others and marked an important stage in the evolution of a system of independent states in Europe.

Zero-Sum Strategy A game plan that assumes that a gain for one side automatically results in an equivalent loss for the other. It encourages selfish or egoistic behavior.

THE BALANCE OF POWER is one of the most widely used expressions in the field of international relations. In fact, it refers not to one, but to numerous, often quite distinct concepts. It conjures up a series of assumptions about a particular style of foreign policy behavior and interactions among states. Balance of power relationships are perceived of as the product of a hard-headed, unsentimental, calculating, and essentially nonideological diplomacy. They are usually associated with the heyday of the old European powers in the 18th and 19th centuries. This entry explores the multiple meanings of balance of power relationships and their implications for the foreign policies of states and for the international system as a whole. Using insights from history and international relations theory, it assesses their past significance and their possible relevance to the post-Cold War international order.

I. CONCEPTUAL ISSUES: POWER AND BALANCES OF POWER

Our first, and most obvious problem in attempting to define balance of power relationships is the enormous ambiguity which surrounds the concept of "power" itself. Although the entries under power elsewhere in this volume provide a more comprehensive treatment of the topic, a few words on its application to balance of power relationships are in order here. Our other problem, of course, is with the notion of a "balance." Since this has been the focus of the debate about the concept of the balance of power among international relations scholars, it is worthy of more detailed consideration.

A. Power

Power can be understood as the ability to ensure that one's own preferences prevail. This can be achieved by controlling the behavior of others, by shaping a favorable consensus of opinion, or by manipulating the environment. It can be exercised through action or inaction, as well as by means of coercion or persuasion. Power is often confused with indicators of power or with the purposes for which power is deployed. Historians have usually spoken of the "balance of power" in terms of the military and economic capabilities of states, those resources that might assist them in waging war or in threatening the use of war to achieve diplomatic ends. Suffice it to say that a mere count of tanks or dollars does not in itself predict the power of any actor. Questions of political will and the ability to set and alter agendas must also be taken into account. The utility of material resources is heavily dependent on the context in which they are deployed. Geography and distance, for example, have important bearings on the value of conventional military forces. Power also depends on the perceptions of those at the receiving end of a transaction. If a government is so fanatical in its beliefs that it is willing to expose its population to external attack and mass annihilation, the threat of military action may not alter its behavior. Economic pressures are less potent if a regime is committed to autarky as a matter of principle. A state that rejected the exchange value of paper money, for instance, would find it difficult to take part in the world economic system but the international community would have difficulty in its dealings with that state too.

It is when two or more actors share the same or similar perceptions of the value of certain resources or the undesirability of certain outcomes, that the game of power politics comes into its own. The changing pattern of rules, expectations, and beliefs held by actors alters the balance of power among them. Changes in the balance of military or economic capabilities are only significant insofar as they are believed to enable or constrain states in particular ways. Just as legal decisions establish precedents, the unfolding of events over time changes the environment of world politics. This "transformational" view of power, as found in the work of David Dessler, reminds us of the importance of nonmaterial factors. On the other hand, we must avoid dismissing traditional approaches to state power and throwing out the baby with the bathwater. As will be seen later, military-strategic resources have always been important and will remain so for some time, in part because most states still believe them to be the key to their national security.

B. Balances of Power

The concept of "balance" has been used in numerous ways, each one with its own specific consequences for our understanding of international relations. A balance of power could refer to

- any relatively stable distribution of power a specific distribution of power giving rise to an equilibrium effect among several states and actors;
- a state of equilibrium involving two actors or two opposing coalitions of actors;
- a particular configuration of the international system in the 18th or 19th century;
- the theory and practice of power politics in general.

Paul Schroeder found as many as 11 definitions of a "balance of power" and of the related concept of a "European equilibrium." We could give preference to one or more of these over all the others. But, as will become apparent later in the article, a wide range of concepts has its merits and each has its own particular application. Now let us examine some of the more common interpretations in greater detail.

1. The Audit of Power

The expression can be used to refer to any distribution of power among a number of actors, as in the phrase "balance of forces," even if the capabilities of the actors involved are not evenly "balanced." Thus we could say that China did not act in this or that way because "the balance of power was unfavorable." It might even be possible to quantify such a balance by counting the number of actors and by calculating the relative concentration of power measured in terms of military and/or economic resources. Of course, what we are describing here could just as easily be called the distribution of power. Used in this way, the concept merely refers to an audit of capabilities, as understood, for example, in the title of *The Military Balance*, an annual compilation of military data produced by the International Institute for Strategic Studies.

2. The Equilibrium Balance

Alternatively, a balance could be thought of as a state of equilibrium in which two roughly equal forces balance each other out. The focus here is the blocking effect of equal but opposite forces which is understood to provide a basis for stability. That is the logic behind much of deterrence theory. The principle of Mutually Assured Destruction (MAD) relied on a balance of terror between the Americans and the Soviets during the Cold War, as well as on an assumption of rough strategic parity after 1970. Deterrence, of course, can also be provided through the threat of overwhelming defeat by vastly superior force, rather than by means of an equilibrium balance. Thus, the United States could deter Iraqi incursions into Saudi Arabia in the post-Gulf War situation, not because of any equal balance of forces but due to a preponderance of American power in the region.

The general effect of a balance of power involving several actors of roughly equal strength is that no one actor will be able to overwhelm another major actor and, more importantly, that no actor will be able to establish itself as a hegemon that could eliminate the others from the scene and create a world empire or world state under its control. Such a balance could exist among several actors or simply between two major players. The optimal number of participants in the game has always been a bone of contention. It is even possible to disagree on what constitutes a relevant actor. Are we talking about individual states? Should we count alliances and coalitions of states as, in effect, single actors? The answers to these questions are also dependent on our assessment of the polarity of the system, that is, on the relative concentration of power. There were at least six Great Powers involved in the European strategic contest before the First World War, suggesting a multipolar system. However, in practice, they were organized into two quite rigid alliances: the Triple Alliance of Germany, Austria-Hungary, and Italy, and the Triple Entente comprising Britain, France, and Russia. Consequently, the European order was actually bipolar, with the alliances likely to behave almost as predictably as single actors.

3. The Traditional European Balance of Power

In its purest form, a balance of power system does not tend toward bipolarity. In other words, the players involved have no permanent allies and no permanent enemies. They enter shifting coalitions, as in a game of musical chairs. At first glance, and taking account of individual states as opposed to coalitions of states, such balances of power might appear to have been quite common in European history, especially since the consolidation of the international states system after 1648. The 18th century has been characterized as a period in which balance of power relationships took the place of ideological war and rigid religious alliances. States formed coalitions to counterbalance the power of others regardless of traditional enmities or creeds. The complex system of relationships among Britain, France, the Habsburg Empire, and Russia, subsequently extended to include the Ottoman Empire and Prussia/Germany, is described as the "classic" European balance of power. Although it is dangerous to generalize across time periods and civilizations, a similar mutiplolar system could be said to have operated in China during the Warring States Period and in Renaissance Italy. These systems are usually contrasted with universal empires such as the Roman or later Chinese empires, on the one hand, and with the polarized ideological battlegrounds of post-Reformation Europe or the Cold War, on the other.

But although European politics in the 18th and 19th centuries was characterized by prolonged periods of multipolarity, it is doubtful whether an equilibrium balance of power really prevailed for much of this time. The early years of the 19th century, for instance, are often described in terms of a contrived "concert" of powers arrangement rather than a mechanical balance of power. Such a "concert" is a group of states attempting to coordinate their actions, playing together "in concert," in spite of their many differences, in order to preserve overall system stability. The rhetoric of the European Concert suggested that it was somehow "balancing" French power. The reality was quite different. France was a defeated actor. The Concert was an alliance of victors keeping weaker states at bay working to preserve the new status quo. It was only when France had time to recover and tensions arose among the anti-Napoleonic allies that you could glimpse the possibility of a new multipolar equilibrium.

It is also doubtful whether the European order in the second half of the 19th century could be characterized as a balance of power system. The emergence of Prussia-Germany altered the distribution of power and created a new source of instability. Germany's perceived military lead over its protagonists increased rapidly. Bismarck was certainly conscious of balances of power among individual states or groups of states but he did not always want to preserve a systemic balance. He was concerned with German interests first and foremost. Shifting coalitions and balances were merely instruments to be deployed to enhance national power with minimal risk in the game of Realpolitik. Kissinger sums up the relationship between Bismarck's conception of "balances" and his pursuit of the national interest in this way:

> Enhancing the power of the state became the principal, if not the only objective, restrained solely by the forces massed against it (Kissinger, 1994: 129).

Realpolitik was seen exclusively in terms of national policy rather than as a systemic requirement which also served long-term national interests. The survival of the fittest and the potential for hegemony was the name of this very Darwinian game in which local balances of power were fleeting and expendable tactical devices. In a genuine balance of power system, on the other hand, the balance would assume such significance that it might have to be deliberately created and preserved and would acquire long-term value for all major participants. Such a convergence of expectations was never a foregone conclusion, not even in the era of the Classical European Balance of Power.

4. Intentionality: Contrived versus Automatic Balances

The question of how a balance of power comes into existence and is maintained is just as important as the number of actors involved in it. At the outset, we can see two possibilities: the equilibrium happens by accident, as a consequence of the historical evolution of forces, or it is deliberately created and maintained to serve systemic purposes. As summarized by Bull, the balance of power has traditionally served three purposes: it has facilitated international order, protected the sovereignty of the leading states in the system, and prevented world empire. These were deemed to be positive byproducts of balance of power relationships and for much of the time, good reason to nurture them. They were observed and extolled as "principles" of international relations by the 18th-century European philosophers such as Emmerich de Vattel, Jean Jacques Rousseau, and Edmund Burke. Doubtless, many saw parallels with Newtonian physics, another arena where stability and natural order depended on carefully constructed equilibrium and delicate balances among the competing forces of magnetism, motion, and gravity. In an almost mechanical response, a power vacuum or the prospect of an imperial hegemon would prompt states to preserve an existing balance of power or to create a new one.

Balances of power are more informal regulators of the international system than international law or global institutions. The rules by which they operate are essentially tacit rules, shared understandings based on a convergence of expectations among the participants. Although weak states can be sacrificed, the sovereignty and independence of the major actors are preserved. The rules of behavior are like the "laws of the market," imposed on states by the logic of their situation rather than enforced by any identifiable world policeman.

For writers such as Kenneth Waltz, the balance of power is a natural and almost an automatic feature of the international system. He suggests that states wishing to survive in an anarchic system will probably engage in balance of power behavior anyway. With no world policeman, they must survive or go under. To survive, they will copy other survivors and form balances and alliances to counter threats to their security. Hegemony is difficult: world empire extremely difficult. Consequently,

> States balance power rather than maximize it. States can seldom afford to make maximizing power their goal. International politics is too serious a business for that (Waltz, 1979: 127).

Hedley Bull argued that a fortuitously arrived-at balance of power may not be a solid guarantee of long-term stability. The same forces of economic and technological change that give rise to the equilibrium in the first place may eventually work to undermine it. Rising powers, emboldened by their new parity with the old giants, will want to go farther. Previously dominant powers will want to regain their advantage. So, on their own, the principles expounded by the philosophers could not prevent the balance from breaking down. When a number of relatively powerful states become locked into such a high-stakes game, stability is all-important. The horrors of universal religious warfare and the benefits accruing from longer periods of peaceful trade and commerce ultimately taught European leaders that a contrived balance might be more attractive than none at all.

It came to be believed that, for a balance to succeed, states must coordinate their actions, not only at the moment of its inception but on a continuous basis thereafter. There must be a desire to avoid excessive disruption. Even the dominant powers must show restraint. In this situation, power is something possessed collectively by all states in a system, not just by one. For Richard Little, this "associative" conception of the balance of power enables all the major players to safeguard their security by averting international crises and global war. Where such a power stalemate effectively precludes outright hegemony, nobody can secure freedom and peace by their own efforts alone but only by carefully playing world politics according to the rules of the game. As summarized by Kaplan, these stipulated the conditions under which states would go to war, form alliances, or act with restraint. They suggested that it was in everyone's interest that no major power be eliminated. Vacuums tempted ambitious states into adventurism, so they must be avoided. The key to balance of power relationships in such an scenario is an awareness of how much pressure the international system can take and a realization that even states involved in strategic competition are interdependent.

This sensitivity to the needs of the international system was best exemplified by Britain's role as a "balancer" in the 19th century, a role much admired by Henry Kissinger in his various writings on European history published between 1957 and 1994. Britain had a non-ideological foreign policy, enabling it to form flexible coalitions with weaker powers against potential hegemonic blocs. It felt relatively secure and it had no claims on the European territories of the other major players in the system. It had interests beyond the central balance in Europe, namely in its overseas possessions. Thus, her caution in Europe contrasted with a more aggressive stance in Asia, the Middle East, and Africa, and especially in her efforts to counter Russian expansionism southwards toward to the Indian subcontinent through Central Asia and Afghanistan.

Valuing the balance of power was one thing: preserving it was another. Few countries were in such a fortunate position as Britain. Restraint was not always easy. Moreover, the balance often required considerable risk-taking. Limited wars of adjustment were necessary if major war involving all the Great Powers was to be avoided. These corrective actions, such as the Crimean War, curtailed the ambitions of potential upstarts and "updated" the share of spoils to reflect the evolving power distribution.

II. BALANCE OF POWER RELATIONSHIPS: CAUSES AND CONSEQUENCES

Conceptual nuances aside, there has been much criticism of late of the dominance of power politics in the academic literature on international relations. During the late Cold War, for instance, critics charged that this only reinforced or intensified East-West conflict. The reaction against power politics has led specialists to explore new dimensions of global politics including gender issues, the environment, international political economy, and cross-cultural communication. For many, this broadening of the international relations agenda was long overdue. But debate persists over whether we can simply equate power politics with war and violence and thus dismiss it as an outmoded and undesirable preoccupation.

To assess the implications of balance of power relationships for the international system, we can ask two recurring questions that have been of concern to the IR community: does the balance of power have any effect on the behavior of individual states and, if so, what kind of balance is most conducive to peace and security? In specifying the latter, we might ask how many actors should be involved in the system and investigate its polarity or concentration of power. Our concern here is with questions of polarity in the context of balance of power relationships; the wider implications of this variable are discussed in the entry on bipolarity and multipolarity.

A. The Significance of System Structure

The first question that has to be addressed is the extent to which structural factors, that is, the arrangement of states in the international system and the distribution of power among them, can explain state behavior. This is a wider issue in international relations that cannot be dealt with in great detail here. But if we believe that domestic, state-level factors are more important than global power structures, the balance of power may not be all that important anyway. Clearly, much of the drive behind the foreign policies of, say, the Islamic Republic of Iran or North Korea come from domestic ideological movements and experiences. Such states will often risk challenges to the superpowers even when the odds are against them because their belief systems or internal political factors suggest that is the "right" thing to do. They may forgo militarily or economically profitable alliances with ideologically "impure" partners for the same reason.

On the other hand, even the most ideological decisionmakers must give some thought to the strategic consequences of an unfavorable distribution of power. Their policies will at least be influenced by an awareness of structural constraints. Indeed, faced with this reality, they may even violate their own declared rules and cover their forays into power politics with a neat ideological justification, just as the superpowers often do. To understand this, one has only to recall the commonalties of interest that drove the antiterrorist Ronald Reagan, revolutionary Iran, and the conservative Likud government in Israel into tacit collaboration in the Iran-Contra Affair.

These considerations reflect the wider but interminable debate between those who believe that international politics is essentially a tactical game in which ideology is either a sign of irrationality or a cloak for deep strategy, and those who would attach more weight to the declared beliefs of the participants. But even those who believe that a state's location in the international hierarchy is important have moved away from crude deterministic approaches that claim to predict behavior from a single variable such as wealth or military power. Keeping an open mind on the resolution of this debate, we can at least explore structural elements without investing blind faith in them or assuming that they will provide watertight explanations of events.

B. The Number of Players

With these caveats on board, let us now consider the impact of the number of major powers participating in the system on balance of power relationships. The traditional European balance of power had a certain appeal when US-Soviet rivalry was resulting in what many perceived to be a dangerous polarization of the international system. Morton Kaplan, for instance, suggested that as many as five reasonably strong states were necessary for a working balance of power arrangement.

Bipolarity reduces the number of crosscutting cleavages. All effort goes into the core confrontation and every issue forces even the independent states to side with one camp or the other. A multipolar system, on the other hand, was believed to induce moderation by giving states more partners from which to choose. Critics of bipolarity, like Inis Claude, raise the prospect that the resulting crescendo of confrontation may end in war, as it did in the case of the standoff between the two opposing alliances in 1914. For Kenneth Waltz, however, the singular focus of bipolar confrontation has its advantages. If the two sides want to avert Armageddon, they must learn to deal with each other. They are not distracted by the multiple games that must be played in a more extensive political system. There is only one relationship to manage and the buck cannot be passed to others.

Multipolarity could lead to greater instability. In a multipolar system, no one actor has sufficiently preponderant power to overwhelm its neighbor. Thus, in the absence of the collective will to coordinate state behavior, individual states can be tempted to settle their own scores at the expense of others. Regardless of political will, more states are materially capable of initiating aggression. This is especially evident if we enter weapons of mass destruction into the equation. To appreciate this point, just consider the implications of a world in which every state had an equal number of nuclear weapons and roughly equal delivery capability. Would such proliferation of weapons produce a stable balance of power based on all-round deterrence? Or would it increase the probability of the use of such weapons by one rogue state?

Multipolarity can also greatly increase the level of complexity of the system. In a bipolar arrangement, there is only one major conflict to keep under wraps.

In a multipolar system, there are numerous bilateral and multilateral relationships to consider. The number of bilateral relationships is given by the factorial equation

$$\text{D (number of dyads)} = \frac{(n-1)n}{2},$$
where n = number of actors

The consequences of this can be seen in Figure 1. With two players, there is only one relationship to manage. With three actors, there are three bilateral relationships. But four participants raise the number of bilateral relationships to six.

When these are plotted, we see that the complexity of the system increases very rapidly once we move beyond a three- or four-actor game (Fig. 2).

The resulting uncertainty over likely future alliances was a positive factor when the consequences of war were limited by the available technology. But it would be more difficult to gauge the outcome in today's environment when preemptive strikes over long distances can be undertaken with split-second decision-making.

The link between the relative concentration of power and global stability is another hotly debated topic. Of course, those who see the balance of power as a relationship among equals will not even recognize an asymmetrical system as relevant to our discussion. But relative parity can also be dangerous. Organski, writing in 1958, and Scharpel, writing in 1993, found evidence for the proposition that rising powers are tempted to challenge states that are marginally stronger than themselves but less willing to disrupt the security regime when there is a clear power asymmetry.

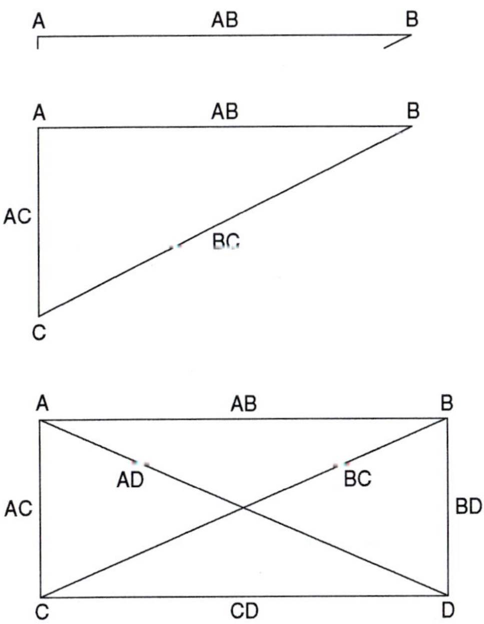

FIGURE 1 Bilateral relationships involving two, three and four actors

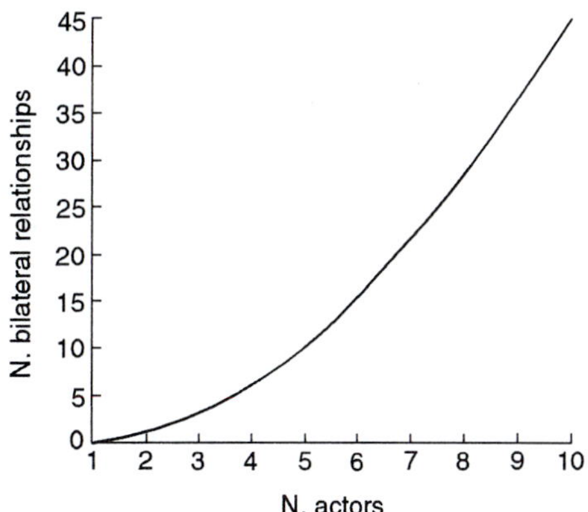

FIGURE 2 Multipolarity and system complexity

If the evidence appears inconclusive, it is because balance of power relationships cannot be seen in purely mechanical or numerical terms. Their efficacy also depends on the manner and purpose of their creation.

C. Contrived Balances of Power and Security Regimes

Discussion of contrived and automatic balances of power has been given a new lease of life by the growing literature on international regimes, the sets of both formal rules and decision-making procedures governing specific issue-areas in international politics. Like the Highway Code, regimes involve voluntary restraint on the part of actors who fear the collective risk and uncertainty that would prevail in their absence. Regimes are therefore intentionally created structures. As Robert Jervis has suggested, a balance of power system would generate regime-type behavior if it was consciously created and nurtured rather than an unintended consequence of the blocking power of others. Furthermore, regime theorists argue that regimes alter the perceived interests of states. They stick to the rules because they fear the consequences of a ruleless world. Insofar as balance of power relationships become institutionalized in this way, regime theory can be helpful. However, as we have seen, the requirements of the international system do not always coincide with the perceived interests of national elites. The circumstances under which estimated costs of a nonregime situation might outweigh the benefits of preemptive action or aggression are not easy to predict and they change over time. The predictability of security regimes is attractive on paper but much more difficult to create in practice. This is because, although complex balance of power relationships do exhibit features of interdependence and mutual restraint, most people still conceive of security issues in terms of zero-sum relationships. The balance of power is all very fine but if it does not favor me today, it might favor my enemy tomorrow.

III. BALANCE OF POWER RELATIONSHIPS IN THE POST-COLD WAR WORLD

A. A Return to Balance of Power Relationships?

There are some reasons to believe that the study of balance of power relationships may be of renewed relevance in the post-Cold War World. The Cold War balance was a rather rigid, bipolar structure. It was also marked by the high salience of ideology. We are now assumed to have reached the "end of history," as Francis Fukuyama called it, a time when global ideological crusades no longer threaten world peace. A preoccupation with the decline of American power since the early 1970s has been accompanied by evidence of the rising economic potential of Germany and Japan, and the emergence of a concerted European trading bloc. There has been a proliferation of missile and mass destruction weapons technology to the Middle East and South Asia. These trends point to a more multipolar world in the next century.

On the other hand, there is also evidence of a trend toward unipolarity, with one major actor, the United States, calling the shots. This is bolstered by perceived American military preponderance since 1989. International military actions ranging from the policing of Bosnia-Herzegovina to the Gulf War were heavily dependent on U.S. military firepower and logistics. Americans are confident that their vision of capitalist democracy is in the ascendancy. Developing nations have expressed alarm at this prospect in the context of the U.S.-inspired "New World Order" promulgated by the UN.

There are two principal counterarguments to the Unipolar World Thesis: those resting on assumptions about longer term American decline and the neorealist proposition that power begets resistance and competition. It could also be argued that it is the balance of political and ideological alignments that has changed and that the actual balance of military capabilities has not altered very much since 1989. Russia has certainly lost territory, population, and strategic resources but retains the ability to initiate a global thermonuclear war that both superpowers would lose. Russia is probing rather than resisting American foreign policy purposes only because she has changed sides in the political game.

Declinist arguments originated in research on the American response to defeat in Vietnam and growing interdependence in international economic relations. They peaked with Paul Kennedy's study of *The Rise and Fall of the Great Powers*. America's share of world economic activity has fallen sharply since 1945 and the U.S. indebtedness is portrayed as symptomatic of a superpower exhausted and overstretched from its global military commitments. But critics of the declinist school, such as Samuel Huntington and Henry Nau, for instance, have pointed to American economic resilience, noting that both the size of the U.S. lead in the 1950s and the scare over deficits in the 1980s were temporary and exceptional cases. Indeed, the gap between U.S. and European economic performance formed the essential backdrop to the G7/G8 summits of the 1990s.

Citing balance of power theory, neorealists predict that a countervailing force will inevitably emerge to curb any trend toward long-term hegemony. Waltz, writing in 1993, argued that the most likely scenario in the post-Cold War world is not a "bandwagoning" effect around American preferences but ultimate resistance to U.S. leadership. Since the early 1990s, a culturally and ideologically diverse group of countries, notably Iran, China, India, Zimbabwe, Cuba, and Malaysia, has indeed dissented from the emerging global consensus on human rights, UN military intervention, weapons proliferation, and trade. But, even when it has the backing of Russia, this grouping still lacks the cohesion to act consistently against American policy. We can only conclude that while the global power structure is still undergoing some kind of transition, the pace and ultimate extent of change remains uncertain.

B. Balance of Power Relationships and Regional Politics

Perhaps we will find better evidence of the renewed salience of balance of power relationships at regional level. The Gulf Crisis of 1990 and 1991 certainly suggested a U.S. concern with balance of power dynamics. To begin with, the ideologically incoherent anti-Iraqi coalition contained some unusual bedfellows: the United States, Saudi Arabia, Egypt, and Syria, and, tacitly at least, Israel as well. The endgame was even more telling. The United States chose to leave Saddam Hussein in power because it feared the consequences of the fall of Iraq. The dismemberment of such a significant regional power might drag Turkey and Iran into a conflict over the carcass. The Turks would intervene to curb Kurdish guerrilla activity; Iran might want to establish a Shiite satellite state in the southeast. The optimal solution, in this view, was a delicate balance of power in which Iraq was strong enough to survive as a state but too weak to launch any new military adventures. A similar logic drove Western countries to favor a stalemate in the earlier Iran-Iraq War, since a victory by either side would pose a new strategic threat to the rest of the region.

Another region where balance of power relationships are assuming new importance is East Asia. The rise of Japan and the tiger economies adds weight to the prospects of multipolarity in the world economy. There has been speculation about a new post-Cold War military-strategic balance within the region itself. If the United States were to withdraw from the area because of the declining Russian threat, Japan and the other East Asians might fear Chinese opportunism. China is already building a blue ocean navy capable of projecting power in the western Pacific. There are conflicts over territorial seas and resources around the Paracel and Spratly Islands. Beijing might use military coercion to resolve its unfinished business in Taiwan. In the more distant future, any failure on the part of the United States to protect South Korea or Japan might induce Tokyo to translate its technological advantages into military applications in a way that significantly alters both the regional and the global balance of military power. Tokyo and Beijing would then court the other East Asians in an attempt to get them on side or to neutralize those that might be initially tempted to support the opposing power. Conscious of these dynamics, the medium-sized states would shift alliances as their threat perceptions altered. Much as they fear Chinese hegemony, they also retain painful memories of a militarily aggressive Japan. They too might feel more secure in a true balance of power system.

The behavior of all participants in this regional subsystem already echoes the curious mixture of military preparedness and diplomatic caution that we found in Europe in the past. Whether in the fields of human rights or trade, many Western leaders follow Henry Kissinger's advice and pursue pragmatic policies toward China and the Southeast Asian nations in anticipation of their increasingly important role in the regional and global power structure of the 21st century. Policymakers tread gingerly lest they might need their opponent of today as a friend tomorrow. As for the United States, it could play the role of balancer that Britain performed in 19th-century Europe. Washington wants good relations with both China and Japan, while wishing to constrain them as well. It also wants to lessen its overall military involvement in the region.

This neat scenario is not without its problems. To begin with, it is still difficult to determine whether all of this reflects genuine efforts to construct a stable regional balance or merely reflects inertia and confusion in a time of strategic transition. Moreover, Michael Sheehan argues that the balancing role performed by Britain in the 19th century arose under a specific set of historical circumstances and is not a useful model for contemporary politics. In the case of East Asia, past American involvement and partisan commitments in regional conflicts render it less acceptable as a systemic balancer. Britain's land forces were not sufficient to pose a serious threat to the European powers. Her capabilities were primarily relevant to the oceans-based politics of naval warfare and the global political order rather than to military campaigns on the continental landmass. American power is so much greater and more wide-ranging that it poses a potential all-round threat to other essential actors in the system.

The pull of interdependence and trade may also favor regional integration rather than power politics, as it has done in Europe. In a recent survey, Renato Cruz de Castro found little statistical evidence of a regional arms race or an action-reaction cycle typical of balancing behavior. But this analogy with Europe could also be taken too far. For, despite all of the progress toward European integration, the triangular relationship among Germany, Britain, and France still provides ample room for shifting coalitions and alliance behaviour in the internal politics of the European Union.

Balance of power relationships are also evident in South Asia. Despite India's clear military superiority, the fear of chemical and nuclear war has produced a balance of terror on the subcontinent. Conscious of the need to prevent a systemic breakdown, both sides have agreed to mutual restraints under the 1972 Simla Accords, especially regarding Kashmir and their border areas. Moreover, Pakistan and India have cultivated external and subregional alignments in an attempt to preserve or alter the balance according to their needs. Thus, Pakistan has sought links with both the United States and China, while India is struggling hard to ensure continued Russian support in the post- Cold War setting. As Russia and China strengthen their ties, India has moved to improve its relations with Beijing too, lest Sino-Russian rapprochement develop to her disadvantage. Again conforming to the rules of power politics, the improvement in Sino-Indian relations reflects the logic of shifting alliances in circumstances where China, rather than Russia, could lead the challenge to American hegemony much desired by Indian leaders.

C. Competing Ideas: The Ideological Balance of Power

It would be premature, of course, to announce the death of global ideological conflict. Samuel Huntington has predicted a new "clash of civilizations" involving the liberal West, the Islamic East and the socially authoritarian Far East. Conflicts over values and human rights have not abated. The new power struggle in Central Asia may well be about access to regional mineral resources or geopolitics. But it is also, at least in part, a contest between those who put their faith in secularism and those who welcome an overtly Islamic influence.

It is all too easy to represent balance of power relationships and ideological competition as quite distinct and even mutually exclusive phenomena. Competing ideas often provide those intangible elements of political will and motivation that make all the difference. The balance of power among ideas is an important factor in the overall power balance. This is especially significant when the ideas in question concern the nature of the international system itself. Stephen Kocs, for instance, argues that the 19th century balance of power persisted, not because of the deterrent effect of military alignments but because of a shared adherence to international law. But he has still missed the point. It is the law of practice, the expected rules of behavior based on experience, rather than the formal Law of Nations written in treaties that is paramount. There was another balance of power at work here: that between those who believed that the strategic balance was important and those who would have undermined it.

The great philosophical questions in international relations have practical significance. Should security be dependent on balance of power relationships? Or should we attempt to build collective security through the United Nations? Has the sovereign state had its day? Should the global economy be run on free market lines or a more regulated basis? The prevailing answers to these questions create shifting balances of power which favor some states or actors at the expense of others. This kind of balance may change as a consequence of a single dramatic development. But more often than not, change will be evolutionary as the ebb and flow of ideas runs its course.

The prevailing norms of the international system are also power resources that can be used by states. Thus, while the norm against infringements on state sovereignty does not prevent superpower aggression against small states, it does restrain Great Power behavior in many circumstances. Likewise, as Krasner has shown in his 1985 work on North-South structural conflict, Third World states exploit the rules of conference diplomacy in international institutions and the collective ideology of Third World solidarity as a resource to generate bloc cohesion and as a counterweight to the Western advantage in material capabilities. Similarly, shifts in the prevailing mood have favored either free market or interventionist economic policies that, in turn, have had important implications for overall balance of power in the world economy.

As with the balance of material capabilities measured in terms of tanks or dollars, the ideological balance can be loosely defined as any relationship among competing ideas, including situations in which one set of ideas constitutes an orthodoxy. Thus, the norm of state sovereignty is deeply embedded in the main body of Western thought on international relations. However, there can also be delicate equilibrium balances that are easily upset and that require great care and attention. So even if the military capabilities of the 19th-century Great Powers were not evenly balanced, there was what Paul Schroeder called "a balance of satisfactions and rights, performance and payoffs." These "satisfactions" and "rights" were intangible variables but no less critical to European stability.

Our focus on nonmaterial considerations echoes the so-called "constructivist" approach to power and international institutions. In this view, it is not the material resources themselves that constrain behavior but their meaning to the actors involved. This meaning is "constituted" or constructed through the experience of interaction among states. The system socializes actors and creates rules of practice. Where these rules are intentionally created, we have international regime, the norms and rules governing specific issue areas in international politics. We have already met these regimes in the context of intentionally created balances of power where rules governing mutual restraint and power relations are in effect. A key element here is the belief that one's own interests are in some way bound up with the health of the system: not necessarily of other individual states but of the system as a whole. The balance of power held together not only because of mutual fear but also because of an even greater fear of the consequences of systemic crisis. Again, we must emphasize that rules, expectations, and fears are nonmaterial, perceptual, or cognitive rather than purely material factors. Perhaps the greatest contest over rules and expectations arises between status quo powers and rising challengers. Challenges to the status quo can result from shifts in the distribution of military or economic resources, but they can also be cultural and ideological. Moreover, as in conventional balance of power relationships, some actors can swap their partners as we move from one issue to another, thus creating cross-cutting cleavages of the type that we saw in the "musical chairs" of 18th- and 19th-century power politics.

The Cold War ended in the capitulation of one of the ideological blocs, a paradigm shift in which one perspective e displaced another. The increasingly bitter contest between Western value systems and Islamic influences in much of the Arab World, the Middle East, and Central Asia also appears quite intractable. So the prospects for balance of power—style flexibility and "musical chairs" in the relationship among cultural warriors do not look particularly good. But they are not impossible. East Asians, for instance, have much in common with the West and may dislike Islamic fundamentalism. They also dislike Western preaching about human rights. On the other hand, there are social and cultural issues on which Western conservative leaders and Islamic or East Asian governments might agree. Who will these emerging nations support when it comes to the construction of global regimes? Likewise, Latin Americans have followed the U.S. example in much of their political and economic life. They have a love-hate relationship with the United States. On the other hand, many of them would like to import European-style social democracy in order to deal with problems of poverty and inequality. In a global debate between U.S.-style free market liberalism and European social regulation, the Latins are in an intriguing position.

Rather than dismissing intangible resources like rules and value systems as "another" arena of inquiry, we can incorporate them into our calculation of the overall balance of power. Given the methodological problems associated with quantifying material power resources, this will not be easy. On the other hand, the exclusion of these variables as mere residual factors does little to enhance our understanding of balance of power relationships, the object of the research in the first place.

IV. CONCLUSION

The concepts of a balance of power and balance of power relationships remain elusive. A pure multipolar equilibrium balance of the type preferred by the 18th-century philosophers, will be difficult to establish and even more difficult to maintain over long periods of time. Nonetheless, many of the norms and expectations born out of earlier attempts to sustain such balances are still relevant today. Attention to local, regional or global balances can foster a concern for system stability, alongside the usual focus on national interest. It also encourages actors to learn more about the strategic vulnerabilities perceived by others. These aspects of balance of power relationships contribute to global or regional community-building in a practical sense but without the usually futile macropolitical engineering associated with utopian plans for World Government and Universal Law.

At the same time, however, power politics, whether directed at systemic or individual state goals, can blind policymakers to the rights of individuals and other moral and ethical dimensions of international relations. As we saw in the case of Bismarck's Germany, balance of power relationships can be misused to mask longer-term expansionist, zero-sum strategies. Balance of power relationships do not prevent war. At best, they confine it to a limited sphere of corrective action and legitimate it under specific circumstances. The danger is that, for the most ambitious states, a delicate equilibrium balance of power may represent an obstacle to be overcome at the earliest possible opportunity.

The looser conception of balance of power as any stable configuration of forces will continue to be used to describe and even to quantify the structural features of the international system at any given time. But if this is to be accurate, we must add nonmaterial variables to our calculations. The ideological balance of power is just as important as any raw count of material factors. Its incorporation into the wider concept represents an interesting challenge to both empirical and theoretical research in the years ahead.

The various interpretations of balance of power relationships described here will continue to be used by academics. As with any other concept, this is not problematic provided that we specify our terms in advance and indicate how they are to be used. Moreover, though the patterns we discover in those relationships can be interesting, they do not produce iron laws. Researchers can avoid a crude and deterministic approach to the predictive utility of the distribution of resources. The real world of international politics is much more complex than allowed for by any model. Nonetheless, balance of power theory can be a useful yardstick or framework of analysis for assessing many instances of state behavior.

Also See the Following Articles

ALLIANCE SYSTEMS • COLD WAR • COLLECTIVE SECURITY SYSTEMS • INTERNATIONAL RELATIONS, OVERVIEW • POWER, SOCIAL AND POLITICAL THEORIES OF

Bibliography

Bull, H. (1977). *The anarchical society: A study of order in world politics*. New York: Columbia University Press.

de Castro, R. C. (1997, April). Is there a Northeast Asian arms race? Some preliminary findings. *Issues and Studies*. *33*(4), 13–34.

Claude, I. (1989, April). The balance of power revisited. *Review of International Studies 15*(2), 77–85.

Dessler, D. (1989, Summer). What's at stake in the agent-structure debate? *International Organization*. *43*(3), 441–473.

Fukuyama, F. (1990). *The end of history and the last man*. New York: Free Press.

Gulick, E. (1955). *Europe's classical balance of power*. Ithaca, NY: Cornell University Press.

Huntington, S. P. (1988, Winter). The U.S.—Decline or renewal? *Foreign Affairs, 67*(2). Reprinted in Stiles, Kendall and Akaha, Tsunea (Eds.). (1991). *International political economy: A reader*, pp. 481–498. New York: Harper-Collins.

Huntington, S. P. (1997). *The clash of civilizations*. Hemmel Hempstead: Simon and Schuster.

Kaplan, M. (1966). Some problems of international systems research. *International Political Communities: An Anthology*. Garden City: Anchor. Reprinted in J. Vasquez (ed.), *Classics of international relations* (2nd ed.), pp. 277–282. Prentice Hall, Englewood Cliffs.

Kennedy, P. (1987). *The rise and fall of the great powers: Economic change and military conflict from 1500 to 2000*. New York: Random House.

Kissinger, H. (1994). *Diplomacy*. London: Simon and Schuster.

Kocs, S. A. (1994, December). Explaining the strategic behaviour of states: International law as system structure. *International Studies Quarterly, 38*(4), 535–556.

Krasner, S. D. (1985). *Structural conflict: The Third World against global liberalism*. London: University of California Press.

Little, R. (1989, April). Deconstructing the balance of power: Two traditions of thought. *Review of International Studies*, 15(2), 87–100.

Moul, W. (1989, April). Measuring the "balances of power": A look at some numbers. *Review of International Studies*. *15*(2), 101–122.

Nau, H. R. (1990) *The myth of America's decline: Leading the world economy in the 1990's*. Oxford: Oxford University Press.

Organski, A.F.K. (1958). *World politics*. New York: Knopf.

Scharpel, J. (1993, December). Change in material capabilities and the onset of war. *International Studies Quarterly, 37*(4), 395–408.

Schroeder, P. (1989, April). The nineteenth century system: balance of power or political equilibrium? *Review of International Studies, 15*(2), 135–154.

Sheehan, M. (1989, April). The place of the balancer in balance of power theory. *Review of International Studies, 15*(2), 123–134.

Waltz, K. (1979). *Theory of international politics*. London: McGraw-Hill.

Waltz, K. (1993, Fall). The emerging structure of international politics. *International Security, 18*, 44–79.

Behavioral Psychology

Kenneth R. Murray
Armiger Police Training Institute

Dave Grossman
Arkansas State University

Robert W. Kentridge
University of Durham, U.K.

GLOSSARY

Acquired Violence Immune Deficiency Syndrome (AVIDS) The "violence immune system" exists in the midbrain of all healthy creatures, causing them to be largely unable to kill members of their own species in territorial and mating battles. In human beings this resistance has existed historically in all close-range, interpersonal confrontations. "Conditioning" (particularly the conditioning of children through media violence and interactive video games) can create an "acquired deficiency" in this immune system, resulting in "Acquired Violence Immune Deficiency Syndrome" or AVIDS. As a result of this weakened immune system, the victim becomes more vulnerable to violence enabling factors such as poverty, discrimination, drugs, gangs, radical politics and the availability of guns.

Behavior Modification (also behavior therapy and conditioning therapy) A treatment approach designed to modify a subject's behavior directly (rather than correct the root cause), through systematic manipulation of environmental and behavioral variables thought to be related to the behavior. Techniques included within behavior modification include operant conditioning and token economy.

Behavioral Psychology (also behaviorism) The subset of psychology that focuses on studying and modifying observable behavior by means of systematic manipulation of environmental factors. In its purest form behaviorism rejects all cognitive explanations of behavior.

Classical Conditioning (also Pavlovian and respondent conditioning) A form of conditioning in which a neutral stimulus becomes associated with an involuntary or autonomic response, such as salivation or increased heart rate.

Conditioning A more or less permanent change in an individual's behavior that occurs as a result of experience and practice (or repetition) of the experience. Conditioning is applied clinically in behavior modification. There are generally two types of conditioning: operant conditioning and classical conditioning.

Operant Conditioning (also conditioning) A form of conditioning that involves *voluntary* actions (such as lifting a latch, following a maze, or aiming and firing a weapon), with reinforcing or punishing events serving to alter the strength of association between the stimulus and the response. In recent, *human* usage operant conditioning has developed into a type of training that will intensely and realistically simulate the actual conditions to be faced in a future situation.

Effective conditioning will enable an individual to respond in a precisely defined manner, is spite of high states of anxiety or fear.

Reinforcement The presentation of a stimulus (i.e., a reinforcer) that acts to strengthen a response.

BEHAVIORAL PSYCHOLOGY is the subset of psychology that focuses on studying and modifying observable behavior by means of systematic manipulation of environmental factors. This article examines the history and origins of behavioral psychology, the role of behavioral psychology in creating a revolution in military training and combat effectiveness during the second half of the 20th Century, and the contributions of behavioral psychology in helping to understand one of the key causal factors in modern violent crime.

I. INTRODUCTION: A BEHAVIORAL REVOLUTION IN COMBAT

Behavioral psychology, with its subsets of behavior modification and operant conditioning, is a field that is ripe for use and abuse in the realm of violence, peace and conflict. Perhaps the least subtle or most "directive" of all the fields of psychology, in its purest form behaviorism rejects all cognitive explanations of behavior and focuses on studying and modifying observable behavior by means of systematic manipulation of environmental factors. In its application, behavior modification and other aspects of the behavioristic approach are generally considered best for use on animals and children (who tend not to resent or rebel against such overt manipulation as reinforcers and token economies), *and* for the preparation of individuals to react immediately and reflexively in life threatening situations such as: children in fire drills, pilots repetitively trained to react to emergencies in flight simulators, and law enforcement and military personnel conditioned to fire accurately in combat situations.

Throughout history armies and nations have attempted to achieve ever higher degrees of control over their soldiers, and reinforcement and punishment have always been manipulated to do so. But it was done by intuition, half blindly and unsystematically, and was never truly understood. In the 20th century this changed completely as the systematic development of the scientific field of behavioral psychology made possible one of the greatest revolutions in the history of human combat, enabling firing rates to be raised from a baseline of 20% or less in World War II to over 90% among modern, properly conditioned armies.

In the post-Cold War era the police officers and the soldiers of the world's democracies are assuming increasingly similar missions. Around the world armies are being called upon for "peace making" and "peacekeeping" duties, and law enforcement agencies are responding to escalating violent crime with structures, tactics, training and weapons that have been traditionally associated with the military.

Some have observed that this process may be resulting in the creation of a new warrior-protector class similar to that called for by Plato in that first, fledgling Greek democracy more than 2000 year ago. If there is a new class of warrior-protector, then one factor which is profoundly unique in its modern makeup is this systematic application of behavioral psychology, particularly operant conditioning, in order to ensure the warrior's ability to kill, survive, and succeed in the realm of close combat.

Today the behavioral genie is out of the bottle, and in life-and-death, close-combat situations any soldier or police officer who is not *mentally* armed may well be as important as if he or she were not *physically* armed. Governments have come to understand this, and today any warrior that a democratic society deems worthy of being physically armed is also, increasingly, being mentally equipped to kill.

When this is done with law enforcement and military professionals it is done carefully and with powerful safeguards, yet still it is a legitimate cause for concern. But the final lesson to be learned in an examination of the role of behavioral psychology in violence, peace, and conflict is that the processes being carefully manipulated to enable violence in government agencies can also be found in media violence and violent video games, resulting in the indiscriminate mass conditioning of children to kill, and a subsequent, worldwide explosion of violence.

II. THE BIRTH OF BEHAVIORAL PSYCHOLOGY

Around the turn of the century, Edward Thorndike attempted to develop an objective experimental method for testing the mechanical problem solving ability of cats and dogs. Thorndike devised a number of wooden crates which required various combinations of latches, levers, strings, and treadles to open them. A dog or a cat would be put in one of these puzzle boxes and, sooner or later, would manage to escape.

Thorndike's initial aim was to show that the anecdotal achievement of cats and dogs could be replicated in controlled, standardized circumstances. However, he soon realized that he could now measure animal intelligence using this equipment. His method was to set an animal the same task repeatedly, each time measuring the time it took to solve it. Thorndike could then compare these learning curves across different situations and species.

Thorndike was particularly interested in discovering whether his animals could learn their tasks through imitation or observation. He compared the learning curves of cats who had been given the opportunity to observe other cats escape from a box, with those who had never seen the puzzle being solved, and found no difference in their rate of learning. He obtained the same null result with dogs and, even when he showed the animals the methods of opening a box by placing their paws on the appropriate levers and so on, he found no improvement. He fell back on a much simpler, "trial and error" explanation of learning. Occasionally, quite by chance, an animal performs an action that frees it from the box. When the animal finds itself in the same position again, it is more likely to perform the same action again. The reward of being freed from the box somehow strengthens an association between a stimulus (being in a certain position in the box) and an appropriate action. Rewards act to strengthen these stimulus-response associations. The animal learned to solve the puzzle-box not by reflecting on possible actions and really puzzling its way out of it but by a mechanical development of actions originally made by chance. Thus Thorndike demonstrates that the mind of a dog, or a cat, is not capable of learning by observation, then can only learn what has been personally experienced and reinforced.

By 1910 Thorndike had formalized this notion into the "Law of Effect," which essentially states that responses that are accompanied or followed by satisfaction (i.e., a reward, or what was later to be termed a reinforcement) will be more likely to reoccur, and those which are accompanied by discomfort (i.e., a punishment) will be less likely to reoccur. Thorndike extrapolated his finding to humans and subsequently maintained that, in combination with the Law of Exercise (which states that associations are strengthened by use and weakened by disuse), and the concept of instinct, the Law of Effect could explain all of human behavior in terms of the development of a myriad of stimulus-response associations.

Thorndike, his laws, and trial-and-error learning became the foundation for behavioral psychology, and the behaviorist position that human behavior could be explained entirely in terms of stimulus-response associations and the effects of reinforcers upon them. In its purest sense this new field of behavioral psychology entirely excluded cognitive concepts such as desires or goals.

John Broadhus Watson in his 1914 book, *Behavior: An Introduction to Comparative Psychology,* made the next major step in the development of behavioral psychology. Watson's theoretical position was even more extreme than Thorndike's. His rejection of cognition, or "mentalism" was total and he had no place for concepts such as pleasure or distress in his explanations of behavior. He essentially rejected the law of effect, denying that pleasure or discomfort caused stimulus-response associations to be learned. For Watson, all that was important was the frequency of occurrence of stimulus-response pairings. Reinforcers might cause some responses to occur more often in the presence of particular stimuli, but they did not act directly to cause their learning. In 1919 Watson published his second book, *Psychology from the Standpoint of a Behaviorist,* which established him as the founder of the American school of behaviorism.

In the 1920s behaviorism began to wane in popularity. A number of studies, particularly those with primates (which are capable of observational, monkey-see, monkey-do, learning), appeared to show flaws in the law of effect and to require mental representations in their explanation. But in 1938 Burrhus Friederich Skinner powerfully defended and advanced behaviorism when he published *The Behavior of Organisms,* which was arguably the most influential work on animal behavior of the century. B.F. Skinner resurrected the law of effect in more starkly behavioral terms and developed the Skinner Box, a technology that allowed sequences of behavior produced over a long time to be studied objectively, which was a great improvement on the individual learning trials of Watson and Thorndike.

Skinner developed the basic concept of "operant conditioning" claiming that this type of learning was not the result of stimulus-response learning. For Skinner the basic association in operant conditioning was between the operant response and the reinforcer, with a discriminative stimulus serving to signal when the association would be acted upon.

It is worth briefly comparing trial-and-error learning with classical conditioning. In in 1890s, Pavlov, a Russian physiologist, was observing the production of saliva by dogs as they were fed, when he noticed that saliva was also produced when the person who fed them appeared, even though he was without food. This is not surprising. Every farm boy for thousands of years has realized that animals become excited when they hear the sounds that indicate they are about to be fed. But Pavlov carefully observed and measured one small part of the process. He paired a sound, a tone, with feeding his dogs so that the tone occurred several times right before and during the feeding. Soon the dogs salivated to the tone, as they did to the food. They had learned a new connection: tone with food or tone with saliva response.

In classical conditioning, a neutral stimulus becomes associated with an involuntary response, such as salivation or increased heart rate. But operant conditioning involves voluntary actions (such as lifting a latch, following a maze, or aiming and firing a weapon), with reinforcing or punishing events serving to alter the strength of association between the stimulus and the response.

The ability of behavioral psychology to turn voluntary motor responses into a conditioned response is demonstrated in one of Watson's early experiments which studied maze-learning, using rats in a type of maze that was simply a long, straight alley with food at the end. Watson found that once the animal was well trained at running this maze it did so almost automatically, or reflexively. Once started by the stimulus of the maze its behavior becomes a series of voluntary motor responses largely detached from stimuli in the outside world. This was made clear when Watson shortened the alleyway, which caused well trained (i.e., conditioned) rats to run straight into the end of the wall. This was known as the Kerplunk Experiment and it demonstrates the degree to which a set of behaviorally conditioned, voluntary motor responses can become reflexive, or automatic in nature. Only a few decades after Watson ran these early, simple experiments, the world would see the tenets of behaviorism used to instill the voluntary motor responses necessary to turn close combat killing into a reflexive and automatic response.

III. THE PROBLEM: A RESISTANCE TO KILLING

Much of human behavior is irrefutably linked to a mixture of operant and classical conditioning. From one perspective grades in school and wages at work are nothing more than positive reinforcers, and grades and money are nothing more than tokens in a token economy, and the utility of behaviorism in understanding daily human behavior is significant.

Yet the purist position (which holds that behavioristic processes explain all aspects of human behavior), is generally considered to be flawed in its application to humans, since humans are able to learn by observational learning, and humans tend to strongly oppose and negate blatant attempts to manipulate them against their will. But in emergency situations, or in the preparation of individuals for emergency situations, behaviorism reigns supreme.

Those in power have always attempted to utilize the basic behavioral concepts of rewards, punishments, and repetitive training to shape or control, and in many cases they would hope, predict the responses of military and law enforcement personnel throughout history. Certainly in ancient times when there was no formal understanding of the underlying precepts of conditioning, military leaders nevertheless subjected their troops to forms of conditioning with the intention of instilling warlike responses.

Repetition played heavily in attempting to condition firing as seen in Prussian and Napoleonic drill in the loading and firing of muskets. Through thousands of repetitions it was hoped that, under the stress of battle, men would simply fall back on the learned skill to continue firing at the enemy. While this may have accounted for some increase in the firing of muskets in the general direction of the enemy, statistics from the Napoleonic era do not bear out the hit ratios that would indicate success in the method, success being determined by increased kill ratios.

In tests during this era it was repeatedly demonstrated that an average of regiment of 250 men, each firing a musket at a rate of four shots per minute, could hypothetically put close to 1000 holes in a 6-foot high by 100-foot wide sheet of paper at a range of 25 yards. But Paddy Griffith has documented in his studies of actual Napoleonic and American Civil War battles that in many cases the actual hit ratios were as low as zero hits, with an average being approximately one or two hits, per minute, per regiment, which is less than 1% of their theoretical killing potential. While these soldiers may have been trained to fire their weapons, they had not been conditioned to kill their enemy.

In behavioral terms, to prepare (or train, or condition) a soldier to kill, the stimulus (which did not appear in their training) should have been an enemy soldier in their sights. The target behavior (which they did not practice for) should have been to accurately fire their weapons at another human being. There should have been immediate feedback when they hit a target, and there should have been rewards for performing these specific functions, or punishment for failing to do so. No aspect of this occurred in their training, and it was inevitable that such training would fail.

To truly understand the necessity for operant conditioning in this situation it must first be recognized that most participants in close-combat are literally "frightened out of their wits." Once the arrows or bullets start flying, combatants stop thinking with the forebrain (which is the part of the brain that makes us human) and thought processes localize in the midbrain, or mammalian brain, which is the primitive part of the brain that is generally indistinguishable from that of a dog or a rat. And in the mind of a dog the only thing which will influence behavior is operant conditioning.

In conflict situations the dominance of midbrain processing can be observed in the existence of a powerful resistance to killing one's own kind, a resistance that exists in every healthy member of every species. Konrad Lorenz, in his definitive book, *On Aggression,* notes that it is rare for animals of the same species to fight to the death. In their territorial and mating battles animals with horns will butt their heads together in a relatively harmless fashion, but against any other species they will go to the side and attempt to gut and gore. Similarly, piranha will fight one another with raps of their tails but they will turn their teeth on anything and everything else, and rattlesnakes will wrestle each other but they have no hesitation to turn their fangs on anything else. Lorenz suggests that this non-specicidal tendency is innately imprinted into the genetic code in order to safeguard the survival of the species.

One major modern revelation in the field of military psychology is the observation that this resistance to killing one's own species is also a key factor in human combat. Brigadier General S.L.A. Marshall first observed this during his work as the Chief Historian of the European Theater of Operations in World War II. Based on his innovative new technique of postcombat interviews, Marshall concluded in his landmark book, *Men Against Fire,* that only 15 to 20% of the individual riflemen in World War II fired their weapons at an exposed enemy soldier.

Marshall's findings have been somewhat controversial, but every available, parallel, scholarly study has validated his basic findings. Ardant du Picq's surveys of French officers in the 1860s and his observations on ancient battles, Keegan and Holmes' numerous accounts of ineffectual firing throughout history, Paddy Griffith's data on the extraordinarily low killing rate among Napoleonic and American Civil War regiments, Stouffer's extensive World War II and post-war research, Richard Holmes' assessment of Argentine firing rates in the Falklands War, the British Army's laser reenactments of historical battles, the FBI's studies of nonfiring rates among low enforcement officers in the 1950s and 1960s, and countless other individual and anecdotal observations, all confirm Marshall's fundamental conclusion that man is not, by nature, a close-range, interpersonal killer.

The existence of this resistance can be observed in its marked absence in sociopaths who, by definition, feel no empathy or remorse for their fellow human beings. Pit bull dogs have been selectively bred for sociopathy, bred for the absence of the resistance to killing one's kind in order to ensure that they will perform the unnatural act of killing another dog in battle. Breeding to overcome this limitation in humans is impractical, but humans are very adept at finding mechanical means to overcome natural limitations. Humans were born without the ability to fly, so we found mechanisms that overcame this limitation and enabled flight. Humans also were born without the ability to kill our fellow humans, and so, throughout history, we have devoted great effort to finding a way to overcome this resistance.

IV. THE BEHAVIORAL SOLUTION: CONDITIONING TO KILL

By 1946 the U.S. Army had completely accepted Marshall's World War II findings of a 15 to 20% firing rate among American riflemen, and the Human Resources Research Office of the U.S. Army subsequently pioneered a revolution in combat training that replaced the old method of firing at bull's-eye targets with deeply ingrained operant conditioning using realistic, man-shaped pop-up targets that fall when hit.

The discriminative stimulus was a realistic target popping up in the soldier's field of view. For decades this target was a two-dimensional silhouette, but in recent years both the military and police forces have been changing to mannequin-like, three-dimensional, molded plastic targets; photo realistic targets; and actual force-on-force encounters against live adversaries utilizing the paint pellet projectile training systems pioneered by The Armiger Corporation under the name of Simunition. These are key refinements in the effectiveness of the conditioning process, since it is crucial that the discriminative stimulus used in training be as realistic as possible in its simulation of the actual, anticipated stimulus if the training is to be transferred to reality in a crucial, life-and-death situation.

The operant response being conditioned is to accurately fire a weapon at a human being, or at least a realistic simulation of one. The firer and the grader know if the firing is accurate, since the target drops when hit. This realistically simulates what will happen in combat, and it is gratifying and rewarding to the firer. This minimal gap between the performance (hitting the target) and the initial reinforcement (target drops) is key to successful conditioning since it provides immediate association between the two events. A form of token economy is established as an accumulation of small achievements (hits) are cashed in for marksmanship badges and other associated rewards (such as a three-day pass), and punishments (such as having to retrain on a Saturday that would have otherwise been a day off) are presented to those who fail to perform.

The training process involves hundreds of repetitions of this action, and ultimately the subject becomes like Watson's rats in the Kerplunk Experiment, performing a complex set of voluntary motor actions until they become automatic or reflexive in nature. Psychologists know that this kind of powerful "operant conditioning" is the only technique that will reliably influence the primitive, midbrain processing of a frightened human being, just as fire drills condition terrified school chldren to respond properly during a fire, and repetitious, stimulus-response conditioning in flight simulators enables frightened pilots to respond reflexively to emergency situations.

Modern marksmanship training is such an excellent example of behaviorism that it has been used for years in the introductory psychology course taught to all cadets at the U.S. Military Academy at West Point as a classic example of operant conditioning. And in the 1980s, during a visit to West Point, B.F. Skinner identified modern military marksmanship training as a near-perfect application of operant conditioning.

Throughout history various factors have been manipulated to enable and force combatants to kill, but the introduction of conditioning in modern training was a true revolution. The application and perfection of these basic conditioning techniques appear to have increased the rate of fire from near 20% in World War II to approximately 55% in Korea and around 95% in Vietnam. Similar high rates of fire resulting from modern conditioning techniques can be seen in FBI data on law enforcement firing rates since the nationwide introduction of modern conditioning techniques in the last 1960s.

One of the most dramatic examples of the value and power of this modern, psychological revolution in training can be seen in Richard Holmes' observations of the 1982 Falklands War. The superbly trained (i.e., conditioned) British forces were without air or artillery superiority and were consistently outnumbered three-to-one while attacking the poorly trained (i.e. nonconditioned) but well equipped and carefully dug-in Argentine defenders. Superior British firing rates (which Holmes estimates to be well over 90%) resulting from modern training techniques has been credited as a key factor in the series of British victories in that brief but bloody war.

Today nearly all first-world nations and their law enforcement agencies have thoroughly integrated operant conditioning into their marksmanship training. It is no accident that in recent years the world's largest employer of psychologists is the U.S. Army Research Bureau. However, most third-world nations, and most nations which rely on large numbers of draftees rather than a small, well trained army, generally do not (or cannot) spare the resources for this kind of training. And any future army or law enforcement agency which attempts to go into close combat without such psychological preparation is likely to meet a fate similar to that of the Argentines.

V. CONDITIONING KIDS TO KILL

Thus the tremendous impact of psychological "conditioning" to overcome the resistance to killing can be observed in Vietnam and the Falklands where it gave U.S. and British units a tremendous tactical advantage in close combat, increasing the firing rate from the World War II baseline of around 20% to over 90% in these wars.

Through violent programming on television and in movies, and through interactive point-and-shoot video games, the developed nations are indiscriminately introducing to their children the same weapons technology that major armies and law enforcement agencies around the world use to "turn off" the midbrain "safety catch" that Brigadier General S.L.A. Marshall discovered in World War II.

U.S. Bureau of Justice Statistics research indicates that law enforcement officers and veterans (including Vietnam veterans) are statistically less likely to be incarcerated than a nonveteran of the same age. The key safeguard in this process appears to be the deeply ingrained discipline that the soldier and police officer internalize with their training. However, by saturating children with media violence as entertainment, and then exposing them to interactive "point-and-shoot" arcade and video games, it has become increasingly clear that society is aping military conditioning, but without the vital safeguard of discipline.

The same sort of discipline that sets boundaries for members of the military is also part of the hunting subculture, the other sector of society that is familiar with guns. In this environment there are: strict rules about not pointing guns at people, extreme cautions regarding the safety of individuals, and often even respect for their prey, all of which hunters pass on as part of their socialization process and which are reinforced by strict laws. Video game players are not instilled with the same values.

The observation that violence in the media is causing violence in our streets is nothing new. The American Academy of Pediatrics, the American Psychiatric Association, the American Medical Association, and their equivalents in many other nations have all made unequivocable statements about the link between media violence and violence in our society. The APA, in their 1992 report *Big World, Small Screen,* concluded that the "scientific debate is over." And in 1993 the APA's commission on violence and youth concluded that "there is absolutely no doubt that higher levels of viewing violence on television are correlated with increased acceptance of aggressive attitudes and increased aggressive behavior." The evidence is quite simply overwhelming.

Dr. Brandon Centerwall, professor of epidemiology at the University of Washington, has summarized the overwhelming nature of this body of evidence. His research demonstrates that, anywhere in the world that television is introduced, within 15 years the murder rate will double. (And across 15 years the murder rate will significantly underrepresent the problem because medical technology developments will be saving ever more lives each year.)

Centerwall concludes that if television had never been introduced in the United States, then there would today be 10,000 fewer homicides each year in the United States, 70,000 fewer rapes, and 700,000 fewer injurious assaults. Overall violent crime would be half what it is. He notes that the net effect of television has been to increase the aggressive predisposition of approximately 8% of the population, which is all that is required to double the murder rate. Statistically speaking 8% is a very small increase. Anything less than 5% is not even considered to be statistically significant. But in human terms, the impact of doubling the homicide rate is enormous.

There are many psychological and sociological processes through which media violence turns into violent crime. From a developmental standpoint we know that around the age of 18 months a child is able to discern what is on television and movies, but the part of their mind that permits them to organize where information came from does not fully develop until they are between ages five and seven. Thus, when a young child sees someone shot, stabbed, beaten, degraded, abused, or murdered on the screen, for them it is as though it were actually happening. They are not capable of discerning the difference, and the effect is as though they were children of a war zone, seeing death and destruction all around them, and accepting violence as a way of life.

From a Pavlovian, or classical conditioning standpoint, there is what Dave Grossman has termed the Reverse-Clockwork Orange process. In the movie, *Clockwork Orange,* a sociopath is injected with a drug that makes him nauseous and he then is exposed to violent movies. Eventually he comes to associate all violence with nausea and is somewhat "cured" of his sociopathy. In real life millions of children are exposed to thousands of repetitions of media violence, which they learn to associate with not nausea but pleasure in the form of their favorite candy, soda, and a girlfriend's perfume as they sit and laugh and cheer at vivid depictions of human death and suffering.

Finally, from a behavioral perspective, the children of the industrialized world participate in countless repetitions of point-and-shoot video and arcade games that provide the motor skills necessary to turn killing into an automatic, reflexive, "kerplunk" response, but without the stimulus discriminators and the safeguard of discipline found in military and law enforcement conditioning.

Thus, from a psychological standpoint, the children of the industrialized world are being brutalized and traumatized at a young age, and then through violent video games (operant conditioning) and media violence (classical conditioning) they are learning to kill and learning to like it. The result of this interactive process is a worldwide virus of violence.

A hundred things can convince the forebrain to take gun in hand and go to a certain point: poverty, drugs, gangs, leaders, radical politics and the social learning of violence in the media. But traditionally all of these influences have slammed into the resistance that a frightened, angry human being confronts in the midbrain. With the exception of violent sociopaths (who, by definition, do not have this resistance) the vast, vast majority of circumstances are not sufficient to overcome this midbrain safety net. But, if you are conditioned to overcome these midbrain inhibitions, then you are a walking time bomb, a pseudo-sociopath, just waiting for the random factors of social interaction and forebrain rationalization to put you at the wrong place and the wrong time.

An effective analogy can be made to AIDS in attempting to communicate the impactof this technology. AIDS does not kill people, it destroys the immune system and makes the victim vulnerable to death by other factors. The "violence immune system" exists in the midbrain, and conditioning in the media creates an "acquired deficiency" in this immune system, resulting in what Grossman has termed "Acquired Violence Immune Deficiency Syndrome" or AVIDS. As a result of this weakened immune system, the victim becomes more vulnerable to violence enabling factors such as: poverty, discrimination, drugs, gangs, radical politics and the availability of guns.

In behavioral terms this indiscriminate use of combat conditioning techniques on children is the moral equivalent of giving an assault weapon to every child in every industrialized nation in the world. If, hypothetically, this were done, the vast, vast majority of children would almost certainly not kill anyone with their assault rifles; but if only a tiny percentage did, then the results would be tragic, and unacceptable. It is increasingly clear that this is not a hypothetical situation. Indiscriminate civilian application of combat conditioning techniques as entertainment has increasingly been identified as a key factor in world-wide, skyrocketing violent crime rates. Between 1957 and 1992 aggravated assault in the United States, according to the FBI, went up from around 60 per 100,000 to over 440 per 100,000. Between 1977 and 1986 the "serious assault" rate, as reported to Interpol:

- Increased nearly five-fold in Norway and Greece, and the murder rate more than tripled in Norway and doubled in Greece.
- In Australia, and New Zealand the "serious assault" rate increased approximately four-fold, and the murder rate approximately doubled in both nations.
- During the same period the assault rate tripled in Sweden, and approximately doubled in Belgium, Canada, Denmark, England-Wales, France, Hungary, Netherlands, Scotland, and the United States; while all these nations (with the exception of Canada) also had an associated (but smaller) increase in murder.

All of these increases in violent crime, in all of these nations, (which Dave Grossman has termed a virus of violence) occurred during a period when medical and law enforcement technology should have been bringing murder and crime rates down. It is no accident that this has been occurring primarily in industrialized nations, since the factor that caused all of these increases is the same factor that caused a revolution in close combat, except in this case it is the media, not the military, that has been conditioning kids to kill.

VI. CONCLUSION: THE FUTURE OF VIOLENCE, SOCIETY, AND BEHAVIORISM

The impact of behavioral psychology on combat in the second half of the 20th century has been truly revolutionary. It has been a quiet, subtle revolution, but nonetheless one with profound effects. A healthy, self aware, democratic society must understand these processes that have been set in play on its streets and among its armed forces. Among government institutions this is being done with great care and safeguards, nevertheless it should trouble and concern a society that this is occurring and (far more so) that it may well be necessary.

In a world of violent crime, in a world in which children around the globe are being casually conditioned to kill, there may well be justification for the cop and the peacekeeper to be operantly conditioned to engage in deadly force. Indeed, Ken Murray has conducted pioneering research at Armiger Police Training Institute that concludes that, even with conditioning, the psychology of the close combat equation is still badly skewed against the forces of law and order. Building on the Killing Enabling Factors first developed by Dave Grossman, Murray's widely presented findings have been instrumental in a major reassessment of the need for a comprehensive, systematic approach to law enforcement training.

But if the carefully safeguarded conditioning of military and law enforcement professionals is a necessary evil that is still a legitimate cause for concern, how much more should a society be concerned about the fact that the exact same process is being indiscriminately applied to our children, but without the safeguards?

The impact of behavioral technology in the second half of the 20th century has been profound, closely paralleling the timeframe and process of nuclear technology. Behavioral psychology has done to the microcosm of battle what nuclear weapons did to the macrocosm of war. Just as our civilization is entering into the 21st century with a determination to restrain and apply itself to the challenges of nuclear proliferation, so too might the time have come to examine the indiscriminate proliferation of violent behavioral conditioning distributed indiscriminately to children as a form of entertainment.

Also See the Following Articles

AGGRESSION AND ALTRUISM • ANIMAL BEHAVIOR STUDIES, NONPRIMATES • ANIMAL BEHAVIOR STUDIES, PRIMATES • PSYCHOLOGICAL EFFECTS OF COMBAT • EVOLUTIONARY FACTORS • RITUAL AND SYMBOLIC BEHAVIOR • WEAPONRY, EVOLUTION OF

Bibliography

American Psychiatric Association (1975). *A psychiatric glossary*. Washington, DC: APA. Washington.

Boakes, R. A. (1984). *From Darwin to behaviorism: Psychology and the mind of animals*. Cambridge: Cambridge University Press.

Bower, G. H. & Hilgard, E. R. (1981). *Theories of learning (5th ed.)*. Englewood Cliffs, NJ: Prentice-Hall.

Centerwall, B. (1992). Television and violence: The scale of the problem and where to go from here. *Journal of the American Medical Association*, 267 (10 June 1992): 3,059.

Grossman, D. (1995, 1996). *On killing: The psychological cost of learning to kill in war and society*. New York: Little, Brown, and Co.

Holmes, R. (1985). *Acts of war: The behavior of men in battle*. New York: The Free Press.

Lorenz, K. (1966). *On aggression*. New York: Harcourt Brace.

Schwartz, B. & Robbins, S. J. (1995). *Psychology of learning and behavior (4th ed.)*. New York: W. W. Norton.

Skinner, B. F. (1938). *The behavior of organisms: An experimental analysis*. New York: Appleton Century Crofts.

Watson, J. B. (1930, 1963) *Behaviorism*. Chicago: University of Chicago.

Biochemical Factors

David LeMarquand, Chawki Benkelfat, and Robert O. Pihl
McGill University

GLOSSARY

Agonist A compound that binds to a receptor and initiates intracellular processes.

Amino Acids Monomers that are the structural building blocks of proteins; a small minority function as neurotransmitters.

Androgens Male sex hormones; one class of steroid hormones in mammals.

Antagonist A compound that binds to and occupies a receptor but does not initiate intracellular processes.

Central Nervous System Part of the nervous system composed of the brain and spinal cord.

Cerebrospinal Fluid Liquid produced by the choroid plexuses of the lateral, third, and fourth ventricles that fills the ventricular system of the brain and the spinal subarachnoid space.

Hormone A compound released from neuronal or non-neuronal cells that circulates and acts at a site distant from its release site.

Monoamines A class of neurotransmitters, along with amino acids and peptides, consisting of three catecholamines (dopamine, norepinephrine, and epinephrine), an indoleamine (serotonin), a quaternary amine (acetylcholine), and an ethylamine (histamine).

Monoamine Oxidase An enzyme that degrades biogenic amines.

Neurotransmitter A compound synthesized and released from the presynaptic membrane upon nerve stimulation of a neuron in the nervous system, inducing a physiological response on the postsynaptic membrane.

Platelets Disc-shaped blood cells formed in the bone marrow whose primary physiological function is haemostasis.

Receptor A protein in the neuronal membrane of a cell that is a binding or recognition site for a neuroactive compound that may result in a change in the activity of the cell.

Reuptake Inhibitor A compound that blocks the reuptake of a neurotransmitter into the presynaptic membrane.

VARIOUS NEUROCHEMICAL FACTORS have been strongly implicated in the regulation of violence as well as prosocial behavior. This article will review the neurochemical findings to date, focusing on hormonal and neurotransmitter influences on aggressive and violent behavior in humans.

I. INTRODUCTION

The experimental study of the biochemistry of human aggression and violence is a relatively young field. The first report of an association between a neurochemical (cerebrospinal fluid [CSF] 5-hydroxyindoleacetic acid [5-HIAA]) and aggression was published only 25 years ago. Much less research has been done on the biochemistry of human prosocial and affiliative behavior (e.g., cooperation, altruism, friendship). As such, the focus of this review will be the biochemistry, and primarily neurochemistry, of aggression and violence in humans.

The primary dependent measures used in the study of the biochemistry of human aggression and violence include: (a) hormones and their precursors/metabolites, measured in saliva, blood and urine; (b) neurotransmitters and their precursors/metabolites, measured in blood, urine and CSF; (c) neurotransmitter uptake and receptor functioning on blood platelets; and (d) neurotransmitter physiology and its effects on hormonal responses using neurotransmitter precursor, reuptake inhibitor, and direct receptor agonists/antagonists. The latter technique has been particularly useful in elucidating which specific neurotransmitter receptor subtypes may be involved in aggression, particularly with the development of agonists and antagonists with greater receptor specificity. Some experimental studies assessing human aggressive behavior following the administration of hormones or neurotransmitter precursors, agonists or antagonists have also been done.

Many of these measures are limited in what they indicate about central nervous system (CNS) function. Urinary biochemicals (e.g., neurotransmitter metabolites) primarily result from metabolism in the periphery; therefore they tend to be less reflective of CNS function. The relationship between neurotransmitter (and precursor) concentrations in the blood and the function of CNS neurotransmitter systems is not well understood. As well, some cellular structures and physiological processes on blood platelets are thought to be analogous to those in synaptic membranes in the CNS. However, the environment of blood platelets is substantially different than that of neurons in the brain with potentially important consequences. It is not entirely clear how the levels of CSF neurochemicals, sampled from the lumbar spinal cord region, relate to brain neurochemical *functioning*. Studies have demonstrated correlations between CSF and levels of neurotransmitter metabolites in some brain regions. It is unlikely though, that CSF levels of metabolites reflect neuronal activity in specific brain regions. This limitation also applies to the psychopharmacologic challenge paradigm. Despite their limitations, many of these measures have been correlated to CNS processes, and thus are held to be reflective of brain processes. As such, they are extensively utilized. It should also be noted that peripheral biochemicals may provide information on important peripheral processes pertinent to the understanding of the biochemistry of aggression and violence.

The biochemistry of violent behavior is primarily studied by comparing aggressive/violent and nonaggressive/nonviolent groups on biochemical indices. Alternatively, measures of aggression/violence are correlated with biochemical indices in a study sample. As such, the majority of studies in this literature are correlational. Correlational studies cannot specify the direction of the relationship between aggression/violence and biochemical variables. Biochemical differences interpreted as important in the etiology of aggression/violent behavior may, in fact, be a consequence of such behavior (or the result of third variables). Human experimental studies in which hormones, neurotransmitter precursors, agonists, or antagonists are administered and aggressive behavior is assessed offer the best evidence for causal relationships. Experimental animal studies are also invaluable in the interpretation of the human literature on the biochemistry of violence.

A further difficulty in this field concerns how aggression and violence are defined, operationalized, and assessed. Aggression has been variously defined as any behavior directed toward the goal of harming or injuring another individual who is motivated to avoid such harm/injury, or any behavior that is capable of damaging or degrading the integrity of other individuals or objects and that occurs within a social context. Violence has been defined as purposeless, antisocial aggression exhibited out of context: aggressive behavior that is no longer regulated by situational and social stimuli. The variability in the assessment of aggressive and violent behavior is equally great. Assessment techniques and measures include official records of violent and nonviolent criminal offenses, self-report questionnaires of aggressive/violent traits and behaviors, and self-reported feeling states associated with aggression and violence (e.g., anger, irritability). Between-study differences on these parameters tend to hinder interpretation of the data, and may obscure relationships between certain biochemicals and specific types or components of aggressive/violent behavior (e.g., fighting, irritability, impulsivity).

II. STUDIES ON VIOLENT OFFENDERS

A. Hormones

1. Gonadal Androgens

Hormones are secretions of endocrine glands that are transported through the bloodstream and act on target tissues throughout the body (including the central nervous system) to effect physiological and behavioral changes. Androgens, a particular class of steroid hormones, are primarily produced in the gonads (i.e., the testes and ovaries of men and women) and in adrenal glands. They have two distinct sets of effects: androgenic (differentiation, growth, and development of the male reproductive tract) and anabolic (stimulation of linear body growth). During the pre- and perinatal organizational stage of sexual differentiation, androgens masculinize the fetus through the development of the male reproductive tract. At puberty, the activational stage begins, and androgen levels increase, leading to increases in bone growth, muscle mass, growth of the genital organs, development of the secondary sex characteristics, and increases in sexual motivation. The absolute levels of testosterone, one of the primary androgens, are substantially lower in women than in men, and decline with age in both sexes.

Testosterone is the most abundant androgen, and is generally thought to have the greatest impact on behavior. Other less abundant androgens include 5α-dihydrotestosterone, androstenediol, dehydroepiandrosterone, and estradiol. Most of the behavioral effects of androgens are mediated through binding to androgen receptors widely distributed in the brain and other sites in the body. Hormonal action is terminated through the dissociation of the androgen from its receptor. Androgens are known to modulate the functioning of a large number of neurotransmitters and neuropeptides. Testosterone is metabolized into dihydrotestosterone, androsterone, etiocholanolone, and 5-α-androstanediol (estradiol), the latter of which may act at the estrogen receptor to mediate androgen effects. Thus, how a steroid is metabolized will have important functional consequences.

A number of comprehensive reviews demonstrate that violent males have higher testosterone levels relative to nonviolent control males. This holds true for criminals with histories of violent crimes compared to those with histories of nonviolent crimes, as well as violent sex offenders relative to nonviolent sex offenders and adult volunteers. Also, incarcerated offenders with higher testosterone levels misbehave more in prison. Interestingly, studies with women have noted higher testosterone in aggressive versus nonaggressive groups. Some studies with offenders have found no differences in testosterone levels between, for example, adolescent males convicted for repeated assault compared to those convicted for assault or for property offenses, or men charged with murder or assault versus those charged with property offenses. Even in the former study, however, adolescents from the most violent group tended to show higher testosterone levels than the other two groups. A higher than expected proportion of XYY individuals are involved in violent crime; these individuals also have higher testosterone levels than their adolescent peers.

In more recent studies, impulsive alcoholic violent offenders with antisocial personality disorder had high levels of free CSF testosterone relative to healthy volunteers, whereas impulsive alcoholic violent offenders with intermittent explosive disorder and nonimpulsive alcoholic violent offenders did not. In these violent alcoholic offenders, high free CSF testosterone was correlated with self-report aggressiveness and sensation seeking. The authors suggest that increased CSF testosterone may result from a lack of inhibition of luteinizing hormone-releasing hormone and luteinizing hormone by circulating cortisol. Alcoholic, impulsive violent offenders have been reported to have low urinary free cortisol outputs (see below). Cortisol has negative feedback effects on anterior pituitary function, where luteinizing hormone, responsible for stimulating production of testosterone in the testis of males, is produced. Interestingly, one previous study found no differences in CSF testosterone between impulsive and nonimpulsive violent offenders.

There have also been a number of studies investigating hormone-aggression correlations in offenders. Many of these studies investigated total plasma (blood) testosterone rather than unbound (physiologically active) testosterone levels. Salivary testosterone levels are thought to provide a measure more reflective of unbound testosterone. In those studies that measured salivary testosterone in violent offenders, positive correlations were found with indicators of aggression. Studies using total plasma testosterone also found, by and large, positive correlations with aggression in violent individuals. Unfortunately, wide between-study variation in the measures of aggression and sample characteristics hinders interpretation.

Finally, socioeconomic status (SES) and age appear to moderate the testosterone-aggression relationship. Among military veterans with high SES, high testosterone did not predict higher risk of engaging in antisocial behaviors. Among military veterans with low SES, however, higher testosterone predicted a higher risk of antisocial behavior. A study of incarcerated females found that increasing age was related to lower testosterone levels, reductions in violent crime, and less aggressive dominance in prison. Among young men, an earlier age of onset of criminal activities is correlated with higher testosterone levels.

2. Adrenal Hormones/Neurotransmitters

Cortisol has been studied as method of indexing physiological activation of the hypothalamic-pituitary-adrenal (HPA) axis. Some studies have demonstrated that violent offenders have lower levels of HPA axis biochemicals, possibly indicating underarousal, an overregulated HPA axis, or an increased threshold for stress. For instance, urinary cortisol has been shown to be lower in habitually violent criminals relative to nonviolent offenders. Impulsive alcoholic violent offenders with antisocial personality disorder also had lower CSF adrenocorticotropic hormone (ACTH, or corticotropin, which regulates the synthesis of glucocorticoids such as cortisol) relative to healthy volunteers, with no differences in other adrenocortical stress response-associated neuropeptides (diazepam-binding inhibitor, corticotropin-releasing hormone, and arginine vasopressin). However, there have been opposing findings; violent alcoholics had elevated cortisol levels relative to depressed alcoholics and nonviolent, nondepressed alcoholics.

Cortisol levels have been shown to moderate the testosterone-aggression relationship. The correlation between testosterone and the violence of a crime in late adolescent male offenders was higher in those below the mean in cortisol levels. Cortisol may moderate the testosterone-aggression relationship by inhibiting testosterone production directly (see below).

Consistent with the notion that violent individuals may show reduced physiological activation under stress, several studies have demonstrated that violent offenders have reduced levels of plasma and/or urinary epinephrine. Epinephrine (adrenaline) is a neurotransmitter in the sympathetic nervous system and adrenal medulla; epinephrine levels may provide an index of peripheral sympathetic nervous system arousal. Plasma and urinary epinephrine were lower in men convicted of violent personal attack versus those convicted of arson, sexual or property offenses. Urinary epinephrine and cortisol were also lower in violent offenders relative to nonviolent offenders, mentally ill, and healthy men following stressful environmental procedures.

Conversely, a series of studies assessing urinary norepinephrine (NE) output found higher levels, particularly when anticipating a stressful experimental event, in violent incarcerated males relative to nonviolent controls. As well, recent work with rhesus monkeys suggests that increased noradrenergic reactivity may be associated with state measures of aggressiveness and irritability. These results suggest greater peripheral NE levels, and possibly function, in violent individuals, particularly under stress.

B. Neurotransmitters

1. Serotonin

Serotonin (5-hydroxytryptamine, 5-HT) has been hypothesized to play an inhibitory role in the expression of aggressive and violent behavior. This neurotransmitter is primarily concentrated in neurons of the raphe nuclei of the brainstem, whose processes project to a wide variety of subcortical and cortical areas. Serotonin is formed from the amino acid tryptophan. The primary pathway of 5-HT metabolism leads to the formation of 5-hydroxyindoleacetic acid (5-HIAA), which is commonly measured in the CSF and employed as an indicator of brain 5-HT turnover.

Violent offenders and fire-setters, incarcerated personality disordered individuals with XYY, and homicidal offenders who had killed a sexual partner or their own child have been shown to have low CSF 5-HIAA levels, which suggests reduced brain 5-HT function. Low CSF 5-HIAA also predicts recidivism in violent offenders and impulsive fire-setters. Additionally, low CSF 5-HIAA in violent offenders and impulsive fire-setters is associated with a history of serious suicide attempts and paternal alcoholism. In several of these investigations, violent offenders have been classified as either impulsive or nonimpulsive based on the qualities of their index crime (impulsive crimes being those in which the victim was unknown to the offender, the offender was not provoked, and the crime was committed with little chance of monetary gain). In these studies, it is the impulsive violent offenders that show reduced CSF 5-HIAA levels relative to nonimpulsive violent offenders and healthy controls. Thus it may be impulsivity, a characteristic of a subset of violent acts, that is related to low 5-HT functioning. These findings have contributed toward 5-HT being conceptualized as regulating behavioral inhibition/disinhibition.

Some characteristics of the studies investigating the relationship between CSF 5-HIAA and impulsive aggression/violence suggest caution in the interpretation of their findings. For example, a number of the studies on CSF 5-HIAA and impulsive aggression have been carried out with samples of Finnish offenders; independent replication by other research groups with other samples is warranted. These violent offenders were comorbid for a number of other disorders (alcoholism, personality disorders), thus CSF 5-HIAA may be related to one of these characteristics rather than impulsive aggression. As well, in relating low CSF 5-HIAA to *impulsive* aggression, impulsivity has been defined as a quality of the index crime rather than a stable personality characteristic. The accuracy of such a characterization can be questioned; the description of the index crime may have been falsified by the offender in order to avoid more severe punishment. Despite these difficulties, a review of the studies judged to be the most methodologically rigorous concluded that low CSF 5-HIAA is related to aggression, particularly for relatively young, White, personality-disordered male criminal offenders.

The reduction in CSF 5-HIAA in impulsive violent offenders may be mediated genetically. The gene for tryptophan hydroxylase, the rate limiting step in the conversion of the tryptophan to 5-HT, has at least two alleles designated U and L. The L allele of the tryptophan hydroxylase gene has been associated with low CSF-5-HIAA in impulsive alcoholic violent offenders but not in nonimpulsive alcoholic violent offenders or controls. It has also been related to a history of suicidal behavior in the alcoholic violent offenders, irrespective of impulsivity. This suggests a possible reduced capacity to hydroxylate tryptophan to 5-hydroxytryptophan, the precursors of 5-HT. (In healthy men, however, the U allele has been associated with lower CSF 5-HIAA levels.) Questions remain as to whether the tryptophan hydroxylase polymorphism is associated with aggression/violence or suicidal behavior, as other studies have found conflicting results (e.g., no association between the tryptophan hydroxylase gene and suicidal behavior, or an association between the U allele and suicidal behavior in individuals with major depression).

An alternate method of assessing central serotonergic functioning is through the measurement of the neuroendocrine hormones following the administration of a serotonergic compounds. This method reflects the dynamic functioning of the serotonergic system in the limbic-hypothalamic pituitary system that regulates neuroendocrine hormones. Blunted prolactin responses following the administration of fenfluramine, a 5-HT releaser and reuptake inhibitor, have been noted in murderers with antisocial personality disorder, suggesting a subsensitivity of central serotonergic systems, possibly due to reduced postsynaptic receptor numbers or functioning. This interpretation is supported by the findings of a peripheral indicator of 5-HT function, platelet receptor binding. Platelet receptor binding studies assess the density (B_{max}) and affinity (K_d) of plasma platelet receptors using various 5-HT ligands. Significantly lower ketanserin binding to platelet 5-HT_2 receptors was found in adolescent violent delinquents compared to controls, possibly indicative of lower receptor binding in the central serotonin system in violent individuals.

Other putative peripheral indicators of central 5-HT function have been studied although their significance remains equivocal. The availability of plasma tryptophan, the amino acid precursor of 5-HT, for uptake across the blood-brain barrier in violent individuals has been studied. Tryptophan competes with other large neutral amino acids for the same carrier for brain uptake. Contrary to expectation, increased concentrations of tryptophan and competing amino acids were found in violent offenders compared to nonviolent offenders and nonoffenders and in violent male offenders with intermittent explosive disorder compared to those with antisocial personality and healthy controls. In one of these studies, there was no difference in the relationship between tryptophan and its amino acid competitors between the violent offenders and controls. Additional studies are needed on this subject.

Studies of blood serotonin have generally noted a positive correlation with aggression. This relationship has been noted in violent male juvenile offenders, and with violence in an epidemiological study as well. One study, however, found no difference in whole blood 5-HT between violent offenders and controls, while another found lower whole blood 5-HT in aggressive versus nonaggressive patients. A final study measured plasma 5-HIAA and found no association between it and self-report measures of anger and hostility in seven violent criminals.

2. Catecholamines (Norepinephrine, Dopamine) and Related Compounds

The catecholamines, norepinephrine (noradrenaline) and dopamine (DA), are formed from the amino acid tyrosine, which itself is derived from the amino acid phenylalanine. Cell bodies of the noradrenergic system are primarily located in the locus ceruleus. High concentrations of norepinephrine are also found in the hypothalamus. Dopamine is present in high levels in the neostriatum, nucleus accumbens, and olfactory tubercules. In the central nervous system, the major metabolite of norepinephrine is 3-methoxy-4-hydroxyphenylglycol (MHPG). In the peripheral sympathetic nervous system, vanillylmandelic acid (VMA) is the primary metabolite of norepinephrine. In the human brain, the primary metabolite of dopamine is homovanillic acid (HVA), with a smaller amount of 3,4-dihydroxyphenylacetic acid (DOPAC) and 3-methoxytyramine. Free MHPG diffuses from the brain into the CSF and general circulation, so estimates of its concentration in the CSF are thought to reflect central nervous system noradrenergic neuronal activity. A proportion of CSF MHPG derives from the plasma, because free MHPG diffuses readily through membranes, so correction for the plasma contribution must be made. Plasma and urinary free MHPG may be useful indices of total body NE metabolism, but are not valid indices of brain NE metabolism, as the brain accounts for only approximately 30% of the total body production of MHPG. CSF HVA levels are taken as an index of DA metabolism in the central nervous system.

The few studies that have been done investigating CSF MHPG in violent offenders suggest reduced levels of this neurochemical are associated with violent behavior. Impulsive arsonists (relative to habitually violent offenders and nonviolent controls) and alcoholic violent offenders and impulsive fire-setters with histories of violent suicide attempts (relative to those without) have low CSF MHPG. Low CSF MHPG also predicted recidivism in these individuals. Two other studies have found no differences in CSF NE or MHPG concentrations between groups of impulsive versus nonimpulsive violent offenders, so the relationship between violence and CSF MHPG remains to be confirmed.

The noradrenergic system contributes to the regulation of arousal and responsiveness to the environment. Increased locus ceruleus activity has been associated with reactivity to novel and particularly threatening stimuli, decreased activity with self-restitutive or vegetative activity such as eating, self-grooming, and sleeping. The few studies that did find lower CSF MHPG in arsonists and impulsive violent offenders may imply reduced arousal and reactivity in these individuals. This is consistent with psychophysiological studies of psychopaths showing reductions in sympathetic nervous system arousal (e.g., skin conductance activity) compared to nonpsychopaths.

Less evidence in humans implicates the dopaminergic system in violent behavior. Studies on violent offenders have found no differences in CSF HVA levels in arsonists versus habitually violent offenders and nonviolent controls, convicted violent criminals who committed impulsive versus premeditated crimes, violent offenders and impulsive fire-setters with histories of serious violent suicide attempts compared to those with no such histories, or impulsive alcoholic violent offenders, with antisocial personality disorder, impulsive alcoholic violent offenders with intermittent explosive disorder, nonimpulsive alcoholic violent offenders, and healthy volunteers. Violent criminals with antisocial personality disorder had lower levels of CSF HVA compared to those with paranoid or passive-aggressive personality disorders. CSF DA levels and turnover were not different between five XYY assaultive patients and controls. No differences in CSF DOPAC or HVA have been found between convicted violent criminals who committed impulsive versus premeditated crimes.

One study has found that violent alcoholic offenders had slightly higher striatal dopamine reuptake site densities compared to nonviolent alcoholic offenders and nonalcoholic controls, suggesting that violence is associated with increased dopaminergic activity in the brain.

Finally, two studies suggested that violent male offenders may be either higher or lower in their levels of free or conjugated plasma phenylacetic acid, the major metabolite of phenylethylamine following its breakdown by monoamine oxidase (MAO) B, compared to nonviolent offenders. Phenylethylamine, structurally related to amphetamine, has a similar pharmacological response to the latter when administered following pretreatment with a MAO inhibitor. It is synthesized from the amino acid phenylalanine. It has been posited that increased phenylacetic acid levels in violent offenders may indicate increased phenylethylamine levels, the latter representing a compensatory increase to reduce aggressive tendencies, much the way amphetamine reduces hyperactivity in attention deficit and hyperactive children.

C. Other Neurochemicals

1. Monoamine Oxidase

Monoamine oxidase (MAO) is one of the enzymes that metabolizes monoamine neurotransmitters. There are two forms of this compound; MAOA primarily oxidizes 5-HT, NE and epinephrine, while MAOB primarily oxidizes phenylethylamine and benzylamine. DA, tyramine and tryptamine are oxidized by both forms. Human blood platelets express primarily MAOB.

Recently, a mutation in gene coding resulting in deficient MAOA activity has been associated with borderline mental retardation and aggressive/impulsive behavior (verbal threats, aggressive posturing, exhibitionism, attempted rape, arson) in several males of a large Dutch kindred. This MAOA deficiency was associated with decreased urinary 5-HIAA, HVA, and VMA. This finding compares well to a report of a similar MAOA deficiency in a line of transgenic mice associated with increased aggression in males and high levels of brain

5-HT, NE, and DA. These findings suggest a different neurochemical mechanism leading to aggressive/violent behavior than commonly put forward (i.e., that *low* 5-HT is associated with aggressive/impulsive behavior). A prenatal MAOA deficiency resulting in increased brain 5-HT in early development may alter receptor densities and/or serotonergic innervation, possibly resulting in an overall reduction in serotonergic functioning.

Platelet MAO (primarily MAOB) has been measured as a marker of the functional capacity of the serotonergic system, despite the lack of a correlation between platelet and brain MAO activities. CSF 5-HIAA and platelet MAO are positive correlated in healthy volunteers and pain patients, however, suggesting some basis for interpretation. Studies suggest that violent offenders may have lower platelet MAOB activity compared to nonviolent offenders, although some studies suggest no differences. Lower platelet MAO is also associated with psychopathy. Furthermore, platelet MAO is also inversely correlated with general aggressiveness and feelings of anger or frustration, as well as behavioral patterns associated with violent or nonviolent criminal behavior, including defiance of punishment, impulsivity, childhood hyperactivity, poor academic performance, sensation seeking, recreational drug use, alcohol abuse, and extraversion. Clinical studies in children reveal somewhat contradictory findings, with lower platelet MAO in youth with dual diagnoses of conduct disorder and attention deficit disorder compared to those with conduct disorder alone, but higher platelet MAO activity in conduct-disordered sons of substance-abusing fathers relative to non-conduct-disordered sons of substance-abusing fathers and conduct-disordered sons of non-substance-abusing fathers. Also, impulsivity in children with disruptive behavior disorders is positively correlated with platelet MAO activity. These discrepancies may be explained by developmental changes that might occur in MAO functioning. In sum, although evidence suggests lower MAO activity is associated with aggression/violence, contradictory evidence exists, and further clarification is needed, particularly concerning the functional significance of low MAO activity.

2. Glucose Regulation

Violent offenders and impulsive fire-setters have low blood glucose concentrations following the oral glucose tolerance test. This hypoglycemic response may be a consequence of enhanced insulin activity also noted in these samples. A low blood glucose nadir following oral glucose challenge predicts recidivism (however an extension of this sample failed to replicate this finding). These studies should be interpreted with caution, as between-group differences in diet and alcohol use/abuse may have accounted for the observed findings. In particular, the violent offenders in these studies had histories of alcohol abuse; alcohol is known to enhance insulin secretion. The low glucose nadir/violence relationship was not replicated in drug abusers, suggesting that recent ingestion of drugs may affect responses on the glucose tolerance test.

Nevertheless, these findings, together with those suggesting reduced CSF 5-HIAA in violent offenders, have led to a model of serotonin involvement in the production of impulsive aggression. In this model, reduced serotonergic innervation from the dorsal and median raphe nuclei to the suprachiasmatic nucleus leads to a disturbance in circadian rhythms, resulting in increased dysphoria or dysthymia, which prompts excessive alcohol use (and the acute release of serotonin) to ameliorate this subjective state. Reduced suprachiasmatic serotonergic functioning disturbs glucose metabolism, which results in lowered blood glucose levels and an increased propensity for impulsive, aggressive behavior. Excessive alcohol use subsequently lowers serotonergic functioning which further increases the propensity for impulsivity. Further experimental tests of this theory are warranted.

3. Cholesterol

A small number of studies have found low serum cholesterol levels in violent individuals relative to controls, particularly in those under the influence of alcohol. Low fasting cholesterol concentration did not predict recidivism in alcoholic violent offenders and fire-setters. The relationship between cholesterol and violence is discussed further in the section on studies with healthy individuals.

III. STUDIES IN OTHER CLINICAL SAMPLES

A. Hormones

1. Adrenal Hormones/Neurotransmitters

The findings on the relationship between cortisol and aggression in children are equivocal. Some studies find lower levels of cortisol to be associated with aggressive behavior in children, which suggests reduced HPA activity. For instance, a negative correlation between the number of conduct disorder symptoms and salivary cortisol concentrations in preadolescent boys has been noted. In this study, boys whose fathers had conduct disorder followed by antisocial personality disorder had lower salivary cortisol compared to boys whose fathers had conduct disorder but not antisocial personality disorder, and boys whose fathers had neither diagnosis. Two additional studies have found lower cortisol at baseline to be associated with aggression/hostility. In another study, children with conduct disorder but no DSM-III-R anxiety disorder had lower cortisol levels when compared to children with conduct and a comorbid anxiety disorder, but not relative to children with neither diagnosis. Similarly, low-anxious/high-externalizing boys demonstrated stress-induced cortisol decreases, while high-anxious/high-externalizing boys demonstrated large increases. In contrast, three other studies found no relationship between cortisol and aggression in disruptive children. This may be due to a failure to measure cortisol in children with aggressive and nonaggressive conduct disorder symptoms separately.

Plasma NE, a measure of peripheral presynaptic NE function, was positively correlated with risk-taking and self-report impulsivity in personality-disordered individuals. As well, plasma NE in borderline hypertensives with suppressed aggression was higher following one of two mildly stressful laboratory tasks (mental arithmetic, Stroop task), with no changes in plasma epinephrine, relative to participants without suppressed aggression. These two studies are consistent with the studies on urinary NE in violent offenders, and suggest a positive relationship between peripheral indicators of NE function and aggressive behavior, particularly under conditions of stress.

B. Neurotransmitters

1. Serotonin

The role of serotonin in aggression in personality-disordered individuals and other clinical groups has been extensively investigated. As one might expect, a similar inverse relationship between indicators of central serotonergic function and aggression has been noted in these populations as in violent individuals. For example, some of the earliest studies investigating the 5-HT/aggression relationship found an inverse relationship between CSF 5-HIAA and life histories of aggression and suicide attempts in personality-disordered men with no affective illness. Depressed individuals and alcoholic males who self-report high aggression have low CSF 5-HIAA. Low CSF 5-HIAA is also related to Rorschach ratings of hostility and anxiety in depressed and suicidal individuals. These results suggest that the CSF 5-HIAA/aggression relationship represents a biochemical and behavioral trait association that cuts across clinical groups. There have been incongruous findings, however. Recent studies have found a positive association between CSF 5-HIAA and aggression in personality-disordered men, no association in borderline personality disorder individuals with a history of violence towards others versus those without such a history, and no differences in CSF 5-HIAA between violent and matched nonviolent patients with schizophrenia. The inverse relationship between CSF 5-HIAA and aggression may be dependent on the severity of aggression, with the relationship being found in individuals with more severe aggression.

Cerebrospinal fluid 5-HIAA has also been negatively correlated with aggression in children and adolescents with disruptive behavior disorders (characterized by hyperactive, impulsive and aggressive behaviors), and was lower in these young people than in a comparison sample of pediatric patients with obsessive-compulsive disorder. CSF 5-HIAA significantly predicted the severity of physical aggression at 2-year follow-up in these individuals.

Congruent with the studies in violent offenders, blunted neuroendocrine responses to challenges with various central 5-HT reuptake inhibitors, releasers, or receptor agonists have been found in personality-disordered patients as well as those of other clinical groups. Blunted prolactin and/or cortisol responses to 5-HT agonist (fenfluramine, meta-chlorophenylpiperazine) challenges have been noted in individuals with past histories of suicide attempts, impulse control disorders (bulimia, substance dependence, pathological gambling), and personality disorders (borderline, narcissistic), borderline personality disorder patients with histories of impulsive and aggressive behavior, patients with histories of self-mutilation or suicide, and men with antisocial personality disorder relative to healthy controls.

Other studies have correlated the neuroendocrine response to 5-HT agonists with self-report aggressivity. Prolactin responses to fenfluramine challenge have been inversely related to impulsive aggression in patients with personality disorders, Buss-Durkee Hostility Inventory "direct assault" in personality-disordered individuals, a laboratory measure of aggression in personality-disordered men, and self-report life histories of aggression in personality-disordered individuals. Reduced neuroendocrine responses to other 5-HT agents, such as the mixed 5-HT receptor agonist meta-chlorophenylpiperazine, and the 5-HT_{1A} receptor agonists buspirone and ipsapirone, have similarly been correlated to aggression and impulsivity. Interpretation of reduced neuroendocrine responses to 5-HT agonists is difficult at present. Blunted neuroendocrine responses to fenfluramine suggest decreased presynaptic availability of 5-HT. Blunted neuroendocrine responses to 5-HT receptor agonists may indicate decreased postsynaptic 5-HT receptor numbers or function; alternatively, they may be the result of adaptive changes in 5-HT receptor numbers/function in response to altered presynaptic 5-HT availability.

Reduced serotonergic function in aggressive individuals may be partly genetically determined. Twin studies with indicators of serotonergic functioning suggest that this neurotransmitter system is partly under genetic control. A genetic vulnerability to aggression has been demonstrated as well. Furthermore, indicators of reduced serotonergic function have been correlated with family histories of impulsivity and aggression. Reduced prolactin responses to the 5-HT releasing/reuptake inhibiting agent fenfluramine in personality-disordered individuals are correlated with a greater prevalence of impulsive personality disorder traits in their first-degree relatives. As well, reduced prolactin responses to the fenfluramine in aggressive boys are associated with a parental history of aggressive behavior. Also, the density of platelet 5-HT_{2A} receptors was lower in boys with parents with histories of incarceration or substance abuse compared to family history-negative boys, suggesting decreased central 5-HT_2 postsynaptic receptor function. Finally, CSF 5-HIAA levels in newborns with family histories of antisocial personality disorder were lower than in those with no family histories of antisocial personality disorder.

By and large, these studies suggest that low central 5-HT function is associated with aggression, and perhaps impulsive aggression. However, there have been conflicting results. Patients with *compulsive* personalities had higher impulsive aggression scores than noncompulsive patients, and had blunted prolactin responses to fenfluramine compared to noncompulsive patients and nonpatient controls. Additionally, there have been at least five studies showing no association, or a positive relationship, between neuroendocrine responses to 5-HT agonist challenge and impulsivity or aggressivity.

Recent evidence suggests that 5-HT systems in aggressive boys may show a different developmental trajectory than those in nonaggressive boys. Prolactin responses to fenfluramine challenge in younger aggressive attention deficit hyperactivity disorder boys were *greater* compared to attention deficit/hyperactive nonaggressive boys. Also, prolactin response to fenfluramine was related positively to self-report aggressivity and adverse-rearing environmental conditions in younger brothers of convicted delinquents. However, in an older cohort of boys, prolactin response was slightly higher in the nonaggressive boys (and therefore slightly blunted in the aggressive boys), suggesting that normal boys may show a developmental increase in serotonergic functioning not found in aggressive boys. This potentially interesting finding awaits replication. In one other negative study, preadolescent and adolescent males with disruptive behavior disorders showed no differences in prolactin or cortisol release following d,l-fenfluramine challenge relative to controls. The neuroendocrine response was unrelated to aggression levels in those patients with disruptive behavior.

Peripheral measures of 5-HT function also suggest that a 5-HT dysfunction is associated with aggression. Platelet 5-HT uptake studies are consistent in their finding of a negative association between 5-HT uptake and aggression/impulsivity (although there are two studies finding no relationship, and one finding the opposite relationship). Platelet B_{max} (number of binding sites) was reduced in conduct-disorder children, highly aggressive mentally retarded adults and suicide attempters, and male outpatients with "episodic aggression," compared to controls. The number of platelet binding sites has been inversely correlated with measures of aggression in a combined sample of conduct-disordered children and healthy controls, personality-disordered individuals, and schizophrenic and conduct-disordered adolescents. Platelet serotonin uptake has also been negatively correlated with impulsivity. It has been postulated that reduced 5-HT uptake might lead to increase synaptic availability, reduced sensitivity of terminal 5-HT autoreceptors, a greater release of 5-HT per neuronal impulse, and a subsensitivity of postsynaptic 5-HT receptors, with the net effect being reduced 5-HT neurotransmission.

Studies of blood serotonin have generally noted a positive correlation with aggression, whether it be in depressed inpatients, hyperactive or conduct-disordered youth, children or adolescents with behavior disorders, or individuals with episodic aggression. Still, there have been two studies that have found the reverse: lower blood 5-HT levels related to aggression. Taking into account the studies in violent offenders reviewed above, a positive relationship between blood 5-HT and aggression is suggested. This appears paradoxical when compared to the negative relationship between CSF 5-HIAA and aggression. This paradox may be reconciled if serotonergic neurons and blood platelets share increased serotonergic transport.

Contrary to the findings in violent offenders, tryptophan has been negatively related to aggressive behavior in studies with other clinical groups. One study with a small sample found preliminary evidence that impulsive adolescents have low tryptophan levels and a reduced ratio of tryptophan to the other large neutral amino acids competing for brain uptake. Two reports have indicated that a low ratio of tryptophan to the other amino acids which compete for brain entry is associated with increased aggression in alcoholics, particularly early- (<20 years old) as opposed to later-onset. A final report found a positive relationship between tryptophan levels and self-report extroverted aggression. Clearly, more studies measuring the ratio of tryptophan to the other large neutral amino acids in aggressive individuals are needed. One study has looked at the effect of an acute dietary depletion of tryptophan on self-report aggressiveness in small sample of aggressive patients. No effect of tryptophan depletion was found, possibly due to a lack of provocation.

2. Catecholamines

The relatively few studies investigating NE functioning in personality-disordered individuals suggest a positive correlation with aggression. CSF MHPG levels were positively correlated with self-report aggression in personality-disordered military personnel (although the variance in aggression explained was low after controlling for CSF 5-HIAA). Growth hormone responses to the alpha-2-adrenergic agonist clonidine were positively correlated with sensation-seeking and risk-taking behaviors, and self-report lifetime irritability (but not assaultiveness) in both personality-disordered patients and normal controls. Note that there was no correlation between growth hormone responses and overt aggression or impulsivity in this study. In another study with personality-disordered individuals, growth hormone responses to clonidine were associated with irritability and verbal hostility.

These results are difficult to reconcile with those found in violent offenders, which suggest that increased NE function is related to aggression and violence. It has been suggested that reduced presynaptic *and* increased postsynaptic NE function are related to aggression. Increased presynaptic alpha-2 NE receptor activity in the locus ceruleus (as has been suggested by increased locus ceruleus alpha-2 agonist binding in violent, but not nonviolent, suicides victims) may lead to reduced NE outflow (and thus reduced CSF MHPG) and an upregulation of postsynaptic alpha-2 NE receptors, thus increasing growth hormone responses to clonidine. Overall, this might lead to an augmented alpha-2 NE signal in NE pathways in the presence of aversive, provocative stimuli, resulting in a heightened behavioral arousal (fight/flight response). Furthermore, alpha-2 heteroceptors terminating on presynaptic 5-HT neurons may be supersensitive, leading to greater inhibition of 5-HT firing. Such a synthesis is intriguing and provides a number of testable hypotheses.

3. Peptides

A recent study found a positive relationship between CSF vasopressin and lifetime aggressive behavior in personality-disordered individuals. CSF vasopressin was inversely correlated with prolactin responses to d-fenfluramine, but not CSF 5-HIAA. Animal studies suggest an interaction between 5-HT and vasopressin, as 5-HT compounds reduce brain vasopressin levels and decrease aggressive behavior. A hyposensitive 5-HT system may result in enhanced CNS vasopressin and increased aggressive behavior. Yet, as mentioned previously, no difference in CSF vasopressin was found between impulsive alcoholic violent offenders with antisocial personality disorder, those with intermittent explosive disorder, nonimpulsive alcoholic violent offenders, and healthy volunteers.

IV. STUDIES WITH HEALTHY INDIVIDUALS

A. Hormones

1. Gonadal Androgens

A number of studies have investigated testosterone-aggression correlations in normal volunteers including both men and women. As mentioned earlier, wide variability exists between studies on the hormone assessed (total plasma versus salivary [unbound] testosterone) and the measures of aggression used (self-report questionnaires, peer ratings, diary assessments). Overall, similar to studies with offenders, small positive correlations between testosterone and aggression have been noted (approximately $r = 0.15$). The magnitude of this relationship is smaller for studies using self-report measures of aggression, and slightly larger for studies using observer ratings (teacher, peer measures). Self-report inventories of aggression commonly measure aggressive traits or dispositions, suggesting that testosterone may be more related to aggressive behavior per se, rather than self-reported aggressive traits.

A number of studies find no relationship between testosterone and aggression in normal volunteers, and some find a negative relationship. In a recent study, aggressiveness in women was negatively correlated with both testosterone and estradiol. These incongruities are difficult to reconcile. Another study found estradiol to be significantly positively related to aggression in young men. This is not entirely unexpected, given that testosterone is aromatized into estradiol.

There have been a handful of studies on boys at puberty, a time when an increase in aggressiveness might be expected to occur due to a rise in testosterone in males. These studies have provided only modest evidence of an association between testosterone and aggression. A longitudinal study using path analysis found that testosterone in boys at 16 years of age was associated with provoked aggression at age 16. Also, there was evidence that provoked aggression at age 13 was related to testosterone at age 16, suggesting that earlier experiences of provoked aggression may have led to subsequent elevations in testosterone. More recent analyses have shown that testosterone had a direct causal relationship with provoked aggressive behavior from grade six to grade nine. There was an indirect effect of testosterone on unprovoked aggression mediated by low frustration tolerance at grade nine. More longitudinal studies such as these are needed in order to test for causal relationships between testosterone and aggression.

Recently, it has been suggested that the mechanism of testosterone's effects on dominance and aggression may involve serotonin. Studies in rats have shown that serotonin agonists reduce testosterone-induced increases in dominance. There is, at this point, no evidence supporting such a mechanism in humans.

The major limitation of correlational studies is the difficulty in specifying the direction of the relationship. It is commonly hypothesized that higher testosterone leads to increased aggression through some as yet unspecified biochemical pathway. Alternatively, the effects of testosterone on muscle mass and body hair may lead to a more intimidating appearance, which may affect interactions with others, lead to changes in one's self-perceptions, and ultimately increase aggressiveness. Alternatively, or additionally, aggression may increase testosterone. Increases in testosterone in male judo competitors were correlated with anger and violence during the competition, suggesting that these behavioral reactions produced the hormonal changes. Plasma testosterone was elevated in healthy males following a laboratory point subtraction aggression task.

Other findings suggest that elevated mood may increase testosterone levels. In one study, testosterone levels increased prior to a sports competition and remained high in the winners compared to the losers. In this study testosterone levels correlated more closely with the individual's mood than with performance; those with a more positive mood prior to the competition had higher testosterone. Also, among the winners, those most satisfied with their performance had the highest testosterone levels. Another study demonstrated elevated testosterone levels in the winners of a contrived laboratory competitive reaction-time task. There was no such increase in losers, which suggests that physical competition is not necessary to demonstrate hormonal changes. Thus, it may be more the cognitive/affective experience of the event that affects androgen levels rather than androgen levels affecting performance.

Additionally, dominance may be associated with testosterone. Testosterone levels in humans rise after victory and fall after defeat in competitions. Testosterone levels rose in winning male tennis players and wrestlers relative to the losers. Testosterone levels in chess players at a tournament rose and fell following wins and losses, with the likelihood of winning increased with higher testosterone. In new recipients of an MD degree, testosterone rises, and this increase is related to elevated mood in these individuals. Moreover, vicarious success and failure are associated with elevations and reductions in testosterone, respectively. Soccer fans whose team won showed an increase in salivary testosterone, while those supporting the losing team showed a reduction in testosterone. Testosterone is also positively associated with self-rated elevated mood, well-being, and alertness, and decreased anxiety, fatigue, and tension. These findings suggest that increases in testosterone may result from the internal experience of dominance, or having dominance socially attributed ("eminence"), and concomitant increases in status and subsequent feelings of well-being. Bi-directional influences are also possible. Higher testosterone levels may increase the likelihood of engaging and achieving success in competition; the increased status attained through victory might then increase testosterone levels.

A longitudinal study of adolescent boys supports the notion that testosterone is associated with dominance and social success rather than physical aggression. Thirteen year-old boys concurrently rated by unfamiliar peers as "tough" and "leaders" had higher testosterone compared to "tough-not leaders" and "not tough" groups. Conversely, longitudinal analyses revealed that those boys teacher-rated as physically aggressive from ages 6 to 12 (particularly those also rated as anxious) had lower salivary testosterone levels than nonaggressive boys. These physically aggressive boys were not socially dominant, as they were rated as less popular by their peers compared to nonaggressive boys, and were failing in school. Thus, high testosterone was found in boys who were successful in imposing their will on their peers (perhaps through aggression at times), but who remained socially attractive. The stress of social rejection in physically aggressive boys may have led to higher anxiety and activation of the adrenal axis, which suppresses the hypothalamic-pituitary-gonadal (HPG) axis.

Aside from the effects of competition on testosterone levels, a number of other factors can impact on testosterone and other androgens. Stress decreases these neurochemicals; sexual stimulation and exercise can increase them. Alcohol can also alter testosterone levels, although the direction of the relationship is not clear. These factors also must be considered when interpreting studies in this area.

Some studies with adolescent males have shown that aggressive behavior is related to *lower* levels of gonadal hormones (e.g., testosterone) and higher levels of adrenal hormones. It has been suggested that lower concentrations of gonadal steroids and higher adrenal androgens are related to antisocial behavior through: (i) a heightened sensitivity of the hypothalamic-pituitary-gonadal (HPG) axis to stress-related secretion of HPA axis hormones, resulting in HPG suppression, or (ii) a predisposition in some individuals to heightened arousal following environmental stressors, resulting in HPA axis activation. The HPA axis impacts indirectly on testosterone levels through modulation of the HPG axis. Stress-induced HPA activation suppresses the HPG system, resulting in decreased androgen production.

Finally, studies of aggressive behavior following androgen administration provide limited support for the notion that androgens increase aggression. A randomized, double-blind, placebo-controlled cross-over trial in which depo-testosterone or conjugated estrogens were administered to adolescent boys or girls, respectively, demonstrated increased self-report physical aggressive behaviors and aggressive impulses in both boys and girls, with no changes in verbal aggressive behaviors or inhibitions in both boys and girls. However, in a number of other studies in which testosterone has been administered to either hypogonadal men or men with normal gonadal function, no increases in mood correlates of aggression (e.g., anger) were noted following testosterone treatment. At least one study reported that, following testosterone treatment, anger decreased in hypogonadal men who were significantly more angry than controls at baseline. Healthy volunteers administered an anabolic steroid (methyltestosterone) in a double-blind, placebo-controlled study experienced increases in negative mood symptoms, such as irritability, violent feelings, anger, and hostility, but also increases in euphoria, sexual arousal, and energy.

2. Adrenal Hormones/Neurotransmitters

A few additional studies support the notion that aggression is related to reduced HPA axis function. Corticotropin-releasing hormone is released from the hypothalamus following a stressor. It induces the release of ACTH in the anterior pituitary. In pregnant adolescents, corticotropin-releasing hormone is negatively correlated with conduct disorder symptoms assessed postpartum. This finding is consistent with lower salivary cortisol in preadolescent males whose fathers had conduct disorder that later developed into antisocial personality disorder compared to boys whose fathers had no Axis I disorders or antisocial behavior. Also, prepubertal boys and girls characterized by low plasma cortisol levels at baseline that increased following a stressor had more conduct disorder symptoms than adolescents who either showed no changes or reductions in cortisol levels over time. Conversely, one study found a positive correlation between plasma cortisol and self-report irritability and resentment (but not global aggressiveness) in healthy males. By and large, these studies, along with those reviewed in previous sections, suggest that reduced activity of the HPA axis is correlated with, and may be causally related to, aggressive and violent behavior.

Similar to studies in violent offenders and personality-disordered individuals, peripheral indicators of NE function are positively correlated with measures of aggression in healthy individuals. Self-report irritability and resentment, as well as global aggressiveness reported by spouses and first-degree relatives, were positively related to plasma NE in healthy males. As well, plasma cortisol and growth hormone levels (but not prolactin) increased following a point-subtraction aggression laboratory task in healthy males with higher (versus lower) basal aggressiveness. This was interpreted as a secondary response to increased plasma NE levels following the aggression task in these men. In another study, aggression on a laboratory task involving the administration of aversive noise to another person was weakly correlated with urinary methyladrenaline (methylepinephrine), but not with methylnoradrenaline (methylnorepinephrine) or creatinine, in healthy adolescent boys.

Taken together, the findings of studies on adrenal hormones and neurotransmitters in healthy individuals, as well as those in violent offenders and other clinical groups, tentatively suggest that aggression is associated with reduced basal HPA axis function coupled with hyperresponsivity during stress. Second, the findings on cortisol in aggressive children suggest the need to distinguish between aggressive individuals with and without anxiety symptoms, as hormonal/neurotransmitter and aggression relationships may be different in these two groups.

B. Neurotransmitters

1. Serotonin

Studies investigating the relationship between 5-HT and aggression in normal volunteers are generally consistent with the relationship found in violent offenders and personality-disordered individuals. One study noted an inverse relationship between self-report aggression and CSF 5-HIAA levels in normal volunteers, although a second study found that this relationship disappeared after controlling for age. Cortisol responses to fenfluramine challenge are negatively correlated with self-report Buss-Durkee Hostility Inventory total and aggression factor scores in healthy males with no relationship between prolactin responses and aggression, and no relationships in females.

A number of studies have found increased aggressive responding on laboratory tasks following acute dietary depletion of tryptophan in healthy males, particularly following provocation and in individuals who are higher in baseline aggression (e.g., normal males high in hostile or antisocial traits, and young men who score high on aggression on the Buss-Durkee Hostility Inventory). In another study, aggressive responding on a laboratory aggression paradigm was reduced in healthy males following administration of the $5\text{-HT}_{1A/1B}$ agonist eltoprazine; however, nonaggressive responding was also reduced, suggesting an overall sedative effect. Future experimental studies in humans using serotonin precursors, reuptake inhibitors, and receptor agonists in combination with receptor antagonists may provide more detailed information on the serotonergic regulation of aggressive and violent behavior.

Finally, in one of the only studies to look at social affiliation in humans, 4-weeks' administration of the 5-HT reuptake inhibitor paroxetine (double-blind, placebo-controlled) in healthy volunteers reduced hostility (and more generally negative affect), had no effect on positive affect, and increased a behavioral index of social affiliation (cooperative behavior during a puzzle-solving session). Changes in negative affect and affiliative behavior were significantly related to plasma paroxetine levels.

2. Peptides

The only study in humans to investigate the role of endogenous opioids in aggression has found a positive correlation between CSF opioid binding protein and self-report assaultiveness in healthy males.

3. Acetylcholine

Evidence linking brain acetylcholine and human aggression/violence is limited to the effects of nicotine. Nicotine is an agonist of nicotinic cholinergic receptors in the central nervous system. Nicotine cigarettes decrease experimental aggression in a competitive task in healthy humans. Experienced aggressive smokers titrate their nicotine intake in part to reduce their anger. Withdrawal from smoking is associated with increased hostility and irritability. Conversely, one study found that the frequency of weekly cigarette smoking was weakly correlated with scores on the Buss-Durkee Hostility Inventory in healthy men.

C. Other Neurochemicals

1. Monoamine Oxidase

Some personality traits and behavioral dispositions commonly associated with aggressive and violent behavior have been inversely associated with platelet MAO levels in studies with normal volunteers. These include disinhibition, impulsivity, externalizing behaviors, and sensation-seeking.

2. Glucose Regulation

Congruent with the studies in violent offenders, a tendency toward reactive hypoglycemia was correlated with self-reported aggressiveness in healthy males.

3. Cholesterol

An association between low plasma cholesterol concentration and violence has been prompted by the observation that programs designed to reduce total and low-density lipoprotein cholesterol reduced heart attacks and sudden cardiac deaths, but did not decrease total mortality. Total mortality remained high due to an increase in noncardiovascular deaths, including those due to suicide, homicide, and accidents. It has been hypothesized that lowered cholesterol may cause increased accidental and violent death directly, and that factors such as alcohol use, smoking, disease, medications, or socioeconomic factors may reduce cholesterol. Alternatively, these factors may cause increases in accidental or violent death as well as lowered cholesterol, with low cholesterol not causally implicated in accidental or violent death. While a 1990 meta-analysis demonstrated significantly greater deaths from accidents, suicide, or violence in groups being treated to lower cholesterol relative to controls, more recent follow-up studies with large sample sizes have not confirmed an association between low cholesterol and death due to accidents, suicide, or violence.

It has been suggested that low cholesterol may lead to low impulse control, increasing the chances of violent death. Furthermore, the association between low cholesterol and accidental and violent death may be mediated by reduced brain serotonergic activity. There is limited evidence for the link between lowered cholesterol and reduced 5-HT function; in separate studies with macaques monkeys put on a low-fat, low-cholesterol diets, blunted prolactin responses to fenfluramine, and lower CSF 5-HIAA concentrations, possible indicating reduced central serotonergic function, were found relative to monkeys on high fat, high cholesterol diets. Monkeys on the low fat diet were more aggressive and less socially affiliative as well. Additionally, platelet serotonin uptake in humans increases in the presence of low serum cholesterol, possibly leading to decreased serotonin availability. Lowered cholesterol might also reduce brain serotonin activity by altering cell membrane permeability and microviscosity, reducing serotonin receptor numbers.

Despite this suggestive evidence, the link between low cholesterol and violent behavior is tenuous. Confounding variables, such as side effects of cholesterol-lowering drugs, disease, or psychiatric disorders, may be responsible for the increase in accidental and violent deaths observed in some studies through mechanisms other than lowered cholesterol. It is also important to emphasize that low cholesterol concentrations have been linked to deaths due to violence, not violent behavior.

V. SUMMARY

Clearly, the empirical study of the biochemistry of aggressive and violent behavior in humans has just begun. The most well-replicated relationship appears to be the inverse association between indicators of central serotonergic function and aggressive/violent behavior, or perhaps more specifically, *impulsive* aggressive/violent behavior. This general finding is supported by a large animal literature showing that experimental increases in 5-HT function result in decreases in aggression, while decreases in 5-HT function increase aggression. A positive relationship between testosterone and aggression/violence is also suggested by a large number of studies. The magnitude of this relationship appears to be small, and it may be due, at least in part, to increases in testosterone *following* commission of aggressive or violent behavior. The inverse association between platelet MAO activity and aggressive/violent behavior is also intriguing, however its significance remains in question. It is important to note again that the large majority of studies on the biochemistry of aggression and violence in humans are correlational in nature; the direction of the brain-behavior relationship can not be specified from these studies.

A neglected area of research is the biochemistry of prosocial, affiliative behavior in humans. Presumably these relationships would be the inverse of those found for aggressive and violent (i.e., antisocial) behavior (e.g., the serotonin reuptake inhibitor paroxetine increasing affiliative behavior in healthy volunteers). Higher order relationships are certainly possible, however. Greater emphasis also needs to be placed on experimental studies in humans in which neurotransmitter or hormonal functioning is altered and the effects on behavior observed. Such studies will elucidate causal biochemical mechanisms controlling human aggression and violence.

Investigators are only beginning to map out possible neurotransmitter/neurotransmitter and neurotransmitter/hormone interactions in the regulation of human aggressive and violent behavior. Serotonin/norepinephrine and serotonin/testosterone interactions have been hypothesized, however experiments designed to test these relationships in humans have only just begun. One of the difficulties in this field is the lack of easily measurable peripheral indicators of central neurotransmitter function. Hormonal responses to neurotransmitter agonist challenges represent one such indicator; whole blood serotonin may yet prove to be another. Future investigation of adrenal/gonadal hormonal interactions promise to provide a greater understanding of the relationship between hormones, stress, and aggressive behavior.

Biochemical by environmental interactions will also need to be a focus of future investigation. A biochemical system may be tuned in such a fashion that it provides a template for the occurrence of aggression or violent behavior given the occurrence of certain environmental stimuli. For example, individuals with low serotonin may exhibit aggressive behavior specifically when provoked. Studies designed to demonstrate person by environment interactions will help to illuminate the multitude of interactions that likely occur in the expression of aggressive and violent behavior in humans.

An array of newer techniques have the potential to further enhance our understanding of human aggressive, violent, and prosocial behavior. In vivo imaging of brain neurotransmitter synthesis and receptor function will clarify the neurochemical systems regulating prosocial and aggressive behavior. Groups of well-defined individuals selected for specific behavioral characteristics (e.g., physical aggression, impulsivity) should be studied in order to advance our knowledge of the biochemistry of the components of clinical disorders (e.g., conduct disorder). Only through such fine-grained analyses will the biochemical underpinnings of prosocial, aggressive, and violent behavior be illuminated.

Also See the Following Articles

DRUGS AND VIOLENCE • MENTAL ILLNESS • NEUROPSYCHOLOGY OF MOTIVATION FOR GROUP AGGRESSION

BIBLIOGRAPHY

Archer, J. (1991). The influence of testosterone on human aggression. *Br. J. Psychol. 82,* 1–28.

Archer, J. (1994). Testosterone and aggression. *J. Offend. Rehab. 21,* 3–25.

Berman, M. E., Tracy, J. I., & Coccaro, E. F. (1997). The serotonin hypothesis of aggression revisited. *Clin. Psychol. Rev. 17,* 651–665.

Brain, P. F. (1994). Hormonal aspects of aggression and violence. In: Reiss, A. J., Jr., Miczek, K. A., & Roth, J. A. (Eds.), *Understanding and preventing violence, Volume 2: Biobehavioral influences.* National Academy Press, Washington, DC, pp. 173–244.

Coccaro, E. F. (1996). Neurotransmitter correlates of impulsive aggression in humans. *Ann. N.Y. Acad. Sci. 794,* 82–89.

Coccaro, E. F., & Kavoussi, R. J. (1994). Neuropsychopharmacologic challenge in biological psychiatry. *Clin. Chem. 40,* 319–327.

Coccaro, E. F., Kavoussi, R. J., Trestman, R. L., Gabriel, S. M., Cooper, T. B., & Siever, L. J. (1997). Serotonin function in human subjects: Intercorrelations among central 5-HT indices and aggressiveness. *Psychiatry Res. 73,* 1–14.

Eichelman, B. (1987). Neurochemical and psychopharmacologic aspects of aggressive behavior. In: Meltzer, H. Y. (Ed.), *Psychopharmacology: The third generation of progress. Raven Press, New York, pp. 697–704.*

Ellis, L. (1991). Monoamine oxidase and criminality: Identifying an apparent biological marker for antisocial behavior. *J. Res. Crime Delinq. 28,* 227–251.

Kanarek, R. B. (1994). Nutrition and violent behavior. In: Reiss, A. J., Jr., Miczek, K. A., & Roth, J. A. (Eds.), *Understanding and preventing violence, Volume 2: Biobehavioral influences.* National Academy Press, Washington, DC, pp. 515–539.

Linnoila, M., & Virkkunen, M. (1992). Aggression, suicidality, and serotonin. *J. Clin. Psychiatry 53 Suppl.,* 46–51.

Mann, J. J. (1995). Violence and aggression. In: Bloom, F. E. & Kupfer, D. J. (Eds.), *Psychopharmacology: The fourth generation of progress.* Raven Press, Ltd., New York, pp. 1919–1928.

Miczek, K. A., Haney, M., Tidey, J., Vivian, J., & Weerts, E. (1994). Neurochemistry and pharmacotherapeutic management of aggression and violence. In: Reiss, A. J., Jr., Miczek, K. A., & Roth, J. A. (Eds.), *Understanding and Preventing violence, Volume 2: Biobehavioral influences.* National Academy Press, Washington, DC, pp. 245–514.

Potter, W. Z., & Manji, H. K. (1993). Are monoamine metabolites in cerebrospinal fluid worth measuring? *Arch. Gen. Psychiatry 50,* 653–656.

Rubinow, D. R., & Schmidt, P. J. (1996). Androgens, brain, and behavior. *Am. J. Psychiatry 153,* 974–984.

Santiago, J. M., & Dalen, J. E. (1994). Cholesterol and violent behavior. *Arch. Int. Med. 154,* 1317–1321.

Virkkunen, M., Goldman, D., & Linnoila, M. (1996). Serotonin in alcoholic violent offenders. *Ciba Found. Symp. 194,* 168–182.

Volavka, J. (1995). *Neurobiology of violence.* American Psychiatric Press, Washington, DC.

Chemical and Biological Warfare

Howard S. Levie
Saint Louis University Law School and U.S. Naval War College

GLOSSARY

Bacteriology The science that deals with bacteria, the microscopic organisms whose influence in the biosphere is incalculable but some of which cause disease.

Biology The science of life or living matter in all its forms and phenomena.

Biological Warfare Warfare that makes use of bacteria, viruses, toxins, and so on, to disable or destroy man, animals, and food crops. Anthrax and nerve gases are examples of these weapons.

Chemical Warfare Warfare that makes use of disabling and deadly chemicals that disable or kill members of the enemy community, military and civilian, and that contaminate territory. Phosgene, chlorine, and mustard gases are examples of these weapons.

Precursor Any chemical reactant that takes part at any stage of the production by whatever method of a toxic chemical.

Toxins Any of a group of poisonous, usually unstable, compounds generated by microorganisms or plants or of animal origin, the causative agents of a number of diseases, including tetanus, diphtheria, and so on.

CHEMICAL AND BIOLOGICAL WARFARE generally refers to the use of chemical and biological agents as weapons of war. Chemical weaponry in the form of poison gas (e.g., chlorine) was a significant feature of World War I, and though gas warfare was generally condemned afterward, it has been noted, or at least alleged, in various subsequent conflicts. In the current era, the term chemical warfare has been extended to apply to, among other actions, the use of herbicides to destroy foliage on a large-scale basis. Biological warfare refers to the use of harmful organisms, chiefly pathogenic bacteria or viruses (e.g., the anthrax bacillus). At the present time, the intentional deployment of toxic microorganisms as weapons of war remains a potential threat rather than an actual strategy. Nevertheless, the devastating effect of disease on wartime populations, as in the flu epidemic of 1918, is well documented, and the world community has taken steps to outlaw biological warfare.

I. INTRODUCTION

The first specific reference to either chemical or bacteriological (biological) weapons contained in the conventional international law of war appeared in **Declaration IV of the 1899 International Peace Conference**, which met in The Hague from May to July of that year on the initiative of Czar Nicholas II of Russia. That **Declaration** stated:

> The Contracting Powers agree to abstain from the use of projectiles the sole object of which is the diffusion of asphyxiating or deleterious gases.

France, Germany, Great Britain, and Italy all ratified that Declaration. The United States neither signed nor ratified it. [Article 70 of the **1863 Instructions for the Government of the Armies of the United States in the Field** (the so-called "**Lieber Code**") had prohibited the use of poison in any manner. However, this applied only to the Union Army during the American Civil War (1861–1865) and had no international status although the **Code** itself served as a source for subsequent international conventions on the law of war.]

II. CHEMICAL WEAPONS

A. World War I

Despite its adherence to **Declaration IV of the 1899 International Peace Conference**, the German Army used gas shells in Poland on 31 January 1915. However, because of the frigidity of the atmosphere the gas projectiles proved ineffective. The Germans next used chlorine gas against the French at Ypres on 22 April 1915. This time its effect went far beyond any expectations, with the result that the Germans were unable to capitalize on their success. (It is sometimes alleged that the German action at Ypres was not a violation of the **Declaration** because the gas was released from barrels, not projectiles, and was carried over the French lines by the wind.) During the remainder of World War I both sides used various types of gas (chlorine, phosgene, mustard, etc.) and there were more than 1,000,000 gas casualties, more than were caused by any other form of warfare. (Despite this, there are those who claim that it is the most humane method of warfare!) The **Treaty of Versailles**, which ended World War I, contained a provision forbidding Germany all such weapons.

The **1922 Treaty of Washington**, while basically a treaty dealing with submarine warfare, contained a provision prohibiting the use of "asphyxiating, poisonous or other gases and all analogous liquids, materials or devices." As France failed to ratify this treaty, it never became effective.

B. World War II

In 1925 an international arms control conference meeting in The Hague drafted a **Protocol for the Prohibition of the Use in War of Asphyxiating, Poisonous or Other Gases, and of Bacteriological Methods of Warfare**. Its operative provisions stated:

> Whereas the use in war of asphyxiating, poisonous or other gases, and of all analogous liquids, materials or devices, has been justly condemned by the general opinion of the civilized world;
>
> . . . . . .
>
> Declare:
>
> That the High Contracting Parties, so far as they are not already Parties to Treaties prohibiting such use, accept this prohibition, agree to extend the prohibition to the use of bacteriological methods of warfare and agree to be bound as between themselves according to the terms of this declaration.

A number of the more than 100 nations that ratified this **Protocol** did so with a reservation that it was only binding as regards other parties to the **Protocol** and with the so-called "first-use" reservation pursuant to which a party was released from its obligations under the **Protocol** in the event that its enemy failed to respect its obligations thereunder. Italy admittedly used poison gas against Ethiopia in the 1935–1936 war between those two nations, justifying it as a reprisal against violations of the law of war by Ethiopia. Despite the provision of the **Treaty of Versailles** mentioned above, Nazi Germany had chemical weapons in its arsenal during World War II. However, on the advice of his military leaders, Hitler wisely refrained from using them because of the knowledge that the Allies also possessed large supplies of chemical weapons and could devastate Germany with them should they find it necessary to retaliate. As a result, gas was not used during World War II.

While the United States signed this **Protocol** at the time of its drafting in 1925, it did not ratify it until almost 50 years later, in April 1975. Its ratification included the "first-use" reservation. However, contrary to the position taken by the **International Committee of the Red Cross** that herbicides and riot control weapons are both chemical weapons and that fire weapons such as napalm burn oxygen and are, therefore, "asphyxiating," an executive order issued by the president prior to the effective date of the 1975 ratification, contains the following provisions:

> The United States renounces, as a matter of national policy, first use of herbicides in war, except under regulations applicable to their do-

mestic use, for control of vegetation within U.S. bases and installations or around their immediate defensive perimeters, and first use of riot control agents in war except in defensive military modes to save lives such as:

(a) Use of riot control agents in riot control situations in areas under direct and distinct U.S. military control, to include rioting prisoners of war.

(b) Use of riot control agents in situations in which civilians are used to mask or screen attacks and civilian casualties can be reduced or avoided.

(c) Use of riot control agents in rescue missions in remotely isolated areas, of downed air crews and passengers, and escaping prisoners.

(d) Use of riot control agents in rear echelon areas outside the zone of immediate combat to protect convoys from civil disturbances, terrorists and paramilitary organizations.

The reasons for these reservations are obvious. Herbicides had been widely used in Vietnam, not as an antipersonnel weapon, but to clear away foliage around U.S. military installations so as to prevent sneak attacks (their usage is claimed to have adversely affected the growth of millions of tons of rice). Riot control agents (basically, gas grenades) had been used to overcome rioting prisoners of war in Korea and to clear openings for helicopters to rescue downed airmen in Vietnam. They consist of a temporary disabling tear gas that causes no permanent harm, only temporary disability, and they are used by police all over the world. No specific mention of napalm, a chemical fire weapon, was made at the time, and the United States continues to consider it a legal weapon. While **Protocol III** to the **1980 Convention on Prohibitions and Restrictions on the Use of Certain Conventional Weapons Which May be Deemed to be Excessively Injurious or to Have Indiscriminate Effects** does not specifically mention napalm, it does place restrictions on the use of incendiary weapons. The United States has not ratified this **Protocol**.

C. Post-World War II

While, as noted above, gas was not used in World War II, it was used by belligerents on several occasions thereafter. For example, Egypt has been charged with using gas against Yemen; the Soviet Union is alleged to have used gas in Southeast Asia; Iraq is reputed to have used gas against the Kurds; and so on. It was well known that a number of countries had been experimenting with nerve gases, gases that are far more deadly than any previously known gas. The international community continued its efforts to effectively outlaw the use of all chemical weapons. As early as 16 December 1969 the General Assembly of the United Nations adopted Resolution 2603A (XXIV) in which it

> Declares as contrary to the generally recognized rules of international law, as embodied in the *Protocol for the Prohibition of the Use in War of Asphyxiating, Poisonous or Other Gases, and of Bacteriological Methods of Warfare*, signed at Geneva on 17 June 1925, the use in international armed conflicts of:
>
> (a) Any chemical agents of warfare—chemical substances, whether gaseous, liquid or solid—which might be employed because of their direct toxic effects on man, animals or plants;
>
> (b) Any biological agents of warfare—living organisms, whatever their nature, or infective material derived from them—which are intended to cause disease or death in man, animals or plants, and which depend for their effects on their ability to multiply in the person, animal or plant attacked.

(This Resolution was adopted by a vote of 80 to 3, with 36 abstentions. The United States cast one of the 3 negative votes. Most of its allies abstained.)

As we shall see, in 1972 a convention with respect to bacteriological (biological) and toxin weapons was drafted and widely accepted by States. Article IX of that Convention provided:

> Each State Party to this Convention affirms the recognized objective of effective prohibition of chemical weapons and, to this end, undertakes to continue negotiations in good faith with a view to reaching early agreement on effective measures for the prohibition of their development, production and stockpiling and for their destruction, and on appropriate measures concerning equipment and means of delivery specifically designed for the production or use of chemical agents for weapons purposes.

It required 21 years for this undertaking to reach fruition!

In January 1989 a **Conference of States Parties to the 1925 Geneva Protocol and Other Interested States**

on the Prohibition of Chemical Weapons adopted a **Declaration** that stated in part:

> 1, The participating States are determined to promote international peace and security throughout the world in accordance with the Charter of the United Nations and to pursue effective disarmament measures. In this context, they are determined to prevent any recourse to chemical weapons by completely eliminating them. They solemnly affirm their commitments not to use chemical weapons and condemn such use. They recall their serious concern at recent violations as established and condemned by the competent organs of the United Nations. They support the humanitarian assistance given to the victims affected by chemical weapons.

Finally, the international efforts with respect to outlawing chemical weapons culminated in the drafting and adoption on 13 January 1993 of a **Convention on the Prohibition of the Development, Production and Stockpiling of Chemical Weapons and on Their Destruction**. It is a very lengthy Convention (24 articles covering 36 pages and Annexes that exceed 100 pages). A few of the most relevant provisions follow:

Article I
General Obligations

1. Each State Party to this Convention undertakes never under any circumstances:

(a) To develop, produce, otherwise acquire, stockpile or retain chemical weapons, or transfer, directly or indirectly, chemical weapons to anyone;

(b) To use chemical weapons;

(c) To engage in any military preparations to use chemical weapons;

(d) To assist, encourage or induce, in any way, anyone to engage in any activity prohibited to a State Party under this Convention.

2. Each State Party undertakes to destroy chemical weapons it owns or possesses, or that are located in any place under its jurisdiction or control, in accordance with the provisions of this Convention.

3. Each State Party undertakes to destroy all chemical weapons it abandoned on the territory of another State Party, in accordance with the provisions of this Convention.

4. Each State Party undertakes to destroy any chemical weapons production facilities it owns or possesses, or that are located in any place under its jurisdiction or control, in accordance with the provisions of this Convention.

5. Each State Party undertakes not to use riot control agents as a method of warfare.

Article III
Declarations

1. Each State Party shall submit to the Organization, not later than 30 days after the Convention enters into force for it, the following declarations, in which it shall:

(a) With respect to chemical weapons:

(i) Declare whether it owns or possesses any chemical weapons, or whether there are any chemical weapons located in any place under its jurisdiction or control;

(v) Provide its general plan for destruction of any chemical weapons production facility it owns or possesses, or that is located in any place under its jurisdiction or control, in accordance with Part V, paragraph 6, of the Verification Annex;

(e) With respect to riot control agents: Specify the chemical name, structural formula and Chemical Abstract Service (CAS) registry number, if assigned, of each chemical it holds for riot control purposes. This declaration shall be updated not later than 30 days after any change becomes effective.

Article IV
Chemical Weapons

1. The provisions of this Article and the detailed procedures for its implementation shall apply to all chemical weapons owned or possessed by a State Party, or that are located in any place under its jurisdiction or control, except old chemical weapons and abandoned chemical weapons to which Part IV(B) of the Verification Annex applies.

3. All locations at which chemical weapons specified in paragraph 1 are stored or destroyed shall be subject to systematic verification through on-site inspection and monitoring with on-site instruments, in accordance with Part IV(A) of the Verification Annex.

4. Each State Party shall, immediately after the declaration under Article III, paragraph 1(a), has been submitted, provide access to chemical weapons specified in paragraph 1 for the purpose of systematic verification of the declaration through on-site inspection. Thereafter, each State Party shall not remove any of these chemical weapons, except to a chemical weapons destruction facility. It shall provide access to such chemical weapons, for the purpose of systematic on-site verification.

5. Each State Party shall provide access to any chemical weapons destruction facilities and their storage areas, that it owns or possesses, or that are located in any place under its jurisdiction or control, for the purpose of systematic verification through on-site inspection and monitoring with on-site instruments.

6. Each State Party shall destroy all chemical weapons specified in paragraph 1 pursuant to the Verification Annex and in accordance with the agreed rate and sequence of destruction (hereinafter referred to as "order of destruction"). Such destruction shall begin not later than two years after this Convention enters into force for it and shall finish not later than 10 years after entry into force of this Convention. A State Party is not precluded from destroying such chemical weapons at a faster rate.

Article VI
Activities Not Prohibited Under This Convention

1. Each State Party has the right, subject to the provisions of this Convention, to develop, produce, otherwise acquire, retain, transfer and use toxic chemicals for purposes not prohibited under this Convention.

2. Each State Party shall adopt the necessary measures to ensure that toxic chemicals and their precursors are only developed, produced, otherwise acquired, retained, transferred, or used within its territory or any other place under its jurisdiction or control for purposes not prohibited under this Convention.

11. The provisions of this Article shall be implemented in a manner which avoids hampering the economic or technological development of States Parties, and international cooperation in the field of chemical activities for purposes not prohibited under this Convention including the international exchange of scientific and technical information and chemicals and equipment for the production, processing or use of chemicals for purposes not prohibited under this Convention.

Article IX
Consultations, Cooperation and Fact-Finding

Procedure for Challenge Inspections

8. Each State Party has the right to request an on-site challenge inspection of any facility or location in the territory or in any other place under the jurisdiction or control of any other State Party for the sole purpose of clarifying and resolving any question concerning possible non-compliance with the provisions of this Convention, and to have this inspection conducted anywhere without delay by an inspection team designated by the Director-General and in accordance with the Verification Annex.

10. For the purpose of verifying compliance with the provisions of this Convention, each State Party shall permit the Technical Secretariat to conduct the on-site challenge inspection pursuant to paragraph 8.

Article XII
Measures to Redress a Situation and to Ensure Compliance, Including Sanctions

1. The Conference shall take the necessary measures, as set forth in paragraphs 2, 3 and 4 to ensure compliance with this Convention and to redress and remedy any situation which contravenes the provisions of this Convention. In considering action pursuant to this paragraph, the Conference shall take into account all information and recommendations on the issues submitted by the Executive Council.

2. In cases where a State Party has been requested by the Executive Council to take measures to redress a situation raising problems with regard to its compliance, and where the State Party fails to fulfil the request within the specified time, the Conference may, *inter alia*, upon the recommendation of the Executive Council, restrict or suspend the State Party's rights and privileges under this Convention until it undertakes the necessary action to conform with its obligations under this Convention.

3. In cases where serious damage to the object and purpose of this Convention may result from

> activities prohibited under this Convention, in particular by Article I, the Conference may recommend collective measures to States Parties in conformity with international law.
>
> 4. The Conference shall, in cases of particular gravity, bring the issue, including relevant information and conclusions, to the attention of the United Nations General Assembly and the United Nations Security Council.

The Annexes include one on **chemicals**, one on **verification**, and one on **confidentiality**.

When President Clinton of the United States and President Yeltsin of Russia met in Helsinki in March 1997, before either country had ratified the **Chemical Convention**, they issued a joint statement that included the following commitment:

> The Presidents reaffirmed their intention to take the steps necessary to expedite ratification in each of the two countries. President Clinton expressed his determination that the United States be a party when the Convention enters into force in April of this year, and is strongly urging prompt Senate action. President Yeltsin noted that the Convention had been submitted to the Duma with his strong recommendation for prompt ratification.

By December 1997, 106 nations, including the People's Republic of China, India, Iran, the Republic of Korea, Mongolia, the Russian Federation, and Vietnam, had ratified the **1993 Convention.** Notable for their absence from the list of signers and/or ratifiers were Iraq, Libya, North Korea, and Syria. Although the United States did not wait 50 years before ratifying the **1993 Convention**, as it had done in the case of the **1925 Geneva Protocol**, in finally giving its advice and consent to the ratification of the **Convention** by the president in April 1997, the Senate attached 28 "Conditions," conditions that in some instances largely rewrite the **Convention.** (It should be pointed out that, contrary to most newspaper and other reports, the Senate *does not ratify treaties*. The Executive Branch drafts a treaty with other nations, either bilateral or multilateral, and the president then submits it to the Senate for the latter's advice and consent, by a two-thirds vote of those present and voting, to ratification by the president, an authority that he may decide not to exercise, but that he, of course, usually does, barring some major development in the intervening period. See Article II, Section 2, of the Constitution of the United States.)

Originally, there were 33 Conditions contained in the Senate's advice and consent to ratification, the last 5 being so-called "killer conditions" as they would have made it impossible for the United States to become a party to the **Convention**. Many of the remaining 28 Conditions are completely internal, being concerned with the constitutional relationship between the president and the Congress. (See S. RES. 75, 105th Cong., 1st Sess., 24 April 1997.) On 25 April 1997 the president certified to the Congress his compliance with the Conditions and immediately submitted the ratification of the United States to the depositary, the Secretary-General of the United Nations, before the 29 April 1997 date of the entry into force of the Convention, thus making the United States eligible to participate as a voting member in the **Conference of States Parties to the Convention** which met in The Hague on 6 May 1997. (The Russian Federation did not ratify the **Convention** until October 1997 when the Duma approved it unanimously.) The nature of a few of the more controversial Conditions adopted by the United States Senate were as follows:

> **Condition 1:** The Senate reserved its Constitutional right to include reservations in its advice and consent to ratification, despite the fact that Article XXII specifically prohibited reservations to the Convention. (This right was also to apply to amendments to the **Convention.**)

What the Senate is saying here is that it has a Constitutional right to take an action forbidden by an international agreement to which the United States desires to become a party. (Although Article I(5) of the **Convention** prohibits the use of riot control agents as a method of warfare, Condition 26 requires the president to certify to the Senate that the Convention does not prohibit the United States from using riot control agents in a number of specified circumstances. This is, in effect, a reservation. However, Article III(1)e), above, appears to indicate that despite the provision banning riot control weapons, it is contemplated that states parties will continue to possess them.

In his letter to the Congress, dated 25 April 1997, prior to the filing of the ratification, the president stated that all states parties to the **Convention** had been advised of the retention by the United States of a right to make reservations, notwithstanding the provisions of Article XXII of the **Convention**.

> **Condition 2:** The Executive Branch is prohibited from making any payment to the Organization for

> the Prohibition of Chemical Weapons (OPCW) without the authorization and specific appropriation by Congress.

Here the Senate is, in effect, admonishing the Executive Branch that all expenditures must be authorized by the Congress, a matter that obviously is an internal constitutional matter and not one with which the states parties to the Convention can be concerned. The president did not even deign to refer to this Condition in his letter to the Congress!

> **Condition 9:** The President is required to certify before ratification and annually thereafter that the "legitimate commercial activities" of the affected industries in the United States are not being "significantly harmed" by the limitations contained in the **Convention**.

The president so certified in his letter to the Congress. This is undoubtedly the intent of Article VI, quoted above.

> **Condition 15:** The President is required to certify to the Congress that the United States will not contribute to a fund, nor provide assistance, for States Parties which are ineligible for United States assistance under certain laws of the United States.

The president certified in his letter to the Congress that no assistance, other than medical antidotes and treatment, would be provided for states parties that are ineligible for assistance under certain specified laws of the United States.

> **Condition 26:** Requires the President to certify to the Congress that the United States is not restricted in the use of riot control agents for specifically mentioned purposes.

The president so certified in his letter to the Congress. This Condition is, of course, directly contrary to Article I, paragraph 5, of the **Convention**, *supra*, which flatly prohibits the use of riot control weapons as a method of warfare. This Condition actually amounts to a reservation as it enables the United States to do something that the Convention appears specifically to prohibit. Nevertheless, the president certified compliance with this Condition in his letter to the Congress inasmuch as the Condition relates only to instances where the United States is not a party to the conflict, but is acting in a peacekeeping capacity.

> **Condition 28:** Requires the President to certify that an appropriate search warrant will be obtained before any search of any facility in the United States unless the owner or operator consents.

In his letter to the Congress delivered before the filing of the ratification, the president certified that appropriate search warrants would be required.

As of 29 April 1997, when the **Convention** became effective, 165 States had signed the **Convention** and 87 of those States had ratified it. It is interesting to note that Egypt, Iraq, Lebanon, Libya, North Korea, and Syria had neither signed nor ratified this **Convention.** (This was the basis for one of the so-called "killer" conditions.) Iran, Russia, and Yemen had signed it but had not as yet ratified it. (Russia has since done so.) While North Korea is not a member of the United Nations and is not recognized by most other nations, this would not prevent it from becoming a party to the Convention, as has the Republic of Korea. However, it has not done so.

III. BACTERIOLOGICAL (BIOLOGICAL) WEAPONS

A. Historical

While the **1925 Geneva Protocol** included a ban on bacteriological weapons, that **Protocol** was generally regarded as solely a limitation on the use of gas in warfare and the fact that it likewise contained a ban on bacteriological weapons is rarely mentioned. This is likewise true of many of the other actions taken with regard to gas warfare, which likewise contained references to bacteriological weapons. This was probably because little experimentation had been made in the bacteriological field and no national army actually had usable bacteriological weapons at its disposal.

B. World War II

During World War II both sides experimented with bacteriological (biological) weapons, but fortunately these were never used in the European war. The Japanese Army had two units in China that conducted experiments with bacteriological weapons, allegedly using Chinese prisoners of war as guinea pigs, and in 1949 the Soviet Union conducted a war crimes trial in Khabarovsk of 12 Japanese, all of whom confessed and were found guilty of preparing bacteriological weapons (germs of plague, cholera, gas gangrene, anthrax, typhoid, paratyphoid, and other diseases) for use by the Japanese Army in China. In 1982 the Japanese government officially acknowledged that during the war a detachment of the Japanese Army in China had engaged in experiments with bacteriological weapons. It did not admit that prisoners of war had been used in the experiments.

C. Post-World War II

After the war a number of nations were known to be experimenting with bacteriological weapons, particularly anthrax. There was apparently less reluctance on the part of nations to ban bacteriological weapons than there was to ban chemical weapons, perhaps because far fewer nations had conducted experimentation in this field and far fewer were technically competent to do so. Accordingly, with considerably less controversy than in the case of gas warfare, on 10 April 1972 the General Assembly of the United Nations adopted a resolution recommending that states ratify a convention drafted by the Committee on Disarmament entitled **Convention on the Prohibition of Development, Production and Stockpiling of Bacteriological (Biological) and Toxin Weapons and on their Destruction**. The most important provisions of this **Convention** state:

Article I

Each State Party to this Convention undertakes never in any circumstances to develop, produce, stockpile or otherwise acquire or retain:

1. microbial or other biological agents, or toxins whatever their origin or method of production, of types and in quantities that have no justification for prophylactic, protective or other peaceful purposes.

2. weapons, equipment or means of delivery designed to use such agents or toxins for hostile purposes or in armed conflict.

Article II

Each State Party to this Convention undertakes to destroy, or to divert to peaceful purposes, as soon as possible but not later than nine months after the entry into force of the Convention, all agents, toxins, weapons, equipment and means of delivery.

Article IV

Each State Party to this Convention shall, in accordance with its constitutional processes, take any necessary measures to prohibit and prevent the development, production, stockpiling, acquisition or retention of the agents, toxins, weapons, equipment and means of delivery specified in Article I of the Convention, within the territory of such State, under its jurisdiction or under its control anywhere.

Article VI

1. Any State Party to this Convention which finds that any other State Party is acting in breach of obligations deriving from the provisions of the Convention may lodge a complaint with the Security Council of the United Nations. Such a complaint should include all possible evidence confirming its validity, as well as a request for its consideration by the Security Council.

2. Each State Party to this Convention undertakes to co-operate in carrying out any investigation which the Security Council may initiate, in accordance with the provisions of the Charter of the United Nations, on the basis of the complaint received by the Council. The Security Council shall inform the States Parties to the Convention of the results of the investigation.

Article VII

Each State Party to this Convention undertakes to provide or support assistance, in accordance with the United Nations Charter, to any Party to the Convention which so requests, if the Security Council decides that such Party has been exposed to danger as a result of violation of the Convention.

Article X

1. The States Parties to this Convention undertake to facilitate, and have the right to participate in, the fullest possible exchange of equipment, materials and scientific and technological information for the use of bacteriological (biological) agents and toxins for peaceful purposes. Parties to the Convention in a position to do so shall also co-operate in contributing individually or together with other States or international organizations to the further development and application of scientific discoveries in the field of bacteriology

(biology) for the prevention of disease, or for other peaceful purposes.

2. This Convention shall be implemented in a manner designed to avoid hampering the economic or technological development of States Parties to the Convention or international co-operation in the field of peaceful bacteriological (biological) activities, including the international exchange of bacteriological (biological) agents and toxins and equipment for the processing, use or production of bacteriological (biological) agents and toxins for peaceful purposes in accordance with the provisions of the Convention.

As of October 1997 142 states parties had ratified this **Convention** and 16 had signed but had not yet not ratified it. Among the ratifiers are the People's Republic of China, the Republic of Korea, Mongolia, the Russian Federation, and Vietnam. Strange to relate, also among the ratifiers are Iran, Libya, and North Korea. Several of the other nations that are not considered completely trustworthy have signed the **Convention** but have not as yet ratified it. The cease-fire that ended the Gulf War authorized representatives of the United Nations to make inspections in Iraq to ensure that it had no bacteriological (biological) weapons or means to produce them. Iraq has used every available subterfuge to circumvent these inspections, which would appear to indicate an intention to disregard the obligations specified in the **Convention** and that is likely to result in military action to enforce the relevant provisions of the cease-fire agreement.

IV. CONCLUSION

From the foregoing it is clear that the world community as a whole desires to eliminate from the use in war of chemical, bacteriological (biological), and toxin weapons and has taken action to accomplish this purpose. It remains to be seen whether, in the event some outlaw nation, counting on the inability of its enemy to retaliate in kind, makes no commitment or violates its commitment with respect to these weapons, the other parties to the conventions will unite in taking action against the renegade nation.

Also See the Following Articles

ARMS CONTROL • NUCLEAR WEAPONS • WARFARE, MODERN • WARFARE, STRATEGIES AND TACTICS OF • WEAPONRY, EVOLUTION OF

Bibliography

Aronowitz, D. S. (1965). *Legal aspects of arms control verification in the United States.* Oceana.

Fyodorov, Y. (1987). *The silent death.* Progress Publishers.

Harbour, F. V. (Ed.). (1990). *Chemical arms control.* Carnegie Council on Ethics.

Levie, H. S. (1991). Nuclear, chemical and biological weapons. In H. B. Robertson (Ed.), The law of naval operations. Naval War College, 64 *International Law Studies, 331.*

(1975). Weapons of warfare. In P. D. Trooboff (Ed.), *Law and responsibility in warfare, 153.* Honolulu: Univ. of Hawaii Press.

Roberts, B. (Ed.). (1992). *The Chemical Weapons Convention: Implementation issues.* Center for Strategic and International Studies.

United Nations. (1969). Report of the Secretary General. *Chemical and Bacteriological (Biological) Warfare and the Effect of Their Possible Use.* (A/7575/Rev. 1, 1969).

Child Abuse

Kristin L. Anderson
Drew University

Debra Umberson
University of Texas at Austin

GLOSSARY

Child Neglect Acts that endanger the welfare of children, including leaving a child unsupervised in a dangerous situation, failure to provide shelter, nutrition, education, or medical care, and abandonment.

Deprivational Dwarfism (psychosocial short stature syndrome) Stunted growth of children resulting from physical or emotional neglect.

Emotional Abuse Acts that endanger children's psychological well-being, including verbal abuse, belittlement, rejection, and practices designed to terrorize children.

Genital Mutilation (female circumcision) The partial or complete removal of external female genitalia, including the clitoris and labia.

Munchausen by Proxy A rare behavior in which an adult will induce or affect illness in a child in order to elicit medical attention.

Nonorganic Failure to Thrive The absence of age-appropriate weight gain and growth among infants due to nutritional and emotional deprivation.

Physical Abuse Acts that endanger the physical well-being of children, including beatings with an object, burning or scalding, severe physical punishment, deliberate poisoning, suffocation, and Munchausen by proxy syndrome.

Ritual Abuse Abuse occurring in a context of religious, magical, or supernatural group activities.

Sexual Abuse Sexual assaults, incest, genital fondling, exposure to indecent acts, and involvement in child pornography.

Sociopolitical Abuse Negative consequences for children resulting from political violence, socioeconomic inequality, and gender inequality, including child labor, dowry deaths, homelessness, and genital mutilation.

CHILD ABUSE entails acts of omission or commission that may have harmful physical or emotional effects on a child. This article presents a multidisciplinary view of issues characterizing the field of child abuse research, and summarizes research on the prevalence, etiology, and effects of this pervasive social problem.

I. DEFINING ABUSE

Defining child abuse is a challenging endeavor. Because standards for the appropriate care of children differ across cultures and historical periods, definitions of abuse must be placed within a given cultural and environmental context. Within societies, definitions of child abuse are controversial due to limited social consensus about harmful parenting practices, conflict over whether definitions should be based on standards of endangerment or harm, and differences in the meaning of a particular act based on the age, gender, ethnicity, and developmental level of the child.

A. Types of Abuse

Research literatures have developed around four general categories of abuse in Western industrialized nations: (1) physical abuse; (2) sexual abuse; (3) child neglect; and (4) emotional maltreatment. Physical abuse entails beatings with an object, burning or scalding, severe physical punishment resulting in actual or probable injury, deliberate poisoning, suffocation, and Munchausen by proxy syndrome. Sexual abuse includes sexual assaults, incest, genital fondling, and other activities, including exposure to indecent acts and involvement in child pornography, designed to lead to the sexual gratification of a sexually mature person. Child neglect involves acts that endanger the physical and psychological welfare of children, including leaving a child unsupervised in a potentially dangerous situation, failure to provide shelter, nutrition, education, or medical care, and abandonment. Emotional or psychological abuse entails verbal abuse and belittlement, rejection, and acts designed to terrorize children. Early child abuse research and policy efforts focused on physical abuse, largely in response to work on the "battered child syndrome" conducted by medical practitioners in the United States and Britain. In recent decades, researchers have documented the occurrence and prevalence of child neglect, emotional abuse, and sexual abuse, although physical and sexual abuse have been the focus of the largest number of empirical investigations.

Other types of abuse, including ritual abuse and moral/legal/educational abuse, are more controversial. The extent of ritual child abuse perpetrated and sanctioned by religious or supernatural groups has been the focus of recent controversy within Western industrialized nations; some scholars contend that ritual abuse is a common occurrence while others argue that this type of abuse is extremely rare. Moral/legal/educational practices such as failing to enroll children in school or exposing children to deviant behaviors have been identified as abusive by some scholars. However, others argue that the identification of these forms of abuse is arbitrary and biased by racial and social class differences. Recently, scholars have proposed that children who witness the physical and emotional abuse of their mother are victims of child abuse.

Research among Western scholars has concentrated on abuse perpetrated by parents and other caretakers. However, scholars in many nations propose that political violence and socioeconomic inequality are forms of sociopolitical abuse that result in substantial harm to children. Sociopolitical forms of child abuse and neglect include child labor, genital mutilation, dowry deaths, poverty, homelessness, and injuries to children resulting from political violence. A growing research literature documenting the negative effects of sociopolitical abuse on children can be found in the international journal *Child Abuse and Neglect* and in the *American Journal of Orthopsychiatry*.

Although particular acts form the basis of abuse definitions, issues of intent, duration and chronicity of abuse, and cultural variations complicate the actual classification of a given incident as abusive. Particularly in the case of child neglect, intention is relevant to designations of abuse, as the failure to provide adequate nutrition and shelter may result from changing economic and social conditions over which parents have little control. Duration and chronicity are also salient factors in designating abuse because large numbers of parents may perpetrate isolated incidents of child neglect or emotional abuse. Cultural practices such as genital mutilation, facial tatooing or scarring, and pressing coins into the skin are defined as abusive among some scholars in Western industrialized nations, while strict feeding schedules and isolating children in separate rooms for sleeping fall outside of normative definitions of appropriate child care among many cultures in the southern hemisphere.

Abuse is often defined differently in the legal and medical professions and in diverse disciplines such as psychology and sociology, reflecting the particular agenda and goals of the given profession or discipline. Medical definitions often concentrate on injuries resulting from abuse that are the basis for identification by physicians, while legal definitions contain emphasis on balancing the possible harm of separating the child from his/her caregivers against the need to protect the child from future harm. Academic definitions used in clinical research reveal disciplinary differences. Sociologists tend to emphasize socioeconomic inequality and other social and environmental predictors of abuse and physical punishment and psychologists focus on personal characteristics of sexual and physical abusers and their victims. Disciplinary and cultural differences make it difficult to achieve consensus on definitions of child abuse. A failure to develop consistent definitions of abuse often precludes comparisons across studies. As a result, scholars have identified the construction of a clear operational definition of abuse as a research priority.

II. DEMOGRAPHICS/EPIDEMIOLOGY

A. Prevalence

Data on the prevalence of child abuse comes from four primary sources: cross-national comparisons, mortality studies, regulatory agency data, and community and national surveys. Although most prevalence research has been conducted in Western industrialized nations, particularly the United States, recent efforts in many countries have contributed data on the number of children affected by abuse.

1. Cross-Cultural Rates

International studies of child abuse are rare, reflecting the methodological difficulty of obtaining valid data on child abuse rates that are comparable across nations. Even within nations, different regions may establish different criteria for identifying abusive incidents or classifying deaths as due to maltreatment, complicating calculation of national prevalence estimates. Several attempts at cross-national comparisons identify substantial variation in child-rearing practices across cultures. Drawing on anthropological reports from small-scale folk societies, David Levinson found that severe physical punishment is common among some cultures in rural Jamaica and extremely rare among others such as the Central Thai. Social class, religious, and ethnic group differences in the use of physical punishment characterize Western industrialized nations. These variations may reflect cultural differences in the legitimacy of physical means of control, the extent of household and parent isolation, and degree of emphasis on conformity and obedience.

The relatively high levels of child abuse and violence in the United States as compared to other industrialized nations have been the focus of scholarly concern among U.S. researchers. These relatively high rates may reflect more rigorous monitoring in the United States or they may reflect a cultural emphasis on violence as a legitimate tool of child rearing. However, the number of children affected by sociopolitical violence in some areas of the Middle East, Europe, Africa, Central America and South America is dramatically higher. Large numbers of children experience beatings or torture by police, or are seriously injured by gunfire, beatings, or tear gas in areas of intense political conflict. Amnesty International identified 624 press reports of violent killings of street children in Guatemala City and in Brazilian cities from 1988 through 1989; 130 of these deaths were attributed to death squads, including off-duty police officers.

2. Child Abuse Mortality Rates

World Health Organization data allow for international comparisons of child mortality resulting from physical abuse. Since cross-cultural mortality comparisons are complicated by different procedures for the classification of death across countries, World Health Organization figures combine categories for deaths attributed to homicide and "deaths from undetermined external causes" to determine a "presumed child abuse death rate." A 1993 study by Mark Belsey estimated that the presumed child abuse death rate for infants under one year per 100,000 live births ranges from 0 in several nations, including Greece, Cuba, and Columbia, to a high of 46.7 in Chile. On average, the international child abuse mortality rate for infants under one year is 6 to 7 deaths per 100,000 live births. These figures suggest an estimated abuse mortality rate of between 13 and 20 per 100,000 live births for children under the age of 5. However, the number of "hidden" child abuse deaths across countries is unclear; large differences across nations are likely due to different reporting and classification criteria for child deaths.

Mortality attributable to child neglect is more difficult to identify than mortality resulting from physical abuse. However, general infant mortality rates are a useful gauge of the living conditions of children across countries and serve as an approximate measure of the number of child deaths resulting from the neglect of children's nutritional and medical needs in addition to deaths resulting from physical injury and abuse. Infant mortality rates for selected countries are presented in Table I. In less industrialized nations, particularly equatorial Africa and parts of Asia, infant death rates are generally over 100 deaths per 1000 live births. Infant mortality rates are generally under 10 per 1000 live births in developed nations. However, infant mortality rates in developed countries ranged from a low of 4.2 in Japan to a high of 7.5 in the United States in 1996; these differences primarily reflect practices leading to higher risks of premature births such as alcohol, tobacco, and drug usage as well as unequal access to medical care within the United States.

International differences in infant mortality rates are in large part due to global socioeconomic inequality. Wealthy nations can provide their populations with clean water, adequate sanitation, food, shelter, and access to health care. In developing and less developed

TABLE I

1996 Infant Mortality Rates, Selected Countries

Country	Infant mortality rate[a]	Country	Infant mortality rate[a]
Africa		Europe	
Algeria	55	Denmark	5.4
Western Sahara	152	Estonia	15
Benin	86	Sweden	4.4
Niger	123	France	6.1
Mozambique	148	Austria	5.5
Zimbabwe	53	Bulgaria	15.5
Chad	122	Czech Republic	7.9
Lesotho	79	Russia	18
Asia		Albania	33.2
Cyprus	9	Greece	8.3
Iraq	67	Italy	8.3
Israel	6.9	Spain	7.2
Yemen	83	South America	
India	79	Belize	34
Pakistan	91	Honduras	50
Turkmenistan	46	Mexico	34
Cambodia	111	Barbados	9.1
Philippines	34	Cuba	9.4
China	44	Haiti	74
Japan	4.2	Martinique	6
Mongolia	61	Bolivia	71
Oceana		Chile	13.1
Australia	5.8	Peru	60
Guam	9.7	Uruguay	20.1
Papa New Guinea	63	North America	
		Canada	6.2
		USA	7.5

[a] Infant deaths per 1000 live births.

Source: Population Reference Bureau (1996). *World Population Data Sheet 1996*. Washington, DC: Population Reference Bureau.

nations, the extreme poverty, lack of sanitation, and pollution associated with high levels of infant mortality may be exacerbated by economic and development practices of industrialized nations. Moreover, the number of deaths resulting from child physical abuse and intentional child neglect is associated with the quality of health care within nations. Due to these problems, mortality rate data should be carefully examined and a discussion of potential biases should accompany reports of international variation in child abuse mortality.

3. Regulatory Agency Data/Child Abuse Reports

National reporting systems for child abuse and neglect exist in at least 30 nations, including 16 developed and 14 developing countries. However, reporting policies differ regarding the mandatory or voluntary nature of reports and the responsibilities of different individuals or sectors to report child abuse, making cross-national comparisons difficult.

Where available, data drawn from agency reports constitute a rich source of child abuse data, although scholars agree that this data source may uncover only a portion of abuse and overrepresents abuse cases among disadvantaged groups. Data from national incidence studies of child abuse in the United States completed in 1980, 1986, and 1995 identify from 8 to 15 per 1000 children as victims of abuse or neglect that can be verified by agency personnel. In 1991, 4 out of every 1000 British children were on national child abuse registers. Reports to child abuse agencies increased substantially during the 1980s and 1990s in both the United States and Britain, with most of the increase in reports of sexual abuse. The majority of this increase is believed to be due to greater public awareness of child abuse and neglect due to educational initiatives, yet the possibility of real increase cannot be dismissed due to a lack of accurate historical data. In recent years, child neglect cases constitute roughly half of all reported cases, while physical, sexual, and emotional abuse are less frequently reported.

4. National Survey Data

Several national probability studies of child physical abuse have been conducted in Canada, the United States, and Britain. National surveys of U.S. families conducted in 1975 and 1985 by Murray Straus and Richard Gelles found a rate of severe physical abuse between 107 and 140 per 1000 children annually and a very severe physical abuse rate of between 19 and 36 children per 1000 annually, with the lower rates reflecting 1985 figures. Severe physical abuse was defined as parental reports of their perpetration of one of the following acts against a child in the previous year: kicked, bit, hit with fist, hit, or tried to hit with something, beat up, threatened with a knife or gun, or used a knife or gun. The very severe physical abuse category was limited to the severe abuse acts most likely to produce injury to a child, including kicking, biting, hitting with a fist, beating up, or using a knife or a gun. A 1995 telephone survey of U.S. parents estimated the physical abuse rate at 49 per 1000 children. These rates are approximately double the reporting agency data rates, suggesting that at least half of all child abuse cases do not come to the attention of investigators in the United States.

Several national surveys have focused on the prevalence of sexual abuse. A 1985 British national survey of sexual abuse found that 12% of women and 8% of men reported that a sexually mature adult involved them in one or more of the following activities before the age of 16: intercourse, touching, exposure of sexual organs, showing pornographic material, or talking about sexual things in an erotic way. Fourteen percent of these individuals reported abuse by a family member, resulting in a intrafamilial abuse rate of 13 per 1000 children. A 1990 report of national survey research conducted in the United States by David Finkelhor revealed that 27% of women and 16% of men reported childhood sexual victimization defined as contact and noncontact abuse by any person. Four percent of women and 10% of men experienced actual or attempted sexual intercourse. A 1995 telephone survey of U.S. parents estimated the annual sexual abuse rate at 1.9 per 1000 children. Although prevalence rates vary substantially depending upon definitions of sexual abuse, these studies suggest that sexual abuse is prevalent within Western industrialized countries.

5. Sociopolitical Abuse Rates

Although rates of physical and sexual abuse perpetrated by adults against children appear high, substantially larger numbers of children are victimized by sociopolitical violence and socioeconomic inequality. Available data on the numbers of children affected by participation in child labor, genital mutilation, dowry deaths, political violence, and homelessness suggest that a large proportion of the world's children suffer from abusive and neglectful practices.

a. Child Labor

In newly industrializing and less developed countries, children work in factories and as street traders, outworkers, or seasonal agricultural laborers. An estimated 10 to 30% of children between the ages of 6 and 14 work in rural Iran, rural Argentina, and Pakistan. In India, children comprise approximately 10% of the work force in factories of the lock industry. Poor children in Western industrialized nations are also part of the labor force; a 1973 U.S. study found that 25% of all farm workers were underage. Although legislation prohibiting child labor is in place in many nations, including India and in Western industrialized nations, government statistics in India show that at least 5% of children continue to labor as full-time workers.

b. Genital Mutilation

Female children and adolescents are victimized by social and cultural practices placing them at high risk of death, injury, and infection. Genital mutilation of female children is commonly practiced among some populations in Africa and the Middle East. Female children in the United States have also been victimized by clitoral excision due to parental desire to control sexual behavior, although the practice is rare. The World Health Organization reports that more than 84 million African women alive today have undergone circumcision. Political movements against female genital mutilation have led some African countries to outlaw the practice and the United States and Canada to offer amnesty for young girls. However, strong support for genital mutilation as a form of cultural expression has hindered efforts to end this practice.

c. Dowry Deaths

Young brides suffer abuse at the hands of husbands and in-laws on the Indian subcontinent if their families fail to meet escalating and ongoing demands for dowry money or goods. Severe harassment often ends in the woman's suicide or homicide, which frequently takes the form of burning the woman. Although dowry deaths are commonly recorded as accidents rather than homicides in official data, mortality data indicate that one out of four deaths to women ages 15 to 24 in urban Maharshtra and Mombai (formerly Bombay) are caused by "accidental burns."

d. Child Homelessness

Rates of child homelessness around the world are extremely difficult to estimate due to the mobility of homeless populations and the variety of living conditions labeled "homeless" around the world. In developing countries, the term "children *on* the street" is used to describe children who work on the streets during the day selling flowers, shining shoes or begging and return home at night, while "children *of* the street" refers to children who live primarily on the street and have only occasional contact with their families. Although difficult to estimate the true number of street children, an estimate supported by UNICEF suggests that 100 million children live or work on the street around the world.

In the United States homeless children typically live in shelters with their parents, while in Eastern Europe the term "homeless" generally refers to children living in institutions due to abandonment or disability. In the United States estimates of the number of homeless children range from 100,000 to 750,000. Around 1% of Western European children live in institutions, while from 2 to 3% of children are institutionalized due to homelessness in Eastern Europe.

B. Characteristics of Perpetrators

Personal characteristics of individual perpetrators reveal little about the etiology of abuse when considered in isolation from other potential causal factors. However, past studies have consistently identified demographic, social, and psychological factors associated with abuse. The presence of multiple demographic, social and psychological risk factors among parents has been linked to particularly high rates of maltreatment.

1. Demographic

Sociological studies document associations between child abuse and indicators of structural inequality, including social class, poverty, and unemployment. Maternal age, marital status, and household density are also associated with child abuse; young, single parents in crowded living conditions have particularly high risks of abusing their children. Membership in non-White racial or ethnic groups is associated with maltreatment when reporting agency data are examined, perhaps reflecting racism among reporting physicians, teachers, and neighbors to a greater degree than actual racial-ethnic differences in rates of abuse. Moreover, comparing rates of child abuse across racial-ethnic groups is problematic due to the strong association between non-White ethnicity and poverty in Western industrialized nations. Two similar national surveys of U.S. parents conducted by Murray Straus and Richard Gelles did not find racial group differences in rates of physical punishment of children. Sexual abuse rates do not significantly differ across ethnic groups based upon findings from reporting agency and national survey data.

Gender has also been the focus of research on perpetrator characteristics. Although men engage in substantially more interpersonal violence than women outside of the home, women perpetrate physical child abuse and neglect at rates similar to or slightly higher than men. However, women may be less likely to perpetrate violence when time spent with children is taken into consideration; studies indicate that men have higher abuse rates than women within two-parent families. Women's relatively high rates of child maltreatment in the United States may be due to their greater time spent with children as well as the cultural construction of mothers as responsible for the behavior of children, which may lead women to become more frustrated by perceived child misbehavior.

The vast majority of sexual abuse incidents are perpetrated by males. Some research suggests that reports of women's perpetration of sexual abuse are increasing and that the finding of different rates by sex may be due to a lack of focus on women in past sexual abuse research. However, research conducted by David Finkelhor in the United States suggests that men are the perpetrators in 95% of sexual abuse incidents involving female children and 80% of abuse incidents involving male children. Additionally, sexual abuse cases are exceptional in that the demographic correlates of physical abuse and neglect such as poverty and unemployment have not been associated with sexual abuse rates in past research. This finding suggests that the etiology of sexual abuse may differ from that of other forms of child maltreatment. In particular, sexual abuse may be less likely than physical abuse and neglect to be associated with stressful social and economic conditions.

Very little is known about the demographic correlates of emotional abuse due to the lack of research on this form of maltreatment. Future child abuse studies should develop measures of psychological and emotional abuse to contribute to an understanding of the social and psychological correlates of emotional abuse.

2. Social and Cultural

Environmental, neighborhood, and community factors may facilitate child maltreatment. Maltreating families are often isolated from social support networks, although whether social isolation is a cause or consequence of abuse is currently unknown. The higher maltreatment rates among single parents within industrialized societies and among cultures with polygynous marital forms in which women and children often live apart from the male parent suggest that social isolation may be conducive to higher levels of maltreatment. Moreover, research conducted with maltreating and nonmaltreating parental groups who are matched on other variables (e.g., poverty, IQ) suggests that maltreating parents receive less social support than nonabusive parents. Child physical abuse has been associated with high levels of family conflict and domestic assaults between adults living in the home.

The role of substance abuse in child maltreatment is the focus of substantial controversy. Contradictory findings concerning an association between alcohol abuse and child maltreatment have been attributed to methodological shortcomings, including failure to consider severity of substance abuse. Few studies have examined the relationship between drug use and child maltreatment, and this research is complicated by the potential confounding effects of poverty on the relationship between drug and child abuse. Richard Gelles contends that alcohol and most drugs do not play a causal role in familial violence; however, particular drugs such as amphetamines raise excitability and muscle tension and may contribute to impulsive behavior. Currently, the relationship between substance abuse and child maltreatment is poorly understood. However, one clear finding is that alcohol is often involved in abuse incidents.

The role of ethnic culture in the incidence and treatment of abuse has been neglected by child abuse researchers. Culture affects family organization and the climate in which abuse occurs, the likelihood that abuse will be disclosed, and whether families seek or accept social or mental health services. Future research should play close attention to the ways that cultural beliefs deter, facilitate, and maintain abusive family interactions.

3. Psychological

In its early years, psychopathological models dominated the field of child abuse research. As a result, many studies focus on identifying psychological causes of abuse. Although the evidence concerning psychopathology among abuse perpetrators is contradictory, research has identified consistent psychological correlates of abusive behavior. Cross-sectional and prospective studies find that neglectful and abusing parents are characterized by low self-esteem, impulsiveness, depression, and anxiety. Physically abusive parents have higher levels of reported anger, external locus of control, and antisocial behavior. Moreover, abusive parents exhibit different cognitive processes in comparison to nonmaltreating parents, including expressing greater annoyance and irritation in response to children's behavior and unrealistic expectations regarding children's abilities. Other research demonstrates an association between mother's negative attitudes regarding the coming birth of a child and maltreatment following birth. Men's domestic assaults of wives or female partners often begin to occur during women's first pregnancy and may result in miscarriage or birth defects. Research on the psychological characteristics of sexual abusers suggests that timidity and low impulse control characterize a minority of this population. Psychological factors associated with emotional maltreatment have not received significant research attention.

Overall, psychological research suggests that while some psychological characteristics may be linked to abusive behavior, these characteristics must be examined in tandem with social and demographic variables. Recent models emphasize the importance of examining the interactive effects of social, psychological and demographic variables in the etiology of maltreating behavior. For example, particular psychological characteristics may be associated with abuse only under conditions of high stress due to poverty or unemployment. Examining the interactive effects of perpetrator characteristics, child characteristics and the environmental context represents an important avenue for future research.

C. Victim Characteristics

Although most scholars agree that victim characteristics play a limited causal role in child maltreatment, research suggests that abused children may develop traits that place them at increased risk of abuse by other caretakers such as day care workers or foster parents. Moreover, abuse rates are linked to sociodemographic child characteristics such as age and gender, although the relationship between these characteristics and maltreatment is poorly understood.

1. Sociodemographic

Child age is associated with differential risk of specific types of maltreatment. Child abuse deaths and physical abuse are most common among young children under the age of 3, while children from age 8 to 12 face greater risks of sexual abuse. Results from national surveys of the United States conducted by Murray Straus and Richard Gelles find the greatest rates of severe physical violence are directed at toddlers and adolescents.

Gender is a risk factor for some forms of abuse. International comparisons reveal that children are at increased risk of abuse and neglect across cultures if they are disabled, handicapped, or born under difficult or stigmatized conditions (such as illegitimacy), have poor health, or are female. Female children have higher risks of child neglect and physical abuse in some countries, including China, India, and Pakistan, while rates of abuse do not differ substantially by gender in industrialized nations. Infanticide of female children among several cultural groups within the Middle East and Asia has garnered international concern. Female children face particularly high risks of homicide, abuse, and neglect within cultures that value male children due to their greater traditional economic obligations to parents. Some studies indicate that female children receive lower qualities and quantities of food, are breast-fed for shorter lengths of time, and are less likely to receive medical care than male children. Among 1 and 2-year-old children in Pakistan, Sri Lanka, Bangladesh, Trinidad, Tobago, and Columbia, the female mortality rate is 1.3 to 1.5 times higher than that of male children.

Female children experience much greater risk of sexual abuse than male children. In Western industrialized nations, female children are roughly two times more likely to be victimized by sexual abuse than male children. In newly industrializing and underdeveloped nations, female circumcision or genital mutilation contribute to girls' mortality and morbidity.

2. Disability

Although retrospective studies find that prematurity, low birthweight, disability, and difficult child temperament (e.g., irritability, frequent crying) place children at higher risk for abuse, prospective studies that include controls for social and demographic variables have not replicated these findings. Additionally, low birthrate and prematurity are associated with poverty, making it difficult to separate the distinct effect of child physical characteristics from contributing sociological variables. Difficult temperament ratings of infants made by mothers and nurses are not associated with maltreatment, although some evidence supports an association among older children.

The causal role of child characteristics in maltreatment is controversial. Some scholars suggest that physical disability is a probable consequence of abuse rather than a causal factor. Moreover, abused children may learn characteristics that lead to revictimization. Some research indicates that following abusive incidents, sexually abused children begin to exhibit sexualized behaviors, physically abused children may become more aggressive than nonabused peers, and neglected children may become withdrawn and sickly. These characteristics contribute to difficult interactions with other adults and may place children at increased risk of future abuse by other adults in addition to their original perpetrators. However, emphasizing the role of child characteristics in abuse may imply that children have some responsibility for their victimization, a notion that is clearly unfounded. Child abuse scholars generally agree that child characteristics do not cause abusive practices.

D. Effects of Abuse

Substantial research documents the negative effect of child abuse on children's physical, psychological, and social development. Yet only a minority of children who experience abuse exhibit severe disturbance, suggesting that many children are highly resilient. The interplay between parent characteristics, child characteristics, and the environmental context, however, complicates efforts to disentangle the pathways through which abuse leads to minor versus severe disturbance among children. Moreover, abuse outcome research is based primarily on retrospective data from clinical samples rather than general population studies. Clinical samples of abused children may differ from the total population of child victims of abuse. Despite these methodological limitations, research has identified negative consequences of abuse and neglect for children's physical, cognitive, psychological, and social development.

1. Physical Outcomes

The physical outcomes of abuse and neglect can range from minor skin markings and scars to severe neurological damage and death. Child neglect is linked to nonorganic failure to thrive and deprivational dwarfism as a result of nutritional deficiencies in early life. Physical abuse may result in mild or severe neurological damage including speech disorders, mental retardation, and cerebral palsy. Abused children also suffer from higher levels of skin markings, bone fractures, and other physical defects when compared to nonabused peers. Higher rates of suicide, substance abuse, and self-mutilation have been linked to child abuse among older children in industrialized nations. Sexually abused children are at risk of infection by sexually transmitted diseases and may suffer genital injuries. Although physical abuse is typically the focus of social concern, numerous scholars contend that the emotional maltreatment that often accompanies physical abuse has serious negative consequences. Research on the prevalence, etiology, and consequences of emotional maltreatment will contribute to an understanding of the dynamics of physical abuse, sexual abuse, and child neglect.

Sociopolitical forms of child abuse have severe consequences for children's physical health and well-being. Child laborers experience injury due to accidents and illness resulting from exposure to chemicals. Factory work may have especially negative effects on children's health and physical development, as working conditions often consist of long hours (12–14 hours daily) and involves running dangerous machinery. Food shortages produced by political conflicts lead to higher rates of malnutrition and disease among children. Female victims of genital mutilation suffer health risks due to complications arising from the procedure, including hemorrhage, tetanus, and blood poisoning resulting from the use of unsterile instruments, and shock due to pain. Doctors in Sudan estimate that between 10 and 30% of young girls die due to complications resulting from infibulation, an extreme form of genital mutilation in which both the clitoris and labia are removed and the sides of the vulva are sewn together.

Studies conducted in the United States find that homeless children suffer from malnutrition, increased rates of infection, developmental delays, and psychological problems. Homeless adolescents have higher risks of drug abuse and contracting sexually transmitted diseases, including HIV/AIDS than do children living with families. Street youth in impoverished regions do not have access to clean water, sanitary facilities, or places to rest. Moreover, homeless children are at high risk for physical abuse victimization; vigilante groups have beaten and killed street children in Columbia and Brazil on suspicion that street children are carriers of AIDS.

2. Cognitive Outcomes

Abused children exhibit cognitive difficulties including deficient verbal language skills, poor school performance, and deviant social information processing. Of these cognitive outcomes, poor school performance is the most consistent research finding. Negative cognitive outcomes vary by type of abuse; child neglect appears to be associated with the most severe outcomes. Findings for child sexual abuse are inconsistent; some studies show an association between sexual abuse and poor school performance, while other research does not find an association between sexual abuse and cognitive outcomes. Physical abuse is associated with the development of deviant social interaction styles including increased aggression among child victims. The necessity of child labor among poor families in some countries keeps large numbers of children out of schools. Because child abuse occurs during a time in which children are forming initial cognitive views of the world, it is not surprising that abused children see the world as unpredictable, unjust, dangerous, and uncontrollable.

3. Psychological Outcomes

Children victimized by adult caretakers have difficulty developing secure attachment patterns to significant others and may exhibit a variety of other emotional problems, including low self-esteem and depression. Although cross-cultural analyses of abuse outcomes are rare, available studies suggest that child neglect and emotional maltreatment lead to decreased self-esteem and insecure attachment patterns in a range of cultures. Exploratory work on the effects of Munchausen by proxy victimization suggests similar psychological outcomes such as posttraumatic stress symptoms, reality-testing issues, and insecurity. Recent studies indicate that exposure to political violence lowers self-esteem and increases neuroses among children, although these effects may be temporary. Posttraumatic stress disorder symptoms also characterize child victims of sociopolitical violence.

Sexualized behaviors such as frequent masturbation, inappropriate sexual overtures toward others, and play including sexual content characterize children victimized by sexual assault. Additional consequences of sexual assault include posttraumatic stress disorder, dissociation, nightmares, neurosis, running away, and a lack of empathy. Studies employing retrospective reports of childhood experiences suggest that sexual abuse may be linked to eating disorders among young females and to anxiety, depression, attachment disorders, low self-esteem, and sexual dysfunction among young adult males.

Overall, the research indicates that children victimized by abuse and neglect suffer from emotional problems during childhood, including difficulty in trusting others and low self-esteem. The appearance of psychological consequences may be submerged for some developmental periods and reemerge later in life, presenting a challenge to abuse outcome investigations. Recent literature reviews identify studies of the differential effects of abuse on children of varying developmental levels as a research priority.

4. Social Outcomes

Prospective longitudinal data show that children experiencing physical abuse exhibit consistently higher rates of aggressive and antisocial behavior than nonabused children. Although the relationship between child physical abuse and violent criminal outcomes is hampered by methodological problems such as retrospective reports of child abuse, there is some evidence that abused children are more likely to engage in violent activities as adolescents and young adults. Other studies document greater difficulty with social and peer relations among maltreated children.

However, the resiliency of some children has also garnered recent attention. Resilient responses such as adaptive coping strategies characterize some victims of abuse, while other children seem to be more vulnerable. Research on the processes that support resiliency among children is a fruitful direction for understanding etiology as well as the development of effective treatment and intervention efforts. Future research should center on disentangling the consequences of different types of abuse on children of varying age and developmental status. In particular, research examining the effects of abuse on children's worldviews about mastery over the environment, relations with others, and cognition about violence may facilitate an understanding of connections between the various abuse outcomes described above.

5. Intergenerational Transmission of Violence

The notion that violence begets violence is a prevalent explanation for the occurrence of child abuse. However, research on the transfer of abusive practices across generations is controversial due to a reliance on retrospective reports of childhood abuse by adult perpetrators. Such studies do not include abuse survivors who do not replicate abusive practices with their own children, and thus some scholars argue that the intergenerational transmission of abuse is overstated.

Drawing on the available evidence which includes a few prospective studies, researchers estimate that between 20 and 40% of adults who were victimized as children will abuse their own children. Although these rates suggest that a history of abuse is an important risk factor for child abuse, many childhood victims do not abuse their own children and some nonabused adults initiate abusive practices. Recent scholarly attention has focused on identifying processes that diminish the risk of intergenerational transfer. These studies suggest that social support plays an important role in ending the cycle of violence: adults victimized as children who were supported by a nonabusive adult during childhood and/or have a supportive partner in parenting are less likely to be abusive toward their children. Moreover, adults who are able to express anger about their childhood victimization and those who have participated in psychotherapy have decreased risks of perpetrating abuse against their own children, while those who dissociate from their abusive experiences are less able to end the violent cycle. Future research on pathways to abuse among adults who did not experience abuse as children and on the processes that mitigate the intergenerational transfer of abusive practices will aid understanding of the complex etiology of abuse.

III. ETIOLOGY

Child abuse has been studied by scholars trained in psychology, sociology, anthropology, medicine, social work, and law. The various theoretical frameworks formulated to explain child abuse reflect this interdisciplinary research interest. Psychological and sociological theories have dominated the field since its inception. More recent approaches include the public health/ecological framework.

A. Psychological Theories

Early explanations of child abuse emphasized psychological and psychiatric factors. Contending that child maltreatment is rooted in parental psychopathology, early investigations focused on comparing maltreating and nonmaltreating parents on psychological indicators. These studies did not find greater levels of psychopathology among maltreating parents than within the general population, and thus the early emphasis on pathology has shifted toward identification of specific psychological risk factors. More recent psychological models draw upon attachment, trauma, and social learning theories.

1. Attachment Theories

Attachment theories propose that psychological attachment between parent and child leads to a sense of physical and psychological security. Nonresponsive or rejecting interactions with a caretaker lead the child to feel anxiety, insecurity, and low self-esteem. These psychological insecurities inhibit the child's formation of satisfying relationships with others, including his or her own children. Thus, attachment theorists propose that neglecting and abusive behaviors are transmitted across generations. The high (20–40%) rate of intergenerational transmission of abusive practices in the United States provides some support for the attachment perspective. Attachment theory has been criticized for a failure to conceptualize family dynamics other than the mother–child dyad and to integrate social and cultural factors such as poverty and unemployment. However, attachment theory's emphasis on psychological security and interpersonal relationships is an important contribution to an understanding of the psychodynamics of child abuse.

2. Trauma Theories

Trauma theories propose that abuse and neglect represent acute forms of trauma that may result in extreme and potentially permanent emotional injury to children and adolescents. Because a child's personality is in a constant state of development, the physical and emotional injuries resulting from abuse and neglect may be particularly disruptive because coping with the trauma diverts energy away from healthy development into potentially dysfunctional forms of survival or self-protection. Trauma theorists propose that external trauma may penetrate the core of the psyche due the constant interchange between external events and internal unconscious processes. A child victimized by abuse and neglect may feel guilt for the traumatic incident, develop pathological defense mechanisms, or identify with the aggressor or perpetrator of abuse. Because child abuse and neglect are usually not isolated to a single incident, victims experience repeated traumatic incidents. Moreover, trauma theorists contend that witnessing the abuse of a caretaker is highly traumatic for children even if they are not themselves victimized. Traumatized children often do not have the verbal or developmental skills to convey their problems to adults and their symptoms may go unrecognized. If the resulting pathologies are left untreated, the traumatized child may be at greater risk of perpetrating aggressive or abusive behavior upon reaching adulthood. Trauma theory is susceptible to similar criticisms to those directed against attachment theories. However, trauma theorists focus on the entire family system and the variation in child responses to trauma, and thus represents a broader and more inclusive approach to explaining child abuse than the attachment perspective. Because children may respond to trauma in a variety of ways, empirical investigations of the role of trauma processes in child abuse present a challenge to researchers.

3. Social Learning Theories

Social learning theories reject the emphasis on internal mental processes that characterize attachment and trauma theories of child abuse. Rather, learning theories suggest that behavior, including abuse, is shaped through individual interaction with the environment. In this framework, child abuse results from dysfunctional child-care practices that are modeled by succeeding generations of children. Interventions drawing upon learning theory attempt to change the child-rearing behaviors of abusive parents through education and behavior modification. However, some studies indicate that these interventions are inadequate without a corresponding emphasis on attitudinal and relational changes.

4. Contributions and Limitations of Psychological Theories

Some scholars speculate that psychological explanations are culturally popular because they set up abusive parents as scapegoats and allow us to ignore the violence done to children through poverty and "normal discipline." Moreover, psychological theories often ignore the effects of the social environment on psychological well-being. However, the emphasis on interactive mental processes and personality disorders within psychological explanations represents an important contribution to an understanding of child abuse.

B. Sociological Theories

Sociological theories focus on structural and cultural aspects of societies that encourage or mitigate child abuse rather than individual characteristics of perpetrators or victims.

1. Structural Theories

Structural sociological theories of child abuse suggest that elements of structural inequality such as poverty, unemployment, and racism influence propensities for child maltreatment. Some sociologists contend that the state plays a role in creating conditions that lead to abuse through supporting or ignoring substandard housing, education, and health among poor families. The stresses that accompany material deprivation lead to greater substance abuse, overcrowded conditions, and the abuse and neglect of children. Sociopolitical violence is rooted in structural inequities between nations that contribute to extreme poverty within some countries. The structural perspective is supported by empirical findings that intrasocietal abuse and neglect are more common within poor families and among the unemployed. However, this perspective fails to address the etiology of sexual abuse, physical abuse, and neglect that occurs within middle- and upper-class families and wealthy nations.

2. Sociocultural Theories

Sociocultural explanations of child abuse propose that societal approval of violence as a means of obtaining order and socializing children may facilitate abusive violence. Normative support for intrafamilial violence within some cultures can create a climate in which child abuse is simply an extreme form of culturally sanctioned behaviors. Cultural values such as family preservation and privacy and religious beliefs about the willful and defiant nature of children have been cited by some researchers as creating a climate in which child maltreatment will go unnoticed and unpunished.

Moreover, sociocultural theories emphasize the contribution of socialization practices and age-based power differentials to child abuse. In cultures wherein biological offspring are considered the property and responsibility of parents, the state bestows dominant rights and power upon the adult. The cultural construction of children as the sole responsibility of parents may contribute to higher rates of child abuse. Findings from cross-cultural research indicate that child maltreatment is less prevalent in cultures wherein child-rearing responsibilities are shared by several people. Additionally, the research finding that most abuse occurs in the context of "normal" discipline situations provides evidence that sociocultural norms about discipline may be salient to an understanding of abuse.

3. Contributions and Limitations of Sociological Theories

Sociocultural and structural explanations are not sufficient to an understanding of child maltreatment. The continuing incidence of abuse within nations with societal norms against parental violence suggests that additional risk factors should be incorporated within sociological models. Further, sociocultural explanations of sexual abuse, emotional maltreatment, and child neglect have not been formulated. However, empirical findings that socioeconomic inequality and cultural beliefs about child-rearing contribute to some forms of child abuse suggest that sociological explanations provide important insights into child abuse etiology. Moreover, sociocultural and structural explanations are necessary to an understanding of the abusive consequences of sociopolitical violence, socioeconomic inequality, and gender inequality.

C. Public Health/Ecological Approaches

Recent scholarship on public health outcomes of child abuse and neglect and on the interplay of social, environmental, and psychological factors in child abuse has led public health scholars and social psychologists to develop new theoretical approaches to child abuse.

1. The Public Health Approach

In the United States, homicide is one of the five leading causes of death for children between the ages of 1 and 18 years. The U.S. General Accounting office estimated that more than $5 billion annually go toward services for abused and neglected children. These findings have led scholars in the United States to classify child abuse as a national health issue. The public health policy approach to child abuse differs from sociological and psychological perspectives in its emphases on national surveillance, epidemiologic techniques, and the development and implementation of preventative strategies. Rather than drawing upon existing theoretical paradigms to guide research, epidemiologic models emphasize controlled experimental research methods designed to isolate factors associated with child maltreatment. In practice, they seek to identify social, environmental, and psychological factors that may contribute to violent behavior.

Like sociocultural theorists, public health scholars propose that family violence will remain a problem until social norms reinforcing violence are redefined as unacceptable. The federal research funds designated for violence research constitute only a small percentage of those marked for other public health issues, although injuries account for more years of life lost prior to age 65 than other health problems such as heart disease. The emerging public health perspective calls for collaborative efforts among health departments, regulatory agencies, and criminal justice systems to develop integrated prevention and intervention programs. To this end, the Centers for Disease Control in the United States identified the reversal of the rising incidence of child maltreatment in its statement of health objectives for the year 2000.

2. Ecological Theories

Although scholars generally agree that abuse results from the complex interaction between social, cultural, and psychological factors, the relations between these factors are poorly understood. Recent proposals for a developmental/ecological approach to child abuse highlight the need to identify causal characteristics at the individual, familial, neighborhood, community, cultural, and societal levels. Ecological models propose that abuse occurs in the context of transactions between children, parents, and the social environment. The form and content of these transactions will be shaped by the developmental level of the child, personality characteristics of those interacting with the child, and the environmental context within which transactions occur.

Ecological models further propose that the interactive effects of child and parent characteristics are salient to the occurrence of abuse. For example, a parent with substantial psychological and social resources may not be at risk for abusing a child that is difficult to rear due to temperament or physical disability, while a parent with a history of childhood abuse who is dealing with the constraints of poverty or unemployment may be at high risk for abusing such a child.

3. Contributions and Limitations of Public Health and Ecological Theories

Public health and ecological perspectives are supported by research suggesting that single risk factors, whether demographic or psychological, are not consistently associated with maltreatment. These approaches are limited by a lack of theoretical explanation of how individual, familial, community, and sociocultural levels interact in child maltreatment. However, the growing theoretical emphasis on the interplay of individual, community, and cultural factors in child abuse etiology represents a promising development for future research.

IV. POLICY AND TREATMENT

Although ending child abuse is the common goal of maltreatment researchers, they disagree about the most appropriate strategies for intervention and prevention. Sociologists emphasize the normative cultural supports for violence within some nations, the socioeconomic conditions contributing to pervasive poverty among children, and the lack of social policies designed to reduce these problems and to support parents with children. Psychologists focus on the identification of at-risk parents and counseling to prevent future abuse. Public health perspectives emphasize surveillance and the development of integrated national prevention programs. Ecological frameworks suggest that protective factors should be strengthened through interventions that are targeted toward the particular environmental context in which the abuse occurs.

Intervention for child abuse varies widely across cultures, ranging from informal sanctions by relatives and neighbors to formal legal prosecution. Although political campaigns against maltreatment characterized several historical periods, the formation of centralized social policy to combat child abuse is generally confined to the late 20th century. The vast majority of intervention research has been conducted in industrialized nations and has focused on treating individual perpetrators and victims. Political movements designed to end dowry deaths and genital multilation have formed in India, Zimbabwe, Nigeria, and Uganda. Organizations dedicated to eradicating child abuse such as the International Society for the Prevention of Child Abuse and Neglect have increased global awareness of the problem. Although research on intervention is relatively rare, studies suggest that some programs may be effective in reducing child maltreatment.

A. Social Policy Initiatives

Within industrialized nations, social policy efforts to prevent and intervene in child maltreatment cases are operated by governmental agencies. National and state or province agencies have been formed to investigate child abuse cases and provide services to families at risk of maltreatment. In rare cases of documented risk, abuse, or neglect, children are removed from the parental home. These formal interventions have been the source of enormous controversy in some countries, arising in part due to the lack of empirical research documenting the effectiveness of agency interventions.

1. Mandatory Reporting

Findings that teachers, neighbors, and physicians often do not report cases of suspected abuse to regulatory agencies have led several countries, including Canada and the United States, to mandate child abuse reporting. Certain professionals, including teachers and physicians, are required to report suspected maltreatment incidents to regulatory agencies. Within the United States and Britain, abuse reports have increased dramatically since the 1970s.

2. Regulatory Agencies

Agencies charged to investigate the validity of child abuse reports, perform risk assessment of families, and monitor cases are a substantial component of child abuse intervention. At least 30 developed and developing nations currently have national child abuse reporting agencies. Approximately half of all reported maltreatment cases are substantiated by agency workers in the United States, resulting in a risk assessment of the family that may lead to the provision of counseling or other supportive services to parents and children. In rare cases (less than 25%), the risk assessment leads to the removal of the child from the home. Many of the children removed from the home are placed in foster care and remain in foster care programs for a median of 1.5 years. A minority of children are adopted following legal terminal of parental rights in cases where agency workers do not see an improvement in family conditions.

Regulatory agencies are caught in the middle of contradictory cultural values regarding abuse, children, and families. Within the United States and Britain, the value of individual children's right to protection from harm clashes with the value of family preservation. Agencies are simultaneously criticized for failing to remove children from situations in which they are mistreated and for violating the rights of parents accused or suspected of child maltreatment. A political movement against agency intervention has gained force within recent years within the United States, as parents claim they were unjustly accused of abuse and that their parental rights were violated by agency workers.

Although regulatory agencies are required to meet legislative guidelines regarding investigation, monitoring, and placement of children at risk of child maltreatment, insufficient resources often prevent agencies from meeting requirements. An understaffed system, the lack of employment, training, and counseling services to which caseworkers can refer families, and the growing number of child abuse reports hamper regulatory agency efforts.

Few studies have examined the factors that influence agency responses to particular child maltreatment reports or the effectiveness of agency interventions. Some studies suggest that poverty and ethnicity influence agency decisions to remove children from parental care regardless of the nature of abuse. Additionally, research concerning the effectiveness of regulatory agency interventions in preventing future abusive incidents is limited.

3. Education/Counseling

A variety of intervention efforts attempt to change individual parental characteristics associated with maltreatment. These interventions include home-based services, individual and group therapy, and self-help programs. Other interventions attempt to treat child victims and adult survivors of abuse through therapeutic day-care and counseling programs. Parental enhancement programs focus on training physically abusive parents in child-rearing and anger management and neglecting parents in nutrition and child care. Treatment programs for child sexual abusers include group therapy, behavior therapy, and educational approaches.

Research on the effectiveness of intervention programs is minimal. Although a few evaluation studies demonstrate that intervention efforts can improve individual and family functioning, findings also suggest that treatment programs are relatively ineffective at reducing or ending abusive behaviors. Interventions with victims appear to be somewhat more effective. Therapeutic day-care programs have documented improvement in the cognitive, language, and social and emotional development of physically abused children as compared with control groups. Programs for adult survivors of sexual abuse have been associated with some positive outcomes such as anxiety relief and improved social adjustment.

The role of caseworker and psychotherapist characteristics in the success of intervention efforts has only recently come to the attention of researchers. Some studies suggest that regulatory agency caseworkers in the United States bring social class and racial biases into risk assessment decisions. Others find that insufficient understanding of cultural diversity hampers counseling interventions. Within the United States, a growing research emphasis on cultural diversity is an important trend that should facilitate the development of more effective intervention programs. Although evidence finds only weak and inconsistent links between psychopathology and child abuse, treatment efforts remain primarily psychotherapeutic. The effectiveness of interventions addressing multiple individual and social risk factors should be an additional focus of future research.

B. Alternatives to Abuse

Alternatives to abuse include policies designed to change cultural norms regarding the use of violence by parents, the provision of conflict resolution and sexual abuse prevention programs for school-aged children, and the adoption of nonviolent alternatives to sociopolitical conflict. While relatively new, some of these policies promise to help reduce the incidence and prevalence of child abuse and neglect.

1. Nonviolent Parenting: The Case of Sweden

In 1979, the Swedish government passed a law stating "A child may not be subjected to physical punishment of other injurious or humiliating treatment." The law carries no penalties, but in cases where physical assault on a child is confirmed, the Swedish Criminal Code penalties apply. The law is primarily intended to encourage the development of societal norms against family violence. Following the passage of this legislation, early reports suggested that parents in Sweden initially questioned whether they could effectively parent without the use of corporal punishment and believed that the law was a joke. However, by 1988 most parents reported that they no longer believed corporal punishment is an effective and necessary form of discipline. Swedish parents tend to report a reliance on time-outs, positive reinforcements, and verbal conflict resolution. In addition to the anti-corporal punishment legislation, Sweden has very low rates of poverty and unemployment in contrast to other countries. Cultural concern with violence is indicated by strict gun control and a substantial effort to monitor violent television programming. Parents in Sweden are supported by extended maternal and paternal leave policies, excellent national child-care programs, and neighborhood family centers designed to provide assistance with child-rearing.

An international comparison conducted by Richard Gelles and Ake Edfeldt found that while Swedish parents reported lower rates of mild physical violence compared to U.S. parents, overall rates of abusive violence did not differ between the two nations. However, some scholars contend that it is too early to gauge the long-term effects of changes in normative attitudes toward the use of physical violence in parenting and that reductions in child abuse may not appear for several generations. Others contend that these findings support the view that abuse rates reflect psychological disorders among a minority of the population rather than sociocultural or structural factors. More recent international evidence from a study conducted by Mark Belsey indicates a decline in Swedish child abuse mortality rates from 4.2 presumed child abuse deaths per 100,000 live births in 1985 to 0.9 presumed deaths in 1989.

The Swedish example has led many other Northern European countries to enact anti-corporal punishment legislation. Additionally, Britain passed a law banning physical punishment in schools in 1981, and most states within the United States have outlawed school-based corporal punishment. In the United States, some commentators have advocated licensing parents and requiring women convicted of abuse and neglect to use contraception to prevent risks to additional children. Others have argued that such policies violate human rights and fail to address the root causes of abuse. Moreover, some scholars warn that these policies would contribute to social class and racial biases.

The slow trend toward an exploration of alternatives to physical discipline within some nations should provide opportunities for research regarding the relationship between societal norms about violence and child maltreatment. Prospective and cross-cultural studies will be particularly important in future etiological research on social and environmental causes of child abuse.

2. Conflict Resolution and Sexual Abuse Prevention Programs

School teachers and counselors in the United States have noted that peer mediation conflict resolution programs have been effective at reducing conflict in school settings, but the impact of these programs on children's abilities to manage conflict situations with parents or on future risks for child maltreatment has not been adequately assessed. Peer mediation has been lauded as a way to teach children role-taking skills, empathy, self-regulation, critical thinking, and problem-solving skills. Although reports from schools where such programs have been implemented suggest that conflict resolution programs may change children's attitudes about the use of aggression, research has generally focused on the overall reduction in amounts of conflict requiring adult intervention within schools rather than attitudinal or cognitive outcomes. However, conflict resolution programs present an important opportunity to intervene with young children who may be at risk for physical abuse victimization and eventual perpetration. Moreover, participation in program discussions of violence and conflict may encourage abused children to recognize and report their victimization and thus receive protective services.

Sexual abuse prevention programs include community awareness, parent and teacher education, and age-appropriate and culturally informed programs designed for children. Implemented widely in the United States, such programs have been the subject of controversy. Proponents argue that these programs educate about sexual abuse and empower children and parents to recognize abusive situations. Critics contend that current evidence about the effectiveness of these programs is limited and that programs with school children may disseminate the view that children are responsible for protecting themselves against victimization. Although the evidence is inconclusive regarding the effectiveness of sexual abuse prevention programs for reducing the incidence of abuse, these programs have educated substantial numbers of children, teachers, and parents, and created a climate in which sexual abuse issues may be openly discussed. Moreover, potential perpetrators may be discouraged if they believe children will be more willing to report sexual abuse incidents. However, limited parental participation in some cases (particularly among fathers) has hampered comprehensive prevention efforts. Future prospective studies should provide additional knowledge of the effectiveness of preventative efforts in the case of sexual abuse.

3. Nonviolent Alternatives to Sociopolitical Violence

Although rarely articulated in mainstream academic work on child abuse within industrialized nations, a growing body of international scholarship proposes that extreme poverty, war, and global inequalities constitute a form of structural violence which is particularly damaging to children. High rates of starvation and malnutrition, the beating and torture of children in regions of intense sociopolitical conflict, and the child labor necessary for survival in some nations affect children at potentially staggering rates. Recent national and international evidence documents the negative consequences of poverty and exposure to political and social conflict for children's social, emotional and physical development.

Research on alternatives to structural and sociopolitical violence conducted by scholars of peace studies, liberation theology, and nonviolent conflict resolution suggests that structural changes will be necessary to address conflicts created by global economic inequalities and racial and religious antagonisms. This work contends that nonviolent activism for civil rights and an end to economic exploitation is an important means to a reduction of violence against children.

V. CONCLUSIONS

Children suffer from child abuse and neglect resulting from parental and societal characteristics. However, defining abuse remains a challenge due to political and cultural differences in normative beliefs about appropriate child-rearing. Although physical abuse, sexual abuse, emotional maltreatment, and child neglect have severe and often similar negative consequences for children's physical, emotional, and social development, the research literature on abuse etiology and outcomes remains divided by these four types of abuse. Future studies should concentrate on the identification of similarities and differences between the types of abuse to further knowledge about the causation and consequences of abuse.

Recent research on the negative effects of political violence and global socioeconomic inequality on children's development represents an important trend within child abuse scholarship. Future studies should examine the prevalence of child victimization resulting from war and poverty and the impact of international sociopolitical conflict on the well-being of children.

A recognition of the importance of culture in the identification, definition, consequences, and etiology of abuse is a recent advance within child abuse research. Cross-cultural research examining variations in family structure, socioeconomic conditions, social norms, and abuse and neglect rates across cultures could further knowledge about factors that mitigate or promote child abuse.

Also See the Following Articles

ANTHROPOLOGY OF VIOLENCE AND CONFLICT • CHILDREARING, VIOLENT AND NONVIOLENT • FAMILY STRUCTURES, VIOLENCE AND NONVIOLENCE • PUBLIC HEALTH MODELS OF VIOLENCE AND VIOLENCE PREVENTION

Bibliography

Belsey, M. A. (1993). Child abuse: Measuring a global problem. *World Health Statistics Quarterly,* 46, 69–77.

Corby, B. (1993). *Child abuse: Towards a knowledge base.* Buckingham: Open University Press.

Everstine, D. S., & Everstine, L. (1993). *The trauma response: Treatment for emotional injury.* New York: W. W. Norton.

Finkelhor, D. (1984). *Child sexual abuse: New theory and research.* New York: Free Press.

Fontes, L. A. (Ed.). (1995). *Sexual abuse in nine North American cultures: Treatment and prevention.* Thousand Oaks, CA: Sage.

Gelles, R. J., & Loseke, D. R. (Eds.). (1993). *Current controversies in family violence.* Newbury Park, CA: Sage.

Glasser, I. (1994). *Homelessness in global perspective.* New York: G.K. Hall & Co.

Hunter, M. (1995). *Child survivors and perpetrators of sexual abuse.* Thousand Oaks, CA: Sage.

Kempe, C., Silverman, F., Steele, B., Droegemueller, W., & Silver, H. (1962). The battered child syndrome. *Journal of the American Medical Association,* 181, 17–24.

Koblinsky, M., Timyan, J., & Gay, J. (1993). *The health of women: A global perspective.* Boulder, CO: Westview Press.

Korbin, J. (Ed.). (1981). *Child abuse and neglect: Cross cultural perspectives.* Berkeley: University of California Press.

Lavalette, M. (1994). *Child employment in the capitalist labour market.* Aldershot, England: Avebury.

Levinson, D. (1989). *Family violence in cross-cultural perspective.* Newbury Park, CA: Sage.

Levinson, D. (1994). *Aggression and conflict: A cross-cultural encyclopedia.* Santa Barbara, CA: ABC-CLIO.

National Research Council. (1993). *Understanding child abuse and neglect.* Washington, DC: National Academy Press.

Rosenberg, M., & Fenley, M. A. (Eds.). (1991). *Violence in America: A public health approach.* New York: Oxford University Press.

Straus, M. A., and Gelles, R. J. (Eds). (1990). *Physical violence in American families: Risk factors and adaptations to violence in 8,145 families.* New Brunswick, NJ: Transaction Publishers

U.S. Department of Health and Human Services. (1997). *Child maltreatment 1995: Reports from the States to the National Child Abuse and Neglect data system.* Washington, DC: U.S. Government Printing Office.

Childrearing, Violent and Nonviolent

Joanna Santa Barbara
McMaster University

GLOSSARY

Caregiver/Parent/Mother These are used somewhat interchangeably. Where "mother" is used, the research underlying the text has been done on the mother–child dyad.

Childrearing The myriad processes by which adult caregivers influence children to acquire the knowledge, behavior, values, and attitudes necessary to be well-functioning members of their society

Corporal Punishment The use of physical force (violence) with the intention of causing the recipient to experience pain, but not injury, for the purpose of correction or control of the recipient's behavior.

Nonviolence The principle of refraining from the use of violence.

Violence The use or manifestation of physical force; in this article, the use of physical force by one person on another for the purpose of achieving the user's ends (as distinct from, e.g., hurling a child out of the path of a moving vehicle).

I. A FRAMEWORK FOR THINKING ABOUT CHILDREARING

We begin with a model of childrearing broader than parents' deliberate strategies intended to influence their children's behaviors. Childrearing occurs in a context of relationship to the caregivers. Important dimensions of this relationship on the parent's side appear to be the physical proximity, responsiveness, and emotional accessibility that enable secure attachment; the parent's empathy with the child; the parent's capacity for sustained cooperative behavior with the child; the parent's level of moral development; the absence or presence of parental depression. On the child's side innate temperamental variables may influence the quality of the relationship, especially the fearful/fearless dimension, the child's adaptability, and capacity for inhibitory control.

Childrearing is influenced by the family's structure and function, especially in terms of the number of children, economic stresses, exposure to actual, media and fantasy violence, and the opportunities available for prosocial behaviors (sharing, caring, helping, cooperating).

The behavior across all domains of parents as models for children will have a powerful influence on outcome. In the interpersonal sphere, the style of the parent's relationship to the child and his/her siblings, as well as to the other parent, may well be the most powerful determinants of outcome for the child.

Finally, there are those actions taken deliberately by the parent to influence the behavior of the child that are referred to as discipline or control functions. Much of the research in this area classifies disciplinary actions into the categories *inductive* and *power-assertive*.

Inductive discipline presents the child with reasons for the desired behavior. These may focus on the benefits of compliance or the disadvantages of noncompliance. The reasons may focus on costs and benefits to the child, to the parent and family, to the person(s) affected by the behavior, or may make reference to accepted rules or norms, such as:

"Your friend won't want to play with you if you don't share."
"Mummy doesn't like it when you don't share with your friend."
"Your friend is crying. She feels unhappy because you didn't share."
"In this family, we always share with our friends."

The inductive strategy that focuses on the recipient of the behavior can be seen as likely to strengthen the child's capacity for empathy.

Another kind of information that influences the development of desired behavior is attribution of enduring positive qualities to the child. This information presumably becomes incorporated in the child's concept of him/herself and then influences subsequent behavior.

"I do like the way you're sharing with your friend You're such a generous child."

Power-assertive discipline relies on the capacity of the parent to create pleasurable or aversive experiences for the child. Rewarding experiences are signs of the parent's approval of the child, such as praise, a hug, privileges, (such as staying up later at night), and material rewards (such as food or money). The salience of the parent's approval will depend on the strength of the good relationship between parent and child. (There are children who are so alienated from or angry with their caregivers that they either do not care about their approval or wish to upset them.)

Aversive experiences include withdrawal of the parent's benign regard or their social response, withdrawal of privileges, deprivation of needs such as food, confining a child to a closet or room, fining, frightening with threats of pain or separation, and infliction of pain by hitting, punching, pinching, shaking, pricking, or burning. Yelling, banging furniture, or throwing objects may be strongly associated with being hit in households where hitting is used. In some cultural settings, power assertion may include the evocation of imagined highly aversive experiences such as burning in hell, or being captured and eaten by a supernatural monster. Violent childrearing in this discussion refers only to the use of physical force but some of the outcome research must be discussed in reference to the whole cluster of power-assertive strategies.

Internalization refers to the child's building reasons and motivations for desired behavior into his/her concepts of him/herself and the world. It is as if the child who is motivated by external controls complies because s/he thinks, "I'll share because I'll be punished if I don't and/or rewarded if I do." The child who has internalized a precept about sharing might be supposed to think, "I'll share because I'm a generous person; that's the way we do it in my family; my friend will like me better; my friend will feel happier."

Internalization of behavior precepts means that the child (or adult) will follow them when there is no external supervision, and that s/he will be relatively resistant to attempts by others to induce noncompliance. It may also mean that the child is better able to apply the precepts in new situations.

To internalize precepts the child requires social understanding of the required behavior and its reasons, the capacity for self-control, and internal motivation to comply.

There is a body of research that bears upon the relationship between reward and internalization. Where there is some intrinsic motivation for behavior, (e.g. reading stories, producing art), being rewarded actually diminishes the manifestation of the behavior. As there appears to be some intrinsic motivation for much prosocial behavior, it would be useful to know the impact of rewarding sharing, caring, helping, and cooperating. It is as if the child might say, "I must be doing this for the reward I know I'll get. It must not be such an intrinsically pleasant behavior." This research is extrapolated by some to recommend that where rewards and punishments are used, that they are designed to be the minimum required to induce or maintain the behavior.

Caregivers behave in a goal-oriented way to rear children who are well-adapted to their cultural environment. One relevant dimension is the degree of obedience to external control required in the adult environment versus the degree of internalized self-control. This dimension is known to affect the degree to which physical punishment is used in any society. Other goals of socialization that have been the subject of some research are being liked by others, the capacity for empathy, manifesting prosocial behavior, and the capacity for moral reasoning.

II. WHAT ROLE DOES VIOLENCE PLAY IN CHILDREARING?

The socialization of a child comprises innumerable experiences over the years of childhood. Some are quiet and slow, such as the experience of being raised in a tidy or chaotic house, and others are short and sharp, such as hearing angry arguments between parents. Some influences are deliberately arranged, such as rewards for compliant behavior, and others are not, such as observing how a parent cares for a new baby. Some experiences give pleasure and others are aversive. Experiences involving violence are often highly salient, and engender strong emotion. They may occur suddenly, causing high arousal, the child may experience pain, directly or in empathy with another, and there may be loud noise and fast action. They will often occur in contexts involving meanings highly significant to the child, such as, "Am I still loved or am I rejected? Am I worthy or worthless?" Experiences involving violence are likely to be highly influential on the child's developing understanding of him/herself and his/her social world.

A. Types of Violence in Childrearing

Violence may be a theme in a child's rearing environment in the following ways:

- child as recipient of corporal punishment from adult caregiver;
- child as recipient of other violence from adult caregiver;
- child as recipient of violence from sibling;
- child as perpetrator of violence on parent or sibling;
- child as witness of violence between parents or others;
- child as recipient or observer of threats of violence within the family;
- child as observer and participant in media, video-game, war-toy, and other fantasy violence.

In some cases violence by parent to a child, often begun with punitive intentions, will cross a boundary and be seen by authorized institutions as "child abuse." What defines the boundary? This differs between jurisdictions. In some jurisdictions, this social construct will include force that leaves a visible injury on the child. It may include criteria of frequency and severity. In some jurisdictions it includes the use of an object such as a belt or a brush to hit the child. Formal regulation to limit violence by parents to children is recent in history and is not now universal in extent.

B. History of the Use of Violence in Childrearing

If the Book of Proverbs in the Old Testament can be considered an example of childrearing advice, harsh physical punishment was recommended in some societies by the 6th century B.C. Under both Mosaic and Roman Law, a child could be put to death for incorrigible behavior. Wang Fu, a 2nd-century Chinese scholar recommends death for seriously delinquent youth. Chinese writers from that century described being whipped, often with bamboo rods, and usually for inadequate performance in school.

In medieval Europe, some writers of advice on childrearing recommend indulgent practices up to the age of 7, considered the first of four stages of development. The child was to be allowed to play and was only gradually required to study after that age. (This advice was presumably intended for the small literate elite.) After 7, it seems that the Biblical advice on use of the rod held sway, but little is known of prevalence, severity, and how much physical discipline crossed the boundary into what we would now consider child abuse. Certainly intimidation by the threat of fantasy violence was used in the form of frightening folk tales of child-eating monsters or of the Devil who seized bad children. Pictures of frightening creatures were used to add vivacity to the threat.

Lloyd de Mause, in his *The History of Childhood* (1974), presents a horrifying picture of often severe and frequent physical punishment of children in Europe from medieval to recent times.

Russian elite society was especially severe. Rigidly hierarchical from monarch to serf family, each level held almost absolute power over the one below, and extreme obedience was demanded and enforced by flogging or other physical punishment. The "Domostroi" was a guide to household management compiled by 16th-century churchmen and continued to be recommended in ensuing centuries. It counseled:

> Do not spare your child any beating, for the stick will not kill him, but will do him good; when you strike the body, you save the soul from death. . . . If you love your son, punish him often so that he may later gladden your spirit . . . . Raise your child in fear.

From literary and autobiographical accounts up to the 19th century, the counsel seems to have been well followed.

Studies of Norwegian childrearing provide an interesting case study, as it is one of the countries in which it is now illegal to hit children. In Viking times, fathers wielded power over the lives of their children. Men's power to flog children, wives, servants, and farmhands continued until legally limited in 1833. Lutheranism as a strong determinant of culture from the 16th century was characterized by patriarchal families and much emphasis on control, guilt, and shame. Corporal punishment was enjoined. In the early 19th century, the ideas of Rousseau, encouraging respect for the child and guidance rather than chastisement, enjoyed brief influence. This was countered and occluded by more writings on the sinful nature of children and the need to bend their wills to absolute obedience to authority.

In the 1930s a change of ideology began, focusing on more permissive educational practices. In 1947 a survey showed that half the parent population spanked their children. In 1970 a survey showed that three-quarters of the adult population thought parents should have the right to hit children, with a higher proportion of conservative Christians wishing to retain that power. This makes it surprising that in 1972 this right was repealed by parliament. In 1982 a survey showed that 26% of children were spanked, 44% had their hand slapped, and 25% had no violent discipline. After 1986, it was forbidden by law to hit children.

In early colonial families in the United States, physical punishment was strongly enjoined. A child over 16 who cursed or hit his parents could suffer the death penalty. The reminder of violent punishment was incorporated in teaching young children the alphabet in the *New England Primer*:

> F The Idle *Fool*
> Is Whipt at school
> J *Job* feels the Rod
> Yet blesses GOD

An important study by Sears, Maccoby, and Levin 40 years ago showed the following practices by parents of preschoolers in the United States:

never hit	1%
occasionally slaps hands	12%
2–3 spankings per year	35%
often slaps, occasionally spanks	29%
often spanks, sometimes severely	15%
frequently spanks severely	7%

A contemporary reader of this study might be struck by the nondefensive acknowledgment of beating and whipping children, selecting switches to do it, how it is an expression of the parents' anger and is often quite arbitrary. Only half the parents thought that corporal punishment was effective. Some of the children in the study were seen to have bruises or switch-marks. This decade marked the beginning of awareness of child abuse.

C. Contemporary Data on Corporal Punishment

Most contemporary societies, agricultural, industrial and "postindustrial," incorporate some hitting of children in their socialization practices. There appear to be great differences in frequency and severity of use, together with differences in supporting ideology, but there is little quantitative data to clarify this.

U.S. data were gathered by Murray Straus (1994) from National Family Violence Surveys in 1975 and 1985, based on interviews with parents. They show that almost all U.S. parents hit young children. From age 2 through 6, about 90% of U.S. children are hit. The rates decrease with the child's age, but at age 17, more than 20% are still being subjected to corporal punishment.

How is this done? Of those who used corporal punishment, 50% slapped or spanked, 31% pushed, shoved, or grabbed the child, 10% used a hairbrush, paddle, or belt, and 3% threw something at the child.

How often? Twelve percent said only once in the year of the survey, 46% said two to seven times, and 42% used corporal punishment eight or more times in the year.

Were there changes over time? Between 1975 and 1985, there was a small decrease in the number of parents using corporal punishment, and substantial decreases in the frequency of use. If the Straus figures can be compared with the 1957 Sears figures, the percentage of parents hitting preschoolers declined from 99% to 90% in 1985.

More boys are hit than girls, and a little more often.

Asking adults to recall their teen years it was found that 50% remembered being hit at least once a year, more by mothers than by fathers. Middle-class parents were more likely to hit adolescents than lower or higher classes.

The more a parent approves of physical punishment for an older child, the more likely they are to use it on their teenagers. However, there is discrepancy between belief and behavior. Of those who think corporal punishment of a 12-year-old is never necessary, 25% still hit their 16-year-old children.

Older parents hit their children less. The more a parent was hit as a teenager the more likely s/he was to hit his/her own teen.

Mothers who have been hit by their husbands are much more likely to hit their children. This variable has a greater influence on the probability of hitting than any other studied.

There is some evidence that among U.S. parents, African-Americans hit their children more than do European Americans. In addition, the use of spanking is related to lower rule-setting by parents, less use of praise, and a greater tendency to yell at their children.

How does this almost universal mode of childrearing in the United States relate to child abuse? It is judged that perhaps 90% or more of the episodes of child abuse occur within the context of corporal punishment. It seems clear that child abuse and corporal punishment are on the same continuum of parental behavior, with no clear boundary between one and the other.

There are few cross-cultural data comparable to the detailed U.S. studies. Qualitative descriptions suggest that, in many cultures there is less resort to physical punishment.

Japanese childrearing provides an interesting example. There is less emphasis on obedience to authority or to rules and a great deal of emphasis on awareness of the impact of one's behavior on others (as in "victim-oriented" discipline, described later). This is conveyed in dialogue between mother and child. Apparently, there is little hitting.

Political circumstances may affect degrees of violence in childrearing. There is evidence for an increase in harsh discipline in periods of social violence or war. This is likely to be mediated by various parental factors, especially maternal stress and depression. There is some evidence for an increase in wife abuse by military men engaged in active service and possibly for military men in general, which, in turn, raises the likelihood of mothers hitting children. There is a good deal of evidence for higher levels of aggressive behavior (presumably provoking disciplinary action) in children exposed to the phenomena of war—bombing, shelling, loss of dwelling, and loss of family members. It may also be that parents resorted to a more authoritarian style of discipline in order to keep their children safe in a dangerous environment.

Some of the most extreme examples of the use of physical punishment of children in a highly deviant version of childrearing derive from accounts of the training of child soldiers in contemporary wars. The children live in military camps in the care of armed men. They have described being beaten, tortured, and raped, and watching peers raped and killed in training them as fighters and killers or forcing them to function as porters and sexual objects. Such descriptions have come from recent wars in Mozambique and Liberia, for example.

D. Attitudes on Spanking

Adjusted data from seven U.S. surveys between 1968 and 1994 show a decline in approval of disciplinary spanking from 94% to 68%, or 26 percentage points in 26 years. The question used in all but the 1968 survey was "Do you strongly agree, agree, disagree or strongly disagree that it is sometimes necessary to discipline a child with a good hard spanking?" Blacks, rural dwellers, and conservative Protestant Christians approved of spanking especially strongly. Men approved it more than did women, and graduate school education reduced approval. Approval increased with the number of children in a family. Living in northeastern states reduced approval.

Straus and Mathur (1996) suggest that the steady decrease in approval (and probably use) of corporal punishment over three decades is related to a shift in the U.S. economy from industrial to post-industrial society. Whereas the former demanded obedience and low internalization of rules and norms, the latter demands interpersonal and managerial skills. Nonviolent childrearing provides anticipatory socialization for new roles.

However, increased awareness of social norms proscribing child abuse may also lower rates of reporting on approval of spanking. Ultimately, though, this is likely to affect actual parental behavior, with a tendency to become congruent with reported attitudes.

The attitudes of Swedish colleges students in 1988 (nine years after Sweden legally prohibited physical punishment of children) were strikingly different from their U.S. counterparts. Some 29% of young men and 19% of young women believe in spanking. The comparable figures for U.S. students were 62% and 60%. And 75% of Swedish men and 77% of women agreed with their country's new law. Of U.S. students, 22% of men and 31% of women would support such a law.

E. Assaults by Siblings

Violence at low levels between siblings in a family must be universal. In some situations it is serious and results in physical and psychological injury.

F. Assaults by Children on Parents

Formerly a heavily proscribed behavior, this seems to be emerging as a problem in a small proportion of poorly socialized youth, and largely in the context of serious family dysfunction.

G. Children Who Witness Spousal Violence

Spousal violence is unhappily common in many cultures—it occurs in about one in ten Canadian families and is very much higher in cultures where gender inequality is greater. In Canadian families husband and wife are equally likely to initiate an assault, but women are far more likely to be injured. Such violence ranges from mild to murderous. All of this means that for a substantial number of children in almost all cultures, their rearing environment includes witnessing or being aware of frighteningly violent behavior between their parents. The outcomes of these experiences will be discussed later.

H. Exposure to Fantasy Violence

The way in which children's view of the world and their engagement in fantasy has been mediated by adults has changed sharply in this century. Previously, the media were direct encounters with adults in conversation, oral story-telling, songs and poetry, reading books, and engagement in fantasy with toys and games. Now, the media are largely electronic, particularly television, with the addition of movies, rock videos, and video games. Children's use of these media is enormous. In North America it increases to about four hours per day by age 10 or 11, decreasing somewhat thereafter. A considerable proportion of the material involves the depiction of violence. This is highest in the United States where more than half the programs contain violence. Three-quarters of violent scenes contain no remorse, criticism, or penalties for violence. The typical script divides the players into "good" and "evil"; the "evil" ones are dehumanized and are frequently trying to take over the world or some portion of it. Violence is the necessary way for the "good guys" to resolve the conflict, often with high technology. Apart from the "justified" bringing down of the enemy, there are no other significant effects of the violence on the innocent or the environment. It is hard not to see this typical script as congruent with certain political ideologies.

Japanese television also contains high levels of violence, but it is said to be more often the "bad guys" who commit the violence as a villainous act, with the "good guys" suffering the consequences—a very different meaning context.

Canadian and European children's television have lower levels of violence, but the levels are still considered significant contributors to outcomes to be discussed later.

III. WHAT IS NONVIOLENT CHILDREARING?

Children won't do what they ought
If you beat them with a rod.
Children thrive, children grow
When taught by words, and not a blow . . .
Evil word, words unkind
Will do harm to a child's mind.

(Vogelweide, around 1200, quoted in deMause, 1974)

- Narrow definition: All other processes of family socialization of children except for the use of violence.
- Expanded definition: Some parents (and perhaps many children) see it as desirable to minimize all power-assertive discipline strategies in their childrearing and to socialize their children by inductive and other means.
- Broad definition: Some parents strive also to minimize the valuing and expression of violence by their children. For them, nonviolent childrearing connotes, in addition to the above meanings, efforts to control the exposure of their children to fantasy violence in television and war toys, training to avoid the use of

violence to peers at school, at play, or in sports, and censure of violence to other species such as frogs, cats.

All parents, even those who approve and make much use of hitting, use nonviolent methods of childrearing. The most fundamental of these is based on the child's attachment to its caregivers. In a process known as social referencing, babies from about 9 months of age regulate their behavior by monitoring the facial and vocal expressions of their mothers. Experimental work on this process has particularly focused on situations that can be seen as safety issues—touching an interesting object, crawling over the edge of a simulated cliff, and response to a stranger. Safety socialization, in which parental protectiveness may be aroused, may be a particular situation in which parents feel they must slap infants, because they are too young for reasoned explanations. However, an infant encountering a novel situation scans the mother's face for her emotional response. Fearful or angry facial expressions and tone of voice are powerful inhibitors of exploratory behavior and happy or interested expressions appear to encourage the baby's motivation to explore further.

In the second half of the first year, parents add cognitive information to their emotional expressions to control behavior: "No," "Don't touch," "Hot," and "Hurts" are frequent meanings used, and these are steadily expanded with the baby's cognitive development.

As will be shown in Section V, much of the success of these parent control strategies depends on parental behaviors outside the realm of deliberate discipline. Security of attachment of the infant to the parent, a mutually responsive relationship with rich exchanges between the two, and a happy mood in the relationship appear to be the foundations of good functioning of the above-described control system. Threats and harsh discipline have been shown to disrupt it. Mothers high on empathy, who have the ability to "read" their child's emotional state, are better able to establish this reciprocal system. Its functioning also requires that mothers are emotionally accessible to their infants, that is, not only nearby, but also with their face visible so that the infant can see her emotional expression.

Out of the parent's accurate reading of the child's emotional state and respect for the child emerges a quality of parent cooperativeness with the child. The parent may act as if by a rule, "I'll say yes whenever it's reasonable." There is evidence that child cooperativeness with parents is greater under these circumstances.

Parents and other adults modeling consistent mundane examples of desired behaviors probably accounts for a large proportion of successful socialization. Hygiene, tidiness, politeness, and helping, as well as the many skills of interpersonal relationships, are partly learned this way. Care of house, yard, and garden, crafts, and some trades are learned as the child develops. Some societies regard this kind of learning as the sole or main mode of childrearing and socialization. It seems obvious, and is supported by evidence, that such learning will occur most effectively when there is a strong, warm relationship between the child and the relevant adults.

Parents arrange the young child's environment to minimize access to fragile objects or dangerous situations. They divert a child's attention from a desired but forbidden situation to minimize frustration. They begin to convey behavioral expectations in words, often using easily remembered repetitive formulas. These may become the beginning of the child's self-talk repertoire, another pillar of early self-control: "Turn off the tap," "Be careful," "No hurting." Matching the child's developing capacity, parents set clear expectations for good behavior.

Parents react positively to desired behavior, with happy expressions, exclamations of pleasure, hugs, and other affectionate exchanges. For some purposes, this may include a material award. Where the parents' pleasurable reaction to the child includes a positive attribution of an enduring characteristic of the child such as "What a generous girl you are," "What a kind boy!," the behaviour is particularly likely to be repeated.

Parents react to undesirable behavior. This may range from a sharp expression of displeasure to a calm request for correction of the behavior. Parents may remove the child from the site of social interaction, thus depriving him/her of attention, stimulation and affection temporarily. This is known by many as a "time out." Its use seems most effective when preceded by an escalating but time-limited warning to exert self-control, as with a count of 1 . . . 2 . . . 3, with several seconds between counts to give the child time for inhibitory control.

Social shaming is used in many cultures to control undesired behavior. Some of the following meanings are conveyed to the child: the child will not be a proper member of this family if the behavior continues, or will be looked down upon by relatives, peers, teachers, society in general; the child will not be marriageable; people will laugh.

Parents may rehearse desired behavior, such as how to act while shopping, ahead of anticipated difficult situation. Parents engage in explanations to the child of why the behavior is required or forbidden. Such dialogues may involve eliciting understanding of the impact of the behavior on the feelings of the other person involved. They may issue in an apology when warranted, and actions to make restitution for harm done. With older children, restitution may also involve extra chores done for parents to compensate for time and other losses occasioned by the child's misbehavior. Parent conversations with children for the purpose of influencing their behavior are often referred to as "inductive" methods of discipline as described above.

Perhaps the most attractive style of socialization by induction is story-telling as used in many traditional cultures. B. Bradbury (1992) gives an account of a Methodist missionary family in northern Canada in the mid-nineteenth century. The two young children of the family had a Cree nurse who was horrified by the parents' practice of whipping their children, locking them in a dark closet, and depriving them of food. She stealthily sought to mitigate the harsh punishment at every opportunity. She also told them countless Cree stories and socialized them rather successfully into Cree values and practices. When the family moved into Salteaux native territory the nurse went with them. The children were then exposed to Cree-Salteaux story-telling duels. The parents eventually moved south again because the children had become too "Indian."

The system of natural and reasonable consequences entails allowing children to experience the outcome of their negative behavior. The natural consequence of coming home late is a cold dinner and no time to watch television. The natural consequence of losing a desired object is not to have it; it is not replaced by parents. The reasonable consequence of losing or damaging someone else's property is to have to replace it from one's own resources. This is a very flexible system, adaptable to many kinds of undesired behaviors, and is intended to promote the child's consideration of the consequences of behavior and awareness of his/her responsibility for choices.

Parents can create opportunities for prosocial behaviour by children—for sharing, caring, helping, and cooperating. For young children this will be within the family; for older children it can extend outside the family. For teenagers it may involve formalized volunteer service to others.

Parents may apply the principles of behavior modification to influence their child. These are:

1. Rewards contingent on behavior will increase the frequency of that behavior.
2. Punishments contingent on behavior will decrease the frequency of that behavior. Systematic application to childrearing is more often based on rewards than on punishments. It is likely to involve greater awareness by the child and supervision by the parent of the targeted behavior, as well as the application of contingent rewards.

Parents monitor and supervise children's behavior, thus enabling many opportunities for contingent praise and correction. The need for supervision is considered to apply until well into teen years, with continual adjustments to allow for the child's developing need for autonomous functioning.

Some families use family meetings or less formal equivalents to enable all family members' participation in setting expectations, attaching consequences, assigning chores, solving problems, and reaching decisions. This may strengthen internalization of rules and acceptance of consequences and be a route to minimizing violent conflict resolution in the family. It also may be considered as training in the practice of democracy.

Parents valuing a nonviolent family are likely to apply negative consequences to inter-sibling or inter-peer violence displayed by the child.

Parents can teach their children constructive (nonviolent) conflict resolution by example, instruction, rehearsal, and coaching, as well as mediating their conflicts when necessary. This is likely to reduce the frequency of sibling violence as well as provide the child with valuable training for other settings.

On the grounds that exposure to fantasy violence is known to increase aggressive behavior in children, parents may use various strategies to limit such exposure. This will involve limits on television watching, video games, and rock videos, on the use of war toys and the playing of war games. Strategies include limits to media and toy choices, discussion of media and toy choices, and watching and discussing content with the child.

Team sports can present problems to parents with nonviolent values, since many sports tolerate violence and some even train children in it, such as ice hockey.

A parenting attribute thought to promote good socialization of children is consistency of expectations and consistency of application, and follow-through of consequences. Consistency between parents and consistency day by day over time are thought to be important, and to reduce the need for correction.

In summary, enduring parental characteristics shown to promote successful socialization are:

- providing the conditions for the establishment of secure attachment in the child;

- emotional accessibility of the parent to the young child;
- fostering a rich, positive, interactive environment for the child;
- empathic relationship with the child.

Parental behaviors known to be effective are:

- emotional facial and vocal expression to inhibit behavior of very young children;
- Cooperative behavior toward the child;
- adult modelling of desired behaviors;
- contingent praise and other rewards for desired behavior;
- contingent positive attribution of enduring good qualities to the child;
- provision of opportunities for prosocial behavior;
- verbal guidance and explanation;
- consistent contingent negative consequences for undesirable behavior;
- supervision of child;
- structuring the environment to minimize misbehavior and redirecting behavior when misbehavior is likely;
- maintenance of calm parental demeanor in parent control interactions (not yelling).

Parental behaviors thought to contribute to successful socialization but not yet clearly evaluated are:

- use of natural and logical consequences;
- use of family meetings;
- the teaching of nonviolent conflict resolution;
- intervention in children's exposure to violent fantasy or sports;
- ignoring trivial misbehavior.

A. Prevalence of Nonviolent Childrearing

There are several societies in which children are apparently not hit at all and some in which probably only a minority of families hit their children. In societies in which most families hit their children, there is still a segment that does not use violence in childrearing.

Societies in which children are not physically punished include the hunter-gardener Fore of New Guinea, the !Kung of the Kalahari Desert, some Inuit groups in Canada, and the Semai of Malaysia. It must be noted that their childrearing practices were described when their cultures were fairly intact. In these societies, nonviolence to children was merely one feature of the socialization of the young to be members of remarkably nonviolent cultures. Some of the features of the cultures that may have been conducive to nonviolent childrearing were very close physical proximity and emotional accessibility of the mother; clarity and uniformity of social rules conveyed by everyone in the child's social environment; easy access to relief for frustrated mothers from other adults in the community, usually in a transient way, but including adoption of unwanted babies; high levels of indulgence and cooperative relationships between adults and children; highly developed adult skills of managing one's own anger, together with social shame attached to loss of control in anger and in some cases belief in the damage to oneself of angry, hostile feelings.

Beginning in 1979, the following nations have enacted legislation to ban spanking of children by parents: Sweden, Switzerland, Finland, Denmark, Norway, Austria, Cyprus. The law in Sweden is supported by a clear majority of the population, and a majority believe that children should not be spanked. Although there are no data on how this is expressed in parent behavior, other research shows a fairly close correlation between belief and behavior on this issue.

In the United States, where there is a strong culture of physical punishment for children, one in five adults does not agree with spanking children and one in ten young people reaches adulthood without ever having been hit!

In mid-twentieth-century Soviet society, nonviolent childrearing was set as the ideal. Childrearing manuals proscribed physical punishment and recommended verbal reprimands, deprivation of privileges, cold parental behavior or, for severe misbehavior, not speaking to the child for several hours. In collective childrearing situations, high standards of cooperative behavior were set and encouraged by the provision of toys and materials requiring cooperation, and by rewards and public praise of cooperative behavior. Misbehavior was dealt with by peer group disapproval and problem solving, peer monitoring and reporting, encouragement of self-criticism and parent criticism of the child to the school, deprivation of privileges, compensatory work, shaming, and expulsion from the peer group.

IV. IDEA SYSTEMS RELATED TO VIOLENT AND NONVIOLENT CHILDREARING

Modes of childrearing occur in cultural contexts, and when there is cultural stability, may be considered adaptive, at least for the segment of society with power to define its culture. Cultural practices are very often supported by values and beliefs. It has been shown that cultures or subcultures in which success as an adult is likely to depend on conformity to rules and obedience to those on higher levels of the power hierarchy consciously value conformity and obedience. These cultures make significantly greater use of physical punishment in rearing their children than do others. The more a culture values self-reliance in successful adult roles and internalization of social rules without the need for surveillance, the less that culture endorses hitting children.

It might be expected that religious belief systems in which conformity and obedience to authority are highly valued would endorse physical punishment of children. This value might be further strengthened by belief in a punitive God, a hierarchical social structure, and a belief in "original sin," that is, that children are born bad and must have goodness inculcated. That segment of Christianity that purports to take the Bible literally and conservative Protestants (these groups have much overlap) have been shown in the United States to favor hitting children even more strongly than does the population average. There are many passages in the Bible, especially in the Book of Proverbs, that urge the beating of children.

> He that spareth his rod hateth his son: but he that loveth him chasteneth him betimes.
> Foolishness is bound in the heart of a child; but the rod of correction shall drive it far from him.

Conservative Protestant writers on childrearing assert that the parent who beats a child for "willful rebellion" is conveying a spiritual lesson about the nature of God. Many recommend the use of a stick or a belt for the beating.

Let us now turn to values associated with nonviolent childrearing; these have been less systematically studied. The tribal societies in which children were not hit at all were ones with extremely little in the way of hierarchy and in which personal freedom and autonomy were valued. Cooperation, interpersonal sensitivity, caring for others and skilled management of personal anger had survival value in these societies.

In contemporary Euro-American writings on childrearing, those that endorse a nonviolent approach generally embrace a view of children as fully worthy beings whose autonomy must be respected. Some invoke the moral standard of the golden rule—that we ought not treat children in ways we ourselves dislike. A somewhat different framing of this is in the form of children's rights—the claim that children have the right not to be assaulted. It is argued that this is a right that has been progressively won by other groups low in hierarchical systems—wives, servants, apprentices, low-ranking military men (in some countries), even prisoners in some countries. This leaves children as the last group to claim this right. It has been noted that this right is now embedded in the legislation of seven countries.

In addition, the proponents of nonviolent childrearing often endorse democratic values within family functioning. The idea of a family council is often promoted. Here all members of the family participate in decision making, including decisions about rules and control systems. Proponents may claim that such a family system is a good training for participating as a citizen in a democratic society.

Some proponents of nonviolent childrearing have a general belief in the value of nonviolence beyond the realm of family functioning. They believe the family is a setting where there is early training in dealing with necessary conflicts constructively. The child can then apply these skills in broader settings and perhaps contribute to the proportion of people who will not endorse the large-scale violence of war as a response to conflicts.

V. WHAT IS KNOWN OF OUTCOMES IN CHILD DEVELOPMENT OF VARIOUS STRATEGIES OF VIOLENT AND NONVIOLENT CHILDREARING?

A. Outcomes of Power-Assertive vs. Inductive Strategies

Certain qualities of the parental relationship appear to cluster together and to go with certain discipline styles. Parental acceptance and approval, warmth, nurturance, support, and responsiveness to distress are positively related to parental "demandingness," that is to the expectation of child responsibility, independence, problem solving, and self-control. Both of these sets of qualities are related to the use of inductive methods of discipline and democratic practices in the family. The use of power assertion by parents is related to less use of induction, less demandingness, and a less supportive relationship with the child.

In terms of child outcome, inductive techniques are more likely to produce children who have greater capacity for prosocial reasoning and for empathy and who are liked more. Power assertive techniques are negatively related to these outcomes. Children beginning school for the first time who have been reared with a high degree of power assertion are the least well-behaved in the new setting. Children of power-assertive parents have less motivation for intellectual achievement than children of parents using gentler methods. Much research confirms that inductive techniques promote internalization of precepts, and that power-assertive techniques may undermine it. Power assertion however, is just as effective (but no more so) at gaining immediate compliance. Secure attachment in the child and high responsiveness in the mother are related to high degrees of child compliance with requests. Internalization induced by explanations maintains the desired behavior longer than do reprimands with no explanations. Interestingly, explanation of the effects of behavior on another may induce longer-lasting compliance than explanation of the effects on the child's self.

In one experiment, parents were taught to use "victim-oriented induction" with their children. This involved inducing the child to take the perspective of the "victim" of their misbehavior, making an apology and reparation to the "victim." In the hands of mothers this enhanced moral internalization in children. The effect was not shown for fathers.

There is some evidence that most parents are discriminating with their disciplinary methods. They use power assertion when they want immediate compliance and explanation when they aim for long-term compliance in the absence of adult supervision. Abusive parents do not discriminate but use unexplained punishment for everything, with ready resort to violent punishment.

There is research evidence of a relationship between parents' and children's levels of moral reasoning. People believe they behave in the "right" way because of instrumental rewards and punishments (being hit or going to jail), social rewards and punishments (being liked or rejected), the wish to maintain an orderly and caring society or consistency with principles such as human rights. Evidence suggests that power-assertive techniques are used by parents who largely reason with principles of reward and punishment and inductive techniques are used by parents who make more use of social contract and moral principles in their reasoning. In turn, the experience of these disciplinary modes is shown to affect the young person's level of moral reasoning. In addition there is a direct effect of the mother's type of moral reasoning on the child's, possibly mediated through direct discussions, observations of the mother's interactions with siblings, and other aspects of family functioning. Although there are important situational influences, moral reasoning is related to moral behavior.

Not only does internalized compliance correlate with a positive, rich relationship with a parent using inductive guidance, but defiant behavior is *more* likely to emerge in children who are disciplined with threats and physical punishment. One of the mediators of this may be the child's response to parental anger. While some children respond with fear, others respond with reciprocal anger. This obviously undermines any capacity to care about the impact of their behavior on others, and in some children arouses a motivation to punish their caregivers. This can begin a very vicious cycle.

Security of attachment and gentle discipline are both important in inducing internalization but appear to have different degrees of influence on young children of different temperaments. Relatively fearful children internalize motivation for desired behavior more strongly than do fearless children. For fearful children gentle discipline is the predominant factor; security less so. For fearless children, the opposite holds. The worst outcomes are in fearless children without close affectionate relationships.

In the preschool years, girls show higher degrees of internalized motivation than do boys. This may be related to the fact that mothers and daughters have a more strongly developed mutual relationship and that girls are disciplined a little more by induction and a little less by power assertion and physical punishment than are boys.

Soviet children reared in the ways described above (nonviolent power assertion with much induction of cooperative behaviour) were compared with U.S., English, and West German children on indices of prosocial behavior. They tested higher than the other nationalities, girls higher than boys, and children from boarding schools higher than day-school children. Interestingly, in one test condition in which peers would know of an antisocial choice by the child, this decreased the probability that a Soviet child would make such a choice, but *increased* the chance that a U.S. child would.

B. Outcomes of Corporal Punishment

Murray Straus and his colleagues have done decades of work on correlates of corporal punishment of children and adolescents. Their work shows the following:

- Adults whose parents hit them as adolescents are more likely to be depressed than those whose parents did not. The effect is proportionate to the amount of hitting, and independent of the effects of poverty and heavy drinking.

- Adults whose parents hit them a lot as adolescents are more likely to have thoughts about killing themselves.
- Children whose parents used corporal punishment are more than twice as likely to severely attack a brother or sister than children whose parents did not. Physically abused children are even more likely to attack a sibling.
- Adults hit as adolescents are more likely to hit their spouses. The effect is proportionate to the amount of hitting and is much the same for women as for men. There is evidence that the effect is mediated through social learning, depression, and inadequate development of nonviolent conflict resolution skills.
- The more a parent hits a child, the greater the chances that that parent will also hit his/her spouse.
- The more corporal punishment parents use on teenagers, the greater the chances of delinquent behavior in the teens. This effect is enhanced by marital violence.
- Adults who were hit as adolescents are more likely to physically assault someone outside the family.
- The more children are hit by parents, the greater the probability that they will experience masochistic sexual arousal in adulthood.
- The more corporal punishment was experienced as an adolescent, the lower the chances of being in the top fifth of the population economically. The mediators proposed are depression, violence, alienation, and diminished initiative and creativity.
- Children who are spanked are more likely to show antisocial behavior. When the same sample of children was tested for antisocial behavior 2 years later, the degree to which antisocial behavior had worsened was proportionate to the frequency of spanking at the time of first sampling. Children who were not spanked at first sampling had improved in antisocial behavior over 2 years. This last piece of research strongly suggests that the direction of causality goes from spanking to antisocial behavior and not the reverse direction. The effect was found to be independent of the degree of parental emotional support of the child.

Other researchers have confirmed many of the above findings and have shown in addition:

- College students who were physically punished in childhood have fewer friends and a greater frequency of negative social interactions.
- People who were physically punished as children are less likely to see themselves as acceptable or to feel any personal control over life outcomes.
- Corporal punishment is a significant psychological stressor for youth, even at low levels (once or twice a year). Its effects are partly mitigated by high parental support, except when corporal punishment is very frequent.
- The intellectual development of young girls may be particularly vulnerable to the effects of parenting. Three-year-old girls who had experienced harsh discipline had IQ scores 8 points below controls. Where harsh discipline occurred with low maternal warmth, IQ was depressed by 12 points.

While there seems to be an overwhelming volume of findings suggesting a causal relationship between the use of corporal punishment and a number of undesirable outcomes, there are some research findings that suggest a respectful approach to the complexity of the process of socializing children:

- In one study, spanking of children (4–7 year olds) deterred the development of subsequent aggressive behavior. It had the same deterrent effect on Black children. However, for White children 8 to 11 years old, spanking fostered the subsequent development of fighting behavior.
- Another study has replicated the above differential results for African- and European-American children. Why should this be so? One suggestion is that spanking is seen as culturally normal by Black children. Since it is the norm for almost all ethnic groups, this is a dubious explanation. An alternative explanation is that among African American families, the lack of physical punishment may indicate an abdication of the parental role, leading to unfavorable outcomes.
- In a study of the effects of parental involvement and corporal punishment on adolescent aggressiveness, delinquency, and psychological well-being, the quality of parental involvement was significantly associated with all three outcomes. Once the effect of parental involvement was removed, corporal punishment had no independent effect on outcome. However, the authors pointed out that the use of corporal punishment was negatively related to the quality of parental involvement and to children's feelings that the same-sex parent cared about them.

- There is also the issue of the child's construction of meaning around the event of being physically punished. There may be a difference for the child in experiencing a controlled spanking and being beaten by an out-of-control, furious parent. Some children may accept the system of ideas around the use of physical punishment. A Tibetan court calligrapher described being caned to the point of bleeding by the Thirteenth Dalai Lama when he was 13 years old. He then expressed the belief that his good health and long life had resulted from these "blessing" beatings.

The child's perception of acceptance and being loved and cared for versus being rejected and viewed with hostility is a major determinant of outcome in psychological development. This will be influenced by how much the child is physically chastised, the parent's demeanor while punishing, and the child's perception of justice and benign or malign intent in the punishment. The child's construction of meaning around the events of discipline is finally what is important in outcome.

C. Outcomes for Children Witnessing Spousal Abuse

This phenomenon is included as an aspect of violence in childrearing as it involves the exposure of the child to violence in the immediate rearing context. A variety of poor outcomes have been described for children who have seen their parents assault each other—withdrawal, dependence, sleep difficulties, distress, poor impulse control, anger, depression, poor academic adjustment, and delinquent behavior. There is substantial evidence for significantly higher levels of developmental delays and behavioral problems. Because there is also evidence for an association of less emotional support for the child and for decline in effective parenting in the presence of spousal abuse, it is unclear whether the effect is relatively direct, mediated by other parenting factors, or both.

Some describe boys who have witnessed parental violence as aggressive, having learned that violence is an acceptable interpersonal strategy, and girls as passive, having learned what it is to be a victim and that men are not to be trusted. Other workers do not find these differences.

There is considerable evidence for long-term adverse effects on boys who witness parental assaults. They develop less effective conflict resolution strategies. This increases rates of marital distress in their adult life and issue in higher rates of wife beating. There is also a direct effect of witnessing spousal abuse as a child on subsequent wife beating, presumably through a learned pattern of behavior.

D. Outcomes for Children's Exposure to High Levels of Media and Fantasy Violence Abuse

> And shall we just carelessly allow children to hear any casual tales which may be devised by casual persons, and to receive in their minds ideas for the most part the very opposite of those which we would wish them to have when they are grown up?
>
> —*Plato, The Republic*

Hundreds of studies have made clear that exposure to television and video game violence and to war toys increases aggressive behavior in children. The greater the exposure, the more marked the effect. There appears to be a relationship between early violent television watching and later social violence and criminality. Exposure to media violence desensitizes watchers to the effects of violence on its victims and reduces empathy. This induction of callous attitudes is seen in both children and adults. Media violence watchers also tend to hold attitudes that favor the use of aggression to solve conflicts.

VI. HOW DO CULTURAL PRACTICES OF VIOLENCE AND NONVIOLENCE IN CHILDREARING RELATE TO DIFFERENCES IN THE ACCEPTABILITY OF STATE AND OTHER LARGE-SCALE VIOLENCE?

Consider the experience of a child with violence from infancy on. The child's first experience is almost certainly to be in the form of parental discipline, with the exception of some cultural minorities, and this is likely to increase steeply in the second and third year. The child is likely to experience some sibling violence and his/her own violence in anger with siblings and parents. Television violence then becomes part of the experience of children, not only in industrialized countries, but in cities, including slum areas, throughout the nonindustrialized world. Violence in interactions with peers enters the child's experience, and may be either tolerated or disapproved by parents. For some children disciplinary violence from a new source begins on school entry. Sports violence may become part of the youngster's experience—in some cases, encouraged by coaches. Parents in some settings continue disciplinary hitting into adolescence. In high school, the teen may be part of gangs that espouse the use of violence and carry weapons, or he may simply live with increased anxiety about peer violence and possibly feel the need for a "defensive" weapon.

As the youth becomes politically acculturated, s/he will become aware of larger scale violence associated with crime, and violence used in pursuit of political ends by nonstate and state actors. The state-legitimated violence the young person will be exposed to may include use in parental discipline, use in school discipline, use as a sentence in criminal justice (e.g., caning, capital punishment), use by police, endorsement of gun ownership and use by citizens, use of the military to repress dissidents within the nation, to pursue constructed national interests outside the nation's borders, or for real security purposes. Societies differ greatly in the degree to which violence is legitimized.

There is heavily reinforced learning about violence in this experience, which will be countered in varying degrees by other cultural influences in the family, school, religion, media, and peer culture. Some of the possible lessons about violence are:

- Violence is legitimate, even good, in controlling bad behavior;
- When reasoning has not succeeded, violence must be used;
- Violence is effective in securing compliance, as long as the user's strength is superior;
- Threat of violence is effective as a deterrent to undesirable behavior;
- It is important to make good occasionally on the threat of violence, to remind subordinates that the threat can be realized;
- Violence by legitimated authorities (parents, the state) is good; violence by others is bad.

Are these lessons carried outside the family arena, into the arena of unorganized social violence or the acceptability of high levels of state violence? There is very little research evidence that can be applied to this question.

Conversely, we can imagine a child reared with little or no use of disciplinary violence by parents, no exposure to spousal violence, strong negative values attached to violence in entertainment, school, sports, the judicial and military spheres, and the expectation of applying nonviolent means to deal with conflicts. Does this affect the young person's subsequent political role in supporting or protesting state and large-scale violence?

Some of the lessons about nonviolence might be:

- Violence is rarely or never an acceptable strategy in controlling bad behavior;
- The threat of violence is not acceptable,
- There is a range of alternative ways of dealing with conflict or the control of behavior;
- Violence by the state is unacceptable and must be protested;
- In some cases, the child might learn that civil disobedience is warranted to protest state-regulated violence (e.g., military conscription).

This linkage between a society's endorsement of the use of violence and power over others at the "micro" level of the family, and at the "macro" level of society and nation remains quite unclear on the basis of present evidence. It is an area inviting research. Some evidence suggesting linkage follows:

- Children reared by violent methods with low parental support are more likely to commit criminal violence outside the family and subsequently to assault their spouses;
- Military men in combat divisions have higher rates of wife abuse than other men;
- War-affected mothers are more violent to their children (but this could be mediated by stress rather than a culture of violence);
- War-affected children are more aggressive to their peers (but this could be mediated by parental disciplinary methods and by stress);
- Exposure to violence in entertainment is followed by greater use of violence by children, and by an attitude of callousness toward others' suffering in adults;
- Countries that favor corporal punishment have higher infant homicide rates and higher military expenditure per capita.

Straus uses the term "cultural spill-over" to refer to the theory that a culture that is high on legitimating various forms of violence may tend to acculturate its members toward greater frequency of illegitimate violence.

Evidence against micro–macro linkage should be considered:

- The Semai, a Malaysian tribe that uses no violence in childrearing, with whom social and intergroup violence are at extremely low levels, were said to be highly motivated and effective fighters in counterinsurgency forces in the 1950s when their livelihood and existence were at stake.

- Apparently, ordinary people in a wide range of cultures can be induced to cooperate in genocide, sometimes in a convulsive crisis, as in Rwanda, 1994, and sometimes in a sustained, bureaucratized effort, as with the Nazis during the Second World War. They may proceed with benign family relationships while engaging in organized killing.

Complicating the issue of linkage is the fact that, while most current wars continue to expose the frontline combatants to the immediate effects of violence in terms of victims' suffering, the development of war technology is increasingly distancing war fighters from war victims. Much of the 1991 war against Iraq was of this nature. The pain inflicted on the population was caused by weapons activated by people operating control panels at great distances from the site of suffering. The pain becomes an abstraction, and the emotional linkage with other forms of violence may become less clear.

It seems reasonable to leave the question of micro–macro linkage as an open one.

VII. ARE THERE INTERVENTIONS AND ORGANIZATIONS ATTEMPTING TO INFLUENCE CHILDREARING WITH RESPECT TO VIOLENCE OR NONVIOLENCE?

The reasons for opposing the use of violence in childrearing include:

- It causes immediate pain and humiliation to the child. Some people consider it intrinsically wrong to inflict pain and humiliation on another.
- A different perspective on the same moral issue is derived from a human rights framework—that children have the same rights as other citizens not to be assaulted.
- Being physically punished as a child is associated with a number of socially undesirable outcomes, particularly antisocial aggressive behavior and spousal abuse.
- Most instances of physical abuse of children begin with corporal punishment. The phenomena are on a continuum.
- Corporal punishment is known to induce obedience under supervision, whereas inductive discipline promotes internalization of rules, standards, and values. The latter is thought to be the more desirable outcome, especially given the need for adaptation to nonroutinized, less hierarchical ways of organizing livelihoods in the late 20th and early 21st centuries.
- Beginning with the premise that exposure to legitimated violence increases a person's tendency to choose or support violence as a solution to conflict, it is proposed that the reduction of legitimated violence in spheres such as childrearing may influence our capacity to choose and devise nonviolent solutions to larger-scale conflicts that might issue in war.

Reasons for supporting the use of violence in childrearing are:

- It is effective in securing obedience in the short-term.
- Some consider it a way of teaching children about the nature of God.

Citizens have acted in various ways to promote one or other of these positions. It must be noted that despite the perceived urgency of reducing rates of child abuse, there is an odd gap in public perception and public policy. The continuum between physical punishment of children and child abuse does not enter public discourse for the most part except presumably in those countries where all assaults on children are illegal. Nevertheless, much of the frontline work in child protection agencies has to do with teaching parents nonviolent methods of childrearing. Authorized foster parents in many jurisdictions are not allowed to hit children, and many child protection workers are explicitly forbidden to endorse physical punishment by parents in general.

Some long-standing and respected researchers take a strong stand advocating delegitimating violence in childrearing, at least in their own nations. Others, faced with the broad cultural acceptability of hitting children, and the less than completely watertight body of evidence, suggest setting a dividing line (e.g., six spankings a day) between culturally appropriate and inappropriate physical punishment as a guide to intervention.

In 1989 an organization called EPOCH (End Physical Punishment of Children) began in Britain and has since become a multinational federation. Other organizations, such as the Canadian Foundation for Children, Youth and the Law promote similar goals.

The United Nations Advisory Committee on the Rights of the Child that oversees implementation of the United Nations Convention on the Rights of the Child recommended in 1995 that legislation allowing corporal punishment of children in the home and elsewhere be prohibited.

It is likely, however, that where there are serious moves to legislate against physical punishment by parents, there will be organized countermoves, especially by conservative religious groups. One example is the Canadian group Focus on Family, which insists on the necessity of physical punishment.

As childrearing practices in Europe change, it is possible that North America will next see a lively debate on this issue.

Most recent childrearing books for popular readerships refrain from advocating corporal punishment. Many do not mention the topic, but there is a recent shift in clarity of position toward clear support of nonviolent childrearing.

VIII. CONCLUSION

Caregivers behave in goal-oriented ways to rear children well-adapted to their cultural environment. All modalities of childrearing have costs and benefits. Violent strategies in childrearing have benefits of rapid short-term obedience and obedience under surveillance. Such strategies are prominent in societies where these qualities have adaptive value. Other advantages may be that such strategies are easily learned and require less investment of parental time. The costs of such strategies are lower intelligence in girls, greater sibling violence, and antisocial behavior in childhood; more delinquent behavior and psychological distress in teens; and in adulthood, lower-self-esteem, worse social relationships, more depression, suicidality, social violence, and spousal abuse.

It seems that while some part of these outcomes is a direct effect of violence in childrearing, much is mediated by the associated factor of low parental support and involvement and the child's perception of parental rejection and hostility.

Nonviolent methods of childrearing, especially inductive strategies, produce greater internalized compliance that is more enduring, better prosocial reasoning, higher empathy, and greater social attractiveness in the child. Disadvantages may be that such strategies demand a higher level of parental time investment, especially early in the child's life, and require parental capacity for empathy. It is also possible that attempts at inductive strategies without parental demandingness, consistency, and follow-through may result in a poorly socialized child.

Many contemporary societies are making the transition from industrial society, requiring compliance under surveillance, to postindustrial society, requiring internalized standards, adaptability, and creativity. This has been a rapid transition and there may be a cultural lag in childrearing practices, especially if they are bolstered by religious beliefs.

Some contemporary societies have continued with physical punishment entrenched in childrearing practices. Others have sharply reduced social tolerance for it.

There is much speculation about the relationship of legitimated violence within the family to participation in a support of legitimated violence on a larger scale, such as war. There is little clear evidence on this linkage.

Since violence within the family and beyond is seen throughout the world as a major social and health problem, it is likely that the debate about modes of childrearing will continue to be lively.

Also See the Following Articles

BEHAVIORAL PSYCHOLOGY • CHILD ABUSE • FAMILY STRUCTURES, VIOLENCE AND NONVIOLENCE • PEACEFUL SOCIETIES • PUBLIC HEALTH MODELS OF VIOLENCE AND VIOLENCE PREVENTION • TELEVISION PROGRAMMING AND VIOLENCE • VIOLENCE AS SOLUTION, CULTURE OF • VIOLENCE TO CHILDREN, DEFINITION AND PREVENTION OF

Bibliography

Bradbury, B. (1992). *Canadian family history*. Toronto: Copp, Clark, Pitman, Ltd.

Coloroso, B. (1994). *Kids are worth it! Giving your child the gift of inner discipline*. Toronto: Somerville House Publishing. [This is one of the recent books on childrearing that takes a clear position against physical punishment.]

deMause, L. (Ed.). (1974). *History of childhood*. New York and Toronto: Harper.

Dobson, J. (1986). *Temper your child's temper tantrums*. Wheaton, IL: Tynedale House. [In this and many other titles, the author recommends hitting children with a stick or belt, and presents a Christian theological argument for doing so]

Dreikurs, R. (1964). *Children: The challenge*. Dutton, NY: Hawthorn. [This writer took an unusually strong position against all punishment, including physical, for children. Many subsequent writers of books on childrearing worked from his ideas.]

Montagu, A. (Ed.). (1978). *Learning non-aggression.* New York: Oxford University Press. [This is a series of anthropological studies of nonviolent societies]

Sears, R. R., Maccoby, E. C., & Levin, H. (1957). *Patterns of child rearing.* New York: Harper and Row.

Sponsel, L. E. & Gregor, T. (Eds). (1994). *The anthropology of peace and nonviolence.* Boulder, CO: Lynne Rienner.

Straus, M. A. (1994). *Beating the devil out of them: Corporal punishment in American families.* New York: Lexington Books.

Straus, M. S. & Mathur, A. K. (1996). Social change and the trends in approval of corporal punishment by parents from 1968 to 1994. In Frehsee D., Horn W. & Bussman K-D. *Family violence against children: A challenge for society.* New York: Walter de Gruyter.

Children, Impact of Television on

Edward L. Palmer
Davidson College

GLOSSARY

Aggression/Violence Behavior intended to cause pain or harm.

Cable Penetration The degree to which a given culture or country has access to cable.

Callousness A child's desensitization to violence in her or his everyday life—related to frequently having seen violence within television programming.

Co-viewing When an adult watches a television program with a child.

Educational Television Television programming designed to teach a child specific concepts—generally within an individual-viewing, home setting.

Instructional Television Television programming designed to teach a child specific concepts—generally within a group or school setting.

Mass Marketing Selling a product or a program to a mass audience or group.

Modeling A child's imitation of behaviors seen on television.

Prime-Time Television Television programming which is shown in the prime viewing hours for adults, generally 7 to 10 p.m. weekdays.

Prosocial Television Television programming designed to teach a child specific positive interactive values such as cooperation, appreciating diversity, and so on.

Psychoanalytic Based on the work of Freud, this perspective takes the premise that behaviors are unconsciously motivated and aggression is instinctual.

Psychodynamic Based on the work of Adler, Jung, Erikson, and others, this theoretical position gives credence to a learned aspect within aggression.

Total Saturation Medium A communication medium such as television when the potential to receive its transmission is present in virtually every household.

VIOLENCE, PEACE, AND CONFLICT form a trilogy that has prevailed since the dawn of human history. Conflict has provided the fulcrum, and violence and peace have provided the basic end points for conflict resolution. Historically, humankind has shown a penchant for violence, and within that penchant the major markers of human history have been far more frequently its battlefields than its peacefields. This history has spawned countless academic works and interdisciplinary debates on the question of whether humans are innately aggressive and violent or whether these predispositions are learned. Perspectives such as the psychoanalytic consider aggression instinctual whereas psychodynamic perspectives consider aggression to be learned. Placed in the child context, the latter perspective gives prominent credence to the premise that children mirror the environment in which they live and grow. Correspondingly, the major reflections within that environmental mirror will shape the child's development, learning, and behavior.

I. INTRODUCTION

A. Child Socialization and the Advent of Television in the U.S.

Neither violence nor children's early learning are new within the human experience, but the vehicles through which children learn have changed and evolved across time. From basic hunting and survival skill learning through oral traditions passed from older to younger and, more recently, the printed word, children's socialization has always relied upon the family, the larger societal group, and peers. A recent addition to this socialization context has been the advent of television. Technologically available prior to World War II, this medium resembled a lumbering giant that had slept through the 1930s and much of the war and would awaken only gradually from its drowsy state. While radio scheduled feverishly on the hour and half-hour throughout the days and evenings, television in the early 1940s slept on. It would awaken sporadically for a ballgame perhaps, or a newsreel, but then it would promptly go back to sleep. There was little reason for it to stay awake for long intervals. Radio was entertaining and informative, and everyone listened to it regularly while television lacked the resources to stay awake throughout the day and evening. For all kinds of reasons—some vested, some technological, some programming—it was radio's era and a formative time for television.

After World War II, radio remained the dominant medium. Television was caught in the circular dilemma of needing resources to develop programming and needing revenues to provide those resources. To compound the dilemma, virtually every household in the country had radio receivers while very few had television sets. So both production and marketing faced major challenges—how to program without resources, and how to reach a mass audience not yet equipped to receive the programming. This cycle of challenge compounded for the retail set dealer who was faced with the prospect of trying to motivate customers to buy sets to receive programming that did not yet exist. Both to create a market and to sustain one, television programming needed to span more of the day.

To create its mass market, television programming appealed to families. Many bought sets for the chance to see NBC's *Texaco Star Theater* with Milton Berle; and its landslide success ushered in the variety show format and soon-to-be household names such as Sid Caesar and Imogene Coca, *The Ed Sullivan Show*, and *I Love Lucy*. Although television had not yet reached all the masses, it was well on its way, and the follow-up marketing strategy spotlighted children. The basic appeal very closely paralleled a more recent marketing strategy for computers—namely, their educational value for children. Families were encouraged to buy sets for the educational welfare of their children. The combined marketing strategies met with marvelous success, and set ownership mushroomed from one-household-in-a-hundred in 1947 to one-household-in-ten by 1950. Ten years later, 9 out of every 10 households owned a television set, and today it has become a total-saturation medium reaching virtually every household in the country. Many are now multi-set households. Table I provides major growth figures across the time period from 1961 to 1997.

Television's mass-market entry into households and families brought major changes in the ways families

TABLE I

Profile of U.S. Television Growth

1961	1997	Description
47.2	245	Million television sets in U.S. homes
5	98	Percent color sets
1	64.8	Million homes served by cable television
543	1,196	Commercial television stations
62	365	Public television stations
150	263	Million people in the U.S.
2.17	7.2	Hours per day spent watching television
1.2	42.5	Billion dollars in television advertising revenues
51 million	24 billion	Dollars in cable subscription revenues
0	3.2	Billion dollars in cable advertising revenues
4	30	Dollars per month paid by cable subscribers
0	74	Million U.S. homes owning videocassette recorders
0	14	Billion dollars video revenues for movies

TABLE II
Daily Average Time Spend Viewing Television by a U.S. Household

Year	Hour-level newly reached/1997 hour-level
1956	5 hours, 1 minute
1971	6 hours, 2 minutes
1983	7 hours, 2 minutes
1997	7 hours, 11 minutes

spent their time. Table II provides a glimpse of viewing patterns as television gained increasingly more of families' time. Note within the table the significantly shorter time frame between the 6-hour and 7-hour viewing-time benchmarks. Where it took 16 years for television viewing time to move from 5 to 6 hours, it required only 12 years to move from 6 hours to 7 hours. The numbers readily suggest that television commands more of a household's time than virtually any other activity except sleep, and children's viewing time parallels this overall pattern. As television viewing time has increased, time spent in other activities such as play, reading, and family interaction have correspondingly decreased. This trend has been of major concern to educators and health care professionals as well as other community-based and religious groups, for not only does the trend have implications for learning and health, but it carries subtle implications for community gathering and civic involvement.

1. Children's Viewing Patterns: A Close-Up Perspective

Children begin watching television between $1\frac{1}{2}$ and 2 years of age. By age 12 a child is watching television 4 hours per day, with the heaviest viewing times on Saturday morning, after school, and during adult prime time. One million young children in the United States are watching television after 10 p.m. each school night. A set is on in the typical U.S. home an average of 7 hours per day, and by the time a person is 18 that person will have spent more time watching television than he or she has spent in school.

Lower socioeconomic group children, on average, watch 5 or 6 hours per day—notably more than the national average. And these children, along with the children of ethnic minority families and immigrants, rely heavily upon television as their primary socializing tool for learning the language, customs, and social mores of the culture. For them, television is the equivalent of their window to the social and cultural world, and they accord it this level of reality and credibility.

For the culture-at-large, television has become the primary information source. Young people, adolescents, and adults rely upon television for news and information. Newspapers are unable to compete with its visual appeal. Television newscasters, however, draw heavily upon newspaper coverage for their news clips and summaries.

2. Parental Role in Children's Viewing

Surveys indicate that the parental role in children's television viewing is one of expressing verbal concern while at the same time paying little attention to the amount of time a child spends viewing. When a limitation is imposed, it generally is a bedtime cut-off rather than a restriction on the amount of viewing. Dr. George Comstock of Syracuse University has concluded that for all practical purposes television and its viewing is governed by children's authority rather than parental guidance. When children and parents disagree on program and viewing choices, the child's preference prevails as often as the parent's. And when the parents themselves disagree on program and viewing choices, the child's preference is the decisive one. In these instances, the child is attributed an air of television-expertise and, within it, a corresponding authority.

With an increasing number of households now having more than one television set, the decentralization has created yet another family/demographic change and within it a diminished awareness/guidance role for parents. The set in a child's bedroom, den, or playroom greatly decreases the likelihood that parents will know either the programs or the amount of time their children spend watching television. And the decentralized viewing context itself means families are much less likely to be viewing programs together. Adult co-viewing with children has frequently been research-cited as a critically important ingredient in the impact of viewing upon children. Not only does it provide an interaction and sharing-context, but it also provides opportunity for adult and child to discuss what they have been viewing together. The loss of such opportunities constitutes a major loss in child socialization.

II. VIOLENT/AGGRESSIVE PROGRAMMING

A. Introduction and Definitional Distinctions

As one thinks of violence and aggression, a broad range of interactions and definitional perspectives readily come to mind. The football player completing a flawless tackle, the flower pot accidentally knocked off the window sill and hitting an unsuspecting passerby, the gangster who says, "Let's Talk!" and opens fire on those whom he has just addressed. For purposes of this discussion, neither the football player nor the flower pot knocker will qualify as aggression and violence. They lack the critical ingredient of intent to inflict harm. For purposes of this discussion, aggression/violence will be defined as behavior intended to cause harm or pain.

B. Contents of Children's Program Viewing

1. What Children See

In the 1500 hours of television U.S. children watch each year, they see primarily a violent face. The average child will see 8000 murders and 100,000 acts of violence before finishing elementary school. By the time that same person reaches high school graduation, he or she will have seen 18,000 murders and more than 250,000 acts of violence. The violence is "sanitized"—clean, neat, and tidy with no pain and no suffering. There is a distinct identity pattern among perpetrators and victims with initiators tending to be Anglo-American, male, single, and of middle-class socioeconomic status while their victims tend to be minority ethnic group members, women, the elderly, and members of lower socioeconomic status groups.

The prevalence of violence in any given year depends heavily upon the Nielsen ratings for the previous season's programming. Where highly violent programming has received high Nielsen ratings in a given season, there will be more of these look-alike programs the subsequent season. Being primarily a conservative medium playing economically "close to the vest," television networks and producers seek to ride the economic "coattails" of the previous year's successes.

Across the last 20 years, the overall prevalence of violence in programming has remained relatively constant at 8 episodes of violence per hour. Within that relative constancy, prime-time television violence has increased dramatically across that same 20-year period. Where the most violent prime-time programs of 1980 registered 22 acts of violence per hour, their most violent counterparts now register 45 to 60 violent acts per hour. Children's programming contains significantly more violence-prevalence than the overall average of 8 hourly acts across all programming. The children's sector reached an all-time record high in 1992 with 32 acts of violence per hour. Much of this prevalance occurs within animation and cartoons.

2. What Children Learn: Violence Viewing Impact

For heavy television-viewing children, three major impacts of viewing have been observed—modeling, fear, and callousness. With regard to modeling, heavy viewers behave more aggressively than do light viewers. This finding relates both to immediate behavior modeling after viewing a specific act of violence and to long-term patterns of violent behavior. A growing body of longitudinal research data now links heavy viewing in the 8-year-old child to juvenile delinquency at age 18 and criminal activity at age 30. Where this linkage has been most pronounced among male viewers, the delinquency and criminal linkage has now surfaced among female viewers as well. These findings have been replicated cross-culturally in countries such as Australia, Britain, Finland, Israel, and Poland. (See Part IV for more detailed cross-cultural discussion.) Modeling is most prevalent among heavy-viewing children with aggressive predispositions. In a closed-loop cycle that feeds upon itself, the more aggressive child watches more violent television programming and the viewing, in turn, engenders more aggression. To profile a child most likely to be affected by television violence, it is a boy or girl who frequently watches violent programs, thinks that they portray real life, feels a strong identification with the shows' aggressive characters, engages frequently in aggressive fantasies, and—in the case of girls—prefers stereotypically boys' activities. Another avenue of violence-effect research has focused on those unique settings where television has been introduced to a town or village and comparisons can be made between the pre- and post-television time periods. Where such comparisons have been made (e.g., a remote Canadian north community of Manitoba Cree Indians), significant differences in aggressive attitudes were found among heavy-television-viewing children pre- and post-television introduction.

Fear is notably increased among heavy-television-viewing children. These children overestimate by 10-fold the likelihood that they will be victims of aggression within their daily societal activities. A corollary to this expectation is the tendency of such children to believe that people take advantage of others and cannot be trusted. Within such a belief system, these children "act like victims" when they move through their days, and such action and expectation can, in some instances, prove self-fulfilling.

Callousness or desensitization as a product of violence viewing relates to a heavy-viewing child's tendency to be television-hardened to acts of violence.

These children develop a kind of "heat shield" that desensitizes them to emergencies, help-requiring situations, and violence occurrences in their daily lives. For them, television is reality, and their daily experience is merely an extension of that reality.

The broader, underlying lesson children learn relates directly to this encyclopedia's theme of conflict and its resolution either peacefully through communication and negotiation or aggressively through violence. The major lesson conveyed within commercial television programming is that violence is the way to resolve conflicts.

III. PROSOCIAL/INSTRUCTIONAL PROGRAMMING

A. Introduction and Definitional Distinctions

This area of programming can be broadly labeled "educational." It is distinct from the prevalent commercial programming outlined within Section II, and sets out to convey positive interactive/social patterns or cognitive learning concepts. The term, prosocial, relates specifically to programs designed to convey positive interactive/social patterns and skills. Instructional programming is designed to teach a given set of learning concepts. It is, in effect, a lesson plan and it communicates the lesson through the design of the program. If an instructional program had the goal of promoting children's reading readiness, for example, a given episode in the series might set out to teach specific letters or words. Correspondingly, a mathematics program might set out to teach numbers or operations such as addition and subtraction. By contrast, the prosocial program might socialize children in cooperative attitudes and values, promote their familiarity with and appreciation of service personnel in their society, or introduce them to children of other cultures. Generally, a program is either prosocial or instructional, but in some notable instances (e.g., *Sesame Street*) a program is both prosocial and instructional.

B. Historical Perspective

1. Early Instructional Television

Instructional television had begun in the late 1950s. With crude closed-circuit technology or a transmission aircraft circling overhead, programming could be beamed to single school systems or to systems in several contiguous states. The programming itself tended to be "talking head." A master teacher in a given subject area would present the lesson before the television camera, and students would watch this teacher on their classroom monitors. The within-class teacher would then follow up with any questions or necessary clarification.

The early instructional television process met with mixed reviews. It had been borne of necessity—overcrowded schools, teacher shortages, and poor quality teacher training in the 1950s. And while it spoke to these necessities and beamed a gifted teacher beyond a single classroom, many of these teachers were not readily adaptable to effective television programming, and the "talking head" took on a reputation for sameness and boredom. Instructional television had not yet reached its potential as an effective communication medium.

2. Later Instructional/Educational Television

A new mission and, with it, a venture into unexplored programming terrain came in 1968. The Carnegie Commission Report recommended establishing a Corporation for Public Television and an increased level of state and local support for Educational Television (ETV) stations. With the adoption of these recommendations, the Corporation for Public Broadcasting (CPB) was formed. The mechanism and vehicle were now in place to move beyond primarily instructional television to programming that would broaden children's horizons and stimulate their imaginations. Now ETV would be challenged to develop and effectively use the high-quality, sophisticated production techniques prevalent within commercial television broadcasting. This challenge required money, time, and an effective working relationship between scholars and producers—two groups that heretofore had lived worlds apart.

The Children's Television Workshop (CTW) was created in 1968 to respond to the ETV challenge. Its flagship production, *Sesame Street*, had an unprecedented $8 million funding base and 2 years' lead time before airing. With its clearly focused goal, a solid funding base, a strong research commitment, and a blend of professional production talent and scholarship, it had all the ingredients necessary to meet its challenge with notable success. Program components were child-tested for their ability to hold attention. And within the "Sesame Street Model", educators developed the program "lesson plans" while producers were given the freedom of their own creativity and imagination in providing the programming vehicle. Adopting all the techniques of commercial television advertising, the program targeted inner-city children with the goal of conceptually preparing them for the elementary school classroom. The program aired in 1969 and quickly found a broad child-audience stretching well beyond its inner-city target group. Now translated and adapted in cultures throughout the world, the program continues to be a flagship standard in its field. With its use of puppetry and animation, coupled with its capacity to have segments continually changed and updated, it has the potential to remain an effective standard.

Mister Rogers' Neighborhood has brought preschoolers a long-running, prosocial program that stands in sharp contrast to *Sesame Street*. Far from the sophisticated production, ad techniques, and fast pace of its public broadcasting colleague, *Mister Rogers' Neighborhood* is relaxed and slow-paced. Child-viewers relate to Fred Rogers as they would to a good friend, and Rogers aims to identify with them and their feelings, creating an atmosphere of acceptance while building their self-esteem and self-worth. As he changes from his coat into his sweater, removing his street shoes and putting on sneakers, children relate to him. And within this relationship, together they get to know many service people, artists, sports stars, astronauts, musicians, and others in society who drop in as guests. A football star wide receiver tells about his other life as a ballet dancer, an astronaut tells children how astronauts "go potty" in space, and children hear direct and open talk about concerns such as divorce, conflict, peaceful resolution of differences, moving to a new neighborhood and school, or the death of a loved one. Together on a small trolley, they also travel to "The Land of Make-Believe" where puppets such as Lady Elaine (a lovable mischief-maker of Make-Believe), King Friday, Prince Tuesday, and Lady Aberlin greet them and mirror the many distinct differences in children's own personalities. In one of the Make-Believe episodes, for instance, King Friday wanted Prince Tuesday to swim miles and miles. Lady Aberlin reminded King Friday that this was not their goal. Their goal was to have fun. The episode went on to say, "Whether you are first, middle, or last, you are you and people can like you just the way you are." It is a central and ultimate expression of individual acceptance and caring.

Beyond these two standards, many child-directed programs have aired at different points in commercial and public television's history with goals to stretch imaginations, expand cross-cultural horizons, and promote understanding and appreciation of diversity. The *Big Blue Marble* highlighted the lifestyles of children around the world. Each half-hour program featured 7- to 10-minute portraits of children, a "Dear Pen Pal," and serialized dramas promoting international understanding. Sponsored by International Telephone and Telegraph (ITT) as a public service, the program premiered in September 1974 and was carried on 180 commercial and public television stations in the United States and in 60 countries around the world. No other multicultural program has attained a comparable level of international popularity and impact.

Other multicultural programs have included *Vegetable Soup* and bilingual programs such as *Villa Alegre*, *Carrascolendas*, and *Rebop*. *Carrascolendas*, for example, targeted Mexican-American children in the Southwest United States, helping them to enculturate while simultaneously helping other child viewers to gain appreciation and understanding.

Another group of programs have addressed special populations and specific social concerns. *Inside-Out* was geared toward elementary school children with learning disabilities, helping them cope with challenges such as expressing their feelings, making new friends, practical jokes, embarrassment, peer acceptance, emotional abuse at home, and bullies. Any child could readily identify with these topics and challenges, and the program held important lessons about conflict and conflict resolution. While reaching the learning-disabled child with special poignancy, the program carried much broader messages to all children about understanding and acceptance. *Freestyle* targeted elementary school girls in Grades 4 through 6 and sought to counter sex-role and career stereotypes with a message to these girls to "think career" in broad, nonsexist terms. As an important corollary to the program's primary goal, boys were encouraged to broaden their perspectives and move beyond their own gender-stereotypical career images.

Two of the longest-running commercial programs for children were *Captain Kangaroo* and *Fat Albert and the Cosby Kids*. Targeting preschoolers, *Captain Kangaroo* has been revived by Saban Entertainment (producers of *The Power Rangers*). Given the profits realized from *The Power Rangers*, Saban has sponsored the return of the "Captain" as a public service. *Fat Albert and the Cosby Kids* beamed toward African American teens in the inner city. Like many of its contemporaries, the show reached well beyond its target audience, addressing human feelings, ethics, values, conflicts, and challenges experienced by all teens and, indeed, by all humans. The show never feared nor avoided the opportunity to address a broad range of topics including ethics and values, morality, divorce, mental retardation, handicaps, personal hygiene, and social responsibilities, nor did it sidestep controversial issues such as mixed marriages, death, the Ku Klux Klan and Nazi bigots, teenage sexuality, or drugs and alcohol. The *Cosby Kids* spanned a range of personalities as diverse as the issues themselves, and the core focus was always prosocial.

"Fat Albert," for instance, was a big, lovable optimist who, despite his great size and strength, was very sensitive and would go to great lengths to help a friend or stranger. "Bucky" was a mild-mannered peace lover who usually agreed with both sides of an argument. What better recipe for peaceful resolution of the many conflict-ridden challenges the *Cosby Kids* encountered. The recipe and its lessons stretched well beyond their inner-city roots.

Other children's program initiatives have included *Barney and Friends* for preschoolers; *Reading Rainbow*, *Ghostwriter*, and *Wishbone* for developing children's literary awareness and interest; *Bill Nye, the Science Guy*, and *Mr. Wizard* for relating science to the daily lives of children; *Where in the World is Carmen Sandiego*, for developing geography knowledge and awareness; *Square One TV*, using a variety of familiar commercial-programming formats for upper elementary school mathematics; *Zoom*, as a show by kids for kids, focusing on the prosocial and broadening children's awareness and appreciation of diversity; and *Blue's Clues*, a recent, popular initiative from Nickelodeon. Both Nickelodeon and The Discovery Channel on cable have made major programming initiatives oriented toward children and their development of knowledge as well as prosocial awareness and sensitivity.

3. "Drop-Ins" or "Pop-Ups": Prosocial Advertising

Commercial television's programming for children drew public criticism and federal regulatory heat in the late 1960s. With the prospect of a governmental ruling hanging in the balance, the networks introduced a significant Saturday morning first for children in the 1970 season. Variously called "pop-ups," "drop-ins," "snippets," "mortar messages," or "educational activities," they were educational commercials that used a phonics method to teach vowels, consonants, and sentences. Others addressed mathematics concepts, social studies, and news. NBC-owned stations were the first to introduce this innovative feature, and ABC and CBS quickly followed suit. CBS, for example, had $2\frac{1}{2}$ minute newscasts for children at the end of each Saturday morning half-hour of cartoon programming. This longest running series, *In the News*, had a 10-year track record. ABC premiered a series of brief consumer information messages, *The Dough Nuts*, that taught children how to wisely use their "dough." ABC also aired several 4-minute drop-ins featuring a popular singing group (Menudo) and Cap'n O.G. Readmore, an animated purring cat encouraging youngsters to "Oh, gee, read more!" ABC's all-time classic, *Schoolhouse Rock*, used catchy tunes and words with animation to teach mathematics, social studies, and history. In addition to drop-in sequences, each network produced and aired brief spots on nutrition, health, and safety. Within this ratings-free environment between programs, networks dramatically demonstrated their capacities to be creative on behalf of children.

4. Impact on Child Viewers

Research demonstrates that both educational and prosocial programming have an impact on child viewers. Summative research on *Sesame Street* demonstrated that its target group of inner-city children was learning the concepts and increasing in reading readiness. Because the program was widely viewed by all children, the concepts and reading readiness were being enhanced among children in all settings and at all socioeconomic levels. Similar summative research effectiveness has been shown for programs such as *Square One TV*.

Research has demonstrated a comparable effectiveness in communicating prosocial messages to child viewers. Eight- to 10-year-olds demonstrated effective retention and understanding of message content in lab-tested episodes of *Fat Albert and the Cosby Kids*. Similar results were found in summative research relating to *Mister Rogers' Neighborhood*. Behavioral effects have been most notable in laboratory studies and less evident in correlational or field-study settings.

Studies further indicate that prosocial programming with a broad, global perspective influences children's attitudes toward different ethnicities and toward children who in other ways are different from themselves. Fourth- through sixth-grade children viewing *Big Blue Marble* demonstrated a post-viewing effect of more positive attitudes toward children from other parts of the world. These viewing children also became less ethnocentric and developed a positive respect and appreciation of children globally. Brief program-viewing exposure produced major changes in children's perceptions of the world and its people.

IV. CROSS-CULTURAL AND WITHIN-CULTURE PERSPECTIVES

A. Introduction and Definitional Distinctions

Several cross-cultural and within-culture elements impact the nature and the degree of television-presence. For purposes of this discussion, the cross-cultural categories of developed, developing, underdeveloped, and undeveloped will be used. Each category is necessarily broad and will encompass a variety of characteristics and culturally unique settings. Note that the term culture is used rather than country. Even the most developed country (e.g., the U.S.) may have an underdeveloped or undeveloped culture (e.g., an Indian tribe in the remote, northern regions of Alaska). Such a tribe would have more in common with the undeveloped than with the developed. As a rule-of-thumb—somewhat precarious to venture or state in this landscape—urban areas tend to be more developed than rural areas, settings with product marketability and higher economic levels per capita tend to be more developed than those without such product marketability and economic means, cultures with higher educational levels and technological expertise/sophistication tend to be more developed than those of lower educational levels and technological expertise, free-market/competitive economies tend to be more developed than centralized/government-run economies, and the geographically accessible areas tend to be more developed than the remote and relatively inaccessible. There will be natural variations within this heuristic, but it provides a helpful framework for this discussion.

Developed cultures include most areas of the larger industrialized nations of the so-called "G7" plus Russia (e.g., Canada, France, Germany, Italy, Japan, United Kingdom, United States) and most areas of the smaller developed countries of Western Europe and geographically scattered areas, including such countries as Australia and South Korea. With the notable exception of Russia, these countries and the majority of their cultures have an overall standard of living and level of technological expertise that lends itself to an advanced level of television presence and television programming. Developing cultures encompass several of the former Communist-bloc countries of Eastern Europe (Poland, the Czech Republic, Hungary, Slovenia), Communist China (with the notable exception of Hong Kong, which is developed) and other areas of Asia (e.g., India, the Philippines), areas of Africa (e.g., South Africa), much of Central and South America. Underdeveloped cultures include major areas of countries that are in whole or in-part rural and agrarian or politically unstable (e.g., Zaire; Zimbabwe; Haiti; areas of Mexico; and several of the East European Communist bloc countries including Armenia, Tajikistan, Georgia, and Serbia). Undeveloped cultures by reasons of geography, remoteness, or strong cultural/tribal traditions (e.g., remote areas of Canada and Alaska, outlying islands in the Philippines) have remained insulated from outside influences and have maintained their centuries-old mores, traditions, and lifestyles. In their own ways, these cultures either have remained oblivious to outside developmental influences or have said, "No, thank you" to them.

A detailed analysis of each culture lies far beyond the purview of this discussion. Indeed, a large encyclopedia dedicated to that topic alone would be severely challenged in accomplishing such coverage. This overview provides a bird's-eye glimpse of the globe and some of its major cultural contours. Within that view, case-study close-ups will provide some of the major dynamics as they relate to television access and the content and nature of television programming.

For close-up purposes this section will view in greater detail the major dynamics and television access within a developed culture of the "G7" or "Group of 8" (United Kingdom) and a developed culture in the Middle East (Israel); developing cultures within the East European Communist bloc (Czech Republic, Poland), China, and the Philippines; underdeveloped cultures (Armenia, Tajhikistan); and undeveloped cultures (remote Philippino and Northern Alaskan tribes).

B. Television Presence: A Cultural Close-Up

1. Developed Cultures

a. United Kingdom

Television presence in the United Kingdom (U.K.) has closely paralleled its timetable and presence in the United States (U.S.A.). While U.S. television emanated from a commercial framework and base with public television and educational outreach being secondary considerations, the U.K. established a solid funding base for public television from the outset. Television sets were taxed, and these taxes supported the high-caliber production and programming of the British Broadcasting Corporation (BBC). The Children's BBC has produced a wide range of high-quality programming for children including *Blue Peter, Fully Booked, Studio 9,* and *Short Change.* There is a Children's BBC on Prime, designed for viewers throughout Europe. Cable availability and satellite transmission are readily available, and the combination of Children's BBC, commercial television, and access to resources such as The Discovery Channel, provide a broad spectrum of prosocial/educational programming for child viewers. Consonant with the society's overall perspective on nonviolence and weapons availability (e.g., British "bobbies" not carrying weapons), television programming is closely monitored for aggressive content deemed potentially harmful to children. Next to the U.S., the U.K. is a major "exporter" of television programming to other countries in Europe and throughout the world.

As in the U.S., television viewing is a child's most prevalent daily activity beyond sleep. Television-viewing time has been borrowed from such activities as movie going, radio listening, and outdoor activities. Commercial television programming has become a stronger "draw" for children than educational programming, and viewing time is inversely correlated with intelligence, personal adjustment, friendship, and school performance.

b. Israel

From 1968 till the 1990s, Israel had only one television channel—the Israeli Broadcasting Authority. Rapid transition occurred when the Israeli Parliament approved the introduction of cable and a second national channel (a commercial channel). Thirty-one cable area concessions were sold, and cable penetration within the society followed swiftly. By 1993, there were 400,000 cable households (40% penetration); and this number doubled to 800,000 cable households by the end of 1995 (67% penetration). These households received 40 channels—mostly foreign stations received by satellite dish in the cable station and transmitted to the subscribing households.

Comparing cable and noncable households before and after its introduction, the most significant differences in viewing time occurred among children 6 to 15 years old and retirees. Children in cable households watched significantly more television than their noncable counterparts, with a notable difference between male and female viewers. Where boys in cable households were watching an average of 56 minutes per day, girls were watching only 33 minutes. The gender difference was even more pronounced in noncable households—boys, 43 minutes; girls, 21 minutes. When compared with child viewing in the U.S., all of these child-viewing figures are quite modest.

A much broader issue relates to changes in viewing audience perceptions, values, and attitudes. What has been termed the foreign "cultural invasion" or "media imperialism" has had a far-reaching impact which will be discussed in more detail within a later section of this chapter.

The kibbutz stands in sharp contrast to the television and cable households of Israel. Children of the kibbutz do not watch television. The primary focus within these settings is interpersonal interaction, creativity, and the group.

2. Developing Cultures

a. East European: Czech Republic and Poland

East European countries are emerging from a state-owned broadcasting background, and while the state owned have the strongest financial base, superior transmission systems, and the financial ability to do more news gathering, recently emerging commercial television stations have attracted more viewers than their state-run counterparts. An example of this pattern can be found in the Czech Republic, where the first private broadcasting system was introduced in 1990 and Nova TV became the Republic's first privately owned commercial television station in 1994. Owned by Central European Media Enterprises (CME) whose majority stockholder is Ronald Lauder, heir to Estee Lauder Cosmetics Company, Nova TV has surpassed Czech TV's viewership in less than two years. Private partnerships in other East European countries have followed similar patterns.

b. China

China has been a unique developing culture in the sense that it continues to be a centralized, communist country that promises to be both a major consumer and a major exporter within world markets. Few would doubt the role of China as one of the world's most extensive emerging markets, and large enterprises worldwide have been vying for a significant foothold in this major new market.

Television prevalence has followed this overall development pattern, rapidly penetrating the Chinese society. With 202 television stations in 1985, the country now has almost 700. Where the 1985 "audience reach" was 45% of the population, television now reaches 80%. The vast majority of these stations are either local or municipal, and many of them have been created to serve a given industrial community with local news and public affairs programming. There is virtually "total saturation" within these closed-circuit industrial-community cable systems.

With its first radio station arising in 1945, its first *People's Daily* edition in 1948, and its first television station in 1958, media had the role of defining the objectives of the Chinese Communist Party. Media continue to be operated from a central Ministry of Radio, Film, and Television under the Central Propaganda Department of the Communist Party Central Committee on Programs. More than 600 commercial cable television stations have begun operations in China's urban areas, reaching approximately 30 million households. Most of these stations carry 24-hour sports programming, news, community affairs, ads, music videos, and feature programs along with imported movies and TV serials—mostly from Hong Kong and the U.S. There are limitations on what Chinese viewers are permitted to see. Ironically, China's own 1993 Cannes Film Festival Winner, *Farewell, My Concubine,* could not be shown in its native country.

China's own television production tends to be rudimentary and basic. As the society becomes more globally aware, there is a growing market for foreign-import programming. Under Chairman Mao such programming imports were limited to Albania, the former Soviet Union, and North Korea. Under Chairman Deng the foreign import market broadened to include Japan, the U.S., Australia, West Germany, the U.K., and developing noncommunist countries. China now imports from 23 countries. Because television authority is decentralized—resting primarily with non-media-trained managers in provinces and municipalities—the selection and prevalence of foreign programming varies widely from one section of the country to another.

Children's programming has been notably slow to be imported. No children's programming was being imported prior to 1980 and this programming has gradually increased to 10%, but overall children's programming has not been a priority with Chinese television.

c. The Philippines

The Philippines portrays both ends of the developed/undeveloped spectrum. While 91% of the households in metropolitan Manila have television, only 18% in the rural areas are set owners. This stark contrast stems from several sources including income levels, population distribution and location, availability of electricity and television reception. Manila—the urban center—has notably higher per capita income than the rural population. And once one goes beyond Manila, the population of 75 million is spread over 7,107 islands—1000 of them inhabited. The geographical "scatter" itself poses a major problem in reaching these people and in bringing electrification to these diverse locations and remote villages. Among the many villages without electrification, a rare few have their own generator. All the programming these villages can receive originates in Manila. Because it is the third largest English-speaking population in the world, the Philippines has attracted prominent cable interest. Cable penetration overall has been minimal—250 operators and 250,000 subscribers in a population of 75 million—and centers virtually exclusively within Manila. Programming viewed by set owners is predominantly domestic, with special focus on public affairs and educational programming. Those households with cable have access to a broad spectrum of programming from other countries, and within this spectrum children's programming is an inclusion. For the population at large, children's programming has not become a priority or an available reality, as indeed television itself is not a reality for much of the country and its many scattered islands.

3. Underdeveloped Cultures

a. Armenia

Unlike some of its former communist-bloc country "neighbors" such as the Czech Republic, Poland, Hungary, and Slovenia, Armenia has not begun the process of television change and is unlikely to do so for quite some time to come. Two of the major underlying reasons are economic and political. The desperate economic and societal straits leave little hope for television expansion in the near term. The basic unmet human needs are far more pressing.

b. Serbia

War-torn and divided with very tenuous prospects of long-term political stability, Serbia has many of the characteristics mentioned for Armenia. Compounding the problems experienced by Armenia, Serbia has ongoing tensions, ethnic divisiveness, large displaced and dispossessed portions of its population, and major uncertainty about its prospects for peace and prosperity once the UN peacekeeping force leaves. For this country, television is an arm of the ruling parties and can be nothing more. Similar prospects to those of Armenia and Serbia prevail in former communist-bloc countries such as Tajikistan and Georgia.

4. Undeveloped Cultures

The term "undeveloped" itself warrants clarification because, in a very real sense, these cultures are the most developed. While many of the traditionally termed developed countries lose sight of their heritage and roots, these cultures retain these unique and distinguishing characteristics. They may be termed "undeveloped" in the economic and technological sense, and it is within this context that the classification is here made.

a. Remote Islands in the Philippines

With their challenges of remote location and inaccessibility, these areas remain pristine in the technological sense. Having no electricity and no media acess, they remain insulated from external influences. Earlier tribal ways and customs prevail.

b. Remote North Alaskan Villages

Like their counterpart in the Philippines, these villages have both remote location and inaccessibility. Outside development efforts and influences have been effectively countered, and these villages continue much as they have for several generations. Although television is a possibility theoretically in the airwaves around them, these villages do not receive and have no desire for such reception. Their cultural integrity has been preserved—no small feat in an ever-shrinking, increasingly sophisticated technological world.

V. GLOBAL ISSUES AND CONCERNS RELATING TO TELEVISION AND CHILDREN

A. Preserving Cultural Integrity

1. The Production Issue

The production aspect of cultural integrity relates to issues surrounding the practice of "outsourcing" production work on programming. As a case in point, most U.S. children's program production work has been outsourced to facilities in Japan for reasons of cost and competitiveness. The major question raised within this practice has been whether the production facilities will insert their own culture's interpretations and character depictions. As the outsourcing practice is initiated, the consumer country's own production facilities and expertise dry up, making it impossible for the consumer country to "retool" quickly and readily bring production back "in-house."

2. The Reception Issue

The reception aspect of culture integrity relates to a country's receiving most of its television programming from another country or group of countries. Some have termed this "cultural invasion," and the fact that the vast majority of satellite and cable-transmitted programming comes from the U.S. has led several countries to fear what they call "media imperialism." If most of the world's television originates in the U.S., what is the likelihood that U.S. cultural values will erode cultural values and norms in the receiving country, homogenizing the globe into one U.S. "world culture"? The concern has been significant enough to prompt some countries to place program-import limits. And in still other countries, evidence of native culture erosion has been observed when cable programming has been introduced. For example, in Israel traditional drama and folk culture programming have become victims to the so-called "cultural invasion." Israel's experience has not been unique.

3. The Transmission-Ownership Issue

In several emerging countries within the former East European communist-bloc, for example, their privately owned commercial television stations have majority foreign investor ownership. The question remains open regarding the impact of this ownership on the people and the culture of the host country. In the case of the Czech Republic's Nova TV, majority owned by Ronald Lauder, will it mean a promising new market for Estee Lauder Cosmetics? Or a vast array of other products from foreign countries rather than the host country? Will there be similar potentials within the programming itself? It is too early to know the nature and extent of this impact, but it seems relatively certain there will be notable and significant impact.

B. Attitudinal/Behavioral Effects

1. Negative Effects

The major viewing effects that have been found within the U.S. have been found among heavy television-viewing children worldwide. Imitating aggressive television models, resorting to aggression as the prescription for resolving conflicts, overestimating the likelihood of violence occurring in their own daily experience, and identifying with prime-time program models who are aggressive—each of these has been found in the global context. Also evident have been the effects of advertising wherein child viewers translate personal worth into product ownership and wealth. To the extent that individuals then become viewed as commodities, the perception and its implications become disturbing and problematic.

2. Positive Effects

The same positive effect potentials observed within U.S. programming to children have been found worldwide as well. *Sesame Street* has been translated and adapted in more than 60 countries around the world—extending globally the reach of this very effective prosocial/educational program. This program and others in this genre carry the potential to be "peace ambassadors" throughout the world. To the extent that they can communicate prosocial values to a broad spectrum of the world's children, they will be a major ingredient in the quest for an evanescent and elusive world peace. And to the extent that current program sequels to the classic *Big Blue Marble* can foster international awareness, understanding, and communication among the world's children, these initiatives also will be major ambassadors for peace.

Television itself resembles a car in the sense that the vehicle is neither intrinsically good nor bad, positive nor negative. The same car can be used to stage a bank robbery and get-away or to take physically challenged children to their Special Olympics. What makes the difference is how the vehicle is used.

The ultimate arbiter of television's value on the global stage will depend on the priority given its prosocial potentials, the commitment countries will make to programming for their children within the broadcast-day, and—much later in this scenario—the capacities of countries to move beyond the specter of so-called "media imperialism" with high-quality production of their own children's programming.

Also See the Following Articles

JUVENILE CRIME • MASS MEDIA, GENERAL VIEW • POPULAR MUSIC • TELEVISION PROGRAMMING AND VIOLENCE

Bibliography

Asamen, J. K., & Berry, G. L. (Eds.). (1997). *Research paradigms, television, and social behavior*. Newbury Park, CA: Sage.

Berry, G. L., & Asamen, J. K. (1993). *Children & television: Images in a changing sociocultural world.* Newbury Park, CA: Sage.

Bryant, J., & Zillmann, D. (1994). Media effects: Advances in theory and research. Hillsdale, NJ: Lawrence Erlbaum.

Cornfield, M., Gomery, D., & Lichty, L. W. (Eds.). (1997). *A media studies primer*. Baltimore: Johns Hopkins University Press.

Liebert, R. M. (1992). *The early window: Effects of television on children & youth*. Boston: Allyn & Bacon.

Silj., A. (Ed.). (1992). *The new television in Europe*. London: John Libbey.

Zillmann, D., Bryant, J., & Huston, A. C. (1994). *Media, children, and the family*. Hillsdale, NJ: Lawrence Erlbaum.

Civil Society

Martin Shaw
University of Sussex

GLOSSARY

Civil Society A sphere of association in society in distinction to the state, involving a network of institutions through which society and groups within it represent themselves in cultural, ideological and political senses.

Global Civil Society The extension of civil society from national to global, regional, and transnational forms, involving the development of globalist culture, ideology, and politics.

Global Political Crises Local crises, typically wars, that come, often through media coverage, to have global political significance.

Hegemony The cultural, ideological, and political dominance, in civil society, of a social class or group or bloc of social classes and groups.

Postmilitary Society A society that has ceased to be dominated by war preparation, and in which mass military mobilization and participation are replaced by high technology professional militaries.

Social Movements Collective actors in civil society distinguished by mass mobilization or participation as their prime source of social power, typically concerned to defend or change society or the relative position of a group within society.

Total War A mode of warfare based on the mobilization or participation of society as a whole, in which society becomes both a major resource and a major target and warfare tends toward total destruction and genocide.

CIVIL SOCIETY refers to a sphere of association in society in distinction to the state. The term has been used in a variety of ways, and this article will explore the meaning of civil society by examining the understanding of it in the modern social sciences and its relevance to the understanding of violence, peace, and conflict in major periods of modern history.

I. THE MEANING OF CIVIL SOCIETY

The origins of the concept of civil society lie in key phases of modernity in the late 18th and early 19th centuries. Then writers in classical philosophy and political economy began to distinguish systematically between the spheres of state and society. In feudal society, the same social relations between superiors and inferiors had embraced both production and family life, on the one hand, and political and military authority, on the other. With the dissolution of feudal relations, these two areas of social life became more clearly demarcated in modern conditions as "society" and "state." The term civil society was first used to distinguish a sphere in which social relations were based on the free association of individuals, rather than a fixed hierarchy of legal institutions. For classical writers like the philosopher Georg Hegel and the revolutionary theorist Karl Marx, civil society was an inclusive concept of "society minus the state," and very definitely included what we would now call "the economy." Civil society was defined, indeed, by the emergence of a distinct political economy in which individuals related to each other as independent agents rather than as people who filled prescribed social roles.

The major classical theorists had, however, different ideas about civil society and about its relation to the state. Hegel saw civil society as a sphere of contradictions that could be resolved in the higher institution of the state, which embodied the highest ethical ideals of society. Marx believed, in contrast, that civil society was a sphere of conflicts between competing private interests, and that far from being reconciled in the state, these conflicts would take the form of class struggles in which the state itself would be overthrown. (In Marx's later work, the concept of civil society is largely replaced by that of the capitalist mode of production.)

Although these classical ideas of civil society are still influential, as we shall see, the concept has been refined by later writers in ways which have made it, while still a broad concept, arguably more relevant to contemporary social analysis. The Italian Marxist Antonio Gramsci, writing in the 1930s, referred to civil society in a more specialised sense than that of "society minus the state." He argued instead that "*between* the economic structure and the state with its legislation and coercion stands civil society" (Gramsci, 1971). Civil society for Gramsci was a set of institutions through which society organized and represented itself autonomously from the state. Although representative institutions of the economic sphere, such as employers' associations and trade unions, were among the institutions of civil society, there were also churches, parties, professional associations, and educational and cultural bodies. The economic sphere itself, with its functional institutions (firms, corporations) responsible for organizing production, was not on this definition part of civil society.

Gramsci built a comparative theory of political change on this concept of civil society. He argued that whereas in the East, where civil society was weak, revolution might have succeeded through a direct violent assault on the state (as in Russia in 1917), in the West, where civil society was strong, this would not be possible. The institutions of civil society formed the "outer earthworks" of the state, through which the ruling classes maintained their "hegemony" or dominance in society. It was necessary to transform civil society, indeed to create an alternative hegemony of the subordinate classes, before it would be possible to challenge state power.

Gramsci's hegemonic theory of civil society saw transformation as a cultural, as well as political, process, and specified an important role for intellectuals. According to Gramsci, each class developed its own intellectual groupings. While some traditional groups, such as priests and lawyers, continued from previous phases of society, many new groups had been created "organically" through the development of capitalism—managers, educators, social workers, and so on. These groups, playing central roles in the institutions of civil society, contributed to maintaining the existing hegemony. A counterhegemony, which Gramsci conceived of in Marxist terms as led by the working class, would require its own organic intellectuals and beliefs.

Gramsci's ideas were newly influential in the 1970s, both among Western social science academics and in inspiring the "Eurocommunist" strategy of the Italian and some other West European Communist parties. Another strong stimulus to the development of civil society thinking came around the same time from oppositional thinkers in the Communist states of East-Central Europe. In an interesting advance on Gramsci's ideas, many oppositionists believed that because the authoritarian character of the Communist regimes made a direct challenge to their legitimacy very difficult, it would be easier to develop civil society based on cultural institutions that made an indirect challenge to the values of the system.

In the repressive atmosphere of the late 1970s and early 1980s, even this was difficult—although in Poland the autonomous trade union Solidarity developed as a mass national movement. In the more liberal situation of the later 1980s, however, civil society mushroomed in many Communist countries. The growth of autonomous cultural and social institutions played the role of preparing the foundations for a challenge to political power—very much as Gramsci had argued. As Communism collapsed and competitive party politics developed, however, key intellectual elites often moved from civil society to parties and the state, leading to a crisis of civil society practice and thinking. Nevertheless, the more advanced Central European countries, especially, are characterized in the late 1990s by much more extensive civil societies based on voluntary associations than was the case a decade earlier, although the political significance of these civil societies has changed.

Implicit in these ideas of civil society was the notion of it as a sphere of peaceful civility in contrast to the coercion, authoritarianism, and violence of nondemocratic states. At the end of the 20th century the development of civil society is coming to be seen, therefore, as a significant criterion of the development of democracy. Democracy is seen as involving not merely the formal establishment of certain rights, institutions, and procedures—important as these are—but also the consolidation of the social relations that support these. These supports include the development of an educated middle class and a framework of civil institutions that can support democracy. Just as in former Communist states, so in many countries of the "Third World": as democratization has advanced in the last decade of the 20th century, the creation of civil society is widely viewed as a concomitant of democratic change.

Similarly in the West, the strength of civil society is often seen as a criterion of democratic health and stability. A central question in Western analysis, however, is the role of mass media in civil society. Traditional representative institutions of civil society, such as trade unions, parties, and churches, have decayed in many Western societies, with membership and participation rates often (although not always) in decline. Even where some of these institutions remain strong, they exercise their representative functions to a large degree through mass media, above all television. Participation in Western civil societies (and democracies) increasingly depends on the openness of communications media. Media can be seen both as constituting the framework of contemporary civil society and as powerful actors within it. The centralized mass media of the early 20th century are partially giving way to more participatory media, in which civil society is renewed.

There are key differences between media and other institutions, to do with the informational character of much media activity and the quasi-instantaneous communication between communicators and audiences. Most other institutions largely take for granted the information that their members or audience possess and are more concerned with influencing the value framework within which information is evaluated. Media, on the other hand, are always heavily concerned with communicating information, and have highly divergent relationships to evaluation. Much television eschews open commitment to value frameworks (except those concerned with information), while at the other extreme, many newspapers are highly committed to propagandizing particular values. In participatory new media like the Internet, a diversity of both information sources and opinions transforms these tensions.

Frequency of communication between media and audiences is another key differentiator between them and other institutions. Many newspapers publish daily, and television and radio broadcast continuously, sometimes updating news and interpretation hourly or even more frequently. Computer communication is virtually instantaneous. Political and religious leaders, educators, movement activists, and other civil leaders, on the other hand, communicate with their audiences intermittently and update their analyses of specific situations episodically; they are not required in the same way to inform or comment regularly on any given situation. A related difference is that media news analysis claims, implicitly or explicitly, to provide a total context of information relevant to given situations (whether or not media do this is, of course, another matter). The views of political and religious leaders, educators, activists, and others are "parts" while the media provide the "whole" picture. In this sense media contextualize and relativize the outputs of other institutions.

II. CIVIL SOCIETY ON A GLOBAL SCALE

A primary tension in the development of civil society has been between the universal values that civil institutions have often professed—and that some see as characteristic of civil society as such—and the national forms of civil society that supplies much of their real content. Both religious ideologies such as Christianity and secular political ideologies such as liberalism, socialism, and conservatism have fostered universal beliefs. Nevertheless, institutions such as churches, parties, trade unions, schools, and media have characteristically been highly national institutions during the 19th and 20th centuries. Indeed, civil society as a whole has been a national sphere, generally involved in mutually sustaining relationships with the nation-state. Civil institutions have generally fostered national versions of universal belief systems and values, including loyalty to the state, and have been supported in turn by states.

In the second half of the 20th century, much of the nation-state framework of civil society has been transformed. During the Cold War, both state and civil society changed in the West. National forms were maintained, but they lost much real significance. There was a huge internationalization of Western military, economic, cultural, and ideological power. Western states increasingly shared frameworks for organizing their monopoly of violence and their management of economic life. They created the conditions for massive processes of economic and cultural globalization. In this context, the old national civil society declined. The weakening of many of the forms that were most characteristic of it in midcentury—churches, mass political parties, and trade unions—was partly related to this transformation of the national context.

Civil society has been partially renewed in new institutions that are less formal, less tied to particular social interests, and less national. Sociologists have given most attention to "new" social movements (i.e., those based not on class but around other social axes or issue interests). Mass-participatory social movements tend to be episodic, but there are other institutions—single-issue campaigns and voluntary organizations, especially global development and human rights agencies—that are more enduring if often less activist based.

These nongovernmental organizations (NGOs) are particularly important not only in that, although based in the West, they operate across the globe, but also because many (e.g., Amnesty, Greenpeace, *Médicins sans Frontieres*) are "globalist" organizations with a specifically global orientation, membership, and activity. There are, however, other major types of institutions that comprise the emergent global, regional, and transnational civil society. These include formal organizations linking national organizations of parties, churches, unions, professions, educational bodies, media, and so on.

The growth of mass media has also tended to transcend the nation-state context, and not simply because of trends toward transnational ownership and diffusion. Media also have different relationships to the tension between the universal values (religious, political, educational, informational, etc.) on which civil society institutions claim to be based, and their essentially national character, based on the aim of representing nationally defined social interests and viewpoints. Insofar as media fulfill their function of providing information on the widest possible (i.e., global) basis, they inevitably tend to transcend the national limitations of state and civil society.

Although the worldwide expansion of civil society in eastern Europe and the former Soviet Union, and parts of Africa, the Middle East and elsewhere—has often taken highly national forms, it has rested on the globalizing forces of education and cultural diffusion. The present growth of civil society combines global and particularistic aspects—even the nation is a universal idea in the modern world.

These changes in civil society—the decline of some traditional national forms, the rise of global (or globalist) social movements, NGOs, and media, and its worldwide expansion—have led many to discuss a movement from national to global civil society. Recent debates in international relations have extended the analysis of civil society to the transnational and global levels. They have often ascribed to it considerable normative and political importance, although they have not always dealt with the empirical problems involved in hypothesizing "global civil society."

Civil society and social movements have become leading concepts of critical theory, more sociologically based approaches and especially of radical political visions in international relations. As international theorists have moved beyond not just realism but also neorealist ideas based on economic interdependence, they have increasingly seen social movements as a third major category of international actor after states and transnational corporations. These movements have been seen as especially significant forms through which society outside the state is represented in the global and international arenas.

Social movements are seen as having unique characteristics, but in reality they have many features in common with the other civil society institutions to which we have referred. It cannot be assumed that social movements are more effective than other bodies in civil society: their relatively informal, spontaneous character brings advantages but also disadvantages in both the mobilization of support and the achievement of leverage. Linkages of social movements and informal networks (e.g., of women's, gay, and peace groups and movements) are only one kind of global development.

A particular problem in the definition of global civil society is to specify its relationship with state forms. The emergence of global civil society can be seen both as a response to the globalization of state power and a source of pressure for it. There is no one, juridically defined global state to which global civil society corresponds, even if a de facto complex of global state institutions is coming into existence through the fusion of Western state power and the legitimation framework of the United Nations.

The emergence of global civil society in fact corresponds to the contradictory processes of globalization of state power, and the messy aggregation of global and national state power that comprises the contemporary interstate system. The forms of global state power are often inadequate from the point of view of civil society organizations—for example, power can be mobilized to deal with what is seen as a problem for Western strategic interests (e.g., Iraq's invasion of Kuwait) but not coherently to deal with genocide, environmental crises, or world poverty. Civil society organizations often find themselves, at the end of the 20th century, arguing for a different kind of crystallization of global state power from those favored by state elites.

The development of global civil society, as of the global state, is moreover still limited. Civil society institutions are still generally defined in terms of national bases, and because of this there is a deep structural difficulty in their relationship to interstate relations, let alone transnational forms of state power. These problems are especially significant in the case of social movements. Whether social movements are demonstration based or mobilize utilizing a wider range of methods, they rely more on cultural impact than on articulated connections with the political system. The cultural strength of social movements derives partly from their location outside the formal party and parliamentary structures of the state; but this can also be a weakness when it comes to seeking particular concessions from the state.

The political power of social movements does not arise from occupying positions within formal political institutions (as in the case of parties) but largely depends on their cultural mobilizing power, that is, the extent to which they can achieve symbolic impact on the streets and/or in the media. In the case of demonstration-based movements, leverage is dependent on the relationships between physical mobilizations and media coverage. There are cycles of mobilization within social movements, mediating the internal momentum of the movement and the politico-cultural context in which it is operating. It is very difficult for the leaders of a movement to ensure that the peak of the mobilizing cycle coincides with the greatest opportunity for influence on the state. Leverage is often a somewhat hit-and-miss affair.

If social movements generally have such difficulties with the state, then clearly they are greatly magnified in relation to interstate (rather than intrastate) politics. To influence interstate relationships, social movements need to move beyond the national base that is still their most common framework. They need, implicitly, to influence all of the states involved in a particular set of interstate relations, which in turn requires equivalent movements within each state and developed transnational linkages, including ideally a common strategy. All of these requirements represent an inherent strain on the resources of social movements, which typically respond locally, regionally, and nationally to issues, expressing feelings and beliefs within these limited frameworks. The problem of international leverage expresses the general contradiction between the modes of bottom-up and top-down politics in its most extreme form, since interstate relations have traditionally been the area of politics most removed from popular or electoral influence.

Given these structural limitations of social movements within interstate politics, how should their role be understood? From the point of view of states (and hence also of statist theorists of international relations), social movements represent a relatively unpredictable (often even "irrational") intrusion into the balance of power. From the standpoint of a broader conception of international politics, in which states are the organizing but not the only level of analysis, the effects of including social movements (and other civil society organizations) are to complicate "pure" interstate relationships. James N. Rosenau (1991) has gone so far as to argue that we need to talk of "postinternational" rather than international politics.

In this perspective, international politics is one subcontext of the larger framework of global politics. States can be seen as parts, in Justin Rosenberg's (1994) phrase, of the "empire of civil society" within which they originated and on which they depend. In this context, rather than seeing social movements or other civil society organizations as intruders, or categorizing them residually as "nonstate actors," they are recognized as normal actors within global politics. As the increasing "turbulence" of global politics and the relative decline in state autonomy break down the insulation of international politics from politics in civil society, international relations theorists are finding the "conceptual jailbreak" to postinternational—indeed global—concepts more and more necessary.

Within recent international theory, both substantive and normative arguments have been developed concerning the significance of global civil society. It has been argued that international governance, in the late 20th century, involves international organizations and global civil society as well as the system of states. The moral and political significance of global civil society has also been elaborated, in two principal ways.

On the one hand, writers like the Marxist Rosenberg and the Hegelian Mervyn Frost (1995) have revived classically inclusive concepts of civil society and argue correspondingly (in the former case) for a broad social transformation as the context of changing international relations and (in the latter) for an "ethical" approach to international order. On the other hand, however, a broader range of radical writers have argued for approaches to global politics based on a concept of civil society closer to the narrower Gramscian approach. Richard Falk (1995), for example, argues for a "humane global governance" based mainly on civil society, in the sense of civil associations and especially social movements, as opposed to the "inhumane global governance" of states and multinational corporations. In his project, civil society is the core of a democratic "globalization from below" to be counterposed to the dominant trend towards an authoritarian "globalization from above." In this humane alternative, the development of civil society is seen as working against the militarism of the state system towards a democratic world peace.

III. CIVIL SOCIETY, VIOLENCE, AND WAR IN HISTORICAL PERSPECTIVE

This positive reading of the role of civil society in war and violence is only partially supported by a reading of the historical evidence—although is not to deny that the emerging global civil society of the early 21st century may have different relationships to war from those of the national civil societies of the 19th and 20th centuries. Perhaps because of the positive reading of civil society that characterizes most of the literature, virtually nothing has been written on the role of civil society as such in the violence of the European empires and the world wars. We can, however, construct an argument from the vast historical literature on all aspects of social life in the wars of this period.

The study of "war and society" has been a staple of modern historiography. Vast literatures analyze the ways in which warfare has hardly been an exclusive concern of states and armies, but has transformed and been transformed by social relations. From the mid-19th century especially, warfare has been industrialized—adopting technologies from the civilian economy, as well as functioning as a motor of technological change in the economy as a whole. The relations between states and arms corporations have been a central facet of political economy since the late 19th century.

Beneath the surface of the pacific commerce that mostly reigned in Europe from 1815 to 1914 (if not in the United States where the Civil War foretold later horrors), the industrial capitalist societies that developed in the 19th century engendered the classic modern form of militarism. Everywhere in Europe toward the end of the century, militarist ideologies flourished in social life: from the propagandist militarism of army and navy leagues to new paramilitary youth organizations and the militarist saturation of popular culture.

In this climate, no institution or profession of the national civil societies of the 19th and early 20th centuries escaped militarization, although the degree and forms varied. Industry, schooling, and religion showed the influence of military methods and values. Newspapers and advertising, and later radio and cinema, were often enthusiastically and voluntarily militarist, before they were conscripted to the cause of the nation-state. The paradigmatic social movements of the late 19th and early 20th centuries, the social-democratic parties and trade unions, fell under the sway of militarism, putting aside the pacifist tendencies of their ideologies once war was declared.

In total war, civil societies took almost wholly national forms. The internationalization of professions and science, which had a long history even before the 19th century, largely succumbed to the nationalism of the early 20th century. As in almost all civil institutions, national content prevailed over universal forms. Internationalization prevailed only within military alliances, and even then was often limited by nation-state interests. The most that could be claimed was that the universalizing values of civil society lent a special character to the war aims (and later Cold War aims) and political-intellectual culture of the democracies—as opposed to totalitarian Fascist and Communist states, where autonomous civil societies ceased to exist.

The historical sociologist Michael Mann (1996) has pointed out, moreover, that civil society hardly had a pacific character in colonial wars. Settler civil societies were often more militaristic (and racist) even than colonial empires. They generated their own systematic violence against indigenous populations across the continents wherever Europeans migrated, whether in North or South America, Africa, or Australasia. Settler societies were often more aggressive toward preexisting societies than were colonial states. They continued as sources of violence into the era of decolonization, playing key roles in wars to defend White "European" power from Algeria to South Africa.

Guerrilla war involved a special version of the total-war militarization of civil society. Guerrillas fought directly in and through civil society, hiding behind civil institutions just as states sought to secure them against guerrilla takeovers. Guerrilla war, even more than total war between conventional state military forces, was a form of warfare centered on the shape and control of civil society.

Total war, in both its major interstate and minor guerrilla forms, transformed civilian populations and their institutions into factors in warfare. Civilians and civil society became both instruments and targets of war. Total war thus developed an implicitly—and in cases like the Nazi Holocaust, explicitly—genocidal character. Wars were fought against peoples and cultures (for Hitler, the war was against the Jews as well as his conventional state adversaries). Attempts were made to physically exterminate peoples, to eliminate their ways of life and histories, and to abolish their civil society and institutions. In the militarization of civil society by total war, some versions of civil society triumphed, others were destroyed; all changed.

IV. CIVIL SOCIETY AND THE COLD WAR

We have already seen that during the Cold War there was a significant internationalization of economy and society as well as of the state in Western countries (in the Soviet bloc, Communist internationalism was experienced as forced and led therefore to the reassertion of nationalism on the system's demise). There was also, moreover, a major transformation of warfare. Total war in the form that had dominated the first half of the 20th century declined. On the one hand, the total destructiveness and the genocidal character of war were accentuated by the development of nuclear and other weapons of mass destruction. On the other, however, these same systems made redundant the mass mobilization and participation of the total war era, inaugurating a "postmilitary society." Civil society began to develop therefore beyond its dominant national and militarized forms in international and global directions, in which a new postmilitarist character was strong.

We also noted that during this period, "new" social movements developed often with implicitly or explicitly transnational and global reference. Some, such as women's movements, were movements with broad social and cultural aims that had a wide-ranging influence on international politics. Others, however, such as peace movements, represent the opposite case: movements with very specific political goals designed to affect the workings of the interstate system and particularly to affect the dangers of war and the possibilities of peace. The genocidal character of nuclear warfare, with its total threat to society, stimulated new mass participatory movements against state strategies.

Although peace organizations of various kinds have existed continuously for many decades, peace movements have tended to arise because of particular conflicts or crises. In recent times, they have been of two main types: to halt or prevent particular wars (most notably the Vietnam war) and to oppose particular weapons developments (chiefly nuclear weapons). Where women's movements have grown in diffuse ways since the 1960s, peace movements have tended to rise and fall quite dramatically in conjunction with particular international crises. Nuclear disarmament movements for example emerged, primarily in Western Europe and North America, in two main periods (1958–1963 and 1979–1985) but almost disappeared in the intervening years and again in last years of the 20th century. The movement against the Vietnam war, peaking from about 1966–1972, was a quite distinct movement from the two nuclear disarmament movements, with as many political and organizational differences as similarities.

I shall concentrate on the example of the most recent phase of nuclear disarmament movements. These movements arose almost simultaneously in 1979–1980 in a number of Western European countries, following the NATO decision to introduce new nuclear systems, especially cruise missiles, into five states (the United Kingdom, the Federal Republic of Germany, Italy, the Netherlands, Belgium). From the beginning, although antinuclear campaigns arose locally and nationally within each of the states, the common framework of the NATO decision, while varied according to the missile installation timetable and national political situation, imposed a common agenda on the new European peace movements: to prevent the deployment of the new systems. In European states not directly affected, such as France and Spain, parallel movements arose with different national agendas. In the United States, a similar movement arose around the broader demand for a "nuclear freeze."

These movements were successful in mobilizing large-scale demonstrations and influencing public opinion. While they imposed some delays in implementation, they failed however to prevent deployment of the new missiles, which was mostly completed by 1984; or in the American case, to secure a general freeze on new nuclear deployments. Ironically, new disarmament proposals between the superpowers, which developed beginning in 1986 after the coming to power of Mikhail Gorbachev in the USSR the previous year, appeared after the peace movement had gone into fairly rapid decline as a mass movement.

On a short-term balance sheet of the peace movements the failures were substantive and the successes, largely symbolic. Their influence on European public opinion was substantial: in all states designated for the deployment of cruise missiles, opinion poll majorities consistently opposed the deployments. They also influenced established civil-society institutions such as social- and liberal-democratic parties, media, and churches. The movements partially succeeded in their cultural goals: movement culture, in which pacifist, environmentalist/green, and feminist strands were strong, that had a powerful impact on some groups of young people.

At a deeper level, the peace movements were less successful in shifting support for existing nuclear systems or for NATO, or in deflecting the broad U.S. and Western nuclear strategy. The movements stimulated a different political climate around nuclear weapons issues, forcing governments to justify and debate their policies; the bottom line, however, was that they failed in their manifest political aim of preventing missile deployments. A major reason for this is revealing: despite the movements' influence on both public opinion and opposition parties, the parties that adopted or were more influenced by their demands were resoundingly defeated in national elections (notably the German Social Democratic Party and British Labour Party in 1983, the American Democrats in 1984).

The structural problems of social movements in the context of interstate politics largely account, too, for the failures of the peace movements. The mutual solidarity of NATO governments helped them to withstand the separate (and variable) pressures of their national peace movements. The European peace movements faced the difficulty that the major center of NATO decision making, the United States, was outside their reach. The difficulty of stimulating a largescale parallel peace movement in the Warsaw Pact states was a major additional factor, since it enabled NATO governments to claim that for them to halt their deployments would be "one-sided" disarmament in the face of Soviet weapons modernization.

Nonetheless, although the disarmament of the later 1980s arose primarily from interstate politics and from the domestic politics and economics of the Soviet Union, the peace movements were an important part of the context that produced these changes. First, the peace movements stimulated strong popular support in Western Europe for détente and disarmament and so ensured Gorbachev of a positive Western European response to his disarmament proposals. Second, Ronald Reagan's "zero option" proposals for eliminating intermediate nuclear missiles, initially produced as a propaganda measure to help counter the peace movements, were picked up by Gorbachev and became an important element in the move towards agreement. Third, the small independent peace and human rights movements in Eastern Europe, stimulated by deliberate actions of the Western movements, helped to lay the foundations for mass opposition to the Communist regimes. This led in turn to the East German and Czechoslovak revolutions of 1989 that overthrew the system and completed the ending of the Cold War.

The 1980s began with one kind of social movement, the peace campaigners, on the streets of Western European capitals, and ended with another, the movement for democracy, on the streets of Eastern European capitals. These two movements, together, represented important moments in the complex processes—both within civil society and within and between states—that unraveled the Cold War system. Neither set of social movements could by itself claim direct and decisive responsibility for this change; but their actions contributed both directly and indirectly to the change. Any account of the end of the Cold War that seeks to interpret it without reference to them is certainly lopsided. Peace movements and the wider civil society context that they helped to transform were significant factors in the processes of transformation.

V. CIVIL SOCIETY IN CONTEMPORARY WAR AND PEACE

With the end of the Cold War, there have been new, dramatic transformations of global politics, the longer term results of which it is difficult to foresee in the late 1990s. Economy and culture have become significantly more globalized, due particularly to the removal of the major political barriers between the former Communist states and Western-led world economic and communications systems. War between Russia and the West has become almost as unthinkable as war between the major states of North America, Western Europe, and Japan had become during the Cold War, although relations have not been fully stabilized (nor has the internal political structure of Russia).

The power of states has been widely seen as in relative decline—although these remain the pivotal and in many senses still the most powerful institutions of global politics. Many states have been subject to fragmentation. The Communist multinational states of the USSR, Yugoslavia, and Czechoslovakia have broken up—the first two amidst major wars. Many African states, including Somalia, Liberia, Sudan, Sierra Leone, and Zaire, have disintegrated at least partially through largescale violence. Even Western states like Canada, Belgium, Italy, and the United Kingdom have been subjected to disintegrative strains, even if those have so far been managed largely by peaceful political means.

The trends toward, and debate about, global civil society have developed significantly in the last decade of the 20th century. Civil society has also had a new centrality to what have been called the "new wars" of the 1990s. With the diminution of classic interstate conflict, most major wars of this first post-Cold War decade have been wars of state fragmentation. In these wars, the central issues have often been the very composition of society and the character of civil society, as well as of the state. Two visions of civil society and its relations with the state have been in contest. On the one hand, ethnic nationalists have sought to define civil society and state in exclusivist terms. On the other, pluralists and democrats have contended for open and inclusive ideas of society and the state.

Ethnic nationalism has arisen because political elites—in many cases fragments of old (especially Communist) elites in new guises—have sought to maintain or carve out political power. They have exploited old ethnic differences to mobilize support and maintain legitimacy, and have utilized parts of the state and military apparatuses to create ethnically homogenous ministates or fiefdoms. Many wars have been, like Hitler's war against the Jews, wars against civilian populations and against civil societies and cultures. While these wars have often been against "other" ethnic cultures, plural civil society has also been a key target of ethnic nationalism. In Bosnia, multi-ethnic Sarajevo, where intermarriage and "Yugoslav" identification was relatively high, were a prime target of the Serbian nationalists. Intellectuals who organized pluralist civil institutions—local officials, teachers, and so on—have often been prime victims of the new genocidal politics. So-called "ethnic cleansing"—since the term derives from the Serbian practitioners of mass killing it is hardly adequate for social science—has targeted pluralists as well as people of other ethnicities.

Although many of these elements of the "new wars" are not really novel—the history of the last 100 years is littered with genocides—the particular configuration of the genocidal fragmentation wars of the late 20th century is distinctive. The trends toward global and transnational forms of civil society work in these wars in a number of different ways. On the one hand, protagonists in these wars typically mobilize ethnic-national civil society in a transstate and global manner. The Israeli state, for example, has long been dependent on the American Zionist lobby. More recently the Palestinians have also organized themselves with increasing effectiveness as a diaspora—not merely in the refugee camps of neighboring states but in the wealthier West too. Irish Republicanism has long depended on Irish-American support; there have also been signs recently of its Unionist opponents organizing in the United States. Serbian and Croatian ethnic-nationalisms were transstate in the dual sense of being organized on a transrepublican basis within the former Yugoslav territory, and in drawing on the global Serb and Croat diasporas, again in North America but also in Western Europe and Australia. In these and in other contemporary cases, the organization of civil society on an ethnic-national basis threatens to undermine the idea of a plural, often panethnic civil society not only in the zones of conflict but also in areas of the advanced West where diaspora communities are strongly organized. The role of these civil societies in wars and even genocide shows a heightened tension between national and universal interpretations of civil values, which we noted existing in earlier periods.

On the other hand, some new wars have been transformed into global political crises in which civil society linkages have generated real support for victimized groups. Not only the protagonists of plural civil society, but the representatives of abused ethnic minorities, have begun to pressure Western states and legitimate international institutions to provide aid against genocide and violence. Because Western states often fail to perceive traditional strategic interests in the plights of victims of war and genocide, and are reluctant to commit people and resources to helping them, the appeal of the oppressed is often directed at Western civil society, and linkages between civil society in zones of crisis and in the West are strengthened. These links can be seen as elements in the forging of global civil society.

Two kinds of responses originating in Western civil societies have been crucial in generating support and protection. On the one hand, mass media have been the main agencies through which some (but by no means all) wars have become recognized as global crises, and through which political pressure for aid and intervention has developed. While the attention of mass media, especially television, to wars is undoubtedly selective, brief, and episodic, and is often led or circumscribed by the access for cameras and portable satellite dishes that determine picture availability, there is no doubt that it can have powerful effects. The intensive television campaign by news broadcasters during the Kurdish refugee crisis following the Gulf War, for example, helped push the American and British governments toward an unprecedented "humanitarian intervention" in northern Iraq, which reversed their previous stance of nonintervention. The possibility and success of this campaign depended very much on the prior nexus of responsibility between Western leaders and Iraq, and in this sense was atypical. But elsewhere, media have still nudged governments, however unevenly, toward interventions, and once intervention has taken place, have made them aware of the responsibility that goes with it.

On the other hand, humanitarian agencies and campaigns and other nongovernmental organizations

(NGOs) have been principal means both of mobilizing political pressure within Western societies, and of delivering aid within zones of crisis. Aid organizations mediate between donors and victims: in the zones of crisis, they are the physical representations of a substantial minority of Western publics who donate and raise funds for the downtrodden in war zones; within Western societies, they are the symbolic representatives of the victims, seeking to mobilize support. Aid organizations have some of the aspects of social movements: the goal of mobilizing a large popular base, and the aim of changing (if only in a limited ameliorative sense) social conditions. Of course, many agencies have longer term development as well as short-term aid objectives, and some seek to organize people in a more campaigning mode to alter general perceptions of Third World problems. To this extent, these organizations operate in a social movement mode; and yet their primary relationship to their supporters is a passive financial one. To this extent, they fail the participatory or mobilizing test of a social movement.

The international crises of the 1990s have indeed failed to precipitate classic social movement responses in Western societies. The Gulf War produced only brief intimations of antiwar movements of the kind seen in previous Western wars (above all Vietnam); there have been few significant social movements in response to other global crises. It seems that movements arose over nuclear weapons and the Vietnam war because these issues could be presented as simple moral-political questions, in which the issues of responsibility were direct. Despite the enormity of the mass killings in Bosnia, Rwanda, and so on, which were extensively publicized in the mass media, these sorts of situations neither appeared as simple, nor was there a clear nexus of responsibility involving Western governments. Their challenges did not fit, moreover, into established Cold War ideological paradigms: Western governments could not be represented so easily as "imperialist," nor could the demand for military intervention to protect victims of genocide be accommodated simply within the pacifist, or at least antimilitarist, traditions of most social movement activism.

Traditional representative institutions in national civil societies, however, have hardly proved very responsive to global crises. Just as the zones of crisis, nationalist definitions of civil society have been partly reinforced, so in the West most civil institutions remain national rather than global in orientation. National ideologies are much more passive and open than in war zones, but parties, churches, and other groups respond more to those crises that have national significance, for example where national troops are involved, than to the problems of victims. The transition from national to global civil society appears, from the experience of the new post-Cold War crises, to be in its early stages.

On the edge of the 21st century, therefore, profound changes in world politics are posing new dilemmas of war and violence in which the nature and role of civil society is very much a contested issue. Civil society is central to the new world politics of peace, but the relations between the plural, democratic idea of civil society and the national framework in which it has been cast require radical rethinking in a global era.

Also See the Following Articles

ARMS CONTROL AND DISARMAMENT TREATIES • COLD WAR • ETHNIC CONFLICTS AND COOPERATION • INTERNATIONAL RELATIONS, OVERVIEW • MASS MEDIA, GENERAL VIEW • MILITARISM • PEACE ORGANIZATIONS • TOTAL WAR, SOCIAL IMPACT OF • WARFARE, TRENDS IN • WORLD GOVERNMENT

Bibliography

Cohen, J. L. Arato, A. (1992). *Civil society and political theory*. Cambridge, MA: MIT Press.

Falk, R. (1995). *On humane governance*. Cambridge, England: Polity.

Frost, M. (1996). *Ethics in international relations: A constitutive theory*. Cambridge, England: Cambridge University Press.

Gill, S. (Ed.) (1993). *Historical materialism and international relations*. Cambridge, England: Cambridge University Press.

Mann, M. (1996). Authoritarian and liberal militarisms. In S. Smith, K. Booth, & M. Zalewski (Eds.), *International theory: Positivism and beyond*. Cambridge, England: Cambridge University Press.

Rosenau, J. N. (1991). *Turbulence in world politics*. Princeton: Princeton University Press.

Rosenberg, J. (1994). *The empire of civil society*. London: Verso.

Scott, A. (1990). *Ideology and the new social movements*. London: Unwin Hyman.

Seligman, A. (1992). *The idea of civil society*. New York: Free Press.

Shaw, M. (1996). *Civil society and media in global crises*. London: Pinter.

Shaw, M. (1996). *Post-military society*. Philadelphia: Temple University Press.

War Report (Journal) (1991–98). London: Institute of War and Peace Reporting.

Civil Wars

Errol A. Henderson
University of Florida

GLOSSARY

Civil War A major, sustained, violent conflict between the military forces of a state and insurgent forces comprised mainly of residents of the state.

Insurgency An armed conflict, wherein opponents of the government (insurgents) from within the state use organized violence against government forces to achieve their political aims.

Internationalized Civil War A civil war in which a third party intervenes on the behalf of the government forces or those of the insurgents.

Rebellion An armed uprising, or insurrection, of citizens against their government.

Revolution A violent attempt to overthrow both the political leadership of a state and the political system, itself.

Secession Separation from a political union usually with the intent of establishing an independent state.

I. DEFINITION OF CIVIL WAR

A civil war is a sustained, violent conflict between the military forces of a state and insurgent forces comprised mainly of residents of the state. Civil war is not synonymous with internal or intrastate war. The latter also includes conflict between groups in the state that does not involve the armed forces of the state, such as recent conflicts between warlords in Somalia, which are internal wars but not civil wars. In addition, civil war is characterized by a much higher scale of violence than riots or civil disturbances, which are more often sporadic and relatively disorganized forms of civil violence that are often of short duration. Therefore, the urban riots that spread throughout the United States in 1992 and the mass civil disturbances in France in the 1960s fall well short of the level of sustained violence present in civil wars. Also, civil disturbances are often directed at groups and institutions in the society other than the central government, which is the main protagonist in civil wars. Violence directed specifically at the regime in power, such as coups d'etat also often fail to attain the threshold of civil wars. While such conflicts often involve the armed forces of the society, coups d'etat are more explicitly extralegal executive transfers aimed at overthrowing the sitting regime's leaders. Coups are rarely accompanied by the sustained violence that occasions civil wars; however, coups can often spawn civil wars as in the case of the 1966 coup in Nigeria that gave rise to the Biafran Civil War the following year.

It is widely agreed that civil wars have three clear attributes: (1) they are primarily internal conflicts as opposed to conflicts between states; (2) the participants include the central government's forces pitted against an insurgency as opposed to violence between groups in the society that does not include government forces (e.g., communal conflict); and (3) the insurgents must be capable of effective resistance—which is absent in cases of massacres and genocides that are prosecuted by states but often do not involve non-state groups capable of effective resistance. Civil wars may also become internationalized, involving the intervention of third party states on behalf of either the government or insurgents. Examples abound during the Cold War era, including civil wars that escalated into major interstate wars such as the internationalized civil war in Vietnam.

It has been observed that civil wars have become increasingly destructive in the post-World War II era. For example, the Chinese Revolution from 1946 through 1950 resulted in approximately 1,000,000 battle deaths in this conflict between Chiang Kai-shek's government forces and those of Mao Zedong's communist insurgents. Yet it is not simply the greater availability of more destructive weapons of war in the modern era that has given rise to the prevalence of civil war. For example, the civil war in Rwanda in 1994 witnessed the massacre of more than 500,000 persons carried out largely with machetes and small arms. The vast increase in the number of states in the global system since the end of World War II may be partly to blame for the greater frequency of civil war during the postwar era; however, even controlling for the increased number of states in the world, the incidence of civil war during the postwar period has been greater than during the period from the end of the Congress of Vienna to the onset of World War II. Not only have they been more frequent, but many civil wars in the post World War II era have been quite long. In fact, of the 15 longest civil wars in the period from 1815 until 1980, more than half occurred in the postwar era. All told, it is probably a combination of the severity of these wars, their greater frequency, and their protracted nature that has contributed to the perception of their increasing importance.

From the end of World War II until the end of the Cold War in 1989, most civil wars occurred in the recently decolonized, or postcolonial, regions of Africa, Asia, and the Middle East and to a lesser extent in the Caribbean and in Central and South America. Civil wars during this period were virtually absent from North America and Europe, which experienced, at most, only two (the Greek Civil War and that in Cyprus). Only with the end of the Cold War and the fall of the Soviet Union did the regimes in Eastern Europe experience the paroxysms of civil violence similar to those which have continued to ravage the postcolonial states. During the Cold War era, the poverty and minimal institutional development of postcolonial states reduced their ability to provide effective governance for their countries and often left them ill-equipped to deter the insurgency of their disaffected citizenry (especially their armed forces). Many of these states became highly militarized and their citizens suffered under authoritarian generals who often used their troops as agents of internal repression. Meanwhile, modernization also induced social change in these states as they attempted to industrialize. The record of successful industrialization among postcolonial states was mixed (though largely poor) and development was strained by bloated militaries, burgeoning bureaucracies, and rapidly expanding populations. Political elites in postcolonial states faced increased demands from both their military counterelites and their increasingly urbanized citizenry who were both potential sources of insurgency. In addition, fissures in the culturally diverse and often rapidly urbanizing newly independent states often increased their susceptibility to institutional breakdown.

Cultural diversity within the postcolonial states often provided a basis for ethnic, linguistic, or religious mobilization by political elites who appealed to ethnic nationalism, or religious fundamentalism—often euphemisms for chauvinism and demagoguery—to mobilize their followers for political protest and insurgency. Further, the mixture of ethnocentrism, nationalism, and the arbitrariness of colonial boundaries appeared to foment civil war—especially secession—throughout Africa, Asia, and the Middle East. The weak regimes in the former colonized states often lacked legitimacy, thereby reducing their ability to mediate intercultural conflicts borne of rising expectations among the diverse groups in their states. As it were, most state elites catered to their preferred ethno-linguistic audience(s) whom they relied upon for support. Abrogating their role as impartial arbiter, they often evinced a penchant for repression rather than representation.

In addition, Cold War intrigue and exigency contributed to the escalation of conflicts in the postcolonial world. Since the United States and the Soviet Union were effectively deterred from engaging each other directly, the Third World became the battlefield upon which they prosecuted wars in attempts to solidify and expand their respective spheres of influence. Whether their policies were driven by fears of falling dominoes or imperialist expansion, the destructiveness of superpower intervention in the domestic politics of postcolonial states gave truth to the African saying that "when two elephants fight it is the grass that suffers."

Nevertheless, there is an emerging consensus that civil wars in the postcolonial world—even those during the height of the Cold War—resulted largely from internal factors. Fundamentally, postcolonial states were faced with the simultaneous challenges of state and nation building. State building involves the creation of effective institutions of government and the development of societal infrastructure to provide, at minimum, coordination for the executive, legislative, judicial, and military functions of the state as well as the establishment of institutional channels for political and social mobilization. In addition, state building requires the development of the physical infrastructure of the society to include transportation networks, hospitals, schools, housing, sanitation facilities, and other public welfare assets that are necessary for the functioning of the society. State building involves both coordinated planning and sacrifice; most importantly, it assumes a degree of social cohesion that generates among citizens a sense of identification with the state and a willingness to commit to the process of state building and the sacrifice of parochial interests to more collective ones. Nation building involves the creation of a national identity that supersedes local identities and loyalties that might compete with and preclude broader identification with the state. The objective in nation building is to make the nation the primary political unit to which citizens swear fealty.

Postcolonial states, especially, were almost always forced to build functional state institutions at the same time that they were attempting to galvanize a national consciousness and identity among the often diverse amalgamations of peoples in their territories. Where Western states were able to take each of these challenges (state and nation building, respectively) in turn, often over several centuries, postcolonial states were forced to accomplish both simultaneously. Without the glue of a common sense of national identification, there was little motivation for individuals to sacrifice their local institutions in order to contribute to the establishment of the often competing institutions of the state. Rival elites fed this recalcitrance since they often viewed state institutions as competitors to their traditional positions of leadership. The result was fissures within postcolonial states across cultural, class, and regional lines. In addition, postcolonial states were obliged to forge their national identities and promote state institutions during the cold war era and in an international political economy that often put draconian limits on their autonomous development.

While the incidence of civil war has become more pronounced in the postwar era—especially among the former colonies, one should not assume that civil wars that occurred prior to World War II had only a negligible impact on world history. For example, the U.S. Civil War (1861–1865) is often considered as the first modern war where the full weight of industrialization in the form of machine-made arms and the use of railroads to move troops and supplies was applied to warfare. Not only that, this war of attrition that basically turned on the North's success in disrupting the transportation and administrative systems on which the Confederacy relied for support of its troops in the field, actually presaged developments in World War I. Contemporaneous with the U.S. Civil War, the Manchu government in China fought the forces of Hung Hsiu-ch'uan in the most destructive civil war in the last two centuries, the Taiping Rebellion, which ravaged China and led to the deaths of millions. In this century, the Spanish Civil War began as a revolt of elements in the army led by Franco and conservative Catholics against the Republican government of Spain. While the Western democracies, especially France and Britain, demurred from aiding their democratic brethren, the fascist governments of Italy and Germany assisted Franco's forces. Ironically, much of the support for the Republicans came from the USSR. Only after Germany entered into a short-lived rapprochement with the Soviet Union through the Nazi-Soviet Non-Aggression Pact of 1939 did Soviet aid to the Republicans end and Franco's forces triumph. This internationalized civil war presaged the most destructive war in the history of humankind—World War II.

II. TYPES OF CIVIL WAR

There are generally three types of civil war as defined by the objective(s) of the insurgents: rebellion, revolution, and secession. Rebellion, or insurrection, refers to an armed uprising of citizens against their government, and it usually involves attempts to redress grievances with respect to a state's policies. For example, the recent rebellion in the Chiapas region of Mexico was initiated by Zapatista rebels seeking a greater degree of autonomy and better representation of their predominantly indigenous populations, but it did not seek to overthrow or to separate from the Mexican state. During the civil war in Lebanon in 1958, Sunni Muslims mobilized for a more equitable distribution of government resources, but not to overthrow the political system or to erect different political structures.

Where rebellion seeks the reform of the political system or a redress of grievances, revolution has as its objective the overthrow of both the political leadership of the state and the political system, itself. For example, the French, American, and Russian revolutions had as their objective the overthrow of the monarchical system, British colonial government, and Tsarism, respectively. The Cuban revolution had as its objective not only the overthrow of the Batista dictatorship but also the incipient capitalist system on the Caribbean island. Revolutions are often intended to overthrow colonial domination in pursuit of national self-determination for the colonized people(s). However, all of these cases of anticolonial conflict, or independence conflicts are not clearly civil wars. As a case in point, the independence struggle in Gandhi's India pursued a relatively nonviolent strategy (although the British were quite violent) in their attempt to overthrow British colonial domination in a conflict that would not be categorized as a civil war. On the other hand, revolutionaries in Algeria, Angola, and Kenya utilized less nonviolent measures in their pursuit of self-determination and fought what were more clearly civil wars (technically, anticolonial civil wars) to extirpate themselves from French, Portuguese, and British colonial domination, respectively.

Unlike rebellion and revolution, secession has as its objective the separation of a political entity from a larger political unit, usually with the intent of establishing an independent state. The U.S. Civil War of 1861–1865 was a prototypal secessionist civil war. Because of the centrality of territory and population to a state's power calculus, secession is often the most severe form of civil war because states rarely accede to the loss of their territory without resort to arms. For example, in 1971 the eastern region of Pakistan was wrestled free from the state of Pakistan, becoming the independent state of Bangladesh, in a bloody civil war that turned on the intervention of Indian troops in support of the insurgency. Secession wars are often of long duration such as the attempt by Eritreans to secede from Ethiopia, which precipitated a civil war that lasted more than 30 years. Often secession struggles involve a strong cultural component where culturally dissimilar groups attempt to separate from culturally heterogeneous societies—such as in the case of the Kurds, who have for decades fought civil wars in their attempt to secede from Iraq, Iran, and Turkey in order to form an independent Kurdistan.

III. CORRELATES OF CIVIL WAR

One can distinguish between human agency and contextual factors that increase the likelihood of civil war. The former relate to the individual and collective dispositions to insurgency that are the more immediate causes of civil war: these may derive from relative deprivation or rational actor motivations for collective action. The latter refers to the characteristics of the state, region, and global system that may be more remote, or permissive, factors associated with civil war. There is an absence of theoretical consensus on the role of human agency factors in civil war and this largely reflects the ongoing tension between relative deprivation and rational actor explanations of civil violence. Research findings on the role of contextual factors in civil war are less disputed but they are not conclusive. For example, it appears that states with higher levels of economic development are less prone to civil war than poorer states. In addition, more mature states are less likely to experience civil wars than younger states. States that are more militarized and those that have a history of past civil wars are more vulnerable to insurgency. Moreover, while there does not appear to be a direct relationship between the cultural diversity of a state and its likelihood of experiencing civil war, states in which ethnic, religious, linguistic or racial groups are culturally polarized seem to be at greater risk for civil war.

An interesting relationship emerges with respect to the association between a state's level of democracy and its likelihood of civil war. Recent studies suggest an "inverted U" relationship between a state's level of democracy and its likelihood of experiencing civil war. The assumption is that states with higher levels of democracy are unlikely to experience civil war because of the availability of alternate channels for protest within the political system. States that are more autocratic, also, are less likely to experience civil wars because governments in those states are more likely to effectively repress dissent and stifle protest. However, states with intermediate levels of democracy, "semi-democracies," such as those undergoing democratization—the transformation of a regime to a more democratic form of government—have the highest probability of experiencing civil war. These relationships are evident, for example, in India where the spread of democracy has increased access to education, technology, and political power for previously disenfranchised groups such as Muslims and "untouchables" while also generating a backlash from segments of the Hindu community. This relationship is even more apparent in Africa, where autocratic regimes appear to enjoy greater stability than more democratic regimes that often fall prey to insurgency. For example, Uganda's nascent democracy was terminated by the civil war in the summer of 1966, Nigeria's Third Republic was overturned by the civil violence of 1984, and more recently, the civil war in Congo-Brazzaville began shortly after the country's first democratically elected president took office. While African autocracies have endured for decades and the continent's more mature democracies such as Botswana and Mauritius, have not experienced civil wars, Africa's "semi-democracies" are often victims of insurgency.

It is important to remember that these state level factors do not operate in a vacuum. To be sure, both regional and systemic level factors also play important roles in dampening or exacerbating civil conflict. In particular, the intervention of a major (or regional) power in civil disputes may reduce the levels of civil conflict in a state. For example, the intervention of NATO forces and the implementation of the Dayton Accords helped to reduce the level of conflict in the civil war in the former Yugoslavia. Similarly, the intervention of Vietnam in the civil war in Cambodia (Kampuchea) brought an end to the vicious regime of Pol Pot and the slaughter of millions of Cambodians in that country's "killing fields." What is no less likely is that the intervention of third parties may intensify ongoing civil wars as in the case of the Indian intervention in Sri Lanka's civil war, U.S. intervention in Vietnam's civil war, the Soviet Union's intervention in Afghanistan's civil war, and South Africa's intervention in Angola's civil war.

While maybe less straightforward, systemic level factors are no less important in understanding the onset and spread of civil wars. The most important of these systemic factors is the distribution of power in the global system, for example, whether there is a bipolar distribution of power such as during the Cold War standoff between the Soviet Union and the United States, or a multipolar distribution of power as was evident in the interwar period where power was clustered about several states including the United States, Great Britain, France, Japan, Italy, and eventually the Soviet Union and Germany. The most significant impact of system level variables on civil wars relates to their influence on the spread of civil violence beyond the initial participants to include the major powers. In bipolar systems, there appears to be a decreased likelihood that the major powers will be dragged into civil conflicts that expand to full-scale major power war (e.g. the United States and the Soviet Union never fought each other during the bipolar cold war era). In addition, in bipolar systems, the two major powers may dominate their respective spheres to such an extent that they can stifle potential insurgency in the states within their blocs. This conflict dampening impact of systemic factors appears less obvious in multipolar systems. In multipolar systems, the likelihood of interstate war resulting from major power intervention in civil war is increased because the greater number of major powers in the system increase the probability of the intervention of at least one of them and the subsequent intervention of others. The multipolar scenario is consistent with explanations of the onset of Word War I insofar as the civil violence resulting from South Slav nationalism in Bosnia compelled Austria-Hungary to attack Serbia, which was viewed as the nucleus of South Slav nationalism, following the assassination of the heir to the Austro-Hungarian throne in Sarajevo. Austria-Hungary was supported by Germany and later Turkey and Bulgaria, while Russia—allied with the Serbs—came to their support and through its alliance ties brought in the major powers of France, Great Britain, Japan, and ultimately the United States and Italy to offset the Central Powers. In this way, one can appreciate the impact of a systemic level factor such as multipolarity contributing to the escalation and diffusion of the civil conflict in Bosnia into the most destructive war in the history of the world up to that time. In sum, the major impact of regional and systemic factors is their contribution to the expansion of civil wars. It is to these matters that we turn in the next section.

IV. EXPANSION OF CIVIL WARS

Civil wars expand, or escalate, as a function of several factors that can be conceptualized in terms of vertical and horizontal escalation by both insurgents as well as governments. In vertical escalation, there is an intensification of the civil war usually resulting from changes in the political goals and opportunities of either the government forces, the insurgents, or both. For example, civil wars can expand vertically when insurgents, encouraged by early victory, abandon more reformist objectives and strategies of rebellion and attempt full scale revolution instead. In one case, the Hukbulahup (Huk) rebellion in the Philippines emerged from an anti-Japanese guerrilla movement in central Luzon that pushed for inclusion in the postwar Philippines government. The movement only turned to armed struggle when their reformist goals failed to materialize; however, the combination of land reform by the Magsaysay government, U.S. assistance to the regime, a governmental policy of land reform, and the failure of the insurgency to expand beyond its original constituency served to undermine the rebellion. The popular insurrection against the Somoza dictatorship in Nicaragua gained in strength and eventually resulted in Somoza fleeing the country; however, an element of the insurgents, the Sandinistas, transformed the larger reformist objectives of the insurgency and pursued a Marxist style revolution of the Nicaraguan political system.

For the government, expansion may involve a change of policy from accommodation or mediation of rebel demands to repression of dissent and destruction of the insurgency. For example, the genocide of hundreds of thousands of Tutsis and moderate Hutus by the Hutu-dominated Presidential Guard in Rwanda in 1994 was preceded less than a year before by the settlement of that country's civil war and an agreement on a power sharing arrangement between the parties. In Bangladesh, Yahya Khan's attempt to deny Bengalis in east Pakistan an electoral victory and their quest for a degree of autonomy within the Pakistani state quickly became a policy of brutal repression of the Bengalis including the torture, rape, murder, and imprisonment of resistance members and sympathizers and ultimately a full-scale civil war.

The more conflict intensifying form of expansion, horizontal escalation, results from the intervention of third party states (through the introduction of military forces or weapons transfers) on the side of the government or insurgent forces. What results is an internationalized civil war such as occurred in the following cases from the turn of the century to shortly after the end of the cold war: Morocco (1907, 1911), Iran (1909), the USSR (1918), China (1927), Spain (1936), Greece (1944), Vietnam (1961), Zaire (1960), Yemen (1962), Laos (1964), the Dominican Republic (1965), Lebanon (1958, 1975), Angola (1975), Cambodia (1979), Mozambique (1979), Chad (1980), Sri Lanka (1983, 1987), Iraq (1985), Liberia (1989, 1992), Russia (1991), and Bosnia (1992).

Civil wars expand as a function of several factors, and the most important appear to be (1) the spread of refugees into bordering states; (2) the presence of ethnic, linguistic, or religious confreres in neighboring states; and/or (3) shared ideology or alliances between the participants and potential patrons (or a combination of several or all of these). First, civil wars are more likely to spread in cases where they create refugees who flee across international borders to safer havens in adjacent states as in the case of Rwandan Tutsis who, in 1994, fled the genocide in their homeland into neighboring Uganda, which then provided support for the Tutsi-led forces who subsequently wrestled control of the Rwandan state from the perpetrators of the genocide. In 1971, India's Indira Gandhi was spurred to intervene in the conflict in East Pakistan as much by geopolitical reasons as her concern that more than 10 million Bengalis had fled into northeast India to escape the brutal repression of Yahya Khan's forces in the civil war in eastern Pakistan (now Bangladesh).

Civil war may also spread into adjacent states as part of the purposive policy of one of the belligerents. For example, after West African states had established a regional multinational force, ECOMOG, to help quell the devastating civil war in Liberia, Charles Taylor's faction formed a spin-off group composed of mainly dissidents in neighboring Sierra Leone who spread the war to that country in an effort to pressure that state into withdrawing its military support for ECOMOG. Conflict between these forces and Sierra Leonean troops ultimately led to the overthrow of Sierra Leone's president. South Africa's apartheid regime followed a clear policy of destabilizing the Frontline States (Angola, Botswana, Mozambique, Tanzania, Zambia, Zimbabwe) not only to support their clients in the civil wars raging in several of them, but also to prevent aid from those states from reaching insurgent forces in South Africa.

Second, the presence of ethnic or religious confreres in a warring state may compel leaders to intervene on behalf of their cultural cousins. For example, the Russian Federation has intervened in the civil conflict in Moldova on behalf of ethnic Slavs who organized a secession struggle to establish the Dniester Republic. Muslim-dominated Pakistan continues to support Muslim rebels in the Indian province of Kashmir. Similarly, predominantly Hindu India has intervened on behalf of predominantly Hindu Tamils in Sinhalese dominated Sri Lanka.

Third, shared ideology, as well, is often a pretext for intervention as in the case of Soviet and Western intervention in many of the civil wars during the Cold War era epitomized in the cases of Vietnam and Afghanistan. But minor powers may also intervene in civil wars in order to support their ideological fellow travelers. For example, Nasser's intervention in the Yemeni Civil War was largely spawned by his antimonarchical stance and his vision of pan-Arabism. South Africa's policy of white supremacy allowed it to find common cause with Rhodesia's pariah regime and to support it in its civil war against the indigenous African-led insurgency in Zimbabwe. What is often more common is the support of international diasporas to their cultural kin abroad. For example, Chinese American, Greek Americans, Jewish Americans, African Americans, Polish

Americans, and Irish Americans have provided material support for parties in civil conflicts in their cultural homelands. Similarly, various global diasporas including ethnic Chinese in Malaysia, ethnic Indians in Africa, Jews in South Africa and Europe, Arabs outside the Middle East, and Africans in the West are among the important sources of aid to parties of conflicts throughout the world's regions.

Importantly, just as civil wars expand they can also contract. This contraction involves the limiting of the goals or objectives of the parties of the dispute, for example, from secession to rebellion for the insurgents, as in the case of the Sudanese Civil War, or from repression to accommodation for the government, as in the case of the Russian response to the civil war in Chechnya. Contraction may result from several factors including a change in leadership toward one that seeks to resolve the conflict, the termination of military assistance to the belligerents, war weariness on the part of the belligerents, the successful intervention of third party mediators, or the military defeat of one of the parties. If there is a successful contraction of the civil war then the opportunity for resolving the conflict is increased. In the next section, we discuss some of the factors associated with the resolution of civil wars.

V. RESOLUTION OF CIVIL WARS

The resolution of civil wars can take the obvious form of the cessation of hostilities due to the military defeat of either party; nonetheless, even in the case of a clear military outcome, the manner by which the civil war ends might encourage dissatisfied factions to splinter off and generate further insurgency in pursuit of objectives denied by the outcome. This may occur even in the case of an actual settlement between the disputants. For example, dissatisfaction with the political settlement that allowed for the partition of Ireland following the armed conflict between Irish nationalists and British occupation forces in the 1920s split the insurgent forces between supporters of Michael Collins who (albeit reluctantly) accepted partition and those of Eamon de Valera who opposed it. This dissension within the insurgency following a settlement of the major conflict precipitated further civil war on the island, which continues in various forms up to the present. In another example (as noted above), while the civil war in Rwanda appeared to be settled, extremist Hutu elements who were dissatisfied with alleged government overtures to Tutsis assassinated the Hutu president and then set upon a coordinated plan to massacre hundreds of thousands of Tutsis and moderate Hutus. Often, splinter groups may continue the civil wars years after the initial conflict has ended, as in the New People's Army rebellion in the Philippines in 1972, which emerged from many of the unresolved issues related to the earlier Huk rebellion. In fact, the leader of the military arm of the insurgency, Commander Dante, was a former Huk guerrilla leader who had seceded from the Huk army.

The clearest resolution of civil wars arises from the establishment of a clear preponderance of military power on the part of the government forces or the insurgents. For the government, this is usually a matter of reestablishing its authority and military preeminence within its territory such as was the case with the Union forces over those of the Confederacy in the U.S. Civil War, or alternatively, the Russian Civil War is an example of insurgents overcoming the forces of the government—and as is often the case in these instances—with a sizable number of government forces switching sides in favor of the insurgents. In the nuclear era—where there was a real fear that civil wars would draw in the superpowers—there was an increased impetus for third party resolution of civil wars whether through the good offices of outside parties, the mediation efforts of intergovernmental or nongovernmental organizations, or through the intervention of international peacekeeping forces. In one case, Zaire's dictator, Mobutu Sese Seko, was an unlikely—and unsuccessful—mediator of the Angolan Civil War, which was exacerbated by, among other things, superpower support for the opposing sides. More successful third party conflict resolution was practiced by Costa Rica's head of state, Oscar Arias, who formulated the peace plan that bears his name and provided the blueprint for the resolution of the civil wars in Guatemala, Nicaragua, and El Salvador. To be sure, conflict resolution does not have to be generated by the actions of third parties; for example, in Colombia's protracted civil war known as La Violencia, the rival political parties, themselves, adopted a consociational arrangement in which it was agreed that each would rotate in power from 1958 to 1974. The implementation of this agreement in 1958 did not end the conflict, although it helped to moderate the country's protracted civil war.

Negotiated settlements, however, may fall apart as a result of changing power relations among the factions involved. For example, the Lebanese Civil War of 1975–1976 emerged, in part, from changing demographics among the primary communal groups within the state. These changes undermined the legitimacy of the power-sharing arrangement, the National Pact of 1943, which relied on a census from the 1930s to determine the dispensation of important political offices in the state. The agreement determined that Christians comprised half of the population of the country and that Maronite Christians, in particular, were the preponderant communal group and therefore they were allowed to dominate the presidency. Seats in parliament were allocated in favor of Christians, with Sunni Muslims accorded a smaller role in the legislature. Shia Muslims were marginalized in this arrangement; however, by 1975, the Shias were the largest of all the communal groups and the Muslims, altogether, comprised a greater share of the total population than Lebanese Christians. What is more, the socioeconomic marginalization of the burgeoning Shia community in the context of these changed demographics was an important factor precipitating the civil war in Lebanon in 1975.

What is required for the successful resolution of civil conflicts, according to Zartman (1995), is the presence of a mutually hurting stalemate, which is a condition wherein the parties are deadlocked and neither can gain effective advantage through further fighting. At this point, it is argued, both begin to search for alternatives and it is here that third party intervention may contribute to the separation of the disputants, the effective deployment of peacekeeping forces, the mediation of the dispute, and the resolution of the conflict. For example, the South African government's military forces were not militarily exhausted nor were they defeated in their civil war with African insurgents but they came to realize that the costs of maintaining the apartheid state was much too great to sustain. Similarly, the insurgents led by the forces of the African National Congress and the Pan-Africanist Congress realized that they did not have the military capability to defeat the government's military forces even while they realized that the government could not destroy their movement. From this stalemate, a mediated settlement was forged that dramatically transformed the country, although economic and military power still remains primarily in the hands of white South Africans—those who profited most from apartheid—and that does not bode well for the peace process in that country. In a similar situation, the Sandinista regime was not militarily defeated although it was compelled to accede to popular demands for free elections during the U.S.-supported insurgency in Nicaragua. Therefore, it is clear that civil wars can be resolved even where the parties have not won a clear military victory or suffered a clear military defeat.

In recent years, the United Nations has intervened in several civil wars as peacekeepers and they have contributed (if in some cases only moderately) to the dampening of the conflicts in El Salvador, Mozambique, Nicaragua, Haiti, Namibia, South Africa, Cambodia, Tajikstan, and Western Sahara. The UN has been more successful in preventing civil wars from developing into superpower confrontations as in the civil wars in Congo, Cyprus, Lebanon, and Yemen; however, it has been less successful at preventing hostilities from reemerging later, as each of these cases demonstrates. In addition, there have also been some glaring UN failures, as in the civil wars in Burundi, Liberia, and Rwanda. UN peacekeeping initiatives have played more of a conflict constraining role than a conflict resolution role. Moreover, it appears that when the interests of the five permanent members of the Security Council (P-5) are not at stake, there is relative inaction on the part of the UN as in the recent civil wars in the interlacustrine region of Africa. When the interests of P-5 members (or their allies) are at stake—as in the case of the conflict in Cyprus or the former Yugoslavia—UN intervention is more likely.

All told, the resolution of civil wars requires a nuanced strategy of multinational peacemaking and peacekeeping including the separation of the combatants, establishment of cease-fires, the promotion of confidence building measures, reductions in arms sales to the belligerents, and mediation. However, the cessation of hostilities does not necessarily portend the actual termination of the conflict unless the underlying factors that gave rise to the conflict are adequately addressed. These issues might be quite extensive and complex, therefore, the best strategy for decreasing the probability of the recurrence of civil wars is to provide an environment for the peaceful resolution of civil disputes in the first place. This entails, inter alia, the development of democratic political systems, open and productive economic systems, civic—as opposed to racial, ethnic, or religious—requirements for citizenship, the professionalization of the armed forces, the teaching of a non-chauvinist curriculum in schools, the development of responsive institutions to redress citizen grievances, and the demilitarization of society.

In addition, the occurrence of civil wars often suggests that the process of state or nation-building in the affected country is far from complete. This was as much the case in the U.S. Civil War in the nineteenth century as in the Biafran Civil War of the 20th century. In some cases, it suggests that independent state building has not been successful and that secession may be necessary, as in the case of Eritrea or the Czech Republic. Although it is not always clear whether the nature of a civil war suggests the need for integration or secession, the interests of the international community should be geared to what is in the best interests of the parties to these conflicts instead of what is the preferred strategy of the superpowers who, in the past, often seemed more interested in recruiting new states to their respective blocs and destabilizing states in the rival camp. What is important to remember is that civil wars often result from the internal demands on societies; nonetheless, an international environment that is conducive to the nonviolent resolution of such conflicts remains an indispensable element in promoting peace and preventing civil war.

VI. CONCLUSION

Civil wars have become increasingly prevalent in their incidence and increasingly deadly in their result. For the most part, factors that give rise to civil wars seem to be related to the problems associated with state and nation building in many of the world's younger states. As noted above, postcolonial states, especially, are often forced to simultaneously attend to state and nation building and the problems related to both. Civil wars in the post-Cold War era emerge from a variety of factors and even the process of democratization—that is often viewed as a panacea for civil conflict—is implicated in some degree in the incidence of civil war. While mature democracies seem to be less prone to experience civil wars (as do mature autocracies), "semi-democracies," or states with only moderate levels of democracy, evince an increased likelihood of experiencing civil war. Nonetheless, the development of democratic political systems is an important ingredient in the building of viable and less war-prone states; however, we are cautioned that violence often accompanies this process. Our challenge is to attempt to find more nonviolent avenues for political and economic development. The international community has an important role to play in support of these objectives; nonetheless, the states themselves—their policies, practices, and programs—will ultimately determine their prospects for development and their likelihood of experiencing—or avoiding—civil war.

Also See the Following Articles

COLD WAR • COLONIALISM AND IMPERIALISM • ETHNIC CONFLICTS AND COOPERATION • MILITARISM AND DEVELOPMENT IN UNDERDEVELOPED SOCIETIES • PEACE AND DEMOCRACY • WARFARE, MODERN • WARFARE, TRENDS IN

Bibliography

Brown, M. (Ed.). (1996). *The international dimensions of internal conflict.* Cambridge: MIT Press.

Lichbach, M. (1995). *The rebel's dilemma.* Ann Arbor, MI: University of Michigan Press.

Licklider, R. (Ed.). (1993). *Stopping the killing: How civil wars end.* New York: New York University Press.

Midlarsky, M. (Ed.). (1992). *The internationalization of communal strife.* New York: Routledge.

Small, M., & J. D. Singer (1982). *Resort to arms: International and civil wars, 1816–1980.* Beverly Hills, CA: Sage.

Small, D., & Singer, J. D. (1996). *International and civil wars. Correlates of War project data.* University of Michigan, Ann Arbor.

Zartman, I. W. (1995). *Elusive peace: Negotiating an end to civil wars.* Washington, DC: Brookings.

Clan and Tribal Conflict

Keith F. Otterbein
State University of New York at Buffalo

GLOSSARY

Cultural Unit An ethnic unit composed of contiguous political communities that are culturally similar. In most instances the cultural unit is the same as a society or culture.

External War Warfare between political communities that are not members of the same cultural unit; that is, they are culturally different. There are two aspects of external war that can be measured separately: political communities of a cultural unit can either attack or be attacked by culturally different political communities.

Feuding A type of armed combat occurring within a political community in which, if a homicide occurs, the kin of the deceased take revenge through killing the offender or any member of his kin group.

Feuding with Compensation Feuding that occurs if the relatives of the deceased sometimes accept compensation in lieu of blood revenge.

Feuding without Compensation Feuding that occurs if the relatives of the deceased are expected to take revenge through killing the offender or any close relative of his. The possibility of paying compensation does not exist.

Fraternal Interest Groups Localized groups of related males who can resort to aggressive measures when the interests of their members are threatened.

Internal War Warfare between political communities within the same cultural unit.

Matrilocal Residence Marital residence rule that requires the groom to reside with the bride, either nearby or in the home of the bride's parents.

Military Organizations A type of social organization that engages in armed combat with other similar organizations in order to obtain certain goals.

Neolocal Residence Marital residence in which the bride and groom establish a household independent of the location of the parental home of either partner. Unlike matrilocal and patrilocal residence, a rule requiring an independent location is rarely specified.

Patrilocal Residence Marital residence rule that requires the bride to reside with the groom, either nearby or in the home of the groom's parents.

Political Community A group of people whose membership is defined in terms of occupancy of a common territory and who have an official with the special function of announcing group decisions—a function exercised at least once a year. There is usually more than one political community in a cultural unit.

Polygyny The marriage of one man to two or more women at the same time.

War, Causes of The causes of war—that is, the reasons that military organizations go to war—include subjugation and tribute, land, plunder, trophies and honors, revenge, and defense. These are goals of war.

Warfare Armed combat between political communities.

Warriors, Nonprofessional Military personnel who have not had intensive training in the art of war.

Warriors, Professional Military personnel who devote a substantial part of their time during their early adulthood to intensive training, which may involve not only practice in the use of weapons but also practice in performing maneuvers. They may be members of age-grades, military societies, or standing armies.

CLAN CONFLICT is feud; tribal conflict is war. Feuding takes place within a political community, war takes place between political communities. War between culturally similar political communities is internal war, while war between culturally different political communities is external war. Figure 1 shows the interrelationship among these several forms of armed combat. Armed combat is fighting with weapons.

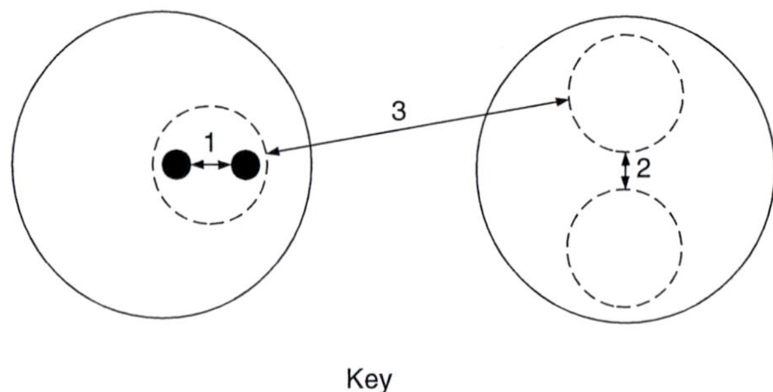

FIGURE 1 Diagram of major concepts.

I. FRATERNAL INTEREST GROUPS

A. What They Are

Fundamental to the understanding of clan and tribal conflicts is the recognition that when conflict of a violent nature arises among nonliterate peoples, as well as among ethnic groups in modern nations, localized groups of related males—fraternal interest groups—pursuing their own interests are likely to be responsible for the conflict and violence. These fraternal interest groups constitute the vengeance parties that engage in feuding in tribal societies as well as in modern polities, and they form the backbone of the military organizations of the majority of tribal societies.

B. Cause of Feuding and Internal War

In 1960, in one of anthropology's seminal papers, H. U. E. Thoden Van Velzen and W. Van Wetering demonstrated that the presence of fraternal interest groups is responsible for the conflicts that occur within local groups. Fraternal interest groups—power groups of related males—arise through following a rule of patrilocal residence and/or practicing polygyny. In a cross-cultural study, that is, a study examining ethnographic descriptions of practices of a sample of societies, K. F. Otterbein and C. S. Otterbein showed that fraternal interest groups, using either patrilocal residence or polygyny as an index of the presence of fraternal interest groups, predict feuding. K. F. Otterbein, in other cross-cultural studies, showed that the presence of fraternal interest groups in a society predicted rape, often a cause of feuding, and internal war. In another study Otterbein showed how fraternal interest groups, feuding, and capital punishment were interrelated in tribal society. In tribes with fraternal interest groups executions of wrongdoers are carried out by members of the wrongdoer's own clan. The homicides that occur between feuding clans are not capital punishment. In tribes without fraternal interest groups but with councils of elders, executions are performed only by political leaders; thus, capital punishment in these tribes can serve to limit the occurrence of homicide.

C. Types of Societies

Although societies with fraternal interest groups based on patrilocal residence are a majority of those described by ethnographers (about 70%), there are nevertheless numerous societies without fraternal interest groups, which have matrilocal or neolocal residence. Thus two categories of societies can be delineated and contrasted: (1) societies with fraternal interest groups have much conflict, rape, feuding, internal war, and intraclan executions, whereas (2) societies without fraternal interest groups have little conflict, no rape, no feuding, no internal war, and politywide executions. These are ideal types; not all societies neatly fit into one of them. Yet, fraternal interest groups, rape, feuding, internal war, and capital punishment are interrelated; rape can lead to feud, while the military organization whose core is a fraternal interest group can on one day attack a member of a kinship group within the political community (an act leading to feuding or continuing a feud) and on the next day ambush a member of another political community (an act of internal war). Thus, the emergence of category (1) societies helps to explain the widespread occurrence of violence in tribal societies. These are the societies that W. T. Divale and M. Harris argue have the male supremacist complex.

II. FEUDING

A. Essential Elements

A recent review by K. F. Otterbein of definitions of feuding revealed two essential elements. First, kin groups are involved, homicides occur, and the killings occur as revenge for injustice (the terms *duty, honor, righteous,* and *legitimate* appear in discussions of the motivation for the homicides). Second, three or more alternating killings or acts of violence occur. Nonetheless, if an unsuccessful attempt at a counterkilling leads to the killing of one of the attackers, as occurred in the Turner-Howard feud in 19th-century Eastern Kentucky on several occasions, I would classify the sequence of killings as feuding. Incidentally, mortality in that feud was one-sided: 13 Turners died, and no Howards. However, one element of feud is in dispute: whether the unit within which feuding occurs is political or ethnolinguistic. It appears that in politically developed societies the unit is the political community, and that in acephelous (meaning headless) societies without any formal overall political authority (the identification of headmen is nearly impossible) the unit is the ethnolinguistic group. Nevertheless, in only a small number of societies is it difficult to identify the political community.

B. Compensation

In many feuding societies the feud can be ended by the payment of compensation. Indeed, feuding societies can be classified into two categories: (1) Feuding without compensation, in which there is no institutionalized means by which compensation can be paid. (2) Feuding with compensation, in which payment of compensation can either prevent a counterkilling or stop a feud. In a sample of 50 societies, Otterbein and Otterbein found that 16% fell into the first type, while 28% fell into the second type. The majority of cases (56%) fell into a third category that included societies in which homicides were rare, or in which, following a homicide, a formal judicial procedure came into effect, leading to settlement through compensation. Or the killer might be executed. Christopher Boehm argues that feuding with compensation is a means of controlling conflict—in his view it is an alternative to warfare. Feuding arises, Boehm suggests, because the potential combatants realize that uncontrolled warfare at close quarters would be disastrous.

C. Legitimacy of and Target of Vengeance

In addition to whether compensation can by paid, two other dimensions to feuding have been considered. Karen Ericksen and Heather Horton in 1992 used a range of six categories to describe the legitimacy of kin group vengeance: (1) moral imperative; (2) most appropriate action; (3) circumstantial; (4) last resort; (5) formal adjudication only; and (6) individual self-redress. The second dimension used three categories to describe possible targets of vengeance: (1) anyone in the wrongdoer's kin group; (2) the wrongdoer if possible, otherwise selected members of his kin group; (3) wrongdoer only. In 1985 Otterbein questioned whether feuding was a legitimate course of action for a kin group that believed itself to be wronged. For some researchers feud occupies an intermediate position between law and crime, and thus has been designated quasi-law or self-help. Although feuding may be carried out following a large body of culturally defined rules, the political leaders and members of kinship groups not involved in the feud are usually highly desirous of seeing the feud end or be settled. Political leaders—it is the nature of the status role—almost always attempt to abrogate to themselves the exclusive right to judge whether a crime has been committed and to do the punishing. For these reasons, Otterbein views feuding not as a legal action, but rather as a highly disruptive sequence of antisocial acts. Actions taken by political leaders to prevent feuding are viewed as legal, the revenge killings of kinship groups as extralegal. The feuds of 19th-century Eastern Kentucky illustrate this well. Wilson Howard, who admitted to killing five Turners, was hanged. In the French-Eversole feud, Tom Smith, a French supporter and killer of six Eversoles was also hanged. Furthermore, in the Martin–Tolliver and Baker–Howard feuds, the governor of Kentucky sent in books to prevent further killings.

D. Extent of Feuding

The extent of feuding can be inferred from two cross-cultural studies, one by Otterbein and Otterbein, the other by Ericksen and Horton; each examined ethnographic descriptions of the feuding practices of a sample of societies. The former found that 44% of their sample societies had feuding, the latter found that 54% of their sample viewed violent action as legitimate. A cross-cultural study of homicide conducted by Martin Daly and Margo Wilson found that 95% of their sample societies harbored the idea of taking a life for a life. To achieve near universality the researchers needed to include capital punishment as evidence of the desire for blood revenge, a result which is not surprising since Otterbein found, using the same sample, that 51 of the 53 societies, or 96%, for which there was information had the death penalty. The results of these studies lead to the conclusion that although approximately 50% of the world's societies practice feuding, the desire for revenge—a life for a life—may be nearly universal.

E. Feuding versus Internal War

Can feuding be distinguished from warfare in small-scale societies? Otterbein believes that these two types of violent conflict can be distinguished if a political community can be identified. He looks for a political leader who announces group decisions. The group is often small. Some researchers have despaired of distinguishing feuding from warfare and include feuding under the rubric of internal war (war within the same cultural or ethnolinguistic unit). But to most researchers feuding and warfare appear to be qualitatively different.

One of the few societies whose armed combat had not been influenced by Western contact when they were first studied by anthropologists is that of Bellona Island, a small Polynesian outlier. Rolf Kuschel recorded "feuds" stretching back 21 generations and ending only in 1938. Application of the concept of political community to a specific case leads to reclassification of Bellona feuding as warfare. On Bellona Island the clans were politically autonomous fraternal interest groups. The feuding of these clans can thus be classified as warfare. Further support for this interpretation arises from Kuschel's contention that the intent of a raid was not to "even the score" but to reduce enemy manpower. Once a pattern of mutual raiding was set in motion it was likely to continue until one group was nearly annihilated.

III. MILITARY ORGANIZATIONS

A. What They Are

Military organizations, which can be viewed as a type of social organization, engage in armed combat in order to obtain certain goals. They differ, however, from other organizations in that the goals or objectives they pursue are usually directed at military organizations in other political communities. The goals of war include subjugation and tribute, land, plunder, trophies and honors, defense, and revenge. All these objectives can be achieved only at the expense of other political communities. When two military organizations engage in an armed combat, the outcome will depend upon the efficiency of their respective military practices. A victorious military organization makes a political community militarily successful and increases its likelihood of survival in conflicts between political communities. The successful political community will almost undoubtedly expand territorially.

B. Composition of Military Organizations

The warriors comprising a military organization may be either professionals or nonprofessionals. Professionals, in contrast to nonprofessionals, devote a substantial part of their time during their early adulthood to intensive training, which may involve not only practice in the use of weapons but also practice in performing maneuvers. They may be members of age-grades comprising all males of a given age, of military societies, or of standing armies, or they may serve as mercenaries employed for a specific purpose. Political communities with age-grades, military societies, and standing armies are considered to have military organizations composed solely of professionals. Political communities that employ mercenaries to lead, train, or assist untrained warriors are considered to have both professionals and nonprofessionals in their military organizations. If all members of a military organization are warriors who have not had specific intensive training in the art of war, the military organization is considered to be composed solely of nonprofessionals. If both professional and nonprofessional warriors are absent, there is of course no military organization. Otterbein's cross-cultural study of war examined the military practices of 50 cultures. It was found that 9 political communities had military organizations composed of professionals, 13 had military organizations that included both professionals and nonprofessionals, 24 had military organizations composed of nonprofessionals, and only 4 had no military organization. The vast majority of tribal peoples have military organizations composed only of nonprofessionals. These military organizations are frequently composed of fraternal interest groups.

C. Why Military Organizations?

The fact that few political communities have no military organization raises the fundamental question: Why do most political communities have military organizations? The answer seems to be that if a political community is to have contact with other political communities and yet to remain a social entity, it needs to have the means to defend itself from the attacks of neighbors and to retaliate if the attacks have been successfully made against them. The four political communities without military organizations, mentioned above, are all found in isolated locations. Their members are descendants of groups that had been driven from other areas and had taken refuge on an island, in arctic wasteland, or on the top of a mountain. Relocated in an area where they were protected by their isolation, they no longer found it necessary to maintain a military organization. Thus a political community that does not have a military organization capable of defending it will probably be annihilated and absorbed into other political communities unless it is able to flee and protect itself, not by arms, but by hiding in an isolated area. Robert Dentan's "geographic refuge" inhabited by foragers who adapt to slave raids by their ability to disperse and regroup elaborates this theme. The foragers in Dentan's "geographic refuge" become nonviolent and develop values of peaceability. The Sewai of southeast Asia are his prime example. This does not always occur. The Waoroni of the western Amayon who occupy a geographic refuge were until recent years able to keep foreigners at bay with their long thrusting spears. A further indication that a military organization is a necessity, if a political community is to persist through time, is to be found in the fact that defense and revenge are universal causes of war. Several studies have shown that all known military organizations go to war at some time or another for defense and revenge.

The destruction of a political community does not necessarily mean the disappearance of tribesmen. The conquest and incorporation of peoples without written language creates dependent native peoples. Feuds may continue. Groups of warriors may try to seize by force the government into which they have been incorporated, or they may serve as soldiers in their new nation. Native Americans are an example of the latter situation. By the 20th century only in a few remote places in the world could anthropologists find native peoples who had not been deprived of their political autonomy. They included Amazonia, Highland New Guinea, and the Central Sudan spanning East and West Africa.

IV. WARFARE

A. Types of Warfare

Warfare, which is defined as armed combat between political communities, is conducted by military organizations. If the political communities are culturally the same, the armed combat is classified as internal war. But if the political communities are culturally different, the armed combat is external war (see Fig. 1). Two types of external war can be distinguished: a political community can either attack (offensive external war) or be attacked by (defensive external war) a culturally different political community. In tribal societies, the military organizations that carry out the armed combat are apt to be fraternal interest groups. If the members of such a military organization make an attack on someone who is a member of their own political community, they are engaged in feuding or the initiation of a feud. If the next day these warriors ambush a member of another political community, they are engaged in war. Thus, a fraternal interest group, employing ambushing tactics, can be responsible for both feuding and warfare. Otterbein showed in a cross-cultural study that fraternal interest groups lead to frequent internal war. This apparently occurs because most cultures with fraternal interest groups probably contain a large number of such military organizations because of the large number of localized kinship groups in the constituent political communities. The presence of a large number of small-scale military organizations creates the strong likelihood that there will frequently be internal war in a society. Presumably because of the greater distance between most political communities that are in different cultures, fraternal interest groups do not produce either the offensive or the defensive type of external war.

B. Goals of War

Wars occur when military organizations do battle in order to obtain certain goals. These goals may vary from war to war, and they may change over time. Thus for the military organizations of a political community there will probably be several goals of war. At a given period in the history of a political community—if sufficient ethnographic information is available—the order of the importance of the goals can probably be ascertained. The political leader of the political community may determine the goals and send the military organizations to war in order to achieve these goals, or the leaders of the military may make the decision as to which goals will be pursued. Thus it can be argued that wars are caused by the decisions of men as members of organizations, whether they be military organizations or political systems. There are six basic reasons for going to war: subjugation and tribute, land, plunder, trophies and honors, revenge, and defense.

Some social scientists have argued that states, which are political communities headed by kings or dictators, go to war for subjugation and tribute. On the other hand, political communities headed by chiefs and headmen go to war for economic, social, and defensive reasons. These reasons for going to war are likely to be pursued at one time or another by the military organizations of states. They also constitute the major reasons stateless political communities go to war. An important economic reason for attacking other political communities is to capture land by defeating and driving back or killing the inhabitants. The land may be used for fields, hunting, or grazing. Another goal of war, primarily economic, is to obtain plunder. Plunder includes forms of wealth, such as animals, material goods, and money and also captives for use as wives, slaves, hostages, adoption, or sacrifice. Trophies and honors are social or prestige goals. Military organizations and political communities often go to war, just as individual warriors do, to obtain honors. Simply the prestige of victory in armed combat may be the sole reason for going to war. The capturing of trophies, cherished items usually of little economic value, is another way of obtaining prestige. Revenge—the desire to retaliate for the killing of a member of one's political community and even the score—is another reason military organizations go to war. And the final reason military organizations engage in war is defense—the organized attempt by a group of armed men to defend from enemy attacks their own lives, the lives of their families, their property and homesteads, and their political community.

C. Basic Pattern of Warfare

The ambush and the line are two components of the warfare pattern of most tribal peoples who engage in war. In his study of warfare Otterbein distinguished between each type of tactic and classified each society in terms of whether its warriors used ambushes only (23 cases), lines only (5 cases), or both (18 cases). Detailed analysis of numerous cases since has revealed, however, that both tactics are probably used by all societies with war. An ambush consists of either laying a trap or surrounding the enemy, usually a village at night. A line consists of warriors drawing parallel to the enemy forces. A distinction that is important, but that was not made in the original study, separates mutually arranged battles, perhaps on a traditional fixed battlefield, from encounter battles. An encounter battle arises when a raiding party intent on laying an ambush encounters a band of warriors either hunting or intent on laying their own ambush. When two raiding parties meet in the field, they line up facing each other and a battle that is often more noise than combat ensues. If the sides are relatively equal, they may withdraw before there are serious woundings or fatalities. If one side greatly outnumbers the other, the smaller side may be annihilated except for the warriors who can run the fastest. Whether battles are prearranged or unexpected encounters, they constitute one of the two components of the warfare pattern of all warring peoples. Since ambushes are part of the basic two-component warfare pattern, Otterbein now considers attacks by a group of armed men on a single individual or on a group of individuals from a different political community to be examples of war, even if the object of the attack is unarmed, and thus armed combat has not occurred.

When groups attempt to destroy each other, they will choose the most effective means they can find to accomplish the task. The basic pattern provides two ways of waging war; if one way is not effective, the other may be. If neither is effective, another means may be developed. For example, the Dani of Highland New Guinea had arranged battles that produced few casualties, ambushes that produced a few more, and massive dawn raids that killed hundreds. Battles were a means of testing the strength of an adversary. If one polity appeared weak, two others might join forces and annihilate the weaker in a dawn raid.

V. SUMMARY

A. Major Conclusions

1. Fraternal interest groups are a major cause of rape, feuding, and internal war in many societies. Military organizations in tribal societies are frequently fraternal interest groups. Defense and revenge are universal reasons for going to war.

2. The peoples of the world fall into two categories: those with fraternal interest groups, which are violent and conflict ridden, and those without fraternal

interest groups, which are relatively peaceful within their culture.

3. Feuding peoples may or may not use compensation to terminate a feud. Revenge for injustice drives feuds. Without the means to settle feuds they may persist for centuries.

4. Political communities with neighbors have found it necessary to have military organizations to defend themselves. Those that cannot defend themselves will be annihilated and absorbed into other political communities or driven into refuge areas. Those with efficient military organizations are likely to expand territorially.

5. The warfare pattern of most tribal peoples consists of the ambush and the line. In a confrontation the more effective tactic will be chosen.

Also See the Following Articles

ANTHROPOLOGY OF VIOLENCE AND CONFLICT • CULTURAL ANTHROPOLOGY STUDIES • ETHNIC CONFLICTS AND COOPERATION • ETHNICITY AND IDENTITY POLITICS • INDUSTRIAL VERSUS PREINDUSTRIAL FORMS OF VIOLENCE • MILITARISM • PEACEFUL SOCIETIES • RITUAL AND SYMBOLIC BEHAVIOR • WARRIORS, ANTHROPOLOGY OF

Bibliography

Boehm, C. (1984). *Blood revenge: The anthropology of feuding in Montenegro and other tribal societies.* Lawrence: University Press of Kansas.

Daly, M., & Wilson, M. (1988). *Homicide.* New York: Aldine de Gruyder.

Dentan, R. K. (1992). The rise, maintenance, and destruction of peaceable polity: A preliminary essay in political ecology. In J. Silverberg and J. P. Gray (Eds.), *Aggression and peacefulness in humans and other primates.* New York: Oxford University Press.

Divale, W. T., & Harris, M. (1976). Population, warfare and the male supremacist complex. *American Anthropologist, 80,* 379.

Ericksen, K. P., & Horton, H. (1992). "Blood feuds": Cross-cultural variations in kin group vengeance. *Behavior Science Research, 26,* 57.

Ferguson, R. B., & Whitehead, N. L. (Eds.). (1992). *War in the tribal zone: Expanding states and indigenous warfare.* Seattle: University of Washington Press.

Heider, K. (1997). *Grand Valley Dani: Peaceful warriors* (3rd ed.). Fort Worth: Harcourt Brace College Publishers.

Keeley, L. (1996). *War before civilization: The myth of the peaceful savage.* New York: Oxford University Press.

Kuschel, R. (1988). *Vengeance is their reply: Blood feuds and homicides on Bellona Island,* pt. 1. Copenhagen: Dansk Psykologisk Forlag.

Otterbein, K. F. (1970). *The evolution of war: A cross-cultural study.* New Haven: Human Relations Area Files.

Otterbein, K. F. (1986). *The ultimate coercive sanction: A cross-cultural study of capital punishment.* New Haven: Human Relations Area Files Press.

Otterbein, K. F. (1994). *Feuding and warfare: Selected papers of Keith F. Otterbein.* Langborn, PA: Gordon and Breach.

Otterbein, K. F. (1996). Feuding. In D. Levinson & M. Ember (Eds.), *The Encyclopedia of Cultural Anthropology.* New York: Henry Holt and Company.

Otterbein, K. F., & Otterbein, C. S. (1965). An eye for an eye, a tooth for a tooth: A cross-cultural study of feuding. *American Anthropologist, 67,* 1470.

Pearce, J. E. (1994). *Days of darkness: The feuds of Eastern Kentucky.* Lexington: The University Press of Kentucky.

Robarchek, C., & Robarchek, C. (1998). *Waorani: The contexts of violence and war.* Fort Worth: Harcourt Brace and Company.

Thoden Van Velzen, H. U. E., & Van Wetering, W. (1960). Residence, power groups, and intra-societal aggression. *International Archives of Ethnography, 49,* 169.

Class Conflict

Larry W. Isaac
Florida State University

GLOSSARY

Capitalism A particular class-based system of organizing society in which wealth and valued goods are produced by subordinating human labor in the wage relation while virtually everything is converted into a commodity to be bought and sold.

Capitalist Class The dominant class in capitalist society whose accumulation of wealth is based on the process of expropriating the labor of others.

Capitalist Contradictions Capitalism is structured in such a way as to produce fundamental (i.e., deep-rooted) processes of conflict and opposition; for example, the extraordinary capacity to produce enormous material wealth on the one hand, and poverty, despair, and inequality on the other. Related opposites that are structured by capitalism include: value-for-use vs. value-for-surplus; socialized production vs. private appropriation; community vs. individualism; labor vs. money.

Class Exploitation The particular social form and process by which surplus-value is extracted from the subordinate class by the dominant class. In capitalist society this takes place primarily through the wage relation that binds working class to the capitalist class.

Class Inequality Social inequality, such as wealth and poverty, that is systematically structured by class power relations.

Commodity-Form of Social Organization The capitalist organization of social life based on the two-sided form of the commodity in which virtually everything with a use-value to humans is structured into production for market (exchange)-value designed to obtain surplus-value.

Interclass Conflict The conflict and struggle between classes such as the capitalist and working classes in a capitalist society, or slaveowners and slaves in a slave society.

Intraclass Conflict The conflict or divisiveness among factions of a given class that work against solidarity in the class formation process.

Social Classes Antagonistic power relations that are shaped by and in turn shape the social organization of labor, work, production, circulation, and distribution of value in society.

Surplus-Value That portion of the total social product produced by the direct producers (working class) but appropriated by the owners of wealth and productive property (the dominant or capitalist class). This is surplus-value because it exceeds the reproduction costs of the class system at any given historical moment and represents newly expanded value; that is, money as capital makes new money through the indirect coercion of the labor of others. Profit is one concrete form of surplus-value.

Working Class The subordinate class in capitalist society whose members must sell their labor-power (i.e., labor capacity or potential) for a wage in order to survive.

CLASS CONFLICT refers to a broad set of social actions that are manifested in direct and indirect, violent and nonviolent, institutionalized and noninstitutionalized struggles between social classes. At root, classes are defined by social relations that bind people into the social organization of labor, production, circulation, and distribution processes. These relations simultaneously involve objective and subjective dimensions, and appear in economic, political, and ideological forms. In capitalist societies, the employer–employee (or wage) relationship is central. Hence, we speak of labor-management conflict as a basic dimension of contemporary class conflict.

Class analysis has a long, rich, and contentious history that spans the development of capitalism, social science in general, and sociology in particular. During the late 19th and early 20th centuries, important class analytic studies of modern capitalist society were advanced in the impressive works of Karl Marx, Max Weber, Rosa Luxemburg, Georg Lukacs, and Antonio Gramsci, to name a few. Taking their lead from these early theorists/activists contemporary class analysts believe that class conflict is significant because it: (a) is grounded in the exploitation of human labor; (b) permeates and shapes virtually all social values and institutions; and (c) is an important force in the dynamic trajectory of capitalism as a whole.

I begin this article with a discussion of the structured but indeterminate social bases of class conflict (Section III), progress into an inventory of concrete dimensions of class conflict (Section IV), and then examine comparative national trends in forms of class conflict across different institutional arenas in recent decades (Section V). I conclude with brief speculative comments about possible directions of class conflict in the coming century (Section VI).

I. SOCIAL BASES OF CLASS CONFLICT

Class conflict—its causes, consequences, significance—are all rooted in how we understand social class. Two basic approaches have dominated class analytic scholarship: (a) class as hierarchical position; and (b) class as antagonistic relational social process.

A. Class as Hierarchical Position

Much of modern social science has conceptualized class as structured space, a position or slot within an overall hierarchical ranking. Following the ideas of Max Weber, classes are traditionally conceived as gradational hierarchy and measured in quantities of social status, income, or wealth. In the recent neo-Marxist stratification approach of Erik Wright, classes have also been conceptualized as differentiated positions to be filled. Class structure is rooted in certain occupational types that, based on their job characteristics, define the class to which a person belongs.

While both traditional and neo-Marxist stratification approaches have their own merits—offering a picture of resource distribution or yielding a static map of aggregated occupational characteristics—neither is particularly useful for understanding the dynamics of class conflict and related social change. How, then, might we understand the conflictual dynamics of social class?

B. Class as Antagonistic Relational Process

Social class is at the core of any class-based society. In a particular historical era, a subordinate class (e.g., serfs, slaves, workers)—so defined by the social conditions that differentially separate them from the control of the means of life, wealth, and coerce their labor—is compelled to produce at a rate beyond that necessary for its own survival or reproduction. This social surplus (value) is the source of new wealth and is expropriated by a corresponding dominant class (e.g., lords, slave-owners, capitalists) of nonproducers, whose ownership of productive property allows them to live off the labor of those beneath them. The relationship between rulers and ruled—the basic antagonistic classes of any society—is shaped by the manner in which this surplus is extracted from the direct producers. Thus, class refers to a power relation and class conflict is about the determination of power to shape social life in particular directions.

Capitalism is so named because capital is the foundation, the core, of this mode of social life. But what, then, do we mean by capital? In the most impressive answer to this question, Karl Marx filled three lengthy volumes, entitled *Capital*. I draw on those ideas in brief form and begin with this premise: Capital is a form of social power relation that involves the subordination and exploitation of human labor through the social organization of the commodity-form, is continuously expanding, and is personified in the capitalist and worker.

But why is this social relation necessarily antagonistic or conflictual? The fundamental unit of capital is the commodity. The social relations that comprise the commodity (i.e., simultaneously use-value and exchange-value organized to acquire surplus value) and capital in its expanded form, undergird, envelope, and shape all spheres of social life. Hence, "things of value" that appear as self-contained objective entities are really given their "value" by the social relations among people. Market processes, for example, are not driven by mysterious "laws," but are rather dynamic and volatile social relations.

Capitalism's ever-expansive and cumulative quality has a tendency to turn virtually everything into the form of a commodity in a relentless drive to expand surplus value. Surplus value, in turn, becomes the social basis for the monetary accounting category called "profit." Commodity relations that comprise capital come to commodify people in a host of different ways. However, this happens most fundamentally through the wage relation, through the buying and selling of human labor-power (potential) for definite periods of time (e.g., working hour, working day, work week). But this process of commodifying human beings in which employers convert labor-power into capital by treating it as an object (e.g., "factor of production") like any other commodity leads, over time, to resistance.

All commodity relations are two-sided, simultaneously constituted by use-value and exchange-value. When people are commodified (proletarianized) through the wage relation, exchange-value appears as the buying of the worker's labor-power for a money wage. This sort of exchange on the labor market appears as freely chosen by both employer and employee in which the rules of equality, ownership, and individualism prevail. But labor-power (potential) that the employer purchased is not what is actually desired by the employer. Once purchased, the labor-power is assembled (classically) in what Marx colorfully termed the "hidden abode of production." Here in the workplace all pretense to equality ceases as capitalist management settles down to extract maximum labor from labor-power, the purchased commodity. It is this actual labor (productivity) that is the use-value of the human commodity purchased (actually rented for a period of time) by the capitalist.

However, unlike inanimate commodities utilized for their maximum contribution to expanded value (profit), labor-power is embodied in human beings with subjectivity; that is, workers have culturally established senses of justice, time, value, life; and they often protest and resist in various ways if they are treated as objects, driven too long, too hard, or too fast. On the one hand, the capitalist is under pressure to exploit labor-power to its fullest due to market pressures. On the other hand, workers attempt to protect/conserve their labor-power, the only thing of value they have, by attempting to resist the wholesale consumption of it. Each attempts to get the most for her/his commodity: For labor it is the wage and conditions of the labor process (e.g., autonomy, safe working conditions) while the capitalist focuses on maximum use-value in the form of actual labor expended (i.e., productivity).

Table I displays this antagonistic foundation of the basic cell of capital, the commodity-form as wage relation. The relationship embodies a dual basis for conflict: Differential interest between the employer and employee over the market-based money wage and differential interest between employer and employee over the

TABLE I

Work in the Wage Relation as Commodity-Form: The Basis of the "Effort-Reward Struggle"

	Commodity-form	
	(Exchange)-value	Use-value
	Labor market relations	Labor process relations
	(A)	(C)
For capitalist:	Buys labor-power for a definite period of time via monetary wage (wage for potential)	Attempts to consume/extract as much labor as possible from worker per period (working day)—actual output or productivity
	(B)	(D)
For worker:	Sells labor-power for a definite period of time in return for money wage	Gives up labor, but also attempts to preserve/protect labor as life-energy and major value resource being consumed

Note: Cells A and B define the terms of the money exchange (wage contract) between employer and employee in the labor market. There is a definite material basis for conflict here: for the employer, the money wage is an expense or cost of production and is therefore to be subjected to downward pressure; for the employee, the wage rate is revenue and therefore subject to upward pressure. Hence the basis of conflict over the terms of the money wage.

Cells C and D define activity within the labor process housed within the "hidden abode" (private workplace). For the employer, actual labor (productivity) is a source of value/revenue and therefore always subject to more by management; for the employee, this labor is a liability, a drain, a means to an end, and therefore needs to be limited to preserve one's life energy as the major resource.

actual labor expended in the workplace. This twofold class-based conflict is also known as the "effort-reward struggle." Outcomes—wage levels and labor as well as the ratio of the two—are indeterminate at any given point in time. The conflict is inherent in the class relation that ties labor and capitalist together and is predicated on the drive for more surplus value (profit) through the exploitation of human labor. This is a struggle that pits "right against right," in which the relative balance of power decides the answer to a host of socially significant questions, including: What is a fair wage? What is a fair day's work? What is the normal length of the working day/week/year/lifetime? What are safe working conditions? How much environmental degradation is acceptable?

Hence, capitalism is a social system based on the imposition of work through the commodity- form. Class struggle (whether overt or latent conflict) is in, through, and about the way the commodity-form is imposed on the majority of the population by forcing them to sell portions of their lives as labor-power in order to gain access to the means of life that have themselves been commodified. Capital's totalizing tendency creates a social condition of (abstract, indirect, impersonal) coercion through markets, commodities, money—that is, through capitalistic control over the means of producing social wealth. This generalized imposition of the commodity-form through capitalist history has created class dependency and forced work as the principle means of organizing and directing society.

The opposition between capitalists and workers is significant not only because the many are exploited for the enrichment of the few, but also because these exploitation relations (and endemic conflict) are key elements in the dynamic development of capitalist social formations as a whole. Capital's incessant drive to accumulate—to expand and mold more human life activity into the commodity-form—produces a conflictual reaction that, in turn, forces capitalists to innovate and the state to reform. Consequently, the dialectical relation between class conflict and systematic restructuring creates a constantly shifting "contested terrain" on which future class conflicts will unfold. This shifting terrain produces a recomposition of class combatants (i.e., what the working class looks like changes) and spawns new forms, sites, targets, and demands for subsequent struggles.

C. Intraclass Conflict and Class Formation

Each conflict between classes is also simultaneously a struggle within classes. Intraclass conflict happens because classes do not appear on the scene ready-made—collectively organized with immediately clear interests. Questions of interests, solidarity, community, goals, strategy, tactics, are always sources of contention within classes and the immediate agents of class self-organization (or formation) are particular leaders, parties, and factions. In fact, a central part of this intraclass struggle is about the very meaning of class and even whether combatants are involved in a class conflict or some other non-class form of struggle.

Capital, too, goes through processes of class formation, although it also works diligently to deny its class character. For example, the lines of potential division within capital can issue from a number of important dimensions such as corporate size, type of capital (finance, commercial, industrial), market orientation (consumer/producer, local, national, international), profit distribution. Certain levels of agreement—solidarities, coalition formation, alliances—must be created for concerted collective actions. But class formation does not take place on an even field. Capital possesses organizational, cultural, material, and political advantages that are structurally unavailable to the working class. For example, capital: (a) operates as "organization" (corporate firm) rather than individual from the outset and corporate laws enhance that supra-individual status; (b) creates a culture of superiority by virtue of society's employment and economic growth dependency on it; and (c) has an enormous economic resource advantage. Moreover, as class analyst Nicos Poulantzas argued in his *Classes in Contemporary Capitalism* (1975), the state's use of policy, laws, and national offensives typically contributes to solidifying multiple forms of capital while weakening, fragmenting, and disorganizing the working class. This usually means that effective working class formation meets with more difficult and divisive forms of intraclass struggles (e.g., racial, ethnic, gender) than does capital.

When the famous British labor historian E.P. Thompson wrote in his *Making of the English Working Class* (1966) that class is something that happens when people "as a result of common experiences (inherited or shared) feel and articulate the identity of their interests as between themselves, and as against others whose interests are different from (and usually opposed to) theirs," he was pointing to this concrete historical process of class formation. Sphere of production relations are most important but not the only relations in this process and certainly should not be understood in a rigid, deterministic fashion. Class is not merely an economic category that expresses itself politically through class struggle. Instead it is cultural experience that forms the crucial fibers linking laboring activity, critical class consciousness, and collective (class) action. Culture is central to the constitution of class and it is in the formation of class culture, solidarity, and community that class conflict—over wages, working conditions, autonomy, poverty, inequality—becomes possible for the working class. Therefore, class and thus conflict between classes is not simply a function of where one stands, but most importantly, what one stands in relation to and for as Howard Kimeldorf has put it.

Cooperation in the capitalist labor process—increasingly important as modern capitalism becomes more socially interdependent—has dual channels: Cooperation with capital allows labor to be a significant use-value to capital (the goose that can lay the golden eggs), yet labor is also a potential nightmare—as Marx wrote in the 1857 manuscripts known as the *Grundrisse*—because, as living subject, labor is "the only use-value that can form the opposite pole to capital." The dual character of cooperation generates prospects for two generally corresponding work cultures: (1) a culture of loyalty and compliance with capitalist demands, purposes, and terms; and (2) an oppositional culture of labor resistance. The latter requires some degree of worker solidarity and is usually present within the former, although the range of its development can be quite wide.

Solidarity among working people runs contrary to the dominant values and themes of competitive, possessive individualism cultivated by pervasive capitalist culture. It is created and expressed by mutual association bonds, organizational capabilities, institutional arrangements and social values that arise within these relations. Most importantly, "cultures of solidarity," as Rick Fantasia (1987) calls them, are forged by workers in the course of collective struggle as new "maps of meaning" become expressive of a dynamic form of symbolic action. This processual unfolding of oppositional class cultures never occurs in a vacuum but rather is mediated by and contingent on other important social relations, such as gender, race, skill levels, occupational divisions, and so on.

While the twofold character of the commodity-form of value and its expanded form as capital generates the inherently conflictual basis for struggle between capital and labor, this process is always conditional on within-class struggle; that is, whether class conflict actually takes place, the forms it assumes, the extent to which it grows, its successes and failures are all dependent on intraclass struggle in the process of class formation. Thus, division and competition is a problem of class formation for both capital and labor. The next section concentrates on the concrete dimensions and forms of class conflict that have grown out of various oppositional cultures established in the contentious soil of class relations.

II. CONCRETE DIMENSIONS OF CLASS CONFLICT

The scope of class conflict is complex and multidimensional in historical phases, levels, arenas, and forms. Moreover, the internal composition of each form of struggle is multiplex: It consists of multiple-actor (collective) phenomena composed of multiple actions; that is, within each collective event multiple actors come together to shape cultural bonds of solidarity and engage in an array of contentious and often quite risky actions. While important historical commonalities exist, class conflict also displays significant historical differentiation in fundamental issues, institutional contexts, and repertoires of collective contention.

A. Major Historical Phases of Capitalist Imposition

Each historical phase of capitalist development has had its own central point of contention, from capital's point of view, that shapes the repertoire of struggle as well as the institutional formations of particular periods: For example, class conflict has revolved, according to Harry Cleaver, around the fundamental questions of *whether* the commodity-form could be imposed, *how much* it could be imposed, and *at what price* it could continue to be imposed.

1. Primitive Accumulation and Early Extensive Regimes

This was the period of initial class formation in nascent capitalist society that first occurred through the imposition of work in capitalist agriculture and small-scale commodity production. These processes were carried out in a massive way in England and parts of Western Europe in the "rosy dawn" of capitalism, which was subsequently extended through the restructuring of the existing society and colonialism. However, it certainly was not a foregone conclusion that laboring activity (as a source of new value) could be accomplished as "free" wage labor in the New World. A central axis of struggle and often bloody conflict revolved around precisely this question: Could the commodity-form of human life activity be generally imposed? Could labor-power be subsumed (organized and controlled) as "free" wage labor on a sufficiently large scale? Forcefully clearing the land and extending the wage form (from Europe to the Americas) involved a tremendous amount of coercion, violence, and bloodshed. In the New World during this early formative period, "clearing the land" meant more than just removing trees and underbrush; it also meant directly coerced labor of indigenous populations or their removal as well as directly coerced labor of imported peoples in the form of indentured and slave labor. By contrast, there was relatively little "free" wage labor. The key point is that the commodity-form's spatial extension (across Europe and the New World) and temporal extension (lengthening the working day) was an extraordinarily conflictual and violent process.

For the working classes during this early period, the commodity-form of life was still quite alien. Because capitalist society was not yet thoroughly institutionalized as the normal state of affairs, recently or partially proletarianized workers would struggle with the real prospect of escaping this form of labor imposition. For some, death as mode of escape was preferable to life in the new alien form.

2. Working Day, Time Discipline, and Intensive Regimes

In locations where the possibilities of avoiding the imposition of wage labor had been reduced or eliminated, the struggle for capital shifted to the question of how much (how intensively) it could be imposed. The first response to this quantitative quest was addressed by extending the length of the working day—the temporal analogue to extending the commodity-form across space in, for example, opening the frontier and extending "the market" from Atlantic to Pacific. Capital's unfettered prolongation of the working day, and accumulated human suffering, violence, and worker resistance it brought in its wake, forced capital (via state regulation) to serially shorten the working day, eventually moving to the 8-hour norm. But that temporal work norm was established only after decades of struggle. Eventually the shorter working day put pressure on capital that spawned, in turn, a new offensive of productivity/efficiency drives that revolutionized the social organization of the labor process by introducing new machinery, employing day and night shift work, and increasing the intensity of the labor process (i.e., the rate at which labor is pumped out of labor-power) through "scientific management," "Fordism," and other productivity enhancement schemes. The generalized imposition of time discipline in the form of the clock and machine pacing profoundly altered the rhythms of work and nonwork life.

3. The State, Distributional Struggles, and Productivity Deals

By the 20th century, capitalism had been largely institutionalized in the advanced industrial nations such as the United States. In these locations the dominant forms of class conflict took place within an already imposed wage form of work. Most workers had been thoroughly proletarianized and the general aim of class struggle was no longer escape (although escape did take individualistic forms such as mobility into the ranks of the small entrepreneur or even escapist entertainments), but rather a more equitable distribution of value within the institutions of capitalist democracy. For capital, once the intensive regime of production was established, the fundamental concern shifted to questions of distribution and cost: What price would have to be paid to elicit continual compliance with commodified work on a massive scale? Here the relative relation between the price of labor-power (money wage) and level of productivity (labor extracted per time interval) determines the relative distribution of power in the workplace. At first, large mass production industry dealt with this issue through individual firm strategies (e.g., early Fordist approaches). But during the "long New Deal" (ca. 1935–1950), capital (via the state) restructured and institutionalized this intensive regime through the new industrial relations system, the Keynesian welfare state, union contracts, "productivity deals" or "accords." By linking wages and productivity, capital and state attempted to structure institutional conditions such that the working class struggle to drive up the wage level would become the growth motor for a stagnation-prone capitalism. But in this context workplace discipline and cooperation became more significant and its absence substantially more costly to capital.

4. Globalization and the Contemporary Capitalist Offensive

By the mid-1970s, the labor-capital accord established at the end of World War II began coming apart. The system that, for two to three decades, made it possible for at least the unionized sector of the American working class to attain middle class consumption patterns had come to an end. The very success of organized labor in economic distributional conflict with capital was one reason for this transformation. At the end of the war the terms of United States capital accumulation could tolerate, even benefit from, the presence of conservative unions in some major industries. But as conditions of world market competition and workplace technologies expanded, unions (always only weakly tolerated in the United States) became major obstacles to capital accumulation and profit levels established during the years of the accord. Gradually during the 1970s, more rapidly in the 1980s and 1990s, corporations began to decouple the productivity deal through what has become known as the "contemporary capitalist offensive" against working people. Globalization of markets has generated pressures on capitalist profitability. In turn, corporations launched offensives to transform work and workplaces, "downsizing" the organization to create "lean" (and mean) production processes. Capitalist restructuring—international competition, lean production, neoliberal policies for state austerity—are now bearing down with increasing weight on larger fractions of the working classes in more and more nations of the world.

The severe decline in unionization in the United States was one result of the destruction of the labor-capital accord. It was also importantly a function of overt class assault by corporations against workers, unionized or not. This assault was launched by business and conservative politicians using weapons that included: (a) threat and actual use of permanent replacement of strikers; (b) union decertification procedures; (c) threat and actual use of capital migration and other forms of disinvestment; (d) hiring specialized union-busting consulting firms; (e) common violations of fair labor standards (e.g., illegal intimidation and firing of workers and violations of NLRB regulations); and (f) converting corporate anti-unionism into government policy, especially during the Reagan administration years.

While all capitalist nations have been exposed to an intensified global competition in the 1980s and 1990s, the extent to which this translated into large losses, moderate losses, or no loss for particular national labor movements depended heavily on the historical trajectory of the movement (especially how unionized it was), the degree of centralized bargaining, and the extent to which organized labor controlled the terms of the labor market such as unemployment compensation. The countries that have these conditions and have best weathered the recent attacks on organized labor are the social democratic and, to some extent, the strong corporatist regimes of Western Europe. These are also countries that have relatively low average strike volumes. However, worker militancy may promote unionizaton in countries (e.g., the U.S.) where labor's institutional control is weak.

Across all four phases of capitalist development, the character of class conflict changed as a result of the extent to which the social environment had been commodified, moving first from direct, personal, often violent coercion to more indirect, impersonal abstract forms of domination. Importantly, this was and remains a continuous two-sided struggle, not simply a one-way manipulation. The level of capitalist productivity entails class conflict over the terms of the labor process—that is, over the duration of labor, the intensity of labor, and the conditions of labor. As a result of this conflict, the commodity-form of life in capitalist society undergoes a metamorphosis through time, a key source of social change.

B. Levels, Arenas, and Forms of Labor Struggle

Oppositional cultures developed from class domination and degradation spawn diverse forms of resistance that are dependent on historical conditions. Such working class resistance varies by level of intensity, institutional arena, and form.

1. Everyday Resistance

One meaning of class struggle is the simple recognition that life for the working class, under terms of socially structured class inequality, is a continuous struggle; finding employment, maintaining employment, facing the indignities of class dictatorship in the workplace, acquiring a living wage, fighting class-related health problems, and much more are part of the mundane daily rigors of working class life. Class conflict in the form of everyday resistance—individual and collective—by working people is a common response to these conditions in the workplace; sometimes resistance manifests itself in arenas other than the workplace; for example, in consumer actions against corporations that make and market particular products.

It is important to recognize that class conflict in the form of everyday resistance by working class people directed against power and authority in the workplace is mostly noninstitutionalized, covert, or subterranean. These "weapons of the weak," as John Scott calls them, include such acts as: soldiering, "working to rule," intentional shoddy work quality, undeclared slowdowns, feigned ignorance, pilfering, accidents, sabotage, and others. Precisely because these "hidden acts of resistance" are covert and undeclared, they are often not identified as class conflict.

If dramatic, romanticized, and infrequent revolutionary upsurges are the tip of the class conflict iceberg, these everyday forms of resistance constitute its submerged, unseen mass. From capital's point of view, these are the "human problems" of production that must be solved by management and (physical and social) engineering "solutions."

2. Politicized Movements and Organizations

Class conflict also appears in more overt, highly politicized organizational and social movement forms. These collective actions—for example, strikes, protest demonstrations, and the like—are aimed at achieving political, economic, and even broad social goals through mass mobilizations that agitate for change. The targets of such mobilizations are most frequently capitalist employers and the state. This category of actions can take on noninstitutionalized forms—for example, social movements, general strikes, rallies, wildcat strikes—or more routinized, institutional forms of grievance delivery—such as democratic electoral politics (including lobbying, campaign contributions) and unions (including institutionalized strikes, grievance procedures, and arbitration). Often class movements will simultaneously use both noninstitutionalized and institutionalized forms of struggle. The Irish movement, Sinn Fein, is a good example of a strategy that combines both electoral/party and insurgent social movement actions.

There is also a very complex relation between forms of organized labor as unions and labor movements focused on fundamental forms of social change. Organized labor—both local and international leadership—can play important conditioning roles in forming cultures of cooperation and opposition. However, worker militancy and labor unions are not necessarily isomorphic through time and space. Militant worker cultures have developed in the absence of unions, with the support of unions, and sometimes even despite unions.

Capital, for its part, uses a wide repertoire of actions in class struggle and open conflict. Moving along a continuum of relative intensity, capital is involved in class warfare (which may take the rhetorical delivery of "problems of management," "business decisions," "managerial prerogative," "maintaining order," and so on) through: (1) ideological representation and inculcation; (2) electoral politics, lobbying, control/domination of various parts of the state apparatus; (3) social organization of production and technical design of the labor process (e.g., "downsizing," "outsourcing," "flexible production"); (4) formal business associations (e.g., National Association of Manufacturers, Chamber of Commerce); (5) capital investment or disinvestment (e.g., investment strikes against government policies that may be relatively pro-labor or redirect capital away from segments of workers—capital flight—to avoid, discipline, weaken labor); and (6) repression, both direct (violent and nonviolent) and indirect (through the state). For example, in United States history capitalists often did not hesitate to use their own private armies, hired guns (e.g., Pinkertons, Baldwin-Felts agents), local vigilantes, or state agents to repress labor, especially during the 19th century and first half of this century. Similar processes of repression by corporate interests and state agents are all too common in many parts of the contemporary world economy.

3. Revolutionary Action

The intensive and overtly dramatic forms of labor revolt or revolutionary action constitute only a small fraction of the conflictual reality inside the commodity-form of social life. These actions are noninstitutionalized mass struggles, often violent, that seek fundamental change in the social organization of society. Radical and revolutionary mobilizations are most likely to take place in defense of established cultures of thought and action, a reaction by a community with some social resources that are sufficient to confront social transformations that threaten to take everything from them, as Craig Calhoun has argued in *The Question of Class Struggle* (1982).

Although relatively infrequent, revolutionary forms of class conflict are important for a variety of reasons. Sidney Tarrow (1993: 302–3) captures the significance of revolutionary fervor that often grows *inside* peak cycles of mass protest:

> Few people dare to break the crust of convention. When they do during moments of madness, they create the opportunities and provide the models for others. Moments of madness—seldom widely shared, usually rapidly repressed, and soon condemned even by their participants—appear as sharp peaks on the long curve of history. New forms of contention flare up briefly within them and disappear, and their fate of absorption into the ongoing repertoire is slow and partial. But the cycles they trigger last much longer and have broader influence than the moments of madness themselves; they are, in Zolberg's (1972: 206) words, "like a flood tide which loosens up much of the soil but leaves alluvial deposits in its wake."

In the advanced capitalist countries, the last major protest cycle, containing potentially revolutionary mass actions occurred during the late 1960s; for example, spring 1968 in France, the 1969 *autunno caldo* ("hot autumn") in Italy, and much of 1968 and 1969 in the United States. However, in none of these instances were major waves of madness constituted solely of workers' movements. Rather they were sometimes broad analgams of separate movements merging into a massive movement wave, while at other times they were marked by deep internal division (e.g., some "hard hat" opposition in the U.S.).

III. COMPARATIVE TRENDS IN CLASS CONFLICT

How are the class bases of political actions and collective struggles altered, if at all, by the various institutional developments and trajectories of capitalist nations? In other words, are the class bases of politics and collective conflict becoming more or less salient with the historical development of capitalist society? These and related questions were an integral part of capitalist history at the beginning of this century; they have reemerged at its end.

During the middle of the century, this question was posed in the wake of depression, fascism, and world war. By the late 1950s and early 1960s, models of industrial progressivism and proclamations of the "end of (class) ideology" became hegemonic on both sides of the Atlantic. Much of the working class had acquired what appeared to be stable, long-term incorporation, representation, and citizenship rights in the institutional forms of trade unionism and reformist political parties. Old models of class polarization were pronounced dead; many working class children could aspire to middle class occupations or at least consumption patterns. America became the premier "middle class society" while much of Europe became the home of the "affluent worker." According to Gösta Esping-Andersen, radical politics of all sorts—left and right—had been replaced by pluralist havens (America) or forms of corporatist representation (Europe).

By the mid-1970s, the institutional foundation of the Fordist-Keynesian regime of production—the productivity/wage deal that made the relatively stable middle class style occupation/consumption trajectory of the working class possible—came undone in global economic crises. In the midst of restructuring of institutions and markets created by transformations in globalized capitalism, new questions have appeared regarding the trajectory of class conflict in capitalist society and world economy.

Two major opposing lines of argument regarding trends in class conflict have been posed. On one hand, there is the "end of class" thesis which maintains that the political significance of class and class conflict are rapidly declining, if not already totally eliminated. Post-Fordist industrial shifts have diminished the (manual, blue-collar) industrial working class and its traditional class values, attitudes, political affiliations, and actions. The alternative claim, found in the "re-emergence of class" thesis, argues that new social divisions are growing out of the ashes of the old class divide. Key social processes cultivating new class polarizations are connected to: (a) the emergent segmentation between core and periphery workers within nations and between regions of the world; and (b) growing inequality, poverty, and marginalized "outsider" underclasses.

Central to the "decline of class and class conflict" argument are claims that entail one or more of the following: (1) the class bases of electoral politics (the arena of "peaceful, democratic class struggle") are weak and have been deteriorating for some time; (2) unions are weak, outmoded, and have been in decline for some time; (3) forms of collective working class militancy, such as strikes, have been waning in effectiveness and use; (4) subjective class identification, language and rhetoric has been eclipsed by physical attribute identities (such as gender or race); and (5) new social movements (said to be nonclass-based or post-materialist) are crowding out the old class-based movements like the labor movement.

However, comparative evidence across nations and arenas of struggle suggest a scenario that is decidedly different from and more complicated than that painted by the universal "decline of class conflict" argument: It is reasonably clear that the conditions, substance, locus, and meanings of class conflict may be changing but there is no general decline and certainly no absolute disappearance of class conflict. These points can be illustrated by examining comparative empirical trends.

A. United States and Capitalist Core Nations

Violent class conflict has declined dramatically within the capitalist core nations since the 19th century rise of the modern bourgeoisie and working classes. The use of violence by single industrialists, capitalist organizations, and the state was present in the early phases of labor-management relations in all capitalist countries. It was especially severe in the United States. In fact, violence by capitalists and state against workers' attempts at self-organization in the period from the First Reconstruction to World War II is one of the main processes that decisively shaped the U.S. working class into a relatively weak, apolitical trajectory. After World War

II, modern industrial relations systems were established which channeled and contained much (not all) class conflict into the relatively nonviolent arenas of electoral politics and union representation as American society in particular was thought to be the pluralist middle class haven in a capitalist world.

1. Electoral Politics: The Nonviolent Democratic Class Struggle

The relationship of class conflict to institutionalized electoral politics has a long history in capitalist nations. Around the turn of the century, the question of whether socialism could be achieved through the electoral process was very much on the minds of the working class and their class superiors. By the middle of the century, the issue of the "democratic class struggle" in America and Europe had become a major focus of political sociology. In recent decades, a number of studies analyzing the significance of class in American or European electoral politics have sounded a note of weakening class impact. In the new orthodoxy, class has been dealigned from party conflict in electoral arenas as part of the broader decline in the salience of class and class conflict. The empirical basis for this orthodoxy centers, however, on the use of a single flawed measure, the Alford Index.

When measurement of the class basis of voting takes into account important factors like changing occupational distributions and simultaneously examines multiple electoral outcomes (e.g., nonvoting), the data yield a very different picture. Figure 1 reports the strength of class bases in total vote, party, and turn-out using just such a measure developed by Hout and colleagues that avoids the problems of the Alford Index. Using this measure, U.S. presidential elections from the end of World War II into the early 1990s show historical fluctuations, but no evidence of a declining trend in class foundations of the vote that is yielded when the Alford Index is employed. Using data from 1952 to 1992, Brooks and Manza (1997: 400) find the class cleavage in U.S. presidential vote choice "exhibits a robustness that appears likely to persist into the future."

Esping-Andersen (1994) summarized major patterns from a variety of studies of European electoral politics. Among the Scandinavian nations, Sweden shows the greatest stability in the left vote: Approximately two-thirds of the electorate voted for the Social Democrats in 1968, during the 1970s, and as recently as 1988. In Norway and Denmark, where the Social Democrats were traditionally less dominant than in Sweden, there has been some decline in working class support (e.g., in Norway the base diminished from about 60–63% in the 1970s to 42% in 1990). However, the social democratic decline in these two cases has been offset by a modest shift in working class support to the more leftist Socialist Peoples' parties in those two countries.

There is also a mixed pattern for the corporatist states of continental Europe from the mid-1970s to mid-1980s, according to Esping-Andersen: Belgium and Germany experienced increased working class support

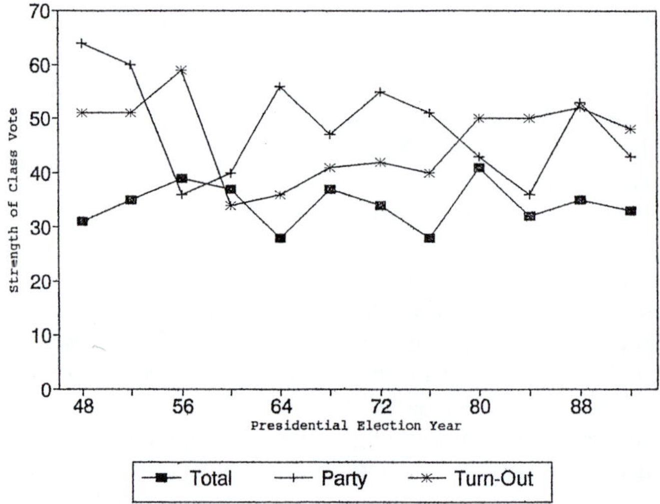

FIGURE 1 Class bases of electoral politics: United States, 1948–1992. *Note:* Data are from Hout, M., Brooks, C., and Manza, J. (1995), Class voting in capitalist democracies since World War II. *American Sociological Review, 60* (December): 805–828.

for the left; Italy's working class shows stable support; while the Netherlands and France experienced small and modest declines, respectively. But the left parties in these countries also gained some white-collar support. Britain, on the other hand, appears to have undergone more dramatic deterioration in working class support for the left.

2. Unions: Comparative Trends

Unions matter in class relations because they serve as the self-organization of workers, a vehicle for mobilizing resources in class struggles in the workplace and beyond. In particular, unions matter because they: (1) offer some protection against blatant workplace despotism—that is, arbitrary and capricious actions by employers; (2) contribute to societal well-being by increasing economic equality; (3) struggle to improve the quality of working conditions and the rights of workers as citizens; and (4) give workers a collective voice that can foster dissent, the cornerstone of democracy.

Data on unionization for core capitalist democracies from 1950 to 1985 followed roughly three basic trajectories. First, high levels coupled with increasing trend are best reflected in the paths of Belgium, Denmark, Finland, and Sweden. By the mid-1980s, between 70 and 90% of the work forces in these countries were unionized. Second, a large and diverse group of countries such as Australia, Austria, Canada, Germany, Ireland, New Zealand, Norway, and the United Kingdom have experienced relatively stable unionization with between 35 and 60% of their labor forces unionized. The third group of nations has relatively low unionization. These countries, including France, Japan, Holland, Switzerland, and the United States have suffered the greatest unionization declines in recent decades. Finally, Italy is a major exception to these three relatively consistent trends. Italian union density (percentage of the labor force unionized) declined through the 1960s and then began increasing into the early 1980s. Figure 2 shows union density trajectories for one country reflecting each of these four broad patterns—Sweden, The United Kingdom, the United States, and Italy.

But both worker self-organization and disorganization show variable time-paths even when driven by globally intensified hypercompetition beginning in the late 1970s and 1980s. Those countries where unions were able to grow under adverse global competition were those with already high union densities nurtured by strong centralized corporatist bargaining institutions and union control of unemployment insurance arrangements. Conversely, those countries where labor organizations were most seriously weakened had relatively low union densities to begin with, decentralized bargaining, no union control of unemployment insurance, large shifts to service sector employment and unfavorable economic conditions. Within this group of nations, the United States stands out for its antilabor industrial relations system and class assaults launched against workers (organized or not) in recent years.

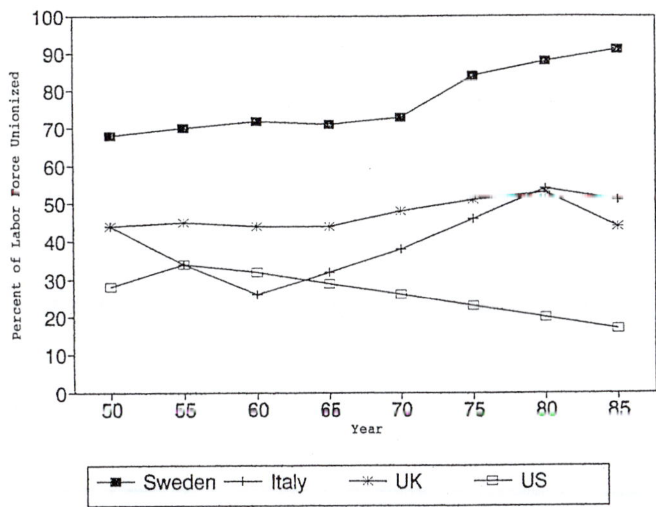

FIGURE 2 Union density: Select capitalist core nations, 1950–1985. *Note:* Data are from: Goldfield, M. (1987), *The decline of organized labor in the United States,* University of Chicago Press; Visser, J. (1989), *European trade unions in figures,* Kluwer; and Western, B. (1993), Postwar unionization in eighteen advanced capitalist countries, *American Sociological Review, 58* (April): 266–282.

Electoral politics and unions are both institutional manifestations of class and other forms of conflict. But what about the trajectory of more blatant conflict like strikes and other dimensions of working class militancy?

3. Strikes: Comparative Trends

The modern strike began to appear in most Western countries at various points in the 19th century. This form of collective action developed out of the ongoing struggles and conflicts between key class actors—wage workers, employers, state officials—that were forged by the development of modern industrial capitalism. These conflictual relations ultimately defined the rules and institutionalization of acceptable forms of protest. But what of the general trajectory of the strike in recent decades?

Figure 3 illustrates comparative strike patterns for four different advanced capitalist countries—Sweden, Germany, the United Kingdom, and the United States. In particular, this figure plots country-specific temporal strike density—that is, the number of strike days annually per 1000 workers in a particular country.

Since World War II, the country-specific strike trajectories show substantial variation. Sweden, characteristic of the Scandinavian social democratic regimes, has had a low average strike activity level with no real trend over the postwar decades. The only deviation from this pattern occurred in 1980 when strike volume spiked as a result of accumulating worker grievances under deteriorating economic conditions and the first non-Social Democratic administration in decades.

Germany, a relatively strong corporatist regime, has also been marked by a low average annual strike level, characteristic of France as well. On the other hand, Italy, a weak corporatist regime, has had a remarkably high average annual strike level. In fact, it is the highest postwar average of all the 18 major OECD capitalist core nations. As for trends, both France and Italy have experienced fluctuating declines since the peak protest waves of spring 1968 and autumn 1969, respectively. Germany has experienced a modest increasing trend although the level of strike activity is low relative to other countries.

The liberal market-centered regimes, such as Canada, the United Kingdom and the United States, display generally high average annual levels of strike volume. However, trends across these nations vary: Canada and the United States have both followed relatively smooth declining trajectories since the early 1970s, while the United Kingdom shows an increasing trend punctuated by major spikes in 1972, 1979, and 1984. By 1996, Spain, Italy, Germany, France, and Britain have all shown significant signs of an upward trend in levels of industrial strike actions.

In the east, Japan is an interesting and important case. Throughout this century, the Japanese labor movement was plagued by two prominent divisions. On the one hand, the moderates supported the capitalist system, viewed labor and capital's interests as one, and

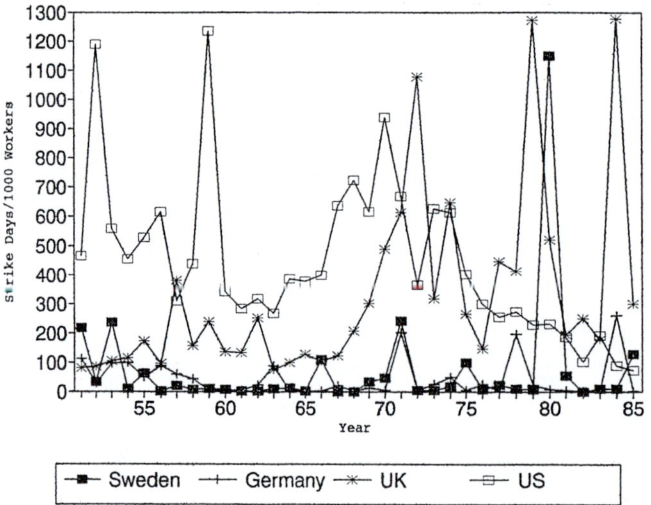

FIGURE 3 Strike volume: Select capitalist core nations, 1951–1985. *Note:* Data are from: Western, B. (1996), Vague theory and model uncertainty in macrosociology, *Sociological Methodology 1996*, Washington, D.C.: American Sociological Association; data can be accessed at: http://www.stat.cmu.edu/datasets/strikes.

deprecated strike actions. On the other hand, the radical faction sought the abolition of the capitalist system and advocated the use of strikes to achieve worker rights and social justice. For cultural and political reasons, the moderates gained the upper hand. Partially as a result, Japan developed "enterprise unionism" organized on a paternalistic-company basis rather than a geographic, industry, or trade foundation. Moreover, strike action became widely perceived as intimately associated with antisocial, antistate, and anticapitalist views. More recently, Japan has been reasonably successful in containing overt class conflict within the core industries (e.g., autos) through corporate strategies that combine the "dualistic approach" (good working conditions, wages, life-time employment security for some, while many others work in smaller outsourcing firms with the opposite conditions) and the "lean and mean approach".

Some strikes turn violent, while others that are also highly contentious do not. What do we know about the variability in strike violence? Beyond the general recognition that the level of violence between workers and employers tended to be much more widespread during the 19th and early 20th centuries, there are few studies that have analyzed the conditions that cause strike violence. Table II summarizes the key findings from four prominent studies.

In general, strikes tend to become violent when (a) they are large, long, and involve multiple issues, especially union organization and recognition issues; (b) they are staged mostly by low-skilled workers who are weakly organized or undisciplined; and (c) either labor or management engages in aggressive or provocative tactics. On the other hand, repression and presidential election periods appear to be political regime characteristics that mute strike violence. While reigning pro-labor administrations tend to also be associated with greater violence in Grant and Wallace's Canadian study, this tends to contradict the well-known evidence that strikes (violent or not) are much less likely under long-term social democratic labor regimes. This finding may, therefore, be peculiar to Canada or political economies in which labor parties do not control power for lengthy periods of time. Although these several studies are useful, more detailed comparative-historical case studies are necessary to gain greater insights on the strike violence question.

TABLE II

Studies of the Conditions of Strike Violence

Study	Location	Major findings
Taft & Ross (1969)	U.S., 1880s–1960s	Strikes over union organization and recognition are more likely to be violent
Shorter & Tilly (1971)	France, 1890–1935	Larger and longer strikes are more likely to be violent
Snyder & Kelly (1976)	Italy, 1878–1903	Multiple issue strikes are more likely than single issue strikes to be violent Weakly organized and poorly disciplined workers are more likely to use violence Regime repressiveness mutes strike violence
Grant & Wallace (1991)	Ontario, Canada 1958–1967	Aggressive tactics by labor or management increases violence Higher proportion of low skilled workers increases likelihood of violence Pro-labor party in power increases the likelihood of violence Presidential election year mutes probability of violence

Source notes:

Taft, P., and Ross, P. (1969). American labor violence: Its causes, character, and outcome. Pp. 270–376 in *Violence in America: Historical and comparative perspectives,* H. D. Graham and T. R. Gurr (Eds.). New York: New American Library.

Shorter, E., and Tilly, C. (1971). *Strikes in France, 1830–1968.* New York: Cambridge University Press. Snyder, D., and Kelly, W. R. (1976). Industrial violence in Italy, 1878–1903. *American Journal of Sociology, 82,* 1: 131–62.

Grant, D. S., and Wallace, M. (1991). Why do strikes turn violent? *American Journal of Sociology, 96* (March): 1117–50.

4. Strikes: U.S. Patterns

The history of the modern strike in the United States began on a large, national scale in the decade following the Civil War. The first major national-level action, signaling the emergence of a militant national working class, occurred in the 1877 general railroad strike. This massive work stoppage not only required state militia, national army, and substantial violence to quell it, but in its aftermath it also led to the proliferation of the armories across U.S. cities and the establishment of local elite militias and vigilante groups.

From the late 19th century to the final years of the 20th, long-term trends in U.S. strike frequency show no general upward or downward pattern. However, this long history has been punctuated regularly with major strike waves. Edwards (1981) documents major strike waves in 1886, 1887, 1903, 1933, 1934, 1937, and 1944. Other extremely important wave years (not meeting

Edwards strict quantitative criteria) include the World War I wave (1916–1922, especially 1919); the post-World War II wave (1945–1946); and the wave from 1967 to 1971.

Prior to the institutionalization of the modern industrial relations system (circa 1947–1950), labor-management confrontations were certainly much more violent. Quite commonly workers would confront the powerful forces of employer militias, state militias, and even the army, with bloody consequences resulting disproportionately for workers. A number of these events were so severe that labor historians refer to them as "massacres." But workers learned, too, the power of their numbers and strategic location in the production system when solidarity could be maintained on a broad level. The "general strike" that overflows single workplaces to involve large portions of whole communities or even multiple communities, is a major example of this process of extensive working class solidarity. Many of the general strikes involved considerable bloodshed as industrialists and state agents attempted to intimidate workers and break the communal culture that sustained the strike. In fact, some labor massacres happened in the context of a general strike (e.g., Chicago 1886); and general strikes are typically embedded within mass strike wave years (e.g., 1877, 1886, 1894, 1919, 1946) and broader "cycles of mass protest" that often produced important social change in American society. Table III summarizes major cases of these two classes of extraordinary events—labor massacres and general strikes—in U.S. history between 1877 and 1947.

TABLE III

Labor Massacres and General Strikes: United States, 1877–1947

Labor massacres		General strikes	
Year	Location	Year	Location
1886	Chicago (Haymarket), IL	1877	National Rail Strike
1897	Lattimer, PA	1886	Chicago, IL
1914	Ludlow, CO	1892	Homestead, PA
1916	Everett, WA	1892	New Orleans, LA
1919	Centralia, WA	1894	Pullman, IL
1922	Herrin, IL	1910	Philadelphia, PA
1937	Little Steel Strike Memorial Day (Chicago)	1919	Seattle, WA
		1934	San Francisco, CA
1938	Hilo, HA	1934	Textiles (AL, GA, NC, SC, New England)
		1934	Toledo, OH
		1934	Minneapolis, MN
		1935	Terre Haute, IN
		1936	Pekin, IL
		1946	Stamford, CT
		1946	Lancaster, PA
		1946	Rochester, NY
		1946	Oakland, CA
		1946	Pittsburgh, PA

Source notes:

Taft, P., and Ross, P. (1969). American labor violence: Its causes, character, and outcome. Pp. 270–376 in *Violence in America: Historical and comparative perspectives,* H. D. Graham and T. R. Gurr (Eds.). New York: New American Library.

Brecher, J. (1972). *Strike!* San Francisco: Straight Arrow Books.

Lipsitz, G. (1981). *Class and culture in Cold War America.* New York: Praeger.

Fillippelli, R. (1990). *Labor conflict in the United States.* New York: Garland Publishing.

As the United States was transformed from an agricultural to manufacturing to service-oriented economy, there have been important shifts in the industrial distribution of strike activity. Labor historian, Melvyn Dubofoky, points out that from the 1880s to World War I, strikes were typically local in character and most likely used by skilled workers concentrated in construction, needle, printing, mining, and transportation trades. During the war years of 1916–1919, strikes began to move increasingly to the factories and became substantially more national in scope. Through the decades of the 1930s, 1940s, and 1950s, workers in mass production factories grew increasingly strike-prone and likely to participate in multi-plant, multi-employer nationwide stoppages. Workers in the construction trades continued to employ frequent local strikes, while strikes in rails, mines, and clothing trades were diminishing in frequency. Since the mid-1960s, strikes have declined in all the extractive and manufacturing sectors of the economy while expanding substantially in the service and professional sectors, especially among public sector workers. While overall strike levels in the United States have been rather low, in 1996 they rose for the first time in years.

Finally, there is the issue of strike effectiveness as a worker tactic used in class conflict. While there is every reason to believe that the strike will continue to be an important form of collective action within the working class repertoire of class contention, there is evidence that it has been weakened since the establishment of the modern industrial relations regime after World War II. As McCammon (1994) has shown, the state's legal intervention into workplace conflict through major legislative acts (e.g., Wagner Act of 1935 and especially Taft-Hartley of 1947) and Supreme Court decisions have disorganized (by making illegal) precisely those forms of collective worker action that posed the greatest challenge to employer authority and capitalist institutions. Consequently, strikes over the right to unionize or over work rules ("control strikes") have declined dramatically in the post-World War II decades. Simultaneously, worker challenges have been structured into strikes over wages and other remunerative issues prompting the characterization of narrow economistic "business unionism." Workplace class conflict has also been directed away from more spontaneous and unpredictable forms of labor contention such as midterm contract and wildcat strikes as well as broad-based solidarity actions—for example, sympathy and general strikes. Instead, worker actions have been channeled into collective bargaining, arbitration, and even wage strikes that tend to occur in a ritualistic, regularized fashion at contract expirations. Since the early 1980s and the advent of concessionary bargaining, even these relatively conservative wage strikes have lost what little sting they might have had in many industrial sectors.

As with class bases of electoral politics and unionization, there have been those who have claimed that capitalist development would also cause the strike to "wither away." However, there is no convincing evidence for such a general conclusion. Instead, the comparative strike data show quite mixed trajectories that seem to have a generalized global component, but depend most heavily on nation-specific histories and conditions—labor movements, labor laws, industrial relations and state regimes. In fact, the evidence suggests that strike activity declines and tends to stabilize at relatively low levels only when labor-oriented social democratic parties are successful in acquiring stable, long-term control over government and industrial relations apparatus; that is, labor movements tend to deradicalize with, not so much capitalism per se, but rather with the expansion of the welfare state and institutionalized class conflict that is labor-oriented. The Scandinavian social democracies are major cases in point. However, even within these strong corporatist social democratic regimes, large annual spikes of strike activity, albeit infrequent, indicate that the strike, as a form of class conflict, has not been extinguished.

Evidence regarding trends in class voting, unionization, and strike activity are summarized for several major capitalist nations in Table IV. The weight of the comparative data indicates a highly mixed set of trajectories in conventional forms of class conflict. Within the advanced capitalist core nations, anyway, there have been important shifts in the form, location, and composition of these arenas of class conflict. However, it would be foolish to suggest that class conflict is withering away. But what about global patterns that extend beyond the most wealthy capitalist core nations?

TABLE IV

Summary of Trends in Class Conflict: Select Capitalist Core Nations

	Arenas of class mobilization		
State type/country	Electoral[a] politics	Union[b] density	Strikes[c]
Traditional corporatist			
Germany	increase	small increase	low level, modest increase
Italy	stable	sizeable increase	high level, fluctuating decline
France	small decline	modest decline	low level, stable
Social democratic			
Denmark	shifting	sizeable increase	low level, spike (1985)
Norway	shifting	small increase	low level, stable
Sweden	stable	sizeable increase	low level, spike (1980)
Liberal market-centered			
Canada	increase	small increase	high level, smooth decline
United Kingdom	decline	sizeable decline	high level, fluctuating increase
United States	stable	sizeable decline	high level, smooth decline

Notes:
[a] Trend in working class support for left parties mid-1970s through 1980s.
[b] Trend in union density across 1970s and 1980s.
[c] Trend in strike volume from 1975 to 1985.

B. Global Patterns of "Labor Unrest" in the 20th Century

Comparable and reliable data on unionization and strike activity are even more difficult to come by for countries outside the capitalist core nations. But some crude patterns can be discerned. In general, within the increasingly important developing Pacific-rim Asian countries, unionization patterns are mixed but do show slow growth trends. Unionization data for several of the non-core Asian countries, often termed "Asian Tigers" because of their rapid economic growth, offer interesting examples. Table V reports union density by decade from the 1950s through the 1980s for Hong Kong, Singapore, South Korea, and Taiwan. While the trends across these decades are not particularly clear in the cases of Hong Kong and Singapore, both South Korea and especially Taiwan show signs of union growth although their unionization levels are below those of Hong Kong and Singapore.

Official industrial strike militancy also follows mixed paths in these four countries. Table VI reports the average annual number of work stoppages from the 1950s through the 1980s. A clear declining trend is apparent only in the case of Singapore. The other three countries indicate rather stable patterns—Hong Kong and Taiwan—while South Korea has been experiencing a dramatic increase in strike militancy.

Because class conflict can manifest itself in so many different ways, each subject to temporal and cultural transmutations, our focus on electoral, union, and strike activity is not without limitations. Both electoral politics and unions are institutionalized forms born of prior conflicts, but they can also serve to shape and contain subsequent class conflicts in certain ways. Even the more overt form of conflict found in the strike has limitations for mapping class conflict; for example, it is a narrow form of class conflict; there are problems of equivalent meaning across time and space; and there are very limited data available for long-term, global comparisons.

TABLE V

Union Density in Several Noncore Asian Countries

	Country			
Decade	Hong Kong	Singapore	S. Korea	Taiwan
1950s	NA	NA	NA	7.5
1960s	15.1	NA	3.2	8.7
1970s	18.2	23.2	6.3	13.4
1980s	15.3	19.2	7.0	18.9

Note: Figures represent union members as a percentage of the total employed work force. "NA" indicates data not available.

Source: Frederic C. Deyo. *Beneath the miracle: Labor subordination in the new Asian industrialism.* Berkeley: University of California Press, 1989. Re-stylized from tables 10 and 11.

TABLE VI

Industrial Strikes in Several Noncore Asian Countries

	Country			
Decade	Hong Kong	Singapore	S. Korea	Taiwan
1950s	6.8	41.5	43.4	48.8
1960s	15.1	39.3	52.0	22.0
1970s	37.6	4.4	43.8	32.3
1980s	22.0	.2	176.1	NA

Note: Figures represent industrial conflict in the form of average annual number of "work stoppages." "NA" indicates data not available.

Source: Frederic C. Deyo. *Beneath the miracle: Labor subordination in the new Asian industrialism.* Berkeley: University of California Press, 1989. Re-stylized from tables 5, 6, 7, and 8.

The World Labor Group (WLG) at the Fernand Braudel Center at Binghamton University has been working to overcome these problems and has produced a more comprehensive measure of "labor unrest" as an important indicator of class conflict (see Special Issue of *Review*, Volume 18, Winter, 1995). They define their measure of labor unrest as "all the observable resistances and reactions by human beings to being treated as a commodity, both at the point of production and in the labor market. It includes all consciously intended, open acts of resistance. It also includes 'hidden' forms of resistance when these are widespread, collective practices" (Silver, 1995b: 20). These scholars point out that the main strength of their measure resides in its ability to identify and map waves of labor militancy as turning points in class conflict.

Data on "labor unrest" from the WLG project are displayed annually in Figure 4 from 1906 to 1990. Two series are shown: One represents the capitalist core nations (here that includes: Australia, Austria, Belgium, Canada, Denmark, Finland, France, Germany, Holland, New Zealand, Norway, Sweden, Switzerland, the U.K., and the U.S.); the other series combines indices for the semiperiphery and periphery regions of the world (see Silver, 1995b: Appendix B for the noncore countries).

Figure 4 illustrates several important points. First, there is no clear overall or long-term trend in labor unrest for either core or noncore areas of the world over this century. Second, major global labor unrest

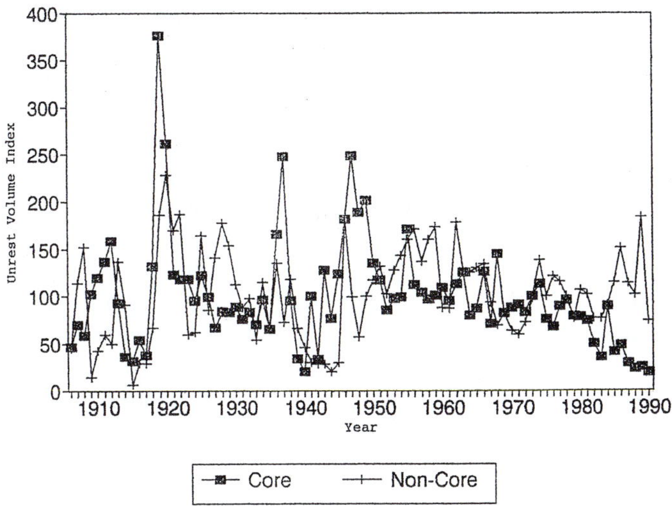

FIGURE 4 Global labor unrest, 1906–1990: Capitalist core & Noncore countries. *Note:* Data are from: Silver, B. J. (1995). World-scale patterns of labor-capital conflict: Labor unrest, long waves, and cycles of world hegemony. *Review, XVIII* (Winter): Appendix 2.

troughs occurred during the two world wars while major peaks happened in the immediate wartime aftermaths. Third, since the 1970s the core showed some reduction of labor unrest as the noncore regions registered a substantial upturn in activity.

Global and zonal labor unrest waves are significant beyond simply gauging the relative intensities of class conflict. For example, plausibly important links exist between such waves and global war as well as other major processes of social change—such as, new state policies, shifts in institutional structures, transformations in the location and social organization of labor processes. Restructuring and relocation processes are very much part of the reversal in labor unrest change patterns between core and noncore countries in recent years. Silver (1995b: 181) captures this spatial redistribution of conflict in the following words:

> The upturn in labor unrest in the semiperiphery and periphery can be interpreted as "the other side of the coin" of the continuing downward trend in the core. The geographical relocation of capital—as a mechanism for evading and undermining the bargaining power of labor—has played an important role in containing overt militancy in the core. The (threatened and actual) elimination of jobs in mass production industry has become an increasingly potent weapon on the side of capital since the early 1970's. Relocation, however, has proved to be a double-edged sword: labor movements in areas from which capital emigrates are undermined, but new working classes are created (and over time strengthened) in the sites to which capital migrates.

The successes of these conflict-containment aspects of class struggle undertaken by capital and core states depends on: (a) their ability to continually "externalize" or "export" the most contradictory elements of class conflict to the noncore regions of the world, and (b) the willingness of Third World regimes to repress labor and human rights.

The level of labor exploitation by employers was, in general, higher in the semiperiphery and periphery than in the core even before globalization processes began over the last two decades. But that gulf is growing. The contemporary system of global capitalism produces grotesque inequality (between enormous wealth and dire poverty) and growing class conflict of both the latent and overt varieties. The rhetoric of economic globalization has taken on a force of its own as corporate power brokers use their formidable propaganda machines to sell workers and ordinary citizens on the inevitable and beneficial "primacy of markets over politics, and of capital over labor" (Piven and Cloward, 1997: 9) in a globally linked economy.

The new business globalization refers most centrally to multinational capitalist enterprise moving through a process of serial capital migration around the globe. Firms move into labor surplus regions to enjoy the labor cost advantages that exist until upward wage pressures and worker militancy begin to develop. They, then, move on to other poorer regions and repeat the process. In this great surge of "flexible" open, free-market migration, multinationals "cream" the poor countries for cheap and relatively docile labor, and they do so with the collaborative repression provided by governing elites in those countries. As William Greider (1997: 32) recently put it: "The economics of globalization . . . relies upon a barbaric transaction—the denial of individual rights—as a vital element of profitability."

Globalization is swelling conflict in the peripheral and semiperipheral poor regions of the world. In country after country, clashes between workers and authorities, often violent in form, are happening with increasing frequency as people struggle collectively for human rights, worker rights, and to demand political and economic improvements. Thousands of wildcat strikes, "flash protests," and riots have been reported in the press but these often do not get reported in the official strike statistics.

These new working-class militants are disproportionately young, inexperienced, women who toil in sweat shops making shoes, shirts, watches, toys, and electrical appliances for export. They brave the enormous odds erected by companies, police, paramilitary squads, military troops, their own government officials, and often cultural norms that prohibit any form of aggressive action by women. Since strikes and other labor actions are typically illegal in developing countries, these workers are defying the law. Yet their actions occur with increasing frequency even when these simple collective expressions of defiance can easily be repaid with long prison terms or much worse.

Repressive labor regimes and authoritarian politics tend to be characteristic magnets for globalized capital expansion. What draws corporations to many locations around the world is the recognition that labor surpluses allow extraordinarily low wage rates along with governments that prevent workers from doing anything about it. As William Greider (1997: 32) recently put it: "Corporations and governments, such as Indonesia's, seek prosperity for the few by curbing unions and suppressing workers." In fact, many of the national economic "miracles" of the past decade (the "Brazilian miracle," the "Asian Tigers") have been aided and abetted by the repression of basic human rights. Examples are, sadly, all too abundant. This was the case in China's democracy rebellion in 1989. And now that Hong Kong is ruled by the Beijing regime, workers there are confronting hostility from both the new government and the business tycoons. Within weeks of the summer of 1997 takeover, basic workers' rights were suspended. Days before the 1997 Christmas holidays, 45 men, women, and children were massacred in the Chiapas region of Mexico. Those slain were reportedly supporters of the left-wing (i.e., worker, and Indian friendly) Zapatista National Liberation Army (ZNLA); the assailants were state-trained paramilitary units in the region (*New York Times*, December 28, 1997).

As powerful as the rhetoric of globalization is today, we must understand that it does not happen through automatic motion of inexorable economic laws or imperatives. Economic globalization is driven by political-strategic decisions rooted in material interests that seek superprofits. Corporate exits, or threats to exit, to play the widening serial capital migration game, may be given their possibility through changing economic and technical conditions, but their realization is contingent on politics—government policies that facilitate the exit in the country of origin and government repression of workers in country of destination.

This "globalization" strategy will extract a price at home and abroad. The time necessary for a significant accumulation of the costs associated with contradictory containments poses an important remaining question: What direction is class conflict likely to take in the future?

IV. CLASS CONFLICTS INTO THE 21st CENTURY

Capitalism contains an enormous transformative capacity. But no single class is *the* transformative agent of the future. It is not capitalists as such, not state agents, not the proletariat, but rather the inherently contradictory dialectical character of the class *relation* itself that is the transformative dynamic of society. The problem is that capitalist dynamics do not have a single concrete trajectory or a single potential future. The path actually taken depends heavily on past history and current class struggles that are shaping the terrain on which future struggles will unfold. What, then, might be the most likely future for class conflict in the early 21st century?

One possibility, in line with the "decline of class and class conflict" prognostications, is that class conflict would disappear. Based on the evidence reviewed in the previous section, this does not seem a likely scenario. In fact, there are two very serious conceptual errors in the withering away of class conflict theories. For one, they mistake a downward movement in a cycle (e.g., 50–60 year longs cycles in global capitalist boom and bust) of militancy for a long-term trend. The second problem is that they fail to grasp the multidimensionality and fluidity of class conflict; that is, it does not always manifest itself in precisely the same locations and in the same forms. In fact, in the very process of class struggle the meaning of class might be transmuted into a conflict that is thought to be based on race or gender relations rather than class. The main point is that so long as the world is organized on principles of class domination, exploitation, and extreme inequality, class conflict will not simply "wither away." In fact, if past long waves of capitalist reorganization and massive class conflict are any indication, the next large wave of class confrontation will occur early in the next century, likely between 2005 and 2020.

A second possibility is the construction of a new institutionalized "class truce," "accord," or new "social contract," perhaps similar to the one put in place in the aftermath of the Second World War. This could conceivably happen within the next generation, but is not likely without other major social changes taking place first. For such an institutional reordering to have a real chance, capital must be generally and seriously threatened; that is, there must be a major crisis (e.g., global economic disaster or world war induced by a major North-South conflict over the distribution of world surplus-value) combined with a mobilized working class that is sufficiently strong to be taken seriously.

For the working class to gain in strength, substantially more class conflict will likely have to take place. We can read the signs in current social circumstances. The face and actions of the working class will continue to change following some of the patterns that are already becoming clear. Globalization processes will likely continue to batter workers. Unless the working people of the core nations, such as the United States, want their living standards to continue declining toward the global lowest common denominator, the labor movement must gain enormous national strength and forge relations of solidarity with labor movements in other parts of the world. The goal should be a leveling-up of the living standards in the periphery and semiperiphery, not a leveling down in the core. With the resurgence of organized labor in the past several years, there are some hopeful signs. Organized labor in the United States, for example, is attempting to regain its activism and movement vigor, to once again become a social movement unionism rather than the conservative business unionism of the past several decades. Yet much remains to be done.

Forms of class conflict will change, too. New technologies, strategies, and organizational forms often used to more efficiently subordinate, discipline, and displace labor, will produce new contradictions as they are turned against capital. Several recent instances illustrate the point. First, there have already been class conflicts played out in cyberspace. For example, in response to the recent downsizing at Bridgestone/Firestone, members of the technically sophisticated International Federation of Chemical, Energy, Mine and General Workers' Union (ICEM) fought back with mass salvos of e-mail protests to CEOs and "hotlinks" into Bridgestone's home page that announced to the world the workers' story of struggle with their company. Second, "just-in-time" (JIT) production schemes are proving to be more vulnerable to strikes than previous Fordist mass production. Especially in industries such as autos, the JIT approach to minimizing production inventory costs has meant that strikes in parts supply plants have a much greater impact than old arrangements in which inventories contained substantial buffer stock. The series of successful strikes against General Motors during the first half of 1997 is a good example. Third, part of the new "flexible production" ensemble is capital mobility. As capital roams the globe settling in regions where labor is most exploitable (i.e., weakest), it cultivates precisely the conditions it seeks to avoid—the antagonist is brought on stage. In location after location, capital plants the seeds of new labor movements.

Capitalism recomposes social classes through time. In recent decades the working class within advanced capitalist nations has changed in composition and appearance. For example, in the United States, the traditionally male, blue-collar, mass production worker is being replaced by female (and minority) service workers. Signs of discontent are especially high among public sector service workers and many professionals. Even physicians are beginning to organize. But if the potential for a new, more vibrant, working class formation is to be realized, working people, *as always*, must overcome serious divisions (e.g., race, gender, occupational) that weaken them as a class. If this fundamental goal of class formation is unsuccessful, an all too likely future is one in which race, ethnic, and gender hatreds are cultivated in even more virulent strains than those we now face.

What will the working classes of the next century struggle to attain? In general, these are likely to be old goals. An important part of the agenda will include expanded democracy. In the peripheral regions of the world, this will take the form of struggles for basic human rights and civil rights necessary for even meager political democracy. In the advanced core nations, where forms of political democracy already exist, the drive will be toward an expanded socioeconomic democracy that attempts to weaken the ravages of capital and market vagaries while giving more autonomy and power to working people. For many the dream remains a democracy that overcomes capitalism. This would involve nothing short of the elimination of the working class through the destruction of the wage form of social value. The withering away of class and class conflict would necessitate the end of commodified laboring arrangements in which people work *for* and *as* capital and all that is sacred within that form of social organization—for example, destructive "work ethics" and productivity expansions as the panacea for all social ills.

The old struggles and conflicts that started with the emergence of capitalism continue today and will undoubtedly be with us in the next century. Throughout the history of this class conflict capital has not always won, but it has generally held the upper hand. At the current historical moment that hand is squeezing especially hard and political conditions are generally quite grim. In today's world, the enormous imbalance between profit growth and wage work, or between the fortunes of the stock market and those of average workers are only the more obvious signs that the "free" market economy heavily favors capital over work. Within the developing countries, labor movements are struggling to emerge in areas in which capital has penetrated. They battle for basic human rights in general and worker rights in particular. These rights can be achieved in one of two ways: through orderly global politics that enlist the power and authority of core nation-states, or through the road that takes decades of bloody conflict. Within parts of the capitalist core (e.g., the U.S.), social arrangements won by working-class and poor people over this century, reforms that helped humanize Western capitalism, are facing serious threats. Current trends—assaults by corporations against working people, threats of business migration, rollbacks of social programs, prominent racialized ideology, widening inequality, growth in child, sweatshop, and slave labor globally—reflect a fragmentation and weakening of working class and democratic forces on the eve of the 21st century. The forces of class exploitation, inequality, and suffering are as extensive and deep as ever. Postindustrial trends (hailed in core nations) have been harbingers of a more harsh class reality veiled by a softer class ideology.

Taken together, these trends presage more, not less, class conflict in the next century. However, due to the indeterminate quality of class conflict, we cannot know for certain what shape it will take in the future. But surely the greatest failure of insight and sociological imagination is to assume that there will be none.

Also See the Following Articles

COLONIALISM AND IMPERIALISM • INDUSTRIAL VS. PREINDUSTRIAL FORMS OF VIOLENCE • POLITICAL ECONOMY OF VIOLENCE AND NONVIOLENCE • SOCIAL EQUALITY AND INEQUALITY

Bibliography

Amsden, A. (1981). An international comparison of the rate of surplus value in manufacturing industry. *Cambridge Journal of Economics* 5 (September): 229–249.

Brooks, C., & Manza, J. (1997). Class politics and political change in the United States, 1952–1992. *Social Forces* 76 (December): 379–408.

Brym, R., Gillespie, M., & Lenton, R. (1989). Class power, class mobilization, and class voting: The Canadian case. *Canadian Journal of Sociology* 14 (1): 25–44.

Budrys, G. (1996). *When doctors join unions.* Itaca, NY: ILR Press, Cornell University.

Chomsky, N. (1996). *Class warfare.* Common Courage Press, Monroe, Maine.

Clark, T. N., Lipset, S. M., & Rempel, M. (1993). The declining political significance of social class. *International Sociology* 8 (September): 293–316.

Cleaver, H. (1979). *Reading capital politically.* Austin: University of Texas Press.

Dubofsky, M. (1995). Labor unrest in the United States, 1906–90. *Review* 18 (Winter): 125–135.

Edwards, P. (1981). *Strikes in the United States, 1881–1974.* New York: St. Martin's.

Esping-Andersen, G. (1994). The eclipse of the democratic class struggle? European class structures at fin de siecle. University of Trento, Italy.

Fantasia, R. (1987). *Cultures of solidarity.* Berkeley: University of Califoria Press.

Fantasia, R. (1993). The assault on American labor. In *Social Problems* (C. Calhoun and G. Ritzer, Eds.). New York: McGraw-Hill.

Fillipelli, R. (1990). *Labor conflict in the United States: An encyclopedia.* New York: Garland Publishing.

Fusfeld, D. R. (1984). Government and the suppression of radical labor, 1877–1918. In *Statemaking and social movements* (C. Bright and S. Harding, Eds.), pp. 344–77. Ann Arbor: University of Michigan Press.

Greider, W. (1997). Why the global economy needs worker rights. *Working USA* 1 (May–June): 32–44.

Griffin, L., Botsko, C., Wahl, A., & Isaac L. (1991). Theoretical generality, case particularity: Qualitative comparative analysis of trade union growth and decline. *International Journal of Comparative Sociology* 32, 1–2: 110–136.

Griffin, L., & Korstad, R. (1995). Class as race and gender: Making and breaking a labor union in the Jim Crow South. *Social Science History* 19 (4): 426–454.

Griffin, L., Wallace, M., & Rubin, B. (1986). Capitalist resistance to the organization of labor before the New Deal. *American Sociological Review* 51 (April): 147–67.

Hibbs, D. A. (1978). On the political economy of long-run trends in strike activity. *British Journal of Political Science* 8: 153–175.

Hout, M., Brooks, C., & Manza, J. (1995). The democratic class struggle in the United States, 1948–1992. *American Sociological Review* 60 (December): 805–828.

Isaac, L., & Christiansen, L. (1997). Degradation of labor, cultures of co-operation: Braverman's "Labor," Lordstown, and the social factory. Forthcoming in *Labor and monopoly capital in the late twentieth century: The Braverman legacy and beyond* (M. Wardell, P. Meiksens, T. Steiger, Eds.). Albany: State University of New York Press.

Isaac, L., & Griffin, L.(1989). Ahistoricism in time-series analyses of historical process: Critique, redirection, and illustrations from U.S. labor history. *American Sociological Review* 54 (December): 873–890.

Kimeldorf, H. (1994). Class not strata: It's not just where you stand, but what you stand for. In *From the Left Bank to the mainstream* (P. McGuire and D. McQuarie, Eds.), pp. 13–28. Dix Hills, NY: General Hall.

Lind, M. (1995). To have and have not: Notes on the progress of the American class war. *Harper's Magazine* (June): 35–47.

Marsland, S. E. (1989). *The birth of the Japanese labor movement.* Honolulu: University of Hawaii Press.

Marx, K. (1967). *Capital.* Three Volumes. New York: International Publishers.

Marx, K. (1973). *Grundrisse.* Translated by M. Nicolaus. New York: Vintage Books.

McCammon, H. J. (1994). Disorganizing and reorganizing conflict: Outcomes of the state's legal regulation of the strike since the Wagner Act. *Social Forces* 72 (June): 1011–1049.

Moody, K. (1997). Towards an international social-movement unionism. *New Left Review* #225 (September–October): 52–72.

Myles, J., & Turegun, A. (1994). Comparative studies in class structure. *Annual Review of Sociology* 20: 103–124.

Piven, F., & Cloward, R. (1997). *The breaking of the American social compact.* New York: The New Press.

Postone, M. (1993). *Time, labor, and social domination.* Cambridge: Cambridge University Press.

Scott, J. C. (1990). *Domination and the arts of resistance.* New Haven: Yale University Press.

Selden, M. (1995). Labor unrest in China, 1831–1990. *Review* 18 (Winter): 69–86.

Silver, B. J. (1995a). Labor unrest and world-systems analysis. *Review* 18 (Winter): 7–34.

Silver, B. J. (1995b). World-scale patterns of labor-capital conflict. *Review* 18 (Winter): 155–192.

Silver, B. J. (1988). Turning points of workers' militancy in the world automobile industry, 1930s–1990s. *Research in the Sociology of Work* 7: Forthcoming.

Stepan-Norris, J., & Zeitlin, M. (1989). "Who gets the bird?": Or, how the communists won power and trust in America's unions: The relative autonomy of intraclass political struggles. *American Sociologist Review* 54 (August): 503–523.

Stillman, D. (1997). Working USA interview: Hong Kong union leader Lee Cheuk Yan. *Working USA* 1 (November–December): 40–47.

Tarrow, S. (1993). Cycles of collective action: Between moments of madness and the repertoire of contention. *Social Science History* 17 (Summer): 281–307.

Tucker, J. (1993). Everyday forms of employee resistance. *Sociological Forum* 8, 1:25–45.

Weber, M. (1978). *Economy and society.* Re-issue edited by G. Roth and C. Wittich. Berkeley: University of California Press.

Western, B. (1993). Postwar unionization in eighteen advanced capitalist countries. *American Sociological Review* 58 (April): 266–282.

Wood, E. M. (1995). Democracy against capitalism. New York: Cambridge University Press.

Woolman, W., & Colamosca, A. (1997). The Judas economy. *Working USA* 1 (September–October): 51–61.

Wright, E. (1985). *Classes.* London: Verso Books.

Cold War

Brigitte H. Schulz
Trinity College

GLOSSARY

Cold War Denotes the struggle between the United States and the Soviet Union for global power and influence during much of the 20th century.

Marshall Plan Also called the European Recovery Program, committed $17 billion in U.S. aid for the reconstruction of war-torn European economies after World War II.

Military-Industrial Complex A term coined by President Eisenhower in his farewell address to the nation, in which he warned of the dire consequences of an alliance between the defense industry and the Pentagon.

Mutual Assured Destruction Emerged as a strategic doctrine in the 1960s in recognition that nuclear war between the superpowers would amount to mutual suicide.

NATO Founded in 1949 as a trans-Atlantic military alliance to guarantee the the security of Western Europe. NATO continues to exist and is accepting formerly communist countries in Central Europe as new members.

Nixon Doctrine Ended the American commitment to contain communism anywhere by transferring primary responsibility for defense to the countries directly involved.

Truman Doctrine Enunciated in March 1947 and linked the global containment of communism to American national security.

Warsaw Pact Founded in 1955 as a military alliance between the Soviet Union and Eastern European countries against foreign threats. It formally dissolved on July 1, 1991.

THE TERM COLD WAR is generally credited to Walter Lippmann, a prominent American journalist and early critic of U.S. foreign policy after World War II. The Cold War was a period of intense global competition and unprecedented arms build-up between the two superpowers, the United States and the Soviet Union. There is some disagreement about when precisely the Cold War began, but general agreement exists that it ended in 1990 with the collapse of communism in Eastern Europe and the unification of Germany. The Cold War led to massive military spending, with $21 trillion spent globally between 1960 and 1990 alone. The Cold War also coincided with the onset of the nuclear age, forever changing the nature of warfare and introducing new strategies such as deterrence and mutual assured destruction to military planning.

I. THE ORIGINS AND CAUSES OF THE COLD WAR

Given the scale of the Cold War, both in terms of military spending and the ever-present danger of nuclear confrontation, the question of how and why it started has been a matter of considerable scholarly debate. This debate can be grouped into two broad categories: the traditional American and the revisionist perspectives.

A. The Traditional U.S. Perspective

Proponents of this perspective tend to hold a deep ideological commitment to free market capitalism and Western-style democracy. This standpoint is coupled with a view of the United States as basically isolationist, peace-loving, and generous toward the rest of the world. From this perspective, Americans only get involved in foreign conflicts reluctantly in order to fight a dictator, an evil force threatening freedom and democracy. As soon as a foreign dictator is either eliminated or effectively subdued—from Adolf Hitler to Saddam Hussein—Americans go back to concentrate on domestic matters.

According to this view, the rise of the United States as a global power thus has its roots in *external* causes, driven by the expansionist appetites of ruthless dictators. Joseph Stalin met this prerequisite more than any other. He was ruthless and driven by traditional Russian expansionism as well as a communist ideology certain of its ultimate historical victory. A return to isolationism was impossible for the United States after World War II, since this would jeopardize Western European peace and security. The wartime alliance thus quickly turned into a relationship of bitter and protracted antagonism—the Cold War.

Supporters of this view see ample evidence of Stalin's expansionist appetite after World War II, from his refusal to leave Iran, to the domination of Eastern European countries by communist regimes propped up by the Red Army, to civil wars in Greece and China involving communists, to the Soviet Union putting pressure on Turkey regarding the Dardenelles. George Kennan's analysis of Soviet foreign policy behavior, sent in a long telegram from the American Embassy in Moscow on February 22, 1946, confirmed American suspicions: The Soviet Union's appetite for expansion was indeed limitless, requiring constant vigilance on the part of the United States in order to keep it in check. Winston Churchill, in his famous Iron Curtain speech delivered in Fulton, Missouri, on March 5, 1946, reminded Americans that Russians only understand force. Harry Truman, who became president after Franklin D. Roosevelt's death on April 12, 1945, had already shown that he was not afraid to be tough with the Russians. As Nazi Germany advanced into the Soviet Union, *The New York Times* quoted his reaction on July 24, 1941: "If we see that Germany is winning the war we ought to help Russia, and if Russia is winning we ought to help Germany, and in that way let them kill as many as possible." After Truman met with Soviet foreign minister Molotov at the White House on April 23, 1945, the Russian observed: "I have never been talked to like that in my life." And at the final Allied conference in Potsdam Conference in July, 1945, Truman reportedly treated Stalin with utter contempt.

On March 12, 1947 President Truman addressed the joint houses of Congress to outline America's response to Soviet foreign policy behavior. This policy response, usually referred to as the *Truman Doctrine*, called for an American commitment to contain communism and to defend democracy and freedom wherever it may be threatened. President Truman thus tied American *national* interest to the nature of domestic governments around the globe. This policy, said Truman, "is no more than the frank admission that totalitarian regimes imposed upon free peoples by direct or indirect aggression, undermine the foundations of international peace and hence the security of the US." Truman simultaneously committed $400 million in aid to Greece and Turkey, two countries whose security the United States saw as most immediately in need of American assistance in fighting communist aggression.

On June 5, 1947, Secretary of State George C. Marshall announced during a commencement speech at Harvard University that the United States would commit a total of $17 billion over a 4-year period to help in the reconstruction of European economies and societies. By 1952, more than $12 billion had been disbursed by the Marshall Fund. The newly created Central Intelligence Agency also helped in the effort by covertly aiding anticommunist trade unions and political parties, especially in Italy and France. The United States viewed the Soviet Union's refusal to accept help from the Marshall Fund, or to allow any Eastern European government to receive these funds, as further proof of Stalin's ill will and intransigence.

Events in Germany during 1947 and 1948 cemented the Cold War division of Europe. The Soviets had begun to implement a series of reforms in their zone of occupation shortly after the war ended. The United States and Great Britain also took steps to bring their zones of occupation in line with Western thinking on the future of Germany. The fusion of their zones into *Bizonia* as one administrative unit became effective on January 1, 1947. A currency reform was carried out on June 18, 1948, in the Western zones to prepare for Marshall Plan funds. France, the United States and Great Britain simultaneously recommended the creation of a separate West German state. In response, the Soviets blocked off all land access to Berlin, located deep inside the Soviet zone of occupation. The West responded by initiating a huge airlift operation. The United States and Britain flew a total of 277,569 missions with 2,325,510 tons of cargo, including 1,586,029 tons of coal and 536,705 tons of food that presented a lifeline for West Berlin's 2.5 million inhabitants. The Soviets lifted the blockade on May 12, 1949. The transition from wartime alliance to a relationship of profound mutual antagonism, fueled by deep distrust and suspicion, was complete.

On August 30, 1948, the American government instituted its first peacetime military draft. A few months later it joined its first major peacetime military alliance by becoming a signatory to the North Atlantic Treaty Organization (NATO) on April 4, 1949, along with Belgium, Canada, Denmark, France, Great Britain, Iceland, Italy, Luxembourg, the Netherlands, Norway and Portugal. NATO committed itself to the defense of Western Europe against communist expansion. It represented the organizational recognition to the deep division that now characterized Europe. An Iron Curtain had indeed descended upon Europe that would not open again until 1989.

B. The Revisionist Perspective

According to revisionist historians, the changing nature of the American economy doomed isolationism long before the Cold War began. Revisionists do not deny the ruthless nature of Stalin's rule, but argue that, given the level of destruction in the Soviet Union, the country was committed to postwar reconstruction, not foreign expansion. World War II had cost more than 27 million Russians lives. In addition, the Germans had destroyed most of the material infrastructure of the country, from 35,000 miles of railroad tracks and 56,000 miles of main highways to 84,000 schools and colleges and 43,000 libraries. Revisionists argue that Stalin was not driven by the ideological desire to support the growth of communism abroad as much as by a keen appreciation of the need to safeguard communism inside the Soviet Union itself.

Why then did the Soviets dominate Eastern Europe after the war? Revisionists agree with political realists such as Winston Churchill and Walter Lippmann that the creation of a *cordon sanitaire* in Eastern Europe was based on legitimate Soviet security concerns along its Western borders. A history of invasions, particularly from the Germans, convinced the Soviets of this necessity. Domination over Eastern Europe did not equal an attempt to subject the entire globe to Soviet rule. Nor was it evidence that the Soviet Union intended to jeopardize its relationship with the Western allies. Winston Churchill reported to the House of Commons on February 27, 1945, upon his return from Yalta:

> The impression I brought back from the Crimea, and from all my other contacts, is that Marshal Stalin and the Soviet leaders wish to live in honorable friendship and equity with the Western democracies. I also feel that their word is their bond. I know of no government which stands to its obligations, even in its own despite, more solidly than the Russian Soviet Government.

Revisionists point out that it is a matter of historical record that FDR well understood Soviet security concerns and made important concessions to Stalin at the Yalta Conference in February 1945. FDR and Churchill at that point saw Soviet domination over Eastern Europe as *defensive* in nature. After FDR died in April 1945 subsequent American leaders, from President Truman to Secretary of State James Byrnes (who had actually attended the Yalta Conference and took copious notes) denied this understanding had ever been reached and publicly denounced Soviet postwar policies vis-à-vis Eastern Europe as communist expansion.

Why this duplicity, revisionists ask? Why this insistence on explaining to the American people that they must make continued sacrifices to defend freedom and democracy around the world because of Soviet expansionism? Revisionists argue that the answer lies in America's new role as hegemon within the capitalist world economy for which the Bretton Woods conference in July 1944 laid the groundwork. At this conference, the International Monetary Fund and the World Bank were founded as multilateral institutions designed to regulate economic challenges under American control and guidance. The U.S. dollar became the most important international currency and thus became a crucial pillar of the postwar global financial system.

The United States thus committed itself to becoming a global power well before the war ended.

American Fordism, based on the assembly line, had clearly established its superiority over foreign competitors with spectacular increases in productivity in the interwar period. For example, in the 1920s a worker in the Ford Motor Company produced 20.5 cars annually, while a European automobile worker made only 2 cars during the same time period. Industries making electrical appliances such as washing machines, refrigerators, and radios also began applying continuous-flow production, making them highly competitive on the world market. Fordism also fundamentally altered American foreign policy. The traditional sectors of the American economy such as railroads, iron and steel, and coal, as well as Midwestern agriculture, were domestically oriented and deeply committed to isolationism. In contrast, the emerging leading sectors, from the automobile to electrically powered machinery as well as the oil companies, rapidly developed an appetite for global markets and investments. Revisionists argue that this constituency pushed for a strong U.S. presence overseas, drawing American foreign policy into a more interventionist posture. Revisionists point out that foreign intervention in defense of economic interests have formed an integral part of U.S. relations vis-a-vis Latin America since the enunciation of the Monroe Doctrine in 1823, largely to protect the interests of American agricultural firms such as the United Fruit Company. Now that American manufacturers traded and invested in all corners of the planet, American foreign policy also had to span the globe.

FDR's fear of another economic depression once the war ended became another factor fueling a future interventionist American foreign policy. As early as 1940, a study conducted by the influential Council on Foreign Relations concluded that, "at a minimum, the American 'national interest' involved free access to markets and raw materials in the British Empire, the Far East, and the entire Western hemisphere." The Council, in turn, heavily influenced the Roosevelt administration in its conceptualization of the postwar international order.

Revisionists thus argue that the United States became a global power when *domestic economic considerations* called for such a change. However, given the nature of domestic politics and alliances inside the United States, it became necessary to create a foreign enemy that would tip the political balance away from those who wanted to return to isolationism. The United States invented the myth of limitless communist expansion to mobilize domestic support for America's global hegemonic role. Officials who disagreed with the insistence that the Soviet Union represented an aggressively expansionist power, or with the American military buildup and nuclear weapons testing, or any other aspect of the changed global role of the United States, were silenced. For example, in a private memorandum dated July 23, 1946, Henry A. Wallace, Secretary of Commerce, challenged President Truman on a number of U.S. actions after the war, including appropriating $13 billion for the War and Navy Departments, the atomic tests on the Bikini Islands, and "efforts to secure bases spread over half the globe from which the other half of the globe can be bombed. I cannot but feel that these actions must make it look to the rest of the world as if we were only paying lip service to peace at the conference table." When Henry Wallace began discussing his views publicly the following September, President Truman asked for his resignation. James Byrnes was forced to resign as Secretary of State on January 20, 1947, because President Truman felt that Byrnes was "babying the Soviets." The House Committee on Un-American Activities (HUAC) conducted its first hearings on October 20, 1947, in order to find communists in Hollywood. In February 1950 Senator McCarthy announced that he had "proof" that hundreds of communists were employed by the State Department. During a speech to the Senate on June 14, 1951, McCarthy spoke of a "great conspiracy, a conspiracy on a scale so immense and an infamy so black as to dwarf any previous such venture in the history of man." A communist conspiracy threatened freedom and democracy not only abroad, but also in the United States itself. Anticommunism, coupled with a blanket approval of American global military expansion, had become the litmus test for the embodiment of a good and loyal American.

The corporate and political leadership of the advanced capitalist countries had keenly understood the threat to capitalism from the inside since the Bolshevik Revolution. Marxism/Leninism enjoyed a certain amount of support among workers and intellectuals in the United States as well as in Europe. The first Red Scare in the United States in 1919 failed to eliminate this support entirely and the Depression in the 1930s actually fueled it. The elites in the advanced capitalist countries welcomed fascism, with its militant anticommunism, as an antidote to the Bolshevik menace. Two full decades before the enunciation of the Truman Doctrine, Winston Churchill congratulated the Italian people for Benito Mussolini and Italian fascism at the end of a visit to Italy in 1927:

> If I had been an Italian I am sure that I should have been wholeheartedly with you from start

> to finish in your triumphant struggle against the bestial appetites and passions of Leninism . . . Externally, your movement has rendered a service to the whole world . . . Italy has shown that there is a way of fighting the subversive forces which can rally the mass of the people, properly led, to value and wish to defend the honor and stability of civilized society. She has provided the necessary antidote to the Russian poison.

Moreover, in 1933 Churchill called Mussolini "the greatest law-giver among living men" in recognition of his anticommunism.

It is evident to revisionist historians that the Cold War began immediately after the Bolshevik Revolution in 1917 with the deliberate and systematic attempt to crush this challenge to capitalism's vision of modernity and progress. In the immediate aftermath of the Revolution, the Western powers, including the United States, intervened in the civil war in Russia. On September 27, 1920, President Woodrow Wilson explained his administration's refusal to grant diplomatic recognition to the Soviet Union this way: "Bolshevism is a mistake and it must be resisted as all mistakes must be resisted . . . It cannot survive because it is wrong." After Hitler came to power Stalin repeatedly warned the Western powers of Germany's growing rearmament efforts in violation of the Versailles Treaty. The West ignored these warnings. Instead, France and Great Britain consented to Hitler's annexation of the *Sudetenland* in Munich in 1938, a move that turned the German military East. Given Hitler's bellicose stand toward Bolshevism, including sending communists and trade unionleaders to concentration camps very early on, this "appeasement" of Hitler and acquiescence to the *Anschluß* was not as simple-minded as it might appear. According to revisionists, Nazi Germany's goal of eradicating communism was absolutely compatible with the wishes and objectives of the major Western powers. With Germany's defeat and the Soviet Union's victory, the struggle against communism metamorphosed into yet another form: the Cold War.

Revisionists argue that the West primarily fueled the developments between 1945 and 1948 that led from the wartime alliance to bitter and protracted antagonism. The United States had emerged from the war with the world's strongest economy and as the sole nuclear power. As Gar Alperovitz has pointed out, the atomic bomb gave the United States an absolute strategic advantage that explains President Truman's refusal to honor FDR's agreements reached with Stalin at Yalta. Possession of the bomb, its use in Hiroshima and Nagasaki, and threat of its renewed use in other conflicts made the United States the real aggressor in the creation of the Cold War.

II. FROM ANTAGONISM TO DÉTENTE

Hardening positions on both sides of the Iron Curtain after 1948 largely prevented direct negotiations on improving relations between the two superpowers for well over a decade. In the meantime, much of the struggle between them took place by proxy.

A. The International Context

In Europe, the Cold War contributed directly to the division of Germany into two separate states. West Germany, or the Federal Republic of Germany (FRG), was founded on May 23, 1949, with the intent of making it a showcase for capitalism. In fact, the monetary reform undertaken by the British and Americans in their zones of occupation in June 1948 had precipitated the Berlin blockade. The eastern part of the country, under Soviet occupation, became the German Democratic Republic (GDR) on October 7, 1949. The Soviet Union did not recognize the GDR as a sovereign nation until March 26, 1954.

The Warsaw Pact came about on May 14, 1955, in response to the admission of the FRG into NATO on May 5. Although Stalin had died 2 years earlier, the new Soviet leadership under Nikita Khrushchev shared his fears of a renewed threat emanating from Germany. Albania, Bulgaria, Czechoslovakia, the GDR, Poland, Hungary, Romania, and the USSR became signatories to the Warsaw Treaty Organization, an alliance that defined itself as acting in self-defense against external threats. The Warsaw Pact also served the purpose of integrating Eastern European militaries on the basis of a new modicum of equality with Moscow.

Most important developments in the first two decades after the war occurred in Asia. China became a communist nation on October 1, 1949, after defeating the Kuomintang government. On June 25, 1950, the Korean War began when communist North Korea invaded the southern part of the country. It ended when both sides signed an armistice on July 27, 1953, but the country has retained its division at the 38th parallel to the present. In Indochina, communist forces under the leadership of Ho Chi Minh defeated their French colonial masters in Dien Bien Phu on May 7, 1954. John Foster Dulles had warned a year earlier of a "domino effect" in Southeast Asia, one that would engulf the entire region in communist dictatorships. Negotiations in Geneva on July 21, 1954, established a "provisional demarcation line" across the middle of Vietnam and elections were set in both parts of the country within 2 years. Ho Chi Minh, the communist leader of North Vietnam, enjoyed overwhelming support in all of Vietnam and fear of a communist victory in the South prevented the election from being held. Vietnam sank into an escalating abyss of violence. The United States began to provide military advisors to the South under President Eisenhower. By John F. Kennedy's assassination in 1963, the United States had sent 16,000 American combat troops to South Vietnam to fight against communist insurgents from the North. By early 1968, President Johnson had dispatched roughly 500,000 men to Vietnam. In 1973 the United States signed a peace accord with the North Vietnamese in Paris in recognition of the North's victory.

Recently decolonized countries such as Indonesia and India openly defied the United States in Bandung, Indonesia, in 1955 by advocating a policy of nonalignment with either the East or the West. They characterized their problems as largely economic and attributable to colonial exploitation. The United States viewed this critique as unjustified and communist-inspired. John Foster Dulles called nonalignment immoral and cowardly in the face of the great evil of communism. The decolonization process and discourse about postcolonial political and economic development thus became an integral part of the Cold War. Just as opponents of the Cold War had been silenced inside the United States, Washington either overtly or covertly neutralized or eliminated any Third World leader challenging the status quo. In this environment, the litmus test for the eligibility of any Third World government to receive Western support became a commitment to anticommunism, not to democracy. As a result, the West supported a string of ruthless dictators, from Mobuto Sese Seko in Zaire to Suharto in Indonesia. The Soviet Union, with an ideology based on antiimperialism, became the center for antisystemic struggles directed against Washington and the global economy.

B. Bilateral Superpower Relations

Extreme hostility marked bilateral relations between the two superpowers throughout the 1950s. The United States continued to oppose the Soviet presence in Central and Eastern Europe and to demand the "rollback" of communism. On January 12, 1954, John Foster Dulles announced "massive retaliation" with the use of nuclear weapons as the future American response to Soviet advances anywhere in the world. Although the Soviet Union had entered the nuclear age in September 1949, its ability to threaten the U.S. mainland did not come until its first successful testing of an intercontinental ballistic missile (ICBM) in August 1957. The Soviets launched Sputnik I on October 4, followed by Sputnik II on November 3, 1957. The National Aeronautics and Space Agency (NASA) was founded in 1958, as American policymakers pondered the strategic implications of the Soviet Union having entered the missile age. Deterrence based on massive retaliation had lost its effectiveness. American security experts now advocated a strategy of "flexible response" that would involve the use not only of nuclear weapons but also of conventional forces should armed conflict with the Soviet Union break out. The introduction of a second-strike capability further enhanced American nuclear deterrence strategy. This policy required keeping solid-fuel Minuteman missiles in underground silos and Polaris missiles on submarines in order to protect them from a Soviet strike. Military spending rose by 30% under the Kennedy Administration in order to pay for these new strategies.

Studies about Soviet capabilities conducted by think tanks such as the RAND and Mitre corporations for the Pentagon added to concerns about the Soviets. These think tanks, with their heavy reliance on Pentagon contracts, various military intelligence organizations, as well as the Central Intelligence Agency, consistently overestimated Soviet military capabilities, from the "bomber gap" of the early to mid-fifties to the "missile gap" after the Sputnik launches. A powerful alliance emerged between the defense industry, military planners in the Pentagon, and politicians with large military industries in their districts. President Eisenhower grew increasingly worried about this development and warned of the negative consequences of this "military-industrial complex" in his presidential farewell address. The Pentagon nevertheless continued with its procurement of intercontinental ballistic missiles (ICBMs) based on the alleged missile gap. By 1964 the United States had 834 ICBMs, compared to 120 deployed by the Soviet Union. Clearly a gap existed, but it was in America's favor.

Neither domestic nor foreign considerations gave the Soviet elite reasons to deny the exaggerated American projections of Russian military strength. The Soviet leadership routinely published falsified statistics of the country's economic progress and military might in order to create the impression that the socialist experiment was succeeding. The Kremlin had important reasons for hiding the true state of country. Domestically, admission of the truth might well have led to destabilizing uprisings, while overseas any hint of failure would have tarnished the carefully fostered image that Soviet socialism represented a viable alternative to capitalism. Exaggerated American claims of Soviet capabilities thus played into the hands of the Soviet leadership. Emboldened by its new reputation of invincibility after the Sputnik launchings, the Soviet Union began a game of brinkmanship with the West. In 1958, Nikita Khrushchev demanded the withdrawal of the allies from West Berlin within 6 months. The ensuing crisis eventually culminated in the building of the Berlin Wall in August 1961, a visible reminder of Germany's division. Despite its outward appearance of strength, however, the Wall came to symbolize a humiliating defeat for the Soviets and the socialist system. The Western allies refused to give in to the Soviet demand for withdrawal and the Wall became a visual symbol for the unpopularity of communism throughout the Soviet bloc.

In October 1962 Khrushchev gambled again, this time by attempting to install Soviet missiles on the island of Cuba, only 90 miles from the U.S. mainland. Fidel Castro had successfully ousted the Cuban dictator Fulgencio Batista, a close U.S. ally, on January 1, 1959. In one of the worst fiascos of his administration, Kennedy had unsuccessfully sought to overthrow Castro in the Bay of Pigs invasion on April 17, 1961, with the help of almost 1500 CIA-trained Cuban exiles. The Soviet leadership's decision to deploy Soviet missiles on Cuban soil represents one of the only moments in Soviet history driven principally by proletarian internationalism, a rhetorical cornerstone of Marxist-Leninist ideology. Khrushchev, in his deep commitment to Castro and his revolution, hoped that Soviet missiles would deter any further American military aggression against the island nation. Instead, the U.S. government imposed a naval blockade on Cuba on October 22, 1962, forcing Soviet ships to turn back without being able to unload the missiles. In return, the United States promised to refrain from future attacks on its island neighbor. The Cuban missile crisis, more than any other event in Cold War history, brought the world to the brink of a thermonuclear war. It was also a turning point in U.S.-Soviet relations.

In 1963, the superpowers installed the Hot Line to enable direct communication between the White House and the Kremlin, and passed the Limited Test Ban Treaty. The recognition of shared vulnerability and the relative stalemate between the superpowers led to yet another security concept—Mutual Assured Destruction (MAD). The MAD doctrine arose in the late 1960s in recognition that nuclear war was mutual suicide. This balance of terror now constituted the best guarantor of peace.

Détente, or the growing rapprochement between the two superpowers, began to evolve slowly under the leadership of President Nixon and Henry Kissinger, his foreign policy advisor and subsequent secretary of state. Kissinger, a brilliant tactitioner deeply steeped in traditional balance-of-power thinking, began the process by gradually normalizing relations with the People's Republic of China (PRC). He visited Beijing secretly in mid-1971, followed by an official visit by President Nixon in February 1972. Given the depth of the Sino-Soviet rift, Kissinger clearly hoped that playing the China card would give important advantages to the United States in negotiations with the Soviet Union. The United States was willing to grant de facto recognition to the Soviet sphere of influence over Eastern Europe in return for significant concessions from the Soviets in military capabilities. President Nixon signed the Anti-Ballistic Missile Treaty (ABM) on May 21, 1972, culminating 3 years of Strategic Arms Limitation Talks (SALT I). In 1974, the United States granted diplomatic recognition to the German Democratic Republic. In 1975, the United States, the Soviet Union, as well as all countries of Eastern and Western Europe signed the Helsinki Accord, committing its signatories to respect the territorial integrity of European borders and well as to the repudiation of the use of force.

The Iron Curtain had begun to open slightly for the first time since the beginning of the Cold War. The opening was to be shortlived.

III. REVOLUTION IN THE THIRD WORLD AND THE SECOND COLD WAR

It is now clear that neither superpower viewed détente as the beginning of a true rapprochement. SALT I brought some reprieve to the arms race, undoubtedly to the relief of the Soviet leadership. Recently declassified sources show that by the 1970s the Red Army was in terrible shape: Battle readiness and morale were low, alcoholism and the mistreatment of conscripts rampant, while theft and corruption had eroded its material infrastructure. The struggle between the two superpowers nevertheless continued unabated in the Third World. Anticolonial movements in Angola and Mozambique were fighting against Portugal, a member of the NATO alliance. Unable to receive help from the West, they had turned to the Soviet Union and the People's Republic of China for material assistance and weapons. On April 24, 1974, a military coup ended the fascist government in Lisbon. The new socialist government of Portugal granted independence to its African colonies in 1975. This victory for these explicitly Marxist/Leninist liberation movements led the Soviet leadership to conclude that the "correlation of forces" had finally turned in its favor. In 1978, a revolutionary group brandishing Marxism/Leninism as its official ideology overthrew the ancient kingdom of Haile Selassie in Ethiopia. South Yemen also became a socialist country with Soviet assistance in 1978. While conditions worsened at home, Moscow quite openly celebrated these victories for socialism abroad. It simultaneously emphasized its desire to continue a policy of peaceful coexistence with the West.

The Nixon-Kissinger team refused to delink superpower relations from developments in the Third World. Détente granted belated recognition to the status quo in Eastern Europe as well as Soviet security concerns in its immediate sphere of influence. It did not give the Soviets a carte blanche for supporting anticolonial and antisystemic revolutions. The East-West conflict thus continued unabated. After its defeat in Vietnam, the United States responded to socialist victories in the Third World mainly with covert support of opposition movements from Angola to Chile. This was in line with the Nixon Doctrine enunciated in 1969 that a country's defense was the primary responsibility of its own military. From now on, the United States would provide military and economic aid but refrain from direct military involvement.

Soviet activities in the Third World lent support to powerful forces in the United States that had rejected détente from the beginning. An important figure in this fight, Senator Henry Jackson from Washington State, staunchly advocated American military superiority. Jackson also strongly supported the Boeing Company in Seattle, Washington, a major defense contractor that produced the B-52 bomber, and the Minuteman and Cruise missiles. He worked closely with the Committee for a Democratic Majority, a group fiercely opposed to détente. Another group, the Committee on the Present Danger, founded in November 1976, pursued the same ends. It was a bipartisan organization having a membership of 60% Democrats and 40% Republicans and standing united in its commitment to take a firm stand against the Soviet Union. The Committee implored the newly elected President Jimmy Carter to take a harder stance than his predecessor. This plea did not fall on entirely deaf ears, as President Carter's presidency was marked by a concern for human rights. The lack of political freedom in the Soviet Union entered political discourse and the East-West struggle once again became couched in moral terms.

On June 18, 1979, President Carter and Leonid Brezhnev signed SALT II in Vienna but the American Congress never ratified it. The Sandinista victory over the U.S.-installed Somoza dictatorship in Nicaragua in July 1979 further fueled anxiety in Washington over Soviet successes. The Soviet intervention in Afghanistan on December 25, 1979, gave opponents of détente their final piece of evidence that Soviet expansionism remained strong. The Soviet Union, on the other hand, felt increasingly threatened by Western policies, including the NATO decision on December 12, 1979, to deploy Cruise and Pershing II missiles in West Germany.

President Carter lost the 1980 election to Ronald Reagan, a man who had based his political career on militant anticommunism going back to the persecution of communists (real and imagined) in Hollywood 1946. He was also a member of the Committee on the Present Danger and 31 members of the Committee went on to hold important positions in his administration. With the Second Cold War in full swing, President Reagan increased military spending by 40%, much of that on borrowed money that changed the role of the United States from being the world's largest creditor to largest debtor nation. The Reagan administration also actively supported antisocialist groups around the world, from Angola to Afghanistan to Nicaragua. In November 1982 Reagan announced his decision to deploy MX intercontinental missiles, and in March 1983 he proposed the Strategic Defense Initiative (SDI), also known as Star Wars, which he saw as a viable alternative to MAD. Relations between the superpowers had deteriorated to such an extent, and the use of nuclear weapons had been advocated with such enthusiasm by the Reagan administration, that in October 1983 an international group of scientists warned against the devastating effects of a "nuclear winter" should nuclear war become a reality. By November 1983, arms limitations talks between the United States and the Soviet Union had completely broken down.

Mikhail Gorbachev became General Secretary of the USSR on March 14, 1985. British Prime Minister Margaret Thatcher had met him a few days earlier and announced: "I like Mr. Gorbachev. We can do business together." This marked the beginning of a rapid and astonishing turnaround in superpower relations. Between March 12 and April 23, 1985, the two superpowers began a new round of arms reduction talks (START) in Geneva. Reagan and Gorbachev met in November 1985 for the first time, followed by a mini-summit in Reykjavik, Iceland, in October 1986. On December 8, 1987, the two leaders signed the Intermediate Nuclear Forces Treaty (INF) that called on both countries to reduce their nuclear arsenals and to eliminate all intermediate-range nuclear missiles from Europe. One year later Gorbachev announced unilateral troop reductions of 500,000 men and the graduate withdrawal of Soviet troops from Eastern Europe during a speech to the United Nations. Before the Iron Curtain had a chance to open between the two sides, it rapidly disintegrated. On May 2, 1989 the "Green Border" opened between Hungary and Austria, leading to a mass exodus of East Germans throughout the summer of 1989 amid an escalating sense of crisis. In June, Poland's Solidarity Movement won the election. By October, the Hungarian Communist Party renounced Marxism/Leninism in favor of social democracy. On November 9, 1989, the East German leadership, confused after the departure of its longtime general secretary Erich Honecker, opened the Berlin Wall, the most visible and hated symbol of the Cold War division of the continent.

In September 1990, Great Britain, France, the United States, and the Soviet Union signed a peace treaty with East and West Germany, formally concluding World War II. This agreement laid the groundwork for the unification of Germany on October 3, 1990. At a meeting in Paris from November 17 through 19, 1990, all of the countries of Europe, plus Canada, the United States, and the Soviet Union signed a new charter to regulate relations in the new era. President George Bush said of the occasion: "We have closed a chapter of history. The Cold War is over."

IV. THE LEGACY OF THE COLD WAR

According to the traditional U.S. perspective, the collapse of communism, as well as the disappearance of both the Warsaw Pact and the Soviet Union, represent the ultimate vindication of the West. Woodrow Wilson's assessment of September 1920 that communism "cannot survive because it is wrong" had proved to be correct. All efforts on the part of the Soviet Union to export the communist revolution abroad, not only to Eastern Europe, but also around the world, had failed. The United States and its NATO allies accept much of the credit for this victory, as the Western alliance steadfastly guarded against the Soviet Union's westward expansion, giving Europe the gift of 40 years of peace, stability, and economic prosperity.

Those who advocated and supported the Second Cold War go even further. They argue that beyond NATO, President Ronald Reagan's determined efforts in the 1980s to achieve strategic superiority are largely responsible for bringing the Soviet Union down. Soviet-era records now available suggest that this assessment may not be wrong. The size of the Soviet economy was not two-thirds that of the United States, as had been claimed by Moscow and agreed to by Western intelligence experts. Instead, in the early 1980s the size of the Soviet economy was roughly 14% that of U.S. GNP. As a result, the level of Soviet military spending necessary in order to achieve and maintain any type of parity with the United States imposed an enormous burden on the Soviet economy.

The traditional U.S. perspective views the end of the Cold War not only as a vindication of huge military spending and the use of nuclear deterrence to achieve a political objective, but also as proof of the superiority of Western capitalism. One analyst writing in this genre, Francis Fukuyama, went so far as to announce in the early nineties that with the collapse of communism the end of history had finally arrived.

Revisionist historians also see themselves vindicated by many events since 1990. They point to the many differences that have arisen among the Western allies since the end of the Cold War, from the war in Bosnia to frictions with the Japanese, that the invocation of the Soviet threat had greatly aided American hegemony in contracting compliance from often reluctant allies. The Cold War not only provided the glue that held the Western alliance together but also served as the umbrella under which the United States could construct a liberal postwar order.

The inability of the American economy to convert from military to civilian production to any significant extent since 1990 is further proof to revisionists that the concentration on military production begun during World War II has given the United States a permanent war economy. Since the end of the Cold War there has been an escalation in American arms sales to the rest of the world and the United States is now, in Jimmy Carter's words, "arms merchant to the world." Between 1991 and 1994, the top 10 arms exporting countries sold weapons worth $98.7 billion, 81.9% of them to the Third World. The United States sold 50.1% of these weapons, from tanks to missiles to submarines.

Revisionist critics of the Cold War view the militarization of conflicts around the world and the huge fiscal expenditures associated with the global arms trade as the single most important consequence of the Cold War. In 1995, 5 full years after the end of the Cold War, world military spending still amounted to $797 billion, 1.75 times more than in 1960, and at the rate of more than $1.5 million a minute. Military spending in the industrialized countries actually increased from $636 billion to $643 billion between 1985 and 1995.

In 1995, well over 21 million people served in the military, 14 million of them in the Third World. This, according to the revisionists, has added tremendously to the use of violence to resolve conflicts around the world.

Revisionists juxtapose the level of military spending to United Nations figures that show that toward the end of the 20th century, a quarter of the world's people live in severe poverty, 1.3 billion of them on less than the equivalent of $1 a day. Nearly a billion people are illiterate, 160 million children are chronically malnourished and 110 million are out of school, and well over a billion people lack access to safe drinking water. In the postcommunist countries of Eastern Europe and the successor to the Soviet Union, the Commonwealth of Independent States (CIS), poverty has spread to about a third of the population and about 120 million people live below the poverty line of $4 a day. In the advanced capitalist countries, 37 million people are jobless.

The UN estimates that it would cost about $40 billion a year over a 10-year period to provide basic social services such as primary education, basic health care, sanitation, and access to safe water supplies for all in the developing world. As a share of GNP, that represents half of what the United States disbursed annually between 1948 and 1952 in Marshall Plan funds. To bring everyone out of absolute poverty by providing minimum incomes would cost an additional $40 billion a year and would help establish a pattern of self-sustaining growth. This would represent roughly 10% of the amount spent annually on the military worldwide, but so far the international community has lacked the will to fund such programs.

V. CONCLUSION

As this brief analysis has made clear, it is extremely difficult to reach a definitive conclusion as to the causes and consequences of the Cold War. Much of the evidence presented by either of the two opposing camps, the traditionalists and the revisionists, is compelling. It is notoriously difficult to speculate counter-factually about profound turning points in human history. What if Cleopatra had been ugly? What if President Roosevelt had not died in April 1945, only weeks before the end of World War II? Would the Cold War still have happened? To what extent was ideology the driving force behind the Cold War? Given the size and importance of both the United States and Russia, is a lasting peace between them possible in the future?

As documents dealing with the Cold War become declassified in both the former Soviet Union and the United States, some of our questions will find answers. Others, however, may never reach a definitive conclusion, making the Cold War era at once one of the most studied and enigmatic periods in human history.

Chronology

1945	
Feb 4–11	Yalta Conference
Apr 12	FDR dies
May 7	Germany surrenders
Jul 17	Potsdam Conference begins
Aug 2	Potsdam Conference ends
Aug 6	Atomic bomb dropped on Hiroshima
Aug 9	Atomic bomb dropped on Nagasaki
Aug 14	Japan surrenders
1946	
Feb 22	Kennan's Long Telegram sent from Moscow
Mar 5	Churchill's Iron Curtain speech in Fulton, Missouri
Dec 2	Great Britain and the U.S. decide to create *Bizonia*
1947	
Mar 12	President Truman announces containment policy
June 5	George C. Marshall announces Marshall Plan at Harvard commencement
July	George Kennan's analysis is published in *Foreign Affairs*
Oct 20	House Committee on Un-American Activities (HUAC) conducts first hearing
Oct 23	Ronald Reagan testifies before HUAC
1948	
Jun 18	Currency reform in Western part of Germany
Jun 24	Berlin Blockade begins
Aug 30	Peacetime draft begins in US
1949	
Apr 4	NATO founded
May 5	Federal Republic of Germany (FRG) founded
May 12	Berlin Blockade ends
Jun 21	CIA established
Sep 23	Soviets explode first nuclear weapon
Oct 1	People's Republic of China established
Oct 7	German Democratic Republic (GDR) founded
1950	
Jan 1	$1 billion in military aid to Europe released by U.S.
Apr 7	NSC-68 makes containment a military doctrine
Jun 25	Korean War begins
Jun 30	American troops enter Korean War
1951	
Sep 8	War with Japan ends formally
Oct 22	Greece and Turkey join NATO
1952	
Oct 2	Britain explodes first atomic weapons
Oct 31	U.S. explodes first thermonuclear device
1953	
Mar 5	Stalin dies
May 31	John Foster Dulles warns of "domino effect" in Southeast Asia
Aug 14	Soviets explode first thermonuclear device
Sep 13	Khrushchev becomes 1st Secretary of Soviet Communist Party

1954	
Jan 11	U.S. announces massive retaliation via use of nuclear weapons
Mar 26	Soviets recognize GDR as sovereign nation
May 7	French defeated at Dien Bien Phu
Jun 7	U.S.-sponsored coup topples reformist government of Guatemala
1955	
Jan 12	John Foster Dulles announces doctrine of massive retaliation
Apr 17–24	Bandung Conference starts Non-Aligned Movement
May 9	West Germany officially joins NATO
May 14	Warsaw Pact founded
1956	
Feb 16	Khrushchev denounces Stalin at 20th Party Congress
May 21	U.S. explodes first airborne hydrogen bomb
Nov 4	Soviets invade Hungary
1957	
Mar 25	Treaty of Rome creates European Economic Community (EEC)
Aug 26	Soviets successfully test an intercontinental ballistic missile
Oct 4	Sputnik I launched by Soviets
Nov 11	Sputnik II launched by Soviets
1958	
Jan 1	EEC goes into effect
Mar 23	Khrushchev becomes Soviet Premier
1959	
Jan 1	Fidel Castro wins in Cuba
Jan 15	Eisenhower and Khrushchev meet in Washington, D.C.
Sept 15	Khrushchev visits US for more talks
1960	
Feb 13	France explodes first nuclear device
May 1	U.S. U-2 spy plane shot down over Soviet Union
Nov 8	John F. Kennedy elected American president
1961	
Apr 12	Cosmonaut Yuri Gagarin becomes first human to orbit Earth
Apr 17	Bay of Pigs invasion of Cuba
May 5	Astronaut Alan Shepard is first American in space
Jun 3	Kennedy and Khrushchev meet in Vienna
Aug 13	Berlin Wall built
1962	
June 16	Robert McNamara announces new policy of "flexible response"
Oct 14–28	Cuban Missile Crisis
Nov 20	Blockade of Cuba ends
1963	
Aug 5	U.S., Great Britain and Soviet Union sign first test-ban treaty
Aug 30	U.S. and Soviet Union establish Hot Line
Nov 22	President Kennedy assassinated
1964	
Aug 7	U.S. Senate passes Tonkin Gulf Resolution
Oct 15	Khrushchev ousted, Brezhnev and Kosygin new leaders
Oct 16	China explodes first atomic bomb
Nov 3	Lyndon B. Johnson elected president
1965	
Mar 8	U.S. combat troops arrive in Vietnam
1966	
Jul 1	France withdraws from NATO
1967	
Jun 17	China explodes first hydrogen bomb
Jun 23	Johnson and Kosygin meet in Glassboro, New Jersey
1968	
Jan 4	486,000 American troops in Vietnam
Jan 5	Aleksander Dubcek becomes 1st Secretary of Czech Communist Party
July 1	62 nations sign Nuclear Non-Proliferation Treaty
Aug 20	Warsaw Pact forces invade Czechoslovakia
Aug 24	France explodes first thermonuclear bomb
1969	
July 25	Nixon Doctrine—U.S. no longer accepts primary responsibility for the defense of other countries
Nov 17	President Nixon initiates strategic arms limitation talks (SALT I) with Soviet Union
1970	
Mar 19	West German Chancellor Willy Brandt initiates *Ostpolitik*
Apr 16	SALT talks begin in Vienna
1971	
Jul 15	President Nixon announces visit to China
Oct 20	China admitted into United Nations, expelling Taiwan
1972	
May 22–30	President Nixon first American president to visit Soviet Union
May 26	Nixon and Leonid Brezhnev sign SALT I in Moscow
Oct 3	SALT I and ABM Treaty signed in Washington, D.C.
Nov 21	SALT II negotiations begin in Genea
1973	
Jan 27	U.S. and North Vietnam sign ceasefire agreement in Paris
Jul 3	Conference on Security and Cooperation in Europe (CSCE) opens
Sep 11	Salvador Allende ousted in military coup in Chile
1974	
Apr 24	Military coup in Portugal ousts fascist dictatorship
May 18	India explodes first atomic weapon
Jun 27	Nixon-Brezhnev summit begins in Moscow
Aug 9	Nixon resigns over Watergate scandal
1975	
Aug 1	CSCE Accord signed in Helsinki
Nov 11	People's Republic of Angola declared
1976	
Jul 2	Vietnam officially united
Nov 2	Jimmy Carter wins presidential election
1977	
Feb 3	Mengistu seizes power in Ethiopia
Jun 16	Brezhnev becomes president of Soviet Union
1978	
Mar 10	Nuclear Non-Proliferation Treaty signed by Carter
Apr 27	Afghan president Daud ousted in coup
1979	
Jan 1	U.S. and China establish diplomatic relations
Jan 16	Shah flees Iran
June 18	Carter and Brezhnev sign SALT II in Vienna

July 19	Sandinistas overthrow Somoza dictatorship
Dec 12	NATO votes to deploy intermediate range nuclear missiles
Dec 25	The Soviet Union invades Afghanistan
1980	
May 4	Yugoslav president Tito dies
Aug 14	Massive strikes in Poland
Nov 4	Ronald Reagan elected president
1981	
Nov 30	Intermediate-range Nuclear Force (INF) talks open in Geneva
Dec 10	Spain joins NATO
Dec 13	General Jaruzelski declares martial law in Poland
1982	
Jun 30	Strategic Arms Reduction Talks (START) open in Geneva
Nov 10	Brezhnev dies
Nov 12	Yuri Andropov named General Secretary
Nov 22	President Reagan announces decision to deploy MX missiles
1983	
Mar 23	Reagan proposes "Star Wars"
Oct 25	Reagan orders invasion of Grenada
Oct 31	Scientists war about "nuclear winter"
Nov 22	Superpower arms limitation talks break down in Geneva
1984	
Feb 9	Andropov dies
Feb 13	Konstantin Chernenko replaces Andropov
1985	
Mar 10	Chernenko dies
Mar 11	Mikhail Gorbachev becomes General Secretary of the USSR
Mar 12	New round of arms reduction talks (START) begin in Geneva
Nov 19–21	Reagan and Gorbachev hold summit in Geneva
1986	
Feb 26	Ferdinand Marcos deposed in Philippines
Sep 22	Stockholm security conference on conventional arms
Oct 11–12	Reagan and Gorbachev meet in Reykjavik, Iceland
1987	
Dec 8–10	Washington Summit—Reagan and Gorbachev sign INF Treaty
1988	
May 26	Reagan and Gorbachev begin Moscow Summit
Dec 6	Gorbachev announces unilateral Soviet troop reduction
Nov 8	George Bush elected president
1989	
Feb 15	Soviets complete withdrawal from Afghanistan
May 2	Green Border opens between Hungary and Austria
Jun 4	Chinese government crushes pro-democracy movement
Jun 5	Solidarnocz wins election in Poland
Nov 9	Berlin Wall opens
Dec 10	Noncommunist government sworn in Czechoslovakia
Dec 25	Ceaucescu and wife Elana executed in Romania
1990	
Mar 18	First free election in East Germany
Sept 12	Great Britain, France, the U.S., the Soviet Union, and East and West Germany sign peace treaty officially ending World War II
Oct 3	German unification
Oct 15	Gorbachev receives Nobel Peace Prize
1991	
July 1	Warsaw Pact dissolves formally
Dec 31	USSR officially ceases to exist—replaced by Commonwealth of Independent States

Also See the Following Articles

ALLIANCE SYSTEMS • ARMS PRODUCTION, ECONOMICS OF • ARMS TRADE, ECONOMICS OF • BALANCE OF POWER RELATIONSHIPS • MILITARY-INDUSTRIAL COMPLEX, CONTEMPORARY SIGNIFICANCE • MILITARY-INDUSTRIAL COMPLEX, ORGANIZATION AND HISTORY • NUCLEAR WARFARE • NUCLEAR WEAPONS POLICIES • WORLD WAR II

Bibliography

Alperovitz, G. (1995). *The decision to use the atomic bomb and the architecture of an American myth*. New York: Knopf.

Chilton, P. A. (1996). *Security metaphors: Cold War discourse from containment to common house*. New York: Peter Lang Publishing.

Dalby, S. (1990). *Creating the Second Cold War: The discourse on politics*. London: Pinter.

Gaddis, J. L. (1997). *We now know: Rethinking Cold War history*. Oxford: Oxford University Press.

Goldfischer, D. (1993). *Policy alternatives for U.S. nuclear security from the 1950s to the 1990s*. Ithaca: Cornell University Press.

Harbutt, F. J. (1986). *The Iron Curtain: Churchill, America, and the origins of the Cold War*. New York: Oxford University Press.

Johnson, R. H. (1994). *Improbable Dangers: U.S. conceptions of threat in the Cold War and after*. New York: St. Martins.

Kennan, G. & Luckas, J. (1997). *George F. Kennan and the origins of containment, 1944–1946*. Columbia, MO: University of Missouri Press.

Lechuga, C. (1995). *In the eye of the storm: Castro, Khrushchev, Kennedy and the missile crisis*. Melbourne: Ocean Press.

Leffler, M. (1992). *A preponderance of power: National security, the Truman administration, and the Cold War*. Stanford: Stanford University Press.

Naimark, N. (1995). *The Russians in Germany: A history of the Soviet Zone of Occupation, 1945–1949*. Cambridge, MA: Harvard University Press.

Pisani, Sally (1992). *The CIA and the Marshall Plan*. Lawrence, KS. University of Kansas Press.

Powaski, R. E. (1998). *The Cold War: The United States and the Soviet Union 1917–1991*. New York: Oxford University Press.

Schulz, B. H. (1995). *Development policy in the Cold War era*. Münster. Lit Verlag.

Smith, G. (1994). *The last years of the Monroe Doctrine 1945–1993*. New York: Hill and Wang.

Collective Emotions in Warfare*

Thomas J. Scheff
University of California, Santa Barbara

GLOSSARY

Alienation Separation between individuals and between groups. Solidarity is the opposite of alienation, since it implies trust, understanding, and mutual identification. Alienation implies distrust, lack of understanding or misunderstanding, and misidentification. Alienation comes in two forms: isolation (own person or group overwhelmingly dominant) and engulfment (other person or one's group overwhelmingly dominant.

Denial and Acknowledgment Emotions are acknowledged when they are named correctly and expressed respectfully. They are denied, in the psychological sense, when they are defended against by projecting them onto others, ignored and avoided. Denial does not dispel emotions; on the contrary, since when they go underground, they lead extended lives independently of conscious individual or collective intent.

Emotions Feelings that have a genetic basis. Commonly named emotions are joy, interest, surprise, love, fear, grief, anger, contempt, and disgust. Although the genetic basis of emotions is universal to the human species, it is acknowledged that the management of emotions, and therefore their manifest appearance, is culturally conditioned. In particular, the patterns of suppression and denial of emotions are culturally learned.

Shame and Humiliation Shame is genetically determined signal of threat to the social bond. It is therefore of premier importance in understanding the make-up of social bonds, and in identifying the state of bonds between individuals and between groups. Humiliation is usually understood to be an intense form of shame, originating in public exposure of self or group. The occurrence of shame is not always obvious, since in Western societies it is usually disguised, denied, or ignored.

EMOTIONS are little favored in current explanations of the causes of war. If they are referred to at all, it is

* This article is based in part on Chapter 3 of my earlier book (Scheff, 1994).

only indirectly and casually. Frequently used concepts such as prestige, honor, and morale are directly linked to emotions, but this link is never investigated. If emotions are mentioned directly, they are not indexed or theorized. For example, the emotion of humiliation is often mentioned in studies of quarrels, feuds, vendettas, and wars. But none of these studies see this emotion as part of the process of causation. Fear of opponents is another emotion that is often mentioned, but again is seldom part of the central argument. Most serious studies of warfare seem to presume that although emotions are present among the combatants, they are not a significant causal force.

Current explanations of the causes of war and peace are dominated by a "realist" ideology. This view assumes that human behavior is motivated by "objective," that is, nonemotional elements, and that conscious calculation of material benefits and losses figures prominently in the instigation of war. In this article, I will not argue against the importance of objective motives and calculation in human affairs, but I will try to frame the "realist" view within a larger perspective that includes both emotional and non-emotional elements.

Michael Billig (1995) has brilliantly made the point that nationalism, a strong emotional attachment to one's own nation, is probably the single most significant causal element in wars between nations. That is to say that the leading motive for killing in the modern world is not in the name of one's self or family, one's city or state, but one's nation, an imagined community, rather than the people who one actually knows. Billig's thesis points toward the necessity of understanding collective emotions: why are so many so desparately and intensely attached to their homeland that they deem it more important than their own lives and those of the "enemy?" Although this question seems shockingly obvious, most current studies do not ask it, much less provide a plausible answer. We may need an analysis of the dynamics of individual and collective emotions in order to answer such a question.

Billig's book points toward one important reason for the cataclysmic power of nationalist emotions: they are so taken for granted that they are seldom noticed. The most powerful forms of nationalism, he argues, go completely unnoticed. Nationalism is so much a fabric of our everyday life that we are not aware how frequently and how fervantly we reaffirm it. For this reason, he calls this most prevalent form "banal nationalism." Of the many dramatic examples he offers, I give only one from the life of Samuel Johnson, scholar, poet, novelist, and maker of the first English dictionary, as reported by his biographer, Boswell. In a conversation at the house of a friend (Mrs. Dilly) Johnson stated "I am willing to love all mankind, except an American." At this point, according to Boswell, Johnson's highly charged nature was bursting "into horrid fire." This particular episode occurred at the time the American colonists were rebelling against England. To quote Billig: "Johnson was, of course, expressing his own views and emotions. But he was doing more than that; he was repeating commonplace themes of his times: the virtues of loving all mankind and being brimful of patriotism; and the naughtiness of enjoying an explosive hatred of Americans. All these matters stretch beyond Johnson, the individual; they reach into the ideological history of nations and nationalism" (Billig, 1995: 18–19).

Billig's comment on Johnson's intense feeling of hatred exactly catches the confluence between individual and collective emotions in moments of crisis, the taken-for-granted character of the emotion, and its insult to logic (universal love and hatred for the enemy are expressed in the same sentence).

The example of Johnson's outburst against Americans suggests a potentially important link between Billig's concept of banal nationalism and the emotion analysis to be described here: Johnson was probably unaware of the intensity of his nationalistic emotions, since they were so habitual to him, and fit so perfectly with the emotions of his associates. His emotions, as powerful as they were, went unacknowledged by him and by others. I will return to the issue of unacknowledged emotions in the analysis below. Before doing so, it is necessary to discuss the background for it provided by the avoidance of emotions in most contemporary research on warfare.

I. EMOTIONS IN CURRENT STUDIES OF WARFARE

Billig makes an important point about research on international relations. He points out that banal nationalism is so taken for granted that even scholars are ensnared in it; their attachment to their nation is so much part of the fabric of their lives that they are oblivious to it. Their obliviousness can be seen in many contemporary studies.

Although there are several broad surveys of studies of warfare, I will single out one by Vasquez (1993), because it seems to be the most precise and comprehensive. It references almost 400 studies, most of which are empirical investigations of actual wars. From these studies, the author generates some hundred propositions about the causes of war. Here is an example:

7. More interstate wars will occur between contiguous states than non-contiguous states (Vasquez, 1993: 310).

All of the propositions cite studies which provide supporting evidence. The list of propositions is broken down into several sections, Territorial Contiguity (from which #7 above was selected), Rivalry, Alliances, Arms Races, Crises, and Domestic Politics. The style of reasoning is atheoretical, that is, inductive and correlational (#7 implies only a correlation between warfare and contiguity of the opponents). But the large number of studies that use one or more of the section headings suggests a view of causation that is part of the habitus of the political scientists and others who study war. That is to say, they believe that territorial contiguity, rivalry, alliances, arms races, crises, and domestic politics are causes of wars.

The massive number of studies actually tells us little about the causation of war because they are low-level generalizations, perilously close to being truisms. They are too abstract to include any of the ambient details in the social and psychological process that leads to war. But it may be these very details that are needed to develop a useful theory. Does one need careful empirical studies to find that wars are more frequent between states that are contiguous, or rivalrous? Or that arms races, crises, and domestic politics figure in the instigation of war? These "findings" can be seen as a variation of the cargo cult science that Feynman complained about.

The only direction not flirting with truism are the 15 propositions about the types of alliances that precede wars, as against the types of alliances that do not precede wars. But even these propositions are stated in vernacular, rather than theoretical terms, and tell us little about causal process: "15b. When the global institutional context limits unilateral acts through the establishment of rules of the game, alliances tend not to be followed by war." Once again, this proposition is only correlational, and does not furnish any information about the step-by-step process which leads to war.

No studies that provide step-by-step details are included in Vasquez's study, since he favors generalizing studies over case studies. Kennan's brillant study (1984) of the political process that led to the formation of what he called "the fateful alliance" between France and Russia prior to the First World War is not referenced. The idea of nationalism, which Kennan and many others have named as a powerful cause of war, is mentioned only once in the proposition section of Vasquez's book. Nationalism is not actually involved in any of the hundred propositions; it is mentioned in a query following 44c, and then only along with several other factors. It appears that the idea of nationalism as a powerful force for war is not part of the conceptual equipment of the political scientists of warfare, perhaps because, as Billig suggests, they take it for granted.

Even those concepts that imply that nationalism involves emotions are used in a way that glosses over this link. An example of such a gloss is provided by the idea of ethnocentrism. This concept was introduced into social science by Sumner (1911), who apparently borrowed it from Gumplowitz. He defined it as the practice of viewing all matters from the standpoint of one's own group. This usage is still current in social science, as in the discussions by Levine and Campbell (1971), and Staub (1989).

The concept of ethnocentrism masks several significant dimensions of social process and social structure. First of all, it is static, individualistic, and simplistic. As the term is usually used, it refers to a fixed attitude of individuals, rather than one aspect of a complex social process. Secondly, it subsumes only the perceptual and cognitive aspects, excluding emotions. As did Sumner, current discussions assume that ethocentrism is a viewpoint or a set of beliefs, with no concern for the emotions that may also be present.

Current studies of ethnocentrism gloss emotions in their analysis of the genesis of conflict, particularly the emotions of pride and shame. The distinction made in this article between pride and false pride is particularly important in understanding the causes of conflict. Most current discussions of "national pride," "race pride," "group pride," and so on, confound pride with false pride, that is, authentic, justified pride, with a show of pride that is only a disguise. A person or group in a state of normal pride is usually not hostile or disparaging toward others. False pride, however, a mask for shame, generates hostility toward others.

Finally, classic and current discussion usually do not attempt to assess the intensity of ethnocentrism relative to other forces, and therefore their importance in relationships between groups. This flaw is apparent in the idea widely held in current social science that ethnocentrism is universal. Although this doctrine may well be true, it avoids a crucial issue: what are the conditions in a society that encourage runaway, exploding ethnocentrism? That is, when does ethnocentrism become the leading force in a society, to the extent that other issues, even survival, seem to fade from consciousness? In order to explore this issue, it will be necessary to review some basic ideas from family systems theory and from the sociology of emotions.

II. FAMILY SYSTEMS THEORY AND THE SOCIOLOGY OF EMOTIONS

I begin with communication tactics and alienation in family systems. Family members are alienated from their own conflicts, to the extent that they are deceptive with each other, and self-deceptive. To the degree that the basis of their own conflicts is invisible to them, they see them as exterior and constraining, as inevitable. This attitude toward conflict provides a strong link with Durkheimian theory: nationalism and warfare are social facts, social institutions that are reaffirmed in the day-to-day organization of our civilization. To the extent that individuals and groups deny conflict and/or their own part in conflict, it will be seen as inevitable, a self-fulfilling prophecy.

Although family systems theory is useful, a necessary component is missing if we are to understand interpersonal and intergroup conflict, the role of emotion sequences. In our theory (Scheff and Retzinger, 1991), we emphasize the way in which the emotion of shame is managed. Pride and shame are crucial elements in social systems. Pride signals and generates solidarity. Shame signals and generates alienation.

The emotion of shame can be directly acknowledged by referring to one's inner states of insecurity, or feelings of separateness or powerlessness. Often it goes unacknowledged to self and others. Following the important distinction discovered by Lewis (1971), unacknowledged shame takes two different forms; overt shame is signaled by furtiveness, and emotional pain that is misnamed. In bypassed shame, one tries to outface the other, masking one's shame by hostility toward, or withdrawing from, the other.

Acknowledging shame helps connect parties; admissions of feelings of weakness or vulnerability can build solidarity and trust. Denial of shame builds a wall between parties. If shame signals are disguised and/or ignored, both parties lose touch with each other. Pride and shame cues give instant indications of the "temperature" of the relationship. Pride means the parties are neither engulfed (too close), a "we" relationship, not isolated (too far), an "I" relationship, but are emotionally and cognitively connected in what Elias called interdependence (1972). Overt shame usually signals engulfment, bypassed shame, isolation.

Unacknowledged shame appears to be recursive; it feeds upon itself. To the extent that this is the case, it could be crucial in the causation of interminable conflict. If shame goes unacknowledged, it can loop back upon itself (being ashamed that one is ashamed) or co-occur with other emotions, such as grief (unresolved grief), fear (fear panics), or anger (humiliated fury). Unacknowledged shame seems to foil the biological and cultural mechanisms that allow for the expression and harmless discharge of these elemental emotions. In the absence of shame, or if it is acknowledged, grief may be discharged by weeping, under culturally appropriate conditions of mourning. But if shame is evoked by grief and goes unacknowledged, unending loops of emotions (shame-grief sequences) may occur. The individual will be unable to mourn.

If shame is evoked but is unacknowledged, it may set off a sequence of shame alternating with anger. Shame-shame sequences are probably much more prevalent than shame-anger sequences. Elias's (1978, 1982) analysis of changes in advice manuals over the last 5 centuries implies that shame-shame sequences are a central core in the development of modern civilization, to the extent that they occur in the socialization of children.

Another direction in the management of shame is to mask it with anger. Shame/anger may be interminable in the form of "helpless anger," or in the more explosive form, "humiliated fury." The shame-anger loop may be central to destructive conflict. If one is in a shame state with respect to another, one route of denial is to become angered at the other, whether the other is responsible or not. That is, if one feels rejected by, insulted by, or inferior to another, denial of shame can result in a shame-anger loop of unlimited intensity and duration.

One difficulty in communicating the new theory is that emotions have virtually disappeared as creditable motives in modern scholarship, as already indicated. One would hardly know they existed from reading the analyses of causes of conflict in the social sciences. When references to emotions are made, they are likely to be abstract, casual, indirect, and brief. For example, emotions are sometimes invoked under the rubric of "nonrational motives," but with little attempt to specify what this category might contain.

III. EMOTIONAL SOURCES OF VENGEANCE

The identification of shame-anger sequences in the causation of conflict may help to solve the problem of the causation of revenge. Although there is a very large literature on vengeance, it is almost entirely descriptive in nature. The largest literature is the anthropology of duels, feuds, and vendettas. Another source concerns the revenge genre in world literature, especially in drama. A third, smaller and less defined literature is on conflict in families.

These literatures testify to the way in which the revenge motive leads to interminable conflicts in human affairs, and to the widespread popular appeal of dramatic portrayals of this motive. However, these sources limit themselves to descriptions of the behavior involved. None offer substantive theories of the causation of revenge. A similar paucity of explanations of revenge is also found in theories of human behavior. Surprisingly, there is only one book-length treatment of revenge in the entire human science literature, by Marongiu and Newman (1987). Although these authors attempt an explanatory formulation, it sheds little light on the problem. Rather than ask the critical question, the specific conditions under which revenge occurs and the conditions under which it does not occur, this book offers a general and vague explanation for the existence of revenge in the human species.

Predicatibly, given their framing of the problem, one explanation they offer is genetic; they propose an evolutionary account of the origins of revenge. They also offer a what they think of as a psychological alternative, drawing upon Freud's mythic formulation of the primal crime of the sons against the father (*Totem and Taboo,* 1918). Freud's formulation is basically another version of the genetic explanation. He thought that the revenge motive might arise out of genetically driven sexual and aggressive instincts. For reasons already given, this approach is useless for explaining specific acts of vengeance. In this article I propose that a viable explanation should deal with emotions. In particular, my formulation suggests that emotional arousal leads to vengeful actions only if that arousal is denied.

IV. EMOTIONS AS EXPLANATIONS

There is a strong tradition in modern scholarship in the human sciences of ignoring emotions as causes. Even when words that reference intense emotions are used directly, the author often obscures the specifically emotional component by confounding it with a more rational motive. An example of the kind of confounding that frequently occurs involves humiliation, one of the most direct ways of referring to shame (Jervis, Lebow, and Stein, 1985: 140): "The dangers of humiliation, of conveying the appearance of weakness to real adversaries, were too great to permit acquiescence in the triumph even of apparent ones." The analysis is referring the American government's tendency to react a communist nation that is not dangerous (China) in the same way as to one that is dangerous (USSR).

At first glance one might think that the analyst is implying that governments, like individuals, sometimes act in the way that they do because they are attempting to avoid shame. Although a word is used that is clearly in the family of shame terms, invoking an emotional motive, the sentence also invokes the idea of avoiding not just shame, but the appearance of weakness. This is the modern lexicon of military strategy, of credibility and deterence. By invoking this lexicon, the analyst managed to avoid the "nonrational" implications of his statement, that is, the specifically emotional components of motivation. The entire literature on the strategy of deterrence is pervaded by exactly this confound.

In the narratives of these texts, such as the one by Jervis, Lebow, and Stein (1985), there are many references to humiliation, particularly in the discussions of concrete instances of conflict, as in the case of the Falklands War and Israeli-Arab conflicts. But this word does not appear in the introduction, conclusion, or index. It does not have the conceptual status of a real motive. It is too useful to avoid entirely, but too embarrassing to elevate to the status of a concept.

There are a number of psychoanalytically derived approaches to conflict that treat emotions directly. For the most part, however, following Freud, these studies ignore shame. An example is provided by a study of the need to have enemies and allies (Volkan, 1988). This work focuses on the inability to mourn (unresolved grief) in the exacerbation of conflict. Other studies emphasize the other two emotions which Freud recognized, anxiety and anger.

Emotion is widely recognized as a cause of conflict in only one area, conflict and war among traditional peoples. Students of feuds and vendettas are apt to see humiliation and revenge as causal agents among premoderns, not "us," but "them." In his assessment of the causes of primitive warfare, Turney-High gives revenge pride of place (1949, pp. 149–150, and passim 141–168):

> Revenge is so consistently reported as one of the principal causes of war that it requires detailed analysis. Why should the human personality yearn to compensate for its humiliation in the blood of enemies? The tension-release motives plays a part here: Revenge loosens the taut feeling caused by the slaying or despoiling of one's self, clan, tribe, nation. Even the hope for revenge helps the humiliated human to bear up, enables

> him to continue to function in a socially unfavorable environment. Fray Camposano wrote of the Mojos of southwestern Amazonia to Phillip II of Spain that, "The most valiant were the most respected and their patience under injuries was only dissimulation for subsequent vengeance." Revenge, or the hope for revenge, restores the deflated ego, and is a conflict motive with which mankind must reckon with universally.

Even in this realm, explicit analysis of emotions as motives is an endangered species. Turney-High's explicitness occurs in a volume published 42 years ago. In the next generation of analysis, reference to avoidance of shame is considerably blunted.

In 1966, Peristiany edited a volume on feuds in Mediterranean society. It contained the word shame in its title, and mentions in the chapters, but most of the authors carefully refrain from considering emotions to be motives. The exception is Pitt-River's chapter on honor and social status. In his analysis of honor and shame (*verguenza*) among the peasants of Andalusia, he is direct to the point of bluntness about emotion words and their cognates (1966: 42): "As the basis of repute, honor and shame are synonymous, since shamelessness is dishonorable; a person of good repute is taken to have both, one of evil repute is credited with neither."

For most current scholars, the way in which Pitt-Rivers identified honor and shame as interchangeable parts of a larger cultural system of motivation and action would be utterly unacceptable. Pitt-Rivers must have been an entire generation older than the other contributors, putting him in the same cohort as the equally blunt Turney-High. In recent treatments of primitive warfare, references to emotions have all but disappeared. Even more indirect references, for example, to actions such as revenge, which are closely related to emotional motives, are less frequent and more dispersed. This is not to say that the analysts completely avoid the consideration of emotional motives. What has happened is that such motives are treated, but distantly and briefly, in terms that are more diffuse: prestige, face-saving, and status-competition. The vagueness of these terms facilitates the kind of confounding already mentioned above: emotions lead only a shadow life these days. Shame, particularly, has dropped out of the discussion, along with other emotions and personal motives. Lust for possessions or power is seen as real, for honor, unreal.

It is difficult to locate the exact time in which shame and humiliation dropped out of the lexicon of respectable motives. Strong decrements seemed to occur in the two eras just preceding and during the two World Wars. In the 19th century, it was still possible to name "national honor" as a reason for going to war, as in the origins of the Spanish-American War. But by the beginning of World War I, this kind of motive no longer had full legitimacy. Even in pre-WWI France, where there was still much public talk of the honor, glory, and triumph associated with war, revenge was seen as too coarse a motive to countenance openly.

This timing might correspond to the lowering trajectory of shame thresholds that has been traced by Elias (1978, 1982), which he proposes to be one of the key characteristics of modernity. Increasingly, as shame thresholds and open acknowledgement of shame both decrease, social scientists, like most others in our civilization, are too ashamed of emotions to give them serious attention as causal elements.

This one change may have wrought havoc with our understanding of human motives in general, and specifically with analyses of the causes of conflict. Governments and their analysts seem forbidden to talk or even think about emotional motives. Instead, duplicity, indirection, and silence reign. If we cannot talk openly about the emotional causes of conflict, we may embarrass ourselves to death.

In one of the press conferences during the Iran hostage crisis (Nov. 28, 1979), a reporter bluntly asked President Carter about an emotional motive: "How can you satisfy the public demand to end such an embarrassment?" Most of Carter's response sounded as if he had not heard the question, since he talked in the main about abstract legal and ethical issues, in an extremely detached manner.

Only toward the end of his statement, and obliquely, did he respond to the emotional content of the question, saying that "... acts of terrorism may cause discomfiture to a people or a government." Discomfiture is one of many codewords for shame (Gottschalk and Gleser, 1969), but its use and the indirection of the sentence (not "us," but a hypothetical people or government) essentially denies the existence of shame. This stance is expressive of the isolated form of alienation, and the bypassing of shame.

Where Carter favored denial and silence, not just in this instance but in all of his press conferences, Reagan was more duplicitous. One example will give the flavor. In his statement of September 5, 1983, regarding the downing of a Korean jetliner by a Russian fighter, he said: "With our horror and our sorrow, there is a righteous and terrible anger. It would be easy to think in terms of vengeance, but that is not a proper answer."

Reagan's statement has it both ways; it acknowledges anger and vengeance but also denies it. Especially in the Iran hostage crisis, he used this maneuver to great advantage. This stance is expressive of the engulfed style of alienation, and the overt, undifferentiated style of shame (Lewis, 1971, and Gottschalk and Gleser, 1969; both list self-righteous anger as one of the many cues for hidden shame.)

Elsewhere, Retzinger and I (1991) have suggested an emotional basis for charisma; it may be the ability of a leader to express the dominant emotions of his or her public, and anti-charisma, a leader's penchant for denying or even condemning these emotions. The contrast drawn above between Reagan's and Carter's style illustrates this proposition, as does my analysis of the emotional basis of Hitler's appeal to the German people (Scheff 1994).

The stance of the analysts of the actions of governments is virtually always that of the isolated, bypassed style: emotional motives are mentioned only casually and distantly (e.g., prestige) or not at all. None of the many governmental and scholarly discussions of the strategy of deterrence even acknowledge the possibility that there might be an emotional, "nonrational" component in this strategy. Emotions have disappeared not only from the statement and actions of governments, but from the writings of most scholars. Humiliated fury is not a creditable, respectable motive like power, territory, or other objectified motives. As Emerson said, "Things are in the saddle; they ride humankind." Objectification sets the stage for, and reflects alienation between persons and between nations.

V. PRIDE AND SHAME

The psychoanalytic idea of repression may be helpful in understanding defenses against inadequate bonding. If the ideology of the self-sufficient individual is a defense against the pain of threatened bonds, what is being repressed is the idea of the social bond. Freud, however, argued that repression concerns not only ideas, but also the feelings that accompany them. He thought that repression could be lifted only if both idea and emotion were expressed. If modern societies repress the idea of the social bond, what are the associated feelings that are also repressed?

I follow the lead of Cooley (1922), who implied that pride and shame are the primary social emotions. These two emotions have a signal function with respect to the social bond. In this framework, pride and shame serve as intense and automatic signs of the state of a system otherwise difficult to observe. Secure social bonds were unknown to Hitler, and also seem to have been in short supply in the society in which he grew up. To understand how this situation might have led to implacable vengefulness, it will first be necessary to once more review how emotions can cause continuous conflict.

VI. UNENDING EMOTIONS

I propose that unacknowledged alienation leads to interminable conflict. Like Watzlawick and colleagues (1967), I argue that some conflicts are unending, any particular quarrel being only a link in a continuing chain. What causes interminable conflict?

There are two forms of interminable conflict, the quarrel and impasse. Both forms grow out of unacknowledged shame. Shame is pervasive in conflictful interaction, but invisible to interactants (and to researchers), unless Lewis's [or Gottschalk and Gleser's (1969)] approach is used. I connect the two forms of conflict with the two forms of unacknowledged shame; quarrels with the bypassed form, impasses with the overt, undifferentiated form. The two forms of shame are polar opposites in terms of thought and feeling. Overt shame involves painful feeling with little ideation, bypassed shame, the opposite pattern: rapid thought, speech, or behavior, but little feeling. The two forms correspond to a distinction in Adler's (1956) theory of personality: children lacking a secure bond at critical junctions respond in two different ways, either with an "inferiority complex" (chronic overt shame), or the drive to power (behavior masking bypassed shame). Lewis's analysis parallels Adler's, but also represents an immense advance over it. Unlike Adler, she described observable markers for the theoretical constructs, and specified the causal sequence, the unending spiraling of emotion in "feeling traps."

Overt shame is marked by furtiveness, confusion, and bodily reactions: blushing, sweating, and/or rapid heartbeat. One may be at a loss for words, with fluster or disorganization of thought or behavior, as in states of embarrassment. Many of the common terms for painful feelings appear to refer to this type of shame, or combinations with anger: feeling peculiar, shy, bashful, awkward, funny, bothered, or miserable; in adolescent vernacular, being freaked, bummed, or weirded out. The phrases "I felt like a fool," or "a perfect idiot" are prototypic.

Bypassed shame is manifested as a brief painful feeling, usually less than a second, followed by obsessive and rapid thought or speech. A common example: one feels insulted or criticized. At that moment (or later in recalling it), one might experience a jab of painful feeling (producing a groan or wince), followed immediately by imaginary but compulsive, repetitive replays of the offending scene. The replays are variations on a theme: how one might have behaved differently, avoiding the incident, or responding with better effect. One is obsessed.

Lewis (1971) referred to internal shame-rage process as a feeling trap, as "anger bound by shame," or "humiliated fury." Kohut's (1971) concept, "narcissistic rage," appears to be the same affect, since he viewed it as a compound of shame and rage. Angry that one is ashamed, or ashamed that one is angry, then one might be ashamed to be so upset over something so "trivial." Such anger and shame are rarely acknowledged, difficult to detect and to dispel. Shame-rage spirals may be brief, a matter of minutes, but can also last for hours, days, or a lifetime, as bitter hatred or resentment.

Brief sequences of shame/rage may be quite common. Escalation is avoided through withdrawal, conciliation, or some other tactic. Wars are generated by a less common process. Watzlawick and colleagues (1967:107–108) call it "symmetrical escalation." Since such conflicts have no limits, they may have lethal outcomes. In this theory, unacknowledged shame is the cause of revenge-based cycles of conflict [this formulation was anticipated in the work of Geen (1968) and Feshback (1971)]. Shame-rage may escalate continually to the point that a person or a group can be in a permanent fit of shame/rage, a kind of madness.

VII. STUDIES OF SHAME AND AGGRESSION

The theory outlined here is supported by several exploratory studies. Katz (1988) analyzed descriptions of several hundred criminal acts: vandalism, theft, robbery, and murder. In many of the cases, Katz found that the perpetrator felt humiliated, committing the crime as an act of revenge. In some of the cases the sense of humiliation was based on actual insults:

> [A] ... typical technique [leading to a spouse being murdered] is for the victim to attack the spouse's deviations from the culturally approved sex role.... For example, a wife may accuse her husband of being a poor breadwinner or an incompetent lover ... or the husband may accuse his wife of being "bitchy," "frigid," or promiscuous (Ch. 2, p. 8).

In other cases it was difficult to assess the degree to which the humiliations were real and/or imagined. Whatever the realities, Katz's findings support the model of the shame/rage feeling trap. In his analysis of the murder of intimates, he says: "The would-be-killer must undergo a particular emotional process. He must transform what he initially senses as an eternally humiliating situation into a blinding rage" (p. 11). Rather than acknowledging his or her shame, the killer masks it with anger, which is the first step into the abyss of the shame/rage feeling trap, which ends in murder. Katz reports similar, though less dramatic findings with respect to the other kinds of crimes he investigated.

One issue that Katz's study does not address is the conditions under which humiliation is transformed into blind rage. Since not all humiliations lead to blind rage, there must be some ingredient that is not indicated in Katz's cases. Studies of family violence by Lansky suggest this extra ingredient. In order to lead to blind rage, the shame component in the emotions that are aroused must be unacknowledged.

Lansky has published three papers on family violence. The first paper (1984) describes six cases, the second (1987), four. The third (Lansky, 1989) analyzes one session with a married couple. In most of the cases, he reports similar emotional dynamics: violence resulted from the insulting manner that both husbands and wives took toward each other. Although some insults were overt, in the form of cursing, open contempt, and disgust, most were covert, in the form of innuendo or double messages.

Underhanded disrespect gives rise to unacknowledged shame, which leads in turn to anger and violence, in the way predicted by Lewis. It is difficult for the participants to respond to innuendo and to double messages; these forms of communication confuse them. Instead of admitting their upset and puzzlement, they answer in kind. The cycle involves disrespect, humiliation, revenge, counter-revenge, and so on, ending in violence.

The way in which both spouses seem to be unaware of the intense shame that their behavior generates can be illustrated in one of the cases (Lansky, 1984, 34–35, emphasis added):

> A thirty-two year old man and his forty-six-year-old wife were seen in emergency conjoint consultation after he struck her. Both spouses were horrified, and the husband agreed that hospitalization might be the best way to start the lengthy treatment that he wanted. As he attempted to explain his view of his difficult marriage, his wife disorganized him with repeated humiliating comments about his inability to hold

a job. These comments came at a time when he was talking about matters other than the job. When he did talk about work, she interrupted to say how immature he was compared to her previous husbands, then how strong and manly he was. The combination of building up and undercutting his sense of manliness was brought into focus. As the therapist commented on the process, the husband became more and more calm. . . . After the fourth session, he left his marriage and the hospital for another state and phoned the therapist for an appropriate referral for individual therapy. On follow-up some months later, he had followed through with treatment.

The disguising of the wife's humiliation of the husband in this case is not through innuendo, since her disparagement is overt. Her shaming tactics are disguised by her technique of alternately praising her husband, by stating how "strong and manly" he was, then cutting him down. Perhaps she confused herself with this tactic as much as she did her husband.

Lack of awareness of shaming and shame can be seen in Lansky's report of a conjoint session with a violent man and his wife (1989). In this session, Lansky indicates that the wife was dressed in a sexually provocative way, and that her bearing and manner was overtly seductive toward the interviewer. Yet neither spouse acknowledged her activity, even when the interviewer asked them whether the wife was ever seductive toward other men. Although both answered affirmatively, their answers concerned only past events. The lack of comment on what was occurring at that very moment in the interview is astounding. It would seem that blind rage requires not only shaming and shame, but blindness toward these two elements.

The relationship between collective violence and unacknowledged shame is suggested by an analysis of the Attica riots (Scheff, Retzinger, and Ryan, 1989). The violence of the guards toward the inmates began with a series of events that the guards perceived as humiliating: without consulting the guards, a new warden intent on reform increased the rights of the prisoners, which resulted in a series of incidents with prisoners that the guards experienced as humiliating. Since the guards did not acknowledge their humiliation, their assault on the prisoners follows the sequence predicted by the Lewis theory: insult, unacknowledged shame, rage, and aggression.

This formulation does not discount the importance of the topic of conflict, be it scarce resources, cultural differences, or any other issue. But it argues that in the absence of unacknowledged shame, human beings are resourceful enough to be able to find a compromise to any dispute, one that is most beneficial to both parties, or least harmful. If shame is evoked in one or both parties, however, and not acknowledged, than the content of the dispute becomes less important than the hidden emotions, which take over. Unacknowledged shame is the basis of what Goffman (1967) called "character contests," conflicts in which the topic of dispute becomes subordinate to the issue of "face," which is a disguised way of referring to matters of pride and shame, honor and disgrace.

VIII. SUMMARY

The theory outlined here may provide a solution to the problem of interminable and destructive conflict. It can be summarized in terms of three propositions:

1. Bimodal alienation (engulfment within, and isolation between groups) inhibits cooperation both within and between groups. Understanding, trust, and cooperation become increasingly difficult to the extent that social bonds are insecure (Persons on one or both sides of a relationship feel threatened with rejection).
2. Bimodal alienation leads to interminable conflict if, and only if, alienation and its accompanying emotions are denied. This proposition may be true independently of the gravity of the differences in interests between the two groups. That is, the most beneficial or the last harmful compromise on differences of interests can be found if alienation is acknowledged.
3. The denial of alienation generates an emotional process which leads to escalation of conflict, a triple spiral of shame-rage between and within parties to a conflict. Acknowledgement of alienation and shame de-escalates conflict, independently of the differences of interests between the parties.

This formulation has a number of advantages over existing ones. Rather than being based on the assumption that groups are made up of isolated individuals, it assumes a structure/process composed of social relationships. It is not static, since it proposes that the degree of conflict at any moment is based on the state of social bonds in and between the contending parties at that moment. The formulation is exceedingly complex, since it suggests an analysis of solidarity and alienation in terms of actual social relationships between and within the parties to a conflict. Unlike many theories of conflict, this one offers a description of the causal chain that links social and psychological conditions to the generation of conflict. Communication practices that serve to deny alienation and emotion generate spirals in which emotions escalate to the point of intolerable tension, explaining the origin of "war fever" and other highly irrational behaviors by individuals and groups.

Finally, this theory is potentially testable, since it provides detailed descriptions of its elemental components, alienation and emotion. For this reason, it might be seen as a "grounded theory" (Glaser and Strauss, 1967). In our study of videotapes of game shows, Retzinger and I (1991) have shown that markers of solidarity and alienation can be rated systematically, and that alienation interferes with the ability of contestants to cooperate, and therefore, to win. In her work on marital quarrels, Retzinger (1991) has shown that shame and anger can be systematically rated in videotape recordings. Her findings in each of four quarrels suggest that unacknowledged shame always precedes rather than follows the disrespectful anger which leads to escalation. At an interpersonal level, her work supports Simmel's (1955) conjecture that separation leads to conflict, rather than the other way around.

I do not argue that the material bases of conflict are unimportant, or that alienation and shame alone explain all interminable quarrels. Rather I propose that these two interrelated components are always present in destructive quarrels, feuds, vendettas and wars, but have been neglected. Alienation and emotion are intergral to the kind of internation conflict that is a central feature of our current world, and need to be studied directly, along with the other components that cause conflict.

Also See the Following Articles

AGGRESSION, PSYCHOLOGY OF • BEHAVIORAL PSYCHOLOGY • ENEMY, CONCEPT AND IDENTITY OF • ETHNIC CONFLICTS AND COOPERATION • ETHNICITY AND IDENTITY POLITICS • EVOLUTIONARY FACTORS • FAMILY STRUCTURE AND FAMILY VIOLENCE AND NONVIOLENCE

Bibliography

Adler, A. (1907–1937). *The individual psychology of Alfred Adler*. New York: Basic Books (1956)

Billig, M. (1995). *Banal nationalism*. London: Sage.

Elias, N. (1972). *What is sociology?* London: Hutchison.

Elias, N. (1978). *The history of manners*. New York: Pantheon.

Elias, N. (1982). *Power and civility*. New York: Pantheon.

Freud, S. (1918). *Totem and taboo*. New York:

Moffat and Yard Ferguson, B. (1988). *The anthropology of war*. New York: Occasional Paper of the Herman Guggenheim Foundation.

Feshbach, S. 1971. The dynamics and morality of violence and aggression. *American Psychologist, 26,* 281–292.

Geen, R. G. (1968). Effects of frustration, attack, and prior training in aggressiveness upon aggressive behavior. *Journal of Personality and Social Psychology, 9,* 316–321.

Glaser, B., and Strauss, A. (1967). *The discovery of grounded theory*. Chicago: Aldine.

Goffman, E. 1967. *Interaction ritual*. New York: Anchor.

Goffman, E. (1972). *Relations in public*. New York: Harper

Gottschalk, L., and Gleser, G. (1969). *Manual for using the Gottschalk-Gleser content analysis scales*. Berkeley: U. of California Press

Haas, J. (1990). *The anthropology of war*. Cambridge: Cambridge U. Press.

Jervis, R., Lebow, N., and Stein, J. (1985). *Psychology and deterrence*. Baltimore: Johns Hopkins U. Press

Katz, J. (1988). *The seductions of crime*. New York: Basic Books.

Kohut, H. E. (1971). Thoughts on narcissism and narcissistic Rage. *The search for the self*. New York: International University Press.

Lansky, M. (1984). Violence, shame, and the family. *International Journal of Family Psychiatry, 5,* 21–40

Lansky, M. (1987). Shame and domestic violence. In D. Nathanson (Ed.), *The many faces of shame*. New York: Guilford

Lansky, M. (1989). Murder of a spouse: A family systems viewpoint. *International Journal of Family Psychiatry, 10,* 159–178.

Levine R. T., and Campbell, D. T. (1971). *Ethnocentrism: Theories of conflict. New York: Wiley*

Lewis, H. B. (1971). *Shame and guilt in neurosis*. New York: Internat'l. Universities Press.

Lynd, H. (1958). *Shame and the search for identity*. New York: Hartcourt Brace.

Marongiu, P., and Newman, G. (1987). *Vengeance: The fight against injustice*. Towota, NJ.: Rowman and Littlefield.

Peristiany, J. (1966). *Honor and shame in Mediterranean societies*. Chicago: U. of Chicago Press.

Retzinger, S. M. (1991). *Violent emotions: Shame and anger in marital quarrels*. Newbury Park: Sage Publications.

Riches, D. (1986). *The Anthropology of Violence*. Oxford: Basil Blackwell.

Scheff, T. (1990). *Microsociology: Discourse, emotion and social structure*. Chicago: U. of Chicago Press.

Scheff, T. (1994). *Bloody revenge: Emotions, nationalism, and war,* Boulder: Westview Press.

Scheff, T., and Retzinger, S. (1991). *Emotions and violence: Shame and rage in destructive conflicts*. Lexington: Lexington Books

Scheff, T., Retzinger, S., and Ryan, M. (1989). Crime, violence and self-esteem: Review and proposals. In A. Mecca, N. Smelser, and J. Vasconcellos (Eds.), *The social importance of self-esteem*. Berkeley: U. of California Press.

Simmel, G. (1955). *Conflict and the web of group-affiliations*. New York: The Free Press of Glencoe.

Staub, E. (1989). *The roots of evil: Origins of genocide*. New York: Cambridge U. Press

Sumner, W. G. (1911). *Folkways*. Boston: Ginn

Tavuchis, N. (1991). *Mea culpa: A sociology of apology and reconciliation*. Stanford: Stanford U. Press.

Turner, P., and Pitt, D. (1989). *The anthropology of war and peace*. Granby, MA: Bergin and Garvey.

Turney-High, Harry H. (1949). *Primitive war*. Columbia: U. of S. Carolina Press.

Vasquez, John. (1993). *The war puzzle*. Cambridge: Cambridge U. Press.

Volkan, Vamik. (1988). *The need to have enemies and allies*. London: J. Aaronson.

Watzlawick, P., Beavin, J. H., and Jackson, D. (1967). *The pragmatics of human communication*. New York: Norton.

Collective Security Systems

Mira Sucharov and Victor D. Cha
Georgetown University

GLOSSARY

Alliance A formal association of states aimed at increasing the security of its members, usually targeted against an external threat.

Anarchy The absence of a governing authority in the international system.

Balance of Power Theory The idea that international stability is best achieved through a roughly equal distribution of power across five or more great powers, and whereby defensive alliances arise to counter potential threats.

Bipolarity The distribution of material, economic, and industrial capabilities among two major states within the international system (contrasted with **multipolarity** and **unipolarity**).

Collective Action Problem The dilemma of encouraging consumers of **public goods** to contribute to their production.

Collective Defense A joint coalition of states that designates the external threat to be balanced against.

Concert System A security arrangement of major powers that join together to maintain the international status quo, the most prominent example being the 19th-century Concert of Europe.

Liberalism A perspective within international relations theory that places primary importance on the rights and liberties of the individual, and that understands human nature as essentially benign.

Public Good A benefit from which no actor may be excluded, and that cannot be divided up among its members.

Realism A perspective within international relations theory that understands state behavior as governed by the pursuit of power.

Revisionist Power A state that seeks, by acquisition of territory, to alter the international status quo in its favor (contrasted with **status quo power**).

Self-Help The assumption that under anarchy, states must provide for their own security.

Sovereignty An attribute of the modern state; the supreme authority to command within the state's territory.

COLLECTIVE SECURITY is an inclusive, formal interstate arrangement aimed at deterring aggression through the display of joint and preponderant power.

It represents a form of "organized security," the cohesiveness of which is based on moral obligation and enlightened self-interest, and the effectiveness of which is based on military force. Collective security embodies the notion that security is a joint obligation among those committed to nonaggression. The concept gained popularity in the interwar years, particularly since World War I severely undermined the belief among policymakers in the efficacy of unchecked power balancing. As Woodrow Wilson stated, "the day we left behind was a day of alliances. It was a day of balances of power. It was a day of 'every nation take care of itself or make a partnership with some other nation or group of nations to hold the peace of the world steady or to dominate the weaker portions of the world.'" Collective security provided the answer to this search for a new and superior means of achieving peace.

I. BASIC PRINCIPLES

Collective security rests on several interrelated principles:

One. Collective security encompasses the notion that peace is indivisible and nonexcludable, in the sense that aggression against one is considered aggression against all. States join together in a formal arrangement in which they renounce war as a means of statecraft, except through participation in a joint coalition to punish any member who violates this pledge. As with any public good—one that is indivisible and nonexcludable—collective security often leads to a collective action problem that precludes states from cooperating. Collective security is therefore premised on the idea that if peace is to be enjoyed by all, every state must contribute to the collective effort to preserve it. Collective security systems thereby are intolerant of neutral or nonaligned stances or isolationist policies of states; states that are members of a collective security system are expected to come to the aid of any victim state.

Two. Collective security emphasizes the importance of institutions in achieving and maintaining security. It accepts the centrality of military power in shaping international relations, but sees the need to manage this power in order to achieve peace. While balance of power theory sees peace achieved through a process of atomistic balancing which ultimately gives rise to an equilibrium, collective security understands peace as best achieved through the establishment of formal structures. The objective is to seek "communities of power" rather than balances of power. This logic reflects the classic liberal view that sees humans as the seat of moral virtue, and that understands the conflict-ridden nature of the anarchical international system as manageable through human efforts. Collective security organizations monitor gradual military build-ups by potential aggressors, codify definitions of aggression, and stipulate a series of countermeasures—including sanctions leading up to the use of force—to be taken by members of the collective security system to thwart aggression.

Three. Collective security explicitly renounces force as an acceptable instrument of statecraft, except in instances of self-defense and collective security implementation. Like traditional balance of power logic, the threat to use force is understood to be necessary to discourage potential aggressors; however, under collective security, force is seen as an option of last resort. A state can be a member of a collective security organization and at the same time be dissatisfied with the status quo; however, as a member of the organization, it has renounced force as a means by which to deal with its dissatisfaction. Throughout history, collective security systems have relied on three tiers of persuasion to ensure compliance. The first was moral pressure, stemming largely from institutionalization of the collective security norm. The second was economic sanctions pursuant to an act of aggression (as discussed below in the cases of the League of Nations). The third and last resort was military force. This sequence of actions *theoretically* gave collective security an "automaticity" absent in other forms of security organization; *in practice*, however, the steps were far from automatic, requiring deliberation and often resulting in hesitation among the organization's members.

Four. Collective security differs from bilateral alliances and collective defense arrangements in its inclusiveness. While the latter two forms of security formally or informally designate the external threat, thereby excluding that state or bloc from the institutional arrangement, the domain of action for collective security systems is bounded only by its own membership. Cold War groupings such as NATO, the Warsaw pact, the Sino-Soviet alliance, or the U.S.-Japan alliance were collective defense and bilateral alliances rather than collective security arrangements because they aimed primarily at deterring and intimidating outside powers rather than preventing violations of peace within the group. Put another way, alliances may provide security, and a series of alliances may make up a collective defense arrangement, but for collective defense to be collective security, the "adversaries" in the former two instances must become "allies" in a universal effort to oppose all violations of the peace. It follows then that the moral imperatives of collective security and the realist imperatives of collective defense may sometimes conflict, particularly when a state is called upon to counter aggression on the part of one of its allies.

Five. The causal mechanism for peace under a collective security system is balancing, in that an act of aggression by one results in all the other members of the system joining together in a display of predominant force. However this differs from balance of power logic, in that the norm of collective balancing is formally agreed upon, institutionalized, and internalized among the members rather than being *ad hoc* and based on expediency. Thus, while critics of collective security point to the problem of underpreparedness that could result from a state not actively seeking alliance assurances against potential threats, proponents of collective security maintain that a collective security coalition promises to generate a counterforce *at least as* great as the natural coalition that would result under anarchy.

Six. In addition to inclusiveness, collective security de-emphasizes the self-help imperative enshrined by realism. Unlike realism's assumption that states will act only to further their own short-term self interests, collective security assumes that states will equate the interests of the other member-states with their own. As Woodrow Wilson described the nature of American responsibilities under such a system, "... the interests of all nations are also our own. *We* are partners with the rest. What affects mankind is inevitably *our* affair as well as the affairs of the nations of Europe and of Asia" (Mearsheimer, 1994/1995: 29). A key condition of any collective security system is therefore that states commit themselves to action even if it runs contrary to their myopic self-interests.

II. PHILOSOPHICAL UNDERPINNINGS

Collective security is often associated with the liberal tradition in international political thought, while the shifting alliances, secret pacts, and mutual suspicions that characterize balance of power politics are manifest within realism. Collective security envisions a virtuous spiral dynamic flowing from a formal security institution with prescribed rules and obligations. As members internalize these rules, a pattern of collective self-regulation results in which the state grows more confident in the organization's security-producing benefits, and believes itself to be more obligated to punish all violators regardless of myopic self-interests. This reflects the liberal conviction that humans are not destined to seek domination over one another. It does not deny that war occurs and that military power is an important determinant of interstate relations, but it does assert that individual efforts at coordination, rule-making, and institution-building can manage these forces and lead to stable patterns of cooperation, thereby transcending a Hobbesian state of nature. However, more recent proponents of collective security who attempt to embed their arguments within the anarchy assumption do not attempt to posit a more benign view of human nature, but rather attempt to show how the "all against one" logic of collective security may be more effective in maintaining peace than is the inherent unpredictability of balancing under anarchy.

Among the earliest advocates of international organizations intended for peace was the early 18th-century thinker Charles Francois Irenee Castel de Saint-Pierre. Although not wholly inclusive (Saint-Pierre called for excluding Turkey from the arrangement), Saint-Pierre's version of global security paved the path toward what would emerge as a more inclusive collective security arrangement following World War I. Moreover, collective security, particularly as envisioned in the interwar years, was seen to be normatively superior to the balance of power logic of 18th- and 19th-century Europe. The notion of "one for all and all for one" offered a path to peace that cultivated an accountability and sense of justice that was absent in balance of power systems where self-help imperatives reigned. Under the latter system, peaceful, status quo powers could become victims, and aggressive, revisionist powers could benefit. However, within collective security, one could expect that even under anarchy, aggression would be punished and victims would have recourse to justice through their peers.

The normative superiority of collective security was also evident in its inclusiveness. Balance of power and concert systems (the most often cited example being the Concert of Europe; 1815–1854) served only the security interests of the major powers. These were not inclusive, but exclusive, elite security systems, often operating at the expense of minor powers. Thus, in the 1820s, concert powers such as Great Britain and France permitted cohort powers Austria, Prussia, and Russia to suppress domestic threats to their influence in places like Italy, Germany, and Poland. Smaller powers were easily sacrificed for the balancing imperatives of larger powers. On the other hand, under collective security systems—at least in their most ideal form, the norm of unconditional egalitarianism came with membership. Membership entitled all powers—large or small—to the security guarantees of the organization.

III. COLLECTIVE SECURITY SYSTEMS: THE LEAGUE OF NATIONS AND THE UNITED NATIONS

There have been two large-scale, institutionalized efforts at establishing collective security systems in the 20th century: the League of Nations and the United Nations. The League was established in the wake of the First World War, and represented the Allied powers' vision of a new global order based on the norms of self-determination and liberal democracy. One of the early articulations of this vision was Woodrow Wilson's Fourteen Points, drafted in 1918. Of particular significance was the 14th point, which called for "a general association of nations [to] be formed under specific covenants for the purpose of affording mutual guarantees of political independence and territorial integrity to great and small States alike."

The League's membership ranged from 42 states at its establishment in 1920 to 57 states in 1938. The organization consisted of the General Assembly, in which all member-states participated, and a smaller guiding body in the League Council (originally to be composed of the United States, Britain, France, Japan, Italy, and later Germany as permanent members, and four nonpermanent members). League membership was, in theory, open to all who accepted the League's principles, but in practice a bias toward liberal democracies was apparent. The rationale for this was that democracies were much more likely to have the power of public opinion as a check against governments that sought to renege on League obligations. For example, Germany was not granted membership until 1926; Russia only joined in 1934, and many Asian and African states were not granted membership as colonial dependents.

States acquired membership by ratifying the League Covenant, which laid out the basic principles of collective security. In particular, Article 10 of the Covenant established the "all for one" principle, committing members to preserve and respect the territorial integrity of each of the other member states. States pledged to submit all disputes to arbitration rather than use force. Most importantly, Article 16 stated that war in violation of the Covenant was deemed an act of war against all other members, after which the violator would be automatically subject to economic sanctions. The actual clause stated, "should any Member of the League resort to war in disregard of its covenants ... it shall, *ipso facto,* be deemed to have committed an act of war against other Members of the League." The League Council would then determine, based on the principle of unanimity, what further military actions would be taken. The focus on economic sanctions as the primary enforcement tool reflected both pragmatic and philosophical lessons learned from World War I. First, the Allied victory was largely believed to highlight the decisive importance of economic power rather than military might. Second, economic sanctions were believed to be a more "humane" act against aggressor states than was war (a debatable point). Third, logistically, economic sanctions were believed to be the most effective and immediate response, given the slower process of organizing a military response. This last point highlights the difficulty and slowness of multilateral coordination and intervention, a notion that precludes the principle of "automaticity" envisioned by ideal collective security.

Founded in 1945 at the end of World War II, the UN represented the second major attempt at institutionalizing collective security. The UN was similar to the League in several ways. First, it consisted of two major bodies: the General Assembly and the Security Council. The latter group, composed of five permanent members (the United States, Great Britain, France, the Soviet Union, and China) held the same guiding role over the organization as did the League Council. The principles of collective self-regulation, indivisible peace and nonaggression were enshrined in the UN Charter. The scope of membership was global, and given the United States' willingness to join the UN, was more successful in this regard than was the League. However, despite the UN's professed universalism, the organization has been described as institutionalizing a 19th-century-type balance-of-power arrangement among the Great powers in the form of the Security Council, whereby the status quo that the UN is intended to uphold is that which is acceptable to the major powers.

Where the UN differed from the League is in its enforcement mechanisms. While the emphasis on collective action against aggression remained, the UN Charter did not call for automatic economic sanctions by member-states. Moreover, Articles 42 and 43 of the Charter laid out more specifically than the League Covenant how an act of aggression would be determined (i.e., by the Security Council) and how collective force would be administered (i.e., to be decided by the Council's mandates to member-states). Like the League, UN decisions were also implicitly based on the condition of unanimity as each Security Council member was granted veto power.

The founders of the UN in 1945 successfully addressed the failures of the League of 1920; nevertheless, the path of collective security still remained relatively untrodden in the ensuing decades. In retrospect, the League's shortcomings stemmed less from the effectiveness of its enforcement mechanisms (although this was a problem in theory), than from the absence of leadership and universal participation. Most importantly, the United States, despite President Woodrow Wilson's exhortations, saw membership in the organization not as a ticket to world peace but as an invitation to American entrapment in distant wars, and opted against participation. While the American presence was not the critical missing element in resolving the crises commonly associated with the League's demise (discussed below), its absence presaged the sort of self-help behavior that contributed to the League's inability to function as had been originally envisioned.

The UN remedied the problems afflicting the League. It enjoyed universal membership (i.e., including the United States) and a new decision-making and enforcement structure (i.e., the Security Council) that gave it the "teeth" and great power commitment to enforce collective security. Ironically though, this long-sought full participation of the major powers in the UN stymied the organization as the Cold War divided the Security Council's permanent members on virtually all issues, and effectively prevented the body from carrying out its intended functions. For this reason, many argue that the UN has had less-than-expansive experience as a collective security organization, although it has adapted itself to performing different forms of peace-related functions. The most successful of these has been peacekeeping and preventive diplomacy. An innovation arising out of the Security Council's incapacitation during the Cold War, this UN action did not center on the collective repelling of aggression by peace-breakers (which required a unanimous Council vote) but on neutral interventions to stop fighting and maintain the status quo between combatants. With the end of the Cold War, the UN's ability to act in collective ways as originally envisioned in 1945 is manifest in its more active use of enforcement mechanisms. The number of economic sanctions and military authorizations (some for humanitarian reasons) that are outlined in Chapter VII of the UN charter have increased, for example—from 2 during the Cold War to well over 10 since its end.

IV. ATTEMPTS AT COLLECTIVE SECURITY

A. The League of Nations

The empirical record of the League and the UN as collective security organizations is at best mixed, a point acknowledged even by the theory's proponents. The early years of the League were marked by some modest successes. In the 1920s, the League resolved minor disputes between Greece and Bulgaria (border dispute); Sweden and Finland (over the Aaland Islands); and in Albania (withdrawal of Greek, Italian, and Yugoslav troops). However, these successes should be assessed in the context of a decade that saw no major power attempting revisionist policies, thereby increasing the chances for peace. The League was unsuccessful, however, in resolving a host of other conflicts. In the 1920s, the League was unable to prevent the Greco-Turkish War (1920–1922), and the Russo-Polish War (1920). In the 1930s, the League failed with regard to the Chaco War (1932–1935), the German militarization of the Rhineland (1936), Germany's annexation of Czechoslovakia and Sudentenland (1938–1939), the Soviet invasion of Finland (1939), and the division of Poland (1939).

Two early and critical challenges revealing the League's shortcomings occurred in Asia and Africa in the 1930s. Japan, as part of its great power aspirations, had long sought to add Manchuria to its empire. In September 1931, the Japanese Imperial Army used a staged explosion on a railway it administered in Manchuria as the pretext for a massive, premeditated intervention into the area. Ostensibly, this was to protect Japanese nationals and economic interests, but in the process, Japanese troops occupied the resource-rich area and established the puppet government of Manchukuo in February 1932. The 1931 Manchurian Incident thus represented the first serious large-scale challenge to the League. China appealed to the League Council on the grounds that Japanese actions violated the League Covenant. The Council investigation (the Lytton Report) found that Japanese actions were indeed unjustified and that the forced seizure of territory was a violation of the spirit of the Covenant. However, because Japanese actions in Manchuria were not taken as a formal declaration of war, it was not technically a violation of the Covenant. As a result, the League did not invoke Article 16 and call for collective force to repel Japanese aggression. Instead, it advocated a policy of nonrecognition among League members of the Manchukuo government, and recommended that China and

Japan negotiate a joint administrative arrangement over the territory under question. This resolution effectively represented a failure of the League's collective security mechanism.

Another major challenge to the League came in the form of Italy's invasion of Ethiopia (Abyssinia) in 1935. Italy had a history of failed attempts at colonizing in northern Africa in the 19th century and had failed miserably in its last attempt in 1896 at the battle of Adowa where Italian troops were massacred. With the rise of fascism under Mussolini, there was a growing desire to annex Abyssinia to both avenge the defeat at Adowa, and to demonstrate the strength of the new fascist state. In December 1934, Mussolini built up forces along the Abyssinian border of Eritrea, launching a small attack. Abyssinia's appeals to the League for counteraction met with no response on the grounds that no actual territory had been seized. A few months later, in October, 1935, Italy launched a larger scale attack which the League was forced to contend with. This was a clear act of aggression by Italy, and both disputants were members of the League. However, the League's response was again weak. In accordance with Article 16, the League imposed a series of economic sanctions against Italy. However, these were largely cosmetic, as the most effective punitive measures—sanctioning oil and denying Italy access to the Suez Canal—were not undertaken. Moreover, the League later lifted sanctions and recognized the Italian victory in Abyssinia. The inability of the League of Nations to deal effectively with these two early challenges thus demonstrates the inherent limits of collective security as an effective mechanism for maintaining peace.

B. The United Nations

The UN has fared better as a collective security organization than did the League of Nations. The post-1945 period has indeed seen a correlation between the organization's existence and the absence of systemwide war. Moreover, two events are often pointed to as examples of successful collective security mechanisms at work: UN actions in Korea (1950–1953) and the U.S.-led coalition against Iraq during the 1991 Persian Gulf War. However, critics find problems with these propositions—both that the existence of the UN explains the absence of systemwide war, and that either the Korean War or the Gulf War are actual examples of collective security. First and foremost, there are numerous alternative explanations for the absence of major conflict in the post-1945 era, aside from the collective security efforts of the UN. Furthermore, while Korea certainly had the appearance of a collective security action, it might be better termed "collective defense." Finally, although a multimember coalition assembled under the auspices of the UN managed to quell Iraqi aggression in Kuwait, critics posit that Operations Desert Shield and Desert Storm were merely UN-bestowed "subcontracts" that effectively had the United States defending its own interests in the Gulf.

V. ALTERNATIVE EXPLANATIONS FOR THE ABSENCE OF SYSTEMWIDE WAR IN THE POST-1945 ERA

Three alternative conditions to explain the absence of systemwide conflict since World War II present themselves as a counterpoint to collective security arguments: structural bipolarity, nuclear deterrence, and the emergence of a normative shift against war as a legitimate means of statecraft. The particular structure of the international system in a given era, measured in terms of the distribution of capabilities among the system's members, has long been regarded as predicting relative levels of systemic stability. Specifically, bipolarity—the concentration of military, economic, and industrial capabilities among two states or regions—is widely considered to be more stable than is multipolarity. In bipolar systems, the symmetry of the two roughly equal coalitions elicits a self-equilibriating mechanism, as each bloc monitors the power of the other, and constantly attempts to match it. Conversely, multipolar systems are subject to power fluctuations among a handful of major powers; uncertainty reigns as today's allies may become tomorrow's adversaries. The bipolarity of the post-1945 era—with the United States and the former Soviet Union having shared a preponderance of the world's military and economic power—can thus be said to account for the so-called "long peace."

A second alternative explanation for post-1945 stability is contained within the logic of nuclear deterrence. That is, with the advent of nuclear weapons came the trend toward acquiring second-strike capabilities and the probability of "mutually assured destruction" should nuclear war break out. Under this argument, states fear escalation to the nuclear level and are therefore more hesitant to initiate large-scale conflict. Nuclear deterrence arguments extend across the system, as even states contemplating nuclear attack on another, non-nuclear state must necessarily fear the possibility of nuclear retaliation from an ally of the victim state.

Third, scholars have raised the issue of whether a worldwide conceptual shift has taken place since World War II regarding the normative legitimacy of war as an instrument of statecraft, the idea being that the notion of war has now become "unthinkable." As John Mueller writes with regard to the conceptual shift which began to evolve even after World War I, there was a "bone-deep revulsion;" a "colossal confirmation [of] the repulsiveness, immorality and futility of war and of its uncivilized nature" (1989:55). He further argues that it was only the emergence of three sets of leaders who fell "outside" of the dominant culture—Hitler, Mussolini, and the leadership of Japan—that led to the outbreak of World War II. This argument presents an interesting converse of the Wilsonian idealism underpinning collective security. While Wilson stressed the need to entrench the newly acquired postwar norms into an institutional arrangement, the likes of Mueller would argue that collective security organizations are redundant and perhaps unnecessary, as they merely reflect the already widespread revulsion toward war.

VI. THE UNITED NATIONS AND KOREA, 1950

In the case of the Korean War, critics of collective security argue, collective defense rather than collective security prevailed. While both are joint interventions against aggression, the former implies different motives for action. In particular, collective security implies a joint obligation to take action even if it is not in one's myopic self-interest. On the other hand, collective defense implies collective intervention stemming from a confluence of myopically self-interested individuals, and the fact that the aggressor is not part of the collective security system from the outset. The North Korean invasion elicited a multination U.S./UN force committed to repel aggression; however, American reasons for intervention were widely perceived as being based on the emerging bipolar competition with the Soviets rather than on any ideal of collective security.

Similarly, Western European intervention was largely seen to be motivated by analogies drawn with Germany and the perceived need to show resolve in Korea in order to deter similar aggression in Europe. Finally, Korea made clear the broader problem that the Cold War posed for the efficacy of UN collective security. Like the League, the UN was established for collective security based on the principle of unanimity. In the Security Council, this unanimity was almost impossible to achieve due to Cold War rivalries among the five permanent members. In this sense, the Korean intervention in particular (the Security Council decision to intervene was facilitated by the absence of the Soviet representative during the voting), and UN collective security in general, did not operate as originally envisioned.

VII. THE UNITED NATIONS AND THE GULF WAR, 1991

The Iraqi invasion of Kuwait on August 2, 1990, resulted in the most recent attempt to test the limits of collective security in the post-World War II era. Saddam Hussein's incursion into a neighboring oil-rich state, clearly as a military corollary to economic warfare as Iraq bemoaned its falling oil profits resulting from Kuwaiti sales, represented a classic violation of territorial sovereignty. Within a purely collective security calculation, the UN could hardly eschew the opportunity to thwart the aggression. And for the first time in the history of the UN, all five members of the Security Council (including the Soviet Union, despite its friendly ties with Iraq) agreed on countersecurity measures to repel the attack. The Security Council passed 12 resolutions, including Resolution 678 passed on 29 November 1990, authorizing member states "to use all necessary means" to restore the status quo ante. Furthermore, the joint action on the part of the U.S.-led coalition would also serve to unravel Iraq's chemical, biological and potentially nuclear weapons production capabilities—another longer-term goal of collective security measures.

However, what makes Operation Desert Storm less than ideal collective security is the fact that the UN delegated the counterforce operation to one of its members—the United States. Article 24 of the UN Charter mandates that the Security Council, rather than a given member-state(s), assume "primary responsibility for the maintenance of international peace and security." Moreover, during Desert Storm, coalition forces did not fight under the UN Flag (as they had done in the Korean War), nor were the U.S.-led forces answerable to UN authority. And it was only after Iraqi capitulation that a UN peacekeeping force was organized. An additional way to test whether the Gulf War represented a case of collective security is to determine whether the members of the U.S.-led coalition acted contrary to their respective myopic self-interests and in pursuit of the broader goal of maintaining the peaceful status quo. In the case of Iraq's invasion of Kuwait, securing American access to Middle Eastern oil was clearly a short-term, selfish interest motivating the United States to apply force to Iraq. Furthermore, those Arab states who joined the coalition could expect to receive increased financial aid levels from the United States. Finally, and in the interests of alliance politics, the United States was not going to stand by idly while Iraq threatened to shower chemical weapons upon Israel—the United States' closest ally in the Middle East. In the end, Iraq fired 30 SCUD missiles at Israeli cities, some of which were shot down in the air by American-operated Patriot missiles, and all of which had conventional tips only. Thus, while usually touted as an instance of collective security, the Gulf War was not a case whereby states were necessarily forgoing satisfaction of their short-term interests in favor of joint, long-term interests. Moreover, the Gulf War represented an evolution of post-World War II collective security as a system whereby the task is "jobbed-out" to the party with the most immediate interests in the conflict. This is partly due, no doubt, to pragmatism: an increasingly cash-strapped UN requires states with the most vital interests to assume responsibility for carrying out the task. Thus, in the post-Cold War era, the UN may be increasingly seen as the primary *facilitator,* rather than necessarily the *implementor,* of collective security.

VIII. CONCEPTUAL AND EMPIRICAL PROBLEMS

The attempts at collective security throughout the history of the League of Nations and the UN highlight some conceptual obstacles to the functioning and feasibility of collective security. First, events in Europe, Asia, and Africa in the 1930s showed that nations did *not* view peace as indivisible. If anything, later aggression by Germany, Japan and Italy showed that war does tend to spread. In theory, collective security stood on the principle that threats to peace could not be viewed as affecting the interests of certain states only; rather, a threat to one was to be considered a threat to all. In practice, however, states did prioritize threats to peace in terms of those that did and did not involve myopic self-interests. In the cases of Manchuria and Ethiopia, League members saw little incentive for expending the energies and resources to entangle themselves in conflicts in remote, peripheral places that did not involve direct material or strategic interests. For example, in the Manchurian case, some form of embargo in accordance with the League Charter would have been appropriate. Britain was the only power capable of leading the embargo, as Russia sought to appease Japan after its defeat by the Japanese navy in 1904–1905, as well as to attend to its own domestic problems, while the United States was dealing with domestic groundswells of isolationist sentiment (discussed below). However, the British were not willing to expend the resources.

This case highlights how the sense of community and general congruence of interests, often assumed to underpin collective security systems, are difficult to achieve in actuality. The desirability of maintaining the status quo or about what constitutes a stable and acceptable international order are essential yet hard-to-achieve components of collective security. However, this dilemma is not limited to collective security systems, but is endemic to any international organization or arrangement with the maintenance of peace as its goal. These, more often than not, have an inherent status-quo bias and thereby benefit only those members already satisfied with the status quo.

Second, in the absence of the conditions for congruence and community, the empirical record of collective security shows that balancing imperatives still reign. This was particularly true in the Ethiopian case. In the end, Italy met with no opposition from the League because many members were more concerned about the actions of Nazi Germany in Europe. By the time of the Ethiopian invasion, Hitler had withdrawn from the League of Nations (1933); denounced the armament clauses of the Versailles treaty (1935); and re-occupied the Rhineland (1936). As a result, countries like Britain and France shelved collective security norms, and instead sought to appease Italy in Ethiopia to gain a potential ally to check Germany in Europe (e.g., the Hoare-Lavall Pact). This balancing behavior essentially meant that small states were not protected under the League, but rather, were pawns of great power rivalries. The Haitian delegate to the League summed up the concern of small powers after the events in Africa: "Great or small, strong or weak, near or far, white or colored, let us never forget that one day, we may be somebody's Ethiopia" (Walters, 1952:653).

Third, the empirical record clearly illustrates the problem of collective action. Collective security is premised on the notion that peace and transparency constitute public goods that benefit all. A public good is defined as one which, once produced, cannot be enjoyed by some and not others, and therefore must be provided communally. However, the rational incentive is to "free-ride" off the efforts of others to provide the good, while still enjoying its benefits, which ultimately results in the good no longer being provided. This dynamic is referred to as the "collective action problem." Historically, states have chosen the free-ride option, buck-passing responsibility for responding to the threatening power's actions to the party with the most direct interests in the conflict.

The free-rider problem means that collective security's success depends greatly on the participation of the major powers. Their willingness to underwrite the costs imposed by free-riders and buck-passers helps to ensure that the good is provided. In the case of the League, this leadership requirement was conspicuously absent. In spite of Woodrow Wilson's commitment to the principles of collective security as embodied in the League, isolationist sentiment in Congress and the American public after the First World War eventually led the Senate not to ratify the League covenant.

Fourth, and linked to the leadership issue are membership requirements. Collective security's fundamental flaw is that it clashed with the sovereign prerogatives of its members. Perhaps more than any other principle, and consonant with the 1648 Peace of Westphalia, which divided the international system into individual nation-states, sovereignty—the principle by which states hold supreme authority over their internal and external affairs—has shaped interstate relations. With sovereignty comes the precepts of nonintervention and territorial integrity. While the latter principle is consistent with the principle of collective security that explicitly sanctions territorial incursions other than those performed for the purposes of self-defense or collective defense, the principle of nonintervention can be seen to be at odds with the principle of collective security, whereby aggressor states can expect to have a third-party coalition intervene on behalf of the victim. In this sense, collective security systems impinge on notions of sovereignty to a lesser degree than would a system of world government, but to a greater extent than unrestricted balance of power systems. Thus, while intervention exists in collective security systems as well as under balance of power systems, the intervention under the former is prescriptive while under the latter it is *ad hoc*—states balance (sometimes intervening) out of myopic, self-interests. Collective security may therefore be seen as a middle ground between unchecked anarchy and wholly binding and centralized multilateralism.

Fifth, the obligation by member-states to come to the aid of any victim can be seen to impinge on the right of states to choose when and where to deploy military force. A related critique of collective security is that of the escalation dilemma: a small, localized conflict is more likely to escalate into a system-wide war as some states will fulfill their collective commitment and come to the aid of the victim, while others might choose to side with the aggressor out of particular alliance loyalties. The potential result is therefore a conflict much larger than would have occurred had the original warring parties been left alone.

Alongside the sovereignty principle as defined by international law is the aspect of self reliance. While a collective security system attempts to establish itself as an international adjudicator, force remains the only arbiter in the eyes of states adhering to balance-of-power politics. If push came to shove, states would—and in the case of the League's failed attempts at collective security implementation, did—choose the option of self-help. When Japan objected to the League's recommendations in response to its invasion of Manchuria, it unilaterally withdrew from the League (as did Germany over its renouncing of the Versailles armament clause the same year). When France occupied the Ruhr in 1923, any League measures were thwarted by the French threat to simply withdraw from the League.

Sixth, and an additional operational problem with the collective security mechanism that has become evident empirically is the inherent difficulty in defining aggression. Collective security operates on the assumption that there is a common and clearly perceived act of aggression that sets the League's collective security mechanism into motion. For example, in the Ethiopian case, the League could not act in response to Italy's buildups on the Eritrean border the year prior to the actual attack because this was technically not an act of aggression as defined by the covenant (i.e., an actual seizure of territory). The problem is that collective security responds to acts of aggression rather than to the capabilities or perceived intentions of the actors. This can have the counterintuitive effect of actually encouraging rather than discouraging aggressors, particularly in the form of "biding time" strategies. Aggressor states build up and are then encouraged to carry out attempts to revise the status quo before the collective security organization has time to respond. Stated otherwise, the problem of underpreparedness results from arrangements that do not explicitly require would-be victim states to build up their internal balancing capabilities to counter potential, long-term threats.

A final criticism of collective security is methodological. Arguments both against and in favor of the viability of the concept generally assume an extremely narrow and specific definition of what constitutes collective security. The result is an unnecessarily stringent test of when collective security occurs. According to the principles laid out above, collective security operates only when there is collective action taken against an aggressing party *and* (1) the decision is unanimous; (2) the aggressor is a member of the collective security community; and (3) the motives for undertaking the obligations of the organization do not derive solely from myopic self-interest. The last condition is both methodologically and empirically difficult to verify. Flexible and more relaxed conditions for collective security are more useful, and will be discussed below.

IX. ANALYTICAL RESPONSES

Proponents of collective security, especially in the post-Cold War era, are cognizant of the conceptual limits of the theory, but adhere to differing assumptions about the dynamics of international relations. First, while critics of collective security view it as requiring states to trust one another, proponents of collective security—even operating within a strictly rationalist view of international politics—argue that trust is *not* intrinsic to the maintenance of a collective security system. That is, critics argue that the degree to which states comply with the obligations of the system, identify with it, and entrust their security to it, is a function of the degree to which they are confident that other members sincerely renounce force as an instrument of statecraft and that others will come to their aid if they are a victim of this aggression. However, collective security's proponents respond in two ways: first, would-be defector states are dissuaded from shirking from their collective security commitments by the imperatives of reputation—states fear a loss of face should they fail to come to the aid of a victim state under collective security's obligations. Second, proponents of collective security view such arrangements as merely *augmenting* the counteraggressive coalition that would be expected to result even within an anarchic, balance-of-power system. Thus, should a state, or group of states, fail to uphold their commitment to join the coalition, it is expected that, *at the minimum,* those states whose interests are most threatened by the aggression will come to the aid of the victim. In other words, collective security should not be any less stable than the unpredictability inherent in a world governed by shifting alliances and balancing dynamics.

There is one problem with this line of reasoning, however, which illustrates the limitations of long-term collective security implementation in an international system whose conditions of anarchy and self-help are understood as being fixed and immutable. That is, as a collective security system garners increasing successes, states may become complacent about their need to balance—either internally (military build-up) or externally (acquiring allies) against potential threats. As discussed above, this danger of underpreparedness may lead to a fatal window of opportunity for would-be aggressor states. Thus, the more collective security succeeds, the more it may be setting the stage for subsequent failures, as even a preponderant number of coalition states may not have the joint resources necessary to counter every act of aggression.

A second issue-area both illustrates the differing assumptions between collective security's adherents and critics, as well as offers the possibility of resolution to the success-complacency-underpreparedness dilemma. That is, the question of the formation of interests and identity cuts further to the core of international relations debates than does the latter critique of balancing dynamics. Implicit in debates over the role of institutions in international relations is the degree to which interests and identity are shaped by institutional interaction. One criticism of collective security leveled by scholars who view interests as fixed from the outset (i.e., prior to any interstate interaction), is that collective security systems—when they do work—do not *cause* peace; rather, collective security systems are merely institutionalizing an international order *already agreed upon* by the members of the international system—or at least by the great powers. This view leads one skeptic to write, "collective security works only when it need not" (Joffe, 1992:44).

However, a view of international relations that ascribes international institutions the power to shape state interests would see collective security systems as not only institutionalizing an already existing norm, but in so doing, strengthening it. In other words, through the continued existence of a collective security system, and by states adhering to the membership requirements by avoiding proscribed aggression, the interests and identities of states *evolve* in keeping with the encoded norms of nonbelligerency and international stability. Here, even interactional aspects such as discourse can serve to shape and consolidate existing norms; conceiving of and proclaiming oneself as a member in good stead of a collective security system can therefore serve to encourage peaceful, status quo behavior. Seen in this light, a collective security arrangement which serves to further the identity and interests of participating actors may serve to mitigate the problem of underpreparedness, as would-be aggressor states come to internalize the norms of the system.

X. PROSPECTS FOR COLLECTIVE SECURITY IN THE POST-COLD WAR ERA

With the dissolution of the Soviet Union and the subsequent end of the Cold War, some scholars have begun to revive variants of collective security as an appropriate security prescription for maintaining international order. However, given the historical failures of collective security in overcoming aggression, it has become clear that collective security is an ideal-type arrangement to which it is unfair to subject the challenges of interstate competition in an anarchic, international system. Thus, more tempered versions of collective security prescriptions have emerged, namely that of a Great Power "concert," similar to the nineteenth century Concert of Europe.

Chief among the conditions of the post-Cold War era that bode well for an adapted collective security arrangement, proponents argue, is a general consensus among the major powers to uphold the territorial and ideological status quo. Institutionalizing such a collective arrangement among the major powers not only approaches the ideal of collective security, but allows for a group of great powers to assume responsibility—and have an incentive to do so—for underwriting the public good of collective security, thus moving towards overcoming the collective action problem. Other authors have pointed to the possibility for implementing versions of "collective conflict management"—systems that are far less restrictive than ideal collective security, but nevertheless institutionalize the potential for multilateral action to prevent and respond to conflict.

It is clear, therefore, that the conditions of the post-Cold War world lend themselves to exploring the potential for more relaxed versions of collective security. While the empirical record reveals the potential pitfalls in implementing collective security, it is possible that collective security might still remain a viable strategy for institutionalizing presently held norms of relative ideological consensus and stability. Whether policymakers restrict themselves to adhering to a stringent Wilsonian ideal, or whether they allow themselves to experiment with alternative collective arrangements for conflict response may well determine the level of peacefulness we can expect as the post-Cold War era unfolds—and whether or not collective security will even be needed.

Also See the Following Articles

ALLIANCE SYSTEMS • BALANCE OF POWER RELATIONSHIPS • COLD WAR • MILITARY DETERRENCE AND STATECRAFT • PEACEKEEPING • PEACE ORGANIZATIONS • WORLD WAR I

Bibliography

Bennett, A., & Lepgold, J. (1993). Reinventing collective security after the Cold War and Gulf conflict. *Political Science Quarterly, 108,* 2.

Betts, R. K. (1992, Summer). Systems for peace or causes of war? Collective security, arms control, and the new Europe. *International Security, 17,* 1.

Claude, Jr., Inis L. (1996). *Power and international relations,* Chaps. 4–5. New York: Random House.

Claude, Jr., Inis L. (1971). *Swords into plowshares; The problems and progress of international organization* (4th Ed.). New York: Random House.

Downs, G. W. (Ed.). (1994). *Collective security beyond the Cold War.* Ann Arbor: University of Michigan Press.

Finkelstein, M. S., & Finkelstein, L. S. (Eds.). (1996). *Collective security.* San Francisco: Chandler Publishing Co.

Hinsley, F. H. (1967). *Power and the pursuit of peace: Theory and practice in the history of relations between states.* Cambridge: Cambridge University Press.

Jervis, R. (1985, October). From balance to concert: A study of international security cooperation. *World Politics, 38,* 1.

Joffe, J. (1992, Spring). Collective security and the future of Europe: Failed dreams and dead ends. *Survival, 34,* 1.

Kupchan, C. A., & Kupchan, C. A. (1991, Summer). Concerts, collective security, and the future of Europe. *International Security, 16,* 1.

Lepgold, J., & Weiss, T. G. (Eds.). (1998). *Collective conflict management and changing world politics.* Albany: State University of New York Press.

Lyons, G. M., & Mastanduno, M. (1995). *Beyond Westphalia? State sovereignty and international intervention.* Baltimore: The Johns Hopkins University Press.

Mearsheimer, J. J. (1994/95, winter). The false promise of international institutions. *International Security 19,* 3.

Morgenthau, H. J. (1985). *Politics among nations: The struggle for power and peace* (6th Ed.). (with Kenneth Thompson). New York: Knopf.

Mueller, J. (1989). *Retreat from Doomsday: The obsolescence of major war.* New York: Basic Books.

Nye, J. S. Jr. (1997). *Understanding international conflicts: An introduction to theory and history* (2nd Ed.). New York: Longman.

Ullman, R. H. (1991). *Securing Europe.* Princeton: Princeton University Press.

Walters, F. P. (1952, 1960). *A history of the League of Nations.* (London: Oxford University Press.

Weiss, Thomas G. (Ed.). (1993). *Collective security in a changing world.* Boulder: Lynne Rienner Publishers.

Walters, F. P. (1952). *A history of the League of Nations,* Vol. 2. London: Oxford University Press.

Wolfers, A. (1962). *Discord and collaboration: Essays on international politics.* Baltimore: The Johns Hopkins Press.

Colonialism and Imperialism

Dierk Walter
University of Berne

GLOSSARY

Chartered Company Joint-stock company, vested by a state charter with trade monopolies and quasi-governmental rights.

Frontier Shifting area between a territory under firmly established colonial rule and the neighboring indigenous societies.

Men on the Spot Protagonists of imperialism acting on the periphery.

Metropolis Capital of an imperialist state; figurative: the totality of central driving forces of imperialism.

Monopoly Privilege of exclusive trade in a certain area.

Periphery Remote field of imperialist action; the colonial spot.

Preventive Imperialism Occupation of a territory with the main purpose to prevent its occupation by a competitor.

Subimperialism Imperialist action undertaken by men on the spot or dependent governments without state permission.

NO GENERALLY ACCEPTED DEFINITION is available for either the term "colonialism" or "imperialism." Both are frequently used with various meanings as a description of historical processes and phenomena, but also for political polemics (see "Theories"). In the context of this article, *imperialism* means the political process leading to the integration of new territory into an expanding economy. As an important part of imperialism, *colonialism* means the establishment of formal political control over such territory; thus it includes the setting up of protectorates, colonies, and so on.

I. THEORIES

The word imperialism refers to the Latin term *imperium*, which originally indicated unrestricted authority of a single person. In the middle ages this term had come to describe the idea of a universal Christian monarchy or, in practice, the rule of a single monarch over several kingdoms. "Imperialism" was first used by the critics of Napoléon III to denounce the political system of imperial France (*système impérial)*. Eventually applied to the prestige-seeking foreign policy by British prime minister Benjamin Disraeli in the 1870s, after the beginning of the "scramble for Africa" (1882–1914) the term was increasingly used in its modern meaning, namely as the expansion of a European nation-state, especially into the non-European world.

Theories of imperialism have been brought forward by economists, historians, and sociologists for more than a century, but still there is not even agreement on which subject is to be covered. Theories usually confuse definition, description, and explanation, and therefore they tend to be incomparable.

Non-Marxist theory offers several political, economic, or social explanations for European expansion. For J. A. Hobson, financial interests seeking investment opportunities were driving British politicians into expansion in Africa. One model commonly used among historians is that of evergrowing European industries looking for new sources of raw materials and for new markets overseas, which have to be protected against third parties through political control by the metropolis. Others saw the reason for expansion in the rivalry of great powers, where colonies give prestige to the mother country, act as bases for a worldwide pursuit of interests, or are used as objects in diplomatic bargaining. H.-U. Wehler explained German expansion as the attempt of social elites to relieve themselves of domestic pressure by means of a successful colonial policy. He called that phenomenon *social imperialism*.

Marxist(-Leninist) theory dogmatically identified imperialism with "the highest stage of capitalism," where the aggravated rivalry of monopoly-dominated capitalist states finally caused World War I and thus the breakdown of capitalism. Having had to admit that this self-destruction of capitalism had obviously failed to materialize, Western neo-Marxist writers, especially following World War II, focused on the role of economic factors in preserving the domination of the "First" World over the "Third" after the disbanding of the colonial empires. Joined by scholars from the newly independent countries, several theories of dependency and of "neocolonialism" have eventually emerged within this school of thought. These emphasize that economic structures continue to keep the Third World dependent on the First even after the end of colonialism.

More or less coincidentally, Marxist and non-Marxist writers originally met in the assumption that "imperialism" was a phenomenon restricted to the time from 1880–1890 through 1914–1918, when most of the non-European world came under the control of European states. Neo-Marxists applied the term to the period after World War I (and II), whereas others increasingly found structural links back in the early 19th century. J. Gallagher and R. Robinson created the term "informal empire" for territories dominated by an expanding country without colonial rule and thus were able to show continuities that had so far been ignored by concentrating on formal control. By stressing the importance of the specific situation on the spot for the choice between informal and formal means of domination, they shifted the scholars' debate to the colonial periphery. For a long time other writers have demanded to look at the process of European expansion as a whole, albeit without calling it "imperialism." Recently both schools of thought have met in applying the term without too much theoretical restraint to dominance relationships throughout the history of European expansion. Some authors even undertake comparisons with ancient or non-European expansionist societies. Therefore, the old distinction between modern "imperialism" and early modern "colonialism" has lost most of its meaning.

A certain agreement has been achieved as to the fact that the underlying motivation of imperialism is economic, which does not mean that each single step of expansion has to be undertaken with hope for immediate economic gain—strategic factors may play an important role, too—nor that expansion is necessarily led by economic or financial lobbies in the metropolis.

II. PROTAGONISTS

Imperialism was not always primarily a matter of metropolitan governments. People of different social groups and professions acted as protagonists of expansion, with the majority of them not in the metropolis but on the colonial spot (for one example, see Table I). The scope of their action depended on their position within the imperial system.

State officials (viceroys, governors, administrators of all kinds) in existing colonies often had a key interest in further expansion, which would earn them promotion, merits, popularity, and often immediate material gain as well. Prior to the availability of modern means of communication, the higher ranking of them especially had to be vested with vast powers and the right to exercise them without first asking for permission. Thus continuous expansive processes were sometimes completely initiated on the spot by successive governors (early Spanish America; British India). Lower ranking officials had to rely on more subtle means of carrying through their plans, for example, exerting influence on their superiors, warranted by more intimate knowledge of country and people.

Soldiers (high-ranking army and navy officers) were not just the instruments of conquests or of acts of gunboat diplomacy ordered by the home or colonial government. Instead, by exceeding their authority they frequently used their forces for the conquest of territory, eventually justifying this as peace making or peace keeping. Whether they could get away with that depended on the structure of the armed forces and the

TABLE I

British Imperial Expansion, 1783–1815

Period	Area	Protagonists	Government involvement	Aim/Result
1807–1810	Brazil	Government	Decision, diplomacy	Informal empire
1804–1821	Canada's Northwest	Chartered companies	Assistance, arbitration	Penetration, bases
1795/1806	Cape Colony and Ceylon	Government soldiers	Decision, military	Conquest
1793–1810	Caribbean islands	Government	Decision, military	Conquest
1787–1793	China	Merchants	Diplomacy	Penetration (failed)
1798–1801	Egypt	Government	Decision, military	Expelling the French
1793–1815	India	Officials, Soldiers	Attempt to restrain	Conquest
1788–1814	Interior of West Africa	Scientists	Assistance	Penetration (failed)
1809–1810	Mauritius	Officials	Agreement	Conquest
1787–1808	Sierra Leone	Chartered company	none	Freed slave settlement
1787–1811	Southeast Asia	Merchants, Officials	Diplomacy, Military	Penetration/conquest
1806–1825	Spanish America	Merchants, Politicians	Decision, Military	Informal empire

colony, and, increasingly in modern states, on whether the public would appreciate their (successful) action. If so, this would even protect them from being court-martialed. The goals in military expansion were glory, merits, promotion, and immediate material gain—pillage.

From the beginning *merchants* were among the most important protagonists of expansion. The initial aim of European expansion was to expand trade, even prior to conquest, and consequently merchants were often the first to explore an overseas territory and to open it for trade. During most of the European expansion the flag followed the trade—merchants only turned to their government for protection when they felt an urgent need to do so. However, because they lacked official authority as well as military force, merchants rarely had the means to carry out expansion on their own, and they had to rely on exerting influence on political or military institutions. On the other hand, merchants' interests were often used by (colonial) governments as a pretext to justify expansion.

Chartered companies, composed of many merchants and working with their joint capital, were the spearhead of expansion in many parts of the world. Especially in early modern times, governments vested them not only with trade monopolies as an economic basis, but with vast quasi-governmental powers for certain areas, including even the right of war and peace and of concluding international treaties. In turn, the state expected financial contributions to the treasury. The end of the companies came with the introduction into politics of free trade principles, or, alternatively, with bankruptcy. Their governmental rights reverted to the state, which in some prominent cases (British and Dutch East India) also implied the responsibility for extended territories. Chartered companies witnessed a short revival as relatively cheap instruments of expansion in the "scramble for Africa."

Industrialists and financiers invested in colonial enterprises that opened and developed territories for the world market. Like the merchants, they occasionally had to turn to their government for protection, which often simply meant protective tariffs. Their interests were also frequently used to justify expansion.

Settlers played an important part mainly in those regions where the climate allowed European-style agriculture. Their evergrowing need for more area under cultivation led them to expand into new territory by force. In doing so on their own, the settlers usually ignored the rights of indigenous peoples, even when those rights were guaranteed by their government. Eventually the settlers induced the same government to provide them with protection from indigenous reaction. Thus, large areas were brought under European control (both Americas; southern and eastern Africa; Australasia).

In some regions *the clergy* was the instrument of comparatively peaceful penetration of frontier areas (Spanish and French America, sub-Saharan Africa) by means of "civilizing" indigenous people. By teaching them European culture and religion as well as the advantages of protection from their enemies by European weapons, missionaries paved the way for the eventual takeover by colonial governments. There were, however, great differences between colonial empires; some were intimately intertwined with the church (Spain), others excluded it completely from vast areas (early British India).

Led by a diversity of personal motives, *adventurers, explorers, and scientists*, acted as the vanguard of expansion in unknown territory. Their prospects and means were as diverse as their appearances, ranging from the 16th-century pirate in the Caribbean to the 19th-century explorer traveling alone through Central Africa. But their reports usually made eventual expansion look promising.

European expansion would have been impossible without *indigenous collaboration*. In only a few cases did Europeans simply conquer territory; instead, imperialism began as bargaining terms for trade or rights of settlement. Even conquest usually began as "assisting" one indigenous party in an external or internal conflict with another, thus subjugating the enemy and obliging the ally. The more "collaboration regimes" had to rely on European support to stabilize their power, the more they became alienated from their subjects, which in turn made them even more dependent on their European allies. Finally, this vicious circle could cause the breakdown of a regime, thus forcing the imperialist power to take over in order to preserve its interests.

In many cases, *resistance* emerged only decades after the takeover, when the subjects felt colonial rule in their daily lives. Often the subjugated indigenous people have later been accused of "disunity," which had made conquest possible, but that is largely beside the point: for example, inhabitants of the Indian subcontinent prior to the British conquest did not consider themselves to be "Indians," but Bengalis, Gujaratis, Marathas, and so on, and certainly they were Hindus, Muslims, and Sikhs. To think in terms of nationality was usually the result of a combination of the experience of European rule, contact with European ideas, and social changes.

III. STRUCTURES

A. State

The part played by state governments in imperialist ventures varied greatly. Although originally initiated by individuals, the expansion of Spain and Portugal in the Americas and in Asia was primarily a state enterprise; the British conquest of India, on the other hand, was undertaken by men on the spot, often consciously sabotaging London's explicit policy. Between these extremes, all forms of governmental action are to be found (see Table I for examples). The state vested merchant companies with governmental rights and trade monopolies; it gave assistance of all kinds (bases, forts, diplomacy, military force, drawing up borders or demarcation lines), partly beforehand in order to encourage individual undertakings, partly in case of emergency, when existing enterprises of state subjects were threatened. But while governments could do a lot to support the expansionism of their subjects, they could do little to restrain it, and what already had happened on the periphery was almost impossible to undo.

B. Administration

The various types of colonies can be distinguished along three lines:

1. Purpose/Economic and Social Structure

a. *Colonies of domination* with large non-European populations, governed by a small European administration, with marginal presence of merchants, soldiers, and clergymen. Colonies of domination were mainly reserved for trade, exploitation of natural resources, or gaining wealth from the indigenous subjects through taxation or tributes (British India, French Southeast Asia, parts of Africa).

b. *Colonies of Settlement* had a dominant European population, and were largely dependent on agricultural production. The work force could be recruited primarily from the indigenous population (Africa), from imported slaves (Caribbean, South America), or from the Europeans themselves (North America, Australasia). In both the latter cases the original inhabitants were first expelled or exterminated.

c. *Naval Bases* made possible worldwide communication, trade, and exertion of power, and often served as instruments to control a vast hinterland by informal means (early bases in Africa; Hong Kong, Singapore, Malacca).

2. International Law Status

In theory, European control led to different degrees of limiting the sovereignty of the indigenous entities: from (unequal) treaties on specific matters over control of foreign affairs (protectorate) to complete takeover (colony). In some cases, territories were integrated in the political structure of the mother country (many French colonies; Russian Asia).

3. Internal Administration

A colonial government could either install a bureaucratic administration at all levels (direct rule), or rely to various degrees on precolonial power structures (indirect rule). The latter comprised everything from restricted jurisdiction of local chieftains to the incorporation of large principalities with the entire political system surviving (British India). From existing colonies a third type eventually emerged: Certain or all subjects could be given political participation in democratic forms. Colonies of settlement could thus be transformed into *dominions* (Canada, South Africa, Australia, New Zealand).

But colonies were not always directly governed by the state. Remnants of feudal structures were also to be found (early modern America), and private companies could possess governmental rights as well and could act as sovereigns for all practical purposes, even if sovereignty in theory rested with their respective home government.

C. Economy

The economy of imperialism was characterized by various structures, but overall it was a trading system.

1. Trade

From the first voyages to India in search of spices, trade was the aim and the means of expansion. Even where expansion began with conquest, destruction, and pillage, trading systems eventually evolved under the protection of the new colonial governments.

The classical *pattern of colonial trade* was the exchange of colonial produce, either natural resources or agricultural produce, for manufacturing commodities from the mother country. A key feature was the global trade network, which connected the specific trading potential of several continents. Thus, for instance, the Atlantic triangular trade (16th to 19th century) typically exchanged cheap manufactured goods and firearms from Europe for slaves in West Africa, brought them to the American plantation colonies, where the profit from their sale would buy colonial goods for the journey home or would be transferred to Europe in bills of exchange.

Where even an imperial trade network could not provide for adequate exchange commodities, bullion gained overwhelming importance. The economy of Spain as well as the bulk of European trade in Asia until well into the 19th century was based on large shipments of Peruvian silver, benefiting from the fact that silver was comparatively cheaper in America than in Asia. Until the 19th century, trade with Asia was also the most important exception to the classical pattern: Europe imported not only raw materials but also manufactured goods (dyed textiles, porcelain) from there.

Through systems of *trade regulations* governments attempted to maximize the share of their subjects in world trade, thus supporting both the home economy and the treasury (tariffs, taxation). Until the 19th century, the theory of *mercantilism* dominated these attempts. Typically, a mercantilist trade system confined colonial trade to shipping raw materials and cash crops to the mother country, and receiving in turn manufactured goods. Many commodities (the classical "colonial" produce such as sugar, tobacco, coffee, dyestuffs) were also re-exported. Colonial manufacturing was restricted to domestic needs. But the differences between the powers were great: Whereas British mercantilism was comparatively liberal and marked by exceptions, Spain and Portugal surrounded their colonial empires with almost impregnable walls of regulations.

The second half of the 19th century witnessed the introduction by Great Britain of *free trade* principles into the world economy. Britain's superior industries needed vast, open markets worldwide rather than protection. Other colonial empires followed only reluctantly. By the end of the century, new *protective tariffs* began to regulate trade with their respective colonies in favor of the colonial powers. Nevertheless, only in the case of Great Britain was the share of trade with its own colonies of any significance. Even here the bulk went to the Dominions (see Table II).

2. Agriculture

Except when the indigenous population already produced export commodities (as in some African regions), colonies with favorable natural conditions were adapted for the world market through the establishment of plantations or farming. The various forms of colonial agriculture, from sheep or cattle breeding (Australasia, South Africa, South America) to European-style farming (North America), to sugar, tobacco, oil, rubber, coffee,

TABLE II

Share of Own Dependencies in Export Trade of Colonial Powers

	ca. 1870	ca. 1900	ca. 1930
France		10%	12.7%
Germany		less than 1%	
Netherlands (East India only)	40.6%		16.8%
UK: whole empire	26.8%	34.1%	37.2%
UK: dominions only	12.0%	16.7%	20.6%
USA			5%

or tea plantations (tropical climates in America, Africa, and Asia), all had an immense need for cultivable land in common. But whereas plantations were capital- and labor-intensive, farming was not. And while the farms produced at least partially for domestic consumption, plantations merely provided cash crops for the world market.

3. Industry

Although few manufacturing branches (armaments, textiles) had produced at least partially for the colonial export trade since the 17th century, industrial production as a whole only began to play a part in imperial expansion in the early 19th century, and even then it was not a major driving force. Undeveloped world regions were not a profitable market, and the bulk of the industrial output of the colonial powers went to other industrial countries. The development of *colonial* industries did not really begin before World War II.

4. Finance

Investments on the periphery were more important. From the early Caribbean plantations to the great infrastructural projects of the 20th century (railroads, channels, roads), investment in the colonies was a risky, but, if successful, highly profitable business. Still, investment was not necessarily confined to the colonies of the respective country (see Table III). But where investments of its subjects were, or appeared to be, threatened, an imperial power had a very good reason for intervention.

5. Service Sector

Shipping, banking, and insurance were key branches of the global trade network. They benefited from its existence, but even more from its expansion. This did not necessarily involve advocating formal rule, but the service sector could not lose where it was established.

6. Taxation

The state also profited from the colonial economy through taxation of its subjects in the colonies. Some possessions with large indigenous populations first seemed to be goldmines for the state that had the opportunity to siphon off the profits of the colonial economy and tax the inhabitants. Eventually, most colonies turned out to be very costly in terms of running and defending them, so that the home government, in contrast to businessmen, benefited little or not at all.

TABLE III

Share of Own Dependencies in Foreign Investment of Colonial Powers 1913–1914

France	8.8%
Germany	2.1%
UK: whole empire	47.3%
UK: dominions only	34.6%

D. Ideology

The effect of ideologies, whether religious or secular, on imperialist ventures has often been overestimated: ideologies rarely caused imperialist expansion, but in many cases they supported it or helped to justify it against external rivals or internal critics.

1. Christian Mission

The obligation to convert the pagans was used over the centuries by all European powers, Catholic or Protestant, to justify expansion. This concept had its most prominent appearance in power politics when a papal grant in 1493 gave imperial Spain the lion's share of both Americas as fief, linked to and justified by the duty to proselytize.

2. Claim to World Power

The medieval idea of universal monarchy in the tradition of ancient Rome survived well into the modern age. Imperial Spain pursued it in the form of the claim to unite all Christendom in one empire. In later centuries this ideology was partially secularized. Increasingly, great powers propagated their duty to police the world as a whole or at least in part to bring about order, peace, civilization, free trade, democracy, socialism, or other advantages.

3. (Natural) Superiority

Partially based on Aristotle's theory of natural slavery, the idea of superiority over indigenous peoples accompanied European expansion from the beginning. It appeared in two shapes:

a. Overemphasizing their own lead in technical, organizational, scientific, or cultural development could lead colonial powers to formulate a commitment to share it with the less developed, if necessary, against their will: Civilization as "*the White man's burden*" (R. Kipling).

b. The other variation was social Darwinism or simply racism: people who were less fit for survival, who were unable to adopt a European way of life, or who were marked by a non-European outward appearance were designated by nature for subjugation, expulsion, or extinction.

4. Nationalism and Chauvinism

In the 19th and 20th century nationalism and chauvinism could be transferred from the European power rivalry to the wider world in order to divert domestic pressure to areas where success might be achieved more easily. Thus, for a comparatively short period in the history of imperialism, considerations about popular opinion at home could lead to expansion.

E. The World System

The most striking feature of European expansion was the emergence of a European-style, European-controlled world system. Over five centuries, the growing dominance of European states over most of the world restyled international relations along European lines. While global trade and communication, carried on by Europeans, linked continents formerly living apart, European rules of conduct in economic as well as diplomatic affairs, together with European thought and European legal traditions, increasingly became binding for the non-European world. No matter how much European powers competed for their share of the world, they acted resolutely together to carry through these principles, if necessary. Thus, European states developed a system of international law in their favor, and ruthlessly applied it to societies that had never seen a written law. They convened international conferences and staked claims to vast territories that were largely unknown to them. Beyond that, the European-style world economy was a structural force that left individual non-European societies with no choice but to adapt themselves to it, to be adapted by European force, or to be reduced to economic insignificance.

IV. THE COURSE OF EVENTS

A. From Contact to Colonies

As an ideal type, the way to full-scale colonial rule over an extended territory would go through the following phases: (1) exploration of unknown coasts; (2) first contact with indigenous population; (3) barter; (4) setting up trading posts through treaties with local authorities; (5) exploration of the hinterland; (6) economic penetration of the hinterland; (7) extension of political influence through diplomatic interventions and military actions in indigenous conflicts; (8) increasingly unequal treaties with political authorities (collaboration regimes); (9) establishment of protectorate or colonial rule after breakdown of collaboration regimes or because of threat of intervention of another European power; (10) construction of a colonial administration and economy.

In historical reality, one or several steps might have been missing. In particular, colonies of settlement adopted a rather different approach, but Europeans also acted less hesitantly where conquest was the aim from the beginning. Nevertheless, the phases described above apply to the majority of colonies established throughout the history of European expansion.

B. Phases of European Imperialism

The global history of European imperialism was too diverse and heterogeneous to be more than very roughly divided into periods. The most frequently used caesuras are: the first wave of decolonization (the Americas, 1776–1825); the beginning of the "scramble for Africa" 1881–1882; the start of the third wave of decolonization in 1945. Thus, four phases are commonly distinguished: (1) the "first" colonial empires in the Americas; (2) an intermediate period, where apparently very little happened in terms of establishment of formal rule; (3) the "second" colonial empires, the "new imperialism"; (4) decolonization. Admittedly, this periodization is rather superficial. It concentrates mainly on the development of formal rule and neglects strong trends even in this context.

1. The Roots of European Expansion

Antecedents of European expansion are to be found in the crusades, in the expansion of the Italian merchant cities into the eastern Mediterranean (13th to 15th century), and in the *reconquista* (the reconquest of the Iberian Peninsula before 1492). In these cases basic techniques of expansion, of colonial economy and colonial rule were developed.

The competition of Castile, Portugal, and Genoa for bases on the northwestern coast of Morocco, for Madeira, the Canaries, and the Azores beginning in the 14th century formed the prologue to European expansion. This process began to intensify with the Portuguese conquest of Ceuta on the mainland of Morocco (1415). An important reason for this conquest was an extreme scarcity of bullion in Europe since 1395, which made an attempt to break or circumvent Arab control of the trade routes through the Sahara to the gold-producing regions of the upper Niger look desirable. While further attacks on Morocco failed, Portuguese sailors succeeded in finding a way around the coast of West Africa after 1434.

2. The Colonial Empires of Spain and Portugal

Toward the end of the 15th century the expansion of Castile-Spain and Portugal took different directions. While Portuguese sailors explored the route to India around Africa, Spain after Columbus' "rediscovery" of America in 1492 concentrated on this part of the world. This was sanctioned (1) by papal bulls of 1452–1456, which granted Portugal exclusive rights on the sea route to India (yet to be discovered at this time); (2) by an analogous grant of 1493 for Spain in the Americas; (3) by the treaties of Alcáçovas 1479 and Tordesillas 1494, which drew demarcation lines restricting Portugal to the area south of the Canaries and east of 46°30′ W, respectively.

Spanish occupation of the Americas began in the Caribbean Islands. In 1519 and 1520 the mighty Aztec confederacy in Mexico and in the period from 1531 until 1534 the vast Inca empire in the Andes succumbed to a few adventurers who cunningly took advantage of cultural differences, technological gaps, and indigenous strife. By 1580 Spanish viceroys ruled from New Mexico to the Rio de la Plata. Meanwhile, the Portuguese Vasco da Gama finally reached India via the Cape of Good Hope in 1498. Soon the Portuguese realized that they had no chance of getting a share in the closely woven trade network in the Indian Ocean without force. But unlike the Spanish they could not even think of conquering extended territories, because their adversaries in Asia were among the most developed societies of the time. However, no power in the East except the Ottoman and Chinese empires could challenge the Portuguese warships, and thus they were able to bring the lion's share of the trade in the Indian Ocean under their control by capturing nearly all important ports and bases between Mozambique and Malacca by 1518. In the course of the century, this network of Portuguese bases was extended to regions as remote as Japan and the Moluccas, while Spain began to occupy the Philippines in 1565 in order to secure a backdoor to the spice markets of Southeast Asia.

En route to India, Portuguese sailors happened to discover Brazil in 1500. In order to exclude French competitors from the exploitation of tropical timber, Portuguese administration was established there between 1532 and 1534.

While the profitable Portuguese trade missions to India remained a state enterprise, the Spanish and the Portuguese in the Americas had to rely at least partly on private undertakings once the initial looting was over. Thus, their aims shifted from short-term profits to long-term development. Silver mining and sugar plantations emerged as the most important branches. Both had an immense need for labor, and after the indigenous population had largely died while working in the mines, African slaves were imported in growing numbers. While several Caribbean islands were lost in continuous wars with England, France, and the Netherlands in the 17th century, Spanish America generally preserved its territorial extent until its breakdown was caused by the independence movements of the white settlers (1810–1825). Portuguese Brazil became an independent empire in 1822.

3. The Early Colonial Empires of the Netherlands, Great Britain, and France, 1583–1815

In the 17th century new competitors began to challenge Portugal's and Spain's exclusive claim for world trade. Imperialism now became increasingly a matter of constant wars among European states, but these occurred mainly on the periphery. Eventually new plantation colonies evolved from the initial period of pillage at the expense of Spain in the Caribbean, while North America witnessed the rise of colonies of European settlement.

The prosperous merchants' republic of the *Netherlands* established its naval supremacy in the East by seizing the bulk of the Portuguese chain of bases (1605–1662). In its attempt to secure exclusive control of the spice trade, Dutch imperialism, unlike the Portuguese, carried with it the germ of colonial rule, which was eventually to unfold in the shape of Dutch East India (Indonesia). As a stepping-stone on the way to Asia, a settlement at the Cape of Good Hope was established in 1652. In the West, Dutch occupation of large parts of Brazil remained a short-lived intermezzo (1630–1654), and the Netherlands' new Caribbean possessions (Curaçao, Guyana, Surinam) were of limited significance. Her merchants, however, retained control of the Atlantic slave trade until the end of the century.

British imperialism started in 1583 with the occupation of Newfoundland. By 1732, all of the 13 colonies of settlement that were eventually to form the United States had been established. In the Caribbean, several important Spanish islands were conquered (1623–1655), including Jamaica. Emerging as the most successful nation from the continuous warfare in the Atlantic Ocean, Britain gained almost complete control of the slave trade after 1713, secured the lion's share of both North America (French Canada) and the Caribbean at the end of the Seven Year's War (1756–1763), and finally, despite the loss of the 13 colonies in 1783, ended the French Wars (1792–1815) as the world's superpower, thereby collecting still more Caribbean islands, the Cape Colony, Guyana, and practically all islands in the Indian Ocean, including Ceylon. The British East India Company had meanwhile succeeded in conquering virtually all of India (1793–1819), but only after British ships had already brought trade in South Asia under their control in the 1780s, in spite of bitter resistance by the French. After 1788 a prosperous settlement began to evolve from the convict colony in Australia.

France also established herself as a colonial power at the expense of Spain in the Caribbean beginning in 1635 (Martinique, Guadeloupe), and for a short period she secured supremacy in the slave trade (1695–1713). With Saint-Domingue, the bulk of world sugar production came under French control in 1697. But like her ailing colony of settlement in Canada (1608–1763), France's position in the Caribbean fell to the British in 1763 and 1815, respectively. Nor could France keep a foothold in the East: in 1763 she could only retain an extremely weak position on the Indian mainland at the mercy of the British, and most of her remaining bases in the Indian Ocean were lost in the wars between 1792 and 1815. Several attempts to set up a colony on Madagascar failed in the 17th and 18th centuries, but these succeeded later.

4. British Supremacy and Imperialist Cooperation, 1815–1881

Following the French wars, British world supremacy, both economic and political, was unchallenged for decades. With a third of world trade carried by British vessels and protected by the mightiest navy the world had ever seen, there was obviously no need for more costly colonies, and other states largely lacked the strength to establish new ones. However, the necessity to safeguard existing colonies strategically, the growing need for cultivatable land in colonies of settlement, and subimperialism kept the process of colonial expansion alive though. But economic penetration by informal means gained in relative importance. The most prominent case was British economic predominance in most of the newly independent states of Latin America. A new phenomenon was large-scale cooperation by several imperialist powers in order to open up countries that resisted European imperialism: the Ottoman, Chinese, and Japanese empires. All in all, this was the period where European domination of the world was finally carried through.

5. The Partition of the World, 1881–1945

Toward the end of the century, this picture began to change rapidly. Within a few decades after the French occupation of Tunis 1881 and the British intervention in Egypt in 1882, European powers subjugated most of the non-European world. By 1914, only 15% of the surface of the globe were not under the control of Europe or her former colonies. This partition process began in Africa, where until well into the second half of the 19th century trading posts and naval bases had dominated the scene. By 1914, only Ethiopia (where an Italian attempt had failed in 1896) and Liberia (which was a colony until 1847) were not under the rule of one of the several European countries involved. But the rest of the world was also affected: Britain and France subjugated Southeast Asia except Thailand; Japan began her expansion in the Far East; the United States advanced into the Pacific Ocean and the Caribbean (Philippines, Cuba, 1898). Most of China was partitioned into European spheres of influence. This enormous expansion has been mainly attributed to (1) the relative decline of British economic and political predominance, which forced her again to preserve her merchant's interests through formal rule; (2) the aggravated rivalry of European powers, which necessitated preventive occupation of territories; (3) the rising influence of nationalist/chauvinist movements in European politics; (4) the collective breakdown of collaboration regimes on the spot. The formerly exclusive circle of imperialist powers was also opened for newcomers: Germany, Italy, Belgium, Japan, and the United States entered it now.

Having contributed to the origins of World War I, imperialist expansion did not end with it. In 1919, the German colonies were divided (as League of Nations' mandates) among the victorious powers. World War II witnessed the intensified imperialist expansion of the Axis powers.

The 20th century also experienced the first attempts to develop systematically the economy and infrastructure of existing colonies. But decades of European education and culture also helped to bring about national independence movements.

6. Decolonization

Three waves of decolonization are usually counted: The first, from 1776 through 1825, brought about the independence of most of the colonies in the Americas; the second was a British peculiarity: the autonomy of the white settler societies in Canada, South Africa, Australia, and New Zealand (from 1867 until 1910–1931) as *dominions*; the third began from 1945 through 1947 in Asia, reached its peak in 1960, when 17 African colonies gained independence, and was largely over in 1975, when Portugal finally let go of Angola and Mozambique. But even in the 1990s some microcolonies have become sovereign states, and Hong Kong and Macao revert to China in 1997 and 1999, respectively.

7. The Special Cases

Some seemingly imperialist expansive processes fit in with the usual patterns only with difficulties:

Russia (Siberia, Central Asia), the United States (the American West), and China (Tibet) expanded primarily into the mainland beyond their own backyard. Sooner or later most subjugated territories became integral parts of the mother country.

Japan (Korea, North China, Taiwan, Pacific Islands) was certainly not a "European" power; the United States is at least largely inhabited by Europeans. To cover their expansion, one may categorize them as "Europeanized" countries to a certain degree. A problem remains with the Chinese expansion though, for example, in Tibet.

Whether the economic, political, and military predominance of the United States over the Western hemisphere after 1945 can be described in terms of an informal empire, is a matter of debate.

V. SPECIAL FEATURES

A. Violence

Because it is a relationship of (pre)dominance, imperialism cannot do without at least structural force and the threat of open violence. But of course actual violence was frequently applied in various forms, including extreme forms such as genocide. Colonial rule over indigenous populations relied to a large degree on open violence, occasionally including ruthless military operations, but relied even more on structural violence: i.e., the rapid transformation of economy and society in favor of European interests. In frontier areas, individual violence dominated the expansion. Basically, the application of violence distinguishes imperialism from "peaceful" trade relations: It enters the scene along with political actions. An extreme form of violence against individuals in the context of imperialism was *slavery*.

B. Inequality

A keyword of imperialism is *inequality*. Unequal relationships were not only the aim of imperialism. On the contrary, imperialism was to a large degree only possible through unequal possibilities. Imperialist powers could rely on their technical lead—only slightly developed in the early stages, but overwhelming in the 19th century—their organizational advantages (bureaucratic principles), their superior knowledge of the world as a whole, and above all, on the European-style world system.

C. Transformation

The world system and colonial rule subjected non-European regions to a transformation process unprecedented in history. Within a rather short period, European political processes, legal traditions, economic principles, and property conditions were imposed on the various societies on the globe. European agriculture, architecture, and infrastructure changed the face of the earth to a uniform view.

Exploitation of natural resources transformed landscapes and caused ecological disasters. Plants and animals of various origins were spread all over the world. But more: Immense migration processes were caused by the imperialist world system. Emigration, slave trade, and other forms of labor migration, but also individual mobility aroused by the opportunities of global empires created many of the multi-ethnic societies of the present world. The enormous problems caused by these global processes are to be dealt with for generations to come.

Also See the Following Articles

ECONOMIC CAUSES OF WAR AND PEACE • INDIGENOUS PEOPLES' RESPONSES TO CONQUEST • TRADE, CONFLICT, AND COOPERATION AMONG NATIONS

Bibliography

Cain, P. J., & Hopkins, A. G. (1993). *British imperialism* (2 volumes). London & New York: Longman.

Gallagher, J., & Robinson, R. (1953). The imperialism of free trade. *The Economic History Review, 6*, 1953, 1–15.

Hobson, J. A. (1902). *Imperialism: A Study*. London: George Allen & Unwin. (6th edition, 1961.)

Lenin, V. I. (1951). *Imperialism, the highest stage of capitalism: a popular outline*. Moscow: Foreign Languages Pub. House (1st Russian edition: Petrograd 1917.)

Olson, J. S. (Ed.). (1991). *Historical dictionary of European imperialism*. New York & Westport, CT: Greenwood.

Osterhammel, J. (1995). *Kolonialismus. Geschichte, Formen, Folgen.* München: Beck.

Pagden, A. (1995). *Lords of all the world. Ideologies of empire in Spain, Britain and France c. 1500–c. 1800.* New Haven, CT, & London: Yale University Press.

Porter, A. (1994). *European imperialism, 1860–1914.* Basingstoke & London: Macmillan.

Reinhard, W. (1983–1990). *Geschichte der europäischen Expansion.* (4 volumes). Stuttgart, Berlin, Köln, & Mainz: Kohlhammer.

Wallerstein, I. (1974–1989). *The modern world system.* (3 volumes). San Diego: Academic Press.

Wehler, H.-U. (1969). *Bismarck und der Imperialismus.* Köln: Kiepenheuer und Witsch.

Combat

James R. Kerin, Jr.
United States Military Academy

GLOSSARY

Action A combat encounter of less than a day's duration between forces relatively small in size.

Battle A large-scale combat encounter that involves multiple engagements over a period of days or weeks between forces of large size.

Campaign A prolonged phase of war that involves combat in the form of numerous battles fought over extended distance and time.

Combatant One who engages directly and willfully in the armed conflict of combat.

Duel A combat encounter of very brief duration between two persons or two individual fighting systems, such as vehicles or aircraft.

Engagement A combat encounter between forces of relatively large size that in its scope and duration is greater than an action but less than a battle.

Single Combat Armed conflict between two individual combatants, either in the context of a larger military encounter or, historically, as a kind of duel in response to a challenge.

Trial by Combat A duel sanctioned by law as a means of formally deciding a cause, claim, or dispute.

COMBAT is, in a general sense, a state of focused conflict between two opposing forces—such as ideals, persons, or military formations. More specifically and typically, the term describes a direct and physical fighting encounter between two armed adversaries, whether individual combatants or larger forces. In the larger context of warfare and its prosecution, combat as a matter of active fighting is often distinguished from other military operations—such as logistical activities—that do not involve actual conflict.

I. OVERVIEW

The word "combat" derives ultimately from the Latin: the prefix *com-* (together, with) and the verb *battere* (to beat). The latter form is an alteration of *battuere,* through which "combat" is connected etymologically with "battle." Certainly the two English words are linked in common use as well. In this case the path of linguistic development wound its way from Latin through French en route to English, such that "hors de combat"—meaning disabled or out of action—now occupies its own place in the English lexicon.

According to the *OED,* "combat" first appeared as both verb and noun in the 1560s; however, the behavior that it describes is very likely as old as humankind itself. Although the word can refer generally to any kind of oppositional encounter, for the most part it signifies a dimension of armed conflict; from that, of course, can stem other figurative or metaphorical applications of the term. In this primary usage, it specifically represents the actual conflict of military forces in action as opposed to other duties or periods of service that do not involve fighting.

By definition, then, combat is incompatible with the condition of peace, finds its essence in the expression of violence, and exists as a particularized form of conflict. In its most common sense connected inextricably with war, combat has taken forms through the centuries that reflect the developing history of warfare itself. War's origins date back to primitive times when tribesmen fought others to satisfy the most basic of human needs by acquiring food, mates, and perhaps territory. In that era there was no differentiation between the warrior and other members of the group, the specialization of functions that includes a hierarchical military structure and a warrior class being a later product of civilized societies. As the nature of war and the means of war-making evolved over time, combat—the direct and violent engagement of opposing forces on the ground, at sea, and (eventually) in the air—remained a sine qua non of warfare. Certainly its forms have changed: from the literally face-to-face encounters of infantry in the Greek phalanx to the present-day spectacle of sophisticated battle tanks engaged in deadly dueling at a mile's distance from each other.

The essence of such encounters has changed very little, though. Indeed, the technological developments that have dramatically altered the techniques and distances of combat are relatively recent; the skirmishers of the American Civil War arguably had more in common with Roman legionnaires than with the Israeli and Egyptian tankers who battled in the Sinai little more than a century later. Indeed, one rather ironic development in the history of warfare is the modern disappearance of clear distinctions between those who are combatants and those who are not. Just as every tribesman in the primitive culture was (or, in some parts of the world, is) a warrior in potential if not in fact, so it is in the age of long-range bombing and cruise missiles that apparent noncombatants of a nation at war can find themselves as directly affected by combat operations as any frontline soldier.

Although combat as a concept generally suggests the idea of military encounters between organized groups, the term also embraces the idea of armed conflict between individuals—perhaps in the context of a larger fight, perhaps not. In addition, combat has applications in and connections to various sports and games that serve as analogues, often violent themselves, to the world of war.

II. MILITARY COMBAT

As suggested by the subtitle of his work *Understanding War: History and Theory of Combat,* T. N. Dupuy views combat not only as a principal feature of warfare, but as its very essence. He defines military combat as "a violent, planned form of physical interaction (fighting) between two hostile opponents, where at least one party is an organized force, recognized by governmental or *de facto* authority, and one or both opposing parties hold one or more of the following objectives: to seize control of territory or people; to prevent the opponent from seizing and controlling territory or people; to protect one's own territory or people; to dominate, destroy, or incapacitate the opponent" (63–64). According to Dupuy, the fighting that occurs between adversarial armed forces—the combat between them—occurs at various levels, characterized in what he calls a "hierarchy of combat." Table I depicts these levels of combat and their characteristics in terms of general duration, the size of organizations involved, and the informing purpose of combat action at each level. In general, each level of combat is a component of the one above it; and at each level the crux of the enterprise is the physical encounter between warring opponents in a quintessentially lethal environment.

Susan D. Moeller strikes the same note at the beginning of her book *Shooting War: Photography and the American Experience of Combat.* The introduction to her study begins with this simple sentence: "War is about combat" (3). If war is about combat, then combat is about fear. Dupuy makes this point quite clearly in his aforementioned study, as does John Keegan in his well-known *The Face of Battle.* Citing the earlier work of both the 19th-century Frenchman Ardant du Picq and the 20th-century American S. L. A. Marshall, Keegan underscores the essential nature of combat as a matter of terror—such that a major concern for military leaders is their need to anticipate the tremendous fear that will accompany their soldiers into battle.

The nature of combat involves a number of related constants: fear, violence, and both the threat and the reality of death—in addition to both physical and psychological wounds of possibly lifelong significance. At the same time, the encounters that inflict such wounds and cause such death have varied over time with the

TABLE I

Hierarchy of Combat

Level of combat	Duration	Units involved	Common thread
War	Months–years	National Forces	National goals
Campaign	Weeks–months	Army groups or field armies	Strategic objectives
Battle	Days–weeks	Field armies or army corps	Operational mission
Engagement	1–5 days	Divisions–companies	Tactical mission
Action	1–24 hours	Battalions–squads	Local objective
Duel	Minutes	Two individuals, people or mobile fighting machines	Local objective

Source: T. N. Dupuy (1992). *Understanding War: History and Theory of Combat.* London: Leo Cooper.

evolution of both the tactics and the weaponry of warfare. Keegan's essential work illustrates one way of organizing the experience of combat by considering three pivotal battles in British military history in terms of what he calls the "categories of combat."

In this respect, the battle of Agincourt (1415) can represent the means of combat that existed for centuries before in the form of individualized face-to-face fighting—what one might call "single combat"—between soldiers either mounted or on foot. Keegan establishes two other categories in his analysis: missile-firing infantry against regular infantry, and missile-firing infantry against cavalry. The latter two cases signaled the increasing importance of weaponry that can kill from a distance, the archers of Agincourt representing a significant improvement over the cruder forms of indirect weapons (such as the catapult) employed theretofore.

Four hundred years later, Waterloo demonstrated what Keegan sees as seven different kinds of combat encounters: single combat (any kind of one-on-one, hand-to-hand encounter); cavalry versus cavalry; cavalry against artillery; cavalry against infantry; infantry versus infantry; missile-firing infantry against its enemy counterpart; and artillery versus artillery. One of the most significant differences between Agincourt and Waterloo was the presence at the latter of artillery in significant numbers. While the cannon had not yet become a weapon of indirect attack from great distances, it brought to the field a tremendous increase in lethality. Any sword, arrow, lance, or even rifle could normally produce only one casualty at a time, but artillery could wound or kill groups of people in but a moment.

A century later, at the Battle of the Somme in 1916, the nature of combat was distinguished by the virtual absence of single combat, the presence of the machine gun, and the employment of artillery as an indirect-fire weapon that functioned from much greater distances than before. Keegan notes only three distinct kinds of combat encounters at the Somme: artillery versus artillery, artillery against infantry, and infantry against other infantry. (It is possible, he also observes, to categorize machine gunners separately from infantry and consider the employment of those automatic weapons against both the other two capabilities.) Significantly absent from combat in this battle was cavalry. The horse was all but obsolete on the front lines of what was then called the Great War, and the tank—the cavalry of the next great conflict and beyond—was not yet much more than an experimental oddity.

Two enormously important developments in the technology of warfare found their first expression in World War I and created new kinds of combat encounters in the conflicts fought since then. These were the growth and eventual dominance of mobile armored warfare on the ground and the introduction of the third dimension represented by aerial combat in its various forms. Both these areas of modern military combat have produced striking changes in terms of speed, distance, and lethality on the battlefield. While some geographical contexts will always present the need for simple infantry and the possibility of close encounters, mobile warfare informed by the latest technology serves to distance the soldier, the sailor, or the airman from his adversary. Tanks can now kill enemy tanks that are hardly visible to the naked eye; cruise missiles enable warships to engage targets—at sea or on land—that are many miles distant; combat aircraft view their targets from great vertical and even horizontal distances. Nonetheless, mutual threats posed by engaged forces preserve both the fear and the lethality that have characterized the experience of combat from its beginnings.

A notable aspect of the word "combat" in its military sense is its adjectival usage, in which the term modifies some other word to denote a person, item, entity, or condition whose existence or importance derives from its association with the experience of combat. One of the best known of such terms is *combat fatigue,* a nervous disorder produced by the stress and exhaustion of battle, a syndrome in which the victim experiences some combination of anxiety, depression, and irritability. The word "combat" as modifier can also describe a person not a soldier whose occupation has become specialized by his or her employment in a combat environment. In this respect such terms as *combat correspondent, combat photographer,* and *combat artist* are familiar. Another common expression that describes a familiar item is *combat boot,* a form of heavy leather footwear either laced or with a buckled cuff above the ankle typically worn by frontline soldiers since the era of the Second World War. Other such terms abound; and the more technical the source or context, the more terms of this nature one is likely to encounter. Examples include *combat air patrol, combat day of supply, combat information center, combat intelligence, combat power, combat service support,* and *combat zone.* Expressions such as these all have specialized meanings in the world of military science that have emerged from their relevance to the engagement of armed forces in active conflict with the enemy on the battlefield. In the United States Army, one of the more exclusive awards for service is the Combat Infantryman Badge (CIB), which can be earned only by an infantry soldier who has served in active ground combat.

Not only does the concept of combat usually find its context in military operations, but it also refers most often—thanks largely to the nature of modern warfare—to the experience of groups: military units or formations of various sizes and kinds. Nevertheless, as portions of the foregoing discussion have suggested, there is a relevance to the notion of combat as a strictly personal experience—sometimes in a setting of actual warfighting, sometimes not.

III. PERSONAL COMBAT

While the primary application of the word "combat" is indeed to military operations, which have involved progressively larger formations and more sophisticated weaponry over time, the role of personal combat—both within the context of warfare and otherwise—is not without significance. From the Bible comes the famous story of David and Goliath, an example of personal combat that doubles as one of the great victories by an underdog of all time. From the mythology of classical antiquity we preserve the memorable encounter between Achilles and Hector in the Trojan War as depicted in Homer's *Iliad.* Cultural artifacts such as these and the Bayeux Tapestry indicate that before and through the era of the battle of Agincourt already mentioned, warfare was rather more individualized an enterprise than it became later—and certainly more than it is now. The nature of combat as a group activity and the weaponry with which combatants were armed had much to do with the relative incidence of personal combat within a larger battle; whether dismounted or astride a horse, the fighting man of those days must needs have been within a sword's length of his adversary (a lance's or a pike's distance at most). In such close quarters, as John Keegan has observed, one could expect a variety of personal encounters involving the various kinds of combatants.

One can follow Keegan's lead in characterizing any such encounter as "single combat," but the term more specifically refers to the kind of encounter by challenge that was not uncommon during the period of chivalry that flowered in the 15th century. Something of an historical precursor to the duel, this kind of combat evolved into an elaborate proceeding that began on horseback and concluded on foot with the victor's dispatching of his vanquished opponent with the coup de grace, the rather ironically titled "stroke of mercy." Such a victim would typically have been unseated by his opponent's lance, debilitated on the ground by a war hammer or mace, then killed with a narrow dagger called a misericorde—a weapon designed to pierce him fatally at a vulnerable point on his otherwise armored body.

An interesting version of single combat was the "trial by combat," in which the guilt or innocence of a person was determined by the outcome of his or her actual or vicarious encounter with an armed opponent—the notion of vicarious representation applicable to a contest involving the judgment of a woman or an elderly man who by their status would require a designated champion. This was actually one of several ways of clearing oneself of charges or resolving disputed claims. The procedure was quite simple; the winner, or survivor, was demonstrably in the right. In the 12th century, King Henry II of England decreed that the plaintiff could himself not actually fight but must instead appoint to represent him a vassal who believed his claim. For a time this judicial procedure received sanction by the church, until the Fourth Lateran Council in 1215 forbade the clergy's role in such proceedings.

Although trial by combat and horse-mounted duels eventually ran their historical course, it remained the case from the Middle Ages through the Renaissance and beyond that men of societal station were commonly armed with swords, or at least proficient in their use, such that sword fighting became an art in itself, an art formally taught at schools of defense. Experts such as the "Master of Defence" in England and the "Master of Arms" elsewhere instructed others in what survives today as the sport of fencing. This was a very serious and sometimes lethal business, and it involved a variety of weapons and techniques. Over time the weapon of choice evolved from the heavy broadsword to the more elegant rapier. Since real or perceived insults to personal honor were still not matters to be taken lightly, the duel evolved from the armored knight on a charger to the sword-bearing individual on the ground. The end of Shakespeare's *Hamlet* and the middle of his *Romeo and Juliet* depict versions of this kind of personal combat encounter. Although societal disapproval of such behavior found expression in legislation against it beginning in the 17th century, the practice hardly ceased.

Eventually, however, swords gave way to sidearms; and the pistol made its appearance in personal conflicts in the early 18th century. The state of firearms in that day meant, though, that even a pistol-based encounter was still a matter of very close combat. By the 19th century, the pistol—now more sophisticated—had become more common as the weapon of choice for a duelist. Employment of such a weapon enabled adversaries to engage from a greater distance, and with that greater distance came the slightly lesser importance of skill. Forms of personal combat in this regard ranged from the ritualistic, almost courtly, duel of two gentlemen—a form of personal combat characterized by various rules, procedures, and techniques—to the much less formal encounter of the gunfight in the American West. Meanwhile, the dagger and other kinds of knives survived the demise of the sword to play a role in personal combat. One famous example is the "Bowie knife" developed by the American James Bowie, possibly better known for his death in 1836 at the besieged Alamo in Texas. A form of military knife called the bayonet has a continuing relevance to personal combat insofar as that kind of encounter can still apply in certain circumstances. The bayonet can either be affixed to the end of a rifle or wielded by the soldier in hand-to-hand combat.

Today there is little left of personal combat as such. Laws forbid such encounters in the forms they traditionally assumed; and, by its nature, modern warfare generally offers little opportunity for such things as the bayonet assault. There is, however, one kind of encounter that serves as a notable exception: the aerial combat of fighter pilots. It is still quite possible during military operations for such warriors to engage in one-on-one clashes that bear significant resemblance to personal combat as waged in earlier eras. Central to the concept of personal combat have always been the notion of equality and the importance of personal skill. To be sure, the jet pilots of today—operating at supersonic speeds and firing sophisticated radar-controlled missiles from a distance—differ significantly from their pioneering counterparts of World War I, who fired machine guns at adversaries whose faces they could see. The advent and improvement of high technology, whether characterizing high-performance aircraft or sophisticated main battle tanks, might well cause one to wonder if indeed the term "*personal* combat" is appropriate for even those kinds of one-on-one encounters still possible on the field or in the skies of modern warfare.

IV. ANALOGUES: SPORTS AND GAMES

Humankind's aggressive tendencies and the propensity for violent expression thereof not only have led to war and combat but have also resulted in various nonlethal analogues to combat that provide outlets for those urges even as they reflect the values and interests of a given culture. While there is doubtless an important link between competitive urges and the very existence and nature of combat, most sports and games are not of interest in this context. However, some athletic pursuits merit consideration within the larger discussion of "combat" because they foster and reward physical aggression and violent bodily contact. Two such sports—wrestling and boxing—find their origins in the ancient world and live on today. Others are more recent developments.

In different ways we have evidence of the existence and importance of combat sports in the ancient world. Various forms of art and artifacts tell us that the ancients, especially the Greeks, prized physical prowess and the competitive spirit. Surviving sculptures have preserved the legacy of boxers, and many a classical vase depicts wrestlers in postures and holds strikingly similar to those employed by athletes today. The epic Sumerian story of Gilgamesh tell of its protagonist's wrestling match with his adversary Enkidu, while the Book of Genesis from the Old Testament paints a memorable picture of Jacob wrestling with a mysterious emissary from God in order to achieve a blessing on the eve of his encounter with Esau.

Besides the well-known sports of boxing and wrestling, which still exist today, the ancients engaged in a combat sport called *pankration* (the Latin form is *pancratium*), a term that translates roughly as "complete victory" or "total fight." This was a virtually no-holds-barred approach to personal combat in the guise of sport; only biting and gouging were proscribed. Thus unfettered, athletes engaged in that sport must have inflicted a tremendous amount of violent damage on each other—in an age, however, that was much more receptive to such violence in such a context. This was a culture that might well, for example, have lionized the loser of a contest whose brutal defeat turned fatal rather than deplore the excessive violence of the sport. Curiously, and unfortunately, recent years have seen the emergence of the so-called "ultimate fighting" match that is rather reminiscent of *pankration* in its relatively unrestricted (and thus very violent) nature.

The athletes of classical antiquity trained in a facility called the *palaestra* and, later, in the *gymnasion* (or *gymnasium*). The linguistic legacy of the latter term is obvious, and the former survives in a large athletic complex called The Palestra on the campus of the University of Pennsylvania in Philadelphia. Much of the athletic competition took place in conjunction with large festivals—the most famous, of course, being the Olympic Games. Both wrestling and boxing have continued to play prominent roles in the Olympics of the modern era.

Both sports were much less regulated—thus much more violent—than their present-day counterparts. Boxing was, naturally, the most physically damaging since it featured repeated blows to the head and body in the absence of much protection for anything. The kind of physical trauma that would stop a fight today was an expectation in that more brutal world. It was, after all, a world in which the violence of the boxing ring or the wrestling room was not so far removed from the nature of combat itself. Moreover, for the Greeks especially, these sports and others played a major role in the culture. These were serious and very competitive enterprises that embraced the interest of all.

While other ancient cultures, including the Romans, also featured these sports, their cultural significance seems to have been diminished. Indeed, for the Romans combat-like sports were largely matters of entertainment. A notable legacy of that tradition is the violent spectacle of single combat between gladiators, who would fight to the death as they entertained an audience watching and cheering at a phenomenon that conflated personal combat with sport.

A later historical connection between true combat and combat-as-game was the medieval tournament, in which mounted knights fought mock battles in groups or, later, singly in the form of jousting. Having commenced in the 12th century as a serious kind of training for war (the first recorded tournament held at Wurzburg in 1127), the tournament eventuated into essentially a theatrical event or pageant by the 15th century. Blunted weapons in these mock battles lessened the possibility of injury, both in the group melees and in the one-on-one jousts that began in the 14th century. If there is a modern counterpart to the tournament of the Middle Ages, it would be the re-creation of battles designed and enacted by historical societies. On the other hand, since these contemporary efforts focus on the replication of historical events, they lack the kind of open-ended competition that must have characterized the medieval tournament.

As mentioned above, the two most important combat sports of the ancient world—wrestling and boxing—have survived and occupy prominent positions in the world of modern sport. While the version of wrestling called "professional" is but a parodic caricature of the sport's more violent early days, amateur wrestling is a true sport that emphasizes the controlled application of violence and aggressive behavior such that injuries are minimal and bloodshed virtually nonexistent. This is true of the Japanese Sumo tradition as well as the Greco-Roman descendant practiced in the modern Olympic Games. While boxing is still very much about the infliction of pain and physical damage, it is nonetheless still a highly regulated sporting activity—especially at the amateur level. The smaller gloves and the absence of headgear that characterize the professional level of the sport—prizefighting—make it closer in nature to its ancient origins. The incidence of brain damage in professional boxers and the occasional death in the ring cause critics to label it uncivilized despite the rules that govern its existence.

A discussion of combat-like sports must include two team sports that occupy places of prominence in the current popular culture: ice hockey and American football. The former has traditionally prized and celebrated, at least at the professional level, a kind of aggression involving physical contact that is arguably not essential to the playing of the game. Interruption of play for a full-blown fistfight is not unusual; and, although the combatants are penalized for their behavior, there is a kind of informal sanction to such activity that underscores the violent nature of the game. The combination of the sport's attack-and-defend flow and the emphasis upon physical contact make it more analogous to combat than most other team games.

An even greater analogue, however, is the distinctly American version of the game called football. There is much about this sport that is closely related to the world of warfare. Football players gird themselves for action by donning protective helmets and wearing padding that constitutes a form of body armor designed to protect them in the prolonged physical encounter that is the essence of the sport. The game itself is conducted like some kind of military maneuver, in which one side attacks and the other defends. Prominent within the parlance of the sport are terms lifted directly from the lexicon of war and combat. The quarterback, sometimes described as a "field general," implements his team's "strategy." Typically employing both a passing ("aerial") or running ("ground") "attack," he may attempt to strike deep into the enemy's rear with a "long bomb." As he does so, he will maneuver to avoid the "blitz" employed by one or more members of the opposing team. And just as modern warfare has seen a striking increase of speed and lethality over simpler forms of combat from years past, so this game—especially in its professional form—is characterized by a kind of speed and violence (resulting to some extent from the speed) that might well impress its early devotees just as warriors of old would be astonished by the state of combat technology today.

V. CONCLUSION

One way to think about the idea of combat, and to conclude a discussion of it, is to consider it against the three principal terms of this larger work.

First, peace. While simple assertions about human behavior are often problematic, and while the so-called "spectrum of conflict" suggests that confrontation, conflict, and violence can exist at various levels, it is still the case that war is more or less the opposite of peace. Combat in its primary sense—actual fighting between armed opponents—is the essence of war. If there is no war at whatever level, there is no combat. Accordingly, "peace" and "combat" are mutually exclusive terms. That which makes combat what it is cannot be peaceful.

Next, conflict. This, on the other hand, is a term most compatible with the notion of combat. Indeed, combat is very much about conflict, and conflict sometimes finds its expression in combat. That is not always so, of course; and it is always desirable to achieve conflict-resolution short of combat.

Finally, violence. If combat is the essence of war, then violence is the essence of combat. Whatever its metaphorical applications or its athletic analogues, combat is ultimately a matter of armed physical confrontation that thrives on aggression and violence resulting inevitably in the loss of life, the destruction of property, and the despoiling of natural resources. While the weapons of war and the accouterments of warriors have changed dramatically over time, the core of the combat experience is essentially unaltered. Once initiated, its purpose remains the defeat of an enemy, an end still best accomplished by the application of violent means.

Also See the Following Articles

MILITARISM • MILITARY CULTURE • PROFESSIONAL VS. CITIZEN SOLDIERY • SPORTS • WARFARE, TRENDS IN • WEAPONRY, EVOLUTION OF

Bibliography

Dupuy, T. N. (1992). *Understanding war: History and theory of combat.* London: Leo Cooper.

Dyer, G. (1985) *War.* New York: Crown.

Ellis, K. (1971). *Warriors and fighting men.* London: Wayland.

Gray, J. G. (1970). *The warriors: Reflections on men in battle.* New York: Harper & Row.

Keegan, J. (1976). *The face of battle.* New York: Viking.

Keegan, J. (1993). *A history of warfare.* New York: Knopf.

Keegan, J., and Darracott, J. (1981). *The nature of war.* New York: Holt, Rinehart and Winston.

Keegan, J., and Holmes, R. (1985). *Soldiers: A history of men in battle.* New York: Viking.

Keen, M. (1984). *Chivalry.* New Haven: Yale.

Moeller, S. (1989). *Shooting war: Photography and the American experience of combat.* New York: Basic.

Poliakoff, M. B. (1987). *Combat sports in the ancient world: Competition, violence, and culture.* New Haven: Yale.

Preston, R. A., and Wise, S. F. (1979). *Men in arms: A History of warfare and Its interrelationships with Western society.* (4th ed.). New York: Praeger.

Wise, A. (1971). *The art and history of personal combat.* Greenwich, CT: Arma.

Young, P. (1981). *The fighting man: From Alexander the Great's army to the present day.* New York. Rutledge.

Communication Studies, Overview

Mike Berry and Howard Giles
University of California, Santa Barbara

Angie Williams
Cardiff University, Wales

GLOSSARY

Bargaining Moves and countermoves, concessions and counterproposals in quest of a zone of reasonable outcomes for both parties.

Communication Studies Investigations of, and theories about, the exchange of messages in terms of information, ideas, and feelings. Given analyses can attend to the microscopic features of an interaction (e.g., nonverbal reactions) as well as to its more macroscopic associations (e.g., the historical antecedents of an event), researchers' affiliations are as often outside that of the interdiscipline of communication (e.g., psychology, sociology, political science) as within it.

Conflict From a communication perspective, the interaction of interdependent people who perceive incompatible goals and interference from each other in achieving these goals.

Media Literacy Program An umbrella term to describe a variety of educational interventions designed to increase awareness of the roles, functions, and conventions of the mass media.

Verbal Aggression Overt, negative, and attacking comments to another person in order to cause them psychological pain.

WE CANNOT POSSIBLY DO JUSTICE to the ways in which aggression and conflict are communicated across societies or in the plethora of social contexts in which they are enacted. Herein, we examine violence and conflict as they have been studied in two of the major components of communication: the interpersonal and the mass media arenas. We shall begin by looking at how everyday conflicts are managed moving thereafter to examining how more serious verbal abuses can cause relational stress and can ultimately lead to physical violence. We then engage how violence is depicted in the media and what consequences can arise as a result of this in terms of sustaining our views of various social groups and social reality itself. Next, we look at how the media's reporting of critical events can be constrained by both private and public institutions, and how this process defines our understanding of these very events. Throughout, we attend to incisive theory, overviewing work from different methodologies and ideologies. We conclude by highlighting issues that should inform future research agendas.

I. INTERPERSONAL CONFLICT, CULTURE, AND ORGANIZATIONS

We all experience conflict as a natural, integral part of our social lives and the ways we manage it can have a great impact on the health of our relationships. Researchers have (variously labeled) three kinds of strategies for engaging in such conflict. First, a competitive (or controlling) style is characterized by high engagement and low positive affect, manifest in a range of communicative behaviors, including personal criticism, hostile imperative, presumptive remarks and so forth. Second, a cooperative (or solution-oriented) style is characterized by high engagement but also by positive affect, manifest in descriptive, nonevaluative statements, concessions, acceptance of responsibility, and so forth. This style is construed to demonstrate a desire for mutual resolution. Third, a nonconfrontational (or avoidance) strategy is characterized by implicit or direct denial of conflict, evasive remarks, topics and shifts.

The selection of one particular style over another has been the subject of a great deal of research in the interpersonal, organizational, and intercultural areas. In general, people from collectivistic East Asian and Middle Eastern cultures prefer to resolve conflicts more by avoidance than direct confrontation whereas those of us in individualistic societies (e.g., Australia, The Netherlands) incline the opposite way. An analysis of the 1950s Suez Crisis attributed the cause of that traumatic international conflict to the fact that the U.S. secretary of state directly informed the Egyptian ambassador, after protracted negotiations, that financial aid to build the Aswan Dam was not forthcoming after all. Such interpersonal and immediate directness (rather than an indirect, long-term unfolding of events) was an anathema to Arabic cultural expression leading the ambassador to communicate back that not only had he been insulted but that Egypt's integrity had been cast asunder.

Intercultural differences in conflict norms and rules as well as emotional expression and conflict styles abound. Individualistic cultures tend to emphasize the norm of equity—and a "what's in it for me mentality"—which leads to a focus on short-term outcomes for self. This leads to self-protection, expressions of pride, vulnerabilities, and hurt. Conflict among collectivists, however, is driven by a communal orientation, a concern for the other, and relational harmony (at least within their ingroup, be that family, neighborhood, or work organization). There is also a different notion of time-span in such cultures such that conflict is seen in a continuous spiral and lifelong context involving complex patterns of facework and compromise. Hence, collectivists mask or downplay the expression of negative emotions; an honorable individual should be self-disciplined, restrained, and composed. That said, collectivists do distinguish between their own ingroup and that of outgroups and when communicating with the latter may well opt for equity in managing conflict situations.

However, even in individualistic communities, a variety of factors determine strategic choices including dialectical tensions such as a pull between underlying dimensions of cooperation and assertiveness. In general, people choose their strategies dependent on attributions about the partner's intent to cooperate, the perceived locus of responsibility, and the stability of the conflict. For example, people who believe that they may be responsible for the conflict are more likely to cooperate whereas when time constraints are intense or when a work partner has more expertise than another, competition might well ensue.

As the last factor implies, relational conflict can evolve longitudinally and along a variety of dimensions. One of these, for example, is "variety" and refers to the possibility that negative behavioral routines can be established as a result of unresolved dissatisfaction leading to a spiral of further dissatisfaction; these are hard to break. Another dimension, "symmetry," occurs when partners reciprocate each other's conflict strategy (the quid pro quo principle). Dissatisfied couples have often been found to engage in such "quid pro quos" and research has shown important gender differences here. Many females are more able or willing than males to de-escalate conflictual affect once it has emerged from their partner, and the latter in distressed relationships often appear unable to decode their partner's communication. Not surprisingly, communication satisfaction attends cooperative tactics of conflict resolution and least satisfaction is associated with tactics involving personal threat, blame, and criticism. There is also evidence that relational happiness is associated more with those who believe conflicts should not be avoided and that brooding upon it in silence can actually exacerbate the problem. Interestingly, having the flexibility and spontaneity to mix styles can ultimately engender collaboration and the diversion of destructive patterns. Such adeptness at employing different forms of conflict management, however, appears to feature in younger married couples' conflict than those who are older. Recent studies suggest that while retired couples evince more confrontation when issues were salient to them, in general, they were more avoidant and noncommittal, although this could simply mean that they have learned to "choose their battles." Midlife couples have been found to be somewhere between the passivity of retired couples and the intensity of the young.

The gender issue often surfaces in organizational communication research, particularly when one has to manage a supposed "difficult subordinate." For instance, when the supervisor is female and the difficult subordinate male, the latter was reported by the former as often using confrontational tactics in ways he would not when the supervisor was male. However, when the supervisor is male and the difficult subordinate female, she would be more avoiding than when the superior was female too. Females often find themselves skilled in a particular workplace role as "peacekeepers"—and usually played out in the wings. When successful—and hence valuable to the company—this can be a very satisfying activity, albeit not always recognized nor rewarded by management. One important element of peacemaking—that is, at least stereotypically, associated with females, is the ability to accommodate the positions and feelings of others.

Being correct in understanding your opponent's view—referred to as "co-orientational accuracy"—can be an ingredient of successful conflict exchanges. A number of theories (e.g., principled negotiation, and the 5A model) point to the importance of this capacity in the workplace advocating a refocusing of any dispute away from the invested parties themselves onto the conflictual issue per se. All too often parties rigidly take the moral high ground in their rhetorical stances—a process (called "positional bargaining") that is not often persuasive in its appeal to the other party. Moreover, bargainers in disputes often rely on stories, fantasies, and rituals in order to promote the "good-guy"–"bad-guy" dichotomy. In contrast, negotiators need to understand the validity of the other's perceptions and needs and work towards mutually-beneficial outcomes. Linnda Putnam has been a prime theorist here investigating the need for, and value of, *reframing* a conflict in innovative ways than either party originally brought to the table; such a process would seek to unite the disparate viewpoints and goals while also underscoring common values. This is obviously a difficult process when the interests of conflicting parties are networked out and embedded in other interest groups. Communication is, therefore, at the heart of conflict management. Recent scholars—in both the marital and organizational spheres—have begun to focus on how the family and the workplace can be political arenas with conflict being caused by, a resource for, and outcome of maintaining or acquiring social power. Indeed, communication scholars have pointed to the ideological need for all parties to understand the macrocontext in which an immediate small-scale dispute occurs. Disputes cannot be adequately resolved if the management of them merely centers on the superficial bones of contention rather than on the sometimes longstanding, power asymmetries between the individuals or the groups which they represent.

A. From Conflict to Aggression

Clearly in the foregoing, we have painted conflict in rather negative terms. Furthermore, negotiations can be undertaken in order to strategically hinder and stymie the other. In the organizational communication sphere, however, conflict can often be construed in more positive terms, such as the catalyst for producing improved ideas. Yet there is, of course, a difference between conflict in everyday work and family relationships that can be considered culturally normative and even healthy, and relational conflict that is physically or psychologically damaging. Clearly, verbal and physical aggression are frequently used as an attempt to control the relationship and or the partner. According to Roloff (1996), data has emerged showing that 53% of victims of physical aggression report that verbal aggression was a precursor to the latter whereas 33% of the protagonists cited verbal aggression as the cause. Given a supposed aggressor and the apparent victim often have different perceptions of the situation, less argumentation (expressing one's emotions giving vent to powerful feeling without striking out) and more verbal aggression is typical of violent relationships.

As Vissing and Baily (1996) describe, verbal aggression has been linked to a number of negative, long-term health outcomes such as suicidal thoughts, depression, and poor physical health. There have been an array of attempts to define, conceptualize, and operationalize verbal aggression and yet it still seems to be a "catch all" of negative relational communication. Typologies, such as Vissing and Bailey's, include saying unfavorable things about a person's character, animosity, accusations, ridiculing, swearing as well as certain nonverbal behaviors such as rolling eyes, various obscene gestures, and even failing to respond. Nonetheless, insults have been considered the most frequent form of verbal aggression.

A link between verbal and physical violence in relational disputes is proposed in the "catalyst model." This claims that people who are unskilled at arguing may resort to the use of verbal aggression that, in turn, leads to retaliatory aggression including physical violence. For example, and taking a dyadic approach, Sabourin, Infante, and Rudd (1993) studied verbal aggression and argumentativeness in violent-distressed, nonviolent-distressed, and nonviolent-nondistressed couples. The strongest discriminator between violent and nonviolent couples was "inferred reciprocity" (when the husband said the wife used a message and the wife said that the husband used that message) and it is suggested that this leads to an escalation of verbal aggression in violent relationships. Nonviolent couples' perceptions of each other's aggression and argument strategies tended to be in agreement and they reported using less verbal aggression and more argumentation in their disputes. Husbands' reports in nonviolent/nondistressed and distressed but nonviolent relationships were considerably more in agreement with wife's self-reported aggression, indicating that they were better at decoding these messages than were violent husbands. These findings suggest that skill-deficient husbands might interpret argumentativeness as aggressiveness and may not be able to distinguish between the two—akin to what has been termed a "hostile attribution bias."

In sum, the combination of lack of skill in argumentation and reciprocity of aggression is a key determinant of whether marital disputes turn violent, although other causative factors such as individual psychopathology, disdain for the other, and social learning are clearly acknowledged. Related to the foregoing, scholars have recently documented aggression in marriages that were self-reported as satisfying. This was manifest in negative reciprocity where the two partners strove for relational control. It has been suggested that such patterns may identify potentially troubled relationships in the early stages and therefore may be useful for intervention that can head off violence before it begins.

II. DEVELOPMENTAL AND INTERGROUP PARAMETERS OF INTERPERSONAL CONFLICT

Family aggression is of course not confined to spouses. United States national survey data has shown that verbal aggression has been found so prevalent in child abuse that occasional instances of verbal assault (even up to 10 incidents) are not considered abusive. This study also suggested that two out of three American children are victims of verbal aggression from their parents. Yet there are dangers here in that the lack of an adequate working definition can lead to classifying any negative communication directed at children (e.g., verbal discipline) as abusive. Research suggests that parental verbal aggression produces a number of short-term effects (e.g., poor self-image, introversion) as well as long-term effects (e.g., drug abuse, delinquency) in children. While both physical and verbal aggression can cause both physical and psychological traumas, researchers believe that the latter can be severely detrimental to children's developing social and interpersonal skills.

A recent study analyzed interactive play tasks within family groups. Fathers who were aggressive to their wives were found to be more authoritarian, less authoritative, and used more negative affect in dyad tasks (i.e., father and son) and were more controlling in triadic tasks (i.e., father, mother, and son). This pattern did not hold for fathers and daughters, but fathers did seek alliances with their daughters against their wives. Although mothers' physical aggression was not associated with any hostile or controlling behavior toward the child by the mother, mothers' emotional aggression was linked to fathers' negative affect with their sons. Father marital aggression was linked to mothers' negative affect toward daughters and attempts to establish alliances with daughters. Thus, one parent's physical or emotional aggression in the marital dyad was linked to the other's parent's communication with their children in a series of feedback loops that seem to reinforce coercion and aggression within the familial network.

Such abusive effects can be quite far reaching. People who report high levels of parental verbal aggression may seek out relationships that are lacking in support and solidarity leading to a transmission of negative relational patterns. Yet still further, those who have been past recipients of parental abuse can become abusers and neglectors when they themselves become parents.

Verbal aggression and violence can also be levied, of course, outside the family context to outgroup strangers and acquaintances (e.g., homosexuals, mentally handicapped, political interest groups). Verbal aggression is increasingly being studied now in the domain of sexual harassment, as in sexist remarks, taunts, and jokes, inappropriate but sanction-free sexual advances, coercion of sexual activity, and so forth. Many ethnic groups have received negative stereotypical images in the media—both in terms of outgroup labels (e.g., faggots, bitches) and visual depictions (e.g., in advertising). Inescapably, the history of intercultural relations has been all too tragic and complex. While the workplace has allowed the cataloguing of numerous ethnic epithets and slurs that can be used to derogate ethnic groups, civil rights laws in many cultures now legally prohibit their expression. This does not mean that racism has dissipated because of its less frequent verbal and nonverbal invocation. In fact, some scholars argue that because any expression of prejudice is frowned upon, people now favor disguised, ambiguous, and indirect ways to express their bigotry. Ethnic minorities often argue that indirect expressions of racism are more common and more problematic—as they can be dismissed as an overreaction by the recipient and can be easily misattributed. Indeed, our own work with Laura Leets suggests that minority recipients of verbal abuse (sometimes called "dignatory harm" when it communicates inferiority to the recipient) can find indirect forms of abuse more deeply wounding than overt messages. Moreover, individuals concede that ethnic (and other) slurs can be as psychologically damaging as forms of physical harm. Teun van Dijk, in his editorial to a special issue of *Discourse and Society* (vol. 6 [3]) on the "discourse of violence" argues that "the increasingly overt but 'merely verbal' aggression against immigrants, refugees and minorities in political and media discourse may effectively curb immigration, encourage discrimination, legitimize inequality and generally violate the human rights of millions of people." A particular interest of research at the interface between communication and the law is concerned with if and how harmful speech can be legislated against. The courts will not prohibit nor punish speech merely because it can be lewd, profane, or otherwise vulgar and offensive. Nonetheless, scholars have argued that the core of hate speech is a desire to subordinate another group. On these grounds, some have argued that hate speech (and pornography) should not receive First Amendment protection in the United States.

A. A Cognitive-Communication Model

Overall, it is suggested that verbal aggression is a necessary yet not sufficient cause of physical aggression. At least four factors have been proposed to mediate this relationship such as face loss, a desire to control, violence potential, and the loss of control (i.e., anger). Some of these factors are echoed in Daphne Bugental's cognitive-communication model of child abuse, which is relevant for placing verbal aggression in the context of ongoing familial processes. Paradoxically, parents who exercise dominance, power, and control over their children see themselves as relatively powerless in the relationship. In a series of studies using experimental, computer-simulation, and field methods, Bugental and associates have shown that high-risk adults matched with high-risk children constitute a problematic combination. What makes adults high risk is their perception of their own relative lack of power that, in turn, provides them with a schema making them hyperalert and vigilant to threat. A threat orientation here is where the adult assigns high importance to factors that they perceive as controlled by the child and uncontrollable by adults; even low-level danger signals may be overestimated. Additionally, there is a tendency to rely on stereotypical categorizations (e.g., a "troublesome child") rather than to individuate the child. At-risk children, on the other hand, tend to be less responsive than those who are not at risk.

According to Bugental, the child's unresponsive behavior results in the threat-oriented parent or other adult initiating a series of strategies that almost invariably begin with what is termed "opening diplomacy." This is a stage of impression management whereby the adult uses placating or ingratiating behavior such as insincere smiling. This rapidly gives way to increasing levels of anxiety as measured by acoustic analysis of verbal patterns. This, in turn, stimulates increases in child unresponsiveness, most probably because the child, at varying levels of awareness has noticed the insincerity of the adult's advances and the subsequent rising levels of anxiety and defensiveness. As this sequence unfolds, the child remains unresponsive and the adult mobilizes his/her defense systems cognitively as well as physiologically. As a result of decreased cognitive processing, adults experience decreases in attention and information processing which can induce impulsive acts. (Note, in relation to the above, this suggests that argumentation "skill" may decline as arousal increases.) In line with this, threat-oriented adults begin to withdraw positive reinforcement, together these factors form a feedback loop, reinforcing the original threat and lower power orientation (e.g., "my attempts at being positive didn't work"), and increasing the possibility of coercion.

B. Accounting for Aggressive Acts

Finally, one of the major contributions that communication scholars can make to this area of inquiry is through analyses of the ways that people account for aggressive and violent acts. As might be expected, perpetrators' accounts of violent episodes include a variety of self-serving attributions. A number of different studies have shown that men tend to attribute violence to external factors (i.e., the wife's behavior or personality), jealousy (rivalry with others who took the wife's attention, previous partners, etc.), her verbal and/or physical abuse, and to control issues. Stamp and Sabourin (1995) have investigated the linguistic resources used to accomplish this including excuses (admission of guilt, but a denial of responsibility), justifications (acceptance of responsibility, yet denial of the pejorative nature of their behavior), and minimization or even denial that violence occurred. Even a casual observer reading the transcripts of such accounts can notice that they are very vague, abstract, and nonspecific—seemingly indicating highly managed (avoidant and censored) accounts. By studying the devices that people use to shift responsibility away from themselves and avoid and attribute blame, researchers hope to educate therapists to identify ways in which such people can accept responsibility, come to terms with abuse, and effect change. It is also suggested that such devices perpetuate violence perhaps by allowing the perpetrators to create distance between themselves and the event. Relatedly, research has shown that the language used by the news media to report violent acts against women, mainly in the passive voice, can lead (especially among men) to acceptance of such actions.

III. MASS MEDIA EFFECTS ON AGGRESSIVE ATTITUDES AND BEHAVIORS

The last 40 years have seen in excess of 3000 studies on the relationship between viewing media violence and subsequent aggressive behavior. A number of position papers reviewing findings across different methodological approaches and different measures of aggression (i.e., the 1972 Surgeon General's Report and the 1982 National Institute of Mental Health Report) endorsed a direct causal link between them. Not only were the effects underscored with regard to young children of both genders but exposure to media violence was believed to have other effects beside facilitating aggression, such as overestimating the level of violence within society. Later position papers in 1985 and 1991 (by the American Psychological Association [APA] and the Center for Disease Control, respectively) called upon parents to monitor and restrict their children's viewing of violence that was aggrandized, and they encouraged parents to seek out alternative programming. In addition, the broadcast industry was urged to curb violent programming within children's television and produce more prosocial offerings. The most comprehensive review of the literature by the APA's Commission on Youth and Violence (1993) also concluded that there was "no doubt" that viewing media violence was, cross-nationally, related to increases in subsequent aggression and fear about becoming a victim of violence. In addition, it could lead to a "desensitization" effect whereby individuals become less concerned about viewing violence and increased behavioral apathy (e.g., becoming less likely to come to the aid of a victim of violence). The report also highlighted research showing that when men viewed films depicting women as enjoying rape or sexual coercion, it made them more sexually callous, increasing their beliefs that women do indeed desire rape and deserve sexual abuse. However, this report finished on a positive note by pointing out that studies had shown that "media literacy" programs aimed at children could be effective in mitigating the effects of viewing media violence. Below we examine the kinds of studies these reports had evaluated.

A. Empirical Research

1. Laboratory Experiments and Field Studies

A recent review of laboratory studies concluded that in an overwhelming number of studies, viewing media violence has been shown to lead to increases in subsequent aggression. However, not all types of violence facilitated aggression-the context in which violence is presented is vital; some contextual features inhibit aggression, others facilitate it. These contextual factors are presented in Table I. Therein, it can be seen that violence which is punished within the narrative, or leads to overt pain or suffering for the victim

TABLE I

Contextual Factors Mediating the Relationship Between Violence Viewing and Subsequent Aggression (where + is facilitatory and − inhibitory)

Contextual factor	Effect on likelihood of eliciting aggression
Presence of rewards for violence	+
Presence of punishments for violence	−
Presence of attractive perpetrator	+
Violence seen as justified	+
Similarity between aggressor and viewer	+
Strong identification with aggressor	+
Depiction of victim's pain/suffering	−
Realism of violence	+
Extensive/graphic violence	+
Presence of weapons	+

is not likely to facilitate aggression. Violence that is perceived as justified, rewarded, or perpetrated by an attractive character is, however, likely to facilitate aggression.

Laboratory research has also produced evidence that media violence desensitizes viewers to real-life violence. For example, previous exposure to a stimulus film containing violence caused 8-year-olds to take longer to report fighting between children (to an adult) they were supposed to be monitoring, as compared to a control group who witnessed a neutral film. This effect has been replicated and effects extended to children of up to 14 years of age. Other experiments have shown that exposure to violent media depictions actually leads to physiological desensitization in individuals. Research by Steve Penrod, Dan Linz, and Ed Donnerstein measured the reactions of college-age men to films portraying violence against women, often in a sexual context, viewed over a 5-day period. Comparisons of first and last day reactions to the films showed that with repeated exposure, initial levels of self-reported anxiety decreased substantially. Furthermore, material that was previously viewed as offensive and degrading was considered significantly less so by the end and subjects also felt less depressed and enjoyed the material more. Disturbingly, these effects generalized to the victim of a sexual assault presented after the above exercise in a videotaped re-enactment of a rape trial. The exposure group rated the victim as significantly less injured compared to the no-exposure control group. A further study by these authors also found the exposure subjects were less sympathetic to the rape victim and less able to empathize with rape victims in general, compared to no exposure groups and groups exposed to neutral fare.

In order to overcome some of the accusations of artificiality leveled at laboratory experiments, researchers have conducted field studies in more naturalistic settings, using observations or estimations of real aggressive behavior. In order to ensure control over viewing, most research has occurred in institutional or group settings. For instance, preschool children exposed to violent television fare for 10 to 20 minutes per day for four weeks were more aggressive during free play sessions than those who had been exposed to neutral or prosocial programs. Virtually all these studies have confirmed the same kind of patterns as laboratory studies: viewing violence increases aggressive behavior. The findings are also more generalized to real world conditions because the films are viewed in (a relatively) natural context, actual aggressive behavior is measured, and the aggression occurs under conditions where naturally occurring consequences are present.

2. Longitudinal Studies

Longitudinal studies involve following groups of children over long periods of time and assessing how initial levels of violence viewing relate to aggressive behavior later in life. Such a methodology is useful in effects research since it allows researchers to examine the cumulative effects of viewing violence over long periods of time. Evidence from such studies has generally supported the findings from laboratory and field experiments.

Tannis MacBeth Williams and associates studied the effects of the introduction of television into a Canadian town that had been unable, due to geographical location, to receive television until 1974. Over a 2-year period after the introduction of TV, they compared any changes that occurred in observations and (peer and teacher) reports of aggressive behavior of 45 children with ratings of children in two nearby comparable towns, which had had TV for many years. It was found that children in the town newly receiving television showed significant increases in both physical and verbal aggression while there were no changes in the comparison towns. Furthermore, the effects were not restricted to any subsets: boys and girls, children initially high and low in aggression, and those viewing more or less TV were equally likely to show increased aggressive behavior.

The most comprehensive longitudinal work to date was the set of studies carried out by Leonard Eron and his colleagues over a 22-year period in New York State. The work began in 1960 and involved the entire 3rd-grade (aged 8) population of Columbia county. In 1970, 735 of the original subjects were located and 427 were interviewed. Twenty-two years later, 409 were re-interviewed and criminal justice data were collected on 632 of the original pool. In the initial study, it was found that the aggressiveness of 8-year-old boys, as determined by peer nominations, was significantly correlated with the violence level of the TV show they most frequently viewed (as reported by their mothers). In the second stage 10 years later, no relationship was found between violence viewing at age 18 and current aggressive behavior, but that there was a significant relationship between violence viewing at age 8 and seriousness of aggression at age 18. In the final stage when the subjects were, on average, 30 years old, no relationship was again found between current level of violence viewing and current aggression. There was however a longitudinal effect spanning 22 years. For boys, early exposure to TV violence was predictive of self-reported aggression (particularly under the influence of alcohol) at age 30, and added a significant increment to the prediction of seriousness of criminal arrests accumulated by age 30. These effects occurred independently of class, intellectual functioning, and parenting variables and analyses suggest that approximately 10% of the variability in later criminal behavior can be attributed to the early violence viewing.

Studies focusing on children's reactions to violent media have noted the persistence of disturbed anxiety states for days, including the cued and uncued recollection of the violence witnessed and an increased incidence of nightmares. Types of depictions particularly likely to induce fear, include dangers and injuries, the distortion of natural forms (e.g., monsters for very young children), and the experience of endangerment by, and fear in, others. Such effects are mediated by, and are generally reduced, when (a) there is a lack of realism; (b) viewing with information that effects are not real; (c) the intensity of the effects are not aurally or visually dramatic; and (d) an adult is co-present.

B. Theoretical Models

1. Social Learning Theory

In a series of classic experiments, Albert Bandura demonstrated that children would spontaneously imitate the behavior of an aggressive model they had witnessed on television. The adult model was shown punching and kicking an inflatable clown known as a bobo doll, and when subsequently left alone with a similar toy the children would indulge in identical behaviors. This was used as evidence for social learning theory, which contends that children learn their personalities and behavioral repertoires from experiences and interactions with culture, subculture, family, and peers. It places great emphasis on the role of models in shaping the acquisition of socially sanctioned behavior patterns. With regard to the effects of exposure to violent models, Bandura made an important differentiation between acquisition of aggressive repertoires and performance of those repertoires. If the aggressive television model was praised and rewarded for its violence this was likely to increase the chances of a child imitating it. However if the model's behavior was met with disapproval and punishment children were highly unlikely to imitate it. Social learning theory then suggests that it is the nature of the portrayals of violence on television involving their depicted consequences that may be influential in stimulating aggression. The theory also notes that violent models do not just stimulate the imitation of novel aggressive acts but may also lead to a more general disinhibitory effect, with the viewing of specific behavioral acts (e.g., a "shoot-out" in a Western) leading to the increased likelihood of the display of other different responses that belong to the same class (e.g., rough play or hostile verbalizations).

2. Cognitive Priming Theory

Priming effects theory was developed by Leonard Berkowitz to explain the occurrence of short-term aggression after exposure to media violence. It contends that aggressive ideas stimulated by viewing media violence can prime the activation of other semantically, related thoughts and is based on the notion of spreading activation. This asserts that thoughts of which we are consciously aware send out patterns of radiating activation along associative pathways in the brain. However, this does not only activate related thoughts about violence, it also activates connected emotional reactions and behavioral tendencies. Thus the viewing of violence can set in motion a complex set of processes where thoughts, emotions, and even behaviors compatible with aggression are elicited. However, Berkowitz notes that there are important intervening variables, the most significant being the perceived meaning of the depiction for the audience. Aggression-related thoughts will not be activated unless the viewer considers the depiction aggressive. For example, if two individuals witnesses a football match, the one who perceives the players as deliberately trying to hurt or injure each other is likely to become aggressively primed, while the other who considers the players as athletes involved in a game of skill and determination, will not be. Other factors such as the perceived justification for the portrayed violence are also important, since violence presented as morally commendable, may provide a context whereby viewers interpret their own subsequent aggression within such a light. Levels of identification with the violent perpetrator is another important factor since those who relate strongly to such perpetrators may vicariously commit the latter's violence while viewing, and these aggression-related thoughts are especially likely to prime their aggression-associated mental networks.

3. A Developmental Social Scripts Model

Rowell Huesman has proposed a model that explains how cumulative exposure to media violence in childhood may lead to the acquisition of aggressive behavioral patterns that, once established, may be highly resistant to change, leading to serious, adult antisocial behavior. He proposes that aggressive behavior like other social behavior is governed by "programs" that are learned during early development. These programs—or social scripts—are stored in memory and used as guides for behavior and problem solving in social situations. They are learned by observing the behavior of others, and encoding a representation of that behavior into memory. Whether a viewed depiction of violence becomes encoded into memory as a social script for a child will depend on a number of factors, an important one being the salience of the violent depiction to the child. Realistic violence by highly attractive or similar (to the child) perpetrators is likely to be highly salient, and this may lead to aggressive fantasizing by the child, which involves the rehearsal of social scripts stored in memory. This is likely to strengthen those scripts and increase the likelihood that they will be retrieved and employed as problem-solving strategies in social situations. Other contextual factors in violent narratives, such as the punishments or rewards for violent behavior, are also likely to effect whether children encode violent behavior into their social scripts.

The theory also provides a model illustrating how the relationship between viewing violence and aggressive behavior may, for children, be reciprocal and mediated by social popularity and intellectual achievement. Children who are heavy viewers of television violence regularly view characters who use violence as a social problem-solving strategy. To the extent that children (particularly boys) identify with those characters, they may encode such behaviors into social scripts. The cumulative viewing of such behaviors may lead to the encoding and rehearsal of such social scripts in memory, as general problem-solving solutions applicable to a range of social situations. This process is likely to be strengthened if the violence viewing leads to the child frequently engaging in aggressive fantasizing. If these aggressive scripts lead to aggressive behavior and this aggression leads to desirable outcomes, this may lead the child to become habitually aggressive. However, habitual aggressiveness is likely to lead to the child becoming less socially popular and a poorer academic achiever. Such academic and social failures may frustrate the child and lead to further aggressiveness. In addition, it may also lead to further television viewing as the child attempts to vicariously obtain the satisfactions denied to it in its social life and at school. This further violence viewing may then provide the child with justification for his or her own aggression, and it may lead consequently to more aggression. In this manner the relationship between violence viewing and aggressive behavior may be reciprocal and mutually reinforcing.

C. Interventions to Mitigate the Effects of Media

In a review of intervention strategies designed to reduce the relationship between viewing media violence and aggressive behavior, it was noted that classroom strategies aimed directly at youngsters appear to be the most effective. In particular, a 2-year intervention designed by Huesman and his colleagues was found to be successful in reducing children's aggressive behavior. This occurred despite the fact that the children's level of violence viewing did not decrease over the course of the intervention, suggesting that the intervention had served to "inoculate" the children against the harmful effects of viewing media violence. The intervention used a number of strategies to achieve its aim, such as demonstrations, discussions, and observations of television segments shown to be implausible. It was emphasized to children that individuals in the real world do not use the violent methods employed by television characters to solve social problems. In the second year, a variety of methods that had been proved successful in counterattitudinal advocacy research were adopted, such as stressing the consequences to the children of their own actions on others, and praising the children for possessing attitudes that the researchers wanted them to hold. The children participated in making a film designed to teach other children about the dangers of imitating media violence. They were filmed making a small presentation on why doing so was foolish, and had the opportunity to see themselves and their peers advocating such a position.

Strategies targeted at encouraging parents to monitor their children's viewing habits and cutting down their children's exposure to violent media have proved less successful in reducing children's levels of aggressiveness. There is very little research here and conclusions must be drawn with caution. There is evidence however, that teaching parents how to improve their children's language and social skills may have a small indirect effect on mediating the relationship between violence viewing and aggression.

IV. MASS MEDIA EFFECTS ON PERCEPTIONS AND ATTITUDES TOWARD VIOLENT CRIME

A. Cultivation Theory

Aside from leading to increases in antisocial behavior, there is also research evidence that exposure to mass media can lead to distorted and inaccurate perceptions about the nature, prevalence, and causes of violence within society. The most prominent research within this field has been carried out by George Gerbner. This theory argues that television is a powerful cultural force of unrivaled depth and penetration, which functions as an arm of the established social order. Its main role is to maintain, stabilize, and justify the present social order. Through its narratives, television demonstrates how society works by dramatizing its norms and values. Cultivation theory has been applied to explain how many different aspects of social reality (e.g., views of the elderly, sex-role stereotyping) may be shaped by television. With regard to violence and conflict, television is hypothesized to teach lessons about the power structure of society, and in particular who are the legitimate purveyors and recipients of violence. Due to the fact that violence is massively overrepresented in the television environment as compared to its occurrence in the real world, heavy viewing of television will lead to an overestimation of the level of violence within society and an increased (and unrealistic) fear of becoming a victim of violence. The theory also hypothesizes that heavy television viewing will lead to increased interpersonal mistrust and suspicion, a condition dubbed the "mean world syndrome."

In the 1970s and 1980s, George Gerbner and associates provided empirical support for their hypotheses by examining how perceptions of crime and victimization differed between light and heavy television viewers in large U.S. regional and national surveys. Australian support has been found for many aspects of cultivation including relationships between television viewing and misconceptions about crime rates and belief in a mean world. However, studies conducted in Great Britain, Holland, and Sweden provided qualified support on only a small number of cultivation indices. Furthermore the theory has received substantial academic criticism on both conceptual and methodological grounds. Critics have argued that the theory's use of total television viewing, rather than particular genres, makes the mistaken assumption that television viewers are television violence viewers per se. They also questioned whether the research adequately controls for other extraneous variables that may be responsible for the relationships proposed. The current consensus is that, although there is evidence that some cultivation effects do exist, the model fails to take account of mediating factors, such as differential individual perceptions of the reality of television, or the effects of living in areas with different crime rates. Furthermore, it is likely, and there is empirical support for this, that heavy viewing of television and personal distrust is bidirectional, with highly fearful individuals choosing to seek out certain television shows (e.g., crime dramas) where there is usually "a triumph for the forces of good."

B. The Agenda-Setting and Framing Effects of Television News

The agenda-setting functions of mass media refer to the tendency of individuals to cite issues recently featured in the news media when asked to cite the most significant issues of the day. Such effects have been found consistently for both local and national issues, for different media, across different research methodologies. With regard to effects on perceptions of crime and violence, the prominence and frequency of crime within news reports has been shown to effect how salient individuals consider the issue. Frequent saturation of media airtime with sensational violent crime is likely to lead individuals to overestimate violent crime levels within their communities. Such effects are magnified by the psychological process known as the accessibility bias, which is an individual's ability to retrieve information from memory when making judgments about issues. Thus, when individuals come to make judgments about the frequency of serious violent crime, the frequent media coverage of such occurrences coupled with their highly arousing nature is likely to lead to substantial overestimations in both violent crime levels and chances of victimization.

Research looking at framing issues has examined how the presentational format of news items about crime and violence within society affects both attributions of causal responsibility and treatment responsibility. Most news, for instance, is reported within the episodic or thematic framework. The former involves presenting acts of violence and crime as discreet events and places emphasis on the actions of individual actors. The latter entails presenting a news story within a general context. Network news presents numerous reports on individual acts of terrorism (episodic frame) but very few reports on the political and economic antecedents of terrorism (thematic frame). The overwhelming use of episodic frames by news agencies when reporting crime, violence, terrorism and international conflict, leads viewers to individualize such social problems, and deflects attention away from potential societal interventions to relieve them.

V. MASS MEDIA AND INTERNATIONAL CONFLICT

Communication studies also assesses the role of the mass media during international conflicts (e.g., the Vietnam War, in Bosnia). How do the mass media present modern warfare both symbolically and rhetorically?

What is the relationship between the media presentation of war and the wider public perception? How is international conflict presented differently cross-nationally? What is the public's view on restrictions on press freedom during wartime? This section will focus attention on research efforts examining the functions of the news media during the 1991 Persian Gulf War. Analysis of *this* conflict was chosen for three reasons. First, it was an extremely serious conflict, with catastrophic human, environmental, and economic consequences for the region. Second, it involved more countries than any conflict since World War II. Third, given the conflict involved a protracted ultimatum from President Bush, scholars were granted the rare opportunity to prepare research projects before the crisis actually began.

A. War Coverage: Institutional Functions

Recently, the use of media messages has become as important as the effective use of military weapons. Commentators argue that the Gulf War solidified three important relationships between global politics and television. First, television has become the crisis communication channel of international relations. Due to both technological advances in news gathering capabilities and availability of direct broadcast satellite links, international borders have become increasingly porous with regard to the flow of media messages. Television diplomacy thereby takes center stage. Second, television allows private organizations (e.g. Amnesty International) to influence foreign policy, by speeding up decision-making times for protagonists and diluting the secrecy in diplomacy by allowing governments to frame the enemy's offers. Third, television has become a tool of government as a means to further foreign policy objectives. In the Gulf War conflict, the United States and, to a large extent, global media presented a pro-American, prowar slant by interviewing almost exclusively (prowar) military or administration personnel, and providing uncritical and frequently jingoistic coverage of U.S. operations and policy.

On the home front, the war was conducted as a slickly produced public relations exercise. One of President Bush's closest advisers told the *Washington Post* that during the war they used the same basic principles as used in presidential campaigns. Indeed, the government and military were able to control media output very strictly. Security guidelines emerged over what aspects of the conflict could be reported, and many aspects of news coverage were off-limits—not due to military security, but political policy (e.g., pictures of coffins arriving in the U.S. were banned). Only a few (compliant) reporters were allowed and the military had a public relations person accompany any official who was giving a press interview.

The military appreciated that it had to cater to both its own troops and their dependents in the United States. Hence, they set up extensive television, print, and radio media specifically for the troops, and a network of media professionals who could transmit information to an individual soldier's hometown media, if anything significant happened to the soldier. The government and military approached the war as an exercise in crisis management, provided information and dealt with rumors quickly and frequently, and centralized the source of information with effective spokespersons (primarily Generals Neal and Schwarzkopf).

Arguably, the function of the mass media during the War was to act primarily as a mouthpiece for American foreign policy, by limiting the level of critical media discourse. The media failed in their mandate to serve the public interest by not providing a wide range of opinion on a matter of grave universal significance, such as what was at stake, what the consequences would likely be, who would benefit, and what the alternatives to war were. Although a few dissenting voices were initially raised, these quickly vanished in the months leading up to the conflict. Any attempts to discuss alternative nonmilitary solutions were derided as the "new pacifism" (*New York Times,* August 27, 1996) or as being anti-American. Approximately 1% of the coverage of the Crisis dealt with popular opposition to possible U.S. military intervention, despite mass demonstrations by peace activists across the United States.

B. Assessments of News Coverage and Public Perceptions

In the build-up to the War, adjectives such as "brutal," "merciless," "evil," "savage," and "another Hitler" were used to describe Saddam Hussein and served to focus attention on him as the embodiment of the problem. There was also an irresistible rhetorical drive toward war in the speech-making of President Bush. His repeated invocations that there was "no choice" left but war, that he had "gone the extra mile for peace," and that Hussein was "forcing the hand" of the U.S. military sent a clear message that war was inevitable.

During the war, four ways in which the conflict was framed by the U.S. administration have now been discerned. First, the declaration that "this will not be another Vietnam" was a powerful, but strategically ambiguous, statement that could mean to a conservative that "we will not fight this conflict with one arm tied behind our back" or to a liberal that "dissent will not be tolerated this time around." Second, the administration linked support for the troops with support for the U.S. war policy. That failure to show unanimity as a nation would undermine the morale of "our" troops served to quell dissent and powerfully linked patriotism with conformity. Third, Bush's conception of a "New World Order" served as a secular variant of the millenialist myth present in the three main religions of the Middle East. Such a linkage of sacrifice and tragedy with purpose is a frequent element in discourse that justifies war. Lastly the Bush administration emphasized technical achievement in battle over more searching questions of policy, shifting the focus of debate from "Is it right?" to "Does it work?"

Cross-national analyses of the war coverage were conducted and differences in the presentation of themes and subthemes were noted. For instance, *Le Monde* was unique in being one of the few papers to give emphasis to the overarching moral significance of the war, including the question of whether it was really necessary. The *Allgemeine Zeitung* did not allow the war to dominate its news coverage in the same way that most of the other papers did. Japan's *Asahi* coverage of the war stressed that official propaganda had to be carefully examined and that diplomatic efforts had to be given full consideration.

The agenda-setting function of the media was tested by tracking over time the number of paragraphs devoted to stories emphasizing the likelihood of war in Associated Press and *USA Today* stories. This information was then correlated with public opinion data on the perceived likelihood of war. The process was repeated with coverage relating to the possible assassination of Saddam Hussein, and public opinion data on the issue. For both, the results were unequivocal, the media coverage appeared to have driven public opinion consistently.

Although public assessment of media performance during the conflict was generally positive, there were significant differences in perceived quality among different social groups, the most notable emerging between those who supported and those who opposed the war. Heavy television viewers were more likely to rate the news coverage positively as were conservatives, war supporters, and those financially better off. Education, however, operated in the opposite direction, being positively related to increased dissatisfaction with news coverage. Although war supporters and opposers offered criticisms of new coverage, they did so for different reasons. The former criticized the media for its sensationalism and giving too much coverage to the enemy, while the latter felt the media failed to provide comprehensive coverage and remain detached from the official government line. Research conducted elsewhere (viz., British and Australia) also documented that significant caveats were expressed particularly on overglorification of the war. Viewers felt the conflict could have been framed more in terms of its socio-historical antecedents and they expressed a desire to see "different sides of the story" (particularly the Arab point of view). The most significant criticism of media reporting was that it relied too much on action-oriented matter, speculation, and interviews with "experts," and was "padded out" by continual reports on the movements of domestic and foreign dignitaries.

VI. EPILOGUE

In sum, communication scholars have explored interpersonal conflict strategies, attributions, evolution and relational outcomes in the family and in the workplace. Of the three main conflict strategies identified, confrontational strategies are thought to be highly related to physical aggression. However, the exact pathways from verbal to physical violence are still under study. That said, we need to understand, in the words of Patricia O'Connor, "discourses of violence-language that accompanies acts of violence, language that reports or reclaims acts of violence, language that leads to violence and violation, language that is itself a violation." We have also seen that there has been much work conducted on examining the controversial issue of the effects of viewing media violence and on the news reporting of international events, both suggesting that there is considerable cause for concern.

Emerging from this overview are four themes. First, that the meaning of violence—be it face-to-face or portrayed on the media—is often a function of the context in which it occurs. For instance, although the movies *The Killing Fields* and *Terminator 2* were both highly violent, most would agreed that their messages about violence were very different. Relatedly, the media reporting of the urban riots in Brixton, South London, in the early 1980s, revealed very different patterns of contextualization across media outlets. While right-wing sections of the press presented the riots as due to mindless criminality, individual Black psychopathology, and the inevitable consequence of attempts to create a multiracial society, left-leaning sections focused more on questions of poverty and deprivation, police brutality, and racism. Clearly, such different framings of conflict inevitably proscribe very different measures for dealing with conflict and preventing its possible future occurrence. Second, while the communicative effects of violence are enhanced or reduced by various situational factors (e.g., prior anger is much more likely to lead to aggression after viewing violence), the effects can be very long-term. For instance, the best predictor of adult aggressiveness is childhood aggressiveness and this is correlated with early childhood exposure to media violence as we have noted. The most pernicious aggressive scripts learned early in life are highly resistant to modification. Third, communication plays crucial roles in our understanding of the causes, forms, and alleviation of conflict; communication consultants are now key players in conflict mediation and arbitration. How events are framed for us (as above) in others' reporting of events and how people negotiate and bargain over conflicts of interest in organizations and through diplomacy are all communicative processes. Fourth, whether the conflict is between subordinates and superordinates in industry, between parents and children, or in the reporting of international crises, we can see that the constructs of control and power account for a significant amount of the variance. In sum, violence is a contemporary problem in part by the ways in which some people have problems resolving it via appropriate communicative means and also in part by the ways in which it is depicted in the media. A recent section of 1996 *American Psychologist* (September) was devoted to a call for a better understanding of how we communicate risk assessments of violence; obviously, we contend that communication studies has a profound role to play therein for the future.

Note we are not claiming that the media is wholly or even largely responsible for violence in society. We believe it is a potent force that accounts for a small yet significant proportion of the variance. However, censoring or legislating the media may not be the short- or long-term answer. The recent focus on television V-chips could be a technical fix for a rather larger scale social problem. For instance, it will probably censor out violent programs per se without differentiating between what social science research suggests is harmful and what is not (e.g., *Shindler's List* versus *Terminator*). Also the parents of those most at risk of being influenced, such as so-called "latchkey" children, may not be interested or able to afford the new technology on new television sets. Experts are also split on whether introduction of the V-chip will lead to less or more TV violence. Some argue that it will lead to more extreme and common violence because it may replace more generalized control. Programmers then excuse extreme violence on the grounds that it can be blocked if desired. Others anticipate that TV will become utterly bland as commercial pressures will force off the screen anything that is likely to earn a rating. Whatever, communication scholars will be monitoring new technologies—and especially so in the organizational context where different group decision-making possibilities have opened up—as they relate to conflict and aggression and suggesting appropriate policies.

The links between interpersonal aggression and media violence—two separate domains for the most part as we have seen—require further research. For example, relationships in soap operas are constantly portrayed as aggressive and conflictual, and people commonly parade their relational conflicts in the ever-increasing number of TV chat shows that are being shown. What are the effects of this—as well as watching sexual violence on the media—on young people's relational expectations and norms when starting off their romantic relationships? Presumably quite impactful, and especially so if their parents and friends provide role models that themselves involve aggression. In tandem, we also ought to be moving away from individualistic accounts of aggression to begin looking at network and system level variables and processes. Aggression is more likely when we are aroused and feel in low power/ control positions so that perhaps each one of us has the potential to be aggressive under particular circumstances.

Sociolinguistic scholars have recently been looking at the ways in which some social groups are subordinated in society given they are silenced in the media and do not have an appropriate voice. Lack of attention to groups and individuals is as pernicious and as strategic as biased attention on occasion. This is clearly the case when it comes to elderly neglect. Future theory might also look more comprehensively to the positive aspects of violence and conflict: under what conditions is conflict unavoidable and socially necessary? When are depictions of violence useful and supportable? When do community standards about, thresholds of, and tolerance for violence and aggression change? Indeed, there needs to be far more attention paid to how people can use different conflict strategies with varying success rates in different contexts. Some contexts do not call for collaboration and in others, collaboration will never really work. Likewise, in some contexts aggression may be called for and be highly successful.

We also need to rethink our disciplinary boundaries wherein "conflict studies" assumes the status of the core curriculum, such as in elementary school where it could be an interdiscipline. Rather than relegating it to the attention of later remediation, therapy, and counseling, we should engage it and its various, changing, and evolving forms as we develop. Moreover, we should begin to investigate and theorize about the ways in which interpersonal, organizational, intercultural, and media (and other) conflict and violence studies intersect. At the moment, they are largely segregated from synthesis and mutual understanding. Certainly there is a dire need for more meshing of communication with socio-legal studies. For instance, some commentators argue that hate speech is more effectively battled through persuasion and education on the values of tolerance, civility, and social respect than through punishment and coercion. Deprecating and violent speech is a rape of human dignity that needs to be vigorously confronted, but not through the heavy hand of the law. How to manage hateful speech directed at one as an individual or as a depersonalized member of a social category is a complex process—and this can occur face-to-face, in writing, or via the media. What is deemed a successful, defensive outcome here is also multidimensional and contentious and communication scholars have a compelling challenge to face here theoretically as well as pragmatically. Finally and conceptually, we might seek to dissuade ourselves from conveniently dichotomizing "communication" from "conflict," and vice versa. Virtually all forms of conflict are communication—and many forms of the latter are conflictual, an appreciation of which (positive and negative) may yield important payoffs.

Also See the Following Articles

AGGRESSION, PSYCHOLOGY OF • CHILDREN, IMPACT OF TELEVISION ON • LINGUISTIC CONSTRUCTIONS OF VIOLENCE, PEACE, AND CONFLICT • MASS MEDIA AND DISSENT • MASS MEDIA, GENERAL VIEW • TELEVISION PROGRAMMING AND VIOLENCE, INTERNATIONAL • TELEVISION PROGRAMMING AND VIOLENCE, U.S.

Bibliography

Bugental, D. (1993). Communication in abusive relationships: Cognitive constructions of interpersonal power. *Amer. Behav. Sci.,* 36, 88–308.

Cahn, D. D., & Lloyd, S. A. (Eds.). (1996) *Family violence from a communication perspective.* Newbury Park, CA: Sage.

Donnerstein, E., Slaby, R. G., & Eron, L. R. (1994) The mass media and youth aggression. In L. R. Eron, J. H. Gentry, & P. Schlegel (Eds.), *Reason to hope: A psychological perspective on violence and youth* (pp. 219–250). Washington DC: American Psychological Association.

Gerbner, G., Gross, L., Morgan, M., & Signorielli, N. (1994). Growing up with television: The cultivation perspective. In B. Jennings and D. Zillman (Eds.), *Media effects: Advances in theory and research* (pp. 17–41). Hillsdale, NJ: Erlbaum.

Greenberg, B. S., & Gantz, W. (Eds.). (1993) *Desert Storm and the mass media.* Creskill, NJ: Hampton Press.

Iyengar, S. (1991). *Is anyone responsible? How television frames political issues.* Chicago: University of Chicago Press.

Putnam, L. L., & Roloff, M. E. (Eds.). (1992). *Communication and negotiation.* Newbury Park, CA: Sage.

Roloff, M. E. (1996). The catalyst hypothesis: Conditions under which communication leads to physical aggression. In D. D. Cahn & S. A. Lloyd (Eds.), *Family violence from a communication perspective* (pp. 20–36). Thousand Oaks, CA: Sage.

Sabourin, T. C., Infante, D. A., & Rudd, J. I. (1993). Verbal aggression in marriages: A comparison of violent, distressed but nonviolent, and nondistressed couples. *Hum. Comm. Res.,* 20, 245–267.

Sillars, A. L., Wilmot, W. W., & Hocker, J. L. (1993). Communication strategies in conflict and mediation. In J. M. Wiemann and J. Daly (Eds.), *Communicating strategically* (pp. 163–190). Hillsdale, NJ: Erlbaum.

Stamp, G. H., & Sabourin, T. C. (1995). Accounting for violence: An analysis of male spousal abuse narratives. *J. of App. Comm. Res.,* 23, 284–307.

Ting-Toomey, S. (1994). Managing conflict in intimate intercultural relationships. In D. D. Cahn (Ed.), *Conflict in personal relationships* (pp. 47–77). Hillsdale, NJ: Erlbaum.

Vissing, Y., and Baily, W. (1996). Parent-to-child verbal aggression. In D. D. Cahn and S. A. Lloyd (Eds.), *Family violence from a communication perspective* (pp. 85–107). Thousand Oaks, CA: Sage.

Whillock, R., & Slayden, D. (Eds.). (1995). *Hate speech.* Thousand Oaks, CA. Sage.

Conflict Management and Resolution

Ho-Won Jeong
George Mason University

GLOSSARY

Alternative Dispute Resolution Settlement out of court; emphasis on compromise.

Basic Needs Food, shelter, freedom, identity, and other elements needed for development and growth.

Conflict Management Efforts for preventing escalation of conflict or reducing the destructive nature of conflict; less concerned with structural conditions.

Conflict Resolution Dealing with root causes; satisfaction of basic needs; change in enemy perceptions; institutional changes or new social relations often required.

Deterrence An authoritative way of exercising power to maintain order.

Third Party Intervention Adjudication, arbitration, ombudsmanry, negotiated rule making, a problem-solving workshop

THE PURPOSE OF THIS ARTICLE is to review recent developments in the effort to promote our understanding of how to manage and resolve conflict. The way we deal with conflict has broad implications for human well-being and social change. After discussing conceptual issues, the article examines three different models of interpreting conflict. Then it explains diverse ways of dealing with a broad range of problems. These include negotiation, adjudication, mediation, arbitration, problem-solving workshops, and consensus decision making. The final section looks at issues relevant to the application of these methods.

I. CONFLICT AND SOCIETY

As modern societies grew complex, problems of managing conflict have become enormous. In tribal societies, the issues facing elders and religious leaders were less complicated. In the contemporary world, conflict over distribution of resources can occur between individuals, organizations, and nations. The growth in the gap between the rich and the poor has become inevitable with the emergence of industrial societies and free market economic systems. The development of more destructive technologies and the willingness to use them indiscriminately increased the costs for forceful solutions of conflict.

Arguments and disputes are inherent in human society. A husband and wife can argue about the education of their children. Neighbors fight over the use of land. In a tenancy relationship, complaints about late payment of rent, noise, and pets are not unusual. Lawsuits result from challenges to rules and regulations, and disagreements over responsibility and liability. Nations can be in dispute over economic, security, and environmental issues. Interest groups have high stakes in policy outcomes. If conflict is not properly managed, it can generate violence and lead to the destruction of a community. Protracted conflict in various areas has proven unproductive and costly in terms of human life and economic losses.

The nature of conflict can be understood in terms of how problems are defined and framed. In general, struggles between opposing forces touch on differences in opinions and contending interests. Conflict reflects relations within a family, a community, and an international system. Bitter disputes over wages may develop into emotionally tense relations. Disadvantaged groups may initiate and maintain a conflict with more powerful adversaries in order to achieve social and political reform. As we have observed in anticolonial struggles in the Third World, labor movements, and civil rights movements in the 1960s, conflict often tends to escalate because those in power refuse to respond to the grievances of the exploited or disadvantaged. The less powerful parties raise the stakes when their voices are not heard.

Competition between different groups of people over resources, rights, and power often results in challenges to existing norms and relationships and rules of decision making. Long-term grievances over economic and social inequities can derive from a failure to enhance the quality of life. Compromise is not possible in a situation where the fundamental rights of people are not recognized. Demand for justice can reflect problems with the institutional structures, practices, and beliefs. A highly centralized political system, which does not allow self-determination and autonomy, represents the failure of a modern state system. In dealing with conflict, it is important to understand sources and remedies that address structural inadequacies.

Military and police interventions can crack down on protests against social injustice and economic inequality. Under these circumstances the absence of overt conflict can be explained in terms of the ability of state elites to impose their own will on society. A lack of civil strife in authoritarian regimes often results from fear. Social order in Nigeria, Indonesia, and China, for example, is based on repression of freedom to express popular sentiments from below. However, repressive conflict management is reactive and on an ad hoc basis. Coercive means hardly deal with the main source of problems, and ignore inevitable changes. The suppression of people's discontent does not bring an end to conflict.

Conflict, as interpreted as a problem to be solved, can offer opportunities for communication between adversaries and it can bring positive changes in the relationship. An effective response to conflict helps reduce a sense of isolation, a fear of abandonment, as well as generating a strong belief in others. Disagreements and arguments can be managed in such a way to avoid extreme polarization, physical violence, and rancor. The efforts to limit escalation of disputes can lead to build interpersonal trust that prevents the interpretation of the situation in extreme terms. As a result of conflict, an integrated society can emerge.

II. CONCEPTUALIZATION

There are no precise definitions of conflict management and resolution. Some believe that resolution of conflict is not possible given its intrinsic nature in society, and they prefer the term management in explaining any effort to deal with conflict. Others argue that even a protracted conflict can be resolved if changes in behavior, policies, and institutions are made to satisfy the interests and needs of parties. If conflict in ordinary relationships is not properly managed, it can develop into a situation in which the existence of anger and hatred requires a deeper level of analysis and intensive efforts for overcoming misperceptions. In general, it can be argued that understanding the root causes of problems is essential for conflict resolution whereas conflict in a given system cannot be managed without changes in social norms and institutions.

A. Conflict Management

Conflict can be related to specific interests or processes within organizations and social systems. It is not difficult to find arguments and disputes in normal relationships. In everyday life, people encounter disagreement, for example, on room temperature and salaries. Interest disputes are readily provoked by broken agreements, unobserved norms, and competition in the use of resources. Problems in commercial relations may be caused by pursuit of incompatible monetary and other material interests, breach of contract, dissatisfaction with quality of goods and services, and the ignorance of consumer rights. Individuals can argue about the implementation of specific policies and the fairness of government authorities without questioning the fundamental nature of economic and political systems.

This type of conflict does not necessarily challenge the legitimacy of dominant norms, values, and institutions. Disputes within an existing system can be easily settled by established rules and institutional processes. The provocations that give rise to such problems are part of the system, and the arguments are part of ordinary social and organizational relationships. Management problems may emerge from inadequate knowledge, misperceptions, and differences in preferences. At the work place, some form of organized discussion and leadership direction can handle misunderstanding and arguments. Communication assisted by someone may be able to eliminate problems within a factory or a family. In other cases, the remedies are sought through sanctions, punishment, and arbitration. Disputes can be easily managed when the sources of the problem are found within the system.

In some cultures that emphasize collectivist values, avoidance and withdrawal are encouraged as nonconfrontational conflict management techniques. Some tribes in the South Pacific ocean islands have a culture where group survival traditionally depends on close cooperation among family and community members, making the overt expression of hostile feelings to others a threat to the group. An avoidance strategy can also be adopted under other circumstances. If the matter is not worth fighting over, conflict tends to be ignored. When faced with a stronger opponent or a potentially hostile environment, people are more reluctant to raise an issue. In this situation, the costs of action are perceived as greater than any possible returns, or there may be no hope for changes in the situation. In general, avoidance is not a healthy way of dealing with tension if ignorance of anger and other feelings can lead to more serious relationship problems.

Cooperative and confrontational behaviors are mixed together even in intense conflicts. Conflictual events have more impact on determining the consequent strategies of groups. Escalation of hostile actions can more easily happen in polarized communities where leaders pursue contentious goals. On the other hand, inappropriate processes of interaction are likely to turn functional problems into more serious conflicts. Substantive issues are transformed into differences of principles, hence making any concession look like defeat. When conflict is escalated, it is more difficult to address the concerns of each party. The steps for conflict management may require initiating and maintaining communication between the parties.

Violent confrontations can be avoided by appropriate forms of third-party intervention. Community policing in urban areas can reduce youth violence and bloodshed among gang members. In international conflict, peacekeeping operations have frequently been used to maintain a fragile cease fire agreement between belligerent parties. Humanitarian assistance contains and controls explosive situations with urgent relief work. Good offices, whose function is to deliver messages, serve as a communication channel between parties who, because of legitimacy reasons, do not sit at the same table. To build a more satisfactory relationship, however, more direct contacts need to be restored. Tension reduction measures may make the conflict more bearable in the short term, but they do not necessarily deal with the sources of the problems. Although the management of hostile relationships is necessary for creating an environment for resolving problems, it can, at the same time, help prolong the entrapment of conflict by removing an urgent need to take immediate action.

B. Conflict Resolution

Conflict resolution involves a far more complex process than mere conflict management. As conflict unfolds, old identities change and new groups are formed. Compromises between parties may not last long if the parties do not feel that their problems have been satisfactorily dealt with. Settlement of specific cases and issues may not involve changes in the relationship that was the main source of contention. As the result of a constructive way of dealing with conflict, all the parties should be better off than before. Conflict resolution requires changes in the psychological environment. At the same time, descriptions that focus only on an individual's motives miss the fundamental nature of social conflict. Conflict cannot be managed within a given system if social norms and political processes are questioned. The goals of conflict resolution lie in helping alienated parties analyze the causes of the conflict and explore strategies for changes in the system that generates it.

One of the criteria for successful conflict resolution includes the satisfaction of nonnegotiable needs and cultural values. Changes in perceptions result from the recognition of the other side's legitimate needs, and shared interests should be redefined by participatory, but not judgmental, processes. Collaborative processes rather than power bargaining can help discover accommodations that bring net advantages to all concerned. Removing the causes of conflictual behavior results from the transformation of relationships. Dealing with a particular conflict situation does nothing to prevent the occurrence of another incident of the same kind unless the broad causal problems are understood. For instance, settlement of landlord and tenant disputes without concerns of equity in impoverished areas can set patterns that would, in the end, aggravate the housing problems for the poor. Successful conflict resolution has a preventive effect on future conflicts by eliminating the possible causes of problems without using threats.

In general, any given conflict's susceptibility to a win-win solution depends on the nature of the issues, the constellation of interests, and the availability of alternative options as well as the commitment of parties to problem solving. Conflict over interests can be more easily resolved than conflict over values and basic needs. Options can be invented to find win-win solutions for labor-management problems and the division of resources in the global commons. The economic aspirations of individuals and groups, which alter with circumstances, can be negotiable. Disputes over material goods and role occupancy are transitory but not inherent as human needs and values might be. If competing interests are the prime motivator of the conflict, a compromise can be easily bridged.

Conflicts affecting the security of personal identity, the autonomy of an ethnic group or a nation cannot be resolved by conflict management techniques. The resolution of deep-rooted conflict, which reflects long-term hostilities, requires more intensive efforts to understand perceptions, emotions, values, and needs of parties. Parties should be helped with assessing the costs of conflict and exploring conditions for resolution. In contrast with conflict over material interests, issues over values and basic needs cannot be compromised. Highly emotional and value-oriented issues are not for trading and cannot be handled easily by the imposition of third party decisions. Group identity, autonomy, and freedom cannot be bargained away, and conditions for realization of human dignity and self-fulfillment should be understood and recognized. Elimination of discrimination and other sources of social inequality requires changes in political institutions and social norms.

III. APPROACHES TO CONFLICT

Depending on the interpretations of human nature and the goals of society, there are different approaches to dealing with conflict. Diverse interpretations of relations between individuals and authorities also have an impact on the conceptual frameworks of three different conflict management and resolution models, including deterrence, alternative dispute resolution, and basic needs.

A. Deterrence Model

A deterrence model suggests a hierarchical way of solving problems. Deterrence theory provides the basis of domestic enforcement and international strategic policies. The goal of society is to maintain order and to punish those who do not conform to its values. Many governments use coercive mechanisms to prevent challenges to dominant political and economic interests. The construct of evil human nature justifies the conventional wisdom that an authoritative way of exercising power at all social levels, from parents to the state, is the foundation of peace, for only power can control inherently antisocial human behavior. Punishment and constraints of deviant persons and groups are a primary strategy of deterring others from taking nonconformative behavior in the future as well as a means of dealing with the present situation.

Ample evidence suggests that dissident behaviors result from alienation and other consequences of frustration of certain ontological human needs. In the framework of social control and containment policies, however, more police measures are believed to offer solutions to gang violence with little consideration of economic conditions in poor urban areas. For instance, in efforts to reduce drug trafficking and consumption, there is no understanding of deeper causes of problems such as a lack of opportunities for development. Human dimensions are ignored in solving pressing social problems. According to this approach, the death penalty and long-term sentences replace rehabilitation. Little emphasis is put on education and training, and no proper attention is paid to social and economic well-being of individuals.

In dealing with international conflict, this model suggests a state centric approach. As was exemplified in the Persian Gulf War, maintaining international order is enforced by military operations rather than negotiated solutions. A conventional response to terrorism is another example of deterrence strategies. Israeli bombing in Lebanon caused suffering to the civilian populations while failing to deter Hezbollah guerilla attacks. Greater powers seek to impose their institutions and values on peoples of other countries in the name of democracy and freedom, but there is little analysis of the oppressive circumstances that have led to the present condition. Some Middle Eastern countries such as Iran and Libya have been condemned as terrorist states, and their behavior is considered irrational. However, the long-term domination of the West in the region has often been ignored as one of the main causes of their challenges to the Western hegemony.

Deterrence strategies do not appear to be an effective means to prevent conflict. First of all, a continuing level of violence in protracted conflicts often derives from repressive measures. Deterrent and coercive approaches do not lead to the discovery or removal of causes of conflict and fail to stop the occurrence of similar events. In the superpower conflict during the Cold War period, the uncertainty of nuclear deterrence policies increased insecurity, while the problems were never resolved by the threat of nuclear weapons. Secondly, the cost of deterrence policy is too high given the level of destructiveness of weapons technology. In considering the nature of modern warfare, the majority of victims of the deterrence policy has become civilian populations. The complex nature of modern society makes the prevention of terrorist attacks by extreme religious and nationalist groups very difficult without building a police state. In considering the attacks on Paris by Algerian terrorist groups, suppression and containment prove more costly but less effective than a change in the French interventionist policies toward the region.

Conflict in modern society emerges from various forms of social control. Threats of punishment and adversarial institutions are major characteristics of an elite controlled society. Collaborated problem-solving approaches are resisted by power holders since they are fearful of institutional changes. In a deterrence model, conflict can be settled without the elimination of real causes of problems. Forced compromise can generate more issues to be resolved in the future. Conflict at all societal levels—family, community, industrial, and international—reflects the failure of traditional power elite deterrence strategies.

The conceptions of power politics still dominate official policies of many governments. State centric and unitary decision-making models do not easily explain such questions as whose interests matter in society. Conflicts are built in a framework that attaches significance to the socialization of individuals into dominant social norms, to the preservation of institutions, and to a hierarchical decision-making process. Coercion and containment policies do not fit into the social and political adjustments needed for peaceful relations. Authorities seek to preserve existing structures, institutions, and policies despite the fact that these are a source of conflict. They are traditionally reluctant to admit that coercive power does not work, and insist that there cannot be a dialogue with enemies. The hint of a willingness to negotiate can be perceived as an admission of defeat or, at the very least, as a sign of weakness. When negotiation is seen as part of the power process, a willingness to negotiate is considered as a surrender.

B. Alternative Dispute Resolution Model

Based on the observation that the costs of war and litigation are too high, the proponents of Alternative Dispute Resolution (ADR) argue that rational individuals should be able to resolve their differences without depending on coercive means. In congruence with the notion of social contract interpreted in terms of the Enlightenment philosophy, this model suggests a more voluntary form of cooperation under conditions of free speech and rationality. Neighborhood disputes can be more easily handled by a participatory mode of decision making. There has been a great emphasis on training and education. The goal was to stop violence with a broad implication for social change. At an international level, mediation can help two countries fighting over territories avoid a war. With good will, parties to a dispute can settle their differences by negotiation and compromise. In difficult cases, some skilled third party intervention may be needed to help dialogue, and to move toward an informed consensus. Problems can be resolved by consensus rather than threats. The process is generally seen as nonconfrontational and nonadversarial.

The origin of Alternative Dispute Resolution movements goes back to the early 1970s with the establishment of community dispute resolution centers. However, before the emergence of community projects, the federal government of the United States took initiatives in the early 20th century. The Federal Mediation and Conciliation Service was founded in 1917 under the aegis of the Department of Labor and was reorganized as an independent federal agency in 1947. Its jurisdiction includes other federal agencies, private industries engaged in interstate commerce, and private nonprofit health facilities. In the midst of racial conflict in the South, the Community Relations Service of the Department of Justice was created in 1964 with a mandate to intervene in disputes related to discrimination based on race, color, or national origin, school desegregation problems, issues of fair housing, economic development, education, communications, and protests against White supremacists. In response to growing violence and conflict at schools, there also have been efforts to introduce peer mediation to various levels of students. All these efforts were made to maintain an orderly society without relying too much on law enforcement forces.

The recent expansion of mediation to commercial disputes represents a growing trend to look for alternatives to lengthy, expensive judicial processes. Mediation is recognized as cost effective, and many mediation businesses have emerged to profit from the demand of a corporate world. Specialists on organizational development advise big corporations in setting up conflict management systems to avoid expensive sexual harassment and discrimination lawsuits. Some differences exist between the community-based mediation and professional mediation services. In general, community-based dispute resolution programs emphasize empowerment of individuals with their traditional roles of advocacy. Their main focus is on building a harmonious community and sharing decision-making power. The community-based models not only utilize nonprofessionals as mediators but also involve the volunteers in staff work, outreach, and training.

In recent years, as the legal system is congested, mediation has become more popular in achieving settlement out of court. In some states of the United States, it is mandatory to try mediation on specific problems such as divorce and child custody before court hearings. Court officials utilize the system of Alternative Dispute Resolution to reduce their backlogs and speed processes through court referrals. Compared with the original goal of empowerment, its function has turned out to be supplementary to and supportive of the existing legal system. In other countries such as Australia and South Africa, ADR has also been developed at more or less the same pace and in the same areas as the United States.

ADR has been criticized for several reasons. Given its emphasis on how to settle disputes without regard to power disparities, it can be seen as another mechanism of social control. The supposed neutrality of a third party favors compromise and conceals the biased impact of power imbalance on the outcome. Since ADR is embedded in individualism, it is not looking to structural inequalities in the society as a reason for conflict. The underlying assumption is that the parties themselves have a sufficient insight into the nature of their conflict, and can reach an agreed outcome that will be lasting. All that is required is a process that helps conduct discussion and points out the misunderstandings in communication between disputants. These techniques are not adequate to the resolution of conflict that represents sharply contrasting views about fundamental public values such as abortion and environmental protection. Since the basic social structure is rarely questioned, grievances are trivialized and personalized. ADR has lost sight of its original purpose, including its concern for the poor who do not have access to the law. Recent development can be seen as the privatization of dispute settlement.

C. Basic Needs Model

As opposed to the traditional thinking of the deterrence model that conflict is inherent to human nature, the basic needs model of conflict resolution stresses that unfulfilled needs are the main causes of violence. It is assumed that the normal human being is not typically aggressive when basic needs are met. Conflict between groups is the consequence of a lack of institutionalized means that guarantee identity and security. Needs, in particular, are inherent drives for survival, identity, recognition, and development. These elements cannot be suppressed by socialization, threats, or coercion. The merits of punishment in a deterrence strategy have been limited in maintaining social control when an individual defies social norms and enforcement authorities. Ontological and genetic needs—comprised of the desire for development and biological necessities of food and shelter—should be fulfilled within the context of the social good. Contrary to values acquired through education and socialization, needs are universal and primordial. To trade basic needs is not within a range of free decision making of an individual since needs, which reflect universal motivations, are an integral part of the human being.

Separate cultures and identity groups emerge from linguistic, religious, class, ethnic, or other features. These can be bases for discrimination, and also turn into a means of defensive identity against the consequences of such discrimination. Wars are often fought to preserve cultural values and identity. Leadership emerges to defend them. As we observed in the former Yugoslavia, aspirations for national identity can also be manipulated for political purposes. It was a quest for self-autonomy that divided Lebanon, Northern Ireland, and many other multi-ethnic societies. The past history shows that a small Catholic minority community in Northern Ireland could not be controlled by a large British army. The failure to recognize the separate identity of Tamils has sustained ethnic conflicts in Sri Lanka. No relative power differences can eliminate these problems as we saw in secessionist movements and colonial struggles. The satisfaction of basic needs is essential to nonadversarial problem solving. Social justice and equity are important elements.

Overall, the conditions of social stability and peace require the satisfaction of human needs. A conflict resolution model should focus on the redefinition of issues in a broad social context and the assessment of costs derived from repression of needs. Since needs can be universally applied across cultures, they transcend separate compartments of knowledge. Understanding human dimensions of conflict takes a holistic view of conflictual behavior. An identity group, defined in terms of a class, ethnicity, and race, is an important unit of analysis in examining sources of conflicts and exploring options. Human development is a major concern in dealing with critical problems of conflict and survival. Conflict cannot be contained within an existing framework when the appropriate remedies suggest changes in norms, institutions, and policies.

IV. METHODS FOR DEALING WITH CONFLICT

Depending on the nature and sources of conflict, there are different ways to deal with conflict. In negotiation, parties can reach an agreement through compromise. If negotiations between two parties are not possible, third parties can be involved to promote communication, make proposals for solutions, or impose decisions. Negotiated rule making is designed to help multiple interest groups reach consensus. Facilitators in a problem-solving workshop assist adversaries in exploring options that can satisfy basic needs. This section discusses major aspects of negotiation and various types of third party intervention, including adjudication, arbitration, mediation, negotiated rule making, and a problem-solving workshop.

A. Negotiation

Bargaining existed from the ancient period when people began to exchange goods to satisfy their material interests. In the modern economic system, negotiation is an inevitable part of daily life, ranging from buying rugs in a foreign country as a tourist to making decisions on the purchase of a new car. Negotiations settled trade disputes between Japan and the United States before the issue generated animosity in their relationship. Successful international negotiations might have prevented the Gulf War, which inflicted so much pain on the population of Iraq. The reason for negotiating is that people want to achieve something better than could be obtained without negotiation.

There are different ways for negotiators to achieve their goals and objectives. In bargaining, two sides may have a bottom line to be satisfied before they accept any deal. Negotiations are successful when both sides find a compatible range of points that they are willing to agree on through compromise. In other situations, interests can be satisfied by the trade-offs of priorities in different issue areas. Compromise of different positions is encouraged in interest-based negotiation. Sometimes concerns with face saving can be an obstacle to make concessions needed for reaching a final agreement. Face saving reflects a person's need to reconcile the stand she or he takes in a negotiation with past words, deeds, and principles. Revealing motivations and goals can reduce the other side's fears and clear up misperceptions. Efficient and amicable agreements may be reached by using principled negotiation that emphasizes separation of emotions from interests, cooperation for maximization of mutual gains, and the use of fair procedures and standards.

In positional bargaining, negotiating parties stick with positions and make slow concessions toward reaching a compromise. Failure of negotiation can often be attributed to a contest of will. In the Cyprus conflict in the 1960s, the talks between the Greeks and the Turkish broke down at the prebargaining stage. Each had preconditions that its own draft constitution would be the basis for discussion. In this kind of bargaining environment neither side is willing to give up its position by accepting the draft of the other. As is often the case, parties believe that they cannot afford to negotiate from positions of weakness. Insisting on positions endangers an ongoing relationship while each side tries through sheer will power to force the other to change its position. Resentment inevitably emerges in a situation where one side sees itself bending to the other side's rigid will whereas its own concerns go unaddressed. Power imbalance between parties leaves fewer options for a weaker party. When negotiators take win-lose strategies, the outcome often reflects power differences.

B. Adjudication

As a formal legal process, adjudication can handle disputes in the areas of property rights, constitutional interpretations, and criminal offenses. Parties in disputes have little control over the process. They cannot choose a judge or jury who delivers a verdict on the case. The decisions are formal, and generally, enforced. Court arguments are guided by precedents and legal norms rather than an analysis of the values and needs of the disputants. Under the condition that the law is based on equity and justice, a court system can protect rights of individuals. The European Court of Human Rights protects individual citizens' civil rights by allowing them to sue their own government. The ruling of the International Court of Justice has a better chance, than power-based negotiation, to yield a favorable result to a small country in its disputes with a strong neighbor.

An old example of adjudication is a tribal council.

Currently about 15% of cultures still rely on councils as the primary means to settle disputes among individuals or groups in the community. The council is normally composed of men who draw respect because of age, status, or other criteria that are important in the culture. To settle disputes, councils hold hearings to ascertain the facts. Disputants are permitted to present their cases through speeches, witnesses, and testimony from supporters. Consensus is needed to make the decision on punishment and compensation. An informal aspect of this process is that the council has no means of enforcing its decision. It is usually adhered to not only because the disputants respect the status of the council members but also because the community supports the council's procedure.

Theoretically, the modern court system serves justice for all, but the costs of formal litigation do not offer realistic opportunities of guaranteeing fairness to everyone. To predict formal court decisions, parties can use a minitrial where private judges make nonbinding decisions after hearing the evidence and arguments presented by each side. The predicted outcome can help parties reach some form of mutual agreement instead of going to litigation. Litigation is an adversarial process since parties are forced to oppose each other without direct communication. As a traditional method, court settlements and police intervention help maintain law and order. Given that their primary purpose is to control, a judicial process is not an effective means of revealing the roots causes of problems. Formal and binding decisions of the court do not always reflect immediate social concerns and human well-being. In international conflict, legal settlement is not possible without the enforcement power of supranational authority. An authoritative exercise of power by the international court is opposed by states that do not accept such limitations on their sovereignty. The U.S. withdrawal from the jurisdiction of the International Court of Justice in 1985 over Nicaraguan action against the U.S. was a dramatic evidence of this.

C. Arbitration

Arbitration can be considered as an informal category of adjudication. In some cases, arbitration exists as a quasi-judicial process within a legal system. Contrary to a court system, parties can choose arbitrators who determine the outcome. Otherwise the parties at least should accept the authority of the system which appoints the arbitrator. The bottom line is that an arbitrator should be acceptable to both parties. Arbitrators make a decision based on presented evidence and arguments. At a hearing both parties present arguments, respond to the other side, and answer arbitrators' questions. Since participants do not make decisions on the outcome, good will, trust, and cooperation between parties are not required.

With the stress on the objectivity of the process, arbitration avoids issues of feelings. The major concerns for arbitrators should be fairness, impartiality, equity, good conscience, the merits of the case, and natural justice. Suitable cases include a question of legal interpretation or technical assessment of problems in such areas as property damages. Arbitration can deal with practical problems, including commercial contracts where objective criteria exist and are required. Expert arbitration focuses on complex questions of facts that are central to the conflict. In international trade disputes, the World Trade Organization has a wide range of authority to hear complaints and make binding decisions. While some decisions have an advisory effect only, parties may sign a formal agreement to accept biding decisions. While a decision regarding material interests can be made by arbitration, it does not prevent an irreconcilable breakdown in the relationship between the parties. Stable and long-term personal relations will not emerge from a decision in favor of one party. In addition, arbitration is not effective in resolving value-oriented conflict.

D. Ombudsmanry

The bulk of ombudsmen's work comes from individual citizen complaints about administrative decisions made by public agencies. The ombudsmanry system protects individuals against possible government abuse of public trust. It can also work within other organizational settings. The main concerns are the protection of the rights of clients served by the organization such as children, college students, employees, prisoners, and health care patients. Functions similar to those of an ombudsman can also be found in some newspaper sections, and television and radio programs that deal with individual complaints. The threats of large-scale publicity about an institution's failures have a compelling impact on corrections of problems.

The main idea behind ombudsmanry is the notion that all power is accountable and responsible to the public. Reforms in policy and practice can be generated by the hearings of grievances related to a pattern of neglect, incompetence, or inadequate implementation procedures of policies. As a result of the investigation, efforts can be made to find remedies within established procedures and systems. Ombudsmen may make legislative recommendations and suggest new policy-making procedures. Since they are not in a position to make changes in laws or policies by themselves, their power is indirect. Their political independence is important in investigating complaints and preparing a report. The procedure is normally objective, informal, inexpensive, and quick.

The Swedish experience, which goes back to the early 19th century, has offered a model of the modern type of ombudsmanry for Western industrialized countries. In many countries, ombudsmanry performs traditional roles of fact-finding and investigating the sources of a complaint. In most cases, problems might be presented, as an initial step, to the head of the department or agency with responsibility and power to respond to the complaint. Ombudsmen can take a public advocacy role in a particular field or a specific geographical area. In general, the modern practice of ombudsmanry emphasizes that elected officials and public institutions should be subject to public scrutiny and evaluation.

E. Mediation

The assistance of a neutral third party in a negotiation can help produce a mutually acceptable solution. Consent to a mediation process is voluntary, and the disputants make final decisions on the issue. It is assumed that reasonable compromises can be reached through good will and mutual confidence. The third party would create that good faith and confidence by assisting communication. An impartial third party has no authoritative decision-making power since the disputants are the major players. Parties are allowed to express their concerns and feelings directly or indirectly at meetings facilitated by mediators. A third party is mostly concerned with the process rather than the content. Mediators organize meetings, provide clarity in communication, and keep records.

The profiles of mediators range from tribal chiefs, world religious leaders, and former politicians to school children. Especially active in international mediation have been peace churches, including the Quakers, Mennonites, and Brethren. Due to its geopolitical interests, the U.S. government mediated the negotiation between Israelis and their neighbors such as Egypt and Palestine. The UN Secretary General also successfully conducted mediation in ending the Iran/Iraq war at the end of the 1980s. Such involvement has also become a common form of social intervention in domestic arenas. Mediation has been heavily applied to intracommunity problems such as consumer merchant relations as well as divorce and child custody issues. In addition, it has been applied to labor management problems and intercorporate disputes. Schools and prisons use mediation programs to prevent inmate uprisings and campus violence. Mediation is often advocated as a more amicable way of ending conflict. It can generate mutually satisfactory outcomes in an efficient manner. Since voluntary agreement is necessary for a settlement, parties have a great degree of control and expect predictable outcomes.

All forms of mediation are more democratic in their nature than judicial or arbitration processes. People can learn a new process of resolving their own disputes, and the new knowledge is self-empowering. All that is necessary is to interact in good faith. If there is a prior agreement between parties, failure of mediation is followed by arbitration. A third party acting as a mediator can have power to move into the role of an arbitrator when mediation is not successful. Parties are more willing to reach an agreement since they face the risk of arbitration. On the other hand, the possibility of arbitration inhibits honest expression of feelings and opinions. Questions can be raised about the application of rigidly defined processes to a variety of settings, including public policy and community development. Some mediators are obsessed with success rates, and they tend to repress discussion of larger problems such as social injustice and unrepresented interests.

F. Negotiated Rule Making

Negotiated rule making can be adopted when there are multiple parties arguing over complex issues. Decisions made by public authorities often lead to policy disputes. Even though people share common goals, they can disagree on the choices as to how to achieve them. In public policy areas, there are often many parties contesting different issues. It is often unclear who represents stake-holding interests. In addition, as issues alter rapidly, the parties change their positions in unexpected directions. This is different from a classic bargaining situation where two parties fight over a single item. While the process of decision making is more complex due to the existence of multiple parties, trade-offs for mutual gains may be made more easily across multiple issues.

To reach consensus among multiple parties requires a collaborative decision-making process facilitated by a third party. Consensus would be found when everybody in the group feels that they can live with and support actively the decision. They have to be able to believe that the decision is a win for everyone in the group. Designing a process for consensus decision making starts with identifying key stakeholders. They can work together step by step, continuously checking back with their constituencies. The participants first work for agreements on the definition of the issues and then move on to solutions. The initial stage of facilitated meetings discusses the nature of issues and advice from specialists such as engineers on technical issues and facts. A third party assists parties in assessing the scope of problems and exploring the options available. It is essential that the key stakeholders agree to participate in a collaborative process. They have to see it as an integral part of their decision making.

Negotiated rule making was applied to the formulation of the Clean Air Act by the U.S. government's Environmental Protection Agency, which determines penalties on manufactures of air-polluting truck engines violating the industry leader standard. Many aspects of consensus decision making are also reflected in the complex negotiations in Law of the Sea Conference, which discussed the allocation of mineral resources on the sea bed. At the 1992 Rio Environmental Summit, free trade issues were compromised with those of protection of endangered species and preservation of resources in the treaty making process.

Because there is no voting, one of the most important factors in consensus decision making is that each party should be able to understand its own and the other side's interests. In addition, creativity in inventing solutions is critical in bridging gaps between different positions. Obstacles to negotiated rule making include insufficient resources of low income groups for full participation, different levels of expertise among participants, and costs to hire technical consultants for joint fact finding. Most importantly, value conflicts cannot be resolved through a consensus decision-making process. It is more helpful in dealing with conflict over interests and questions of how to achieve certain goals.

G. A Problem-Solving Workshop

A problem-solving workshop is geared toward enabling the parties to identity and understand each other's needs. Representatives of parties confidentially meet in the presence of a small panel of disinterested consultants in order to analyze the causes of conflict and examine conditions for its resolution. Compared with mediation that seeks an acceptable compromise, facilitators help participants identify suppressed and hidden human needs.

Ideal participants for the workshop are individuals who are influential within their respective communities. The analysis of the situation leads to the new definition of the relationship, which helps create the joint frame of references. Unless participants can identify something relevant to their experience and belief systems, they cannot easily internalize new information and knowledge, and learn from interaction. Workshops are designed for participants to see the impact of their action on the other side. Parties can develop a common universe of discourse in order to cooperate. As the workshop proceeds, participants can develop alternative roles first as analysts and later as partners.

A panel, which may consist of half a dozen facilitators, encourages parties to get to the bottom of the problem that is not easily understood in power bargaining situations. In their sponsoring role, the third party facilitates clarifications and interpretations of facts and events by offering knowledge about relevant patterns of behavior drawn from other situations. The workshop approach has been applied to the civil wars in Africa and conflicts between Palestians and Israelis by a number of scholars who were interested in action-oriented research. Most of these workshops focused on the conditions of perceived victimization that stemmed from denial of separate identity and culture as well as the absence of effective political participation. The status of the panelists as academics provided a basis for credibility and legitimacy in the eyes of the parties.

Starting within the participants' frame of reference, interactive decision making will screen out false assumptions and implications from existing knowledge, cultural and ideological orientations, and personal prejudices. A detailed outcome of this process is unknown in advance since the workshop does not advocate particular solutions. Enduring solutions result from the principles of reciprocity and equity. Parties are more eager to look for possible outcomes acceptable to all if each side is informed of the perceptions of the other, and realizes the existence of alternative means of attaining their goals as well as the costs of pursuing present policies. The workshop is supposed to generate new ideas, knowledge, attitudes, and altered perceptions. Problem-solving workshops can prove effective in intractable conflicts with a history of intense hostilities. The success of the workshop may be judged by the eventual transformation of relationships between long term adversaries. New knowledge and information produced at the informal workshop meetings should be able to feed into an official process.

H. The Context of Applications

Theories and skills can be applied to various types of problems at different levels of analysis, including personal, communal, and international. Given the absence of an overriding power in the international scene, adjudication is less frequently used than mediation and arbitration in settling disputes between states. In the domestic arena, mediation has become more popular due to deficiencies in the legal system. Peer or voluntary mediators can deal with arguments between people at a workplace as well as ordinary problems within a family. Organizational disputes need to be professionally handled by administrators, managers, or industrial arbitrators who are familiar with the issues. Given their destructive impact on public life, strikes of public employees can be referred to arbitration for quick solution. Emotional problems and personality conflicts may require the expert knowledge of social workers and psychiatrists. On the other hand, there are cases such as sexual harassment and child abuse that need to go to court since seeking justice is an important issue. In such areas as environmental and industrial conflicts where power imbalance is prevalent, advocacy roles may be required before any negotiation or mediation takes place. Given their focus on basic needs, problem-solving workshops can be applied to the resolution of protracted conflict between hostile ethnic and racial groups in various parts of the world.

The nature of negotiation and different types of third party intervention influences the conditions for dispute settlement and conflict resolution. The settlement process may involve threats and coercion as well as persuasion. A negotiated solution based on a power-bargaining process would not last long as the discontented party wants to change the settlement terms in the future. Third party intervention can be assessed in terms of the degrees of their decision making power, types of their roles and other attributes (see Fig. 1). In judicial settlements and arbitration, the imposition of a third party decision does not help mend relations in considering a lack of direct form of communication between protagonists. Parties have more pressure in compulsory mediation ordered by courts than in voluntary settings. In negotiated rule making, consensus among different issues can be forged through technical analysis of problems and trade-offs of priorities. The merit of problem-solving workshops is related to its unconventional ability to change socio-psychological environments of participants.

Problem-solving Workshop — Consensus Decision Making — Mediation — Arbitration — Litigation

←——————————————→

Decrease — Increase

1. Degree of an authoritarian mode of decision making.
2. Chances of win/lose outcomes.
3. Significance of legal norms and facts.
4. Coercive implementation of decisions or agreements.

FIGURE 1 Third party intervention: Decision-making power, types of roles, and other attributes.

Mediation, court procedures, and arbitration can fit in a conventional framework of dispute settlement. Adjudication and arbitration support existing laws and norms. Especially in situations where a minority group develops nonconformity with the dominant values, courts, lawyers, public officials, and mediators tend to treat disputes in a superficial way. Adjudication is an adversarial process since the outcome often reflects a win-lose, zero-sum solution to the problem. Arbitration is not successful when value differences of participants exist. Facts and law cannot deal with emotional problems and incompatible values. While mediation often helps communication between parties, the process does not necessarily generate an understanding of the main cause of problems. Negotiated rule making is a better way to deal with policy disputes that have a broad impact on multiple stake holders. Harmonious social relations can be built by building a broad level of consensus in key public policy areas.

The adoption of specific skills depends not only on the sources of conflict but also the nature of the existing relationship between the parties. Building sustainable relationships is important in many of prenegotiation interventions. In negotiation, the perception and understanding of the situation are affected by the degree and quality of communication between negotiators. Disputes over material interests can be managed by clarifying facts or expanding resources. In some cases building communication may be enough to manage conflict. The existence of a contentious relationship hampers an analytical process of problem solving. The application of conflict management techniques to historical animosities produces limited, short-term solutions. Some conflict will never be resolved unless parties are willing to change the patterns of their interactions and realize the need for structural changes. Getting to the root causes of problems requires the analysis of perceptions, motives, and basic needs by parties. A nonauthoritarian and nonjudgmental mode of decision making is more helpful for reaching consensus. Facilitated methods are essential for finding options acceptable for different parties. A facilitator needs a wider knowledge base if the goal of conflict resolution is understood as problem solving. Mutual satisfaction requires innovative and flexible solutions made by the maximum involvement of participants.

V. CONCLUSION

If it is assumed that human beings are inherently evil and biologically aggressive, conflict management mechanisms based on control are likely to be seen as more appropriate. However, if conflict is considered innate in society, research on conflict resolution should pay more attention to broad social relationships. Conflicts need to be tackled at the source by an adequate understanding of human behavior and by appropriate processes. Much of the research and practice has not paid adequate attention to cultural issues, questions of social justice, and economic inequality as sources of conflict and problems to be resolved. For the last three decades, knowledge and practice of conflict analysis and resolution have been developed by educated, verbally skilled, middle-class professionals in Western industrialized societies. As we are entering the 21st century, the nature of human diversity is such that a creative approach to problem solving is essential. To this end, exposure to a wide range of theories and practices is important to the development of conflict management and resolution mechanisms.

Also See the Following Articles

CONFLICT THEORY • CONFLICT TRANSFORMATION • COOPERATION, COMPETITION, AND CONFLICT • MEDIATION AND NEGOTIATION TECHNIQUES • PEACEMAKING AND PEACEBUILDING • SOCIAL CONTROL AND VIOLENCE

Bibliography

Burton, J. W. (1996). *Conflict resolution: Its language and processes.* Lanham: The Scarecrow Press.

Burton, J. W. (1990). *Conflict: Resolution and provention.* New York: Macmillan.

Burton, J. W., & Dukes, F. (1990). *Conflict: Practices in management, settlement & resolution.* New York: MacMillan.

Caplan, P. (1995). *Understanding disputes: The politics of argument.* Oxford: Berg Publishers.

Fisher, W., & Ury, M. (1991). *Getting to yes.* (2nd Ed.). New York: Penguin Books.

Hampson, F. O. (1995). *Multilateral negotiations: Lessons from arms control, trade, and the environment.* Baltimore: The Johns Hopkins University Press.

Mitchell, C., & Banks, M. (1996). *Handbook of conflict resolution: The analytical problem-solving approach.* London: Pinter.

Ross, M. H. (1993). *The management of conflict: Interpretations and interests in comparative perspective.* New Haven: Yale University Press.

Sandole, D. J., & van der Merwe, H. (Eds.). *Conflict resolution theory and practice: Integration and application.* Manchester University Press: Manchester.

Conflict Theory

Roderick Ogley
University of Sussex and University of Bradford

GLOSSARY

Cardinal Payoffs Payoffs to a player expressed in terms of some absolute unit, as of money or years in jail.

Conflict a. An incompatibility in the interests, aims, or goals of two individuals or social units.

b. (or conflictful behavior) A reciprocated tendency, on the part of two individuals or social units, to hurt, damage, frustrate, or destroy the other.

Dogmatism Resistance to changing one's belief system, or world image.

Dominant Strategy In game theory, one strategy dominates another strategy for a player if it either yields better results, regardless of the choice of the other player, or is better for at least one choice of the other, and not worse for any.

Drama Theory A representation of conflict as a series of episodes, allowing for imperfect perceptions by the parties (characters), as in hypergames, and, between one episode and the next, changes in the parties' preferences among outcomes.

Hypergame A variation of game theory that abandons the assumption of perfect knowledge, allowing for situations where at least one party perceives options, for itself or for the other party, that had not occurred to the latter; or misperceives the other's preferences.

Metastrategy A strategy open to a player in a sequence of plays (repeated games), specifying the choice to be made in each play in the light of the choice of the other player in the preceding play.

Ordinal Payoffs Indications of a player's order of preference for the various possible outcomes of a game, the highest number being given to the most preferred and 1 to the least preferred.

Rational Choice Given the preferences of, and the options open to, the other party, a course of action that will yield to the party choosing it an outcome at least as good as that resulting from any other choice.

Strategy Any option open to a player in a game.

Unwilling Threat An indication by a threatener (source) that, unless the target meets its wishes, it will act disagreeably toward the target, where the action threatened is more punitive than the source's response to noncompliance would have been if it had not made the threat.

I. DEFINITION AND RAISON D'ETRE

Familiar though the word "conflict" is, it can in different contexts mean quite different things. On the one hand, it can refer to an incompatibility in the aims, goals, or interests of two or more individuals, groups, or other units ("actors"); on the other, to a kind of behavior, involving a proneness to hurt, damage, frustrate, or destroy some other actor or actors.

This is, essentially, the distinction Robert Axelrod made between "conflict of interest" and "conflictful behavior". This conflict of interest (or other incompatibility) can be seen as well-nigh ubiquitous in human life, and not, in itself, inherently destructive. Cultures differ in their appraisal of it. Western societies exalt such manifestations of conflict of interest as economic and political competition, or confrontational court proceedings (prosecution versus defense and plaintiff versus defendant), seeing its absence as conducive to inefficiency and worse. Many Eastern societies, especially those that have fallen under the influence of Buddhism, emphasize the importance of community, and when domestic and industrial disputes occur, adopt procedures designed to generate outcomes that all will find acceptable. It is, however, not with conflict of interest, as such, but with *conflictful behavior*, that this article is primarily concerned. Its occurrence, in any given situation, may or may not be explicable in terms of incompatibilities of aims, goals, or interests; it can even be wholly unilateral, as is shown in its extreme form by the Holocaust. The word conflict tends to be used of such behavior only when it is reciprocal, but that is merely a matter of usage. One-sided behavior of this kind should not be seen as a different phenomenon. In order to understand why people behave aggressively or ruthlessly *in a conflict* we may need to know what makes people aggressive in general.

Conflictful behavior may occur in many different contexts, such as family rows, bar brawls, strikes, kidnappings, or wars. Conflict theory assumes that it is instructive to explore the common elements and the differences that are observable in all these different manifestations of conflict.

The impetus towards conflict theory derived, historically, from revulsion against the destructiveness of the two world wars of the 20th century and awareness of the even greater devastation that, after the invention of nuclear weapons and their use against Japan in 1945, might attend a third. If war is one form of a more general phenomenon, conflict, then by understanding conflict it was thought that we might be better able to understand and thus control war.

Lewis Fry Richardson's pioneer works first appeared (but only in learned journals) in the interwar years. Otherwise, the subject took off with the 1957 launch of the *Journal of Conflict Resolution*, and the publication shortly afterwards of Anatol Rapoport's *Fights Games and Debates*, Thomas Schelling's *The Strategy of Conflict*, and Kenneth Boulding's *Conflict and Defense*.

II. CLASSIFICATION

Of the many scholarly classifications, that embodied in the title of Rapoport's book is perhaps the most penetrating. Rapoport sees these three categories as types of dyadic conflict, but they apply just as well, with simple changes of nomenclature, to unilaterally malign dispositions.

In fights, Rapoport says, we are dealing with "the operation of blind forces," where "it is ... altogether impossible to express the 'positions' of the opponents in words," and "the rational components of behaviour" do not come into play. Party A seeks to hurt, damage, frustrate, or destroy Party B—in short, to make Party B suffer—for its own sake, and vice versa. The hurt can be physical, financial, or even merely verbal, but what makes it a fight is that it cannot be explained as serving some other end.

The names Rapoport gave his other categories, though vivid, can mislead. He adopts the game theory concept of a game, implying *not* frivolity and relaxation, but seriousness, strategic calculation, and cold-bloodedness. This becomes less of a paradox if we keep in mind the distinction between the *activity* of game playing, and the behavior games model. Acting in the play *Macbeth* might be enjoyable, but being in the real situation depicted in the play would be terrifying. The game *Diplomacy*, based on the rivalries and crisis behavior of the European powers in the early years of the 20th century is fun to play, but the situation it depicts was momentous in its significance and catastrophic in its consequences. In a situation modeled as a game, then, any given player may act with great cruelty or ruthlessness, but it will be, for that player, a rational choice—that is, given the preferences of, and the options open to, any other player(s), it will produce an outcome that player would prefer to those resulting from any alternative choice. Conversely, a player may play cooperatively, but only if the results are at least as good for him or her as those attending any competitive alternative. The rationality attributed to the players is not deemed to be governed by any form of moral scruple.

The category of debates, too, can be far more savage than the image conjured by the word. Debates arise because parties differ in their beliefs about something they see as vitally important. The issue may be mundane, while still being a matter of life or death, such as whether smoking causes lung cancer or whether the building one is now in happens to be on fire; or it may be profound, and concern the direction the whole of the human race should take, as in the Crusades, or in the 20th-century conflicts over the spread or roll-back of Communism. In a debate, though, the brutality with which adherents of one creed will treat those they believe to have contradicted or defied it, or even slightly diverged from it, is directed toward the conversion of the renegade or heathen, or the vindication of the behaver's truth.

A given conflict may fall into more than one of these categories. Awareness of the classification liberates us from persisting in what otherwise proves a sterile line of reasoning. For instance, if we assume every conflict to be essentially a game, when we become embroiled in one the only questions we will ask will be how to deter the other side from doing X (which we do not want them to do) or how to reward them for doing Y (which we want them to do). Allowing for the possibility that it might be a fight or a debate, we may also ask "Is X something they do at a time of great emotional tension, without counting the consequences, and if so how can we reduce the chances of their again falling into this emotional state (thus seeing it as a fight)?" or "What are the beliefs they hold that lead them to do X or refuse to do Y, and is there any way in which we can show them, either that their beliefs are wrong, *or* that such beliefs do not require them to do X or abstain from Y (thus seeing it as a debate)?" Similarly, by assuming that all conflicts are fights, or (as Rapoport confesses he did earlier) that they are all debates, we neglect possibilities of analysis and amelioration which might be prompted by the categories they exclude.

As indicated earlier, Rapoport's three categories of dyadic conflict have obvious unilateral counterparts. One person may be more prone to engage in fights (whether with weapons, fists or words) than another; the same person may be more prone to do so in some circumstances than in others, or more disposed to choose certain targets than other targets; to understand why, we need to study aggressiveness. One person may be more cold-blooded than another, good at getting others to do what he or she wants, less susceptible to the pressures of emotional and ideological ties, and have no, or fewer, qualms about betraying friends and principles—in other words, that person may be more Machiavellian. Again, we need to know why. And some people, or groups, or institutions may be more inspired with missionary zeal than others, more liable to believe that they have learned a truth that needs to be taught to the rest of the world, and, in the course of seeking to impose their truths on others, to resort to such malign practices as inquisitions and brainwashing.

Thus to the three categories of dyadic conflict, namely fights, games, and debates, we may add three corresponding sources of unilateral ill-will; aggressiveness, manipulativeness, and ideological coerciveness, which lead us into the themes on which A.G. Davies focuses in his "psychoanalytical contribution to the study of politics," *Skills, Outlooks and Passions* ("skills" for manipulativeness, "outlooks" for ideological coerciveness, and "passions" for aggressiveness).

III. FIGHTS AND AGGRESSIVENESS

Since fights are bilateral manifestations of aggressiveness, we first need to account for human aggressiveness and the variations in its incidence. Five theories can be identified:

A. Aggression as a need
B. Aggression as a product of frustration
C. Aggression as socially learned
D. Cognitive theories of aggression
E. Aggression fanned by ambivalence toward violence.

A. Aggression as a Need

It is often argued that human beings, like animals, have a need for aggression. For this to be plausible, either aggression must be very widely defined (to include, for instance, digging the garden), or the need can be met by low levels of it. In any case, it is not clear that animals have such a need. The aggressiveness of baboon troops, for instance, varies markedly with their history and geography. Nor, among human beings, are the inhabitants of countries that have kept out of war for long periods, such as Sweden and Switzerland, more than averagely aggressive, or those who engage in physically aggressive sports less so in other contexts. There does seem, however, to be a phenomenon of overcontrol. The perpetrators of some particularly violent and brutal crimes were reported by those who did not know what they had done or had gone on to do as "well-behaved and unaggressive." Their explosions into violence could be explained in two ways. Either we do all have some modest need to express aggression, and theirs was not being met, or, in their "overcontrolled" state, they were frustrated in respect of other needs, such as those for sex and for self-esteem.

B. Frustration-Aggression Theory

Evidence that aggressiveness is often, if not always, a consequence of frustration is more convincing. The lynchings of Blacks in the U.S. "cotton" states in the interwar years, for instance, were consistently more frequent in times of economic depression than in times of prosperity. Frustration is not, however, simply the denial of needs, such as those of food and sleep, but includes interference with a goal-response, which depends on expectations. If expectations are low, frustration with a given state of affairs will be low. What it does is to create *instigations* to aggression, which may be inhibited by social and prudential restraints.

C. Social Learning Theory

One great strength of social learning theory is that it promises to explain aggressiveness we engage in for sport, such as teasing, bullying, or hunting, or for sexual stimulation, that is, sadism. We behave, it says, as we have learned to behave, either by imitating those presented to us as models or by being rewarded for some kinds of behavior and punished for others. We do either what everyone else is doing—tease the new boy, or the odd one out—or what wins approval or some other reward. Punishment *can* teach us not to do things, particularly if it follows the forbidden act immediately and with near certainty; but corporal punishment offers a model of violence that could weaken and even outweigh its deterrent effect. Social learning theory is thus good at explaining how we may come to enjoy hurtful acts, if psychologically rewarded for them, and it can also explain, not *why* we become angry, but what we do when we *are* angry—punch, snap, swear, or sulk. We learn our habits from others and they are hard to break without help.

We do not merely *imitate* others in their aggressive behavior. As Stanley Milgram showed in a chilling series of experiments in the United States and elsewhere, we can be induced to harm people for no good reason when told to do so by others conveying an impression of authority. His subjects were supposedly participating, a pair at a time, in an experiment designed to test the effectiveness of punishment in learning. In each pair, one was a stooge, and he was assigned the role of "learner." When the "learner" answered wrongly, the subject, as "teacher" was asked to press buttons giving shocks of ever-increasing voltage, culminating in one labeled "extremely dangerous." In the United States, when the "learner" was in a separate room, 26 out of 40 subjects complied, in spite of the victim's screams and pleas of heart trouble. In fact the "victim" was an actor, and no actual shocks were given, but the deception was effective. Many subjects protested, in some distress, at what they were told to do, but still did it. By embarking on an experiment in a hierarchical setting, Milgram explains, they had entered a "state of agency" where "conscience is diminished and they define themselves as instruments for carrying out the wishes of others."

There is, however, more to learning than simply following models, or obeying orders, or even seeking rewards or avoiding punishments. Kittens raised in the company of rats do not kill them, even when hungry, or when observing adult rats killing them. Habits of bullying and jeering at those with obvious disabilities can be unlearned if we mix with them in such a way as to become conscious of them as people, and thus empathize with them. But social learning theory cannot explain *all* aggression. Not all ill will manifests itself by the use of learned techniques. The malicious can invent their own by, for instance, deliberately or absent-mindedly omitting to transmit information important to someone else's goals or welfare.

D. Cognitive Theories of Aggression

Aggressiveness can also be triggered by a belief that someone has, without adequate justification, violated some norm we value; but whether this will lead to our feeling slighted and bearing long-standing grudges will depend on personality factors such as whether we are prone to jump to conclusions, inclined to blame people rather than situations for disasters, and feel vulnerable. At the extreme, there are those who respond to some political laxity or wrong doing with what Heinz Kohut has called "narcissistic rage". The offender is seen as "a flaw in the narcissistically-perceived reality." The ferocity of such reactions needs explaining, at least in part, in terms that go beyond the nature of the offence that provoked it, that is, as aggression displaced from elsewhere.

E. Aggression Fanned by Our Ambivalence toward Violence

Psychiatrists often stress the damaging consequences of our inability to accept the ambivalence with which we view violence. While professing political or religious views that explicitly forbid it, we remain fascinated by it, and when it appears to have been suddenly given legitimacy, as in war, there can be huge swings of mood and people are ready to endorse much violence that serves no instrumental purpose. To control our behavior we need to be aware of and accept the ambivalence of our emotions.

Not surprisingly, a manifestation of aggressiveness by A toward B may elicit a similar response by B toward A. This may stimulate increased hostility of A to B, and, in turn, of B to A. This reciprocated growth in aggressiveness, otherwise known as escalation, is the essence of a fight.

One measureable approximation to the phenomenon of explosively expanding mutual hostility is the bidding in a "both-pay auction". This game, where a prize is auctioned and sold to the highest bidder, while the two highest bidders *both* have to pay what they have bid, neatly encapsulates the logic of wars, strikes, and other destructive conflicts. Experiments with such auctions show that the two highest bidders usually bid more between them, and often more individually, then they think the prize is worth. Thus if they have bid 95 cents for the "prize" of a dollar, and seen "the other bidder" bid a dollar, they will already have lost 95 cents if they pull out. Rationally, at any given point they should coolly consider: "Am I likely to have to bet a *further* dollar, or more, in order to win the dollar?" and if the answer is yes, they should pull out. In fact, they often do what parties to a war or a strike often do in such circumstances, and, impelled by the emotional pressure of the loss they have already incurred, fight, that is bid, on. They have "too much invested to quit." Of course, any inference about real-world conflicts drawn from the results of experiments must be treated with caution. If monetary gains are trivial, for instance, subjects' choices may be made out of boredom, curiosity, or playfulness; but the phenomenon here described seems well substantiated.

IV. GAMES

Game theory explores the question of how far conflictful behavior, as defined earlier, can be explained through analyzing the *structure* of the participants' situation, that is, by identifying and even, where meaningful, measuring incompatibilities in their aims or interests, or incentives for one or more of them to act to the disadvantage of the other or others. Thus to classify a situation as a game is to imply that it is these incompatibilities and incentives that are important, and not their emotional vicissitudes, or philosophical, religious, or moral beliefs.

Before we can present a conflict or some aspect of it as a "game," we have to specify, first, how many players there are in it; second, what options (strategies) are open to each; third, in what order of preference each player would rank the consequences of each theoretically possible combination of choices, that is to say, each outcome; and finally, whether the situation involves simultaneous or successive moves by the parties. The simplest game would be one in which there were two players, each having two strategies (which could simply mean that there was something that the player could either do or not do). This would give four outcomes for each player. The payoffs for each outcome can either be ordinal, simply indicating where that outcome ranks in the player's order of preference, or cardinal, that is specifying how much money or other "good" or "bad" the player would receive from it.

Take the Chicken Game, for instance, where cars hurtle toward each other in the middle of the road, and crash, unless at least one swerves. Simultaneously, each driver has to choose whether or not to swerve. While a crash would be the worst outcome for both drivers, each would lose face by swerving and gain face by making the other swerve.

The matrix in Figure 1, uses ordinal payoffs, since cardinal payoffs would be arbitrary. (How much is "face" worth, compared with the cost and injuries a crash might inflict?) It represents the situation at the point where each driver has his last chance of swerving. For each player, "4" is the best outcome and "1" the worst. Thus the outcome in which neither driver swerves is the worst for both parties. Similar structures

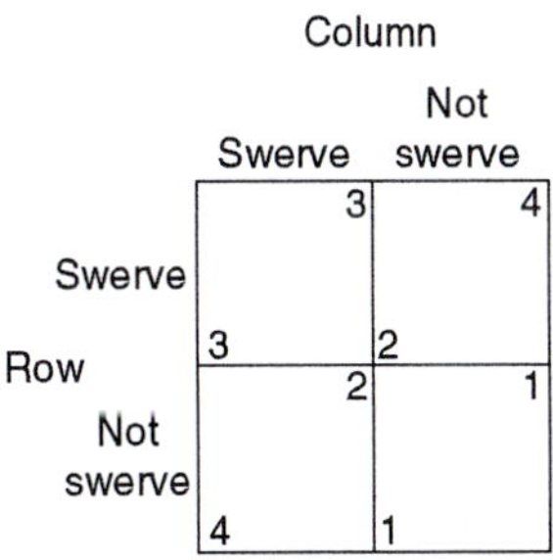

FIGURE 1 The Chicken Game. The two players are Column, who chooses between the left and right columns and Row, who chooses between the top and bottom rows. The payoff to Column for each combination of choices is in the top right-hand corner of the appropriate small square, and that to Row in the bottom left-hand corner.

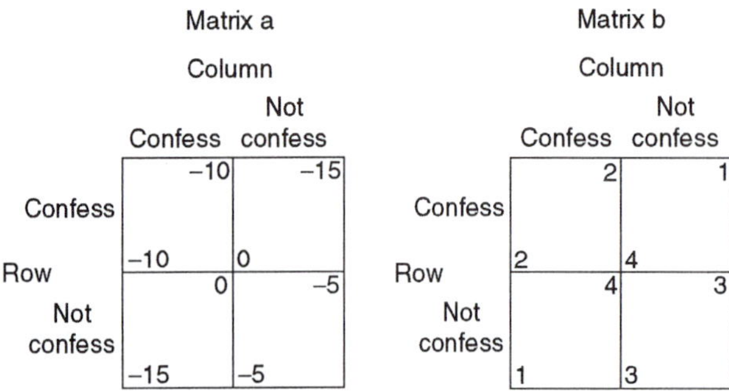

FIGURE 2 The Prisoner's Dilemma.

Matrix a: A matrix consistent with the original story, with negative cardinal payoffs.

Matrix b: The Prisoner's Dilemma matrix in ordinal form.

can frequently be seen in international, intercommunal, industrial, and even interpersonal confrontations, where at least one party has to "swerve" to avoid what both recognize as mutual disaster, and each decides not to out of a misplaced confidence that the other will.

A game with a rather different structure is the Prisoner's Dilemma. Two suspects are interrogated separately and invited to confess to a major crime they committed together; for one to "confess" will provide the police with the evidence they need to convict the other. If each confesses they will get 10 years; if neither, they can be convicted of a less serious crime and get 5 years each; if only one confesses, enabling the nonconfessing partner to be convicted, the latter gets 15 years, while the confessor, in return for "helping the police", goes free. We thus get the matrices shown in Figure 2.

Here (negative) cardinal payoffs make sense—they represent years in jail. Here a rational player will confess. If we first consider Row, his calculation would be: if Column confesses (chooses the L column), I get 10 years for also confessing, and 15 years for not confessing—better confess, in that case; if Column *doesn't* confess (chooses the R column), I get free by confessing, and thus implicating Column, and 5 years for not confessing. Again, better confess. So, I don't need to know what Column will do; I am better off confessing in either case. Column, of course, calculates similarly. The result is, they both get 10 years when, had neither confessed, they could have escaped with 5.

A strategy that is best for a player no matter what the other chooses, like that of confessing in the Prisoner's Dilemma, is said to be dominant. Game theory assumes rationality, meaning that, at least in a game played only once, players with dominant strategies will always choose them.

Chicken and Prisoner's Dilemma can be seen, in their ordinal forms, as two families of games. Rapoport and Guyer have shown that there are 78 of these families of two-person, two-strategy games where each player can put the four possible outcomes in a strict order of preference—that is, one in which no two, or more, outcomes are ranked equally.

Conflict theory can use game theory in two ways. It can either take a real-life "game-like" situation and try to construct a matrix that represents it as closely as possible, and then analyze the game that emerges; or it can experiment with very simple abstract games, using either human subjects, or computers playing according to pre-set strategies, and thereby test hypotheses about the conditions that might be most conducive to conflict behavior, as opposed to cooperation.

The Prisoner's Dilemma has become the most popular tool for the latter project, since choice of the "Don't Confess" strategy can be seen as the epitome of cooperation. Suppose we add 15 units to every payoff in Matrix a of Figure 2. Although the original story would not now apply, this is still within the Prisoner's Dilemma family of games since it leaves the *order* in which each player would rank the outcomes unaffected. (See Fig. 3.)

Experiment has confirmed two broad propositions suggested by a priori speculation. First, choice of the dominant, selfishly rational, strategies (here Top or Left) rather than the cooperative ones (Bottom or Right), which we can regard as conflictful behavior, is more likely, the greater the conflict of interest in the matrix. In a matrix with cardinal payoffs, conflict of interest can be measured by comparing the gaps between a party's best and second-best payoffs (the temptation to defect), and between its third-best and worst payoffs (the vulnerability to the other's defection) with that between its second-best and third-best payoffs (the incentive for cooperation). When the incentive to cooperate is low relative to either or both of the other two

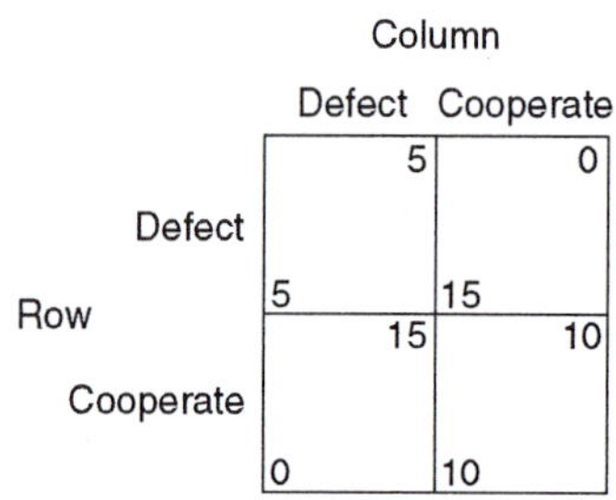

FIGURE 3 The Prisoner's Dilemma with positive cardinal payoffs.

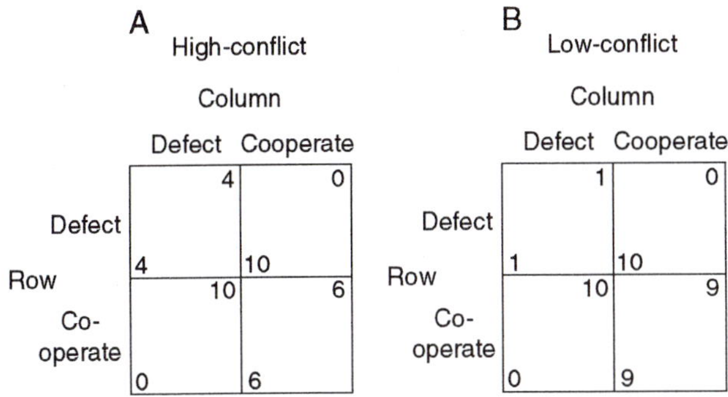

FIGURE 4 High Conflict and Low Conflict Prisoner's Dilemma Games.

In (A) the players each gain 2 units more if they both cooperate than if they both defect, but for any given choice of the other, each would gain 4 units by defecting.

In (B) the players each gain 8 units more if they both cooperative, but for a given choice of the other each would gain only 1 unit by defecting.

gaps, the degree of conflict of interest can be said to be high, and vice versa. (See Fig. 4.)

Second, for any given matrix, cooperation by rational players requires a *linking* of the players' choices. If they could communicate, they could agree to choose cooperatively; but at the point of choice, they could still go back on their agreement, unless it is enforceable. If, however, the parties expect to play this same game a large number of times, there is another route to cooperation. Rapoport proposed that either, or both, parties follow a "Tit-for-Tat" principle—cooperating on the first move, and thereafter choosing on each move what the other player chose the previous move. In this way each player can give the other an incentive to cooperate. Cooperation thereby becomes rational.

Tit-for-Tat is a metastrategy, that is, a strategy that specifies the choices a player will make in a *sequence* of plays of the same game, given, at each play, a knowledge of the choices of the other player on the previous play. Axelrod showed that in a computer tournament open to all metastrategies anyone cared to propose, it was the most successful in eliciting cooperation. However, in all these experiments with repeated games, one condition most conductive to cooperation was maintained. The matrix for each play remained exactly the same, in scale as well as in other respects, throughout. The gain from defecting in any one trial would be small compared with the gains from continued cooperation in a large series of subsequent plays. If in some plays the payoffs for all outcomes were much higher than in others, say by a factor of 20, the temptation to defect in those plays would be greatly increased.

The success of Tit-for-Tat in "iterated" Prisoner's Dilemma games has two practical applications. First, if two parties can see a Prisoner's Dilemma-like situation recurring indefinitely in their relations, either or both could proclaim a Tit-for-Tat metastrategy and offer the other an incentive to cooperate, with little risk, and with a good prospect of developing a pattern of cooperation. Second, if a single momentous arrangement with a Prisoner's Dilemma structure, such as a comprehensive disarmament agreement between superpowers, could be broken down into many stages, so that each party would know whether the other had done what it promised to do at one stage before implementing the next, and no one stage is so crucial that one party, by cheating on it, could establish a significant strategic advantage, either party could adopt a Tit-for-Tat metastrategy and give them both incentives implement the agreement, stage-by-stage. (It is assumed that both prefer a "disarmed" parity to a heavily armed parity, but that what each would *most* prefer would be an outcome where *it* remained armed while the other side was disarmed, and what it would *least* like would be the reverse, where *it* disarmed while the other remained armed.)

V. THREATS

Threats typically commit the threatener (the source), in the event of noncompliance by the threatened party (the target), to respond to it more punitively than they would otherwise have done. (Similarly, promises—"If you do this, I will give you that"—commit the promiser, in the event of *compliance*, to respond more favorably than they otherwise would have). Three stages are involved. First, the threatener (the source) indicates, tacitly or explicitly, that it will do something disagreeable to the target if the latter fails to comply with the latter's wishes or commands; then the target either conforms to those wishes or commands, or does not; and if not, then the source either implements, or does not implement, its threat. (See Fig. 5.)

If a target is rational (in the game theory sense), a threat must meet two requirements if it is to influence that target to comply with the threatener's wishes. First, assuming the threat was necessary—that there was some possibility that, without it, the target might have disregarded these wishes, it needs to be adequate. The target must prefer the situation constituting compliance to the situation that would follow if it did not comply and the threat was implemented. Second, it must be

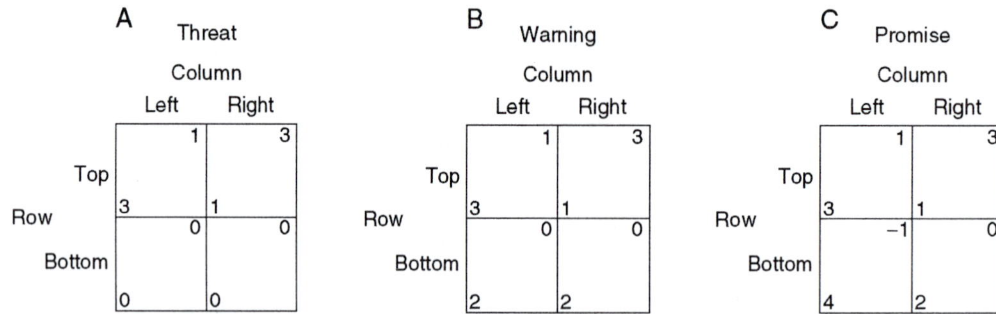

FIGURE 5 Threats, warnings, and promises

In (A), for Row to say to Column "If you choose R, I will choose Bottom" would be to depart from the logic of the matrix, since if Column *did* choose R, Row would be better off choosing Top (and getting 1) rather than Bottom (getting 0). This is what makes it a threat.

In (B), for Row to make the same statement to Column as in (A) would now simply explain the implications of the matrix, since if Column *did* choose R, Row would get a higher payoff (2) for choosing Bottom than for choosing Top (1). It is thus a warning.

There is also scope for "assurance." Row can assure Column that if Column chooses L, Row will choose Top, giving Column 1 instead of 0.

In (C), Bottom is dominant for Row and Right is dominant for Column. To persuade Column to choose L, Row would need to do two things: *warn* that if Column chooses R, Row will choose Bottom (which accords with the logic of the matrix), and *promise* that if Column chooses L, Row will choose Top (which does not). That is what makes it a promise rather than an assurance.

credible. The target must believe that, in the event of noncompliance, it will, or at least *may*, be carried out.

Schelling suggested that to make a threat credible, the threatener needs somehow to worsen the payoff to himself that would follow if he failed to implement it. The more public the commitment and the better the source's reputation for carrying out threats or other undertakings it may have made, the more it would lose by nonimplementation of a threat once made. Alternatively, it could bet that it would implement it, and so lose money if it did not; or it could create a situation in which, in the event of noncompliance, it might be unable to prevent implementation even if it wanted to. But while all these devices might well increase a threat's credibility, for a rational target they also all tend to worsen the source's predicament if the target does *not* comply.

Even if a threat can be made both adequate and (objectively) credible, in the sense that the target has been given good reason to think it would be implemented in the event of noncompliance, it may not work. First, the target may not receive the threat or it may fail to interpret it correctly; or it may be unable to control its behavior; or it may panic; or it may regard the very fact that the demand is accompanied by a threat as a violation of its integrity, and as opening it to the possibility of having to comply with other demands under threat in the future. Finally, even if a threat *does* work, it may sour the source's relationship with the target.

That is not to say that threats are never advisable. All penal sanctions are threats. So are fines for the late return of library books. Some arouse little indignation and almost certainly improve law-abidingness and other forms of rule observance. Others seem to have little, if any, effect on the incidence of the crimes for which they are imposed.

Nevertheless, threats address *symptoms* of noncompliant (and often aggressive) behavior, rather than *causes*. They epitomize a relationship of power, in the sense used by Karl Deutsch, as implying "the ability not to have to learn." Securing acceptable behavior by means of threats can be, for the threatener, a substitute for the more crucial task of discovering *why* the target tends to behave so unacceptably.

Personality also seems to have some effect on the likelihood of a person using, or complying with, threats. Those who, in response to questionnaires, revealed an outlook on life consistent with Machiavelli's—"High-Machs"—were adept at threatening and exploiting others in other ways; and were prepared to comply with the adequate and credible threats of others. They are, predictably, less sensitive to norms; whereas others—"Low-Machs"—will retaliate against breaches of norms even at cost to themselves, "High-Machs" would not, and would indeed be likely to breach the norm themselves if they could get away with it.

VI. HYPERGAME THEORY AND DRAMA THEORY

More recently, theories of conflict have emerged that spring from game theory but relax one or more of its characteristic assumptions. Among the most promising of these are hypergame theory and drama theory.

Hypergame theory, developed by Bennett (1977), abandons the assumption of perfect knowledge, and explores cases where at least one party perceives options for itself or for the other party that had not occurred to the latter; or misperceives the other's preferences, believing it to prefer Outcome O_1, to Outcome O_2, when it in fact prefers O_2 to O_1. (See Figure 6.)

Thus, if this hypergame analysis of the crisis were correct, each party was making a rational decision according to its own perception of the crisis.

Drama theory, developed by Howard, Bennett, Bryant, and Bradley (1992), not only follows hypergame theory in allowing for differing perceptions by different players (or "characters"); it also allows for characters to change their preferences as the drama unfolds. It sees a conflict as passing through a series of stages—scene-setting, build-up, climax, resolution, and denouement. Initially, some characters may see the drama through different "frames". As they enter "the stage," communicate and interact, they come to approach a common frame but without, so far, any changes in preferences among the possible outcomes. This process is called an "episode," but it culminates in a climax in which there will be change in the characters' positions (that is, preferences).

In this theory, a conflict has times of stability (or attrition) and times of change. In the latter, a character's preferences will be affected by the "unwilling" threats and promises it makes. (An unwilling threat is simply a threat, as opposed to a warning, as explained earlier in Fig. 5, and an unwilling promise, similarly, is a promise as opposed to an assurance). The theory claims that having made a threat or a promise, a character tends to change its preferences so that it does actually want to fulfill it. Thus in a Chicken game, one driver

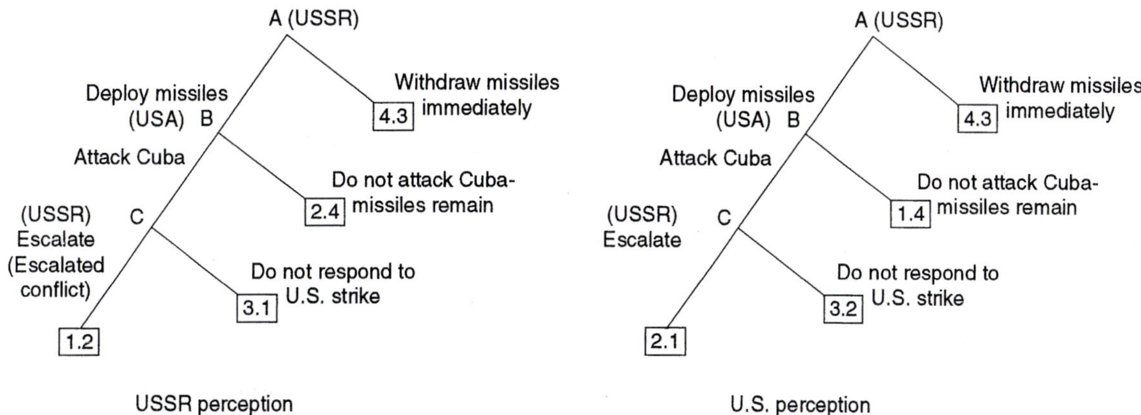

FIGURE 6 A Hypergame Explanation for the Soviet Decision to Continue to Deploy Missiles in Cuba after their Presence had been Discovered by the United States.

The left-hand "tree" represents Soviet perceptions and preferences, the right-hand, American perceptions and preferences. In each case, the "game" starts at the top, and has three decision points, A, B, and C. The right-hand choice, in each case, would end the crisis; the left-hand choice implies escalation. The numbers in the rectangular boxes represent the supposed (ordinal) payoffs to the United States (given first) and the USSR.

The left-hand tree implies that Soviet decision makers judged that the most-preferred outcome of the United States would be where the USSR withdrew the missiles immediately (payoff 4), its second-best would be where, although the USSR did not withdraw them, the United States attacked Cuba without provoking Soviet retaliation (payoff 3), its third-best would be where it allowed the missiles to remain and did *not* attack Cuba (payoff 2), and its *least-preferred* outcome where it attacked Cuba and provoked Soviet retaliation (payoff 1). The right-hand tree, however, showing U.S. perceptions, implies that while the USSR was right about the first and second preferences of the United States, the U.S. decision makers would have preferred the escalatory outcome resulting from Soviet retaliation against a U.S. attack on Cuba (payoff 2) to allowing the missiles to remain in place without launching such an attack (payoff 1). This was crucial. Figure 6 also implies an American misperception of Soviet preferences, whereby they judged that the USSR would also prefer not to respond to an American attack on Cuba (payoff 2), to escalation (payoff 1), whereas in reality, the contrary was the case. Thus each side believed its own decision to stand firm would *not* lead to escalation.

might "threaten" to drive straight on, without swerving, in order to get the other driver to swerve, while still preferring to swerve rather than crash, but the very act of making the threat ("If you don't swerve, I'll make sure we crash"), could cause a change in his preferences so that he now prefers the crash to the dishonor of being the one to swerve first, coupled now with the further dishonor of being shown to be bluffing. Conversely, promising a "cease-fire" in return for some other concession could make a character actually want to deliver it, even if strategic gains could have been made by the continuation or resumption of hostilities.

These changes in preferences are accompanied, according to drama theory, by changes in one's attitude to the other side. One's threats increase one's hostility, one's promises diminish it. In contrast to traditional game theory, where words are seen as no substitute for actions, and one's rational choice was determined by the actual options and payoffs, here words are potent. Even if deceitful and insincere, they do not leave a character's position unchanged. They have their cost.

If drama theory is right in positing an alternation between "build-up" and "climax," the timing of proposals becomes important, leading to attempts to specify the features of a conflict that indicate that it is ripe for change. It also suggests that the acceptability of a given action in a conflict may depend on its dramatic appropriateness, in terms of the way the characters view themselves and each other.

In terms of our original classification, drama theory tries to *include* the fight and debate elements with the strategic or gamelike ones, rather than subjecting each to separate analysis, according to the extent to which either would fit a given case of malign or conflict behavior. It should not, however, let us forget that a party's, or character's perception of a situation, or manifestations of aggression, may derive from factors outside the situation.

VII. DEBATES AND THE IMPOSITION OF TRUTH

That we frustrate, damage, hurt, or even kill others as a result of our beliefs is, as indicated earlier, painfully obvious from any survey of the Crusades, the religious wars, the Inquisition, and the 20th-century political practice of "brainwashing". This fact prompts two questions: (A) Why do beliefs, or "belief-systems" come to be so entrenched in people? (B) Why do such "believers" use such malign methods to spread their beliefs?

A The Entrenchment of Beliefs

Beliefs enable us to make sense of the world, but once we have adopted them we tend to hold onto them, particularly if we are prone to two aspects of this trait, mental rigidity or closed-mindedness (also known as dogmatism). Rigidity describes the extent to which we stick to *specific* beliefs, dogmatism our resistance to changing our belief systems, or world images. Changing the latter is particularly difficult, because of the emotional commitments with which they have been shored up. We hold them because they offer us security, and often dare not look at alternatives. Rigidity tends to impair our analytical skills, dogmatism our capacity for creative synthesizing.

Our beliefs, and our values, are affected by much that is irrational. If we try to make sense of something prematurely—that is, before we have the necessary evidence—and our belief happens to be false, we persist in it even when we have the evidence with which to correct it. We also stick to views that comfort us—such as that the city that we live in is healthy, or that the make of car we have just bought is far superior to its rivals; and we are particularly prone, in accordance with what is known as "justification of effort" theory, to value highly experiences that cost us much effort, pain, or embarrassment to qualify for.

The belief systems of the closed-minded tend to be compartmentalized, and even inconsistent. What holds the constituent beliefs together is the fact that they emanate from a source believed to be authoritative. To find out about other belief systems they would go to their fellow believers, not to adherents of the belief in question. These features are signs of anxiety, "mechanisms ... designed to shield a vulnerable mind." The closed-minded avoid ambivalence, and tended to see their parents as perfect, rather as mixtures of good and bad.

In its extreme form closed-mindedness can prompt arbitrary reinterpretations of seemingly contrary evidence. One group believed that North America would be wholly destroyed on December 21, 1955. When this did not happen, they announced that the continent had been saved by their faith and unprecedented virtue, and immediately sought new converts.

B. Hostile Action in Support of Beliefs

There are several reasons why people's belief systems might lead them to take hostile action against those with different views. They might hope for forcible conversion. They might want to silence them, thus preventing them from converting others, or to punish them so as to deter others from dissenting openly. The plan might be to ensure that future generations will be brought up in the orthodox faith rather than in that of the dissidents; or they may, like those in the throes of the "narcissistic rage" mentioned earlier, see such action (the *fatwa* against Salman Rushdie, for instance) as in itself being demanded by their faith.

Three characteristics would tend to make a belief system likely to lead its adherents to engage in violent or harmful action toward others: being seen as universal in its application (that is proclaiming a "truth" everyone should accept); including among its tenets a belief in an enemy—the AntiChrist, or capitalism—who could be blamed for all internal opposition and dissent; and urgency—the eschatological view that the universe is about to be transformed, so that drastic, immediate remedies must be applied before it is too late.

Naturally, a belief system with such characteristics would tend to alarm those who did not share it. *Satyagraha* campaigns, like those of Gandhi in India and Ghaffar Khan in Pashtunistan (now split between Pakistan and Afghanistan), in the years before and during the Second World War, sought, by renouncing violence and initiating supportive acts aimed at winning over opponents to persuade all with whom they dealt that *their* belief system did not have this hostile dimension to it. As Gandhi put it:

> Satyagraha is a process of conversion. The reformers ... do not seek to force their views on the community; they strive to touch its heart.

This conversion process often involved civil disobedience, prompting severe and violent reactions from opponents, but such conversion, as Gandhi interpreted it, was *not* a one-way process. Though a protagonist of *satyagraha* was expected to withstand such manifestations of hostility to the death, if need be, he or she was entitled to revise opinions and goals, if persuaded of their falsity.

Thus with *satyagraha*, the underlying theory of conflict attributed wrongdoing to ignorance. When officials, and others, behaved callously or unjustly, it was because they did not fully understand what they were doing. One could say that their consciousness needed to be raised. The prescribed remedy was to oppose actions deemed to be unjust in ways that never ceased to acknowledge the humanity of those responsible for such unjust actions.

Such theory was part of a worldview, developed as a basis for action; it was not thought of as being subject to a process of empirical testing.

VIII. THE RESOLUTION OR MITIGATION OF CONFLICT

Attempts to resolve or mitigate conflict, or indeed even asymmetric or wholly one-sided hostile behavior, depend for their success on accurately diagnosing the category or categories into which it falls.

In a fight, where hostile action is primarily attributable to hostile emotions such as resentment or hatred, and where it is not possible physically to restrain the participants, it is necessary to induce a change in the feelings of one or both of them.

In gamelike bilateral conflicts, tacit or explicit bargaining can sometimes create capsules of restraint. Gas, in the Second World War, was tacitly outlawed because both sides knew that, if either used it, the other could and would have retaliated in kind and neither would gain. Explicit bargaining gives the parties the chance to gauge each other's underlying concerns (though they will be tempted to misrepresent those concerns for strategic purposes). They may then have scope, not merely for *distributive* bargaining—deciding, for instance, what percentage payraise a category of workers should have, with one side wanting the highest possible and the other the lowest, but also for *integrative* bargaining, where the deal reached is, for both sides, an improvement on what they originally contemplated.

Debates are resolved, according to Rapoport, only when those trying to impose their views are able to grasp the element of truth in the outlooks of those who disagree with them. To do this, he contends, they must feel that their own views have been understood and acknowledged to have a "region of validity," which moves the discussion onto where the boundary lies between the regions of validity of the contending truths.

Also See the Following Articles

AGGRESSION, PSYCHOLOGY OF • CONFLICT MANAGEMENT AND RESOLUTION • CONFLICT TRANSFORMATION • DECISION THEORY AND GAME THEORY • DETERRENCE THEORY • DIPLOMACY • NONVIOLENT ACTION

Bibliography

Allan, P., and Schmidt, C. (Eds.). (1994). *Game theory and international relations: Preferences, information and empirical evidence.* Aldershot: Edward Elgar.

Axelrod, R. (1970). *Conflict of interest*. Chicago: Markham.
Axelrod, R. (1984). *The evolution of cooperation*. New York: Basic Books.
Bennett, P. G. (1977). Towards a theory of hypergames. *Omega*, 5: 749–751.
Bennett, P. G. (1987). *Analysing conflict and its resolution*. Oxford: Oxford University Press.
Bennett, P. G. (1995). Modelling decisions in international relations: game theory and beyond. *Mershon International Studies Review*, *39*, 19–52.
Bondurant, J. V. (Revised Edition 1965). *Conquest of Violence: The Gandhian Philosophy of Conflict*. Berkeley: University of California Press.
Boulding, K. (1963). *Conflict and defense*. New York: Harper Torchback.
Christie, R., and Geis, F. L. (1970). *Studies in Machiavellism*. New York: Academic.
Davies, A. G. (1980). *Skills, outlooks and passions*. Cambridge: Cambridge University Press.
Galtung, J. (1996). *Peace by peaceful means*. Oslo: International Peace Research Institute.
Howard, N., Bennett, P. G., Bryant, J. W., and Bradley, M. (1992). Manifesto for a theory of drama and irrational choice. *Journal of the Operational Research Society*, *44*:99-103, and *Systems Practice*, *6*: 429-434.
Kohut, H. (1972). Narcissism and narcissistic rage. *Psychological Study of the Child*, 360-400.
Megargee, E. I., and Hokanson, J. E., (Eds.) (1970) *The dynamics of aggression*. New York: Harper and Row.
Milgram, S. (1974). *Obedience to authority*. New York: Harper and Row.
Nicholson, M. (1992). *Rationality and the analysis of international conflict*. Cambridge: Cambridge University Press.
Ogley, R. (1991). *Conflict under the microscope*. Aldershot: Avebury, (Also Brookfield, USA.)
Rapoport, A. (1960). *Fights, games and debates*. Ann Arbor: University of Michigan Press.
Rapoport, A., and Guyer, M. (1966). A taxonomy of 2×2 games. *General Systems*, *11*.
Rokeach, M. (1960). *The open and closed mind*. New York: Basic Books.
Schelling, T. (1963). *The strategy of conflict*. Oxford: Oxford University Press Galaxy Books.
Teger, A. I. (1980). *Too much invested to quit*. New York: Pergamon.

Conflict Transformation

Louis Kriesberg
Syracuse University

GLOSSARY

Conflict De-escalation A decrease in the scope or number of parties engaged and/or in the severity of the means used in a conflict.

Conflict Resolution, Problem-Solving The process of concluding a dispute or conflict in which the adversary parties, with or without the assistance of mediators, negotiate or otherwise strive toward a mutually acceptable agreement or understanding, taking into account each other's concerns. It often entails reframing the conflict so that it is regarded as a shared problem.

Constructive Conflicts Conflicts are waged constructively insofar as the means are not violent, but rely on persuasion and positive sanctions as well as coercive ones and insofar as the adversaries recognize each other as legitimate and seek a mutually acceptable outcome of their conflict; that recognition may refer to the entity the leaders purport to represent, but not to the leaders.

Destructive Conflicts Conflicts are conducted destructively insofar as the means used are severe and many participants suffer great harm, insofar as the scale of conflict expands, insofar as one or more sides believes that its survival is threatened, and insofar as the conflict becomes self-perpetuating.

Hurting Stalemate When none of the primary adversaries in a struggle is winning and none expects that the situation will change so as to enable it to triumph, and the situation is unsatisfactory and even painful.

CONFLICT TRANSFORMATION refers to a fundamental and enduring change away from a protracted, destructive struggle between adversaries toward a constructive accommodation between them. That changed relationship may be a mutually satisfactory resolution of their conflict and may lead to reconciliation between them; or the new relationship may be embodied in an ongoing conflict, but one that is conducted more constructively. Conflict transformation refers to the process of change and also to the relationship resulting from that process. At various points during the transformation process, a conflict may be regarded as having become transformed.

Among the many cases of conflict transformation, several large-scale transformations may be cited illustratively. In the United States, labor-management struggles at the end of the 19th century and during the early part of the 20th century were marked by violence and the refusal by employers to recognize trade unions, but these struggles were transformed in the 1930s as collective bargaining became institutionalized. The struggles by African-Americans to achieve equality of civil rights was particularly intense in the 1960s; consequently, the numerous local struggles in the South and national legislation transformed that struggle. In South Africa, the struggle to against apartheid and the disenfranchisement of Blacks was transformed in the early 1990s. Internationally, the ending of the Cold War between the United States and the Union of Soviet Socialist Republics during the late 1980s marked a fundamental transformation, ending with the dissolution of the USSR.

There are, of course, other kinds of fundamental changes in a conflict that are not generally termed transformation. Thus, a conflict may escalate into a great violence after a long period of well-regulated struggle; but in this discussion, transformation refers to a particular kind of conflict de-escalation. Some forms of de-escalation are not regarded as transformations; for example, the crushing defeat of one side by the other can result in a fundamental de-escalation of the struggle; but that is regarded here as the terminating culmination of a struggle, not its transformation.

Conflict transformation has structural-behavioral and subjective-attitudinal features, varyingly emphasized by different partisans and analysts. Structurally, the process is a joint one and not a unilateral imposition. It involves a change in the mixture of behaviors, from large components of violence or other coercion to large components of cooperation or exchanges indicating mutual dependence. Subjectively, feelings and beliefs also tend to change, with the adversaries having increased mutual acceptance, and even mutual respect.

I. ANALYZING CONFLICT TRANSFORMATIONS

Although conflicts have always undergone transformations in human experience, systematic analysis of the phenomenon is recent, as illustrated in the books by Louis Kriesberg, Terrell A. Northrup, and Stuart J. Thorson, by Raimo Vayrynen, by Robert A. Baruch Bush and Joseph B. Fogler, and by Kumar Rupensinghe. Beginning in the 1980s, several developments converged to focus attention on the transformation of social conflicts. First, attention to protracted and recurring conflicts had increased, spurred by seemingly intractable ethnic conflicts. Second, the growth in the practice of problem-solving conflict resolution and in research and theorizing about conflict resolution were challenged by such intractable conflicts. Third, some major conflicts that had seemed intractable underwent profound changes, notably the Cold War and the struggle about apartheid in South Africa. The idea of conflict transformation seemed to capture an important but neglected aspect of social conflicts and their resolution.

Since theory and research about conflict transformations is so recent, this article does not review their histories. We examine the current analyses of various transformations, the stages of transformation, the underlying sources of transformation, and the policies fostering transformations. This examination draws from relevant evidence and theorizing in many fields, whether or not they previously have been identified as contributions to conflict transformation work.

The conflict transformation process has many commonalities, regardless of its occurrences in different kinds of conflict. Thus, transformation generally requires that adversaries recognize each other's claims and humanity to a significant degree. The antagonists also begin to regard their previously conflicting goals as reconcilable. At some time in the transformation process the primary adversaries come to believe that the conflict is irreversibly moving away from destructive conflict and toward an accommodation. During this process, unilateral conciliatory gestures, confidence-building agreements, and partial settlements are likely. The adversaries reduce or cease conduct that tends to cause the other party humiliation and pain.

The process of transformation is rarely a smooth, uninterrupted passage. A few of the many reasons for the likely difficulties should be noted. The conditions that fostered de-escalation and termination may change again and undermine the process; the terms of the conflict's settlement may appear unacceptable upon closer inspection; and parties to the fight who were excluded from the termination proceedings may obstruct and sabotage the process. The difficulties in making peace between the Israeli government and the PLO, even after the transforming Declaration of Principles of September 13, 1993, is illustrative. Rejectionists on each side committed actions to derail the process, including the assassination by an Israeli Jew of the Israeli Prime Minister Yitzhak Rabin in November 1995 and the suicide bombings of Israeli buses by Hamas supporters prior to the elections of May 1996. This resulted in a new Israeli government which in the name of security and ethno-nationalist claims acted in ways that countered PLO and Palestinian expectations about the ultimate terms of a peace agreement with the Israeli government. Unlike the leaders of the ANC and the Nationalist Party in South Africa, the leaders of the Israeli government and of the PLO were not seeking a common political union, but separation. Therefore, the leaders had little immediate interest in appealing to the constituency on the other side and building a cooperative relationship.

Conflict transformations, moreover, vary in many other fundamental regards. Many variations are reviewed as they occur in different kinds of conflicts, starting from different conflict conditions, and moving toward different kinds of accommodations.

A. Kinds of Conflicts

Conflicts vary notably by the social context in which they are waged, by the means used in the struggle, by the issue in contention, and by the units engaged in the struggle. This discussion is organized in terms of the variation among adversaries, but the other kinds of variations are also relevant for understanding conflict transformation, and many will be noted.

1. Between Persons

Conflicts between individuals are universal, whether in a family, community, or organizational setting. Interpersonal conflicts are often viewed as fights between two isolated persons in a dyadic relationship; but individuals are never wholly isolated in their fights. To some degree each person sees herself or himself as a representative of others, with whom she or he feels kinship due to for example, ethnicity, age, or gender; furthermore each person is likely to see the other as a representative of other categories or groups of persons.

Persons who are engaged in a persisting struggle are also generally involved in an enduring relationship. That relationship exists within a larger social system such as a country, family, community, or university whose members usually have common identities and shared interests. Such underlying considerations inhibit a conflict from becoming protracted and destructive; furthermore, other persons in the community, organization, or family system in which the disputants are functioning often try to restore relations that the conflict has disrupted. That is an important basis for transformation, particularly in cultures where individualistic concerns are not prominent.

2. Between Organizations

Organizations, here, refer to entities such as political parties, corporations, trade unions, churches, and governments. They tend to be clearly bounded and internally differentiated. What is particularly significant about the internal differentiation is that leadership roles usually exist, and their incumbents represent the members in external relations and have the authority to make certain kinds of commitments, binding the members. The persons playing these roles must, to some degree, satisfy their constituents as they represent them in contentions with other organizations. This greatly complicates the course of a struggle. For example, leaders often mobilize and commit their constituencies to wage a fight and then feel constrained by constituency pressure from ending it on terms that are acceptable to the opposing sides.

Organizations operating within a society generally compete and struggle with each other within mutually agreed upon rules. For example, trade unions and business managers anticipate and conduct recurrent disputes often within an institutionalized conflict management system.

But some organizations based on ethnic, linguistic, or religious identities may make claims that seem to challenge government agencies and a struggle erupts and escalates, using relatively noninstitutionalized methods. Furthermore, many organizations survive beyond the life of any individual members and therefore have the potentiality for protracted, even intergenerational fights. Finally, although organizations consist of humans filling social roles, partisans who view each other as formal entities my find it easier to depersonalize each other. Minimizing the humanity of the opponent permits inhumane conduct toward the opponent and hampers de-escalation and problem-solving conflict resolution.

3. Between Communal Groups

Communal groups range from a few persons regularly interacting and sharing a common identity to large collectivities or social categories whose members believe or are attributed to have common interests or identities. Such large-scale groups often have ambiguous membership boundaries and lack an elaborate and differentiated structure. These characteristics make resolving a struggle constructively very difficult. Organizations generally exist that claim to represent these large collectivities or social categories and their activists may develop a vested interest in continuing to wage the struggle.

Communal groups often are based on the presumption that members have shared interests derived from their common occupation or location in the labor market. As a result, they may conduct various forms of industrial or class struggles, including revolutions. Interests also may be based on shared values or beliefs and the desire to advance them. Large-scale groups may also arise from shared identities based on ethnicity, religion, language, or other communal identifications, and they may wage national liberation struggles.

4. Between States

In many ways, the world is organized as a system of independent, sovereign states, with the earth's territory divided into countries ruled by a government. Each government claims exclusive dominion over the affairs within its territory and the right to use force to impose its rule on the people within its territory and against external governments. Of course, such unbridled sovereignty has never been fully realized and in many ways is decreasing. The peoples of the world are increasingly economically and socially interdependent and more and more live in the context of transnational organizations and institutions.

The state system, nevertheless, makes protracted and destructive conflicts possible: many states control resources that enable them to fight on and on and peoples are socialized to be loyal to their state and hostile to its rivals and enemies. But even seemingly intractable interstate conflicts become transformed, as happened between France and Germany, after the Second World War.

5. Linkages Among Conflicts

Many struggles are conducted between different kinds of units. For example, conflicts frequently are waged between states and organizations, groups, and persons, or between persons and organizations, or between groups and organizations. The asymmetries in some ways hamper reaching a mutual accommodation; for example, one side may be able to so dominate the other that it simply imposes its will or one side does not accord legitimacy to the other. On the other hand, the variety of units may enable those who think their conflict can be accommodated to do so, bypassing those who are relatively intransigent.

Every conflict is interlocked with many others. Often several lines of cleavage dividing partisans in a conflict coincide and reinforce each other, making the conflict more likely to be intense and difficult to resolve; this is the case when ethnic, class, and regional cleavages in a society coincide. Conflicts also may cross-cut each other and from the vantage point of the partisans in one conflict, that conflict may be more salient to one side than to the other. Shifts in the salience of a conflict can contribute greatly to the transformation of another conflict, as when adversaries find themselves confronting a common enemy of greater threat and subordinate their antagonism in order to fight against the shared enemy number one; thus, antagonistic social classes in a society tend to unite against a foreign attacker.

This contribution gives particular attention to the transformation of seemingly intractable destructive conflicts between large-scale units. Illustrative material, for example, is drawn from the transformation in relations between Whites and Blacks in South Africa, between the United States and the Union of Soviet Socialist Republics, and between the Palestinian Liberation Organization (PLO) and the state of Israel.

B. From Varied Circumstances

Transformation can only be understood by taking into account the nature of the conflict that is being transformed. The term is usually used to refer to fundamental changes in conflicts marked by long-lasting enmity and waged in a destructive fashion. Conflicts are protracted and destructive to varying degrees and the possibility and the process of transformation vary accordingly.

1. Long Lasting

Many conflicts persist for very long periods, some for generation after generation, as was the case between the French and Germans. Many of these protracted struggles come to be regarded as intractable, their intractability often marked by failed efforts to resolve them. Furthermore, the leaders of the primary adversaries in the struggles consider their goals to be irreconcilable. Finally, some persons engaged in intractable struggles have vested interests in continuing them.

2. Destructive

Many conflicts are conducted in ways that are destructive to one or more of the adversaries and to their relationship. Destructive conflicts are marked by three characteristics. They result in extensive physical and mental damage to humans, often to noncombatants as well as combatants. In addition, they are frequently waged in ways that tend to evoke feelings of rage and hate, and the desire for revenge. Finally, how they are waged tends to create enduring obstacles to eventual reconciliation. On the other hand, conflicts may be waged in a relatively constructive fashion, as discussed by Morton Deutsch and Louis Kriesberg. Conflicts are never wholly destructive or constructive, but are complex and ever-shifting mixtures of both qualities.

3. Combinations

Conflicts can be protracted, and marked by recurrent struggles, but not be conducted destructively. Thus, class or ideological conflicts may be waged for generations, but conducted through legitimate political institutions using electoral procedures. Long-standing labor-management conflicts may also be waged without recourse to destructive means, for example, when conducted in institutionalized ways through collective bargaining.

Other conflicts may be relatively brief, but the eruptions are destructive. This is likely to be the case when the adversaries do not have an on-going relationship and their encounter produces a fight, but the parties then go their separate ways afterwards. Some personal and intergroup fights may be of this character. Even adversaries in an ongoing highly interdependent relationship may engage in an intense struggle and afterwards find ways to quickly re-establish an accommodative relationship.

Conflicts of particular interest here are those that are both protracted and destructive. They tend to appear intractable and are characterized by developments that sustain the struggle. Thus, the adversaries may tend to dehumanize each other and the mutual animosity perpetuates the struggle, as exemplified in many conflicts related to ethnic antagonisms, marked by feelings of humiliation and wishes for vengeance.

C. To Varied Accommodations

Conflict transformations vary not only by the stage of a conflict when they begin, but also by the kind of new relationship toward which the partisans are moving. One possibility is that the conflict ends, with one side's conversion, dissolution, or assimilation. A transformed conflict, however, need not mean that the adversaries no longer are in any conflict. The adversaries may engage in disputes, waged constructively; they may be embedded in a highly integrated relationship and conduct the disputes according to institutionalized conflict management procedures. These possible relations may be best understood in terms of two dimensions of relations between possible adversarial sides: the degree of integration and the degree of unilateral dominance.

1. Degree of Integration

The integration between adversaries varies in the degree to which they are mutually dependent on each other and they interact with each other. Parties with high interdependence and interaction are highly integrated behaviorally. The cessation of a struggle may lead to high levels of integration and also to a subjective sense of common interest and identity. It may be that former enemies become reconciled with each other. For example, after generations of enmity and recurrent wars, the French and German peoples and governments have established an enduring relationship in which war between them seems impossible.

At the other end of the continuum, the parties become more independent of each other after a conflict between them. The acceptance of increased separation may mark a new relationship. For example, the people of East Pakistan, with the assistance of India, forced their independence from Pakistan and established Bangladesh in 1971.

2. Degree of Unilateral Domination

Some fundamental changes in the relations between adversaries are largely imposed by one side in a conflict, for example, when one side forces the other to accede to its rules about the relationship, as occurred with the American Civil War. However, we are concerned here with those changes that have large degrees of mutuality in shaping the new relationship. The mutuality may occur as a result of internal changes, such as conversions in one of the parties, or to a new balance of power between the adversaries, or to changed views of their relationship as a result of changes in the social context.

Depending on the nature of the relationship taken as the starting level, the extent of transformation varies from a small modification to a fundamental restructuring. Relatedly, the magnitude of the change will appear to differ, depending on the time interval that is being considered.

II. STAGES OF TRANSFORMATION

Transformations often seem abrupt, but they generally occur over an extended time, as the adversaries move step by step toward a new relationship. The transformation occurs through cumulative little changes, as many factors converge toward a new mutually acceptable accommodation. The transformation processes include several steps, varying in duration and irreversibility.

A. Exploratory

As a conflict persists, some events raise doubts about the advisability of persisting in the conflict. The costs of waging the struggle tend to mount, and often the burdens are borne disproportionally by different groups within each side. In very large, highly differentiated conflict units this is especially likely. Consequently, in large groups, in societies, and in large organizations, some factions often express dissent as the struggle persists. Alternative courses of action, including various paths of de-escalation are discussed, and factions may advocate a new line of action. As the ostensible goals of the struggle remain out of reach, members of the constituency may shift away from supporting escalation or even persistence and toward supporting policies of de-escalation.

Members of one side, in the early stages of conflict transformation may explore the possibility of moving toward an acceptable accommodation. For example, peace feelers are tentatively put forward to test whether the other side might accept what is offered as part of the conflict's resolution. Such overtures are often made indirectly and with ambiguity so that they can be denied if rejected. The reasons for such tentativeness are obvious. The adversary leaders making such probes may fear that if the response is rebuffed, their effort will be seen as naive and foolish by their constituents or the rebuff is a sign that the probe was interpreted by the other side as a sign of weakness and its leaders increase their demands.

De-escalating probes, therefore, are often conducted by low-ranking or unofficial representatives of the opposing camps. They can be discounted by the side they represent, if the response is not acceptable. Another vehicle for such probes is provided by intermediaries, who may intervene at the request of one side or by their own initiative. They often represent interested parties such as international organizations or governments that are not engaged in the struggle, but they may also have little stake in the conflict's outcome. In any case their feelers are easily repudiated, if they fail to reveal enough common ground to undertake further explorations and negotiations.

B. Initial Signals and Actions

Tentative probes may be dismissed as tricks or discounted as not representing the position of authoritative representatives of the other side. To be effective, they generally need to be followed by relatively unambiguous words and deeds. An important body of literature has emerged on these matters, much of it related to ways of transforming antagonisms such as the Cold War. Two general strategies have received considerable attention: graduated reciprocation in tension-reduction (GRIT) and tit-for-tat. According to the GRIT strategy, as developed by Charles E. Osgood, mutual tension and fear can be interrupted and de-escalation begun by one side announcing that it is making a concession, inviting reciprocation, but persisting with additional cooperative moves, even if they are not immediately reciprocated. According to the tit-for-tat strategy, as analyzed by Robert Axelrod, cooperative relations tend to develop and be sustained if one side initiates a conciliatory move and then matches the other side's conciliation with conciliation and coercive act with coercive act.

In addition to public gestures and actions, secret meetings are sometimes conducted by very high level representatives of the opposing sides. Often they are the prelude to a dramatic public event taking a large step toward mutual accommodation, enabling that event to be taken and ensuring that further steps will follow. For example, prior to Egyptian President Anwar Al-Sadat's historic visit to Jerusalem in November 1977, the Egyptian Deputy Premier, Hassan Tuhami and the Israeli Foreign Minister, Moshe Dayan, met secretly in Morocco and discussed possible peace arrangements.

C. Reaching Agreements or Understandings

Accommodations between adversaries in protracted conflicts tend to develop by a gradual transition and transformation, often marked by agreements about specific issues in dispute. Explicit agreements are useful in settling some matters of contention, in fostering mutual understanding, commitments, and trust, and in reducing fears and antagonisms among each side's constituencies.

Special attention has been given by policymakers and analysts to confidence-building measures (CBMs). These are agreements directed, for example, to provide antagonists with assurances that neither side will take surprise military action against the other or that neither side will pursue policies preparing for such actions. Such CBMs played an important role in providing stability and security in Europe and fostering the transition ending the Cold War, as analyzed in Louis Kriesberg's *International Conflict Resolution.*

D. Implementation and Institutionalization

The transformation of protracted conflicts requires that agreements reached are carried out and not violated. Adherence to agreements and the perception of adherence are enhanced by establishing mutually agreed upon monitoring and verification procedures. In addition, joint commissions or other bodies may be created to review any disputes about the interpretation of the accords made, as was done for some American-Soviet arms control agreements.

It is also helpful to formulate treaties and other agreements that have self-sustaining qualities. This may mean constructing them so they foster vested interests in sustaining the accords reached for at least some segments of each side's constituents.

Finally, intermediaries often play a crucial role in

sustaining an agreement once it has been reached. They help monitor it and assist in its implementation, for example helping to plan for and to conduct elections and to demobilize former armed fighters. This has been notably important in El Salvador and Namibia.

III. UNDERLYING CHANGES

Reaching a new mutual accommodation occurs through many courses of development; and the pathways are accorded differing importance by various analysts of conflict transformation. Analysts emphasize diverse sources of change, whether those are primarily within one of the adversary parties, in the relationship between them, or in the social context of the adversaries. Analysts also differ in the importance attributed to large-scale trends and impersonal forces or to the policies pursued by specific persons. Finally, they differ in the importance attributed to power relations and other structural conditions or to ideas and other subjective factors. To review the theories and evidence pertaining to these varying emphases, each source of change will be considered. Then, short-term and long-term policies will be reviewed as they are directed to each arena of possible change.

A. Internal

Many fundamental changes occur within each party in a conflict that affect the possibility that the conflict will persist destructively or will become transformed. Often, the leading persons of one or more sides advocate varying perspectives toward an external antagonist. Consequently, a change in the leadership of one of the adversaries often provides an opportunity to explore and realize new steps that lead to a conflict's transformation. The new leader is less identified with or committed to the old policies and in addition, the opposing side may assume that the new leadership provides an opportunity to de-escalate the conflict. This is illustrated by the changes that were implemented by Mikhail Gorbachev for the Soviet Union and by Henderik de Klerk for the Whites of South Africa.

A change in leadership often reflects a shift in the prevailing views among the people and elites of the conflict party toward supporting a de-escalating transformation of the struggle. The shift may occur as doubts rise about the likelihood of prevailing if the policy of confrontation continues. The cost of persevering may come to be seen as too great to be borne for what is increasingly unlikely to be won. This seems to have gradually occurred in the early 1990s for both sides in the Israeli-Palestinian conflict. The shift in prevailing views may also involve a re-evaluation of the importance or even the correctness of what is being sought. A kind of creeping conversion may spread among the constituents of one or both sides. In many ways, this happened among the Whites of South Africa, who lost the moral certainty that apartheid was right. Internal changes are affected by and in turn influence changes in the relations between adversaries, as discussed next.

B. Relationship and Interactions

As a conflict persists, the balance of resources between adversaries and of the burdens of the conflict change and begin to be experienced differently. An influential argument made by I. Wiliam Zartman is that conflicts begin to move toward resolution when the adversaries are in what they regard as a hurting stalemate and a better option seems possible. A hurting stalemate arises when neither side anticipates defeating the other and the current circumstances are highly unsatisfactory. Movement toward de-escalation and transformation also requires, by this reasoning, that the antagonists can envisage an attainable better option.

C. Social Context

Adversaries always wage their conflicts within a larger social context that is in constant flux. We stress three kinds of changes in the social environment that may foster transformation of a given struggle. First, conflict linkages may change as other conflicts become more or less salient for the adversaries. Second, the overall social system may change in structure, norms, or other patterns. Third, other parties may increase or decrease their interventions.

1. Conflict Linkages

Members of each side in any struggle are engaged in many other conflicts and they may also regard their struggle with each other as embedded within a larger conflict. The increased salience of a new common enemy may reduce the primacy of the struggle they are waging against each other, allowing for a transformation of that conflict. Thus, internal struggles may come to be subordinated in the face of an external threat.

Another kind of change in conflict linkage occurs when a conflict that is superimposed on another becomes dormant or is resolved. That can facilitate the transformation of the other conflict. This happened for many regional and civil conflicts after the Cold War ended. For example, in South Africa, the anti-Communism rationale for the governing National Party's hostility to the African National Congress (ANC) was undermined with the end of the Cold War, as was a justification for waging wars in neighboring countries. Moreover, the ANC's reassurances about the economic policies it would pursue if it gained political power seemed more credible under the new conditions. Furthermore, the expectations of the U.S. government's support of the South African government were reduced. Consequently, South Africa's government could then recognize the need and see the possibility of reaching an accommodation with the ANC.

The end of the Cold War also weakened support for both the Israelis and the Palestinians. Thus, assistance for the PLO from the USSR and from many Arab governments who themselves had received support from the Soviet Union was considerably reduced. The end of the Cold War also lessened the value of Israel to the United States and therefore threatened reduced support. All of this contributed to the mutual acceptance by the Israeli government and the PLO that an accommodation between them was necessary.

2. Systemic Patterns

Many global social, economic, and cultural changes impact intrastate and interstate conflicts, often facilitating their transformation. For example, the increasingly integrated global economy meant that the sanctions against South Africa were becoming more and more burdensome to the peoples of South Africa. The growing international recognition of human rights claims and the propriety of intervening in domestic affairs to protect such claims also helped undermine White South Africans' sense of legitimacy for apartheid.

3. Intervention

Actors who are not one of the primary adversaries often play crucial roles in the transformation of a conflict. They often apply pressure to one side or give aid to another, thus hastening a conflict's resolution by making an accommodation seem necessary. On the other hand, external support for waging a struggle by one of the parties often prolongs a conflict, and only the cessation of such assistance contributes to the adversaries' acceptance of a mutual accommodation. Thus, the end of the Cold War and external support for opposing sides contributed to the transformation of the lengthy and brutal civil wars in Central American countries.

Intervention also takes the form of providing mediating services that enable the adversaries to construct new options, thus helping to transform their conflict. This too is illustrated in the ending of the Central American civil wars. For example, in the 1980s, several Central American countries were racked by long-lasting and interlocked conflicts, making it difficult to settle any one of them in isolation. A large move toward resolution was made by the accord reached among the presidents of the five Central American countries, meeting in Esquipulas, Guatemala, as analyzed by Terrence Hopmann and by Paul Wehr and John Paul Lederach. Sometimes called the "Arias Plan," recognizing the great contributions of the president of Costa Rica, Oscar Arias, the accord included three components to be implemented simultaneously and according to a fixed time schedule. The formula included ending the violent conflicts, promoting democracy, and fostering economic integration.

IV. POLICIES FOR TRANSFORMATION

Many persons and organizations undertake efforts that they believe will foster conditions conducive to the transformation of a protracted and destructive conflict. The policies tend to differ for each stage of the transformation process: exploring possible transformations, initiating actions, reaching understandings, and implementing agreements. The policies may be directed at changing internal characteristics of one of the adversaries, the relationship between them, or their external context; effective strategies often combine efforts in all three areas.

A. Effecting Internal Changes

Many efforts to transform a conflict, understandably, are attempts to influence one or more of the primary adversaries. Each side is likely to think and act on the idea that peaceful relations depend on the other side changing itself. But changes in one's own side are often where transformation starts. Policies aimed at bringing about the desired change may be long term as well as short term.

1. Long Term

In considering policies of transformation within an adversary party, it is important to recognize that policies are made not only from the top down, but also laterally, and from the grass roots, as discussed by John Paul Lederach. We begin by noting policies undertaken by the elites, that may promote a transformation process. Such policies from above include leaders mobilizing popular support for de-escalation. In social systems with heterogeneity in the elite ranks, some of them may offer alternative policies to initiate and to foster de-escalation and conflict transformation. Those alternatives may be offered for discussion within the confines of the ruling group, or they may be set forth to gain constituent support. In the latter case the advocates may win office to carry out the policies or they may be regarded by the opposing side's leadership to be offering a possibility that a de-escalating deal might be struck. Top-down policies may also be directed at the opposing side's rank-and-file, encouraging them to pressure the other side's leadership to de-escalate the struggle.

At the middle-rank leadership level, policies of education and providing information about the other side are often undertaken. Many analysts believe that the demonization of the enemy through schooling, the mass media, and other channels must be interrupted in order to transform and resolve seemingly intractable conflicts. Often one side insists that the other side's leaders undertake such campaigns. Efforts to improve the image portrayed of the other side therefore has some immediate benefits for de-escalation, even aside from possible long-term effects.

Grass roots efforts also play a long-term role in conflict transformation by affecting members of each of the adversary sides. This includes the kind of socialization children experience in their families. There is evidence that harsh socialization can generate diffuse anger that tends to be displaced or otherwise expressed in hostile behavior toward external targets; raising children lovingly, therefore, is a contribution to later transformations because more adults will be available to seize the opportunities to make them happen.

2. Short Term

Some policies bringing about internal changes that affect external conflicts are significantly undertaken from the top down, and individual leaders often play critical roles in bringing about these changes. For example, undoubtedly, Mikhail Gorbachev, as the leading figure in the Soviet Union in the mid-1980s, initiated profound changes that set the stage for ending the Cold War. He promoted openness for organizational activity from below and public discussion of many issues; he convinced military and other Soviet elite groups that reducing the antagonism of the Cold War was necessary for modernization and was possible to undertake safely; and he advocated an acceptance of universal standards of human rights and the rule of law. All his helped prepare Gorbachev's constituents for accommodation with the West and also provided powerful signals to the West that a transformative accommodation was possible.

The formulation and implementation of such policies also required the activities of leaders at the middle rank. Many leading Communist Party members, Soviet intellectuals, high-ranking government officials, and other middle-level leaders supported the choice of Gorbachev to head the Communist Party and to reform the Soviet system. Some of them used the opportunities then created to press for even faster and more fundamental reform. The transformation of the Soviet Union had a dynamic of its own and went farther and faster than its originators anticipated, thus it resulted in irreversible changes and the end of the cold war.

Grass-root leaders, at the local level or in the lower ranks of organizations, often contribute to the transformation of a conflict, and even to the initiation of the transformation process. They may arouse and mobilize opposition to the struggle being waged by the larger society or organization to which they belong. Their actions include demonstrations and protests against destructively waged struggles. For example, peace movements often play critical roles in halting a conflict's escalation or speeding de-escalation. They also can play crucial roles in implementing and sustaining agreements that have been reached.

B. Effecting the Relationship

Policies that contribute to the transformation of a protracted destructive conflict are often directed at altering the relationship between the adversaries. Policies may be long term and short term, and they may be pursued by intermediaries or by members of the opposing sides themselves.

1. Long Term

Changing the relationship between the adversaries is the goal of many long-term policies. The goals vary in the degree of integration or separation that is sought, but what is critical in moving toward an accommodation is the degree of mutuality in the goals. Several specific policies with implications for a mutually accommodative transformation are worth noting. They too may be undertaken and pursued from the top down, laterally, or from below.

Policies to increase the well-being and power of the relatively weaker side may be expected to reduce the underlying conditions sustaining an intractable conflict. But not all such policies always serve to interrupt or limit destructive conflicts. Thus, when the leaders of a dominant group offer some redress to the less advantaged, there is the risk of evoking a backlash from their constituents. Furthermore, the members of the disadvantaged community may have their expectations raised only to have them fail to be fulfilled, and consequently feel more frustrated than before. Thus, too, when members of a communal group, feeling that they are disadvantaged, pressure members of what they regard as the relatively advantaged communal group to improve their conditions, the members of the advantaged group are likely to feel threatened. This means that to effectively limit destructive conflicts, such policies must be carefully crafted, and probably need to be conducted in concert with other long-term policies.

Strengthening shared identities, such as American or Nigerian, may help limit communal conflicts within the United States or Nigeria. But here too, that may be experienced as domination by one communal group of others, as the effort to create a Soviet identity was felt by many in the former Soviet Union to be barely disguised Russian chauvinism. One solution to this dilemma is to frame the overarching identity in inclusive terms, and actualize that view in practice. Thus, national identity may be presented in nonethnic terms; for example, in the United States, being American is ideally open to anyone born in the country or who immigrates and swears to uphold the constitution. Insofar as some American citizens do not experience that as the reality, due to ethnic, racial, or other discrimination, the common identity is denied.

Increasingly, policies instituted from the top down as well as advocated from the middle and grass-roots leadership levels are directed at improving individual and collective rights of communal groups and their members. They help provide standards of conduct that contribute to formulating generally acceptable conflict outcomes, thus fostering conflict transformation. Support for such policies is to be found among groups whose members feel at risk, but among members of other groups as well. Furthermore, they provide a basis for external actors to intervene and help shape the relationship in a mutually acceptable manner. For example, the Organization on Security and Cooperation in Europe's (OSCE) High Commissioner on National Minorities, based in The Hague, The Netherlands, convenes meetings, makes visits, advises, and through other procedures helps develop legislation, norms, and practices relating to minorities in member countries of the OSCE, including Kazakstan, Estonia, and the former Yugoslav Republic of Macedonia.

Finally, some policies are aimed at increasing the interaction between members of the opposing sides. This tends to enhance mutual understanding and dependence. Soviet-American cultural exchanges, for example, were initiated and conducted at several levels of leadership in the two societies. For members of each side, the exchanges tended to undermine the demonization of the people in the other side. The establishment of international nongovernmental organizations (INGOS), bringing together people engaged in the same occupational, humanitarian, or recreational activity, is another way bonds are created between members of countries which may be in conflict. Similarly, groups within a society, based on a particular interests or identities, may include members with diverse and cross-cutting concerns.

In addition, dialogue groups, interactive problem-solving workshops, and other nonofficial ways of bringing representatives of adversarial sides together are often undertaken by middle-rank persons, for example from the academic or religious worlds. Through such experiences, representatives of adversarial sides are better able to analyze the conflict, reach better mutual understanding, imagine solutions, and develop relationships that become relevant for official negotiations, as examined by Herbert Kelman. The initiators of such policies are often based outside of any of the adversarial camps.

2. Short Term

Many short-term policies are directed to improve the relationship between adversaries, when partisans or interveners seek to de-escalate a struggle. One fundamental element, as a protracted and destructive conflict becomes transformed, is mutual recognition and reassurance. This generally takes many steps. One step often is mediated or direct conversations at the personal level between leaders of the opposing sides, who come to see each other as full human beings.

In addition, public events at which the mutual recognition or gesture of reconciliation is celebrated demonstrate and deepen the commitments previously made and increase the visibility of the commitments. For example, the well-choreographed handshake between Yasir Arafat and Yitzhak Rabin at the signing of the Oslo Accords on September 13, 1993, in Washington increased their and their peoples' commitment to the Accords. Such ceremonies increase the visibility and grass-roots support for the move toward transformation, helping to make the changes irreversible.

In the case of conflicts within a society, actions taken by middle-range or grass-roots leaders from opposing sides to solve immediate tasks at the local level can serve as a superordinate goals, and so help overcome the antagonisms of the conflict, as analyzed by Muzafer

Sherif. Widely shared common goals may be the basis for top-down policies of mutual accommodation. For example, in Malaysia, the conflict between the Malay and Chinese communities erupted in riots in 1969, but has been managed by policies of accommodation, including affirmative action policies. These policies have been premised and sustained by the widely shared desire to improve earnings and not allow ethnic struggles to disrupt economic progress.

In the case of conflicts involving different societies, efforts to find and advance superordinate goals generally need to be undertaken from the top down. The ideas, however, may be formulated and advocated by middle-range leaders. The efforts may pertain to regional developments relating to water or to particular industries. For example, the development, beginning in the mid 1950s, of the European Coal and Steel Community played a crucial role in the transformation of Franco-German enmity.

Middle-rank leaders can often provide alternative channels of communication between high-rank leaders and other middle-rank leaders of the opposing sides. This can be important in the early stage of conflict transformation, when the possibilities of conflict de-escalation and transformation are being explored. This was the case, for example, in the arrangements for meetings, outside of South Africa, by Afrikaner students and business leaders with ANC officials, as facilitated and analyzed by Henderick van der Merwe. Later, when negotiations are underway, such unofficial channels, sometimes called Track II diplomacy, help the transformation process by generating new options to overcome barriers.

C. Affecting the Context

1. Long Term

Partisans as well as external actors may undertake policies to modify the social context of a seemingly intractable conflict. One policy is to reframe the conflict and locate it in a changed context. High-ranking leaders may be able to institute policies that change the context as a way of achieving their goals and transform a conflict that they despair of winning. For example, Anwar Sadat, soon after succeeding Gamal Nasser as president of Egypt, in 1970, began to orient Egyptian policy away from an alliance with the Soviet Union toward the United States. By moving the Egyptian-Israeli conflict from being overlaid by the Cold War, to lie within the Western side, he thought the United States would help resolve the Egyptian-Israeli conflict on terms he could accept. This did contribute in many ways to the transformation of that protracted struggle. Another kind of top-down reframing of a conflict may be seen in the shift by President Richard M. Nixon to détente with the Soviet Union and improved relations with the People's Republic of China in the early 1970s; this was part of a strategy to end the war in Vietnam on terms acceptable to his administration.

Another context-changing policy is to establish new institutional structures that consist of many members, including adversaries. For example, during the Cold War, NATO and Warsaw Pact negotiations about European relations were ultimately successful in reaching the Helsinki Accords in 1979 when the negotiations were conducted in a broader setting that included European countries not members of either NATO nor Warsaw Pact. That setting was the Conference on Security and Cooperation in Europe (CSCE, later the OSCE). The development of the institutions of Western Europe help ease national conflicts within European countries because of their emphasis on regions and because increasingly decisions about various matters are made in the headquarters of European institutions and not wholly in the country capitals.

The external context is an important source of intervention to transform a conflict. Partisans and/or external agents may try to arouse attention from others in the social context to act so as to help transform the conflict. For example, they may seek to expose human rights abuses, killings, and other forms of oppression so that official and nonofficial action may be taken to stop such repression. The mass media are an increasingly important agency for calling attention to erupting destructive conflicts. Such attention helps spur intervention by external actors, often undertaken from the top down. Within each country, government officials often take actions to control industrial, ethnic, and other conflicts. Increasingly, this is also true for external official intervention in ethnic and other conflicts in foreign countries.

2. Short Term

The preceding discussion is also relevant for short-term policies. Once the conflict has become protracted, policies are generally focused on ending the violence that is being committed. External sanctions and arms sales limitations can affect the balance of power and reduce the prospects of a future imposed settlement. That tends to foster movement toward a negotiated settlement.

External actors can also provide resources which make a mutual accommodation less risky than it otherwise would appear to be. For example, the U.S. government provided benefits that gave some reassurance to Israel and Egypt upon their signing a peace treaty in 1979. This support was crucial for implementing and sustaining the treaty.

Many policies, particularly by intermediaries, are intended to provide services that facilitate communication and problem-solving work between adversaries. This includes using informal, nonofficial channels to transmit information about each side's views of the other. It also includes top-down policies by officials who try to reconfigure a conflict, changing the combination of stakeholders. For example, the 1991 Madrid conference on peace in the Middle East was part of a process brokered by U.S. Secretary of State James A. Baker, that ingeniously combined three negotiating fora, each with a different set of parties: a brief multilateral conference of the primary adversaries, bilateral negotiations between Israel and Syria, Jordan, and the Palestinians, and regional negotiations about shared problems.

V. CONCLUSIONS

The transformation of conflicts is neither the result of immutable, large-scale forces nor of the actions of a few brave and wise persons. Several circumstances converge and interpretations of those new circumstances transform a conflict. It is not the result of one party imposing its will, but neither is force and coercion irrelevant.

Even protracted, destructively waged conflicts often become transformed in a mutually acceptable manner. This is generally the consequence of a confluence of changing conditions within one or more of the adversary sides, in their relationship, and in their social context. In some cases, changes in one of these sets of conditions are especially important; but changes in the other conditions also make contributions to the transformation process. People in various positions within each of the contending sides, or even outside them, must take advantage of those new conditions to actually transform the conflict. In varying degrees, conflicts are transformed by policies intentionally conducted by some of the partisans in the struggle and/or by external agents. Although undertaken, the process is not irreversible; thoughtful and persistent work by many people is needed to sustain the process of transformation.

All policies are affected by value preferences. They are directed to achieve purposes that are deemed desirable by those conducting them. In actuality, everyone has many goals and any given policy implies an ordering of their relative priority. Thus, in transforming a protracted, destructive conflict, many people generally want to reduce or to stop killings, to achieve a just outcome as they conceive it, to achieve an enduring accommodation, to have the wrongs they experienced in the past acknowledged, and to attain many other objectives. No policy can maximize the attainment of all such goals simultaneously, although they may be advanced sequentially.

Conflict outcomes are never fully symmetrical. One side's goals may be more realized than another's, and its members must accommodate to the current realities. The accommodation, nevertheless, can include the attainment of some of what each stakeholder had wanted. Even new shared goals may take on high priority and be the source of shared gratification. The transformation of the conflict in itself can sometimes be the cause of celebration and pride by most of the people who had previously been engaged in a struggle they had waged too long.

Also See the Following Articles

COLD WAR • CONFLICT MANAGEMENT AND RESOLUTION • CONFLICT THEORY • DIPLOMACY • INTERNATIONAL RELATIONS, OVERVIEW

Bibliography

Axelrod, R. (1984). *The evolution of cooperation.* New York: Basic Books.

Bush, R. A. B. & Fogler, J. P. (1994). *The promise of mediation.* San Francisco: Jossey-Bass.

Deutsch, M. (1973). *The resolution of conflict: Constructive and destructive processes.* New Haven, CT: Yale University Press.

Goldstein, J. & John R. F. (1990). *Three-way street: Strategic reciprocity in world politics.* Chicago: University of Chicago Press.

Hampson, F. O. (1996). *Nurturing peace: Why peace settlements succeed or fail.* Washington, DC: United States Institute of Peace Press.

Hopmann, P. T. (1988). Negotiating peace in Central America. *Negotiation Journal, 4,* 361–380.

Kelman, H. C. (1995). Contributions of an unofficial conflict resolution effort to the Israeli-Palestinian breakthrough. *Negotiation Journal, 11,* 19–27.

Kriesberg, L. (1989). Transforming conflicts in the Middle East and Central Europe. In L. Kriesberg, T. A. Northrup, and S. J. Thorson (Eds.), *Intractable conflicts and their transformation* (pp. 109–131). Syracuse, NY: Syracuse University Press.

Kriesberg, L. (1992). *International conflict resolution.* New Haven, CT: Yale University Press.

Kriesberg, L. (1998). *Constructive conflicts.* Lanham, MD: Roman & Littlefield.

Kriesberg, L., Northrup, T. A., & Thorson, S. J. (Eds.). (1989). *Intractable conflicts and their transformation.* Syracuse, NY: Syracuse University Press.

Lederach, J. P. (1997). *Building peace: Sustainable reconciliation in divided societies.* Washington, DC: United States Institute of Peace Press.

Merwe, H. W. van der (1989). *Pursuing justice and peace in South Africa.* London and New York: Routledge.

Osgood, C. E. (1962). *An alternative to war or surrender.* Urbana, IL: University of Illinois Press.

Rupensinghe, K. (Ed.). (1995). *Conflict transformation.* New York: St. Martin's Press.

Sherif, M. (1966). *In common predicament.* Boston: Houghton Mifflin.

Ury, W. L., Brett, J. M., & Goldberg, S. B. (1988). *Getting Disputes Resolved.* San Francisco/London: Jossey-Bass.

Vayrynen, R. (Ed.). (1991). *New directions in conflict theory: Conflict resolution and conflict transformation.* London/Newbury Park/New Delhi: Sage.

Wehr, Paul, & Lederach, J. P. (1991). Mediating conflict in Central America. *Journal of Peace Research, 28,* 85–98.

Zartman, I. W. (1989). *Ripe for resolution: Conflict and intervention in Africa* (2nd ed.). New York: Oxford University Press.

Conformity and Obedience

Sheldon G. Levy
Wayne State University

GLOSSARY

Authoritarianism A set of beliefs about authority. High authoritarians rely upon authority, defer to it, and support a hierarchical social structure.

Cohesiveness A set of relationships among individuals that includes liking, acceptance of common goals with voluntary effort toward them, and willingness to sacrifice to maintain the group as an integral unit.

Conformity Behavior that matches the actions of one or more others.

Frame of Reference A set of related beliefs that operates as a standard for the assessment of information and evaluation of behavior.

Obedience A response that is consistent with the requests or demands of another.

Social Facilitation Increased rate of response on the part of a member of a species in the presence of conspecifics.

Social Norm A standard or typical belief or point of view held by a group.

CONFORMITY AND OBEDIENCE are intrinsic components of most social behavior including group violence. Conformity represents behavioral uniformity within a collectivity while obedience identifies behavior that implies hierarchical distinctions. Both frequently result from coercive forces that undermine individual expression. Both simplify the social environment and therefore reduce anxiety in many individuals. Conformity may reduce intragroup conflict. Obedience may also achieve this end but through unequal distribution of rights and privileges. While social organization is probably impossible without some degree of both, the frequent consequence of each has been to decrease individual rights within the group and to increase the likelihood of hostility toward outgroup members.

I. INTRODUCTION

A. Dimensions of Social Organization

Social existence is dominated by two components, solidarity and status as described by Roger Brown in his classic 1965 text, *Social Psychology*. The former is observed in groups by behavior such as sociability, cohesiveness, and altruism. The second is represented in hierarchical relationships that derive from wealth or power, perceived competence (including scientific, religious, and artistic) or attractiveness. Obedience generally, but not always, derives from hierarchical relationships while conformity is more closely associated with solidarity.

B. Conformity and Obedience as Behavior

Similar behaviors may occur for different reasons and therefore a distinction is necessary between the observed behavior and the inference about its cause. Conformity is behavior that parallels the actions of one or more others. Its inferred cause is usually the motive to obtain social approval which also implies a hierarchical relationship—obedience to the implicit demands of the group. Several types of conformity may be distinguished based on the reason for the behavior.

The variations in obedience are similar to those in conformity.

C. Types of Conformity

Power conformity occurs when the parallel behavior is to obtain rewards and avoid punishments from the larger group. Groupthink is a special case of power conformity and represents an unwillingness by members of a small group, such as a set of advisors, to criticize the leader even when they believe that the decisions are erroneous.

Informational conformity imitates the group's behavior for the purpose of obtaining information. If the behavior is similar to but unrelated to the group's actions, it is coincidental conformity–for example, the crossing of a street at the appropriate change of the pedestrian signal. Normative or value based conformity is based on a prior set of beliefs about the appropriate conduct in a situation. If the actions are believed to be most appropriate for solving a problem then the conformity is functional.

Nonconformity can be individualistic or minority. The former is unique behavior of the individual while the latter differs from the dominant group but parallels that of the subgroup. Dissent implies nonconformity as a result of conscious disagreement.

Conformity is generally identified in static terms, that is, a comparison of behavior to that of the group. Dynamic conformity results from behavioral changes that are closer to the group's position.

There may also be conformity to inaction. The individual attempts to obtain cues from the group for the appropriate response in a situation and, if no action is observed, the inactivity may be imitated.

D. Types of Obedience

Power obedience is based on a motive to obtain rewards and/or avoid punishment for disobedience, the failure to carry out the request.

If there has been prior acceptance of status differentiation and of obligations to obey one who is of higher rank, the obedience is normative or value based. It is functional when the hierarchical relationships have been accepted as best serving the achievement of particular goals and it is merely coincident when an independently reached decision leads to actions that follow a request for the behavior. In conforming obedience, the individual obeys to fulfill the expectations of the group.

In almost all discussions of obedience, power relationships are implied. However, both conformity and obedience may be shaped by at least three different attributes of the influencing agent (following the analysis of Kelman): Power or resource control, which induces compliance to obtain rewards and avoid punishments, credibility, which induces the motive to hold the same beliefs, and attractiveness which motivates the observer to identify. (This line of analysis was suggested to the author by Holly Bowen.)

While the definitional distinctions are necessary to differentiate between behavior and motive, determining the source of the behavior is difficult and frequently only inferred.

II. HISTORICAL BACKGROUND

Although social psychology as an experimental science is a 20th-century phenomenon, the important roles of conformity and obedience have been understood and discussed for millennia.

A central theme in Socrates' arguments for obeying the laws of Athens, as discussed in Plato's *Crito,* is that the acceptance of the authority of the city (state, polity) during one's life incurs a moral obligation to obey that authority's decisions. This obligation remains even when the decision is a death penalty (as for Socrates), unless one can persuade the authorities that the sentence is unjust (normative obedience). He also argued that failure to obey would result in social disapproval in Athens or in any other city to which he might flee (conforming obedience). On the other hand, Socrates also held, for example in the *Apology*, that one is justified in disobeying unjust authority.

During the latter part of Europe's Middle Ages, obedience to both church and state were challenged. For example, the English king's almost total power carried with it reciprocal obligations. Perceptions of unjust acts were the basis for disobedience. Since church and state were closely allied, once the state (church) was perceived as not fulfilling its responsibilities, the individual was freed from the normative obligation of obedience. Authority was particularly questioned in England at the end of the 14th century, for example, the Lollard Heresy, which stemmed indirectly from the teachings of John Wycliffe.

The Puritan view that subsequently arose was essentially that political obligation was functional. Christopher Goodman, and to a lesser extent John Ponet, both of whom along with the Puritans in general opposed Catholic rule, rejected any argument that the individual subject was bound to obey authority. Ponet during the mid-1500s specifically claimed that earthly power derived from God but its purpose was functional, to achieve or administer justice. He further held that it is the people who give authority to the rulers (and, therefore, hold ultimate judgment, that is, reserve the right to disobey unjust laws). On the other hand Sir Robert Filmer (late 1600s) defended without reservation the authority of kings and argued that it was "unnatural" for the people to govern or to chose governors.

Ultimately, as discussed by Ervin Staub, the English tradition sided with individuality while the German tradition for at least 200 years prior to the Second World War valued obedience and devotion to authority.

The normative basis for challenging obedience was present in the American Civil Liberties Union's court case against the Vietnam War. The Union argued that the war was illegal since the president's decision to engage in it violated the Constitution. The pressures of conformity to the principle of "supporting our fighting men" led many congressional liberals of the day to support the appropriation while maintaining that this was not an expression of support for the war (a position that was rejected by the Supreme Court). Although the Court refused to declare the war illegal, elements of its decision became the basis for later resistance to authority.

Dissent (nonconformity) and disobedience derive from psychological bases that encourage, facilitate, or justify the individual's resistance. These include the perception of symmetry, in this case the observer's right to engage in actions similar to those of others (even of higher rank), and a derivative of this, the perception of injustice. (Symmetry and conformity may derive from a more fundamental process, that of imitation, extensively studied by Albert Bandura.) One basis for injustice is the failure, as by authority, to fulfill an agreement. As a consequence the right to demand obedience is relinquished.

III. BASIC RESEARCH

A. Research on Conformity

1. The Emergence of Social Norms

The norms of a communal group frequently emerge from shared experience. Individuals conform to these standards because they wish to achieve solidarity (cohesiveness), which provides greater protection from external forces and also reduces ambiguity about the social environment through consensus. Sherif tested a hypothesis that social ambiguity is reduced through norms that emerge from group experience and that, once established, become comparable in many respects to physical reality.

To mirror the ambiguity of the primordial social environment, he capitalized on the autokinetic phenomenon. In a darkened room, eye muscles relax and a pinpoint of light moves on the back of the eyeball. The individual perceives the object as moving because of the relative insensitivity to the physical state of the eye muscles. (Under ordinary circumstances, the presence of peripheral stimuli result in the tensing of the eye muscles and the object is accurately perceived as stationary). Sherif showed that individual variation was reduced when a group viewed the light and discussed its degree of movement. Further, the new "norm" that emerged persisted when individual participants were returned to the room to again judge the light. It is not unreasonable to suppose that denigration of a target, for example, a minority group, may sometimes also represent an emergent norm. The attributes of the target group may thus be viewed by members of the ingroup as a physical reality thus facilitating intergroup conflict.

B. Conformity and Dissent

1. The Asch Experiments

Solomon Asch conducted the defining research on conformity. He provided college students with a series of lines that differed in length. They were asked to judge which of these was similar to a displayed standard. His preliminary investigations had demonstrated that correct matches were made without error. (Subsequent work by S. S. Stevens established the power law for human perception. Judgments of changes in lengths of lines were shown to be quite accurate).

Asch's experiment was conducted in a group setting. Except for the naive subject, the students were accomplices of the experimenter and had been primed to select an incorrect answer on some occasions. (Sometimes the accomplices answered correctly to prevent raising suspicion.) The experiment was constructed so that, one at a time, they expressed their judgments before the naive subject. Under these conditions subjects frequently provided an answer that was the same as that of the group. In the original experiments, the greater the size of the group, the greater the likelihood of conformity, but this influence reached an asymptotic value when the number of accomplices was between three and five.

The powerful effect of dissent was also demonstrated because a single accomplice who disagreed with the group's incorrect answer resulted in a large reduction in conformity even when the number who provided the incorrect answer was greater than five.

The powerful role of dissent has been implicitly understood for centuries as evidenced by the consistent effort by rulers to eliminate any signs of dissension. If a dissenter can be eliminated as a symbol, the effect is obviously reduced. This was the case under the Argentine military dictatorship in the 1970s. Journalists were regularly assassinated, and, in 1977, Jacobo Timmerman, editor of *La Opinion,* was arrested without charges and described as "missing." Timmerman was released from prison after a year and was placed under house arrest. The case received international notoriety and ultimately the regime solved the problem of the dissenter by expelling him from the country.

In other instances, dissent may emerge in surprising ways and with substantial consequences. For example, in 1978 the Somoza regime in Nicaraugua assassinated Pedro d. Charmarro Cardenal, the editor of the main opposition paper in Managua, *La Prensa.* However, at his funeral, 30,000 citizens appeared. This presented evidence to many that, in fact, there was substantial dissatisfaction with the regime. By July of 1979, the 45-year rule of the Somozas had been overthrown by the Sandinistas. A similar sequence of events occurred in the Philippines in 1983 after the assassination of Benigno S. Aquino, Jr., the main opposition candidate. Finally, the Hungarian revolution against Soviet rule in the 1950s may be cited. Here the revolt began slowly. But as citizens realized that others were also opposed to the regime, the revolution gained momentum until the Soviet army subdued the rebellion.

2. The Nature of the Stimuli and the Role of the Dissenter

Groups are rarely concerned with the proper judgment of the relationship between two lines and its members are not likely to feel a great deal of subjective pressure to agree, although the desire to appear competent is an important one. On the other hand, opinions about social issues are understood to be of vital importance and the attitudes of others are of substantial concern. In addition to the substantive considerations, a dissenter may occupy a role of either compromiser (a position between the individual's and the group's) or of extremist (a position even further from the group's than the individual's).

Research by Allen and Levine sought to extend the understanding of conformity by varying both the nature of the stimuli and the role of the dissenter. For objective stimuli (similar to those employed by Asch) both the compromiser and the extremist dissenter reduced the likelihood of conformity even when the dissenter was not credible, that is, claimed to be unable to clearly see the stimuli. However, for the social issues only the compromising dissenter had this effect.

In real life, it is quite likely that the extremist dissenter may increase conformity. For example, opinions expressed publicly by U.S. communists during the McCarthy era in the 1950s may have influenced some noncommunists who disagreed with McCarthy to express opinions closer to his. Since McCarthy's views did not necessarily represent the majority in the country, the conformity influence was toward a perceived powerful minority.

3. Pressures toward Conformity

Solomon Schachter examined conformity contemporaneously with Asch but prior to the publication of Asch's research. Earlier research, much of it in natural environments, had established the existence of group standards and of sanctions against those who violated them. Two factors were primary in accounting for the pressure the group exerted upon the individual. The first was the cohesiveness of the unit and the second was the amount of deviance expressed by the person. When groups are very cohesive, there is likely to be greater agreement upon values. The pressure for agreement increases with increasing importance of the values and with increasing ambiguity or lack of external referents for establishing the social reality. Under these conditions, the pressure on a dissenter would be expected to increase the greater that person's deviance.

Schachter further hypothesized that the initial attempt would be to convert the deviant. However, the recalcitrant dissenter was likely to experience subsequent exclusion. The study was designed so that subjects believed they were in real organizations, for example, a radio club or a film critic's club. Results supported the basic hypotheses.

4. Groupthink

A special form of conformity may occur in some highly valued groups; this was labeled groupthink by Irving Janis. Those with decision-making ability, for example, advisors to a chief of state, defer to the leader even though they question the quality of the decisions. The factors that increase the likelihood of such deference may include the desire to retain membership in a highly valued group, a history of successful decisions, a devotion and unwillingness to criticize the leader, and a lack of encouragement or actual discouragement by the leader for the presentation of alternate points of view. Among the examples cited by Janis was the decision of the Kennedy administration to support the Bay of Pigs invasion of Cuba in 1961.

5. The Group as an Information Source

Stanley Milgram examined the effect of the group upon passersby in New York City. Groups varying in size from 1 to 15 looked up at a skyscraper. The likelihood a passerby would also look up reached its peak at a group size of 5, comparable to Asch's findings. This might be an example of informational conformity. The behavior of the crowd may merely be a cue for information, somewhat similar to that of a newspaper stand with copies of the daily edition displayed. (The likelihood of stopping and standing alongside the group continued to increase to the maximum crowd size of 15.)

6. Social Facilitation

Social facilitation, discussed by Robert Zajonc, was identified early in the history of experimental social psychology (late-19th and early-20th centuries). Organisms such as ants and cockroaches were observed to increase their response rate in the presence of conspecifics. It is not necessary that these conspecifics be co-acting, as first thought, but merely present. This presence appears to increase arousal. Because the phenomenon is observed in submammalian species, there is reason to argue for a biological basis although the most intelligent species may also be consciously concerned about their public appearance (evaluation apprehension).

In some instances it is difficult to determine whether the response is due to social facilitation or to conformity. In a study of audiences in a movie theater by this author and William Fenley, the likelihood of laughter to a humorous scene (from the movie *M.A.S.H.*) on the part of unobtrusively observed members of the audience increased directly as a function of audience size. The number at a showing varied unpredictably during the 2-week period of observations from a low of 175 to a high of 976. Some implicit conformity is possible since individuals may prefer behavior that is similar to that of a large social group even though that person's presence is essentially anonymous. However, the primary factor appears to be social facilitation with the degree of arousal directly related to the audience size.

C. Research on Obedience

While conformity is an expression of solidarity, obedience for the most part derives from status differences. The most important instances of obedience are not those of bland adherence to the request of others but to behavior that may be morally offensive and that may occur in the context of group conflict.

1. The Milgram Studies

Obedience to malevolent authority was extensively explored by Milgram in one of the most important series of studies in the history of the social sciences. Adults were recruited from the general New Haven, Connecticut, area through a newspaper advertisement. There was one naive subject in each session. The subject's task was to be the "teacher" in a learning experiment in which the "learner," an accomplice of the experimenter, was given an electric shock for a wrong answer. The experimenter was also present and provided instructions to the subject. Unknown to the subject-teacher, no shocks were actually administered. However, the subject believed that they were being received and that they were painful. This belief was reinforced by the administration of a painful sample shock to the subject prior to the formal "learning" session at a level identified as 45 volts. The mock shock machine had labeled levers for dispensing the "punishment" that increased to 450 volts. In addition, the machine contained verbal warnings of danger at the higher levels.

In the main experimental condition, the accomplice-learner was unseen by the subject-teacher since each was on a different side of a room wall. In spite of shouts from the accomplice-learner to stop, repeated warnings from him of a previously indicated heart condition and eventually total silence, a majority of subjects proceeded, at the insistence of the experimenter, to administer increasing levels of shock to the highest level.

There were a large number of variations of the above experiment and altogether several hundred subjects participated. Results indicated that: (a) the subjects were not sadistically inclined; (b) obedience increased with increasing physical distance from the learner; (c) obedience declined the further the experimenter was from the subject; (d) there was practically no resistance to the experimenter's orders when the subject performed a subsidiary role and someone else controlled the shock machine; (e) there was almost complete reduction in obedience when there was dissent (that is, either two experimenters disagreed with each other or a group of accomplices argued over cessation of the shocks; and (f) the experimenter's prior status was of little importance when the experiment was contrived so that a former experimenter became a subject and a new experimenter led the learning session.

The likelihood of obedience was only somewhat reduced when the experiment was not conducted on the Yale University campus but in an office in an unpretentious section of downtown Bridgeport. In this instance, the credibility of the experimenter was dependent solely upon his dress, self-proclamation of the purposes of the experiment and his role, and the pseudoname of the organization and position titles displayed in the office.

Milgram's basic findings, including the levels of obedience, have been replicated both in the United States and in other countries. An example is the research by Mantell and Panzarella in Germany. (Thomas Blass has investigated how the Milgram research is viewed by others through the presentation of sections of the film of the original studies. In addition, the Milgram research has achieved international fame among audiences other than professionals. For example, Alexander Voronov, at the Russian State University of the Humanities in Moscow, in association with U.S. colleagues, developed a film about the Milgram research, which has been presented to the Russian public on television.)

Milgram described the basic experimental procedure to a group of psychiatrists. Their average prediction was that only one of a thousand subjects would comply whereas more than 20 of the 40 in the baseline experiment did. This was one of the factors that led Milgram to propose that people are socialized to obedience throughout their lives. They, therefore, develop two sets of moral values: one is their private morality, the autonomous mode, and another, the agentic mode, which is automatically engaged when in organizational-institutional environments.

2. Nurses and Doctors

Contemporaneously with Milgram's work, and without reference to his early publications in 1963 and 1964, a research team conducted a study of nurse–physician relationships which provided support in a natural setting for Milgram's findings.

The investigation was constructed around an irregular order from a doctor to a nurse that included the following components: an excessive dose of a drug (based on labels on the drug box) was requested by a doctor by telephone, the voice of the doctor was unfamiliar, and the phone request represented a violation of hospital policy since the drug itself was unauthorized. To protect the patients, the actual pills were placebos and were never administered because a member of the research team, a psychiatrist, was in the ward at the time of the phone call.

The call was placed when there were few if any supervisory personnel present. Twelve wards in a public hospital and 10 in a private one were included. Although 18 of the 22 subjects indicated a general awareness of the impropriety of the nonemergency telephone request (based on postexperimental interviews), 21 of the 22 offered no delay in their actions at the conclusion of the call. A majority (15) recalled that they had experienced naturally occurring situations comparable to that mirrored in the experiment.

Consistent with Milgram's findings and theoretical distinction between the autonomous and agentic modes, both senior as well as student nurses stated, in questionnaires administered to supplementary samples, that they would have resisted. However, the description in the questionnaire did not precisely parallel the experiment since it explicitly identified conditions that were implicit in the actual ward study.

3. The Utrecht Studies

The Utrecht studies by Meeus and Raajimakers represent another cross-cultural replication of the Milgram studies but with a modification in procedure. A central thesis was that most violence is mediated; the offender does not immediately see the consequences of the action. Based on the Milgram studies, this mediation may be interpreted as increasing the distance between the attacker and the victim and would be expected to result in higher levels of obedience.

The research was conducted in the Netherlands during the early 1980s and consisted of 17 experiments encompassing a total of 352 subjects. (In 1985, 60 subjects were involved in a replication of 2 experiments that were designed to be comparable to Milgram's.)

The basic procedure was to emulate the Milgram roles of experimenter, accomplice, and naive subject. The accomplice was presumably taking a test to determine fitness for a job. If the test were failed then the "applicant" would remain unemployed. During the testing session, the subject was to "administer" 15 negative and disruptive comments to the applicant who would express objections to the remarks. As in the Milgram research, there were 4 verbal prods utilized by the experimenter to encourage resistant subjects to continue to execute all 15 remarks. The control group experienced the same conditions but subjects were able to decide the number of remarks to execute.

In the baseline condition, 91% of the subjects fully complied, that is, administered all 15 of the negative remarks. When personnel officers were the subjects, the expectation was that their ethical code would inhibit them but the results were the same. This finding is consistent with Milgram's distinction between autonomous and agentic morality.

On the other hand no one in the control group in which subjects were not prodded to continue, administered all of the stress remarks. (Milgram had observed, in one of his experimental variations, that if subjects were allowed to choose their own shock levels, they uniformly selected the lowest levels throughout the session.)

Three other conditions imitated Milgram's procedures. In one, subjects were asked to anticipate whether they would administer all of the stress remarks. Only 9% said yes. In the second, the experimenter was absent after providing the instructions. Compliance decreased to one-third of the subjects. In a variation in which two peers began to object to a continuance, compliance decreased further to one-sixth of the subjects. Providing advance information to the subjects about the experiment prior to participation did not lower compliance.

Two important variations provided further insights. In one, subjects were led to believe that they would be personally liable for damages. Compliance decreased to about one-quarter of the participants. However, if they were informed that the legal liability would be "covered" by the academic department, two-thirds complied. (Milgram had discussed the importance of personal responsibility in his experiments.)

Finally, there were role-playing variations. In one, the subjects were simply asked to be nonactive but imagine the outcomes. Here obedience, as expected, decreased. But when the role playing was active, that is the subject actually performed the experimental sequence, two-thirds complied.

A finding that deserves further investigation was that under some circumstances subjects who were measured as highly authoritarian obeyed the requests to a substantially greater extent than did nonauthoritarians.

D. Obedience and Disobedience in Groups

William Gamson and his co-workers examined disobedience in a group that was asked by a company to provide essentially false testimony. A major goal was to investigate the processes through which rebellion against authority emerges in a collectivity. Such rebellion requires both a redefinition of the social environment that undermines the obligation to obey authority as well as the development of group solidarity for collective action.

Subjects were recruited through newspaper advertisements from the general population in small- to medium-sized cities in southeastern Michigan. The experimental groups ranged in size from 6 to 10. They reported to a local hotel and were asked to be videotaped by a consulting firm hired by an oil company. The oil company was being sued by a former manager of one of their franchised gas stations. The manager had been relieved of his position shortly after criticizing major oil company pricing policies in a man-in-the-street interview. The company claimed this was irrelevant and that he was let go because of nonmarital cohabitation with a woman. The company argued that this violated community standards and interfered with his ability to manage the gas station profitably. The members of the experimental group were supposed to pretend that they were members of the community who were offended by the individual's behavior. Their statements were to be videotaped and, as the scenario unfolded, presented in court with signed affidavits by the participants but without any identification that they were merely playing a role requested by the consulting firm.

The members of the group consisted of strangers. The authorities themselves (consulting company) had no real ability to apply sanctions for disobedience and the experimental staging was complex enough that it was not immediately apparent to most of the participants that they were being asked to engage in any questionable activities.

Successful rebellion against authority (refusal to continue to participate) developed in 16 of the 33 groups. There were two important factors that appeared to emerge. One was the characteristics of individuals that existed prior to becoming part of the experiment. When the group lacked individuals with prior skills relevant to protests against authority, group rebellion was very unlikely. Under these circumstances only 1 of 11 groups rebelled and in only 2 of the others was there "fractional success," that is, some individuals but not the group as a whole resisted.

In addition, if the attitudes of the individuals toward authority and oil companies were positive, rebellion was less likely particularly if coupled with the lack of prior skills.

Another important factor appeared to be the development of some form of resistance to authority early in the group's experience. That is, the group dynamics predicted whether a rebellion would occur. In successful groups, someone was likely to question publicly whether what they were being asked to do was right, or to speak on behalf of other group members.

The research is valuable because its design incorporates the dynamic sequence of events that unfold within a group, including the realization that an injustice exists, and the process by which the members of the group become mobilized for rebellion.

Although the context is quite different, elements of the above processes may be identified in the resistance of French villagers, many from Huguenot backgrounds, to the Nazi deportation of Jews, as discussed by Rochat and Modigliani.

E. Authoritarianism

It is usually recognized in psychology (and elsewhere) that there are some traits for which there are consistent individual differences. The question of whether some people are more prone to conformity and especially to obedience to authority arose in a series of studies that began with Stagner's research in the 1930s. Through examination of writings by those who were fascists or who sympathized with fascism, a questionnaire was developed and, based on data analyses from a number of samples, Stagner concluded that intense nationalism and support of big business and antilabor sentiments were among the primary characteristics of those whose views were similar to those of the fascists.

1. The Authoritarian Personality

The most famous work on authoritarianism, however, is *The Authoritarian Personality,* written by a group of psychologists at the University of California, Berkeley. They believed that a number of "traits" clustered in the authoritarian person. These were encapsulated in questions that formed the following scales: the F-scale (fascistic tendency), the A-S scale (anti-Semitism), the E-scale (ethnocentrism) and the PEC scale (political-economic conservatism). The data supported the original hypothesis that a person who is high on one will tend to be high on the others. The work was strongly criticized on methodological grounds, particularly because questions (except those on the PEC scale) were worded in the same direction. Later research established that there were individuals who tended to either agree with an item independent of its content (yeasayers) or disagree consistently (naysayers). Nevertheless, a large number of subsequent studies have incorporated the original measures and the F-scale in particular appears to provide some valid measure of deference to authority. (Altemeyer has reinvestigated authoritarianism.)

2. The Open and Closed Mind

Milton Rokeach extended both the theoretical and empirical foundations of *The Authoritarian Personality* by positing an authoritarianism of the left as well as of the right. He developed the D-scale (dogmatism) to measure a rigidity of thinking and endorsement of authority independent of political direction. Although most subsequent research reported similarity in F and D scores, there is a possibility that this derives, at least in part, from the fact that very few on the extreme political left have been included in the samples.

3. Research Linkages to Reliance on Authority

Investigations have established a number of linkages to authoritarianism that are consistent with some of the original hypotheses in *The Authoritarian Personality.* For example, high authoritarians tend to be more punitive to dissimilar others, stress (anxiety) increases reliance on authority, authoritarians are more likely to be influenced by communications from those with high status and (in the United States) are less likely to believe that their government might engage in unjust or oppressive acts.

In a series of studies in the 1970s, Sales examined the relationship between stress and authoritarianism in some extremely informative unobtrusive studies that analyzed archival material. Based on the prediction that there should be greater authoritarianism during more stressful historical periods, he compared the 1930s in the United States with the 1920s, an economically low-stress period. Consistent with hypotheses in *The Authoritarian Personality,* the 1930s provided evidence of greater punitiveness, emphasis on power, and demands for conformity and loyalty to the government. Although the results might possibly be accounted for by a secular trend (one occurring through time independent of specific events), evidence from a number of investigations has established the relationship between stress and authoritarianism.

F. The Theory of Reduced Alternatives

The present author's *Theory of Reduced Alternatives* incorporates a number of empirical findings into an overall understanding of the factors that lead to both authoritarianism and the support of oppressive government. The reasoning is that those who are systemically punished in a society (receive the fewest rewards in institutional settings–income, education, housing), experience increased stress, resulting in a reduction in cognitive and behavioral alternatives. This reduction creates additional anxiety because of the reduced ability to cope with the complex social environment. Reliance upon authority is an important means by which the anxiety may be resolved. Such reliance leads to identification with authority with additional consequences. These include greater ingroup ties and greater antagonism to outgroup members. The relationships move in both directions. Thus a leader who creates scapegoats may enhance his leadership position through increasing ingroup identification and reliance on authority to solve problems (even if imaginary) of the society.

The consequences of this process are somewhat counterintuitive. It is those who have the least, the systemically punished, who are psychologically most dependent upon authority. Therefore, they are more likely to be supportive even when that authority is engaged in repressive actions against them. Opposition to authority is more likely to arise from those who have gained the most since the availability of resources has not led to the debilitating reliance upon authority to cope with social complexities.

A number of exceptions and countertendencies can exist. For example, there may be specific socialization to obedience as in Germany prior to World War II. Those who are defined to be ineligible for membership in the society may not identify with that society's leadership, and those who have great wealth and power, although systemically rewarded, are likely to rely upon authority for protection of privilege. However, this latter group is more likely to retain psychological independence from authority and rebel if actions are taken against their interests.

G. Competition, Cohesiveness, and Hostility

Sherif conducted a series of studies frequently referred to as Robber's Cave, the name of one of the camps to which he recruited teenage boys. These summer camps were comparable to those traditionally supervised by nonpsychologists. However, the environment was manipulated in a number of ways. The boys were first divided into two groups that were housed in separate dorms. They were then placed in competition through athletic and other contests. The most immediate consequence was an increase in hostility between the groups and an increase in ingroup cohesiveness. Second, different internal structures developed based on the group's achievements. The less successful one was more hierarchical and appeared to be less cohesive than the more successful one. Thus the research suggests that one source of conformity and obedience may be competition and the subsequent development of ingroup cohesiveness. (It is reasonable to suppose that competition is a form of external stress that increases individual anxiety. The effects should be greater in the less successful group and, under these circumstances, one would predict, based on the previously discussed *Theory of Reduced Alternatives,* greater reliance on the leader.)

IV. CONFORMITY AND OBEDIENCE IN POLITICAL MASS KILLING

Although Sherif's autokinetic experiment preceded World War II, most of the research on conformity and obedience not only postdates that war but the war itself motivated social scientists observing, in some cases directly, the processes and outcome of the war. The initial investigations of conformity and obedience, therefore, were closely related to beliefs about armies and mass killing. Subsequently, however, investigations have frequently not been linked to actual events.

A. Crimes of Obedience

Kelman and Hamilton were motivated by the incident at My Lai during the Vietnam War in which U.S. soldiers massacred approximately 300 unarmed Vietnamese civilians whom they had gathered in the center of the town. Their report, *Crimes of Obedience,* is a major contribution to this area of inquiry.

A national sample in 1971 and one of Boston area residents in 1976 included questions about obedience to authority along with specific questions about My Lai and the conviction of Lieutenant Calley. A key differentiation in attitudes toward the massacre and toward the trial and conviction of Lt. Calley was between those who believed that a soldier cannot be held responsible for actions ordered by superiors and those who believed in individual responsibility for one's own actions. The relationships among the variables were replicated in the Boston area survey in 1976. Hamilton extended the research to Moscow in 1990 and included questions about the Soviet war in Afghanistan and individual responsibility that paralleled those for the U.S. subjects. The Moscow residents indicated as much resistance to authority as did the US respondents. (The data were gathered at a critical time in Russian history and may index the disintegration of the Soviet regime.) The Moscow data represent an important cross-national contribution in attempts to understand psychological factors that may be involved in mass killing.

B. Questioning the Obedience Explanation

Goldhagen reexamined the Holocaust and concluded from archival data that none of the extant theories for explaining the destruction of European Jewry are well supported. These consist of obedience to authority, lack of emotional involvement (Arendt's the banality of evil), conformity to the ingroup, extreme sadistic tendencies, and fear of punishment for failure to engage in the killing process (obedience). His conclusion is that the Jews became a hated group over a long period of time and that in Germany for at least 100 years prior to the Holocaust a mentality of a "Jewish problem," which might be solved only by their elimination, had developed. Goldhagen views the motives of those who engaged in the devastation to be similar to those in other instances of mass killing–hatred of the outgroup with a belief that its destruction is justified.

Las Casas, a Catholic priest and eyewitness to the devastation of the native peoples of the Americas by the Spaniards in the late 1400s and early 1500s, detailed the slaughter of millions of people. His experiences were primarily in the islands of the Indies and in Central America. (In all, it is estimated that about 100 million of the 112 million native peoples in North and South America were destroyed by the European invasion.) In this instance, there was: (a) little fear on the part of the conquerors (the native peoples were very cooperative even as slaves); (b) ultimately little religious difference (they were in many instances easily converted); (c) obviously no prior development of hatred although there is little doubt that they were viewed as inferior; and (d) no orders necessary for engaging in the killings. There were group pressures upon those who disagreed with the destruction as evidenced by the negative treatment of Las Casas. However, the conformity among the actors was probably normative; a large group of Spaniards agreed that the actions that were being taken were legitimate and this was fueled by their greed for gold and other possessions including the native women. In this instance, the dissenting position of Las Casas, although vigorous, public, and expressed to the highest authorities in European Spain, resulted in little reduction in the actions against the Indians. It may, however, have mobilized leaders of other European nations to engage in colonization in the Americas as a counterforce to Spanish influence.

C. Obedience in the Military

There is little controversy that military service entails respect for authority and obedience. Armies are hierarchically organized. Obedience to orders is inherent in military discipline and is based on power—there are sanctions for disobedience. However there are also functional and normative influences. Coordination on the battlefield is necessary for both the successful accomplishment of goals against the enemy and preservation of the individual soldier's life. Agreement about the decision-making process is required including a recognition that roles defined prior to battle include differential rights and obligations with respect to order-making capacities. (Of course, the soldier who is drafted has no choice but to adhere to the rules. Nevertheless, that does not prevent a development of normative and functional obedience.)

However, battlefield actions, while coordinated through hierarchical relationships, also result from motives other than those related to obedience to orders. The work of Benjamin Shalit and others who preceded him provide some tentative generalizations.

Shalit's findings indicate that soldiers are motivated by a number of factors. In addition to the obvious apprehension over self-preservation, those of lower rank are concerned about serving the best interests of their comrades while higher military officers identify serving those under them as a major stress. The data therefore suggest functional goals and role requirements may be more important than obedience due to power differentials (at least, in the Israeli army).

The functional component of obedience in military life is illustrated by famous instances in which the individual's assessment of the requirements of battle led to actions contrary to orders. One example is that of Nelson of the British Navy during the Napoleonic wars. But even Nelson, who died in battle, expressed satisfaction at normative obedience—"Thank God, I have done my duty."

Disobedience may also be functional. If the punishment from disobedience, such as prison, is less than the expected risk from obedience, death on the battlefield, some soldiers may disobey.

Shalit's conclusions include some support for the position that obedience may not be a major factor in mass killing. "I have observed–as have others–that behavior contrary to the rules of war was much more often exhibited by soldiers of the support forces who came to the battle scene after the real conflicts were over" (p. 44).

Of course, a functional source does not imply a functional application. Soldiers learn to obey based on principles of classical conditioning. The stimulus is the order, the response is the behavior that is consistent with the order. Yet the soldier is expected to retain, at the same time, the ability to discriminate among orders since some may so obviously offend basic human, moral or military principles that rebellion is justified.

V. PUBLIC VIEWS OF THE ROLE OF OBEDIENCE IN POLITICAL MASS KILLING, CORRUPTION, AND CRIME

An ongoing research project by the author of this article is an attempt to understand how the public evaluates the role of obedience across a variety of real situations. Two levels of inquiry are included. First, the extent to which there is public support for the principles of international law that govern restraint in war is being explored. Second, it is clear that even when there is agreement on general principles, specific instances do not lead to uniform application of the principle. Therefore, the evaluation of actual historical incidents is also being investigated.

A. Views of the Role of Obedience and of Individual Responsibility

Recognizing obedient behavior is relatively easy but determining why it occurred is much more difficult. Inferences are possible about whether observers believe that obedience is a mitigating factor by comparing answers to questions that include orders from a superior to those in which orders are not a component. Thus, students at Reading University in Great Britain were presented with a series of general items all of which included the killing of innocent civilians. The data were obtained by Peter Jones who is a coinvestigator in the British component of the project.

When orders from a superior were included in the description, the act was judged, on average, as neutral or not a war crime but in the other instances it was considered a war crime. Thus there appeared to be some attenuation of soldier responsibility when orders were involved.

B. Assigned Responsibility in the Evaluation of Historical Events

In this portion of the research, respondents were requested to assign penalties, if any, to the attackers based on a short description of an actual historical incident. Three levels of command were included, for example, soldiers, officers, and generals. Assignment of a large penalty suggests both a judgment of responsibility and also moral accountability. (A person may be responsible for a positively viewed act but the judged penalty would be "none"). If an officer is assigned a higher penalty than a soldier, it may be inferred that the respondent views the officer as carrying a greater responsibility. However, higher penalties assigned to soldiers in itself suggests a judgment of responsibility even if the commanders are judged more severely.

The full cross-cultural research project, which is currently being conducted in the United States, Great Britain, New Zealand, The Netherlands, Japan, China, and Russia, includes events that range in historical period from the sacking of Jerusalem by the crusaders in the first crusade in 1099 to contemporary incidents. Some generalizations have emerged based on data from New Zealand (through the cooperation of Pat Regan), Great Britain, and the United States.

When the described act was conducted by a member of the Western allies, for example, the Panama invasion or the atomic bombing of Japan, judged penalties for soldiers or air force pilots were either absent or very small. However, there was, on average, a more severe penalty assigned to those in command (although the penalty was still relatively small). These results in combination with responses to other questions about individual responsibility suggest that the soldier's actions were considered legitimate responses to orders. Penalties were substantially higher for comparable behavior of participants from other countries. Nevertheless, judged penalties for officers were again higher than for the soldiers.

There were circumstances in which obedience did not mitigate individual responsibility. Among war events, mass rape resulted in equal or higher penalties for soldiers compared to commanders.

Further, the hierarchical structure seems to be viewed with greater legitimacy in some environments than in others. In a data collection in the United States, social offenses provided substantial differences in judgments. Business corruption, for example, was not as subject to obedience excuses as was war behavior. The data, however, do suggest that hierarchical legitimacy was greater for the business environment than for other nonmilitary situations such as riots, terrorism, or criminal acts even when it was clear that the actions occurred within a hierarchically structured group.

Because of the complexity of the issues and the fact that the research is still in progress, the above conclusions are tentative but the findings suggest a more refined role for obedience in the explanation of mass killing.

VI. FURTHER RESEARCH

Increased understanding of both the nature of conformity and obedience and the role they play, particularly in intergroup conflict, will require additional research in a number of areas. These include investigations of the relationship of experiments to actual phenomena as well as of group dynamics.

From time immemorial pressures have existed upon individuals to conform and to obey. It is also clear that both conformity and obedience can be facilitators of group conflict—from riots to wars. Their ubiquitous presence, however, does not demonstrate that they are fundamental to the occurrence and intensity of the violence. In fact, their constant existence includes substantial periods in which such violence is not present. The human tendency to assume that the nearness in time of two conditions implies a causal relationship also exists for the interpretation of the relationship between conformity and obedience to conflict. But there is evidence, for example, the work of Las Casas and of Goldhagen, that such aggression involves other more determinative forces such as greed and hate, which exist simultaneously with the everpresent pressures toward conformity and obedience.

Thus a fundamental requirement of future research is to examine other sources of group conflict and to relate these to conformity and obedience. An illustration of this may be riots. The forces that predispose to an outbreak exist prior to the event. A precipitating event acts as a catalyst. In the process, conformity as well as obedience may be observed. But they are not the proximate causes of the violence, although they may channel and intensify it.

An additional need is to incorporate other clearly related variables. For example, the Utrecht studies suggest a potentially important role of authoritarianism and this is consistent with the Gamson research that examined the relationship of prior attitudes toward authority to the likelihood of rebellion. The Kelman and Hamilton research also incorporated a measure of authoritarianism and found a relationship to their obedience measures. The Robber's Cave studies identify an important role for competition and the ensuing development of ingroup cohesiveness. Investigations are further complicated by the effect of knowledge about prior studies on subsequent behavior. In the Gamson explorations, for example, a number of participants cited the Milgram research as a basis for resistance to authority.

Social science and physical science experiments are comparable in that both attempt to fix the state of all possible influences except those being manipulated. However, in social science particularly, the relationships of the variables may depend substantially on the levels at which the others are set. As a result it is necessary not only to vary experimental conditions as illustrated in the Milgram research, but to approach the problem from different perspectives as demonstrated in the study of doctors and nurses and in that of Gamson and his co-workers.

In addition, the group process is itself insufficiently understood. The research by Sherif, Schachter, and Gamson illustrate the value of such studies and present frameworks for the design of subsequent inquiries.

Behavior for the most part is embedded within a group and unfolds through time. In a number of instances the conduct of the subject in the experiment was filmed (for example, Milgram and Gamson). Others have also specifically focused on changes over time, for example, the cited Schachter and Sherif's Robbers Cave research. However, formal models that incorporate time and rates of change in behavior are noticeably absent.

An illustration of a potentially valuable approach may be provided by the Richardson models. Richardson (1960) hypothesized a feedback relationship between two hostile countries. Exploiting the calculus, he was able to derive predictions such as an arms race that escalates to violence. (He correctly predicted the outbreak of war between Great Britain and Nazi Germany). Although the model has been extensively evaluated and modified, it remains an important example of the formal treatment of the time variable in social science. The Richardson model, it should be noted, incorporates a dynamic process between two countries without recourse to either conformity or obedience. Instead, the variables include the mutual hostility of the parties, the rate at which each is arming, and costs.

VII. CONFORMITY AND OBEDIENCE IN THE 21ST CENTURY

The social science of conformity and obedience is barely 60 years old. Complex human phenomena will require a great deal of additional study if precise understandings are to be achieved. It therefore should not be surprising that social influences may either increase or decrease both conformity and obedience and subsequently their effect on the degree of group conflict depending on the direction and strength of those influences.

A. Forces that Increase Conformity and Obedience

The direction of many developments in the 21st century has already been determined. Technology of weapons of mass destruction will continue to affect obedience to military authority. The "advances" increase the distance of the individual from the target and a direct prediction is an increase in obedience to orders.

Economic concentration increases the power of the wealthy and thus, even in nonmilitary environments, increases their ability to demand obedience. To the extent that such economic interests can influence the media, for example, by rewards for appropriate information and the withholding of resources otherwise, conformity is increased and the likelihood of dissent decreased. Cultural homogenization reduces the points of view that are available and thus also reduces dissent. Although rebellion against unjust authority almost always occurs in groups, such rebellion requires dissenters as shown in the research of Asch, Allen and Levine, and Gamson.

Poverty, as a form of systemic punishment, also increases dependence and subsequently both conformity and reliance on leadership.

A final economic factor may be the depletion of natural resources. The limited supply, almost totally consumed by the already developed nations, places these nations in competition with those that are attempting to develop, particularly large countries such as China or India. Understanding the likely outcome is well informed by Sherif's Robber's Cave investigations. That research suggested that competition increased ingroup cohesiveness and hostility toward the outgroup with subsequent differences in group structure. Under most circumstances competition may reasonably be considered stressful and the effect should be greater on the less successful group. The theory of reduced alternatives argued that these factors increased reliance on authority. The line of reasoning would suggest that, in the competition for natural resources, the already developed countries will be more successful and this will lead to increased reliance on established political leadership in those that are less developed.

B. Forces that Decrease Conformity and Obedience

Urbanization should allow greater opportunity for group formation and therefore provide a vehicle for dissent or disobedience. Group membership has been shown by Tilly to be related to rebellion in France and may itself be considered a resource within the framework of the Gamson research. Of course, any increase in poverty that occurs along with urbanization is a counterforce. In addition, increases in education may increase psychological independence from authority unless the socialization within the educational environment is oriented toward conformity and/or obedience. In general, economic well-being should increase independence from authority and, therefore, increase the likelihood of dissent when injustice is perceived.

Finally, it is important to realize that cultural norms may favor or diminish individual independence as the history of Great Britain compared to Germany prior to World War II illustrates. If the norm of the rights of the individual becomes more widespread, a force for a decrease in conformity and obedience will be established.

Also See the Following Articles

BEHAVIORAL PSYCHOLOGY • COOPERATION, COMPETITION, AND CONFLICT • CULTURAL STUDIES, OVERVIEW • GENOCIDE AND DEMOCIDE • MILITARY CULTURE • MASS CONFLICT AND THE PARTICIPANTS, ATTITUDES TOWARD • POWER AND DEVIANCE • POWER, SOCIAL AND POLITICAL THEORIES OF • WAR CRIMES

Bibliography

Goldhagen, D. J. (1996). *Hitler's willing executioners: Ordinary Germans and the Holocaust.* New York: Alfred A. Knopf.

Miller, A. G., Collins, B. E., & Brief, D. E. (Ed.). (1995). Perspectives on obedience to authority: The legacy of the Milgram experiments. *Journal of Social Issues, 51,* 3 (whole issue).

Kelman, H. C., & Hamilton, V. L. (1989). *Crimes of obedience.* New Haven: Yale University Press.

Meeus, W. H. J, & Raajimakers, Q. A. W. (1995). Obedience in modern society: The Utrecht studies. *Journal of Social Issues, 51,* 3, 155–175.

Shalit, B., (1988). *The psychology of conflict and combat.* New York: Praeger.

References to Classic Research

Adorno, T. W., Frenkel-Brunswik, E., Levinson, D. J., & Sanford, R. N. (with Aron, B., Levinson, M. H., & Morrow, W.) (1950). *The authoritarian personality.* (1969). New York: Norton.

Asch, S. E. (1955). Opinions and social pressure. *Scientific American, 193,* 31–35.

Brotzman, B., Dalrymple, S., Graves, N., & Pierce, C. M. (1966). An Experimental study in nurse-physician relationships. *The Journal of Nervous and Mental Disease, 143*(2), 171–180.

Gamson, W. A., Fireman, B., & Rytina, S. (1982). *Encounters with unjust authority.* Homewood, IL: Dorsey.

Kelman, H. C. (1958). Compliance, identification and internalization: Three processes of attitude change. *Journal of Conflict Resolution, 51–60,* II(1).

Milgram, S. (1974). *Obedience to authority.* New York: Harper and Row.

Richardson, L. F. (1960). *Arms and Insecurity.* Chicago: Quadrangle Books.

Rokeach, M. (1960). *The open and closed mind.* New York: Basic Books

Sales, S. M. (1973). Threat as a factor in authoritarianism: An analysis of archival data. *Journal of Personality and Social Psychology, 28*(1) 44–57.

Sherif, M. (1937). An experimental approach to the study of attitudes. *Sociometry, I,* 90–98.

Sherif, M. (1956). Experiments in group conflict. *Scientific American, 195*(5), 54–58.

Stagner, R. (1936). Fascist Attitudes: An exploratory study. *Journal of Social Psychology,* 7, 309–319.

Conscientious Objection, Ethics of

Michael W. Hovey
Iona College

Gordon C. Zahn
University of Massachusetts, Boston

GLOSSARY

Absolute Conscientious Objection In the United States, this refers to objection to combatant military service in "war in any form," but allows for participation in alternative service. In the British context, the term "absolutist" includes those who refuse *all* forms of participation in war (including alternative service). In the U.S. context, these persons are known as "war resisters" (see below).

Alternative Service The mandatory performance of nonmilitary service to the community or state in lieu of participation in war and the armed forces. Some nations offer this alternative to conscientious objectors, rather than prosecuting or imprisoning those who refuse conscription in the armed forces for reasons of conscience.

Conscientious Objection Broadly, the objection to performing some action for reasons of conscience. Common usage usually relates this term to objection to participation in activities related to war and military service—for example, objection to the payment of taxes used for military expenditures; the refusal of scientists to engage in war-related research or industry; objection to registration for possible conscription; objection to participation in *all* war and *all* forms of military service or to *particular* wars (including guerilla or other forms of internal war) or *particular* roles within the armed forces—for instance, those involving the use of nuclear weapons. Conscientious objectors (or "C.O.s") may or may not be formally recognized as such by governments; many C.O.s have been forced to endure imprisonment or worse because of their refusal to perform military service or to otherwise cooperate with their government's preparations for war.

Conscription The formal, legal enlistment of citizens into the armed forces. Also commonly called "the draft."

Crystallization of Conscience A term used by the U.S. Department of Defense to describe the process through which a member of the armed forces becomes a conscientious objector while serving in the military; when vague thoughts and feelings against war and killing become clear and solid as a result of further reflection on the experience of serving in the armed forces.

Selective Conscientious Objection Objection to participating in the armed forces during a *particular* war, or to serving in a *particular* military unit or engaging in a particular type of activity during a war—for example, involving the use of weapons of mass destruction (nuclear, biological, chemical).

War Resister In the American context, a person who "conscientiously objects" to war and military service but who also rejects other forms of cooperation with governmental avenues of recognition for those opposed to war (such as alternative service); these persons opt for either prison or exile from their country rather than participation in nonmilitary or noncombatant roles established by their government.

THE ETHICS OF CONSCIENTIOUS OBJECTION refers, in the first place, to the moral principles or values, often of a religious or philosophical nature, upon which an individual bases his or her objection to participation in war and military service. It also refers to the ethical treatment of conscientious objectors by society and civil/military authorities. This article first examines the various ethical bases of conscientious objection. It then briefly sketches the religious and philosophical roots of conscientious objection. Next, it explores the relationship of conscription and conscientious objection globally and, as a case study, within the United States. Next, a brief consideration of war resisters is presented. Finally, the article examines the significance of the United Nations recognition of the universal human right of conscientious objection to military service.

I. THE PERSONAL AND SOCIAL ETHICS OF THE CONSCIENTIOUS OBJECTOR

The most basic ethical foundation of conscientious objection to war is the profound conviction that it is morally wrong to intentionally kill another human being. This conviction can be reached as a result of religious training and belief. Christian and Jewish conscientious objectors, for example, might cite the book of Genesis in pointing out their belief that every human being is "created in the image and likeness of God," and is therefore to be treated with dignity and respect. Christian conscientious objectors might also point to the injunction of Jesus to "love your enemies, do good to those who hate you" (Luke 6:27).

The conviction that it is wrong to kill others might also be derived from moral or philosophical precepts and training. A respect and value of every person's unique personality, for example, could lead to a refusal to snuff out the life of any individual for any reason. A conscientious objector might also resist the notion that one's nationality or ethnic identity are grounds for killing, or more generally object to transforming a "person into a thing," as the philosopher Simone Weil once wrote. Likewise, a conscientious objector might find a particular war to be inimical to the nation's well-being, or might embrace the concept of the universality of the human family and reject the proposition that, in being considered as "other," one loses one's "right to life."

While there has been some support for basing a claim of conscientious objection on "political" grounds over the years, this form of objection has been generally rejected because it is not considered to be based on the sort of deeply held beliefs found among those whose conscientious objection springs from religious or philosophical convictions.

For the conscientious objector, it is the distinct possibility, if not probability, that he or she will be compelled to participate in acts of killing other human beings that leads to the objector's refusal to participate in war and military service. Common interpretations of such participation—"defending the homeland," "protecting the innocent," "restoring the peace," and so on—do not obscure the fundamental reality that soldiers are trained to kill other human beings, even perhaps for "good" reasons; nevertheless, the conscientious objector cannot, in good conscience, engage in what he or she considers to be a profoundly immoral act.

This conscientious refusal to kill another human being at the behest of government authorities—who also lay claim to another ethical "good": the duty to defend the community or society from harm and destruction—frequently leads to the quintessential struggle between the individual and the state regarding rights and obligations. It is here that a new set of questions is posed concerning the "ethics of conscientious objection." Does the individual have the right to "withdraw" (at least in terms of the use of violent force) from the duty to participate in the defense of the nation? Does the state have the right to compel an individual, under pain of various sanctions—ranging from fines and imprisonment to execution—to participate in acts that the individual finds morally reprehensible? Should the state be allowed to require some other form of service to the community that does not offend the conscience of its citizens? Should a conscientious objector freely offer to perform nonmilitary forms of service to the community as an indication of his or her understanding and acceptance of the duties of citizenship? As these questions illustrate, the ethical questions facing both conscientious objectors and society are varied and complex, even though the temptation of all parties concerned is often to see conscientious objection as a simple "no" to war.

II. THE RELIGIOUS/PHILOSOPHICAL ROOTS OF CONSCIENTIOUS OBJECTION

Although the term "conscientious objection" was not used until the 1890s (regarding the objections of some to mandatory vaccinations), the religious and philosophical advocacy of opposition to the use of force can be found at least as far back as the 6th century before the Common Era (B.C.E.). In fact, some social scientists, predominant among them Ashley Montagu, have noted the "non-aggression" of some preliterate societies. While it would be incorrect to label such resistance to organized social violence "conscientious objection," it is important to recall that the practice of refusing to engage in warfare and of seeking instead nonviolent methods to resolve conflicts is truly ancient.

The following is a brief overview of the major world religions' teachings on nonviolence and on participation in violence and war.

A. Early Eastern Religious/Philosophical Teachings

Lao Tzu, the Chinese Taoist philosopher, advocated a "way" (Tao) of restraint and acquiescence to the courses of nature, while at the same time recognizing a role for military force, according to Mayer (1966). He sums up the teachings of later Chinese writers such as Confucius and Mencius regarding their advocacy of patience, sympathy for the other, and a rather utilitarian form of the Golden Rule: "Do good to others and others will do good to you. Hate people and be hated by them. Hurt them and they will hurt you. What is hard about that?"

Jainism, "the oldest philosophy based on nonviolence" (1965), is based upon the Great Vow of Nonviolence; all other ethical principles flow from this. The Buddhist and Hindu traditions also embrace a spirit of nonviolence, a spirit that some notable adherents of these traditions tried to incorporate into their lives. Proceeding from the Buddhist ethical foundations of love and compassion, in particular the Precept against Killing, the 3rd century B.C.E. ruler, Asoka, rejected the use of force in his efforts to convert his subjects to Buddhism. In the Hindu tradition the Bhagavad Gita—even with its sanctioning of war—led Mohandas K. Gandhi to embrace the value of "desirelessness," a fundamental element in his later commitment to *ahimsa* (literally, "no-violence") and *satyagraha* (truth- or soul-force).

B. Jewish Teachings

Jewish tradition has likewise sanctioned certain types of warfare over the centuries, but a central *mitzvah* or teaching of Judaism is "seek peace—*shalom*—and pursue it." While it is true that the exploits of some military heroes are celebrated in the Hebrew Scriptures, the Book of Deuteronomy, for example, speaks of various exemptions from military service, including some for those who are "afraid and tender-hearted." Axelrad (1986) interprets this to mean "those who are physically robust but so gentle and compassionate as to be unsuitable for service as warriors."

In the 20th century, Jewish teaching on war and peace was greatly affected by the genocidal *Shoah* (Nazi Holocaust), the establishment of the State of Israel in 1948, and the later wars and military engagements with Arabs/Palestinians. On the one hand, the profound trauma which resulted from the attempted annihilation of the Jewish people by the Nazis and the consequent desire to safeguard the existence of the State of Israel make it rare to find *absolute conscientious objectors* among the Jewish people—although various official Jewish organizations (e.g., Synagogue Council of America and Jewish Peace Fellowship) are on record with their support for C.O.s. (NISBCO 1983)

On the other hand, during the 1980s and '90s, small but increasing numbers of Israeli soldiers became *selective conscientious objectors* as a result of governmental/military policies in Lebanon and toward Palestinians during the *Intifada* ("uprising"). While no official recognition was extended to these C.O.s, claimants were informally removed from their posts and transferred to noncombatant duties in some cases.

C. Christian Teachings

1. Early Nonviolence

The first three centuries of Christianity were characterized by a near total commitment to nonviolence. Taking their cue from accounts in the gospels where Jesus called on his followers to "love your enemies" and "to him who strikes you on the cheek, offer the other also" (Luke 6:27–29), some major early Christian writers, such as Tertullian, Justin Martyr, Origen, and Lactantius, insisted on the "absolute incompatibility" of

Christ's teachings with violence, according to Mayer. Reliable accounts of Imperial Roman tribunals tell of third and fourth century Christians who were executed for their refusal to serve in the army, based not only upon their refusal to shed the blood of another human being but also their resistance to offering incense to the Roman gods—and thus committing idolatry—which was a duty required of soldiers, as explained by Hegeland and colleagues (1985).

2. "Just War" Tradition

Following the Emperor Constantine's conversion to Christianity in 313 C.E. and the end of imperial persecution of the followers of Christ, Christians began to find ways to integrate themselves as full citizens of the empire—including as soldiers. The development of the concept of the "just war theory" in the Middle Ages provided answers to questions that arose for the individual and the governing authorities concerning participation in war and military service. Theologians such as Ambrose, Augustine, and Thomas Aquinas, clerics such as Vitoria and Suarez, and the secular philosopher Hugo Grotius laid out the rationale and criteria which would allow for the participation of Christians in war under limited conditions. While there is no single list of criteria accepted as the "classical just war tradition," a useful summary was presented by the United States Catholic bishops in their 1983 pastoral letter on war and peace ("The Challenge of Peace: God's Promise and Our Response"). Under the traditional category of *jus ad bellum* (the purpose or reason for war), the bishops list the following elements: War must be waged for a *just cause*; it must be declared by *competent authority*; it must be waged with the *right intention*; it must be a used only as a *last resort*; there must be a *probability of success*. Under the traditional category of *jus in bello* (the manner and methods used in waging war), the bishops insist that there must be *proportionality* between the way in which the war is fought and the good expected to be the result of the war, and that any use of force must be proportionate to the outcome desired (i.e., never total destruction of enemies or their societies). Finally, every act of war must be *discriminate*—that is, aimed only at combatants, never intentionally at innocent noncombatants.

Medieval commentators on canon (church) law struggled with the implications of such decisions for princes and subjects; some of the fruits of the scholarly debates which began back then can be seen in the development of the "laws of war" drawn up in the 19th and 20th centuries. It is the application of these criteria to actual wars that could lead one to become a *selective conscientious objector*, when the demands of the criteria are not met.

3. Continuing and Later Christian Nonviolence

The nonviolent witness of Christians continued throughout the medieval era, even during the Crusades, when popes enticed soldiers to fight by offering forgiveness of their sins and eternal salvation. At the same time, however, lay followers of St. Francis of Assisi included in their Rule explicit prohibitions against the bearing of arms.

The 16th and 17th centuries gave birth to the "historic peace churches"—the Church of the Brethren, Mennonites, Society of Friends (Quakers) and others—whose distinguishing witness was their abhorrence of war and adamant conscientious refusal to participate in it. The influence of these churches on the evolving recognition of the conscientious objector position continues to this day.

In the 20th century, particularly in the aftermath of the unprecedented destruction of World War II, as illustrated by the Nazi Holocaust and the atomic bombings of Japanese cities, the mainstream Protestant and Roman Catholic communities sharpened their teachings on war and peace. After giving scant approval to conscientious objectors during the war, the Catholic Church praised those "who renounce the use of violence" and condemned any indiscriminate act of war as "a crime against God and man himself" at the Second Vatican Council in 1965. Firm support was given to both *absolute* and *selective* conscientious objection by most Christian bodies.

D. Islamic Tradition

Similar to the traditions described above, Islam recognizes both the legitimate use of force and some forms of nonviolence. Far from being the impetus to war that many non-Muslims mistakenly believe it to be, *jihad*—a type of war aimed at the restoration of justice and the alleviation of suffering of the weak—includes strict conditions regarding the conduct of war. Islam also recognizes a form of nonviolence known as *quietism*, a "prudential postponement of adopting offensive measures when the probability of success is outweighed by the likelihood of destruction and suffering," according to Smock (1995). There is also a small but significant following among Muslims of Gandhian nonviolence, although officially, according to Smock, "Islam grants no place to absolute or principled pacifism." In the 20th century, no Islamic country made any legal provision for conscientious objection.

III. CONSCRIPTION AND CONSCIENTIOUS OBJECTION

The story of the ethics of conscientious objection does not end with an understanding of the personal beliefs of a conscientious objector or a simple recounting of the religious and philosophical teachings on nonviolence and conscientious objection. The historical experience of those who renounce violence and participation in war and military service throughout history has been, more often than not, one of persecution, imprisonment, exile, or execution. While it is true that various societies and governing authorities throughout the centuries have made some allowance some of the time for those opposed to war and participation in armed forces, the fact is that the question of the ethical treatment of conscientious objectors took on a new significance with the introduction of *conscription* in the late 18th century by Napoleon in France—and many nations that followed his example.

A. The Global Status of Conscription and Conscientious Objection

According to the most recent (at this writing) comprehensive study of conscientious objection around the world, a 1997 report of the United Nations Secretary-General to the U.N. Commission on Human Rights on "The Question of Conscientious Objection to Military Service" (E/CN.4/1997/99) stated that of 173 countries responding, 102 countries had programs of mandatory conscription, 69 did not conscript their citizens, and 2 (Mauritius and San Marino) have no system of military service. Seventy-eight countries responded to the question of recognition of conscientious objection. Thirty-seven explicitly recognize conscientious objection; 36 do not (see Table 1). Most of the nations that do recognize conscientious objection require alternative service, except Switzerland, which requires compulsory labor for one and half times the length of the military service refused. The United States makes provisions for *absolute* conscientious objectors even though military service is voluntary; C.O.s may be either discharged from the armed forces or serve in noncombatant military roles. The Netherlands explicitly recognizes *selective* conscientious objection.

In the case of Israel and Ireland, even though conscientious objection is not legally recognized, exemptions may be granted for those opposed for reasons of conscience to military service. At the time of the report, El Salvador and Romania were revising their laws to

TABLE I

Global Survey of Conscientious Objection

Nations that recognize conscientious objection	Nations that do not recognize conscientious objection
Angola	Afghanistan
Argentina	Albania
Austria	Antigua & Barbuda
Belarus	Bolivia
Brazil	Bosnia and Herzegovina
Bulgaria	Cambodia
Croatia	Chile
Cyprus	China
Czech Republic	Colombia
Denmark	Cuba
Estonia	Democratic People's Republic of Korea
Federal Republic of Germany	Dominican Republic
Finland	Ecuador
France	Egypt
Greece	Ethiopia
Guyana	Guatemala
Hungary	Iran
Italy	Iraq
Latvia	Kazakstan
Lithuania	Kuwait
Moldova	Lao Democratic People's Republic
Netherlands	Libya
Norway	Mexico
Paraguay	Morocco
Poland	Mozambique
Portugal	Peru
Russian Federation	Republic of Korea
Slovakia	Senegal
Slovenia	Singapore
Spain	Somalia
Sweden	Syria
Switzerland	Tunisia
Macedonia	Turkey
United Kingdom	Venezuela
United States of America	Viet Nam
Yugoslavia	Yemen
Zimbabwe	

Notes: Ireland and Israel do not officially recognize conscientious objection, but permit exemptions for those claiming reasons of conscience as grounds for discharge or transfer to noncombatant duty.

El Salvador and Romania are rewriting laws in order to recognize conscientious objection.

From *Secretary-General's Report to United Nations Commission on Human Rights on The Question of Conscientious Objection to Military Service (E/CN.4/1997/99) of 16 January 1997.*

include recognition of conscientious objection and provision for alternative service.

As Table 1 illustrates, the great majority of nations recognizing conscientious objection are found in Europe (including most of the former Soviet bloc nations); conversely, most of the nations which do not recognize conscientious objection are found in Latin America, Asia, and among the Islamic countries. Clearly, religious and cultural traditions contribute to the acceptance or refusal of the claims of conscientious objectors.

Penalties for those whose claim of conscientious objection is not recognized can range from stiff fines to imprisonment. The Secretary-General's report states that C.O.s were known to be imprisoned in Cyprus, Greece, Kazakstan, Switzerland, and Turkey. It is unknown how many individuals are forced into exile and seek asylum in other countries as a result of their conscientious refusal to perform military service. Also, although the report did not address the issue, it is believed or known that some countries apply the death penalty to those who refuse military service on grounds of conscience. Perhaps the most well-known case comes from World War II, when an Austrian farmer, Franz Jaegerstaetter, refused to report for military duty in the Nazi army, and was executed by beheading on August 9, 1943 in Berlin.

B. Conscription and Conscientious Objection in the United States

The history of conscription and conscientious objection in the United States, while not typical, can be instructive, because it illustrates the various forms of conscientious objection and the ways governments can and do choose to deal with them. Since space limitations make it impossible to examine the practice of every nation, a focus on the experience of conscientious objectors in the United States throughout its history can serve as a "case study" and a means of understanding the experience of others around the world.

1. The Civil War

Conscription came to the United States, North and South, during the Civil War (1861–1865) and in 1864, legal recognition was granted to conscientious objectors who were members of religious denominations prohibited from bearing arms by the rules and articles of faith and practice of their religious denominations, provided they agreed to perform alternative (noncombatant) service, according to Schlissel (1968).

2. World War I

Similarly, conscientious objection in the United States during World War I was limited to men who belonged to "well-recognized sects" whose "creed or principles forbid its members to participate in war in any form [i.e., *absolute conscientious objectors*], and whose religious convictions are against war or participation therein," writes Schlissel. Those conscientious objectors who did not belong to well-recognized pacifist sects, such as the Quakers, were imprisoned.

3. World War II

As U.S. involvement in World War II approached, the Draft Act of 1940—which introduced peacetime conscription to the nation—created important new distinctions in the definition of conscientious objection. A concerted effort on the part of the "traditional peace churches" (Brethren, Mennonites, and Society of Friends), along with secular antiwar groups and organizations, succeeded in assuring that exceptions would be made for various types of conscientious objectors. For the first time, provision was made for both those who objected to military service completely and those who would accept military duty only in a noncombatant role (often as a medic). The headquarters of the national agency charged with the responsibility for conscription, the Selective Service System, reported that between 25,000 and 50,000 men applied for and were granted this classification (known as "1-A-0"). Selective Service also advised local conscription or "draft" boards—the members of which determined an individual's draft classification status—that religious training and belief was to be accepted regardless of sect or creed, thus making one's personal beliefs more important that one's membership in a particular religious sect or denomination when claiming conscientious objector status. Those who gained this classification were assigned to *alternative service* "work of national importance" in Civilian Public Service (CPS) programs, in jobs ranging from health care workers to forestry projects.

World War II also brought new concerns to the fore concerning participation in modern war. The atrocities committed by the Nazis, chief among them the genocidal Holocaust, compelled the world to take a fresh look at the generally unquestioned military duty to follow orders without question. The Nuremberg War Crimes Tribunal ruled that individuals have a responsibility to observe international laws of war, regardless of orders from superiors, and it defined the "crimes against peace," "war crimes," and "crimes against humanity" that are justiciable among nations. In such cases, they ruled, the conscientious refusal to follow orders is not merely a right; it is a duty.

The atomic bombings of Hiroshima and Nagasaki produced a new genre of objectors to war—"nuclear pacifists"—who categorically labeled any war that involved nuclear weapons "unjust" because of its obvious violation of the "just war" criteria of proportionality and discrimination between combatants and civilians.

4. Vietnam War

Conscientious objectors to the Vietnam War in the 1960s and '70s brought about a change in the understanding—and legal definition—of conscientious objection in the United States in two landmark Supreme Court rulings. In *United States v. Seeger*, the requirement that an individual's conscientious objection be based on "religious training and belief" was construed in such a way that a belief in a "Supreme Being" was no longer required. The new test required a "sincere and meaningful belief which occupies in the life of the its possessor a place parallel to that filled by the God of those admittedly qualifying for the exemption."

In a more dramatic break with the centuries-old tradition of basing acceptance of a claim of conscientious objection on religious training and belief, the Supreme Court ruled in *Welch v. United States* that nonreligious yet "moral or ethical beliefs" met the test of sincerity for classification as a conscientious objector.

Two other Vietnam War-era Supreme Court cases also contributed to the shaping of the tradition and definition of conscientious objection to military service. Guy Porter Gillette was a draft registrant who, based on a humanist approach to religion, objected to participating in the Vietnam War, but not in a war in defense of the United States or a war sponsored by the United Nations as a peacekeeping measure. Louis Negre, a soldier in the U. S. Army, also claimed *selective conscientious objector* status due to his conviction that, as a Catholic, he must refuse to participate in a war he deemed to be "unjust." Both men lost their cases, based on the Supreme Court's adherence to the regulatory requirement that any objection must be against "war in any form" or *absolute conscientious objection.*

5. War in the Persian Gulf

The U.S. government ended mandatory conscription in 1973; since then, all members of the armed forces have entered their respective branches (Army, Navy, Air Force, Marine Corps) voluntarily. However, voluntary enlistment does not necessarily preclude a later change of heart or, as the Pentagon describes it, a "*crystallization of conscience*" when persons serving in the military are faced with the imminent (as opposed to theoretical) possibility of receiving orders to kill the adversary. The war in the Persian Gulf (1991) produced an estimated 2500 men and women who refused to participate in the war for reasons of conscience, according to a report of the War Resisters League. A number of these individuals were imprisoned for varying lengths of time—some as many as 2 years—which lead Amnesty International to declare some "prisoners of conscience."

IV. WAR RESISTERS

As noted above, an unknown number of men—and more recently, women—have served time in prison, been persecuted, exiled from their countries, or even executed as a result of their refusal, for reasons of conscience, to accept military service and participation in war throughout history. The heroic "solitary witness" against war of these often ignored or forgotten individuals stands in sharp contrast to the frequent accusation made of conscientious objectors by many in society and government that such persons are "cowards." Far from shrinking from dangerous situations, war resisters have often found themselves facing more painful and, at times, lethal situations than they might have if they had quietly accepted induction into the armed forces of their nation.

V. CONSCIENTIOUS OBJECTION AS A UNIVERSAL HUMAN RIGHT

Since 1987, when the United Nations Commission on Human Rights first recognized the universal human right to conscientious objection to military service, any consideration of the "ethics of conscientious objection" must include attention to the way in which nations deal with their citizens who claim conscientious objector status. Since 1989, the members of the UN Commission on Human Rights have regularly reaffirmed, in resolutions passed by consensus, the right of "everyone to have conscientious objections to military service as a legitimate exercise of the right to freedom of thought, conscience and religion as laid down in Article 18 of the Universal Declaration of Human Rights as well as Article 18 of the International Covenant on Civil and Political Rights." In 1994, the United Nations Human Rights Committee (the body charged with overseeing the implementation of the International Covenant on Civil and Political Rights and interpreting the provisions of the Covenant) stated in a General Comment that, although the "Covenant does not explicitly refer to a right of conscientious objection, . . . the Committee believes that such a right can be derived from Article 18, inasmuch as the obligation to use lethal force may seriously conflict with the freedom of conscience and the right to manifest one's religion or belief" (UN Document HRI/GEN/Rev.1 at 35 (1994)).

The Commission on Human Rights has urged the nations of the world to permit persons already serving in the armed forces to become conscientious objectors, to establish programs of alternative civilian service "not of a punitive nature," to establish independent decision-making bodies to take on the task of determining whether claims of conscientious objection are valid, and to promulgate information about this now-recognized human right to young people who face decisions about performing military service and participating in war.

Non-governmental human rights organizations such as Amnesty International, the Society of Friends, Pax Christi International, War Resisters International, and others also devote efforts to supporting and defending both the recognized rights of conscientious objectors, as mentioned above, as well as the derivative right of asylum (in cases where claimants of conscientious objection face exile, deportation, or unjust prosecution because of their claim), which is not yet (at this writing) accepted as an important part of the human rights package for conscientious objectors.

The UN Commission on Human Rights recognition of the right of conscientious objection to military service is not, however, legally binding on nations; therefore, efforts continue to enact national legislation where possible to insure that conscientious objectors can enjoy—at long last—the right of freedom of thought, conscience, and religion which lies at the heart of their refusal to participate in war and the killing of fellow human beings.

Also See the Following Articles

COMBAT • DRAFT, RESISTANCE AND EVASION OF • NONVIOLENCE THEORY AND PRACTICE • PEACE CULTURE • PEACEFUL SOCIETIES • RELIGIOUS TRADITIONS, VIOLENCE AND NONVIOLENCE

Bibliography

Axelrad, A. S. (1986). *Call to conscience: Jews, Judaism and conscientious objection.* Hoboken, NJ: Ktav Publishing House, Inc., and Nyack, NY: Jewish Peace Fellowship.

Bondurant, J. (1958). *Conquest of violence: The Gandhian philosophy of conflict.* Princeton, NJ: Princeton University Press.

Flessati, V. (1991). *Pax: The History of a Catholic peace society in Britain, 1936–1971.* Doctoral Dissertation, University of Bradford.

Hegeland, J., R. J. Daly, & J. P. Burns. (1985). *Christians and the military: The early experience.* Philadelphia: Fortress Press.

Hornus, J. (1980). *It is not lawful for me to fight.* Scottdale, PA: Herald Press.

Khadduri, M. (1955). *War and peace in the law of Islam.* Baltimore: The Johns Hopkins University Press.

Mayer, P. (Ed.). (1966). *The pacifist conscience.* New York: Holt, Rinehart, and Winston, Inc.

Montague, A. (Ed.). (1978). *Learning non-aggression.* New York: Oxford University Press.

Moskos, C. C., & Chambers II, J. W. (1993). *The new conscientious objection: From sacred to secular resistance.* New York: Oxford University Press.

NISBCO (1983). *Words of conscience: religious statements on conscientious objection.* (10th Ed.) Washington, DC: National Interreligious Service Board for Conscientious Objectors.

Sharma, I. C. (1965). *Ethical philosophies of India.* Lincoln, NE: Johnsen Publishing Co.

Schlissel, L. (Ed.). (1968). *Conscience in America: A documentary history of conscientious objection in American history, 1757–1967.* New York: E. P. Dutton & Co., Inc.

Seeley, R. A. (1982). *Handbook for conscientious objectors* (13th Ed.). Philadelphia: Central Committee for Conscientious Objectors.

Smock, D. R. (1995). *Perspectives on pacifism: Christian, Jewish, and Muslim views on nonviolence and international conflict.* Washington, DC: United States Institute of Peace Press.

United Nations Commission on Human Rights. (1997). *The question of conscientious objection to military service: Report of the Secretary-General (E/CN.4/1997/99) of 16 January 1997.* Geneva, Switzerland: United Nations.

Walzer, M. (1970). *Obligations: Essays on disobedience, war and citizenship.* Cambridge, MA: Harvard University Press.

Zahn, G. (1986). *In solitary witness: The life and death of Franz Jaegerstaetter* (Revised Edition). Springfield, IL: Templegate Publishers.

Cooperation, Competition, and Conflict

Sheldon G. Levy
Wayne State University

GLOSSARY

Coalition A group of individuals who combine for the purpose of joint effort. A coalition is, therefore, cooperative.

Competition A form of conflict in which the parties seek to improve their relative position. Such competition may pertain to the division of goods but it can also occur to increase the overall level of available resources.

Conflict Antagonistic or incompatible behavior that defines the opposite end of the cooperation-conflict dimension. The conflictual behavior may be verbal or physical.

Conflict Resolution Any continuing reduction in antagonistic or incompatible behavior. The reduction does not require overt or mutual agreement and it may be partial or complete.

Cooperation Joint action that may be for mutual economic or other benefit, or, in ecology, that has survival value for the parties. Coerced cooperation can exist since the party that is coerced benefits by avoiding penalty.

External Validity (also referred to as ecological validity) The extent to which a research effort replicates or represents the conditions that exist in the real world. Although the concept most frequently refers to experiments, it may also be applied to other research investigations, for example, questionnaire surveys.

Frame of Reference A set of related beliefs that operate as a standard for the assessment of information and evaluation of behavior.

Mobilization The activation of individuals or groups toward a common goal. Mobilization almost always arises within a larger social context of conflict, although it may develop to solve a mutual problem. Although analytically mobilization can evolve without cooperation, it is almost always associated with coalitions.

Structural Factors Those attributes external to the individual that characterize the physical or social environment.

Zero-Sum Linked outcomes that involve a loss for one party when there is a gain for another.

COOPERATION is a continuous but frequently obscure part of social life. All social interaction is based on roles in which behaviors of the participants attempt to fulfill the expectations of both the role player, for example, the president of a country, and those in complementary roles such as the citizens. Members in each role have expectations about behavior that is appropriate for their own role as well as for those occupying the complementary role. To the extent that these expectations are fulfilled, social life is cooperative; without such cooperation no social organization could exist. Since mutual dependence does not require conscious awareness, cooperation may occur in lower animals such as insects. Conflict is theoretically not inevitable although it is difficult to imagine any social organization in which the actors do not at times disagree about appropriate behavior or goals, or engage in overt action to achieve incompatible objectives.

I. GENERAL OVERVIEW OF COOPERATION AND CONFLICT

Since groups consist of individuals, psychological processes are important in any discussion of group behavior. Two major sources for behavior are emotion and information. The emotional component leads to activity that is expressive of feelings as well as to goals that are affective states, for example, reduced fear or increased pleasure. Therefore, although awareness and cognition are important, behavioral choices are not soley or in many cases predominantly determined by "rational" decisions in which choices, outcomes, and probabilities are logically assessed. In animals lower than man, decisions are substantially determined by the biological apparatus; those species with members that reacted automatically in the correct (life-saving) fashion are those that remain extant. Man's evolution includes such biological predisposition, but the more elaborate memories and increased ability to process information and to reason allow such responses, even under emotional severity, to be subject to a reduced level of biological control. Group interaction constitutes a set of stimuli that both provides information and also results in emotional consequences.

The greater capacity of humans to solve problems allows creative employment of both cooperation and conflict. However, even during conflict, cooperation is frequently a means through which the conflictual problem is addressed. A most important arrangement among humans is that of coalitions. Each worker cannot greatly influence the owner of a business, but a coalition of workers forming a labor union or otherwise agreeing on joint action may. The single warrior is unlikely to be successful in defense against an invading army but a coalition forming an army might be.

For cooperation through coalitions to occur, there must be recognition of a common problem and/or authority. The problem may consist of a physical obstacle and thus lead to joint efforts to build a tower of Babel, or it may be social, such as economic exploitation, in which case the purpose of the common action is to challenge the distribution of goods. Effective coalitions require mobilization and both coalitions and their mobilization are integral to the evolution of cooperative and conflictual behavior.

Almost all social organization involves hierarchy. Therefore, the roles of leaders and followers must be distinguished, and the influence of each on the cooperative or conflictual endeavor explored. Finally, the structural circumstances within which the event itself is embedded must also be investigated. Such structural factors overlap several other categories since they range from environmental conditions to the nature of the society.

When conflict exists, the parties may desire to alter the state of affairs but find it difficult to do so. This difficulty can arise from several sources. First, one or more participants may not have sufficient insight to develop alternatives to the intractable problem. Secondly, there may be so little trust that neither side is willing to initiate cooperation and incur the risk that the other side will take advantage of a conciliatory move. Third, concepts of the two parties about what constituted a fair process or resolution may be incompatible and the grievances may be so serious that the participants are unable to even agree on a starting point. Within this context, resort to third parties in the form of arbitration, negotiation, and mediation arises. One step in negotiation and mediation is to lower the intensity of the emotions by reducing the immediate provocation. A cease-fire in war, even if short, facilitates resolution. Another move may be to increase the contact among the contesting factions so that stereotyped images and limited understanding of the other points of view may be altered. Such changes are often necessary prior to conflict resolution.

Recourse to conflict management introduces complex cognitive processes but much conflict results from emotional factors. Once these have become amplified, the disruption of the conflictual process is far more difficult. Therefore, management of conflict is more efficient when it is preventive rather than interventional.

Cooperation exists in large part because individuals wish to be part of a group (conformity) or to avoid negative sanctions (obedience). The slaves who built the pyramids cooperated with the pharaohs; the American slaves cooperated with the plantation owners; soldiers cooperate with officers.

The German apparatus of the Second World War utilized fear and deception to increase the cooperative behavior of the Jews of Europe, who were marked for extinction. Their desire to live coupled with such tactics led to cooperation by the victims at the Theresienstadt (Terezin, located near Prague) concentration camp. Among the inmates were many European Jewish musicians who had been organized into an orchestra and choir. Many believed if they performed exceptionally well for the German high command, they would be salvaged because of their value as entertainers. After an impeccably accomplished performance for the High Command, for which the group had practiced for months, they were shipped to Auschwitz. Their experience, including interviews with survivors, has been extensively studied by Amy Lowenhaar, who directs the Terezin Project in New York City.

Egocentrism interferes with conflict resolution by hindering the recognition of the problem. The master may not imagine the resentment of the servant, the comfortable that of the working poor or unemployed, the guard that of the prison inmates. Under these circumstances, if other forms of communication appear ineffective, conflict serves as communication even if its incitement is not for that purpose. Noise from people, as from wheels, elicits awareness.

Research efforts are scant that attempt to incorporate both emotion and information and to include multiple levels of the system—individual, group, larger political entity—and the historical experience. However, William Gamson, a sociologist, has investigated diverse factors as they combine within the person. The research centered on the representation of the Arab-Israeli conflict in the minds of members of different subcultures in the United States. He obtained data on a set of attributes that included the manner in which the issue was defined, historical events that supported the point of view, and the principles, images, and reasoning that were involved. This approach allows some understanding of the personal emotional and cognitive factors, including the perception of history, which combine with the judgments of others to form a common definition, or frame of reference, of the social issue.

A preliminary requirement for the integration of the various factors is the assessment of the methods and conclusions of the relevant social sciences. Walter Isard, an economist, has discussed the separate approaches of several of the social sciences (*Understanding Conflict and the Science of Peace*). The complexity of the problem is illustrated in a discussion of conflict management. A representative list of 60 variables is provided from a larger set of those that should be considered, particularly by third party negotiators or mediators. The major categories that encompass the variables include: information requirements, structural and time-related properties, motivational and other psychological properties, and solution properties.

The emphasis in this article is on the development, escalation, and de-escalation of conflict and on associated cooperation. The central concern is of relationships between groups rather than between individuals and on armed conflict rather than within other contexts such as labor-management relations. However, much of the research is experimental and, therefore, does not directly investigate the clash between groups. Further, only a portion of the relevant material can be discussed and only some of the disciplinary approaches represented. The reader will obtain much additional information by reading the remainder of this encyclopedia.

II. FRAMEWORK FOR PRESENTATION OF RESEARCH

The following selected studies may be classified into experiments, events analysis, and anthropological-historical investigations. Two major forms of experiments may be differentiated. First are those in which the manipulations occur within a natural environment, represented by the Robbers Cave and the jigsaw classroom studies. More commonly, the research is in the laboratory and these investigations often consist of simulations that may be characterized as games, as will be illustrated in the Deutsch and Krauss trucking problem. An important variation consists of formal games; the Prisoner's Dilemma is one version that has been extensively employed. In addition to experiments, political scientists have utilized actual events data in an attempt to identify causes of conflict and circumstances associated with its resolution. Significant contributions have been provided by anthropologists and historians through the study of other societies, particularly those that are rather continuously peaceful.

Each approach embodies associated concepts. These are partially determined by the design of the investigations but also result from the conceptual development within that academic discipline. The naturalistic experimental studies have focused on competition as it affects the evolution of ingroup-outgroup distinctions and conflict, and on the utilization of superordinate goals as a means of reducing intergroup hostility. The simulation game and formal game designs have frequently been concerned with cooperation, defection, and the role of communication, with the concepts of threat, self-interest, and risk entering the analyses and explanations. The formal methods may also allow some insight into conflicts that involve large amounts of emotion, such as panic. Experimental attempts to study such highly emotional situations are obviously limited because of the physical danger to the participants.

Sometimes two approaches are combined. The Prisoner's Dilemma paradigm coupled with Richardson's formal mathematical model of the arms race led to a creative proposal by Osgood. He argued that the findings and concepts might be employed to de-escalate a conflictual environment and obtain peace in the absence of idealogical agreement. The synthesis of approaches is also illustrated in research by Pilisuk and Skolnick, who investigated the propositions formulated by Osgood through a formal game.

Quantitative political science frequently reverses the dominant investigative process just described. The data are the events themselves as recorded in history. These become the basis for evaluating the patterns of cooperative and conflictual behavior among political states, including the escalation and de-escalation of wars and rivalries. Both psychological and structural concepts are employed, including grievances, power of the disputants, regime type, threat, and transitions in culture and political organization.

Psychological explanations that are tested against actual events are more likely to be developed by political scientists than by psychologists. The relationship of frustration, relative deprivation, and justice to group conflict, and the effects of stress on the decision-making process are examples.

Finally, the anthropological-historical investigations are predominantly structurally oriented with emphasis on environmental circumstances, social organization, and ingroup interaction patterns. Their valuable contributions include the identification of societies that are relatively conflict-free. A fascinating irony is that these investigations return full circle to some of the principles derived from the Robbers Cave observations.

III. DEFINING RESEARCH

A. Competition, Conflict, and Superordinate Goals

1. The Robbers Cave Studies

During the 1950s, Muzafer Sherif conducted a series of investigations that remain distinctly informative. Rather than a laboratory, the sites chosen were boys' camps, one of which was the Robbers Cave State Park in Oklahoma. To the participants, the experience was indistinguishable from any other 3-week summer camp even though it was staffed and engineered by social scientists. The camp session was divided into distinct stages, each lasting about a week. The results contributed to the understanding of the development of conflict as well as processes that may be important for its resolution.

The boys were assigned to two groups that were brought separately to the camp. Each unit was housed in a different cabin and, for the first few days, did not know of the existence of the others. Strong personal ties developed along with identifying group names and emblems. Shortly before the second phase, the formal competitive period, each cabin became aware of the other's existence. The competitive "tournament" consisted of a range of contests that included sporting events. During this competitive stage, friendship patterns were almost exclusively ingroup and overt hostility emerged, including fights and dormitory raids.

The final phase attempted to engineer conflict resolution and demonstrated that mere integration, that is, bringing the boys together, was not sufficient in itself to lower ingroup-outgroup hostility. Such reduction, which also led to the development of friendships in the outgroup, required cooperative efforts to achieve mutually desired (superordinate) goals. These occasions for cooperation were unobtrusively arranged by the experimenters. On one, it was necessary for each person to contribute money to defray the cost of a movie that everyone wished to see. In another instance, a truck carrying the boys broke down requiring the joint effort of everyone to remobilize it.

A number of principles may be derived from this research. First, ingroup-outgroup distinctions may develop based on relatively minor considerations such as physical proximity. Secondly, competition not only increases the difference between ingroup and outgroup but is also associated with (a) overvaluation of the ingroup and derogation of the outgroup and (b) an increase in hostility toward the outgroup. Third, mere integration, that is, meeting together in a common physical environment, does not appear to be sufficient to reduce hostility. Fourth, cooperative effort toward mutually desired goals may be an important conflict resolving strategy. It may be that such cooperation redefines the unit so that all are now contained in an overarching group. This reduction in boundaries between the collectivities may mediate the resolution process.

2. Classroom Cooperation to Achieve Individual Grades

One of the difficulties in reducing hostility between groups is that higher status may be associated with membership in one unit compared to the other. Thus, integration in housing or schools has not automatically resulted in a reduction in intergroup conflict. One community may consider itself as superior to the other and that may combine with the other's perception of it's own inferiority.

Aronson creatively adapted some of the principles derived from the Robbers Cave research to develop cooperative efforts among members of different ethnic groups. The research was conducted in a large number of classrooms in Texas. Academic projects were designed that could not be completed without cooperation since each individual in a group was only provided with a part of the assignment. The superordinate goal was the grade and, although received by the individual, mastery of the assignment required that everyone provide the respective pieces to the "puzzle," with each person learning from the others. Thus, each contributed to and was dependent upon the members of the unit. The approach was labeled the Jigsaw Classroom. Although some improvement between White and Hispanics views toward each other was observed, the results were not as strong as one might have anticipated.

A number of factors may interfere with achieving the desired improvement in intergroup relations. The Sherif superordinate goals were such that everyone brought approximately equal abilities to the task. Money is money when donations are sought and the boys contributed equally in the remobilization of the trunk. In a classroom, there are differential abilities. A study group may have underperformed in the view of some members because others were simply not able to provide adequate contributions. Even when individuals of approximately equal academic ability are placed together, perceptions and evaluations are not always consistent with reality. There is sufficient research in psychology to demonstrate that prior judgments of a person or the group to which that person belongs affect the interpretation of that individual's contributions. Strong prior negative opinions may minimize the equal contributions of others. Further, if the overall level of the members of the group is low, or for some other reason they do not do well on the task, there is less likely to be group cohesiveness. A scapegoat may be sought in which the victimization would be of someone toward whom prior negative opinions existed.

Research supports a number of these contentions, for example, the dislike of less competent members of a team, the distortion of minority group member contributions, and the lowered cohesiveness of nonrewarded groups. Further, under some circumstances, attempts to increase competence of minority group members may increase the conflictual relationship. Thus, if a minority group members violates an expectation, for example, through being trained to be more competent in a particular task, there may be resentment.

In 1954, prior to the publication of the Robbers Cave studies, Allport (*The nature of Prejudice*) concluded that the most effective combination of conditions for reducing prejudice included equal status contact with joint effort toward superordinate goals aided by institutional support.

A number of fairly reliable findings have emerged from several jigsaw classroom studies many of which are consistent with this formulation. These have been summarized by Stephan. For example, there are practically no findings that suggest intergroup relations deteriorate. Interethnic relations improve, when an effect is observed, in many categories, such as attitudes, mutual helping, lessened conflict and increased participation and influence of the minority members. There are a number of conditions that facilitate positive results, for example, strong institutional support for the team process conducted in real settings over a fairly long period of time with members of the group who are equal in status. The circumstances conducive to a lessening of conflict also include: minimization of competition, comparability in belief and values as well as status, similar levels of competence, positive outcomes as a result of the group effort, emphasis on each individual as distinct rather than a member of a category, representation in about equal numbers of the various ethnic groups, efforts that occur in a variety of contexts, and participation that is voluntary.

While the Sherif research is an important contribution to understanding the role of competition in the emergence of hostility and the means by which intergroup antagonisms are likely to be reduced, many real social conflicts involve factors that are more comparable to those faced in the Aronson research. Sherif deliberately minimized many of these influences by selecting well-adjusted White-Anglo-Saxon-Protestant middle class 11-year-old males with average academic performance and by further matching the groups on both academic and athletic ability. Consequently, the effects of the experimental procedures were not confounded by demographic variability among participants.

3. The Factor of Threat

Deutsch and Krauss developed a simulation game with rewards for rapid delivery of goods by truck. The faster the delivery, the greater the payoff. There were two routes, a direct one and an alternate. Three conditions were examined: in the first, neither party possessed a threat, in another the threat was available to only one, and in the third it was available to both. The subjects who answered the research call were females at a telephone company.

In actuality, there was always some threat available to both since a route could only be traveled by one truck. Thus it was possible for one player to block the main route. A blocked player on the main route could simply back up and use the alternate road but then the other player would have unimpeded access to the main route, which took a much shorter amount of time. Of course, if both were intransigent, neither would receive a reward.

Explicit threat was incorporated by providing one or both players with a gate that closed the main road. A gate-endowed player could, if necessary, travel the longer alternate route while depriving the other player of the main road. In the bilateral threat condition, each player possessed a gate.

The game itself was not zero-sum since the speed determined the amount of payment. The conflict existed at one level as a game against nature, that is, beating the clock. At another level, there might have been competition because of interpersonal comparisons of relative gain (although participants were instructed to maximize their own payoff and not attend to that of the other player.) Cooperation, represented by alternating access to the main road to reduce trucking time, was greatest when neither side had the gate threat and it was least when both did.

The research exhibits the value of controlled experimental studies while at the same time demonstrating limitations in capturing real conditions. Individuals were specifically instructed to be motivated by self-interest. Their goal was to make as much money as possible without regard to the amount accumulated by the other person. Second, they were aware of the fact that all earnings were imaginary. Finally, subjects were placed in separate booths and were not allowed to verbally communicate. The only communication was from the display on a board that provided information about the actions of the other player.

Subsequent research has demonstrated that changes in procedure alter observed results. For example, a person's antagonism can alter the focus to maximizing the loss to the other player independent of one's own outcomes or to maximizing the difference between the two payoffs. (One such instance might be the Nazis' efforts, detailed in Lucy Dawidowicz's *War Against the Jews,* in which, even at the cost of moving necessary war materials away from the German armies, the destruction of the Jews was of such importance that it was their losses that were to be maximized.) Gallo found that when real money was involved, competition lessened and the total amount of the payoffs increased.

It is clear, however, that experimental findings are often not consistent with real world experiences. Early labor unionizing occurred when the threat was unilaterally held by management. There was little cooperation between the two sides as evidenced by the high level of conflict during these periods. Only when the workers achieved comparable intimidation, namely that of a strike coupled with the ability to deter scabs, did management become interested in reaching an accommodation with the workers. The importance of these issues will become evident in the discussion of recent studies of international conflict.

B. Formal Games as Research Devices

The complexity of real social interactions has led to employment of tools that allow for a definition of key variables while providing control over them. An extensively investigated paradigm is based on von Neumann and Morgenstern's *Theory of Games and Economic Behavior* and a particular derivative, a seemingly simple game designated the Prisoner's Dilemma (PD).

1. Games and Payoffs

The Prisoner's Dilemma may be represented as a two-person game in which each has two choices. The exact outcome is indeterminate because the payoff is dependent on the combination of decisions. The structure of the payoffs creates the possibility of cooperation or defection and suggests explanations that include trust and/or threat. The most elementary form of the game is one in which both players must make a choice simultaneously. In expanded versions, it is possible to include sequential choices and other factors such as communication.

Consider two suspects in a crime who are interrogated separately by the police. The police have limited information and require a confession to obtain a maximum penalty. Each prisoner may be offered lenient terms if he confesses. Nevertheless, it is in the interest of both that neither confesses, in which case they will either go free or suffer a light sentence. Not confessing, however, requires some degree of trust because of the risk; if one confesses and the other does not, the confessor will get a light prison term while the other will be sentenced to a long one. However, if both confess, they will receive long prison terms but less than the maximum. The dilemma is created because the outcomes are dependent and because one avenue of reasoning leads both to confess.

The PD (prisoner's dilemma) is easily represented by a matrix in which the rows represent choices of prisoner I and the columns those of prisoner II. The outcomes are in the cells:

		Prisoner II	
		Confess	Don't confess
Prisoner I	Confess	Player I, 5 years Player II, 5 years	Player I, 3 months Player II, 10 years
	Don't confess	Player I, 10 years Player II, 3 months	Player I, 6 months Player II, 6 months

This payoff matrix is far more complex than it might appear. The rule that is frequently employed in its analysis may be called a minimax strategy; that is, the player tries to minimize his maximum penalty.

Prisoner I might argue: if my colleague confesses (column 1), it would be better to confess and receive a 5-year sentence rather than 10 years. Even if my friend does not confess, I am still better off confessing and receiving the 3-month term rather than 6 months if I do not confess. (The reasoning is, of course, identical for prisoner II). Under these circumstances, both players have a dominating strategy, that is, no matter what the other player decides, it is better to choose to confess. Of course, they would be far better served if neither confesses. However, choosing the "cooperate" strategy requires trust. Since gains for one are not necessarily losses for the other, the PD is not zero sum.

Rationality, as in the prisoner's dilemma, is dependent on the goal. If it is to maximize one's individual gain, then certain precise procedures can be defined that increase the likelihood of achieving that end. However, there are other goals, for example, to maximize the benefit to the other party even at cost to one's self (altruism), to maximize the joint benefits (community interest) without regard to individual distribution, or to increase the degree to which one dominates even if it means that the outcomes will be negative.

These different philosophies lead to differences in "rationality." Reference to the previous PD payoff matrix suggests that the altruistic player will not confess since this would allow his colleague to escape with either a small 3-month or at worst a 6-month sentence. If both are altruistic, neither will confess. They face no dilemma. A person interested in overall community welfare would not confess since the only distinguishing outcome is a total of 12 months in prison. All of the other combinations of decisions are similar since the total deprivation of freedom is very close to 10 years. If both players are community-spirited, neither confesses. A player motivated to dominate will confess as the only route to obtaining a clear advantage over the other. If both seek domination, they both confess. A more sophisticated analysis would also require assessment of likelihoods of particular choices, but the point is to merely suggest that there are objectives other than the frequently assumed one of self-interest and these alternate goals carry with them their own "logics."

2. The Theory of Moves

Steve Brams (*Theory of Moves*) has expanded the applicability of the formal game approach. The deductive system is limited to 2 × 2 games but may be extended to more elaborate versions. First, Brams notes that there are 78 ordinal versions of the 2 × 2 matrix when only relative payoffs between the players are considered. Of these, 57 may be classified as conflict games. By introducing a starting point, history is included in the decision making. Other aspects of the theory provide the game with a dynamic property and allow incorporation of concepts such as frustration in addition to those already established.

3. Panic: A Prisoner's Dilemma Interpretation of an Emotional Environment

The PD paradigm has some very important applications even when the decision making is not conscious or cognitively reasoned. The environment may lead to fear, as in a panic, and the attempt to escape may result in negative consequences for both parties, whereas "cooperation" might have led to a far better outcome.

For example, as illustrated by Roger Brown (*Social Psychology*, 1965), a person in a theater when a fire occurs can choose to rush to the exits to escape thus competing with others motivated similarly, or "cooperate" in an orderly exit (comparable to the alternating use of the main route in the Deutsch and Krauss study.) The essential structural feature is that there are insufficient escape routes if everyone rushes. However, if one hesitates while the others rush, the hesitator may be trapped while the rushers may escape.

Panic with limited escape routes represents conflict in which the forces in the environment are so strong that they activate emotional reactions that almost automatically result in incompatible behavior.

Mintz attempted to capture the elements of panic in a laboratory. Participants held strings that were attached to cone-shaped objects. The objects were in a single bottle with a narrow neck. Orderly exit from the bottom was required to avoid jamming the "exit." Threat was introduced by requiring that the cones be withdrawn before water entering at the bottom of the bottle reached them. The prevention of communication resulted in a large number of "jams" that were all but eliminated when communication was allowed. Mintz concluded that the ability to communicate, rather than emotion, was the key variable. As described later in this article, emotional factors do interfere with "rational" thought whether in panic or in interstate conflict.

Financial panic in which the individual fears losing his assets has many of the same elements as a theater panic. If everyone rushes the exists (sells at the same time) the price will drop precipitiously since there will be insufficient buyers (exits) to accommodate the market. Sellers are better off not to rush the exits. However, if one waits while the others rush, the hestitant party will be left holding the bag of devalued stock certificates.

During the U.S. stock market debacle of October 1987, "rational" players (employing computerized trading) combined with "irrational" fear of financial loss to create an instant reduction in wealth of hundreds of billions of dollars. To deter such a combination of circumstances, the New York Exchange instituted procedures for halting the panic spiral. The process involves taking away the exits (closing the markets). During the much less severe, but nevertheless important, stock market loss during October 1997, such "collars" went into effect. There are arguments that such procedures exacerbate the problem and risk all being "burned" since there are no exits. Such reasoning is fallacious. Fear interferes with rational decision making and stimulates further fear. Closing the markets, comparable to Roosevelt's Bank Holiday in the 1930s, provides an opportunity for emotions to dampen and allows time for rational decision making. During the earlier 1987 stock market collapse, the lack of collars still resulted in the loss of exits: the panic led to such a great flood of orders that it was not possible to match buyers with sellers and the market opening was delayed. This is advantageous to the buyers who can lower their offer of purchase thus further increasing seller fear.

C. Emotion in Decision Making: Psychologically Closing the Exists

Emotion is clearly an interfering factor in resolving conflict since it may decrease the ability to identify less conflictual solutions including cooperation. Psychological research has shown that high levels of stress reduce problem solving proficiency. This hypothesis was tested in the real world by political scientists at Stanford University headed by Robert North and reported in part by Ole Holsti. Under conditions of increasing stress, decision makers' cognitive alternatives were expected to narrow and result in reduced flexibility in dealing with a crisis. The data were based on communications among key decision makers just prior to the First World War. As mobilization of men under arms increased (mobilization was the index of stress and occurred rapidly prior to the outbreak of war), decision-makers showed a decrease in the alternatives they considered for dealing with the crisis. The data were derived from the meomoranda of key decision-makers—heads of state and cabinet officers or their equivalent.

This research supports the importance of the psychological consequences of external stress that influence decision making in conflict prone environments. During a real crisis, there is also a physical structural factor, namely the shortening of time available for evaluating alternatives, which further increases the stress. Under these circumstances, biases that normally exist would be expected to increase in importance in decision making, for example, increased suspicion, reduced sensitivity to the relevance of new information, overvaluation of past performance, and overconfidence in a prior preferred strategy.

Even without external stress, other essentially emotional factors interfere with conflict resolution. Some were discussed by Janis as group think, in which members of a highly cohesive group seek unanimity. Among the elements that add to dysfunctional decison making are the desire to remain a part of a valued group, assumed unanimity of the members, both imposed and self-censorship of critical ideas, an illusion of invulnerability in decision making and derogating stereotypes of the adversary. All of these would be expected to narrow the range of available alternatives and reduce the ability to reverse the conflict spiral.

Faulty judgments may also occur when the goal of a leader or group is to engage in conflict or to cope with conflict already engendered. Under these circumstances there is an increased importance of neutral third-party intervention as an aid in overcoming the psychological disabilities.

D. Reversing the Conflict Spiral: The Osgood Proposal

Charles Osgood proposed a strategy to increase cooperation between the United States and the Soviet Union during the Cold War. The procedure required communication, a sequential set of decisions, and a safeguard so that a country's safety was not dependent on the goodwill of the other country. The process was called "graduated reciprocated unilateral initiatives for peace." Its acronym is GRIT, where the T represents tension reduction.

Osgood recognized, as did Richardson earlier in his mathematical model of the arms race, that mutual fear led to escalation, which in turn increased the chances of war. Therefore, it was important to employ principles that would induce the opponent to cooperate in arms de-escalation. The proposal assumed that both sides preferred the ideological conflict to a physical war in which the use of nuclear weapons was likely.

The plan required that the initiator assume some risk through a small reduction in military forces that was to be announced publicly and contain the promise of future reductions if there were reciprocation. In addition, the arrangement included inspection to confirm the reduction as well as the reciprocation. Although such a proposal would be ineffective if the parties did not find it to their mutual advantage, it was designed so that the reduction could easily be reversed. Thus the initiator was not placed at undue risk. The process would also be aided if the initiator could incur another small reduction should the first effort not be reciprocated, thereby increasing the credibility of the overture.

In the utilization of game procedures, as illustrated by the Prisoner's Dilemma, a matching strategy is frequently referred to as Tit-for-Tat. Axelrod, based on a large number of computer simulations in which various strategies were pitted against each other, argued that this is the most effective strategy for inducing cooperation. The Osgood plan encouraged Tit-for-Tat but also required one side to initiate the conciliatory process (the Tat), thus indicating the direction of the other player's Tit. It included the promise to then provide another Tat and to continue doing so as long as the opponent provided matching Tits. If successful the result would be a spiraling de-escalation of arms. The extent to which such ideas entered international negotiations between the United States and the Soviets is difficult to assess. It appears that there may have been some influence but the efficient application of the theory was not evident.

E. Pilisuk and Skolnick: Converting Missiles

A number of elements of the Osgood strategy were incorporated into a formal game by Pilisuk and Skolnick. The game was conducted as a sequential multiple play Prisoner's Dilemma, rather than simultaneous single play. It included communication, since communication had already been shown to be an important influence in increasing cooperation. A player could indicate an intention prior to a move and also was provided the opportunity to inspect the other's resources. However, since inspection was not continuous, the possibility of deception existed. Cooperation was signified by the conversion from missiles to factories, the payoffs were identified as economic and decisions were to represent those of a country.

The results suggested that early substantial unilateral initiatives provided increased likelihood of cooperation. Further, intentions with honesty tended to be followed by cooperation but deceptive communication, engaged in by some, lessened cooperation. Although these results provide support for the Osgood suggestions, the amount of cooperation was quite similar (marginally greater) when the strategy was merely a matching one.

In these experiments, the parties possess comparable levels of resources. Only under these conditions does each have a viable threat. It then becomes in the self-interest of both to decrease the conflict. Other research has shown that, under some conditions, unilateral martyrdom, trust, or reliance on power or threat do not lead to cooperation. Martyrdom and trust may at times be ineffective and power and threat may lead to belligerence.

The limitations of the matrix approach led to its omission in a subsequent study by an international team of investigators. The investigators were conducted in eight different laboratories, three in Europe and five in the United States. The simulation involved a complex set of negotiations with systematic variation of a number of variables. These included: the payoffs, sometimes points and other times money, the difficulty level of the problems, and the degree to which subjects were dependent on others in reaching agreement. Consistent with the Gallo variation on the Deutsch and Krauss trucking game, higher stakes resulted in increased importance of negotiation when cooperation yielded clear gain in both parties, provided that exploitation by one party of the other was difficult.

IV. PEACE SCIENCE AND THE STUDY OF INTERNATIONAL CONFLICT

The study of cooperation and conflict attempts to understand real-world interactions. The investigation of real events among political actors contrasts sharply with the experimental approach.

A. The Effectiveness of Credible Threat

Philip Schrodt at Kansas State University has developed a data base of interactions between political states. The interactions vary in the degree to which they represent cooperation or conflict. More than 15,000 events are incorporated for the period from 1992 through 1995. Jon C. Pevehouse and Joshua Goldstein examined interaction patterns represented by these events. Their focus was on three actors in the conflict in Bosnia: the United States (which was actually an aggregation of the world community), Serbia, and Bosnia. The basic question was whether a credible threat (labeled bullying) was most effective in reducing conflict. It appeared that if the Serbs were threatened, they reduced their conflictual behavior. On the other hand if the United States lessened its pressure, then the Serbs increased their aggression. The Bosnian Serbs paid little attention to the UN and Europe but did respond to the United States and to NATO. The findings were based on a 1-week delay between the action and the assessed response.

The research identifies the complexities of actual compared to simulated studies. In the present case, power was asymmetric. The United States and NATO could mount credible threats that were not able to be matched by the Serbs. In many instances of conflict ranging from interstate to ethnic, asymmetric power results in the ability of one party to coerce the other into actions that are in the dominant power's interest. Humanitarian intervention, however, may employ coercive power to aid others, and Bosnia is one such example.

B. Disappointment of Individual Expectations and the Likelihood of Revolution

James Davies hypothesized that disappointed expectations increased the likelihood of internal conflict (civil war). This was most likely to occur when a period of rising expectations of economic well-being was followed by a sudden decrease in actual payoffs. He found support for his hypothesis in the history of three important events, the French Revolution, the U.S. Civil War, and the rise of Hitler.

Ivo K Feierabend and Rosalind L. Feierabend developed a statistical data base of the characteristics of members of the UN during the period 1948 to 1965. These data were utilized to test Davies' hypothesis. Education was employed as an index of expectations on the reasonable assumption that those who are educated anticipate improved economic well-being. In those countries in which there were large annual increases in levels of education without corresponding increases in actual payoffs (measured by per capita income), a large gap between expectations and payoffs was expected to develop. It was therefore predicted that these nations would have the highest levels of internal turmoil; analyses supported this proposition.

The Feierabends also examined the nature of the regime—coercive (dictatorial), democratic, or in-between—and found that those countries at mid-levels were most likely to experience internal political turmoil as were those societies in transition between traditional and modern cultures. With slight variation and utilizing a different data set, Haavard Hegre, Tanja Ellingsen, and Nils Petter Gleditsch recently reported that those states in political transition (rather than the cultural transition of the Feierabends) were also more likely to be involved in civil war.

C. Relative Resources and the Evolution of Interstate Rivalry

Among the data sets developed by J. David Singer's Correlates of War project is one of militarized interstate disputes (MIDs). When combined with the project's set of interstate wars, examination of the evolution of rivalry (defined by military actions) and transition to war is possible. The current vernacular divides interstate relationships into two classes: not enduring or enduring rivalries. Arbitrary decisions about when a rivalry should be considered as enduring might be avoided if instead the degree of rivalry were defined based on a combination of frequency and intensity relative to time. Nevertheless, valuable research on enduring rivalries has been conducted.

D. Termination of War

As important as understanding the development of conflict is the study of the means by which it ends and the relationship of that means to the likelihood of its resumption. Suzanne Werner examined the termination of war, specifically, negotiated compared to imposed settlements. Although the results suggest that an imposed settlement reduces the probability of future conflict, there is a likely selection bias in cases since stalemates induce a recourse to negotiation. However, dealing with the real world requires examining events as they exist. A research question yet to be addressed is the importance of negotiation in conflicts that are not stalemated.

E. Justice and Conflict

The perception of injustice is a source of conflict. There are several bases on which fairness may be evaluated and these may vary depending on the circumstances. Comparisons are one basis for judgment. The Davies hypothesis about disappointed expectations suggests an important comparison between actual and expected payoffs and the rate of change in the discrepancy. At other times fairness may be judged relative to others. The theories of distributive justice and of equity hypothesize that the comparison process adjusts for the person's investments which may include time, effort, and status.

Two distinctions in research on perceptions of justice have been between the outcome and the process through which the decision is reached. Tyler concludes that individuals are motivated to support their institutions and view institutional relationships as continuing. As a consequence, the judgment of fairness is heavily influenced by an individual's treatment and treatment has more in common with process than with outcome.

It may, however, be argued that if the result is extremely important and/or the decision is not one that is likely to involve continuing relationships, outcome may receive greater weight. Someone accused of murder may view justice as being served only if the jury decides "not guilty" and this may be true whether or not the person is guilty. Being judged guilty (and being hanged) allows no future interaction with the institution. It therefore may not be surprising that nations are more prone to evaluate justice by the outcome. Perhaps an outcome is judged as final and if not "fair" the grievance continues and forms a basis for the reemergence of conflict. Since it is not nations, but individuals with roles in them, who judge fairness, both role and issue are important for understanding the perception of fairness in the resolution of intergroup conflict.

Finally, the perception of justice may depend upon the balance between motives for solidarity and those for status or control. Self-control is a very important motivating factor for individuals. In intergroup relationships as well, a repeated observation is a preference for self-determination. Process is less important if the outcome leads to one of domination. The Versailles Treaty is one of innumerable examples.

V. PEACEFUL SOCIETIES

Important understanding and hypotheses may be derived from the examination of societies that are peaceful. Although disagreements exist within these groups, they are resolved, in almost all cases, with minimal physical violence.

Although the groups identified as peaceful appear to be relatively small in numbers with sufficient physical space generally available so that unresolved disagreements may lead dissidents to separate, at least temporarily, from the main group, the structure of such societies and their values do not seem to be totally dependent on these physical circumstances. Central to their existence are several components that are consistent with the findings of the Robbers Cave studies.

First, the societies are organized on a basis of equality in both authority and economic distribution. These may be derivatives of the emphasis on cooperation and the absence, to the extent of abhorrence, of competition and conflict, especially that which takes overt physical expression. Even sporting activities are generally in the direction of play rather than competition. This contrasts sharply with the industrialized societies. Among these, the research evidence reveals the United States as the most competitive.

Examples consistent with the above characterization were observed among the Zuni Indians, among whom there was an emphasis on community possession of material goods and the free circulation of wealth. In a major sporting event, the four-mile footrace, the winner was not announced and someone who repeatedly won was excluded from future races. The Iroquois obtained individual pleasure from group efforts rather than from dominance. The Bathonga of South Africa are essentially noncompetitive both socially and economically and react negatively to any expression of competition.

These attributes are present in groups that are geographically quite dispersed and include the Mixtecans of Mexico, the Inuit of Canada, the Tangu of New Guinea (among whom the goal of one game is a draw), and the Australian Aborigines who demonstrate a great deal of cooperation with members of other tribes as well as their own.

The presence of such societies, although representing only a small fraction of the human species, argues for the importance of socialization in governing conflict and for the nondeterminative consequences of biological predispositions toward aggression.

VI. CURRENT CONFLICT DOMAINS

A. Ethnic Conflict

1. Quantitative and Propositional Approaches

Among the investigators who are currently involved in developing quantitative ethnic data bases are R. Rummel, whose focus is "democide" (politicide, ethnicide, and genocide), T. R. Gurr, ethnic conflict, and J. D.

Singer's specialized collection within the Correlates of War project of ethnic attributes of political states.

Two previous efforts at formalizing the influence of ethnicity are those of Levine and Campbell, (*Ethnocentrism: Theories of Conflict, Ethnic Attitudes, and Group Behavior*), and of Richardson (*Statistics of Deadly Quarrels*). The first developed a set of propositions based on examination of cross-cultural information and represented an important step in producing testable principles related to ethnic conflict. Richardson's work remains a landmark contribution to the quantitative study of conflict. Conflicts during the period between 1820 and 1945 were categorized by the number who were killed. Attributes of the parties were included such as language and religion. Based on statistical analyses, Richardson concluded that those who spoke the Spanish language were more likely than statistically expected by chance to have engaged in conflict and that Christian-Muslim conflicts were also more likely. The Chinese language was underrepresented. The conclusions of Richardson must only be considered suggestive but this approach is a model for research in this domain.

2. Psychological Aspects

The observations of peaceful societies suggest that there is no inevitable conflict between groups that differ in language, religion, or custom. Nevertheless, such differences are frequently associated with conflict. One difficulty in assessing the role of ethnicity is that frequently there are concomitant differences, such as economic or political, that may be the actual source of the grievance. On the other hand, to the extent that societies are competitively oriented, the role of ethnicity may be major. There are psychological reasons for this.

Group identification is an important basis for self-worth. Since thought processes occur in language, the importance of language in group identification should not be surprising. Systems of beliefs (religion) are of great significance because they define worth. As a consequence of group identity, destruction of the integrity of the group is also a destruction of the self.

Language and religion along with physical proximity, social custom, dress and food, distinguish the in-group from the outgroup. Whether such distinctions result in conflict depend on the extent to which there is perceived threat. This perception may be objective or imagined and the source can be either physical or social. Unfortunately, the mere presence of different others frequently leads to a feeling of danger. This may be reduced by increasing physical distances between groups, elimination or domination of one by the other, or through tolerance.

A history of conflict almost inevitably leads to a view of continuing risk and also results in outgroup impressions that are passed from generation to generation. Coupled with competition either for a resource, such as water, or for ideas, such as religion, conflict is almost inevitable.

The prognosis, therefore, is that for the great bulk of humanity group identification will remain important and "threat" will continue to be perceived. The reduction in ethnic conflict will most likely require tolerance at levels of understanding that have rarely been reached.

B. Ecological Conflict

Ecological competition overlaps ethnic differences. Such competition is not likely to be resolved amicably.

1. Overcrowding, Birth, and Aging

A number of observations, including the research of Calhoun, suggest that overcrowding is associated with aggression and social disorganization.

The total number of humans increases by about 100,000,000 persons a year, in spite of the deaths of approximately 10,000,000 children per year from starvation and related causes. To generalize from high population density regions such as the Netherlands, Japan, Israel, and Rhode Island is of limited value because of their high degree of economic development. For these populations, the physical living quarters as well as the psychological living space (the perceived opportunity for physical mobility and individual expression), is greater than among the crowded impoverished of Third World Countries.

In addition to overcrowding, the economic levels of the total human population cannot be raised to the current levels of the most developed unless massive new resources become available. The history of atomic, solar, and wind energy do not give promise that such will occur very soon. If the poor wish to emulate the rich, competition for resources exists.

2. Consumption of Natural Resources

Can't see the forest without the trees. Dissipation of forests is occurring far more rapidly than replacement, with per capita consumption in the United States leading the world. The result is a threat to the available oxygen supply. Were everyone in the world to consume at this rate, there would no longer be a problem of being unable to see the forest for the trees.

Emissions, global warming, and energy consumption.

With 4% of the world's population, the United States provides 25% of the emissions. Were other nations to operate at this industrialized level, oil supplies would be depleted and ice caps would melt. Breathing would also be difficult.

Industrial pollution, acid rain, and water purification. Pollutants from emissions and pesticides contaminate the ground and the water. Most of the world does not have potable water and that may partially explain the fact that 90% of the sales of Coca Cola are outside the United States.

3. The Likelihood of Conflict over Resources

Solutions to resource depletion currently seem unlikely. First, those societies that have been identified as peaceful generally shared economic wealth: the hope for such munificence by the developed countries is forlorn. Second, the elevation of other peoples to the levels of the developed nations is physically impossible since there are insufficient resources to accommodate such massive industrialization. Nor is there much possibility that the industrialized nations will scale back their consumption in a fit of mass altriusm. Third, economic power is becoming more and more concentrated in a very limited number of corporations that operate on a global scale. The effect may be to also concentrate political power. The pessimistic view is that the 21st century will provide its share of conflict and exploitation.

VII. FUTURE RESEARCH

The development of empirical generalizations about conflict is aided by focusing on a particular source such as disputes over religion, over territory, or over economic distribution. Some general principles may be discovered but they are more likely to emerge if similar patterns are shown in separate analyses employing disparate research strategies.

A. The Role of Emotion and External Validity

The research cited in the section on Peace Science demonstrates that the problem of external validity may be bypassed by studying actual events. However, variables cannot be controlled and this leads to the attempt to extract important components and subject them to experimentation. Unfortunately the two-way street rarely carries traffic in the other direction. That is, the generalizations obtained in the experimental environment, although employed to explain the external world, are infrequently tested through prediction to real events. The emotional basis for conflict and conflict resolution suggests that such tests are important since the relevant emotional component and intensity are difficult to duplicate in the laboratory.

B. The Unit of Analysis

It is true that the behavior of individuals combines to provide the behavior of the group. However, it does not follow that the study of individuals will automatically, or even likely, lead to an understanding of the group or that the study of subgroups will lead to understanding of processes in larger units, such as the state.

Another difficulty is the language of explanation. Reifications and anthropomorphisms are endemic. Political and social units do not perceive nor do they experience frustration or assess risk. Actors in distinct roles do. Experts will greet such statement with academic horror since "everybody knows that." These terms are employed, it is argued, because they are a shorthand for the fuller understanding. Unfortunately, the shorthand has missing fingers. The specific roles/individuals must be identified as well as the relationship of their perceptions, feelings and decisions to those in other roles in the society. Then there must be some statement that converts these relationships to group action. The lack of such precision increases the difficulty of subjecting hypotheses to scientific test.

C. The Terminology of Discourse

Construction of research questions is influenced substantially by the terminology of discourse. Two brief examples will suffice. First, there is a phenomenon called social loafing (similar to that of "free riding"), which refers to the ability of some to obtain benefits because of the efforts of others. Of course, if no one contributed then there would be no gain for anyone. Social welfare might be an example of social loafing and/or free ridership. However, these labels imply socially disapproved motivation. Such a priori value judgments reduce the likelihood of objective design and analysis.

Another example is the concept of a social dilemma. A social dilemma is said to exist because the individual must balance self-interest against community interest. However, in most social existence, there is no dilemma. The individual organism, whether at the level of the ant or human, has no balance to achieve—it is given. For insects the determination is biological. In humans, the balance results from social values that have developed based on experiences within the family and larger social institutions. A dilemma implies a cognitive, decision-making problem that is not necessarily consistent with the essentially automatic balance achieved by many. The concept influences the construction of the research problem. That such distinctions and generalizations can be obtained does not justify the conclusion that they are important in real environments.

D. Forced versus Casual Observations

There may be a large difference between casual and forced environments. Laboratory research generally creates a forced environment in which the participants' attention and perception are concentrated on a particular task. In the real word, the processes are much more casual, matter of fact, automatic. The cognitions, perceptions and reasoning in such environments may be substantially different, if not in kind than in emphasis, than those obtained in the forced environments.

E. "When . . . Then" Not "If . . . Then"

Related to the above point and particularly important in research on conflict is the incomplete analogy between the role of the physical science compared to the social science laboratory. The general scientific model is that control of variables allows one, with proper experimentation, to determine the effect of one variable on another. This leads to generalizations of the form, if X changes in the specific direction, then Y will change in a predictable manner.

However, this model omits an important factor. The relationship between X and Y hold *when the conditions in the laboratory are at the identified levels.* In physical science, altering these fixed conditions may still result in the same relationship between X and Y, for example, the pressure on a closed container will increase when heat is applied. Even if that were not the case, it is conceivable to construct physical environments that mirror the laboratory levels. This leads to the "if . . . then" reasoning.

However, in social science, the relationship of X to Y interacts with the other variables and may change substantially when the level of one or more of the fixed variables is altered. Therefore, the relationship that is observed is only a "when . . . then," that is, the relationship is correct *when* the variables are fixed at the specified levels. In the real world, the variables, however, are not and cannot be fixed at these levels. This does not argue against experimentation in the social sciences. It does suggest that such research is only a first step.

F. The Integration of Disciplines

Finally, there is a need for greater interdisciplinary research without which the development of analytic tools is limited. Although the separate components are important, it is necessary to also develop testable hypotheses that predict from individual perception, decision strategies and emotions to group interaction that ranges from low levels of intensity to riot, interethnic hostility and war. The extent to which such propositions are supportable requires predictions to objective events.

Also See the Following Articles

ANTHROPOLOGY OF VIOLENCE AND CONFLICT • CONFLICT THEORY • CONFLICT TRANSFORMATION • CONFORMITY AND OBEDIENCE • DECISION THEORY AND GAME THEORY • ENEMY, CONCEPT AND IDENTITY OF • MASS CONFLICT AND THE PARTICIPANTS, ATTITUDES TOWARD

Bibliography

Brams, S. (1994). *Theory of moves.* Cambridge: Cambridge University Press.

Isard, W. (1992). *Understanding conflict and the science of peace.* Cambridge, MA: Blackwell.

McAdams, D., and Snow, D. A. (1997). *Social movements: Readings on their emergence, mobilization and dynamics.* Los Angeles: Roxbury.

Pruitt, D. G., and Carnevale, P. J. (1993). *Negotiation in social conflict.* Pacific Grove, Ca: Brooks/Cole.

References to Classic Research and Ideas and Summaries

Axelrod, R. (1984). *The evolution of cooperation.* New York: Basic Books.

Coser, Lewis A. (1956). *The functions of social conflict.* Glencoe, Ill.: Free Press.

Gamson, W. 1981. The political culture of the Arab-Israeli conflict. *Conflict Management and Peace Science, 5*(2), 79–84.

Deutsch, M. (1973). *The resolution of conflict: Constructive and destructive processes.* New Haven: Yale University.

Kohn, A. (1986). *The case against competition.* Boston: Houghton Mifflin.

Levine, R. A., & Campbell, D. T. (1972). *Ethnocentrism: Theories of conflict, ethnic attitudes, and group behavior.* New York: Wiley.

Osgood, C. E. (1962). *An alternative to war or surrender.* Urbana, Illinois: University of Illinois.

Pruitt, D. G. (1998). Social conflict. In Gilbert, D. T., Fiske, S. T., and Lindzey, G. (Ed.), *The handbook of social psychology* (Vol. 2, pp. 470–503.) Boston: McGraw-Hill.

Richardson, R. F. (1960). *Statistical of deadly quarrels.* Chicago: Quadrangle.

Pilisuk M., & Skolnick, P. (1968). Inducing trust: a test of the Osgood proposal. *Journal of Personality and Social Psychology, 8,* 121–133.

Sherif, M. (1958). Superordinate goals in the reduction of intergroup conflict. *American Journal of Sociology, 63,* 349–356.

Stephan, W. G. (1985). Integroup relations. In Lindzey, G., and Aronson, E. (ed.), *The handbook of social psychology* (Vol. 2, pp. 599–638). New York: Random House.

Correlates of War

J. David Singer
University of Michigan

GLOSSARY

Agnostic The belief that we do not have sufficient evidence to believe that a given set of statements is or is not true.

Bivariate A statistical correlation or covariation embracing only two variables or factors.

Epistemological A set of beliefs as to what constitutes sufficient evidence to support a conclusion.

Etiology The processes and conditions that lead up to and perhaps "cause" a given class of outcomes.

Hegemonic A social or political system that is dominated by a single person, group, or nation.

Hemogeniety The characteristic of some group or collection of people, events, or conditions such that they are highly similar to one another, as opposed to heterogeniety.

Nomothetic The belief that regularities exist and are thus worth searching for, as opposed to ideographic, which assumes that all cases and conditions are unique.

Ontological Beliefs about the nature of the universe.

Operational Procedures of observation, measurement, or reasoning that are explicit, clear, visible, and reproducible by others.

Sensate A mood or orientation that emphasizes the sensory and the emotional rather than the cognitive and rational, as in ideational.

Teleological The belief that a given set of behaviors is goal-oriented and purposive, and that a sequence of events and conditions must culminate in a specified outcome, as distinct from teleonomic, which permits us to temporarily assume that people and groups behave *as if* their behavior is goal-oriented and purposive.

THE TITLE OF THIS ARTICLE can be understood in three different ways. First, it is the name of a research project in quantitative history begun in 1964 at the University of Michigan, and still under way. Second, it means the extent to which a wide variety of factors rise and fall with fluctuations in the incidence of war: whether they correlate or covary with war, strongly or weakly, positively or negatively. And, third, it describes a research strategy by which we can make the transition from a stage in which the efforts to account for war were largely speculative and anecdotal to a stage in which well-articulated theoretical models can be subjected to the most rigorous scientific scrutinizing. Let me begin with a brief look at the intellectual history of the human effort to understand the "causes" of war and thus to reduce its frequency or severity, or even perhaps to eliminate it entirely from the face of the earth.

I. THE FIRST STAGE

The first stage—speculative and anecdotal—might be reflected in the writings of Thucydides after the Peloponnesian Wars, Machiavelli in the Middle Ages, Clausewitz after the Napoleonic War, and perhaps Norman Angell in the period between the two World Wars. Regardless of the motivation, the steady outpouring of writings on war was thoroughly pre-scientific in method. These authors were typically in pursuit of generalizations on the causes, conduct, and consequences of war, but rested their arguments and inferences on isolated historical incidents or some assortment of such incidents. While the literature that emerged from that humanistic intellectual style was usually fascinating and suggestive, it could never provide the basis for any law-like generalizations, and for two good reasons. One is that we never knew what the population of cases included, or whether the resulting assertions rested on a reasonable sample from a reasonably identifiable population of cases. The other problem—equally serious—was that the factors that allegedly accounted for wars of a certain type, region, or epoch were rarely well-defined, or in the language of social science, they were not operationalized. Simply put, the authors seldom told us which criteria they were using to include or exclude which historical cases, conditions, or episodes in their explanatory categories.

II. THE SECOND STAGE: DEMONSTRATING THE SCIENTIFIC POSSIBILITY

But after World War I, something happened that would lead to an important scholarly advance, and the key figure was a British meteorologist by the name of Lewis Fry Richardson, who was also a religious pacifist. He refused to serve in the army but volunteered to be an ambulance driver for the French forces during that most bloody and foolish of wars. The terror and devastation that he witnessed led him to wonder what we knew about the causes of war, but after reading the most famous of the military and diplomatic historians, he decided that the inadequacy of their methods made their conclusions utterly suspect. As a scientist, he immediately noticed the absence of well-defined populations (or "universes") of historical cases, along with the vagueness of their concepts, and he thus began some studies of his own in his spare time.

These studies during the late 1920s and 1930s took two forms. One reflected his suspicion that military preparedness was hardly an effective deterrent to war, but might well be the sort of activity on the part of one state that would typically encourage the same sort of activity on the part of its rival or opposition state; posthumously entitled *Arms and Insecurity* (1960) it was the first effort to capture the dynamics of an arms race in mathematical language. The other collection, later called *The Statistics of Deadly Quarrels* (1960), represented the first attempt to identify the statistical correlates of war. While neither of these projects gave us much in the way of conclusive evidence, they certainly persuaded many of us that scientific method could be brought to bear on conflict, rivalry, and war.

Almost as important was the work of two other interwar social scientists: Pitirim Sorokin and Quincy Wright. The former, a Russian sociologist, was hoping to put to the test the hypothesis that ideational (or cognitive) periods in the evolution of given cultures were more war-prone than the sensate periods; and while his ability to measure the degree of ideational-sensate was rather limited, his efforts to measure the incidence of armed violence going back to Roman times was nothing short of brilliant (1937). On the other hand, Wright (1942) was one whose work nicely complemented that of Richardson and Sorokin. He and his graduate students showed what could be done by first-rate historians once they had discovered what it meant to be "operational" in their observation and measurement of scores of factors that were thought to be the correlates of war.

This second stage—appropriately located in time between the First and Second World Wars—is remarkable not for its discoveries as to which factors systematically correlated or covaried with war, but for the demonstrations that mathematics could help to capture international interactions, that statistics could reveal the extent to which certain conditions and events can and do rise and fall together, and that careful and systematic historiography could move us from the anecdotal and impressionistic to the operational and reproducible.

III. THE THIRD STAGE: NATURAL HISTORY IN THE SOCIAL SCIENCES

One might expect that the incredible devastation of World War II would have led to an immediate and dramatic effort to build on the earlier research of Richardson, Sorokin, and Wright, but it was not to be; nor is the explanation especially elusive. First, this war was understood on almost all sides as one between the forces of good and the forces of evil. Unlike most of the sustained combat following the Napoleonic War and the Congress of Vienna, this was typically not seen as a dynastic war or the plaything of royalty. The viewpoint in the Berlin-Tokyo-Rome Axis was that of revenge and overturning the draconian treaties following World War I, and among the Allies the dominant perspective was that of preserving the essential virtues of Western civilization and turning back the revisionist barbarians. When good is arrayed against evil, there is little need for rigorous research, and one reason for the hostility toward peace research in the West during the Cold War was the sense that its advocates were not sufficiently enthusiastic in the struggle against the "godless atheistic Communists."

This leads, as a matter of fact, to the second factor in the long delay between the onset of World War II and the beginnings of the peace research movement. In one sense the Cold War can be traced back to 1848 and the Communist Manisfesto; this Marxist statement elicited considerable anxiety and hostility within the economic and political elites of the West, calling as it did for armed insurrection on the part of the working class as the Industrial Revolution gained momentum. Particularly in America, antisocialist and anticommunist sentiment took root early, was moderated briefly in deference to the anti-Nazi coalition, but was resurrected eagerly within months of V-J Day in 1945. Despite the renewed propaganda war, the rapid series of East-West confrontations, and the willingness of social scientists on both sides to enlist in the ranks, there were some fortunate exceptions. Appalled at not only the alarming rate of weapons development and acquisition and the destruction of the Korean peninsula from 1950 to 1953, but also the easy recruitment of the universities to the Cold War, a small group of concerned social scientists in America began to coalesce around the need for a morally and scientifically disciplined resistance. As a result, some of the serious discussions at the Center for Advanced Study in the Behavioral Sciences, and the arrival of a critical mass of such scholars at the University of Michigan shortly thereafter, the Center for Research on Conflict Resolution was established in 1957.

Attracted by this new center and its staff of lively and distinguished behavioral scientists, I moved to Michigan in the autumn of 1958 and quickly became involved in the center and its *Journal of Conflict Resolution,* and began to discuss the need to build on the pioneering work of those described in the above section. Having acquired some modest methodological competence during a post-Ph.D. fellowship at Harvard's Social Relations Department, along with some appreciation of the history of the more advanced social sciences, I was ready to launch into a new research enterprise; it would be, I was sure, very quantitative and operational in its methods and very agnostic in its theoretical basis. If there was a central reference figure, it was probably Charles Darwin, whom I recognized as a master of systematic observation, and a thoughtful hypothesizer who preferred to work outside of the laboratory; my interpretation of his career and that of his contemporary, Alfred Wallace, was that of "natural history" from the title of his first book (1839) based as it was on his famous journey aboard the *Beagle.*

The basic idea was to begin by identifying and then measuring the key characteristics of all interstate wars since the Congress of Vienna—widely recognized as the beginning of the modern interstate system; the result of that effort was *The Wages of War* (Singer and Small, 1972). The next step was to decide which variables and clusters of variables were the most likely candidates for correlates of interstate war. Those flowed from the voluminous traditional literature on the "causes of war," and were heavily influenced by the classical realpolitik (a.k.a. "realist") perspective. The reasoning was quite conventional: if most of the historians and political scientists of the past two centuries believed that geographical contiguities, material capabilities, and alliance commitments were the key factors in accounting for the onset and escalation of interstate disputes, and there was virtually no data-based research to contravene the conventional wisdom, why not start there?

There was, however, a less conventional approach emerging from our sister disciplines of psychology, sociology, anthropology; most of the pioneer peace research scholars around the late 1950s and early 1960s came from these fields and demonstrated a greater breadth, stronger commitment, and superior sense of research strategy than the political scientists. Recognizing that, in 1964 when the Correlates of War Project was getting underway, a few of my students and I completed an anthology designed to look at the ways in which those three disciplines might contribute to our knowledge of world politics via their concepts, their methods, and their findings (Singer, 1965). These certainly did not exhaust the possible places to search for the possible correlates of war, and in the years since, a good many scholars have either urged that we examine their particular fields, or have actually tried to do so themselves (Kelman, 1965; Bernard, 1965). From economics has come a very suggestive trio of studies: Blainey (1973), Boulding (1962), and Russett (1968), and not surprisingly, there were quite a few modern-day followers of Richardson, suggesting all sorts of models and metaphors from the physical and biological sciences.

While there is little doubt in my mind that the empirical domain to be studied should be the international system from 1816 to the present, that choice is far from inevitable. Whether one leans toward the nomothetic or ideographic end of the spectrum—and I clearly tilt toward the former—there is no question that the international system is in a fairly constant state of flux; it is an evolving system, and thus not quite similar from year to year, decade to decade, or century to century. Consequently, the system of 10 or 12 decades ago is not identical to its present-day self; it is merely analogous. And, without too much of a stretch, so is the labor-management bargain, urban politics, small group crisis, animal ecology, or tectonic shift an analogy to today's international system. To carry this argument further, so is a computer simulation, a psychological experiment, or a mathematical model. Thus, the correlates of war approach—using the historical patterns of the past two centuries as our laboratory—seems perfectly sensible, but it need not rule out these alternative research strategies.

Let me close this part of the discussion, then, by describing the research that unfolds under the "natural history" rubric. Simply put, we tend to eschew any energetic search for the "causes" of war on the ground that we do not yet know enough; we just do not know very much as to "what goes with what." In the next section, we will discuss what might come next, but more needs to be said about the correlates of war/natural history stage. The literature that purports to explain—or worse yet, get at the "causes" of interstate war—rests all too heavily on a blend of flimsy evidence, plausible argument, and casual speculation, all of which is shaped by one's ideological stance and/or prior experience. One could readily assemble a "rogues' gallery" of authors who have written at great length and with charming enthusiasm or touching faith on the causes of war, but what needs to be said here is not only that one or another explanation is wrong, but rather what we need to know as to the processes that lead from biological preconditions and childhood socialization at one end of the process to the onset of disputes, domestic factors that exacerbate, and elite decision processes that often transform the most routine inter-state dispute into a threshold of war crisis.

And at every stage on the road to war, our knowledge base is alarmingly slender. We do not really know the extent to which most humans tilt toward the "fight" or "flight" response under conditions of scarcity or danger. Nor do we have much persuasive evidence as to which child-rearing practices make our young adults more or less chauvinistic or cosmopolitan. And as we move from the domain of biology and psychology to that of diplomacy and politics, the story becomes even more depressing; our knowledge base is alarmingly thin when it comes to knowing "what goes with what." On the other hand, the systematic research of the past three decades has not been entirely fruitless. We turn, thus, to a summary of what we think—as the result of the scores of data-based studies since the early 1960s—best captures what we now believe to be the correlates of interstate war.

IV. RESULTS OF THE THIRD STAGE: SOME TENTATIVE CORRELATES OF WAR

In this section, we summarize a fraction of the published correlates of interstate war that have emerged from data-based research since the demonstration stage in our development. It is not necessary to go back over or refer to all these several hundred articles and book chapters, or even to examine the two collections of abstracts (Jones and Singer, 1972, and Gibbs and Singer, 1992), for the very good reason that Geller and Singer have recently done so in *Nations at War* (1998). But in summarizing these findings, we should note that they are not entirely consistent with one another, nor do they all point in the same theoretical direction. Equally important, we reiterate that these essentially bivariate correlations do what needs to be done *on the road to* explanatory theory: they tell us the extent to which two or more variables (one of which is the amount of war getting started or underway) rise and fall or appear and disappear together. Of course, as such correlations accumulate to give us more and more information about the etiology of war and are increasingly integrated into coherent and more complete narratives, we begin to approach theoretical explanation. With these considerations in mind, let us begin with a sampling of what we think we know about the correlates of war at the individual state level.

A. Correlates of War-Proneness in States

While it does indeed take at least two states to carry on the sustained and deadly combat that qualifies as war, we do know that certain states are considerably more war-prone than others during some part of their history. For instance, for the period from the Congress of Vienna in 1815 until 1990, the rank order—based on fatalities sustained—was: Russia, Germany, China, France, Japan, Britain, Austria-Hungary, Italy, Turkey, and the United States. As this list suggests, the traditional major powers have tended to initiate and enter into bloodier wars far more than the middle or minor level states, but recent evidence suggests that this pattern may be disappearing. Be that as it may, let us look at some of the more suggestive regularities.

Beginning with the demographic dimension, the above list reminds us that the more populous states also tend to be more war-prone, but we do not find, however, that this holds for the population growth rate or the population density. Somewhat more surprising, we find no correlation, either positive or negative, between war involvement and the state's level of economic development.

Shifting to the political dimensions, regime type turns out to be unimportant, with autocratic and democratic regimes showing an equal propensity to enter into or to initiate war over the past century and three-quarters, although there is some evidence that states with more contiguous neighbors and more alliance partners will experience higher frequencies of war involvement.

B. Correlates of War Prone Pairs

As suggested above, the correlates of pair-wise war are far more interesting than those of individual states, and it makes sense to begin with one of the more powerful predictions to dyadic war, that of geographical contiguity; nor has modern technology changed this. The big exception is, of course, the major powers whose capabilities permit them to wage war far from home. In the context of relative capabilities, we also have fair evidence that the more equally balanced the protagonists, the greater the likelihood that their disputes will escalate to war; further, the more rapidly their capabilities become more equal, the more likely they are to go to war.

Returning to the question of regime type—a factor that did little to distinguish between high and low war-prone states—it turns out to be a fairly powerful factor at the dyadic level, and the data-based literature is massive and growing; since 1815 we find very few wars between democracies (Small and Singer, 1976). There are quite a few plausible explanations for this dramatic correlation, but it may simply be a spatial-temporal artifact in the sense that up to 1945 there were very few democratic regimes in the interstate system, and few of them were geographically contiguous. And since World War II, most of the world's democracies were bound together in a U.S.-dominated collective defense and collective security coalition (Gates *et al.,* 1996). On the economic side, the popular and plausible notion that high levels of trade between states inhibit war between them is still under investigation, with the results quite inconclusive to date (Barbieri, 1996). But when it comes to economic development, the expected pacifying effect of pairs of highly developed societies is borne out, with such pairs experiencing very infrequent wars.

C. Correlates of War-Proneness in the Interstate System

While it takes two or more states to produce a war, there are two good reasons for finding regional or systemic correlates of interest. First, many scholars believe that the structural configurations and psychocultural distributions in the system will exercise considerable influence on the ways in which states handle their disputes. The policy implication is that all states should have a strong interest in heading off those conditions that are thought to increase the eventuality of war. In light of recent research, what do we think are the correlates? We use the word "think" here because there is considerably less consensus among quantitative researchers on the correlates of war at the systemic and regional level than at the state or dyadic levels.

Perhaps the most heavily examined factor here is that of alliances: while they are often consummated to head off war—as well as to increase the likelihood of victory if it comes to war—they play an important part in accounting for war, and with different results in the past two centuries. That is, for the 19th century, the higher the level of alliance aggregation, the *lower* the amount of war in the system in the following decade or so, and vice versa. But in the 20th century to date, the pattern is quite the opposite, with *more* war as we find an increase in the percentage of the system's members involved in alliance. One nearly inevitable consequence of alliance making is an increase in the system's division into two opposing coalitions: a high degree of bipolarity. The historical evidence bears this out, and furthermore shows that high bipolarity predicts away from war in the earlier period and toward war in the present century.

Given that alliances are typically sought after as a supplement to inadequate material and military capabilities, it should not be surprising that the distribution of such capabilities among the states might also affect the frequency and magnitude of war. The theoretical debate is an interesting and complicated one, but its essentials can be summarized here. The classical balance of power argument is that we will experience less war when there is approximate parity among the major powers or their alliances, when any trend is toward greater parity among the major powers or their alliances, and when the power hierarchy is fairly fluid. The opposing view, often labeled "hegemonic stability" suggests that peace requires a preponderance of one major power or its coalition, any changes toward heavier concentration, and a minimum of fluidity in the pecking order. A key assumption in this debate is that parity and fluidity lead to uncertainty as to the outcome of a military confrontation, while preponderance and stability make for relatively clear certainty. But the issue is whether uncertainty makes states behave more cautiously and prudently and war-avoiding, or whether a clearer and *less ambiguous* state of affairs will deter aggressive tendencies. Once again, the intercentury difference arises, with the typical balance of power model, based on parity and fluidity, capturing the reality of peacefulness in the nineteenth century. But for the best part of the contemporary century, we find that the clarity that arises out of preponderance and stability in the capability distributions does a better job of minimizing the frequency and severity of war. To be sure, it should matter whether the preponderance is on the side of the more conservative and status quo states or that of the dissatisfied revisionists, but at this juncture there seem to be no conclusive findings.

While the number of data-based investigations into the correlates of interstate war has grown over the past three or four decades, a great deal more remains to be done. The above summaries may offer a useful review, but they only capture a fraction of the research already completed; furthermore, they merely suggest what remains to be done within the natural history stage of the scientific effort to explain and possibly reduce the incidence of interstate war. But as already suggested, while we continue to build up our knowledge as to what goes with what on the road to war, it is essential that we begin to move into the fourth stage.

V. THE FOURTH STAGE: INTEGRATING OUR FINDINGS

As already indicated, if the purpose of quantitative, data-based research is to not only satisfy our normal scientific curiosity, but to generate knowledge that might be brought to bear in the policy communities of the world, we need to do more than continue our search for the correlates of war. While every new finding is useful, equally useful is the ability to bring these findings together into well-integrated theoretical models that might give us a better handle on explaining the etiology of war. What we need to know is not only what goes with what in the natural history sense, but also under what specific conditions at the state, dyadic, and system levels of social aggregation, what sorts of moves and counter-moves will likely generate what sorts of processes and what sorts of outcomes (Jones *et al.*, 1996, and Leng, 1993). To move toward that more ambitious goal, we need to develop and invent or discover (or rediscover) stories that might explain how the initial conditions surrounding the onset of a modest dispute between two states might move their relationship down the road to war or along a less destructive path. That will require a better understanding of the connections between certain conflict-prone conditions and the subsequent behavior of the protagonists. This would include both the ways in which conditions affect behavior *and* the ways that state behavior affects the conditions surrounding the protagonists and related states in the region. This in turn calls for a fuller understanding of the oft-underrated domestic context and the characteristics of their decision-making process. And while I incline toward the assumption of considerable uniformity among states in regard to these two sets of considerations, this homogeneity need not be exaggerated. At different times in the evolution of societies and their local regions, and across a wide range of cultural, religious, and linguistic propensities, there is the perpetual need to identify, and account for, the similar as well as the dissimilar. The implication here, of course, is that these explanatory stories need to avoid the provinciality of given cultures as well as given disciplines. Not only do Muslims, Hindus, and Christians tend to bring different and often incompatible assumptions—empirical, ethical, and epistemological—to their efforts to learn from history, interpret correlational findings, and explain the onset of war. But, in a similar vein, the efforts of economists and other devotees of "rational choice" models can also lead us astray. Their particular bias is to perceive all of the actors—individuals, factions, agencies, foreign ministries, and even states themselves—as not only capable of understanding and agreeing upon their particular interests, but also knowing how to pursue and maximize those interests. This approach typically ignores not only the role of the irrational but also of the extra-rational—that is, the parochial priorities of individuals and groups in a larger aggregation—often incompatible with the alleged interests of the aggregation. It also tends to assume a high level of shared information, including the very dubious "information" as to which particular moves and policies will generate which responses in other actors and lead to which particular outcomes. If that were already known by this time, all of the above-described research would not be necessary. In other words, the rational choice models make all sorts of assumptions that may hold in major corporate decision making, for example, but are often quite divergent from the rough and tumble of foreign policy politics around the world.

Having said this, and recognizing that most efforts to develop formal and well-integrated models tend to work from these overly simple assumptions, I would nevertheless emphasize the importance of formal model construction (Bueno de Mesquita and Lalman, 1992; Nichcolson, 1992). But while being highly attentive to logical consistency among the axioms and propositions that constitute the model, and to precise and operational definitions of the key variables embedded in such propositions, nothing says that we need build on such misleading empirical assumptions. The more carefully we read the psychological and anthropological literature—not to mention diplomatic and military history—the more likely we are to construct more realistic models. Worth noting in this criticism of rational choice models is the point that they can be used to make predictions and historical postdictions of an "as if" sort. Such teleonomic models can tell us what *would have* happened were the decisions taken in accordance with the rules of rational choice, and can thus serve as a base line against which to compare what actually did happen, and to provide clues and indicators as to the decision rules that *were* applied. And we cannot emphasize too strongly how little we know of the war-peace decision process, even if we are getting more and more memoirs, interviews, and even tape recordings of the relevant participants. While such materials are valuable, they can often be doctored, mis-remembered, or otherwise misleading; in other words, to get a better handle on the decision process in different countries and different eras, we need all the help we can get.

VI. THE FIFTH STAGE: APPLICABLE KNOWLEDGE

To repeat a point made earlier, this research into the correlates of war is not only a response to scientific curiosity and an exciting intellectual challenge. Most of us—especially those of us who launched the peace research movement in the early 1960s—hold the belief that the resulting knowledge can be applicable to the conflicts that arise in the global system now and in the relevant future. This may seem naive, for several reasons.

At the more abstract end of the argument, there is the possibility that we may never come up with anything more than a growing catalogue of correlates of war, and that many of these will only hold for a given epoch, region, or functional subpopulation. This could be because the regularities are fewer than we have assumed, meaning that there is so much variety in the types of interstate wars and the ways in which they begin that any effort to generalize is doomed to frustration. An extreme version of this argument is that "no two wars are the same," or "each war is totally unlike any other." We have already demonstrated that the similarities are numerous, but that still leaves us in a state of uncertainty. Closely related to this is a slightly less pessimistic view: that our research will be able to demonstrate that most of the existing explanatory models are seriously, or perhaps fundamentally, flawed—especially those embraced by the world's political and military elites. But going on to refine and replace them—it could be argued—will allegedly frustrate us; the complexities are too great, the research methods too primitive, and the important variables too elusive to ever be validly and reliably measured.

An extension of this is an ontological argument typically associated with such antihistoricists as Popper (1959). The view there is that even if we do come up with fairly credible explanatory models resting on very solid historical and empirical correlations, there still remains the problem of historical discontinuity. It is said that we never know when "the clock might strike thirteen!" Given the historical discontinuities that our research has uncovered already, this is not an argument to be dismissed out of hand. On the other hand, we have also demonstrated remarkable continuities across the decades and the centuries. Without embracing the fatuous French dictum "plus ca change, plus c'est le meme chose," we now have a fair amount of systemic research that not only goes back to the Napoleonic Wars and the Congress of Vienna, but back to the War of the Spanish Succession in 1704 (Rasler and Thompson, 1983), to the peace of Westphalia in 1648, or even further back to 1495 (Levy 1983), and beyond that to the wars of ancient China (Cioffi-Revilla, 1995). All of these studies reveal similarities and dissimilarities in conditions and events that belie the notion of great historical transformations so radical that nothing we know about one period (or region) can tell us anything about some subsequent period. The problem with this rejoinder is that it sets up the straw man of extreme historicism, which allegedly claims not only highly repetitive historical patterns but a strong suggestion of teleological determinism.

Then there is the political and psychological problem. That is, even if we achieve a modicum of scientific success and come up with fairly solid feats of postdiction and prediction, political elites and their courtiers will not find any of it credible. This is partially due to the fact that social science is still not taken seriously and that the elites are thus utterly unschooled in scientific method. Even more, there is the matter of their own legitimacy; competence and expertise in politics and diplomacy is their major claim to fame, and recognizing the value of all these arcane quantitative studies might erode that claim.

Finally, even if perchance the foreign policy elites might begin to take our research findings seriously, the likelihood is very strong that the policy implications would run counter to the conventional wisdom in regard to the virtues of military preparedness, xenophobic propaganda, alliance formation, heavy reliance on threats, and of course the frequent resort to force as a major instrument of statecraft. Bearing in mind that the conventional wisdom is conventional not so much because it works, but because it is highly beneficial to its advocates, we would not be surprised that weapons producers, the military establishment, the so-called research institutes, and of course those who have become the court astrologers to defense ministers, foreign ministers, and heads of state, will all have reason enough to reject and dismiss all of this "pseudo science."

VII. SUMMARY

To reiterate, we can understand the correlates of war not only as a body of established associations between certain factors and war, but also as a research strategy and the name of a project using that label. Such a strategy was a long time coming, given the centuries that elapsed between the beginnings of organized human combat and the emergence of the social sciences, more than a century behind the physical and biological sciences. But with the pioneering work of Richardson, Sorokin, and Wright—plus the stimulus of the two world wars—the scientific study of war got underway in the late 1950s, first on the part of psychologists and ultimately on the part of political scientists in the following decade.

And as economists, mathematicians, and others of a more abstract and less empirical turn of mind became interested, we have seen an interesting mix of two research strategies since the early 1980s, with these formal modelers trying either to integrate the findings of the correlates of war researchers, or their own ideas about the etiology of war, or both. As indicated by the growth and readership of the more scientific journals, the increasing number of such books (sadly, almost all are in English and by native English speakers), and the size and number of the relevant scholarly organizations, the research pace is clearly quickening. But in contrast to the efforts to understand cancer, black holes, traffic safety, or tropical storms, this enterprise remains miniscule. Thus, the slow pace in Stage Four results from the indifference of our political and academic elites to social science and in turn assures that we are still decades away from Stage Five.

Also See the Following Articles

AGGRESSION, PSYCHOLOGY OF • ALLIANCE SYSTEMS • CONFLICT THEORY • ECONOMIC CAUSES OF WAR AND PEACE • EVOLUTIONARY THEORY • INTERPERSONAL CONFLICT, HISTORY OF • MILITARY-INDUSTRIAL COMPLEX • PEACE AND DEMOCRACY • TRADE, CONFLICT AND COOPERATION AMONG NATIONS

Bibliography

Barbieri, K. (1996). Economic Interdependence: A path to peace or a source of interstate conflict? *Journal of Peace Research, 33*:29–49.

Bernard, J. *et al.* (1965). *The nature of conflict.* Englewood Cliffs, NJ: Prentice-Hall.

Blainey, G. (1973). *The causes of war.* New York: Free Press.

Boulding, K. (1962). *Conflict and defense.* New York: Harper and Row.

Bremer, S. (1992). Dangerous dyads: Conditions affecting the likelihood of interstate war, 1816–1965. *Journal of Conflict Resolution, 36*:309–341.

Bueno de Mesquita, B., & D. Lalman, D. (1992). *War and reason: Domestic and international imperatives.* New Haven, CT: Yale University Press.

Cioffi-Revilla, C. (1995). War and politics in ancient China, 2700 BC to 722 BC. *Journal of Conflict Resolution, 39*:467–494.

Darwin, C. (1839). *Journal of researches into the geology and natural history of various countries visited by H.M.S. Beagle.* New York: Harper.

Gates, S., Knutson, T., & Moses, J. (1996). Democracy and peace: A more skeptical view. *Journal of Peace Research, 33*:1–10.

Geller, D., & Singer, J. D. (1998). *Nations at war: A scientific study of international conflict.* Cambridge, UK: Cambridge University Press.

Gibbs, B., & Singer, J. D. (1993). *Empirical knowledge on world politics.* Westport, CT: Greenwood Press.

Jones, D., Bremer, S., & Singer, J. D. (1996). "Militarized Interstate Disputes, 1816–1992: Rationale, Coding Rules, and Empirical Patterns." *Conflict Management and Peace Science, 15/2*:163–213.

Jones, S., & Singer, J. D. (1972). *Beyond conjecture.* Itasca, IL: F.E. Peacock.

Kelman, H. Ed. (1965). *International behavior.* New York: Holt.

Leng, R. (1993). *Interstate crisis behavior, 1816–1980.* Cambridge, UK: Cambridge University Press.

Levy, J. (1983). *War in the modern great power system, 1495–1975.* Lexington, KY: University of Kentucky Press.

Nicholson, M. (1992). *Rationality and the analysis of international conflict.* Cambridge, UK: Cambridge University Press.

Popper, K. (1959). *The logic of scientific discovery.* New York: Basic Books.

Rasler, K., & Thompson, W. (1983). Global wars, public debts, and the long cycle. *World Politics, 35/4*:489–516.

Richardson, L. F. (1960). *Arms and insecurity.* Pittsburgh, PA: Boxwood Press.

Richardson, L. F. (1960). *Statistics of deadly quarrels.* Pittsburgh, PA: Boxwood Press.

Russett, B. (1968). *Economic theories of international politics.* Chicago, IL: Markham Publishing Co.

Singer, J. D. (1965). *Human behavior and international politics.* Chicago, IL: Rand-McNally.

Singer, J. D., & Small, M. (1972). *The wages of war: A statistical handbook.* New York, NY: Free Press.

Sorokin, P. (1937). *Social and cultural dynamics.* New York, NY: American Book Co.

Wright, Q. (1942). *A study of war.* Chicago, IL: University of Chicago Press.

Crime and Punishment, Changing Attitudes toward

Angela Y. Davis
University of California, Santa Cruz

GLOSSARY

Abolitionism The theories, policies, and advocacy of ending the practice of capital punishment; the theories and advocacy of decarceration and of replacing punitive with peacemaking approaches to crime.

Crime Legally prohibited action regarded as detrimental to the public welfare or to the interests of the state.

Criminalization The ideological process of linking presumptions of criminality to specific groups and communities; legal prohibition of actions, thereby rendering them crimes.

Decriminalization The elimination of legal restrictions on actions previously treated as crimes.

Penitentiary A 19th-century prison model emphasizing solitude, religious self-reflection, and self-reform; a U.S. prison operated by the state or federal government.

Prison An institution for the involuntary confinement of individuals convicted of committing crimes; an institution (U.S., jail) for the involuntary confinement of individuals awaiting trial.

Prison Industrial Complex A term referring to the exponential expansion of prisons and jails in the U.S. and the rising number of prisoners from communities of color, as well as to the increasingly symbiotic relationship between private corporations and the prison industry, the reliance of many communities on corrections for economic vitality in the aftermath of corporate migration to the Third World, and the mounting political influence of the correctional community.

Punishment The penalty imposed by law on those convicted of committing crimes.

ATTITUDES TOWARD CRIME AND PUNISHMENT historically have been informed by prevailing ideas about class, gender, race, and nation. They rarely have reflected strict legal definitions of crime, but rather have been influenced by political discourses, economic conditions, ideological circumstances, and the means by which ideas are publicly disseminated. In the late 20th century, representations of crime through the mass media have encouraged an uncritical attitude of fear toward racially- and class-defined communities as the main perpetrators of crime, deflecting attention away from corporate, white collar, government, and police crime, as well as domestic violence against women. The history of the prison reveals that this institution, which has emerged as the dominant mode of punishment, has been unable to solve the problem of crime, but rather has become a site for violence, assaults on human rights, and the perpetuation of racism. Nevertheless, it has expanded in the industrialized countries—especially in the United States—to the extent that we now can speak of an emergent prison industrial complex. Oppositional attitudes toward penal systems have emerged in transnational organizations, including abolitionist perspectives toward both prisons and the death penalty.

I. REPRESENTATIONS OF CRIME

During the late 20th century, increasing evocations of "the crime problem" in the discourse of elected officials, the centrality accorded crime reportage in the print and electronic news media, and the mounting popularity of literary, televisual, and cinematic representations of fictionalized crime all have tended to create a crime-saturated social environment. New genres such as *Court TV* have helped to transform high-profile trials, such as that of O.J. Simpson, into global media events. The formation of popular attitudes toward crime—and specifically the fascination with and fear of crime—in fact is more an outgrowth of these representational practices than of the actual risk of becoming a victim of crime.

Crime, as it is perceived on the level of common sense, is only indirectly related to its legal definition, which covers a range of actions so vast as to make it difficult to identify commonalities among them beyond the fact that "criminal actions" are those proscribed by law and those for which courts can impose punishments. What is considered a crime during one historical period in another may become neutral behavior in which criminal justice systems have no apparent interest. The penal codes of different countries, as well as state penal codes within the United States, frequently are at variance with each other. Moreover, while numerous surveys indicate that a vast majority of most populations have engaged at one point or another in behavior proscribed by law, only a small percentage of these acts ever is addressed by criminal justice systems. In some countries, spousal battery, a historically sanctioned behavior, has been recognized relatively recently as a punishable crime. Although this and other crimes committed by victims' relatives and acquaintances over time have constituted the great majority of violent crimes, the widespread fear of crime is directed not toward such commonplace events, but rather toward the specter of an assault by a stranger. Historically, the construction of this imagined anonymous stranger has been class- and/or race-inflected.

The deployment of military metaphors in governmental anticrime policy has helped to legitimize a discourse on crime that constructs the criminal as an enemy to be conquered. In the United States, the "war on crime," as articulated by former president Richard Nixon, developed alongside—and, in many ways, as an appendage to—the war against communism. If communism was represented as an external threat to the security of the nation, crime represented the internal threat. During the era of the 1960s, when the U.S. Civil Rights movement and social movements that opposed the Vietnam War and raised demands for student rights acquired a dramatic visibility throughout the world, anticrime campaigns frequently were conflated with strategies to counter political dissent. Through the law-and-order themes that, since the Nixon presidency, have become recurring ingredients in U.S. election campaigns, crime and the call for ever-more stringent punishments have become increasingly politicized. Similar patterns can be found throughout North America and in many European, African, South American, and Asian countries. China's 1996 "Strike Hard" campaign, which specifically targeted drug-related crime, has been associated with the more than 4000 state-sanctioned executions that year. Japan, on the other hand, has thus far avoided official "tough on crime" postures and, in recent years, has reduced its rate of imprisonment, which is less than one-tenth that of the United States. Although President Nelson Mandela has described crime in the new South Africa as "out of control," he insisted in 1996 that his government's "short-term tactics to deal with crime" should not eclipse the fact that their most effective long-term anticrime strategy resides in their plans to eradicate poverty. Moreover, under Mandela's leadership, the death penalty was abolished in South Africa.

As criminologists and historians have pointed out, the "crime waves" that, according to public officials, demand the staging of wars against crime, almost always have referred to specific kinds of crime, usually anonymous, violent, and—in the late 20th century—drug-related street crime. White collar crime, corporate crime, police crime, and government crime rarely have been included in evocations of crime waves or in the statistics produced to evidence the rise and fall of crime. British sociologist and cultural critic Stuart Hall has emphasized that crime statistics function in deeply ideological ways, seeming to ground elusive information for the media and the public at large by transforming complex, disparate, and often contradictory information into numerical data and incontestable facts. In reality, statistics do not always reflect the actual volume of crime committed.

The history of anticrime campaigns in the United States is closely linked with the production of FBI crime statistics. Despite serious weaknesses in the FBI's Uniform Crime Reports, some of which were detected immediately after the UCR began to be issued in 1930, these figures—which measure reported crime as it is mediated by police interpretations—have continued to be the primary source upon which public perceptions about crime are based. Police information forwarded to the FBI is based on citizens' reports and may include crimes for which no suspect is identified, as well as crimes that go uninvestigated. That factors related to race, class, gender, and sexuality often determine what crimes are reported, and how law enforcement officials respond to reports of crime, is not reflected in crime statistics.

II. CLASS, GENDER, RACE, AND THE PRODUCTION OF CRIME

Crime as a legal category is defined as behavior proscribed by law and subject to governmental punishment. Poverty and crime often have been conflated in the popular imagination—as well as in public policy—as a result of punishment historically being meted out disproportionately to poor populations. Vagrancy laws frequently have functioned to reinforce the idea that poverty is synonymous with criminality. In 1798, Thomas Malthus published his *Essay on the Principle of Population,* lending support to political efforts to revise the English Poor Law, which provided for welfare assistance by the parishes of those in need. Malthus contended that state charity was little more than a public encouragement of poverty, and that the state should leave the poor to their natural fate. The English Poor Law of 1834 embodied Malthus' idea and, according to Karl Marx, reflected the view that workers are responsible for their own poverty. Moreover, Marx claimed, the passage of this law encouraged the attitude that poverty is not a misfortune but rather a crime requiring punishment. The new Poor Law called for confinement in workhouses or poorhouses, where labor was coerced and unpaid.

The earliest model of imprisonment as punishment rather than detention was the workhouse opened in Brideswell, London, in 1555, which later inspired the Act of 1576 calling for the creation of workhouses or "brideswells" in other counties. On the European continent, the Rasphuis of Amsterdam, opened in 1596, was used as a place of confinement and forced labor for beggars and young people labeled as malefactors. In the United States, the poorhouse developed during the early 19th century; it was not entirely differentiated from the jail either in its function or in the way it was popularly perceived. Both impoverished people and criminals were viewed as dangerous elements who threatened social stability and needed to be locked away.

A. Patriarchy and Criminality

Patriarchal structures and ideologies also have tended to produce assumptions of criminality, particularly in relation to women who have violated social norms defining women's "place." The most popular examples of this patriarchal production of criminality can be found in the figure of Jeanne d'Arc, in the witch hunts in Europe during the Middle Ages, and in the execution in 1792 of accused witches in Salem, Massachusetts. From the 14th to the 17th centuries, among the many thousands of people accused of witchcraft, 80 to 90% were women. Moreover, feminist historians have uncovered evidence of severe corporal punishments inflicted on women accused of adultery, while the behavior of male adulterers simply was normalized. With the rise of professionalized medicine, women healers in Europe and the United States often were criminalized and punished.

The conflation of criminal and immoral, that is, sexual, activity among girls rendered permeable the borders between "crime" and "unfeminine" behavior. In the late 19th century, one girl was committed at the Lancaster Reformatory, the first girls' reformatory in the United States, because her father accused her of engaging in masturbation. As it turned out, she merely was trying to alleviate, by scratching, the chronic genital rash from which she suffered. Adult women tended to be treated similarly. Rather than legally being accused of crimes, many deviant women were locked away in almshouses, workhouses, or asylums for the insane. Prevailing social attitudes during the 17th and 18th centuries reflected a belief that most women were incapable of intentionally violating the law—and that there was no hope of reform for women who were deemed depraved and criminal—but that they *could* be afflicted with poverty and madness, both of which were sufficient grounds for incarceration. In the 20th century, women inclined toward or engaging in lesbian sexual practices still could be committed to mental institutions in many countries. In Egypt in 1981, feminist writer and physician Nawal El Saadawi, the first African woman to speak publicly against genital mutilation, was arrested for alleged "crimes against the state."

B. Race and Criminalization in the United States

Particularly in the United States, race has played a central role in constructing presumptions of criminality. After the abolition of slavery, former slave states passed new legislation revising the Slave Codes in order to regulate the behavior of free Blacks in ways similar to those that had existed during slavery. The new Black Codes proscribed a range of actions—such as vagrancy, absence from work, breach of job contracts, the possession of firearms, and insulting gestures or acts—that were criminalized only when the actor was Black. In light of the provision in the Thirteenth Amendment that abolished slavery and involuntary servitude "except as a punishment for crime, whereof the party shall have been duly convicted," there were crimes defined by state law for which only Blacks could be "duly convicted," and thus sentenced to involuntary servitude. Black people thereby became the prime targets of the developing convict lease system, in many ways a reincarnation of slavery. The Mississippi Black Codes, for example, declared vagrant "anyone/who was guilty of theft, had run away [from a job, apparently], was drunk, was wanton in conduct or speech, had neglected job or family, handled money carelessly, and . . . all other idle and disorderly persons." Thus vagrancy was coded as a Black crime, one punishable by incarceration and forced labor, sometimes on the very plantations that previously had thrived on slave labor.

Identifying the racialization of crime, Frederick Douglass wrote in 1883 of the South's tendency to "impute crime to color." When a particularly egregious crime was committed, he noted, not only was guilt frequently assigned to a Black person regardless of the perpetrator's race, but White men sometimes sought to escape punishment by disguising themselves as Black. Douglass would later recount one such incident that took place in Granger County, Tennessee, in which a man who appeared to be Black was shot while committing a robbery. The wounded man, however, was discovered to be a respectable White citizen who had colored his face black.

Legal scholar Cheryl Harris has argued that a property interest in Whiteness emerged from the conditions of slavery. According to Harris, since White identity was owned as property, rights, liberties, and self-identity were affirmed for Whites while being denied for Blacks, whose only access to Whiteness was through "passing." Douglass's comments indicate how this property interest in Whiteness was easily reversed in schemes to deny Black people their rights to due process. Interestingly, cases similar to the one Douglass discusses above emerged in the United States during the 1990s: in Boston, Charles Stuart murdered his pregnant wife and attempted to blame an anonymous Black man, and in Union, South Carolina, Susan Smith killed her children and claimed they had been abducted by a Black carjacker. The racialization of crime—the tendency to "impute crime to color," to use Frederick Douglas' words—is not only operative in the United States, but in other countries such as Brazil and South Africa, which have their own distinct histories of racial subjugation.

C. The Drug Wars

A racialized disjuncture further characterizes the relationship, in contemporary campaigns against drugs, between illicit drug use and interventions of the criminal justice system. The general context of this disjuncture has resulted from the ways in which the multinational pharmaceutical industry advertises a range of licit drugs—particularly those that have psychotropic effects, such as Prozac—as panaceas for emotional disorders, while the use of drugs that circulate outside of corporate and governmental sanctions is defined as criminal. Because of the prevailing association of drug use and illegal drug-dealing with people of color, Black, Latino, and immigrant communities in the United States, Canada, and Europe have become disproportionately vulnerable to prosecution. "Wars on drugs"—which, like the various "wars on crime," evoke the violence of military maneuvers—have thus played a pivotal role in criminalizing these populations. The Dutch Ministry of Justice, for example, which until the 1980s had managed to prevent increases in—and, during many years, to reduce—its incarcerated population, has begun to construct more prison space largely in response to drug trafficking. Among those sentenced to prison on drug trafficking charges, a disproportionate number are first- or second-generation immigrants from the Netherlands' former colonies in the Carribean and Asia, as well as Latin Americans involved in the drug economy. In the United States, the war on drugs is responsible for soaring numbers of imprisoned individuals. In 1996, drug defendants made up 61% of the U.S. federal prison population, up from 23% in 1980. In the state prison systems, by 1991, nearly one in three women were incarcerated for drug offenses.

In the United States, sentencing disparities in cases involving crack and powdered cocaine result in much more prison time for crack users than for cocaine users. This distinction is highly racialized: the majority of crack cases involve Black defendants—according to a 1992 report by the U.S. Sentencing Commission, 91.3% of defendants sentenced for federal crack offenses were Black—and the majority of powdered cocaine cases involved White defendants. The result is the criminalization and incarceration of many more people of color for offenses comparable to those committed by their more leniently treated White counterparts.

D. Violence against Women

Another disjuncture between crime commission and the response of the criminal justice system can be discovered in the historical treatment of women who have been targets of domestic violence. Before the advent of feminist movements, spousal assault—and in earlier eras, gynocide—was not addressed within the realm of criminal law. Thus violent assaults in the public sphere were criminalized, while male violence enacted within the domestic sphere was privatized and thus shielded from state intervention. This historically dichotomous relationship between the public and private realms has positioned gender at the center of many contradictions in the ideological production of crime and the practical implementation of punishment. One particularly dramatic example is the pattern of murder convictions and excessively long sentences—currently contested by feminist movements in many countries—meted out to battered women who have killed their male batterers. For much of the history of criminal justice, men have killed and assaulted their wives and partners with impunity, whereas women who fight back have been defined as assailants and murderers. Currently, feminist movements are calling upon state and national governments to recognize "battered women's syndrome" as a viable legal defense.

III. PUNISHMENT AND THE PRISON: A HISTORICAL OVERVIEW

Although noncapital corporal punishment still prevails in some countries, imprisonment is by far the most widely employed mode of punishment. Fines, and in some cases (the U.S., for example) the death penalty—the most violent state assault on the body—complete the spectrum of punishment. However, the prominence of incarceration is a relatively recent historical development and incarceration itself has been theorized during different eras as accomplishing very different goals. Prison reform movements have criticized the brutality associated with imprisonment for as long as prisons have existed.

The United Nations' Standard Minimum Rules for the Treatment of Prisoners, approved in 1957, reflect many decades of organizing and advocacy of international prison reform toward the reduction of, among other things, torture and injurious living conditions. In this context it is ironic that the institution of the prison itself originally emerged in part as a response to Enlightenment-era opposition to the cruelty of corporal punishment. Michel Foucault opens his germinal study, *Discipline and Punish: The Birth of the Prison,* with a graphic description of a 1757 execution in Paris. The court had sentenced the unfortunate murderer to undergo a series of formidable tortures before he was finally put to death. Red-hot pincers were used to burn away the flesh from his limbs, and molten lead, boiling oil, burning resin, and other substances were melted together and poured onto the wounds. Finally, he was drawn and quartered, his body burned, and the ashes tossed into the wind.

This gruesome execution reflects the extent to which the body was a target of torture, which in this instance—although not always—was terminated by death. Other modes of corporal punishment have included the stocks and pillories, whippings, brandings, and amputations. Prior to the historical birth of the prison, such punishment was designed to have its most profound effect not so much on the person punished as on the crowd of spectators. Punishment was, in essence, public spectacle.

When women were punished within the domestic domain, instrumentalities of torture were sometimes imported by authorities into the household. In 17th-century Britain, women whose husbands identified them as quarrelsome and unaccepting of male dominance were punished by means of a gossip's bridle or branks, a headpiece with a chain attached and an iron bit that was introduced into the woman's mouth. Although the branking of women was often linked to a public parade, this contraption was sometimes hooked to a wall of the house, where the punished woman remained until her husband decided to release her.

Although the conceptualization of punishment as the infliction of physical pain on the body is associated with precapitalist eras, there are conspicuous exceptions to this pattern. The extralegal lynching of Black Americans well into the 20th century, although not directly sanctioned by law, was nonetheless condoned by the political structures of the southern states. These lynchings, like the community spectacles of the U.S. colonial period and Europe of the Middle Ages, were frequently public events with a carnivalesque character.

Other modes of punishment that predated the rise of the prison included banishment, forced labor in galleys, transportation, and appropriation of the accused's property. The punitive transportation of large numbers of people from England facilitated the initial colonization of Australia. The North American colony of Georgia also was settled by transported English convicts. During the early 1700s, one in eight transported convicts were women, and the work they were forced to perform often consisted of prostitution.

Imprisonment was not employed as a principal mode of punishment until the 18th century in Europe and the 19th century in the United States. European prison systems were instituted in Asia and Africa as an important component of colonial rule. In India, for example, the English prison system was introduced during the second half of the 18th century, when jails were established in the regions of Calcutta and Madras. In Europe, the penitentiary movement reflected new intellectual tendencies associated with the Enlightenment, activist interventions by Protestant reformers, and structural transformations associated with the rise of industrial capitalism. In Milan in 1764, Ceasare Beccaria published his essay *On Crimes and Punishments,* which was strongly influenced by notions of equality advanced by the philosophes—especially Voltaire, Rousseau, and Montesquieu. Beccaria argued that punishment should never be a private matter, nor should it be arbitrarily violent; rather, it should be public, swift, and as lenient as possible. Beccaria identified what was then a distinctive feature of imprisonment, its imposition prior to the defendant's guilt or innocence being decided. Eventually, when incarceration became more a function of the sentence rather than of pretrial detention, it emerged as the predominant form of punishment, revealing a shift in the valuation of the individual. Prior to the Enlightenment, before the individual was perceived as a bearer of formal rights and liberties, the deprivation of rights and liberties through imprisonment could not be understood as punishment. The prison sentence as punishment invokes the abstraction of time in a way that resonates with the role of labor-time as the basis for computing commodity value. Marxist theorists of punishment have noted that the historical period during which the commodity form arose is the same one in which the penitentiary emerges as the paradigmatic mode of punishment.

Georg Rusche's and Otto Kirchheimer's *Punishment and Social Structure,* first published in 1939 by the Institute for Social Research, attempted to establish a relationship between penal policy and labor market conditions, particularly those prevailing during different phases of capitalist development. While their model has been criticized for its economism and reductionism, it has greatly influenced Marxist criminologists and historians of punishment, some of whom argue that Rusche and Kirchheimer underestimated the role of ideology. Feminist critics such as Adrian Howe, author of *Punish and Critique: Toward a Feminist Analysis of Penality,* have observed that most political economies of punishment are profoundly masculinist, failing to account for the women who are in prison and ignoring feminist contestations of traditional Marxist categories.

The fact that convicts punished by imprisonment in emergent penitentiary systems were primarily male reflected the deeply gender-biased structure of legal, political, and economic rights. Since women were largely denied public status as rights-bearing individuals, they could not be punished by the deprivation of those rights through imprisonment. This was especially true of married women, who had no standing before the law. According to English Common Law, marriage resulted in a state of "civil death," as symbolized by the wife's assumption of the husband's name. Consequently, she tended to be punished for revolting against her domestic duties rather than for failure in her meager public responsibilities. The relegation of women to domestic economies, where use value prevailed, prevented them from playing a significant role in the emergent commodity realm, which was defined by exchange value. This was especially true because the wage reflected the exchange value of labor power, typically gendered as male and racialized as White. Thus corporal punishment for women survived long after these modes of punishment had become obsolete for (White) men. The persistence of domestic violence painfully attests to historical modes of gendered punishment.

A. The Penitentiary

Ironically, as some scholars have argued, the word "penitentiary" may have been used first in connection with plans outlined in England in 1758 to house "penitant prostitutes." In 1877, John Howard, the leading Protestant proponent of penal reform in England, published *The State of the Prisons* in which he conceptualized imprisonment as an occasion for religious self-reflection and self-reform. Between 1787 and 1791, the utilitarian philosopher Jeremy Bentham published his letters on a prison model he called the panopticon, which would facilitate the total surveillance and discipline he claimed criminals needed in order to internalize productive labor habits. Prisoners were to be housed in single cells on circular tiers, all facing a multilevel guard tower. By means of blinds and a complicated play of light and darkness, the prisoners—who would not see each other at all—would be unable to see the warden; from his vantage point, on the other hand, the warden would be able to see all of the prisoners. However—and this was the most significant aspect of Bentham's mammoth panopticon—because each individual prisoner would never be able to determine where the warden's gaze was focused, each prisoner would be compelled to act, that is, work, as if he were being watched at all times. Howard's ideas were incorporated in the Penitentiary Act of 1799, which opened the way for the modern prison. While Bentham's ideas influenced the development of the first national English penitentiary, located in Millbank and opened in 1816, the first full-fledged effort to create a panopticon prison was in the United States. The Western State Penitentiary in Pittsburgh, based on a revised architectural model of the panopticon, opened in 1826.

Pennsylvania's Walnut Street Jail housed the first state penitentiary in the United States when a portion of the jail was converted in 1790 from a detention facility to an institution housing convicts whose prison sentences simultaneously became punishment and occasions for penitence and reform. Walnut Street's austere regime—total isolation in single cells, where prisoners lived, ate, worked, read the Bible (if, indeed, they were literate), and supposedly reflected and repented—came to be known as the Pennsylvania system. This regime would constitute one of that era's two major models of imprisonment. Although the other model, developed in Auburn, New York, was viewed as a rival to the Pennsylvania system, the philosophical basis of the two models did not differ substantively. The Pennsylvania model, which eventually crystallized in the Eastern State Penitentiary in Cherry Hill—the plans for which were approved in 1821—emphasized total isolation, silence, and solitude, whereas the Auburn model called for solitary cells and silent congregate labor. Because of its more efficient labor practices, the Auburn model eventually achieved hegemony.

B. Women's Prisons

The relatively small proportion of women among incarcerated populations is often invoked as a justification for the scant attention accorded women prisoners by policymakers, scholars, and activists. In most countries, the female percentage of prison populations usually hovers around 5%. Ideologically, the small numbers of women prisoners tend to bolster the view that imprisoned women must be a great deal more aberrant and far more threatening to society than their numerous male counterparts.

That women, historically, have constituted a far greater number of inmates in mental institutions than in prisons suggests that while jails and prisons have been dominant institutions for the control of men, mental institutions have served a similar purpose for women. That is, deviant men have been constructed as criminal, while deviant women have been constructed as insane. Prior to the emergence of the penitentiary and thus of the notion of punishment as "doing time," the employment of places of confinement to control beggars, thieves, and the insane tended to conflate these categories of deviancy. As the discourse on criminality and the corresponding institutions to control it distinguished the "criminal" from the "insane," the distinction focused largely on men, leaving deviant women in the category of the insane.

Quaker reformers in the United States—especially the Philadelphia Society for Alleviating the Miseries of Public Prisons, founded in 1787—played a pivotal role in campaigns to substitute imprisonment for corporal punishment. Following in the tradition established by Elizabeth Fry in England, Quakers were also responsible for extended crusades to institute separate prisons for women. Fry formulated principles governing prison reform for women in her 1827 work, *Observations in Visiting, Superintendence and Government of Female Prisoners,* which were taken up in the United States by women such as Josephine Shaw Lowell and Abby Hopper Gibbons. Prevailing attitudes toward women convicts differed from those toward men convicts, who were assumed to have forfeited rights and liberties that women generally could not claim. Although some women were housed in penitentiaries, the institution itself was gendered as male. As a consequence, male punishment was linked to penitence and reform. The very forfeiture of rights and liberties implied that with self-reflection, religious study, and work, male convicts could achieve redemption and could recover these rights and liberties. Since women were not acknowledged as ever in possession of them, however, they were not eligible to participate in this process of redemption.

According to the prevailing views, women convicts were irrevocably fallen women, with no possibility of salvation. If male criminals were considered to be public individuals who had simply violated the social contract, female criminals were seen as having transgressed fundamental moral principles of womanhood. The reformers who, following Elizabeth Fry, argued that women were capable of redemption, did not really contest these ideological assumptions about women's place. In opposing the idea that fallen women could not be saved, they advocated separate facilities and a specifically female approach to punishment. Their approach called for an architectural design replacing cells with cottages and "rooms" designed to infuse domesticity into prison life. This model facilitated a regime devised to reintegrate criminalized women into the domestic roles of wife and mother. A female custodial staff, the reformers argued, would minimize the sexual temptations that they believed were often at the root of female criminality.

The U.S. women's prison reform movement unfolded within the context of a larger developing social movement demanding women's rights. Like the woman suffrage movement, it tended to accept the prevailing class- and race-inflected discourse on womanhood, which privileged the social conditions of White middle-class women. Since imprisoned White women came largely from working-class communities, the domestic strategy associated with the women's prison reform movement—while putatively training female convicts to be better wives and mothers—in fact tended to mark them as domestic servants. This outcome of domestic prison regimes was even more pronounced for women of color.

Although it is widely assumed that women prisoners are most often incarcerated in separate women's facilities, in many countries—and indeed in local jails in the United States—they are housed together with men. In a widely publicized case in the mid-1970s, Joanne Little was charged with the murder of a male guard, who had raped her in her cell in a men's jail where she was being held. India is one example of a country where there are very few separate institutions for women, although there are women's sections of central prisons that primarily house men.

C. The Punishment Debate: Deterrence, Retribution, Rehabilitation

The history of the prison and attendant attitudes toward punishment have been shaped by debates regarding the ultimate objective of imprisonment. Does it deter those in the "free world" from committing the crimes that will lead them to prison? Is its primary purpose that of rehabilitating the individual who has broken the social (or domestic) contract by committing a crime? Or is it simply meant to ensure that the person convicted of criminal behavior receives his/her just desserts? In the fields of criminology, penology, and philosophy of punishment, myriad discussions have been devoted to justificatory arguments rationalizing imprisonment on the basis of one or more of these objectives. These scholarly concerns have directly influenced policymaking, especially with respect to sentencing practices and prison conditions. Rehabilitative strategies, for example, may demand educational and vocational programs, as well as more humane living conditions than retributive imprisonment. However, as some critics have pointed out, rehabilitation has led to coercive psychiatric treatment and indeterminate sentences, since the prisoner may not be released until he/she has been "rehabilitated." As the limits of modern discourses on punishment have been established by this conceptual triumvirate of deterrence, rehabilitation, and retribution, popular attitudes toward punishment also have tended to move along these triangular axes.

At the beginning of the intellectual tradition of advocating imprisonment as the primary mode of punishment, the prison was represented as a site for the reformation of the individual. Reformers who opposed the violence and cruelty of corporal punishment proposed confinement under conditions designed to morally reshape the offender. According to Foucault, with the birth of the prisons, the locus of punishment shifted from the body to the soul or psyche and the prison became the disciplinary apparatus par excellence, one that was most appropriate to historical era in which a disciplined working class was required by the developing industrial capitalist economy. In this sense, the institution of the prison had the same aim as educational and military institutions. Bentham claimed that his panopticon could be applied to any institution in which people were subject to surveillance—penitentiaries, workhouses, poorhouses, insane asylums, places of quarantine, factories, hospitals, and schools. As Foucault would observe, it is not surprising that prisons recall schools, factories, military barracks, and hospitals, all of which, in turn, recall prisons.

For a number of reasons—among them recidivism and the continued lack of proof that prisons curtail crime—the great historical penitentiary projects in England, France, and the United States have been acknowledged as failures by advocates and critics alike. Foucault points out that this failure did not follow a period during which the penitentiary was recognized for its successes, but rather it was denounced as a monumental failure from the very beginning of its history. He further argues that reform campaigns were so inextricably tied to ideological assumptions that the prison was the only effective strategy for countering crime, that the prison repeatedly is proposed as the remedy for its own failure. Thus even in its failure to inhibit crime—indeed, to rehabilitate criminals—the prison is self-perpetuating.

The project of rehabilitation itself underwent transformation—from the religious model of the early penitentiaries to the medical model of the 20th century—without any significant increase in the effectiveness of the prison. The philosophical debate about the purpose of the prison has been deeply ensconced in this dilemma—the failure of the prison combined with the inability to conceptualize penal strategies that move beyond the discursive and material space of the prison. Popular attitudes also reflect the assumption that as brutal as prisons may appear, public order will always depend on the existence of prisons, whether they are represented as places of rehabilitation, deterrence, or retribution.

The dominance until the 1970s of arguments for rehabilitation can be explained by the seductiveness of the medical model, which defines criminals as "ill" and thus in need of a cure. However, with the increase and globalization of drug trafficking—which some scholars and journalists have linked to government involvement or sanction—and the attendant "wars" on drugs and crime, imprisoned populations soared to unprecedented heights. As the primary but ineffective weapon in these "wars," the prison again tends to perpetuate its own failures, thereby becoming self-perpetuating.

D. Proliferation of Imprisoned Populations

The United States and other industrialized countries have experienced what John Irwin and James Austin call an imprisonment binge. Between 1980 and 1995, the U.S. federal and state prison populations increased 235% (from 329,821 to 1,104,074). They point out that in 1995 the imprisoned population in the United States equaled or exceeded the populations of 13 states and many major U.S. cities. While the United States, South Africa, China, and Russia have had the highest rates of incarceration, the incarceration rate in a country like the Netherlands—which has an international reputation for a humane penal system and for implementing strategies of decarceration—has increased from 20 per 100,000 in 1975 to 40 in 1988, and is in excess of 50 in the 1990s. Dutch criminologist Willem de Haan has observed that the corresponding tendency to build more prisons in the Netherlands may well interrupt a 125-year-old pattern of decarceration, or consistent reduction of prison populations.

In the United States, there has been great resistance to the idea of decriminalizing drug use, while in the Netherlands, drug decriminalization has been an important part of criminal justice policy for many years. Moreover, while many states in the United States have implemented "three strikes and you're out" sentencing policies providing for long mandatory sentences after the commission of three felonies, Dutch sentencing policies call for much shorter sentences and emphasize prisoners' rights to move to "half-open" and "open" prisons after completion of a certain percentage of their sentences. (Other countries, including Cuba, use similar rehabilitative strategies of progressive reintroduction of prisoners into the "free world.") In general, U.S. criminal justice policies have all but discarded the traditional goal of prison rehabilitation, emphasizing unembellished punishment as the objective of imprisonment. In the Netherlands, on the other hand, rehabilitation, and the ultimate reincorporation of the individual into society, remains the goal of the Dutch penal system.

Even with these vast differences between the United States and the Netherlands—and although the rate of incarceration in the Netherlands is 50 per 100,000, while in the United States it is more than 10 times that amount—both countries have embarked upon a path of prison construction, to which there is no apparent end in sight. Furthermore, in spite of progressive approaches in the Netherlands, a disproportionate number of incarcerated individuals in both countries have been convicted on drug charges, and both the Dutch and U.S. prison populations consist of a preponderance of people of color.

IV. THE PRISON INDUSTRIAL COMPLEX

Social historian Mike Davis first used the term "prison industrial complex" in relation to California's penal system, which, he observed, already had begun in the 1990s to rival agribusiness and land development as a major economic and political force. The United States has the largest prison complex in the world. According to the 1995 Census of State and Federal Correctional Facilities conducted under the auspices of the Bureau of Justice Statistics, between 1990 and 1995 more than 280,000 beds were added in 213 prisons, representing a 41% increase in prison capacity. In 1995 there were 1500 state facilities (up from 1287) and 125 federal facilities (up from 80). The Census indicated that 327,320 persons were employed by these facilities, up from 264,201 in 1990. Almost two-thirds of correctional employees were in custodial or security positions.

The U.S. penal system differs from that of most other countries in that county jails, which are excluded from the BJS Census, are used to detain accused persons awaiting trial as well as to house misdemeanants whose sentences are less than 1 year. In 1994, there were more than 9.8 million admissions to the more than 3300 county jails. Irwin and Austin have calculated that nearly 1 in every 25 adults in the United States goes to jail each year.

Punishment has developed into a vast industry and its presence in the U.S. economy is expanding continually. This presence not only includes the federal and state prison facilities and county jails, but also a significant population under the direct supervision of correctional authorities such as parole and probation officers. If these latter figures are added to those representing prison and jail populations (over 1.5 million), then in 1994 over five million adults were under the direct surveillance and supervision of the U.S. criminal justice system. In other words, 1 in 37 adults was marked in this way as "criminal." The corresponding ratio in 1980 was 1 in 91 adults. (It should be pointed out that these statistics do not reflect the increasing imprisonment of teenagers and children). In the United Kingdom a similar trend can be detected. The 1994/1995 prison population of England and Wales was 49,300—6000 higher than in the previous two years. In 1997, that population had risen to 56,900 and was rising at a rate of 1000 per month.

Such statistics as have been reported in this section do not create a full picture of the emergence of a U.S. prison industrial complex. As astounding as they may appear by themselves, they do not reveal the disproportionate surge in the population of incarcerated women and the phenomenal rise in the numbers of Black men who are under the direct control of correctional systems. Although women in the United States—as in every other country—constitute a relatively small minority of convicted persons, during the last two decades of the 20th century, the number of women sentenced to state and federal prisons increased by 386%, as compared with a 214% increase among their male counterparts. The 20th-century history of women's prison facilities reveals that between 1930 and 1950 only 2 or 3 prisons were built or established per decade. In the 1960s 7 more were created, 17 in the 1970s, and 34 in the 1980s.

In 1990, the Washington-based Sentencing Project published a study of U.S. populations in prison and jail and on parole and probation that concluded that 1 in 4 Black men between the ages of 20 and 29 were among these numbers. Five years later, a second study revealed that this percentage had soared to almost 1 in 3 (32.2%). Moreover, more than 1 in 10 Latino men in this same age range was in jail or prison, or on probation or parole. The second study also revealed that the group experiencing the greatest increase was Black women, whose imprisonment increased by 78%. According to BJS, African Americans as a whole now represent the majority of state and federal prisoners, with a total of 735,200 Black inmates—10,000 more than the total number of White inmates.

The concept of the prison industrial complex, first employed by Mike Davis—or the correctional industrial complex, the term used by Irwin and Austin—attempts to capture not only the phenomenal expansion of prisons and jails and the enormous increase in the numbers of people of color subject to the surveillance and supervision of the criminal justice system, but also the increasingly symbiotic relationship between the corporate structure and the prison industry, the relationship between corrections and economic vitality in many communities, and the mounting political influence of the correctional community.

A. Prisons and Private Industry

Recapitulating the 19th-century postslavery leasing of mostly Black convicts to individuals and companies in the southern states, the contemporary pattern of privatization has established prisons as a source of corporate profit. By the late 1990s, there were approximately 50,000 private prison beds in the United States, the largest private prison company being Corrections Corporation of America. CCA managed 21 prisons in the U.S., Australia, and Britain. Wachenhut, the second largest private prison corporation, was also under contract in Britain, where, as of 1997, there were plans for at least 12 private prisons.

Private corporations not only seek out prison labor, prisons also constitute markets for their goods and services. In 1993 among the many advertisements in a prominent trade journal, a cellular phone company proposed that convicts under house arrest and monitored by electronic bracelets—but possessing no home telephones—could be provided with cellular phones to facilitate constant contact with authorities. The growth of privately run operations within prisons throughout the United States further consolidates connections between the corporate economy and prisoners who are perceived in this context as constituting attractively cheap labor pools. Structurally, prison labor is vulnerable to exploitation in much the same way as Third World labor, which has become a seductive alternative for U.S.-based transnational corporations seeking relief from the demands of domestic organized labor. While the U.S. labor movement has forcefully protested prison labor in China and has spoken out against the use of prison labor by private corporations in the United States, by and large, it has not been persuaded to demand the unionization of prison labor.

In Britain, advocates of privatization have pointed to the fact that privately managed prisons have introduced progressive changes that have been taken up by the public sector, such as more lenient visiting policies. Moreover, they claim that the privatization of entire institutions has not introduced profit into the penal realm, but rather is merely an extension of the solidly anchored presence of private enterprise, long a provider of goods and services to prisons. Among those who have expressed opposition to privatization is criminologist Sir Leon Radzinowicz, who counters this argument by pointing out that provision of goods and services by private companies whose primary interest is commercial is quite a different question from possession by these same companies of the power of coercion over human beings.

V. PRISON ACTIVISM AND ABOLITIONIST STRATEGIES

The concept of the prison industrial complex has been taken up by intellectuals and activists in the United States whose work focuses on issues of criminalization and punishment. The term's growing popularity among these groups in the 1990s is linked in part to its historical resonance with the concept of a military industrial complex, a term first employed by Dwight Eisenhower and appropriated by radical activists and scholars in the 1960s who invoked it in their opposition to the military build-up during the Vietnam War and to the resulting ties between the corporate, academic, and military sectors. While radical prison activism has its most immediate roots in this same period, it should be acknowledged that the tradition of prison activism is as old as the institution of the prison itself. What differentiates the contemporary activist tradition from its predecessors is its attempt not only to protest inhumane conditions of imprisonment, but to challenge the very necessity of prisons as the major mode of addressing such social problems as poverty, drug use, and racial dominance.

In the 1960s and 1970s, activist movements took shape around political prisoners associated with antiracist, antiwar, and anticolonialist movements, including the campaigns for civil rights in Northern Ireland and against apartheid in South Africa. In the United States, governmental repression of civil rights leaders, student organizers, Native American activists, and Black power advocates led to the formation of campaigns to free political prisoners such as Huey Newton, Leonard Peltier, myself, and Ericka Huggins. The more generalized opposition to the prison structure began to form as a result of growing awareness of the political character of imprisonment.

In September 1971, a rebellion of prisoners at Attica Correctional Facility was put down militarily by the New York National Guard, under the command of then-Governor Nelson Rockefeller. Forty-three people, including 11 guards, were killed during the retaking of the prison yard. An inquiry into the events revealed that none of the prisoners were directly responsible for any of the deaths. The prisoners had seized control of the institution by taking civilian hostages, and had presented a list of demands that included, alongside demands for improved prison conditions, the rights to reading materials and religious freedom. The demands were prefaced with an appeal to "conscientious citizens" to help abolish prisons as institutions that "would enslave and exploit the people of America."

The Attica rebellion was the most publicized—and most brutally suppressed—of a great number of similar episodes during that period in prisons throughout the United States and in Europe. In connection with a series of uprisings in French prisons during the early 1970s, Michel Foucault helped to establish a center for information on prisons and in the process was inspired to write *Discipline and Punish: The Birth of the Prison.* A member of the Norwegian pressure group KROM during the late 1960s, Thomas Mathiesen later emerged as a prominent theorist of prison abolitionism. In the United States, some prisoners developed their own theories of imprisonment. George Jackson, for example, linked his analysis of criminality to a transformative strategy whereby the political education of prisoners would seek to abolish criminal mentalities and encourage radical consciousness and resistance. Assata Shakur's autobiography includes important insights on the gendered nature of imprisonment. Puerto Rican political prisoners such as Alexandrina Torres, Ida Luz Rodriguez, and Dylcia Pagan have addressed race, nation, gender, and imprisonment. Mumia Abu-Jamal, a Black journalist who in 1997 had spent 15 years on Pennsylvania's death row, has emerged as a prominent opponent of the death penalty. The extensive international campaign organized around his case has helped to publicize widely his critiques of capital punishment.

A. International Prison Activism

Worldwide campaigns to support political prisoners often have been linked to transnational movements for penal reform. The most prominent transnational prisoner-oriented organization, Amnesty International, seeks the release of prisoners of conscience, defined as individuals who have not used or advocated violence and are detained on the basis of their beliefs, race, ethnic origin, language, and/or religion. Historically criticized for failing to take up cases such as Nelson Mandela's, it now calls for fair and prompt trials for all political prisoners. Moreover, Amnesty International opposes the death penalty, torture, and other forms of cruel and degrading treatment of all prisoners. The organizing principles driving AI's work are taken from the United Nations Universal Declaration of Human Rights.

Other transnational organizations have organized around more specific UN policies. The nongovernmental organization Penal Reform International, for example, has developed a campaign based on the UN's Standard Minimum Rules for the Treatment of Prisoners (SMR). Approved in 1957 by the Economic and Social Council, the SMR encompass a broad range of principles governing conditions of imprisonment and treatment of prisoners, based on the notion that while prisoners are deprived of their liberty, they should not be divested of their human rights. The most fundamental principle of the SMR is that individuals convicted of crimes are sent to prison *as* punishment, not *for* punishment. It is the loss of liberty—not the treatment meted out by the institution—that is meant to constitute the penalty. According to the SMR, when a court sentences an offender to imprisonment, the punishment it imposes is inherently afflictive; prison conditions should not intentionally aggravate this inherent affliction. Thus, prisons should not constitute a danger to life, health, or personal integrity.

Specifically, the SMR require that prison activities focus as much as possible on assisting prisoners to rejoin society after the prison sentence has been served. For this reason, the SMR state that prison rules and regimes should not limit prisoners' freedoms, external social contacts, and possibilities for personal development more than is absolutely necessary. They recommend that prison regimes attempt to reduce as much as possible those differences between the prison world and the free world that render prisoners dependent or violate their dignity as human beings. In general, good prison practice should not accentuate prisoners' isolation from the community, but rather should facilitate their continuing connections with it. Although some countries, such as the Netherlands, use these principles as the basis for developing their own penal practices, many others—the United States among them—are in perpetual violation of the Standard Minimum Rules.

B. Prison Abolitionism

An international conference of activists and academics who associate themselves with campaigns to abolish prisons met eight times between 1982 and 1997. Originally designated as the International Conference on Prison Abolition, its advocacy has extended to penal abolition since 1987—when it became the International Conference on Penal Abolition. ICOPA thus not only opposes prisons, but proposes that all punitive and retributive practices be replaced with criminal justice systems that promote peacemaking, reconciliation, and healing for victims, offenders, and communities. In related contexts, Ghandian strategies and indigenous models of addressing crime associated with peaceful societies have been examined for the lessons they may reveal for such efforts. ICOPA Conferences have been held in Canada, the Netherlands, Poland, Costa Rica, the United States, and New Zealand. Leading theorists include criminologists Herman Bianchi, Harold Pepinsky, Nils Christie, Louk Hulsman, Thomas Mathiesen, and Willem de Haan. While ICOPA emphasizes theories and practices of complete penal abolition, it also encourages theoretical and activist interventions around specific issues relating to penal systems. In the resolutions of its eighth conference, held in Auckland, New Zealand, in 1997, it opposed the privatization of incarceration and detention and demanded an end to killings in and by prisons.

C. Death Penalty Abolitionism

While prison abolitionism is still a minor discourse and movement, death penalty abolitionism has been widely embraced since the organized campaign against capital punishment took shape during the 19th century. Historical opponents of the death penalty have included Cesare Beccaria, considered the founder of the abolitionist movement, Jeremy Bentham, and Victor Hugo. In 1965 only 12 countries had abolished the death penalty, but by 1997, 57 countries had abolished the death penalty entirely and 15 had eliminated it for all but exceptional crimes, for example, crimes committed during wartime. In 20 countries that retained capital punishment there had been no executions for 10 or more years. However, during 1996, according to documentation by Amnesty International, there were at least

5300 prisoners executed in 39 countries. China's 4173 executions accounted for the vast majority, followed by 167 in the Ukraine and 140 in Russia. The United States carried out 45 executions during this same time period. Although South Africa—which, prior to the fall of apartheid, claimed one of the highest rates of execution in the world—abolished capital punishment in 1995, the United States regularly sentences a significant proportion of capital defendants to death. In 1997, there were more than 3000 prisoners on death row, approximately 40% of whom were Black.

Racist patterns in the application of capital punishment have long been central to opposition to the death penalty in the United States. Opponents have pointed out that since 1930 54% of all executions involved people of color, and that 89% of individuals executed for rape when it was a capital offense were Black. In 1972, the U.S. Supreme Court decided in the case of *Furman v. Georgia* (408 U.S. 238)—which involved a Black man who committed a murder in the course of a burglary—that the practice of granting juries the discretion of determining which offenders were to be sentenced to death was "pregnant with discrimination." The impact of *Furman* was to require all prisoners to be removed from death rows. However, because most of the justices joining the majority decision hinged their argument on the due process principle of the 14th Amendment—only a minority among the majority argued that the death penalty was inherently cruel and unusual punishment—the states soon began to develop nondiscretionary and putatively nondiscriminatory principles for the application of the death penalty. Since 1972, new death penalty statutes had been enacted in 37 states.

Although during the late 20th century, death penalty advocacy consistently has been losing ground internationally—and the overwhelming majority of Western industrialized nations have abolished it—public opinion polls indicate that the majority of people in the United States still favor capital punishment, the reason most often evoked for its continued existence. Yet when the framing of questions in such polls is considered, their reliability becomes suspect. More nuanced questions in some surveys have indicated, for example, that a majority of responding death penalty supporters would favor life sentences for murderers if the money earned by prisoners during their incarceration went to victims' families.

Both internationally and within the United States, death penalty abolitionists are far more organized than its advocates. Organized support for capital punishment in the United States tends to develop around specific cases, with family members of murder victims at the center of pro-death penalty campaigns and aided by operations such as the Washington Legal Foundation. On the other hand, numerous organizations such as the American Civil Liberties Union, the NAACP Legal Defense and Education Fund, and the National Coalition to Abolish the Death Penalty, have established long records of abolitionist practice.

VI. CONCLUSION

Ironically, forms of punishment designed to minimize crime—and especially its violent manifestations—themselves promote and perpetuate violence. Capital punishment is only the most extreme example of state-sanctioned violence; many lesser punitive measures—solitary confinement, for instance—represent a form of political violence that rarely receives critical attention because it is obscured by the physical and ideological boundaries that separate the world of the prison from the free world. In the United States, the construction and expansion of state and federal super-maximum security prisons, whose purpose is to address disciplinary problems within the penal system, are structured around the imposition of continuous solitary confinement and sensory deprivation—including extremely limited visiting and telephone privileges—on prisoners deemed a danger to correctional order. The U.S. model of the "supermax" currently is being imported to other countries as well. Moreover, as the phenomenon of prison privatization escalates, more and more punishment—beyond that which is called for in sentencing—is being meted out to prisoners by private companies that have even less public accountability than their public counterparts. This is in direct violation of the guiding principle of the UN Standard Minimum Rules of the Treatment of Prisoners, that individuals are sentenced to prison *as* punishment, not *for* punishment.

Scholars and activists who work toward the eradication of governmental and corporate violence within penal settings have mounted productive campaigns around both prison reform and penal abolition. The limited successes of penal reform and abolitionist campaigns in many countries can be attributed to the degree to which the ideology of crime has eclipsed the social realities that direct vast numbers of people throughout the world into prisons and jails. Critiques of expanding imprisonment should not ignore the existence of individuals sentenced to prison and to death who have committed appalling crimes of violence, nor should they dismiss the importance of security. These problems cannot be solved, however, through the ideological equation of perpetrators of heinous violence with all who are criminalized by virtue of having committed relatively minor criminal acts, having been imprisoned, or belonging to communities that predominate in the prisons. Moreover, the construction of a class- and/or race-inflected "criminal" as the enemy and as a deserving target of often violent punishment—a phenomenon that can result in the false imprisonment of innocent people—diverts attention from social problems such as poverty, homelessness, deteriorating education and health care, and drug use, thereby siphoning off the collective energy needed to solve them.

Also See the Following Articles

CRIMINAL BEHAVIOR, THEORIES OF • CRIMINOLOGY, OVERVIEW • DEATH PENALTY, OVERVIEW • DRUG CONTROL POLICIES • GENDER STUDIES • MILITARY-INDUSTRIAL COMPLEX, ORGANIZATION AND HISTORY • MINORITIES AS PERPETRATORS AND VICTIMS OF CRIME • POLICING AND SOCIETY • PUNISHMENT OF CRIMINALS • WOMEN, VIOLENCE AGAINST

Bibliography

Belknap, J. (1996). *The invisible woman: Gender, crime and justice.* Belmont, CA: Wadsworth Publishing Co.

Cook, D., & Barbara Hudson, B. (Eds.). (1993). *Racism and criminology.* London: Sage Publications.

Churchill, W., & Vander Wall, J. J. (Eds.). (1992). *Cages of steel: The politics of imprisonment in the United States.* Washington, DC: Maisonneuve Press.

de Haan, W. (1990). *The politics of redress: Crime, punishment and penal abolition.* London: Unwin Hyman.

Dobash, R. P., Dobash, R. E., & Gutteridge, S. (1986). *The imprisonment of women.* Oxford: Basil Blackwell.

Donziger, S. (Ed.). (1996). *The real war on crime: The report of the National Criminal Justice Commission.* New York: HarperPerennial.

Foucault, M. (1979). *Discipline and punish: The birth of the prison.* New York: Vintage.

Friedman, L. M. (1993). *Crime and punishment in American history.* New York: Basic Books.

Gaubatz, K. (1995). *Crime in the public mind.* Ann Arbor: University of Michigan Press.

Hall, S., Critcher, C., Jefferson, T., Clarke, J., & Roberts, B. (1978). *Policing the crisis: Mugging, the state and law and order.* New York: Holmes and Meier Publishers, Inc.

Howe, A., (1994). *Punish and critique: Toward a feminist analysis of penality.* London: Routledge.

Irwin, J., & Austin, J. (1997). *It's about time: America's imprisonment binge,* (2nd ed.). Belmont, CA: Wadsworth Publishing Company.

Miller, J. G. (1996). *Search and destroy: African-American males and the criminal justice system.* Cambridge: Cambridge University Press.

Rosenblatt, E. (Ed). (1996). *Criminal injustice: Confronting the prison crisis.* Boston: South End Press.

Simmons, A. J., Cohen, M., Cohen, J., & Beitz, C. R. (Eds.). (1995). *Punishment: A philosophy and public affairs reader.* Princeton: Princeton University Press.

Walker, S., Cassia Spohn, C., & DeLone, M. (1996). *The color of justice: Race, ethnicity and crime in America.* Belmont, CA: Wadsworth Publishing Co.

Criminal Behavior, Theories of

Claire M. Renzetti
St. Joseph's University

GLOSSARY

Anomie A social condition caused by the lack of integration between a society's goals and the institutionalized means to achieve those goals.

Atavism A concept developed by Lombroso to refer to the evolutionary degeneracy of criminals.

Differential Association The process by which an individual receives situational definitions favorable and unfavorable to law violation.

Differential Opportunity The principle that illegitimate opportunities, like legitimate ones, are not equally accessible to all members of a society.

Ego The component of the personality that tries to strike a balance between the impulses of the id and the constraints of the superego.

Multiple Personality Disorder A mental illness that causes an individual's mind to fracture into a number of different selves.

Neurotransmitters Chemical compounds found between nerve cells in the brain that send signals from one neuron to another, influencing mood, emotion, learning, memory, and behavior.

Personality The set of behavioral and emotional characteristics that describe an individual and that individual's reactions to various situations or events.

Phrenology An early biological/physiological theory of criminal behavior that maintained that the development of specific areas of the brain affect personality and behavior.

Psychopathy A mental illness in which the afflicted may appear psychologically healthy, but are callous, selfish, irresponsible, impulsive, and unable to feel guilt or remorse.

Schizophrenia A mental illness that causes those afflicted to be unfocused, withdrawn, apathetic, and delusional.

Somatotyping The notion that one's physique or body build corresponds to a particular temperament that, in turn, affects behavior.

Subculture A social group that shares some of the values and norms of the dominant culture, but also develops its own unique values and norms.

Superego The component of the personality that internalizes society's values and norms; also referred to as the conscience.

IT HAS BEEN SAID that there are as many theories of crime as there are criminals. This is, of course, an overstatement, but social scientists certainly have not been at a loss in their attempts to explain criminal behavior. Nevertheless, all theories of criminal behavior can be classified as one of three types: biological/physiological theories, which look for the causes of criminal behavior in the biological or physical make up of individual offenders; psychological/psychiatric theories, which look for the causes of criminal behavior in the mental or emotional make up of individual offenders; and sociological theories, which look for the causes of criminal behavior in factors external to individual offenders, including the environments in which they live, their relationships with others, and others' reactions to their behavior, as well as their sex, social class, and racial/ethnic identification.

I. BIOLOGICAL/PHYSIOLOGICAL THEORIES OF CRIME

Biological/physiological theories of criminal behavior date to the ancient Greeks and Romans, who believed that a person's character could be determined through a physical examination. Physiognomists, as the practitioners of this approach were called, maintained that certain physical traits were the identifying marks of criminals. Beardless men and bearded women, for example, were untrustworthy, and people with the unusual combination of dark and pallid skin were thought to be naturally violent.

Physiognomy obviously had no basis in scientific fact and finally fell into disfavor by the middle of the 18th century. Historians of criminology generally date the emergence of the scientific analysis of criminal behavior as the early 19th century with the development of the perspective known as phrenology. Phrenologists theorized that the brain is divided into 26 different areas or "faculties," organized into three major regions: intellectual, moral, and base or animal faculties. These regions could be studied through surgery and dissection, but also through physical examination and measurement of the skull, since phrenologists believed that the skull conformed precisely to the size and shape of the brain. If certain faculties of the brain were overdeveloped, they would be seen in bumps on a person's head in the area where these faculties were located. It was the base or animal faculties that phrenologists maintained were overdeveloped in criminals. The faculty of destructiveness, for example, was thought to be located slightly over the ear and was associated with violent criminal behavior, including homicide. But phrenologists also believed that criminal behavior could be inhibited through educational programs and a wholesome social environment that promoted the development of the higher intellectual and moral faculties and simultaneously suppressed the lower animal faculties.

Phrenologists were displaced in the scientific community by Cesare Lombroso (1835–1909) and his followers, who, in the second half of the 19th century, popularized the theory known as atavism. More specifically, Lombroso theorized that the criminal was a biological degenerate or "throwback" to an earlier stage of evolutionary development, more ape-like than human. He called this degeneracy atavism and maintained that atavism manifested itself in certain physical traits or stigmata, which included very large or, conversely, very small ears; premature and abundant skin wrinkles; insensitivity to pain; excessive tattooing; and, in women, muscular strength and hypersexuality. In response to charges that the theory of atavism failed to take into account social and economic causes of crime, Lombroso and his followers developed a typology of criminal behavior that included not only atavists, but also the insane, epileptics, those who committed crimes of passion or self-defense, those influenced by opportunity or circumstance, and those who lacked a good education or parental training. Nevertheless, these theorists remained committed to the idea that criminal behavior is primarily caused by inborn, biological factors.

Twentieth-century biological/physiological theories of criminal behavior can be classified according to their specific focus: body build, genetics and chromosomal abnormalities, nervous system disorders, and hormonal and chemical imbalances.

A. Body Build

Not unlike the notion that criminals are marked by certain physical or anatomical characteristics is the idea that criminals have a specific physique or body build. Perhaps the best-known proponent of this perspective was William Sheldon, whose theory was known as somatotyping. Sheldon maintained that an individual's body build is related to his/her personality which, in turn, affects behavior. He contended that the human body is made up of three components: endomorphy (softness, roundness), mesomorphy (muscularity, skeletal massiveness), and ectomorphy (linearity, frailty). He developed a seven-point scale on which an individual could be rated with respect to each of these components for each of five areas of the body to get an average overall score showing a predominance of one of the components and, thus, yielding the individual's body type. Each body type corresponded to a personality type: endomorphs were viscerotonic (relaxed, sociable, affectionate); mesomorphs were somatonic (assertive, aggressive, domineering); ectomorphs were cerebrotonic (introverted, nervous, inhibited). According to Sheldon, mesomorphs were predisposed to criminal behavior. Moreover, since body build was considered hereditary, so was criminality, and Sheldon supported eugenics programs to prevent mesomorphs from reproducing.

Although somatotyping met with little enthusiasm in the scientific community, as recently as 1972 at least one researcher, Juan B. Cortes, used Sheldon's rating method to classify 100 young male offenders and 100 male high school seniors with no official record of delinquency. Cortes found somatonic mesomorphs disproportionately represented in the offender group. However, reviewers of Cortes's research caution that it does not establish a direct link between criminality and body build or temperament.

B. Genetics and Chromosomal Abnormalities

1. Genetics

Early attempts to demonstrate a genetic cause for criminal behavior examined the criminal histories of members of individual families, but none of these studies successfully isolated genetic factors from environmental factors. More recent attempts focus on the behavior of twins and adoptees.

In studying twins, researchers typically compare the similarity in behavior of monozygotic (identical) twins with the behavior of dizygotic (fraternal) twins. They measure the probability that if one twin has a criminal record, the other twin does too. The rationale underlying this approach is that it allows for some control over environmental factors, since twins experience the same environment contemporaneously, both before birth and afterwards. However, because identical twins are more alike genetically than fraternal twins are, it is assumed that similarities or differences in their behavior are, therefore, attributable to genetics.

Twin studies conducted in the United States and Denmark show remarkable similarity in the tendency toward criminal behavior among identical twins as opposed to fraternal twins. With respect to violent crime, in particular, researchers report that identical twins are significantly more likely than fraternal twins to both be offenders. Still, some scientists question the sampling techniques of these studies and the validity of the methods used to determine zygosity of the twins. Moreover, some reject the assumption of environmental equality for identical and fraternal twins, since research shows that identical twins are treated more alike by others and spend more time together than do fraternal twins. Thus, greater similarity in their behavior could be the result of these environmental influences, not genetics.

Adoption studies look at the behavior of individuals separated from their biological parents at an early age and raised by parents genetically unrelated to them. The logic of this method is that if crime is genetically caused, adoptees will behave less like their adoptive parents and more like biological parents, even though the latter did not raise them. Studies conducted in the United States and elsewhere do indicate that adoptees who have at least one biological parent with a criminal record are more likely to have criminal records themselves than adoptees whose biological parents do not have criminal records. However, these findings do not establish a causal connection between genetics and crime for several reasons. For instance, the research typically relies on the arrest or incarceration records of biological mothers, and these women have often been arrested or convicted of minor offenses, such as prostitution and lewdness, as well as behavior that arguably is not criminal, such as adultery. In addition, the most convincing case for a genetic cause of crime would be made by those adoptees separated from their mothers at birth, but in the majority of these studies, as many as half the adoptees spent several months to more than a year with their biological mothers and many also lived in institutions before being adopted. Consequently, the trauma of parental-child separation and/or institutional living could have seriously influenced their later behavior.

2. Chromosomal Abnormalities

There are many different chromosomal abnormalities, but the one most frequently associated with criminal behavior, especially violence, has been XYY syndrome. Those with XYY syndrome are men who have an extra Y chromosome accompanying the chromosome pair that determines sex (XY in men, XX in women). XYY syndrome captured the attention of scientists and the public when it was reported that two mass murderers—Daniel Hugon in France and Richard Speck in the U.S.—had an extra Y chromosome, although it was later discovered that Speck was chromosomally normal. It was originally thought that the extra Y chromosome produced abnormally high levels of the hormone testosterone, which has been associated with aggression. However, later research found that XYY males were less rather than more aggressive than XY males. Studies have shown that XYY men are disproportionately represented among institutional populations, but this may reflect biases against them in arrest, conviction, and sentencing because they look "dangerous" and capable of violence.

C. Nervous System Disorders

1. Central Nervous System Disorders

The central nervous system (CNS) is responsible for processing complex sensory information and controlling voluntary muscle movements. CNS functioning is typically examined using electroencephalography (EEGs), which measures what in the vernacular are called brain waves. Studies show a significantly higher rate of abnormal EEGs among incarcerated criminals versus the general population: Incarcerated offenders usually have abnormally slow brain wave activity. Some researchers hypothesize that slow EEGs indicate immature brains, but there is no empirical evidence to support this position. Others have found that slow EEGs are produced by high concentrations of toxins (e.g., lead, cadmium) in the body; such toxins have been associated with violence and other behavioral problems as well. One difficulty with CNS research, however, is that it relies heavily on samples of incarcerated offenders, who are not necessarily representative of all offenders.

2. Autonomic Nervous System Disorders

The autonomic nervous system (ANS) mediates physiological activity associated with emotions. ANS activity is often measured through galvanic skin conductance. Studies of serious criminal offenders, including violent offenders, typically show them as lacking in feelings of guilt or remorse. Furthermore, skin conductance studies with samples of these offenders show fairly consistently that they have low galvanic skin conductance indicative of weak ANS activity. But the precise relationship between ANS disorders and criminal behavior is still unclear; in other words, researchers are uncertain how weak ANS activity may contribute to criminal behavior.

D. Hormonal and Chemical Imbalances

1. Hormones

As noted previously, aggression has been associated with the secretion of the hormone, testosterone, also known as the male sex hormone. Studies of samples of incarcerated violent offenders show them to have higher testosterone levels than nonviolent offenders and/or nonoffenders, although in most cases testosterone levels were still within the normal range. Attempts to treat violent offenders with drugs that lower testosterone have had mixed results: The drugs appear to be successful in inhibiting violent sexual offending, but not in inhibiting nonsexual violent offending. Moreover, research indicates that testosterone levels change in response to environmental stimuli and may actually be elevated by aggression.

In women, flucutations in the female sex hormones, estrogen and progesterone, have been associated with violent behavior. Particularly severe cases of the conditions known as premenstrual syndrome and postpartum depression syndrome, both of which are thought to be caused by hormonal fluctuations, have been found by some researchers to prompt violent outbursts in women. Both syndromes have been considered mitigating factors in trials of women charged with violent crimes. However, like testosterone, the precise ways in which hormonal flucatuations in women contribute to violent behavior is as yet unclear and, with respect to premenstrual syndrome in particular, studies purporting to measure personality and behavioral changes associated with the menstrual cycle have produced methodologically flawed and inconsistent findings.

2. Neurotransmitters

Brain cells called neurons communicate with one another by way of chemical messangers called neurotransmitters. Neurotransmitters are chemical compounds found between nerve cells that send signals from one neuron to another, thereby affecting mood, emotion, learning, memory, and behavior. The body produces many different neurotransmitters, but three in particular—serotonin, dopamine, and norepinephrine—have a hypothesized relationship to criminal behavior because they are thought to be regulators of aggression, impulsivity, risk-taking, irritability, and excitability. Studies of various types of offenders, including impulsive arsonists and habitually violent offenders, indicate that they tend to produce low levels of these neurotransmitters, leading researchers to theorize that the compulsive behavior of these individuals is a means to stimulate the brain to produce more of the deficient chemicals. Still, research with human subjects is sparse and considerably more is needed to tease out the effects of these and other neurotransmitters on human behavior.

3. Diet

The production and efficient use of neurotransmitters by the body is largely dependent on diet. Serotonin, for example, is produced from trytophan, an amino acid found in high protein foods. Consequently, some theorists suggest that various behavior problems, including some violent crimes, may be caused by low serotonin production that can be corrected with a high-protein diet.

Another hypothesized relationship between diet and criminal behavior focuses on refined carbohydrates, dominant in sweets and most "junk" foods, such as cake, candy, soft drinks, and potato chips. The ingestion of large quantities of refined carbohydrates causes an excessive level of glucose to enter the bloodstream, triggering a rapid release of insulin, which, in turn, causes a sharp drop in blood sugar. When blood sugar falls to subnormal levels, the brain begins releasing hormones, including adrenalin, increases in which are associated with irritability, anxiety, and destructive outbursts. While provocative, however, scientific research has not demonstrated a clear relationship between blood sugar levels and crime.

Other suggested ways that diet may affect criminality have to do with food allergies or sensitivities, toxicity of specific minerals in food, reactions to dyes and food additives, and vitamin deficiencies. However, the research testing these relationships has been extensively criticized for methodological problems, such as the use of very small, nonrandom samples, and the findings from the research have been inconsistent and sometimes contradictory.

II. PSYCHOLOGICAL/PSYCHIATRIC THEORIES OF CRIME

Explanations of criminal behavior as a product of mental illness or abnormality can be found in the writings of the ancient Greeks and continue to be popular today. Rather than searching for the causes of crime in physical abnormalities, these theories see crime as a product of a mental or emotional deficiency or disorder.

A. Personality Disorders

Personality may be defined as the set of behavioral and emotional characteristics that describe an individual and that individual's reactions to various situations or events. Among the best known psychological/psychiatric theories that postulate a relationship between personality disorder and crime is psychoanalytic theory. In addition, many researchers have attempted to develop theories by isolating personality differences between offenders and nonoffenders.

1. Psychoanalytic Theory

Originating in the work of Austrian physician, Sigmund Freud (1856–1939), psychoanalytic theory sees criminal behavior as typically caused by a malfunctioning superego or ego.

The superego may be described as one's conscience. It is the internalization of society's values and norms transmitted through the process of socialization. It is the superego that produces feelings of guilt when a norm is violated. Criminal behavior, therefore, may be symptomatic of an underdeveloped superego. That is, offenders are individuals who, because of parental neglect, did not adequately internalize society's values and norms. However, criminal behavior may also be symptomatic of an overdeveloped superego that produces constant and intense feelings of guilt. An individual with an overdeveloped superego engages in crime because of his/her intense need to be punished to allay the guilt. Consequently, this type of offender usually (and unconsciously) leaves a trail of clues that ensure apprehension.

The ego is the part of the personality that tries to strike a balance between the superego and another element of the personality, the id, which is composed of powerful, unconscious drives and instincts. Either excessively strict or overly indulgent parents may inhibit the maturation of the ego, making it unable to regulate id impulses, with crime as a potential consequence. The ego also uses various defense mechanisms in regulating the id. Psychoanalytic theory postulates that sometimes criminal behavior is a defense mechanism against very threatening id impulses that produce extreme anxiety. For example, the defense mechanism known as displacement may take the form of criminal behavior. In displacement, the anxiety produced by a particular impulse is neutralized when a substitute target or act replaces an especially threatening target or act (e.g., a man rapes and murders a woman who rejected his sexual advances to unconsciously punish his seductive, but rejecting mother).

It is left to the psychoanalyst to determine which personality disorder is responsible for producing criminal behavior in a specific individual, and herein lies the chief weakness of psychoanalytic theory: Its validity is empirically unverifiable. We must rely on the psychoanalyst's interpretations of an offender's words, recollections, and behavior—a highly subjective process at best and one fraught with disagreements among psychoanalysts.

2. Personality Traits of Offenders vs. Nonoffenders

Numerous attempts have been made to identify particular personality traits that distinguish criminals from noncriminals. Usually this is done by administering one of various personality inventories, such as the Minnesota Multiphasic Personality Inventory (MMPI) and the California Psychological Inventory (CPI). These inventories are composed of scales designed to identify clusters of specific personality traits, such as social introversion, self-control, and dominance. In the vast majority of recent studies assessing the personalities of criminals and noncriminals, strong differences emerged.

In studies using the MMPI, for example, criminals differ from noncriminals in that they tend to have deficient attachment to others and to social norms, they exhibit more bizarre thinking and are more alienated, and they engage in more unproductive hyperactivity. However, MMPI scales have been criticized for their low reliability across samples. In studies using the 18 scales that make up the CPI, only 3 distinguish criminals and noncriminals: the former tend to score lower than the latter on the socialization, responsibility, and self-control scales. But the CPI, too, has been criticized, primarily because the items that make up the individual scales are redundant and interdependent.

Additional research has shown criminals to be more impulsive than noncriminals and less able to delay gratification. It has also been argued that criminals are more extroverted than noncriminals. Other studies, however, fail to support these observations, showing no differences in ability to delay gratification and greater introversion on the part of criminals.

B. Mental Illness

There is a widespread belief that individuals with diagnosable mental illnesses (e.g., psychopathy, schizophrenia, multiple personality disorder) are at high risk of committing crimes, especially violent offenses, and that their dangerousness stems from the fact that their behavior is unpredictable and their selection of victims often random. Research only partially supports this belief: Most people who exhibit symptoms of mental illness are not more likely to be involved in serious offending, but there are serious mental illnesses associated with criminal behavior.

One psychiatric diagnosis frequently applied to violent offenders, especially if their crimes were bizarre or heinous, is psychopathy. Psychopaths may give the impression of mental health, but they are selfish, callous, irresponsible, impulsive, emotionally cold and detached, and incapable of feeling guilt or remorse. Nevertheless, while criminality may accompany psychopathy, one does not necessarily follow from the other; most offenders are not psychopathic.

Schizophrenia, considered to be one of the most debilitating mental illnesses, is a form of psychosis. There are several types of schizophrenia, but in general, schizophrenics are unfocused, withdrawn, and apathetic. However, schizophrenics typically suffer hallucinations and delusions, which, some believe, may lead them to commit crimes. Schizophrenics have been convicted of a range of crimes, from minor to serious, but very few are ever arrested for committing violent offenses.

Multiple personality disorder (which is frequently confused with schizophrenia) is a very rare mental illness. The mind of a person with multiple personality disorder fractures into a number of different selves, each of which may be a different age and some even the opposite sex. Some of those with multiple personality disorder have committed serious violent offenses, but the rarity of the condition means that it can explain only a tiny fraction of all crime, including violent crime.

III. SOCIOLOGICAL THEORIES OF CRIME

There are numerous sociological theories of criminal behavior, but every one identifies the causes of crime as factors external to individual offenders, and it is this focus that distinguishes sociological theories from biological/physiological and psychological/psychiatric theories. Among the major sociological theories of criminal behavior are: strain theory, subcultural theories, differential association theory, control theory, labeling theory, conflict or structural theories, and feminist theories.

A. Strain Theory

One of the best known strain theorists is Robert Merton, who began with the observation that every society has a set of culturally defined goals that embody what the members of the society value and strive to achieve. At the same time, every society has a social structure composed of institutions that provide the means for achieving these goals. Under ideal conditions, these two societal elements are integrated: Everyone knows and accepts the goals and also has available the means to achieve them. This does not mean that everyone will be successful in achieving the goals, but rather that the competition is fair and satisfying. But, Merton observed, in most contemporary societies these two elements are not well-integrated. In the United States, for example, where the most important goal is material success, the institutionalized means to achieve this success are not equally available to all. Members of some groups, in fact, find their access to the institutionalized means systematically blocked because of their race/ethnicity or social class.

Merton called the imbalance between a society's goals and the institutionalized means to achieve them anomie, a condition that produces strain in those who experience it. Those who experience anomie develop various coping mechanisms or adaptations to neutralize the strain. The most common adaptation is simply conformity: Conformists accept the goals and try to achieve them through legitimate means, no matter how difficult that may be. Ritualism is another adaptation that involves accepting the institutionalized means to achieve society's goals, but ritualists scale down the goals, satisfying themselves with very modest achievements. Other adaptations, however, are associated with criminal behavior. Innovation involves accepting societal goals, but upon finding institutionalized means blocked, innovators use illegitimate means to achieve the goals. Retreatism, a less common adaptation, is utilized by those who have accepted both the goals and the means to achieve them but, frustrated by their failure to succeed, simply drop out of the game. And a fifth adaptation, rebellion, involves a rejection of both the goals and the means, but an effort to replace them with different goals and means.

Merton's strain theory is considered one of the most influential sociological theories of criminal behavior, although it is not without critics. Some question whether conformity is actually the most common adaptation to anomie, since self-report studies indicate that very few people—even those who are financially successful and so should experience minimal strain—are total conformists. Other critics question the notion of a single, uniform set of societal goals, arguing that most societies today are culturally diverse.

B. Subcultural Theories

A subculture is a group within the dominant culture of a society that shares some aspects of the dominant culture, but also develops unique cultural traits of its own. Subcultural theorists maintain that groups who have difficulty achieving success within the dominant culture develop independent value structures that reflect their everyday experiences and provide them with better opportunities to succeed. Three subcultural theories that have enjoyed considerable popularity are Cohen's theory of status frustration, Miller's theory of the lower-class subculture, and Cloward and Ohlin's differential opportunity theory.

1. Cohen's Theory of Status Frustration

Sociologist Albert Cohen developed a theory to explain the criminal behavior of male street gangs in poor and working-class neighborhoods. According to Cohen, the dominant culture of U.S. and similar Western societies is middle class and consists of such values as delayed gratification, self-control, academic and occupational success, and good manners. Middle-class parents socialize their children to accept these values, but because lower-class parents are more relaxed in their socialization practices, their children do not develop as much self-restraint and, therefore, have difficulty succeeding in school. Their families' limited financial resources further contribute to a sense of failure. In short, they experience status frustration, and to cope they form gangs that develop their own values against which they can be judged successful by their peers. The central values of the delinquent gang subculture that Cohen identified included: nonutilitarianism (crimes are committed not as a means to an end, but for the intrinsic satisfaction derived from criminal behavior); maliciousness (the purpose of much gang activity is to create problems for people, to make them unhappy or uncomfortable); negativism (the goal of gang members is not just to develop values that are different from the dominant culture, but that are the opposite of the dominant culture); short-run hedonism (immediate gratification); and group autonomy (defying authority and resisting attempts by others to control their behavior).

2. Miller's Theory of the Lower-Class Subculture

Walter B. Miller also studied male street gangs, but unlike Cohen, Miller argued that it is not just lower-class boys who develop distinct values, but all members of the lower class. According to Miller, there are six core values or, as he called them, focal concerns that comprise the lower-class subculture: trouble (getting into and staying out of trouble are preoccupations of lower-class people); toughness (physical prowess and bravery in the face of physical theat); smartness (the ability to avoid being duped, outwitted, or conned as well as the ability to dupe, outwit, or con others); excitement (the search for thrills and risk taking); fate (the idea that one's life is controlled by "luck," or forces beyond one's control); and autonomy (resistance to others' attempts to control one's life).

3. Cloward and Ohlin's Differential Opportunity Theory

Richard Cloward and Lloyd Ohlin agreed with Merton that while U.S. culture values material success, the legitimate means to achieve success are not equally available to everyone. They also agreed that those deprived of legitimate opportunities, especially the poor, may use illegitimate means to achieve success. But they observed that even among those for whom legitimate opportunities are blocked, most do not commit crimes, and they sought to explain this. Their theory posited that it is not enough to simply be motivated to commit a crime, one must also know how to commit particular types of crimes and have the chance to commit the crime. In other words, not everyone who finds legitimate opportunities to success blocked has access to illigitimate opportunities. Moreover, Cloward and Ohlin argued that different social environments encourage the emergence of different subcultures. In unstable neighborhoods with rapidly changing populations, a conflict subculture is likely to develop as men and boys use violence to build a reputation and claim "turf." In more stable neighborhoods, where people know one another and role models are plentiful, a criminal subculture may develop because young men can rely on the contacts and experience of older men to teach them criminal techniques.

Cloward and Ohlin's theory, as well as the other subcultural theories, were developed during the 1950s and early 1960s to explain a specific type of crime—street crime, especially by youth gangs—which official statistics showed was predominant in poor and working-class communities with high concentrations of racial and ethnic minorities. However, subcultural theories have been criticized for portraying crime as a problem only of these groups, while overlooking crimes committed by wealthy, powerful members of society. Critics argue that criminal subcultures exist among all social groups, although the types of crime in which they engage reflects their life circumstances and available opportunities. The wealthy may not engage in street crime, but they may engage in white-collar crimes including tax evasion, insider stock trading, false advertising, and price fixing.

C. Differential Association Theory

One theory that can account for crime among all social groups was developed in the 1940s by sociologist Edwin H. Sutherland. Sutherland's theory, differential association theory, maintains that criminal behavior is learned, and it is learned the same way any other behavior is learned: through interpersonal communication and social interaction in small, intimate groups. What is learned through this socialization process is not only the techniques for committing specific types of crimes, but also the attitudes and motivations that justify and encourage criminal offending. However, simple exposure to criminal techniques, attitudes, and motives is not enough to cause an individual to commit crime. Rather, crime results when an individual receives an excess of situational definitions favorable to law violation over definitions unfavorable to law violation. The process of social interaction by which these definitions are acquired Sutherland called differential association.

The term "differential association" underlines Sutherland's point that individuals receive both kinds of definitions, but not all interactions through which the definitions are received are equal; some carry greater weight and, therefore, have more influence on a person. According to Sutherland, associations vary in frequency, duration, priority, and intensity. Associations that occur often (frequency) and are long-lasting (duration) have a greater impact than those that are infrequent and brief. Associations that occur early in a person's life have a greater impact than those that occur later in life (priority), and associations with people one respects or admires have a greater impact than those with people for whom one has little regard (intensity).

Differential association theory is generally considered one of the most influential theories of criminal behavior of the 20th century. It accounts for various types of criminal activity by members of various social groups, even those who are financially successful. However, critics of differential association theory argue that it is essentially untestable, since there is no way to validly measure associations, much less determine frequency, duration, priority, and intensity, while controlling for other intervening variables.

D. Control Theory

In 1969, criminologist Travis Hirschi published a new theory of criminal behavior, control theory. Hirschi began with the assumption that everybody is equally motivated to commit crimes because fulfilling one's desires usually can be done most effectively, efficiently, and pleasurably in ways that are disapproved of or prohibited. Given this, Hirschi asks, why would anyone be law-abiding? His answer is that people's social ties or bonds to conventional institutions, such as family, school, or employer, inhibit them from acting on criminal motivations, even if they have the opportunity to do so.

Central to control theory, then, is the notion of the social bond, which has four interrelated elements: attachment (sensitivity to others' feelings, so that one avoids crime so as not to hurt or offend those one is emotionally attached to); commitment (the more people have invested in terms of time, money, energy, and emotions in pursuing a specific activity, such as getting an education or building a career, the more they have to lose by committing a crime); involvement (people who are active in conventional pursuits, such as studying, working, or playing a sport, do not have time to commit crimes); and belief (the extent to which a person believes that a rule should be obeyed).

Control theory has common sense appeal and also receives empirical support from some studies of juvenile delinquency. But other studies indicate that the relationship between the social bond and criminal behavior may be the opposite of that postulated by Hirschi: It is criminal behavior that affects the social bond rather than vice versa. So, for example, rather than attachment to school inhibiting criminality, criminality weakens attachment to school. Similarly, attachment to friends, especially if they engage in criminal behavior, may promote rather than inhibit criminality.

E. Rational Choice Theory

Rational choice theory takes as its starting point the principle that humans are rational beings who exercise free will in deciding on a course of action. It is based on the classic notion that people will try to achieve the greatest benefits for themselves at the least cost. For the rational choice theorist, even crimes that at first glance appear purely impulsive or pathological are influenced by rational elements, such as the limits of time and personal abilities or skills as well as the availability of relevant information and victims. Each offender has specific individual needs and skills which intersect with situational factors to affect the decision to commit a crime. To prevent crime, then, societies must make the costs outweigh the benefits; that is, the punishment for the crime must be severe enough to deter the potential criminal (an idea known as the deterrence principle).

Rational choice theory has enjoyed considerable popularity, especially among those who believe that the criminal justice system is too lenient with offenders. Critics, however, maintain that rational choice theorists overestimate the extent to which offenders calculate the relative costs and benefits of committing a particular crime. Moreover, critics point out that while committing a crime may be a rational decision under certain circumstances, it does not necessarily follow that severe punishment will deter such criminality. If, for example, an unemployed person decides that it makes more sense to sell drugs than work full-time at a fast-food restaurant for the minimum wage, then the solution is not to impose severe punishment for drug selling, but rather to increase employment opportunities with wages that raise workers above the poverty line. Indeed, most research on the deterrence principle indicates that the decision to commit a crime is not significantly affected by the perceived severity of punishment by the legal system, but rather by peer and parental sanctions.

F. Routine Activities Theory

Another theory that incorporates the principle that the commission of a crime is a rational choice is routine activities theory, originally formulated by Lawrence Cohen and Marcus Felson in 1979. Routine activities theory postulates that crime is the product of a convergence of three types of variables: motivated offenders, suitable targets (i.e., potential crime victims), and capable guardians (i.e., individuals, including the police, witnessess, and even potential crime victims, who can act to prevent or foil a crime against person or property). In short, the risk of crime increases when you have in the same place at the same time a person or persons motivated to commit a crime along with a person or persons who are viable targets, but an absence of "guardians." Cohen and Felson maintain that since World War II, people's routine activities (i.e., their daily work, school, or leisure activities) have increasingly taken them away from home and into the public sphere, thus increasing their chances of victimization.

Routine activities theory focuses primarily on victims rather than offenders, assuming simply that motivated offenders always exist. While such an assumption is likely true, it is nonetheless important to understand criminal motivation in order to explain criminal behavior. Routine activities theory also implies that the more a person stays at home, the lower that person's chances of becoming a crime victim. While this assumption has some common-sense appeal, it may be true only for males. Females are more likely to be victimized by people they know in their own homes than by strangers in public places. In most empirical tests, routine activities theory has received only weak support.

G. Labeling Theory

Labeling theory, also called social reaction theory, was developed to explain behavior considered deviant, which, of course, includes criminal behavior. Labeling theory represented a bold, new approach to explaining crime, and it is not surprising that it gained a following during the 1960s and 1970s, when questioning authority and the status quo was commonplace. Labeling theorists focus on how certain behaviors come to be defined as criminal and on the consequences of these definitions for people found to be engaged in such activities.

Whereas most theories hold an absolutist view of crime, defining it as behavior that violates the law, labeling theorists emphasize the relativity of crime and deviance. That is, labeling theorists maintain that no act is inherently criminal; it becomes criminal only when defined as such by observers. Whether or not a behavior gets defined as criminal depends on several factors, including the situational and historical contexts in which the behavior occurs, the characteristics of the individual engaged in the behavior, and the characteristics of the definers. In particular, labeling theorists point out that members of some groups—those who are socially and economically powerful—have an advantage in the labeling process: They are more likely to escape being defined or labeled as criminal, and they are better able to attach that label to others.

But labeling theorists are especially interested in the consequences of the labeling process. They maintain that being labeled criminal, especially if the labeling is formal, public, and official (e.g., a trial) produces a fundamental change in the labeled individual's identity. Labeling closes off legitimate opportunities and associations with noncriminals, and also destroys an individual's public image and character, thereby forcing him or her to embark on a criminal career. In other words, social reaction actually produces more crime.

Despite its popularity, empirical tests of labeling theory have failed to demonstrate that being labeled necessarily leads to a negative self-image. In some cases, in fact, the deviant or criminal label is valued, even sought after. Moreover, such labels are not indelible, and those labeled often join together to successfully reject the criminal or deviant label.

H. Conflict or Structural Theories

Conflict theorists, like labeling theorists, maintain that crime is relative. Nothing is inherently criminal; rather, it is criminal because it is defined criminal by some members of the society. However, conflict theorists, who have their theoretical roots in Marxist sociology, extend this position by focusing on how particular structural conditions generate crime. An underlying assumption of conflict theory is that an individual's position in the social hierarchy affects his/her life chances and opportunities. Thus, conflict theorists observe that crime occurs among all social groups, but its visibility and the forms it takes vary from group to group. For example, while the poor may steal by muggings and break-ins, the rich may steal by price fixing and insider stock trades. But while the type of crime reflects the opportunities and life chances of members of these groups, the crimes committed by the poor are more visible and receive greater attention than the crimes committed by the rich. Conflict theorists maintain, therefore, that crime is not only relative, it is a product of the inequalities inherent in a particular society.

Conflict theorists have devoted much of their research to the study of crime in capitalist societies, which is the primary source of criticism of this perspective. Critics maintain that conflict theorists largely overlook crime in socialist and other noncapitalist societies. In addition, critics argue that although conflict theory does a good job of explaining economic or property crimes, it is less successful in explaining violent crime.

I. Feminist Theory

There are several feminist theories of criminal behavior, but they share a number of ideas in common. First, feminist theories begin with the observation that women have been largely overlooked by theorists attempting to explain criminal behavior and have been excluded from many studies of crime. By excluding women, traditional theories have failed to consider how criminal behavior is gendered. Gender, for example, influences criminal opportunities as well as social reactions to criminal behavior. Thus, feminist theorists argue that an understanding of criminal behavior must place it squarely in the context of the gender stratification that characterizes a society.

However, feminist theorists recognize that gender stratification intersects with other forms of inequality—social class inequality, racism, heterosexism, ageism, and ableism—to produce differing outcomes for various groups of women and men. Consequently, feminist theorists maintain that understanding criminal behavior requires researchers to examine the simultaneous affects of these multiple oppressions.

Feminist theories of criminal behavior are relatively new, but within the short span of just 20 years, research on the gendered nature of crime and criminal processing has mushroomed. It is expected that feminist social scientists will be at the forefront of shaping theorizing on criminal behavior as we enter the 21st century.

Also See the Following Articles

AGGRESSION, PSYCHOLOGY OF • BEHAVIORAL PSYCHOLOGY • BIOCHEMICAL FACTORS • CRIMINOLOGY, OVERVIEW • GANGS • MENTAL ILLNESS • PSYCHOLOGY, GENERAL VIEW • PUNISHMENT OF CRIMINALS

Bibliography

Becker, H. S. (1973). *Outsiders*. New York: Free Press.

Borowski, A., & O'Connor, I. (1997). *Juvenile crime, justice, and corrections*. Melbourne: Longman.

Braithwaite, J. (1989). *Crime, shame, and reintegration*. Sydney: Cambridge University Press.

Chesney-Lind, M. (1997). *The female offender: Girls, women, and crime*. Thousand Oaks, CA: Sage.

Cloward, R. A., & Ohlin, L. E. (1960). *Delinquency and opportunity*. New York: Free Press.

Cohen, A. K. (1955). *Delinquent boys*. New York: Free Press.

Cohen, L. E., & Felson, M. (1979). Social change and crime rate trends: A routine activities approach. *American Sociological Review, 49,* 588.

Cortes, J. B. (1972). *Delinquency and crime*. New York: Seminar Press.

Curran, D. J., & Renzetti, C. M. (1994). *Theories of crime*. Boston: Allyn and Bacon.

Englander, E. K. (1997). *Understanding violence*. Mahwah, NJ: Lawrence Erlbaum.

Fitzgerald, M., McLennan, G., & Pawson, J. (Eds.) (1981). *Crime and society: Readings in history and theory*. London: Routledge and Kegan Paul.

Henry, S., & Einstadter, W. (Eds.) (1998). *The Criminology Theory Reader*. New York: New York University Press.

Hirschi, T. (1969). *Causes of delinquency*. Berkeley: University of California Press.

Lombroso, C. (1912). *Crime: Its causes and remedies*. Montclair, NJ: Patterson Smith.

Martin, R., Mutchnick, R. J., & Austin, W. T. (1990). *Criminological Thought*. New York: Macmillan.

Merton, R. K. (1975). *Social Theory and Social Structure*. New York: Free Press.

Miller, W. B. (1958). Lower class culture as a generating milieu of gang delinquency. *J. Social Issues, 14,* 12.

Noaks, L., Levi, M., & Maguire, M. (Eds.). (1995). *Issues in contemporary criminology*. Cardiff: University of Wales Press.

Reiman, J. (1990). *The rich get richer and the poor get prison*. New York: Macmillan.

Reiss, A. J. (1993 & 1994). *Understanding and preventing violence, V. 1–4*. New York: National Academy Press.

Sheldon, W. (1949). *Varieties of delinquent youth*. New York: Harper and Brothers.

Sutherland, E. H. (1947). *Principles of criminology*. Philadelphia: J. B. Lippencott.

Toch, H., & Adams, K. (1989). *The disturbed violent offender*. New Haven, CT: Yale University Press.

Criminology Overview

Esther Madriz
University of San Francisco

GLOSSARY

Classical Criminology The theory that maintains that people in society are free to choose criminal or conventional behaviors to meet their needs and that they are motivated by hedonism or the pursuit of pleasure.

Criminology The science that studies crime and criminal behavior.

Critical Criminology A designation for a series of criminological perspectives based on the beliefs that research agendas are influenced by one's values and beliefs and on the advancement of a more progressive agenda that takes the side of disprivileged individuals.

Moral Panics The strong and widespread belief that there are certain individuals or groups in society that are causing harm and fear to members of the general society.

Positivism The belief that the scientific method is best suited to understand social and natural phenomena, and that human behavior is the result of biological, psychological, and environmental influences.

Sociological Criminology The belief that the motivations to commit a crime do not result from individual flaws or from making wrong choices, but from socioeconomic and political forces that are beyond a person's control.

Social Disorganization A situation existing in a neighborhood or area characterized by conflict of values, lack of solidarity, and decaying social institutions.

THE QUESTION "What is criminology?" seems obvious—it is commonly defined as the science that studies crime and the mechanisms to reduce or control it. But this apparently straightforward definition hides the complexity of the subject matter. Gregg Barak, in his recent book *Integrating Criminologies* (1998), claims that there are three different positions on the nature of criminology. The first position is developed by sociological traditionalists, associated with the Chicago School who regard criminology as a subarea of sociology. These sociologically oriented criminologists follow Sutherland and Cressey's definition of criminology as "the body of knowledge regarding juvenile delinquency and crime. It includes within its scope the process of making laws, of breaking laws and of reacting to the breaking of laws."

The second position is held by multidisciplinary specialists who maintain that there are a variety of professions that contribute to the making of criminology as a discipline—biology, political science, law, anthropology, psychology, medicine, and others. Multidisciplinary specialists tend to emphasize the importance of their own field in the study of criminal behavior.

The third position is that of interdisciplinary generalists who believe that criminology must integrate the knowledge coming from other disciplines in an interdisciplinary theory of behavior that can be applied to the study of crime and criminal behavior.

Barak argues that criminology should use an integrative and interdisciplinary approach to the study of crime. The fragmentation that has characterized criminology until recently has resulted in competing medical, legal, psychological, sociological, and anthropological views of crime and criminals. However, some of the most stimulating insights in criminology are now emerging from interdisciplinary studies that are filling the fissures created by the proclivity to use simplistic and solitary theoretical models. Indeed, integrated studies not only will contribute to the understanding of crime and criminal behavior, but also to the development of more holistic policies to alleviate the crime problem.

I. IN SEARCH OF CRIMINOLOGY

The attention given by the media and the public at large to high profile criminal cases, such as O. J. Simpson, Lorena Bobitt, Mike Tyson, the Menendez Brothers, the Central Park Jogger, and Polly Klaas, reminds us of the significant role that crime plays in our lives. During the O. J. Simpson case, for example, most people in the United States and even around the globe were affixed to their TV sets eagerly awaiting to grasp the latest details on the case and the trial: Does the glove fit? Is Mark Fuhrman lying? Who is going to be the next witness for the defense? Who will testify for the prosecution? Is O. J. guilty or innocent? Indeed, most people became very familiar with the names of the many actors involved in the case: Marcia Clark, Nicole Brown, Ronald Goldman, Robert Shapiro, Judge Lance Ito, and Johnny Cochran, among others.

Survey research confirms that people in the United States are more preoccupied with crime than with many other important social issues, such as unemployment or the economy. People not only crave information about heinous crimes, but they also crave news about crime-related issues, such as actions carried out by law enforcement agencies. Furthermore, the high audience ratings that films and television programs dealing with cops, trials, and prisons receive gives further evidence of the public interest in crime and crime-related issues. This fascination with crime makes criminology one of the most popular courses in many colleges and universities around the country. What can be more interesting than a discipline that deals with questions such as, What motivates a person to commit crime? What is the relationship between class, race, and/or gender and crime? Why are most criminals men? What can we do to decrease crime?

In 1962, Leon Radzinowicz published his famous book, *In Search of Criminology*, in which he reported that, during the early 50s, there were 19 terms in use to describe the discipline. Among those terms were criminology, criminal policy, penology, criminal or forensic psychiatry, and criminal anthropology. Radzinowicz argued that although these terms represented different areas in an emerging discipline, they were confusing because many of them had various connotations for different social scientists. Today, the number of concepts used to describe criminology has decreased. However, the discipline has expanded rapidly as new theoretical perspectives are formulated and new avenues of research are opened.

In the early days, criminology was taught within sociology departments in universities and colleges around the United States. Now entire departments and even whole colleges are dedicated to the study of crime and criminal justice. This is the case, for example, with the John Jay School of Criminal Justice in New York City, which is part of the City University of New York. Its curriculum specializes in a variety of courses dedicated to education, research, and service in criminal justice. In addition, the college deals with connected disciplines such as fire science and related areas of public safety and public service.

II. THE HISTORY OF CRIMINOLOGY

Stephen Pfohl, in his book *Images of Deviance*, reminds us that early ideological views of criminal behavior were heavily influenced by religious or theological beliefs. Criminals were believed to be possessed by demonic forces out of their control. The witch trials in Salem, Massachusetts during the late 1700s were based on the premise that crime and deviance were the work of diabolic forces that entered and possessed a person's soul. Although discounted by many today as "superstition," the demonic view of crime still persists in popular culture and among conservative groups. This view is epitomized in the use of popular cultural expressions that compare, for example, serial killers or mass murderers to demons or "folk evils," to borrow Stanley Cohen's famous term. In the social sciences, scholars such as Erich Goode and Nachman Ben-Yehuda, in their book *Moral Panics: The Social Construction of Deviance*, explain how from the late Middle Ages to the Counter-Reformation in Western Europe, uncounted numbers of people were tortured and killed after being stigmatized as "witches." While numerous men and children were executed, estimates indicate that 85% of those executed for such crimes were women. By burning the body of the criminal, the soul would be freed from demonic possession, and the cosmic order that had been disrupted by such crimes, would be restored.

Moral panics, as the one produced during the Inquisition or during colonial times in Salem, are used for boundary maintenance to keep society in check. The burning and killing of witches suggest that one of the major concerns confronted by these changing societies was the delineation of gender roles. In patriarchal societies, women were challenging men's concentrated authority by attempting to gain access to rights such as the right to land ownership or the right to question male authority over matters of health and healing. As a result, they needed to be controlled. Witch hunts kept women under control and preserved male authority in societies that were facing drastic transformations.

The emergence of criminology as a "respected" academic discipline, however, occurred in Europe. During the 17th and 18th centuries, rationalistic philosophical explanations replaced demonic views of crime and punishment. The use of reason and logic to uncover laws that govern society became the favored way to study the material universe and the functioning of society. Rational explanations replaced demonic interpretations of crime among those scientists who studied physical as well as social phenomena.

The ideology of the Enlightenment, as expressed in the writings of French philosophers Rousseau, Montesquieu, and Voltaire, heavily influenced the development of classical criminology. Early criminologists, such as Cesare Beccaria and Jermy Bentham, claimed that crime could only be understood and eventually reduced by using reason and experience.

As a reaction to the cruel and inhuman practices of the time, Cesare Beccaria objected to the brutal and barbarous way in which the criminal law was enforced. He characterized the Italian criminal justice system of the time not only as ineffectual and unscrupulous, but as criminogenic or crime producing. According to Beccaria, barbarism in the administration of justice will result in barbarism in the population.

One of the major premises of classical criminology was that "punishment should fit the crime." Certainty of punishment was seen as more influential in decreasing crime than the severity of the penalty. This view led Beccaria to oppose the death penalty as inhuman and uncivilized. He considered it irrational and senseless that a public that despised homicide would favor state-sponsored homicide.

Classical criminology resulted in substantive penal and legal reforms in Europe and the United States. The invention by Bentham of the Inspection-House, more commonly known as the Panopticon, responded to the need to discipline unruly members of society. The Panopticon was designed to punish the outlaw, to guard the insane, to correct the malicious, to employ the idle, to cure the sick and to train the unemployable. However, the Panopticon must be understood in the broader context of the transition from a feudal to a capitalist society and the need to sustain and discipline the labor force. The Panopticon was thus an admonition to those who did not conform to strict factory discipline. It symbolized the fate that awaited those who did not comply to the heavy demands of an industrial society.

Classical doctrine has recovered its ascendance in our postmodern world. This "new classicism," as represented in choice and deterrence theory, is based on the principle that criminals carefully elect to commit a criminal act. Fear of criminal penalties, preferably confinement in a penal institution, is the only way to deter offenders from choosing a criminal life. According to the new classicists, intelligible and strong laws along with certain and severe penalties are the preferred ways to control crime. The dominance of new classicism in criminal justice practices in the United States has resulted in a heavy reliance on incarceration as the favored response to crime. It has also led to an increase in the severity of punishment.

In the field of juvenile delinquency, the new classicism is reflected in the conviction that the juvenile justice system is too lenient with young people who break the law. The argument is that adolescents know that they will receive less severe penalties for the crimes they commit. Hence the threat of punishment is not sufficient to deter younger offenders from engaging in heinous acts. One of the proposed solutions to the "lenience" of the system for juveniles is to treat them as adults.

III. FROM PUNISHMENT TO REHABILITATION

During the 19th century, positivism gained ascendancy not only in the scholarly work of those concerned with crime, but also among those concerned with other social and scientific issues. In general, positivism is a method of analysis that uses observation and measurement as a way to understand the social and material world. It can be applied to study a whole range of phenomena, from the fall of an apple to the causes of criminal behavior. Thus the term "positivist criminology" refers to the search for consistent and observable factors that help to explain why a person commits a criminal act.

The rise of positivist criminology in Europe, and more specifically in France, coincides with the creation of the French prison system. Surrounded by a scientific "aura," positivism soon gained intellectual recognition and financial support among scholars and citizens who believed that such scientific methods would result in human progress. The deplorable situation of the urban poor, as immortalized in the works of Victor Hugo in *Le Miserables* and Charles Dicken's *Oliver Twist*, had resulted in an array of social problems—from unemployment to crime. The growth in crime, especially, translated in increasing levels of fear among large sectors of the population. The failure of classical criminal justice institutions to discipline the behavior of the "dangerous classes" and to decrease the crime rate encouraged the advent of other possible solutions to the escalating crime problem. In this context, positivistic methods, such as statistical research, gained popularity as a way to understand a variety of urban problems.

In 1876, Cesare Lombroso (1835–1909), an army physician frequently categorized as "the father of criminology," introduced his concept of "born criminal." In his book *Criminal Man*, Lombroso developed the argument that the only scientific criminology that was possible was the one that considered the individual factors that motivated someone to a life of crime. Reporting on autopsies performed in 66 delinquent men, Lombroso found that these criminals had similar biological characteristics to those of "savages" or "pre-humans." Thus the idea that criminals could be recognized by their physical characteristics was born.

Many authors have criticized such sociobiological theories of crime, especially because of their racist undertones. Biological criminologists have been charged with using racial characteristics associated with people of color as indicators of a proclivity to commit crime. Indeed, Lombroso claimed that delinquents had characteristics similar to "Blacks" in the United States and to Mongolian races. In spite of the enormous critical literature, these theories still enjoy preeminence among certain criminologists and policymakers. Some still insist that the causes of crime can be found in the brain, the shape of the body, the nervous system, the extra Y chromosome, the hormonal system, or the genetic make-up of an individual. More recently, biochemical factors, such as chemical and mineral deficiencies, allergies, hypoglycemia, and even dangerous amounts of copper, lead, or mercury have been introduced as plausible explanations of criminal behavior.

Following this biological positivism, political scientist James Q. Wilson and psychologist Richard J. Hernstein, in their controversial book *Crime and Human Nature* argued that a combination of environmental circumstances and biological factors motivate people to engage in criminal behaviors. They suggested that some individuals may be born with physiological characteristics such as low intelligence, mesomorphic body type, and belligerent personality that predispose them to criminal behavior.

Some psychologists also have joined the chorus of such individualistic explanations of crime. They search back into the lives of criminals looking for childhood traumas, maternal deprivation, problems in the development of personality, conflicts between the id, ego, and superego, psychosis and neurosis, or even penis envy in the case of female offenders accused of committing "male crimes." Freudian psychoanalytic explanations dealing with repression, inferiority complex, and latent delinquency have also been added to the long list of psychosocial dynamics associated with violence.

Gabriel Tarde, a critic of Lombroso's positivistic approach, centered his inquiry on the processes by which we learn crime from others through a process of imitation. In his sociopsychological perspective, Tarde explained how the process of imitation operates in a social context, cutting across social, racial, and economic cleavages. Many contemporary learning theories are based on the same principle as Tarde's concept of imitation—crime originates in a learning process in which people model the behavior of others, specially significant others. The cycle of violence perspective, for example, follows this basic axiom of learning theory arguing that by witnessing crime and violence, those who live in violent homes have a much higher chance of becoming violent themselves. Individuals not only learn crime from observing significant others committing criminal offenses, but also from more distant sources such as movies, television, and other media influences.

IV. THE SOCIOLOGY OF CRIME

Until the early 19th century, positivistic approaches to the study of crime and violence focused on individual factors. These studies used persons, small groups, and even families as the unit of analysis. These micro explanations examined everyday face-to-face interactions, individual traits and behaviors, and small group dynamics. During the late 19th century, however, the first macro theories of criminal behavior emerged, which placed the emphasis on social organizations, institutions, and social structures. While micro theories attempted to understand why individuals engaged in offending behaviors, macro theories tried to explain why certain categories of crime were associated with particular types of societies.

Macro theories of crime developed during and after the Industrial Revolution, when rates of crime skyrocketed. Of crucial importance for the structural analysis of crime was the observation that rates of crime and violence were considerably higher in particular areas of cities rather than rural areas. These dramatic discoveries showed that demographic transformations, and not just individual attributes, led to the advent of distinctive crime patterns.

Beginning with Emile Durkheim's pioneering book, *The Division of Labor in Society*, late 19th century criminologists and scholars began to explore such factors as population density and degree of social solidarity as possible clues to the understanding of crime. Durkheimian explanations, for example, associated living in large urban centers—where anonymity is the rule—with a decrease in social solidarity and with increased levels of anomie—or erosion of the normative structure. Anomic situations provided a fertile ground for crime to flourish.

Durkheim's work paved the way for the emergence of disorganization theory in the United States. During the early 1900s, Clifford R. Shaw and Henry D. McKay—both associated with the Chicago School—called attention to the existence of zones in the cities where there were higher rates of juvenile delinquency and crime. Early Chicago researchers concluded that crime tended to be higher as one moves toward the business center of the city, especially in transitional inner city areas. Instead of focusing on criminal people, these ecological theories focused on criminal locations. Following Shaw and McKay's model, studies were carried out in different cities within the United States, including Philadelphia, Boston, Cincinnati, Cleveland, and Richmond. Crime prevention models, based on Shaw and McKay's conclusions, sprouted up all around the country. The Chicago Area Project, for example, received government funding to develop massive prevention programs that led to major changes in the crime policies of the state of Illinois. Using Durkheim's concepts, the project tried to create a sense of solidarity among inhabitants of inner city neighborhoods. The creation of community centers run by people living in the neighborhood were crucial in creating this sense of belonging and solidarity. The Chicago Area Project eventually became a national model for the prevention of crime and violence.

Robert Merton's famous paper, "Social Structure and Anomie" (1938), published in the leading sociological journal, *American Sociological Review*, introduced a theory that played a highly influential role in criminology from the 1950s to the 1970s. Merton strongly opposed the inclination of many social scientists "to attribute the malfunction of the social structure primarily to those of man's imperious biological drives which are not adequately restrained by social control." In his view, crime was explained not by personal traits, but by socio structural forces existing in the broader society. Using the United States—the most "criminogenic" country among the industrialized nations of the world—as a model, Merton developed his theory of anomie. Reconceptualizing Durkheim's ideas, he claimed that anomie was the result of the disassociation existing between culturally prescribed goals, such as financial success, and the institutionalized means of achieving those goals. "Americanizing" Durkheim's concept of anomie, Merton showed how those who lack the opportunities to reach societal goals through socially acceptable or legitimate means will restore to illegitimate or illegal avenues to achieve their objectives. Consequently, the high rates of crime existing in the United States are not exclusively the byproduct of poor social conditions in which large sectors of the population live. High crime rates are rather hastened by the strain produced in poor people as they struggle for wealth and status in a society where it is nearly impossible for large sectors of the population to achieve such economic and social success. People react to this structurally induced strain by assuming certain "role behaviors" or modes of individual adaptation—conformity, innovation, ritualism, retreatism, and rebellion. From these five modes of adaptation, Merton believed that innovation was of central concern to researchers of crime. Moreover, he claimed that this mode of adaptation was frequently used by working class individuals. By accepting the cultural goal of financial success, individuals who lack opportunities to reach this goal will tend to resort to criminal activities such as drug trafficking, burglary, larceny, and armed robbery. In his book *Social Theory and Social Structure* (1957), Merton further elaborated his analysis by detailing the manner in which "some social structures exert a definite pressure upon certain persons in the society to engage in nonconforming rather than conforming conduct."

During the 1960s, new research emerged in an attempt to explain the higher rates of crime present among lower class, African American youth. In their book *The Subculture of Violence*, criminologists Marvin E. Wolfgang and Franco Ferracuti merged several theoretical approaches. They argued that young lower class African Americans have a value system that deviates from that of the larger society, mainly due to the emphasis on crime as an acceptable behavior. Criminal behavior, according to the authors, becomes an important part of everyday life. These behaviors include carrying weapons as an adequate form of protection and survival, as well as the use of violence as an admissible response to verbal insults. In their view, this leads to the creation of a subculture that manifests higher rates of crime and violence by accepting it as "normal" and by creating distrust of other people and of various criminal justice agencies, especially the police.

Criticisms of the work of Wolfgang and Ferracuti abound. Many have questioned the presumption that there is something inherently violent in African American youth subculture. Others have seen this kind of analysis as contributing to the stereotyping of young African American males, ignoring the fact that violence among White young males can be perceived and treated differently by the agencies of criminal justice as well as the mass media.

Other studies have centered on the existence of teenage gangs that typically resort to crime and violence as an important aspect of their everyday activities. Some authors have focused on the relationship between crime and abuse of drugs and alcohol, suggesting the existence of a pharmacological relationship. Paul Goldstein's study, for example, found that as many as 84% of homicides occurring in New York City were motivated by drug trafficking and by interpersonal conflict linked to drug abuse. This cast doubt on the existence of a biological connection between alcohol or drug intake and murder. According to Goldstein, drug users trying to obtain money for drugs account for a very small fraction of homicides.

The availability of firearms has also been included as a major cause of violence. The Uniform Crime Reports indicate that about one-half of all murders and one-third of robberies involve the use of firearms. Moreover, the presence of firearms in the home significantly increases the risk of suicide among adolescents as well as the possibility of being killed by a family member or another intimate person. The logical conclusion of these studies is that gun control would result in a reduction in the rate of violence.

V. THE CRITICAL TRADITION IN CRIMINOLOGY

As one of the representatives of the critical tradition, Elliot Currie, has vividly blueprinted the growth of a criminogenic society. Such society is one that encourages a distribution of wealth that increasingly separates the rich from the poor, denies meaningful and fulfilling employment to large numbers of its population, particularly to its youth, considers people "replaceable," shifting work to those areas in which labor is cheaper, totally disregarding the consequences of these relocations on communities and on people's lives, promotes competition rather than cooperation among its members, and denies basic benefits to those who cannot work or to those who given their lack of skills or discrimination have problems finding fulfilling jobs. To Currie's blueprint it should be added that a criminogenic society also promotes racist and sexist attitudes and makes scapegoats of certain individuals, such as immigrants and people of color, blaming them for many social maladies.

Critical criminology, especially those studies emerging in the 1970s and early 1980s, were based on Marxist analyses of capitalist societies. As in the sociological tradition, these works centered around structural determinants of crime. The conflict view, for example, argued that crime results from unequal power relations. Powerful groups in society criminalize those behaviors committed mainly by the lower classes. Thus street crimes such as robbery and burglary—mainly committed by the poor—are the ones that receive the almost exclusive attention of the criminal justice agencies. Meanwhile, criminal acts committed by dominant groups in society, such as white collar and governmental crimes and dangerous working conditions, are rarely prosecuted.

Contemporary definitions of what is criminal are aimed at controlling the behavior of poor and powerless individuals who are often presented as potentially "dangerous." Therefore, acts of crime directed toward individuals—such as mugging—are portrayed as more harmful than those committed against the collectivity—such as environmental pollution. The latter crimes are typically committed by those holding political and economic power.

Feminists have added their contribution to the criminological enterprise by focusing attention on acts of criminality and violence committed by and against women. Liberal feminists Freda Adler and Rita Simon challenged early biological assumptions concerning female criminals by claiming that sociological variables—

and not biological ones—explained women's criminal behavior. In their view, a rise in crimes committed by women and a change in their criminal patterns could be expected from women's liberation and especially from women's increased participation in the labor market.

Marxist feminists contend that crime is a by-product of the exploitative nature of the relationship between workers and owners of the means of production. Julia and Herman Schwendinger's famous study, *Rape and Inequality* (1983), is an illustration of the Marxist feminist approach. Based on historical and anthropological studies, they maintain that rape is a product of the unequal gender relations existing in capitalist societies. In more egalitarian societies, they contend, rape is almost absent.

Radical feminists argue that male power and privilege, and not economic oppression, are the root causes of violence against women. Gender inequality is to be found in the needs of men to control women's sexuality and reproduction. The focus of radical feminist criminology is on female victims and survivors of male violence. Femicide, which refers to the homicides committed against women because they are women, exemplifies one of the extremes on a continuum of violence against women existing in our society. Other acts of violence against women include rape, torture, sexual slavery, prostitution, stalking, and sexual harassment at work and in the streets.

Blending Marxist and radical feminist views, socialist feminism centers around both class and patriarchy as the key structural variables that explain gender violence. Socialist feminist Piers Beirne and James Messerschmidt contend that both class and gender are inextricably intertwined. In his famous book *Capitalism, Patriarchy and Crime* (1986), Messerschmidt suggested that "the interaction of gender and class creates positions of power and powerlessness in the gender/class hierarchy, resulting in different types and degrees of criminality and varying opportunities for engaging in them."

In their book *Criminology as Peacemaking*, Harold Pepinsky and Richard Quinney claim that the criminal justice system in this country has its roots in the same violence that it is supposed to eliminate. Although peacemaking criminology share some ideas with other critical criminology schools, it is also grounded in anarchism, liberation theology, Eastern religions, feminism, and Marxism. Still in nascent form, it is not fully accepted yet as a criminological school. One of its major premises is that human transformation is possible only through the ending of suffering and the achievement of peace. Violence underlies the criminal justice system and it is also prevalent in the United States' attempts to dominate the world. Internal individual and structural violence, international conflicts in the form of war and warfare, all share the same common denominator—the need to keep intact the national and international overlapping structures of power that benefit the few.

Also See the Following Articles

CRIMINAL BEHAVIOR, THEORIES OF • JUVENILE CRIME • LAW AND VIOLENCE • POLICING AND SOCIETY • PUNISHMENT OF CRIMINALS

Bibliography

Barak, G. (1998). *Integrating criminologies*. Boston: Allyn and Bacon.

Currie, E. (1996). Confronting crime: New directions. In *Crime*. Edited by Robert Crutchfield, George S. Bridges and Joseph G. Weis. *Crime and Society*, Vol. 1. Thousand Oaks, CA: Pine Forge Press.

Foulcault, M. (1979). *Discipline and punish: The birth of the prison*. New York: Vintage.

Goode, E., & Nachman B. (1994). *Moral panics. The social construction of deviance*. Oxford: Blackwell.

Merton, R. (1957). *Social theory and social structure*. New York: Free Press of Glencoe.

Merton, R. (1938). Social Structure and Anomie. *American Sociological Review*, 3, 672–682.

Messerschmidt, J. (1986). *Capitalism, patriarchy and crime: Toward a socialist feminist criminology*. Totowa, NJ: Rowman and Littlefield.

Pepinsky, H. & Richard Q. (Eds.). (1995). *Criminology as peacemaking*. Bloomington: Indiana University Press.

Pfohl, S. (1995). *Images of deviance and social control*. New York: McGraw Hill.

Radzinowicz, L. (1962). *In search of criminology*. Cambridge, MA: Harvard University Press.

Sutherland, E. H., & Donald R. C. (1974). *Criminology*. Philadelphia: J.B. Lippincott.

Wolfgang, M., & Franco F. (1967). *The subculture of violence: Towards and integrated theory in criminology*. London: Tavistock.

Critiques of Violence

Gregory Fried
Boston University

GLOSSARY

Agape God's overflowing love for humanity.

Ahimsa The renunciation of the intent to cause physical or mental injury; nonviolence.

Hubris Overstepping of our proper bounds as human beings.

Just War Theory The exposition of principles for legitimately engaging in, conducting, and ending war.

Karma Action; the law of action that binds the act to consequences in this or a next life and the actor to the cycle of birth, death and rebirth.

Natural Law Principles inherent to the moral fabric of the universe.

Satyagraha The technique of nonviolent action for social and political change, pioneered by Mahatma Gandhi.

Social Contract An actual or hypothetical agreement to form a society and government in order to avoid the anarchy and violence of the state of nature.

State of Nature A hypothetical situation, characterized by violent competition, in which human beings exist without any organized government.

Tao The way; living in harmony with nature.

Wu-wei The effective exercise of virtue through nonaction.

CRITIQUES OF VIOLENCE may be divided between religious, philosophical and political critiques. Such divisions are somewhat arbitrary, since these categories tend to overlap, but they are helpful in making sense of a very complex tradition. Religious and philosophical critiques of violence have ancient roots, while political critiques are a relatively recent development.

Since the problem of the definition of violence cannot be adequately addressed here, for the purposes of this article, in order to accommodate the breadth of potential critiques, violence will be understood to take a number of forms. These include: the infliction of physical or emotional pain or injury; threatening such injury to coerce action; the use of force to compel action; and social, political, or economic conditions that do damage to the quality of life. It must be emphasized that a great deal depends on how broadly one defines violence, and that some traditions would reject calling anything but the illegitimate use of physical force "violent" in a morally objectionable sense. One's view of the distinction between force and violence, and between literal and metaphorical violence, is crucial. Thus, some would distinguish between the use of violence by an individual criminal or an aggressor nation and the use of legitimate force by the police or a defending army.

While accepting that some sports make considerable use of force, many would deny that such entertainment is actually violent, just as they would deny that the force used to restrain a child from entering a dangerous intersection constitutes violence. Some crimes, such as blackmail or extortion, depend on psychological coercion, but one might deny that they are literally violent. But here, for the most part, we will consider violence in its extended senses without passing judgment on the validity of these broader interpretations.

I. RELIGIOUS CRITIQUES

A. Ancient Greece

The tendency to regard Greek epic poetry and drama as merely literary artifacts neglects that these works have a religious significance that has influenced the Western tradition. While clearly not offering a categorical rejection of violence, these works do in general provide a critique of the excessive violence of human hubris. For example, in Homer's *Iliad*, the wrath (*mênis*) of Achilles results in the near defeat of his allies, the death of his own best friend, and the subsequent extreme brutality of his berserk lust for revenge. This riot of suffering induces even Achilles to pray, "I wish that strife would vanish from among gods and mortals."

The hero Odysseus, fresh from the sack of Troy and piracy against the innocent Cicones, is condemned to 10 years of homesick wandering and suffering by boasting of his act of blinding the Cyclops Polyphemos, a son of the god Poseidon. Odysseus' slaughter of the suitors, who plot the overthrow of his house, is sanctioned by Athena only as just retribution against violators of the laws of hospitality and to protect the home; Athena and Zeus himself intervene to prevent the violence from spreading to the blood feud of a civil war.

The *Oresteia* cycle by the tragedian Aeschylus can also be read as an attempt to restrain the private impulse for revenge, which results in the horror of an unending cycle of violence in the blood feud; Athena's institution of the public court of law as the legitimate power with the authority to employ force, circumscribes the need for violence, although it does not eliminate it. Euripides' tragedy, *The Trojan Women*, indirectly criticizes the poet's home city of Athens, which in the winter of 416–415 BCE had put to death the entire adult male population of the neutral island, Melos, enslaving all the women and children, because they refused to choose sides in the war with Sparta.

Although the Athenian historian Thucydides is not a religious author, we may judge the lesson of his history of the Peloponnesian War to be that while violence may at times be a necessity, understanding the proper extent of the need for force in given circumstances can help us to avoid the terrible excesses occasioned by the panic and passions aroused by all forms of conflict. In general, the Greek abhorrence of hubris, the overstepping of our proper bounds as human beings, can be understood as a critique of a violence both against our own nature and against nature and the gods themselves; genuine civilization and piety require the restraint of violence, if not its renunciation.

B. The Hebrew Bible

The book of Genesis declares that "God created man in his own image." Our sharing in God's own nature seems to underlie both our moral freedom in the Hebrew Bible as well as God's wrath when we use this freedom to do violence to our fellow human beings. The first story to follow the expulsion of Adam and Eve from Eden is the murder of Abel by his brother Cain. Even while God condemns this outrage, he forbids anyone from taking revenge upon Cain. Our being created in God's image seems to mean that the human person is inviolate, and that an act of violence against man is then a sin against God. Hence the sixth commandment given by God, through Moses: "You shall not kill."

Nevertheless, God himself kills. In the story of the Flood, God wipes out all human life except for Noah and his family. God predicates this divine act of violence on man's own sinful violence. Furthermore, after the Flood, God now explicitly permits violent punishment for violent acts: "'Whoever sheds the blood of man, by man shall his blood be shed; for God made man in his own image.'" The laws handed down by Moses proscribe death as punishment for numerous offenses. For reasons such as this, some argue that the commandment against killing is in fact a command to show restraint in one's dealings with all life, but that God still expects us to use force, even lethal force, in fulfilling his other commands.

The divine injunction against violence is therefore ambiguous. The distinction arises between legitimate violence, sanctioned as an instrument of God's anger against those who offend him, and illegitimate violence, the assault on the human person not sanctioned by God. Divinely sanctioned violence extends even to those whom we might otherwise consider innocent, such as when Saul is commanded to "utterly destroy" the Amalekites, including men, women, and children. By contrast, Jacob condemns his sons Simeon and Levi for their excessive violence after the two ravaged the entire city of Shechem without the explicit command of God in revenge for a prince's rape of their sister Dinah. While the laws of Moses may legitimate violence in the case of individual criminal acts, violence against entire peoples as collective punishment seems prohibited except in the case of God's express orders.

C. The Christian Gospels

Jesus is known as the Prince of Peace, and considering his most famous teachings, delivered in the Sermon on the Mount, this title seems apt. His critique of violence stems from his claim that he has come, not to abolish the Mosaic law, but to fulfill it. For Jesus, the Ten Commandments given to Moses by God do not only demand an outward conformity with the law, but also an inward overcoming of violent and aggressive impulses towards other human beings. Christ's "completion" of the law condemns a wide variety of both destructive actions and harmful intentions as violence against our acknowledging and embracing the image of God in ourselves and in other human beings. Hence, Christ condemns not only killing, but also anger and insult; he speaks against responding in kind to acts of violence, advises us instead to turn the other cheek, and he commands his followers to "Love your enemies and pray for those who persecute you." Christ's injunction against violence seems to extend to a rejection of the legal system to adjudicate disputes, preferring instead genuine reconciliation. In the Gospel of John, Jesus proclaims a single commandment: "that you love one another as I have loved you." The injunction against violence, broadly interpreted, seems to be a necessary corollary to this single, overarching command. Indeed, when Peter drew his sword to defend Jesus, striking off the ear of one of those who came to arrest him, Christ rebuked Peter. The emphasis Jesus places on the nonviolent resolution to conflict, even to the extent of passively accepting one's own death, thus seems to repudiate the contemporary Jewish expectation of the messiah as one who would lead the people to their salvation through a necessarily violent political struggle against the Roman occupation.

Nevertheless, even Christ is not unequivocal on the subject of violence. Despite his pronouncement that "all who take the sword will perish by the sword," Jesus himself says, "Do not think that I have come to bring peace on earth; I have not come to bring peace, but a sword." Jesus also withers the fig tree that fails to yield fruit. Even if we interpret such passages allegorically, it is clear that Christ believes that a certain degree of painful strife may be necessary for his teaching to bear fruit, even if this means conflict between parent and child as a new faith takes hold. Still, it is possible to believe that this strife can be engaged in without violence, either physical, mental or spiritual, by those who follow the command of Christ's love (*agape*). Nevertheless, all four gospels report Christ driving the moneychangers from the temple by force, in one case using a "whip of cords," and this passage has been employed to justify physical coercion by Christian authorities.

D. Christianity

It is necessary to distinguish between the Gospels themselves and the tradition of Christianity that is based on interpretations of the scriptures and influenced by various schools of theology. Many early Christians interpreted Christ's teachings as prohibiting absolutely any resort to violence, whether in self-defense, or in the defense of loved ones or the state. They were willing to accept martyrdom to serve as witnesses to Christ's teaching on salvation and suffering. Church fathers such as Tertullian and Origen argued that a true Christian could not kill, which led to confrontation with the conscription policies of the Roman military. A famous case of early conscientious objection is the trial of Maximilianus, who was executed in 295 CE for refusing to be entered into the roles of the army: "I cannot be a soldier for the world, I am a soldier for my God." Here we have the Christian paradox: the faithful must fight, but they must fight only against violence in the spirit of love. Violence of all kinds is the mark of cleaving to this world and of losing the world of the spirit, the kingdom of God.

But this categorical rejection of violence gave way to a more qualified critique after Christianity became the official state religion of Rome during the reign of the Emperor Constantine (306–337 BCE). Citing Luke 3:14, St. Augustine argued that a Christian need not renounce military service so long as he serves morally and observes mercy. Although Augustine distinguished between the heavenly City of God, to which we owe our ultimate allegiance, and the earthly City of Man, in which the Christian resides as a pilgrim, he argued that we ought to celebrate the victory of the more righteous side in a war. Here we have the beginnings of the Christian justification of legitimate violence, either in a just war or in the proper exercise of official civil duties, in order to secure justice in this world. Augustine's critique of justified violence extends only so far as to demand that we acknowledge that the necessity of even such legitimate force makes this world a place of misery from which we should earnestly hope to be delivered by the true peace attainable only in the next life through salvation in Jesus Christ.

The Christian tradition thus limited its condemnation of violence to the illegitimate use of force. The Middle Ages saw the beginning of the codification of such illegitimate violence and the justified force used to oppose it. In the *Summa theologiae*, St. Thomas Aquinas relied upon the doctrine of natural law to detail the offenses of violence against both person and property. Because the state has as its natural purpose the preservation of peace, the ruler is entitled to use force to combat both domestic and external threats. Drawing on Augustine, Aquinas offers three criteria for a just war: (1) that it be waged on the legitimate authority of the ruler, not private individuals; (2) that it be for a just cause; and (3) that it be fought with rightful intention. But the ruler himself is guilty of violence against the common good if he becomes a tyrant, and unjust laws constitute violence against the very nature of law. The exposition of natural law in Aquinas led in the 17th century to the just war theories of Suarez and Grotius, which sought to limit to legitimate and rational ends the exercise of force organized by the state.

During the Protestant Reformation, various sects rejected any compromise between what they considered to be basic Christian principles and the violent dictates of state power. These groups held that a notion of the legitimate exercise of violence could only serve to corrupt the idea and the practice of Christian love. The Anabaptists of Switzerland and the Mennonites in Holland insisted on absolute pacifism. Such Protestant movements had predecessors in Catholic groups such as the Waldensians, the Franciscans, and the Hussites, although all of these met varying degrees of hostility from the Catholic orthodoxy. One of the more radical sects in the Puritan movement in England was the Society of Friends, or Quakers, led by George Fox. Recognizing a "divine spark" in all human beings, the Quakers also forswore all "carnal" violence in favor of what they called spiritual weapons.

These pacifist sects suffered persecution in Europe and many emigrated to the British colonies in North America. The Quaker leader William Penn criticized the use of violence against the Indians by his fellow European colonists, and Penn founded Pennsylvania with the explicit understanding that the Quakers would conduct themselves as equals and brothers of the native peoples. The Quakers did not take their opposition to the world's violence to mean that they must retire from the work of seeking justice. Inspired by John Woolman, many Quakers joined the attack on the institution of slavery as violence against the dignity of the human person.

Although most contemporary Christian traditions continue to support the legitimate use of force by the state, many churches have worked against what they deem to be specific violations of this mandate. In the 1980s, Catholic bishops in the United States signed a pastoral letter against the use nuclear weapons, and in 1997 the Catholic Church declared capital punishment an excessive use of state power that itself demeans society. In addition, the question of abortion remains a volatile issue, with religious opponents generally arguing that abortion constitutes violence against the divinely ordained right to life of the child. Others argue that while the act of abortion itself is certainly violent, it cannot be understood as violence against a person because the fetus is not a human being.

E. Hinduism

Although many of the strands of Indian religion have their roots in the ancient Vedic practices (ca. 1500–500 BCE), the early Vedic religion itself offered no obvious criticism of violence. Many scholars account for this by arguing that the Vedic practices were the religion of a warlike population of invaders who conquered the subcontinent, but some recent scholarship disputes the invasion hypothesis. The Rig Veda collects hymns of the Vedic period, and most of these were to be sung as accompaniment to the animal sacrifices that were central to Vedic ritual. While the question of the continuity from the Vedic religion to what developed as Hinduism is controversial, the Mahabharata, one of the core texts of Hinduism, tells the story of an epic war between two families, a war that God, as Lord Krishna, instigates to fulfill the cosmic cycle of time, which entails both the creation and the destruction of the universe. Nevertheless, in the Bhagavad Gita, a poem contained within the Mahabharata, Krishna explains to Arjuna, a great warrior undergoing a crisis of conscience over facing his own relatives and teachers in battle, that to fight with enlightened detachment is not really violent, since the true self cannot die.

Hinduism emphasizes the belonging of all consciousness to the higher Self of *brahman*, the spiritual unity of all existence. Historically, Hinduism can be distinguished from the earlier Vedic religion by its principled rejection of the violence associated with certain animal sacrifices. All life is reincarnated in an endless cycle of life and birth, a cycle whose action is suffering and whose trajectory for any given individual is dictated by the law of *karma*: that one's actions and attitudes in this life will determine a proportionate reaction in one's standing in the life to follow. Full unification with God as *brahman* depends on liberation (*moksha*) from the individual self's cycle of birth and death. Violence, whether in deed, thought, or word, maintains one's attachment to the wheel of reincarnation, and this binds the self to a lower order of consciousness. Hence, nonviolence, or *ahimsa* (literally nonharming, the renunciation of the intent to cause physical or mental injury) began to gain favor as a virtue of the spiritually enlightened. Furthermore, since all life is reincarnated, one may well be harming a deceased relative when committing violence against another human being or even in butchering an animal.

Mainstream Hinduism, while holding to *ahimsa* as a personal ideal, has not discarded violence as a political or even cosmic necessity, and the ancient caste divisions, including the warrior caste (*ksatryas*), have persisted to the present day. In modern times, however, Mahatma Gandhi has argued that *ahimsa* is in fact at the core of Hinduism and must be put into practice in all aspects of life. Gandhi rejected the caste system itself as violence against the spiritual equality of all persons, and he condemned the poverty inflicted by the caste hierarchy as violence, too. Gandhi interpreted the Bhagavad Gita, ostensibly a poem about observing one's duty (*dharma*) to fight in war, as in fact an argument about the futility of war; nonviolence is a necessity in seeking Truth and in doing one's duty without the karmic attachment to the fruits of action. Gandhi spiritualized the Bhagavad Gita, arguing that the true battle is within one's own soul against evil inclinations, not against physical enemies. But even Gandhi insisted on duty over cowardice, and he advised those who think themselves too weak to practice *ahimsa* at least to use force in upholding justice.

F. Buddhism

Based on the life and teachings of Siddhartha Gautama, or the Buddha (the awakened one), Buddhism arose from within the Indian Vedic tradition in the 6th century BCE. Focusing on liberation from suffering, Buddhism understands this suffering as more than the personal experience of physical or mental pain. Suffering is what all conscious existence must undergo as its passes through the cycles of incarnation, death and rebirth, and so Buddhism seeks the interruption of this cycle through an enlightenment which extinguishes consciousness of the self; this state of the extinction of self is known as *nirvana*. Violence is an impediment to this release for several reasons: the anger and greed which accompany most violent acts increases karmic attachment to the world; violence generally proceeds from delusion, since it usually attempts to preserve a self which is in fact only an illusion; violence in and of itself generates karma which binds us to the cycle of rebirth.

Most Buddhists, however, do not observe total nonviolence. Although the incarnated self is an illusion, the body does have its requirements. In one story, the Buddha, in a previous incarnation, gave up his body to feed a hungry tigress and her cubs, thereby showing that compassion for the living must also recognize that life itself involves violence. But the Buddhist must strive to ameliorate suffering in general, not just his own, and so Buddhism acknowledges that we have duties to protect and to serve those for whom we are responsible. Ever since the Indian emperor Asoka (3rd century BCE) gave official recognition to Buddhism, Buddhists have sought political influence, while in principle attempting to minimize the violence employed by the state. Historically, Buddhist nations such as Burma, Cambodia, Laos, and Thailand have made a similar distinction as in the West between legitimate and illegitimate use of violence: military or police force is justified because these intend only to defend; only the aggressor is violent, because he intends to do harm.

G. Jainism

As founded by Mahavira in India in the 6th century BCE, Jainism espouses a particularly stringent interpretation of the dictates of *ahimsa*. Like the Buddhists, Jains seek to liberate the soul from karma, that is, from our attachment, forged through action, to this world. But Jains go so far as to hold that one's very physical existence constitutes violence. Jainism holds that all killing, even of insects and other pests, and even killing by accident, delays true liberation by encumbering the soul with bad karma. Strictly observant Jains go to elaborate lengths to avoid doing harm to other living things, such as using brooms to sweep insects out of the path of one's feet and wearing masks to avoid accidental damage to airborne creatures. Such practices serve to enhance one's mindfulness, that is, the intense awareness of the meaning and consequences of all action. Traditional Jainism has even prohibited agriculture as violence against the earth. Since violence does such damage to one's own soul, vegetarianism is mandated, and since even vegetable matter is alive, the Jain ideal is to perish by ceasing to eat altogether. Even the possession of a physical body does violence, as it competes with others to occupy space and employ resources. But since violence in this existence is inevitable, Jain practice has allowed the use of force in the performance of one's duty, and so even Jains make the distinction between legitimate protection of the community and predatory, unjust violence.

H. Confucianism

In his writings, the Chinese sage Confucius (551–479 BCE) criticized violence as a disruption of the proper harmony in self, society or nature. He did not rule out violence in the exercise of power, but he insisted that the truly cultivated ruler can and will govern by the sheer moral force of his character. By the proper observation of ritual (*li*) and virtue (*tê*), the gentleman can have a far greater influence than by any threat of force. The use of violence in word or deed is a sign that a man is not right with himself and that he cannot lead properly in either familial or political relations. Confucius held that oppressing the people or neglecting one's duties is also a form of violence against the harmony of the social order and is in fact far less efficient than rule which refrains from punishment and coercion, using instead the moral force of goodness (*jên*) to inspire the common people by example.

I. Taoism

With its focus on the *tao*, or the way, as a harmony between self and nature, Taoism intensifies the Confucian notion that the most effective action is a kind of nonaction (*wu-wei*). While also not explicitly abjuring all violence, Lao-tzu in the *Tao Te Ching* viewed the use of force as the symptom of a failure to accommodate oneself and society to the *tao*. Virtue may then be measured by the extent to which both public and private affairs can be governed by non-action, that is, an unreflective harmony with the *tao*: "I do nothing / And the people transform themselves. / I enjoy serenity / And the people govern themselves." Living in harmony with the *tao* is like being a child at play, immersed in an instinctive and intense joy; violence disrupts the play and makes an arrogant, and ultimately counterproductive attempt to force our will upon nature and society.

II. PHILOSOPHICAL CRITIQUES

Critiques of violence can be found throughout the Western philosophical tradition, although as with the religious tradition, these condemnations are seldom absolute. On questions of morality and politics, it must be understood that the philosophical and religious traditions merge substantially in the medieval period. Selected here are thinkers who have had the most influence in respect to the issue of violence.

A. Socrates

The Socratic critique of violence that we may gather from Plato's dialogues focuses on abuse of power and harm to the health of one's own soul. Socrates considered the breaking of the legitimate laws of a just regime to be an act of violence, and so he refused the offers of his friends to help him escape from jail when he had been sentenced to death by Athens. At the same time, he opposed an unconstitutional trial conducted under the democracy when he served on the Council, and, at the risk of his own life, he refused to serve the unlawful execution decrees imposed by the 30 tyrants.

In addition to this opposition to violence against law, Socrates held that the individual does violence to his own soul in doing injustice. He argued against the view of the sophist Thrasymachus that justice is the advantage of the stronger, or that might makes right. The truly just person will prefer suffering violence to harming others unjustly. The healthy soul is ruled by reason, using its fighting spirit not to coerce others but rather to keep its own passions and appetites in order. Socrates even criticized the traditional legends of the gods using violence against one another, holding that perfect beings should not need to use force or deceit against one another and that such tales provide poor examples for the education of society. While Socrates does not seem to have ruled out violence for national or self-defense, he argued that punishment must not harm the lawbreaker, thereby making him worse, but rather serve to rehabilitate and improve him.

Finally, Socrates' practice of philosophy as a disputatious conversation that seeks the truth offers an implicit critique of violence directed against reason itself. At his trial, Socrates took pains to distinguish himself from the sophists of his day, for whom winning an argument was more important than seeking the truth. Socrates realized that his philosophical conversations often caused people pain, but he compared himself to a midwife who brings ideas to light, just as a baby emerges through necessary suffering. Sophistry does violence to the educational purposes of thinking, and it does violence to those who pay to learn its techniques, for they only learn to corrupt the power of reason. For Socrates, ignorance itself, especially willful ignorance, is a kind of violence against the nobility of the human mind. Claiming, during his trial on charges of impiety and corrupting the youth, that "the unexamined life is not worth living," Socrates argued unsuccessfully that the state should support his work to teach the citizens of Athens to question themselves.

Socrates thus offered a vision of philosophy itself as a hedge against the violence of the human condition. Subsequent philosophy in antiquity often owes as much to the example of his conduct in life as to the content of his thinking. The Stoic philosopher Epictetus, making Socrates his model, advised his followers to live according to nature by accepting as fate what is not up to them. Violence, both in action and in spirit, derives from a failure to understand what we properly can and cannot control. No one can coerce you if you cleave only to what is truly your own: your opinions, desires, and aversions, but not externals such as health, friends, family or property.

B. Social Contract Theorists

The social contract theories of early modern philosophy, building to some extent on the tradition of natural law in medieval Christian theology, conceived of the threat of violence as the prime motivation for the formation of civil society and the institution of government. Thomas Hobbes famously described the state of nature as a war in which life is "solitary, poore, nasty, brutish and short," since in the absence of a higher authority, we are all entitled to use whatever violence we deem necessary to preserve ourselves. Reason demands that we find a way out from this insecure situation, seeking peace by erecting a sovereign over us who has the sole right to employ or order violence and who will use this power to enforce the law. The fear of violent death becomes the engine for the formation of a stable and orderly government with the final power over life and death.

John Locke, in the *Second Treatise of Government*, while agreeing that we have a need to institute government to avoid the violence of the state of nature, disagrees with Hobbes' device of the absolute sovereign with a monopoly on violence. If the ruler abuses his authority, the people have the right to rebel against the tyrant's violence toward the ends of good government: the preservation of life, liberty and property. Each of us must be allowed to rely on his own reason to determine whether the legitimate, coercive power of government has degenerated into the oppressive violence of tyranny. Locke's revulsion with the religious wars of his century led him to denounce religious persecution in his *Letter Concerning Toleration*, and he strongly condemned schooling that relied on violence against the mind in rote learning or against the body in corporal punishment. Locke may be counted as the founder of the modern liberal notion that the individual's rights are based on the right to remain free of unwarranted coercion and abuse, as well as all forms of unwarranted interference in the affairs of one's conscience, one's private property and private life. All constraint by law must have its basis in consent, that is, in a social contract to which we have freely agreed.

C. Kant: Human Beings as Ends in Themselves

Although he made use of social contract theory himself, Immanuel Kant offered an alternative to the rights-based critique of violence. Kant argued that man's rational nature means that we must be understood as ends in ourselves, and that unlawful force or deception does violence to the human person (both the actor and the victim) by treating the human being as a mere means. Hence, we have a duty, derived from our own rational, moral nature and not simply from the rights of others, to avoid violence except under very limited circumstances, such as self-defense and service in the military. Kant did not rule out the lawful use of force, either to enforce the laws or to defend the state, and he believed that the often antagonistic competition between individuals and nations is the engine of human progress. But Kant also considered war a profound scandal, given our rational and moral nature. In *Towards Perpetual Peace*, he reasoned that history could be read as moving in the direction of an international federation of republican states, and that we all ought to do what we can to hasten this cosmopolitan future. According to Kant, if wars must be fought, then this must be done in such a way as to promote a stable peace thereafter, and he condemned innovations such as the national debt which allows for accelerated financing of armaments, armies and ever more destructive wars.

III. POLITICAL CRITIQUES

Although political critiques of violence generally rely on religious and philosophical critiques for their inspiration, the former may be distinguished from the others by their appeal to and their mobilization of a mass political movement. As such, political critiques of violence are a relatively modern phenomenon.

A. Peace Movements

In the 19th century, a wide variety of national and international peace movements arose to condemn war either on religious grounds or as an anachronism long overdue for abolition by human progress. In the United States, the work of organizations such as the New England Non-Resistance Society and the League for Universal Brotherhood helped pave the way for the Hague Court in 1899, the first international tribunal and a forerunner to the League of Nations, founded after World War I, and the United Nations, founded after World War II. Many such movements continue their work today around the world, arguing that war, especially given the destructive potential of modern weapons (nuclear, biological and chemical), presents a form of violence which humanity as a whole must learn to overcome in order to survive. Albert Einstein, in an exchange of letters with Sigmund Freud at the inception of the nuclear era, argued that because of such weapons, humanity must evolve to a new level of civilization. Activists such as Dr. Helen Caldicott, the leader of Physicians for Social Responsibility, have pursued this cause.

B. Economic and Social Violence

With the emergence of workers' movements in the 19th century the argument arose, especially under the banner of Marxism, that the economy itself can impose a form of violence against the poor and oppressed. Karl Marx, while embracing violence as a tool of revolution, regarded the social relations fostered by capitalism, with the alienation between competing human beings as well as between worker and work, as violence against what he called humanity's "species-being." The notion of poverty as violence is still very much alive today in the debates over replacing failing welfare or socialist economies with systems based on market forces. Some social critics also argue that the police forces of the state are used mainly to uphold the power of the ruling classes (economic, racial or ethnic). The psychiatrist James Gilligan has argued that the prison system in the United States, with the pervasive physical and sexual abuse of prisoners by other prisoners, and the psychological abuse caused by the prison system itself, generates an ongoing cycle of violence in society as a whole, since these convicts bring their pathologies with them upon release. Others would argue that while poor social and economic conditions are lamentable, they are only metaphorically violent, and, similarly, that the use of force by the system of justice to arrest, restrain and punish criminals is an unfortunately necessary exercise of legitimate authority which cannot properly be called violence.

C. Political Nonviolence

Mahatma Gandhi is largely responsible for the widespread and often successful adoption in the 20th century of nonviolence as a means of political change. Drawing on a wide variety of sources, including his native Hinduism as well as Christianity, the work of Leo Tolstoy and the civil disobedience advocated against unjust authority by Henry David Thoreau, Gandhi offered a critique of violence on two levels: (1) On a personal ethical level, violence causes harm to the actor as well as the victim, even if the violence is in a just cause; (2) In politics and society, violence does not resolve conflict but at best only suppresses it, and violence often simply replaces one form of unjust domination with another. Violence is therefore an ineffective tool for genuine and enduring change.

Gandhi devised a remarkably disciplined technique of political action through nonviolence (*satyagraha*), involving (1) noncooperation with governmental authorities; (2) civil disobedience against unjust laws; and (3) the willingness to suffer violence in the pursuit of a movement's aims. Gandhi's nonviolent action had an enormous influence, through Martin Luther King, Jr. and other activists, on the civil rights struggles of the 1950s and 1960s in the United States. Some political theorists, such as Gene Sharp, drawing on the success of nonviolent action, have attempted to delineate the strategies for using these methods as an alternative, or as a supplement, to armed national defense.

D. Feminism

Modern feminism, which owes its rise in part to the civil rights movement, has sometimes argued that violence is itself a function of patriarchy, that is, the male domination of society and politics. On this view, patriarchy necessarily suppresses and controls women as the corollary of, or even the precondition to, the domination of other human beings through racism, slavery, colonialism, and tyranny. True human liberation therefore demands the overthrow of male supremacy. Some feminists, such as Andrea Dworkin, argue that in a context of unequal power, sexual relations between men and women inevitably constitute a form of violence (that is, rape), despite the illusion of women's consent. The feminist legal theorist Catherine MacKinnon has endeavored to ban pornography as propaganda which does literal, and not just metaphorical violence to women, both in its production and in the attitudes and behavior which it inspires.

E. Technology and Mass Culture

Despite the extraordinary success of modern technology in producing material benefits, this very success has drawn criticism. The reliance on technology itself has been denounced as an assault that does violence to the human spirit. Furthermore, new media technologies, such as television and movies, have been criticized for reliance on sex and violence to attract a mass audience. Researchers, as well as a variety of political movements, have argued that the pervasive violence displayed in the mass media has a direct influence on violence in society and particularly on the aggressive behavior of children.

F. Environmentalism and Animal Rights

In recent decades, environmental and animal rights movements have gained a wide following. While not necessarily opposed to technology, environmentalists have argued that the unchecked exploitation of the earth's resources made possible by modern technology often does irreparable violence to the natural habitat upon which all life on the planet depends. Animal rights groups generally argue that the use of animals for food, adornment (furs, leather, etc.), labor and scientific research constitutes unjustifiable violence against our fellow living beings, who have the same rights to life and liberty as we do. The more radical among both environmental and animal rights activists have at times advocated violence to protect the earth and animals which cannot defend themselves against the violence of human beings. Both movements imply that the violence human beings are capable of constitutes a unique threat to life on the planet and that our species must learn to accept a subordinate role as steward and protector rather than our accustomed position as master and exploiter.

Bibliography

Aquinas, St. Thomas. (1988). *On law, morality, and politics*. Indianapolis: Hackett.

St. Augustine. (1996). *Political writings*. Indianapolis: Hackett.

Bedau, H. A. (Ed.). (1969). *Civil disobedience: Theory and practice*. New York: Pegasus.

Bok, S. (1998). *Mayhem: Violence as public entertainment*. Reading: Addison Wesley Longman.

Bondurant, J. V. (Ed.). (1971). *Conflict: Violence and nonviolence*. Chicago: Aldin-Atherton.

Brock, P. (1991). *Freedom from war: Nonsectarian pacifism, 1814–1914*. Toronto: University of Toronto Press.

Cooney, R., & Michalowski, H. (Eds.). (1977). *The power of the people: Active nonviolence in the United States*. Culver City: Peace Press.

Chapple, C. K. (1993). *Nonviolence to animals, earth and self in Asian traditions*. Albany: State University of New York Press.

Chan, W. (Ed.). (1963). *A sourcebook in Chinese philosophy*. Princeton: Princeton University Press.

Dyck, H. L. (Ed.). (1996). *The pacifist impulse in historical perspective*. Toronto: University of Toronto Press.

Gilligan, J. (1996). *Violence: Our deadly epidemic and its causes*. New York: Grosset/Putnam.

Hamilton, E., & Huntington, C. (Eds.). (1961). *The collected dialogues of Plato*. Princeton: Princeton University Press.

Hobbes, T. (1981). *Leviathan*. Harmondsworth: Penguin Books.

Kant, I. (1983). *Perpetual peace and other essays*. Indianapolis: Hackett.

Locke, J. (Second Edition, 1967). *Two treatises of government*. Cambridge: Cambridge University Press.

Mayer, P. (Ed.). (1967). *The pacifist conscience*. Chicago: Gateway.

Schneir, M. (Ed.). (1994). *Feminism in our time: The essential writings, World War II to the present*. New York: Vintage Books.

Sharp, G. (1985). *Making Europe unconquerable: The potential of civilian-based deterrence and defense*. Cambridge: Ballinger.

Zimmerman, Michael E. (1993). *Environmental philosophy: From animal rights to radical ecology*. Englewood Cliffs: Prentice Hall.

Cultural Anthropology Studies of Conflict

Christos N. Kyrou
SUNY College of Environmental Science and Forestry

Jason Pribilsky
Syracuse University

Robert A. Rubinstein
Syracuse University

GLOSSARY

Culture The customary way in which groups organize and understand their behavior in relation to others and to their environment.

Language A flexible complex system of communication that incorporates structure, sound, meaning, and practice and which can be used to describe conditions internal or external to people.

Meaning Systems The processes, signs and symbols used to create a coherent picture of reality.

Reciprocity Exchange of services and goods.

Reversal Theory A field of study which explores how individuals' internal motivational states are structured, and which investigates the occurrence of cultural inversions, periods of time during which otherwise inappropriate behavior is acceptable and valued.

Symbolism The use of symbols to create and maintain political and social realities.

THIS ARTICLE reviews cultural anthropological approaches to the study of conflict. Anthropologists view conflict as a very general state of affairs in a relationship or as some basic incompatibility in the very structure of the relationship, which leads to specific disputes and sometimes to violence. Other than the literatures that have focused on war, anthropological work treats conflict within the context of more general ethnographic accounts. As a result the data and interpretation of conflict in the literature spans a variety of approaches. In this article six such axes of conflict are reviewed: (1) meaning systems; (2) ritual and symbolism; (3) language and communication; (4) reciprocity and environmental stress; (5) gender; and (6) ethnicity and identity.

Anthropological interest in social conflict has been long standing and varied, producing a literature that is both broad and vast. Considered as whole, it includes a wide range of interrelated but analytically distinct approaches to the study of conflict, violence, dispute settlement, and conflict management. Approaches include the following: the relative importance of human biological heritage; psychological factors; social organizational and cultural aspects that promote conflict or violent behavior; the dynamics of ethnocentrism; the nature and course of warfare, both "primitive" and contemporary; the lived experiences of individuals and groups in settings of violence; the examination of factors promoting nonviolence as a social and cultural norm; and the dynamics of disputing and of dispute settlement. Because of the wide-ranging anthropological interest in conflict studies, a full review of the literature is not possible here. Rather, this article provides a synthetic overview of selective topics in the anthropology of conflict. Extensive, but not exhaustive, it relates scholarly interest in conflict within anthropology with areas of historical interest in the discipline generally.

I. CULTURAL ANALYSIS AND CONFLICT

In 1871 Edward Tylor proposed one of the first technical definitions of culture as socially patterned human thought and behavior. Tylor claimed that culture was a "complex whole which includes knowledge, belief, art, morals, law, custom, and any other capabilities and habits acquired by man as a member of society." Implicit in his understanding was a belief that humans were bound by a "psychic unity," such that people's minds everywhere operated the same way and all people had the same potential for development. People differed, however, according to their stratified positions along a scale of cultural evolution organized around dichotomies of "modern" versus "primitive," and "advanced" versus "uncivilized." Evolutionary thought dominated much of early anthropology from the late 19th through the early part of this century largely through the efforts of American anthropologist, Lewis Henry Morgan.

By the 1920s anthropological thought had developed into two lines of critical reaction to evolutionary models. In the United States, Franz Boas and the students he trained in the first three decades of this century developed a program of what has become known as historical particularism. By stressing specific historical complexity of cultural development over evolutionary models, Boas and his students sought to group cultures only within broad categories of "culture areas" on the basis of shared traits that often reflect adaptive responses to natural environments. These groupings, however, provided no explanatory model, only a means of comparison.

At about the same time, the functionalist schools of thought developed in Britain. British functionalists opted for detailed studies that attempted to understand "primitive" culture on its own terms. The anthropologists most often associated with this school, A. R. Radcliffe-Brown and Bronislaw Malinowski, understood culture in mechanical terms and took as their metaphor the living organism. Like any organism, it is the individuated parts of a culture—specific customs or institutions—that are interconnected and "function" to maintain the total system.

Functionalism, though, forced anthropologists to accept heuristic models that misrepresented the lived reality of the people they studied. Functionalists, their critics charged, treated cultures as closed systems in timeless equilibrium, despite ongoing change and contact with other cultures. Critics also charged that strict adherence to an assumption that each cultural trait exists by design to serve a specific function led easily to tautologies, or circular arguments. Cultural traits are explained by their functions, which in turn are explained by the traits.

Today anthropologists recognize that "culture" consists of both social structures and patterns, which are characterized by variation and independence at every level. The linkage between the two is made through the study of meaning. An emphasis is placed on understanding social patterns and institutions in terms of how people make their daily experiences meaningful and productive. "Meaning-centered" approaches can be traced to the mid-1950s and 1960s and shifts toward anthropological approaches to the study of symbols and symbolism.

Social conflict and collective violence have often appeared in ethnographies as the backdrop against which to better understand the nature of culture rather than as the primary focus of research. In this sense conflict was studied as a foil to help explain aspects of stability in society. Observing conflict provided instances where the normal functioning of culture could be revealed. Various forms of institutionalized conflict that operated to maintain the social order were exposed.

Two exceptions to this exist. First, so-called primitive warfare has been the focus of considerable anthropological study. Second, ethnocentrism as a human universal was the focus of much work in the 1970s. Some of this work is reviewed below. Recently, anthropologists have been studying the effects of violence on individuals and groups. That recent literature is not treated in depth in this article.

By using the culture-as-meaning approach, anthropologists have collected information on institutions, rituals, norms, and other cultural patterns and processes. This approach has allowed them to better understand how these dimensions of human social life relate to collective violence and to social conflict in general.

In the 1980s, anthropological studies of conflict took on an added urgency due to concerns over the threat of global destruction through thermonuclear war. Much of this literature helped theorize the concept of risk taking and its associated behaviors. M. Margaret Clark traced four traditional motivations for "risk seeking": the elements of play, the involvement of social stratification, the incorporation of supernatural elements, and finally the promise for secular rewards. She provided examples of rituals, institutions, beliefs, and behaviors from a variety of cultures, including those with capacity to engage in nuclear warfare, in order to expose the cultural patterns of risk seeking in our society and to show that radical changes are required to eliminate such patterns. In a similar analysis, Mary L. Foster demonstrated that risk-seeking behavior exists at the group level, as well as at the individual level, where it is socially supported and collectively sanctioned through psychological reversals and cultural inversion.

Foster's analysis builds on the theoretical concept "schismogenesis" developed by Gregory Bateson to explain power and control. In Bateson's work two kinds of relationships, the complementary (leader to follower) and the symmetrical (members of the same team) coexist within society. Mechanisms of periodical "shifts of power," or in Bateson's terms, "dynamic equilibrium," are kept in balance through a jockeying between the two.

Participation in institutionalized forms of violence and conflict requires culturally patterned methods of motivation. Walter Goldschmidt traced the relationship between personal motivation and institutionalized conflict in both tribal societies and American society. Goldschmidt suggested that the benefits of such a career motivate the individual to participate. Such benefits include enhanced social standing, social gratification, personal pride, prosperity, and strength. All of these contribute to preserving what he called "vicious cycle" between popular action and war. Carol Greenhouse has helped to recast militarism as something other than social disorder. Rather, she argues that when militarism is understood as a component of the same social order that keeps vital other social institutions such as religion, kinship, and the law, we are better able to explain why joining the military is often an act that is taken for granted by many state societies.

II. SYMBOLISM, RITUAL, AND CONFLICT

While there are points in the history of anthropology that demonstrate an interest in human aggression and the relationship between human biology and social conflict, anthropologists have overwhelmingly argued for the cultural basis of conflict. Both conflict and violence are understood as shaped in response to culturally specific norms, values, ideologies, and worldviews. What motivates societies in conflict arises out of institutionalized social interactions that are mutually defined by members of that society. Often, however, the cultural knowledge that forms the basis of what justifies conflict in one setting and condemns it in another is taken for granted and is assumed to be an objective fact by the participants themselves.

Analyses of how conflict and violence are institutionalized within cultures have received a considerable amount of attention within the anthropological conflict literature. In particular, anthropologists have looked at ways in which conflict relations are maintained, expressed, or as is often the case, masked, by means of symbolism and symbolic behavior. The early work of anthropologist Abner Cohen has proved particularly insightful for the understanding of the relationship between symbolism—the expression or manipulation of symbolic forms and patterns of symbolic action—and the struggle of groups for economic and political power. As Abner argued, symbols do not arise spontaneously, but rather are produced through a process of continuous restructuring in relation to the distribution of resources found in society. The careful study of the interrelationship between these two domains yields important information regarding motivations for conflict and violent behavior.

The study of ritual has provided a fertile territory for analyzing the relationship between political struggle and symbolic behavior. Political speeches, national demonstration, public executions, all examples of political ritual, draw upon meaning structures and symbols to convey powerful messages of legitimacy and to ensure the mandate to exercise power. David Kertzer observes that the meaningful content of ritual is encoded in symbols. Symbols are the words through which rituals make sense to societies. Their weight, sequence, and presence—or absence—help to ensure that the message is delivered.

In the realm of politics, anthropologists note how symbols and symbolism generally operate in such a way to construct social unity where otherwise diverse interests and needs may be present within a single society. Symbols are, in Victor Turner's words, "mulivocal," thus any symbol or set of symbols can encode a variety of different meanings. Because they possess a certain "condensation" of meanings, feelings, and emotions, symbols can speak simultaneously to people differently situated within society.

More than carrying messages, symbols instigate social action and define an individual's place within society. In her exploration of Iranian popular culture, Mary Catherine Bateson identifies different normative themes of choice making, which she argues can affect international affairs. Through an analysis of popular stories and films, Bateson draws a distinction between two Iranian approaches to decision making. One form is rooted in pragmatism and the rules of compromise and calculation and the other in the preservation of honor in spite of the possible negative consequences. Bringing such forms to bear upon understanding international relations between the United States and Iran demonstrates the future need to focus on motivations rather than simply the outcomes for political behavior.

III. LANGUAGE, COMMUNICATION, AND CONFLICT

Language is a human universal—all peoples use a spoken symbolically based system of communication. Indeed, one of the fundamental characteristics of culture is that it is communicated among its people. Language can create boundaries. It can signify membership in the same culture, or it can denote difference and play a serious role in framing the "other."

Ethnolinguistic analysis yields large amounts of often subtle information about the culture under study. Language, in the broad sense of the term, reflects one or another element of a community's social life, including social stratification, sense of space or time, and most of all, narration. For the study of conflict, examination of communication patterns in society can illuminate the subtle ways intracultural conflict is dealt with through language. In her study of the *baladi* women in Cairo, Early explores how quarrels between women serve as vehicles for the transmission of important cultural expectations concerning respectful and appropriate behavior. What is being said, when, and by whom, plays a decisive role in *baladi* conflict management: the level and role of kinship of the people involved, the place being either private or public, the role of social reputation. What at once seems to be a tedious part of *baladi* daily life serves to index social relations and social reputations, and in the process alleviates tension through allowance of personal expression of frustration.

While quarrels and other forms of direct verbal communication yield important information about how information is transmitted during conflict, the study of indirect discourse is equally rich. Fisher's study of the Barbadian communication strategy of "dropping remarks" demonstrates how beyond the speech act itself, careful attention must be paid to the context of discourse. Dropping remarks are subtle forms of a triangular speech event. They are triangular in the sense that speakers "drop" insults to a target individual through conversations overheard with a third party not directly involved in the dispute. In other words, a speaker's intended audience is not the person directly spoken to, but rather an onlooker. Dropping remarks operates to escalate dormant conflict that may or may not break into direct quarreling by allowing a speaker to state a position in a dispute. As aggressive acts that are packaged as relatively harmless, they allow accusations to be made without leading the necessity of outright quarrel.

The study of ethnolinguistics demonstrates how language can serve to both accelerate and ameliorate conflicts within societies. Similarly, the study of language can reveal the sources of conflict between societies. Much of the scholarly work on language and conflict between cultures has benefited from insights of anthropologist Edward Hall's distinction between "high" and "low" context speech communities. In the case of the former, discourse is indirect, with ideas often expressed in abstract and metaphorical form, and favoring broad frameworks rather than minute details. In contrast, low context represents communication predicated on the direct delivery of information, without ambiguity, and often neglectful of particular idiosyncrasies of communication styles.

The low context/high context distinction has far-reaching applications for the study of conflict and negotiation within international politics. Studies of international security outside of anthropology often accept negotiation as an objective process whereby disputing parties share tacit understandings of the negotiation process. When conflicts fail to be resolved, blame is often placed on the issues at hand or the failures of bargaining process. A cultural approach to conflicts in the negotiating process focuses on cross-cultural negotiation as a confrontation between systems of meaning and understanding constructed symbolically. In an effort to account for the continued failures in negotiation between Israelis and Egyptians for nearly 50 years, Raymond Cohen plumbs the social, cultural, and historical differences between the two cultures to demonstrate how different conceptions of time, the role of violence, and the community impede the negotiating process. Most important from an ethnolinguistics of conflict standpoint is Cohen's discussion of how different styles of verbal communication complicate efforts to forge peace between the two countries. In addition to the contrast between a high-context Egyptian communication style and an Israeli form of direct "low-context" discourse style, Cohen notes how different conceptions of time inform the pace and schedule of negotiation.

Careful linguistic analysis can reveal diverse and sometimes competing notions of argument and persuasion. Barbara Koch's analysis of rhetorical speech in contemporary Arabic texts shows that Arabic writers construct "proof" through such high context forms of persuasion as repetition, paraphrasing, and the structuring of argumentative claims in recurring syntactical patterns. This systematic valuing of linguistic forms and actual words in rhetorical speech, Koch argues, runs counter to Western modes of discourse and rules of argument, which privilege the logical structure of arguments over the particular way in which they are packaged.

IV. RECIPROCITY, ENVIRONMENTAL SCARCITY, AND CONFLICT

In their studies of so-called simple societies, early anthropologists noted a fundamental process where even small surpluses are shared with other members of a community. This observation provoked anthropologists to consider how all surplus production is invested in human relations and translated into social assets. The exchange of scarce goods creates bonds of indebtedness between community members which reinforces the cohesion of society. This process anthropologists label "reciprocity." In the history of anthropology, reciprocity has become one of the ethnographic categories *par excellence*.

As inhabitants of ecosystems, humans are vulnerable to environmental changes that threaten lifeways. Climate change, for example, has gradually driven populations from one geographical region to another, in search for what ecologists term "ecological niches," a new location abundant in space and resources. In the modern era, migration due to social and environmental pressure has become a fundamental force in the transformation, creation, and destruction of cultures.

In studies of conflict, the concept of reciprocity has been an important way to understand how societies negotiate and adapt pre-existing social relations to accommodate periods of resource scarcity brought about by these changes. Under conditions of scarcity, social relations are at their most strained, calling upon a society's ability to adapt to new situations. Reciprocity often reflects a society's effort to convert a lack of economic resources into a system of mutual assistance. Residents of marginalized communities, for instance, manage to survive by establishing social networks that ensure the exchange of goods, services, and information otherwise unavailable in society. In her study of shantytown dwellers in Mexico City, Larrisa Lomnitz noted that patterns of reciprocity were anchored in a series of spatially oriented clusters. Within each network, women engaged in daily exchanges of favors, including borrowing food and money, assistance in child rearing, and the exchange of gossip. Men assisted each other in finding jobs, shared labor, and helped one another with expenses to cover emergencies and fund important community celebrations. Lomnitz found that "reciprocity frequently appears in situations that lack many alternatives, and this is a source of its strength and persistence."

Environmental stress, disaster or prolonged scarity may challenge the adaptability of systems of reciprocity. Charles D. Laughlin and Ivan Brady reviewed the ethnographic evidence from societies undergoing such environmental stress. They found that under such extreme conditions, the bounds of exchange and reciprocity may restrict, causing transactions to be more negative and self-interested in nature. Colin Turnbull's study of the Ik in northeastern Uganda, a people who had experienced such severe and prolonged environmental scarcity, provides an exemplar of those processes. Among the Ik, reciprocity relations had become so restricted that food sharing between parents and their children and between husbands and wives had become the normative exception.

V. GENDER AND CONFLICT

Cultures have systematized, ritualized, and even institutionalized women's unequal position to that of men in almost every domain, from language to political power. This "cultural dimorphism" is more exposed today than ever in human history and has become a subject of slow cultural change as well as a source of several conflicts.

Thomas and Beasley raised the issue of domestic violence from the perspective of human rights. They identified patterns of double standards on law application, as well as patterns of nonprosecution against this widespread crime. By identifying those patterns, they exposed the state as responsible for the frequency of rape and domestic violence. By doing so, they transferred the blame from the man in the street to the man in the uniform, and from the unknown thousands of offenders to the well-known formal institution. From a common crime, Thomas and Beasley brought domestic violence to its real dimension, the sociocultural dimension, and to this point the issue of human rights violation has a serious standing. They also applied their model in Brazil, providing a useful account of the methodological limitations they faced and the "human rights approach" as one substantially potential method of challenging social structures that subject their people to inhuman conditions.

It is inevitable that a debate of change in one culture will travel just like any other commodity through the lines of another. The debate on human rights does not have to be seen as a challenge to moral standards but as part of a process of change that is already on the way. Thus the wording in human right declarations is based not on the morality but on the descriptions of generally undesirable human conditions. If such conditions are recognized as universally undesirable, then further substructures are expected to reevaluate, modify, and even replace if not abandon practices that drive toward such undesirable human conditions. The issue is that no culture considers itself a substructure, and changes "from outside" are seen (and legitimately so) with suspicion.

Robert Edgerton has recently shown that anthropological discussions of issues of human rights have too often been paralyzed by an inappropriate understanding of cultural relativism—the view that cultures must be judged only in terms they themselves set. This has led to a false dichotomy between a kind of moral univeralism and a moral isolationist position.

As mentioned earlier some of the most sensitive issues of gender include genital circumcision, abortion, and domestic and even ritualized social violence. Heise demonstrates very graphically the variety of culturally "justified" violence against women using the general term "crimes of gender" and including social inequities and cultural beliefs that leave women economically dependent on men. Sandra D. Lane and Robert Rubinstein go beyond condemnation of the ritual of circumcision. They argue for an approach that that respects local practices, not independently of local resources for cultural self-examination. They claim that ethical universalism and cultural relativism have framed the debate into their own sphere of polarized conflict. They warn that intervention always involves claims about legitimacy, standing, and authority that are socially constructed and culturally mediated and that it takes place within a complex communicative web. They argue that efforts that address such difficult issues must be done in the context of local available resources that should be explored first as means for change, referring to individuals, groups, organizations, and institutions that have already started a campaign to abolish the practice within their own cultures.

In the case of birth control and family planning, especially when precipitated by discourse on overpopulation and the spread of AIDS in most developing countries, anthropology can provide policymakers with substantial knowledge about what seems probable to work or is doomed to fail, what is supported by or lost in the cultural web of the region under question. Caroline Bledsoe demonstrates the cultural limitations that cause African peoples to rise against the introduction and advertisement of the use of condoms in their societies, even under the shadows of threat from the fast-spreading disease, AIDS.

Gender conflict is a good example of how cultural patterns reflect societal, economic, and political power stratification in a social system, and the opposite. The above discussion may mark conflict between gender as a "cultural" phenomenon, but in the eye of an anthropologist it implies neither legitimization nor contingency of the condition of women. Quite the opposite, it implies that this very condition is in transition, because of changes in the societal structures and processes that sustain it. Anthropologists can suggest and advise policymakers of where "normative minefields" are hidden on the path to constructing the new "realities." Today more than ever, institutionalized structures have replaced the norms in the complex and inflexible webs of administrative and bureaucratic monsters, products, and heritage, or even the ghosts of the industrial revolution: the nation-state. Drawing the borderline, the new structure occasionally succeeded, but most frequently it failed to deal with the issue of ethnic identity.

VI. ETHNICITY AND CIVIL CONFLICT

National borders and ethnic boundaries are not necessarily co-terminus. Like many human boundaries they can be either rigid or highly flexible. Fredrick Barth showed that ethnic boundaries are also extremely persistent despite the movement of people across them, and that such boundaries can be purposefully manipulated. The concept of "ethnic groups" is complex and difficult to approach, and it is the source of much debate in anthropology. Sometimes ethnic groups are treated as identical to religion and/or language groups. People of different ethnic groups may share "a" culture, a broader level of a meaning system. Self-ascription may be a distinct, representative feature of ethnicity. Ethnicity is not defined or limited by physical borders, and unlike nation states, it can exist as minority within, or it can be spread over a number of states, depending also on the historical circumstances.

In any case, ethnicity is not temporal, transitional, or circumstantial, but imperative in the same fashion as is gender or religion. Even in multi-ethnic communities ethnic identity persists and is strategically manipulated. These societies exist based on the complementary relations of their ethnic group-members. However, such relationships can be challenged by an external change to which the ethnic group will respond, either by becoming integrated into a broader entity, by existing within the entity as a minority, or by deciding to take its own course and breaking off from the multi-ethnic society to become a distinct entity of its own. The combination of all of these courses is most probable, as in the case of the Balkans, with emerging issues of irredentisms and overlapping territories.

Ethnological accounts of multi-ethnic societies provide invaluable information about hot-spot areas that are about to explode or those that are about to form a new shared future cultural experience. With the end of the Cold War and the collapse—or transformation—of the two major alliances, the "periphery" has expanded so rapidly that time for gradual transition is simply unavailable. The avalanche of restructuring of the new "order" is far from over, and strategic models developed that are based on political realism can only work under a certain degree of complexity. Today, there are more players than ever, in number (e.g., more separatists' movements), methods (terrorism), objectives (religious, nationalistic, etc.) and potential fire power ("home-made" weapons of mass destruction). To leave the process of restructuring the new order in the hands of chaos is a dangerous policy whose consequences we are witnessing already. The dynamics of change in an ethnically diverse environment are based on cultural identities of several different and overlapping kinds; of these, the social sciences are only now developing some understanding. More information can help us facilitate the transitions of multi-ethnic systems to minimal cost in human and natural resources.

The effects of conflict on traditional societies have been studied. Rene Clignet has identified the effects of modes and production, of rules and descent, of the structure of matrimonial exchanges, and of modes of political integration. He also identified conditions that favor a potential integration of conflict, including the sharing of the same territory between ethnic (or tribal) groups that compete for resources; asymmetric interethnic marriages in which one group is "expanding" over the other; conditions under ethnic, residential, and occupational differentiation; the effect of social boundaries as such under certain circumstances. He indicated the role of time, given also its cultural dimension. Eventually, he called for the need for further understanding, for example, of conflict -"triggering" conditions. People give a variety of meanings to their ethnic identity. Anthony Smith classified the different theoretical approaches to ethnicity and nationalism. He described "primordialism" and "instrumentalism," and their variations, as the two basic doctrines of nationalism, namely, the former perceives ethnic ties as universal and ancient, and the latter perceives them as a tool—a means to an attached end. Another distinction is between the notion that nationalism has always existed and the belief that the modern nation is a relatively new phenomenon. According to Ernest Gellner it is only during the so-called modern era that conditions existed in which local cultural groups would join together in a mobile, nation state.

Eric Wolf, after reminding us of Boas' premise on the "plurality" of social patterns, introduced the issue of the ambiguity of the terms relating to culture, including ethnicity end ethnic groups. For methodological purposes, anthropologists may divide groups according to one or another "cultural," "racial," "gender," "ethnic," or other classification, but we should always bear in mind that such classifications can be exploited politically, one way or another, and the experience from such eventualities in the past has gravely marked our history.

Increasingly, cultural anthropological studies of violence take place in the context of violence and ongoing strife. Jeffrey Sluka's study of Divis Flats and Carolyn Nordstrom's recent work on "fieldwork under fire" exemplify this emerging generation of studies. This new context for anthropological work also calls forth new theoretical and moral dilemmas. As in considering issues of gender and conflict, work in settings of ongoing violent conflict calls upon anthropologists to accept new levels of political responsibility. Like everybody else, anthropologists are the products of cultures and nations and all the other social structures. They are accountable both to their discipline and to their own community. Lines can and must be drawn in order to protect both roles. However, the result is more than rewarding, for every study on human conflict may bring us one step closer to the level of understanding required to avoid unnecessary violence and human suffering.

Also See the Following Articles

ANTHROPOLOGY OF VIOLENCE AND CONFLICT, OVERVIEW • CLAN AND TRIBAL CONFLICT • ETHNIC CONFLICTS AND COOPERATION • GENDER STUDIES • PEACEFUL SOCIETIES • RITUAL AND SYMBOLIC BEHAVIOR • WARRIORS, ANTHROPOLOGY OF

Bibliography

Avruch, K., Black, P., & Scimecca, J. (Eds.). (1991). *Conflict resolution: Cross-cultural perspectives.* New York: Greenwood Press.

Barth, F. (Ed.). (1969). *Ethnic groups and boundaries. The social organization of culture differences.* Boston: Little Brown.

Caplan, P. (Ed.). (1995). *Understanding disputes. The politics of argument.* Oxford: Berg Publishers.

Chay, J. (Ed.). (1990). *Culture and international relations.* New York: Praeger Publishers.

Cohen, R. (1990). *Culture and conflict in Egyptian-Israeli relations: A dialogue of the deaf.* Bloomington: Indiana University Press.

d'Aquili, E., Laughlin, C. D., & McManus, J. (Eds.). (1979) *The spectrum of ritual.* New York: Columbia University Press.

Edgerton, B. R. (1992). *Sick societies: Challenging the myth of primitive harmony.* New York: The Free Press

Foster, M. L., & Rubinstein, R. A. (Eds.). (1986). *Peace and war: Cross-cultural perspectives.* New Brunswick, NJ: Transaction Books.

Ginsburg, F. D. (1989). *Contested lives. The abortion debate in an American community.* Berkeley: University of California Press.

Greenhouse, C. (1987). Cultural perspectives on war. *In* R. Vayrynen (Ed.), *The quest for peace*, pp. 32–47. London: Sage.

Hale, S. (1996). *Gender Politics in Sudan: Islamism, socialism, and the state.* Boulder, CO: Westview Press.

Kertzer, D. (1996). *Politics and symbols. The Italian Communist Party and the fall of communism.* New Haven, CT: Yale University Press.

Kochman, T. (1981). *Black and white styles in conflict.* Chicago, IL: University of Chicago Press.

Lane, S. D., & Rubinstein, R. A. (1996). Judging the other: Responding to traditional female genital surgeries. *Hastings Center Report, 26*(3):31–40.

Laughlin, C. D., & Brady, I. A. (Eds.). (1978). *Extinction and survival in human populations.* New York: Columbia University Press.

Manogaran, C. (1987). *Ethnic conflict and reconciliation in Sri Lanka.* Honolulu: University of Hawaii Press.

Nash, M. (1989). *The cauldron of ethnicity in the modern world.* Chicago, IL: University of Chicago Press.

Nordstrom, C., & Martin, J. (Eds.). (1992). *The paths to domination, resistance, and terror.* Berkeley, CA: University of California Press.

Ross, M. H. (1993). *The culture of conflict. Interpretations and interests in comparative perspective.* New Haven, CT: Yale University Press.

Rubinstein, R. A. (1988). Cultural analysis and international security. *Alternatives, 13*(4):529–542.

Rubinstein, R. A., & Foster, M. L. (Eds.). (1997). *The social dynamics of peace and conflict: Culture in international affairs.* Dubuque, IA: Kendall/Hunt Publishers.

Simons, A. (1995). *Networks of dissolution. Somalia undone.* Boulder, CO: Westveiw Press.

Smith, A. D. (1981). War and ethnicity: the role of warfare in the formation, self-images and cohesion of ethnic communities. *Ethnic and Racial Studies, 4*(4):375–393.

Turnbull, C. M. (1972). *The mountain people.* New York: Simon and Schuster.

Turner, V. (1969). *The ritual process.* Chicago: Aldine.

Wolf, E. R. (1994). Periolous ideas. Race, culture, people. *Current Anthropology, 35*(1):1–12.

Worlsey, P. (1984). *The three worlds: Culture and world development.* Chicago, IL: University of Chicago Press.

Cultural Studies, Overview

Philip Smith
University of Queensland

GLOSSARY

Deconstruction A technique used to demonstrate the instability of sign systems that foregrounds ambivalence and the constitutive role of language.

Discourse A term most associated with Michel Foucault, a discourse is a historically and culturally specific pattern of framing and describing things. According to Foucault, these positioned people in particular relations of power and knowledge.

Hegemony A term most associated with Antonio Gramsci and adopted by the "Birmingham School." Hegemonic cultural forms help to reproduce relations of domination, usually by combining and articulating elements of preexisting discourses in contingent and historically specific ways.

Hermeneutics A philosophical position arguing for the need to interpret human action as meaningful.

Modernism A broad intellectual movement emerging from the Enlightenment arguing for the power of reason, science, and universal, foundational principles in building the good society.

Postmodernism A broad intellectual movement reacting against modernist thought and embracing the local, contingent, irrational, and playful. In cultural studies this movement has been associated with the study of identity and difference and has been strongly influenced by poststructuralist theories of language.

Poststructuralism An intellectual movement emerging from structuralism in the 1960s that questioned some of the assumptions of structuralism about the coherence of sign systems and the status of "reason" and "truth." Poststructural perspectives often foreground the role of power in shaping discourses.

Semiotics The study of signs and sign systems, originating with Peirce and Saussure.

Simulacrum A term developed by Jean Baudrillard to describe situations in which representations and images structure reality, thus confusing boundaries between the real and its representation.

Structuralism An intellectual movement opposed to existentialism that explores the role of deep structures in generating social life.

CULTURAL STUDIES is a rapidly growing interdisciplinary field that has emerged out of the French structuralist tradition. Like the broader array of cultural and interpretative approaches in which it is situated, cultural studies argues for the importance of shared meanings, but specifies these in terms of a linguistic and textual model of culture. This article pays particular attention to the broad theoretical traditions informing contemporary research throughout the area, as opposed to middle level theories and empirical findings relating specific topic areas.

I. INTRODUCTION

In every known society, contemporary or historical, we can find implicit or explicit understandings that culture, in the form of belief, morale, custom or "civilization," plays a key role in social life. Notwithstanding this informal recognition, and the existence of very important intellectual antecedents, it is only over the last 20 or 30 years that the study of culture has become a really powerful force in contemporary academic and intellectual circles. This new-found importance has seen the rise of the area known as "cultural studies" and is reflected in the content of research journals, the syllabi of university courses, the output of publishing houses, and the composition of academic departments. It is helpful to differentiate "cultural studies" as a specific field of research from "cultural approaches" more generally. In a sense any approach that asserts that common meanings are important for social life can be thought of as cultural. However, cultural studies has developed a distinctive conception of culture that differs significantly from previous understandings. These earlier approaches have included:

- Seeing culture as an entire "way of life." This was the traditional view in archaeology and anthropology, which compared "civilizations," "tribes," or "cultures." In the violence, peace, and conflict area (hereafter VPC) such a conceptualization remains influential in "cross-cultural" analyses, such as those that attempt to correlate types of society with levels of militarism or propensity to aggression. From the perspective of cultural studies this approach is flawed as it does not analytically separate the cultural sphere of pure meanings from the social structure or from the routine practices of daily life.
- Describing culture in terms of prevalent values and norms. This was the predominant approach under the functionalist paradigm that dominated the social sciences until the 1960s. From the perspective of the cultural studies paradigm this approach lacks hermeneutic sensitivity, describing complex systems of meanings through broad analytic abstractions (e.g., "egalitarian value system," "culture of violence"). However, this understanding of culture remains influential for survey research programs and for social psychology. This is because concepts like values and attitudes lend themselves to operationalization and measurement at the level of the individual.
- Understanding culture as "high culture," which should be analyzed in terms of the moral values and ideals it endorses. This approach was predominant in the humanities, with critics like Arnold, Ruskin, and Leavis asserting that we should study great works in order to become more civilized. From the perspective of cultural studies, this approach is marred by elitist and moralizing tendencies that exclude popular culture and the mass media from analysis.
- Orthodox Marxist understandings of culture as a "dominant ideology." For a long time the major understanding in critical social thought, this perspective saw culture as the reflection and justification of the economic base. Contemporary scholars in the cultural studies area—even those influenced by Marx—argue against this kind of deterministic thinking which relegates culture to a supporting role in explaining social inequality.

By contrast to these perspectives, what is distinctive about cultural studies is an analytic focus on the form and content of culture that draws heavily on French structuralism and its legacy. This approach looks upon culture as being like a linguistic system or text that can be decoded in terms of its constituent signs, symbols, myths, narratives, language games, discourses, and codes. Such an understanding calls for cultural analysis as a form of hermeneutic activity, in which the analyst uncovers and redescribes core features of overarching systems of meaning. Central to this endeavor is a desire to assert the "relative autonomy of culture," that is to say, treating culture as an independent variable that should be understood neither as a simple reflection of hidden interests nor as a set of functionally determined values and norms. The process of analysis therefore involves decoding, interpreting, and reconstructing the cultural system before going on to trace the contingent ways that culture is articulated with concrete social practices and structures.

The rapid expansion of cultural studies throughout the arts, humanities, and social sciences has led, *inter alia*, to a body of innovative work exploring the role of culture in the generating violence, peace and conflict. It is worth noting, however, that the vast majority of this work comes from outside of the "peace studies" discipline as narrowly defined. This is not simply because departments of peace and conflict studies are a minnow in the academic pond. It is also because interest in culture within "peace studies" has failed to keep pace with shifts in other academic areas. Although a slow change has been under way for some years, the contents of the *Journal of Peace Studies* and successful peace-related research grant applications, for example, still manifest a continuing disciplinary emphasis on "hard" issues such as "strategic spheres" and "military technology" rather than so-called "soft" topics such as "images of the enemy" and "peace culture." In looking at the contribution of cultural studies to the examination of VPC, it is therefore necessary to have an interdisciplinary eye.

This is no bad thing, for cultural studies field itself can be described as a broad church characterized by diversity as much as resemblance. The predominant approaches to academic inquiry draw upon theoretical traditions as diverse as hermeneutics, semiotics, structuralism and poststructuralism, deconstruction, and narrative theory as well as participating in debates in broader discursive fields such as Marxism, feminism, interactionism and systems theory. Moreover, contributors can be found in academic disciplines right across the humanities and social sciences such as sociology, anthropology, linguistics, political science, history, English, and religious studies. This diversity has three important consequences worth noting here. First, it makes an interdisciplinary orientation more or less essential not just for understanding the area, but also for working in it. For this reason collaborative projects extending across traditional academic boundaries are probably the norm rather than the exception. Secondly, as debates internal to the field testify, it is potentially misleading to see cultural studies as a single coherent paradigm with common research agenda and a common core of knowledge. To the contrary, the cultural studies area is better seen as a loose affiliation of complex and overlapping theoretical orientations and empirical domains of inquiry. Finally, it makes summing up the field very difficult. Due to the fuzzy boundaries of the area, there is no easy way of drawing a line between cultural studies work and other related research issues. In this article, for example, I touch upon some areas on the boundary—such as the study of mass communications and the exploration of personality.

II. CULTURE AND CAUSALITY

Despite this diversity and fragmentation, cultural studies practitioners share a common set of presuppositions about the causes of social action, pointing to the role of collectively held and socially constructed meanings. It is this focus on publicly circulating social texts that are internalized and acted upon that provides the distinctive hallmark of cultural studies approaches and differentiates them from noninterpretative forms of inquiry on the one hand (e.g., network analysis), and from more individualistic interpretative inquiry into personal meanings (e.g., psychoanalysis, phenomenology) on the other.

Coming from the *geisteswissenshaft* tradition, cultural analysts are often reluctant to talk about in an explicit way about "causality," seeing this as the province of the natural sciences. However, cultural studies approaches usually have an implicit causal model in which culture (the ideal) makes a difference in real world (the material) via human action. We can identify two broad approaches to the question of how culture patterns action. Some cultural theorists, especially those adopting orthodox structuralist thinking, work with a deterministic understanding in which the individual is the pawn of cultural forces of which they might not even be aware. Others have drawn upon pragmatist philosophies and symbolic interactionist traditions to put forward a model of an active, creative, reflexive individual who understands the world, and acts in it, using a cultural tool kit.

In recent years this second model has become the more popular. It sees people responding to and making use of the meanings that come from the society around them. It is a model that downplays the role of conscious rational calculation on the one hand, and blind instincts and drives on the other in favor of an understanding of action as communicative and expressive. Proponents argue that the processes of evaluation and interpretation that are implicated in culture-driven action are underdetermined, thus opening up space for theorizing freedom and moral responsibility.

By linking culture and agency in this way, cultural theorists working in the VPC area have been able to engage in a powerful critique of alternative explanations of violence and conflict. The argument is not just that other theories ignore cultural variables of obvious empirical importance, but also that they are plagued by fatalistic and deterministic thinking that cannot bear any moral weight. Four lines of theory have been at the center of this critique. Sociobiology has been attacked for attributing inescapable genetic causes to behaviors (e.g., fighting) and sentiments (e.g., hatred) that can be better seen as the product of social conditioning. Closely related to this argument have been attacks on psychoanalytic and instinct theories, such as Freud's theory of the "death wish," which claim to detect deeply buried drives that are almost beyond conscious human control and social intervention. A third target for cultural studies has been the range of theories that see conflict as the product of rational choices. From the cultural perspective, the neorealism of Morganthau and its contemporary allies in areas such as game theory and rational choice theory, not only fails to recognize the role of emotion and the nonrational in generating VPC, but also restores agency and choice (and hence moral responsibility) in appearance and rhetoric only. When the logic of rational action is followed to its terminus, what are called rational "choices," "tactics," and "strategies" can be seen as determined by the distribution of resources, the structure of rewards and penalties, and by the rules of the game. The rational actor has no more freedom than a chess computer, which will always make the same move given the same position and the same computational algorithm. Hence, cultural theorists argue, the inner logic of a theory that attempts to restore agency via a presupposition of strategic rationality dooms it to failure. The final types of theory attacked by culturalists are those that point to social structural and institutional arrangements as driving conflict. These include neo-Marxist and world systems theories, grandiose evolutionary theories about stages of social development and theories that point to middle level phenomena such as institutional dynamics or the vested interests of elites in the military-industrial complex. In general these approaches have received more sympathetic treatment, as they understand the importance of arbitrary social arrangements in generating VPC. However, they have still been attacked for deterministic understandings of the causes of war and violence, and for underestimating the power of cultural forces that operate in a combinatorial way with social structures to shape outcomes. In explaining revolutions, for example, cultural theorists argue we have to look at the "subjective" beliefs and discourses held by revolutionaries as well as at "objective" structural factors such as the class system, the distribution of power, and the form of the state.

Within the peace studies area proper the most important call for this kind of multifactor analysis has been Johan Galtung's model of "cultural violence." By this he means "those aspects of culture, the symbolic sphere of our existence—exemplified by religion and ideology, language and art, empirical science and formal science—that can be used to justify or legitimize direct or structural violence" (1990, p. 291). In his analytical frame Galtung refuses to privilege direct violence, structural violence (injustice and social inequality), or cultural violence, arguing that they constitute a mutually reinforcing vicious circle. Most scholars in the cultural studies area would agree with Galtung's assertion that in looking at the interplay of culture and violence we have to take a wide-angle view. It is not sufficient to look at the role of culture in "violent" events per se (such as war or urban unrest) but rather it is necessary to explore the way that culture creates the preconditions for violence by promoting exclusion, suspicion, and hatred on a routine basis. From this perspective, general studies looking at the role of culture in generating boundaries, hierarchies, and definitions of groups (e.g., studies of racism, sexism, nationalism) are just as important as explorations of specific cultures of violence and peace (e.g., gun culture, the culture of violence as a solution, the philosophy of nonviolence).

While it is useful to think of the issue of cultural causality in terms of a binary distinction between material and ideal factors, it is important to note that a good deal of contemporary research in the cultural studies area has been dedicated to transcending this binary distinction. Scholars as diverse as the cultural historian William Sewell, Jr., the neo-Marxist literary critic Raymond Williams, and the postmodern philosopher Jean Baudrillard claim that we need creative new ways of thinking about how culture works and that to do this we need to drop 19th-century conceptual frameworks.

Thus far we have looked at the general characteristics of the cultural studies field and the sorts of arguments it makes. The remainder of this contribution turns toward an exegesis of the particular. Due the complexity of the field and its astonishing breadth of empirical reference, any attempt to scrutinize detail must inevitably cut corners. Here we look at the theoretical traditions that inform the work of contemporary practitioners rather than review the empirical literature. This inevitably entails looking at the work of scholars who had little to say about VPC directly, but who have subsequently informed the development of cultural studies both within and outside the peace studies area. It is, of course, possible to identify antecedents of modern cultural studies in the work of the Ancient Greeks and Enlightenment philosophers. In a sense all cultural explorations drink from the idealist stream that runs from Plato to Hegel. It is also possible to find more recent ancestors like Durkheim, Dilthey, Weber, Simmel, Husserl, Nietzche, and the young Marx. Yet the source of modern cultural studies can be most accurately located in the intellectual tradition that stretches from structuralism to postmodernism. It is this tradition that marks out cultural studies as a domain that is distinctive within the broader area of cultural inquiry. The review that follows begins by tracing this path before looking at a miscellany of other inputs into the field.

III. STRUCTURALISM

Structuralism remains the single most important influence on contemporary cultural studies. With the advent of structuralism in post-World War II France, a powerful tool kit came into place allowing for the more textual understanding of culture that predominates in cultural studies today. With this overarching paradigm culture and society came to be thought of as analogous to a text that could be decoded in terms of its constituent signs, symbols, codes, and myths. But it was not only in terms of theory that structuralism had a major impact. Because it was a broad intellectual movement as much as a body of theory and method, it permitted dialogue to be established between disciplines and specialisms, thus initiating the current interdisciplinary thrust that has become the norm in cultural studies.

When it emerged in the 1950s and 1960s French structuralism took two forms, both of them defining themselves against the individualism of existentialism. One was cultural, while the other constituted a form of structural Marxism associated with Louis Althusser and Nicos Poulantzas. Structural Marxism was for the most part an anticultural form of analysis concerned with politics and the economy. It is the cultural structuralist movement with which we are concerned here. In its initial stages the cultural structuralist position drew heavily upon earlier work in the field of linguistics, particularly the work of Ferdinand de Saussure. Saussure argued that *parole,* or speech was underpinned by *langue.* By *langue* Saussure meant a deep, more or less logical structure that could be explored systematically in terms of the processes through which signs were linked to concepts and opposed to one another in generating meanings. Importantly, Saussure stressed the arbitrary nature of the sign systems at work in language, pointing out that there was no necessary correspondence between an acoustic image and the concept it denoted. This provided the basis for the assertion that linguistic systems constituted a *sui generis* structure that could not be explained with reference to other levels of analysis. To this day this claim lies at the heart of arguments for the relative autonomy of cultural structures.

The work of Saussure and subsequent structural linguists, such as Roman Jakobson, was to exert a decisive influence on the French anthropologist Claude Levi-Strauss. His key works during the 1940s, 1950s, and 1960s explicated the deep structures at work in kinship systems, mythology, and ritual. Treating these institutions as being like language, Levi-Strauss argued that they could be interpreted as systems of signs arranged in patterns of binary opposition. According to Levi-Strauss, complex systems of meaning were built up from chains of simple contrasts, and the role of the analyst was to reconstruct these elementary grammars from the seemingly chaotic materials available to empirical observation. Levi-Strauss has been criticized on a number of fronts, the more important being that his methodology is unclear, his findings are too abstract, and that he ignores the actor's point of view in favor of reconstructing patterns of abstracted meaning that bear the imprint of a transcendental collective mind. Notwithstanding these, it is difficult to underestimate the impact of Levi-Strauss on contemporary cultural studies. His pioneering works changed the way that people thought about culture by bringing forth ideas about codes and coding, signs, and myth to the center of analysis as well as more general understandings about culture working like language.

Saussure was also to influence Roland Barthes, who combined semiotics with a neo-Marxist brand of literary criticism, and Jacques Lacan, who combined Freud with semiotic linguistics in ingenious and complex ways. Central to Lacan's work was the exploration of the ways that the self was constructed in and through language and symbolism. For Lacan the unconscious could be treated like a language with processes of metaphor and signification governing fundamental psychic processes such as denial, counter-transference, and sublimation. This model provided the basis for a re-reading of psychoanalysis in terms of literary and semiotic discourses rather than those of medicine. Although of great importance in the area of psychoanalysis, Lacan's work has also exerted a decisive influence in the area of literary criticism and has recently filtered through to cultural studies more generally. This is especially true for research on gender and culture that has developed from readings of French feminist theorists such as Irigary and Cixous, with researchers looking at the symbolic and textual ways in which women are positioned in relation to men.

Probably the most influential work by Roland Barthes in terms of its subsequent impact on the cultural studies area is his work on popular culture. In a series of magazine articles subsequently collected as *Mythologies,* Barthes drew upon both Saussure and Marx in exploring the world of signs encapsulated in advertising images and everyday objects. Through these studies Barthes argued that we have to distinguish denotation from connotation. Denotation refers to the manifest meaning of a sign or image, while connotation refers to the deeper (usually ideological) meanings that are also at work in the process of signification. For Barthes these connotations provided a subtle means of reinforcing bourgeois definitions of the world, while excluding alternative definitions that might encompass harsher realities such as colonialism and injustice. Just as important as this theoretical contribution is the fact that Barthes' work made a number of resources legitimate for cultural inquiry. While Levi-Strauss and Lacan worked with esoteric ethnographic, theoretical, and clinical materials, Barthes pointed to the centrality of the middle-brow mass media and popular culture as myth making engines for the contemporary world. Today these remain key research focii in the cultural studies area.

IV. POSTSTRUCTURALISM

There is a good deal of argument about where to draw the boundaries between structuralism and the post-structuralism, deconstruction, and postmodernism that arose in the late 1960s. Usually the resolution of these issues depends on the definitions brought into play. In general, structuralism was underpinned by a modernist sensibility that believed in the scientific nature of structuralist inquiry and the coherence of sign systems. In contrast, the later theoretical movements emphasized the inconsistency, openness, or absence of meaning, pointing to the role of the reader, and questioning the ability of academic inquiry to determine truth. These trends are suggested in the later studies of Barthes, but were given their most significant treatment in the work of Michel Foucault and Jacques Derrida.

Michel Foucault stands across the disciplinary boundaries of sociology, history, and philosophy. His historical studies rejected both Marxist class analysis and causal argument, arguing that the truth was an elusive—even dangerous—concept. Instead, his archaeological and genealogical methods sought to trace the ways that power and knowledge were intertwined in local and contextual ways in the construction of human subjects. His studies of asylums, hospitals, and prisons emphasized processes of surveillance and control that accompanied the growth of the modern human sciences and their associated "discourses." According to Foucault, these discourses marked out particular ways of defining and thinking about issues. They both opened and foreclosed certain intellectual and practical possibilities but always linked people in definite relations of power.

Foucault has been criticized on a number of fronts, most notably for the obscure nature of some of his concepts and, like many structuralist, for failing to incorporate an understanding of agency and resistance to power in his theoretical and empirical works. However, his influence on cultural studies has been enormous. In the wake of Foucault it has become standard practice to map out "discourses," trace their links to power and interests, and to discuss their implications whether or not one is a Foucauldian. But aside from the general tool of discourse, Foucault brought a number of other resources and conceptual spectacles to cultural studies. Contemporary thinking in the VPC area about surveillance, the body, punishment, the gaze, classification, repressive institutions, the construction of subjectivity, and the links between power and knowledge has all been decisively influenced by his work.

Derrida, like Foucault, refuses easy classification—he has been described as the last structuralist and as the first poststructuralist and his work has been seen as both philosophy and literary criticism. Building on and confounding earlier structuralist work, Derrida argued that meaning was always unstable and deferred. The meaning of a sign depended on an absent context that had to be supplied by the reader. There is always a multiplicity of possible contexts and hence a surfeit of meanings within any text. Derrida demonstrated the elusive nature of meanings through close reading of canonical texts, pointing to contradictions, ambiguities, or silences or showing that multiple readings can be made of the same passages. Although Derrida's work has been highly controversial, it has grown in influence in recent years. In areas like queer theory and postcolonial studies, especially, his ideas about reading have been adopted as a subversive strategy through which dominant discourses are problematized and alternative visions retrieved.

Derrida's ideas about difference have also been highly influential. Although the concept of difference originated as a technical tool of the deconstructive method, it has since been converted into both a normative goal and a descriptor of the good society.

A major theme in critical poststructural work looks at the forms of cultural violence through which difference is eroded or denied, or artificially coded by dominant discourses. Here Derridean ideas of difference have often been combined with ideas about the "Other" derived from earlier scholars such as Lacan and Levinas, especially in the area known as postcolonial studies. The basic point is that the search for social identity is inherently relational. Defining who or what one is necessarily involves defining models of what one is not.

In the postcolonial area, scholars assert that imperialism and conquest were made possible by discourses that marked out colonized people as different, as the "Other." Such discourses provided a charter for colonialism by asserting the superiority of the colonizing nations or by denying indigenous peoples full human status. An influential and representative text in this regard has been literary critic Edward Said's *Orientalism.* Said's thesis is that the "Orient" was positioned as the antithesis of the West. It was the realm of sexuality, mystery, disorder, and the irrational, while the West understood itself as embodying science, order, and reason. According to Said this false binarism legitimated colonialism by permitting paternalistic discourses to move into place. Aside from studying the exclusionary practices that have legitimated violent conquest and political and economic domination, scholars of difference have attempted to retrieve the experiences of marginalised "others." Elise Boulding's *The Underside of History*, for example, traces women's reality over the centuries.

Like Derrida and Foucault, Pierre Bourdieu is another profoundly influential French scholar who can be rather uncomfortably described as poststructural. The label is appropriate in as far as Bourdieu draws upon, and moves beyond, both structural Marxism and cultural structuralism. The major interest in Bourdieu's diverse ouevre is the way that culture operates to reinforce social domination. Bourdieu used the term "symbolic violence" to describe the processes through which inequalities in power are both obscured and reproduced through the cultural system. Drawing on his empirical research in North Africa and France, and on the theoretical traditions of Marxism, semiotics, and pragmatism, Bourdieu developed the concepts of "habitus" and "cultural capital" to explain symbolic violence. Habitus refers to internalized phenomenological and pragmatic dispositions influencing human actions and expectations. It is derived in part from cultural schemas and in part from the adjustments that individuals make to their objective life circumstances. Bourdieu emphasizes the conservative role of habitus, with dispositions matching social locations in a way that limits possibilities for fundamental reflexivity or social change. Cultural capital is a resource that individuals accumulate through the life course and consists of both formal educational credentials and informal knowledge of high culture with associated taste preferences. Bourdieu argues that in developed society cultural capital is strongly correlated with social class and that it operates as a barrier to upward social mobility. Thanks to various gatekeeping mechanisms, individuals and groups without power are denied access to networks of authority because they are unable to display or mobilize valued forms of cultural capital. Bourdieu's theories of have been criticized as being unable to explain the role of culture in bringing about either innovation or fundamental social change. Nevertheless they have inspired a vast literature that explores the role of cultural capital and symbolic codes in reproducing systems of inequality and stratification.

V. POSTMODERNISM

Talking about "postmodernism" is problematic as it is generally accepted that there is no such thing as postmodernism, but only postmodernisms existing in complex relationships with each other. Notwithstanding these differences "postmodern" perspectives can be broadly seen as a continuation of the line of development initiated by Foucault and Derrida. Typically they emphasize the elusive nature of truth, the links between power, knowledge, reason, and repression, the fragmentary, incomplete and self-referential nature of sign systems, and the failure of science and modernity. Postmodernism also has a normative dimension, seeking to validate the local, hybrid, and contingent, to break down exclusionary boundaries, and to open up spaces for difference, desire, self-expression, ambivalence, and play. The close and explicit interplay of analytic and normative claims makes a good deal of postmodern work challenging reading for those more comfortable working in the modernist paradigm. This tendency to collapse levels of analysis is often accompanied by playful literary devices such as parody, self-contradiction, and ambivalence. Although sometimes frustrating to the reader, these are intended to draw attention to the constitutive (as opposed to representational) nature of language, thus avoiding the perceived pitfalls of binary, logocentric thought.

As a social scientific concept postmodernism got airborne with Jean-Francois Lyotard's *The Postmodern Condition.* Lyotard's central contention was that the grand narratives of progress such as Marxism and science were defunct—an argument that led to lively debate with modernists like Jurgen Habermas. Lyotard had comparatively little to say, however, about the characteristics of postmodern culture. The seminal author in this regard has been Jean Baudrillard. In a series of innovative essays Baudrillard explored the role of signs in the modern world. His central thesis is that the distinction between sign and reality has been confused due to the all-pervasive nature of cultural forces in modern life. This thesis allowed Baudrillard to dispense with traditional distinctions between reality and its representation or between sign value and use value. Playing a central role in Baudrillard's schema was the idea of the simulacrum, a copy of a model or plan that is so perfect it becomes reality itself. In urban studies this idea has been applied to planned communities and shopping malls, while in media studies it has been applied to media events, where it is the volume of media coverage itself that makes the event. The net effect of this position has been to collapse the usual distinction between culture and social structure that is made in cultural studies, pointing to the depth with which culture has penetrated the "real world."

Postmodern and poststructural theories influenced by Derrida and Baudrillard have been attacked by modernists as morally bankrupt by virtue of relativism. For the postmodernist, "truth" and "reality" are fictions that can never be accessed or determined without the intervention of language or bias. Instead postmodernists propose a consensus model, in which truth and reality are nothing more than arbitrary, historically and socially specific beliefs that are held by certain groups at certain times. Modernist critics argue that this leaves us unable to adjudicate between competing worldviews, engage in a moral critique of pain and suffering, or decry bias and falsehood in representations of the world. Scholars such as the Marxist literary critic Fredric Jameson have also attacked postmodern aesthetic forms, arguing that their playful and fragmented nature does not allow critical thinking. Postmodernists retort that what is needed is creative as much as critical thinking in which we envisage new language games to open up the political. They also point in turn to the role of modernist foundational principles in generating repression and intolerance thanks to binarisms that are unable to accommodate ambivalence and difference.

Whatever the merits of these sorts of arguments, understandings drawing upon the debates between postmodernism and its critics have grown in importance in the study of VPC. Even when scholars reject postmodern theory, they have often conceded that the empirical world increasingly exhibits the perplexing qualities described by people such as Baudrillard. An event of particular importance for this rise to authority and plausibility in the study of VPC was the 1991 Gulf War. Cultural studies analyses of the Gulf War pointed to a simulacrum effect in which the war was both conducted and run as if it were a gigantic video game full of technological wizardry and special effects but without reference to concrete human suffering. It has been argued that video game qualities did not permit a coherent narrative of the war to emerge, but rather replaced reason with empty spectacle. Scholars have also pointed to the crucial role of the media, and especially the Cable News Network (CNN), in defining and shaping the war, with political and military leaders drawing upon the media for information about what was "really" happening and then adjusting their policies accordingly. In this simulacrum distinctions between what the media was reporting and what it was constructing were blurred.

The path from structuralism to postmodernism provides the backbone of contemporary cultural studies and explain the centrality of semiotics and discourse analysis to the examination of meaning. Yet they do not make up the whole story. In addition there is a raft of other influences and debates that are at play in the field, but that do not form a direct part of the French tradition. These have interacted with the legacy of structuralism and each other in complex ways to create the contemporary cultural studies field.

VI. WESTERN MARXISM AND BRITISH CULTURAL STUDIES

During the 20th century Marxism has been wrestling with the uncomfortable legacy of economic determinism. What is known as the "Western Marxist" tradition has attempted to introduce a more cultural form of Marxist analysis by drawing upon and elaborating ideas about alienation and ideology. For the purposes of contemporary cultural studies probably the most significant recent contribution has come from the British cultural studies movement. This originated with the Birmingham Centre for Contemporary Cultural Studies (CCCS) in the 1970s. Spearheaded by Stuart Hall, the "Birmingham School" drew heavily upon the work of Antonio Gramsci. Gramsci's key concept of hegemony emphasizes the role of consciousness in maintaining ruling class domination by short-circuiting critical thinking and by defining reality in particular ways. Drawing upon Gramsci's idea of a war of position, Hall argued that it is vacuous to speak of a single dominant ideology (e.g., "capitalism") but rather we have to look at the contingent discourses and struggles through which a plurality of hegemonic discourses are reproduced and challenged. With this credo in mind, the members of the CCCS undertook a variety of empirical studies, many of them ethnographic, charting hegemonic and counter-hegemonic discourses in areas such as racism and immigration, strikes and industrial conflict, law and order politics, and youth subcultures.

Typically these empirical investigations combined Gramsci with other, French Marxist, influences such as Althusser, Barthes, and De Certeau. The common substantive theme, however, was the way that a politics of repression could be legitimated.

In recent years the Birmingham project has diversified both theoretically and institutionally. In terms of theory, Marxist influences have been left behind and there has been an increasing turn toward poststructuralism and postmodernism. In addition theoretical and topical inputs have come from areas such as feminism, queer theory, and postcolonial studies. This is reflected, for example, in Hall's recent work, which is more concerned with identity, hybridity, and multiculturalism than with class and capitalism. Theoretical differentiation has been complemented by institutional differentiation. Although the CCCS was always interdisciplinary in orientation, its power base lay within the discipline of sociology. Today its Marxism—inflected brand of cultural studies has expanded to the extent that the majority of practitioners are in other academic areas such as women's studies, peace studies, literary studies, art history, and communications. Moreover, its influence has become more global, having had a significant impact on academic life outside of the United Kingdom, especially in the United States and Australia. Consequently the sobriquet "British" or "Birmingham" cultural studies is rather problematic as a descriptor of an international intellectual tradition.

What is still known as the "British" cultural studies model has been criticized for making relentlessly political interpretations of the phenomena it investigates, labeling behaviors and texts as manifestations of "hegemony" or "resistance" but without reference to the actor's or author's point of view. However, it is this ability to read the political in the mundane that, along with theoretical eclecticism, has enabled British cultural studies to become the most important interdisciplinary field for the critical study of culture. This especially true for the PVC area, with significant analyses being made of phenomena like Thatcherism and the Falklands/Malvinas War, the Gulf War, domestic violence, racism, and masculinity.

VII. RHETORICAL AND LINGUISTIC STUDIES

Under rhetorical studies we can position a vast repertoire of literature that explores the role of imagery, narrative, and metaphor in social life. What unites this body of work is a belief that the way that things are described, labeled, and classified has an impact on the way that people respond to them. Although there has been a significant input from French structuralism, major influences here have also come from the Anglo-American philosophical tradition, and there has been a greater emphasis on the surface levels of language as opposed to the exegesis of deeply hidden structures. An important early figure was Kenneth Burke, whose works such as *A Grammar of Motives* pointed to the moral and practical consequences of language, metaphor, and literary genres in framing issues. Burke's work has exerted a subtle influence on figures as diverse as George Lakoff, Clifford Geertz, and Hayden White. Another important input comes from the ordinary language philosophy of Wittgenstein and Searl, which prefigured poststructuralism in arguing that language has a constitutive role in shaping social relations, rather than being simply a neutral medium of communication that reflects reality. More recently this sort of position has been reinforced by postmodernists such as Richard Rorty, who draw upon Derrida and see language as creating the social world rather than reporting on it. In formulating his position Rorty has built upon the work of John Dewey, a figure in the American pragmatist tradition who also influenced various theories of the micro-order such as symbolic interactionism, ethnomethodology, and more recently conversation analysis. These have focused their efforts on the "definition of the situation" and, among other things, the ways that actors frame, use, and sustain these definitions through language and interaction. More recently, studies in the rhetorical tradition have turned toward narrative as a key resource. Narratives can be thought of as the stories that people construct to make sense of the world. They assign identities to protagonists and generate sentiments of solidarity or hatred. Figures influencing the turn toward narrative modalities of rhetorical analysis include the French advocate of hermeneutics, Paul Ricoeur, and literary critics such as Northrop Frye and Mikail Bakhtin. It is possible to provide here only a suggestive outline of the kinds of findings relevant to VPC that are made in this vast field by pointing to a sample of work.

- Interactionists pointed to the ways that such morally loaded definitions such as "mentally ill" and "drug user" justify policies of repression and exclusion against those marginal in society.
- Studies of the Gulf War looked at the role of metaphor and analogy in justifying violence. It has been argued that the rhetorical imagery and narrative construction of Saddam Hussein as a madman and

"another Hitler" made war seem justifiable and inevitable, while imagery of war as a video game helped to obscure suffering.

- Explorations of media racism have repeatedly shown that minority groups are associated with negative images and social problems such as violence, riots, drugs, and crime rather than positive images of achievement.
- Research on nuclear issues has pointed to the centrality of rhetorical struggles to define the technology as safe and clean in the process of legitimation.
- Studies by feminists on issues such as rape have pointed to ways that (female) victims are often framed as complicit in the act, or to the ways that grammatical and narratives constructions serve to exscript (male) agency from the crime.
- Research on images of the enemy in war has documented the presence of degrading and dehumanizing metaphors, sometimes depicting the adversary through animal imagery.

VIII. DURKHEIMIAN AND RELIGIOUS STUDIES

The French sociologist Emile Durkheim wrote little himself about conflict and he is usually associated with "consensus theory." However, key ideas in his oeuvre have provided the inspiration for a number of studies that look at violence and exclusion. In his work on sanctions, Durkheim argued that the identification and punishment of deviance was good for society as it enabled moral values to be reaffirmed. In his later work he studied the role of religion. He claimed that ritual activity and distinctions between the sacred and the profane were essential for social life, providing the basis for social integration by generating solidaristic sentiments. These principles have been drawn upon by scholars in pointing to the role of ritual, religion and the symbolic in framing and generating violence. During the 1950s and 1960s a number of works came out drawing on this point of view, and applying it to violence and conflict within the confines of the functionalist paradigm. Anthropologist Max Gluckman, for example, explored how ritualized protest had a cathartic effect by providing a channel through which social tensions could be expressed. Kai Erikson's *Wayward Puritans* looked at "crime waves" in 17th-century Massachusetts. Erikson argued that minority groups were victimized during moments of crisis. These persecutions occurred when the identity and sense of mission characterizing Puritan settlement had come into doubt. According to Erikson the community was able to reaffirm its values by identifying and punishing deviants. Stanley Cohen's exploration of "moral panics" in Britain made much the same point, although it moved away from functionalism toward a more institutional mode of analysis. Cohen showed how minor public order disturbances involving British bikers were inflated in a quasi-ritualistic way by the police, courts, and media to become a cause of major public concern, with the bikers stereotyped as a profane "folk devil."

These earlier works paved the way for a recent explosion of studies of violence, conflict, and symbolic boundaries in the Durkheimian tradition. These have built on the natural affinity between Durkheim's ideas about the symbolic qualities of good and evil and structuralist theories of semiotics. Many of these more recent studies have drawn upon significant theoretical elaborations in the Durkheimian paradigm, most notably Mary Douglas's work on purity and pollution and Victor Turner's work on ritual and liminality. But other influences have come from outside Durkheim's direct intellectual lineage. By picking from the smorgasbord of perspectives available in contemporary cultural studies—especially semiotics, narrative, and rhetorical analysis—scholars have attempted to discover in finer detail the cultural processes through which images of the sacred are constructed and violence directed toward the profane. It is also worth observing that over recent years the functionalist premises of Durkheim's original theory have been generally rejected, leaving only a residue of cultural theory that can be used to study process rather than system. For this reason contemporary Durkheimians place much greater emphasis on agency, power, and historical contingency in exploring the role of symbols and rituals in social life in general, and VPC in particular. Much of this work has involved tracing the links between social solidarity and violence. Gangs, ethnicity, and nationalism, for example, have been understood in terms of a search for collective identity working through the dynamics of social inclusion and exclusion.

There has been a parallel theoretical movement in the humanities. Rene Girard's *Violence and the Sacred,* for example, explored the role of the scapegoat and sacrifice as foundational moments of violence in Western society. Ideas from the comparative study of folklore and mythology also share common ground with the Durkheimian paradigm, especially those looking at sacred and profane figures like the hero and the Devil or at the role of apocalyptic and millenial narratives in legitimating war. Richard Slotkin's *Regeneration*

Through Violence is one of the most sustained analyses in this genre. Slotkin's essential argument is that the frontier mythology of the United States has exerted a decisive influence on the nation's development and politics. Central to this mythology has been a symbolic association of violence with purification that has seen outsiders such as Native Americans persecuted in the belief that this will generate moral renewal in the community.

IX. CULTURE AND SOCIAL PSYCHOLOGY

While the majority of cultural studies work is concerned with decoding and interpreting the world of meanings in and of itself, there is an important area of overlap with social psychology. After all, it is people acting in response to meanings who enable the nonmaterial realm of cultural structures to have an impact on the material world. It is therefore a logical step to look at the ways that culture makes a difference to people's thoughts and actions. Work in the area of social psychology is often quantitative, and pays more attention to mapping the social distribution of particular values and worldviews (e.g., racism, militarism, the culture of violence as a solution) than in exploring the symbolic processes through which they are constituted.

More directly associated with cultural studies are works that look at the links between culture and personality traits. Early studies in this field set the stage for future research by demonstrating that violent behavior by individuals could be seen as a response to social conditioning. In the field of anthropology, for example, Ruth Benedict and Margaret Mead pointed to the role of upbringing and socialisation in determining the way of life of particular peoples and their dispositions. According to Benedict, the individual was a *tabula rasa* onto which society left a decisive imprint. Another influential and representative contribution to the field was Theodore Adorno's work on the *Authoritarian Personality*. In this book Adorno and his associates attempted to discover the characteristics of people who had submitted to fascist authority. The study pointed not only to family background, but also to the social and cultural characteristics of post-World War I Germany as important factors in shaping the personality of potential fascists. To this day these studies remain an important starting point in that they provide a vigorous argument against biological determinist positions that see the desire for conflict as the inevitable product of human nature or genetic programming.

The most important contemporary legacy of this approach can be seen in the growing area of cross-cultural research on the social and semiotic construction of masculinity. Authors in this field typically note that most violence is conducted by men, but reject essentialist notions of male and female traits. Instead they see the masculinities and femininities that are internalized by people as the products of everyday life and mass culture. Scholars in the area draw upon semiotic and ethnographic forms of analysis to argue that dominant forms of masculinity are strongly underpinned by notions of strength, violence, and power, which encourage militarism, misogyny, and other sociopathic attitudes while devaluing the contributions of women. These are reinforced through the semiotic practices of popular domains like sport and the cinema, where male icons exhibit muscular bodies and the ability to inflict pain. They are also reproduced in everyday life, where ethical codes concerning shame, revenge, and honor are linked to violence and to particular gendered roles, such as can be found in the culture of machismo.

X. MASS COMMUNICATIONS

Although most work in the cultural studies area is concerned with decoding texts and exploring their content, another important line of inquiry has looked at the institutional means through which messages are produced and the ways that they are received by people. Although some attention has been paid to other institutions of socialization such as peer culture, schools, the church, and the family, cultural studies scholars usually agree that in the contemporary world it is the mass media that plays the most important role in this process. They disagree, however, on the extent to which the media is free, autonomous, and critical, and on the relative power of the media and the audience.

It was the rise of Nazi Germany and the emergence of nonprint-based forms of communication (radio, cinema) in the early 20th century that provided the stimulus for intense thinking about the role of the media. Observers were struck by the vitriolic and highly symbolized qualities of Nazi propaganda, the quasi-religious dimensions of Nazi ritual, and the centrality of the Ministry of Propaganda to Nazi political strategy. They could also hardly fail to notice the dramatic rise in popularity of the National Socialist Party and, looking at newsreel footage, the wild enthusiasm of party members attending political rallies. The mass society hypothesis arose as a way of explaining this phenomenon. This argued that with industrialization and the erosion of traditional forms of community people had become highly suggestible to means of mass persuasion. The mass society hypothesis saw messages being implanted in an unmediated way. This is sometimes known as the hypodermic model of media effects, with messages being "injected" into the populace.

This model of a powerful mass media has since been criticized on numerous fronts. Early postwar research suggested that "opinion leaders" in the home and workplace interpreted media messages—such as electoral campaign broadcasts—for others. More recently arguments about identity and social characteristics have come to the fore, with comparative ethnographic studies suggesting that people read media texts differently according to their attributes such as ethnicity, gender, age, nationality, and education. Attempts to revive theories of a powerful mass media have focused on the issue of agenda setting. According to one point of view, advocated by Noam Chomsky, for example, the media sets agendas rather than transmits opinions. It tells people what to think about rather than what to think. In a similar vein, Stuart Hall has argued that in looking at the media, we have to study not only how events are framed (as is traditional in rhetorical studies, for example), but also what is left outside the frame. This perspective has been enormously influential in the VPC field. Scholars in the peace studies area have often argued that nonviolent alternatives to war are given inadequate treatment before and during periods of international conflict, while military tactics and technology are discussed at great length. An implication is that the theme of a peaceful solution does not arise as a discursive possibility within public opinion. Feminist scholars have also made use of this approach, showing that masculinity is exscripted from media discussions of phenomena such as rape and war, even though these events are overwhelmingly undertaken by men.

Yet the mechanisms through which the media formulates issues and frames events are unclear. Research has pointed to a number of factors, including the role of government censorship and information control, the values and interests of journalists, editors, and media owners, the practicalities of producing the news day after day, and the culture and preferences of the audience. It is the first of these factors that has come under the most scrutiny in VPC studies, with particularly intense research interest in the ways that governments regulate and control information in times of war. Research suggests that this has changed over recent years—at least in the United States. During the Vietnam War a policy of information freedom was in force. Military leaders believed—rightly or wrongly, but probably wrongly—that this was responsible for undermining public support for the war. As a result during the 1980s media secrecy and intensive regulation surrounded events such as the Anglo-Argentine Falklands/Malvinas War of 1982, and the U.S. invasion of Grenada. During the 1990s a more pro-active stance has been adopted. Cultural studies researchers looking at the Gulf War have pointed to the role of the military in shooting a barrage of vacuous and misleading material at the media via video bites and charismatic press conferences while at the same time allowing little of negative consequence to be released.

XI. NONVIOLENT ALTERNATIVES

When it comes to suggesting nonviolent alternatives there is inevitably disagreement between scholars in a multiparadigm field such as cultural studies. However it is possible to find common ground at a general level. Just as they place meaning at the center of analysis of violence and conflict, cultural studies perspectives inevitably place meaning at the center in working for peace. Proponents of other paradigms, whether arguing from the left or the right, argue the need for economic, social, and political changes to bring about peace. Ideas about the need for a "balance of power," "social justice," "democracy," or the "end of colonialism" typify this line of argument. Similarly received wisdom in the conflict mediation area points to the centrality of institutional and procedural solutions to conflict but is often unable, or unwilling, to talk about the substantive values, ideals, or symbols that might contribute to the process. While by no means deriding these kinds of solutions as irrelevant, culturalists assert that we also need to change the cultural codes and imagery through which people understand one another, thereby encouraging dialogue, solidarity, and intersubjectivity. A common concept used in thinking about these alternatives is that of building a "peace culture." Discussions of peace culture can take a number of forms from the secular and pragmatic to the mystical and quasi-religious. Formulations of the latter kind often draw heavily on the work of Mahatma Ghandi, who asserted that the process of building peace was akin to a spiritual quest. Given such variability it is little surprise that a number of themes have been advocated for building peace culture, such as:

- Transcending the dualistic forms of discourse and binary codings, which create polarized, stereotypical understandings of "us and them" and leave little room for ambivalence or difference.

- Placing higher cultural value on peace, coexistence, and compromise, as opposed to war, domination and militarism.
- Retrieving subjugated knowledges and ways of life that can serve as models for a peace culture, such as those attributed to women and indigenous peoples.
- Replacing violent, sexist, and racist language and imagery with nongendered, nonracist, nonviolent alternatives.
- Encouraging human spiritual growth and self-knowledge.
- Facilitating an awareness of the connectedness of the glove and the common bonds between people with each other and the environment.

Although placing their primary emphasis on cultural change per se, scholars in the cultural studies area realize that culture does not exist in a vacuum. Therefore discussions on building a peace culture often include arguments for structural reforms to support these cultural changes. These include:

- Rethinking traditional institutions of socialization, such as schools and the family and especially their relationship to masculinity.
- Opening up the public sphere, and especially the mass media, to excluded voices.
- Changing journalistic values to encourage the reporting of peace perspectives.
- Building democracy, social justice, and human rights as a platform for equal civic participation.
- Assisting the development of grass roots organizations that can build both local communities and transnational solidarities.

What is important about these sorts of suggestions is that they see peace as something that has to be worked toward and actively maintained rather than just the absence of overt violent conflict. To date scholarship has been focused on the analysis of culture and violence rather than culture and peace. A major challenge for cultural studies in the future is to map out the contours of the cultural and institutional forms that can promote peaceful coexistence as well as dissecting the myths and codes that promote inequality, division, and violence.

Also See the Following Articles

COMMUNICATION STUDIES, OVERVIEW • ENEMY, CONCEPT AND IDENTITY OF • GENDER STUDIES • MASS MEDIA, GENERAL VIEW • PEACE STUDIES, OVERVIEW • RITUAL AND SYMBOLIC BEHAVIOR • STRUCTURAL VIOLENCE • WOMEN, VIOLENCE AGAINST

Bibliography

Adorno, T., *et al.* (1950). *The authoritarian personality*. New York: Harper.

Althusser, L. (1971). *Lenin and philosophy*. London: New Left Books.

Arnold, M. (1960). *Culture and anarchy*. Cambridge: Cambridge University Press.

Bakhtin, M. (1981). *The dialogic imagination*. Austin: University of Texas Press.

Barthes, R. (1970). *Mythologies*. Paris: Editions du Seuil.

Baudrillard, J. (1989). *Selected writings*. Stanford: Stanford University Press.

Baumann, Z. (1991). *Modernity and ambivalence*. Ithaca: Cornell University Press.

Becker, H. (1963). *Outsiders*. New York: Free Press.

Benedict, R. (1937). *Patterns of culture*. Boston: Houghton Mifflin.

Boulding, E. (1987). Learning peace. In R. Vayrynen, D. Senghaas, & C. Schmidt (Eds.), *The Quest for Peace*, pp. 317–329. Beverly Hills, CA: International Social Science Council, Sage.

Boulding, E. (1988). Warriors and saints. In E. Isakkson (Ed.) *Women and militarism*. London: Harvester Wheatsheaf.

Boulding, E. (1992). *The underside of history*. Beverly Hills: Sage.

Bourdieu, P. (1977). *Outline of a theory of practice*. Cambridge: Cambridge University Press.

Bourdieu, P. (1984). *Distinction*. Cambridge, MA: Harvard University Press.

Burke, K. (1969). *A Grammar of Motives*. Berkeley: University of California Press.

Cixous, H. (1978). Castration or decapitation. *Signs*, 7(1), 41–55.

Cohen, S. (1980). *Folk Devils and moral panics*. Oxford: M. Robertson.

Derrida, J. (1976). *Of grammatology*. Baltimore: Johns Hopkins University Press.

Derrida, J. (1978). *Writing and difference*. London: Routledge and Kegan Paul.

Douglas, M. (1969). *Purity and danger*. London: Weidenfeld and Nicholson.

Erikson, K. (1966). *Wayward Puritans*. New York: Macmillan.

Foucault, M. (1972). *The archaeology of knowledge*. New York: Harper and Row.

Foucault, M. (1979). *Discipline and punish*. New York: Pantheon.

Frye, N. (1956). *Anatomy of criticism*. Princeton NJ: Princeton University Press.

Galtung, J. (1990). Cultural violence. *Journal of Peace Research*, 27(3), 291–305.

Gamson, W. (1988). Political discourse and collective action. *International Social Movement Research, 1*, 219–244.

Gates, H.L. (1995). *Colored people*. Harmondsworth: Penguin.

Girard, R. (1977). *Violence and the sacred*. Baltimore: Johns Hopkins University Press.

Greenhouse, C.J. (1987). Cultural perspectives on war. pp. 32–47 In R. Vayrynen, D. Senghass, & C. Schmidt (Eds.), *The quest for peace*, pp. 32–47. International Social Science Council. Beverly Hills: Sage.

Grossberg, L., Nelson, C. Treichler, P. (Eds.). (1992). *Cultural studies*. Urbana-Champaign: University of Illinois Press.

Howell, S., & Willis, R. (1989). *Societies at peace*. New York: Routledge.

Irigary, L. (1985). *The sex which is not one*. Ithaca: Cornell University Press.

Iyengar, S., & Kinder, D. (1987). *News that matters.* Chicago: University of Chicago Press.
Jameson, F. (1993). *Postmodernism.* Durham, NC: Duke University Press.
Lacan, J. (1979). *The Four Fundamental Concepts of Psychoanalysis.* London: Penguin.
Levi-Strauss, C. (1964). *Mythologiques.* Paris: Plon.
Lyotard, F. (1984). *The Postmodern Condition.* Minneapolis: University of Minnesota Press.
McQuail, D. (1985). Sociology of Mass Communications. *Annual Review of Sociology* 11:93–111.
Morganthau, H. (1985) *Politics Among Nations.* Knopf, New York.
Mowlana, H., Gerbner, G. Schiller, H. (1992). *Triumph of the Media's War in the Persian Gulf.* Westview Press, Boulder Co.
Norris, C. (1993). *The Truth About Postmodernism.* Blackwell, Oxford.
Ricoeur, P. (1983). *Le Temps et le Recit.* Editions du Seuil, Paris.
Rorty, R. (1989). *Contingency, irony, solidarity.* Cambridge: Cambridge University Press.
Said, E. (1993). *Orientalism.* London: Routledge and Kegan Paul.
Sewell, W. (1985). Ideologies and social revolutions. *Journal of Modern History, 57,* 57–85.
Sewell, W. (1992) A theory of structure, agency and transformation. *American Journal of Sociology, 98*(1), 1–29.
Sherwood, S., Smith, P., & Alexander, J. (1993). The British are coming. *Contemporary Sociology, 22*(2), 370–375.
Slotkin, R. (1973). *Regeneration through violence.* Middletown, CT: Wesleyan University Press.
Smith, P. (1991). Codes and conflict. *Theory and Society, 20*(1), 103–138.
Soothill, K., & Walby, S. (1991). *Sex crime in the news.* London: Routledge.
Strauss, A. (1977). *Mirrors and masks.* London: Martin Robertson.
Swidler, A. (1986). Culture in action. *American Sociological Review,* 51, 273–86.
Turner. V. (1969). *The ritual process.* Ithaca: Cornell University Press.
van Djik, T. (1991). *Racism and the press.* London: Routledge.
Williams, R. (1978). Base and superstructure. *New Left Review, 82,* 3–16.

Death Penalty, Overview

Hugo Adam Bedau
Tufts University

GLOSSARY

Abolitionists Persons who oppose and want to abolish the death penality.

Capital Crime; Capital Offender A crime punishable (or historically punished) by death; a person guilty of such a crime.

Deterrence The use of the threat of unpleasant consequences (punishment) to persuade would-be offenders not to commit a crime.

Incapacitation The use of physical means (leg irons, prison cells, medication) to make it impossible for a person to commit a crime.

Lex talionis The principle that a punishment ought to be similar to the crime for which it is imposed ("a life for a life").

LWOP Life in prison without possibility of parole.

Recidivism Commission of a crime by a person with a previous criminal record.

Retentionists Persons who support and want to keep and use the death penalty.

Retribution The imposition of a punishment on a person because it is deserved.

THE DEATH PENALTY (capital punishment) has been one of the most widely used punishments; no people or nation seems to have been exempt from some recourse to this form of violence under the law. Today, the death penalty is still in evidence, but many countries have abolished it entirely and others have severely limited its use, preferring instead to sentence capital offenders to long terms of imprisonment. The principal explanation for the decline in the use of the death penalty is twofold: the availability of imprisonment as an adequate alternative punishment, and the increasing influence of international human rights law. Underlying that influence is the belief (more widespread in Europe today than in the United States) that the death penalty is cruel, inhumane, and unnecessary.

I. MODES OF CAPITAL PUNISHMENT

The death penalty has been employed in a wide variety of ways, including beheading, crucifixion, poisoning, drowning, boiling in oil, tearing asunder; none of these methods survives anywhere under current law. (No doubt the cruelty of such modes of inflicting the death penalty played a role in persuading some governments in the 19th century to abolish it entirely.) Two among the most widely used methods of carrying out executions are the firing squad and hanging. Three other methods, still in use, were pioneered in the United States: the electric chair, the lethal gas chamber, and lethal injection. A twofold rationale motivated these developments: less apparent cruelty to the offender (little or no physical disfigurement, pain, or protracted dying) and greater efficiency.

As Jeremy Bentham (1748–1832) pointed out, the death penalty may be used either in an aggravated manner or not. A favorite example of aggravated capital punishment was the sentence meted out in 1757 to Damiens, a French regicide. First he was tortured by having boiling oil poured over his body and bits of his flesh torn away by pincers. He was then drawn and quartered; his limbs were tied to horses so he could be pulled asunder; that failed and so his limbs were hacked off. While he was still alive, his trunk was impaled upon a stake, which finally killed him.

Why were such brutal punishments commonplace in earlier centuries? Why is the deatlh penalty still in use at all? Among the many reasons, five are paramount. First, a dead offender is no longer a threat to the public; a death sentence guarantees incapacitation. Second, the terrifying example of such punishments (especially when carried out in public) may deter others. Third, justice (or at least vengeance) demands extreme punitive measures for heinous offenses. Fourth, the ceremony of death, the ritual sacrifice of a malefactor, symbolically mends the social fabric torn by his crime. Finally, a suitable alternative punishment is not always available.

II. INCAPACITATION

No doubt, the death penalty completely incapacitates; it guarantees that the offender will never again harm the innocent. But banishment can and often has served as a nonlethal alternative to death: Russia exiled prisoners to Siberia, England exported convicted murderers to Botany Bay, France sent criminals to Devil's Island, and in the United States the prison island of Alcatraz in San Francisco Bay, used to house dangerous prisoners convicted of federal crimes, effectively removed offenders from society.

Retentionists will argue that today the only plausible form banishment can take is a life-without-parole (LWOP) prison sentence, and that convicted murderers serving a life sentence remain a danger to other prisoners, guards, and visitors. Abolitionists must concede that no alternative punishment is as reliable and effective a means of incapacitation as the death penalty.

III. DETERRENCE

Common sense tells us that the greater the severity of a punishment, the greater the deterrent effect; assuming that the death penalty is the most severe punishment available, it ought to be the best deterrent as well. Retentionists must concede that it has never been a perfect deterrent, however; if it were, there would be no murders in death penalty jurisdictions. Penologists since Cesare Beccaria (1738–1794) have insisted that the effectiveness of a punishment is not a function only of its *severity*; effective deterrence depends also on two other factors as well: the *celerity* of its administration (the brevity of time between the offense and the punishment) and the *certainty* of its infliction (the frequency with which the punishment is actually imposed on those who deserve it). The problem, at least in the United States today, is that the death penalty is demonstrably neither swift nor certain. Crime statistics show that in the 1990s criminal homicides averaged about 23,000 annually, but death sentences averaged fewer than 300 and executions fewer than 50. As for celerity, the average time served by a prisoner in the United States under sentence of death in the 1990s was about 10 years.

To increase either the celerity or the certainty of the death penalty would require curb-stone "justice" and a sacrifice of civil liberties that no reflective citizen would defend. Experience in abolitionist jurisdictions shows that the death penalty is far less certain and subject to much greater delay than the alternative of any form of prison sentence.

Whether and to what degree the death penalty is an effective deterrent despite its lack of certainty and celerity is an empirical question, which has been subject to extensive research (especially in the United States during the 1970s). The issue that divides retentionists and abolitionists here is whether the death penalty is a superior deterrent to imprisonment. If it is not, then defense of the death penalty must rest on other grounds. Although a few researchers have claimed that they had identified a deterrent effect from actual executions, the preponderance of professional opinion on the point is sharply to the contrary: However much or little the death penalty has deterred would-be murderers, it has not done so to any extent measurably superior to the deterrent effect of imprisonment.

Whether the deterrent effect of executions would be enhanced by conducting them in public (say, nationally on television), or whether it would prove to be a shameful and disgusting spectacle, is an unresolved question. Public hangings in the 19th century in England were the occasion for drunken and disorderly behavior, often accompanied by expressions of sympathy for the doomed offender. Public hangings did little or nothing to foster deterrence, and much less to celebrate the vindication of law and order. In the United States the courts have yet to permit the filming or televising of executions, although print media are always invited to attend.

In general, one must beware of assuming that other things being equal, a more severe punishment (such as death) will always have a greater deterrent effect than a less severe punishment (imprisonment). For all we know, the less severe punishment may still be quite severe enough to deter all those who can be deterred.

IV. RETRIBUTION

A retributive defense of the death penalty is almost always confined to defending this punishment for the crime of murder; capital crimes such as rape, arson, kidnapping for ransom, and treason cannot be defended as capital crimes by relying only on retribution. Interestingly, defense of the death penalty in the United States has shifted from an emphasis on deterrence to an emphasis on retribution, roughly concurrent with decisions from the Supreme Court in the 1970s nullifying statutes imposing the death penalty for crimes other than murder.

A retributivist defense of the death penalty for murder can be seen as a morally superior version of defending the death penalty by appeal to sheer vengeance. The vengeful person typically acts in anger; his revenge knows no upper limit in the severity of the harm he would inflict; vengeance is personal, in that it is most naturally inflicted by the victim (or if he is unable to do so, by relatives or clansmen); and the avenger takes pleasure in the suffering of the offender. A retentionist who defends the death penalty on purely retributive grounds rejects all this in favor of an appeal to justice and desert.

Abolitionists rarely embrace retribution as their preferred theory of punishment, although some have accepted it and proceeded to argue as follows: No doubt the death penalty is the punishment a murderer deserves, taken in the abstract, in a perfectly just world. But the actual world is full of injustices that are inherent in the administration of the death penalty, and these injustices are graver where the punishment is death than when it is some form of long-term imprisonment. Indeed, they are so grave that they override the claims of desert and instead require abolition of the death penalty.

What are these injustices? They are the injustices of class and race: Rich defendants rarely are sentenced to death, and (in the United States) murderers of non-Whites are rarely sentenced to death. (The problem of class bias has been less extensively studied than the problem of race bias.) In both cases the principal form that injustice takes in administration of the death penalty is the incompetence of legal counsel at trial and the cost and unavailability of counsel for appeal. Both are amply attested to by anecdotal evidence from close observers of capital trials and appeals across the nation.

Abolitionists who are not retributivists also point to such injustices, but they often argue directly against a retributive defense of the death penalty. First, they are likely to point out that any form of *lex talionis*—making the punishment fit the crime, by imitating it—is doomed to absurdity if generally applied. How is the multiple murderer to be punished? Is the rapist to be punished by rape, the torturer by torture, the childless kidnapper by—what?

Second, if one retreats to the far more plausible retributive principle that the greater the wrong in the crime, the greater the deserved punishment, the abolitionist will point out that this version of the retributivist principle does not require the death penalty. The principle of proportionality is satisfied so long as the most severe punishment (whatever it is) is reserved for the worst crime. (One of the greatest obstacles to further abolition of the death penalty in the United States is the growing use of life imprisonment as the punishment for lesser felonies—the policy of "Three strikes and you're out." If one believes that murder is the gravest crime, that the gravest crime should receive the severest punishment, and that LWOP should replace the death penalty, then one must also refuse to support having lesser felonies punished by LWOP.)

Third, the abolitionist may argue that we have no clear conception of exactly what it is that offenders "deserve" as their punishment. It is plausibly argued that retributivism tells us *who* deserves to be punished (viz., all and only convicted offenders); but it does not tell us with comparable plausibility *what* punishment each class of offender deserves. Of course, legally, offenders deserve to be punished according to whatever the law provides; but legal desert falls far short of the concept of moral desert that retributivism requires. Finally, the abolitionist may point to the fact that few retentionists actually believe *all* murderers deserve to die; they, too, believe that sometimes other morally relevant considerations override the claims of desert. This conclusion follows from the actual practice of trial courts: In the United States at present, of the annual 23,000 criminal homicides, some 2000 to 4000 involve defendants who "deserve" to die according to the laws of capital sentencing. Yet barely 10% (under 300) are actually sentenced to death.

V. SYMBOLISM

According to a recent study of the death penalty in Germany from 1600 to 1987, this penalty in the late medieval period was largely a matter of "ceremony," in which "religious repentance, conversion, and absolution" for the condemned criminal was uppermost in the minds of those conducting and observing an execution. A similar study can be told about the death penalty at that time in other European countries. Although such religious goals are no longer central to the modern role of the death penalty, there is a symbolic dimension to this punishment that cannot be ignored.

In the United States, this is most conspicuous where the federal death penalty is concerned. Throughout this century, only a tiny fraction of capital crimes have occurred under federal jurisdiction; the vast majority of capital crimes and death sentences have been issued under state authority. Yet in the 1990s, as the death penalty has become more and more a political issue at the local and state levels, Congress has enacted many new death penalty statutes, despite the fact that they either overlap with the capital statutes already enacted by the states or apply to nonhomicidal crimes that the Supreme Court may well rule unconstitutional. What is the point of such statutes and of the political rhetoric used in their defense? It is difficult to resist the conclusion that federal lawmakers want to be seen to be doing something about crime, something that addresses the anger and frustration of the electorate. They support the death penalty as a symbol of public authority and power; such support requires no imagination and seems to be free (although it is not) of any burden on the tax payer. It also diverts attention from the ineffectiveness and arbitrariness readily documented in the use of this penalty.

VI. ALTERNATIVES

With the development of prison systems in the 19th century in western Europe and other nations with a European heritage, society had available an alternative form of severe punishment, a version of banishment, in the maximum security prison. Abolitionists argued for this alternative on two very different grounds. Beccaria and Bentham believed that this form of punishment was in fact more severe (painful) than death, although it seemed to be less severe. Bentham in particular favored the alternative of imprisonment on several grounds, three of which abolitionists since his day have also endorsed: convicting and sentencing a defendant to prison who is later determined to be innocent can be rectified; a great variety of sentences is available in different forms of imprisonment; and efforts in the direction of reforming the prisoner can be undertaken.

The principal objection to imprisonment as an alternative to the death penalty is the risk of recidivism, even if the prisoner is not released. Murder can be committed in prison against other inmates, prison guards or officials, or visitors, by capital offenders who were not put to death. Anxiety over recidivism to the side, what evidence is there of the risk? (Not relevant here is the recidivism by noncapital offenders; it is no argument for the death penalty on incapacitative grounds that violent offenders not subject to the death penalty sometimes commit murder while in prison or after release.)

In the United States, recidivism by capital offenders in recent years is infrequent but not zero: (a) in the early 1970s, the National Council on Crime and Delinquency reported that 0.3% of released murderers were later convicted of another "wilful homicide"; (b) a study of 453 death-row prisoners not executed under rulings of the Supreme Court in 1972 and released in the 1980s showed 4 had committed another murder while still in prison and 2 had committed another murder after release; (c) Bureau of Justice Statistics show that about 1 in 12 of the prisoners on death row in the 1990s had a "prior homicide conviction."

Is it plausible to argue that these data show the risk of fatal recidivism is too high, and that extreme measures—executing all those sentenced to death as promptly as possible—is the only reasonable path to take? (After all, there is no other way to guarantee that a convicted murderer will never murder again.) Or is it more reasonable to argue that other considerations—notably, the risk of executing the innocent—counsel caution in the face of a fairly low risk in the first place? (The same research reported in (b) above showed that 4 of the former death row prisoners were actually innocent and had been released.) Which risk is it better for society to run—executing the innocent or protecting the innocent from being victims of murderers who could have been executed but were not? Or are the numbers in each case so small that it is impossible to use them as a basis for an argument either for abolition or for retention?

VII. THE MORAL BASIS OF ABOLITION

No one denies that the death penalty is a severe punishment, that error in its use is irremedial, and that it affords society the best defense against lethal recidivism. More controversial are the claims that the death penalty is a better deterrent, that it is the deserved punishment for murder, and that its administration is tolerably successful in weeding out the worst offenders from the bad. Apart from criticisms focused on these issues, on what basis do abolitionists argue their case? They typically rest their views on one or more of three normative claims: the death penalty is a cruel punishment, it flouts the value of life, and it violates the right to life.

A. If we think of the "value of life" as shorthand for the value to self and others of a person across that person's entire life span, then it is very difficult to argue that the value of life for *all* convicted murderers is greater than the disvalue (risk of harm to the innocent, deprivation of liberty, privacy, and autonomy for the general public). No doubt some persons guilty of horribly violent crimes have their redeeming virtues; but what needs to be shown empirically is that they *all* do. As a result, it is extremely difficult to defend abolition on the ground that the death penalty *always* does more harm (creates more disvalue) than some suitable alternative.

B. The abolitionist argument does not fare much better if the norm relied upon is the right to life. That right (like other rights) is not absolute; if it were, not even killing another person in justified self-defense would be permitted. Furthermore, many philosophers at least since John Locke (1632–1704) have argued that moral ("natural," "inalienable") rights can be forfeited, and that criminals forfeit their right to liberty and security of person. One can perhaps argue that other moral considerations outweigh the murderer's forfeiture of the right to life, and so murderers ought not to be executed. But appealing to a right to life and nothing more will hardly suffice.

C. The Bill of Rights of the United States Constitution (1791) prohibits "cruel and unusual punishment," and most abolitionists believe that (despite Supreme Court rulings to the contrary) the death penalty as such violates this prohibition. Similarly, the United Nations Declaration of Human Rights (1948) and the International Covenant on Civil and Human Rights (1966), to which the United States is a signatory, prohibits "cruel, inhuman or degrading" punishment; the death penalty violates these provisions in the judgment of most abolitionists.

1. But what is it about the death penalty that makes it "cruel," especially if it is administered by lethal injection? No doubt society needs a fixed upper bound to permissible severity in punishment. Nor will many seriously argue that it would not be cruel to sentence to death a juvenile first offender guilty of unarmed robbery. In the United States the Supreme Court has ruled that the death penalty is cruel because disproportionate when used as the punishment for rape (*Coker v. Georgia,* 1976) or kidnapping (*Eberhart v. Georgia*, 1976). But it is not so easy to argue that death is cruel *because disporportionate* for the crime of murder (and especially serial, multiple, terrorist murder). And it is surely open to dispute where the upper bound of severity in punishment should be placed.

2. One can argue more plausibly that the death penalty is cruel because it is *excessive*, that is, unnecessary as a means to achieve the legitimate goals of punishment. The primary goal is public safety by incapacitation and deterrence, the twin branches of punishment as a preventive of crime. A secondary goal is vindication of the law—in this case, the law that defines murder as the gravest crime. As for retribution, abolitionists can concede that it, too, has a role, not as a goal but as a feature of all punishments by their very nature. On this view, a long prison term is every bit as retributive as a death sentence. Undergirding this line of argument is the principle that the least invasive, destructive, harmful means ought to be employed by society to achieve its legitimate goals.

Put more expansively, society (acting through the authority of its government) must not enact and enforce any policies (and a fortiori any penal policies) that impose more restrictive interference with human liberty, privacy, and autonomy than is demonstrably necessary as the means to achieve important social objectives (in this case, the goal of public safety). Given that the death penalty is much more severe, more invasive, less remediable, and more violent than long-term imprisonment, and given that there is an effective alternative punishment in the form of imprisonment (which also but less severely interferes with the offender's liberty, privacy, and autonomy), the death penalty in a modern society is unnecessary, excessive, and cruel.

3. This argument obviously depends on several claims of empirical fact, which are open to challenge on factual grounds. Take first the claim that the death penalty is more severe than life in prison. Both abolitionists and retentionists believe this; otherwise the former would not oppose executions and the latter would not favor them. More to the point, death-row prisoners themselves evidently believe this: Very few such prisoners dismiss their legal counsel, very few fail to seek clemency, and very few attempt suicide (fewer still try until they succeed).

Take next the more important claim that the death penalty is not necessary to achieve valid social aims. Here again the issue is one of empirical fact. American abolitionists support this claim by pointing to the century of experience without any death penalty in several states (Michigan, Wisconsin, Minnesota, Maine, and Iowa). These states have controlled criminal homicide and managed their criminal justice systems, including their maximum security prisons with life-term violent offenders, at least as effectively as have neighboring death penalty jurisdictions (Illinois, Indiana, Ohio, and New Hampshire). The public hast not protested abolition with riot and lynching; law enforcement personnel have not been at greater risk nor have they abused their power and authority over long-term prisoners any more than their counterparts in death penalty states; visitors are not at greater risk; surviving victims of murdered friends and loved ones have not found it more difficult to overcome their grief and adjust to their irreplaceable loss.

VIII. CONCLUSION

At the end of the current century, well over a million men and women are serving time in the prisons of the United States. Around 3500 of them are under sentence of death. Despite the relatively small fraction these death row prisoners constitute of the total, their fate arouses disproportionate attention. No doubt this is because the death penalty involves deliberately killing (and threatening to kill) people who do not want to die and who are not dying. For retentionists, the death penalty is the only appropriate punishment for murder; it is wiser to bet on its superior deterrent efficacy even if statistics seem not to confirm that belief; and as for its seeming arbitrary and discriminatory use, it is unreasonable to expect perfection in the administration of public policy, including criminal justice. For abolitionists, such a penalty—even for murder—constitutes excessive power over who lives and who dies, death deliberately inflicted in the face of an alternative (LWOP) sufficient for all legitimate purposes, a power that no constitutional liberal republic ought to have.

Also See the Following Articles

CRIME AND PUNISHMENT, CHANGING ATTITUDES TOWARD • CRIMINOLOGY, OVERVIEW • PUNISHMENT OF CRIMINALS

Bibliography

Amnesty International. (1987). *United States of America: The death penalty.* London: Amnesty International.

Beccaria, C. (1764, 1995). *On crimes and punishments and other writings.* Cambridge: Cambridge Univ. Press.

Bedau, H. A. (Ed.). (1997). *The death penalty in America: Current controversies.* New York: Oxford Univ. Press.

Bedau, H. A. (1987). *Death is different: Studies in the morality, law, and politics of capital punishment.* Boston: Northeastern Univ. Press.

Bentham, J. (1830). *The rationale of punishment.* London: Robert Heward.

Berger, R. (1982). *Death penalties: The Supreme Court's obstacle course.* Cambridge, MA: Harvard Univ. Press.

Berns, W. (1979). *For capital punishment: Crime and the morality of the death penalty.* New York: Basic Books.

Davis, M. (1996). *Justice in the shadow of death: Rethinking capital and lesser punishments.* Lanham, MD: Rowman & Littlefield.

Nathanson, S. (1987). An eye for an eye: The morality of punishing by death. Totowa, NJ: Rowman & Littlefield.

Poijman, L. P., & Reiman, J. (1998). *The death penalty: For and against.* Lanham, MD: Rowman & Littlefield.

Schabas, W. (1996). *The death penalty as cruel treatment and torture: Capital punishment challenged in the world's courts.* Boston: Northeastern Univ. Press.

Simmons, A. J., Cohen, M., & Beitz, C. R. (Eds.). (1995). *Punishment.* Princeton, NJ: Princeton Univ. Press.

Sorell, T. (1987). *Moral theory and capital punishment.* Oxford: Basil Blackwell.

Van den Haag, E., & Conrad, J. (1983). *The death penalty: a debate.* New York: Plenum Press.

Decision Theory and Game Theory

Anatol Rapoport
University of Toronto

GLOSSARY

Aggression The tendency to engage in conflict or combat with conspecifics.

Characteristic Function of an n-Person Cooperative Game A function that assigns to every subset of players forming a coalition a minimum guaranteed joint payoff.

Constantsum (Two-Person) Game A game in which the sum of the payoffs associated with each outcome is the same.

Equilibrium of a Two-Person Game An outcome that cannot be improved for either player by shifting to another strategy, while the co-player does not shift.

Imputation A set of payoffs to each of the players of an n-person cooperative game which awards to each player at least his own minimal guaranteed payoff of the game and to the coalition of all players their maximum joint payoff.

Interval Scale A system of measurement that leaves the ratio of any two differences invariant under a positive linear transformation, $x' = ax + b, a > 0$.

Maximin The maximum of the minimum payoffs associated with each of the strategies available to a player.

Mixed Strategy A strategy determined by a random device, which "chooses" among the available strategies with prescribed probabilities.

Normal Form (of a Two-Person Game) A representation of a game by a matrix whose rows and columns represent the strategies available to the respective players and whose entries are the payoffs associated with each outcome of the game.

Nonconstantsum Game A game that is not constantsum.

Pareto-Deficient Outcome An outcome of a game to which another is preferred either by all players or by some, while the remaining players are indifferent between the outcomes.

Pareto-Optimal Outcome An outcome of a game that is not Pareto-deficient.

Social Trap A situation in which each participant acts apparently "rationally" but that leads to an outcome that is disadvantageous for all concerned.

Strategy A program that prescribes to a player the choice among available moves in each possible situation that can occur in the course of a game.

Utility A function that ascribes a numerical measure to each of a set of objects, situations, and so on, representing an actor's degree of preference for each of them. In formal decision theory, utility is usually given on an interal scale.

I. MODES OF CONFLICT

The appearance of game theory on the intellectual horizon (Von Neumann and Morgenstern, 1944) aroused considerable interest in military circles and among researchers at institutes of strategic studies as an impressively sophisticated theory of rationally conducted conflict. An impressive application of the theory was demonstrated in November 1945 at the Chicago Museum of Science and Industry by a computer that played perfect tic-tac-toe, that is, it never lost and invariably won if its opponent made a mistake. A few years later Nobel laureate Herbert Simon predicted that within a decade a computer will be crowned world chess champion. It took longer, but the prediction was nevertheless realized in May 1997 when Deep Blue, a computer, defeated world champion Gary Kasparov. In the decisive sixth game of the match, Kasparov resigned after the 19th move.

The notion of rationally conducted conflict suggests a classification of conflicts. This can be done in several ways, for example, according to aims sought by the conflicting parties, according to the level of rationality characterizing the pursuit of these aims, by the level of their intensity, and so on. A. Rapoport (1960) singled out three basic types: fights, games, and debates.

A dogfight is a good example of a *fight*. Strictly speaking it has no discernible aim, being apparently driven only by escalating noxious stimuli. Among humans, one can, perhaps, identify an aim of a fight, which is hardly more than that of harming, incapacitating, or eliminating the opponent.

Affects prominent in a fight, such as hostility, rage, fear, or blood lust are not essential in a game, but rationality is. The aim in a parlor game, for example, such as chess, is to outwit rather than to harm the opponent.

In a debate, in the sense used here, the aim is neither to harm nor to outwit but to convince the opponent or at least to bring his position on some issue closer to one's own. It follows that unlike the fight or a zero-sum game (one in which whatever one player wins another must lose), the debate potentially induces a common interest in the opponents and possibly widens the area of agreement.

From a certain point of view, these three modes of conflict can be imagined to represent successively higher stages of maturity. Obviously cognitive processes involved in a game are far more complex than those involved in a fight. The game can also be supposed to reflect a higher ethical level than a fight. First, physical violence is not necessarily involved in it (although it may be, as in war, which in its strategic aspects can be regarded as a game). Second, there is a commitment on both sides to adhere to agreed-upon rules. The latter commitment represents at least a minimal area of common interest. Effective debate involves, over and above rationality, also an ability to see some merit in the opponent's position and a readiness to state it, for only if the opponent feels that his position is understood can he be expected to seriously consider modifying it with the aim of increasing the area of common interest.

II. CHANGING CONCEPTIONS OF WAR

A. From Enthusiasm to Ambivalence

In 19th-century Europe, widespread belief in the inevitability of "progress" was often linked to faith in a decline of violence: civilization was tacitly identified with debrutalization of man. S. Amos (1880) wrote that the process of civilization would make wars ever more "humane" and restricted in space and time. Eventually, he suggested, they would disappear altogether, simply because the immorality of killing human beings would be universally recognized and the art of statecraft (presumably based on developments of social science) would become sufficiently advanced to provide ways of settling conflicts between states.

Interpreting this prognosis in terms of the above classification of conflicts, we could imagine that Amos envisaged war as passing through the three stages: from fight to game to debate. Let us see what actually happened.

A few years after Amos's prognosis an eminent German historian wrote:

> It is war which fosters the political idealism which the materialist rejects. What a disaster for civilization it would be if mankind blotted its heroes from memory. The heroes of a nation are the fighters which rejoice and inspire the spirit of its youth, and the writers whose words ring like trumpet blasts become the idols of our boyhood and early manhood (Treischke [1897–98/1916] Vol. 1, p. 87).

In his introduction to the English translation of this work Arthur James Balfour wrote in 1916:

> Political theories from those of Aristotle downwards, have been related either by harmony or contrast, to the political practices of their day; but of no theories is this more glaringly true than of those expounded in these volumes. They could not have been written before 1870. Nothing quite like them will be written after 1917 (Balfour, 1916).

The allusion to 1870 is the absorption of German states into the German Empire and the concomitant hypertrophy of militaristic nationalism, which Bismarck so aptly expressed in his slogan "Blood and Iron" as the wherewithal of international politics. The allusion to 1917 is Balfour's projection of the defeat of Germany and, as he supposed, the concomitant bankruptcy of the "Blood and Iron" mode of international relations.

Treischke's celebration of war as expression of idealism was symptomatic of the predominant European public mood in the decades immediately preceding World War I.

The martial mood of the time was shared by wide sectors of what throughout the 19th century became "the public"—the urban, literate (hence newspaper-reading) sector of the European population. The mood found identical expression in Paris, in Berlin, and in St. Petersburg. Columns marching through the broad avenues of the capitals to the railroad stations were cheered by crowds on the sidewalks. Strangers embraced and congratulated one other.

Nothing resembling that mood marked the outbreak of World War II a quarter of a century later. There were no parades, no cheering crowds. And, indeed, it seemed that Lord Balfour's prediction was at last realized. The romantic and heroic image of war was dissipated. After World War II no ministry of war remained. All became ministries of defense, as if the only recognized functions of armed forces became "deterring aggression" and, in case deterrence failed, repelling aggression. Almost universally "peace" acquired a positive connotation and "war" a negative one. Academic communities, sectors of the general public, in some countries even governments became receptive to sytematized programs of study and research on the "causes of wars"—studies of the sort envisaged over a century ago by Amos, the somewhat premature prophet of the eventual eradication of war or war as a consequence of discovering and removing its "causes."

It would seem, then, that Amos's prognosis with respect to changed attitudes toward war (and presumably violence) was, in some respects, realized. When we examine the actual global level of violence during the following century, a very different picture emerges.

B. Contemporary Levels and Targets of Violence

In the period from 1900 until 1995, 109,745,500 war-related deaths were reported, of which 62,194,000, nearly 60% were estimated to have been civilian. In some countries, for example, Ghana, Mozambique, Rwanda, and Uganda, the proportion of civilian war-related deaths was more than 90% (Sivard, 1996). Were S. Amos still among us, he might have attempted to explain these results by a cultural lag. The African countries, where civilians were routinely slaughtered, could be regarded as laggards in the general progress toward higher rationality and morality. However comparison of analogous data on "civilized" warfare refutes this hypothesis. According to data compiled by R. L. Sivard (1996) war related deaths during World War I numbered 19.6 million persons; the corresponding number during World War II was 38.2 million.

Apparently the dissipation of enthusiasm for war observed in the changed public moods did not have the expected effect of limiting the extent or attenuating the severity of war. Nor has the expectation of a decline in the frequency, extent, or intensity of organized violence (war) as a result of growing rationality associated with developing civilization been justified. The period between the two world wars was marked by severe criticism by specialists in the "art of war," namely, of failure to take advantage of new war technology so as to make war "more efficient." Efficiency, however, can be understood in two ways: (1) attainment of war aims with lower expenditures, say of lives; (2) increasing the efficiency of weapons, that is enhancing their destructive potential. B.H. Liddell Hart (1933), for example, would have it both ways. On the one hand, he decried the ossified Clausewitzian dogma of numerical superiority that sent infantry rushing at fortified positions to be slaughtered by machine guns in World War I;. and he also decried the failure during that war to keep up with "progress" in war technology, of which lethality of weapons is a reasonable measure.

There was certainly no reticence in developing and applying increasingly sophisticated technology in the conduct of World War II. Nevertheless that war cannot be regarded as more "efficient" in the sense of achieving more at less cost in lives and treasure than did World War I. On the contrary, both the new technology and elaborate new strategies were designed and developed with the view of achieving maximum destructiveness.

Projecting the needs of war far into the future became routine in the flourishing development of the "art of war." It follows that whatever inhibitions against the use of war as an instrument of national policy may have been generated by the "de-romantization" or "de-glorification" of war throughout most of our century, these inhibitions were apparently neutralized by the concomitant "intellectualization" or "rationalization" of war. We will examine this process in the light of rapidly developing formal theory, an offspring of theoretical economics, namely, decision theory and its offshoot, the theory of games, which, as was said at the outset, aroused considerable interest in military circles.

III. THE SCOPE OF DECISION THEORY

In the context of decision theory, a decision is a choice among available alternatives. These may be objects (to be bought, concealed, or repaired), persons (to be hired, married, or killed) actions (to be carried out or omitted), beliefs (to be adopted or discarded) or any imaginable entities, provided they can be unambiguously recognized and distinguished. Each choice is associated with envisaged or imagined consequences.

It is convenient to distinguish between normative and descriptive decision theory. A concept central in normative decision theory is that of a rational actor. "Rationality" is conceived differently by different persons and in different situations. However, it can be generally agreed that all definitions of rationality involve taking into account the possible envisaged consequences of one's decision, that is, of one's choice among available alternatives. As we shall see, rationality will encompass considerably more in different circumstances.

Once it is unambiguously defined in a given context, the aim of a normative decision theory is to deduce from a given definition of rationality how a "perfectly rational actor" will choose among the alternatives given in the situation. Descriptive theory, on the other hand, tends to construct, on the basis of observations, experimental data, and the like, how actual actors, who may be described by some explicit characteristics, will actually decide in a given class of situations. In short, normative decision theory is purely deductive and, like pure mathematics, does not refer to events in the real world. Descriptive theory, on the contrary, is largely inductive. It rests on hypotheses suggested by observations and is deductive only to the extent that it generates predictions of further observations deduced from these hypotheses. The "actor," whose choices are examined, need not be a person. The important criterion defining an actor in the context of decision theory is a set of interests, and these can be attributed not only to a person but also to a corporation, a hockey team, a gang, a guided missile, or a state.

The theory of games examines situations in which two or more actors are involved. The interests of these will generally not be identical. In particular, in the case of two actors, they may be diametrically opposed. But this they need not be. Most interesting from a point of view at the confluence of normative and descriptive decision theories are games involving players, whose interests are partially opposed and partially coincident.

Because of general noncoincidence of interests of actors, the tools developed in the theory of games have been used in the analysis of decisions suggested in conflict situations. For this reason the theory of games can be conceived as a normative theory of conflict, that is, conflict conducted in the light of rational decisions. Indeed, situations first analyzed by tools developed in game theory were analogous to those arising in so called "games of strategy," those in which neither fun (as in children's games of make-believe) nor physical skill (as in sport), but only strategic astuteness plays a part. Chess, Go, Bridge, Poker, Monopoly, all so-called "parlor games," are well-known examples.

IV. THE DECISION PROBLEM INVOLVING ONE ACTOR

A. Decisions under Certainty

Of the decision problems involving a finite number of alternatives, the simplest are those where each alternative is associated with exactly one consequence or outcome. It is assumed, further, than the actor can rank the outcomes in the order of preference. Rationality in this context entails asymmetry and transitivity of the preference relation. That is, if outcome O_i is preferred to outcome O_j, then O_j is not preferred to O_i (asymmetry); if O_i is preferred to O_j and O_j to O_k, then O_i is preferred to O_k (transitivity). If the number of available alternatives is small enough to be scanned at a glance, the solution of the problem is trivial: one simply chooses the alternative that leads to the most preferred outcome.

Complications of decisions under certainty arise in two ways: (1) the set of outcomes, hence of available alternatives, may be infinite, for example, all possible numbers in an interval; (2) the outcomes may be characterized by two or more aspects regarded as criteria of choice.

A timing problem, involving a choice of the best moment to perform some action, is an example of (1). An example of a (2) is choosing among several cars to buy. Desirable properties of a car may be low price, economical fuel consumption, safety, and so on. A number of cars can be ranked according to each of these criteria, whereby the rankings along the criteria may all be different. Such "multi-objective" decision problems may induce nontransitive preference relations that do not lead to a straightforward solution.

These difficulties are overcome by introducing a one-dimensional continuous measure (called an *interval scale*) of utility. The point of origin (zero) and the unit of this measure can be chosen arbitrarily, but once these are chosen, the relative "worths" of any two outcomes become comparable. The decision problem then reduces to a maximization (or minimization) problem that can be attacked by powerful mathematical techniques, such as differential and integral calculus, linear and nonlinear programming, and so on. These techniques have become standard tools in operations research, control theory, management science, and related disciplines, in all of which the concept of "rational decision" is central. The effects of this development on global levels of violence will be discussed below.

B. Decisions under Risk

Dropping the assumption of one-one correspondence between alternatives and outcomes, we now formulate our decision problem as a matrix, where rows represent the given alternatives, columns "states of nature." For example, the alternatives may be T (to take an umbrella along on the way to work) or L (to leave it home). The "states of nature" could be R (rain) or S (shine). Four possible outcomes are: (TR), (TS), (LR), (LS). The situation is represented by a 2 × 2 matrix.

	R	S
T	u_{11}	u_{12}
L	u_{21}	u_{22}

The entries represent *utilities* (degrees of the actor's preferences). To fix ideas, suppose $u_{22} > u_{11} > u_{12} > u_{21}$. That is, the actor is happiest in outcome LS, when the sun is shining and he is not encumbered by an umbrella. He is unhappiest in outcome LR, when it rains and he does not have his umbrella. Assuming it does not rain when the actor leaves the house, the choice between T and L is not clear. If it should rain later in the day, T is preferred; otherwise L. A rational decision is suggested if two conditions are fulfilled: (1) the degrees of preference can be determined on at least an interval scale; (2) probabilities p and $1 - p$ can be assigned respectively to Rain and Shine. In terms of these quantities *expected utility* can be defined as the weighted sum of the utilities associated with an alternative, where the weights are the probabilities of the states of nature relevant to the problem, (now an example of decision under risk). Thus, if probability p is assigned to Rain and (1-p) to Shine the expected utility associated with T is $p(u_{11}) + (1 - p)(u_{12})$ and that associated with L is $p(u_{21}) + (1 - p)(u_{22})$. A "rational decision" can now be defined as one that maximizes expected utility. It agrees with conventional wisdom: take the umbrella "if it looks like rain"; leave it otherwise.

From the point of view of normative theory, the solution of a problem of this sort can be identified as the alternative that leads to the largest expected utility. For instance, in the umbrella problem it becomes advisable to take the umbrella if

$$p(u_{11}) + (1 - p)(u_{12}) > p(u_{21}) + (1 - p)(u_{22})$$

but not otherwise.

The problem remains of choosing an appropriate objectively verifiable surrogate of utility. In some situations, such a surrogate may readily suggest itself, for example, in business contexts money; in the practice of medicine relative numbers of patients helped, harmed, or unaffected by a given drug; in war, perhaps, relative numbers of own and enemy's casualties in an operation. The chess-playing computer assigns numerical values to all future positions envisaged at each move (these valuations being determined by chess experts on the basis of experience and recorded games). Perhaps military experts assign similar values to positions lost or won in some operation and determine their expected utilities by assigning estimated probabilities of favourable or unfavourable outcomes. Once this is done strategic planning becomes essentially a matter of cost-benefit analysis.

1. Examples: Cost-Benefit Analysis of Deterrence Strategies

The problem posed is that of finding an appropriate utility measure in allocating funds for a nuclear arsenal (within the limits of a given budget) presumably serving as deterrence of a Soviet attack on the United States. After dismissing megatonnage of bombs, numbers of bombers, and so on, as too crude, the authors consider

> . . . the number and value of enemy targets that can be destroyed (for a given budget) [which] takes into account the numbers of our offense bombers and missiles but also their operational effectiveness . . . It is still, of course, an ambiguous criterion and requires a more precise definition. For example, what target system—population, industry, or military bases—should we use to keep score . . . ? (Hitch and McKean, 1965).

Here may be the answer to the puzzle how it came to pass that as public attitude toward war became increasingly negative in the industrialized countries after World War I, the scope and destructiveness of World War II sharply increased, while World War III, widely expected during the Cold War, was regarded as ushering in the end of civilization, perhaps of humanity. The conception of war as a rationally conducted process analogous to a business enterprise or a sports event (note the allusion to "keeping score") replaced the image of war as an orgy of violence by an image of a sophisticated rational decision process, devoid of either exultation of heroism or of inculcation of hatred of the enemy (which may have been resisted).

An even more crass example is found in the writings of Herman Kahn, a leading civilian strategist of projected nuclear wars.

The problem of choosing a criterion of "disutility" of a nuclear war (assuming deterrence fails) was faced by Kahn when he attempted to determine the limit of "acceptable" cost (in terms of civilian casualties in a nuclear war) associated with credible deterrence. Kahn reports consultation with a number of colleagues. The proposed numbers of "acceptable" civilian casualties clustered around 60 million, which Kahn may have used as a "working figure" in designing an optimal deterrence posture. (Kahn, 1960, p. 15).

V. TWO-PERSON GAMES

The theory of games deals with decision situations involving two or more "rational" actors, whose interests (valuations of outcomes) in general do not coincide. A game of strategy is sometimes represented as a sequence of decisions called *moves*. The decision makers are called *players*. The rules of the game specify which player is to make a move at each particular stage of the game and what choices are available to him, when it is his turn to make it (the rules of the game). A *strategy* is a plan of action, which a player selects *before the game starts* that specifies his choice in any situation that may arise in the course of the game. In almost all parlor games this is practically impossible, since the number of all possible situations, even if it is finite, is usually superastronomical.

A. The Normal Form

If the number of players is two and if the number of strategies available to each player (even though huge) is finite, we can imagine a game of this sort (called a *two-person game*) represented by a matrix with m rows and n columns. These denote respectively strategies available to the first player, henceforth called Row, and those available to the second, called Column.

Each cell of the matrix represents an *outcome* of the game. It contains two numbers, called *payoffs*, the first being the utility of the outcome to Row, the second to Column. This representation is called the *normal form* of a game.

A *play* of the game consists of a choice by each player of one of his available strategies. It is assumed that neither knows the strategy chosen by the other.

B. Constantsum Two-Person Games

As has been said, the fundamental distinction of the *theory of games* as a branch of decision theory is the multiplicity of actors, whose interests, in general, do not coincide. In the case of two-person games they may be diametrically opposed. That is, the larger the payoff is to one of the players, the smaller it is to the other. This is the case if the sum of the payoffs of every outcome is the same. Such games are called *constant-sum games*. Since the payoffs are usually given on an interval scale, invariant with respect to a linear transformation, their sum can without loss of generality be set equal to 0. (Here the win of one is paired with an equal loss of the other). Hence constantsum games can also be called *zero-sum games*.

1. Dominating Strategies and Saddle Points

Consider the following 2 × 2 *zerosum game*:

	C_1	C_2
R_1	0, 0	−2, 2
R_2	3, −3	1, −1

In contemplating the choice between R_1 and R_2, Row notes that if Column chooses C_1, then R_2, which yields a payoff of 3, is preferred to R_1, which yields 0. If Column should choose C_2, then R_2 (yielding 1) is still preferred to R_1 (yielding -2). We say R_2 *dominates* R_1 (yields more than R_1 regardless of the co-player's choice). Similar arguments lead to the conclusion that Column C_2 dominates C_1 ($2 > 0$, $-1 > -3$). If both players are rational in the sense of maximizing their respective payoffs associated with the outcomes of the game, the outcome of the game is R_2C_2, the intersection of strategies R_2 and C_2.

Let us now consider the game in which the outcomes in R_2 have been interchanged

	C_1	C_2
R_1	−2, 2	0, 0
R_2	3, −3	1, −1

Here R_2 still dominates R_1 ($3 > -2$, $1 > 0$), but C_2 no longer dominates C_1 ($2 > 0$, but $-3 < -1$). Row's optimal choice is still obvious (R_2), but Column's is not. His optimal choice depends on Row's choice, which by the rules of the game Column does not know. However, Column's optimal choice can be determined if he ascribes rationality to Row. For if Row is rational, he can be expected to choose his dominating strategy, namely R_2. Thereby Column's optimal choice is also determined, namely, C_1, which yields him -1, while C_1 yields -3. We have established a new criterion of rationality, in the context of the theory of games. Namely, a rational player attributes rationality to the co-player(s).

Consider now the following game:

	C_1	C_2	C_3
R_1	−2	5	−7
R_2	−1	0	6
R_3	−4	−5	10

We have assumed that the game is *zero-sum*, hence only Row's payoffs need be entered. Column's are numerically equal with the opposite sign.

We note that no row dominates the other two, and no column dominates the other two. So neither player's rational choice can be immediately determined. However, a player, say Row, can reason as follows.

> Suppose I choose R_1 and Column assumes that I did so. Which column would he choose? Clearly C_3, since it is in his interest to minimize my payoff. Similarly he would choose C_1 if he thought I chose R_2 and C_2, if he thought I chose R_3. Of these three outcomes, each worst from my point of view, R_2C_1 is the best ("least worst"). I shall therefore, assume the "worst case scenario" and maximize my *guaranteed* payoff by choosing R_2, which yields "the best of the worst" or the maximum of the minima.

Such an outcome is called a *maximin*. If Row's maximin entry in a game matrix is minimal in its row and maximal in its column, as in our example, then Column's maximin entry must be minimal in its column and maximal in its row. Such an outcome is called a *saddle point*. In the light of the reasoning leading to it, it can be called a "rational" outcome of the game (arrived at by two "rational" players).

Note that linkage between "rationality" and the "worst case scenario" in the theory of the two-person zerosum game is congenial to traditional military thinking: It is not what the opponent *may* do in the pursuit of his own interest, but the worst he *can* do to you that matters.

2. Mixed Strategies

Not every two-person zero-sum game has a saddle point, as shown in the following example.

	C_1	C_2
R_1	1, −1	−5, 5
R_2	0, 0	2, −2

Here the "worst case scenario" reasoning leads into a vicious cycle. Assuming again Row's point of view, we see that Column would choose C_2 if he thought Row would choose R_1. But then, if Row thought so, he would choose R_2 for a win of 2. But then, if Column followed Row's reasoning, he would choose C_1 (to make Row receive 0), which would then make R_1 Row's better choice, and so on in clockwise succession. Column's reasoning would also fall into a vicious cycle.

A way out if provided by extending the repertoire of available strategies to *mixed strategies*. The use of a mixed strategy involves the use of a random device calibrated to determine each of the available strategies with a certain probability. For example, in the case of the game represented by the matrix, Row would use a mixed strategy (p, 1-p) if he chose R_1 with probability p and R_2 with the complementary probability $1 - p$. Row's rational choice in this case would be to choose p in such a way that Column's expected gain would be the same whether he chose C_1 or C_2. In this game, (1/4, 3/4) would be such a strategy, since using either C_1 or C_2 or any probabilistic mixture of the two would make Column's expected payoff −1/4. Similarly, Column's optimal mixture in this game would be (7/8, 1/8), since this would give Row an expected payoff of 1/4, regardless of which strategy he chose. It follows that assuming many iterations, the most Row can win on the average playing against a rational Column is 1/4, which is the most Column must lose on the average. Neither player can improve his expected payoff by deviating from his optimal mixed strategy, assuming that the other does not deviate. The solution of the game is a sort of *equilibrium* in the sense described. In fact the use of all the three principles mentioned, namely the choice of dominant strategies when these are available, the choice of maximin strategies in games with saddle points, and the choice of optimal mixed strategies in games without saddle points leads to outcomes that are equilibria. The equilibrium principle is generally recognized as the determinant of rational decision in situations depicted as two-person constant sum games.

The notion of mixed strategy extended the "solvability" of two-person constant-sum games to all finite games (having finite numbers of strategies) and thus vastly increased the scope of game theory. For instance a mixed strategy could represent a probabilistic response to an antagonist's move, thus curtailing the information available to him about one's own strategy. Further extensions were made to extend the method to games with infinite strategy sets, such as games of timing or problems of control involving antagonistic controllers. Indeed much of research in this area of mathematics has been supported in the United States by the Naval Research Academy and by the Rand Corporation (a think tank working among other things on problems arising in contemporary military science).

B. Nonconstantsum Games

As the name implies, in a two-person nonconstant-sum game, the sum of the payoffs associated with each outcome can vary from outcome to outcome. It follows that the interests of the players can be only partially opposed. The situation may have an area of common interest in that some outcomes may be preferred to others by both players.

1. The Game of Chicken

The game of Chicken is represented by the following scenario. The players drive toward each other, both straddling the middle of the road. The first to swerve to avoid collision earns the humiliating soubriquet "Chicken." The driver who stayed on the collision course receives approbation (rates as a "Daredevil"). If both swerve, the score is tied; if neither swerves, both lose heavily. The game is represented by the following matrix. The rows and columns have been relabeled in accordance to established usage. As will appear below, C stands for "cooperation," D for "defection.

	C_2	D_2
C_1	1, 1	−10, 10
D_1	10, −10	−100, −100

The game of Chicken

We note that neither player has a dominating strategy. If each chooses his maximin strategy, C_1C_2 results, which is not an equilibrium, since each can improve his payoff by shifting to D, provided the other does not. Outcomes D_1C_2 and C_1D_2 are both equilibria, but the former favors Row, the latter Column. Neither can be chosen convincingly as the "rational outcome," since the game is completely symmetric (its structure favors neither player).

The game has also a third equilibrium, an intersection of mixed strategies, namely (10/11, 1/11), whereby the expected payoff of each player is 0. It is an equilibrium in the sense that neither player can improve his expected payoff, by shifting to another strategy, pure or mixed, if the other does not shift. This equilibrium is symmetric, hence reflects the structure of the game. Note, however, that it confers on both players an expected payoff (0) that is less than that associated with the choice of maximin strategies, namely 1. In sum, the choice of dominating strategies does not apply in this game; the maximin principle suggests one strategy; the equilibrium principle another. The question which is the rational choice remains open.

In our next example, all three principles suggest the same strategy to both players; yet the outcome, although "rational" by all three criteria is unsatisfactory, as we shall see.

2. Prisoner's Dilemma

Two men are suspected of burglary. There is not enough evidence to convict them but enough to convict them of a lesser crime, namely, possession of stolen goods. The state's attorney, interested in obtaining confessions, explains the situation to them. If both confess to the charge of burglary, for which the normal penalty is 5 years imprisonment, both receive a reduced term of 3 years. If neither confesses, they can still be convicted of possession of stolen goods, for which the penalty is 1 year in jail. If only one confesses, he is set free (for turning state's evidence), while the other (who has not confessed) can be convicted on the strength of his partner's evidence and sentenced to the full term of 5 years.

Let C represent "cooperation," (with the partner, not with the state, that is to say, *not* confessing) and D

"defection" (confessing). The game can be represented by the following matrix, where negative utilities are assigned to prison terms of various durations.

	C_1	D_1
C_1	$-1, -1$	$-5, 0$
D_1	$0, -5$	$-3, -3$

Prisoner's Dilemma

Clearly, both players' strategy D dominates C. Moreover, D is both players' maximin strategy. Finally, outcome D_1D_2 is the only equilibrium of the game. All three principles of rational decision mentioned above dictate the choice of D to both players. Nevertheless, both players prefer outcome C_1C_2 to D_1D_2, which raises the question of whether the choice of D is indeed "rational" in this game. The name of the game was suggested by this dilemma.

The paradox is resolved if in defining "rationality" a distinction is made between *individual* and *collective rationality*. Then it is clear that in *Prisoner's Dilemma* individual rationality dictates the choice of D, collective rationality prescribes C.

C. Social Traps

Prisoner's Dilemma illustrates a situation called a *social trap*. These are situations in which each involved individual acts in accordance with individual rationality, that is, makes decisions designed to maximize the utility he assigns to the outcome, but in which the outcome resulting from all these apparently rational decisions is disadvantageous to every one concerned. An arms race is an often-cited example. In seeking security against potential enemies, a country may increase its military potential. If all countries do so, the security of none is increased, while the funds expended to increase security are wasted. It is in the individual interest of each fishing fleet to maximize its catch. If all fishing fleets do this, the fish population may be depleted entailing losses for all. If a fire breaks out in a crowded theater, it may seem rational to try to get to an exit as quickly as possible. If everyone tries to do this, a panic may ensue, and everyone may perish.

D. Cooperative Games

So far nothing was said about possible effects of communication between the players on the outcome of the game. It is conceivable that in games like Prisoner's Dilemma communication might make the players aware of their common interest and so allow them to achieve an outcome better for each than D_1D_2 dictated by the logic of individual rationality, namely, C_1C_2. This is, indeed, the case if in addition to the opportunity to communicate, the players can also make *binding agreements*. Then the solution of the game would not have to be an equilibrium, since departing from the agreed upon outcome would constitute a violation of the agreement. In Chicken, the players might also agree on the outcome C_1C_2 (both swerve), rather than use a mixed strategy (the "rational" solution of the noncooperative game), which entails a risk of a crash (the outcome that is worst for both players). Note that C_1C_2 is not an equilibrium, but the payoff associated with it to each player is larger than that associated with the symmetric mixed strategy equilibrium outcome. Thus the theory of the cooperative game extends game theory to problems solvable by *conflict resolution*. This approach is most clearly seen in the theory of n-person cooperative games ($n > 2$).

When the rules of the game permit communication and entering binding agreements, subsets of N, the set of players can form coalitions, that is coordinate their strategies so as to achieve the largest possible joint payoff, assuming the "worst case scenario," namely the case when the remaining players likewise join in a coalition and choose a strategy that keep the payoff of the first coalition to a minimum. Thus, each potential coalition $S \subset N$ can count on a certain *security level* of payoff. The function that assigns to each potential coalitions S its security level $v(S)$ is called the *characteristic function* of the game G, which is now defined by its set of players N and its characteristic function v. It is designated by $G = < N, v>$

It is usually assumed that for each pair of nonoverlapping coalitions S and T

$$v(S \cup T) \geq v(S) + v(T).$$

In words, by joining in a coalition members of S and of T can guarantee themselves a joint payoff at least as large as they could guarantee themselves by staying in separate coalitions. It follows that it is always collectively rational for all players to form a single coalition (the *grand coalition*), since $v(N)$ is the most they can jointly get in the game G by cooperating, that is, coordinating their strategies.

Note that the original decision problem posed in game theory, namely, that of determining a strategy that maximizes a player's payoff (assuming other players are trying to maximize theirs) is bypassed in the theory of the cooperative game, inasmuch as the collectively rational strategy is assumed to have been determined.

The problem remaining is that of dividing this maximized joint payoff among the members of the grand coalition.

A particular apportionment of the joint payoff $v(N)$ among the n players is designated by the ordered set $(x_1, x_2, \ldots x_i, \ldots x_n)$ where x_i, the payoff apportioned to player i. It is called an *imputation* if x_i $(i = 1, \ldots n) \geq v(i)$ and $\sum x_i$ $(i = 1, \ldots n) = v(N)$. The first inequality represents individual rationality. It says that player i will get at least as much as a member of the grand coalition as he could get by playing alone against the coalition of all others; thus it is worthwhile for him to join the grand coalition. The second equality represents collective rationality. It says that the players joining in a grand coalition will maximize their joint payoff. The solution of a cooperative n-person game in characteristic function form is conceived as an imputation or a set of imputations, that is apportionments of the joint payoff that satisfy certain stipulated principles of "stability," or "fairness," or "social justice," however defined.

For example, the *core* of the game is a set of imputations that makes it unprofitable for any subset of n players to break away from the grand coalition to form one of their own. This solution has the drawback that in some games, the set of imputations having that property may be empty. Related to the core is the *nucleolus* of the game, which always exists and, indeed, consists of a single imputation. It is, in fact, a realization of Rawls's principle of social justice (Rawls, 1971) in the sense that it identifies the "least advantaged" set of players, (those who are most motivated to break away from the grand coalition rather than accept a proposed imputation) as the set, whose situation is most favored by the solution.

The *Shapley value* of a game, like the nucleolus, is a unique imputation, in which each player's payoff is proportional to the average benefit he confers on a coalition that he joins - a sort of equity principle.

The choice of a solution principle might well induce a conflict. However, the positions taken might be determined not by the particular problem on hand, but rather on how to agree on apportionments of the rewards reaped from cooperation in *all* future situations, so that no one would know in advance which principle would be the most advantageous from his point of view. That is to say, it could induce a debate not on a particular issue, where specific interests of the players are involved, but on how to deal with issues arising in the future, a matter of values, some of which the participants may hold in common.

It seems that the most promising contribution of the theory of games to problems of conflict resolution, and hence ultimately to the reduction of violence, stems from the approaches suggested by the theory of the cooperative n-person game in characteristic function form. The contribution is not primarily to specific techniques of conflict resolution (these can be learned only through concrete experience) but to developing habits of more mature thinking about conflict.

E. Intellectualization of War

As we have seen, the two-person *zerosum game* appears to be an idealized representation of rationally conducted conflict. Associated with the growing prestige of sophisticated rational reasoning characteristic of scientific activity was a growing acceptance of this mode of thinking in the conduct of wars. This conception is stated explicitly already in Carl von Clausewitz's magnum opus, *On War* (1832/1968), in which a clearly envisaged political aim is defined as the stake for which a war is (or ought to be) fought, and where much emphasis is put on the importance of well-thought-out strategy in pursuing victory. Moreover, victory itself is defined (ideally) as achieving total power over the opponent. "War," wrote Clausewitz, "is an act of violence intended to compel our opponent to fulfil our will" (p.101). Here an area of common interests is implicitly excluded. The two-person *zero-sum game* appears to be the most accurate model of a war as, in Clausewitz's opinion, it ought to be. Of the 35 papers presented at a conference on game theory in Toulon, France in 1964 (Mensch, 1966), 17 were on military applications and 14 of these on the two-person zerosum games.

Problems arising in missile warfare stimulated the development of *differential games,* particularly games of pursuit and evasion. In such a game, the role of Player 1 can be played by an attacking missile aimed at an enemy target and equipped with sensors processing information on the position, velocity, acceleration, and so on, of an antiballistic missile (Player 2), equipped with similar sensors, whose task is to intercept the attacking missile. The "payoff" to the attacking missile increases as the distance between the point of interception (if such takes place) and the target decreases. The payoff to the intercepting missile increases with this distance. A strategy in this game is a choice of a program of control of a trajectory dependent on the information received by the sensors. Thus, the two missiles are effectively playing a two-person zerosum game, mathematically vastly most complicated than the matrix games in our elementary examples, since strategies are represented not by single alternatives or by probability distributions on finite sets of alternatives but on "functions of functions" where the domains are continua.

It is hardly surprising that intricate problems in mathematics, information processing, physics, chemistry, and biology associated with the development of advanced offensive and defensive war technology, presented a challenge, not to speak of career opportunities, to young brilliant scientists. At the same time, preoccupation with these problems amounted to complete "insulation" of their activities which, through long chains of application lead to vastly increasing lethality of organized violence.

This, insulation involves not only separation of intellectual activity from its end product, namely, the huge machine which, if activated, could destroy civilization, perhaps humanity. It entails also separation of rational decision making from reality, which it is supposed to control.

In spite of the intense preoccupation with situations faced by absolutely antagonistic opponents, some aspects of two-person cooperative games did not escape the attention of theoreticians of "rational conflict." In particular implications of the possibility of communication with the antagonist were investigated, in particular utilization of communication in "deterrence," the central concept in the rationalization of the "balance of terror," as the supposed equilibrium sought in the conduct of the Cold War was sometimes called. In assessing the contribution of strategic bargaining to the theory of deterrence, T.C. Shelling wrote

> We have learned that a threat has to be credible to be efficacious, and that credibility may depend on the costs and risks associated with the fulfilment for the party making the threat. We have developed the idea of making the threat credible by getting ourselves committed to its fulfilment, through the stretching of a trip wire across the enemy's path of advance, or by making fulfilment a matter of national honor and prestige. . . We have considered the possibility that a retaliatory threat may be more credible if the means of carrying it out and the responsibility or retaliation are placed into the hands of those whose resolute in stronger. . . (Schelling, 1960, p.6).

A particular "commitment to fulfilment" of a threat was suggested by H. Kahn (1965, p.11) in the context of the game of Chicken:

> The skilful player may get into the car quite drunk, throwing whisky bottles out the window to make it clear to every body how drunk he is. He wears very dark glasses so that it is obvious he cannot see much, if anything. As soon as the car reaches high speed, he takes the steering wheel and throws it out the window. If the opponent is watching, he has won.

One can see the force of this reasoning. But what if the opponent is not watching? Kahn has foreseen this contingency too.

> If his opponent is not watching, he [the skilful player] has a problem; likewise if both players try this strategy.

So far only the potentialities of communication (one feature of the cooperative game) have been examined. The other feature, more relevant to conflict resolution, namely the possibility of coordinating strategies to mutual advantage, was examined by H. Kissinger in a discussion of so-called "limited nuclear war."

> It is possible to conceive of a pattern of limited nuclear war with its own appropriate tactics and with limitations as to targets, areas, and the size of weapons used. Such a mode of conflict cannot be improvised in the confusion of battle, however, The limitation of war is established not only by our intention but also by the manner in which the other side interprets them. It, therefore, becomes the task of our diplomacy to convey to our opponent what we understand by limited nuclear war, or at least what limitations we are willing to observe. . . If the Soviet leadership is clear about our intentions, a framework of war limitation may be established by the operation of self interest—by fear of all-out war and by the fact that new tactics make many of the targets of traditional war less profitable (Kissinger, 1957, p. 185).

F. Aggression Regarded as Manifestation of Human Nature

In now ubiquitous discussions about the role of war in human affairs, the opinion is frequently expressed that war is a form of behavior rooted in human nature. It is sometimes based on arguments suggested by theories of evolution driven by natural selection. The phrase "struggle for existence, survival of the fittest" has been frequently interpreted as referring to ubiquitous competition among living organisms, conspicuously manifested in combats, as a result of which the "strongest," "bravest," "most aggressive" have the greatest chance to survive and reproduce their kind.

Actual combats, for example, between males competing for females, are commonly observed among vertebrates. It is noteworthy, however, that these combats are seldom fatal. Among some animals, commonly regarded as "fierce," restraint is observed, as in the effect of an apparent gesture of "surrender" by a defeated wolf resulting in disengagement. It appears, therefore, that along with the so-called "aggressive instinct" another evolved in consequence of natural selection, namely, an inhibition against killing one's own kind. The survival value of such an "instinct" for a species seems obvious.

It may well be the case that both an "aggressive instinct" and inhibition against killing one's own kind co-exist in man. In human collectives, however, biological predispositions are either reinforced or inhibited by socialization, education, and other methods of social control, some in one direction some in another, depending on the way of life adopted by various cultures. Witness the command attributed to a deity by the authors of the Old Testament:

> . . . of the cities . . . that the Lord, thy God hath given thee for an inheritance, thou shalt save nothing that breatheth, but thou shalt utterly destroy them: the Hittites and the Amorites, the Caanites and the Perrizites . . . That they teach you not to do after all their abominations . . . (Deuteronomy 20: 16–18.)

This injunction may well represent an attempt to neutralize the instinctive aversion against killing one's own kind. At any rate we know that *homo sapiens* is one of very few species that engage in massive, severely lethal combats with conspecifics (rats and some species of ants also come to mind). Moreover, the lethality of organized conflict between human groups has grown enormously throughout the evolution of civilization. A conspicuous cause of this development is clearly the growing effectiveness of killing technology but not that alone. War technology, besides becoming enormously "efficient," has successively removed human targets from the awareness of the killers. Firearms removed them from immediate proximity. It is easier to shoot someone than to butcher him. Artillery removed them from sight. Aviation made possible massive destruction of civilians without targeting them specifically. Moreover, killing civilians became an explicit strategic goal in World War II as in attacks on Rotterdam and Dresden, (undertaken with the view to breaking the enemy's morale) or on Hiroshima and Nagasaki (presumably to reduce military casualties during the impending invasion of Japan). One can imagine a nuclear war as a sequence of "exchanges" triggered by operators watching signals on a screen and manipulating appropriate levers. It appears that the infusion of sophisticated "rationality" in the conduct of war (in our terms, the transformation of war from a fight into a game) did not contribute to its humanization; quite the contrary. In the light of this development, Kissinger's conjecture (that nuclear weapons may actually make nuclear war more humane "making traditional targets of conventional war less profitable") is interesting. It rests on the assumption that limited war (more than all-out war) is in the "common interest" of the potential enemies. Note, however, that the obvious next step in this line of reasoning is not made. Although it seems reasonable to assume that refraining from war altogether is even more advantageous to potential enemies, this solution apparently remains beyond the scope of rational decision making. It contradicts the tacit and hence unassailable tenet of "realist" politics: reduction of one's military potential is analogous to reduction of one's competitiveness in the global market and like the latter can never be consistent with "national interest."

G. The Institutional Approach to the Problem of Chronic Violence among Humans

The foregoing may lend support to the belief that aggressiveness, that is a permanent predilection to violence, is an irremovable component of human nature, like self-preservation or sexual libido. However, the persistent efforts to contain or eradicate violence against own kind among humans throw doubt on this belief. Disarmament was prophesied by Isaiah 28 centuries ago:

> And they shall beat their swords into ploughshares and their spears into pruning hooks. . .

Moreover, not only conversion of hardware but also of software was foreseen:

> . . . neither shall they learn war any more. (Isaiah 2:4)

In modern terms, this means not only converting of tanks into tractors and bombers into airliners but also closing military academies and strategic studies institutes. Of course resistance against such programs would be formidable in the present political climate. But it would be a mistake to attribute such resistance to the primacy of "*aggressiveness*" in human nature. The monstrous growth of destructive potential by no means speaks for dominance of aggressiveness in the human psyche, since the activities related to this growth (research, development, organization, strategic planning, administration, lobbying) are completely divorced from acts of violence. In our time one does not have to hate any one in order to kill every one. The resistance of the war establishment to its abolition is like the resistance of any quasi-living system to its demise. Systems that lacked sufficient self-preserving potential are no longer around. History is littered by dead or dying institutions, such as chattel slavery, dueling, hereditary absolute monarchy, human sacrifice. War may someday suffer the same fate. Its demise by no means implies the elimination of conflict from human life; only lifting conflict to a higher level of maturity (here envisaged as a blend of rationality and humaneness) the sort of conflict that is modeled by the *n*-person cooperative game, in which realization of collective interest is taken for granted and where choice of principles of fair apportionments of joint gains is a consequence of an ethically conducted debate.

Also See the Following Articles

AGGRESSION, PSYCHOLOGY OF • ANIMAL BEHAVIOR STUDIES, NONPRIMATES • COLD WAR • CONFLICT MANAGEMENT AND RESOLUTION • CORRELATES OF WAR • NUCLEAR WARFARE • WARFARE, MODERN • WEAPONRY, EVOLUTION OF • WORLD WAR I • WORLD WAR II

Bibliography

Amos, S. (1880). *Political and legal remedies for war. London: Casse, Potter, Galpin & Co. London.*

Clausewitz, C. von. (1832/1968). *On war.* Hammondsworth: Penguin.

Hitch, C. J., & McKean, R. N. (1965). The criterion problem. In M. Berkowitz and P. G. Bock (Eds.), *American national security.* New York: Free Press.

Kahn, H. (1960). *On thermonuclear war. Princeton: Princeton University Press.*

Kahn, H. (1965). *On escalation. Metaphors and scenarios.* New York: Praeger.

Kissinger, H. A. (1957). *Nuclear weapons and foreign policy.* New York: Harper & Row.

Liddell Hart, B. H. (1933). *The ghost of Napoleon.* London: Faber & Faber.

Mensch, A. (Ed.) (1966). *Theory of games. Techniques and applications.* The proceedings of a conference under the aegis of the NATO Scientific Affairs Committee. London: The English Universities Press, Ltd.

Rapoport, A. (1960). *Fights, games, and debates.* Ann Arbor: University of Michigan Press.

Rowls, J. (1971). *A theory of justice.* Cambridge, MA: Belknap.

Sivard, R. L. (1996). *World military and social expenditures.* Washington, DC: World Priorities.

Von Neumann, J., & Morgenstern, O. (1944). *Theory of games and economic behavior.* Princeton: Princeton University Press.

Diplomacy

Noé Cornago-Prieto
University of the Basque Country

GLOSSARY

Diplomacy The conduct of international relations by negotiation and dialogue or by any other means to promote peaceful relations among states, but also a set of institutional practices and discourses that is key to the basic understanding of the historical evolution and the functional needs of the international system.

Diplomatic Good Offices A multilateral method of peaceful settlement of disputes in which a neutral third party tries to facilitate the communication between the parties, without offering any substantial suggestion on the possible terms of settlement.

Diplomatic Mediation A multilateral method of peaceful settlement of disputes in which a neutral third party, required by the parties, can make substantial proposals in order to seek a compromise, or facilitate a political agreement.

Diplomatic Negotiation The most characteristic method of peaceful settlement. It can be defined as the attempt to explore and reconcile conflicting positions among states in order to reach an acceptable outcome for all the parties in areas of common interest.

Inquiry The formal and impartial determination of facts, by a neutral team, required by the parties in conflict, in order to elude misunderstandings and facilitate a peaceful settlement.

Paradiplomacy The involvement of noncentral governments in international relations, through the establishment of permanent or *ad hoc* contacts, with foreign public or private entities, with the aim to promote socioeconomic and cultural issues, as well as any other foreign dimension of their own constitutional competencies.

Summitry Serial or *ad hoc* diplomatic meetings and conferences at the level of heads of government or state, in order to obtain substantial agreements or simply to improve the climate of relations between states.

DIPLOMACY can be defined as the conduct of international relations by negotiation and dialogue or by any other means to promote peaceful relations among states. Besides this widely accepted single definition, diplomacy is also a set of institutional practices and discourses which is key for the basic understanding of the historical evolution and the functional needs of the international system. This article presents a general approach in discussing this topic, including a short note about the historical circumstances in which modern diplomacy was born, an introduction to its more prominent transformations over time, a brief discussion of bilateralism and multilateralism as its basic modalities, and finally some reflections about the relevance of negotiation and other diplomatic methods for the contemporary international relations of cooperation and conflict.

I. THE RISE OF MODERN DIPLOMACY

It may seem that the basic condition for the extension of diplomatic relations through the world was the existence of independent states able to develop political relations among them. Notwithstanding, the history of diplomacy predates considerably that of the modern sovereign nation-state. For that reason, it seems necessary to discuss briefly the circumstances in which a set of practices of public and private communication among different political entities, existing since ancient times, underwent different historical transformations until becoming conventionally defined as an exclusive attribute of the sovereign nation-state.

Of course, various forms of diplomatic behavior among diverse entities were well known during the Middle Ages in American, Asian or African civilizations. However, the most distinctive institution of modern diplomacy, the exchange of resident ambassadors, did not become a reality until the 15th century. This was due to the intensification of diplomatic activity in Europe, and the increasing awareness among the existing monarchies that diplomatic relations were more practical and efficient when establishing, under centralized political control, permanent representation in a foreign country. However, and besides some interesting precedents from the Italian city-states, it can be said that during the Renaissance, the 16th-century French diplomatic system established for the first time some of the basic features of modern diplomacy: (1) the institutionalization of the permanent diplomatic missions and the definition of diplomatic protocolary and procedural rules; (2) the importance granted to secrecy of negotiation as well as to the personal caution and discretion of diplomats; (3) the extension of some important privileges and immunities for the ambassadors; (4) the professionalization and administrative centralization of diplomatic services.

Certainly, the completion of a web of ministers of foreign affairs, undoubtedly one of the basic institutions of modern diplomacy, did not appear until the late 18th century with the progressive consolidation of the modern nation-state. The great thinkers of the Enlightenment devoted considerable attention to the rational prospects for the establishment of peaceful international relations through the reform of diplomatic methods. Even so, the diplomatic world remained during this long period considerably isolated from philosophical discussions. So, it can be said that only after the revision and regulation of existing diplomatic institutions and practices during the Congress of Vienna, under the social and political impact of the French Revolution and its consequences, modern diplomacy was born in 1815. Later, during the classic era of European imperialism, the modern institution of diplomacy would be extended around the world without substantial changes, despite its increasing complexity, until the outbreak of the First World War. Nevertheless, the emergence in this period of numerous international conferences on topics such as industrial standards, intellectual property, international trade, labor legislation, or health, among others, became a way for national governments to explore potential common interests without great political costs. Thus, it can be said that during the second half of the 19th century, the old institution of diplomacy was gradually adapted to the growing functional and legitimizing needs of world capitalism.

II. OLD AND NEW DIPLOMACY

After the First World War, diplomacy experienced a number of important transformations, giving sense to the so-called transition from *old diplomacy* to *new diplomacy*. In a context in which states became more and more aware of their interdependence, and increasingly interested in obtaining popular support, the European and the colonial wars appeared both to politicians and citizens as the clearest expression of the failure classic diplomacy. The postwar crisis consequently opened a period of social, political, and academic debate about the obsolescence of traditional diplomatic methods and the need for reforms. Public opinion, mobilized first by governments in support of war efforts, would later be one of the principal sources of change. From very diverse political positions, including the peace movement, it would be claimed that diplomacy should be more open to public scrutiny, effectively submitted to international and domestic legal constraints, and specifically directed to the peaceful settlement of conflicts and the prevention of war.

The most prominent result of this new climate of opinion in the critical postwar context was the creation of the League of Nations. Although the experience of the League would fail two decades later with the rising of fascism and the outbreak of a new world war, its relevance for the contemporary transformation of diplomacy is fundamental. The League of Nations established some important limitations on the use of force, institutionalizing different procedures for the peaceful settlement of disputes and creating a completely new system of collective security with the possibility of international sanctions. Besides the innovations in the field of collective security, the League of Nations was also very important in the gradual institutionalization of multilateral diplomacy over social, economic, and technical issues. Furthermore, the experience of the League of Nations substantially improved the techniques and methods of multilateral diplomatic negotiation, and created the first political basis to finish with the secrecy of the old diplomacy, in order to restore, as the Enlightenment thinkers had proposed, the duty of publicity for international treaties. Certainly, none of these innovations avoided the outbreak of a new war, but this failure would be precisely the starting point for the next changes of diplomacy.

The transformation of diplomacy after the Second World War, was the result of several prominent factors: (1) the repercussions of the institutional innovations introduced by the United Nations on diplomacy, particularly the new system of collective security, and the strengthening of multilateral diplomacy with the Security Council, the General Assembly, and the creation of diverse specialized agencies and other important organizations; (2) the Cold War impact, manifested in the importance in an ideologically divided world of new international organizations of security, as well as in the prominent diplomatic role of the Soviet Union and China; (3) the increasing role of modern intelligence and espionage, and the diplomatic management of conflicts in the presence of nuclear weaponry; (4) the impact of the decolonization process and the subsequent denunciation by the new independent states of Africa and Asia of the Western bias of contemporary diplomacy and international law; (5) the broadening and reform of the diplomatic agenda due to growing economic and technological interdependence, and the widespread recognition of the need to promote international cooperation through the creation of international institutions; (6) the growing international relevance of nonstate actors, such as the multinational corporations, or nongovernmental organizations and the intensification and diversification, impelled by new technologies of communication, of transnational contacts. Certainly, all these realities have, during the last decades, dramatically changed the environment in which diplomatic dialogue takes place, imposing the need to rethinking the central role of diplomacy in contemporary international relations. In fact, all seems to suggest that diplomacy needs to reconsider its methods and role in global governance, even if it is difficult to foresee its disappearance.

III. BILATERAL DIPLOMACY

For centuries, the most classic form of diplomacy was bilateral relations. However, besides some partial but important precedents, such as the Havana Convention of 1928 for Latin America, it was not until the signing in 1961 of the Vienna Convention on Diplomatic Relations, that the customary rules and practices of international diplomacy were codified. Many of them needed clarification, others required their adaptation to the contemporary conditions of international relations. Moreover, there was a strong feeling among Western states that international law on diplomacy needed the formal acceptance of the new independent states of Africa and Asia, in order to elude possible controversies and political conflicts in their diplomatic relations. The Cold War political context in which the negotiation was developed was particularly clear with the initial exclusion of China and other communist states. But, finally, the Convention achieved considerable success.

The basic contents of the Vienna Convention can be summarized in four topics related with bilateral diplomatic relations: (1) the procedures for the establishment of permanent diplomatic relations between states based on mutual consent, and the required conditions for their unilateral reprieve or severance; (2) the identification of official representation and the promotion of friendly relations and international cooperation as the basic functions of permanent missions; (3) the protection of the legitimate interests of the sending state, and those of its nationals; (4) the inviolability of the mission's premises, assets, or communications as well as the personal inviolability and jurisdictional immunity of diplomatic agents, as the functional privileges required by diplomatic missions. Furthermore, as a clear expression of fear of foreign interference in domestic affairs, the Convention also detailed the duties which missions must observe toward the receiving state.

As some qualified observers have pointed out, the principal reason for the considerable success of the Vienna Convention in a particularly complex political context was surely its functional and pragmatic approach. Of course, the formal regulation established by the Vienna Convention did not reflect the wide variety of practices associated with contemporary bilateral diplomatic relations nor the real political functions fulfilled by resident embassies' daily work. Certainly, the traditional methods of diplomatic communication and practice have suffered important transformations during the last decades. The spectacular development of transport and telecommunications has taken much of significance away from embassies, dramatically transforming the methods of information, and the possibilities of direct personal contact. Nevertheless, some of the most classic diplomatic procedures, such as diplomatic correspondence in the form of letters or memoranda, still play an important role in contemporary international relations. Diplomatic notes, for example, are widely used for a great variety of purposes, ranging from administrative matters to the expression of a formal protest.

The establishment of diplomatic relations among sovereign states is a matter of mutual consent. The correspondent agreement may contain different stipulations, always in accordance with the Vienna Convention, as well as some additional features such as limitations on the number and mobility of personnel at the embassies and consulates. Agreement with a newly independent state on diplomatic relations used to be considered an act of tacit recognition. Similarly, the maintenance of diplomatic relations can be interpreted, unless explicitly indicated to the contrary, as a form of tacit recognition of any change, even unconstitutional changes, in the political system of the receiving state. The severance of diplomatic relations is a discretionary unilateral act by the state that can be an expression of disapproval or dissatisfaction with the other state. Notwithstanding, the ceasing of diplomatic relations does not affect the existing treaty obligations, particularly those related with the legal protection of the citizens of each state in the territory of the other. However, as the citizens of the sending state lose the protection of their home country, a third state, acceptable to both the receiving and the sending states, may be entrusted with their protection.

IV. MULTILATERAL DIPLOMACY

The main field of change and innovation in contemporary diplomacy during recent decades has not been the old institution and the practice of bilateralism, but innovation due to the spread of multilateral and conference diplomacy. Although multilateral diplomacy is far from being an innovation of the present century, its dramatic growth during recent decades merits explanation. Undoubtedly, increasing international awareness of contemporary conditions of interdependence could explain the functional and rational basis for the growing institutionalization of international cooperation. Multilateralism seems to be a tool especially appropriate to deal with current economic, technological, or ecological problems, through the establishment of diverse international regimes. In fact, the growing importance of international institutions and organizations, and the so-called parliamentary diplomacy, with its deep implications on diplomacy and international law, reveals the progressive institutionalization of international society. Furthermore, it can be said that contemporary multilateralism serves both the functional and legitimizing needs of global political economy, establishing new forms of international regulation over economic and technological issues, as well as new ways of managing potential social conflicts.

In response to the growing importance of multilateralism and the new challenges posed to diplomacy by the increasing role of international organizations, in 1975 a new Vienna Convention tried, without success, to establish a regulation for multilateral dimensions of diplomacy. The Convention, which did not come into force, covered topics such as privileges and immunities of missions to international organizations as well as their diplomatic status. But besides these types of formal problems, key to the understanding of the growing role of international organizations, the most important implications of the rise of multilateralism on diplomatic practice are particularly clear in the domain of international negotiation.

Although the most powerful states have always tried to instrumentalize multilateralism, sometimes with unquestionable success, they are usually much more confident in their diplomatic skills in the bilateral field. Alternatively, weak states usually prefer multilateral methods because of the possibility of building coalitions based on functional, regional, or cultural aspects. For this reason, the growth of consensus and majority voting as forms of collective decision making is probably the most prominent feature of contemporary transformation of diplomacy.

V. DIPLOMATIC NEGOTIATION

Diplomatic negotiation can be defined as an attempt to explore and reconcile conflicting positions among states in order to reach an acceptable outcome for all the parties in areas of common interest. Although analysts usually identify a number of different sequential stages in diplomatic negotiations, the basic model can be characterized as a process in which parties first agree on the need to negotiate and then establish an agenda and the rules of procedure. Later, different opening positions are outlined and explored; and finally, compromises are sought in order to find a point of convergence, forming the basis for agreement. However, it cannot be assumed that any of the mentioned stages should be necessarily easier than the rest. At times, states do not recognize the need to negotiate or are unable to agree an agenda for talks, due to either its excessive precision or its vagueness, its eventual propagandistic value, or simply because of their preferences in the order of topics to be discussed.

Another question that is equally relevant is the agreement on procedure. Frequently, more than two parties are involved in the talks and the negotiation could require both bilateral and plenary sessions. This can have the effect of making the election of the delegation members more complex according to their level and competence, as well as complicate the decision-making procedures. The procedure by which decisions are made differs considerably depending on negotiation objectives. But, if the parties seek to obtain substantial agreements, it is necessary to clearly establish the rules of procedure. The preparation and discussion of a resolution is usually a lengthy and laborious process. Moreover, the states can sometimes deploy diverse tactical devices of pressure and persuasion, according to their objectives, or even quit the table, breaking the negotiation.

After discussing different drafts, the proposed resolution can be submitted to final approval. Although the adoption of decisions by consensus is very common, the most frequent method is voting. In fact, the unanimity rule might induce paralysis when large numbers of states are involved. There are three particularly relevant aspects of voting. First, the weight of votes, ranging from the classic system of one vote per country, to diverse forms of vote qualification according to some formulas, such as the country's financial contribution to the agreement, or others related to their size or relevance to a particular topic. Second, the specification of quorum requirements in order to elude controversies among the parties during voting. Third, and the most prominent, are majority requirements. Decisions can be made by single majority or qualified two-thirds majority of those present and voting, but sometimes unanimity can be required, or even the majority of some specified members, as in the United Nations Security Council.

Besides the formal aspects, the parties shall also establish a certain agreement on the level of discretion required in the negotiation, but it must always be developed in accordance with the rules of diplomatic protocol and the general principles of international law. Nevertheless, due to contemporary requirements of legitimacy in the democratic political process, diplomatic negotiation must sometimes be extended to society, eventually establishing consultative meetings with nongovernmental organizations, pressure groups and noncentral governments. A sign of the increasing public interest in multilateral diplomacy is also the growing relevance of the international conferences, organized by nongovernmental organizations, with the objective of achieving influence on the diplomatic agenda, on topics such as development, human rights, or the environment, among others.

Today, a great deal of bilateral and multilateral diplomacy takes place at the level of heads of government. Summitry is certainly as old as any other form of diplomacy, but during the last decades and due to the fast development of transport and communications it has gained considerable prominence. Both serial and *ad hoc* summits are usually subjected to greater public attention than standard multilateral or bilateral diplomacy. For this reason, without denying its diplomatic relevance, summitry may frequently be used as an excellent tool for foreign or domestic propaganda, as was clearly exhibited during the Cold War. Furthermore, unless it would have been prepared meticulously, summitry used to be seen by professional diplomats as a certain intrusion in their daily work, which sometimes creates more inconveniences than advantages.

VI. FROM PEACEFUL TO COERCIVE DIPLOMACY

Probably the foremost role of diplomacy over its long history has been the peaceful settlement of disputes. Indeed, it can be said that some of the basic contributions of contemporary peace research such as the techniques of mediation and reconciliation were well known from the early beginnings of modern diplomatic practice. Notwithstanding, until the innovations established by the League of Nations, the adoption of different means of peaceful settlement of conflict was certainly a choice but never a legal duty for the states. Later, the Charter of the United Nations established the duty of peaceful settlement of disputes as a general principle of international law, considerably developing its institutional aspects without changing substantially its traditional methods. In fact, the United Nations' more prominent innovation was precisely the possibility of nonpeaceful application of international law, through the coercive competencies of the Security Council. Consequently, the contemporary methods of peaceful settlement of disputes, in spite of their adaptation to contemporary institutional and technological conditions, remain similar to their traditional antecedents. Previously we have referred to negotiation as the most prominent and widespread method for settling international differences and the most characteristic method of diplomatic practice. However, not always is it possible to easily achieve direct discussion among the parties in a dispute.

For this reason, over history, the states have developed diverse political and jurisdictional methods of peaceful settlement: (1) *Good offices* is the participation of a neutral third party in order to facilitate the communication between the parties, but without offering any substantial suggestion on the possible terms of settlement. (2) *Inquiry* is the process of obtaining evidence by a neutral team of investigators, requested by the parties in conflict. The clarification of facts can be very important in order to avoid misunderstandings and facilitate a political agreement. (3) *Diplomatic mediation* is another type of third-party intervention that is especially adequate in disputes in which compromise seems to be very hard to achieve, due to the hostility among the parties or the nature of the conflict. Although the mediator ought to be neutral, particularly important is his or her ability to make substantial proposals in order to seek a compromise, even if they could be understood by one party as favorable to the other side. (4) *Conciliation* is another form of mediation in which a particular international institution has been requested by the parties, due to its recognized neutrality and experience in seeking to find an acceptable solution. (5) *Arbitration* is a method of applying legal principles to a controversy in which the parties have agreed previously on legal principles and procedures, and have chosen the court—permanent or *ad hoc*—they prefer. In agreeing to submit the dispute to arbitration the parties are bound by the final decision. (6) *Judicial settlement* implies that the states in conflict consent in submitting, without any previous limitation, their dispute to the International Court Justice.

However, it should be noted that the states are usually more willing to negotiate directly, or even to accept a mediation, than to consent in a judicial settlement the sentence of which is of compulsory compliance. Contemporary international law established the duty of peaceful settlement of disputes, but nothing assures its political success. So, it can be reasonably stressed that a good diplomatic method in dealing with international disputes should be the deployment of different strategies of preventive diplomacy. Those strategies can be of a very different nature, military as well as nonmilitary, according to their diverse objectives, such as crisis prevention, preemptive engagement, or preconflict peace building.

Although diplomacy is generally defined as the conduct of international relations through negotiation and dialogue or by any other means able to encourage peaceful relations among states, it is difficult to deny that threats and coercion have played an important role in international relations. Moreover, despite the contemporary erosion of militarism and the decreasing role of military force in world politics, nothing seems to suggest that coercion will disappear. A possible solution to this apparent contradiction is to reserve the analysis of international coercion to foreign policy analysis, acknowledging its widely accepted incompatibility with diplomacy. Nevertheless, there is also an increasing amount of literature devoted to the study of coercive diplomacy. Coercive diplomacy is a defensive strategy that is employed to deal with the efforts of an adversary to change a *status quo* situation. Coercive diplomacy needs to be clearly differentiated from offensive strategies. The latter employs threats in an aggressive manner against target states. It is also quite different from deterrence, the preventive employment of threats to dissuade an adversary from undertaking a damaging action not yet initiated. This was certainly a type of diplomacy particularly prominent and controversial during the Cold War, but has today lost a great deal of its relevance. According to their proponents there are three basic types of coercive strategy, which should preferably be used after the failed resort of other more peaceful alternatives, such as a negotiated settlement. The first tries simply to persuade the opponent to stop the hostile action. The second seeks the reversal of the action already accomplished. The third, and undoubtedly the most controversial, seeks to terminate the opponent's hostile behavior through a demand for change in the adversary's domestic political system. Certainly, the diplomatic nature of coercive diplomacy can be debated, given that it could be sometimes a form of illegal interference on domestic affairs. However, it is difficult to deny the relevance of these practices for the contemporary understanding of international relations. Precisely for this reason, it must be remembered that the United Nations system of collective security is precisely, in spite of growing importance also given to peaceful means of preventive diplomacy, the only contemporary legal expression firmly established by international law of coercive but multilateral diplomacy.

This brief description of the classic methods of diplomatic settlement of disputes, as well as the short discussion on the importance of preventive and coercive diplomacy, can easily suggest that the theory of diplomacy has invariably considered the relations among states as the source of international conflicts. Notwithstanding, during the Enlightenment it was suggested by some prominent thinkers, and particularly by Kant, that true peaceful diplomacy would only be possible through the complete abolition of absolute monarchies. This type of examination of the existing relation between domestic political systems and international peace has been extensively reintroduced during the past years by an increasing amount of literature. The common point of departure is the empirical evidence that democracies seem to be much less willing to use violence among them than against nondemocracies. There are two prominent explanations to the so-called *democratic peace*. Some scholars have suggested that the reason may be the intrinsic complexity of the institutional procedures of democratic political process. Others find the source of more peaceful diplomacy in normative constraints imposed by social values of the general public in democratic states. Any thorough analysis of this question considerably exceeds the limits of this article, but its mention can suggest an interesting starting point for the analysis of domestic sources of peaceful diplomacy.

VII. CONCLUSION

The ability to conduct diplomatic relations was considered since the beginnings of modern nation-state as one of the basic attributes of state sovereignty. Much more problematic is the associated assumption that it is also an exclusive one. Historical research has unquestionably established that diplomacy considerably predates the modern sovereign nation-state. In fact, the origins of diplomacy were the multiple practices of public and private communication among different political entities existing since ancient times. Certainly, these practices underwent different historical transformations until becoming conventionally redefined as exclusive attribute of the sovereign nation-states.

Today, the conventional study of diplomacy tends to exclude a wide range of practices, such as corporate, nongovernmental, and non-central government involvement in international affairs, in spite of their increasing relevance. Notwithstanding, the widely extended consideration of diplomacy as an exclusive attribute of sovereign state is more an institutionalized political discourse than the corollary of an empirical evidence.

Nevertheless, and besides the increasing number of international actors, public or private, involved in paradiplomatic activities, the main field of change and innovation in contemporary diplomacy during the last decades has been the spread of multilateralism and conference diplomacy. The increasing international awareness of contemporary conditions of interdependence could explain the functional and rational basis of the growing institutionalization of international cooperation, through the establishment of international regimes. Furthermore, contemporary multilateralism serves both to the functional and legitimizing needs of global political economy, establishing new forms of international regulation over economic, technological, or ecological issues, as well as new ways of managing potential social conflicts.

Also See the Following Articles

COLLECTIVE SECURITY • CONFLICT MANAGEMENT AND RESOLUTION • INTERNATIONAL RELATIONS, OVERVIEW • MEDIATION AND NEGOTIATION • PEACE AND DEMOCRACY

Bibliography

Armstrong, D. (1993). *Revolution and world order: The revolutionary state in international society*. Oxford: Clarendon Press.

Anderson, M. S. (1993). *The rise of modern diplomacy,* New York: Longman.

Barston, R. P. (1988). *Modern Diplomacy*. New York: Longman.

Berridge, G. R. (1995). *Diplomacy: theory and practice*, London: Prentice Hall.

Blumann, C. (1989). *Aspects récents du droit des relations diplomatiques*. Paris: Pedone.

Brown, M. E., Lynn Jones, & Miller, S. E. (Eds.). (1996). *Debating the democratic peace*. Cambridge: The MIT Press.

Clavel, J. D. (1991). *De la negotiation diplomatique multilaterale*. Paris: Bruylant.

Der Derian, J. (1987). *On diplomacy: A genealogy of Western estrangement*. Oxford: Blackwell.

Diamond, L., & McDonald, J. W. (1993). *Multitrack diplomacy: A systems approach to peace*. Washington DC: Institute for Multi Track Diplomacy.

George, A. L., & Simons, W. S. (Eds.). (1994). *The limits of coercive diplomacy*. Boulder, CO: Westview Press.

Hamilton, K., & Langhorne, R. (1995). *The practice of diplomacy: Its evolution, theory and administration*. London: Routledge.

Hocking, B. (1993). *Localizing foreign policy: Non-central governments and multilayered diplomacy*. London: Macmillan.

Kaufmann, J. (1996). *Conference diplomacy*. London: Macmillan.

Lund, M. S. (1996). *Preventing violent conflicts: A strategy for preven-*

tive diplomacy. Washington DC: United States Institute of Peace Press.

Moore, R. (1985). *Third World diplomats in dialogue with the First World*, Ottawa: Macmillan.

Murphy, G. N. (1994). *International organization and industrial change: Global governance since 1850*. Cambridge: Polity Press.

Nicolson, H. (1963). *Diplomacy*. London: Oxford University Press.

Plantey, A. (1991). *De la politique entre les Etats: Principles de la diplomatie*. Paris: Pedone.

Strange, S., & Stopford, M. (1991). *Rival states, rival firms: Competition for world market shares*. Cambridge: Cambridge University Press.

Vilariño, E. (1991). *Curso de Derecho Diplomático y Consular*. Madrid: Tecnos.

Watson, A. (1982). *Diplomacy: The dialogue between states*. London: Methuen.

Draft, Resistance and Evasion of

Jesus Casquette
University of the Basque Country

GLOSSARY

Conscientious Objector Conscientious objector is a person liable to conscription for military service, or to registration for conscription for military service, who, for reasons of conscience, refuses to perform armed service or to collaborate in any way in wars or armed conflicts.

Draft (or Conscription) The state's routine of recruiting able-bodied adult citizens (mostly males) to contribute to the defense of the country for a limited period of time.

Pacifism The doctrine opposing all wars and by extension all preparations for war.

Peace Churches Churches that sustain an uncompromising refusal of violence and war. The main bodies historically are the Mennonites, the Brethren, and the Quakers.

Principle of Equivalency The requirement that people refusing military service make some alternative contribution to society. It can take several forms: payment of fines or commutation fees, the hiring of a substitute, performance of noncombatant duties in the military, or, more recently, the performance of alternative civilian service.

Resistance to and Evasion of Conscription Resistance and evasion of the draft refers to all efforts to avoid the performance of compulsory military (or, as may be, alternative civilian) service on the part of the people liable to perform such services.

I. INTRODUCTION

The duty to fight and, if necessary, die for the state is said to be the most serious obligation that the status of citizenship entails. Nevertheless, there have always been dissenters who have contested the obligation to defend their countries. Two different means of expressing dissent may be distinguished: resistance and evasion. Although both stances try to avoid the draft, in analytical terms (in practical terms it is not always easy to disentangle one from the other) there is a difference between them. On the one hand, resistance to the draft entails an organized action on the basis of a common belief against the state's demand that its citizens perform military service. Evasion of the draft, on the other hand, usually lacks any organized or collective character. It is the seeking of an individual solution to the burden of military service. Some forms of evasion to which draftees have resorted in recent history are draft dodging, desertion, simulation of sickness, self-mutilation, migration, purchasing of exemptions, and hiring of substitutes. In what follows, emphasis will be put on the Western experience of resistance and evasion of the draft.

Conscientious objection is the most important form that resistance to the practice of conscription has taken in modern times in Western countries. Although principled resistance to military service is a long-standing phenomenon in Western countries, only in recent decades have the growing figures of conscientious objection made it a major factor affecting the relationship between armed forces and society.

Conscientious objectors can be classified into several subcategories. On the basis of their motivation, conscientious objectors can ground their refusal to perform military service either on religious beliefs (including those coming to their beliefs through historic peace sects, through mainline churches, and through nonmainline denominations) or on secular motives (including those with either political or private motives). In recent decades, social trends such as the growth of individualism and the secularization of conscience, along with the spreading of institutional arrangements that lower the costs of becoming a conscientious objector, have been chiefly responsible for the exponential rise of resistance to military service. The center of gravity of conscientious objection has accordingly shifted from traditional peace churches to the more inclusive mainstream religious denominations to an ever-widening group for whom objection to military service is based solely upon humanistic or private motives.

On the basis of the scope of their beliefs, conscientious objectors can be universalistic or selective. Universalistic COs are those individuals who hold a strong belief that war and killing are wrong in any circumstances, regardless of its expediency. These "pure pacifists" are the kind of COs most likely to be recognized by the state. Selective COs, on the other hand, sustain a qualified condemnation. In their understanding, war and killing are prima facie wrong, but not always so. The target of their objection can either be a specific war, a specific army—for example, Basques or Lithuanians refusing to serve in the Spanish and Soviet armies, respectively—a specific policy—for examples, Israeli draftees refusing to serve in the occupied territories or South Africans unwilling to collaborate with the policy of apartheid—or a specific type of weapon, primarily weapons of mass destruction such as nuclear weapons.

A third taxonomy of conscientious objectors relates to their degree of willingness to cooperate with the authorities. Thus, noncombatant COs are those individuals unwilling to fight or to bear arms but ready to compromise with the state by fulfilling a military obligation, typically by serving in the branch of the military directly dedicated to saving lives such as the medical corps. The formal incorporation of dissidence in this way ensures the legitimacy of the larger duty. Consequently, noncombatant objectors experience the least friction with the military system simply because they help the system function. The second category of conscientious objectors include the group of people who refuse to perform military service but agree to participate in civilian alternative service in public or private agencies. They are known as alternativists. Most typically, they engage in conservation, health, cultural, or social work. Finally, absolutist objectors refuse to follow the call up by taking an unlawful, public, nonviolent, and conscious stance against the draft because they feel that to accept any alternative to military service is synonymous with becoming an accomplice in the working of conscription. From the point of view of a sociology of disobedience, this duty to disobey the authorities arises when obligations incurred in some secondary group with claims to primacy come into conflict with obligations incurred in a more inclusive group such as the state. Because their claim to be morally right in disobeying a law that is morally wrong directly defies the authority of the state, absolutists are the COs most likely to be imprisoned.

II. STATEMAKING AND REJECTION OF THE DRAFT IN EUROPE

A. Rebellion and Evasion of the Draft in the Eighteenth and Nineteenth Centuries

The armed forces of the various European countries in the 18th century all had their own peculiarities. Nevertheless, them all shared a set of features summarized in the following:

1. All states employed foreign troops in vast numbers. This is especially true for the period between the 15th and the 17th centuries—the critical period of state formation—when armies deployed throughout much of Europe consisted largely of mercenaries recruited by great lords and military entrepreneurs. However, with the 18th century the rising costs and political risks of large-scale nonstate forces led the rulers of these states to rely increasingly on their own citizenry, and to use it instead of foreign mercenaries where possible. The reason was straightfor-

ward. As pointed out by Machiavelli at the beginning of the 16th century, a state's own citizens fought more reliably and more cheaply than soldiers of fortune, not to mention that the purely contractual relationship between mercenaries and the crown considerably raised the dangers of foot-dragging, rebellion, and even rivalry for political power.

2. Some people were more likely to be conscripted than others. Recruitment of criminals, vagabonds, and the destitute was standard practice. Although the scope of compulsion to military service varied from country to country, opportunity was usually taken—especially, but not exclusively, in wartime—to channel into the army or the navy men considered socially dangerous and undesirable, whether they were convicted criminals, habitual mendicants, or just serfs deemed expendable by their lords and masters. When war broke out, the convict population became the front line of the military, and when war was over, the troops went back to the prisons and the galleys.

3. Volunteers were welcome in all armed forces, but conscripts were also needed in many instances. The usual method of recruitment was to specify the proportion of liable men they needed, for example, one in twenty-four, and then leave the method of selection to the local authority. If one young man was unlucky to be drafted, but at the same time rich enough to pay a substitute or purchase the exemption, then he could evade the draft. The practice of paying a commutation fee and hiring substitutes was a legal one and very widespread throughout Europe until well into the 19th century.

4. Force was the prevailing argument used by the authorities both to get draftees into their armed forces and to stop them getting out. In order to prevent desertion—an endemic feature of every country despite all attempts to stop it—military authorities resorted to all sorts of measures. Prussian commanders, for example, avoided camping or fighting in wooded, hilly country, and marching by night. Likewise, British sailors were not normally allowed on shore even when their ship was in port, cordons of troops were set round major naval bases, and rewards for deserted-trackers were offered. In spite of all these measures, the desertion rate in Britain was extraordinary: 42,000 out of 176,000 men raised between 1774 and 1780 deserted.

Such was the relationship between armed forces and society in Europe in the 18th century. However, the scenario changed dramatically with the creation of a standing army by the French Revolution and its principle of "nation in arms." More specifically, the foundations of the modern link between conscription and citizenship lie in France with the introduction of the *levée en masse* in 1793. In March of that year, the National Assembly authorized a nationwide call for 300,000 conscripts. According to the call, unmarried men and widowers without descendants between 18 and 40 years old were liable for conscription. Civil servants, the "true patriots," were exempted. This suddenly imposed grievance became very unpopular. The explanation is straightforward: state-making efforts (and conscription falls squarely within these efforts) entailed heavy burdens to the population, since the authorities pressed the population in search of money, separated the individual from his local community and family obligations, cut and intruded into everyday life of local communities. The population reacted accordingly, often in a violent fashion. So in revolutionary France, while some departments returned their quotas very quickly, others never returned any at all. All in all, only about half of the 300,000 looked for ever entered service. Resistance to the draft was especially fierce in the west of the country, occasionally reaching the proportion of true rebellions. This was the case of the Vendée, where some 100,000 men rebelled against the revolutionary government. Although anticonscription riots proliferated all over Europe as recruiting efforts by the state intensified, no 19th-century movement against conscription reached such a large scale of mobilization. In this century, oftentimes conflicts around the issue of conscription (as in Germany, France, and Italy) consisted of local opposition to the forced departure of particular individuals.

A few years after the first *levée en masse,* in 1798, France became a state committed to military activity driven by its expansionist policy. In that year the National Assembly passed the general Law of Conscription (Jourdan Law), according to which 20- to 25-year-old men had to serve for 5 years (or the duration of the war). Although the revolution had ordained that no replacements or exemptions should be allowed, as early as 1799 that attempt at egalitarian democratic principles was abandoned and those who could afford it were allowed to purchase replacements out of a pool of former servicemen (avoidance of service by money payment was formally abolished in France in 1872, later than in Germany or Austria, but it continued for another generation in Belgium and Spain). Evasion practices followed patterns that had to do with physical fitness and were well known from previous times: simulation of sickness (in France, as virtually everywhere else, a very large proportion of men liable to the call-up proved physically unfit), self-mutilation of thumbs or hands, or pulling out of teeth (essential to prepare cartridges). Except during brief periods of patriotic enthusiasm, draft dodging and desertion were widespread practices among the poorer strata of the population that could not afford to buy exemption. According to some estimations, evasion practices of these kinds involved more than one-third of the call-up. It is not surprising then that the revolutionary government worried about evasion rates, so much that from 1799 on countermeasures were being taken, the like of which were to go on until 1814: night raids on houses, the gendarmerie and even soldiers closing escape routes and combing forests, and—probably the most effective device—the seizure of hostages from uncooperative families or the billeting of troops on them until they produced their boy.

In spite of all the innovations she introduced, France did not invent conscription in the modern form. This merit should be credited to Prussia after 1815, and then to Germany, which by the last third of the 19th century had fashioned a model of mass conscript and reserve army, according to which all young men (with whatever exceptions) went through 3 years of military training and then remained liable to recall until they reached middle age. By the time of World War I, this system had been adopted by the great states of continental Europe—Italy, Russia, France, Germany, and Austro-Hungary—as well as Japan. The underlying principle in all cases was the same: conscription was to be one of the pillars of the democratic states, for it was an instrument for developing social cohesion and political docility of the masses, a school of political socialization, and an essential bond between the citizen and the state. By that time, the state had won the argument over conscription. The general right of the government to require military service from its citizens was not ordinarily at issue. Yet evasion attempts did not disappear altogether nor will they ever. Draftees continued to desert and simulate sickness. Furthermore, emigration (temporary or permanent) became a widespread practice in areas such as Russia, Greece, and Italy. It was to escape conscription that many Russian Jews poured into Britain and the United States in the late 19th century. An inquiry among 131 immigrants in the United States showed that 18 of them—5 Russians and 13 Greeks—had crossed the ocean to avoid conscription. An 1888 Italian law sought to prevent men below the age of 32 from leaving the country.

Nevertheless, emigration and resistance to the draft was not completely unknown among the Christian peace sects whose members had been leaving their countries because of the draft for quite a long time.

B. The Christian Stand against the Draft

When the Roman Catholic Church disintegrated at the Reformation in the 16th century, Christendom became divided into Roman Catholic areas, established Protestant areas (mainly Lutheran or Calvinist), and a variety of pacifist Protestants whose common feature was their rejection of the new as well as the old establishments. More specifically, they were divided over the issue of peace and the use of violence as a means of resolving conflicts. To be sure, there were true pacifist individuals in all churches who held the belief that the taking of human life under any circumstances was evil. However, only the third group (which included the Anabaptists, the Brethren, and the Quakers) can legitimately be termed as pacifists. They all rejected the Augustinian doctrine of the just war (further elaborated by Thomas Aquinas in the 13th century), according to which legally constituted authorities are entitled to conduct war for legitimate causes. To them, any notion of justified violence stood against the biblical commandment of "Thou shalt not kill." These sects developed elaborate beliefs of nonresistance and, over time, established a strong tradition of opposition to the draft and, more broadly, to warfare.

Compulsory military service was much less widespread in the principalities and monarchies at the time of the Reformation and immediately after than it became under the later nation-states. During this period, informal arrangements developed between the ruling sovereigns and the dissenting religious sects that opposed the draft. Payment of fines, commutation of military service into other work, and provision of substitutes became established channels of accommodating the will of the authorities and the irreducible pacifist beliefs of the religious draftees. When the situation became unbearable for those sects in their continental European countries, migration, especially to the New World, became a common practice for evading the draft. From England members of the Religious Society of Friends, known as Quakers, arrived in the United States, and politically dominated Pennsylvania for more than 50 years beginning in the 1680s. In the early 1700s the Mennonites (successors of the Anabaptists) and the Amish (a more rigorous splinter group of the Mennonites) arrived in the United States. Some of the Mennonites had migrated to Russia instead, but during the 1870s they moved to America, fleeing Tsarist persecution. Finally, members of the German Baptist Brethren or Dunkers brought their pacifism to America at the beginning of the 18th century. This last group shared with the Quakers an unwillingness to participate in any kind of military activity but, on the other hand, resembled the Mennonites and Amish in remaining aloof from the world. The same was initially true of the Moravian Brethren who first migrated from Moravia to Saxony and then, also in the early 18th century, to America.

The colonies were very much in need of settlers, especially qualified ones such as these nonresistant Christians, as they came to be known at the time. The legislators as well as the local militia officers of the early colonial days also realized that these men would rather obey the law of God than the law of the secular conscripting authorities. Consequently, a number of colonies provided exemptions from militia training and service for members of the historic peace churches, as well as for smaller denominations whose members stubbornly refused to bear arms. However, these religious conscientious objectors had to pay a fine to evade the draft or, like other draftees, they could hire a substitute if drafted into temporary units in wartime. Such provisions were enacted by all of the 13 original colonies except for Georgia. This pattern of exemption for members of sectarian churches through equivalency was maintained in both the North and the South during the Civil War.

III. DRAFT REJECTION IN THE ERA OF MASS WAR

There have always been dissenters who have called the draft into question every time the authorities have resorted to this prerogative. Nevertheless, war is often the greatest test of the convictions of those opposing the resort to violence. Furthermore, at wartime dissent may take on a broader character, occasionally giving birth to large-scale social movements against conscription. Our attention in this section will center on three landmark conflicts: World War I, World War II, and the Vietnam War.

A. The First World War

Prior to the First World War, a considerable number of Europeans were deeply committed to preventing war. Governments did not fear religious pacifism, which might irritate authorities from time to time, but never threatened their power. What they feared most of all was the labor movement, and with good reason. At every congress of the First Socialist International after 1867, and then at all sessions of the Second International after 1889 (in which socialism defined itself as the "only and true party of peace") resolutions were adopted sharply condemning militarism, denouncing modern war as the instrument of competing capitalist states in the imperialist race, and expressing the social democrats' determination to do everything possible to resist a war in which the workers would be the inevitable victims. This self-definition was still adhered to at the end of July 1914, when the leaders of the European socialist parties met in Brussels in a desperate attempt to find a solution to the ongoing crisis.

In spite of its antimilitarist conviction backed by millions of followers, socialism was seized with patriotic fervor. The promise of resisting war was thus never fulfilled. Faced with contradictory appeals to nation, on the one hand, and to class on the other, most socialists followed the colors as did almost everyone else at the time. A movement ideologically committed to internationalism and peace collapsed suddenly into impotence, and a wave of patriotism under the ruling classes swept over the parties of the belligerent countries.

Next we turn to examine the patterns of resistance to the draft during the First World War, focusing on those major contending countries that provided a framework for legal conscientious objection, namely, Britain and the United States. Whereas in countries such as France, Germany, and Russia universal military service was established by the end of the 19th century, in Great Britain after 1860 and in the United States soon after the Civil War militia conscription was finally abandoned, and these two countries went over entirely to the voluntary system. The imposition during World War I of compulsory military service for all adult able-bodied males served to reactivate pacifism in these two countries. At the end of this section, mention will be made to the fate of resisters to the draft in other countries.

1. Great Britain

Great Britain entered the war under a Liberal government, many of whose members and followers openly disliked the idea of the draft. However, due to nationalist pressure from Conservative opposition in parliament and from popular demand in society, the draft was finally introduced in 1916. It was the first experience in Britain of national conscription. In the course of the debates on the conscription acts, the government recognized the right of conscientious objectors to military service to have their scruples respected. The local tribunals created to administer the conscientious objection act were most of the times unsympathetic to applicants' claims. Members of these tribunals showed themselves more ready to recognize religious imperatives than secular convictions. By proceeding in that way, the tribunals were reflecting public opinion, which tended to regard dissenters as playing the German game and consequently felt that they should not be allowed to put their private conscience before the needs of the nation. Secular objectors were therefore forced to enlist in the military and were liable to court-martial if they refused to accept military orders.

Conscientious objectors (or "conchies," as they were derisively called at the time) who made their way through the tribunals were mostly assigned to the Non-Combatant Corps (NCC) or to "work of national importance" (employment in agriculture, forestry, food-processing industries, education, hospitals, etc.). Those objectors allocated to the NCC had to wear uniforms and were subject to army discipline, although they were not required to carry weapons or to take part in combat. For these reasons, many objectors considered service in the NCC to be part of the military machine and chose prison rather than compliance.

Altogether, about 16,000 young men claimed conscientious objector status in Great Britain between the implementation of the draft act in 1916 and the end of the war. In relative terms, they comprised less than 1% of the drafted population. Some 3300 of them accepted service in the NCC; somewhat less than 3000 performed ambulance work or worked under the direct supervision of their tribunals; around 4000 accepted work of national importance; and rather more than 6000 went to prison at least once. Of this last group, 3750 were subsequently employed under the Home Office Scheme, leaving 1500 stubborn absolutists who stood for the right of individual protest against the demands of the state. The remaining objectors compromised in different ways with the authorities. Seventy-three men actually died from prison treatment and another 31 were driven mad. Thirty-four objectors were at one time in danger of execution, although no death sentence was in fact carried out. These figures of resistance to the draft show the marginality in numerical terms of the opposition to the draft when compared with the 750,000 men who volunteered in the first 8 weeks of the war and the additional million in the next 8 months. By February 1916, more than two-and-a-half million men had willingly stepped forward.

The major associations in which resisters to the draft were organized were the No-Conscription Fellowship (NCF) and the Fellowship of Reconciliation. In both organizations, the social background of the members was middle class. The NCF was created shortly after the outbreak of the war, and was the most vigorous organization to resist first the introduction of the draft and then its implementation. It consisted of young men of military age who based their case on the dictates of the individual conscience rather than religious command. Its leaders were on the whole without religious ties. On the other hand, the Fellowship of Reconciliation, founded about the same time, was mainly organized by the nonestablished churches. The Quakers, the most visible religious antiwar group within the Fellowship, reaffirmed as a body its opposition to war, but a third of their male draftees performed military service and most of the conscientious objectors among them accepted alternative service. Small sects, such as Plymouth Brethren, Christadelphians, Seventh Day Adventists, and Jehovah's Witnesses were more rigorously opposed to the draft. Anglican, Roman Catholic, Muslim, Jewish, and other objectors were few.

2. The United States

The United States entered World War I in April 1917. Within 2 months, the first national draft since the Civil War was passed. The draft required all males between ages 21 and 30 to register for military service. Induction at that time was not regulated by local draft boards. Instead, draftees were inducted directly into the army and subjected to military rules. Conscientious objectors could either opt for noncombatant service or resist and face courts-martial.

The draft was not a popular measure. Of 24 million registrants, there were 330,000 draft evaders reported during the war. Some 3 million may have failed to register. Furthermore, as many as 60% of those registering requested exemptions on mental, physical, occupational, dependency, or conscience grounds. Some local riots also took place.

At the start of the war, the government limited exemptions on conscientious objection grounds to members of the traditional pacifist religions whose absolute rejection of war and violence forbade them from participating in the military. However, the Selective Service authorities (the conscription agency) failed to specify which religious denominations qualified. Absolute exemption from military service was not legally possible. Among the 64,700 draftees who applied on registration to be assigned to noncombatant service (against 3 million who volunteered), the local boards certified 56,800 as COs. Thirty thousand of them passed their physical examination, of whom 20,873 were inducted into the army. In military camps, physical coercion and brutality against COs was not infrequent. They were considered as dangerous enemies of the state and treated consequently. Common punishment for COs (and other military prisoners) who would not respond to military orders in the camps consisted of two consecutive weeks in solitary confinement on a bread and water diet in a dark cell, chained or handcuffed to the wall for 9 hours each day, beaten with fists or rubber hoses, scrubbed down in cold showers with stiff brushes until their skin was raw. Wartime repression clearly exceeded that exercised in Britain. There was a widespread feeling that the authorities had endangered American freedoms. The experience of World War I put civil liberties on the agenda and led to the creation of a major watchdog organization, the American Civil Liberties Union.

As a direct consequence of their experience in training camps, approximately 80% of the 20,873 inducted certified COs decided to give up their stand as objectors and to serve as soldiers in the army. Nevertheless, 4000 young men reasserted their compromise not to participate in war and obtained legal CO exemption from active combat duty. Three-quarters of these belonged to the historic peace churches (Quakers, Brethren, and Mennonites). The training camps also held a few young members of two millenarian sects: the Seventh-Day Adventists, and the Russellites, subsequently renamed as Jehovah's Witnesses. The latter were not ready to cooperate with existing secular institutions, refused to fight for them, and unsuccessfully demanded ministerial exemption on the grounds that all its members were ministers. The uncompromising stand of the Jehovah's Witnesses was to create a major problem for the authorities during World War II.

An additional 15% of the COs in World War I belonged to nonpacifist churches. They were mostly middle-class and well-educated liberals. The remaining 10% fall within the category of objectors who opposed the draft and the war for political reasons. This group included socialists, syndicalists of the Industrial Workers of the World union, anarchists, and some young men of anti-Allied ethnic descent who were considered to be dangerous to national security.

Ultimately, the armed services convicted 540 COs at courts-martial. These were the absolutist COs who resisted all military authority. They were charged with offenses such as refusing to carry a rifle, refusal to train or follow orders, and failure to wear military uniforms. Seventeen of them were sentenced to death, 142 to life imprisonment, and 345 to jail terms averaging $16\frac{1}{2}$ years. None of the death sentences was carried out. The imprisoned absolutists were released by the end of 1920, once their offense was deemed to be expunged by the termination of the war. At least 17 of the COs died in jail as a consequence of mistreatment and poor prison conditions.

Repression against resisters to the draft among the general population was no less noticeable. Altogether, more than 2100 persons were indicted under the Espionage and Sedition laws, always for expressing in public opposition to the war, and 1000 of them were convicted. More than 100 were sentenced to jail terms of 10 years or more.

3. Other Countries

Apart from the countries of the British Empire, in which the pattern in dealing with COs was more or less the same as in Britain itself, recognition of the right to exemption on conscience grounds was minimal. Where it did exist, it almost invariably applied solely to birthright members of the pacifist churches.

Australia was the only belligerent country that fought World War I without any form of conscription. Attempts to introduce compulsory military service through referendums failed. Potential draftees opposing the war and the authorities thus avoided confronting each other.

Although they remained neutral, the governments of Denmark (which in 1917 became the first country in mainland Europe that recognized the right of conscientious objection on religious and ethical grounds), Norway, Sweden, and the Netherlands, under pressure from "consistent antimilitarists" (mainly socialists and anarchists), as well as from religious pacifists, adopted provisions for religious objectors during World War I. In the Netherlands, most of the absolutists (totalling around 500) who refused to serve were socialists and political or religious anarchists.

In Germany, resisters to the draft were either declared to be insane and ordered to undergo psychiatric treatment, or accused of incitement to disaffection in the military, and sentenced accordingly. In France, and despite some tradition of popular resistance to the draft, there was no serious discussion of conscientious objection prior to 1920. The French did not even have the concept in their vocabularly until the 1920s, or in their dictionaries until the 1930s. In that country, the few dissenters were court-martialed as deserters and sentenced to as long as 20 years in prison. In Tsarist Russia, COs were sent to jail for 4 to 6 years, but they were released by the provisional government after the Revolution.

B. The Second World War

The experience of World War I led to the foundation of several international organizations specifically opposed to war and conscription. One such international antiwar body, based on resistance to conscription, was founded in 1921 when groups from several European countries met in the Netherlands to form Paco (meaning "peace" in Esperanto). The Dutch group was inspired by anarchism, the rest by a mixture of pacifism and socialism. In 1925 the organization, now renamed War Resisters International (WRI), held a conference attended by representatives from 20 countries. However, the WRI's absolutist position in opposing not only military service but all forms of alternative or noncombatant service limited its following to a small minority (Einstein collaborated with it for a time). Another major organization was the International Fellowship of Reconciliation (IFOR). Founded in 1919, it was an explicitly Christian body, primarily Protestant. The IFOR was a response to the failure of the churches to transcend national interests and an attempt to promote Christian pacifism.

Public knowledge of the harsh treatment of COs during World War I contributed to a more liberal policy during World War II, in both Great Britain and in the United States, once again exceptions among the major contending countries in allowing conscientious objection. Such liberalization towards COs was reflected in two changes with respect to World War I. First, conscientious objectors performing alternative service worked under civilian rather than military authorities. Secondly, both countries recognized sincere religious objectors regardless of the church they belonged to. The recognition of secular conscientious objectors remained problematic in both countries.

1. Great Britain

As was the case during World War I, refusal to serve in the military was recognized in Great Britain, but it was once again unpopular, particularly if the grounds were socialist rather than religious. As in previous conscientious objection provisions, objectors had to be opposed to all wars without discrimination ("selective" conscientious objection was not allowed). Compared with past experience during World War I, there was less persecution inside and outside the armed forces. Figures of conscientious objection in World War II show that between 1939 and 1945 there were 62,301 COs in Great Britain out of a call-up of about 5 million (that is, 1.2% of the draft, a slightly higher figure in relative terms than in the first war). Of these, 1704 were women, after single women between 20 and 30 years old were liable for conscription starting in 1942. All in all, there were more than 1000 absolutists.

2. The United States

The United States entered the war in December 1941. Shortly afterwards, the Selective Service Act enabled the government to draft millions of men. Of the 34,506,923 men who registered for the draft, only 50,000 were classified as COs. That means that around 0.15% of the eligible age group requested exemption on conscience grounds. Concerning the motivation of the draft resisters, according to an estimate as many as 93% of COs claimed a religious affiliation, the only reason that the draft boards were prepared to recognize. Most of them entered the army in noncombatant service. Some 12,000 of them were Seventh-Day Adventists. Another 12,000 COs refused to collaborate with the military in any way, but agreed to work in one of the 70 Civilian Public Service camps now operated by the historic peace churches, and not by the military as in World War I. Although the peace churches provided most of the COs to civilian service (as many as 60% of the total), many of their draft-age young men did not claim CO status, but accepted full military service instead. Ultimately, some 6000 COs were imprisoned for violating the Selective Service Act. The great majority of the imprisoned objectors, more than 3000, were Jehovah's Witnesses. There were also radical activist COs who based their absolutist stance on secular grounds. Also refusing to collaborate with the authorities in the war effort in any way was a disparate group of Black Muslims, Japanese Americans, Native Americans, and Puerto Ricans. Regardless of the motivation for violating the Selective Service Act, the maximum sentence was 5 years (on average, resisters served 35 months in jail).

After the Second World War, both the United States and Britain expanded their definitions of conscientious objection to include secular reasons, and also set up individual alternative service in various public and private agencies. This policy existed until the end of conscription, which occurred in 1963 in Britain and 10 years later in the United States.

3. Other Countries

In Germany, the Third Reich regime initially imprisoned COs. After 1938, and particularly after the beginning of World War II, resistance to the draft was punishable by death. At that time, COs were sent to concentration camps and executed. In France before occupation there were perhaps a dozen COs. In the Soviet Union conscientious objection was abolished by Stalin in 1939 on the spurious reason that no individual had applied for it. In Australia, where conscientious objection was acknowledged, 1% of conscripts applied for this status.

C. Vietnam

By the time the United States escalated its involvement in the Vietnam War and began a massive male draft in 1964, the patterns of draft resistance had secularized and expanded far beyond the narrow pacifist and religious communities which were dominant before.

Opposition to the war mounted along with rising draft calls (100,000 in 1964, 400,000 two years later) and casualty rates. Supported by a broad network of antidraft organizations, such as the War Resisters League (the American branch of the War Resisters International), the Student Peace Union, Peacemakers, and the Committee for Nonviolent Action, and organizations of students, feminists, civil rights, and many other liberal and radical groups, a social movement against the draft grew in strength. This informal coalition promoted a massive campaign of civil disobedience against the draft. It organized demonstrations, sit-ins at draft induction centers (during the late 1960s and early 1970s, in some instances draft resisters broke into local draft boards in order to destroy draft records) and draft card burning. This last form of expressing opposition to the war, the burning of draft cards, became the most visible and controversial symbol of draft resistance, so that in 1965 a law was passed to stop it. The law established a maximum sentence of 5 years for draft card burners. Thousands of people continued to burn their cards, but only 46 youths were indicted under this law, of whom 33 were convicted.

The rejection of war grew as the war developed. The figures on conscientious objection support this argument. As the courts expanded the definition of conscientious objection (in 1970 a court ruled that religious belief was not essential to achieve the status of CO), and as local boards became increasingly sympathetic to CO claims, the number of conscientious objectors grew. Between 1965 and 1970, more than 170,000 registrants obtained CO exemptions, and only around half of them actually performed alternative service. CO exemptions soared from 6.1% in 1966 to 25.5% in 1970. In addition, between 17,000 and 18,000 members of the armed forces applied for noncombatant status or discharge as COs during the war.

The number of criminal defendants also soared during the Vietnam War. Faced with more than 100,000 apparent draft offenders, between 1965 and 1975 the federal government indicted 22,167 young men for draft law violations. Of these, 8756 were convicted and 4001 were imprisoned. For the first time in American history, there were more secular and members of nonpacifist churches (72%) than members of the historic peace churches (7%). The remaining 21% belonged to the Jehovah's Witnesses.

Nevertheless, in absolute numbers the most common form of expressing disagreement with the draft was evasion. Of the 27 million men of draft age between 1964 and 1973, 16 million (60%) did not serve in the military. Of these, 15 million received legal exemptions or deferments. A further 570,000 evaded the draft illegally: 360,000 were never caught; another 198,000 had their cases dismissed. In addition, an estimated 30,000 to 50,000 emigrated in order to escape the draft, mostly to Canada, Britain, and Sweden.

The widespread rejection of the Vietnam war, as expressed in these figures of legal conscientious objection and other forms of evasion (legal and illegal), was consequential in putting an end to this American adventure in Asia. It is fair to say that the end of the war was to a large extent the outcome of the mobilization campaign against the draft and the war carried out by the antiwar movement.

IV. THE FUTURE OF RESISTANCE AND EVASION OF THE DRAFT

The classical model of armed forces based on mass male conscription (still the dominant practice in all but the English speaking countries) is contested at both the functional and social levels in the post-Cold War era. At the functional level, the model of military participation based on conscription is ill-prepared to deal with urgent conflicts in today's world, such as regional conflicts, civil wars, violent ethnic strife, and major military interventions in so-called "military humanitarianism." The major justification for a mass armed force model since the end of World War II—the likelihood of a large-scale war between capitalist and socialist countries—is gone for good. Moreover, as expensive and ultrasophisticated weapons systems develop, the need for highly trained, long-term, relatively well-paid professionals emerges.

At the social level, military service faces a crisis of legitimacy that widens the gap between the armed forces and society. There is less certainty that authorities have the right to compel young men into military service. Popular support for the armed forces is thus no longer a widespread attitude, as it was in the two world wars. Starting in the 1960s, when a cycle of protest spread throughout the Western world challenging existing systems of authority (and the military institution was one of the favorite targets of the protest), citizens began to express widespread doubt that the safety of the state was a reasonable motive for their death. These doubts are reflected in the figures for conscientious objection. Over the last two decades, as policies have become more liberal, and given secular grounds for objection the same standing in law as religious grounds, high figures of conscientious objection have become a permanent feature of contemporary Western societies. For example, in the early 1990s, conscientious objectors account for more than 30% of the draftee population in countries such as Germany and Spain. Society demands a pattern of relationship with armed forces different from the mass army model based on male conscription.

These two different although closely linked developments at the functional and social levels have helped build a broad and heterogeneous coalition pushing for an end to conscription in most but not all Western countries, Israel being the major exception. Within this coalition are traditional peace organizations, religious groups of various confessions, political radicals opposed to the military establishment, libertarian conservatives more confident of the market also for defense purposes, policy proponents willing to transfer military spending to social programs, ethnic minorities who oppose conscription into the armies of their "metropolis," young people imbued with individualism and materialism prevalent in Western youth culture, and even some military professionals who dislike the idea of dealing with reluctant draftees. This demand for putting an end to conscription has been successful in several countries: Belgium, the Netherlands, France, and Spain have already announced their move toward a smaller, voluntary, professional force. More countries might be following the example in the near future. There can be no doubt that if the example spreads, then the issue of resistance and evasion of the draft will lose the outstanding place it has enjoyed in recent centuries in Western history.

Also See the Following Article

JUST-WAR CRITERIA

Bibliography

Best, G. (1982). *War and society in revolutionary Europe, 1770–1880.* London: Fontana.

Ceadel, M. (1980). *Pacifism in Britain, 1914–1945.* Oxford: The Clarendon Press.

Chambers, J. W. II. (1987). *To Raise an army: The draft comes to modern America.* New York: The Free Press.

Cooper, S. E. (1991). *Patriotic pacifism. Waging war on war in Europe 1815–1914.* New York: Oxford University Press.

Eller, C. (1991). *Conscientious objectors and the Second World War. Moral and religious arguments in support of pacifism.* New York: Praeger.

Forrest, A. (1989). *Conscripts and deserters.* New York: Oxford University Press.

Goldstein, R. J. (1978). *Political repression in modern America. From 1870 to the present.* New York: Schenkman.

Haupt, G. (1972). *Socialism and the Great War. The collapse of the Second International.* Cambridge: Cambridge University Press.

Kiernan, V. (1973). "Conscription and society in Europe before the war of 1914–18." In M.R.D. Foot (Ed.), *War and society.* London: Elek.

Kohn, S. M. (1986). *Jailed for peace. The history of American draft law violators, 1658–1985.* Westport, CN: Greenwood Press.

Levi, M. (1997). *Consent, dissent, and patriotism.* New York: Cambridge University Press.

Marwick, A. (1965). *The deluge. British society and the First World War.* Boston: Little, Brown and Company.

Moskos, C. C., & Burk, J. (1994). The postmodern military. In J. Burk (Ed.), *The Military in new times: Adapting armed forces to a turbulent world.* Boulder, CO: Westview Press.

Moskos, C. C., & John Whiteclay Chambers, J. W. II (Eds.). (1993). *The New conscientious objection. From sacred to secular resistance.* Oxford: Oxford University Press.

Shaw, M. (1991). *Post-military society.* Philadelphia: Temple University Press.

Thomson, J. (1994). *Mercenaries, pirates, and sovereigns. State-building and extraterritorial violence in early modern Europe.* Princeton, NJ: Princeton University Press.

Tilly, C., Tilly, L. & Tilly, R. (1975). *The rebellious century: 1830–1930.* Cambridge, MA: Harvard University Press.

Tilly, C. (1992). *Coercion, capital, and European states AD 990–1992* (2nd. ed.). Oxford: Basil Blackwell.

Walzer, M. (1970). *Obligations: Essays on disobedience, war, and citizenship.* Cambridge, MA: Harvard University Press.

Young, N. (1984). "War Resistance, State, and Society." In M. Shaw (Ed.), *War, state, and society.* London: Macmillan.

Drug Control Policies in the United States and in Japan

Thomas M. Mieczkowski
The University of South Florida

GLOSSARY

Chuzaisho *police substation:* The equivalent of the *Koban* in rural and suburban communities.

Koban *police box*: An urban "ministation" for local police officers, situated in urban neighborhoods. Considered the key concept in the Japanese "community policing" philosophy in contemporary Japanese society.

Nolle Prosequi A legal action wherein a prosecutor declines to prosecute a crime brought to the prosecutor's attention by police. A frequent outcome for minor criminal offenses in Japan because many criminal events are mediated with police participation into a private settlement or resolution.

Shinritsukoryo The first nationwide legal code enacted in Japan in 1870 and considered to be the foundation for further criminal codes developed in subsequent decades.

Tyudoku The Japanese term for "drug dependence" or "drug abuse."

Tyudoku-sha The Japanese term for a person who abuses drugs, is dependent on drugs, or takes drugs to induce intoxication.

I. INTRODUCTION

In most contemporary societies the use or abuse of several types of psychoactive substances is treated as a serious social problem. These psychoactive drugs are mainly opiates, such as heroin and morphine, cocaine, cannabis, amphetamines, and sundry others including the hallucinogen LSD. In Islamic countries ethyl alcohol is also included as a dangerous and controlled if not contraband substance. Some of these psychoactive drugs are legally used under medical supervision (e.g., opiates) while others are essentially contraband (e.g., LSD). Abuse of these substances is problematic because it is believed to lead to dysfunctional changes in the individual's personality and behavior. As well, the use of these substances is seen as becoming compulsive leading to addiction or obsessive use. Another problem often associated with drug use is the increased incidence of crime, especially marked by social violence. Violence associated with drug abuse is typically experienced in three forms: pharmacological violence, predatory violence, and organized violence. Pharmacological violence occurs when a drug causes either a direct stimulation of neurobiological rage or causes profound changes in the perception and psychic functioning which then results in violent outbursts by the individual under the influence. The link between the drug's illegal status and its compulsive use leads to substantial if not overwhelming financial pressure to secure money for drug purchases. Predatory, instrumental violence is associated with the crimes committed by drug users to finance their drug consumption, such as robbery. Furthermore, the illegal status of the drug means its production and distribution provides an opportunity for illicit enterprise. Organized violence arises out of the competition of various criminal organizations involved in drug manufacture, importation, or distribution that use violent methods to conduct and regulate their drug business.

While generally committed to drug regulation and control, there is considerable variation in the social and legal responses to the consumption of these substances in the world community. Consequently, the body of law, policy, and ethical and moral beliefs that have taken shape globally are varied and complex. This section will systematically examine this process. The primary aim of this article is to compare two societies, the United States of America and Japan, both of which recognize they have drug abuse problems that require social regulation and action. The U.S. is a country that exhibits relatively high degrees of criminality, especially in terms of violent crimes and homicides. Japan is universally perceived as a country with an extraordinarily low crime rate. They are selected for comparison because, in fact, they have very different underlying crime rates and rates of drug abuse. These two societies, although sharing the perception that drug use is a social evil, are distinctively different cultures whose approach to normative and legal control of behavior is different.

II. THE LANGUAGE OF DRUG ABUSE

The historical origins of the word "drug" are not at all clear. Its modern use can be taken to have several different meanings. Webster's Third New International Dictionary lists drug as both a noun and a verb. Not all of these meanings carry the connotation that the term "drug" has come to bear in contemporary use. For example, the term may refer to a substance used in dyeing cloth. It also has an archaic but still accepted use as a commodity that has lost its market demand and hence is no longer sellable. Thus the expression "a drug on the market" indicates some item of an inventory that is difficult or impossible to sell. Generally, the term "drug" conveys a medical meaning a substance used in making a medicine, or a medicine itself. In law the term is used to denote a substance recognized as a drug in an official pharmacopoeia (such as the United States Pharmacopoeia) or a formulary. In this regard "drugs" are substances intended for use in diagnosing, treating, curing, or preventing some medical condition or disease. The term "drug" also connotes a substance that is taken specifically with the intention of affecting the structure or function of the body and its physiological processes. Sometimes these substances are taken in the sense of "cures" or "treatments" for diseases, but sometimes they are taken for more ambiguous reasons. People may take drugs to suppress appetites as an aid to dieting or take substances to promote strength or youthful appearance. Such uses are not really directed at alleviating disease *per se,* but enhancing some aspect of life.

"Drug," as the term has been used in formulating current social and legal policy, connotes "a narcotic substance or preparation." Historically popular ideas of drug taking were associated with opiate-based preparations. In current use the word has become much broader (as has the repertoire of consumed drugs) and applies to a number of substances that are not narcotics, in the technical sense, and that have widely differing properties. It has led some authors to suggest that the term "drug" has become a "catch-all" for substances that create any sort of physiological or psychological reaction within the user. As a result a term now used is "psychotropic drug," which refers to drugs that have a psychic component of action, usually thought of as affecting subjective states of mood, feelings, and behavior. An analogous term that is coming into wider accepted use is "psychoactive drug."

III. PHARMACOLOGY

The motivation for taking a psychoactive drug is based on the assumption that it produces a recognizable series of pleasurable or desirable effects for the consumer. These drugs can alter or enhance emotional and psychological perceptions, moods, or sentiments. They may relieve anxiety and/or induce euphoria or pleasurable stimulation. The range of these emotional and behavioral changes and their nature is variable from person to person. Thus the colloquial descriptions and attributes attached to the "pleasures" of drugs are variable. It is also recognized that prior beliefs and cultural expectations are also influential in the perspective observers bring to studying the drug experience.

In both American and Japanese law, drugs are conceptualized as unique chemical compounds with specific pharmacological effects. A pharmacological perspective concentrates on basic drug actions, the biochemical mechanisms by which the drug creates it effects, and consequences of these effects on the neural system. The pharmacological view is interested in documenting the types of responses particular drugs invoke, such as sleep-induction, tranquilization, and stimulation. Also, pharmacological analysis identifies collateral and nonpsychoactive effects drugs may produce, such as a change in heart rate. Pharmacological descriptions of drugs document such effects and often help characterize drugs by their reference to these descriptions. Some psychoactive drugs can be dangerously toxic if taken in sufficient quantities and can produce serious injury or death. Pharmacological study determines the degree of toxicity, the effective and lethal dosages, the persistence and excretion of the drug from the body, and similar aspects of the drug-consuming experience. The methods and conventions of pharmacological research are comparable in the United States and Japan as are the scientific classifications of the major psychoactive drugs. As a consequence, the repertoire of substances regulated by law in both countries is virtually identical.

IV. CULTURAL ASPECTS

In understanding the nature of drugs and their use and abuse, information beyond basic biological description is important. Because drugs produce effects, for example, defined as "pleasurable," there are important cultural aspects associated with the drug experience. These cultural aspects create a frame of reference for the interpretation of the physiological and pharmacological effects of a particular drug. In some societies, for example, consumption of psychoactive drugs is explained as a spiritual or religious experience. In some it is seen as therapeutic. In still others it is seen as hedonistic. In yet others as a sign of madness, a threat, or a danger. The culture creates a frame of reference that gives meaningful interpretation to the physiological processes that the drug evokes. Thus two major components are a part of the process of the definition and identification of drugs. One component is the technical aspect, which focuses on a combination of the literal chemical and physiological nature of the substance, while the other emphasizes cultural components.

There are nonpharmacological perspectives on the concepts of drugs, drug use, and drug abuse, of course. These alternatives may restrict or even ignore pharmacology and biology. This perspective represents a phenomenological approach to drug definition. While not necessarily denying that the compounds labeled as "drugs" are physical agents that produce biological effects, the phenomenological view posits that biological effects must have an attributed cultural meaning or interpretation. And it is the sociological and psychological environment in which this meaning is created. Thus the concept "drug" cannot be reduced to a purely biochemical one. Thus societies or cultures may differ in drug use patterns cultures differ on what is pleasurable, what is dangerous, and so on. The different perception of the effects and dangers of ethyl alcohol in Islamic and non-Islamic societies is an example of this phenomenon.

This leads one to ask, then, why particular categories of pharmacological agents become identified as drugs and how drugs become labeled as "psychotropic," and "euphoric," all terms that involve subjective states of perception. Indeed, the notion of "psychotropic" itself becomes problematic to understand without a cultural reference. If such terms as "mood-altering" are taken as a major element of psychotropic activity, then a very large repertoire of items can be considered so, and one must turn to sociology to understand the dimensions of this term. Experts have pointed out that "the gratification aspect of drug use may not be very different from that aspect of the consumption of everyday things, such as food."

One method to evaluate the weight that pharmacology, physiology and sociological interpretation of drug experiences have is to conduct placebo studies. Placebo studies try to determine the conditions under which individuals consuming alternately either a drug or a placebo can distinguish the two. This ability to distinguish can be interpreted as a measure of the importance of set and setting in the drug experience. Several studies have indicated, for example, that exposure to marijuana does not reliably produce "euphoric" or other notable subjective effects in users when exposure occurs in a neutral setting. Researchers have reported substantial numbers of initiating marijuana smokers whom report perceiving no subjective effect. In one such study roughly half of the subjects reported that on their first experience they either did not "get high" or they were unsure if they felt any effect or not. This demonstrates that users of drugs may have to learn to perceive and define the intoxicating effects of the drug, that they are not intuitively tied to biological actions. Alternately, persons given placebo drugs have reported intoxication when no biologically active compound is present. In addition to the ambiguity that may surround perceptions of psychotropic effects with marijuana, studies of a similar type have been done with cocaine. Such studies show that recreational users of cocaine who took small doses of the drug (approximately 30 milligrams) under controlled conditions "often cannot distinguish it from other drugs or even from a placebo." However, at higher dosage levels they indicate a "reliable" reporting of feelings of euphoria. Other research has reported similar confusion about sensing drug effects or identifying drug effects accurately; for example, the inability to distinguish the effects of cocaine from amphetamine.

A further example of the interaction of cultural perceptions and labeling a psychoactive a "drug" is seen in the differential application of the law. The most telling case in point is ethyl alcohol, which is unambiguously psychotropic in sufficient doses and lethal in extreme doses. Alcohol is consumed for the most part precisely to achieve psychotropic effects and yet is rarely referred to as a "drug." For example, it is common to find references to "problems of drug and alcohol abuse," implicitly holding the two as distinct. American society has a wide variety of alcohol policies, ranging from some political jurisdictions that are "dry" (prohibiting alcohol sales entirely) to ubiquitous availability. In Japan alcohol is sold in vending machines. Likewise tobacco use, while seen as a public health menace, is commonly held aloof from "drug problems." Tobacco use is pharmacologically highly habituating or "addicting." While tobacco is not a powerful psychotropic, it clearly has some psychoactive properties. In some cultures it is held to be a powerful "drug." Its psychotropic properties appear to be substantially different than those associated with the "major drugs" such as opiates in current American and Japanese perceptions with effects more subtle, perhaps more akin to a substance like caffeine. Indeed, in Japan the current American movement toward increasing restrictions on tobacco use often is viewed as extreme. The Japanese generally regard tobacco as having beneficial psychotropic effects, primarily as an anxiolytic. While the medical community and in many instances Federal policy have recognized that the use of alcohol, caffeine, and nicotine are "dangerous" (viz., the Surgeon General's warnings), there is no attempt to control the use of these substances by criminal sanction. Caffeine, the active stimulant in coffee, tea, cola beverages, chocolate, and other widely consumed compounds, is not generally conceptualized in social contexts as a psychotropic drug, although it certainly meets the technical requirements to qualify as one. Neither caffeine nor nicotine, for example, is scheduled under the federal drug laws. These situations clearly demonstrate the role of culture in shaping the concept "drug" in ways that simply cannot be understood by mere technical and chemical definitions.

V. DRUG CONTROL POLICY IN THE UNITED STATES

A. Legal Definitions of Drugs

In the law the identification of a drug is highly specific and is established in court by a technical test of the substance alleged to be a drug. This technical identification must be made in any case where a person is prosecuted under such laws for possessing, distributing, or manufacturing a drug. The law is exact and specific about what substances are illegal or controlled and in the event of a prosecution arrest, the substance must be introduced as evidence. The drug evidence must be substantiated as the illegal substance by an unambiguous scientific test.

There are two circumstances, generally, under which the law is invoked in regard to the possession of a psychotropic substance. There are categories of chemicals, such as opiates, that are legal to possess and distribute under controlled circumstances. So, a physician may possess and distribute narcotics to patients, provided the physician is duly licensed and the distribution of the narcotics is based on appropriate medical practice. Doing so is not a violation of the law. There are also substances that are not legal to possess or distribute under any circumstances (e.g., LSD) except in rare cases where a person may be licensed to possess the material for scientific research. Thus persons may be arrested for the inappropriate use, possession, or distribution of a substance which itself is not illegal (e.g., morphine) or they may be arrested for a substance that is "contraband" or intrinsically unlawful to possess. For substances not so specified as either regulated or contraband under the law, the state has no power to arrest or prosecute. For example, the mere proclamation by a person that a substance is a "drug" or the claim that a substance has psychotropic properties has no legal meaning.

B. Drug Schedules and Classification under American Law

In a certain sense, then, the legal view of drugs is quite straightforward. A substance either is or is not regulated, a chemical assay can determine whether a particle unknown material is a regulated substance, and the judicial system responds to the circumstances of the case as presented before it. The primary basis for legal regulation of drugs in the United States is based on the Controlled Substances Act or, as it is often referred to, the CSA (P.L. 91-513; 21 U.S.C. 800 et seq.), initially passed in 1970. This federal act has been updated by periodic modifications, the most important of which were in 1986 and in 1988. The CSA forms the basis, in federal law, upon which control is exerted over narcotics and other substances deemed "dangerous drugs." The law was enacted in order to replace or consolidate existing federal laws, such as the Harrison Act of 1914, the Marihuana Tax Act of 1937, and related legislation. These laws operate in addition to regulation by the Federal Food and Drug Administration, which regulates the manufacture and distribution of legitimate therapeutic drugs.

This act empowers the Attorney General of the United States to enforce drug regulation according to an established "schedule" of dangerous drugs and to act as the chief monitor over the development and classifications of new drugs insofar as they may be considered "dangerous." The Attorney General is empowered to "add to such a schedule or transfer between such schedules any drug or substance if he finds that such drug or substance has a potential for abuse..." (Title 21, Chapter 13, 811 a.1, Controlled Substances Act, as amended, June 1, 1985).

This legislation creates a series of five "schedules" to classify the legal status of regulated drugs. For a given substance the relative penalty legally applicable is determined by its place on the schedule. The major features incorporated into the schedule are whether the drug has potential for abuse, whether it is useful for medical treatments, and the relatively safety with which the drug can be used. "Safety" in this context means the likelihood or potential that a person will abuse the drug or become dependent on it. The same drug also may be classified into different schedules based upon the form in which it is vended or distributed. Drugs can always be treated as a substance by lower ordered categories. Furthermore, drugs are often vended in various combinations and concentrations, so these combinations may also be important in determining the ultimate schedule number under which a particular drug is classified. Under federal law, the legal penalties associated with drug possession and trafficking are related to the schedule level at which the drug is classified, the quantity (by weight) of drug involved in the legal action, and whether the action is a first offense by the convicted individual. In general, the greater the quantity of drug, the more severe the penalty, and multiple offenders are more severely punished than first offenders. The penalties are substantial, including imprisonment up to life and fines that can attain $20 million in total costs. It is also very important to bear in mind that the prosecution of drug cases is almost always done under governance of state criminal law, not federal criminal law. While state laws reflect quite closely the general schema of the federal regulatory system, there are some departures from federal law within state criminal systems. State law cannot supercede federal law, so states are not free to depart significantly or fundamentally from federal policy. Recently, when states have moved to lessen restrictions on the use of marijuana for medical purposes, the federal government has swiftly moved to restrict the state's actions. They have done this by threatening the enforcement of criminal statutes against persons who may be operating within the state law, by outside of federal law, and by pursuing injunctions against state actions relevant to the liberalized policy.

C. Crime and Drug Use in the United States

Crime in the U.S. is, by world standards, substantial and is very high by comparison to Japan. Drug crime in the U.S. is also substantial in sharp contrast to Japan, which has a minor level of drug crime.

1. General Crime Statistics

In 1994 there were more than 14.5 million persons arrested in the U.S. according to the Federal Bureau of Investigations (FBI), and this figure excludes trivial traffic offenses, curfew violations, and minor crimes such as loitering. The rate of arrest per 100,000 citizens in 1994 was nearly 1,150. It is estimated that about 3 million of the 14 million arrests are for crimes that are serious, felony offenses, and more than three-quarters of a million of them are for violent offenses, including homicide. More than 22,000 homicides were known to the police in 1994.

Approximately 1.3 million of these arrests were for drug offenses (1,351,400). Of all estimated FBI arrest rates, drug abuse violations rank only behind larceny/theft (at about 1.5 million) as the most frequently reported type of arrest in the U.S. and this number is actually slightly *more* than the number of arrests for driving under the influence of alcohol. From 1985 to 1994 the percentage of arrests accounted for by drug violations increased by 38%, while all arrests from this period increased 18%. Approximately 83% of the arrestees were males and 17% female. In 1994, 47% of the arrests were for cocaine or heroin (17% sale, 30% pos-

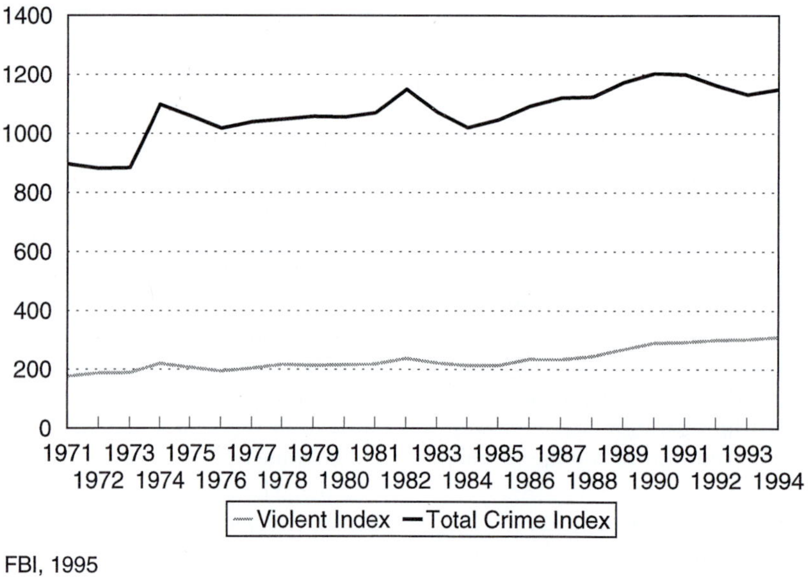

FIGURE 1 FBI crime index rates.

session), 36% for marijuana (6% sale, 30% possession), and the remaining 17% for other drugs.

Since the late 1960s American crime rates generally have increased. Figure 1 shows the long-term trend for serious crimes from 1971 until 1994. The arrest data suggests that illegal drugs play a leading and increasing role in this phenomenon.

2. Drug Crime

Drug abuse offenses are not reported as Federal Bureau of Investigation Part I offenses in the U.S. These crimes are considered FBI Part II offenses, so classified because these crimes are thought of as having a lower level of seriousness. When considered as a component of Part II offenses (excluding traffic and "other" categories) drug offenses are the *most frequent charge associated with Part II arrests*. They are more numerous than any Part I offense except for theft. Drug arrests constitute more than 1 million events in that category. Furthermore, the volume of drug arrests—when compared to the Part I categories of murder and forcible rape—is greater by several orders of magnitude as shown in Fig. 2. Given this large arrest volume, a substantial amount of criminal justice resources are devoted to drug arrests and their consequent judicial processing. The reported arrests are primarily for possession of drugs as opposed to selling or manufacturing drugs. Figure 3 shows the percentages of drug arrests made for possession of drugs compared to arrests for sales or production of drugs. From 1982 to 1994, the percentage of arrests for possession consistently exceeds arrests for sales of drugs.

The emphasis on arrests for possession as opposed to sale reflects the criminal justice-oriented drug control policy at the heart of a "war on drugs" approach. The large relative percentage of arrests for drug possession also demonstrate the effects of the increasing emphasis on "demand reduction." This policy is based on the idea that harsh penalties deter drug users, resulting in a subsequent reduction of demand for drugs and lessening the profit motive for drug importation and sale.

One of the main rationales for an aggressive demand-reduction policy is based on the premise that drug use is associated with general levels of criminal behavior. Data from the National Institute of Justice Drug Use Forecast show that 60 to 80% of persons arrested in major cities are under the influence of drugs when they are arrested. Figure 4 depicts data derived from the *Drug Use Forecast*.

Drug use in the U.S. is high even when the measures do not rely upon arrest or similar criminal justice-dependent data. General population self-reported drug use survey data show that drug use is a part of daily life for many persons in American society. Figure 5 displays data from a recent household-based survey, the National Household Survey on Drug Abuse (NHSDA). This is a random selection survey whose data can be generalized to the household population as a whole. As

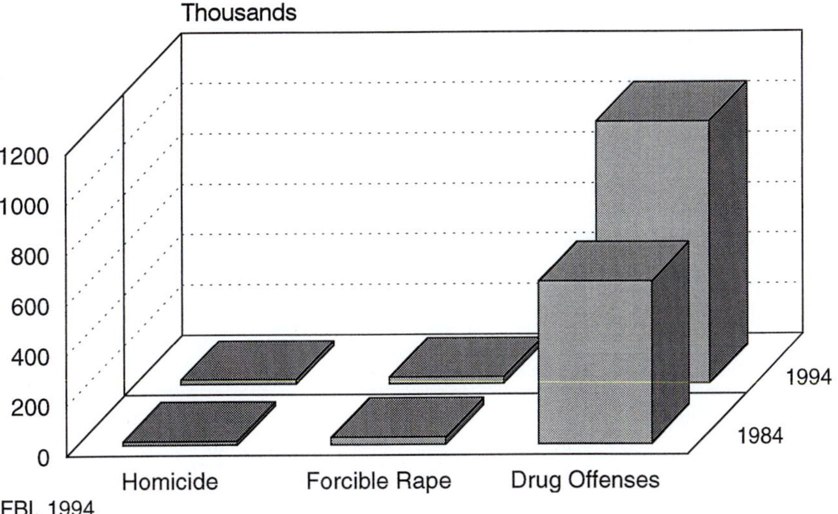

FIGURE 2 Drug arrests and violent arrests.

Fig. 5 shows, a large number of citizens have used some illegal drug during their lifetime, most likely marijuana. However, current use (defined as use in the last 30 days) is significantly less prevalent. Like lifetime use, current use is much more likely to be marijuana as opposed to "harder drugs" such as powder cocaine or crack cocaine.

This same trend is also found among both high school-age students, as well as college students and young adults. Figure 6 shows the most recent data as measured by the Monitoring the Future study, which polls students and young adults on their drug use.

3. Summary

In response to a persistent drug use problem United States drug policy has relied heavily on criminal agencies to control the use and distribution of illegal psychoactive drugs. Even with a heavy investment in this

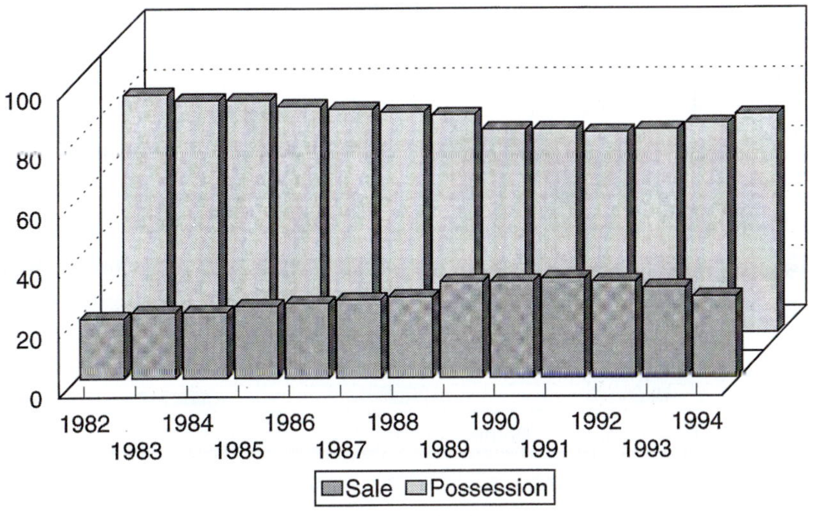

FIGURE 3 Drug charges, possession versus sales.

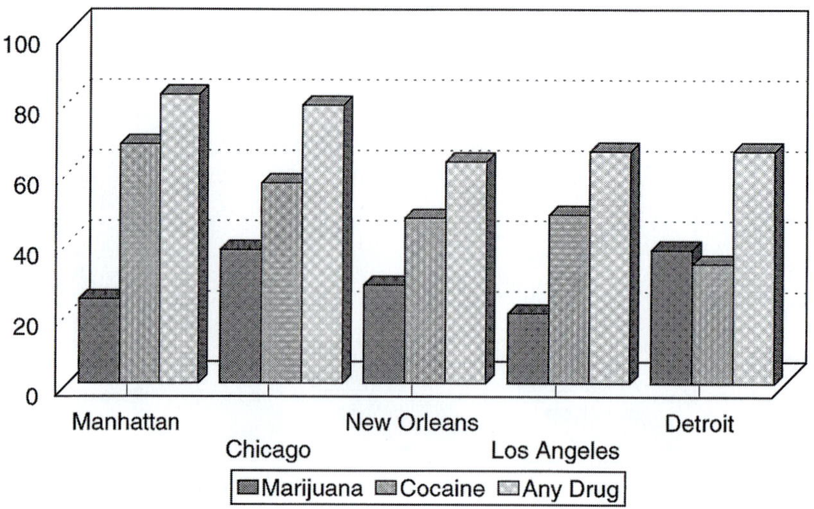

FIGURE 4 Percentage of arrestees testing drug positive.

policy survey data show that drug use is widespread in the general population. Furthermore, data also demonstrate that very large numbers of persons arrested for criminal offenses, at least in major cities, are likely to be drug intoxicated at arrest. Aggressive efforts, dating back more than 20 years, to eliminate or drastically reduce illegal drug use by law enforcement has led to the characterization of this approach as a "war on drugs." This aggressive strategy utilizes both local police agents as well as national military forces to interdict drug distributors and arrest and prosecute drug users with the purported aim of deterring citizens from engaging in drug activities by heightening the likelihood of arrest and punishment. American federal and state law both contain severe penalties for trafficking or possessing drugs. The severity of these sanctions has consistently increased since the late 1970s and the rate of arrests for drug offenses in the U.S. has been and

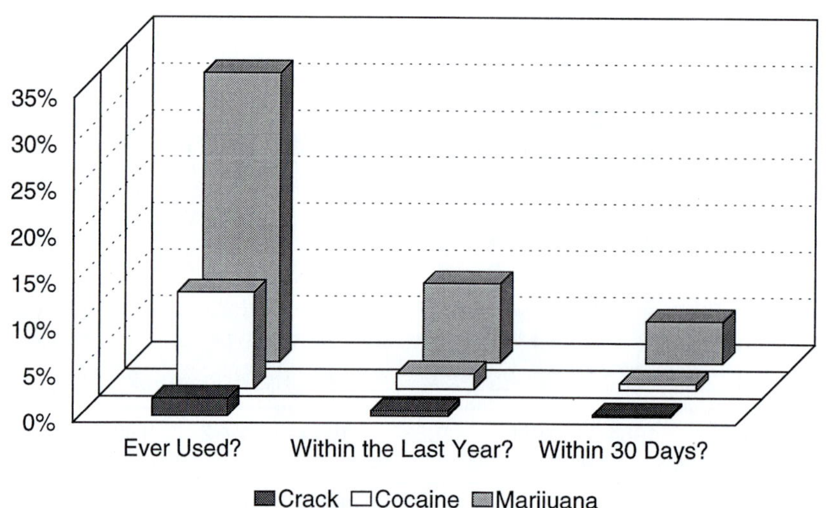

FIGURE 5 Self-reported drug use (1995).

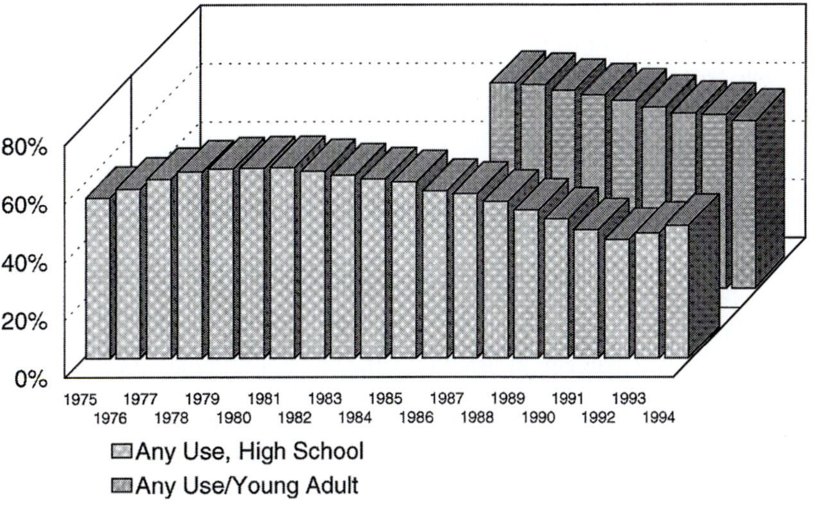

FIGURE 6 Self-reported drug use trends among students and young adults.

remains high. Furthermore, not reflected in the arrest statistics, the use of various types of asset seizure and property forfeiture is also applied against persons arrested for drug possession or sale. Additionally, significant efforts are made to interdict drugs when they are in transit from their sources of origin to the U.S. market, chiefly relying on federal forces such as the Coast Guard. This aggressive posture, with its reliance on criminal prosecution of offenders, is the hallmark of a "war on drugs." The question of whether these policies are effective and appropriate is a matter of intense controversy in the United States. For most of the period of the "war on drugs," drug use as measured by major survey instruments has gone through periods of increase and decline. Whether these changes correspond in a meaningful way to the criminal justice policies cannot be readily determined. Furthermore, this policy is expensive in its requirements for both economic and human resources and also in terms of potential threats and encumbrances on civil liberties and freedoms. Because of these features, the policy approach continues to be debated intensely in American society.

VI. JAPAN

A. The Japanese Legal System

Japan is an island nation located in the eastern Pacific. It is approximately 150,000 square miles with a population of 125 million persons. While Japan is about 1/20th the geographic size of the United States, it has a population about 50% as large. Japan has a very low relative crime rate and is often held up as the best example of an advanced industrial society with a low incidence of serious crime. Drug use is low in Japan in comparison to the United States, but it is not unknown. Recently, experts in Japan have become more concerned with the increase of certain types of drug and intoxicant use, especially amphetamine use and solvent and inhalant abuse among Japanese youth. However, no "war on drugs" approach has emerged in Japan and the use of such a metaphor would be foreign to the culture of Japan and the way in which it deals with control of behavior by its citizenry.

Japan emerged in the mid-19th century from the last remnants of feudal social organization with the passing of the Tokugawa regime. The establishment of the Meiji Restoration of 1868 usually marks its ascendancy to political modernity. The current state is governed by the Constitution of Japan (11 chapters and 103 articles), established in 1946 at the beginning of the rebuilding of Japan following its defeat in World War II. Articles 31 to 40 of the Constitution specifically address fundamental rights of citizens and the principles governing the enforcement of criminal laws. These, in general, are similar to those principles espoused in the American Constitution. Briefly, these principals require legal due process, free access to courts, judicial warrants for arrest and searches, immediate information of charges, rights to counsel, and a judicial review of arrest. Criminal procedural rights are also specified, including the right to cross examination of witnesses, freedom to refuse to self-incriminate, exclusion of *ex post facto* law, and protection against double jeopardy. Two unique provisions in the Japanese Constitution are a prohibition against criminal conviction for a citizen "when the only proof against him is his own confession" and the specific right that "any person may, in case he is acquitted after he has been arrested or detained, sue the State for redress as provided for by law." The Japanese system of governance in includes a bicameral legislative body (the Diet), an executive branch consisting of a Prime Minister and cabinet, and an independent judiciary, which closely resembles the American system of a Supreme Court and a set of lower courts.

B. Japanese Criminal Justice

1. Police

Ordinary enforcement of the law and maintenance public of order is the responsibility of the National Police Agency, a national police force organized hierarchically under the authority of the Prime Minister. The Prime Minister administers it under (successively) The National Public Safety Commission, The National Police Agency, and a series of Regional Police bureaus. The National Police Agency is responsible for police operations and activities and for coordinating the activities of local prefectural police. The policing system in Japan is divided into 47 prefectural headquarters and approximately 1200 police stations. Within each prefecture, the local police separate the police function into an administrative division, a criminal investigation division, a traffic division, a patrol division, a security division, and a communications division. Under the patrol there are a series of community-based "police boxes" or *kobans*. Police officers in Japan are charged with the responsibility of enforcing the criminal laws, including narcotics laws. In general, Japanese policing structures are similar in appearance to United States and European policing systems. They are different in practice, however. The Japanese system reflects a difference in cultural attitudes of appropriate modes of police activity, which for the Japanese relies heavily on a personalization of the system of justice so that the law is enforced in a more discretionary and individuated method than would be found in the United States or Europe.

2. Criminal Law

The origin of the Japanese criminal code, in the contemporary meaning of that term, can be traced to the *Shinritsukoryo* of 1870, which first created a legal code applied to criminal acts covering all of Japan. In the 1880s a new Criminal Law and a Criminal Procedure Law were drafted based upon the French Code. The latter established basic principles identified with the Classical reformation movement in European criminology, such as a strong emphasis on legality of process, fundamental rights, public process, and the like. In addition to borrowing from French law, the Japanese established a number of other legal codes and procedures that were derived from the German legal system; for example, the organization of the court system. In 1907 a revised Criminal Code was enacted, which forms the basis of criminal law until the current time. There were substantial changes made to this Code in 1947, largely in describing procedural rights, as a result of the rebuilding of Japanese society after World War II. A major redrafting of the Criminal Code was undertaken in the mid-1950s.

3. Drug Laws

Japan, like most other nations, relies upon criminal law to regulate the manufacture, distribution, and possession of substances defined as psychoactive drugs, poisons, inhalants, and various substances that may be toxic, abused, or otherwise deemed dangerous. As in most other countries, opiates were the first substance to be regulated as a drug. The Penal Code of 1907 specifically banned the importation, production, or use of opium. No other drug regulation was deemed necessary for nearly 5 decades. Japan experienced a wave of amphetamine abuse in the late 1940s and early 1950s and as a consequence passed in 1951 the Stimulants Control Drug Law, the first of a series of post-WW II drug laws. In 1954 the Japanese Diet revised this law to broaden its control and added in 1954 the Narcotics and Psychotropics Control Law. The legal regulation of cannabis, which had been prohibited since 1948, also was strengthened at this time. With the emergence of novel drugs, such as LSD, and the use by persons of organic solvents as inhalants, the Japanese in 1972 enacted the Poisons and Deleterious Substances Control Law.

Currently there are four major criminal statutes that govern legal control of narcotics and psychotropic substances: The Narcotics and Psychotropics Control Law, The Cannabis Control Law, The Stimulants Control Law, and the Poisonous and Deleterious Substances Law. Drug laws in Japan rely on a mix of punishments, including punishments as severe as life imprisonment for importation of drugs, as well as frequent use of compulsory treatment for simple possession of some drugs for individual use. The Japanese law for compulsory treatment, however, does not apply to inhalant or amphetamine abusers, who receive only conventional criminal sanctions. Persons addicted or abusing these substances may possibly receive treatment if they can be shown to be mentally unstable and dangerous under a separate law, the Mental Health and Welfare Law. However, these two are not formally coupled in the criminal law. The simple use or possession of amphetamines or inhalants does not entitle the person to treatment, as would be the case for an opiate addict.

The Japanese also rely upon monetary fines as part of the criminal sanction process. For example, under current Japanese law, possession of heroin is punishable by up to 10 years in prison (no less than 1 year minimum) and carries a fine equivalent to approximately $50,000 (U.S.), assuming $1.00 U.S. is about 100 Japanese yen. In this regard—considering the severity of Japanese law—it may appear that Japan, like the U.S., could be considered as pursuing a "war on drugs" approach to controlling substance abuse. However, this would be an inaccurate interpretation of Japanese policy and views.

C. Crime in Japan

1. General Crime Data

By American standards and by the standards of many other nations in the world community Japan has very low rates of criminal behavior. The Japanese approach in crime control relies to a great extent on the integration of policing into local communities via the *koban* or "police box" or *chuzaisho* or "police substation." This approach has often been cited as the model for community policing, which is now widely emulated in the U.S. *Kobans* are found in urban setting and *chuzaisho* in the rural or suburban areas of Japan.

TABLE I

Comparative Rates of Crime in Major Industrial Countries

Country	Crime rate
Japan	1427
U.S.	5374
Germany	8038
France	6783
Great Britain	9790

Source: National Police Agency (Japan) (1997).

Crime prevalence is very low in Japan when compared to other major industrial countries. Table 1 shows the comparison of crimes rates per 100,000 citizens for Japan, the U.S., Germany, France, and Great Britain.

Figure 7 shows total crime offense and arrest data for Japan from 1985 to 1995, inclusive.

Japan experiences about 2 million crimes per year. It appears that a slow but consistent increase in reported crime has also occurred over the past decade. The percentage of crimes cleared by arrest has also changed, and the percentage of reported crimes resulting in an

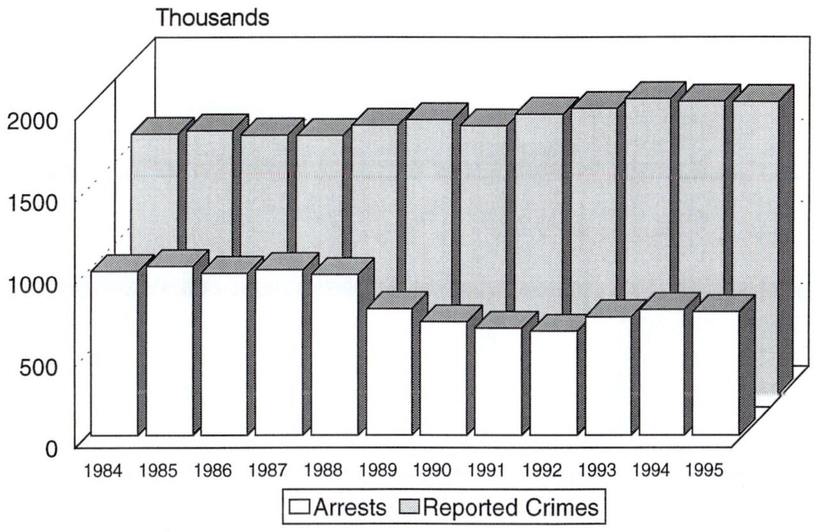

FIGURE 7 Total criminal offences and arrests in Japan (1985–1995).

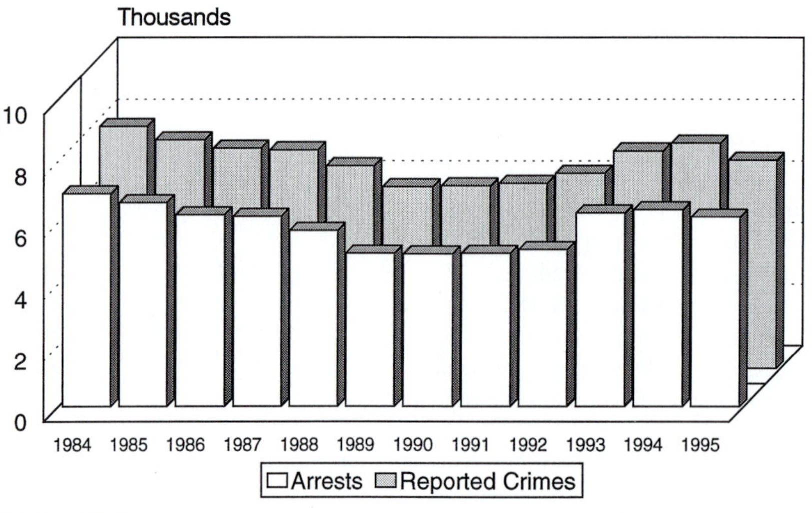

FIGURE 8 Total felony offences in Japan and clearances by arrest.

arrest declined over the same period. In the U.S. about 23% of serious crimes are result in an arrest, and about 60% of violent crimes with the exception of robbery also result in an arrest. In Japan, the percentage of serious crimes resulting in an arrest is larger. In addition, the level of serious or felony type offenses has declined over the past 10 years and, in general, the percentage of these crimes cleared by an arrest is substantial. Figure 8 shows this data for Japan for the decade of 1984 through 1995.

As one can see, while the U.S. measures crimes in the range of millions, Japan counts crimes in the thousands. Equally important, in Japan a substantially larger number of crimes result in an arrest of an offender (the arrest for a crime is usually described as being "cleared" by arrest). Figure 9 indicates the relative difference in arrest clearance between the U.S. and Japan. Percentages of violent crimes in Japan cleared by arrest, as well as felonies in general, range between 80 and 98%. In the U.S. all categories of cleared crimes are much lower

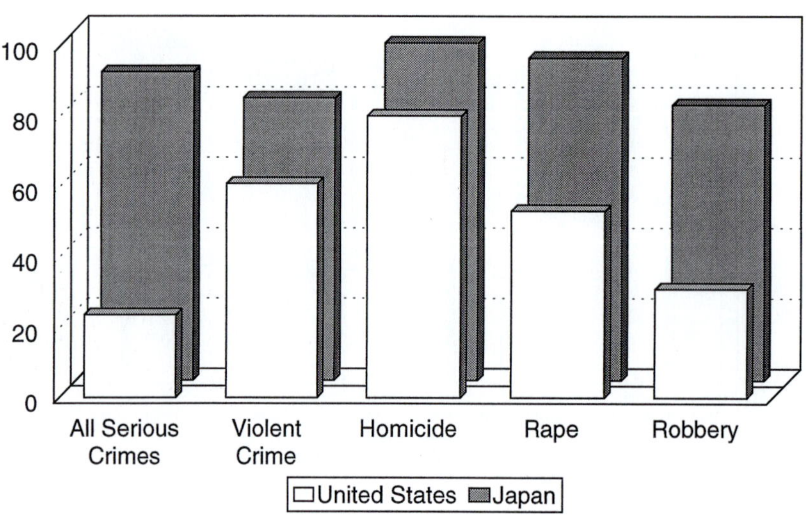

FIGURE 9 Percentage of arrests for reported felonies in Japan (1984–1995).

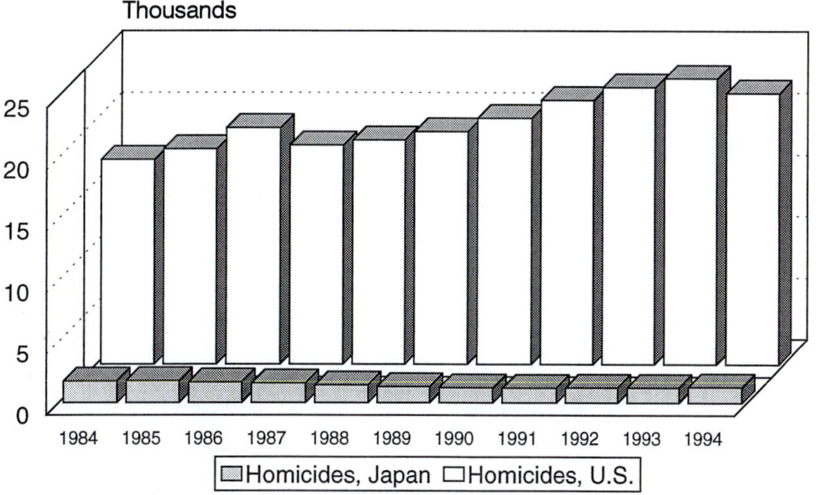

FIGURE 10 U.S. and Japanese homicide rates.

than Japan with the exception of homicide. Figure 10 compares homicide rates in Japan and the U.S. over the 10-year period of 1984–1994. The homicide rate in Japan is approximately 1/15th that in the United States. This ratio holds true for most crimes of violence. Figure 11 presents the rates of a variety of violent offenses in Japan over the 1984–1995 period. Since 1991 robbery has increased, while rapes and gun offenses have declined. Bear in mind that even with these increases the rates compared to the U.S. are still extremely small. In Japan in 1994 there were 7320 felonies reported to police. In the U.S. for that year there approximately 12 **million** felonies reported to the police, approximately 1.7 million of which were major crimes of violence.

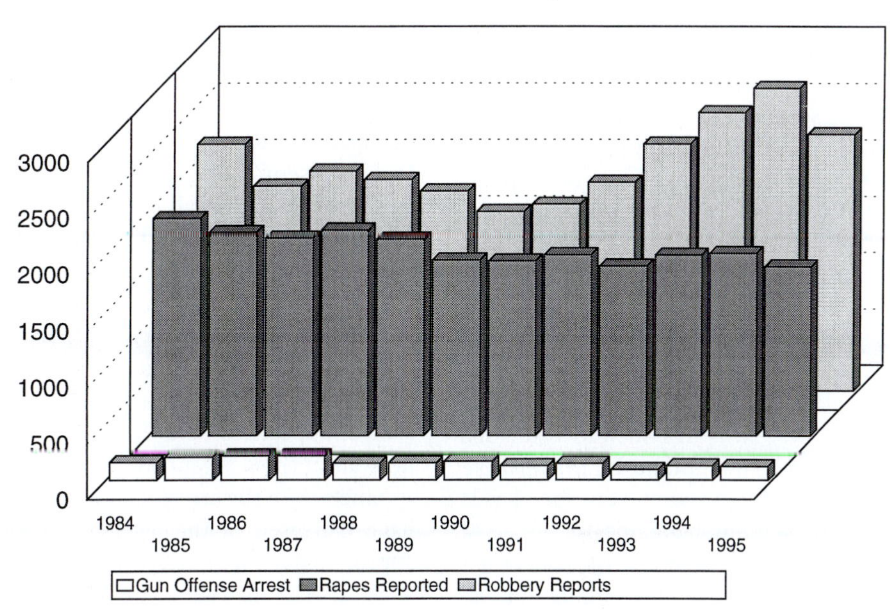

FIGURE 11 Violent crimes in Japan.

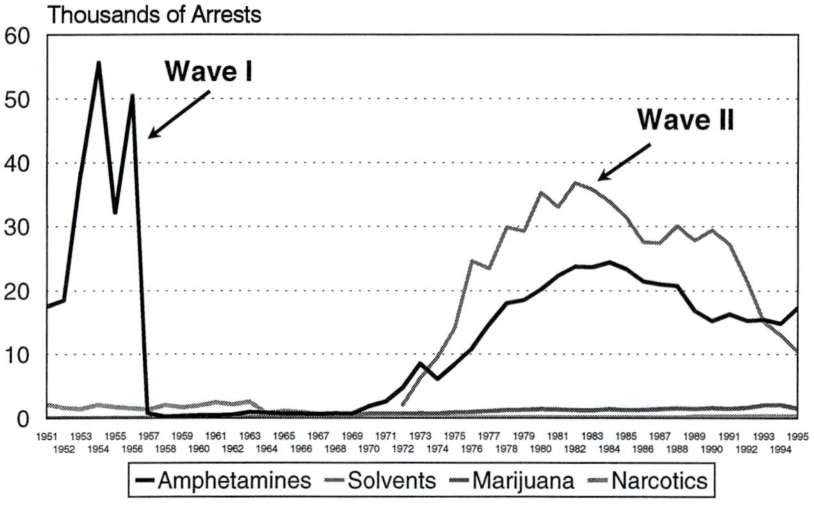

FIGURE 12 Long-term drug abuse prevalence in Japan.

2. Drug Crimes in Japan

Japan does not have a problem with drug abuse that is comparable to the United States. However, the Japanese, like other societies, evaluate the existence of drug abuse problems by gauging the *relative* changes in drug use within their society as a whole. Thus current levels of drug abuse are viewed with alarm by many in Japan despite prevalence statistics that seem extremely low when compared to many other nations. The Japanese, in their own view, have experienced drug abuse problems at several points in the past 50 years. Figure 12 shows that Japan has experienced two distinct waves of drug abuse. The first experience, referred to as "Wave I," occurred in the late 1940s and early 1950s and coincided with the legal over-the-counter sale of amphetamines. This practice was ended by the passage of The Stimulants Control Law, making unrestricted sale of amphetamines a crime. After the legislation amphetamine abuse dropped to a near-zero level. The second wave of Japanese drug abuse concerns began in the late 1960s. "Wave II" coincided with the rise in illegal drug use in the U.S. Inhalant and solvent abuse was a major new component of Wave II. Drugs such as cannabis, cocaine, and opium were not unknown in Japanese society, but their appearance was at very low levels compared to inhalants and amphetamines.

Currently, Japanese officials are most concerned with the apparent increase of drug use among youths, especially with solvent, inhalant, and amphetamine abuse. Use of these drugs is relatively high compared with other drugs. Figure 13 presents drug abuse data for the period 1984–1995, but it excludes solvents and amphetamines. If we include amphetamine, inhalant, and solvent abuse data, the picture is different. Figure 14 shows the relatively larger problem associated with these drugs. When comparing Figs. 13 and 14, one notes that the inhalant and solvent abuse prevalence is at least 10 times the rate of other common drugs. Of course, the amphetamine resurgence has a historical precedent in Wave I, 40 years ago. However, the rather substantial amount of solvent inhalant use represents a development reminiscent of the characteristics of Wave II.

Japan conducted a National Household Survey on Drug Abuse in 1994, similar to the American NHSDA, and reported an overall lifetime prevalence rate of 1.4% for solvent inhalation. The 1994 U.S. Monitoring the Future survey reported a rate of 13.2% for college students and young adults. When considering amphetamines, the Japanese survey reported a 0.3% lifetime prevalence rate for amphetamines, the U.S., 17.1%. As Fig. 14 indicates, the overall trend for these two substances appears to be declining, although not all Japanese authorities accept the accuracy of this data.

Since 1996 the arrest data for drug offenses in Japan have increased to the level of 20,000 per year. This approximates the number of arrests that characterized Wave II. This has led some to consider Japan today to be entering a "Wave III." This sentiment is not based solely on arrest data. Recently, Japan has begun to use

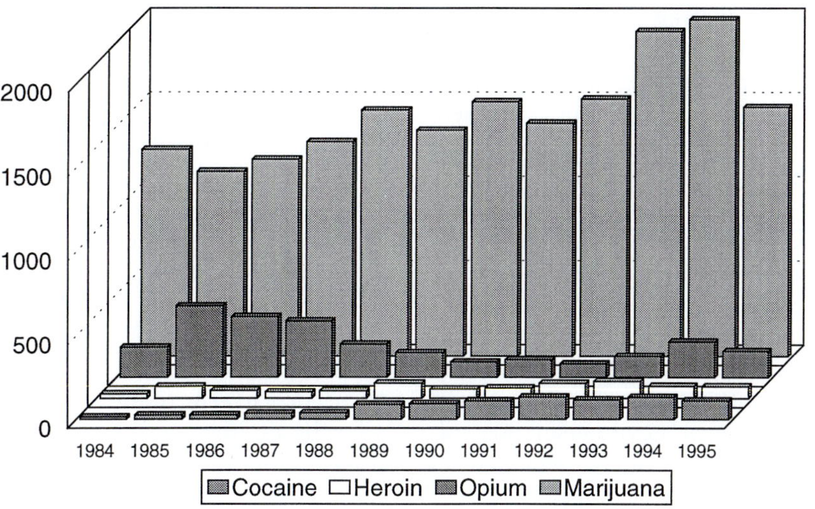

FIGURE 13 Drug law violations in Japan.

survey research to estimated drug abuse potentials in Japan, and some of the findings reported are consistent with a drug abuse problem. The data show that students in Japan have a surprising level of tolerance to drug use. They also express a relatively liberal attitude toward behaviors that could constitute an operational definition of drug abuse. Furthermore, students reported relatively easy access to drugs. The problem is not confined to drug-taking by youths. In order to raise funds to pay for drugs it has been suggested that street mugging (*oyaji-gari*) and schoolgirl prostitution (*enjo kosai*) have increased in frequency.

3. Drug Control Policy in Japan

There are relatively harsh criminal penalties for methamphetamine in the Stimulants Control Law and inhalant and solvent abuse in the Poisonous and Deleterious Substances Law. However, while the Japanese have

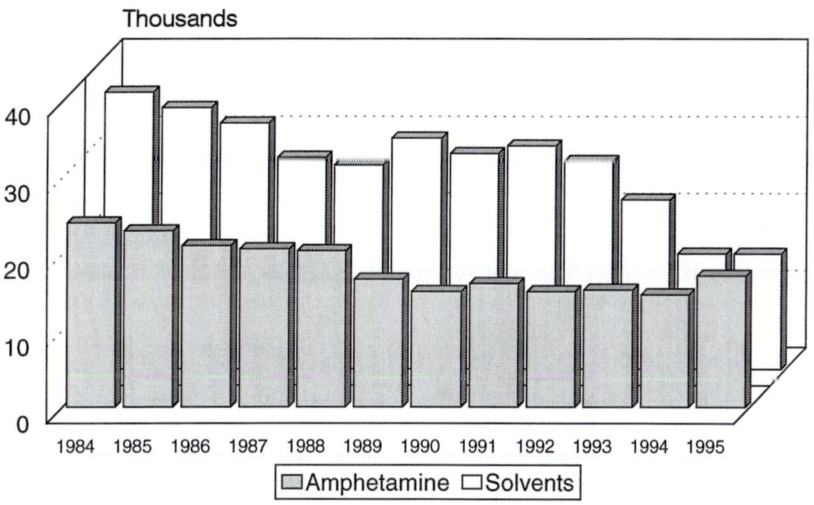

FIGURE 14 Amphetamine and inhalant abuse in Japan.

comparable criminal penalties for the use, trafficking, or importation of all drugs into Japan, it would be inaccurate to consider Japanese drug control policy as comparable to the U.S. "war on drugs" approach. There are two major differences. First, Japanese society has a strong aversion to the metaphor of war in any circumstance, and the term "warfare" as a metaphoric description of response and control of a social problem like drug abuse would not be within the cultural lexicon of Japanese society. Japanese views of social life emphasize balance, duty, obligation, and the requirements of fulfilling familial and communal roles. Drug abusers are more likely to be seen within the context of a person "out of balance" with their social environment. Accordingly, public opinion favors educational treatment to restore the person to a balanced and productive or "normal" life. This is reflected, for example, in a mandated requirement to provide compulsory treatment for certain types of drug abuse problems (e.g., The Narcotic Control Act), although, as noted, treatment is not automatically extended to all drug offenders.

Second, the preference in Japanese society in dealing with issues of drug-related criminal conduct is to try and resolve the problem with discussion and reference to and interaction between authorities and family. The rate of *nolle prosequi* (a decision to not prosecute an arrested citizen) in Japanese society is very high because cases are often resolved via this mechanism as opposed to formal court proceedings. Even when processed through trial, punishment is very unlikely to include imprisonment. There are also very large and historically well-established citizen anticrime groups that help in blending together legal structures and moral structures, resulting in a reliance on normative controls as opposed to physical coercion, imprisonment, and such ancillary procedures as seizure and forfeiture.

While the Japanese system favors the ideas of rehabilitation and educational treatment, it would not be accurate to say that Japan views drug abuse as a purely medical problem or health issue. Certainly there are moral qualities attached to the act of taking drugs, and drug-taking behavior does not escape moral censure. The key to this issue lies in the interpretation of the concept of "dependence," the degree to which drug-taking can be seen as a compulsive act arising out of dependence, and the extent to which drug taking is an act of hedonism and therefore the product of choice. On this matter there is considerable ambiguity in the Japanese orientation.

As we have already noted, the specification of treatment for drug offenders is not uniform in Japanese law. Some drug control laws specify treatment while others do not. In those cases where treatment is not specified in the drug control law, treatment may be compelled by reference and utilization of the Mental Health and Welfare Law, which can be used to compel a person who suffers from a derangement into treatment. This is possible because certain drugs are seen, in Japanese law, as potentially producing psychosis. The terms in Japanese for this are themselves somewhat ambiguous. There is no singular term that corresponds specifically to the English concept of "drug dependence." In Japanese, and in Japanese law, the term *tyudoku* is used, which can be translated as "intoxification," "abuse," and "dependence." The term *tyudoku-sha* refers to a person who abuses drugs, is dependent on drugs, or who uses drugs to become intoxicated. Exactly when the acts of intoxication become seen as a result of drug dependence is variable in Japanese law. Furthermore, the degree to which the drug is seen as capable of producing a psychosis as distinct from a state of dependence is also a critical element in the perception of the meaning of drug-taking and the drug-taker.

For example, The Narcotics and Psychotropics Control Law is directed primarily at the control of heroin, which can produce addiction. Heroin use is not considered as capable of producing a psychosis. It is different for amphetamines. In the Stimulants Control Law, there was no original text reference to *tyudoku* in the law. However, under the provisions of the Mental Health and Welfare Law the chronic use of amphetamine (i.e., a chronic *tyudoku-sha*) can result in a psychotic state of "intoxication psychosis," and thus the abuser can be compelled into treatment under the law. Interestingly, there in no specific provision in Japanese law which relates *tyudoku* to inhalant use. Thus, drug control laws in Japan are to some degree ambiguous when applying the concepts of dependence, abuse, and intoxication to drug-taking. Generally, Japanese drug policy targets demand reduction, through educational efforts, and believes overall that normal and health social and psychological status are protections against drug abuse. The notion of a "war on drugs" in this context is completely alien to Japanese views. There is considerable separation between the concepts of drug abuse and drug trafficking. Trafficking is seen as a purely criminal and entrepreneurial activity whose sole end is to make a financial profit for the trafficker. *Yakuza* or *boryokudan,* which are organized crime groups, are considered to be the major and virtually sole source of major importation and production of drugs in Japanese society. However, despite Japanese concerns with increasing abuse of drugs, the arrests of Yakuza members for drug-based offenses has fallen over the past 12 years and in 1994 and 1995 reached all-time lows. Also, the abuse of inhalants and solvents, which are adaptive uses of legitimate products, is not within the framework of an organized crime paradigm.

VII. SUMMARY

Japan and the U.S. differ radically in the prevalence of drug use and trafficking. They also differ in the social attitudes associated with drug use. The Japanese are more likely to view the problem of drug use as one involving a threat to social stability and as a problem related to social and familial duties and responsibilities. Americans see it as an individual moral failing that carries with it the profound concept of the drug user as an "enemy" upon whom it is necessary to make "war." Japanese find this idea difficult to comprehend. The Japanese do see the drug user as a social failure. But this person is not necessarily fundamentally undone by drugs and is not a person upon whom the state is entitled to make "war." The possibility of rehabilitation overshadows the more radical view that a "war" is the solution to the problem. Thus Japanese authorities are reluctant to respond to individual drug use with harsh punishment. Certainly the notion of a "war on drugs" is completely inappropriate to describe the Japanese viewpoint. A "war" mindset—so intimately tied to the American legal posture—does not appear to be the inevitable outcome of strict legal control and substantive punishment associated with drug-using behavior. The relatively intimate integration between Japanese police and the citizenry, and the preference in Japanese society to first consult and treat problems of disorder by reference to family structure strongly mitigates a purely punitive and impersonal response. Furthermore, the psychological integration of the citizen into a family and community structure facilitate informal and normative control and provide an alternative not often available to American criminal justice institutions.

The Japanese interest in treatment, as exemplified by its written law, is also distinctive. While there are many types of treatment organizations in the United States that provide some degree of drug treatment for offenders, it is not required in American federal or state law. The Japan willingness to extend treatment is more formalized and supported. The Japanese have not experienced the type of violent crime that characterizes many American communities with high rates of drug abuse. This may make the social perception of the drug abuser as a "sick person" easier to sustain in Japanese society. It is also likely that the premium placed on family organization, duty, and obligation in Japanese culture plays a role in deterring drug abuse since it provides some buffering incentives. In effect, the Japanese reduce "at risk" behaviors through this family socialization mechanism. Japanese analysts, in recent commentary, have commented that the alienation of youth from their families may be important in understanding the perceived increase in youthful drug abuse.

While it is important to also note that Japan and the U.S. have substantial differences in the occurrence of drug abuse and their responses to it, they also share some common attributes. As indicated earlier, both countries have essentially the same substances under regulation, and both countries have a comparable ideological view on the dangers of drug use. In neither country is there any official support for decriminalization or significant tolerance of drug use as a matter of governmental policy. The U.S. has a more vocal expression advocating drug tolerance than does Japan, but few policy experts believe the American decriminalization movement will succeed in significantly modifying current policy. Both the U.S. and Japan tend to look to foreign countries as contributors to their drug abuse problems because they believe that the sources of drugs are outside their national boundaries. Recent commentary in the Japanese press has suggested that drugs entering Japan are coming from "foreign sources," often identified as China. And in American society the focus on Colombia, Mexico, Peru, and Ecuador (for cocaine and marijuana) and Southeast Asia (for heroin and amphetamines) as source countries for drugs has led to policies including the direct military cooperation between several of the governments and the U.S. The popular press in Japan overtly identifies drug sellers in Japan as often being "foreigners," although they are seen as working with Japanese *yakuza*. This is also true in the U.S., which portrays an interface between foreign producers and cooperating American and foreign elements who import drugs in substantial quantities and sell them to American criminal enterprises for retail distribution.

Also See the Following Articles

DRUGS AND VIOLENCE • PUNISHMENT OF CRIMINALS

Bibliography

Adler, F. (1983). *Nations not obsessed with crime.* Littleton, CO: Fred Rothman.

Ames, W. (1981). *Police and community in Japan.* Los Angeles: University of California Press.

Becker, H. S. (1953). Becoming a marihuana user. *American Journal of Sociology, 59,* 235–242.

Byck, R. (1987). Cocaine, marijuana and the meaning of addiction. In R. Hamoway (Ed.), *Dealing with drugs* (pp. 221–245). Lexington, MA: Lexington Books.

Clifford, W. (1976). *Crime control in Japan.* Lexington, MA: Lexington Books.

Greberman, S. & Wada, K. (1994). Social and legal factors related to drug abuse in the United States and Japan. *Public Health Reports, 109*(6), 731–737.

Miyazawa, S. (1992). *Policing in Japan: A study on making crime.* Albany, NY: SUNY Press.

National Police Agency (Japan) (1997). *White paper on police.* Tokyo, Japan.

Parker, L. C. (1984). *The Japanese police system today: An American perspective.* Tokyo: Kodansha International.

Thornton, R. & Katsuya, E. (1992). *Preventing crime in America and Japan.* Armonk, NY: M. E. Sharpe.

Wada, K. (1994). Cocaine abuse in Japan. *Japanese Journal of Alcohol and Drug Dependence, 29*(2), 83–91.

Wada, K. & Fukui, S. (1993). Prevalence of volatile solvent inhalation among junior high school students in Japan and background life style of smokers. *Addiction, 88,* 89–100.

Wada, K. & Fukui, S. (1994). Demographic and social characteristics of solvent abuse patients in Japan. *The American Journal on Addictions, 3*(2), 165–176.

Wada, K. & Fukui, S. (1994). Prevalence of tobacco smoking among junior high school students in Japan and background life style of smokers. *Addiction, 89,* 331–343.

Westermann, T. & Burfeind, J. (1991). Crime and justice in two societies: Japan and the United States. Pacific Grove, CA: Brooks/Cole.

Drugs and Violence

Mark S. Gold and Michael Herkov
University of Florida Brain Institute, University of Florida

GLOSSARY

Addiction A disease marked by (1) preoccupation with obtaining and using the drug, (2) continued use despite adverse consequences, and (3) failed attempts to eliminate or cutback drug use.

Antisocial Personality Disorder A character disorder where the person displays a persistent disregard for the rights of others. It is manifested in disregard for societal rules of behavior, impulsivity, irresponsibility, aggressiveness, deceitfulness and lack of remorse. It has an early onset, is chronic, and is highly resistant to intervention.

Crack A cocaine alkaloid that is extracted from its powdered hydrochloride salt by mixing it with sodium bicarbonate and allowing it to dry into small "rocks" that are smoked in a pipe.

Incidence Rate The rate at which new cases of a disease or condition are occurring. It is the number of new cases that occur during a defined unit of time, divided by the number of persons at risk or exposed during the same time.

Post-Traumatic Stress Disorder A mental illness precipitated by an event in which the person is confronted with threatened death or serious bodily harm to self or others. Symptoms include reexperiencing the traumatic event, emotional numbing, and increased physiological arousal.

Prevalence Rate The number of diagnosed cases of a disease or condition within a specific period of time.

PEOPLE HAVE USED SUBSTANCES to achieve altered states of consciousness since the beginning of recorded history. Drugs and alcohol can provide the user with feelings of euphoria, relaxation, or other positive feeling states. However, at some point each culture has also become aware that substance use is a double-edged sword with associated health risks, cognitive impairments, decreases in judgment, and social ills such as aggression and increased violence. The relationship between substance use and violence appears evident, but is deceptively complex. It is well established in the literature that persons under the influence of alcohol or drugs, or involved in the drug distribution system, commit more violent crime and that the prisons are disproportionately filled with substance abusers. However, support for a linear causal link between drugs and violence is elusive. Part of the problem is the finding that a significant portion of alcohol and drug users do not engage in violent behavior. Other studies have shown that expectancies and other situational factors also moderate the drug-violence relationship.

The purpose of this article is to explore what we believe is a clear, but complex, relationship between substance abuse and violence. We will accomplish this by: (1) providing a brief history of the evolution of substance use with emphasis on American attitudes toward drugs; (2) exploring the associated epidemiology between substance use and violence; and (3) examining how drug pharmacology interacts with individual differences as well as social factors to lead to increased in violent behavior. This discussion will utilize Goldstein's tripartite model in examining the drug-violence nexus. This model hypothesizes that drugs lead to violence through three fundamental mechanisms: (1) pharmacological effect of drugs on the brain; (2) violence associated with the addicts' attempt to obtain the money necessary to purchase the drugs; and (3) violence associated with the drug distribution system. To Goldstein's conceptualization we would add the interaction between substance abuse and preexisting, concomitant, or resultant mental illness. We will conclude by exploring new intervention strategies that offer new hope in treating substance abuse.

I. HISTORICAL FACTORS OF ALCOHOL AND DRUG USE

Alcohol and other drugs have been included as part of social interaction, healing, and religion practices since antiquity. The ancient Greeks were known to ferment wine and even had a god of wine making, Dionysus. The Romans worshiped their own god of wine making, Bacchus, and had a yearly feast in his honor. This drunken festival serves as the root of the modern word "bacchanalian." The use of alcohol also has strong traditions in both Jewish and Christian religions. Wine is used as part of the communion service for many Christians, and any Sunday school student can recount Jesus' first miracle of turning water into wine.

Alcohol is not the only intoxicating substance with ties to antiquity. The Incas of Peru viewed cocaine as a gift from the gods and were chewing on coca leaves as early as 3000 B.C. Freud advocated the use of cocaine as an aphrodisiac and as a treatment for hysteria, syphilis, and altitude sickness. Natural opioids have been used for at least 3500 years and were usually either smoked or mixed in solutions of alcohol. Marijuana was referred to as early as the 15th century B.C. in a Chinese medical text for the treatment of a number of physical and psychological ailments, and was introduced into western Europe by Napoleon's soldiers returning from Egypt. References to hallucinogen use occur in Sanskrit writings that are more than 3500 years old. Thus, the use of these substances is not new, although changes in chemistry and pharmacology have resulted in more potent and dangerous drugs.

A. The American Experience

The evolution of drug use in the United States is chronicled by Musto. For the most part, humans used these various drugs for centuries in their natural form or with very little preparation, such as chewing on leaves, smoking dried plants, and so on. However, the advent of organic chemistry in the 19th century allowed, for the first time, the isolation of the active ingredients of the various drugs, resulting in a purer and more potent forms of drugs. For example, morphine was isolated in the early part of the century and cocaine was synthesized by 1860. This new organic chemistry provided a product that demanded more efficient pathways to enter the body. The advent of the hypodermic syringe in the mid-1800s provided a new delivery system for drugs that far surpassed the traditional oral consumption of the drugs both in terms of potency of dose and onset of intoxicating effects.

In the United States, pharmaceutical companies capitalized on these developments and became increasingly adept at marketing these drugs to the general population. During the late 19th and early 20th centuries drugs such as cocaine and morphine were included in a number of over-the-counter remedies purported to cure everything from coughs to pains. In fact, the term heroin was coined in 1898 when synthesized acetylmorphine was introduced by the Bayer Company as a cough suppressant. An early advertisement for the product purported that it "simply stands upon its merits before the profession, ready to prove its efficacy to all who are interested in the advances in the art of medication." In 1886, American druggist John Pemberton patented a concoction of cocaine and caffeine into a drink. This product, which eventually became known as Coca-Cola, was marketed as an "intellectual beverage" and "brain tonic." The use of drugs was so accepted and widespread that many well-known companies such as Parke-Davis manufactured personal "emergency kits" for drug-using consumers. These stylish containers housed doses of cocaine and morphine as well as hypodermic syringes for immediate use.

This permissive and accepting attitude toward drug use began to erode near the turn of the century as more Americans became concerned regarding the addictive properties and other deleterious effects of many of these drugs. Despite strong opposition from over-the-counter manufacturers, in 1905 the Congress outlawed the use of opium for any purpose other than medical use. The Pure Food and Drug Act of 1906, while not preventing the use of addictive drugs, did require accurate labeling for all products sold in interstate commerce. This antidrug legislation culminated with the passing of the Harrison Act of 1914, which severely limited the import, dispensing, and use of narcotics and cocaine.

Opiates and cocaine were not the only substances that came under government control in the early 1900s. Alcohol, long a part of American culture, came under severe attack as a societal evil. In fact, opposition to alcohol was so strong that Congress, in 1920, passed the 18th Amendment prohibiting the manufacture, transportation, sale, and possession of alcohol.

Marijuana represents a somewhat unique chapter in American drug use. It was introduced into the United States much later than the other drugs, after the passage of government legislation restricting drug use. While marijuana cigarettes arrived in the United States during the 1920s with the influx of Mexican immigrants, widespread use did not occur until the 1960s. In response to public concerns over marijuana use the government instituted the Marihuana Tax Stamp of 1937. This act established government control over the sale and transfer of the plant and required a stamp (not available for private use) for buying the plant.

LSD was first synthesized in 1938 and was originally marketed with the suggestion that psychiatrists self-administer the drug to help them better understand psychosis as well as to help patients release repressed feelings and thoughts. It was soon realized that the side effects of LSD outweighed any medical benefits, and its use declined. However, the drug found resurgence with the counterculture of the 1960s, with LSD use purported by such national figures as Timothy Leary.

Societal rejection of alcohol, opiates, marijuana, and cocaine was short-lived. The 18th Amendment was repealed in 1933 with a corresponding increase in alcohol consumption from that observed during prohibition. At the present time alcohol is second only to the drug caffeine in terms of usage. The opiate problem declined in the United States during the 1920s and 1930s until it was mostly confined to the peripheral elements of urban society. However, the last 60 years have been marked with episodes of increased opium usage. For example, between 15 and 20% of American military enlisted personnel serving in Vietnam, where opioids were readily available, reported being addicted. Current statistics show that as many as 2 million Americans abuse opioids, mainly heroin, with 600,000 described as addicts. Attitudes toward marijuana were generally favorable during the 1960s and 1970s, culminating in formal advocacy by the Carter administration in 1977 of the legalization of marijuana in amounts up to 1.8 ounces. However, deleterious effects of the drug on cognitive functioning and its association with illegal behavior have begun to generate a public backlash as evidenced by the state of Alaska recriminalizing marijuana possession in 1990. Examination of marijuana use among high school students showed a general decline from a high in 1979 to a low in 1992. The 1993 statistics revealed a reversal of that trend. Prior to the 1970s cocaine usage was mainly confined to jazz musicians and other artist groups. Use continued to increase during the 1970s, with the synthesis of crack cocaine in the 1980s leading to an explosion in cocaine consumption.

During the last decade, the American public has become exposed to another drug of abuse, flunitrazepam, better known as Rohypnol. This drug, which is a benzodiazapine some 10 times more powerful than Valium, was first marketed in 1975 by Hoffman-Laroche as a sedative hypnotic. While widely prescribed in Europe for insomnia, it has never been approved for manufacture or use in the United States. The illicit use of the drug came to prominence in the United States in the early 1990s, mainly in the South. In fact, Rohypnol use has been identifed as Florida's fastest growing drug problem. The drug is purported to have obtained its street name of "roofies" due to its association with roofers who came to South Florida to work in the construction industry following several destructive hurricanes. Traditionally, Rohypnol was classified under the U.S. Controlled Substances Act as a Schedule IV drug (legitimate medical use with low potential for abuse). However, several states, including Oklahoma, Idaho, Minnesota, and Florida, have reclassified the drug as a Schedule I substance (no legitimate medical value and high potential for abuse) and criminalized its possession and distribution.

This history of alcohol and drug use illustrates the historical use of substances and how societal attitudes toward drugs have varied over time. Analysis of drug use in the United States illustrates how Americans have wholeheartedly accepted and then vehemently rejected drugs several times during our own brief history. Musto discusses how these drug epidemics seem to skip generations, as if the lessons learned by one generation are forgotten and must be learned again. One thing is clear: Drug and alcohol use is rampant among Americans of all ages. In fact, if these prevalence rates were viewed as infectious diseases, we would consider ourselves to be within an epidemic of substance abuse. Next, we will more closely examine the current epidemiology of alcohol and drug use.

II. EPIDEMIOLOGY OF ALCOHOL AND DRUG USE

Alcohol is one of the most-used drugs in America. More than 90% of Americans report using of alcohol at some time during their lives. More than 40% of alcohol users experience some alcohol-related problem in their lives and 10% of men and between 5 and 10% of women meet criteria for an alcohol abuse or dependence diagnosis. It is estimated that alcohol-related problems cost the U.S. economy $150 billion in 1995, with 60% of the costs associated with loss productivity, 15% related to health costs and treatment, and the remaining 25% linked to a variety of alcohol-related damages.

Amphetamine use has fluctuated dramatically in the last 20 years. A 1991 community survey indicated that 7% of the population reported nonmedical use of amphetamines in their lifetime, with approximately 2% of the population meeting *DSM-III-R* criteria for amphetamine abuse or dependence. During the last decade new amphetamine compounds such as MDMA or "ecstasy" have emerged, promising to enhance everything from awareness to sexual sensation.

Cannabis use is widespread in the United States and abroad. In fact, marijuana remains the world's most commonly used illicit drug with between 200 and 300 million regular users worldwide. At present it is estimated that more than 67 million Americans have used marijuana one or more times in their lives, with almost 10 million using the drug within the last month. About 2 or 3% of Americans report daily use of marijuana and 4% meet *DSM-III-R* criteria for cannabis dependence or abuse.

Cocaine usage reached epidemic proportions in 1985 when almost 13 million Americans reported using the drug. Most studies showed a decline in cocaine use between 1985 and 1992, due largely to drug education efforts. Recently, however, this trend appears to have been reversed. National Household Survey of Drug Abuse (NHSDA) 1993 statistics reveal that 1.3 million Americans reported weekly cocaine use while another 3 million reported using the drug monthly. However, changes in the demographics of cocaine consumption have accompanied the advent of crack cocaine. For example, in 1983 the typical caller to the Cocaine National Helpline was a 31-year-old intranasal cocaine user, college educated, and employed with an income of more than $25,000. By 1989, the typical caller was less educated, unemployed, a nonintranasal user, with an income of less than $25,000. Since 1989 these early findings have been replicated. It has become common to consider crack a drug of the urban poor and cocaine Hcl as a suburban and middle-class drug of abuse. It is currently estimated that about half a million persons abuse crack cocaine. This shift is important for understanding the relationship between drugs and violence, which will be explored in more detail below.

Hallucinogen use is mostly confined to lysergic acid diethylamide (LSD) and 3, 4, methylenedioxymethamphetamine (MDMA or Ecstasy). A 1991 community survey revealed that 8% of the population had used hallucinogens at some point during their lifetime, with 2% reporting use in the past month. Still, compared to other drugs, hallucinogen abuse using *DSM-III-R* criteria, approximately .3% of the sample met criteria for hallucinogen abuse. Phencyclidine-related drugs (PCP and ketamine) while hallucinogens are traditionally examined separately from other hallucinogen drugs. PCP use peaked in the U.S. during the late 1970s when 14% of high school seniors reported lifetime use and 2.4% reported use in the last year.

Rohypnol use is seen among persons of various ages and socioeconomic classes. However, its low cost (sometimes as low as $.50 a tablet) has made it particularly popular among young users. It is most often used in conjunction with alcohol and marijuana, and like other benzodiazepines, it has a synergistic effect with alcohol.

III. EPIDEMIOLOGY OF DRUGS AND VIOLENCE

There is considerable confusion regarding the terms violence and aggression. Although the terms are often used synonymously, violence traditionally refers to acts against others or the self that are designed to cause injury. Aggression is a broader term and can include issues of competition, dominance, and so on. Animal research typically uses the term aggression, while violence is applied to human studies. We will use both terms in this chapter as the specific data dictate.

Clearly, the United States has become the "Land of the Violent." Data from the Federal Bureau of Investigation indicate that 23,760 persons were murdered in 1992, making homicide the 10th leading cause of death in the United States. Violence among young Americans is even more frightening. Between 1970 and 1991, more than 50,000 children were killed by firearms, thus equaling the total number of U.S. casualties during the Vietnam War. Thirty children are injured by firearms every day, with one child dying every 2 hours from a gunshot wound.

While violence against others is widely reported in the media, relatively few persons are aware of the enormous amount of violence that persons perpetrate upon themselves in the form of suicide. The Centers for Disease Control (CDC) reported that 30,906 persons committed suicide in 1990 and the National Center for Health Statistics reported in 1991 that more people died from suicide than from homicide, making the former the eighth leading cause of death in the United States.

Alcohol, and to a lesser degree other drugs, have indeed become part of human culture. While humans obviously receive pleasure from their use of these substances, alcohol and drugs also have a deleterious effect on cognitive abilities and on a wide range of human behaviors. In fact, recent rises in violent behavior are highly correlated with rises in substance abuse. The association between substance abuse and violence is compelling. Substance abuse is associated with 50% of traffic fatalities, 49% of murders, 68% of manslaughter charges, 38% of cases of child abuse, 52% of rapes, and 62% of assaults. Below, we examine the relationship between specific drugs and violence.

Of all of the drugs, alcohol has received the most attention in terms of its relationship to violence. These data clearly illustrate the association of alcohol with violence. Much of this is associated with the high prevalence of alcohol use compared to that of other drugs. With more than 90% of all Americans having used alcohol, it is most likely to be the drug used during a violent event. In fact, almost half of all murderers and their victims were intoxicated with alcohol at the time of the murder. Alcohol's association with violent crime, including homicide and rape, is well documented. Alcohol appears to be even more closely linked to family violence with Slade and colleagues (1990) reporting that alcohol was involved in 85% of domestic homicides. Similarly, half of all traffic fatalities involve a driver with a blood alcohol level that is over the traditional legal limit. Alcohol is also linked to perpetrators of physical and sexual abuse.

This relationship between intoxication and violence has long been recognized by the legal system. For example, in the early 17th century English legal theorist Sir Edward Coke defined four classes of persons who did not have the mental element or "non compos mentis" to be responsible for a crime. One class was a category of persons who deprived themselves of memory and understanding from voluntary drunkenness. This concept is still recognized today and virtually all legal jurisdictions make special allowances, either by statute or case law, for crimes committed by intoxicated individuals. In many jurisdictions, including Florida, a person who was *voluntarily* intoxicated at the time of an offense is thought to be functioning under a type of diminished capacity, and by definition, cannot be convicted of a specific intent crime such as first degree murder. Similarly, suicide rates for alcoholics rank only behind depression and schizophrenia in terms of prevalence per 100,000 population.

However, the relationship between alcohol and violence is complex. Some data have shown that dose and individual characteristics are important moderators, with low doses showing no affect or even a reduction in aggression. The type of alcohol used also seems to be important in modulating violence with liquor. Research has shown that nonpharmacological factors such as expectancy, situational context, and disposition play a considerable role in understanding the effects of alcohol on violence.

The association of cocaine with violence burgeoned during the 1980s. The commission of a felony is highly associated with the presence of cocaine or other illicit drugs in the body of the perpetrator. Nearly one in four drug-related emergency room visits involved some combination of drugs (mostly cocaine) and alcohol. By 1989, cocaine was the number-one cause of emergency room visits in major U.S. cities such as Washington, New York, Atlanta, and Los Angeles. Visits for intentional injuries, such as gunshot wounds, were attributed directly to crack, rather than to simple increases in the base rate of violence. Similarly, more than 70% of those arrested in such major cities as New York, Philadelphia, and Washington tested positive for one or more drugs, usually including cocaine. Slade and colleagues (1990) found a strong correlation between drug use and domestic homicides. For example, they found that cocaine and its metabolite, benzoylecgonine, were involved in 35% of these deaths. Interestingly, in many of the cases, both the perpetrator and the victim tested positive for drugs.

The association of cocaine with violence does appear to be linked to the route of administration, with smoked cocaine (crack) more often associated with violence than is snorted cocaine (cocaine hcl). For example, closer examination of emergency room admissions reveals that 37% of admissions involved crack, while only 11% involved cocaine Hcl. In addition, the distribution system of crack cocaine is associated with more violence than is that of other drugs. For example, one study found that between 40 and 50% of dealers selling crack cocaine with other drugs reported being involved in violence, while only 20% of those selling cocaine Hcl and other drugs reported violent events.

Cocaine and alcohol are not the only drugs linked with violence. In fact, the use of almost any substance results in an increase of other or self-directed violence when compared to non-drug-using matched cohorts. There is less data available on the relationship of opioid use and violence. Media representations, however, depict heroin addicts as desperate individuals who are willing to do anything to support their addiction. However, the data that do exist also link opiate use with violence. For example, Gordon and colleagues found that 9% of adolescents who were admitted to an emergency room trauma center tested positive for opiates alone, and 14% had a combination of opiates and cocaine in their systems. Still, other data document that many opiate users have criminal histories prior to their use of the drug. This suggests that the drug may amplify premorbid personality factors.

The relationship of PCP to aggressive, violent, and bizarre behavior is well known. Anecdotal reports from law enforcement officers describe how PCP-intoxicated persons behave in bizarre and unpredictable ways, and seem oblivious to pain. Much of this is undoubtedly related to the anesthetic and dissociative qualities of the drug. This violence is exacerbated by the disoriented, psychotic state evidenced by many PCP-intoxicated persons. Baldridge (1990) and Poklis and colleagues (1990) reported on a sample of 96 persons who had died, and who through postmortem analysis were found to be positive for PCP use. Seventy-five of these persons died from homicide (64 gunshot wounds), 12 from suicide (11 gunshot wounds), and 9 from accidents. More than half of the cases involved use of PCP with another drug, mainly cocaine and ethanol. Gordon and colleagues (1996) found that 5% of adolescents admitted to an emergency room trauma center tested positive for PCP, alone or with alcohol. Interestingly, unlike opiate addicts or other drug users, PCP users who are violent generally do not have a previous history of violence.

While typically thought of as a benign drug, marijuana has a surprisingly high association with violent behavior. This does not necessarily mean that this link is pharmacologically derived. In fact, considerable research indicates that marijuana reduces aggressive responses to provocation. However, while controversial, a cannabis-induced psychosis has been identified. Nonetheless, epidemiological data show a definite relationship between marijuana use and violence. In addition to the information in Table 1, Spunt (1994) reports on the link of marijuana to homicide. This study of 268 persons incarcerated for homicide found that of the prisoners who used marijuana *three-fourths* were under the effects of the drug at the time of the crime.

Amphetamines have been associated with violence since their widespread use of the 1960s. The associated slogan, "speed kills," and the prevalent use of amphetamines by outlaw motorcycle gangs have emphasized this point. The potential of these drugs to cause psychotic-like reactions has been one of the principle reasons for this relationship. However, as noted above with other drugs, persons who commit violent acts while using amphetamines have histories of violence prior to the onset of their drug use.

Rohypnol's association with violence is almost exclusively in the area of sexual assault. It has become known as the "date rape" drug due to its sedative effects and disruption of memory. It is primarily the abuse of Rohypnol that led to the passage of the Drug Induced Rape Prevention and Punishment Act in 1996. This legislation provides sentences of up to 20 years for persons who use controlled substances to facilitate a crime such as sexual assault.

As with drug addiction, young people seem to be at most risk for perpetrating or experiencing drug-associated violence. In fact, of all age groups, those between

TABLE I

Prevalence of Violent-Associated Behaviors among Substance-Using Adolescents

	Alcohol users	Alcohol nonusers	Marijuana users	Marijuana nonusers	Cocaine users	Cocaine nonusers
Physical fighting	51%	33%	63%	39%	74%	42%
Carrying a weapon	34%	17%	48%	22%	71%	28%

ages 16 and 19 have the highest rate for victimization by violent crimes, excluding homicide. One study revealed that 25% of adolescents admitted to an inner-city trauma center had a positive urine test for some drug, mainly alcohol, cocaine, or opiates. This increase in trauma seems to be associated with an increase in high-risk behaviors. For example, in a study of 12,272 adolescents Durkham found that physical fights or carrying a weapon was much more likely by substance-using adolescents than by nonusers (see Table 1). Adolescents who use crack cocaine manifest deficits in school performance and family relationships, and exhibit increased psychiatric symptoms and delinquent behavior.

IV. NEUROBIOLOGY OF VIOLENCE AND AGGRESSION

A. Outward-Directed Violence

All behavior, whether benevolent or malevolent, originates in the neuroanatomy and neurochemistry of the brain. Advances in brain research over the last decade have added considerably to our understanding of the brain mechanisms associated with aggressive and violent behavior. This research has utilized both animal and human models to elucidate the anatomical structures and neurochemical basis of violent behavior.

It is beyond the scope of this article to review, in detail, the neurobiology of violence, and readers are referred to other sources for a more thorough discussion of this research. Nonetheless, some review of the anatomical structures and neurochemistry of violence is needed in order to understand the link between substance abuse and violence.

Much of our understanding of aggression involves animal research. These studies typically involve the development of aggression by manipulating the brain through psychopharmacology, electrical stimulation, or lesioning specific brain sites. Compilation of this research reveals that aggressive behavior is modulated by a number of subcortical structures, including the medial and lateral hypothalamus, lateral septum, pons, raphe nuclei, olfactory bulbs, and amygdala. Lesions to these areas can lead to increases in erratic and aggressive behavior. For example, lesions of the hypothalamus of either male or female rats result in increased aggression.

It is also clear from animal research that neurotransmitters, especially serotonin, are related to aggressive behavior. Generally, decreases in serotonergic activity lead to an increase in aggressive behavior, while increasing serotonin results in a decrease in aggressive behavior. It has been known for a number of years that the serotonin receptor 5-HT2 can lead to decreased aggression. The role of serotonin in aggression is further supported by the finding that deleting the 5-HT1b gene in mice resulted in a reduced latency of attack and in an increase in attacking behavior. These data suggest that the 5-HT1b receptor may mediate the anti-aggressive effects of serotonin. This relationship between serotonin and aggression has also been demonstrated in nonhuman primates. Cerebrospinal fluid levels of the serotonin metabolite 5-HIAA has been found to be lower in dominant monkeys.

Research with humans, however, must be confined to noninvasive procedures, autopsies, or studying persons with known lesions. These methods are less precise than procedures in animal research and are confounded by variables such as sampling bias and multisite lesions. For example, nonsurgical lesions such as stroke or head injury most often involve damage to several brain structures. Similarly, persons referred for diagnostic testing may represent a nonnormative subtype that, because of their behavior, are more likely to be referred. Still, there is sufficient data in the human literature to point to a relationship between aggression and certain brain structures. For example, imaging studies have revealed a link between temporal lobe dysfunction and aggressive behavior. Research has found that 5 of 14 violent patients had lesions in the anterior-inferior temporal lobe. Similarly, PET scan studies revealed that a sample of psychiatric patients with a history of violent behavior all had decreased blood flow in the left temporal lobe. Other data have shown that electrical stimulation of the amygdala and the hypothalamus can result in rage reactions, and tumors in the ventromedial hypothalamus can result in uncoordinated aggressive behavior and hyperphagia in some patients.

Disturbance in the frontal lobes is also associated with aggressive behavior. While lesions to the dorsolateral frontal area leads to apathetic behavior, damage to the orbitomedial frontal lobe had been associated with increased violence. This may be because this section of the frontal lobe has connections to the amygdala and the hypothalamus.

Under normal circumstances, activation or deactivation of the above structures is the result of brain's underlying neurochemistry. Thus, understanding how these structures are linked to aggression requires examination of the neurotransmitters involved in neuronal communication. Many studies link neurotransmitters to aggression. Serotonin and its metabolite 5-HIAA appear to inhibit aggression in a variety of animal species. Thus, low levels of serotonin may be associated with increased aggressive behavior. Indeed, there is some data to support this hypothesis. For example, numerous studies have established a link between low levels of 5-HIAA in the cerebrospinal fluid (CSF) and violence, depression, and suicide. Low CSF levels are believed to reflect a reduction in central serotonergic activity. Other animal studies reveal an association between norepinephrine, dopamine, aminobutyric acid, and endogenous opioid peptides in aggression. For example, research has linked low CSF 5-HIAA with increased irritability, hostility, impulsive behavior, fire setting, and maternal aggression, and it has found that a low level of CSF 5-HIAA was linked to an increase in lifetime aggression.

There is also some evidence that dopamine is involved in aggressive behavior, and that greater dopamine activity is associated with dominance and aggression. While there have been few studies directly examining the role of the dopaminergic system and aggression, pharmacological data examining the effects of amphetamine (dopamine agonist) and the anti-aggressive effects of dopamine antagonists support the hypothesis that dopaminergic activity may underlie some forms of aggression.

There is also data to support the role of the noradrenergic system in aggression. Measurement of CSF levels of 3-hydroxy-4-thehoxphenyglycol (MHPG) reveal a positive correlation with aggressive behavior. Consistent with this the finding that the B-adrenergic antagonist, propranolol, may be effective in the treatment of episodic aggressive behavior frequently associated with head injuries. Animal studies link low levels of brain and brain stem norepinephrine with aggression. This drop in norepinephrine is presumably reflective of decrease of the transmitter within the brain.

B. Self-Directed Violence

There are no models of suicidal behavior in animals, although research on self-injurious behavior in monkeys reveals a link to serontonergic activity. Research in humans has focused on the serotonergic, noradrenergic, GABAergic, cholinergic, and dopaminergic systems. However, most research has examined the serotonergic and noradrenergic systems. Postmortem studies of brain tissue of persons who completed suicide have found reductions of 5-HT or 5-HIAA within the brainstem, and to a lesser extent, the prefrontal cortex. This reduction in 5-HT or 5-HIAA is similar in depressed patients, schizophrenics, and alcoholics. Data on the noradrenergic system are still equivocal, although there is some data to suggest increased binding to B-adrenergic receptors in the cerebral cortex of suicide victims. However, more research is needed.

V. NEUROBIOLOGY OF SUBSTANCE ABUSE

Once ingested into the body, and crossing the blood-brain barrier, alcohol and drugs affect all aspects of brain functioning, including the neurochemistry of the brain structures. While millions of different chemicals exist, fewer than 25 are abused by humans. These chemicals, including opiates, cocaine, ethanol, hallucinogens, and inhalants, while diverse, share the common factor of enhancing endogenous brain reward mechanisms through the release of specific neurotransmitters. Alcohol targets the GABA (gamma-aminobutyric acid) complex, cocaine the dopamine re-uptake transporter, opiates the endogenous opioid systems, and marijuana the endogenous cannabinoid systems. Below, we briefly examine the effects of various drugs on the brain, specifically examining how they relate to the above discussion on the neurobiology of violence.

Alcohol (ethanol) effects several neurotransmitter and neuroreceptor systems. In the adrenergic system it increases the synthesis and release of norepinepherine, with a corresponding decrease in cyclic adenosine monophosphate (AMP) response to norepinepherine. During withdrawal, humans show a marked increase in CSF norepinephrine and MHPG, with return to normal range over several days. While the influences of ethanol on the GABA system have been varied, one consistent finding has been reduced brain GABA after chronic alcohol administration. The relationship of GABA to alcohol abuse is illustrated by the finding that GABA agonists reduce alcohol withdrawal symptoms while GABA antagonists produce pharmacodynamic effects resembling alcohol abstinence syndrome. The effects of alcohol on opiate systems is more controversial. In general, acute alcohol use decreases the bindings of enkephalins to delta receptors while increasing beta-endorphin levels and binding to mu-receptors.

Most germane to our discussion of drugs and violence are the effects of alcohol on serotonin and dopamine. While some studies show a depletion of brain serotonin after chronic alcohol administration, other studies show no such change. However, and most importantly, it is apparent that ethanol shifts serotonin metabolism production from 5-HIAA to 5-hydroxyindoleacetaldehyde and 5-hydroxytryptophol. As will be discussed below, changes in the serotonin system, especially the CSF levels of 5-HIAA are linked to increases in both other-directed and self-directed aggression. The effect of alcohol on the dopamine system is more equivocal and may have to do with the relationship of the alcohol dose to the dopamine system. For example, animal studies reveal that low doses inhibit activity within the dopamine system, while higher doses stimulate activity.

Phencyclidine also alters a number of neurotransmitter systems, including dopamine, serotonin, acetycholine, and the ion channel associated with NMDA. There is also evidence that endogenous PCP receptors and peptides exist within the mammalian brain. Like other drugs, PCP enhances dopamine by inhibiting re-uptake through binding to the receptor that inhibits the dopamine transporter responsible for re-uptake. It enhances presynaptic release of dopamine as well. While it inhibits the uptake of serotonin, it reduces the 5-HT turnover and the CSF 5-HIAAA.

Cocaine primarily effects the dopamanergic system within the mesolimbic and mesocortical areas. This results in an increase in dopamine achieved through cocaine binding to the dopamine transporter and thereby preventing the re-uptake of dopamine. Cocaine also blocks the presynaptic re-uptake of other neurotransmitters, including serotonin, norepinephrine, noradrenaline, and dopamine.

Marijuana's active ingredient, delta-9-THC, has a direct impact on the brain's endogenous cannabinoid system. The interactions between cannabinoids and central nervous neurotransmitters have received considerable research attention. Results indicate that cannabinoids interact with both the dopaminergic and noradrenergic transmitter systems. The THC enhancement of extracellular dopamine within the mesolimbic and mesocortical system is believed to underlie the reward characteristics of the drug. While the effects of THC on the serotonergic system is less clear, there are numerous studies that show that serotonergic agonists enhance the effects of THC. Several research studies have established a link between cannabinoids and the GABAergic compounds.

Opioids such as heroin and morphine act upon the endogenous opioid systems of the brain. Activation of the mu receptor in the thalamus and other areas is believed to underlie the euphoric effects of these drugs. There is research to suggest that Mu-receptor activation may be linked to the release of dopamine from the dopaminergic system originating in the ventral tegmental area and connecting to the nucleus accumbens and frontal cortex. On the other hand, kappa receptor agonists, often associated with dysphoria, may decrease dopamine release.

Substance abuse not only influences brain chemistry, but in some cases actually fundamentally changes neurotransmitter levels in the brain for a period long after drug use stops. Withdrawal from the particular substance may also involve erratic behavior, including many of the negative symptoms associated with intoxication. For example, psychomotor acceleration can be a symptom of both intoxication and withdrawal from cocaine and amphetamine use. One crack addict reported "It doesn't seem to matter whether you're on or off crack . . . you're crazy both times" Also, the biochemical addiction of these drugs in the brain may cause the user to seek out any means possible, including violence, to obtain more of the desired substance.

Finally, many drugs may do more than simply alter the release or re-uptake of a specific neurotransmitter. There is emerging data that long-term use of certain drugs may actually alter brain structures. For example, studies of methamphetamine and MDMA use in nonhuman primates indicate that the drug has neurotoxic effects and actually damages the axon terminals of serotonin producing neurons.

VI. ADDICTION

The cost of alcohol and drugs, along with the associated health, social, occupational, and legal problems, provide in and of themselves a reason for avoiding substance abuse. Therefore, to understand drug use one must understand the power of addiction. As mentioned earlier, there are thousands of different chemical compounds available in the world today, and humans consistently abuse roughly 25 of these substances. It is beyond the scope of this article to give a detailed account of the complete psychosocial and neurobiological process of addiction. We provide a brief outline of addiction in order to help the reader understand how this concept is related to drug violence.

All of the above-mentioned drugs achieve their effects through crossing the blood-brain barrier and altering the neurochemistry of the brain. The chemical compounds of the drugs create their sensations of euphoria, stimulation, sedation, and so on by affecting neurotransmitter systems within various regions of the brain.

The neurologic substrate for addiction is located within the limbic system, where the biologically primitive circuitry for the drive states such as hunger, sex, and thirst are housed. This area, described as the medial forebrain bundle (MFB), contains a number of structures, including the frontal cortex, nucleus accumbens (NA), and ventral tegmental area (VTA). One of the most common ways for drugs to achieve their effect on the brain is to block the presynaptic re-uptake of neurotransmitters, including dopamine, serotonin, and norepinephrine. The surpluses of these neurotransmitters at the postsynaptic receptor sites in the mesocorticolimbic areas of the brain are responsible for the reinforcing and euphoric effects of the drugs.

Brain neurochemistry is further complicated by the fact that most users abuse a variety of drugs, or they may seek to ameliorate some of the unpleasant effects of one drug by concomitantly or subsequently ingesting another. For example, a person may seek to reduce the unpleasant stimulating effects of cocaine with sedating agents, such as alcohol or marijuana. The combined use of cocaine and alcohol is common, with reports that between 62 and 90% of cocaine abusers are also concurrent ethanol abusers. However, concomitant use of these drugs creates a new drug, cocaethylene, with its own unique effects on brain neurochemistry.

These brain neurochemical effects can be followed in the amygdala, which suggests that altered neuronal activity in this brain area underlies drug-seeking behavior. Thus, although the nucleus accumbens plays a critical role in the reinforcing properties of cocaine and other stimulants the amygdala might be invovled in the acquisition of stimulus-reward associations or the motivational aspects of drug seeking. Here, there is a clear interaction between biological and psychosocial processes in which the danger and allure of the streets may actually increase the reinforcing potency of a drug such as crack cocaine.

Addicts can become conditioned to seemingly benign objects in the environment that have become powerful stimuli for drug craving. Vivid, long-term memories of being high tend to persecute the drug abuser by invoking powerful cravings for the next high. For example, cocaine users describe intense craving for cocaine when cocaine is made available to them or when merely seeing places, people or paraphernalia associated with cocaine use.

VII. BEHAVIORAL MANIFESTATIONS OF INTOXICATION

There are a number of different drugs that humans abuse, and each has its own unique neurobiological reaction in the brain. However, as noted below, there are several common pathways within the brain and neurochemical reactions that most drugs seem to share. Thus, it should not be surprising that there is remarkable similarity in behavioral manifestation of various types of drug intoxication. For example, *DSM-IV* lists mood lability, impaired judgment, and aggressive behavior as symptoms of intoxication with alcohol, amphetamine, cannabis, cocaine, hallucinogens (LSD, MDMA), inhalants, PCP, and sedative-hypnotics. Additionally, many of these drugs cause perceptual disturbances, increased paranoia, and psychomotor agitation. Effects can last from minutes to hours, depending on substance, dosage, and abuse history. Chronic cocaine users develop a paranoia that is difficult to distinguish from delusional disorder. Amphetamine and PCP users can demonstrate disorganized thinking and psychotic processes similar to that seen in schizophrenia. Given this impaired judgment, impulsivity, distorted thinking, and disinhibition, violence stemming from substance abuse would seem to be a natural consequence of usage.

A. Neurobiology of Substance-Induced Euphoria and Aggression

While specific in their neurochemistry, the above drugs are used because of their ability to produce euphoria or a high. While diverse in their individual chemical reactions, it is clear from the above review that all of these drugs achieve their results through interaction with one or more of noradrenergic, dopaminergic, serotonergic, or other brain neurotransmitter systems. The result is that these drugs cause alterations in the neurochemistry of the brain reward centers of the medial forebrain bundle (MFB) and the mesolimbic dopaminergic pathway.

The MFB region of the brain, along with the nuclei and projection fields of the MFB, have been found to be primarily responsible for the positive reinforcement associated with drugs of addiction. The MFB consists of a group of interconnected strutures within the limbic system, including nucleus accumbens (NC) and the ventral tegmental area (VTA) with connections to the amygdala and septal regions. The MFB lies within the limbic system, with connections to other limbic structures most often identified as including the limbic lobe, the hippocampal formation, the amygdaloid nucleus, the hypothalamus, and the anterior nucleus of the thalamus. These structures are connected through the alveus, fimbria, fornix, mammillothalamic tract, and stria terminalis. The limbic system extends through parts of the temporal and frontal lobes, septum, thalamus, and hypothalamus.

Identification of the brain structures involved in drug reward is important because many of these brain regions have been identified as being linked to aggressive and violent behavior in animals and humans. Thus, the neurochemical reactions that bring users pleasure may also predispose them for violence. For example, alcohol and drugs also influence brain regions such as the septum and amygdala, which have been shown to underlie aggressive and impulsive behavior. Grinspoon and Bakalan (1985) found that the injection of cocaine into these areas led to increases in aggression in both animals and humans. Histofluorescence mapping techniques have revealed a close association between the brain stimulation reinforcement region and the mesolimbic dopamine (DA) system. Additional studies have confirmed the importance of DA neurotransmission to brain reinforcement (see Table I). These brain neurochemical effects can be followed in the amygdala, suggesting that altered neuronal activity in this brain area underlies drug-seeking behavior. The amygdala receives dopaminergic innervation from the ventral tegmental area and serotonergic innervation from the midbrain and pontine raphe as well as extensive communication from the nucleus accumbens. Although the nucleus accumbens plays a critical role in the reinforcing properties of cocaine and other stimulants, the amygdala might be involved in the acquisition of stimulus-reward associations or the motivational aspects of drug seeking.

Drugs can effect aggression by not only stimulating brain centers associated with aggressive arousal, but also by altering the person's perceptions and judgment. For example, drugs may act on the septum and amygdala to provoke an aggressive response. Activation of the basal ganglia may then lead to increased motor behavior. Mesolimbic influences can lead to paranoid ideation or perception of threat or hostility where none exists. Finally, the effect of drugs on the frontal lobes leads to impairment in the person's insight and judgment, culminating in an aggressive or violent event.

These structures are activated by neurotransmitters that are directly or indirectly influenced by alcohol and drug use. It is clear from the above discussion on neurotransmitters that in many cases the same neurotransmitters associated with violent and aggressive behavior are involved in the subjective feelings of euphoria and brain reward. As illustrated above, neurotransmitters such as dopamine, norepinephrine, epinephrine, serotonin, and gamma aminobutyric acid are all affected by substance abuse. Not surprising, analysis of the neurochemistry of addiction shares many similarities with the neurobiology of violence. One hypothesis of the neurochemisry underlying drug-related aggression is that that repetitive use of drugs and alcohol depletes neurotransmitters such as dopamine, norepinephrine, and epinephrine in the presynaptic neurons, resulting in an increased sensitivity of the respective postsynaptic receptors. Thus, there develops an enhanced sensitivity to dopamine in the postsynaptic receptors. An exaggerated postsynaptic response to dopamine may then lead to suspiciousness and paranoid delusions. Similarly, exaggerated postsynaptic responses to norepinephrine and epinephrine in the hypothalamus, amygdala, and septal regions may lead to increased impulsivity and aggression.

There is emerging research data to support this relationship between dopamine and drug-induced aggression. For example, analysis of striatal dopamine transporter density reveals significantly more DA re-uptake density and the presence of D2A1 alleles in violent alcoholics compared to nonviolent alcoholics and that DA transporter density was higher in violent alcoholics than in nonviolent alcoholics or matched controls. Cocaine, amphetamines, and opiates also alter brain neurochemistry and may in similar ways set the stage for increased aggressive behavior.

Illicit drugs such as alcohol and cocaine influence catecholamine and serotonergic activity, which is also linked to increased aggression. For example, a study of military personnel revealed a positive correlation between 3-methoxy-4-hydroxyphenylglycol (MHPG) and aggression. Alcohol also depletes levels of serotonin and its metabolite 5-HIAA. As noted above, low levels of this neurotransmitter can lead to a disinhibition of aggressive impulses. Chronic self-administration of cocaine in yoked animals is associated with addiction and with markedly elevated dopamine and serotonin levels. These brain neurochemical effects can be followed in the amygdala, suggesting altered neuronal activity in this brain area underlies drug-seeking behavior.

VIII. ECONOMIC COMPULSIVE FACTORS OF DRUG VIOLENCE

For everyone, the first use of drugs or alcohol is voluntary. There is no innate compulsion or drive in humans for alcohol, cocaine, amphetamines, or other drugs. Clearly, the human body can function in perfect health without ever coming into contact with these substances. But for a number of individuals, each successive use of the drug become less voluntary and more a response to drug addiction.

Recent research into brain neurochemistry has clearly delineated alcohol and drug addiction as a disease. As noted above, alcohol and drugs achieve their clinical effect by targeting the primitive reward centers of the brain such as the MFB in the limbic system. This is primarily achieved through blocking the re-uptake of DA into the presynaptic neuron. By preventing DA re-uptake, greater concentrations of DA remain in the synaptic cleft with more DA available at the postsynaptic site for stimulation of specific receptors. Mesolimbic dopaminergic neurons originating in the ventral tegmental area and projecting to the nucleus accumbens and other limbic forebrain areas are well-known substrates of reward and reinforcement, and primary targets for the action of cocaine and other drugs. These neurons are also being studied as responsible for craving and relapse on the basis of the effects of repeat administration and withdrawal. Results indicate that there are major and long-lasting changes in these neurons during withdrawal.

For the drug user the description of normality changes so that the "normal" brain state is one in which alcohol, cocaine, amphetamine, or other drug is present and "abnormal' is defined as lack of the the drug. Withdrawal states from these drugs are extremely unpleasant and are aptly called "crashes," due to the intense and unpleasant feelings experienced. Feelings of drug craving, irritability, dysphoria, impulsivity, insomnia, muscle aches, and nausea and vomiting are reported for a variety of drugs. Thus, the person's addiction to the drug is based both on reward mechanisms associated with usage as well as neurobiological punishment associated with absence of the drug. These symptoms can last for days or weeks, and much of the relapse in substance abuse is associated with withdrawal symptoms.

Thus, the drug user has tremendous motivation to supply his or her brain with the needed drug. With the exception of alcohol and some inhalants, virtually all other drugs must be obtained through illegal means. As discussed below, the costs associated with drug addiction, especially crack cocaine, can be enormous and can quickly deplete the resources of user. Because drug use has a deleterious effect on employment status, users must seek out resources from family and friends. When these sources have been exhausted other mechanisms must be found to meet the brain's demand for the drug. This last resort almost always involves criminal activity.

Miller and Gold (1994) examined crime-related activity in a sample of 200 crack addicts. Their data indicated that 53% of subjects spent more than $200 a week on crack, with 15% spending more than $300 and 14% spending more than $400 a week. However, 53% of the sample reported a total annual family income of less than $15,000, and 38% of the subjects had a family income of less than $10,000. A person who spends $200 a week on drugs would incur an annual cost of $10,400, more than the total family income for almost 40% of the sample. These data clearly illustrate how the drug user must turn to crime to support his or her addiction.

Crimes committed by drug users associated with their quest to obtain drugs can be grouped into five general categorizes: (1) theft; (2) robbery; (3) drug distribution; (4) forgery; and (5) prostitution. Thefts and robberies represent a major method of obtaining money to purchase drugs. Inciardi, in a study of 611 adolescent offenders, found that the following drugs were used on a daily or regular basis: alcohol, 47%; marijuana, 95%; cocaine, 91%. Almost unbelievably, these adolescents accounted for 18,477 felonies, 109,538 property crimes, 43,962 vice crimes, and 257,159 drug-trafficking offenses in the 12-month period preceding the survey. That averages more than 700 offenses per subject. While these numbers seem astronomical, closer analysis reveals that more than half the crimes involved drug trafficking and that almost 93% of the crimes could be accounted for by drug trafficking, prostitution, shoplifting, and dealing in stolen property offenses. Still, these youth were responsible for more than 18,000 felonies. While the majority of robberies represented purse snatchings, a significant number of incidents involved armed robbery in homes, businesses, and on the streets. Of the 611 youths, 59% (361) participated in robberies, the majority of which were committed to obtain drugs.

Prostitution is also a frequently used method to support drug addiction, especially among women. Strek and Elifson found that almost 74% of women involved in prostitution in their sample indicated that drug use preceded their prostitution activities, suggesting that they began their prostitution to support their drug habits. More than 50% of the crack-using prostitutes reported that they were performing sex in exchange for drugs or money to purchase crack. On the other hand, only 22% of male prostitutes reported becoming involved in prostitution after their exposure to drugs, suggesting that this group did not appear to trade sex for drugs.

Hanlon and colleagues examined the criminal histories of drug users over their addiction careers. These authors found a high proportion of thefts, violence, and drug related offenses. Their data did indicate a decrease in criminal activity, both in terms of frequency and profitability of crime, with increasing age. However, their data may be confounded by the fact that their subjects were generally older (mean age of 34.6 years) and in treatment at the time of the survey.

IX. VIOLENCE ASSOCIATED WITH THE DRUG DISTRIBUTION SYSTEM

Violence associated with the selling of illegal substances has been present from the Opium Wars of China through the American Prohibition of the 1920s. In fact, one of the most violent periods in American history surrounds the time of Prohibition. It was during this time that notorious criminals such as Al Capone developed their fortunes and reputations. Bootleg alcohol and private speakeasies emerged to meet popular demand. Even in contemporary society where the sale of alcohol is legal, profits associated with the manufacture and sale of alcohol are staggering.

Not surprisingly, a similar distribution system has emerged for the dispensing of illegal drugs. Violence has also been associated with the production and distribution of other drugs such as marijuana and heroin. However, it has been the manufacture of cocaine, and more specifically, its variant, crack, that has led to an explosion of violence in the drug delivery business.

In 1990, it was estimated that 80 tons of cocaine were imported into the United States. The illicit profits associated with the drug trade are staggering. For example, a kilogram of cocaine that sells for $1200 in Colombia would have a street value of more than $20,000 in the United States. If the cocaine is converted to crack, (at $5 per vial) the profitability triples to more than $60,000. When one multiplies the amount of cocaine imported by its potential street value, it quickly becomes apparent that the sale and distribution of cocaine is a multibillion dollar business. It is estimated that if included with legitimate businesses, the profits of the cocaine cartel would rank the industry as the number seven Fortune 500 company, behind Ford Motor Company and ahead of Gulf Oil.

With the amount of money associated with drug distribution, there is an ample supply of willing dealers. Unfortunately, market share is not decided by clever advertising campaigns and business disputes are not settled in courtrooms through legal representatives. Rather, violence is regularly used for regulation and social control in the cocaine business. Part of this has to do with the enormous amount of profits from crack use compared to other drugs. For example, 15 years ago a person may have achieved a weekend "high" by purchasing an ounce of marijuana for around $40. It takes around 30 minutes to begin feeling high from marijuana, and the clinical effects last at least 2 or 3 hours. Thus, an ounce of marijuana provides the addict with a supply of the drug that lasts for several days. Crack cocaine, on the other hand, costs between $3 and $5 per rock. However, while the person experiences the cocaine high in a matter of seconds, the high lasts less than 5 minutes, leaving the user craving the next use of the drug. It is not uncommon for a chronic crack user to consume more than $500 a day of the drug. With the profits from crack greatly exceeding that of marijuana, it is not surprising that the crack distribution system would create a scenario for violence.

Fagan and Chin discuss how violence became a common mechanism for regulation and social control in the distribution of crack. New York Police Department officials described the crack industry as "capitalism gone wild," with no legal, economic, or social controls. They describe several reasons why more violence was associated with selling crack than with other drugs. First, the selling of crack takes place primarily in blighted, urban neighborhoods where previously existing social controls have been weakened by years of economic and social decline. Second, the profits from crack caused the development of new drug-selling groups, ready to compete with established groups of drug profits. This led to internal violence to maintain control of a relatively new distribution system and external violence to assure market share (turf) and product quality. In a study of drug sellers, only 10% of the dealers who only sold marijuana and 9% of dealers who sold only heroin reported violence with other dealers. However, more than 20% of the sellers of cocaine and crack reported fights with rival dealers. While selling drugs may be profitable, it can be a dangerous career with extremely high mortality rates. For example, Stanton and Galbraith report that of the 414 homicides examined in their study, 179 (43%) resulted from drug trafficking. Of these, 148 (34%) of the victims were drug traffickers. The most common causes of these murders were territorial disputes, robbing of the dealer, and assaults to collect debts. Of the 522 homicides committed in Baltimore in 1990, 166 (31%) were related to drug trafficking.

A tragic consequence of drug selling is the steadily downward trend in the age of the sellers. Stanton and Galbraith report that more than 20% of low income, urban, Black males may have been involved in drug trafficking by midadolescence. Further, a study of 7573 6th and 7th graders from the Washington, D.C., area reveals that 5% of boys were involved in drug trafficking and an additional 17% reported being approached to sell drugs.

This exposure to the drug culture and associated violence has resulted in the traumatization of a number of urban youths. Exposure to violence and witnessing the death of family and friends, the "war zone" climate of many crack neighborhoods, and the special vulnerability of adolescence can lead to PTSD (Post Traumatic Stress Disorder) symptomatology among these youths. It is reported that approximately 10% of adolescents who had witnessed the murder of a friend or relative developed PTSD. Other data have shown that the presence of PTSD is five times higher among chemically dependent youth than among a comparable community sample of non-drug dependent adolescents.

X. DRUG USE, MENTAL ILLNESS, AND VIOLENCE

For much of history, there has been a perception among the general population that people with mental illnesses represent a dangerous, unpredictable, and violent segment of society. In fact, most social science research has demonstrated that the vast majority of mentally ill persons are actually less likely to commit a violent act than a person in the general population. This, however, is not always the case. Research indicates that there is a positive correlation between mental illness and violence, especially when combined with substance abuse. Prevalence of offenses tends to be highest among those with serious psychopathology, especially schizophrenics who use alcohol or cocaine. Results of the NIMH Epidemiological Catchment Area (ECA) revealed that while only 2% of the nondisordered population had exhibited violent behavior in the preceding year, 13% of schizophrenics and 34% of drug abusers were involved in violent acts. These data established a particularly strong relationship between violence and persons with comorbid psychiatric and substance abuse diagnoses.

Schizophrenia is another mental illness that is associated with violence, especially when comorbid with substance abuse. For example, schizophrenics who used multiple substances were 12 times more likely to have engaged in violent behavior than nonusing schizophrenics. Prospectively, substance use led to a 400% increase in the likelihood of future violence. Clinical experience has taught us that other groups of mentally ill persons with diagnoses ranging from mood disorders to personality disorders also exhibit increases in violent behavior when under the influence of drugs of alcohol. Much of this variance is likely caused by the fact that alcohol and drugs decrease judgment and increase irritability and impulsivity in a population that is already experiencing difficulties in these areas.

Of all the psychiatric disorders, antisocial personality is most commonly associated with violent behavior. Studies indicate that as many as 70% of prison immates meet *DSM-IV* criteria for APD (antisocial personality disorder). The comorbidity between APD and substance abuse is high, with 20% of men and 11% of women in treatment for substance abuse meeting criteria for APD. The relationship between APD, substance abuse, and violence may share a common neurobiological pathway. As illustrated abuse, disturbance in serotonergic function, especially, the metabolite 5-HIAA has been found to be linked to substance abuse and violence. New research has also found that persons with APD or with criminal histories tend to have low levels of 5-HIAA in the CSF. As illustrated above, the use of drugs and alcohol may further reduce levels of the serotonin metabolite among this group of disordered patients, thus increasing the likelihood of violence. The implications of these findings in the treatment of violence are clear. The finding that a substantial number of antisocials commit their violent behavior while under the influence of a particular substance has caused many clinicians to decide that the most effective treatment of APD may be substance abuse treatment.

XI. CONCLUSIONS AND RECOMMENDATIONS

It is clear from this discussion that the scientific literature overwhelmingly supports a relationship between violence and alcohol and drug use. While the correlation between drugs and violence can be traced to antiquity, the effects of modern chemistry and more efficient delivery systems have greatly added to this problem.

It was not long ago that experts in the area of drugs and violence minimized the role of neurobiology in drug-related violence. An NIDA monograph on drugs and violence concluded that "there is virtually no evidence that the pharmacological effects of drugs (alcohol excepted) account for a substantial portion of drug related violence." While they cannot explain all of the variance associated with drug violence, new insights into the effects of drugs and alcohol on neurotransmitter systems and brain regions that are often thought to be linked to violent behavior suggests that pharmacological influences may be greater than previously thought. But violence is related not only to the pharmacological effects of the drugs on the brain. As illustrated above, preexisting personality attributes, situational variables, and factors associated with the drug trade also contribute to this problem.

Despite political claims, data from the past decade indicate that criminal penalties and drug interdiction efforts have done little to curb drug usage and associated violence. While some argue that legalization of drugs would reduce collateral violence, the negative consequences of such legislation might be catastrophic for society. Clearly, one ounce of prevention is worth a pound of cure. While "just saying no" may be a solution that is too simplistic in many situations, creating environments where a person can just say no is imperative. This includes the strengthening of family ties, drug education, and economic opportunity.

However, there will always be those who say "yes." And for some of these people, saying yes creates a chemical addiction that makes it difficult to ever say no. For these persons, intensive treatment programs that emphasize abstinence and that view recovery as a process and not an endpoint are needed. In fact, most professionals agree that violence and antisocial behavior can best be addressed by reducing substance abuse.

Treatment planning requires a comprehensive assessment of the psychobiologic, social, and pharmacological aspects of the patient's substance abuse. For many patients, drug use is the focus of their entire life. They become totally preoccupied with drug-seeking and drug-taking behaviors, and they have forgotten what life without drugs is like. Thus, they come to regard the drugged state as "normal" and they may not believe that any treatment is necessary. For this reason they may refuse to acknowledge the need for help. Because of this, many patients enter treatment only under pressure from family, friends, employers, or the judicial system. In severe cases, the patient perceives such pressure to be a threat from "enemies," which only serves to reinforce drug-induced feelings of suspicion, persecution, and paranoia. The initial contact with a patient may occur after the crash and during the withdrawal phase. The numerous health dangers associated with alcohol, cocaine, and other drugs require that the person undergo a thorough physical examination. Any medical treatment that helps relieve withdrawal symptoms is important because many addicts cite unpleasant withdrawal as an important factor in relapse.

Whether it serves as the primary mode of care or as a sequel to hospitalization, a comprehensive outpatient program should include a range of treatment strategies. These include supportive counseling, drug education, peer-support groups, and family meetings. Exercise therapy may also prove to be a helpful adjunct. Severe depression may require psychotherapy and perhaps the use of medications. Regular telephone support should continue for several months. Many treatment centers offer ongoing group therapy sessions for patients and their families for a period of years following discharge.

In all cases, patients should be given frequent urine tests to screen for all drugs. Another crucial element of long-term treatment is participation in a 12-step recovery program. In recent years the medical and psychiatric professions have come to recognize the significant contributions that Alcoholics Anonymous and similiar programs can make to the lives of substance abusers. Members draw strength and security from meeting with others who understand and share their concerns, and who can offer practical strategies for surviving "one day at a time." Any treatment program that does not embrace the 12-step approach, which encourages patients to participate, stands little chance of long-term success.

When it comes to substance use disorders, pharmacotherapy plays a relatively minor role compared with the treatment of affective and anxiety disorders. The 12-step program, the most potent cognitive-behavioral approach, is ascendant. However, for certain classes of drugs, new medications provide a powerful weapon in blocking the effects of the drug as well as reducing cravings and relapse. For example, opiate antagonist drugs such as naltrexone and naloxone can attenuate the brain reward enhancement produced by drugs of abuse such as opiates, cocaine, amphetamine, ethanol, and benzodiazepines. The use of these new medications along with effective treatments such as 12-step programs provides the best hope for the addict and for society to break the drug-violence connection.

Also See the Following Articles

BIOCHEMICAL FACTORS • JUVENILE CRIME • MENTAL ILLNESS • SUICIDE AND OTHER VIOLENCE TOWARD THE SELF • URBAN VIOLENCE

Bibliography

American Psychiatric Association. Diagnostic and Statistical Manual of Mental Disorders, 4th edition: 1994: Author: Washington, DC.

Asberg, M., Traskman, L. & Thoren, P. (1976). 5-HIAA in the cerebrospinal fluid: A biochemical suicide predictor, Archives of General Psychiatry, 33, 1193–1197.

Bigelow, G. E. & Preston, K. L. (1995). Opiods. In Pharmacology: The Fourth Generation of Progress. F. E. Bloom & D. J. Kupfer (Eds.). Raven Press: New York.

Crowley, T. J. (1995). Hallucinogen disorders. In Comprehensive Textbook of Psychiatry, (6th edition). H. Kaplan & B. Sadock, Editors, Williams & Wilkins: Baltimore.

Durkham, C. P., Byrd, R. S., Auinger, P. Weitzman, M. (1996). Illicit substance use, gender, and the risk of violent behavior among adolescents, Archives of Pediatric Adolescent Medicine, 150 797–801.

Fagan, J. & Chin, K. (1990). Violence as regulation and social control in the distribution of crack In Drugs and Violence: Causes, correlates and consequences (La rosa, M. Lambert, E. Y. & Gropper, B. Eds.). (NIDA Research Monograph, 103.

Goldstein, P. J. (1985). The drugs-violence nexus: A tripartite conceptual framework. Journal of Drug Issues, 15, 493–506.

Hanlon, T. E., Nurco, D. N. Kinlock, T. W. & Duszynski, K. R. Trends in criminal activity and drug use over an addiction career. Am J Drug, Alcohol Abuse, 16:3–4, 223–238.

Hatsukami, D. K., Fischman, M. W.: Crack cocaine and cocaine hydrochloride: Are the differences myth or reality. JAMA 1996: 276:19: 1580–1588.

Kandel, D. B. & Davies, M: High school students who use crack and other drugs. Arch Gen Psychiatry: 1996: 53:71–80.

Kingery, P. M., Pruitt, B. E. & Hurley, R. S. (1992). Violence and illegal drug use among adolescents: Evidence from the US National Adolescent Student Health Survey, International Journal of Addictions, 27 (12), 1445–64.

La rosa, M., Lambert, E. Y. & Gropper, B. (1990) Drugs and Violence: Causes, correlates and consequences. (NIDA Research Monograph, 103.

Mann, J. J. Violence and Aggression. In Bloom, F. E. and Kupfer, D. J. (Eds.). Psychopharmacology: The Fourth Generation of Progress. 1995: 1919–28.

Miller, N. S. Gold, M. S., Mahler, J. C. Violent behaviors associated with cocaine use: Possible pharmacological mechanisms. International Journal of the Addictions, 6:10 1077–1088.

Schuckit, M. A. (1995). Alcohol-related disorders. In Comprehensive Textbook of Psychiatry, (6th edition) H. Kaplan & B. Sadoc, Editors, Williams & Wilkins: Baltimore.

Sterk, C. E., Elifson, K. W. Drug related violence and street prostitution. (1990) In Drugs and Violence: Causes, Correlates, and Consequences (M. La Rosa, E. Lambert & B. Gropper, Eds.). 103: 92–111 NIDA Research Monograph 103.

Tonkonogy, J. M. (1991). Violence and temporal lobe lesion: Head CT and MRI data. Journal of Neuropsychiatry and Clinical Neuroscience, 3, 189–196.

Virkkunen, M., De Jong, J., Bartko, J., Goodwin, F. K. Linniola, M. Relationship of psychobiological variables to recidivism in violent offenders and impulsive fire setters: A follow-up study. Arch Gen Psychiatry 1989;46:600–603.

Volavka, J. (1995). *Neurobiology of Violence,* Washington DC: American Psychiatric Press.

Weisman, G. K. Adolescent PTSD and developmental consequences of crack dealing. (1993) Amer J. Orthopsychiatry, 63:4 553–561.

Widiger, T. A., Corbitt, E. M.: Antisocial personality disorder. IN Livesley, W. J. ed. The DSM-IV Personality Disorders. New York: Guilford Press, 1995:103–126.

Ecoethics

William C. French
Loyola University of Chicago

GLOSSARY

Animal Rights An attempt to apply rights theory to affirm the inherent value of sentient animals.

Anthropocentrism Historically dominant Western value scheme that holds only human life has inherent moral value by virtue of humans' unique rationality.

Biocentrism Ethical critique of anthropocentric value schemes by appeal to the priority of ecosystems or the global biosphere.

Biodiversity Ecological emphasis that ecosystems remain vital and stable through the interactions of diverse species.

Biospherical Egalitarianism Affirmation by deep ecologists and others that all life-forms have equal moral value.

Deep Ecology Broad radical environmental movement that critiques shallow, reformist positions and calls for revolutionary changes in modes of production and consumption and for a reduction in human population.

Ecofeminism Movement that wants to ecologize the feminist movement and critique ideologies that support the domination of women and nature.

Prudence Principle Ethical action principle holding that when stakes are high, and outcomes are uncertain, one should always prepare so as to err on the side of safety.

Ranking An ethical approach that tries to establish priorities in cases of conflicts of interest between humans and nonhumans by making assessments of relative levels of inherent value given characteristics of the different species.

ECOETHICS is an emerging discipline that in recent decades has been prompted by alarm about increasing environmental degradation and its impact on human and nonhuman life. Ethics in general is critical reflection on the rightness and wrongness of particular human actions in different spheres of practice to help improve human sensitivity and responsibility in perception, decision-making, and action. Ecoethics concentrates critical attention on humanity's participation within the natural ecosphere, our dependency on its well-being, our increasingly heavy impact on it, and the implications of increasing environmental damage for present and future human and nonhuman well-being.

I. PROBLEMATIC: ECODEGRADATION

Ecoethical concern emerged since the end of World War II as new technologies and industrial innovations gave rise to new types of harm flowing from insecticide use in agriculture, nuclear energy in power generation and weapons advances, new forms of petrochemical effluent and industrial pollution, rising acid precipitation from coal burning, and smog alerts triggered by increasing emissions by expanding auto and truck fleets. Cases such as the 1978 Love Canal toxic scare, the industrial poisoning disaster in 1984 at Bhopal, India, the fire at the Three Mile Island nuclear power plant in 1979, and the disaster in 1986 at the Chernobyl nuclear power station, near Kiev, sensitized a generation to the stakes involved in new ecological threats.

Popular recognition of other ecological concerns emerged in the 1980s and 1990s. Scientific studies began to raise the specter of global warming and climate shift occurring in the next century due to increases in human-caused greenhouse gas emissions such as carbon dioxide given off by fossil fuel consumption, which has been surging in recent decades. Likewise, the discovery in the winter of 1987 of a huge hole in the ozone layer over Antarctica drew world attention to the role the ozone layer in the stratosphere plays in sheltering us from solar radiation and to the way increasing CFCs (chlorofluorocarbons) used in refrigerators, air conditioners, aerosol sprays, and in the production of Styrofoam deplete the ozone shield and cause rising skin cancer rates. The last two decades have seen a growing awareness of the escalation of tropical rainforest clearing occurring in Central America, the Amazon Basin, Central Africa, India, Indonesia, and the Philippines, and how such habitat destruction pushes plant and animal species extinction rates and reduces the biomass sink that is able to sequester carbon from the atmosphere.

Increasingly people around the world have become aware of the changed conditions of life on earth. Where once we viewed nature generally as a vast and stable grounding for human existence, now the very stability of the planet's natural systems and climate patterns appear to be rendered problematic by the vast upsurge in human numbers, industrial powers, economic productivity, and globally rising expectations of rates of consumption. History has accelerated in the 20th century with a tripling of human population and a 50-fold advance in world economic output. Together, these have escalated humanity's destructive impact on the planetary ecosystem to historically unprecedented thresholds. The expanded reach of human action has increased the range of our ability to damage and destroy. Actions and policy decisions today can end ancient natural habitats, consign species into extinction, increase climate instability, and threaten the well-being of future generations. Whole new ranges of realities have been swept into the sphere of human action and power. Thus these must be sheltered by a new and broader sense of human responsibility, care, and loyalty. Ecoethics is the attempt to articulate our heightened obligations for sustaining life on earth.

II. PEACEMAKING GOAL

Ecoethics as a discipline is directly related to peace and conflict studies. The environmental history of this century charts the course that humanity has taken in putting ourselves increasingly in conflict with nature's habitat requirements, environmental structures, and climate patterns. The ruling modern ideology of both Marxist and capitalist societies has been dominated by a valorization of progress understood as the increasing mastery of nature achieved through economic transformation and technological advance. Where many at the beginning of the century could view nature as a passive field to be subdued, we now know that human welfare is inextricably knit into the dynamism of nature's sustaining energies, and actions by humans that do violence to natural habitats and ecosystems or alter climate patterns will redound back destructively on human communities. Actions and policies that are in fundamental conflict with nature will generate massive nonhuman and human casualty rates.

One of the most glaring divides between peoples is the chasm between the global rich and the poor. Generally, pollution, soil erosion, species extinctions, and their attendant harms fall heaviest on the world's poor, for the rich have better means of protection, alternatives, or escape. Irresponsibility to natural ecosystems almost always carries harm and loss to people dependent for their livelihood and health upon those habitats. Human actions that do violence to natural communities usually entail violence being transmitted through the medium of nature to other humans.

One can better grasp the security threats posed by planetary ecological degradation when one uses the analogy of "superpower" taken from international and strategic studies to highlight nature as a vast system of productive and potentially destructive power. Nature is surely a "superpower" in the positive sense that the productivity and consumption of all peoples is ultimately derived from the originating productivity of the planetary ecosystem. Likewise, actions or policies that simplify or destroy natural habitats, incur massive biodiversity loss, deplete the ozone shield, or force climate change will cause a series of natural planetary or ecosystem reactions that can redound back destructively on humanity. The human casualties thus generated by nature's "kickback" capacity suggest that we need to recognize nature's potent "retaliatory capacity" in the face of human abuse.

Understanding nature as a superpower suggests that the century ahead will be dominated by a superpower clash between the agenda of the burgeoning global economy—surging with population and economic growth—and the constraints of the global ecosystem. Surely our national and global security will depend on how responsibly we can restrain ecologically unsustainable human practices. Ecoethics in its attempt to promote environmental responsibility and sustainability is thus a discipline committed to peacemaking between humanity and the rest of the Earth community.

III. REFORMIST AND RADICAL STREAMS

There are reformist and radical streams of ecoethics. The reformist project draws on traditional categories and perspectives from philosophical and religious traditions of ethics and attempts to stretch these terms to cover new environmental realities and responsibilities. The radical stream attempts to recast ethics in light of revolutionary new understandings of the human condition rooted in an awareness of burgeoning human power and the precariousness of natural balances and ecosystems. In this view ecoethics is a "subversive" discipline because it radically critiques a whole series of culturally entrenched assumptions about progress and the uniqueness of the human that have been the animating energy of modern scientific and economic advance.

IV. HUMAN-CENTERED APPROACHES

A. Western Anthropocentrism

1. Historic Roots

Dominant ethical traditions in Western culture have emphasized the value of human life and have failed to voice much concern for the value of other forms of life or the natural environment. Certainly different voices—both philosophical and religious—have at times drawn attention to the need not to be cruel to animals and the importance of caring for them, but the ethical weight has fallen most consistently on a strong affirmation of the uniqueness of human life, its high value, and the moral centrality of its protection. Affirmations of humanity's unique rationality, capacity for language, or possession of an intellectual soul have each grounded at various times an ethical emphasis on the inherent value of human life.

The ancient Hebrews affirmed both animals and humans as God's beloved creatures, but humanity was said to be created alone in the "image of God" and to hold "dominion" over other living creatures. By emphasizing God's transcendence the Hebrews split the sphere of the sacred off from the world of nature. Still their acknowledgment that the Earth is the Lord's checked their understanding of their dominion over nature from sliding into a warrant for complete domination.

Dominant schools of Greek philosophy stressed the purposefulness of nature with its unity, order, and teleology, and the distinctiveness of human rationality to discern nature's order. Stoic thought held that the natural universe constitutes a vast community and that humanity must cohere our actions to the universe's order. Still, the Greek tendency to underscore humanity's rationality tended to justify a belief in human superiority over the rest of nature and a moral justification for humanity's use of animals, plants, fields, and rivers. Aristotle illustrates this view in his *Politics* where he states, "Plants are created for the sake of animals, and the animals for the sake of men . . ." (Bk. 1, ch. 8, 1256b).

The early Christian communities generally followed the Hebraic understanding of humanity's God-given dominion over the rest of nature. As Christianity spread throughout Greece and the Roman Empire, however, it picked up Neoplatonic philosophical and religious emphases on divine transcendence from the physical world of mundane matter, flux, and darkness. Christians followed the general Hebraic view that nature is created by God and thus is good, but over time Christianity came to stress humanity's distinct rationality. A heightened anthropocentric concentration of moral attention went hand in hand with a corresponding ethical depreciation of the value of nonhuman creation.

Various theological schools in Medieval Christianity came to develop a more robust appreciation for the doctrine of creation and the essential goodness of nature, but still this did not displace the dominance of the anthropocentric scale of value enunciated by Aristotle.

Martin Luther (1483–1546) and the other Protestant Reformers focused on the problem of justification of a sinful person before God. This new emphasis in theology intensely scrutinized human emotion, action, belief, and behavior, but its intense focus on one's relationship with God and one's human neighbors left little moral energy to attend to possible human obligations to the natural world and its nonhuman species.

2. Modern Intensification

The rise of modern science in Europe in the 16th and 17th centuries intensified a sense of human separation from, and superiority over, the rest of nature. Francis Bacon (1561–1626), René Descartes (1596–1650), and Isaac Newton (1642–1727), along with other scientists, mathematicians, and philosophers, gave impetus to a new understanding of nature as a vast machine. As the mechanical model took hold, ancient notions of nature as an organic whole animated by inherent, vital energies pushing growth and motion toward certain ends gave way. Where the new philosophy was allowed to account for the motion of human bodies via appeal to mechanism, the essential core of the human—mind and soul—were excluded from mechanistic explanation. Thus the human was understood as radically distinct and unique in a world understood as a vast field of machines and inert forces. By its sharply drawn divide between humanity and the rest of nature this new mechanistic philosophy gave potent sanctions for scientific experiment, technological transformation, and industrialization.

Modern ethical anthropocentrism was given its classic expression by the great German philosopher Immanuel Kant (1724–1803), as he responded to the new sciences and stressed the radical differences between human and nonhuman life. For Kant, only rational beings, deserve the designation of "persons," while other living beings lacking rationality, such as animals or plants, are properly classed as "things." While persons are, ethically speaking, "ends-in-themselves," "things" have value only as a "means" to the service of human ends. Persons enjoy inherent value, while animals and plants have mere instrumental value, value derived from their usefulness in serving human interests and goals. While Kant explicitly rejects cruel actions toward animals, his conceptual framework defines animals, plants, and the rest of nature as a sphere of things devoid of intrinsic moral value or worth in themselves.

Kant and other enlightenment philosophers applied the notion of rights to humans because of humans' unique rationality. Animals and plants, however, devoid of rationality, seemed to lack subjectivity and agency and thus could not be the bearers of rights. By taking humans as the paradigm case of moral value, enlightenment liberalism provided a powerful rationale for extending rights and affirming the dignity and equal moral worth of classes of humans heretofore excluded, such as peasants, slaves, and women. However by enshrining rational agency as the litmus test for admission into the moral community, liberalism provided an easy conscience for not extending direct moral concern to nonhuman life.

B. Anthropocentrism Environmentally Informed

Modern environmental awareness has contributed directly to the recognition that human life, rights, and welfare are threatened by water and air pollution, soil erosion, habitat loss, and species extinction. While many argue rightly that environmentalism requires a radical critique of the anthropocentric ethical tradition, it is nonetheless clear that concerns for human self-interest and welfare, once informed by the findings of the ecological sciences, have been historically the most potent rationale for environmental protection legislation.

In the 1960s the rise of ecological science with its close attention to the complex interrelationships between humanity and the rest of nature broadened our understanding of how environmental trends and developments could impact heavily on human well-being. While the ecological sciences are encouraging many to hold that animals and even plants have significant inherent value deserving of direct moral respect and care, still appeals to human welfare hold potent moral force in pushing for environmental protection and policies aimed at promoting ecological sustainability.

V. ANIMAL WELFARE APPROACHES

Many ecoethicists worry that human-centered approaches to environmental ethics and policy are theoretical half-measures doomed to trying to protect nature while at the same time theoretically undercutting the generation of any direct sense of obligation to nonhuman nature or sense of close connection to the natural world. These ecoethicists argue that we can no longer hold human life alone among all the myriad sorts of life on earth as having inherent moral value. They advocate a shift from human-centered to biocentric ethics and propose we recognize inherent value not just in human life, but in animal and plant life as well. For these theorists ecoethics is primarily an extension project, taking the established moral consensus about the important moral status of human life and extending the border of the class of beings and entities that are said to have inherent value or moral rights or to be deserving of direct moral consideration.

A. History of Emerging Attention to Animals

The Scottish Moralists—Lord Shaftesbury (1671–1713), Francis Hutcheson (1694–1746) and Adam Smith (1723–1790) among others—placed "sympathy," "sentiment," and feelings of compassion at the center of the "moral sense" and thus helped pull ethical theory away from its intense focus on rationality as the key to value. British utilitarians such as Jeremy Bentham (1748–1832) picked up this ethical emphasis on "feeling" and centered their new theory on the concern to maximize pleasure and to minimize pain and suffering. The range of direct moral compassion, Bentham believed, should extend not just to rational beings, but should be expanded to include the entire class of sentient beings, including any being capable of experiencing pain or pleasure.

In England the impact of the utilitarians' reform agenda pushed many to join movements dedicated to the ending of cruelty to animals, along with parallel reformist efforts to eliminate slavery, promote the enfranchisement of women, and regulate child labor practices. In 1824 the Society for the Prevention of Cruelty to Animals was formed and it began to work for the elimination of blood sports like bull-baiting, bear-baiting, and dog- and cock-fighting in addition to passing anticruelty legislation for domestic animals and pets. In the first half of the 19th century such sentiments crossed the Atlantic and in 1866 the American Society for the Prevention of Cruelty to Animals (ASPCA) was founded.

Contemporary animal welfare debates are informed by the scientific study of animals, especially animals observed in their home habitat. By the 1950s and 1960s the emerging science of ethology, the study of animals in their interactions in the wild, gave new appreciation for not only the complex ways animals interact with their habitat, but also for their often formidable powers, adaptive behaviors, and complex sociality. Primate specialists broke new ground in studying chimpanzees in Tanzania and mountain gorillas in Rwanda and Congo. Other ethologists explored chimpazees' ability to learn and use American sign language. These and other important studies have contributed greatly to our understanding of the complexity of many species behaviors, social relations, levels of cognition, and interactions with their environment.

B. Utilitarian Animal Welfare Ethics

Animal welfare ethics was widely popularized by Peter Singer's 1975 book *Animal Liberation*, which develops the utilitarian ethical insight that moral consideration must be extended to not just rational humans, but all sentient life forms, that is, all those capable of experiencing pain or suffering. Since the beginning of this century, mainstream animal welfare societies had focused their attention on humane treatment of cats, dogs, horses, and wild animals, but Singer and others began to examine the inhumane treatment of animals in modern agricultural production and laboratory testing. Singer understands the exclusion of moral concern for animals, what he dubs "speciesism," as directly parallel to other forms of unjust exclusion found in racism and sexism. He holds that the "basic moral principle" is the "equal consideration of interests" and believes that it should be extended to all beings with the capacity of having interests, that is, to all animals that enjoy sentience.

The equal consideration of interests, for Singer, does not entail equal or identical treatment or the extension of equal rights to members of different species. He does not argue that human life and animal life have equal moral value. Singer's goal is not to diminish the value of the human, but to extend our recognition of value to animals, who by virtue of their sentience have significant interests that impose strict duties on humans of moral consideration and care.

Where Singer acknowledges that it is appropriate to give moral priority to the human in most cases where we are forced to save either a human or an animal, still he believes that it is morally wrong to allow minor human interests to override the major interests of a sentient animal. Accordingly, Singer argues that many widespread human uses of animals are morally wrong, including our current factory farm methods of raising animals for meat, our use of animals in many scientific and industrial laboratory experiments, our hunting and trapping of wild animals, and our use of animals in circuses and rodeos. For certain tribal communities Singer holds that killing animals for food may well be a necessity and therefore may be morally justifiable, but he holds that citizens in most industrialized societies can easily sustain themselves through a healthful diet without resorting to the use of meat supplied via factory farm techniques.

C. Animal Rights Approach

A number of theorists have come to join Singer in his rejection of the abuse of animals in factory farming, meat consumption, hunting for sport, and use of animals in laboratory experiments, but they also believe that utilitarianism is not the best ethical theory for supporting moral respect for animals. For utilitarians the main harm of the factory farming system is not so much that it kills animals, but that it causes animals to suffer both in life and in death. Many theorists suggest that deontological traditions of ethical reasoning based on the acknowledgment of strict duties actually articulates better the sorts of obligations and care we owe animals. This approach has been articulated most forcefully by Tom Regan, an American philosopher, who radically revises Kantian ethical reasoning to argue for the inherent value of higher animals and the legitimacy of ascribing rights to such animals, especially the "right to respectful treatment." Whereas Kant held that only humans have inherent value, Regan argues that all beings who are "subjects-of-a-life" have an "experiential welfare" and thus inherent value that deserves respect. Whereas for Kant the moral community consists of rational humans understood as "ends-in-themselves," for Regan the borders of the moral community are expanded to include both rational moral agents and human and nonhuman nonagents, "moral patients"—human infants, young children, the mentally deranged, and normal adult mammals.

Individuals with inherent value cannot be treated merely as "means" to some other ends but must be regarded as moral ends-in-themselves. Thus such individuals are owed "respectful treatment" as a matter of strict justice. This duty is a "prima facie" duty, not an absolute duty, for it exists in the company of other such duties that can, under certain circumstances, legitimately override it. For example, in a case where a lifeboat will only sustain four individuals, yet four humans and a dog are crowding on, Regan thinks it morally justified and not speciesist to push the dog off. He holds that the death of a normal human poses a "greater prima facie harm" (by foreclosing greater opportunities) than the death of the dog.

In practical terms Regan's animal rights approach holds that vegetarianism is morally obligatory and calls for the end of factory farming, which "violates the rights of farm animals." Likewise, he is against the use of animals in scientific, educational, or commercial testing procedures and is against sport hunting and trapping because these, he believes, all violate the rights of animals. Regan and other deontological or rights-based theorists believe that their rejection of the use of animals in laboratory testing is on firmer ground than any utilitarian rejection of animal testing, because for utilitarians if the overall consequence of animal testing would produce the "best aggregate balance of good over evil," then the testing of animals must be judged morally obligatory.

VI. ECOLOGICAL ETHICS

Ecological ethics has developed as moral reflection has attended to three historic developments: the Darwinian Revolution, the rise of the ecological sciences, and the growing visibility of significant cases of ecological degradation. Darwin's theory of evolution based on the principle of natural selection was first promulgated in his classic work *The Origin of Species* in 1859. This book provided a persuasive account of the evolution of discrete forms of life via advantageous adaptations to the conditions and resources of their natural habitat. Darwin drew attention to the historically dynamic exchange between and among individuals, species, and environment. Likewise in 1871 in *The Descent of Man and Selection in Relation to Sex* Darwin explicitly focused on how humanity is subject to the same evolutionary laws governing the rest of nature and that we, like all other animals, have descended from simpler living forms. In stressing our kinship with other apes Darwin forced us to take seriously our animality as an important component of our humanness.

The rise of ecological science in the 20th century offers a new model for understanding the natural world and humanity's place within it, and in so doing challenges the grounds of the traditional anthropocentric restriction of ethical concern solely to matters of human life and well-being. Just as ethology insisted on examining animals in interaction with natural habitat, ecology came to focus on humans, animals, plants, and the nonliving natural environment as a complex system of interaction and interdependency. From its origins ecology focused on the whole system of complex interrelations that sustain individual organisms. The term "ecology," like the term "economy," is derived from the Greek word *oikos,* meaning house. Ecology, as Barry Commoner notes, is the "science of planetary housekeeping" for it studies the patterns, relationships, and structures that sustain species diversity and the richness of life on Earth.

While animal welfare ethics concentrates on the value of animals, ecological ethics expands the circle of moral consideration further to include plants and nonhuman natural entities such as river systems and ecosystems. Some believe any ethic that extends direct moral concern to all living entities should be understood as an ecological ethic, while others would reserve the label of ecological ethics only for those ethical approaches that both extend moral concern to all living entities **and** place a moral priority on the well-being of whole ecological systems—natural communities or aggregates such as habitats, ecosystems, and species. In what follows I distinguish between individualist ecological ethics that extend the range of care to all living beings but continue with an individualist analysis of moral worth, and holistic ecological ethics that both extends the range of care and places priority on the common good of the "whole" over that of individual entities or "parts."

A. Individualist Ecological Ethics

Much of ecological ethics draws its inspiration from the remarkable vision of Albert Schweitzer (1875–1965), a Swiss physician, philosopher, theologian, and musician, who developed an influential philosophical ethic centered in a "reverence for life." Where utilitarians such as Bentham and Singer would draw the line of moral consideration to include only animals with the capacity of sentience, Schweitzer felt that all entities that are alive—animals, plants, insects, and simple organisms—deserve our reverence and moral respect.

Others have followed Schweitzer's lead in extending moral concern beyond the sphere of humans and animals. Kenneth Goodpaster, for example, holds that all living entities have interests in "remaining alive" and these interests are morally significant and deserve moral consideration from humans. Still, he acknowledges that not all that lives shares the same level of moral significance. As one contemplates a path of action, one must directly consider all the sorts of living entities impacted on by one's action. However, it remains appropriate that in some circumstances there may be morally compelling reasons to still opt for a course of action that will kill or injure certain living beings.

Schweitzer and Goodpaster both wish to expand our moral concern beyond a focus on humans or sentient animals to consider the inherent moral value of plant life, insects, and earthworms. However, Schweitzer and Goodpaster, like many animal welfare ethicists, continue to focus on individual living organisms. While their analysis is helpful as far as it goes, still their general approach fails to engage questions of the moral value of ecological communities or "wholes" such as species or forests, marshlands or other ecosystems.

B. Holistic Ecological Ethics

1. The Land Ethic

Aldo Leopold is considered by many to be one of the major contributors to ecological ethics. After training and work in forest management he became a professor of wildlife management at the University of Wisconsin. In 1947 Leopold brought his ruminations about the need to extend ethical consideration to the natural environment to completion in his seminal essay "The Land Ethic," the final chapter of his book, *A Sand County Almanac*. Our relation to land, he notes sadly, typically remains governed by strictly economic considerations of profit, a perspective that entails "privileges but not obligations." All ethics, he believes, is rooted in a "community instinct in-the-making," and he calls for recognition that we are part of the broader natural community and owe it duties of care for both its well-being and our own. "The land ethic simply enlarges the boundaries of the community to include soils, waters, plants, and animals, or collectively: the land" (Leopold, 238–239). He believes that ecological awareness requires dethroning the human from a traditional status of "conqueror of the land-community" to that of "plain member and citizen of it" holding ready respect for one's nonhuman "fellow-members" and for the entire natural community as a whole.

Whereas most of us have been trained by our culture to view humans as active and nature as the passive field of resources awaiting our manipulation and use, Leopold applies ecological insights to describe nature as a dynamic field of energy exchanges that make possible the sustenance of all life forms including the human. He writes of "the land pyramid," whose base is the soil system that in conjunction with the layer of plants captures solar energy and harnesses it for growth. The ecosystem functions, for Leopold, as a "fountain of energy" circulating vital power up from soil through food chains and returning it back to soil as plants and animals die and decay. This ecological perspective suggests directly, for Leopold, a key ethical rule: "A thing is right when it tends to preserve the integrity, stability, and beauty of the biotic community. It is wrong when it tends otherwise" (Leopold, 262).

2. Deep Ecology

Rooted in a strong critique of human-centered ethics, deep ecologists call for a broadening of empathetic identification with the entire Earth community and all of its members. Concerned about surging ecological degradation and species extinction rates, deep ecologists advocate a significant lessening of humans' destructive impact on the natural environment by radical alterations of humans' productive and consumptive practices and a reduction in human population levels.

First outlined by Arne Naess, a Norwegian philosopher, and developed by George Sessions, Bill Devall, and others, deep ecology seeks to move beyond shallow, reform environmentalism based on traditional human-centered concerns. The proponents of deep ecology understand it as an evolving movement open to many insights from many communities and cultures around the globe. The movement's fundamental norms are "Self-realization" and "biospherical egalitarianism." The first refers not to the little self of each individual but to the great Self of the entire Earth community, the global ecosystem including all its members. Deep ecology is committed to an expansion of our sense of identification with, and participation within, the huge living system of this Self.

The second norm, "biospherical egalitarianism," asserts a requirement for a deep and equal respect for all forms of life. This norm flows out of the heightened sensitivity of deep ecologists to understanding all living beings—including humans—as thoroughly interparticipating in a dynamic and complex web of ecological relations that sustains each individual. All living entities—even the "lowest" and simplest plants and animals—contribute to "the richness and diversity of life" and to the stability of the global ecosystem. Accordingly it seems inappropriate to the deep ecologists to hold that some life forms have higher or lower inherent value than others. Still, while deep ecologists hold "in principle" to biospherical egalitarianism, in practice they acknowledge that some killing and suppression of certain living entities is often necessary.

The primary national and international agenda, deep ecologists believe, must shift from ever-expanding profit and growth to ecological sustainability and genuine quality of life concerns. They support decentralization of political and economic power and grass roots efforts to promote policies of ecological sustainability. Deep ecology is as concerned about preserving human cultural diversity as it is concerned about preserving biotic diversity. It encourages people of diverse cultures, religions, and philosophies to provide distinctive and particular grounding and rationales for deep ecological principles and perspectives. Thus deep ecology sees itself as a loose-knit global movement enriched by the distinctive contributions of a wide range of religious, philosophical, and political traditions.

3. Ecofeminism

Beginning in the mid-1970s different feminist theorists began to probe the historical and conceptual linkages between the oppression of women and the domination of nature and to draw attention to women's distinctive potential for promoting ecological care for the Earth. Just as there are liberal, radical, and socialist streams of feminism, there are diverse streams of ecofeminism. Yet all ecofeminist thinking shares the view that the heritage of sexism is interconnected with the ideological heritage supporting the human domination of nature.

Ecofeminism seeks to broaden the agenda of feminism by showing how a concern to overcome sexism necessarily requires a concern to overcome the ideology of the domination of nature, an important ideological support for sexism. Likewise ecofeminism hopes to remind the ecology movement that it is not simply human-centered thinking, anthropocentrism, but more specifically male-centered thinking, androcentrism, that lies at the core of our ecological problems. Ecofeminists believe we cannot begin to respond adequately to the core forces that continue to energize the domination and degradation of the natural world without first dismantling male-dominated patterns of reasoning, privilege, exclusion and hierarchy. Feminist scholars have been leaders in unmasking the ethical distortions rooted in historically reified understandings of nature.

Central to the ecofeminist vision is a powerful sense of our interconnectedness with nature and our common solidarity with other humans and life-forms. Against liberalism with its stress on individualism, personal agency, and rights, many feminists highlight relationality, community, and caring responsibility. Ecofeminists pick up this stress on familial and social relationality and enrich it with an emphasis on our complex interrelationality with the rest of the Earth community.

Given feminists' sensitivity to how value hierarchies have been used to justify patriarchy and sexism, it is not surprising that ecofeminists are deeply suspicious of value hierarchies in ecological ethics depicting humanity as "higher" or primates as "higher" than other living species. Indeed, ecofeminists often join deep ecologists in noting how the simple grasses, plants, bugs, and plankton are more important, ecologically speaking, than the so-called "top" predators and primates. Ecofeminists often construe nature as the "web of life" and stress the weave of relations that sustains the threads and species. Many worry that talk of animal rights simply drags in the individualist bias of liberal traditions of rights language at a time when we need more holistic understandings of nature and relational accounts of our ethical responsibilities.

Many ecofeminist thinkers are suspicious of rationalism as a disengaged stance leading to alienation and insensitivity. Many feminists thus do ecoethics in a new key—one attuned less to discrete decisions, analytical rules, or policy analyses and more to revisioning our sense of human life within an enveloping ecosphere, expanding our sense of interconnectiveness and care, and intensifying our feelings of identification with the rest of the community of life and with future generations.

VII. ONGOING POINTS OF CONTENTION

There remain two major faultlines in ecoethical theory along which disagreement erupts. First, there is the tension between animal welfare ethics, which focuses on the value of discrete individual animals, and holistic models of ecoethics, which place the moral priority on the well-being and stability of ecological "wholes," such as ecosystems and species. Second, there is the faultline between those espousing different sorts of species-ranking procedures and those arguing for biospherical or ecological egalitarianism. Classic anthropocentric ethics and newly emergent animal welfare ethics are both comfortable with enunciations of value-rankings for members of different species based on their levels of complexity of experience and subjectivity. Many deep ecologists, ecofeminists, and others resist such assertions of different relative value because they believe that such claims erode the direct respect and moral consideration owed to every living animal or plant.

Where animal welfare theorists tend to focus on the rights and intrinsic value of each human and animal, often they have little to say about the interests or inherent value of an animal species in general or of an ecosystem, the sustaining habitat of individual animals. Some animal welfare ethicists are concerned that by focusing centrally on the good of species and ecosystems, holistic ecological ethics will allow an easy overriding of the rights and interests of individuals. They worry that an "ecological fascism" will ensue where the good of the aggregate or whole will too easily trump the rights of individuals.

While the concern to maintain vigilance regarding the value of individual animals and humans is an admirable moral agenda, it would seem equally admirable to give some direct moral accounting of the interests of ecological wholes, such as species, wilderness regions, and ecosystems in their own right rather than derived from their support of individuals within. To focus exclusive moral attention on the worth of individuals seems to fly in the face of the most central insights of the ecological awareness emerging over the last 40 years regarding the complex ecological interrelationality that sustains all life on Earth. Against those who believe that there exists a necessary ethical choice between individualism and holism, some ecoethicists are attempting to argue for a pluralist ethical view that attends seriously to the value of both individuals and of ecological wholes. Like a good toolbox, ethics, they remind us, must have different tools for different jobs.

Likewise the crude moral hierarchy of classic anthropocentrism must be critiqued, but that does not require that one opt for a flat-out egalitarian position that affirms the moral equivalency of worms, humans, lichens, and wolves. Between crude anthropocentric value-hierarchy and equally unhelpful biospherical egalitarianism, some ecoethicists, such as Lawrence Johnson, are attempting to articulate critical ranking procedures that heed the full seriousness of all living entities' interest in life and well-being and also the significant anatomical, behavioral, and experiential differences between and among members of different species. Such ranking approaches attempt to provide some concrete guidance for decision and action that is often missing from egalitarian based schemes.

VIII. CONCRETE SPHERES OF POLICY CONCERN

While much energy in ecoethics is devoted to exploring the moral status of animal and plant life and to critiquing anthropocentrism, there are many spheres of environmental concern and policy analysis that engage ethical reflection. While some worry that environmental concerns will pull moral commitment and energy away from pressing human rights and social justice issues, most activists and ethicists now see that ecological degradation hits the world's poor the hardest. Thus many now see a close convergence between concerns for social justice and for ecological sustainability. Accordingly, much policy debate, while attentive to biocentric insights and values, remains in good part governed by human-centered concerns for present and future human well-being.

A. Population Growth

Human population growth has soared in this century due to medical advances, improved sanitation, and increased food production, which have made possible heightened human longevity and lower infant mortality. At the beginning of the 20th century there were roughly 1.6 billion people and by century's end roughly 6 billion. The United Nation's low, medium, and high range projections for the year 2050 are 7.9 billion, 9.8 billion, and 11.9 billion respectively. It is estimated that 95% of that growth will occur in developing countries—African and Central and South American nations, India, Indonesia, and others.

Controversy surrounds the best way to achieve population stabilization. China's notorious one child per family policy slowed its population growth via coercive measures such as enforced sterilization and abortion. This approach has proved deeply unpopular in China and has been regarded as a violation of family rights by many around the world.

In recent years the notion of "birth control" for many has become associated with governmental agendas that too narrowly target birth reduction and too crudely pressure or coerce people. At the International Conference on Population and Development held in Cairo in September 1994, a new program of action was endorsed that seeks to place birth limitation strategies within a broader agenda aimed at increasing family and women's health care opportunities, increasing girls' educational opportunities, and empowering women's employment opportunities. When families are made to feel more secure through better health care and employment prospects, they tend to embrace birth limitation voluntarily. Likewise when girls are given educational opportunities and see employment options before them, they typically delay marriage and want fewer children.

Birth limitation issues remain culturally and morally contested even as they remain of critical importance for future ecological sustainability. The key ethical issue is how to increase access to birth limitation in a way that promotes family and women's empowerment, is culturally sensitive, promotes justice for the poor, and balances attention to population growth in developing countries with close critique of the ecologically disruptive consumption explosion in the developed countries.

B. Consumption Growth and Wealth Disparity

Humanity's remarkable surge of production and consumption shows no signs of slowing down. It places increasing stress on the global ecosystem by pushing wilderness development, forest clearing, soil erosion, species extinction, and climate change. The bulk of ecological degradation is caused by the world's wealthiest one-fifth—the global consumer class—and the poorest one-fifth. Where the global poor act out of necessity, the global rich do not, and that makes all the difference in terms of moral culpability. The United States, for example, with just 5% of the world's population produces roughly 26% of the gross world product and 23% of the world's carbon emissions which increase global atmospheric concentrations of carbon dioxide and increase threats of global warming. Much of America's high per capita fossil fuel usage occurs because the United States has allowed its transportation mix to become excessively dependent on the automobile and light trucks. In 1996 in the United States there were 198 million registered motor vehicles while the world fleet was 650 million and rapidly growing. Because of high American fuel and resource consumption rates, studies estimate that the average American pushes global warming potentials 3 times the rate of the average Italian, 13 times that of the average Brazilian, and 35 times that of the average Indian.

These rates of disparity pose significant moral issues about the ecological unsustainability of common consumer habits in industrialized countries and the middle-class and wealthy elites in developing countries. Habits of high meat consumption impose heavy ecological impacts via the transformation of forest and jungle regions for increased cattle ranges. As more wilderness and jungle are turned into range and farmland, increasing numbers of wild species become endangered or extinguished because of the diminishment of their natural habitat. Increasing overfishing is depleting both ocean and fresh-water fish stocks. Increasing population growth and agricultural irrigation needs threaten many regions with water shortages as aquifers are drained and river waters diverted.

Concerns for social justice as well as ecological sustainability require high consuming nations to develop policies that curtail their overconsumption and heavy negative impact on the global ecosystem. It is the affluent overconsumers who most bear the responsibility for changing practices to ensure ecological sustainability.

C. Habitat Destruction and Biodiversity Loss

Surging growth in human numbers and in production and consumption increases the pressure of human encroachment on wilderness regions globally. Almost half the forest area that once covered the planet has been cleared, and current rates of deforestation are alarming. As more natural ecosystems are converted into human-dominated ones, more of the planet's basic food energy is diverted from sustaining a wide diversity of animal and plant species to sustaining increasing numbers of one dominant species, namely the human. Accordingly, species extinction rates have begun to soar.

The World Conservation Union estimates that roughly 11% of bird species around the globe are now threatened with extinction. Among the world's mammals, 25% are currently threatened. Among the primates—monkeys, apes, lemurs, chimpanzees—almost half are currently listed as "threatened." 37% of hoofed mammals—camels, deer, antelope, rhinos, horses, and so on—are now threatened. For at least three quarters of these threatened mammal species the key factor in pushing their decline in numbers is habitat loss.

As Edward O. Wilson, a noted Harvard University entomologist, observes, there have been only five great extinction spasms over the course of the last 500 million years that produced anything like the scale of extinction that humanity is now causing. Biodiversity loss is an irreversible diminishment of the vitality and stability of the planetary community. Plant diversity is important for its agricultural and pharmaceutical potential and for its basic foundational role in ecosystems as food for diverse animal species. Plant and animal species together perform myriad and often unnoted services within the ordinary functioning of local ecosystems. These services range from improving the fertility of soil, to manufacturing oxygen, to stabilizing watersheds, and degrading corpses back into nutrient cycles. Genetic, species, and ecosystem diversity are precious resources that have evolved down through the eons and they hold the fundamental biological capital of the planet.

D. Climate Change and Global Security

In the last decade scientists have become alarmed that increased fossil fuel consumption is forcing more carbon dioxide (CO_2) into the atmosphere even as agricultural production is emitting increasing levels of atmospheric methane (CH_4) and industrial processes are emitting chlorofluorocarbons (CFCs), ozone (O_3), and other greenhouse gases. At the same time increasing jungle and forest clearing are diminishing the planet's biomass, which functions to draw carbon from the atmosphere. In 1995 the United Nations-sponsored Intergovernmental Panel on Climate Change (consisting of a network of 2500 of the world's top atmospheric scientists) announced that there is evidence of a "discernible human influence on global climate." They project that atmospheric carbon dioxide levels will reach roughly 500 ppmv by the end of the next century, approaching a doubling of atmospheric carbon from the preindustrial era levels. They calculate that by 2100 this will increase world average surface temperatures by 1°C–3.5°C (1.8°F–6.3°F).

It is feared that such a planetary-wide warming trend will not only cause rising sea levels to inundate low-lying island nations and coastal populations, but could also disrupt many ecosystems and natural habitats, causing severe damage to human agriculture and to many animal and plant species. Because hurricanes draw their strength from the warmth of surface air, warmer ocean waters may well increase the wind velocity and destructiveness of such storms. Some plant and tree species would be able to adapt to the new temperature and weather conditions while others would slowly shift their range. Many others would be pushed into extinction along with animal species that do not adapt quickly enough via migration.

Just as some nations and peoples bear a greater burden of responsibility for climate change dangers due to their greater emission rates of greenhouse gases, it is likely that certain nations and peoples will bear a greater vulnerability to the impact of climate change. Wealthy Holland can afford to build up its sea wall of dikes, while Bangladesh and the Maldives, off India's coast, in their poverty cannot. Many ethicists believe that justice calls for countries that consume high levels of fossil fuel to take the lead in mitigating climate change threats by restricting their fossil fuel use and patterns of greenhouse gas emission. Many advocate conservation strategies that shift habits of transportation from high airplane and auto usage to a greater reliance on more energy efficient modes of transit such as rail, bus, bicycling, and walking. At the same time many argue for the importance of halting deforestation and for the need to make a major commitment to reforestation efforts. The long-range goal for many theorists is a shift to a solar-power and wind-power economy of renewable energy that gives off no greenhouse gas emissions.

Many argue that market price structures need to reflect both nature's services and the full ecological costs of certain practices of consumption, such as fuel use. Accordingly, they call for "green" or "carbon taxes" on the use of coal, oil, or gas prorated to the amount of carbon emitted. Increasing fuel taxes would act as a disincentive for high levels of auto driving and provide incentives for energy conservation. However, these taxes need to be introduced with an eye to justice for the poor, who cannot afford higher costs.

IX. RISK ASSESSMENT AND THE PRUDENCE PRINCIPLE

Governments have long applied the prudence principle to justify expenditures of national treasure to ensure national protection in a context of uncertainty regarding a potential threat. Many people hold that it is wrong to be asked to make economic sacrifices at the present time when the prognoses regarding future climate change and biodiversity loss potentials are so uncertain. But needing to act in a context of incertitude is not unusual. When the stakes are high and outcomes uncertain, most people and nations opt to reduce risk. People buy home insurance not because of any certitude about the occurrence of a future fire, but out of a current certitude that a future fire is possible. In terms of threat assessment and response it is the mere possibility, not the certitude, of the threat that matters both morally and emotionally. Prudence suggests that when the stakes are as high as planetarywide security, the possibility of future ecological degradation should justify speedy and forceful action in the present to insure global well-being in the future.

X. CONTRIBUTIONS OF THE WORLD'S RELIGIONS

If the heart of our unfolding ecological drama lies in the need to restrain human practices that are ecologically, unsustainable, then the remedy lies in empowering broad regional, national, and global movements committed to ecological security, habitat and climate stabilization, and social justice. The global effort to achieve ecological sustainability will draw from the distinct traditions of philosophical and religious ethics in two ways. First, the global ecoethical conversation will be enriched by the distinct philosophical and religious ethical emphases of the diversity of the world's peoples. Where the West has been dominated by anthropocentric ethics, Asian, African, and Indigenous traditions have often included animals within the moral community and plants and ecosystems within a sphere of reverence and embodied respect. Much can be learned by listening to the wisdom of other cultures. Second, global ecoethical response must occur through empowering local and national movements that work for ecologically sustainable practices and public policies. The slogan "Think globally, act locally"—requires that the energy of diverse cultural and religious traditions will need to be tapped to provide vital impetus for change. People may well be more engaged to push for ecosustainability if they come to see how new ecological responsibilities connect to their own deeply held traditional moral perspectives and religious beliefs.

Even as biodiversity tends to stabilize and vitalize an ecosystem, so too the world's cultural and religious diversity can be a powerful force for moral vitality and global responsibility. Ecologically concerned Muslims note how the earth and all in it belong to Allah, the sovereign creator, and not to humans. Humans may use the earth to our betterment, but acts of ecosystem abuse are failures to act with requisite piety (*taqwa*). Jews and Christians, too, understand that all of God's creation is loved by God and is good and worthy of respect and care. The ethical imperative to "love the neighbor" suggests to many Christians today that they need to recognize animal and plant species and future generations as "neighbors" whose well-being needs to be secured. Judaism's *bal tashhit*, the injunction against wanton destruction, is seen by many to apply to practices that promote ecological degradation. Indeed, Jews committed to the need for *tikkun olam*, the repairing of the world, see this in new ecological ways.

Asian religions and the religions of indigenous peoples also offer important energies for ecological responsibility. Buddhist emphases on interconnectedness and the necessity of compassion for all sentient beings directly engage ecological concerns. Likewise the Noble Eightfold Path, with its emphases on "right livelihood" and "right mindfulness," offers means for overcoming egoist and consumerist drives. Hindu traditions and rituals stress a sense of divine immanence in mountains, rivers, cows, and trees. Reflection on *dharma* (righteousness, duty, justice) is being expanded today by a growing number of Hindus to include environmental responsibilities. The Chipko movement, for example, whose name is derived from a verb meaning to "hug" or "embrace," is inspired by these views as it gathers women's groups to link arms around trees in the Indian Himalayan region to prevent their being chopped by developers. Jainism, with its traditional insistence on *ahimsa*, nonviolence or noninjury, likewise draws close attention to our actions and impels a potent concern for the entire community of life. So too the close sense of kinship with earth and animals held by the Maya of Guatemala and Mexico, the Lakota of the North American Plains, the Nuer of Sudan, and the Ashanti of Ghana contains an energy of significant ecological potential.

XI. SOLIDARITY ACROSS THE GENERATIONS

Ecoethics seeks to support the values of ecological sustainability, social justice, planetary security, and prudence, but it derives much of its emotional energy and commitment from a critical sense of time and history. It follows Darwin's lead to hold that we—this generation—have been deeply gifted by previous generations of humans and nonhuman life-forms stretching back through evolutionary history. We have inherited a world rich with life but increasingly vulnerable. We cannot return the gift to previous generations. All we can do is act in gratitude to them and seek to pass on their gift to future generations. Ecoethics begins with a sense that the planetary stakes are high, time is short, and our responsibilities extensive.

Also See the Following Articles

ANIMALS, VIOLENCE TOWARD • ENVIRONMENTAL ISSUES

Bibliography

Brown, L. R. *et al.* (1998). *State of the world.* New York and London: W. W. Norton.

Durning, A. (1992). *How much is enough: The consumer society and the future of the Earth.* New York and London: W. W. Norton.

Gaard, G. (Ed.). (1993). *Ecofeminism: women, animals, nature.* Philadelphia: Temple University Press.

Goodpaster, K. (1978). On being morally considerable. *Journal of Philosophy*, 75:308–325.

Gottlieb, R. S. (Ed.). (1996). *This sacred Earth: Religion, nature, environment.* New York and London: Routledge.

Johnson, L. E. (1991). *A morally deep world: An essay on moral significance and environmental ethics.* Cambridge: Cambridge University Press.

Jonas, H. (1984). *The imperative of responsibility.* Chicago and London: University of Chicago Press.

Leisinger, K. M., & Schmitt, K. (1994). *All our people: Population policy with a human face.* Washington, DC: Island Press.

Leopold, A. (1966). *A Sand County almanac.* New York: Sierra Club/Ballantine.

Naess, A. (1989). *Ecology, community and lifestyle.* Rothenberg, D. (Ed.) Cambridge: Cambridge University Press.

Regan, T. (1983). *The case for animal rights.* Berkeley and Los Angeles: University of California Press.

Schweitzer, A. (1964). The ethics of reverence for life. *The philosophy of civilization.* Buffalo: Prometheus Books.

Singer, P. (1975). *Animal liberation: A new ethics for our treatment of animals.* New York: Avon Books.

Sterba, J. P. (Ed.). (1995). *Earth ethics: Environmental ethics, animal rights, and practical applications.* Englewood Cliffs, NJ: Prentice-Hall.

Tucker, M. E., & Grim, J. A., (Eds.). (1994). *Worldviews and ecology: Religion, philosophy, and the environment.* Maryknoll, NY: Orbis Books.

Wilson, E. O. (1996). *In search of nature.* Washington, D.C.: Island Press.

Economic Causes of War and Peace

Jon D. Wisman
American University

GLOSSARY

Financial Capital An ownership claim on real wealth. Stocks, bonds, bills of exchange, and money are examples.

Free-Rider Problem Within a market economy, the problem of not being able (without undue costs or appeal to government) to exclude someone from receiving benefits that others have paid for. It results in the failure of markets to efficiently allocate resources in certain instances.

Game Theory A procedure for mapping the strategies and corresponding payoffs available to competing participants such as two firms, a firm and a union, or two nations where their decision-making is interdependent. That is, the effectiveness of one agent's strategy depends upon the decisions taken by the other agent.

Gene-Culture Co-Evolution An evolutionary theory that argues that genetic change and cultural change mutually affect each other. This is the dominant view among evolutionary biologists of how the human species has evolved.

Negative-Sum Game Where the sum of losses exceed the sum of gains for all parties taken together.

Neolithic Revolution The beginning of humanity's adoption of agriculture about 10,000 years ago. It was the greatest economic revolution in human history.

I. OVERVIEW

Surprisingly, those who have most studied war—specialists in political science and international relations—have typically tended to attribute little causal power to economic variables when analyzing the causes of war and peace. But economic factors play an important role in determining whether social groups are at war or peace.

On the most general level, it should be expected that economic forces have been significant in setting the stage for war and peace, since humans are necessarily and fundamentally economic beings. In order to survive and reproduce in a world of scarcity, humans must struggle with nature. But this very condition of scarcity also establishes a reason why groups of humans might fight for limited resources.

Yet even though economics and war seem related, no general theory of war and peace has evolved that is widely embraced within the study of economics. This may be due in part to the fact that economists have not given a great deal of study to the economic causes of war and peace. It may also be due to the fact that war and peace are such complex social phenomena that economists, like other students of war, have been unsuccessful in formulating a definitive body of theory. Those who have attempted to develop general theories of war and peace have not managed to convince their colleagues—much less the wider body of scholars who study the domain—of the explanatory power of their approaches.

During the earliest part of human existence, war offered little in the way of economic benefits. However, as hunting and gathering territories became more scarce, and especially with the advent of agricultural societies, war came to offer more substantial economic benefits to the victors. Indeed, for likely victors, war could be more economically beneficial than economic production.

Yet war is a negative-sum game. That is, the economic gains of the winner are less than the losses to all participants taken together. Therefore, peace has always offered a higher collective pay-off. There has always been an economic motivation for peace. Where the outcome is obvious, it would be better for the losers to bribe the likely winners not to attack.

It must be emphasized, however, that because humans are *social* beings, the motivations for war or peace are more complex than such mere calculation of advantage. Indeed, as society became more complex, so too did these motivations.

In any event, the evolution of capitalism changed the equation: economic production came to offer greater benefits than waging war. The economic benefits of peace increased. The technological sophistication and social coordination that accompanied the maturation of capitalism made war increasingly destructive. Indeed, the level of destructive capacity of potential combatants eventually came to mean that even a victor would lose economically. Yet, even as war became ever more destructive, and hence ever more economically irrational, it continued all the same. However, in the latest chapter of humanity, a major war has come to mean potential species suicide, and this, combined with the critical self-interested individualism that capitalism nurtures, provides good reason for believing that major wars belong to the past.

To gain a broad appreciation of the manner in which economic forces have generated the conditions for both war and peace, it is useful to survey broadly the history of humanity. To make this task manageable, this history is divided into several stages of economic development. Surveying this history will constitute the first part of this article.

The second part examines the question of whether war is natural. Part three briefly surveys the spectrum of theories that economists have formulated concerning war and peace. Part four focuses on the social dynamics of peoples at war and at peace. The concluding part looks at the future potential for peace from an economic perspective.

II. A BRIEF HISTORY OF THE ECONOMIC CAUSES OF WAR AND PEACE

As human culture has evolved, the specific economic causes of war and peace have not only varied, they have also become increasingly complex. Consequently, a useful overview of the topic can be gained by briefly examining war and peace over the historical stages of economic development. As will become evident, for much of human history—indeed until rather recent times—there was no clear distinction between an economy and warfare.

A. War and Peace among Hunters and Gatherers

It has been suggested that if all of human history were viewed as a 24-h day, then 23 h and 50 min of that day were spent in the preagricultural stone era. Humans survived by hunting and gathering their food supply. This means that only 10 min—1/144th of human history—have gone by since the beginning of the adoption of agriculture about 10,000 years ago.

It has also been argued that, genetically, we are not significantly different from paleolithic peoples, at least those who were members of our species—*homo sapiens*. Consequently, if we are innately war-like—genetically programmed with a proclivity to go to war—then it should be apparent during that period.

Hunters and gatherers were typically nomadic. They would hunt and gather an area until it was fairly well picked-over and then move on, often following the migratory patterns of animals. Because of their nomadic ways, foragers could not accumulate significant material wealth. What material wealth they might possess would be in the form of crude primitive weapons and tools, perhaps clothing and hides for shelter, and ornamental jewelry. Such meager material wealth offered groups little incentive to attack so as to steal others' possessions.

This does not mean, however, that hunting and gathering peoples did not war with each other. Indeed, the personal and social skills necessary for bringing down prey were highly suited for war. And there *were* motivations for belligerence toward other groups. They might fight for women or for hunting and gathering rights to specific territories.

Yet such warring was quite limited in scope and damage was unlikely to be severe. The intensity, and seeming irrationality, with which humans will fight over access to sex is legendary. But unless there was a shortage of promising hunting and gathering territory, groups would not so readily risk death in battle. We might expect a sort of economic form of reasoning to prevail, one balancing the risk of death from starvation against death in battle. And because groups could usually move on to other territories, conflict was more generally in the form of bluffing, an attempt to convince the opposing group of their fighting superiority and their willingness to do battle. Although fleeing might be more rational than fighting, it would nevertheless be rational to try to convince opponents that you would fight rather than flee.

The average foraging group numbered only about 25. This was due to the average food yield and the amount of territory a group could cover (approximately 25 square miles) and still cohere as a group. Again, this small group size, combined with the general dispersion of groups, meant that casualties from combat were likely to be limited. Groups could of course band together for purposes of war, but given how little could be gained, the energy expenditure and time taken away from food procurement could make it a poor economic bargain.

B. War and Peace in the World of Early Agriculture

Although the adoption of agriculture—the so-called neolithic revolution—is typically dated to about 10,000 years ago, it did not begin all of a sudden. Groups planted crops at first to supplement food from hunting and gathering. Nor was agriculture chosen because it seemed to be a superior mode of existence. In fact, evidence suggests that given the choice, hunter-gathers did not voluntarily adopt agriculture. Instead, it is generally believed that the adoption of agriculture was forced by the decline of productivity in hunting and gathering as populations expanded. It was over-hunting and over-gathering that made the adoption of agriculture necessary.

Agriculture results in greater human command over the physical world. Rather than forage for food, humans gained a greater degree of physical control over their food sources. But agriculture introduced a new problem of major importance. Early agriculturalists did not live hand-to-mouth. Instead, they invested long periods of labor in their future food supply. They had to await the harvest; they had to wait until their animals birthed young and nurtured them to an independent age. The problem is that marauders could sweep in and steal the harvest or herd animals. And after they had done so, the victims would be highly vulnerable to starvation. Consequently, the adoption of agriculture created a need for effective defense.

Agriculturalists needed to defend their investment in their future food supply, even to their deaths, since they would likely starve if the marauders should win. Compare this to the hunters and gatherers who had far less to defend. They seldom had more than a few days stock of food, and if it were stolen, they would simply hunt and gather more. Moreover, as noted above, there is little reason for hunters and gatherers to fight to the death. If they are challenged for access to their foraging grounds, they can move on to other grounds. Little wonder, then, that missionaries had such difficulty convincing hunting-and-gathering peoples to settle down to agriculture.

Thus, the evolution of agriculture made war far more economically attractive. Harvests and herd animals could present all but irresistible pickings. Agriculture created greater differentials in group sizes, division of labor, and technological sophistication. Clear military superiority could well enhance the chances of plundering raids or the ability to withstand such raids.

C. Pastoral Nomads and Continual War

One form of agriculture—pastoral nomadism—was especially prone to war-like behavior. Pastoral nomads herded animals from one grazing area to another. Once horses became domesticated and nomads began moving about on horseback, they became ferocious warriors. Their wealth was in their herd animals, and the skills they needed develop to protect this wealth against both animals and other groups of humans kept them continually prepared for combat. Their equestrian skills gave them the capacity to strike with lightening speed and terrifying effectiveness.

Virtually all adult males would serve as warriors. Thus they in effect had two principal means of acquiring their needed resources: They could tend and breed their herds and they could attack agricultural settlements or other nomadic bands to steal all that was worth carrying off. Their economic well-being depended upon both. Not surprisingly, then, the skill and courage required for attack made war a noble activity within their cultures.

Yet their mobility posed serious limits to their economic and cultural development. Without giving up nomadism, they could accumulate only limited wealth. Because of their nomadism, they could not develop a high degree of division of labor or specialization. Consequently, they typically remained poor and illiterate.

Nevertheless, their aggressiveness had serious economic consequences. It was to severely retard economic development in many areas of the world, such as Eastern Europe, which suffered continual waves of nomadic attack from the East. Because of their mobility they were all but impossible for more settled powers to constrain or control.

D. War and Peace and the Rise of the State

As agricultural settlements grew, defense became increasingly specialized. Social power came to be based increasing on political relations as opposed to kinship relationships. Sociologist Max Weber saw this evolution of the state as a consequence of a group gaining a relative monopoly on violence. In a similar vein, economic historian Douglass North has developed a theory of the state according to which a group with a comparative advantage in violence specializes in offering defense in return for a portion of the output of all producers. This group becomes the state.

It should be noted that from the vantage point of economic science, the state can be viewed much like a monopoly business firm, albeit one with unique characteristics. An implicit contract exists between the state and its subjects: in exchange for protection from both external and internal aggression, subjects provide the state with resources in the form of tribute or taxes. Its superior fighting power, and hence its high degree of monopoly on violence, gives the state the temptation and potential ability to extract a maximum of taxes from producers. However, the state's ability to exploit the people within its domain is checked by the threat of revolt and the availability of substitutes. If the state's tax burden is deemed excessive, subjects might be tempted to give their allegiance to a rival group offering to provide protection for less. They might even prefer the assumption of power by a foreign force.

Paradoxically, peace is necessary for economic progress, yet peace can make despotism more readily possible. If a state faces no serious internal or external competition for the allegiance of its subjects, then these subjects have no recourse to substitutes. If the state has no internal competitors, then it need not be so solicitous of the people. If no external competition is in evidence, then factions of subjects cannot flirt with such foreign powers in a manner that places checks on the sovereign's power. Thus, without internal or external substitutes, the state can more readily oppress its people. Its people have no options.

A classic example is pharaonic Egypt. With a sea to the north, deserts to the south and east, and semi-arid lands to the west, Egypt was relatively well insulated from external aggression. There was little or no internal competition. Consequently, the power of the pharaohs was near absolute and their exploitation of their peoples supposedly quite extreme.

A second example is that of Rome. The Roman state developed military technology that was superior to that of other states and peoples. Yet more importantly, it developed the economic power and highly sophisticated social organization that gave it clear military superiority over contending political entities. The consequence was that competing political powers were typically defeated. The evolving Roman Empire had then two sources of income: It could tax its own citizens and it could demand tribute from conquered peoples.

The Roman state developed a fairly high degree of monopoly power over violence for a theretofore unparalleled geographic range. This high degree of monopoly resulted in the *pax romana*, a degree of peace in the Empire that enabled the growth of trade and economic development. This economic development increased the tax base and hence the revenue accruing to the state.

Yet the far-flung nature of the Roman Empire meant that internal competition for power was practically ever-present. This placed a check on the ability of the state to exploit not only Roman citizens but also others within the Empire.

Eventually, however, Rome lost its comparative advantage in violence. The challenge was both internal and external. Internally, factional fighting weakened the state. Externally, political contenders, adopting similar technology and organization strategies, succeeded in opposing Roman forces on the frontiers of the Empire.

If the state is viewed as a unique type of economic agent, then like all other economic actors, the state will attempt to maximize its income. But its power to do so, as noted above, is constrained by the availability of substitutes. If an internal or external contender offers protection for less, then the ruled may switch allegiance. It is for this reason that rulers, like all economic firms, will constantly strive to eliminate all competition. The invasion of the Roman Empire by "barbarians" offered peoples in the Empire substitutes. The invasions may have been successful in part because the invaders offered a better deal—better protection for less taxes or tribute.

Once a state is weakened by competition, it may find itself on a self-propelling decline. The dynamic works as follows: An attack means that more resources must be allocated to defense. At some point these increased costs will force the state to increase the amount of surplus it takes from its citizens. It must increase taxes, tribute, or confiscations. Such highly unpopular measures cause allegiance to waver.

In addition, if the state takes more, economic incentives may be impaired. Why work hard to create a large harvest or amass a large stock of animals if the state is likely to take them away? Instead of putting their wealth into productive assets, people have an incentive to convert it into nonproductive forms of property, such as precious metals, that can be hidden from a confiscating state. Obviously, such behavior reduces a society's potential economic output and thus is also likely to erode the state's revenue base, handicapping its chances of amassing the resources necessary for fending off contenders for power.

Ideology can, of course, play a significant role. The state would wish that subjects express "product loyalty." If possible, the state could be expected to appeal to higher motivations such as defending the "fatherland" or "motherland." It would wish to convince its subjects that its cause is the will of a god or gods, a just cause against the forces of evil. Typically a priestly class helped create and maintain such state-supportive ideology. Rulers might even portray themselves as gods, as was the case with Egypt's pharaohs, or divinely chosen, as was the case in much of medieval Europe.

A state's capacity for waging war is constrained by the amount of surplus output that is produced. For instance, if a people faced such material hardship that they would have to expend absolutely all of their energies producing for bare survival, then no one could be freed from production to engage in fighting. By contrast, if 90% of the population could produce enough subsistence for the entire population, then conceivably 10% could engage in fighting. Of course, the amount of surplus created by those in production limits not only the capacity for waging war, but also the size and luxury of the governing or priestly classes.

E. The Rise of Capitalism

In premodern agricultural societies, war was frequently a more promising route to wealth than economic production. The spoils of war could potentially make the victors instantly wealthy. The two principal factors of production and hence the two principal forms of wealth were land and labor. Both could be obtained through military conquest. To be useful, conquered land had to be controlled and defended against competing forces. Captured peoples could be returned as slaves to work the land. Indeed, the taking of slaves was an especially good economic coup. Those taken would typically be old enough to work. The conquered peoples had paid the expense of raising them to that age. Thus the capturing of adults to become slaves was a better deal than domestically breeding and raising slaves until old enough to work.

Hard work in production, saving, and investment, by contrast, could promise to improve one's lot, were it not for the fact that brigands or the state stood too frequently ready to take it all away. Indeed, a principal reason why economic development has been so slow to evolve in human history is that property rights have been too fragile.

The superiority of war over economic production was expressed in the status relationships of premodern agricultural societies. The highest prestige was held by those in government or in military service. Frequently, the two were indistinguishable. In fact, the only acceptable careers for the nobility were in politics and the military. As the Marquis de Vauvenargues put it in the mid-18th century, "a man of quality, by fighting, acquires wealth more honorably and quickly than a meaner man of work."

Those in production, by contrast, typically commanded little if any esteem. Those in agriculture—the overwhelming majority of the people—were generally unfree, being tied to the land as either slaves or serfs. Those in crafts, although generally freer than cultivators, had relatively little prestige prior to the rise of capitalism. Those in trade and finance were especially looked down upon. Indeed, these domains were viewed with such disdain and distrust that they were frequently not permitted to full members of society. Instead, trading and banking functions had to be performed by metics or aliens. Incidentally, the state periodically found it ideologically useful to blame society's ills on these metics, making it easy to confiscate their wealth.

The slow rise of capitalism in Western Europe became one of humanity's greatest watersheds. It set in motion forces that would not only create unparalleled wealth, but also the eventual promise of the end of war.

As nation states evolved in Europe, fueled by the new technology of gunpowder that could lay waste to feudal castles and by the wealth of expanding trade and commerce, these states found themselves in a unique political situation of a general balance of power. After the fall of Rome, no single political power succeeded in conquering and sustainably controlling all of Europe. Not that there were not notable attempts, such as those of Charlemagne, Napoleon, and Hitler. This prolonged general balance of power was unique to Western Europe and helps explain its economic success.

The consequence of no one power being capable of establishing hegemony over Europe had three major related consequences. First, nations faced the constant insecurity of being attacked by other more or less equally insecure political entities. This nation-state competition created an arms race in which to fall too far behind meant possible conquest by a more advanced enemy. This competition also placed a premium on improving the economic foundations of military might.

Second, nation-states had a collective interest in no one power becoming overly strong. Alliances would thus form to preclude an already strong nation from becoming yet stronger by annexing a neighboring territory.

Third, nation-state competition made it more difficult for individual nation governments to suppress ideas and technological progress. Repressed intellectuals could often flee to neighboring states to find sanctuary. Two of the best known examples of this were Voltaire and Karl Marx. In addition, intellectuals, unable for political reasons to publish a work within their own nation, often successfully sought publishers abroad.

Nations that attempted to repress technological innovations often were forced to relent. A striking example was France's attempt to outlaw the printing press in order to protect the livelihood of copyists. The consequence was that authors sent their manuscripts abroad for publication, thus not only outflanking the prohibition, but also depriving France of an important business. Eventually, France was obliged to permit the evolution of a printing industry within its own borders.

While capitalism makes states stronger by strengthening their economies, it also tends to weaken states' ability to act tyrannically. It does this by dividing authority or power into two spheres: the political and the economic. As capitalism evolves, the state is forced to withdraw progressively from intervention in the workings of the economy. Although this withdrawal has never been total and there have been reversals, it has generally meant that the political sphere occupies itself with the functions of statecraft such as waging wars, making and maintaining alliances, maintaining order, and promulgating laws.

The second sphere of power and authority is the economy. It concerns itself with production and distribution, both of which come to be ruled increasingly by market forces. States have discovered, and are still discovering, that economic dynamism is frequently better promoted by leaving most economic matters to the workings of this market sphere. The market sphere grows to serve as a countervailing power to the political sphere.

The evolution of capitalism has slowly replaced the premodern logic of economic reward. The potential for attaining wealth through war declined as the technology of destruction became ever more sophisticated and widely dispersed. The increasing cost of this technology, along with the rising amount of destruction of wealth that it promised, reduced the probability that the spoils of war could make war economically worthwhile.

Further, under capitalism, growing productivity in agriculture meant that this sector would decline in relative importance. With the exception of a few natural resources such as oil and minerals that are highly unevenly dispersed geographically, capturing land promised too little in terms of wealth.

Two forces were also generated to serve against the capturing of labor in the form of slaves. The growing sophistication of production technology made the use of unfree labor less productive. Second, markets work best if all are free to enter and exit them without coercion. The expansion of markets helped increase the value of freedom generally. Slavery came to be seen as morally wrong.

The logic of reward shifted from war and violence to peaceable production. And, although the potential risks and rewards of a military career would continue to confer social prestige upon its practitioners, leaders in production found their social standing continually improving as capitalism evolved.

The fuller manner in which the maturation of capitalism favored production over war can be seen by examining the changing importance of factors of production. Economists have long identified the three major factors of production as land, labor, and capital. As agriculture declined in relative importance, so too did land. As manufacturing and services increased in relative importance, capital became increasingly important. The traditional aristocratic class held its wealth in and derived its power from land. As land's relative importance declined, so too did the power, influence, and status of the aristocracy. The bourgeois class, by contrast, holds its wealth in and derives its power from capital. The rising importance of capital has meant the ascendancy of bourgeois power, influence, and values.

Unlike land, capital is fairly mobile. Machines can be moved. But even more mobile is the ownership claim on capital, financial capital. This provides the capitalist class with great power vis-à-vis the state. Because this wealth is highly mobile, it can more readily escape the control of any particular government. This was noted by Montesquieu in the early 18th century. He wrote of how with the evolution of a form of financial capital, the bill of exchange, "the richest trader had only invisible wealth which could be sent everywhere without leaving a trace . . . a contrivance which somehow lifts commerce right out of [the ruler's] grip."

This is an example of how the market sphere came to serve as a countervailing power to the political sphere. If government threatens capitalists' freedom or wealth, that wealth threatens to flee to a friendlier location abroad. Because military strength ultimately depends upon economic power, governments had to be careful not to frighten off capital. They had to provide capital with security. Social thinkers were beginning to recognize that this new economy promoted nondespotic government. For instance, in the mid-1760s, political economist James Steuart observed that a "modern economy . . . is the most effectual bridle ever was invented against the folly of despotism."

As governments became increasingly aware that military strength was dependent upon economic strength, property rights were established that provided producers with greater assurance that their property was secure. Property came to be better protected by more clearly defined and better enforced laws. Note, for instance, the concerted efforts to eliminate piracy on the high seas. The state also offered greater assurances that property could not be readily confiscated by the state itself. Note here, for instance, the protections against confiscation provided by the U.S. Constitution. The consequence was, of course, greater economic dynamism, as well as more enduring domestic peace.

Just as the rise of the nation-state centralized political power, the evolution of capitalism has brought about the decentralization of power. The rising wealth of the bourgeoisie prompted this class to demand a share of political power. At times this demand expressed itself violently, as in the English "Glorious Revolution" and the French Revolution. But more frequently, political rights were acquired slowly, piece by piece.

With the rise of industrialization and extensive urbanization, the working class also began to demand political rights and a share of power. Although their struggle was frequently violent, for the most part they gained rights slowly but progressively. Later yet, women and minorities would also petition for their share of political power. The upshot has been that over the history of capitalism, power has come to be ever more widely shared. As a result differences have come to be resolved within a peaceable political arena as opposed to through civil strife or civil war.

III. A BRIEF RETURN TO THE QUESTION: IS WAR NATURAL?

Is war-like behavior part of the very nature of human evolution? Historical, anthropological, and archeological evidence suggest that war and war-like behavior have been an ever-present part of the human experience. As social animals, it would appear that humans have always divided themselves into groups with radically different attitudes toward members and nonmembers. Violence against members has been discouraged, often by violent punishment. Violence against nonmembers, by contrast, has often not only been tolerated, but encouraged and rewarded as well.

A. War as Economic Behavior

As we saw earlier, in a world of scarcity social groups struggle against each other, perhaps war with each other, for control or possession of limited resources such as, first, women and hunting-and-gathering territories, and later cultivable land and slaves. War, then, can be a form of competition for command over scarce resources. Anthropological studies have found that in general, the scarcer the resources, the greater the likelihood of war.

But where resources have been abundant and widely distributed, competition has been rarer. Much has been made of a number of societies, such as the Bushmen of Africa's Kalahari Desert, or the Eskimos, that have been especially peaceful. Clearly resources were not abundant for such peoples. But what explains their peacefulness is that they were uniquely situated in territories where competition through war for scarce resources could not have paid off.

Because the global human population has been rising ever more rapidly since the beginning of the adoption of agriculture, all societies would ultimately face others in competition for scarce resources. The central problem of the science of economics, the problem of scarcity, means that human groups are bound to war against each other whenever the pay-off is adequately attractive.

B. War as Evolutionary Strategy

War also seems natural from an evolutionary perspective. Those groups that were most successful in increasing their command over scarce resources would have a survival advantage which would permit them to increase their populations and thereby pass on their genes or culture to more progeny.

Evolutionary biologist David Barash addresses the naturalness of war by noting the fitness argument: "The fitness of individuals within a group suffers most when that group is forced to share resources with individuals of another group. The personal fitness of these individuals could therefore actually be increased by warfare, provided that the cost of waging war is less than the benefits received."

Thus from both economic and biological vantage points, it would appear that, at least in the early history of humanity, war was not the consequence of some self-destructive passion run amok. Instead, it would appear to have been critical to the very process of human social and cultural evolution. Indeed, Darwin and others since have suggested that the evolution of human intelligence is linked to the pervasiveness of warfare in the human experience. Barash suggests that "Our most dangerous predator may well have been ourselves, and selection would have favored those individuals whose brains were large enough to permit them to enter into workable alliances and to coordinate defense—and aggression—against other groups."

IV. WHAT ECONOMISTS HAVE HAD TO SAY ABOUT WAR AND PEACE

Although war made sense from an economic perspective until fairly modern times, economists have had relatively little to say about it. Indeed, until fairly recently, most economists who expressed an interest in the economic aspects of war and peace were outside the mainstream of the profession. War and peace have simply not been given enough attention within the profession for a general consensus to evolve as to their causes. In this section, the major contributions are briefly surveyed.

A. Heterodox Economic Thinking on the Causes of War and Peace

Karl Marx and Friedrich Engels saw war as part of the process of what they called primitive accumulation in the early evolution of capitalism, whereby violence was used by the capitalist-controlled state to expand profitable opportunities. At the turn of the 19th century, theoreticians of imperialism—some Marxist, others not—believed that imperialism in search of resources and markets was necessary to avoid economic stagnation. State capitalist rivalry for imperial domains would likely lead to war.

Two non-Marxist heterodox economists who discussed war were Thorstein Veblen and Joseph Schumpeter. Both essentially viewed participation in war by capitalist societies as irrational: Veblen saw such participation in war as a cultural perversion, stemming from an earlier predatory stage from which humanity might never escape. Schumpeter also saw such war as atavistic behavior and optimistically as something that capitalistic rationality—which he saw much in the manner of Max Weber's spirit of capitalism—would move us beyond.

More recently, a group of neo-Marxists, often referred to as the monopoly capital school, adopted a Keynesian inadequate-aggregate-demand framework. Keynes had argued that government spending is at times necessary to maintain adequate aggregate demand to prevent an economy from falling into recession or depression. The monopoly capital school argued that the capitalist-controlled state could only spend on those activities that might enhance capitalist profits, and the spending which was most easily justifiable to the greater public was on war. Consequently, they argued that capitalist states were destined to maintain war-like postures towards other states in order to maintain profits and avoid economic crises.

Since the early 1960s, attention has also been focused on what outgoing President Eisenhower termed the "military–industrial complex." The general idea has been that the military and industries that benefit from military spending work together to generate public anxiety concerning external threats to the nation and its interests. This view often shared much with monopoly capital theory, as well as the long standing charge that because war frequently is good for the armaments industry and profits generally, capitalism as a system is prone to war or war-like behavior. Most economic research in this area has been descriptive and not highly theoretical. It has also been performed by mainstream as well as heterodox economists.

B. The Mainstream Economic Theory of War

Within the mainstream of economics, the subject of war has rarely received more than passing mention. Where mainstream economists have discussed war, it has usually been in terms of viewing the state in the same manner that individual behavior is viewed. That is, they have extended the neoclassical economic model to an analysis of the behavior of rivals in war. Central to this model is the assumption that actors are rational, self-interested maximizers and that decisions are made at the margin.

War and war-like behavior are depicted as rational for one or more parties. By rational it is meant that war follows some sort of at least rough-and-ready calculation of the estimated costs and benefits of varying degrees of war-like behavior.

These calculations include assessing the rationality of bluffing, or mere war-like behavior that cannot only be rational, but even more so than actually going to war. For instance, a weaker power, knowing it would lose a war, might nonetheless pretend that it would fight if provoked. Only by threatening the stronger power with losses might the weaker discourage the stronger from actually attacking.

Mainstream economists have also taken note of the parallels between the strategies employed by a small number of firms within an industry (e.g., duopolies and oligopolies) and the behavior of states in potential military competition (incidentally, the famous early 19th-century German military theoretician, Carl von Clausewitz, compared war to business competition). The models of game theory have especially been used in trying better to grasp the options available to military rivals.

Within such models, war is viewed as a negative-sum game. That is, whereas war might be rational for one or more parties, it is irrational for all participants taken together. It might be tempting to think of it as a zero-sum game, whereby whatever one participant wins, the other loses. But war is in fact a negative-sum game because the gains of the winners will be less than the losses of the loser. War costs resources, and thus if war could be avoided, these resources could in principle be allocated to meet other needs.

The particular strength of this sort of modeling is that it makes clear how we would expect rival parties to behave in their strategies toward one another on the field or at the bargaining table. In fact, this basic framework of analysis has been widely used by noneconomist students of international relations and politics such as Robert Gilpin and Bruce Bueno de Mesquita.

Although this model possesses considerable explanatory power, its limitation is that it focuses on individual decision-makers as rational self-interested maximizers. It ignores and thus sheds no light on how individuals are socialized; on how their preference functions are formed. It does not tell us how or what individuals come to understand as their self-interest.

Moreover, although the model of rational maximizing behavior may characterize the strategies rivals adopt toward one another, it appears limited in two interrelated senses. First, it presumes that the self-interests of political leaders and of their constituents are essentially the same. Second, when it comes to actual conflict, the model of rational maximizing behavior does not seem to fit the varied accounts we have of how individual participants behave in battle.

More pointedly, it would appear that when members of one side behave as purely self-interested actors, they decrease their side's chances of success. The reason, of course, is what economists call the free-rider problem. If individuals self-interestedly shirk their fair share of the battle effort, a breakdown in cohesion threatens. Success in battle, and especially those extraordinary upsets where a physically weaker side trounces a stronger opponent, typically is found to involve a certain *esprit de corps*—an especially strong commitment on the part of individuals to the group—which is precisely what the mainstream model has difficulty explaining.

This suggests, then, that whereas war may be rational for a group, it requires nonrational motivation on the part of individual actors. But if this is the case, how might it have come about in term of human evolution?

V. THE SOCIOECONOMIC DYNAMICS OF PEOPLES AT WAR AND AT PEACE

As noted above, war and war-like behavior are understandable from both evolutionary and economic perspectives. Through evolution, war and war-like behaviors were selected. Some evolutionary biologists and ethnologists argue that this selection was genetic. Others, perhaps wishing to hold out for greater optimism, suggest that it was not genetic, but instead that it has been culturally selected. An intermediate view—indeed the dominant view among evolutionary biologists and ethnologists today—is what they term "gene-culture coevolution" by which they mean that there are, as Charles Lumsden and Edward O. Wilson have put it, "reciprocal effects of genetic and cultural change within the human species." Cultural change prompts genetic change and vice-versa.

A. Group Commitment

Just as war-like behavior has been selected, so, too, it would appear, have two correlative social tendencies: The first is the extraordinary commitment of members to the group during war or its threat. This is hardly surprising, since a group for which such commitment was weak would be at a severe disadvantage in a struggle for resources and therefore would be at a disadvantage in terms of survival, in terms of passing its members' genes or culture on to progeny. It is even plausible that our very sociability, at least to some extent, was selected for as a result of the benefits of social cohesion during threats from external aggressors.

Evidence of this group commitment under threat is everywhere in our cultural history: War occasions the most splendid acts of heroism. It is during war that individuals most readily sacrifice their lives for others. Nietzsche and many others since have noted that men are more tightly bonded together in combat than at any other time. This bonding appears to be pleasurable. Indeed, there appears to be an exhilaration in identifying with a group in conflict with others. We also see this proclivity for group commitment in sports. For instance, rarely is anything really to be gained by spectators if their team wins, yet at times there is actual carnage among spectators not content with the outcome of the game. Clearly something other than rational self-interest is at play here.

Indeed, evolution may have selected a tendency always to locate an external foe. Societies rarely seem to be without one. Thus, for instance, is it more than mere coincidence that in the U.S. the two great political purges of this century came in the wake of the two World Wars, when a new serious external threat had not yet been clearly identified? If such a tendency always to locate an external foe had been selected for in evolution, the pay-off would be the social cohesion that would better enable society to minimize the free-rider problem.

B. Loyalty to Leaders

The second corollary of war that appears to have been selected has to do with the degree of loyalty given to leaders when the group is threatened. Such loyalty would enable a more coordinated quick response to an enemy attack or change in strategy. In fact, it seems that leaders rarely achieve as high a degree of loyalty from their followers during peace as during war. As biologist John Alcock has put it, "paradoxically, war depends on the cooperative, group-bonding, authority-accepting aspect of human behavior."

Because leaders more readily receive stronger loyalty and respect from followers when external aggression threatens, they face an all-but-irresistible temptation: They can benefit if they can convincingly keep alive a perception of an external threat. They might even be expected to craft measures against other powers that will provoke a limited amount of real threat. Hegel had made note of this phenomenon when he wrote that "peoples involved in civil strife ... acquire peace at home through making war abroad."

C. Loyalty to Leaders in Modern Times

As to the social functioning of loyalty to leaders, an important difference exists between early human society and quite recent history. As noted above, almost all of the human past occurred prior to the adoption of agriculture (23 h and 50 min of the 24-h-day of human history). Presumably, during this long period of human evolution, a tendency for group commitment and loyalty to leaders in times of danger was being selected for. Note that during war leaders were the most vulnerable to injury or death. They were literally leading the band into battle. Hence, any temptation to reap loyalty and respect by showing courage before the enemy had to be tempered by the risk of serious injury or death.

Since the adoption of agriculture, however, human society has become progressively more complex: differentiated in terms of economic function through the division of labor; and stratified with respect to wealth, status, and power. There are two consequences of this that are of interest for grasping the nature of modern war. First, what is rational for certain segments of society is no longer necessarily rational for all. Some may disproportionately reap whatever benefits there might be from war, whereas others, especially those who go to the front lines, may disproportionately bear the costs.

The second consequence of this explosion in social complexity is that the cost to leaders of yielding to the temptation to seek the loyalty and respect of followers by keeping alive the perception of a threat of external aggression has slowly declined. As societies have become increasingly complex, their leaders have progressively retreated from the front such that failure in war has generally become personally less costly to them.

This does not, of course, imply that leaders could maintain loyalty by generating external hostilities with impunity. If they pushed too hard, a catastrophic war might result, robbing them of power and even life. On the other hand, if members of the group view the alleged threat as either not real or as not sufficient to merit the cost, then the leader loses credibility and possibly also power. In the U.S. during the Vietnam War of the late 1960s, this appeared to have been the fate of President Lyndon Johnson.

It may be the case that leaders do not always consciously and in a calculatingly rational manner weigh the political benefits against the costs of war-like behavior. Such behavior might come forth spontaneously, in a manner akin to group commitment or the followers' allegiance to the leader.

Ideology also comes into play. Since the evolution of complex language, ideology is likely to have been important in maintaining group cohesion and effectiveness in war-like behavior. But in the earliest eras of human history, a threat was generally visible for all to see. In more modern times, by contrast, a threat may be protracted or not always clearly in evidence. Here ideology becomes more critical for maintaining loyalty both to the group and to the leader. Indeed, ideology production becomes an industry, keeping alive depictions of enemies as not actually or fully human; or as godless; or as advocates of barbarian social institutions; or as people of an "Evil Empire." Alternatively, a society's ideology may vest its distant leader with supranatural powers such as quasi-godhood, divine status, or divine rights.

In very modern times there is reason to believe that it has been during periods of economic instability that leaders have been most tempted to use the external threat strategy to achieve support. During economic crises, leaders would be most tempted to craft limited measures against another power in order to provoke a manageable amount of real threat. The reason is that beyond providing for defense and domestic law and order, the most important criterion for judging leadership today is its ability to maintain material or economic prosperity.

A number of events in recent times lend support to this hypothesis. World War II grew out of the worst economic depression in the history of capitalism. By contrast, the widespread peace movement and détente came forth during the extraordinary world-wide economic prosperity of the 1960s. When economic progress began to falter in the 1970s, détente began to be drowned out by rattling sabers. Note also that during the 1960s there was widespread confidence in governments' ability to use Keynesian tools to insure macroeconomic stability, whereas during the late 1970s and early 1980s laissez-faire doctrine resurfaced, arguing that governments are essentially powerless to stabilize economies.

The most successful, long-lasting modern example of how the threat of foreign aggression served to legitimize political power is the former Soviet Union. From 1917 until its fall, it was relatively easy for the Soviet power elite to maintain the credibility of a constant external threat. No sooner had the Bolsheviks taken power than England, France, and the U.S. set out to undermine the socialist experiment, especially by arming and financing the White Russians. Throughout the 1920s there was a perceived threat that the socialist experiment would be undone by hostile capitalist countries. So strongly did Stalin feel this that in 1931 he announced: "We must make good this distance (to become a first-rate economic and political power) in ten years. Either we do so, or we shall go under." His words were to be prophetic—the Germans crossed Soviet borders 10 years later. And then, at the end of World War II, the U.S. dropped atomic bombs on civilian populations in Japan, further suggesting to the Soviet people how ruthlessly inhumane the capitalist U.S. might be in pursuit of its interests.

In good part due to geography, few people have suffered the ravages of war as much as the Soviets—20 to 30 million perished during World War II. Consequently, in a sense, the Soviet political elites had it made. They could justify the lack of democracy or civil rights and the sorry state of their economy as necessary for defense in an aggressively hostile capitalist world bent on their destruction.

VI. THE SOCIOECONOMIC DYNAMICS OF THE CREATION OF PEACE

As noted earlier, the evolution of capitalism made economic production more profitable than war. Indeed, as it made war ever more destructive, it eventually made it economically unprofitable even for the winner. Capitalism generated and fed upon ever more sophisticated technology and ever more sophisticated social coordination. The two World Wars of this century—separated by a mere quarter century—made strikingly clear capitalism's destructive potential. Approximately eight million died in the First, approximately 50 million in the Second.

And then the cost of a major war between the U.S. and the USSR became potentially infinite. The threat of species extinction as a consequence of a U.S.–Soviet war meant that leaders were once again on the front lines. They would also perish in a full war. Their ability to play the external threat card to rally support was thus constrained. And in spite of slogans such as "Better Dead Than Red," popular support for a major war was unlikely to materialize. Indeed "peaceniks" in the U.S. reversed the slogan to "Better Red Than Dead." Quite convincingly, sophisticated atomic weapons and the means of delivering them over great distances are widely credited with effectively ending major wars.

When viewed in the full sweep of human existence; there is an interesting sense that humanity has come full circle. In our earliest history as hunters and gatherers, war did not have a very high pay-off. It was not typically a good economic bargain. There was simply too little to win from military victory. War-like behavior in the form of bluff might pay off, but actual combat with the threat of serious injury or death was not generally a good risk. Today this is again true: war has again become a poor risk. Destruction might be total. But even if more limited, it is likely that no power would win economically. It would appear that there is no remaining economic rationale for war.

However, it is not just the threat of species suicide or the lack of an economic pay-off that is turning people in the more-advanced and wealthy nations against war. Capitalism has set in motion a number of dynamics that serve to increase the probability of peace. In the following concluding paragraphs, attention will be given to these dynamics.

Capitalism took war to its necessary conclusion. It produced the wherewithal that enabled total war and ultimately total destruction. But capitalism has done more than this to give peace a chance. It has changed how people think about the world. It has made them ever more critically minded.

The most frequently noted consequence of capitalism is that it has brought forth a level of affluence that not even the most starry-eyed of visionaries past could have imagined. Less noted is that as people become materially wealthier, they come to value their lives more. Note for instance that with ever-greater wealth, people generally become more cautious. They eat more healthily, they smoke less, drink less, wear seat belts, and in general place a higher value on personal safety. This latter point is strikingly obvious to anyone from a wealthy nation who has the opportunity to drive on the roads of a relatively poor country. With so much more to lose, increasingly wealthy populations might be expected to show less willingness to engage in war.

Karl Marx and Friedrich Engels argued that under the regime of capitalism, "all that's solid melts into air." Economist Joseph Schumpeter referred to this dynamic character of capitalism as "creative destruction." What these social thinkers were alluding to is the tendency of capitalism to destroy all traditional social institutions, beliefs, and attitudes. Believing that the "dead weight of the past" fettered human progress, they by and large thought this was a good thing. However, not all social thinkers have been so sanguine.

Capitalism has acted as a "corrosive acid" upon the extended family, traditional communities, rigid class distinctions, and the authority of traditional religions. In doing so, it has thrust humans into social worlds where they sense themselves as increasingly alone. Capitalism means that individuals relate to each other not as traditional norms dictate, but as markets dictate. And in markets, individuals are encouraged to be rational and calculatingly self-interested. The increasing intensity of competition has meant that those who are most successful in pursuing their own self-interest become wealthy, the least successful, poor.

Traditional values such as honor, glory, courage, patriotism, and sacrifice for the greater good of the whole have suffered as people have become ever more calculating of their own narrow self-interests. The downside of all this is all too obvious and is widely lamented. A clear upside, however, is that individuals are less willing to sacrifice themselves or their economic well-being in war.

In precapitalist societies, a religious framework served as the central referent of all behavior and understanding. The evolution of capitalism slowly eroded religion's dominance and with it the promise of an afterlife. This loss in belief of an afterlife increases the value of this worldly life. Loss of one's life in war means loss of one's total personal existence.

Finally, for reasons discussed earlier, capitalism has tended to decentralize political power. It has, especially in its advanced form, provided a fertile ground for democracy. Yet ironically, democracy increases the ease with which a leader might lose power and thus might enhance the temptation to rattle sabers. However, because a democratic society is, by definition, a more open society, claims about threats can be more openly challenged. Perhaps not surprisingly, then, empirical studies have found no significant differences in the involvement of democratic versus nondemocratic states in war. However, democratic states have not warred against each other.

During the Cold War, both the U.S. and the Soviet Union propped up totalitarian regimes around the globe in a quest to hold them in their respective spheres of influence. Since the end of the Cold War, both capitalism and democracy have been rapidly spreading around the globe. And because modern democratic capitalist regimes appear relatively friendly to peace, may there not then be grounds for optimism that war will, in the not-too-distant future, become extinct?

Also See the Following Articles

ANTHROPOLOGY OF VIOLENCE AND CONFLICT, OVERVIEW • ARMS PRODUCTION, ECONOMICS OF • ECONOMIC CONVERSION • ECONOMICS OF WAR AND PEACE, OVERVIEW • EVOLUTIONARY FACTORS • INDUSTRIAL VS. PREINDUSTRIAL FORMS OF VIOLENCE • MILITARISM AND DEVELOPMENT IN UNDERDEVELOPED SOCIETIES • MILITARY-INDUSTRIAL COMPLEX

Bibliography

Alcock, J. (1978). Evolution and human violence. In L. L. Farrar, Jr. (Ed.), *War: A historical, political and social study*. Santa Barbara, CA: ABC-Clio Press.

Crumm, E. M. (1995). The value of economic incentives in international politics. *Journal of Peace Research*, 32(2), 113–130.

Forland, T. E. (1993). The history of economic warfare: International law, effectiveness, strategies. *Journal of Peace Research*, *30* (2), 151–162.

Gellner, E. (1992). An anthropological view of war and violence. In R. A. Hinde (Ed.), *The institution of war* (pp. 62–79). New York: St. Martin's Press.

Gelven, M. (1994). *War and existence*. University Park, PA: Pennsylvania State University Press.

Kaldor, M. (1992). Do modern economies require war or preparations for warfare? In R. A. Hinde (Ed.), *The institution of war* (pp. 178–191). New York: St. Martin's Press.

Levy, J. S. (1989). Domestic politics and war. In R. I. Rotberg and T. K. Rabb (Eds.), *The origin and prevention of major war* (pp. 79–100). Cambridge University Press.

de Mesquita, B. B. (1981). *The war trap*. New Haven, CT: Yale University Press.

Mueller, J. (1989). *Retreat from doomsday: The obsolescence of major war*. New York: Basic Books.

Neild, R. (1995). Economics and conflict. In R. A. Hinde and H. E. Watson (Eds.), *War: A cruel necessity? The bases of institutional violence* (pp. 126–207). London: Tauris Academia Studies.

North, D. (1981). *Structure and change in economic history*. New York: Norton.

Shaffer, E. H. (1996). Peace, war and the market. *Canadian Journal of Economics*, 29 (2), 639–643.

Tullock, G. (1974). *The social dilemma: The economics of war and revolution*. Blackberg, VA: University Publications.

Economic Conversion

Bernard Udis
University of Colorado

Peter Almquist
US Arms Control and Disarmament Agency

GLOSSARY

Corporate Culture A general term for the elements of decision making, perspective, judgment, and procedure within a company, usually historically established, that characterize this particular company and distinguish it from others.

Demilitarization The fact or process of converting a nation's economy, or the production of a particular company, from an emphasis on military weaponry to civilian or consumer goods.

Diversification In this context, the process in which a company oriented toward military production enters a new civilian market, without necessarily leaving the existing military market; contrasted with *conversion* in which the company replaces a military market with a civilian one.

Economies of Scale In strict usage, a term which refers to a physical relationship in which increases in physical inputs lead to more than proportional increases in output. However, increased output may lead to reduced costs for a variety of other reasons. Thus, volume economies often result where increased *cumulative* output leads to learning economies on the part of labor resulting from increased experience. Larger outputs also permit the spreading of fixed costs leading to lower fixed costs per unit of output. Technically, it is incorrect to lump these phenomena together and label the package as economies of scale, since this ignores the distinction between short and long run periods.

Economies of Scope A term which describes a situation where savings derive from a firm's producing a variety of different products rather than their separate production by different firms. This often permits a fuller utilization of productive factors. Multiproduct firms often reflect the presence of economies of scope.

Oligopoly An economic condition or entity in which a few companies dominate a large market; i.e., trade is less concentrated than in a monopoly but there is a lack of general competition. The production of U.S. military aircraft can be regarded as an oligopoly.

Transaction Costs Likened to friction in mechanical systems, they emerge from "planning, adapting, and monitoring task completion" (Williamson, 1979). They may have a significant impact on decisions within a firm about what should be produced *within* the firm and what should be purchased from outside vendors.

I. INTRODUCTION

This entry discusses economic conversion, as well as why it (and its close relative, diversification) is an analytically challenging issue; why conversion has proven difficult in practice; recent experience in the United States, western Europe, China, and Russia; and the role of government policy.

Economic conversion (or, more commonly, simply "conversion") has come to mean different things since Isaiah's vision 2700 years ago of a world in which people would "beat swords into ploughshares, spears into pruning hooks." Economic conversion has been used to describe retraining demobilized soldiers, applying military technology to civilian needs, reusing military bases for civilian purposes, applying military equipment to civilian uses, or even development of "dual-use" technologies. Its most common meaning and the focus of this entry, however, is the redirection of industrial resources (such as personnel, skills, machinery, technology, and funds) from serving a military market (mainly weapons-related) to serving civilian markets.

In general, conversion efforts are linked with reductions in domestic military spending (after all, firms are unlikely to withdraw by choice from a sector of the market that is stable or growing). The enterprises responsible for military production, whether private or state-owned, have a variety of responses to such reductions, from closing no-longer profitable subsidiaries to increasing efforts to export military goods and technology. Their responses will have implications for political leaders, who must deal with issues such as unemployment and weapons-export decisions. If it were easy to shift to civilian markets, conversion would hold the promise of providing an alternative to the social disruption (such as lay-offs) and security problems (such as proliferation of weapons systems or technologies) of reducing defense spending. However, conversion has also proven one of the most difficult alternatives.

Conversion is an especially complex subject because it is at the intersection of different analytic disciplines and different policy communities. For some, conversion simply describes an economic process of responding to market changes. As defense procurement declines, companies respond in predictable ways: seeking alternative markets, redirecting or shutting down production lines, retraining or laying off redundant workers, and so on.

For others, conversion is a policy goal, desirable because it "demilitarizes" the economy, frees resources that can be used to address other social problems, or provides a way to retain skilled labor in existing firms. Advocates of government assistance for conversion make several, often controversial, arguments: defense spending is less productive economically than other types of spending; a large national defense industry is no longer necessary, making it an expensive luxury; pressure to keep such industries alive will translate into foreign arms sales, perhaps to unstable regions or to rogue nations; a robust defense industry will often be perceived by other states as a real or potential threat; arms control efforts are more difficult when they mean loss of jobs; the government should not allow defense enterprises to fail because of the danger of losing talent; defense industry workers deserve special protection against job losses.

In other words, there are those who *describe the process* of conversion and those who *prescribe a policy* of conversion.

Further complicating the issue of conversion are the different levels of analysis. Analyses vary from micro—at the level of the individual worker or firm—to macro—focusing on national policy to aid the conversion process through monetary (central bank) and fiscal (tax and expenditure) policy. It is important to be aware of these different levels, because an *apparent* success at one level can obscure what is actually taking place at another. For example, a decline in the proportion of a company's output going to the military may reflect simply closing (rather than converting) a subsidiary or the acquisition of a civil subsidiary; no "conversion" takes place, but the balance in the company's annual report between military and civil work changes.

Diversification, whether through acquisition of a new subsidiary or indigenous development, further complicates analyses of conversion. Although related, conversion and diversification are quite different concepts. Both deal with problems of adjustment following significant reductions in military spending and the subsequent release of resources, financial, human, and physical capital (plant, equipment, and materials) with minimum dislocation and wastage. That is where the two concepts diverge. In the narrowest sense, conversion focuses on "in place" adjustment where one bundle of resources previously devoted to production for military purposes is refocused to produce civilian goods and services, transforming the same land, plant, equipment, labor force, management, and materials that had previously created weapons or other military system components into a producer for the civil sector.

Diversification, in contrast, means entering a new market *without necessarily leaving the old.* While conversion implies *substituting* the civil market for the military, diversification implies *adding* the civilian market through, for example, acquisition of a new (civilian) subsidiary. (In some discussions, diversification is also used to describe adding additional *military* markets through, for example, exports.) Diversification into civilian markets can be an important part of the conversion process, helping an enterprise acquire experience, expertise, and market share. However, output for the military customer may continue or even increase in absolute terms as a firm diversifies, even though the military *proportion* might decline.

Conversion would be an ideal resolution to the problem of reduced defense spending. However, although attractive in theory, successful conversion continues to be elusive in practice. Successful transformations require that the resources employed in military production be shifted into civilian production with ease, and that a market exists for the new civilian products. As a result, the converting firm thus faces many of the same hurdles confronting a start-up company.

Conversion provides a challenge to scholars and policy makers. In general, studies show that under *some* circumstances, *some* companies can successfully diversify into other areas, including from military to civilian. *Some* individuals can apply the same skills used in the defense industry to equally desirable civilian jobs. *Some* technologies originally developed for the military can find civil markets or be used to produce for the civil sector.

However, studies also suggest that the very characteristics that contribute to military production may impede success in the civilian market. Most efforts at diversification from military to civilian markets, regardless of country, have been difficult or unsuccessful, making firms wary of undertaking it. Skilled defense workers generally have a difficult time finding comparable jobs in the civilian sector, if only because the sector may already be saturated. As a result, the implications for government policy are ambiguous, and depend more on existing views toward industrial policy and intervention in the market than on the specifics of conversion.

The successful conversion efforts after World War II were the result of specific circumstances that highlight the changes that have taken place since that time. On the supply side, many of the principal producers of war material had established markets to which they were able to return. Indeed, it is for this reason that the term used to describe the situation was not "conversion," but "reconversion," emphasizing a return to their traditional activities. The shift of major vehicle producers in the United States, such as Ford and General Motors to the production of military aircraft was facilitated by the government's use of emergency powers to prohibit the production of new passenger cars during the war. In addition, the long years of denial of desires for consumer goods resulting first from the Great Depression and later from shortages of such items, buttressed by the large accumulation of savings, led to an explosion of consumer demand at war's end. Even then, despite the favorable conditions, not all efforts at conversion were successful. (Sandler & Hartley, 1995; Weidenbaum, 1992; Stewart, 1993).

In the United States, and to a lesser extent elsewhere, World War II involved the sudden redirection of civil industry to serve the military needs of the country for a relatively short period of time. In the course of the Cold War (which lasted more than 40 years), specialized defense companies developed because of the increased peacetime spending on military technology. Such companies cannot "return" to recent prewar civil production. As a result, the post-Cold War conversion has been quite different and, in many ways, more difficult than the post-World War II experience.

II. THE ECONOMICS OF CONVERSION

Any market adjustment, including defense conversion, will be more easily accomplished when the level of economic activity is high and the available supply of labor and other resources are nearing complete utilization in meeting the demand for goods and services in the aggregate. Under such circumstances, resources newly released from the military sector would more easily find employment elsewhere, other things remaining unchanged. In the following discussion, however, emphasis will be focused on microeconomic considerations surrounding an individual firm's response to a loss of some fraction of its traditional market. Decisions at this level in response to changes in purchases of military equipment trigger adjustment problems confronted by individuals and communities.

Figure 1 presents a schematic representation of the resource reallocation process triggered by reductions in defense expenditures (the most likely motive to undertake conversion). It traces the direct and indirect consequences of such cuts as they reverberate through the military, defense industries, and their network of suppliers with consequent local, regional, and international implications.

Much of the conversion literature focuses on public policy options and the possible role for government in spurring or facilitating conversion. However, diversification in general, and conversion in particularly, are

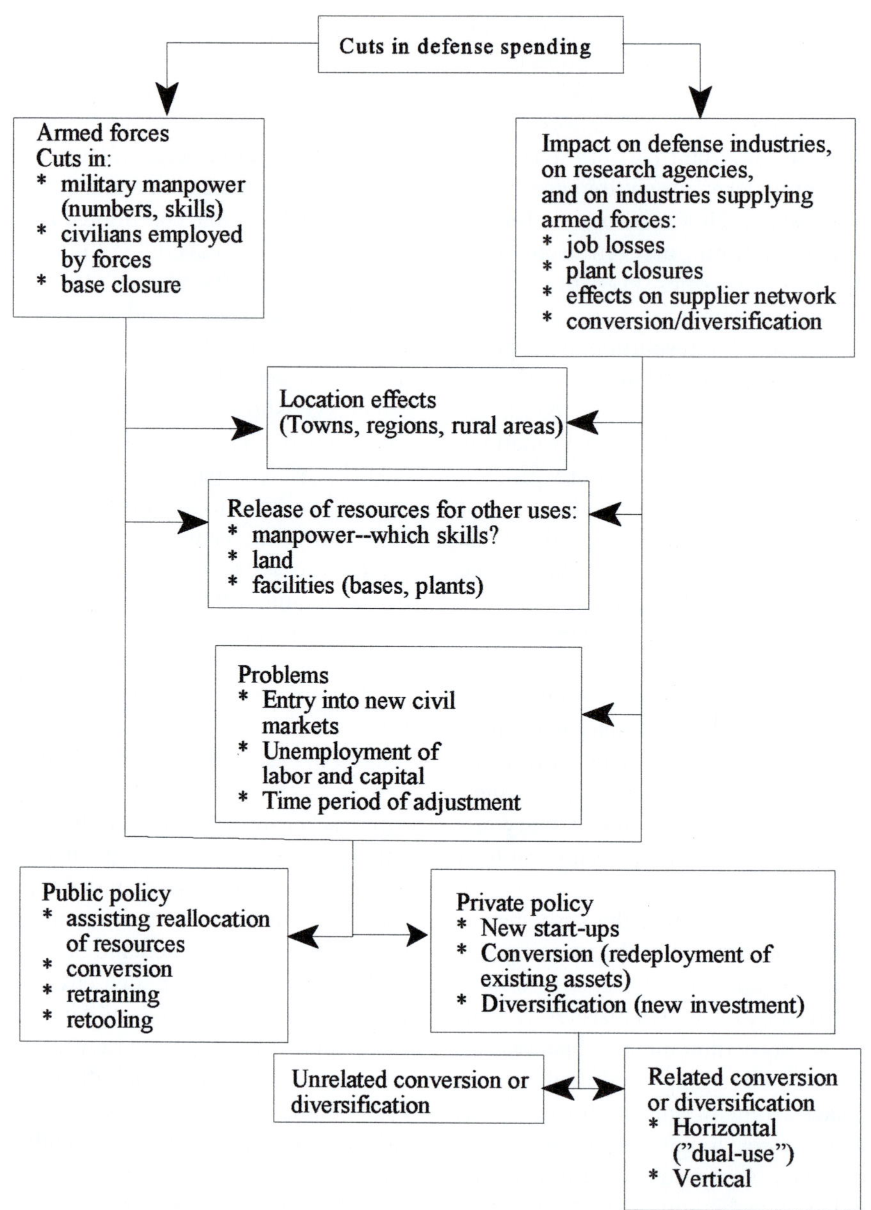

Source: Derived from Sandler and Hartley (1995) and Leech (1993)

FIGURE 1

probably shaped principally by private decision making at the level of the firm in market-based economies; in such economies an optimal policy probably involves some mixture of private and public policies, even if the latter are essentially permissive in nature. In practice, how different countries have addressed the issue of conversion has varied with the degree of dependence on market mechanisms (Sandler & Hartley, 1995). In this sense, adjustment to reduced military spending in market economies is not different in kind from other changes in demand in a dynamic market setting, whether a decline in demand for automobiles (due to trade policies), lumber (due to environmental policies), or tobacco (due to health policies). Like reductions in military spending, each of these examples involves changes in public policy. The principal difference in

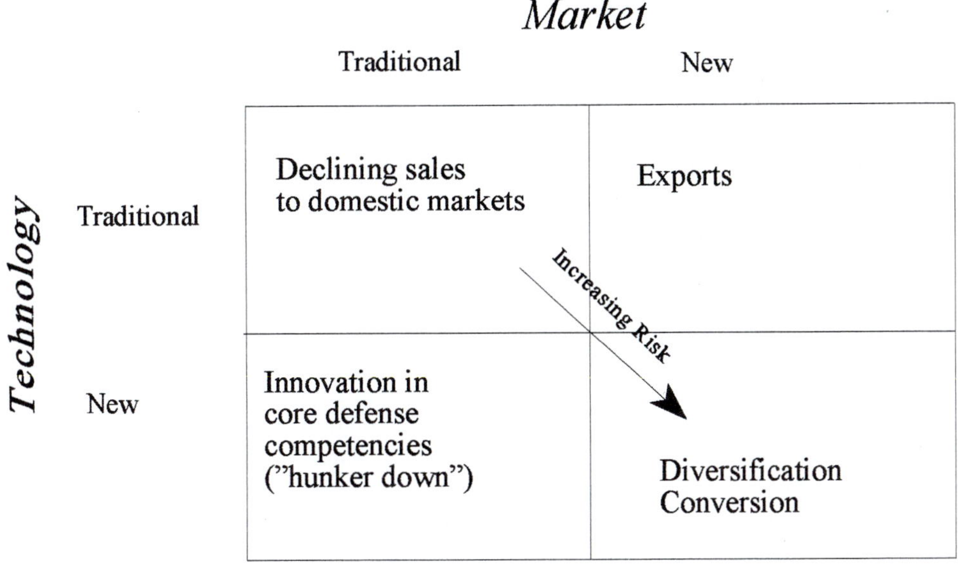

FIGURE 2

conversion is the nature of the customer (typically one government buyer) and the type of market this creates.

Several options are available to military producers experiencing a decline in *domestic* defense spending. In general, the producers must find new markets for existing products, new products for existing markets, or new products for new markets (See Fig. 2). For the defense enterprise, finding new markets for existing products typically entails expanding military exports. Finding new products for the existing domestic defense market might require further concentration on core competencies and a focus on innovation to increase the likelihood of capturing a larger share of a declining market. The riskiest strategy may be the third: seeking new products for new markets.

These approaches (and a firm may try more than one, simultaneously or sequentially) are targeted at replacing declining domestic markets and they represent logical attempts to retain or expand economies of scale or of scope and to minimize transaction costs.

The search for market expansion, however pursued, involves serious consideration by an organization's top management of its core competencies and how and where they should be utilized. As a result, firms are constantly reviewing the boundaries that determine which activities should be conducted within the firm, which outside it, and why (Coase, 1972; Williamson, 1979).

A moment's reflection should indicate the importance of these questions to the issue of conversion. What is it, if not a consideration of what activities might be undertaken within the defense firm (or plant) facing drastic reduction in military contracts? In addition to cost considerations, however, product design, market considerations, and profitability also are important ingredients in the success of conversion attempts. As noted previously, however, most efforts at conversion narrowly defined have failed. Under these circumstances, many firms have turned to export expansion, international collaboration, and mergers and acquisitions.

Defense conversion is difficult for the same reasons that any economic growth is difficult. But these challenges are compounded by the unique position of the defense sector within each country: how the sector affects politics and how politics affect the sector. In the following sections, we will focus on the general problems affecting conversion efforts and some of the varieties of experience in different countries. We will begin by discussing some of the general obstacles and difficulties encountered in attempting conversion and diversification and developments in export efforts by defense firms. Thereafter, we present specific illustrative cases and experiences in Western Europe, the United States, China, and Russia, and we conclude with a discussion of the role of government and general conclusions.

A. Obstacles to Conversion/Diversification

Conversion is nothing new to the defense industries. Many firms and governments have explored or pursued conversion efforts, especially with the winding down of the Cold War from the late 1980s. Global defense spending (in 1994 dollars) peaked in 1987 at about $1.3 trillion, falling to $840 billion in 1994, while military exports had peaked in 1984 at $84 billion, and fell to $22 billion 10 years later. The decline is reflected in the loss of nearly 7 million defense industry jobs worldwide, from the 17.5 million peak in 1988 to the 10.9 million in 1995 (WMEAT; BICC). In addition to shedding employees, defense firms also undertook a process of consolidation, mergers, and restructuring that resulted in a smaller number of larger corporations and holding companies. The deep declines in spending provided a strong incentive to convert; the limited successes in doing so, especially when compared with alternatives such as exports or consolidation, reemphasizes the difficulties of conversion. But what are these difficulties, and where do they originate?

As noted earlier, conversion successes (defined as substituting a civilian market for a military one with minimal changes in personnel, technologies, etc.) are relatively rare. Indeed, entering a new market is almost always difficult for any firm. But beyond the general challenges associated with entering new markets, there are crucial differences in the nature of the military and civilian markets that profoundly affect the firms themselves. The fundamental difference between military production and civilian production has been, and remains, that the former is driven mainly by performance requirements set by (typically) a single buyer, while the civil market is driven mainly by costs (determined by constantly changing market pressures).

The emphasis on performance (quality) for military hardware and the associated escalating costs, plus the radically changed geopolitical situation have led to a situation in which military procurement has dropped precipitously, in contrast with mass production of consumer goods and very large outputs of traditional military products during World War II and the Korean War. Instead of annual outputs numbered in the thousands of items as during the wars of the mid-20th century, output fell to the hundreds and, in some cases, the tens.

Not only did such change in output volume affect the familiar phenomena of economies of scale and scope, but they brought a dramatic change in what might be called the culture of the defense industry. When such firms consider a shift to consumer products, culture shock often will be encountered. This point was made by an executive of a Dutch aerospace firm, who noted that early efforts by his firm to enter new markets through acquisition failed in part because the acquired firms retained their peculiar corporate cultures in the newly merged enterprise. This required the top officials of the newly integrated firm to give up the culture of an aircraft firm and become a more general business-oriented management—a transition they were unable or unwilling to accomplish (Udis, 1993). The chairman of Boeing, discussing the aircraft company's merger with McDonnell Douglas, noted that most mergers do not live up to the expectations of the companies. "The reason is usually that corporate culture issues don't get addressed." (Kitfield, 1997, p. 40)

Other areas in which traditional Cold War military producers experience was different from that of producers in consumer/commercial markets include marketing, advertising, finance, accounting, investment, law and regulation, design, quality control, competition, security, labor relations, intellectual property rights, and many others. Depending on the country, these differences are often so pronounced that firms producing both for military and commercial markets have gone to great lengths to keep the operations completely separate from one another in different departments or plants. While it may be harsh to suggest that the managers responsible to the military customer had developed a "trained incapacity" to survive in commercial markets (Adelman & Augustine, 1992), it is clear that management optimized for the defense market is likely to be "sub-optimal" for the civil. (A very similar conclusion is reached in a recent report of the European Union Commission for Industrial Policy. See Commission of the European Communities, 1996.)

Such incapacity is mainly the result of the unique conditions imposed upon firms and their managers by the military buyers. In the United States, such conditions are imposed by both the military services and the U.S. Congress. Recent studies of the weapons acquisition process in the United States, conclude that the web of regulations is the principal factor preventing the consolidation of military and civil production work in the same facilities (Gansler, 1995; McNaugher, 1989). Any hope of utilizing such consolidation as a key to more easily permitting the shift of production between military and civil work will be largely frustrated by this phenomenon. The transactions costs encountered in such an effort appear to be overwhelming.

While some countries such as the United Kingdom and France have made efforts to reform their weapons acquisition processes, such as the establishment of "procurement executives" to disengage the individual armed services from the details of the actual procurement process, there is little evidence that the basic problem has been corrected. The nature of the military bureaucracy and the art of dealing with it requires that defense firms be highly specialized.

B. Varieties of Experience

Thus far, we have examined conceptual and theoretical aspects of conversion and diversification. We now turn to a review of experiences and "real-world" attempts at conversion and diversification. We shall examine the United States, Western Europe, Russia and China to sample efforts in both market and nonmarket economies.

III. U.S. CONVERSION EXPERIENCE

In the United States, in the 1990s, the defense industry has placed heavy reliance on mergers and acquisitions to attain diversification. At one extreme is General Dynamics, which sold its well-known F-16 military aircraft division to Lockheed and for a while is believed to have considered going out of business after distributing its high cash reserves to stockholders. Instead, it acquired Chrysler's Land Warfare Division, which produced heavy tanks, and Electric Boat Company, a significant producer of nuclear powered naval vessels (submarines). In less than 2 years, it acquired four military speciality houses, including Bath Iron Works naval shipyard. The company purchased another producer of armored vehicles and attempted, unsuccessfully, to buy United Defense, the remaining producer of tracked armored vehicles. Clearly, GD desires to become a major player in armored combat vehicles and nuclear-propelled naval vessels.

GD also purchased Lucent Technologies' Advanced Technology Systems unit, which supplies undersea surveillance systems, signal processing defense systems, and related defense technologies. Referring to the Lucent purchase, the chairman of GD observed that "this acquisition strengthens GD's position as a global leader in total systems integration for marine and ground combat weapons platforms." The president of Lucent Technologies unit making the sale observed he was selling the business because "it doesn't fit well with the core communications operations" (*Washington Post*, August 22, 1997, p. G2). Every completed voluntary transaction involves a satisfied buyer and seller.

While GD is clearly choosing to concentrate on specific defense niches, other companies are taking different approaches involving diversification and even selling defense lines. North American Rockwell has sold its space shuttle operations and its B-1 bomber division to Boeing while keeping its Collins unit, which focuses on communications and avionics. International Telephone and Telegraph is now selling its marine radar units to individual boat owners and its advanced night vision optical equipment to mariners, hunters, and other outdoor enthusiasts. Private and public security organizations have also found such equipment attractive. Raytheon has sold its Amana group, moving it out of the consumer big-ticket white goods field while expanding its involvement in heavy construction, often for governmental units. Lockheed-Martin is utilizing its simulation skills to develop video games, and has apparently completed its search for a partner knowledgeable in marketing to arcade operators. And Hughes, while continuing to produce space satellites for large communications firms, is now manufacturing the small boxes that are necessary to transmit the signals into home reception from direct broadcast. Hughes is also producing automated toll road fee-collection equipment.

Among the least surprising market adjustments is the effort by many military aircraft and components producers to shift resources to the production and control of civil passenger aircraft. Such firms include major aircraft producers such as Boeing and McDonnell Douglas, aircraft engine firms such as Rolls Royce, General Electric, and Pratt and Whitney, and avionics and related producers like Hughes, Rockwell Collins, and Honeywell. Several of the latter are also entering the market for air traffic control systems.

What conclusions can one draw from such disparate examples? For one thing, corporate cultures go a long way to define core competencies. The latter are not just technology-geared as is often assumed. The identification of markets within which corporate executives are comfortable is important. General Dynamics is clearly at ease selling to the military and sees "diversification" as selling to the several different military services. GD's behavior suggests that it may be more difficult to master the art of selling to the military (mastering its web of regulations) than to produce military equipment. For firms like GD, this mastery of marketing to the military may constitute a major comparative advantage.

Another point, not unrelated to the GD case, reflects the concerns of the management with market share as a goal or index of success. Economists have long recognized that in the presence of oligopolies, firm executives may substitute their personal utility functions for the traditional profit maximization goals assumed in perfectly competitive models. Most of America's prime defense contractors qualify as oligopolies and thus, one can easily conceive of managers deciding on market entry and exit to enhance their probabilities of attaining first or second rank in particular market segments.

The risk of overreliance on particular customers has

clearly motivated defense producers to seek greater diversification of markets. One can observe this in several of the above examples. In most cases, the process involves a rather conservative definition of core competency and even selection of new markets. Thus, a focus on selling to the world's major airlines and airports is a far cry from selling to individual consumers and households. In addition, in many cases defense firms venturing into new water (so to speak), move cautiously, for example moving from selling to the Defense Department to civil markets in which the buyers are still government agencies, whether federal, state, or municipal.

The case of Hughes moving from a focus on hardware (producing space satellites) to owning a portion of the resulting communications system may reflect a belief that the latter is permanent, while the particular hardware used may change over time. The North American Rockwell case noted earlier may be another example of the same belief. The IT&T case may reflect a spillover from its sales of marine radar and night-vision equipment to private and public security agencies, in order to experiment in consumer markets.

The principal conclusion to be drawn from recent experience is the corporate preference for mergers and acquisitions to attempts to convert, reflecting the difficulties most firms see in conversion and the corporate predilection for "hunkering down" in response to reductions in defense spending. At the same time, the very merger and acquisition process, when it extends to nondefense firms, may be introducing the managerial skills that the next generation of defense firms will need to enter civilian markets successfully.

IV. EUROPEAN ATTEMPTS AT CONVERSION

An important determinant of behavior is the strength of the national commitment to retain a complete, domestic, defense industrial base. A government may seek to preserve its defense industry by subsidizing defense production, or it may try to retain much of the defense industry's general capabilities by supporting conversion to analogous or comparable civilian goods. Some countries have conceded their inability to afford this luxury across the board, and, as in the case of Switzerland, have abandoned the goal of maintaining a capacity to design and build advanced military aircraft, for example, relying instead on imports of foreign aircraft. Sweden also has shown signs of moving in this direction via the retention of the design role, but attempting to control production costs via innovative partnering with larger foreign firms.

While the number of attempts at conversion in Europe is limited and the number of successes even smaller, the experience mirrors much of that in the United States and elsewhere. One point highlighted by European experience in particular, however, is the usefulness of early notification for firms facing the loss of a significant share of their military markets. Such early warning enables the firm to plan to take compensatory action. The German aerospace firm Dornier acquired subcontracting work on the Airbus project, which required significant investment in infrastructure, special machinery and tooling, largely financed by the company. In addition it invested heavily in R&D and production planning for its Dornier 228 commuter aircraft with a break-even point and return on investment in the distant and uncertain future.

Perhaps most interesting is the case of the Lithotripter, a new medical device to nonsurgically destroy kidney stones. It was derived from military-supported R&D at Dornier. Here one had, it would appear, a classic example of conversion; a highly useful direct transfer of aerospace technology to cure a widespread medical problem. Tracing this case should yield some interesting points. Initially, Dornier's Lithotripter was highly successful and gave the company a monopoly in this slice of the medical equipment market. Its success became well known, and Siemens, which traditionally had been a market leader in the field, entered the market a few years later with a somewhat different machine. Facing increasing competition from Siemens, Dornier responded by establishing a subsidiary in the United States, and investing in a second generation of medical equipment designed to treat gallstones. In the interim, Dornier had been absorbed into the newly formed Daimler Benz Aerospace. From this point, much hinged on whether Dornier's new parent would retain an interest in the medical equipment market. In a subsequent dispute between Daimler Benz and the Dornier family interests, 80% of the Dornier Medizintechnik GmbH (which controlled the lithotripter) was sold to Singapore Technologies, Pte., in March 1996. For the foreseeable future, production (and, thus, employment) will continue in the Munich area. However, some fears were undoubtedly raised concerning the possibility of a future transfer of this production to Asia.

The principal lesson of the lithotripter case is that the innovative use of defense (in this case, aerospace) technology does not assure success in the new market. Other traditional leaders in established markets challenged by the newcomer will counterattack. Unless the new entrant has access to significant financial backing, it may be forced to license its technology to established leaders or to sell out completely.

While Dornier's action was socially desirable in bringing a new and useful device into public use, there is, however, no necessary happy ending which guarantees that the innovating firm or division will succeed. Indeed, in 1996, Dornier Medizintechnik lost DM 8.88 million due to heavy R&D spending and problems with its American subsidiary, Acoustics Imaging Technologies of Phoenix, Arizona. A final point deals with profitability *per se*. Even had lithotripter remained profitable, how far would those profits have gone to replace loss of profits resulting from loss of aerospace business by Dornier? Evidence on this point is difficult to obtain, but several years ago an official of the Dutch aerospace firm Fokker commented that

> As far as my experience goes, the spinoff we have had from commercial aircraft business has been marketable in a limited number of cases. However, these spinoffs, so far, have been special technical applications [for] which the market in the world is very small indeed.... All-in-all, the turnover in these areas is about two percent of total business and one wonders whether that is worth the effort. (Udis, 1993, p. 157.)

A very interesting case of diversification via acquisition is found in the French firm, Matra. In the early 1970s, Matra was completely dependent on defense contracts. The company's chief executive, concerned about the risks of such dependency, sought to use the company's defense profits to diversify by buying or creating new high-technology-based companies. Several of the early efforts, such as those involving clockmaking and automobile components, failed. However, Matra's sponsorship of a Formula 1 racing car team and its development of a sports car led to its design of the highly successful "Espace" vehicle, which is distributed by Renault and which has a Renault engine manufactured at a Matra factory. Matra also merged with Hachette, one of France's leading publishers, which provided a presence in both publishing and press technology. Matra has also developed business lines in space, telecommunications, and the design and production of unmanned metro trains. As a result of these efforts, by 1993, Matra was only 20% dependent on defense contracts.

The general lessons to be drawn from the experiences of Matra (and others) are that successful conversion is likely to take considerable time, effort, and investment; it can be accomplished largely without direct government support, but it is easier when the firm has the security of public contracts during the transition—there is no sudden ending of defense contracts; conversion benefits from the continuous commitment of the top executives of the firm and of centralized ownership interests as well; and conversion is easier when companies were acquired that had a different culture from that of the military industry. These companies brought a market understanding with them that assisted in the process of changing the culture (Udis, 1993).

A few comments on French policy would be appropriate at this point. France has pursued an active industrial policy longer than almost any other state. Intervention by French governments to encourage the growth of new industries and technologies has a long tradition and Jean Baptiste Colbert, minister to Louis XIV of France, has been identified as the first global and consistent industrial strategist. His policies combined protection from foreign competition with incentives (grants of monopoly and patents, subsidies, and training programs) to develop advanced technology and modern industry in France.

It would also appear logical to connect such policies with the problem under discussion here—adjustment to reduced military spending. Both areas face the same challenge: to devise government policies that would help bridge stages in economic life; in the one case from older to newer technologies, and, in the other, from heavier to lighter concentrations on defense production. Indeed, many recommended policies in the conversion literature are borrowed from the broader industrial policy area (Udis, 1987). Such bridging or "pump-priming," to be successful, must help affected industries and sectors move to new activities and ultimately become sufficiently entrenched to no longer require government support.

A careful analysis of French experience with industrial policy identifies a common thread differentiating successes from failures: the nature of the market. Thus,

> In ... three sectors [energy, aerospace, and electronics] French industry has been able to reach an advanced technological level and an internationally competitive position ... Why is this so ... ? A common characteristic is heavy dependence on government procurement and state intervention in industries for which government is the main customer; it appears less successful in those producing consumer goods and general industrial equipment ... The reason is because the main objective of government in the more suc-

> cessful sectors has been national security . . . Even if these industrial policies have subsequently produced applications in non-military areas, their origins can almost always be traced to a desire to preserve national independence. (Stoffaes, 1986, p. 44.)

The experience in Europe in general reflects that of the French: it is a market that makes transformation possible. Conversion in place does not yet sustain much hope in replacing lost defense markets. A string of profitable lithotripter-like or Matra-like successes and a commitment to conversion goals, well-managed by corporate leadership liberated from the heavy weight of military procurement culture, would appear necessary—an unlikely chain of events.

V. THE RUSSIAN EXPERIENCE

When Mikhail Gorbachev came to power in 1985, he inherited an atrophying civilian economy and a defense sector that, while costly, seemed robust and effective. In an effort to invigorate the civilian sector, he undertook a series of steps to transfer skills (mostly managerial and administrative) from the defense to the civilian sector. He shifted defense industry leaders to civilian production; created civilian versions of important defense industry oversight organizations; and, eventually, simply turned more than 200 civilian factories over to the defense industrial ministries to run.

When these steps did not achieve the desired results quickly enough, Gorbachev turned to a large-scale conversion effort, promised in a December 1988 speech to the United Nations. As developed by government officials over the next several months, the Soviet conversion program was to be phased in gradually and on an experimental basis.

The Soviet conversion program was part of a larger economic reform effort undertaken by Gorbachev. The Law on Soviet State Enterprises, starting the process of freeing enterprises from the often-stultifying controls of the ministries, had been passed in 1987. The economic reform debate continued at the same time that conversion was supposed to be implemented.

The original goal of the Soviet conversion program was relatively modest: increase the defense sector's output of commercial goods from 40% in the late 1980s to 60% by 1995. By 1995, some level of conversion was to take place at 422 enterprises throughout the Soviet Union. Military production would be reduced by:

- 10% at 124 enterprises (29%);
- 10–20% in 118 enterprises (28%);
- 20–30% in 56 enterprises (12%);
- 30% or more in 124 enterprises (29%).

Only three plants were to be totally converted.

In other words, a relatively small number of the Soviet Union's 2000 to 5000 defense enterprises (estimates vary) would undertake any reduction in military production as part of the conversion plan, and most would reduce their production by less than 20% over 5 years. Such an approach was designed to be gradual and manageable. And while many of the defense industry managers were hostile to the addition of new civilian goods to their portfolios, most accepted this conversion by the plan.

The process was upset, however, by a series of problems. Economic reform meant that defense enterprises were responsible for covering their own costs, driving the costs of weapons systems up. Spending on military procurement, on the other hand, was being reduced, gradually at first but by a sharp 32% in 1991 and a further 68% the following year. As in other countries, the "psychology" of the defense industry, in which performance was often the paramount consideration, was also quite different from that in civilian industry, where cost is often at least as important. There were frequent press reports of civilian products that were "state of the art," but which were extremely expensive and, thus, for which there was no market. There was also only rudimentary experience in market assessment; in general, the enterprises were unprepared to enter a competitive civilian marketplace (Almquist & O'Prey, 1990).

The problems created by the combination of deep cuts, escalating costs, and inexperience in the civil sector were compounded by the elimination of the centralized planning apparatus and the industrial ministries at the end of 1991. The economic circumstances of the country, ranging from the freeing of most prices to the extremely high inflation rates and the nonpayment or delayed payment by the Ministry of Defense on its defense orders, shifted conversion from being desirable and planned to absolutely critical and almost completely unplanned. As the centralized conversion effort foundered, it became apparent that conversion was taking place "from below." As Julian Cooper noted in 1991,

> for most enterprises of the defense industry the protracted discussion of plans for conversion has become an irrelevance. For up to two years many of them have been attempting to cope with the serious practical problems generated by reduced

> military orders under circumstances of progressive economic dislocation and a breakdown of the traditional structures of authority. (Cooper, p. 139)

A reported 300,000 defense sector workers were made redundant in 1991.

The collapse of the Soviet Union and its defense industrial ministries meant that the managers were suddenly, in a sense, independent. But unlike the Chinese case, in which economic growth and a relative economic stability made it possible to *support* such increased independence, the Soviet (and then Russian) economy was closer to collapse, and the central government was able to provide little or no support to the restructuring of the defense sector. In the Russian case, some managers embraced the new independence and moved quickly to reform their factory and to find new products and markets. A small fraction of these has been successful. Many remained shocked.

The result has been the devastation of the defense sector. By 1997, only a reported 5% of its defense enterprises were stable, mostly due to military exports. From a peak employment estimated at from 7 to 10 million in the late 1980s, the defense industries (excluding the nuclear industry) reportedly now employ 2.5 million people. (VPK Internet) The average number of workers in defense plants declined by more than 12% from 1995 to 1996, while the workers who remain are often those approaching pension age (for whom finding new work is likely to be difficult).

Further, only a fraction of the "employed" people are actually working full time at defense industrial enterprises. Many are working reduced hours, many are on forced leave, and few are paid on time. (Russia was not alone in declining defense industry employment. According to the Bonn International Center for Conversion, global defense industry employment fell from a 1987 high of 17.5 million to around 11.1 million in 1995.)

Overall wages in the defense sector are now substantially below the average wage in Russian industry, and nonmonetary benefits (ranging from health and schooling to vacation resorts and apartments) are being reduced as well. Defense enterprises have often tried to turn responsibility for these services over to the local governments, which, in turn, are often also in financially difficult straits.

New investment in defense industries is rare. When government funds are released to defense enterprises, they are typically used to pay salaries and outstanding debts, not for retooling or updating equipment. The situation of the employees, in particular, is too immediate. At times it has required strikes, or the threat of strikes, to force the government to provide additional money to pay the workers. In early 1997, for example, 30 billion rubles was transferred to the State Nuclear Shipbuilding Center at Severodvinsk to end the strike there. The government owed the Center's enterprises 1.6 trillion rubles, while workers, unpaid for several months, were owed 350 billion rubles.

The national government has proven unable to pay many of its debts or to follow through on its commitments. At the end of 1996, the Russian Ministry of Defense reportedly owed more than 40 trillion rubles, for everything from servicemen's pay to weapons systems, and it is not clear when and how the government will be able to clear this debt. Defense industry, in turn, owes 66 trillion rubles to its creditors. Even the funds allocated in the Russian budget are often not released by the Ministry of Finance, which holds a very tight rein on Russian government spending. Although 20.7 trillion rubles were budgeted for the Ministry of Defense in the first quarter of 1997, the Ministry of Finance released only 11 trillion rubles.

The abrupt collapse of the domestic Russian defense market meant that the defense enterprises had to find new products for civilian markets, find new markets for existing military and civilian products, persuade the government to provide some type of financial protection, or close. Each approach presents Russian decisionmakers with a variety of problems; pursuing all, as has taken place, may only compound the problems.

Converting enterprises—redirecting the resources from military production to civilian—is extremely difficult in the best of circumstances. In many ways, conversion is targeted economic development constrained by the assets and structures that already exist. As a result, it requires major commitments of both time and money, neither of which the Russians have. Making the process even more difficult is the opposition to conversion by those concerned that military capabilities will be lost, that technical development may be hindered, or that civilian work is less challenging or important than military. As a result, conversion is economically and politically daunting.

Two types of conversion have been taking place in Russia's defense sector: workers have left enterprises (sometimes by choice, sometimes not) for more profitable work, and those left behind have tried to find profitable work for their enterprises. While most attention is paid to converting enterprises, it is important to remember that the most successful type of conversion may be taking place *outside* an enterprise, not in it.

The hundreds of thousands of men and women who have left the defense sector have, in a sense, already converted themselves. While data is lacking, it is likely that many of the most talented and flexible personnel have gone on to find work in other parts of Russia's economy where they see greater opportunities. These opportunities may be in areas related to their previous work, but many are likely to be in completely new fields. For these people, conversion has become a fact of life—they are redirecting their talents from military production to work in other areas of the economy.

Where conversion is barely working, if at all, is at the defense enterprises themselves. Redirecting an enterprise from one product line to another, even in a related line of business, is seldom easy, and converting from military production to civilian is even more challenging. Defense enterprises, striving to meet military requirements, are often highly specialized, while management expertise and skills are optimized for a market quite different in both approach and substance from that encountered in the civilian sector. Further, civilian markets are likely to be already highly competitive. As a result, there are few contemporary success stories in any country of an enterprise retaining its workforce and switching to profitable civilian production.

The Russian government's efforts to budget money for conversion has been stalled by the continuing sequestering of funds by the Ministry of Finance (in 1996, only 11% of the budget allocations for conversion was funded). As already noted, some enterprises were barred from privatization, closing off one potential source of new investment. But even if the government were able to allocate funds, it is not clear how the government can best spend the money. For example, should conversion funds be used to invest in specific current projects, sustain individual enterprises with potential, or to develop projects outside existing enterprises?

Domestic private investment in the defense sector has also been limited, mainly because defense industries, already deeply in debt, are likely to be of little interest to private investors (the main exception may be those exporting weapons, discussed below). While interest rates have fallen, they remain at more than 30%, making it expensive to borrow for restructuring purposes in an economy with limited domestic demand.

Private ownership of, and investment in, defense enterprises remains controversial. According to the Russian press, at the end of 1996 more than 400 defense industry enterprises remained fully state-owned, while the state held either a controlling block or a large share of stock in another 1000 enterprises (this state ownership, however, apparently does not bring investment, just control). The remaining 600 were mostly non-state owned. But no clear link between ownership and successful conversion or even enterprise continuity has been established, perhaps because so many other factors, from the limitations on labor mobility to supply problems, affect success or failure at conversion and restructuring efforts.

Enterprises have also sought foreign investment, and while there have been some notable successes (especially in the aerospace area), enterprise managers often have little understanding of how to attract such funds. Foreign investment is also hampered by the complexity and changeability of Russia's laws affecting it.

The lack of government funds and investment has sent enterprise managers scrambling to find opportunities of almost any type, and some have been moderately successful. The Russian press has been very active in reporting apparent successes, such as the Tula Machine Plant's production of motor scooters, the Voronezh Mechanical Plant's oil and gas industry products, and production at various shipyards for the civilian market. Energiya, an enterprise working with foreign companies mainly on commercial space applications, has announced that it will pay dividends to holders of preferred shares, suggesting some success.

But these moderate successes are not the norm. As already noted, more than 300 defense enterprises were insolvent in late 1996. Even Arzamas-16, Russia's first nuclear weapons lab, had bankruptcy proceedings initiated against it (the effort was subsequently dropped). The Director of Chelyabinsk-70, the other main nuclear weapons design institute, killed himself in 1996, apparently in part due to the financial plight of his institute. The Ministry of Atomic Energy, responsible for designing and producing nuclear weapons, is reportedly more than 500 billion rubles in debt to its creditors.

In addition to investment, conversion at an industrial enterprise also takes time. The process of identifying a market, determining the product line, retooling and retraining (if needed), and manufacturing may require years, at a time when day-to-day survival is often in question. And once production is possible, it may take years to turn a profit. The Russian and export markets have thus far had little interest in the products of Russian industry, prompting President Yeltsin's "Buy Russian" initiative of early 1997.

And, finally, the ability to restructure and sustain a converted enterprise depends on the expertise of its management in matching capabilities with demands, finding resources, protecting the interests of the plant, etc. The cadre of Russian defense industrial managers has proven that it is not monolithic; some embrace the opportunities inherent in a conversion effort, while others are wary of the dangers. But most industrial managers are holdovers from the Soviet era, learning "in real time" how a market economy operates.

With such formidable hurdles to conversion, it is not surprising that an enterprise involved in military production would prefer to continue in that line of work, simply changing customers. In contrast to conversion, arms sales hold the promise of foreign revenues, timely payment or government guarantees that can be borrowed against, and minimal changes in managerial expertise.

The Russian experience casts significant light on the "universality" of several fundamental challenges facing conversion efforts. In a planned economy such as existed in the Soviet Union, conversion should have been relatively straightforward: changing the input and output requirements of specific enterprises, with the state absorbing the costs and inefficiencies involved in such a transformation. So long as either the economy was healthy or isolated enough to absorb the inefficiencies or there were few alternatives, the system could make the changes.

But with the collapse of the Soviet economy and the weaknesses of the Russian one, conversion remains dependent on foreign largesse and indigenous scrambling.

VI. THE CHINESE EXPERIENCE

China's defense conversion effort—one of the significant components of Deng Xiaoping's effort to modernize China's economy—is an attempt to rationalize the overbuilt Chinese defense sector. Between 1964 and 1971, China had invested heavily in creating "a huge self-sufficient industrial base area to serve as a strategic reserve in the event of China being drawn into war" (Naughton). The effort was considered so important that Beijing devoted more than half China's total investment during the Third Five Year Plan (1966–1970) to developing this so-called "Third Front." The result was the establishment of nearly 30,000 enterprises in China's remote interior, 2200 of them large- or medium-sized. Fifty-five percent of the country's defense plants are reportedly located in the Third Front region (Frankenstein, 1997).

Conversion has been an attempt by Deng and his successors to turn China's "oversized yet underdeveloped" defense industry from a burden into an asset. Mao's death in September 1976 and Deng's rehabilitation the following year opened a cycle of reforms that included a renewed emphasis on the Four Modernizations (industry, agriculture, defense, and science and technology), originally proposed by premier Zhou Enlai in 1975. The conversion effort, announced in late 1978 and developed over the next few years, was part of the package of economic reforms intended to improve the Chinese standard of living through reforms in agricultural, industrial, and economic policy. In 1979, defense modernization was pushed to fourth place in the hierarchy of modernizations.

By 1981, it was estimated that half the defense industry's capacity was idle (Folta, 1992). The following year, Deng argued that the defense industry should combine military and civilian work, an idea that would be codified in 1982 as the 16 character slogan:

> Integrate military production with civilian production,
> meet the needs of both peace-time and wartime,
> military production has priority, and
> use civilian production to support military production.

That same year, the National Defense Science and Technology Committee and the National Defense Industries Organization were combined to form the Commission on Science, Technology, and Industry for National Defense (COSTIND) to coordinate defense production, and took a leading role in implementing the sector's civilian production.

By 1983, according to one Chinese analysis of the country's conversion experience, the overall conversion situation "was one where it was difficult to either advance or retreat." The period from 1979 to the early 1980s had been characterized by "laissez-faire" or "spontaneous" conversion, in which enterprises, confronted with declines in military orders, chose their civil products. The result was oversupply, production surplus, and idle plants.

In 1985, the Chinese leadership reassessed the country's security situation, and concluded that no major threat loomed for the foreseeable future. China reduced its defense spending, announced the demobilization of a million men, and cut military procurement. Around this time, according to one report, "more than half the military factories stopped or drastically reduced production because of the cut in military procurement" (Crane and Yeh, p. 108). Conversion—finding economically viable alternatives for the country's defense enterprises and defense industrial personnel—became increasingly important.

At the same time, China was undertaking another wave of economic reform, deemphasizing centralized planning and increasing reliance on market mechanisms. As a result of the reforms undertaken since 1978, rural incomes increased, leading to increased demand for industrial production of consumer goods (Dernberger, 1996). Rural industries were freed of many of the restrictions that had limited their development, and quickly grew to compete with the urban state-owned industries. State-owned enterprises were allowed to retain some of profits and sell output above plan targets at market prices. They were also given greater autonomy in making decisions about production, pricing, purchases, and investments. Industry became the primary engine of China's economic growth (Naughton, 1996).

Military production remained under centralized control, but the civilian work in defense enterprises became market driven. But given the unsatisfactory results of the unfettered conversion efforts since 1979, the government decided to intervene to provide some guidance. In 1986, the policy-making Central Military Commission and the State Council approved a list of 126 items to promote the integration of civilian and military production. Special loans totaling 820 million yuan (out of an investment fund of 1.2 billion yuan) were made to the defense sector. In 1988, the government issued another list, this time of 170 items.

In addition, during the Seventh Five Year Plan (1986–1990), the state invested almost 4 billion yuan in loans and built 450 civilian product lines, allowing almost 50% of the enterprises to produce mainstay civilian products. During the Eighth Five Year Plan (1991–1995), the state also supported more than 400 defense conversion technological modification items with loans of 6.3 billion yuan. As a result of these efforts, all military enterprises were producing civilian products, and between 80 to 90% of military industrial enterprises were able to produce one or two mainstay civilian items.

During this same period, Peoples Liberation Army (PLA) units were encouraged to establish or invest in their own enterprises to raise funds to offset budget reductions. In contrast to the state-run military factories, these enterprises typically do not produce military equipment (Anderton, 1996). Serving military personnel were being "converted" to businessmen in PLA-run enterprises, while the separate and distinct defense industry enterprises and factories were trying to find civilian products and markets.

The Chinese have emphasized that their conversion efforts have been successful, noting in their November 1995 Arms Control White Paper that civilian output of the defense sector has increased from just 8% in 1970 to approximately 80% today. However, such data only indicate that the proportion of civil production has increased, revealing nothing about changes in military output. Information about the actual changes in military production that accompany conversion efforts are important for establishing that trade-offs are, in fact, being made, and that civilian production is replacing, not just augmenting, military work (diversification). Indeed, civilian output would appear to grow if the military output were reduced.

Despite China's upbeat claims about its conversion effort, the country's experience indicates how difficult and costly conversion is, even in the best circumstances. China has enjoyed one of the fastest growing economies in the world; changes in Chinese military thinking and the absence of a significant external threat has allowed Beijing to make significant reductions in its military acquisition programs; and the Chinese government has been willing and able to mobilize substantial political and economic resources to support conversion.

Even with these advantages, perhaps two out of three converting enterprises barely break even or take a loss. By the early 1990s, fewer than half the defense-related firms had found either viable commercial goods to manufacture or commercial services to offer, and most had reportedly found only a single product to assemble (Tai, 1992). Most of the products of the conversion effort, such as fans and air conditioners, refrigerators, clothing and shoes, and pharmaceuticals, are in relatively low-technology areas. Only 20% of the civilian production by Chinese defense firms is in machinery, electronics, and other high technology products (Lee, 1995).

The defense industries are regularly cited as among those state-owned enterprises (SOEs) that are losing money. The enterprises of the former Ministry of Ordnance are apparently in the worst shape. According to the Chinese, while industrywide profits were greater than losses in 1992, only 60 industries in the ordnance sector (formerly under the Ministry of Ordnance) made a profit on civilian products, while 96 produced civilian products at a loss. In other words, the few successes were successful enough to offset the losses. A detailed discussion of the ordnance industry in Heijlongjiang Province in Northeast China claimed that 60% of the 68,900 workers at nine ordnance plants are "surplus," and that 6000 people have been either dismissed or "diverted" to other sectors, including farming.

It should also be emphasized that conversion in China is part of at least two complementary efforts. The first is to use the underutilized capacity in the defense sector to support the country's economic development. The second, however, is to use the benefits of conversion—the profits and the technical development—to support China's military capabilities. Thus, Ding Henggao, then-Chairman of COSTIND, noted that "the importation of technology, the utilization of foreign capital, and international technical cooperation and exchange, which takes multiple forms, have all been remarkably successful, giving China a new open look. All these achievements have laid the groundwork for the further development of defense S&T." (*Zhongguo Junshi Kexue,* 1995)

The Jialing Machinery Plant, often cited as a successful conversion effort because of its popular motorcycle line, planned to invest 15 million yuan from its civilian profits into military development and production. Nanjing's Plant 511, the main enterprise of the Jincheng Motorcycle Group, reports that while only 1 percent of the plant's 1 billion yuan was accounted for by military production, *half* the plant's staff are in the military section, subsidized in part by the civilian profits. The Changhong Machine Building Plant, which produced radars and now produces televisions, reported that two-thirds of its technical force is kept for military development even when the military production value has dropped from 90% of the total in 1981 to 2.1% in 1990. Funds from civilian sales are used to keep the military sector in operation.

While converting enterprises suffered from dramatic cuts in military production, they were also protected by the state from bankruptcy or closure, while laying off workers was difficult. There was a political commitment to ensure the survival of SOEs, requiring often substantial investment. At the same time, demand was increasing for many of the consumer goods that made for conversion successes, such as motorcycles, minivans, and appliances.

The apparent success of conversion in China, albeit limited, has been the result of government subsidies, often over years, at a time of significant economic growth that has benefitted the country as a whole. Whether this success can continue as the government reduces support for state-owned enterprises remains uncertain.

VII. THE ROLE OF GOVERNMENT

The role of government in aiding conversion or diversification will clearly vary with the political philosophy of that government and its degree of reliance on the market mechanism. Studies of adjustment to reduced domestic defense spending yield little specific government role other than enhancing macro-stability and growth in the West through general monetary and fiscal policy and providing advance notification of planned decreases in government expenditure programs, such as defense procurement.

Most modern states maintain industrial policies which cover a multitude of areas, such as low-interest loans to industry, aid to research and development, regional development policies, and so on (Udis, 1987). In no cases are these policies identified as a package in aid of military downsizing or diversification, *per se*. Yet they are all capable of influencing that process. If all or many of the problem areas likely to be encountered during defense downsizing are covered by *general* policies, the absence of specifically designated defense conversion policies may be essentially a matter of semantics.

In the European context, two additional factors have to be considered: the activities of a *multinational* level of interest (in the form of the European Union) and of groupings of *subnational* regions that spill across national boundaries. The European Union established an initiative of loans and grants, entitled KONVER, with the goal of speeding the diversification of economic activities in geographical areas with heavy dependence on defense activities. Much of such aid has been directed to communities facing military base closures.[1] The program is still new and the first distribution of KONVER funds began in the mid-1990s. Unlike U.S. efforts (described below), KONVER aid is specifically denied to dual-use or purely military activities that, in effect, funnel assistance only to firms attempting to convert their resources entirely to civilian production.[2]

At the subnational level, the German state of Bremen developed a comprehensive approach to structural change in 1992 that was designed to aid the adjustment of its significant concentration of defense facilities. Although the financial resources originally made available were small (approximately $11 million), the program united various constituencies in the community. Interestingly, the Bremen state government also initiated participation with the regions of Lancashire (in the U.K.) and Zaanstad (in the Netherlands) in an international cooperation group (Network Demilitarised) that

[1] The U.S. has had such a program in the Department of Defense's Office of Economic Adjustment since the Kennedy Administration in the early 1960s. Its significant successes reflect, in large measure, the fact that since these bases are owned by the federal government, they can be used in a wide variety of ways, and often have been made available to local communities at low or no cost.

[2] See the Bonn International Center for Conversion (1996), p. 137.

attracted European Union support for regions economically threatened by reduced military spending (BICC, 1996).

Aside from program details, the question begging to be answered is which policy measures work successfully. Unfortunately, this question is easier to ask than to answer, since there is no precise formula for successful economic conversion. This is clear since similar measures in different countries do not yield similar results. Transfer of resources from military to civil use is an example of adjustment to changing market pressures. Since the challenge to firms in this situation is often to adapt or die, national environments that encourage change and adaptation will enjoy higher rates of success. Therefore, societal views and attitudes to adaptability and change may be as important as specific policy measures in explaining differential success.

In this context, French observers have expressed concern that the French economy's adaptability to change would remain low as long as French society continues to draw its leaders largely from graduates of the Grandes Ecoles, particularly from the Ecole Nationale d'Administration and the Ecole Polytechnique. While acknowledged as outstanding educational institutions, they are criticized widely as stifling to new ideas with their oppressive application of the "old boys' network" and a formulaic approach to problem-solving that often locks the door to the self-made executive who might be more inclined to consider unorthodox approaches to problem solving.

The importance of flexibility applies to workers as well as to managers. European workers have long been noted as tradition-bound and resistant to geographic mobility, a problem that is exacerbated in Russia and China by legal restrictions. Sweden's active labor market policy provides useful and current information on job vacancies and a system of carrots and sticks to motivate unemployed workers to move in search of known job opportunities. In furtherance of the goal of workforce flexibility, a program of industrial apprenticeship training such as that of Switzerland might also be considered in the United States. It would provide alternative career paths for young persons not oriented towards university education and help them acquire genuine craft skills widely used in modern industry. Persons with such training require much less supervision and are more easily adaptable to changes including those resulting from reduced military spending.

Industrial policy in the United States has fluctuated with the political party in control of the government. The Democrats generally have been favorable to intervention, while the Republicans tend to oppose intervention, which they frequently describe as the government "selecting winners and losers." Thus, there have been cycles of activity in support of aid to high technology industry. During the Bush Administration, the director of Defense Advanced Research Projects Agency (DARPA) was dismissed because the Agency's activities in supporting development of computer-related technologies was considered by some to resemble the actions of a venture capital firm too closely.

During the first Clinton Administration, the Democratic Congress passed the "Defense Technology Conversion, Reinvestment, and Transition Act" of 1992. Its Technology Reinvestment Project (TRP) combined the efforts of the Departments of Defense, Commerce, Energy, and Transportation, the National Science Foundation, and the National Aeronautics and Space Administration in the furtherance of conversion. The general aim of the project was to stimulate the development of specific dual-use technologies to promote an "integrated national industrial base" that would simultaneously target displaced defense industry workers while encouraging the evolution of a flexible, advanced technology workforce. Project funds were to be competitively allocated in response to submitted proposals.

The effort demonstrated the difficulty of combining civil and military work under the slogan of conversion. TRP funding was slashed in 1995 and 1996, and the program was eliminated in 1997. It was replaced with the Dual-Use Applications Program (DUAP), a much smaller program that focuses on leveraging commercial technologies for defense purposes. This was only one of the three original objectives of the Administration's program; the other two were to "spin-off" defense technologies to commercial uses and to invest in new technologies that would serve both commercial and military uses. (See Bischak, G., in BICC, 1997.)

VIII. CONCLUSIONS

Conversion defined as "in place" adjustment is exceedingly difficult for technological, bureaucratic, and cultural reasons. While not impossible, conversion remains perhaps the least attractive response for many firms to changes in the defense market. It requires a combination of time, money, skill, will, and flexibility that is often difficult to assemble.

Successful diversification, while less difficult, still provides significant challenges, even in civilian markets. During the 1950s and early 1960s, the trend toward conglomerate enterprises reflected a belief that modern management represented a general purpose tal-

		Characteristics of Demand: Dependence on Defense Sales	
		Low	High
Characteristics of Supply: Asset Specificity	Low	A Relatively easy	B
	High	C	D Most difficult

Source: Sandler and Hartley (1995) (based on Dussauge)

FIGURE 3

ent that could successfully direct almost any organization, regardless of its activities. In more recent years, conglomerate enterprises have been failing, represented by a reversal of trend back toward more narrow specialization. Statistical analyses of the last several quinquenial censuses of manufacturers in the US indicate a movement in the direction of specialization, especially at the *plant* level. As noted by one analyst, "From the perspective of the Standard Industrial Classification System, successful diversification occurs 'close to home,' where resources and expertise can be best used. . . . The central analytical issues for conversion and civil-military integration is the similarity of industrial resources in potentially related markets." (Leech, pp. 12–13).

The similarity of industrial resources combined with dependence on defense sales is reflected in Figure 3, which provides a general analytical approach to predicting the degree of difficulty likely to be encountered by a firm attempting to adjust to reduced military spending. One might also consider a third factor to be incorporated into the analysis—the degrees of dependence of a firm upon governmental support for research and development activities, which does not correlate perfectly with the military share of total sales.[3]

In concluding this survey of conversion, it is worth reiterating that, while the defense sector has many special characteristics, it is not unique in how it deals with decline. Most of our discussion has stressed the factors which make transfer of military producers into civil markets difficult, and which have lead firms producing for both markets to make major efforts to keep these operations separate. But adjustment to reduced military spending is not different in kind from other adjustments faced by firms attempting to adjust to dynamic changes in any market.

Recognizing market changes and reallocating resources to respond is perhaps *the* fundamental challenge for management, whether in defense or fashion, low-technology or high-technology. Andrew Grove, Chief Executive Officer of Intel Corporation, reflected on the general problem when he noted that "As industry becomes more competitive, companies are forced to retreat to their strongholds and specialize, in order to become world-class in whatever segments they end up occupying. Why is this so? . . . Simply put, its harder to be the best of class in several fields than in just one" (Grove, p. 52). He also noted the difficulties Intel faced in refocusing its energies from dealing with a few buyers to a consumer market:

> [S]ince we generally don't sell microprocessors to computer *users* but to computer *makers*, whatever problems we had in the past, we used to handle with the computer manufacturers, engineer to engineer, in conference rooms with blackboards, based on data analysis. But now, all of a sudden, 25,000 computer *users* were calling us every day saying 'Give me a new part, period.' We found ourselves dealing with people who bought nothing directly from us, yet were very angry with us. . . . What had happened? And why now? What was different this time? *Something* was, but in the middle of these events it was hard to tell what" (Grove, p. 17).

In 1997, the telecommunications firm WorldCom offered to buy MCI, a major long-distance company, and suggested that it would jettison MCI's 26 million residential customers to focus on the more profitable business clients. WorldCom's vice chairman noted that ". . . our strategy is not in the consumer business. It's very difficult for us to find a way to make economic sense out of the advertising budgets, the customer service budgets, etc., required to be in the consumer business." (*Washington Post*, October 3, 1997, p. A-1). These comments could just as easily have been made by the vice chairman of a defense firm in the U.S., Europe, Russia, or China.

[3] The Dussauge matrix has also been the base for an expansion by Anderton into five additional dimensions: capital (real and financial), transition mandate, location, industrial policy, and managerial ability. See Anderton, 1996.

Also See the Following Articles

ARMS PRODUCTION, ECONOMICS OF • ARMS TRADE, ECONOMICS OF • ECONOMICS OF WAR AND PEACE,

OVERVIEW • MILITARISM AND DEVELOPMENT IN UNDERDEVELOPED SOCIETIES • MILITARY-INDUSTRIAL COMPLEX, CONTEMPORARY SIGNIFICANCE • MILITARY-INDUSTRIAL COMPLEX, ORGANIZATION AND HISTORY

Bibliography

Adelman, K. L., & Augustine, N. R. (1992). Defense conversion: bulldozing the management. *Foreign Affairs, 71,* 26–47.

Almquist, P., & O'Prey, K. (1990). Beating swords into agricultural complexes: Soviet economic conversion. *Arms Control Today,* April, 17–21.

Anderton, C. H. (1996). Assessing the difficulty of Chinese defense enterprise transition. In *Peace economics, peace science, and public policy, 3.*

Bischak, G. (1997). U.S. conversion after the Cold War, 1990–1997, Brief 9, Bonn International Center for Conversion.

Bonn International Center for Conversion (1996). *Conversion survey 1996: global disarmament, demilitarization, and demobilization.* Oxford: Oxford University Press.

Bonn International Center for Conversion (1997). *Conversion survey 1997: global disarmament, demilitarization, and demobilization.* Oxford: Oxford University Press.

Bonn International Center for Conversion (1998). *Conversion survey 1998: global disarmament, demilitarization, and demobilization.* Oxford: Oxford University Press.

Coase, R. H. (1972). Industrial organization: a proposal for research. In Victor H. Fuchs, ed., *Policy issues and research opportunities in industrial organization.* New York: Columbia University Press, 59–73.

Commision of the European Communities (1996). *The challenges facing European defence-related industry: a contribution for action at the European level.* Brussels: Commision of the European Communities.

Cooper, J. (1991). *The Soviet defence industry: conversion and economic reform.* London: Chatham House.

Crane, K., & Yeh, K. C. (1991). *Economic reform and the military in Poland, Hungary, and China,* RAND Report R-3961-PCT. Santa Monica, California: RAND.

Dernberger, R. F. (1996). China's transition to a market economy: back to the future, mired in the present, or through the looking glass to the market economy. In United States Congress (1996), 57–69.

Folta, P. H. (1992). *From swords to plowshares? Defense industry reform in the PRC.* Boulder, Colorado: Westview.

Frankenstein, J. (1997). China's Defense Industry Conversion. In Jorn Brommelhorster and John Frankenstein, eds. *Mixed motives, uncertain outcomes: Defense conversion in China.* Boulder: Lynne Rienner, 3–34.

Gansler, J. (1995). *Defense conversion.* Cambridge, Mass: MIT Press.

Grove, A. S. (1996). *Only the paranoid survive: How to exploit the crisis points that challenge every company and career.* New York: Currency Doubleday.

Kitfield, J. (1997). Two-minute warning sounds: the realities of the shrinking defense marketplace are transforming the relationship between the Pentagon and its suppliers. *Government executive.* Special annual issue, *Top 200 federal contractors,* August, 31–40.

Lee, W. (1995). China's defense industry invades the private sector. *SAIS review, 15,* Summer-Fall, 177–205.

Leech, D. P. (1993). Patterns of diversification. Supporting material for *Adjusting to the Drawdown: Report of the Defense Conversion Commission.* TASC Report TR-5823411. Washington, DC: Defense Conversion Commission.

McNaugher, T. L. (1989). *New weapons, old politics.* Washington, DC: Brookings Institution.

Milgram, P., & Roberts, J. (1992). *Economics, organization, and management.* Englewood Cliffs, NJ: Prentice Hall.

Naughton, B. (1996). The pattern and logic of China's economic reform. In *United States Congress* (1996), 1–10.

Naughton, B. (1988). The third front: Defence industrialization in the Chinese interior. *China Quarterly, 3,* 351–386.

Sachs, J. D., & Woo, W.-T. (1996). Chinese economic growth: Explanations and the tasks ahead. In *United States Congress* (1996), 70–85.

Sandler, T., & Hartley, K. (1995). *The economics of defense.* Cambridge, England: Cambridge University Press.

Stewart II, W. G. (1993). From War to Peace: History of Past Conversions. Supporting Material for *Adjusting to the Drawdown: Report of the Defense Conversion Commission.* Washington, DC: Defense Conversion Commission.

Stoffaes, C. (1986). Industrial policy in the high technology industries. In William J. Adams and Christian Stoffaes, eds., *French industrial policy.* Washington: Brookings Institution.

Tai, M. C. (1992). On Civvy Street. *Far East Economic Review,* February 6, 40.

Udis, B. (1987). *The challenge to European industrial policy: Impacts of redirected government spending.* Boulder and London: Westview.

Udis, B. (1993). Adjustments to reduced domestic defense spending in Western Europe. In Ethan B. Kapstein, ed., *Downsizing defense.* Washington, DC: Congressional Quarterly, Inc.

United States Congress (1996). Joint Economic Committee. *China's economic future: Challenges to U.S. policy.* Washington, DC.: U.S. Government Printing Office, August 1996.

United States Arms Control and Disarmament Agency. *World military expenditures and arms transfers.* Washington, DC: U.S. Government Printing Office. (Annual volumes).

Weidenbaum, M. (1992). *Small wars, big defense.* New York: Oxford University Press.

Williamson, O. E. (1979). Transaction-cost economics: The governance of contractual relations. *Journal of Economics, 22,* 233–261.

Woo, W.-T. (1996). Crises and Institutional Evolution in China's Industrial Sector. In *United States Congress* (1996), 162–175.

Zhongguo, J. K. (1995). New Defense S&T Strategy to Emphasize Technology transfer to Civilian Use, August 20, 1995, no. 3, 131–136, translated in FBIS-China-95-235, December 7, 1995, 35–42.

Economic Costs and Consequences of War

Carlos Seiglie
Rutgers University

GLOSSARY

External Costs The costs borne by noncombatant nations in a war.

Externality When the action of a nation (individual) affects the consumption or production opportunities available to another.

Internal Costs The cost borne by combatant or participating nations in a war.

Terms-of-Trade The price of commodities that are imported relative to the price of those that are exported by a country.

Value of Life The present discounted value of a person's expected future earnings plus an amount to compensate for the suffering of the victim's family, community, and other nonpecuniary costs.

IN ANALYZING the costs of war, it is convenient to classify or partition costs in two ways. First, a distinction should be made between whether the costs and consequences are internal or external, that is, whether they are borne directly by the participants or by the wider international community, respectively. This distinction is similar to the one made in economics between private and social costs. If the decisions to go to war are based on the calculus of whether the private benefits outweigh the private cost of going to war, then many wars could be prevented if the parties involved internalized the higher social cost imposed by their actions. Once this distinction is emphasized, the importance of developing institutions which provide the proper incentives or mechanisms to account for these external effects becomes evident.

Another useful classification is between the direct and indirect effects or consequences arising from war. Direct effects will involve those immediately arising during and after the war and generally are restricted to the economic effects from casualties, displacement of populations, and destruction of infrastructure and other types of physical capital. The indirect effects are much more subtle and will persist into the future as, for example, famine, disease, and changes in the political and civil society that can occur as a consequence of the event. Since institutions are important to economic activity these events have profound effects on the economy. Finally, we may also make a distinction between a static and dynamic analysis of the consequences of war. Table 1 presents an example of the categorization scheme followed in Section I of the article.

I. MICROECONOMIC ANALYSIS

War leads to the destruction of resources: capital (factories, housing stock, weapons, etc.), human capital (reduction in the population as a result of casualties,

TABLE I

Some Costs of War

	Internal (private) costs	External (social) costs
Direct effects	• Loss of productive resources: Human (due to casualties, emigration, etc.) and physical capital (wealth effects). • Substitution effect from changing prices. • Trade diversion.	• Trade diversion for noncombatants. • Nuclear and biological fallout. • Changes in terms of trade.
Indirect effects	• Famine from increases in food prices and/or decline in income. • Uncertainty reduces capital formation and economic growth as a result of fear of future conflict. • Feedback from economic disruption to political system leads to possible changes in civic and political institutions which may have an adverse effect on social welfare (e.g., the formulation of poor economic policies, restrictions of civil liberties, etc.).	• Uncertainty of future conflict can reduce international trade and investment (capital mobility) leading to loss of welfare as gains from specialization and gains from trade are not fully exploited.

disease, displacement and starvation), and other resources such as the possible loss of land or territory. Historically, if victory is achieved the potential private benefits to the countries involved are the confiscation of resources such as territory (land), slaves (labor), and other resources. Yet, not only does war reduce aggregate resources but the final distribution is generally different. Both the reduction in resources and their redistribution between the participants will lead to changes in the valuation or prices of commodities and factors of production. In effect, there is a wealth effect and a substitution effect from war.

For example, if the nation does not lose territory but suffers a great number of casualties, then labor becomes scarce relative to land. This would lead to the price of land declining and the cost of labor rising in the postwar period. If the economy was closed after the war, the decline in population would also lead to a decline in the demand for many commodities and, therefore, their prices. A new level of prices and returns to factors of production will result. In the event of a victory, the winner may gain sufficient resources, for example, oil, to now have influence over prices. This may lead the victor to decrease production so as to increase price to a more profitable level.

Figure 1 illustrates a possible scenario for Country A. We label its production possibility frontier by AA. It shows all the feasible combinations of commodities X and Y that the country can produce given its endowment and the state of technology available to produce these goods. The country is initially producing the equilibrium amounts given by point E, the point of tangency of the slope of the production possibility curve (which measures the relative cost to society of producing these goods) to the price of commodities X relative to Y given by the slope of the line, p. The amount produced of each commodity is denoted by (X', Y'), whereas the amount consumed by (x', y'). The level of utility or welfare of a representative citizen of Country A consuming this amount is given by U_0. After a war, if the country suffers casualties and loses resources the new production possibility curve is given by BB, that is, the set of feasible choices is reduced. As is shown, if we assume that world prices are unaltered by the conflict (the war is between two small nations), the level of output of both goods as well as the country's comparative advantage has changed. Prior to the war, this country imported commodity Y by an amount (y' − Y') and exported (X' − x'), yet after the war it now exports Y and imports X. In addition, the representative individual of Country A has been made worse off by the amount $U_0 - U_1$.

Note that in this case, only the warring countries are assumed to be affected. Yet generally, wars will have an impact on the international community at large. As such, the social cost of war is greater than the private cost since the war leads to what may be termed a nega-

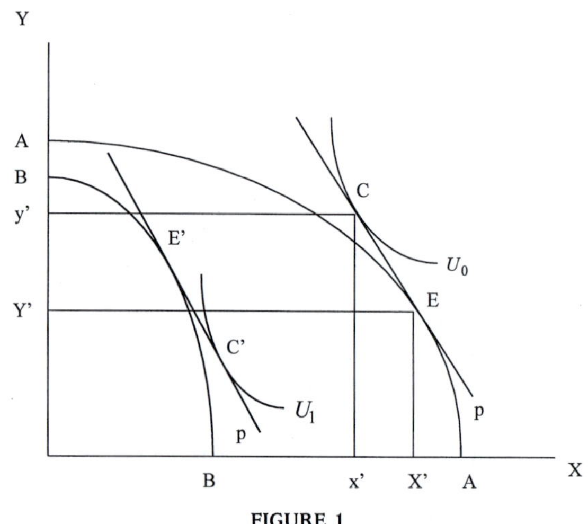

FIGURE 1

tive externality on the world community. Other possible costs may ensue because the terms of trade may change as a result of war. By the very nature of altering the amount and the distribution of resources available in the world, wars will affect prices. The effect of these price changes will be felt by both the participants (internal cost) and the rest of the world (external). As prices change, so will the income of different groups, both domestically in the participating nations and those in the noncombatant nations.

Similarly, wars will divert trade both directly via disruption of commercial trading routes during the conflict and through the alteration of prices. When trade is reduced or diverted, then social welfare declines not only for the participants but also for the many nations that must pay higher prices for the products that have been made scarcer, or whose transportation costs have risen. Those countries exporting the products whose prices have risen may be better off depending on the income and substitution effects created by the war, since the total amount exported may fall during wartime.

There are other internal indirect effects from war such as famine. This results from the disruption of the distribution channels or from a reduction in the income of certain groups. There may also be external indirect effects that we can envision resulting from war. For example, the price of food may increase for the noncombatant nations to a level where starvation and disease in their countries may ensue. If a warring country is a large producer of agricultural products such as wheat and rice, then disruption in their supply of these products raises world prices. The adverse effect is created when the cost of a subsistence diet rises for the poor in parts of the world.

War leads not only to a direct reduction in physical and human capital as it is destroyed, but the uncertainty created by enduring rivalries and the future possibilities of conflict will lead to a reduction in investments in both human and physical capital. This decrease in capital formation will reduce the level of output and economic growth of the participants from the level that would exist if peace prevailed. Conversely, if enduring rivalries induce investments in the military sector, including in weapons and the training of soldiers for war, this imposes a social cost on society since these resources could instead have been used to increase current and future production.

The development of much more destructive weapons seems to have resulted in an increase in the divergence between the private and social cost of war than has been the case historically. When weapons were more primitive, casualties were generally confined to those directly involved in combat. As technology improved, so did the likelihood of casualty to the general population. The recent development of nuclear, biological, and other more destructive weapons has led to the cost of war now spilling over to the larger international community. The extreme example is the case of nuclear war, where the possibility exists for the annihilation of a large fraction of the world's population from nuclear fallout. In the modern era, the realization of this dramatic external effect from war has led many in the international community to demand the elimination of these weapons possessing the potential for inflicting large external costs. Therefore, the weapons or technology employed in war will not only lead to the cost of war varying for the participants, but will also change the size of the divergence between the private and social costs.

Finally, there must be a realization that the economic consequences of war will likely imply changes in the political, social, and civic institutions of the warring countries. Since economic policy is not derived in a vacuum, but is instead formed within political institutions, there are costs and possibly benefits that may thus arise. For example, if war leads to an authoritarian regime coming into power then the general citizenry loses influence in the process of policymaking. This leads to the adoption of economic policies that differ from those that would be adopted under a democratic regime. In addition, the mobilization of resources by governments during war may lead to a reduction in civil liberties, which in many cases persists into the postwar period. The cost of these events, although implicit, must also be factored into account for the total cost of war. There has been a failure to realize that freedom of speech and association, for example, not only are rights that provide direct benefits to those endowed with them, but that they also serve to facilitate trade and therefore, make the economic system more efficient. In summary, since war generally leads to the redistribution of economic and political power there arises the possibility that governments will adopt economic and social policies that impose a higher cost on society than had the event not occurred.

II. MACROECONOMIC IMPLICATIONS OF WAR

It appears that the earliest concern by economists about the effects of war had to do with the financing of military expenditures. In England, the systematic study of inflation and debt financing during the Napoleanic Wars by

Ricardo, Malthus, J. S. Mill, and other British economists led to treatises on monetary and fiscal policy that are the foundation of our knowledge in these areas today. For example, it was as a writer on monetary policy in the discussion of war inflation that David Ricardo first made his reputation.

Wars are generally accompanied by increases in government spending, unless the government reduces spending on nonmilitary goods. Therefore, governments can finance this increase by a combination of either taxing the current generation, that is, by raising taxes, borrowing (levying taxes on future generations to repay the debt), or printing money. The initial concern by economists was on the impact that financing war would have on increases in the general price level or inflation. Like any government expenditure financed by printing money, inflation is the product. If war requires greater amounts of spending at the same time that a country's access to the capital markets or its ability to tax is restricted, then higher rates of inflation would be associated with it.

In fact, the early empirical work in macroeconomics examines the effects of monetary policy on inflation or hyperinflation during and after war periods. Lerner documents that the worst inflation in American history since the Revolution plagued the South during the Civil War. He finds that for 31 consecutive months from October 1861 to March 1864 the Confederate commodity price index rose at the average rate of 10% per month. When the Civil War had ended, the index was 92 times its prewar base. Similarly, Cagan documented the bouts of hyperinflation following World War I in Austria, Germany, and other European countries.

There are two more recent issues in macroeconomics that have led economists to focus research on the consequences of war. The first deals with the tax-smoothing literature that suggests that optimal income taxation requires a smooth tax path and, therefore, unexpected events such as wars are optimally financed by debt. In other words, wars should be financed by fiscal deficits. Although in this literature war plays no special role outside of being assumed to be an unexpected event that governments must deal with, the second literature is more specific to the consequences of war or defense spending in general. This latter work assumes that individuals have a derived demand for national security to protect their well-being, and that of their descendants. Therefore, both temporary increases in defense spending (wars), as well as permanent increases during times of peace will be financed by debt. The key to deriving this result is that bequests, although operative, cannot be fully realized because there exists the possibility that international conflict may break out. If so, then a portion of these bequests may never reach one's heirs since they may be confiscated by an adversary or destroyed during the conflict.

As a consequence of war, a component of government expenditures, defense spending, is perceived by individuals as a form of protecting against these attacks or increasing the likelihood that bequests are realized. Therefore, increases in public debt to finance defense expenditures (which help to ensure that a portion of bequests are received by future generations) will not be fully offset by increases in savings. Consequently, we should expect to observe a positive correlation between increases in the size of the public debt and defense spending in countries where such a concern exists.

Another important implication from this model is that since defense spending lowers the amount bequeathed to future generations it lowers national savings. In particular, using time series data for 11 OECD countries, Seiglie (1998) finds robust results that both aggregate savings as well as the saving rate are reduced by defense spending. Since economic growth is largely determined by the accumulation of both physical and human capital partly financed by inter vivos transfers, then defense spending can affect economic growth.

III. THE TRANSFER PROBLEM AND WAR

Victory in war may lead to not only confiscation of the loser's resources (e.g., territory) as a prize, but a more subtle form of compensation: reparation payments for war damages. For example, France was forced to pay Prussia indemnities after the 1870–1871 war and Germany was made to pay France reparations after World War I. Economic research on the general question of the effects of transferring resources between countries on the terms of trade of the paying or receiving country was stimulated after WWI by debates between Keynes and Ohlin. After WWII, the beginning of the Marshall Plan led to a reexamination of this issue by Samuelson.

The transfer problem refers to the need for real resources to accompany the international transfer of financial resources between two countries or groups of countries in order for the latter to take place. Under standard assumptions, the problem is that for country A that loses a war to make reparations to country B the victor, country A must reduce its expenditures by the same amount as the recipient increases theirs. Otherwise, the transfer would lead to one or the other country's terms-of-trade changing (the price of imports relative to exports) and the transfer would be undereffected or overeffected. Restating the problem differently, when the loser gives the winner $100, the loser's balance of trade will improve as they will reduce their expenditures on imports and the recipient of the transfer will purchase more of the loser's exports. If the improvement in the balance of trade via income changes does not lead to the loser making $100 of transfer in real resources (or commodities) then the terms-of-trade will change to complete the adjustment. For example, if the balance of trade only improved by $90, then the transfer is undereffected and the price of this country's exports relative to its imports would fall. As the price of exports relative to imports falls for the defeated country, this will further encourage their exports and discourage imports until the full transfer is completed. It should be noted that much of the discussion on foreign aid and other transfers in the area of international political economy fails to account for this effect. Therefore, financial transfers that may appear as war reparations (or foreign aid) may lead to dramatic changes in the terms of trade of the recipient country, with varying consequences.

IV. TOWARD MEASURING THE COST OF WAR

Adam Smith was one of the first economists to recognize the costs as well as the potential benefits of the military when used for national defense. In his book, the *Wealth of Nations* he states that "the first duty of the sovereign, that of protecting the society from violence and invasion (by others), can be performed only by means of military force. But the expense both of preparing this military force in times of peace, and of employing it in time of war, is very different in the different states of society (and in) different periods." He recognized that the cost of war, including death, destruction, and other casualties, will vary depending on time and place. In other words, the opportunity cost of the resources employed or destroyed varies depending on the economic conditions of the particular actors.

Jean-Baptiste Say went even farther by noting that the loss of human life is a loss of wealth. This wealth is composed of the total expenditure used up in previous years in maintenance and education. He wrote: "War cost more than its expense; it costs what it prevents from being earned." This is one of the earliest recognition that human beings are embodied with human capital, and therefore a part of the value of a human life is the foregone earnings or the loss to society resulting from the inability of individuals to produce, that is, the reduction in output experienced by society.

In the simple example shown in Figure 1, the cost of war was simply U_0–U_1, since there was no time dimension nor externalities. Yet operationally, measuring the cost of war requires as a first step calculating the present discounted value of the loss in productivity of the dead and wounded. For those who are killed, the base measure is the discounted value of their lifetime earnings. For those who are wounded, we calculate the differential between their potential lifetime earnings prior to the conflict and that after the war. Since casualties during war tend to be young, both as a result of soldiers being young and children being the most vulnerable to some of the spillovers of war such as starvation and disease, these costs based on normal life expectancy would tend to be high. Algebraically, the base amount of the cost of a casualty at time $t = 0$ is

$$C = \sum_{t=1}^{T} \frac{y_t^* - \hat{y}_t}{(1 + r_t)^t},$$

where y_t^* is the individual's annual expected income, $\hat{y}_t$ is the actual income received which is equal to zero if the person is killed, r is the discount rate or cost of capital and T is the expected age of retirement.

It is important to emphasize that in calculating the economic costs of war, we do not just simply total the number of dead and wounded. Each individual has a value to society based on his or her ability to contribute to the production and therefore, wealth of a country. The cost of a casualty of a young person with the same amount of human capital as that of an older one will have a higher value to society, since, for example, his or her death at a younger age results in society foregoing more expected years of production. The amount of the loss or the economic cost is positively related to the life expectancy in the society. This is consistent with Smith's observation that the costs of war varies across time and space since so will economic conditions.

To this base amount, we must then add the value of the foregone consumption of intangibles and the value placed by society on "life itself." In order to arrive at a monetary value for this loss from war requires the use of implicit measures of individuals' valuation for these "goods." We must equally account for the loss of earnings to others as a consequence of war or conflict. For example, there are currently many countries where the presence of relatively low intensity conflict has eliminated certain industries such as tourism. To measure this cost, we calculate the earnings prior to and during the war and the differential is an approximation of the damage to specific industries resulting from the conflict.

Similarly, the adoption of weapons with the potential to impose externalities requires that we factor in these costs. As an example, exposure to chemicals during a conflict reduces the health and life expectancy of those exposed and this amount has to be accounted for in the calculus. Similarly, the environmental damage caused by war has to be factored in. This may include the cost to the environment of oil spills or burning oil wells. As a first approximation, we can estimate the reduction in the income of the affected parties. For example, oil spills resulting from a war may lead to a reduction in the catch of fish. We can then impute some monetary value for this loss. In a similar way, we can calculate the loss generated from increases in infant mortality. This may be done by estimating the loss in production (earnings) for those who do not survive. In addition, we must add the cost of providing health care for those who are casualties of the war.

Other costs of war (or more generally, the maintenance of a military) include the following: (1) the salaries and allowance of military personnel evaluated at their opportunity cost; (2) maintenance of paramilitary forces; (3) payments made to civilians employed in the military sector; (4) operations and maintenance; (5) procurement of weapons; (6) research and development (R&D); (7) construction expenditures related to the military sector; (8) pensions to retired military personnel; (9) military aid to foreign countries; (10) civil defense; and (11) military aspect of atomic energy and space.

All of these components of military spending could be attributed indirectly as a cost of war, even if these expenditures are made during peacetime. The reason is that the existence of war creates the necessity for nations to maintain standing armies and keep stocks of armaments ready for deployment, that is, to divert resources from alternative uses. Therefore, in calculating the cost of war we should include the loss in production of the factors employed in the war effort. For example, we should value the time of soldiers while engaged in war, not by the amount that they are paid by their government, but by the foregone earnings in their prewar employment. In calculating costs, even if soldiers are conscripted their time in the military should be valued at their market wages and not at what they are paid by the government. This is a fundamental issue in the debate on the costs and benefits of the draft versus a volunteer army.

All of the other expenditures listed above should be evaluated at their opportunity cost. For example, we must account for the cost of weapons, expenditures on R & D, and the replacement of capital destroyed during war by the amount required to replace them at market prices. It is important to emphasize that when governments borrow to finance these expenditures (or finance them from tax revenues or seigniorage), care should be taken when determining the appropriate rate of interest used to discount any flow of services. The rate used should be one that reflects the social opportunity cost of capital. As Harberger demonstrates, with distortions such as taxes in the economy the social rate of return will generally deviate from the private rate. But one thing is clear, the rate used should not necessarily be the rate paid by the government to finance expenditures since this rate will generally underestimate the true social cost of capital. Using this lower rate will result in the actual net cost of many different military activities to be understated, leading to the adoption of military projects that have a net social loss to society. For example, if no distortions exist and the government borrows to finance a new weapon system or to fund pension systems, the rate used to evaluate these costs is the marginal productivity of capital in the private sector that without any risk premium and well-functioning capital markets will equal the market rate of interest. More generally, insofar as military expenditures raise claims on factors of production, they should be included in the cost of war.

Also See the Following Articles

ECONOMIC CAUSES OF WAR AND PEACE • ECONOMICS OF WAR AND PEACE, OVERVIEW • MILITARY-INDUSTRIAL COMPLEX, CONTEMPORARY SIGNIFICANCE

Bibliography

Barro, R. J. (1979). On the determination of the public debt. *Journal of Political Economy*, October, 87, 940–971.

Cagan, P. (1956). The monetary dynamic of hyperinflation. In Milton Friedman, (ed.), *Studies in the quantity theory of money*. Chicago: University of Chicago Press.

Cranna, M. (1994). *The true cost of conflict*. New York: The New Press.

Harberger, A. C. (1972). *Project evaluation*. Chicago: The University of Chicago Press.

Kennedy, G. (1975). *The economics of defence*. Totowa, NJ: Rowman and Littlefield.

Keynes, J. M. (1929). The German transfer problem. *Economic Journal*, Vol. XXXIX, (March), 1–7.

Lerner, E. M. (1956). Inflation in the Confederacy, 1861–65. In Milton Friedman (ed.), *Studies in the Quantity Theory of Money*. Chicago: University of Chicago Press.

Ohlin, B. (1929). The reparation problem: A discussion. *Economic Journal* (June).

Say, J.-B. (1803). *Traite d' economie politique*. (1817, English translation edition, *Catechism of Political Economy*). Philadelphia: M. Carey & Son.

Samuelson, P. A. (1952), The transfer problem and transport costs. *Economic Journal*, Vol. LXII, No. 246 (June), 278–304.

Samuelson, P. A. (1954). The transfer problem and transport costs. *Economic Journal*, Vol. LXIV, No. 254 (June), 264–289.

Seiglie, C. (1988). International conflict and military expenditures. *Journal of Conflict Resolution* 32, 141–161.

Seiglie, C. (1998). Defense spending in a neo-Ricardian world. *Economica* (May).

Smith, A. (1776). *An inquiry into the nature and causes of the wealth of nations*. The Modern Library Edition (1937). New York: The Modern Library.

Economics of War and Peace, Overview

Dietrich Fischer
Pace University

Akira Hattori
Fukuoka University

GLOSSARY

Arbitration Two parties resolve a conflict by asking a third party to chose an impartial outcome. The decision is binding.

Conversion Shifting work forces and facilities from military-oriented to civilian-oriented activity.

Global Peace Service Volunteers from around the world working together on the solution of global problems.

Mediation A neutral third party assists parties with a conflict by suggesting solutions that might be reasonably expected to be mutually acceptable. The proposals are not binding.

Optimization Finding the most desirable outcome according to a given criterion.

Pareto-optimal Frontier A situation in which no negotiating partner can gain anything without others losing something.

Peace System A series of mutually reinforcing trends that promote peace.

Prisoner's Dilemma A situation in which two parties seemingly act in their individual self-interest, but end up hurting each other.

Public Good A good that cannot be supplied profitably by private enterprise because nonpayers cannot be excluded from consumption.

Structural Violence Death and human suffering caused by unjust social conditions rather than by military action.

Sustainable Development Economic development that preserves availability of key economic resources and a livable environment for future generations.

Tobin Tax A tax on foreign currency exchange to stabilize exchange rates.

Transarmament A shift from an offensive military posture to purely defensive or nonmilitary defense.

War System A series of mutually reinforcing trends that promote war.

World Treasury A UN agency, proposed by Jan Tinbergen, in charge of raising revenue to help finance the United Nations system.

UNTIL RECENTLY, most economists considered war an external event not amenable to economic analysis that from time to time disrupts more normal conditions under which economic laws apply. But the late Jan Tinbergen, corecipient of the first Nobel Prize in Economic Science in 1969, pointed out, "Warfare affects human welfare to such an extent that economists must raise their voices against it." No issue traditionally addressed by economists threatens the very survival of the human race as immediately as nuclear war. Moreover, economies are adversely affected not only by the destructive force of war itself, but also by military spending, which exceeds $2 billion per day worldwide. In recent years, a growing number of economists have studied the economic consequences of war and military spending and explored causes of conflicts and their nonviolent resolution. They have also examined alternative resource allocations that contribute to peace and sustainable development.

I. CONFLICT RESOLUTION

To a large extent economics deals with methods of accommodating conflicting interests. For example, buyers prefer low prices, sellers high prices, and the market mechanism automatically determines a fair price at which supply and demand are in balance. Any voluntary market transaction is a so-called "win–win" solution in which buyers pay less and sellers earn more than what the item is worth to each. Such win–win solutions, where both sides gain something, are a model for conflict resolution leading to stable outcomes.

The more challenging problems in economics deal not with simple optimization, where a single decision-maker is in control of everything, but with conflicts of interest, where two or more independent decision-makers may seek to frustrate each other's goals or may cooperate for mutual benefit. The theory of games, which was originally developed by John von Neumann and Oskar Morgenstern to explain economic behavior, is a prominent tool to analyze conflicts and their resolution. With the end of the Cold War, the main focus shifted from analyzing war-winning strategies to methods of conflict resolution and global cooperation. Cooperative games have been studied before in other contexts, so there was a body of literature to build on.

Fisher and Ury emphasize that for fruitful negotiations one should express one's goals clearly but be flexible about ways to meet them. It is important to listen carefully to the needs and interests of others. If we make one-sided proposals in our favor, we cannot expect others to agree and thus hurt our own interests. They give the following illustration of that principle: During the 1979 peace negotiations at Camp David, Egypt demanded that the entire Sinai peninsula be returned to it. Israel was willing to give up most but not all of it. The negotiations were on the brink of breaking down. But by exploring the underlying interests rather than the stated positions, President Carter and his advisers were able to find a compromise acceptable to both sides. Egypt's main concern was its sovereignty. It did not want to cede territory again to a foreign aggressor after centuries of colonial domination. Israel's main concern was security. It did not want Egyptian tanks on its border. By giving the territory to Egypt but keeping it free of national military forces and stationing an international peacekeeping force along the border, both sides' principal concerns were met.

Howard Raiffa proposed that negotiations should not stop as soon as a mutually acceptable solution has been found. The search for further mutually beneficial trade-offs should continue until they reach the Pareto-optimal frontier, where neither side can make further gains without the other side giving up something. In negotiating a new contract between management and labor, even after the two sides have reached an initial agreement, both may prefer another solution that offers higher pay in return for longer work hours during a period of unusually high demand. Similarly, even if two countries have settled a territorial dispute, both may perceive themselves better off if one that would otherwise be land-locked gains access to the sea in return for a larger portion of territory elsewhere. The systematic search for new or amended international agreements that can bring benefits to two or more parties can be a major area of economic studies.

Economic cooperation and closer ties should help reduce the threat of war and maintain mutually beneficial relations. After World War II, the French economist Jean Monnet concluded that mutually beneficial economic cooperation between France and Germany might help overcome their century-old hostility. He conceived of the Coal and Steel Union, which has since evolved into the European Union, which has indeed made another war between Germany and France practically unthinkable. Other countries with tense relations can learn from this. Developing mutually beneficial trade and joint ventures is something that is relatively easy to agree to because the benefits are mutual and clearly visible. Such cooperation on easy issues can increase mutual trust and understanding and prepare the way for successful negotiations on more controversial issues later.

A model widely used to explain apparently irrational behavior is the prisoner's dilemma game. A simple illustration is ruinous competition. If one of two gas stations at the same street corner lowers its prices, it may increase its profits by drawing away customers from the competing station. But if both lower their price, they may both have the same number of customers as before, only less revenue. What appears advantageous if one side does it alone may hurt the interests of both sides if they both pursue the same strategy. There are numerous examples of this in real life. If one country arms, it may gain military superiority. But if two rivals engage in an arms race, both become less secure and burdened with heavy military spending. Disarmament negotiations that lead to verifiable and enforceable agreements can help two countries reallocate their resources to meet their people's needs better with neither side risking military inferiority.

National defense is often cited as a textbook example of a "public good" because it protects all citizens of a country, regardless of whether they contributed to it. For this reason it cannot be profitably supplied by private enterprise and has to be funded by governments out of taxes. But as Ruben Mendez pointed out, at the international level, defense may well be a "public bad" because one country's arms acquisitions threaten the security of its neighbors.

Conflicts can probably never be eliminated entirely, but we can develop methods to deal with them without war. For example, there has been an intense struggle between Netscape and Microsoft over providing access to the Internet, but they would never dream of bombing each other's headquarters. Instead, they compete through better quality, lower prices, advertisements, and sometimes battles in court. Governments could learn from that.

A successful businessman once criticized government's often confrontational approach toward international relations. He proposed that to search for areas of common interest was more fruitful than to focus on differences. "If I sit down at the negotiating table and want to strike a deal, I don't begin by breaking the teeth of my counterpart across the table," he said.

II. ECONOMIC CONVERSION AND THE PEACE DIVIDEND

The Stockholm International Peace Research Institute (SIPRI) publishes an annual volume with estimates of each country's military spending. During the height of the Cold War, world military spending reached nearly $1 trillion per year. Since then, it has declined, particularly in the former Soviet Union, but it is still over $800 billion.

Leontief and Duchin used an input/output model of the world economy to analyze the economic implications of various levels of reductions in military spending. All countries would enjoy higher rates of economic growth with lower military spending because they could afford to invest more funds into their civilian economy.

Kenneth J. Arrow considered military spending from four points of view: resource allocation theory, macroeconomic stability, modern growth theory, and political economy.

Emile Benoit found a positive correlation between military spending and economic growth rates in some developing countries. Other authors (e.g., Klein et al., 1995), taking other variables into account, have found the opposite. This question has sparked a long and heated debate. Some believe that military spending increases the level of technical competence of the general population and thus explains higher rates of economic growth. Others argue that it could be a confusion of cause and effect. If people with growing incomes spend more on alcohol consumption, one cannot conclude that drinking raises income level, but rather that higher incomes allow for bigger spending. Similarly, a government that can afford to spend more for military purposes may be tempted to do so.

Some have pointed out that technologies originally developed for military purposes have later been applied to civilian technologies. Others, like Lloyd J. Dumas, argue that if the same engineering and scientific talent were directed to the development of new civilian technologies, the benefits would be far greater.

During the Cold War, a third to a half of the world's physicists and engineers worked on the development of new weapons systems. Dumas has argued that because employers in the defense sector are reimbursed by the government for whatever they spend, they do not hesitate to offer high salaries and state-of-the-art facilities to the top students in engineering and science. Market-based civilian firms do not automatically get their costs reimbursed by taxpayers. They are at a disadvantage in the competition for the "best and brightest" engineers and scientists. This makes the loss to the civilian economy even more serious.

Because many governments are willing to spend lavishly on their militaries, those who make decisions on weapons purchases are less frugal than private consumers, who spend their own hard earned money. Anyone who can reach into the almost bottomless pocket of the public treasury is tempted to spend large sums.

The end of the Cold War has raised hopes for a large peace dividend in the form of reduced military spending that can be reallocated to meet civilian needs. The process has been slower than many expected because of fear of job losses among employees of military industries. However, if the same funds that were previously spent for military purposes were spent for such purposes as education, health care, cleaning up the environment, and the development of renewable energy sources, even more jobs could be created with the same funds. For example, former U.S. Defense Secretary Caspar Weinberger pushed for higher defense spending, saying that every $1 billion spent by the Pentagon created 30,000 jobs. He failed to mention that the same $1 billion spent for education would have created 70,000 jobs so that spending it instead for defense in fact provided 40,000 fewer jobs.

Dumas and many others have stressed the need for systematic planning to convert defense-related jobs to civilian jobs. Weida has estimated that the clean-up of nuclear weapons facilities would create even more jobs than their current operation. The United Nations Institute of Disarmament Research has sponsored a study that emphasized that disarmament can be compared to a process of investment: there may be initial costs of conversion, but the benefits accrue in the long run in the form of higher outputs by the civilian economy.

If political will is present, conversion poses no obstacle to disarmament. For example, as economist and peace researcher Kenneth Boulding pointed out, from 1945 to 1946, fully one-third of the U.S. economy was converted from military to civilian use, and unemployment never exceeded 3%. By demonstrating that this is possible, economists can help generate public support for conversion.

Even a small fraction of military spending could have vastly beneficial effects if spent on the solution of global problems. For example, the World Health Organization's campaign to eradicate smallpox cost $80 million or less than one hour's worth of world military spending. The United Nations Children's Fund, UNICEF, has estimated that inoculating every child against the six most common fatal childhood diseases, from which nearly 3 million children under age 5 die each year, would cost $1.50 per child, or about $200 million per year—less than 10% of the $2.1 billion cost of a single U.S. stealth bomber.

III. INEQUITY AS VIOLENCE

Violence is present not only if people are shot or maimed, but also if innocent children die from hunger or preventable diseases. Johan Galtung has coined the term "structural violence" for unjust social structures that lead to loss of life or human suffering, even if there is no particular individual committing the violence.

Charles Zimmerman and Milton Leitenberg have estimated that if per capita incomes were about equally distributed among countries (even if not within countries), life expectancy in the richer countries would not decline measurably, but the better health care available in the poorer countries could save in the order of 14 million lives per year. This is about 100 times the average annual death toll from all civil and international wars and, according to their estimate, is equivalent to 236 atomic bombs being dropped each year on the poor of the world. But because these avoidable deaths are not concentrated in one moment at one place, they are largely ignored by the news media.

Jan Tinbergen has appealed for more developmental assistance, if not out of compassion, at least out of self-interest, because otherwise the advanced industrial countries will inevitably become inundated with streams of economic refugees.

One of the most underutilized resources for sustainable development is technical knowledge. Unlike material or financial resources, it need not be given up by someone in order to be given to someone else. Knowledge, once discovered, can be copied without limit at very low additional costs. If the most efficient production methods known anywhere on earth—which are least polluting and use the least amount of energy, natural resources and labor—were available everywhere, everyone could be much better off.

Of course, there is a dilemma. If companies that invest in research and development (R&D) of new technologies were required to share their discoveries with everyone else without compensation, the incentive to invest in R&D would greatly diminish, and the stream of new inventions could subside to a trickle. One solution is public funding of research with the results being shared with everyone. The European countries have founded EUREKA in which they pool their resources for research on new technologies in many fields, based on each member country's ability to pay, and share the results among contributing members. If the same principle were extended to the global level, all countries could enjoy higher living standards, and international differences could gradually be reduced.

Such an improvement in living conditions would help eliminate a great deal of unnecessary human suffering and would also reduce sources of conflicts. Conflicts over scarce resources and territory are among the most persistent causes of wars.

Would such a general increase in living standards damage our environment beyond repair? Not necessarily. It is quite possible to supply human needs for nutrition, health care, education, and communications with much less burden on the natural environment than today. To mention just one example, a hair-thin glass fiber can carry as much information as a foot-thick copper cable, at a tiny fraction of the material resources and energy required. If we take care of the environment, people can still gain access to the best available information on health and resource conserving farming and production methods. It is not necessary that everyone consume as much in terms of resources and energy as the average citizens of today's industrially advanced countries for life expectancy and quality of life to improve considerably.

IV. DYNAMICS OF ARMS RACES AND STRATEGIC STABILITY

One decisive factor whether a conflict erupts in war is whether it is preceded by an arms race. Michael Wallace found that among 99 cases of "serious disputes or military confrontations" in the period of 1820 to 1964, 23 of the 28 preceded by an arms race ended in war, whereas 68 of the 71 not preceded by an arms race ended without war.

Selling arms is a highly profitable business, and many private companies and governments sell arms to dictatorships and unstable regimes. Arms merchants profit at the expense of other people's lives. In this respect, the international arms trade resembles the slave trade or drug trade, which have long been declared illegal. Some have proposed a ban on arms exports.

A more modest proposal was advanced in 1995 by former Costa Rican President Dr. Oscar Arias Sanchez, an economist and political scientist, who won the 1987 Nobel Peace Prize for his role in negotiating an end to the war in Nicaragua. He proposed a ban on arms exports to countries involved in armed aggression violating international law or internal violent conflict and to countries violating human rights or governed by illegitimate regimes. He also proposed a global demilitarization fund to promote economic development projects, composed of contributions from reduced military spending, to realize the benefits of the peace dividend. He suggested that the rich nations contribute one-fifth of their savings to this fund with the developing countries contributing perhaps one-tenth of their savings from military budget cuts. Those nations that fail to reduce their military budgets would contribute some stipulated percentage of these budgets directly to the fund. Some developing countries now spend much of their hard-earned foreign exchange on the import of expensive weapons systems, more than for education and health care combined. Arias also proposed regional disarmament talks, where countries can agree to simultaneous mutual arms reductions, and he appealed to countries facing no military threat to abolish their armies, as did Costa Rica in 1948, Panama in 1994, and Haiti in 1995, joining about 30 other demilitarized countries. Costa Rica enjoys a per capita income about twice that of its Central American neighbors, probably because it invests in its civilian economy what others spent for their militaries, and while many wars have gripped its neighbors in recent decades, Costa Rica has remained at peace since 1948.

Arms races are driven by several factors, partly by the lobbying of military industries for weapons sales, partly by dictatorial governments fearful of popular unrest, and partly by mutual fear. To eliminate the last factor, some have advocated an intermediate transition to nonoffensive (or nonprovocative) defense, which is sufficient to resist aggression but cannot be used to carry out aggression. For example, while tanks can be used both for defense and for invading another country, tank barriers in fixed position can be used only for defense.

Purely defensive measures improve the security of the country undertaking them without reducing the security of adversaries. Purely offensive measures reduce the security of others, without contributing a country's own security. One can also imagine "superdefensive" measures that improve the security of two opponents simultaneously; for example, stationing an international peacekeeping force along a contested border. On the other hand, "superoffensive" measures reduce the security of both sides simultaneously; for example, a policy of "launch-on warning." A mistaken "retaliatory" strike based on a false warning would lead to the destruction of both sides. From January, 1979 to June, 1980, the U.S. early warning system generated 3804 false alarms of a possible Soviet nuclear attack. After 1984, the Pentagon stopped releasing these statistics "so as not to frighten the public." No comparable Soviet or Russian figures are available, but on January 25, 1995, Russia temporarily mistook a research rocket launched from Norway to study the polar light as a possible U.S. nuclear attack and readied its missiles for retaliation against the U.S.

A shift from offensive to purely defensive measures, which has also been called "transarmament" (Fischer, 1984), has the advantage that it can be undertaken unilaterally, without risk, whereas disarmament requires mutual agreement because unilateral disarmament could make a country vulnerable and a tempting target for aggression. Sweden and Switzerland, which were able to remain at peace during World War II, deliberately avoided the acquisition of any offensive arms, concentrating instead on a strong territorial defense.

In an arms race with offensive arms, both sides pose a threat to the other and are under pressure to spend a high portion of their total production for military purposes, resulting in a stagnating civilian economy. If the two sides acquire defensive arms, they reach a saturation point where both sides can defend themselves if necessary, but are unable to attack each other. The arms race then comes to a halt, even without any mutual agreement.

Among the most destabilizing weapons systems, which stimulate rapidly escalating arms races and also may lead to the outbreak of hostilities during a crisis, are so-called "first-strike weapons," which are vulnerable and at the same time highly destructive. In an armed confrontation, they give an advantage to the side that strikes first. Examples are unprotected bombers on open airfields. In the 1960s President Nasser believed that acquiring an air force matching that of Israel would make Egypt militarily stronger and therefore safer. He spent vast sums on building a bomber fleet, but it actually made Egypt less secure. Both sides knew that in case of a war, whoever struck first could destroy the bombers of the opponent on the ground before they could take off. When Egypt blocked Israeli ships' access to the port of Aqaba in 1967, which Israel had warned it would consider an act of aggression, Israel was so afraid of an Egyptian air attack that it felt compelled to destroy the Egyptian bomber fleet before it might attack Israel.

Other first-strike weapons are missiles with multiple warheads, such as the American MX missile or the Russian SS-18. If one warhead can destroy a missile site with several warheads, situations can arise where the side that strikes first can disarm the other side in a surprise attack. Instead of giving an opponent the message, "Don't attack us or you face the prospect of retaliation," such weapons implicitly give an opponent the signal, "If you do nothing, you face the danger of being disarmed in a first strike, but if you destroy our weapons, which is easy to accomplish, you face no threat." Instead of deterring an attack, such first-strike weapons may in fact invite an attack, according to the principle "use them or lose them."

This instability would be aggravated if weapons were deployed in outer space, as proposed under the Strategic Defense Initiative or "star wars." Even though these systems have been portrayed as purely defensive, they in fact create instability because space stations are extremely vulnerable, but would be capable of emitting hundreds or thousands of lethal beams or projectiles. In a tense situation, where a war is feared imminent, both sides would know that whoever strikes first can disable the space stations of the opponent and gain strategic superiority.

V. THE RISKS OF NUCLEAR WAR

With the end of the Cold War, the fear of a nuclear war between the United States and Russia has greatly diminished. But India and Pakistan, who have fought three wars with each other since 1947, are believed to have nuclear weapons or to be close to it, and some small nations ruled by dictators, such as Iraq, Libya, and North Korea, are known to have made efforts to obtain nuclear weapons. There is also the danger that terrorist groups may one day gain access to a nuclear device and not shrink from using it. Terrorists have sometimes engaged in suicide missions and may not be deterred by the threat of retaliation. Another danger is that a failure of command and control of safety systems could lead to the accidental explosion of nuclear weapons. Since 1945, there have been dozens of accidents involving nuclear weapons.

Jeanes has calculated the average time until a future nuclear catastrophe under various assumptions. If we assume that there are 10 nations possessing nuclear weapons and each one is as peaceful and technically competent that, on average, it will be able to prevent an intentional or accidental use of nuclear weapons for 500 years (more than twice the time since the American declaration of independence), a nuclear use is still frighteningly close: the probability that nuclear weapons will be used within 50 years is 63%, within 100 years 87%, within 200 years 98%, and within 500 years 99.99% a virtual certainty. Unless we eliminate nuclear weapons, it is only a question of time before they will be used.

French President De Gaulle justified France's development of nuclear weapons by arguing they were cheaper than equivalent conventional weapons. In terms of destructive power, this is true (they yield "more bang for the buck" or "more rubble for the ruble"), but not necessarily in terms of buying security: all of the nuclear powers spend a higher fraction of their income for defense than the world average.

Some have argued that nuclear weapons have helped prevent war. But in fact since 1945 the five declared nuclear powers have been involved in eight times as many wars, on average, as all the nonnuclear countries. Some credit nuclear weapons with having prevented nuclear war, which is preposterous: without nuclear weapons, there could be no nuclear war. The losses in the case of a nuclear war would be so enormous that even if the probability is low, it is an issue that economists cannot ignore. The astronomer Carl Sagan and collaborators discovered in 1983, with the help of a model of the earth's atmosphere, that destruction from a nuclear war would go beyond the impact of heat, blast, and radiation disease. Dust and smoke rising into the stratosphere would linger for months, blocking out sunlight and cooling the earth surface in a "nuclear winter." Harvests would fail, and those who survived the immediate impact could die from hunger and cold. It might well bring an end to civilization and endanger human survival itself. Avoiding nuclear war is a precondition for all other human endeavors.

On July 8, 1996, the World Court declared the threat or use of nuclear weapons contrary to international law under almost any conceivable circumstances and unanimously stated that the nuclear nations have the obligation to conduct negotiations leading to complete nuclear disarmament. Other weapons of mass destruction, such as chemical and biological weapons, have already been banned by treaties. On August 14, 1996, the Canberra Commission on the Abolition of Nuclear Weapons, an international group of leading scientists and former government officials and generals released its final report with a concrete step-by-step plan to eliminate nuclear weapons in a verifiable way. It called on all nuclear nations to adopt immediately a policy of no first use. If nobody were to use nuclear weapons first, they would never be used.

VI. UNITED NATIONS REFORM

According to the principle of subsidiarity, every issue should be decided at the lowest level that involves all those who are affected. Some problems are of a global nature and cannot be solved effectively at any level lower than the world as a whole. One example is preventing the proliferation of nuclear weapons. If only a single country fails to participate in such an effort and sells nuclear weapons technology to anyone willing to pay for it, the whole world is in grave danger. The International Atomic Energy Agency (IAEA) in Vienna, one of the United Nations' many branch organizations, was created to help implement the 1970 Non-Proliferation Treaty that seeks to prevent the spread of nuclear weapons. Currently, it can inspect suspected nuclear weapons plants only with permission of the host governments. If a suspected drug smuggler could tell a border guard, "You may check my glove compartment, but don't open my trunk," such an "inspection" would be meaningless. The mandate of the IAEA should include the right to make unannounced random inspections without the right of a veto from the host government.

Today, most governments would oppose such random inspections as a violation of their national sovereignty. Similarly, when airlines began to search passengers' luggage for explosives after a series of fatal hijackings, many opposed this as a violation of their right to privacy. But today most passengers welcome such precautions, knowing they can be safe only if everybody's luggage is inspected, including their own. Will governments reach the same conclusion before or only after the first terrorist nuclear bomb explodes?

The principal purpose for which the United Nations was founded in 1945 was to prevent another world war by preventing aggression across borders. The UN has been remarkably successful in that endeavor, even though this is rarely acknowledged in the news media, which are quick to focus on any failures but find "good news is no news." Although we still have many wars, almost all of them are now civil wars. Of 39 wars being fought in 1995, all of them were civil wars. A rare exception was Iraq's invasion of Kuwait in 1990, which was decisively repelled by an international force authorized by the UN Security Council.

The UN has been severely limited in preventing civil wars by the provision enshrined in its charter that it is not to interfere in the internal affairs of any member state. If we want to reduce the occurrence of intrastate as well as inter-state wars, it may be necessary to review that stipulation. Under Roman law the head of a household, the "pater familias," had absolute sovereignty over his family. He could sell his children into slavery or beat them to death, and the state had no right to intervene in this internal family affair. Today we consider this concept absurd, but we still cling to the notion of absolute state sovereignty.

One proposal for reforming the UN has been to create an International Criminal Court. Today we have the International Court of Justice in the Hague (also called the "World Court"), but it can only hear cases brought by one government against another and has no enforcement powers. It is unrealistic to expect that citizens can always find justice within their own country, particularly if they are persecuted by their own government and the government controls the courts. For this reason, there is growing support for the creation of an International Criminal Court to which citizens or ethnic minorities who are oppressed by their own government can appeal if necessary.

Many of the international organizations affiliated with the UN provide loans (such as the World Bank and the International Development Association) or give technical advice of various kinds (such as the Food and Agriculture Organization, the World Health Organization, the International Labor Organization, the UN Industrial Development Organization, and many others). These functions play a valuable role in promoting development and helping reduce economic inequality as a source of conflict. But sometimes problems have deeper roots than merely a lack of knowledge or resources. They can be traced to inadequate legal systems and a lack of accountability.

A well-functioning, dependable legal system is one of the most important conditions for peace and development. If people cannot find justice through legal means, they are often tempted to resort to violence. Also, if business profits can be seized with impunity by corrupt officials, this discourages investment and economic growth. If it is easier to get rich by controlling the army or the police than by producing goods that people wish to buy, the most ambitious individuals will plot to seize power by force rather than plan to build business enterprises.

This suggests a new UN agency: a Center for Legal Education and Research (CLEAR). Leading legal scholars and legislators from around the world could work together to exchange insights and study what constitutions and legal codes have worked well, under what conditions, what problems and pitfalls have been encountered, and why. They could make these insights available worldwide and train some of the brightest law students from around the world. This could have the advantage that countries can learn from one another's successes and failures and need not repeat all the mistakes and suffering that others have already gone through.

Another agency that can help promote democratic accountability is the International Institute for Democracy and Electoral Assistance founded 1995 in Stockholm with 14 initial member countries. It seeks to assist countries who request help in monitoring elections and printing ballots. This institute deserves to be strengthened and expanded. Former U.S. President Jimmy Carter, who has participated in many efforts to mediate an end to wars and to observe elections, pointed out that in a civil war, both sides are usually deeply convinced that the vast majority of the people are on their side. If they can be assured of free and fair elections, which they expect to win, both sides are often willing to lay down their arms and settle their dispute through ballots instead of bullets. It is important to make sure that there is no election fraud and that all parties have fair access to the voters via the media before elections. Equally important is to guarantee that the election results will be honored by all parties. If groups who overthrow an elected government by force or prevent it from taking office would automatically face strong sanctions by the international community, there would be fewer military coups. Such an institution could play an important role in helping prevent or end civil wars.

Amartya Sen has observed that serious famines have not occurred in democracies because a government that would allow a famine would not be reelected. Also, some of the worst environmental records have been found in the former centrally planned economies, where any criticism of official policy was punished. A free press, which constantly exposes bad conditions so that they can be corrected, is an essential aspect of democracy. It plays a role similar to that of white blood cells in the human body, which constantly search for infectious agents and eliminate them before they can multiply and spread throughout the body.

The 18th-century German philosopher Immanuel Kant predicted that if the people who have to fight and die in case of war could vote, they would choose governments that would not go to war. This has not been true. Even democracies have engaged in many wars. But it is remarkable that so far there has been no war between two democracies. This leaves open the hope that with the spread of democracy around the world, wars will greatly diminish, if not disappear.

If war erupts despite the best efforts to prevent it, a UN peacekeeping force can intervene to stop the fighting. During the Cold War, few peacekeeping operations took place because the UN Security Council, which needs to authorize such operations, was usually paralyzed by the veto of one or another superpower. Since 1989, more peacekeeping operations have been launched than during the previous 44 years.

Peacekeeping forces have generally been introduced only to observe cease-fires after the conclusion of a cease-fire agreement at the invitation of both sides of a conflict. This is a useful but limited role. If the police could stop a criminal from beating a victim only if "both sides" agreed, it would be powerless. There is a need also for UN peace enforcement, at the request of one side alone, on its own territory, in case of aggression or a perceived threat of aggression.

VII. FINANCING THE UNITED NATIONS SYSTEM

Jan Tinbergen observed that to almost any ministry at the national level, there exists a corresponding international organization, such as the Food and Agriculture Organization corresponding to a ministry of agriculture, the World Health Organization corresponding to ministry of health, The UN Educational, Scientific and Cultural Organization corresponding to a ministry of education, and so on. Most well-run governments also have three major financial institutions: an investment bank, a reserve bank, and a treasury. To the investment bank corresponds the World Bank, to the reserve bank, in a limited sense, the International Monetary Fund, but there is nothing corresponding to a treasury. Yet the treasury, which collects revenue to finance all the other operations of a national government, is its most essential branch. Without a treasury, any government would soon collapse. Tinbergen therefore called for the creation of a world treasury.

Today's arrangement, where countries are assessed on a quota basis for contributions to the UN, but there are no sanctions for late payment or nonpayment, functions poorly. Even though the UN budget ($1.3 billion in 1997) is comparatively modest, less than the annual budget of New York City's police department, for example, the world organization is near bankruptcy. Many countries are late with their payments, particularly the United States, which in 1997 owed $1.3 billion in past dues to the UN, over half of all unpaid dues. Many of the international agencies, whose budgets are independent from the UN, such as the United Nations University, depend on voluntary contributions.

Under U.S. pressure, UN Secretary General Kofi Annan announced a personnel reduction from 10,000 to 9,000 employees in July, 1997. Some have criticized the UN as a bloated, inefficient bureaucracy. Others point out that, for example, in 1997 the U.S. Intelligence Agencies had 80,000 employees and a budget of $26.6 billion. With a relatively small staff, the UN serves 185 member nations, not only a single country, and it does much more than only collect information.

James Tobin proposed a small tax on foreign exchange transactions to calm the highly volatile foreign exchange markets and to give governments more autonomy to pursue socially desirable policies—such as lowering interest rates to overcome a recession or a tight monetary policy to fight inflation—without confronting impeding reactions from the world financial markets. If foreign exchange rates were less erratic and more predictable, this would encourage more international trade and foreign investment and would greatly benefit the whole world economy. As a side benefit, such a tax, which would be collected by national governments on their own territory, could be used—at least in part—to help finance the UN family of organizations. About $280 trillion are exchanged from one currency into another each year or more than 10 times the estimated value of the world's annual economic product. A 0.1% exchange tax, for example, even if it would cut foreign exchange transactions in half, would still yield approximately $140 billion per year. That would be more than sufficient to finance all of today's international organizations, including the World Bank and IMF, and would allow a substantial expansion of funding for sustainable development and peacekeeping.

This tax has never been tried. Given the resistance to new taxes, Ruben Mendez proposed as an alternative that the UN, in cooperation with some major banks, create a Foreign Currency Exchange that would link buyers and sellers of foreign currency at a smaller fee than what banks currently charge their customers. This would be entirely voluntary, giving those who chose to make use of it a financial advantage.

Walter Isard suggested an incremental approach: Some countries might be willing to grant the UN the right to set up such a Foreign Currency Exchange on their territory if the proceeds were shared with the host government and if the UN's share of revenue were spent within that country on a purpose particularly dear to the citizens of that country. Examples include an expansion of the jurisdiction of the World Court in the Netherlands, a research Center on renewable energy and ways to reduce air pollution in Germany, a campus with international students for the UN University in Japan (which now only funds research projects around the world and is not involved in teaching), and so on.

Another potential source of revenue are emission charges, for example a carbon tax, which would help discourage the burning of fossil fuels and save the earth from global warming that may melt the polar icecaps and flood coastal areas, including some of the largest cities. A tax on ozone-depleting gases could help reduce their use, saving the ozone layer that protects us from cancer-causing ultraviolet radiation.

Paradoxically, charging a tax on pollutants would not increase overall taxes, but help reduce them. This is easy to see with the following thought experiment: If gasoline were free at the pump, we would end up paying more for gasoline, not less, because many people would begin to waste it, and in the end the taxpayers would have to cover the costs anyway, regardless of how much gasoline they had used. This is the way in which we generally have dealt with clean air and clean water: by pretending they are free, we have encouraged people to waste them and have paid far too high a price for them—if not always financially, then certainly with our health.

Another potential source of revenue for a World Treasury are auctions of global resources. A 1995 auction by the U.S. Treasury of a small portion of the domestic airwaves spectrum to companies offering mobile telephone services raised nearly $8 billion. Similarly, the limited number of 180 positions for geo-stationary satellites could be auctioned to the highest bidders. Other resources are mining rights on the deep seabed outside of any country's jurisdiction.

Such auctions can also help prevent conflicts. When oil was first discovered in the 19th century in Texas, there were no rules. As soon as anyone had discovered some oil, other companies rushed to the scene and drilled to get a portion of that oil. It occurred that rival oil companies bombarded each other's drilling towers to get at the oil first, but they soon realized that they could never make any profit that way. Today they appreciate that the U.S. government grants exclusive drilling rights to the highest bidder for a parcel of territory. They pay something, but in return they enjoy the security and peace of mind that they can explore without fear that if they strike oil, someone else may take it from them.

A similar service is needed also at the global level to prevent future wars over global resources. No national government can claim the right to auction these global resources to other countries. Only the United Nations, or a World Treasury on its behalf, would be accepted by all countries as a legitimate and impartial auctioneer. Such auctions would also help raise some badly needed funds to address global problems. Of course, an international board of respected personalities, or ultimately an elected world parliament, should oversee the proper use of the funds raised in this way to ensure accountability at all levels.

Developing countries that cannot yet compete on an equal basis in such auctions can be given a fair share, for example, by allocating 50% of global resources according to current population while auctioning the rest. Developing countries would further benefit from such auctions since greater resources would become available to finance development projects.

Such a method to help finance global development, protection of the environment, and peacekeeping has a number of advantages: first, it frees financially pressed governments from paying ever higher contributions. Second, it gives the United Nations and its family of international organizations a more reliable source of funds to meet urgent global needs. Third, it avoids divisive and difficult negotiations over how much each country should contribute, since the richer countries will naturally tend to pay a higher share. Fourth, it uses market principles to improve the efficiency of allocating scarce resources. Fifth, it encourages resource conservation. And sixth, it helps prevent possible future wars over those resources.

Another approach to fund international peacekeeping, proposed by Hazel Henderson and Alan F. Kay, is to offer insurance against aggression. The countries most interested would probably initially be small countries, which are hardly able to maintain military forces that can match potential adversaries. This idea exploits the concept of scale economies: for every country to maintain its own defensive forces is as wasteful as if every house in a community maintained its own fire engine.

Countries that take extra precautions to avoid war, such as having procedures in place to resolve disputes through mediation or arbitration, could get insurance at a reduced rate in the same way as homes built with fireproof materials and having a fire extinguisher can obtain lower fire insurance rates.

A great advantage of a UN Security Insurance Agency over the current situation where the UN Secretary General has to appeal to reluctant member nations to contribute troops for peacekeeping operations is that it would be entirely optional. No country would be required to pay this insurance, but those who did would gain the benefit that anyone who threatened them would face a standing international peacekeeping force that would automatically be committed to the country's defense and would be ready at a moment's notice. Such a swift and certain response should strongly dissuade would-be aggressors and it might therefore be rare that it would actually have to be deployed.

A standing UN peacekeeping force consisting of individually recruited volunteers would have a number of other advantages over military contingents supplied by UN members: the response would be swift, which could save many lives in case of emergencies such as the 1994 genocide in Rwanda. Their primary loyalty would be to the United Nations rather than to their national command structure, and they would train together and work well together. They would be trained to stop fighting and help avoid war rather than winning battles as traditional armies are now trained.

In addition to helping protect countries against aggression and maintaining cease-fires in civil wars, it could also be deployed on short notice to assist refugees and help protect lives in case of natural or industrial disasters, such as earthquakes, floods, accidents at nuclear power plants, poisonous chemical leaks, or other emergencies anywhere on earth.

All of these methods of helping finance the United Nations system would provide a useful service to the world community and as an added benefit help raise funds.

VIII. ECONOMIC SANCTIONS

Given the great destructiveness of modern weapons and, at the same time, the growing economic interdependence of all countries, there has been renewed interest in exploring economic sanctions as an alternative to the use of military force to put pressure on governments to desist from aggression or gross human rights violations. The success has been mixed. Of 103 cases of sanctions examined by Hufbauer and Schott, only about 30% were successful. Sanctions imposed by a single government were rarely successful. However, of the 10 cases of international sanctions approved by the UN Security Council, 9 have so far been successful, including the sanctions against South Africa, which persuaded its business community to join the forces opposing apartheid.

To make sanctions effective, a number of conditions must be fulfilled.

1. Predictability: If sanctions are imposed at will, without clearly known conditions under which they apply, responsibility for the sanctions will be placed by the people on the foreign powers imposing the sanctions, not on their own government that provoked the sanctions with its policies. Galtung has emphasized that arbitrary sanction can provoke nationalist sentiments and rally people behind their beleaguered government.

2. Broad Support: To be effective, sanctions must be tight. Even a few countries that refuse to participate and take advantage of high black market prices can undermine the effect of sanctions. It may be necessary to impose sanctions also on countries that violate sanctions to enforce universal participation. At the same time, neighbor countries that suffer disproportionately from an interruption of trade may need to be compensated to some degree for their losses by the international community.

3. Low Costs: If sanctions impose a high domestic price, like the loss of 150,000 domestic jobs if the U.S. revokes China's most-favored-nation status, they are hard to sustain politically.

4. Compassion: A regime that does not care about the welfare of its people, like Iraq's Saddam Hussein, is not much swayed by economic sanctions that affect the poor. Sanctions should be carefully tailored to hurt only the decision-making elites, e.g., by freezing their foreign bank accounts and refusing their national airline landing rights abroad. In the past, sanctions have often hit innocent people, like democratic opposition forces and vulnerable infants and children and caused heavy loss of life. To punish an entire nation indiscriminately is comparable to blowing up an aircraft with all its passengers to kill a hijacker.

IX. NEW ASPECTS OF INTERNATIONAL SECURITY: SEARCHING FOR PEACE

In December, 1988, an organization called "Economists Allied for Arms Reduction" was founded by Robert J. Schwartz, and today it has branch organizations with a total of well over 1000 members in countries on all five continents. Among its trustees are many Nobel laureates in economics. Its goal is to enlist the special contributions economists can make in the search for peace. Members of every profession have a role and responsibility to do what they can to help assure human survival, even if they have not caused the problems we face.

Economics is perhaps the most developed of the social sciences, insofar as it uses quantification, mathematical models, scientific reasoning, and optimization methods. The concept of human welfare, which is central to economics, needs to include security, to be complete.

Economists can apply their analytical tools to an inquiry into the causes of war and the exploration of nonmilitary strategies to maintain peace. Economists are familiar with the concept of large systems in which many variables interact and may mutually reinforce or weaken one another. We currently live in what could be called a "war system," where a series of interlocking trends, such as poverty, ecological disasters, dictatorships, absence of enforceable international law, and the profitability of the arms trade, among many others, have led to a long series of wars in a vicious cycle. There are also elements of a "peace system" emerging, at least in parts of the world, such as expanding economic cooperation among nations and ways to settle disputes through negotiations and binding legal procedures, e.g., among the members of the Organization for Economic Cooperation and Development, which includes Japan, Korea, the U.S., Canada, and most countries in western Europe. The United Nations also plays an important role in this emerging global peace system.

What are the conditions necessary to guarantee peace, prosperity, and a livable environment for future generations? Few people advocate war, poverty, pollution, or human rights violations. Why do we observe so much of all of these? Is it due to human selfishness, shortsightedness, ignorance, or inadequate legal systems? All of these factors and several more play a role. All of them can be seen as various breakdowns of regulatory feedback systems. Any viable system, whether in nature or human society, needs a series of feedback mechanisms to maintain it in a healthy state or restore that state if the system has deviated.

A regulatory feedback system has three main components: agreement on a desirable goal, methods to detect deviations from the goal, and mechanisms to move the system closer to the goal state if it has deviated. An example is the legal system in which laws define acceptable behavior, courts determine whether someone has violated a law, and the police and prisons serve the function of enforcing the laws.

Such a feedback system can break down in six possible ways: (1) there may be no agreement on the goal (a question of conflict resolution); (2) even if the goal is clear, deviations from it may not be noticed (a question of observation); (3) even if a problem is clear, those who can correct it may have no interest in doing so because others are affected (a question of incentives and also of ethics; whether we care about one another or only about ourselves); (4) even if those who cause a problem ultimately suffer the consequences by themselves, they may fail to prevent it, if the consequences are delayed (a question of future planning); (5) even if the consequences of a mistake are felt immediately, people sometimes act irrationally, against their own best interests, out of hatred or prejudice (a question of psychology and culture); (6) perhaps the most frequent cause of problems is that even though people are fully aware of them and wish to correct them, they may not know how or lack the necessary resources (a question of science, technology, education, and economics). Let us consider these six factors in turn and see what economic reasoning can contribute.

1. Achieving Agreement: Economists' methods to reach agreement consist of negotiations to find mutually beneficial trades and treaties. The use of armed force is not an instrument of economic behavior. A good example of an economic approach to solving international disputes is the Marshall Plan. During the Versailles peace negotiations after World War I, Lord Keynes, as a member of the British delegation, warned that the imposition of huge reparations payments on Germany would create resentment and plant the seeds for another round of war. He resigned in protest when his advice was ignored. The Versailles treaty did indeed help Hitler rise to power with the promise of abrogating it. After World War II, the United States learned that lesson. By giving economic assistance to the war-ravaged countries, including its former enemies, Germany and Japan, it turned them into allies.

2. Observations: Economists are keenly aware that a precondition for formulating and executing good policies is to have reliable data. If we are not aware of a problem, nothing will be done to correct it. Most governments collect extensive economic statistics to detect any deviations from a desired state, such as a rise in unemployment or inflation, so as to be able to take countermeasures. The same type of watchful eye is needed to preserve peace. A 1978 French proposal called for the creation of an International Satellite Monitoring Agency that could detect violations of arms control agreements or preparations for aggression. Because of the Cold War, the proposal was shelved at the time, but it could be revived. Such an agency could also provide early warnings of droughts and other natural disasters. Another inexpensive way to detect threats to peace early could be to have crisis control centers where volunteer citizens could report signs of danger or suspected violations of human rights or international agreements, which could then be investigated and dealt with, if necessary, in the same way as cities have emergency numbers to report fires or crimes.

3. Incentives: A central notion of economics is that people act in their own self-interest. Oskar Morgenstern said that if the politicians and generals who make decisions about war or peace would have to fight themselves at the front line in case of war instead of sending young men to their deaths, we would have fewer wars. Economics also suggests a nonmilitary approach to defense: searching for common security by making peace more attractive. If others see us as a threat, they will naturally seek to counter that threat, which in turn makes us less secure. If we want to be secure, we should seek to play a useful, preferably indispensable role for other coun-

tries so that they wish to maintain good relations with us in their own interest.

4. Future Planning: Economists stress the need for investment. A small payment now may yield big profits in the future. Two examples may illustrate that the same applies to security policy. Alexander Yakovlev, who later became a close advisor to Gorbachev and a key architect of perestroika, which brought an end to the Cold War, was among the first group of 30 Soviet exchange students who came to the United States with a Fulbright Fellowship in 1956–1957. An investment of a few thousand dollars may have contributed more to helping end the nuclear confrontation between the superpowers than billions of dollars in military spending.

Another example shows the benefits of early intervention. Three members of a nongovernmental organization, the Project on Ethnic Relations, were able to mediate an accord between the Rumanian government and representatives of the Hungarian minority in Romania, which ended their conflict by giving the ethnic Hungarians the right to use their own language again in local schools in return for a promise not to seek greater autonomy. That agreement, worked out in two meetings of about 3 days each, may well have prevented another war like in the former Yugoslavia. It is much easier to prevent fighting before it breaks out than to stop it after it has begun. It took nearly 4 years and finally 60,000 foreign troops to end the fighting in Bosnia. This is over 10,000 times as many people for a period more than 100 times longer at a cost far exceeding 1 million times the expense of the Rumanian mediation sessions. Most importantly, preventing war before it erupts can save many lives.

Governments are generally so overburdened that they tend to react to problems only after they have reached crisis proportions, instead of anticipating and preventing them. This is as if we were to drive blindly, waiting until we hit an obstacle and then calling an ambulance instead of anticipating and avoiding dangers. Gorbachev proposed the creation of an international commission of former heads of state and eminent scientists and thinkers who could study potential dangers to human survival and ways to overcome them, free from the pressure to respond daily to the latest crisis.

5. Rational Behavior: Economists advise to carefully weigh costs and benefits of various courses of action, not to act impulsively guided by emotions. A company that practices racism or sexism may fail to hire the most qualified people for a given job. Similarly, nationalism and racism can lead a country to pursue disastrous policies, with Nazi Germany being a prime example. Global education, where children learn to understand and respect other cultures, may be one of the best ways to overcome prejudice and irrational thinking.

6. Resources: Among the most valuable of all resources, as economists have long emphasized, are human resources. Robert Muller, Chancellor of the United Nations University for Peace in Costa Rica, has proposed the creation of a "Global Peace Service" to enlist the talent and dedication of people willing to help solve global problems. Volunteers of all ages from different countries could work together to assist various UN agencies, such as the High Commissioner for Refugees, the Food and Agriculture Organization, the World Health Organization, the UN Environment Program, the High Commissioner for Human Rights, or a new UN Agency for Mediation and Arbitration. They could also work for the thousands of nongovernmental organizations active in promoting peace, development, human rights, and a clean environment. Muller proposed that young people could participate in this Global Peace Service instead of military service, with funding from their own governments. Friendships forged between young people from different countries usually last a lifetime and may later provide valuable links of communication in helping resolve international crises.

Modern science and technology have given humanity unprecedented powers. We can communicate instantly across the globe, and automation has greatly increased the potential for production. Those powers can be used to overcome misery and scarcity—some of the oldest causes of war; they have also enabled us to develop weapons with which we can destroy ourselves. The choice is up to all of us.

Also See the Following Articles

ARMS PRODUCTION, ECONOMICS OF • ARMS TRADE, ECONOMICS OF • COLD WAR • ECONOMIC CAUSES OF WAR AND PEACE • ECONOMIC CONVERSION • MILITARY-INDUSTRIAL COMPLEX, CONTEMPORARY SIGNIFICANCE • NUCLEAR WARFARE • PEACE AND DEMOCRACY • POLITICAL ECONOMY OF VIOLENCE AND NONVIOLENCE •

Bibliography

Arrow, K. J. (1992). The basic economics of arms reduction. In W. Isard & C. H. Anderton (Eds.), *Economics of arms reduction and the peace process* (pp. 57–67) New York: North Holland.

Benoit, E. (1973). *Defense and economic growth in developing countries.* Lexington, MA: D. C. Heath.

Brauer, J., & Gissy, W. G. (Eds.) (1997). *Economics of conflict and peace.* Aldershot, UK: Avebury Press.

Chatterji, M., Fontanel, J., & Hattori, A. (Eds.) (1996). *Arms spending, development and security.* New Delhi: Ashish.

Dumas, L. J. (1995). *The socio-economics of conversion: From war to peace.* Armonk, NY: M. E. Sharpe.

Fischer, D. (1984). *Preventing war in the nuclear age.* Totowa, NJ: Rowman and Allanheld.

Fischer, D. (1993). *Nonmilitary aspects of security: A systems approach.* Aldershot: Dartmouth.

Fisher, R., & Ury, W. (1981). *Getting to yes: Negotiating agreement without giving in.* Boston, MA: Houghton-Mifflin.

Galtung, J. (1969). Violence, Peace and Peace Research. *Journal of Peace Research, 8*(3), 167–191.

Hufbauer, G. C., & Schott, J. J. (1985). *Economic sanctions reconsidered: History and current policy.* Washington, DC: Institute for International Economics.

Isard, W. (1992). *Understanding conflict and the science of peace.* Cambridge, MA: Blackwell.

Jeanes, I. (1996). *Forecast and solution: Grappling with the nuclear.* Blacksburg, VA: Pocahontas Press.

Klein, L. R., Lo, F. C. & McKibbin, W. J. (Eds.) (1995). *Arms reduction: Economic implications in the post-Cold War era.* Tokyo/New York/ Paris: United Nations University Press.

Leontief, W., & Duchin, F. (1983). *Military spending: Facts and figures, worldwide implications and future outlook.* New York: Oxford University Press.

Rapoport, A. (1970). *N-person game theory: Concepts and applications.* Ann Arbor: The University of Michigan Press.

Sen, A. K. (1981). *Poverty and famines: An essay on entitlement and deprivation.* Oxford, UK: Oxford University Press.

Tinbergen, J., & Fischer, D. (1987). *Warfare and welfare: Integrating security policy into socio-economic policy.* New York: St. Martin's Press.

Tobin, J. (1978). A Proposal for International Monetary Reform. *Eastern Economic Journal,* (4), 153–159.

United Nations Development Program (1994). Capturing the peace dividend. In *Human development report 1994* (pp. 47–60). Oxford/ New York: Oxford University Press.

Von Neumann, J., & Morgenstern, O. (1944). *Theory of games and economic behavior.* Princeton, NJ: Princeton University Press.

Wallace, M. D. (1979). Arms races and escalation: Some new evidence. *Journal of Conflict Resolution, 23*(3), 3–16.

Weida, W. (1997). *Atomic Audit.* Washington, DC: Brookings Institution.

Effects of War and Political Violence on Health Services

Anthony B. Zwi
London School of Hygiene and Tropical Medicine

Antonio Ugalde and Patricia Richards
University of Texas, Austin

GLOSSARY

Cold Chain The systems and services required to ensure that vaccines are kept at a cool temperature to ensure their viability during processes of packaging, distribution, and ultimately delivery to the person being immunized.

Primary Health Care The basic level of health care that should be effective, equitable, accessible, acceptable, and affordable to users of services. The primary care approach is closely linked with a multisectoral model of health and development and is community-oriented and accountable.

Secondary Health Care This term usually refers to hospital–level health care, operating at district or local government level.

Tertiary Health Care Institutions that receive referral cases from secondary care facilities. Tertiary care institutions are typically (but not always) located in the large urban areas and will include national referral centers and teaching hospitals.

Vertical Programs These health programs focus on a single condition (for example, malaria or tuberculosis), set of conditions (for example, childhood diseases for which immunizations are available), or set of interventions (for example, those necessary to promote safe delivery of children and the health of their mothers) and are typically organized in such a way that a range of financial control, service delivery, logistics, human resources and training, information systems, and accountability are all located at one key point, often outside of the usual systems for maintaining these activities within the general health system.

I. INTRODUCTION

There is increasing recognition that political violence and war present a significant negative impact on health services and health systems. They also present opportunities, however, for the development of new services and systems; the challenge of confronting adversity allows for innovation, creativity, and the emergence of new technologies and systems that may have some positive benefits for health.

This article examines how political violence of various forms affects health services and health systems. It presents a model (see Fig. 1), reflecting the mechanisms by which war and political violence adversely affect health systems and it seeks to demonstrate the variety of ways in which this occurs. We highlight the challenges facing health systems in their attempts to maintain ac-

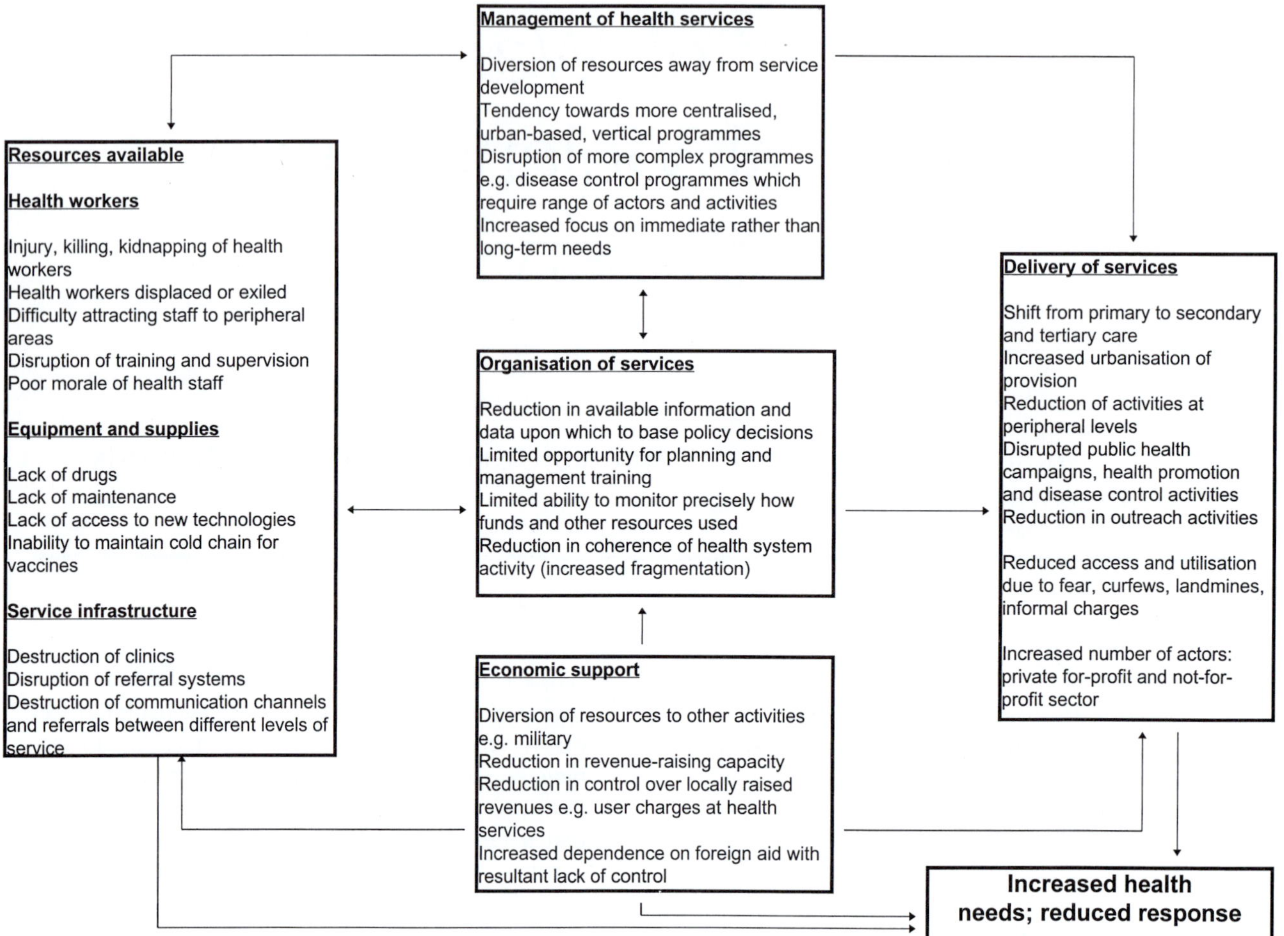

FIGURE 1

tivity despite adversity. Lastly, we focus attention on societies emerging from conflicts and we seek to highlight the role of international aid and nongovernmental organizations in supporting the reestablishment and development of health systems.

A. Trends in Conflict

As described elsewhere in this encyclopedia, the nature and number of wars have changed over time. Each of the last three centuries has revealed an increase in the number of wars and associated deaths. Over 107 million people have died in wars this century alone. While the vast majority of such conflicts have taken place in less developed countries, there have been notable exceptions, such as the 1956 war in Hungary, the 1969 war on the Soviet-Chinese border, and the more recent conflicts in the former Yugoslavia and parts of the former Soviet Union.

A variety of types of struggle, each with different determinants and effects, has been identified. Important factors include anticolonial struggles for independence, struggles based largely on superpower rivalry and the quest for regional hegemony, conflict within states, between classes, religions, ethnic groups, and tribes, often as a result of inequalities in access to political power and decision making, as well as in securing resources for development, and struggles between states over territory, some of which relate to the often arbitrary way in which historically colonized countries and their borders were defined. Violent conflict may also result from populations seeking to redress the structural violence they have experienced: in this sense war and conflict may represent a survival strategy.

For different types of conflict, the extent, form, intensity, and severity of violence varies, as will its effect on health, health services, and systems. Additional influential factors will include the prior development of health services and systems, as well as the nature and form of the conflict, including its scope and geographic extent, its duration, speed of onset (sudden, gradual, chronic); and the level of social preparedness.

B. Impact on Health Reveals Impact on Health System

Examining certain "tracer conditions" or health problems, allows us to identify some of the mechanism by which these adverse effects occur. Aside from the direct effects of conflict on injuries and deaths, many of the other effects are mediated through an impact on health services and systems.

Infant mortality, for example, may be susceptible to the impact of conflict through reduced access to primary care services, the unavailability of drugs for treatable conditions such as respiratory infections, and the disruption of immunization services. Other effects on nutrition, the family structure, and access to water and shelter, will not be described here but clearly have important influences on health, probably more so than health services themselves. During the Ugandan civil war the infant mortality rate rose to above 600 per 1000 in certain war-affected areas; UNICEF has documented the massive impact of conflict on infant and child survival in southern Africa (UNICEF, 1989).

Refugees and internally displaced populations, many fleeing from the effects of conflict, have raised mortality rates, often resulting from the combined effects of poor nutrition, increased vulnerability to communicable diseases, diminished access to health services, poor environmental conditions, anxiety, and stress. In Ethiopia, for example, the sharp decline in immunization coverage during the expansion of the war front in 1991 is likely to have contributed significantly to increasing child mortality; Garfield and colleagues describe a war-related measles epidemic in Nicaragua, attributed in large part to the declining ability of the health service to immunize those at risk in conflict-affected areas. Similarly, the destruction of malaria control activities was instrumental in causing malaria epidemics in Ethiopia in 1991, in Nicaragua, and in Mozambique, suggesting that these complex control programs, which require access to people and their homes, are particularly sensitive to disruption in periods of conflict. Increased rates of malaria may result from war-related population and troop movements, the inability to carry out timely disease control activities, and shortages of personnel for the conduct of control programs in peripheral areas.

Epidemics of louse-borne typhus and relapsing fever have been associated with crowded army camps, prisons, and relief camps, as well as the sale of infected blankets and clothes by retreating soldiers to local communities. Meningitis, dengue fever, and leishmaniasis have all been associated with conflict. Cholera in Africa has been linked with population movements, in great part a response to conflict; sleeping sickness has re-emerged in Angola due to the ongoing civil war, and guinea-worm disease, which is targeted for worldwide eradication, is uncontrolled in South Sudan where an ongoing civil war is underway.

A variety of authors have drawn attention to the "high risk situation" for HIV transmission that occurs in times of conflict. HIV infection has reached high levels in many army forces; the ability of these men to command sexual services from local women, through payment or force, the movement of troops to different parts of the country and front, and their ultimate return to different parts of the country after demobilization, present significant risks to women.

Aside from communicable diseases, nutrition programs and other community-based programs such as the provision of postpartum care may be affected; hospital admissions may decline as a result of services put out of commission or the decline in availability of health service staff. Monitoring these trends may be difficult as the health information system itself may collapse.

Violent political conflict may affect mental health in a variety of ways. The nature of the conflict, the nature of the trauma experienced (or inflicted, as in the case of torture and other repressive violence), the individual and community response to these pressures, the psychological health of those affected prior to the event, the state of community cohesion, and the relationship between the individual, community, and the political struggle taking place will all influence mental health outcomes.

In each of these examples, the impact of conflict on health system activity, whether this be information collection and surveillance, delivery of basic health care services, maintenance of disease control programs, availability of health education and promotion activities, or immunization programs, impedes service delivery and health promotion. These are discussed in more detail below.

II. IMPACT ON HEALTH SERVICES AND SYSTEMS

Lee and Haines (1991) attempted to quantify the impact on health services of the war of the U.S.-led coalition against Iraq in 1991. The prewar Iraqi health system was extensive, accessible to 90% of the population, and it reached 95% of the children requiring immunization. By the end of the war, many hospitals and clinics had been severely damaged or closed; those still operating in the months after the war were forced to cope with massive catchment populations, rendering them unable to provide appropriate care. The damage to infrastructure, such as water supplies, electricity, and sewage disposal, further exacerbated both the determinants of health and the circumstances in which health services operated.

A. Access to Services

The impact of war on health facilities and service delivery is time and location specific. Access will clearly depend on the prior availability of services and their distribution. Users of services are able to utilize them only if they have geographic access (i.e., they are not too far away), economic access (i.e., the services are affordable), and social access (there are no psychological or other barriers preventing use of services). During conflicts all these forms of access to services may be restricted. In Afghanistan following the takeover of Kabul and other towns by the Taliban, women lost access to many services that were previously available to them.

Population movement to access services may be limited as people may be unable to reach services for fear of encountering military personnel or because access to health services is actively hindered. Risk of physical or sexual assault may deter women from seeking care, curfews may prevent people moving about, whether in daytime or nighttime, and the widespread use of antipersonnel landmines may all, directly or indirectly, impede access to health services. People who have been injured may avoid using public services that carry a risk of security force surveillance and in which those with suspicious wounds may be detained or questioned. In South Africa and in the Occupied Palestinian Territories, nongovernmental organizations established alternative health services to allow those injured during uprisings against repressive regimes to seek care without fear of detection and detention.

Many other factors conspire to reduce access: peripheral services may be directly targeted as in Mozambique or Nicaragua. Health workers, anxious to protect their own safety and that of their families, may move to urban areas and may be unwilling to work in more vulnerable peripheral sites. Increasingly, given the absence of drug supplies and logistics support, health workers operating in peripheral services may question whether they are achieving anything at all and may abandon their public sector work in favor of simply ensuring their own survival—either by migration, diversification out of health care provision, or privatizing the care they provide.

In some cases services were not available prior to or during the conflict; in others, there is a rapid decline in service availability, especially where the affected society was fairly well resourced and supported, as in the former Yugoslavia, where the sudden lack of access to good quality medical care was a great shock to the population.

Conflict may seriously disrupt the linkages between different levels of the health service: referrals from clinics to district hospitals, or from districts to provincial centers may be impeded by lack of logistics and communication support as well as by physical and military barriers. Towns and cities may be surrounded and entry into and out of them controlled; experience of besieged cities has taken place over millennia but has more recently been repeated in Sarajevo and in a number of towns in Southern Sudan, such as Juba.

B. Health Services Activity

As mentioned above, health service activity may adapt in a variety of ways. There is generally a tendency to shift from basic primary care activities, where these were provided, toward secondary care services. This partly reflects the shift from peripheral to more urban services, as well as a reduction in peripheral service availability as health workers themselves move to safer areas. In addition, if the military aspects of the conflict intensify, more effort is required to attend to the war wounded, and preventive care and health promotion drop down the list of priorities. Even in situations where there is a desire to promote preventive care, such as in the Tigrayan struggle for liberation, early efforts focused specifically on dealing with the war wounded and making sure that fighting forces were sufficiently well to continue with their campaigns.

In addressing the needs of the war wounded, including rehabilitation, longer term health development and community-based activities may be sacrificed. Scarce health care personnel will be drawn into a more limited range of activities. A frequently disrupted set of services are those concerned with disease control programs. In relation to malaria control, for example, vector control programs, house spraying, the drainage of stagnant water, the availability of information and education activities, and the ongoing development of treatment protocols, training, and supervision necessary to ensure good quality early treatment of disease may all be compromised. The disruption of surveillance and health information systems will further exacerbate these problems and may reduce pressure to ensure that the problem is addressed. Public health programs geared to following up people with communicable diseases, contacting their families and partners, and making advice, information, screening, or care available to them, may be compromised. Community outreach activities invariably suffer as services contract and are offered only in safer, less peripheral areas.

As the public health sector declines for the reasons cited above, other actors increasingly engage in health care provision These include the local indigenous and medical private sector, as well as local and international nongovernmental organizations. Activities become increasingly "projectized," with a lack of overarching direction within a broad policy framework. Aid dependency increases; along with this comes an increase in donor control and a skewing in the nature and types of programs offered. Activities may become increasingly limited to small areas or specific districts and populations. Programs that do operate are likely to become increasingly vertical with a single system operating to assess needs, deliver services, monitor performance, and finance the system. The gap between these better funded vertical programs and the general health services may widen substantially as the former are protected from the neglect and withdrawal of resources occurring elsewhere in the health system.

C. Infrastructure

The destruction of the physical infrastructure necessary for the delivery of health services may wreak havoc on systems attempting to maintain services. The direct targeting of clinics, hospitals, and ambulances may be against international humanitarian law but has frequently been experienced in latter-day conflicts. Increasingly, the delivery of aid, whether in the form of food or health care, has itself been targeted during intense intranational conflicts. In addition, related facilities such as those necessary for storage, water distribution, sewage removal, or electricity have been targeted with adverse health service effects.

The Sudanese army deliberately destroyed hand water pumps in rebel areas, and the insurgency did likewise in government-held territory. During the Gulf War allied bombing damaged sewage treatment plants and water supplies in Iraq. Potable water availability declined from 7 million to 1.5 million cubic meters per day. Shortages of chemicals and electricity required for testing and ensuring water potability led to outbreaks of typhoid, cholera, and gastro-intestinal diseases. In Nicaragua, the insurgency destroyed the main pharmaceutical storage facility of the country in Corinto, creating a severe shortage for months.

The destruction of nonhealth physical infrastructure such as roads, electrical plants, and communication systems has indirect health consequences. In Cape Town, South Africa, transport difficulties prevented health workers from attending work; experiences in the occupied Palestinian territories and other regions of active ongoing conflict have been similar. In some Iraqi hospitals, elevators did not work during energy blackouts and patients could not be moved to surgical theaters, and emergency interventions had to be delayed or take place in suboptimal conditions. The displacement of rural dwellers and health workers from rural areas produced a more urban care system causing a total breakdown of several rural districts.

D. Equipment and Supplies

During violent political conflicts fewer medicines and inputs to health care may be available to the public health sector because of budgetary reductions and import difficulties. The shortage of drugs may translate into an increase in medically preventable causes of death, such as those from asthma, diabetes, and infectious diseases. Shortages also lower the quality of care. In Somalia, amputations performed without intravenous antibiotics produced high rates of infections, and in former Yugoslavia operations were performed with inadequate anesthesia. In Uganda, the Essential Drugs Management Programme, funded by the Danish International Development Agency and organized in the early 1980s, was disrupted by the conflict. Many rural dwellers who for the first time had access to modern medicines were once more deprived of basic drugs. The cold chain, necessary for ensuring that vaccines are kept in appropriate conditions from the time of manufacture to transport and supply and ultimately delivery to the individual, may be disrupted with serious consequences for communicable disease outbreaks.

The availability of basic health care technologies, such as functioning x-ray units or laboratories, may be undermined by lack of maintenance, spare parts, skilled personnel, chemicals, and other supplies. More sophisticated technologies, such as ultrasound, or fetal monitoring, even where previously available, may no longer be present with health workers having to change their practice to less technology-intensive approaches. While this may not, in itself, necessarily be inappropriate, it does increase the levels of stress faced by both health care providers and users alike.

E. Budget

A key concern is the impact of ongoing military struggle on government spending on the social sector. In Ethiopia, the conflict against the Ethiopian Derg led to increases in military expenditure from 11.2% of the government budget in 1974/75 to 36.5% by 1990/91, and to declines in the health budget from 6.1% in 1973/4 to 3.5% in 1985/86 and 3.2% in 1990/91.

The deterioration of the economy during wars implies a reduction in public expenditure. Funds required to support the war shifts budgetary priorities and allocations from social services to the military. The result is a smaller percentage of a smaller budget for health. In Uganda, income per capita was reduced from $500 in 1965 to $250 by 1989 (in constant prices of 1989). In 1986 the public health budget was only 6.4% of what had been in the early 1970s. The drastic reduction of funding at a time when needs were greater, the lack of available health workers and key health administrators, the destruction of physical infrastructure, and the weakening of civil and political institutions all contributed to the collapse of the health system. Before the beginning of political violence Uganda enjoyed health services considered to be among the best in sub-Saharan Africa; by the end of the conflict in 1986 it was near the bottom. In El Salvador the GNP per capita (in constant prices of 1960) was reduced from $839 in 1978 to $619 in 1989, and the proportion of the national budget allocated to health plummeted from 10% in 1980 to 6% in 1990. In the same period the budget available to the ministry of health, as a percentage of the GNP, declined from 2% to 0.9%. Until 1980 the health budget had been higher than the defense budget, but during the first year of the civil war more funds were allocated to the military than to health, and at the peak of the conflict in 1986, the official figures (which probably represented a small part of the real allocations) showed that the military received about four times more than the health sector. During the 1967–1970 civil war in Nigeria the military expenditures rose exponentially. In 1966 only 7% of the national budget was dedicated to defense; by 1970 the percentage was 43%. During the same period, health expenditures as a percentage of the GNP fell from 4% to 0.8%.

F. Human Resources

Injury, killing, kidnapping, and exodus of health workers is common during periods of political violence and war. As in the case of the destruction of the physical infrastructure, there is evidence that in many countries, including Argentina, Guatemala, Mozambique, and Nicaragua, health workers were targeted for destruction. In Uganda, half the doctors and 80% of the pharmacists left the country between 1972 and 1985. After the war for independence from Portugal, Mozambique was left with only 80 of the 500 doctors present before independence. By 1960, one year after the Cuban revolution, half of the Cuban physicians had left that country.

Other times, war-ravaged countries are left without health planning and administrative expertise. Shortage of personnel reduces the availability and quality of services and the control of communicable diseases. As supports to the delivery of health care decline, the morale of service providers is compromised and a vicious spiral of declining quality of care, declining utilization, and increasing privatization ensue. Health workers increasingly seek to protect their own interests, whether by moving to safer areas, by emigration, or by drainage into nongovernmental and private services. The lack of skilled personnel, referral systems, training, and support all detract from the quality of services provided and the satisfaction that service providers take in the care they offer.

G. Community Involvement

In many other struggles, particularly those of the "low intensity" form, there is evidence of community leaders and social structures being specifically targeted for destruction and annihilation. The war against the Marxist Frelimo state in Mozambique was waged, in part, through an attempt to reduce access to health care and educational services that the state had prioritized as a symbol of its commitment to improving the quality of life in rural and peri-urban areas. As a result, these services became specially targeted, for the same reason: in an attempt to undermine the support attracted by the state. In Nicaragua, another country in which the socialist uprising had sought to give priority to education and health services, these were targeted by opposition forces.

The immediate and longer term effect of such action is difficult to quantify: what is clear, however, is that local systems of democracy and accountability will be disrupted and involvement in community affairs discouraged.

H. Health Policy Formation

Violent political conflict tends to undermine national capacity to make decisions rationally and accountably.

On the other hand, conflict may bring communities together to work collectively to solve problems, an issue discussed briefly below.

During periods of conflict, established and routine systems of making decisions, planning, assessing needs, and responding to them may be seriously disrupted during periods of ongoing conflict. As mentioned earlier, normal services may be disrupted and resources, whether human or material, may be required for new needs.

A key problem in conflict-affected settings is the wide range of actors operating and the lack of the usual lines of accountability for action. In regular health systems, decisions taken at a peripheral level are accountable, usually within the health sector, to district or provincial health authorities, and these are, in turn, responsible to central health authorities. During conflicts the system of provision and response to needs may be highly decentralized with few lines of accountability. A related problem is that the policy framework, within which providers and purchasers of services operate, may be entirely lacking. There may be an inability to control and coordinate, or even simply to ensure awareness of, NGO and donor organization activities. There may be a serious lack of data on which to make important health policy decisions.

A longer-term constraint will be the inability of local health service providers and policymakers to relate to the international debates around health care and health system reorganizations that take place all the time. As a result, lessons learned in other settings may fail to be adopted locally and the same mistakes may be made in new sites over and over again. While this is not solely due to conflict, the presence of conflict exacerbates any usual attempt to ensure that systems learn from their own experiences, and that systems of institutional memory are developed, as well as impeding the ability of individuals and systems to learn from the experiences of others further afield. It is notable that during the conflicts in Uganda, and during the period of anti-apartheid political struggle in South Africa, the isolation of the country served to reduce contact with current international health policy developments and debates. This suggests that despite the nature of the struggle, relative isolation and focus on other key political struggles and concerns, detracts from both individuals and systems keeping abreast of developments in the "outside world."

Locally available fora for debate around policy matters may be unavailable. For example, the media may be less accessible to people or may be less willing to take risks in highlighting discrepancies between, for example, what the government might say it does and what it actually does. In the postconflict setting, a key challenge is to reestablish these fora for debate and to facilitate the exchange of ideas between the range of important stakeholders operating in the health environment.

1. Policy Shifts

In almost every country, the dominance of physicians in the health sector sustains policies favoring specialized and tertiary care at the expense of primary care services. By the late 1960s it was becoming increasingly clear among public health scholars that in order to improve the health conditions of the poor in third world countries there needed to be a more even allocation of resources between primary and hospital care, and between rural and urban areas. During the 1970s, in spite of pressure from physicians, some countries had achieved modest gains in making primary care accessible to rural and underprivileged urban populations. In war-torn countries, the tertiary care needs of the wounded and the limited availability of resources reversed earlier changes, while in countries in which the implementation of primary care policies was under discussion, these were postponed, in some cases for extensive periods of time.

The impact of war on the policy process has been studied in very few countries; information and insights into how systems adapt to and respond to ongoing conflict is therefore extremely scarce. (We base this section on work with which we have been involved directly or indirectly in Uganda, El Salvador, Cambodia, Palestine, and South Africa.) In Uganda, the political conflict paralyzed health policy formation. As one informant remarked, during the war years policy "was established by decree, no one knew what health policy really was."

During wars, due to scarcity of resources and government difficulties in accessing populations under the control of insurgents, NGOs fill part of the vacuum left by the public sector. The role of NGOs is extremely important both during and in the aftermath of ongoing conflict. During conflicts, indigenous NGOs and church groups may be among the few service providers who continue to operate during the conflict, especially in rural areas and those more directly affected by violence. A key problem, however, is that these NGOs often provide a patchwork of services that are relatively independent of the state and that do not necessarily fit in with other service provision approaches or priorities. They may communicate poorly with one another, adopt different approaches and standards of care and health worker remuneration, and focus attention mostly at a very local level with some impact on the equity of service availability across large regions.

In the postwar period, NGOs continue to have an important role and may remain the sole service providers in some areas. The link between the services they provided during the earlier emergency period and the services now needed in the postwar period may be at odds with one another, and a gradual transition from a relief mode of operation to one that is development-oriented is required. A number of key problems may emerge in relation to this transition, however. For one thing, different actors, whether donors or NGOs, tend to operate in either the relief/emergency or in the development phase, and there are few organizations with the skills, ability, political insight, and flexibility both in terms of funding sources and in types of activity, that can bridge this divide.

In Uganda after the war, the public sector exhibited extreme weaknesses in planning. Coupled with the proliferation of NGOs (350 were registered in the country) most of which operated largely independently, the result was a degree of policy chaos and persistent fragmentation of health policy and service delivery that had begun during the political conflict. The conflict itself seriously delayed urgently needed policy debates during the reconstruction and development of the country and the form that this should take. Because of a lack of coordination, important programs such as malaria control were not adequately addressed by any of the key donors. In Cambodia, there was a similar neglect of disease control activity, and tuberculosis received inadequate attention during the period under a UN transitional authority. While some services in Cambodia and other conflict-affected countries were neglected, others were offered by a variety of providers. During the period of reconstruction in Uganda, little attention was paid to the more difficult tasks of creating self-sustainability and correcting structural inefficiencies.

The policy process was also altered by war in El Salvador. The insurgency, assisted by foreign volunteers and funding, had developed a remarkable primary health care system based on health promoters, preventive care, and self-reliance. After the signing of the peace treaty in 1992 foreign funding for primary care began to dry up. Because of economic constraints the ministry of health was unable to provide services to the relatively extended and remote rural areas formerly controlled by the insurgency. In the absence of public services, the NGOs that had assisted the insurgents continued to offer services after the war. In the postconflict reconstruction effort, international donors promoted the provision of health services through the private sector and NGOs. In spite of the pressures by international agencies, the ministry was unwilling to coordinate activities with and transfer funds to the NGOs because, as former allies of the insurgency, it considered them to be too leftist. There were also conflicts in the policy approaches between the ministry and the NGOs. The former was more interested in a traditional medical care model, while the NGOs, as a result of the war experience, favored primary care more in line with current international recommendations (use of paramedics, preventive and educational programs, and self-reliance). The result of the impasse were delays in the formation and implementation of policies, friction between international donors and the ministry, delays in the transfer of international assistance, and a deterioration of primary services in the poorest rural areas of the country.

In Cambodia, unique efforts were made by the Ministry of Health, with the support of the World Health Organization, to coordinate international aid to the health sector and to ensure that services offered could be accommodated within a health policy framework on which a wide range of policy actors agreed. While this was an important and innovative effort, the coordination effort was inadequately resourced and had insufficient powers to ensure that coordination actually took place. As a result, much effort was duplicated, unnecessary services were established, conflicts between the NGO community and public sector emerged in some settings, and inadequate attention was devoted to the longer term needs of the health system. More recent discussion of sectorwide approaches to health system development are receiving attention and may present some opportunities for ensuring that the donor community as a group engages with national policymakers to collectively determine how best to assist the reestablishment of the health system and its longer term development.

Almost inevitably, wars reinforce economic dependence in third world countries; Uganda illustrates the consequence of dependence on the health policy process. After the war in 1988, about 50% of health care was provided by church missions. Foreign funding and out-of-pocket payment of health services accounted for four-fifths of health expenditures in the country. Unable to control health funding, the public health sector lost policy-making power, and foreign agencies and donors became the de facto health policymakers. During the reconstruction, the World Bank, contradicting its own international health policy statements, paid lip service to primary care while at the same time advocated the rehabilitation of hospitals. According to the World Bank's Uganda report : "Primary health care . . . will not necessarily be cost-effective . . . it can absorb great amounts of money without yielding results, and may be rejected by consumers . . . immediate future investment in the renovation of hospitals is likely to show a very effective return" (Lee *et al.*, 1987).

Our study in El Salvador found that the Bank preferred to fund hospital construction and rehabilitation because it had more experience in the preparation, administration, and supervision of these types of loans than in primary care. The institutional needs of the World Bank appeared to be more important than the pressing health needs of populations emerging from wars. International banks such as the World Bank have been eager to lend money for reconstruction and rehabilitation of hospitals and other health facilities, in some cases providing opportunity costs and compromising the capability of the health sector for preventive, promotional, and primary care. In the Palestinian territories, donors too have shown a propensity to desire to fund infrastructural projects. In particular, the Japanese government and the European Community have both contributed sizeable sums for the construction of hospitals in Jericho and the Gaza Strip, respectively, despite hospital services not being the priority concerns at this point in time.

III. POSITIVE EFFECTS OF CONFLICT ON HEALTH SYSTEMS

Not all the effects of political violence on health systems are negative. In some cases, adaptations and organizational or political responses might be positive and may allow opportunities for health system and societal development. In the anticolonial liberation struggles in Mozambique, for example, the FRELIMO party encouraged community participation and self-reliance in health; this was a forerunner to more widely promoted primary health care policies in many countries. In the conflict between national groups and the Ethiopian Derg, community-based political movements in Eritrea and Tigray promoted community participation and control in decision making, and facilitated the development of multisectoral health promotion strategies. The system was so sophisticated that an underground hospital, hidden from air raids, was developed in Orota. In Tigray, the Tigrayan People's Liberation Front ensured that health workers were trained and mobile services established. Innovative community-financing systems, operating through elected local governments, the *baitos*, were established, empowering health workers in communities to ensure that drugs and adequate services were available despite considerable constraints. Services that were destroyed during the military struggle were reconstructed, and a functioning referral system was also established.

Similar experiences of the promotion of participation and control by communities over health resources, the promotion of primary health care, and recognition of the social determinants of ill-health have characterized other struggles such as those in Nicaragua and Vietnam.

It is difficult to quantify the impact of conflict on community participation but it is apparent that there are times when it enhanced community mobilization, participation, and control over local decision making. Experiences in Nicaragua, Mozambique, Vietnam, Eritrea, and Tigray suggest that conflict may be an important organizing influence and that communities may come together to respond to this external threat. What is far less certain, however, is whether such participatory activity can be sustained in the longer term. A recent study in Tigray and North Omo, Ethiopia, showed that although the involvement of women in local government and political activity was actively promoted during the war, their ongoing involvement in the postwar period appeared to be declining.

Relatively little is known about how health systems actively adapt to adverse conditions during wartime. This would be a fruitful area for research and warrants attention: if positive adaptations could be more directly supported, it may be possible to ensure that the core elements of health systems are maintained and sustained, or even develop during periods of conflict.

One adaptation that consistently emerges in conflict-affected societies is the development of the private and traditional sectors. These important aspects of the health care system represent an important health care resource that could be usefully incorporated in the delivery of health care in the future. Understanding how this system emerges, what role it plays, and what support can be given it to ensure that the quality of services delivered is appropriate, merit further attention.

In some cases unique adaptations may occur. The WHO assisted the Bosnian and Croatian health care systems to develop a system for registering disabled people during the war. These registration systems can be extended and further developed in the aftermath of the conflict in order to ensure that disabled people retain access to important rehabilitation and social support services. Where services are developed in response to specific war-related needs, for example, the development of war surgery services to care for people with antipersonnel landmine injuries, these services could be extended to other emergency care needs and rehabilitation requirements in the aftermath of conflict.

A variety of forms of health for peace initiatives have been promoted. These include truces to allow for immunization campaigns and other forms of cessation of conflict to perform vital public health activities. Health-related activity may be particularly useful in helping reestablish community functions by allowing a focus on services that all parties agree are beneficial. The extent to which health services reconstruction is able to facilitate a reduction in tensions between factions and a commitment to working together has been underexplored but warrants attention.

IV. POSTCONFLICT CHALLENGES

In the postconflict period, the costs of reconstruction may be staggering. In the immediate aftermath of the Gulf War, it was estimated that Iraq would require $110–$200 billion and Kuwait $60–$95 billion to repair the war damage from the U.S.-led coalition. In contrast, the goals adopted by the World Summit for Children in 1991 required $20 billion for their global implementation.

Some of the key challenges facing postconflict health systems have been referred to earlier. A particularly important issue is to determine the extent to which the prior health system will be reconstituted or the extent to which it will be reformed in an effort to improve efficiency, effectiveness, and equity. It is apparent from studying a number of countries emerging from conflict that the "default mode" is to attempt to reestablish whatever services existed prior to the violence. In Uganda, however, the postconflict resource base was less than 10% of what it was prior to the civil war, making simple reestablishment of prior services totally infeasible. Furthermore, in the period between the commencement of periods of conflict and their resolution, which may last decades, approaches to the nature of health services and who purchases and provides them have changed. In recent years, for example, it has become accepted wisdom (often without careful assessment of local context) that charges be levied for health services and that the state need not be the only provider: where possible the engagement of other providers, including the for-profit and not-for-profit private sector, and the indigenous or traditional sector, have been enlisted in many countries.

An even more important and difficult challenge is to establish the policy framework within which health services and the health system operate. Different stakeholders, including political actors, service providers, and international donors, each have their own agendas and services that they wish to prioritize. A key role of government, when it functions effectively, is to provide a framework within which the different actors can operate. In postconflict countries, this policy framework may be lacking given the inadequacy of government capacity, or challenges to its legitimacy. An important policy role is to facilitate the development of consensus about broad health system direction: in the absence of functioning government this is a particularly challenging task that could be assisted, or (more usually) hindered, by the involvement of the international community.

Among the issues to be debated at such a crucial time in the reestablishment of national policy is the extent to which reform of the health system is possible. Issues such as the extent to which services will be paid for and by whom, how decentralized the system will be, what the role of the private for profit sector will be, and whether third party payment mechanisms will be promoted are all key questions on which debate and direction are required. In the absence of resolving many of these issues amicably, services and systems may develop without any cohesiveness with resultant lack of efficiency and equity.

Ensuring that, to as great an extent as possible, existing inequities in distribution and access to health services are resolved in the aftermath of conflict may be helpful in reducing causes of tension between groups. In the postconflict period, a fundamental concern is to understand and seek to address those factors that contributed to the conflict in the first place. Health may provide an opportunity to bring together community members from different factions. There are a variety of ways in which health services and health-related projects can assist in bringing together different groups. Although the evidence for the effectiveness and sustainability of such initiatives is limited, these deserve attention, experimentation, and careful evaluation.

An additional factor that may contribute to reducing the level of tension between communities is to work toward the establishment of more equitable systems of distributing resources. Improving the proportion of the budget that can be allocated to primary care service provision, to rural areas, and to the poorest areas will all assist in reducing inequities. In seeking to address historical inequities, enhancing the quality of publicly, and where possible, privately provided services, as well as ensuring their longer term sustainability are all important challenges. In seeking to ensure sustainability, some copayment mechanisms may be necessary although appreciating the limited resource base in many postconflict settings is critical. It is important also to appreciate the need for enhancing quality and sustainability.

An appreciation of gender inequalities in society, in health and in access to and utilization of services is crucial to reestablishing a more effective and equitable service. During conflicts gender relations may change, for better or worse: where positive features develop, for example, where women are able to exert more control over household decisions, supporting these positive developments is desirable. In some conflicts, such as the South African, Tigrayan, and Palestinian conflicts, women played an important part in the political struggle and have continued to demand their right to influence ongoing political developments. Postconflict development of civil society and good governance thus reflect opportunities for positive change.

V. CONCLUSIONS

Political violence and conflict have an extensive negative effect on health and health systems. These negative effects are present in all aspects of the health system: their infrastructure, budgeting, planning and management, availability of human and material resources, and service provision.

There is increasing evidence of these detrimental effects. Far less documented and understood are the impacts upon planning and policy-making, and on relationships between services and the communities they serve. An important challenge for researchers is to understand how health systems adapt and respond to conflict and to determine whether those developments that are positive can be further reinforced and sustained. This applies not only to health systems, but to community and local government responses to conflict that may be positive and deserve to be reinforced. Notable among these may be positive changes in gender relations in which women have challenged their domination during conflict and demand that their needs receive attention in any postconflict arrangements.

To examine how systems respond to conflict and if and how they protect key elements of service provision and functioning is an important challenge. To maintain information systems, for example, is crucial to ensuring that ongoing disease control efforts are sustained. The establishment of sentinel sites or areas of heightened surveillance in which ongoing monitoring can be preserved and promoted represent important challenges in urban and rural areas.

Refining rapid assessment techniques that can be used in the aftermath of conflict to establish the extent to which services are able to function and health personnel are actively providing good quality care is another important challenge. How best to integrate a variety of personnel who may have been trained in different systems to different standards has barely been addressed in the literature.

There remain many unknowns regarding how systems and services respond to conflict. Which characteristics of health systems allow them to maintain their activities during conflicts and complex emergencies deserve attention. Are these characteristics of the system of service providers, or alternatively, of the communities in which they function? Here, more research is clearly required: identifying positive developments or mechanisms for bolstering the resilience of health systems will assist in ensuring their survival during disruptive and destructive periods.

A key challenge during and in the aftermath of conflict remains the effective coordination of available resources. A variety of stakeholders operate in these settings: government, private sector, international organizations, and a wide variety of nongovernmental groups. Various mechanisms have been tried in an attempt to ensure a degree of coordination between service providers: a key element is having in place a policy framework within which service providers operate. To stimulate policy dialogue and debate, and to seek to ensure that policy is, at least in part, based on evidence of effectiveness, efficiency, equity, and sustainability, are key challenges to all the stakeholders operating in these highly politicised environments.

It is important that in the postconflict reconstruction priority be given to the reorganization of services with emphasis on preventive and primary care over the physical reconstruction of the infrastructure. In many settings, however, emphasis appears to be mistakenly placed largely on the rehabilitation and construction of hospitals and clinics, with little attention being devoted to the more difficult tasks of improving the policy process, improving management capacity, developing the provision of preventive care, and extending services to the poor.

Also See the Following Artcles

PUBLIC HEALTH MODELS OF VIOLENCE AND VIOLENCE PREVENTION • PUBLIC HEALTH STRATEGIES • WARFARE, MODERN

Acknowledgment

Several parts of this article borrow from previous work by the authors, in particular from A. Zwi and A. Ugalde, 1989, 1991; A. Ugalde and R. Vega, 1989; J. Macrae, A. Zwi and H. Birungi, 1993; A. Ugalde and A. Zwi (Eds.), 1994, 1995; A. Zwi 1996; A. Ugalde *et al.*, 1996.

Bibliography

Barnabas G. A, & Zwi, A. B. (1997). Health policy development in wartime: establishing the Baito health system in Tigray, Ethiopia. *Health Policy and Planning, 12*(1): 38–49.

Cliff, J., & Noormahomed, A. R. (1988). Health as a target: South Africa's destabilisation of Mozambique. *Social Science and Medicine, 27*(7), 717–722.

Dodge, C. P. (1990). Health implications of war in Uganda and Sudan. *Social Science and Medicine*, 31: 691–698.

Dodge, C. P., & Wiebe, P. D. (1985). *Crisis in Uganda: The breakdown of health services.* Oxford: Pergamon.

Garfield, R., & Williams, G. (1992). *Health care in Nicaragua. Primary care under changing regimes.* New York: Oxford University Press.

Garfield, R. M., Frieden, T., & Vermund S. H. (1987). Health-related outcomes of war in Nicaragua. *American Journal of Public Health, 77*: 615–618.

Garfield, R. M., & Neugat, A. I. (1991). Epidemiologic analysis of warfare. A historical review. *Journal of the American Medical Association, 266*: 688–692.

Garfield, R. M., Prado, E., Gates, J. R., & Vermund, S. H. (1989). Malaria in Nicaragua: community-based control efforts and the impact of war. *International Journal of Epidemiology, 18*: 434–439.

Kloos, H. (1992). Health impacts of war in Ethiopia. *Disasters, 16*: 347–354.

Lee, I., & Haines, A. (1991). Health costs of the Gulf War. *British Medical Journal*, 303: 303–306.

Lee, K., Hull, W., & Hoare, G. (1987). The costs and financing of health services in Uganda (Unpublished report). Entebbe: Ministry of Health, AMREF, and International Development Agency.

Levy, B. S., & Sidel, V. W. (Eds.). (1997). *War and public health.* New York: Oxford University Press.

Macrae, J., & Zwi, A. (Eds.). (1994). *War and hunger. Rethinking international responses to complex emergencies.* London: Zed Books.

Macrae, J., Zwi, A., & Birungi, H. (1994). A healthy peace? Rehabilitation and development of the health sector in a post-conflict situation. London: Health Policy Unit, London School of Hygiene and Tropical Medicine.

Ugalde, A., Selva-Sutter, E., Castillo, C., Paz, C., CaZas, S., Oakes, M., & Solas, S. (1996). *Reconstruction and development of the health sector in El Salvador after the 1981–1992 war* (Unpublished report prepared for the European Union, TSA-CT94-0305 (DG 12 HSMU), San Salvador.

Ugalde, A., & Zwi, A. (Eds.). (1994). *Violencia politica y salud en América Latina.* Mexico: Nueva Imagen.

Ugalde, A., & Zwi, A. (1995). Violencia politica. In Vidal, G. (Ed.), *Enciclopedia Ibero Americana de Psiquiatria.* Buenos Aires: Fundación Acta Fondo para la Salud Mental.

Ugalde, A., & Vega, R. R. (1989). Review essay: State terrorism, torture, and health in the Southern Cone. *Social Science and Medicine, 28*: 759–765.

UNICEF. (1989). *Children on the front line.* New York: UNICEF.

Walt. G., & Cliff, J. (1986). The dynamics of health policies in Mozambique 1975–1985. *Health Policy and Planning, 1*(2): 148–157.

Walt, G., Melamed, A. (Eds.). (1984). *Mozambique. Towards a people's health service.* London: Zed Books.

Zwi, A. (1996). Numbering the dead: counting the casualties of war. In Bradby H. (Ed.), *Defining violence: Understanding the causes and effects of violence*, pp. 99–124. Aldershot: Avebury.

Zwi, A., & Ugalde, A. (1991). Political violence and health in the Third World—A public health issue. *Health Policy and Planning, 6*: 203–217.

Zwi, A., & Ugalde, A. (1989). Towards an epidemiology of political violence in the third world. *Social Science and Medicine, 28*: 633–42.

Enemy, Concept and Identity of

Gordon Fellman
Brandeis University

> We have met the enemy, and it is us.
>
> —*Pogo*

GLOSSARY

Alienation Estrangement of the self from feelings of oneness with its work, the product of its work, buyers and users of the product, fellow workers, community, society, nature, and self.

Adversary Compulsion Like addictions, this signifies feelings that one has no choice in nearly all encounters, but to compete to win.

Adversary Paradigm A worldview that assumes that the point of most encounters is to overcome the other. Competition is normative, with appropriate feelings of antagonism, anger, rage, disdain, triumph, hate, failure, loss, and despair.

Ego Advances In contrast to ego defenses (see below), ego advances are strategies by which the self connects with other people, work, nature, and itself, in positive ways that enhance growth and gratifying relationships with others, society, nature, and itself.

Ego Defenses Strategies by which the self avoids facing psychic pain, from external and internal sources, with which it believes itself unable to cope.

Identity Feelings of content and continuity in the self, such that self and others recognize and accept this as the person one is.

Mutuality Paradigm A worldview that assumes that the point of most encounters is to enhance and develop feelings of connectedness, support, nurturance, caring, respect, empathy, compassion, growth, and love.

Neurosis Feelings of incapacity to act on desires, with no apparent objective reasons for such feelings and their deleterious consequences.

THE INTENTION OF THIS ARTICLE is to describe enemy relations in terms that suggest possibilities of moving beyond what we now experience as the all but universal phenomenon of enemy creation and perpetuation. It is not a comprehensive survey of theories of the nature and construction of the enemy. Depending on who one reads, enemy creation can result from the evil nature of humans, from an inborn destructive tendency that inevitably plagues our species, from divine plans not fully fathomable by mortals, from the structure of the state, from the invention and perpetuation of private property, from the peculiar nature of powerful and resilient collective phenomena like nationalism and religion, from the tenacity of ethnic and national identities, from a need for identification with a social-political unit larger than the self, from tendencies to define the self in oppositional contrast with others, from peculiar imperatives of the business of mass media, from the need to avoid anarchy, from the nature and dynamics of patriarchy, from the historical social construction of masculinity across most societies, from unconscious acting out of Oedipal and other universal inner conflicts, from the fear of death and the consequent construction of society, ritual, and war to cope with that fear. And still others.

The Cold War brought to an end a remarkably durable enemy relationship that, whatever its grotesque limits, was at least stable. Each of the two superpowers demonized the other, with the kind of symmetry customary in any enemy caricaturing of the other side. The relationship was costly economically, exceedingly dangerous militarily, exhausting politically, and powerfully destructive of possibilities for transcending the ancient and continuing custom of enemyhood as a central feature of collective life.

With the end of the Cold War, the process of enemy construction did not stop. It went into other modes. In many parts of the world, hostilities between national and ethnic groups, which had simmered throughout the Cold War, exploded. The violence that has ensued has been largely but not entirely within nations and between parts of former nations. Within the United States, social class, immigrant, life style, race, gender, and other enemy constructions, which had been there all along, now waxing, now waning, were renewed. Within the former USSR, social class, criminal, national, and other constructions also succeed that major one provided for over four decades by the Cold War.

Ethnic and national identifications currently offer examples as good as any of how it is that groups can hate each other. But they are only a special case of a general phenomenon.

Undoubtedly enemy construction, like most social phenomena, is overdetermined, that is, there are far more plausible explanations for it than are required by logic alone. This article focuses on three deep, intersecting analyses that might be said to interlink and speak to the foundations of the many possible explanations listed above. Two of them are almost certainly previously familiar to the reader; one is not.

Common sense has it that "enemy" is the opposite of "friend." While in some respects that is true, this formulation misses crucial dimensions of the fuller nature of "enemy." "Enemy" is the opposite of "integrated self," for the enemy is a major but not exclusive symptom of the fractionated alienated, disintegrated, neurotic self.

The enemy represents parts of the self unfulfilled in ordinary daily life. Hated, rejected, loathed parts of the self can be extended, by way of projection, onto others and hated, rejected, and loathed there. That the self is rarely whole is key to understanding the concept and identity of the enemy.

It is those old standbys Marx and Freud who offer the foundation of an analysis that can be used to imagine an eventual reduction of enemy phenomena. The work of Erik Erikson permits fuller development of this analysis of the enemy and also offers glimpses of images of a self that would need no enemies. Finally, a new form of analysis is presented to combine and extend the several that precede and lead into it.

I. "ALIENATION" IN MARX, AND THE CONSTRUCTION OF THE ENEMY

"Class conflict" offers the most easily recognized analysis of the enemy in Marx's work. Throughout history, Marx insists, since the onset of social class divisions in slavery, owners of the means of production and those whom they force in one way or another to work for them, are enemies. The dominated overthrow the dominators, giving way to another system of domination, in a series progressively leading to the end of domination altogether, in a classless society made possible by the material abundance that flows from the full development of industrialization through capitalism.

Enemies are created, thus, from clashes of objective interests. This level of Marx's analysis has inspired socialist/communist movements, parties, and revolutions.

If the enemy is someone whose objective interests compete with one's own, resources defined as scarce are the objects of contention. They may be land, minerals, God's favor, wealth, prestige, or anything else deemed valuable and not available equally to everyone. Heretics are the enemy of the Church; Church authorities are the enemy of heretics. Owners, who want to pay as little as possible in wages, are the enemy of workers. Workers, who want to gain as much as possible in wages, are the enemy of owners. Imperialists and colonialists see people whose land contains valuable minerals as their enemies, and vice versa.

At this level of analysis, the enemy is perceived as an obstacle to the gaining of whatever is defined as desirable and scarce. The enemy relation is managed by overcoming or being overcome by the other party.

In much of social science, as in contemporary psychiatry, objective explanations are preferred. The subjective and the spiritual are removed from consideration. Not to his credit, Marx helped lay the groundwork for this state of affairs, but he was and is hardly alone in assuming that objectivity is more significant in understanding than subjectivity. This is indeed a rule of thumb in much of what is called social science.

Marx himself, in less studied parts of his work, offers hints, even though he does not develop them, of a vastly different analysis of the nature of the enemy. In *Capital,* Marx observes that "The hoarder . . . makes a sacrifice of the lusts of the flesh to his gold fetish." This kind of tidbit is not examined closely by Marx but suggests he saw and felt a social psychological dimension to capitalism that he did not develop. In Marx's very early writings, there are grounds for identifying the enemy as created out of unrecognized, unmet inner needs. The two levels of analysis—objective and subjective—need not clash.

Even though he abandoned the subjectivity option early in his career, in his work on alienation in the 1844 Manuscripts, Marx acknowledges subjectivity. He sees alienation as embodying inner fragmentation sponsored by relations of domination that are inevitable in capitalism. Unlike their medieval predecessors, workers under capitalism lose the relation of producer to consumer, of producer to tools of production, of producer to other producers and to society, human species, nature, and the self itself.

The worker "is related to the *product of his labor* as to an *alien* object." Because they are not masters of what they produce or how they produce it and because they are not connected socially to the people who buy and use the product, workers are wrenched from what could be an integrated sense of self as designers and makers of products and in satisfying relations with customers, fellow workers, everyone. ". . . the estrangement is manifested not only in the result but in the *act of production,* within the *producing activity,* itself." That is, the laborer "is at home when he is not working, and when he is working he is not at home." The sensuous, external world is objectified by processes of production; it ceases to belong to laborers or to be experienced as part of their lives. The producer, thus, potentially a self that feels connections and pleasure in all those areas, deteriorates into a series of fragments, which are dissociated and unrelated to one another; workers can do nothing about the process but suffer it, inevitable victims of capitalist relations beyond their range of control.

If workers do not feel at one with what they are doing, what do they do with the parts of themselves that would relate gladly to tools, production, the product's user, society, humanity, nature, and self? What happens to these desires? Marx does not carry the analysis further except to suggest that this condition is one of enormous pain. It is not just the objective condition of fragmentation but the subjective experience of hurt that motivates the next step, in Marx's understanding of modern capitalism.

Workers who accept their pain as inevitable suffer from what Marx calls false consciousness. Genuine consciousness means understanding the objective conditions that account for the pain. By identifying the owners responsible for alienation as enemies, workers understand the next logical step in the analysis: overturning the relationship that perpetuates the pain.

Marx was convinced that the workers, helped by intellectuals who disidentify with owners, would usher in the new order, either in violent revolution, or in orderly change through the ballot box in societies making that option possible. For some decades, the logic seemed compelling to many people, but this sequence of events has not happened on the broad scale Marx assumed. Perhaps it will, but there is good reason to suspect it will not.

Marx did not foresee complications that would encourage workers to succumb to suggestions that they identify as their enemies groups other than owners. Leaders can turn populations against peoples in other societies and in their own. The criteria of defining enemies can be flimsy and even invented from whole cloth; the important thing is labeling people of another nation, race, class, religion, or ethnicity as threatening. This succeeds in diverting attention from a population's own real concerns. The other is demonized and reviled, and the population's attention is easily diverted from its own real oppressors onto surrogates, suitably identified as simply other, in terms of race, ideology, or anything else. This is the classic scapegoat phenomenon.

By diverting its population thus, a leader can accomplish not a single demonization but a double one. Whoever takes part in demonizing others also takes part in diminishing their own capabilities to judge their life circumstances and, where they find them wanting, act to alter them. The self's desires to act on behalf of itself, then, are shoved away from consciousness and are not acted upon. Those desires become enemies of the self. Anyone outside the self who acts on their own desires or is said to do so, becomes a metaphor for the self's frustrated, denied desires to act on its own behalf. *The self then makes itself into its own enemy,* at the behest of forces encouraging demonization of others. Lacking a suitable foreign enemy, the self can turn against members of its own population, where gender, race, and other classic criteria for demonizing the other also hold.

Drawing on Marx, we can use the concept of alienation to go at least this far: pain leads to efforts to reduce it. The social construction of the enemy is usually an effort to salve pain artificially, by blaming someone not responsible for the pain.

To know more about pain and ways of managing it and to understand the self's susceptibility to political manipulations, we need a more complex theory that includes what happens to people as they are socialized into society, between them and others and also within themselves. For these cues, we turn to Freud.

II. "NEUROSIS" IN FREUD, AND THE CONSTRUCTION OF THE ENEMY

In psychoanalytic theory, neurosis is the bewildered incapacity to act effectively on desires. "Neurosis" corresponds to Marx's "alienation" in that in both systems, the self does not act as it wishes. In Freud, longings to love and work are experienced as mysteriously thwarted. But unlike Marx's system, in Freud's there appear seldom to be objective reasons for this situation.

What the praxis of revolution, violent or nonviolent, is in Marx, the praxis of psychoanalysis (and its numerous derivative psychotherapies) is to Freud. Where the theory of revolution suggests that the external oppressor can be overcome, the theory of psychotherapy identifies internal oppressors with whom one can come to terms. What for Marx is political action, armed or ballot box, for Freud is insight gained through introspection and conversation. Trained listeners—practiced in understanding their own inner lives and behavior—help guide neurotic clients to comprehend contexts that appear to have laid foundations for neurotic behavior and to gain freedom from emotions bottled up in the course of socialization too bewildering and frightening to bear. Through insight and catharsis comes relief from neurotic symptoms and thus access to parts of the self heretofore denied pleasurable release.

Marx locates the self's fragmentation in processes of work. He sees the self as inherently whole but torn asunder by historical circumstances not of its making. Freud spins a more complicated inquiry. He sees the body, desire itself, conscience, and society all as represented within the self in ways that allow parts of the self to be pitted against other parts. Thus, for example, intense desires for sexual pleasure may be censored early on, by constraints—societally based and parentally taught but also internally decided—in response to pulsations of desire too strong for a child to understand and to bear. These pressures are against pleasurably touching the body; against expressing lust, fear, hurt, and rage successfully enough as to move past them; and against thinking and acting on tabooed topics, whether of an incestuous nature or any other, such as criticizing people in authority.

Freud brings attention to inner hurts, fears, anger, and rage. He suggests that those feelings can be so strong as to be felt as terrifying. A self thus fearing feeling overwhelmed, and fearing punishment for wishes and actions learned as tabooed, defends against the feelings. *Parts of the self become enemies of other parts of the self.* It is here that Anna Freud, in a classic work, *Ego and the Mechanisms of Defense,* becomes crucially helpful. "Ego defense" is a way of distorting truth to protect the ego—that part of the self that organizes experience, remembers, plans, assesses, and maneuvers among competing feelings and claims on the self.

The ego has as a major task defending itself against pain and anxiety, from wherever they might come—body, nature, other people, inner psychic processes. Anxiety can be rooted in external reality or in internal reality or both.

The self learns, for example, among its options for how to defend against pain, to distort what are experienced as unbearable feelings into their opposites. Spasms of hate felt as too strong to bear because of anticipated consequences of expressing them or because of an inner censor (conscience, a crucial part of the superego, plays this role in judging) may not only inhibit expressions of hate but may even force out of consciousness (repress) the very feelings themselves. In a deft maneuver, that part of the ego that deals with these troublesome matters may guide the self to feel and express only love toward the hated other. "Methinks the lady doth protest too much" is the suggestion of inauthenticity in a feeling, the possibility that it appears exaggerated because it *is* exaggerated, as a desperate attempt to deny seemingly unbearable opposite feelings.

For understanding construction of enemies, the most important ego defense is projection. This means attributing to others feelings that are actually one's own. Violence toward others is sometimes justified with the cliche, "Force is the only language they understand." Other than the fact that force is not exactly a language, the proclaimer of that seeming truth, appearing to favor force, accuses the other of favoring force. The person who is shouting, who shouts, "I'm not shouting, you're shouting!" offers another example. More subtly, enemies are claimed to have no respect for women, or to be dirty, or to have no conscience. Accusers thereby reveal their own struggles with respecting women and coming to terms with dirtiness and their own consciences.

The mechanism of projection allows insight into a central psychoanalytic insight: ambivalence. Popular culture promotes the mistaken notion that people feel love, fear, respect, hate, and jealousy as if they were unalloyed with other feelings. Part of Freud's radical insight is that people can have opposite feelings toward the same object or phenomenon at the same time; this is what ambivalence means. It is sometimes understood that one can love and hate the same person but less understood that fear and fearlessness, understanding and puzzlement, desire and repulsion can be felt toward the same person or experience at the same time.

There seems to be something in the self, or at least in the Western self as so far socially constructed, that presses for clarity in the form of one feeling without complications. Normatively, for example, children are expected to love and honor parents as if hatred and resentment did not inevitably also accompany close relationships.

Succumbing to pressures, external and internal, to avoid dealing with ambivalence, the self engages in "splitting," whereby positive and negative feelings are divided from each other so that one object receives one feeling and another object receives the other. Culture encourages taking part in normative structures that acknowledge, accept, and encourage splitting in collective ways. Take, for example, the difficulty for a child to permit itself to feel and express hatred as well as love toward a parent. Although wise parents accept this as benefiting them and their children, many—themselves not having experienced the wisdom and relief that accompanies emotional honesty—do not. It is they who socialize children into what might be called culturally normative splitting: Love the parent, family, religious group, ethnic group, nation, and hate the communists, Jews, Blacks, homosexuals, or another ethnic group or religion, or a sports team, people from a nearby city, or virtually any other group for which any reason whatsoever can be found to notice a difference. Alternatively, one can hate the parent, disallowing the love also there, and instead love another person, or a team, a flag, the nation itself. One can also learn to love parents, family, nation, race, gender, and hate other corresponding such units. Differences that are alleged to be the basis for opposition are simply handles, excuses, objects of displacement (to use another item from the vocabulary of ego defense) that are used to justify opposition to other people, that is, the construction of them into enemies.

From a psychoanalytic perspective, then, the enemy is created out of unmet inner needs, not acknowledged and not addressed as such. If one cannot cope with rage, one is told there is someone else (not oneself and not one's people) consumed with rage who is thereby one's enemy. If one cannot cope with lust, one is told there are other people—of a different gender, or sexual orientation, or ethnic or race group, or life-style group—who do not control their lust adequately, and one is encouraged to demonize them as enemies.

Another way of looking at this issue is as one of control. The self loathes the idea that forces inside or outside it might make it act in ways it does not want to. Thus, intricate maneuvers are engaged to ward off that threat.

There are at least three areas where control is experienced as urgent. One is impulses. Lust and rage are the most easily identifiable impulses, but jealousy, spite, spontaneity—any impulse that looms large enough that expressing it fully could lead to trouble and regret—can be frightening. The fear is that one will succumb to a most unwelcome feeling, of being overwhelmed. Although such feelings can be accepted fully and sublimated—channeled into socially useful behavior like work, art, and political action—they can also be defended against in ways not so useful for the self or for society.

Consider spontaneity as an alternative to overcontrol. Acting on whimsical impulses to dance down the street, eat at odd times, wear off-beat clothing, relate to people one has been warned against—make life exciting and full. One might thus find oneself following paths forsworn, getting into unknown territory, risking troubles with one's vulnerabilities, meeting social disapproval.

That brief moment of the counterculture in the 1960s included surfacing and celebrating spontaneity. Most people, rather than joining, warded if off, to the point where it became neutralized by criticism and by the subtle shift of spontaneous commitments to experiment with life to commercial transformation through expensive stylization of such symbols of resistance to cultural norms as jeans and hairstyles.

Lust and rage are especially problematic impulses. When left to free expression, they can sometimes make for big trouble. Rather than accepting and sublimating such feelings when they appear, people are usually encouraged to attribute them to other people and to scorn them there.

An enemy, then, can be constructed out of one's own impulses denied. The so-called "war between the sexes," so intricately deconstructed by many parts of feminism, includes this process of denying in the self what one finds attractive but taboo for whatever reasons, in the other. Thus until very recently and only among some people, with men and weakness and with women and assertiveness. The threat attributed to the enemy is but a projection of something inside onto others and experienced as if it originated and belonged only there. It is easier to condemn an inclination in another than in oneself. The enemy, hence, allows an easy out from many problematic encounters with the self.

A second area where control is problematic is the part of superego called conscience. Although society demands limits on behavior that we may live together at all, people are ambivalent about accepting that mandate. However respected it may be, conscience also stands as a reminder of desires foregone, and for that reason, conscience cannot be experienced only as attractive.

The negative part of one's ambivalence about conscience is projected onto another group, such as children, the other gender, indeed entire race and national groups. Thus for White racists, Blacks are considered without conscience, for anti-Semites the same is true of Jews (who in the Ten Commandments created the groundwork for the Western conscience and thus must be resented, even if also admired and envied, for doing so). Even for Freud, who might have been expected to know better, women, through a tortured and peculiar logic, have weaker consciences than men.

The third control area is the ego itself. It is that part of the self that assesses, organizes, and acts and that is beset by impulses, conscience, and other internal conflicting demands, and external ones as well. How to decide how to act, e.g., on wishes to be female as well as male, gay and straight, adult and child, responsible and carefree? Again, splitting comes in handy, so that the self can ridicule others who intrapsychically and culturally stand for denied parts of the self.

Through projection, splitting, and other defenses, the self perpetuates its own fragmentation. The enemy then is parts of the self unfaced, unmet, unrecognized, unaccepted. It is the self's estrangement from itself that marks its need to define others—in whom, unknowingly and disparagingly, it sees itself—as enemies. In "adversary symbiosis," an unconscious joint collaboration, the creation and maintenance of enemies is a strategy for not dealing with seemingly unfaceable parts of the self.

III. TOWARD REAPPROPRIATING THE SELF

Marx foresees the end of class conflict as the end of alienation. If workers own the means of production, he reasons, they will be able to reintegrate their lives with their work, people around them, humanity, and nature itself. This is an analysis from structure. Change the structure that leads to fragmentation, according to Marx, and fragmentation will end. Marx pays no attention to inner process, socialization, and the body.

Freud, on the other hand, pays no attention to institutions and other forms of structure. He anchors his analysis in the self's growth in family and culture with no reference to social structure. For Freud, reintegration of the self proceeds along lines of inner examination, with the help, often, of a skilled other who helps the self retake and come to terms with its history of pains, confusions, terrors, and lusts. What the child felt it could not handle, the adult has more resources to handle and can. And, if all goes well, does.

This reintegration of the self can be called "reappropriation of the self." It can be enhanced by two theoretical perspectives. One proceeds as an extension of insights of Erik Erikson. The second is a new theory that attempts to combine insights from Marx, Freud, and Erikson into a perspective that allows a vision of ending enemyhood altogether.

In contrast with Freud's theory of ego defenses that ward off threatening feelings and experiences, here is a theory of *ego advances* that indicate ways by which the self unites with others, society, culture, nature, and the planet in ways that enhance them all. Ego advances are also ways in which the self reunites with itself. They are strategies for ending the need for enemies by reappropriating the self.

Freud, and Anna Freud after him, formulate the theory of ego defenses with nouns: projection, repression, denial, displacement, undoing, intellectualization, and the like. The nouns suggest something fixed, a mechanism to be engaged when necessary.

The word defense is from war vocabulary. Freud does not develop words that suggest the ego at peace and preparing for more and better peace, with others, with nature, with itself. I intend now to extend Erikson in this direction of what I see as unfinished Freudian and Eriksonian business.

Although ego defenses imply action, they do so primarily by *protecting the self from others, not enhancing it with others.* Ego advances, by contrast, are efforts to relate, described by gerunds to imply *ongoing work.*

Empathizing, for example, works beyond isolation and responds to pain as well as pleasure in others.

Erikson analyzes aspects and qualities of relationship that allow for engaged, fulfilling connections of people with each other. Although his terms move beyond those of ego defense, they also are limited to nouns, that tend to suggest fixed behaviors rather than ongoing processes.

The notion of ego advances is a variation on terms developed by Erikson for understanding how the self evolves. Erikson refers to "virtues," or strengths of the self that guide it through the complex encounters of development. He sees, for example, "hope" as emerging from the struggle of the self to come to terms with needs to gain both trust and mistrust in learning how to relate to a great variety of other people. By renaming and slightly reconceptualizing what Erikson calls "virtues," or ego strengths, as "ego advances," it is possible to emphasize movement forward, and by using gerunds rather than nouns, to call attention to process.

This exercise promotes the possibility of reintegrating or reappropriating the self, of claiming back for it what has been fragmented off for whatever reason. The main idea here can be called, referring to the discussion above about projection, "deprojection," or bringing back into the self where it belongs, feelings inappropriately attributed to others. If enemies are made by a form of projection, then deprojection is a way to end their creation and perpetuation. To put it another way, if the creation of enemies signals fragmentation of the self, then the ending of unnecessary enemy construction is synonymous with reappropriating the range of what the self feels, means, and is: love, hate, competence, doubt, glory, ambivalence, all. It is helpful to identify major issues facing a self from birth on, to get a sense of what can be kept in the self that is otherwise, normatively, fragmented off and experienced as if located somewhere else.

Erikson identifies the first issue between a new person and its caretaking adult as "trust," a baby's need to learn to trust an adult to meet its needs. But since no one can meet all a baby's needs all the time, it also has to learn "mistrust." Both kinds of learning are crucial in later encountering other people. Without trust, the environment cannot be counted upon to be reliable, safe, and nurturant. At the same time, mistrust is a necessary barrier sometimes against being hurt. It enables one to recognize and respond appropriately to people who are untrustworthy.

Normatively, the definition of other or others as enemy is a way of avoiding the complex reality that any person is in some ways trustworthy and in some ways untrustworthy. This truth is short-circuited by defining one parent as trustworthy and the other as untrustworthy, or more commonly one entire group of people as trustworthy and another as untrustworthy. By contrast, the integrated self's task is to learn to accept both trust and mistrust as appropriate toward the same person, group, nation.

The ego advance at this early stage of development is *trusting*. It is essential as the basis for relationship altogether. It implies a process, never ended, of testing, evaluating, deciding whom to trust and how far, with the attendant pleasures and reassurances of trusting, and reliable knowledge of who cannot be trusted at all or can be trusted under certain identifiable circumstances. If enemies are defined, as they are, as entirely untrustworthy, then working to move beyond enemy construction means learning to accept contradictions and nuances in the trust-mistrust range toward people with whom one has dealings. This includes the laborious process of moving beyond total mistrust, as the Soviet Union and the United States did in the waning days of the former, as Blacks and Whites have begun doing in South Africa and as in their off-again-on-again ways Israelis and Palestinians, Irish Protestants and Irish Catholics have done in recent years.

Erikson's second stage of development is "autonomy," which he contrasts with shame and doubt. Autonomy does not mean simply freedom from restrictions by or ties with others. It suggests mutual recognition of rights to independence. It means a self confident in its strengths and purposes confronting other selves confident in their strengths and purposes.

The negatives of autonomy, in Erikson's phenomenology, are "shame" and "doubt," defensive responses to punishment and humiliation that follow from certain kinds of negations of autonomy in the actions of unnecessary control by others. If we are all beset by shame and doubt as well as autonomy, then it is true if unfortunate that we yield, often, to temptations to define some groups of other people as shameful and some as too pridefully autonomous. Standard systems of discrimination, whether against Jews, people of color, women, homosexuals, or anyone else, define the other as engaging in shameful behavior, the legitimacy of which they should doubt, getting accusers off the hook of recognizing and taking responsibility for their own struggles with shame and doubt. Typically, autonomy is considered legitimate for one's own group, and shame and doubt for other groups. The pride that accompanies autonomy is belittled, ridiculed, dismissed when it appears in groups defined as enemy.

Venturing is the second ego advance, the gerund that

can be considered appropriate for what Erikson calls autonomy. Venturing with pleasure beyond the familiar and secure includes overcoming what could be crippling shame and doubt. It means ending the practice of defining enemies in terms, among others, of what they should feel shame about and about which they should doubt their very goodness and integrity. The capacity for spontaneity, growth, and delight is part of venturing but it cannot be fully integrated into the self without proper accounting also of shame and doubt, to be recognized as parts of oneself rather than as parts only of other people.

The ego learnings of the Oedipal period Erikson calls "initiative" and "guilt." To initiate is to relate to others through the pleasures of competence, imagination, and risk. The child is filled with fantasies of heroism, conquest, and derring-do, and as the healthy child of this age moves into society, it acts out, often in inventive play, whatever projects occur to it. The child unable to achieve full functioning at this stage may expect defeat to be the inevitable outcome of imagined initiatives. Accompanying those feelings of defeat is the feeling of guilt, a feeling of wrongness and inner torment that suggests one has done or thought something forbidden. Rather than cope with guilt as well as delight in initiating, cultures offer normative structures whereby someone else can be defined as guilty. This is part of the collective psychodynamic basis of anti-Semitism in Western cultures. Jews are defined, although less so as time goes on, as having killed Christ and therefore guilty without relief. Guilt is also one of the mechanisms that during the heyday of U.S.–Soviet antagonism underlay capitalist demonization of communism and vice versa. Each side accused the other of being profoundly and irremediably guilty of ignoring fundamental human rights (in the one case political rights, in the other, economic rights). Although both accusations were true, they were intended not as helpful criticisms but rather as rationales for total distancing and demonization. Another piece of enemy construction, then, is attributing guilt to the other rather than to oneself.

When neurotic guilt, which debilitates unnecessarily, is transcended, initiative may include combining with others through joint projects. The reality of guilt is not denied or put onto others but rather accepted and struggled with when it appears. The name of this ego advance, *initiating,* suggests that one can integrate initiating activity and cope with feelings of guilt and still come out with the balance of energies and hope in the process of initiating activities one desires to undertake.

Erikson names the fourth stage of development "industry," effective interaction with the material and social environment at a time when a child begins to acquire its culture's work, play, and interpersonal skills. The unhealthy child suffers from "inferiority," crippling inhibitions that make effective learning and behavior frightening and thus taboo. Feeling inferior is avoided where possible in, among other ways, defining other individuals or whole groups as inferior. This is part of the developmental basis of forms of domination and discrimination. It is another piece of the construction of the enemy as inferior.

Reappropriating the full self, then, includes accepting the reality that in some ways the self is highly competent and in others, it is not. To enjoy and develop competence and neither give way to overwhelming feelings of inferiority nor succumb to the temptation to define others as inferior, in order to avoid the reality that one is not competent at everything one tries, is another way, then, of deconstructing the enemy and no longer needing enemies. The ego advance of industriousness and gaining competence is *learning.*

At the core of Erikson's work is "identity," the consolidation of developing fragments of the self. Although the self is reconsolidated continuously, it is ordinarily in adolescence that one creates a recognizable, more or less predictable self that feels right to oneself and that others can recognize as having meaning, purpose, and continuity. Identity includes family, group, societal, and cultural dimensions that enable feeling part of larger structures that welcome and embrace one as belonging there. The self that fails to achieve a viable identity is beset by "identity confusion," a reflection of bewilderments and pains that prevent pleasurable and meaningful self-integration.

To deprecate another person or group of people is to take part in strategies of attributing to the other not identity confusion but negative identity, wholeness of evil or failure, so to speak. Whereas positive identity implies positive wholeness, to the enemy is given negative wholeness, consisting of numerous parts of the self flaked off from the self and laid onto another. Fragments of mistrust, shame, doubt, guilt, and inferiority are congealed into a working whole of the negative identity of the enemy and experienced as if located only there. The flip side of this demonizing strategy, the ego advance of this stage of development, is *integrating,* bringing disparate pieces into a personal, societal, and cultural whole, even while moving and changing.

With a firm identity, the self can move toward other selves and form deep emotional, intellectual, spiritual, and physical ties, including those of sexuality. What Erikson calls "intimacy" is that capacity and that goal.

Where the self is incapable of establishing intimacy, it suffers "isolation," a defense against the anticipated pain of close involvement with another. While everyone has to handle both tendencies toward intimacy and slides into isolation, defenses allow one to avoid recognizing the latter. Part of the process of enemy construction is to isolate the other. Communists and capitalists tried to isolate each other's worlds. Racism continues in the United States partly through the use of devices like informal segregation and discrimination, whereby groups are isolated from each other.

Intricately, racists not only seek to isolate non-Whites from Whites, they also isolate Whites from non-Whites. Thus, in the pathology of denying parts of the self, the problematic quality laid onto the other is unwittingly also foisted upon the self. To mistrust an entire group of other people is also to set up one's own group as untrustworthy by the other group; as with any self-fulfilling prophecy, the determination to accomplish the separation makes the separation, not necessary at all, appear inevitable.

The gerund for intimacy, the ego advance of the period of mature connections with others, is *loving*. It includes the reappropriation of distancing and isolation, in ways that allow intimacy but do not neglect the problems that sometimes interfere with achieving it.

At some point in the delicate interweaving of lives that intimacy means, people may pass crucial parts of themselves on to others in their species. The cultural continuity this indicates need not be biologically based; it can be managed through parenting nonbiological offspring and by caring for others in teaching, nursing, library work, social work, medicine, and others of what Erikson calls the caring professions. This relationship to coming generations Erikson calls "generativity," and he contrasts it with "stagnation," a later stage of isolation in which one feels stifled, worn out, used up. Demonizing the enemy includes denying virtue in the enemy, denying anything there worth passing on to anyone anywhere anytime. Enemyhood is continued, that is to suggest, by assuming that what is worth bringing to others is one's own heritage and that heritages not one's own are worthless.

In the broadest sense, the ego advance that engages generativity is *parenting*. It means growing as one gives and giving as one grows. It means incorporating one's own tendencies toward stagnation into oneself and learning to cope with them through work, art, political participation, and other forms of activity.

The last stage of life Erikson formulates as "ego integrity" in contrast to "despair." Ego integrity includes forswearing regret and bitterness. If not an enthusiastic acceptance of all one's life has been, it is at least a realistic integration into the self of reasons for sadness as well as joy, renunciation of wistful or angry wishes that the past can be made otherwise and that there is any point in remorse.

Ego integrity is a later stage of identity, its last reworking. Whereas identity is prospective, bringing the experiences of the first two decades into a workable, satisfying whole from which the adult self can develop, ego integrity is an analogous retrospective process. It is the basis for an ego advance that allows the aging person to present a model of closure to younger people, a paragon of completion that feels right and looks right both to the aging person and the community.

It is a characteristic of enemy construction that the effort seems to be made to drive the enemy, by weapons, boycotts, and rhetoric of deprecation and humiliation, to despair. That rarely works; rather, the enemy is driven to renewed determination not to be defeated, not to yield to despair. As despair is perhaps one of the subtler inner issues any person faces, it is understandable that with it, as with other qualities that evoke great discomfort, a serious effort is made to place it away from the self, onto someone else, individual or collective. To retake the despair thus projected outward into the self is to take responsibility for yet another aspect of fragmentation that can be retaken into wholeness.

The ego advance of the latest stage of life is *completing*. One can engage in completing without having to pretend that other people cannot complete, that other people are subject to despair and deserve it, and that one never needs to face despair oneself.

Erikson's ego strengths focus on development of the capacity to enjoy challenge and growth, while learning how to maneuver among numerous temptations and hazards that would keep it from healthy assertion and gratification. If ego defenses ward off attacks on self-esteem, then ego advances actively seek experiences that enhance pleasure in activity and self-esteem. If ego defenses are parts of strategies that fragment the self in an understandable but avoidable effort to refrain from facing problematic parts of self, ego advances are strategies of reintegration of all parts of the self into a functioning, complex whole.

Making the self whole means allowing the self to experience pain and to come to terms with it creatively, no longer needing to manufacture enemies to stand for parts of the self one thinks one is unable to face. Identifying with strengths of the other as well as weaknesses that are like one's own, empathizing with the other in such a way as to extend the range of one's own feelings, initiating activities that challenge and extend one's repertoire of competencies—are another way of looking at ego advances.

The institutions of a society committed to ending the need for enemies would devote themselves, in education, religion, government, the family, medicine, law—every institutional context—to learning how to overcome processes that inhibit the exercise of ego advances. Neither domination nor profit would define the purpose of people in such a society. Purposes would be growth, sharing, and vibrant interdependence.

IV. ENEMIES AND THE POSSIBILITY OF PARADIGM SHIFT

In *Rambo and the Dalai Lama: The Compulsion to Win and Its Threat to Human Survival* I suggest that most encounters in history are organized according to the "adversary paradigm," whereby the point of an encounter is to overcome the other, whether of another age, gender, race, class, nation, sexual orientation, team, school, or any other category that lends itself to zero-sum consideration in terms of encounter and outcome.

Through recorded history (indeed, this may be a crucial way of defining recorded history), this has been the case. Alongside the adversary paradigm, and acting in intricate relationship with it, is the "mutuality paradigm," based on respect for the other, humanization, care, support, delight, nurturance, love.

Religions and political systems idealize mutuality but they forego it by contradictory commitments to imperatives of the adversary paradigm. Political, religious, and virtually all other institutions are based on adversary principles in their organizations far more than on mutuality.

Not only have humans defined other people in numerous contexts as adversaries, so with nature. As an adversary, nature has been seen as a lifeless object to be dominated, used, exploited for human comfort and recreation. But nature, it turns out, is not so passive, and has in the past generation or so put our species on warning that if we mess with it much further, we will be denied essentials of our existence, like drinkable water, topsoil, ozone, and uncontaminated food.

People are socialized into adversarialism and accept that other people and nature are, under numerous circumstances, enemies to be overcome. Our crisis begins in the objective realm. Mastery of nature has led to the nuclear threat, whereby were nuclear devices used fully in an armed confrontation, the users as well as the objects of their use would almost certainly die. Thus does adversarialism bend back upon itself and negate itself. There is no point in opposing if there is no chance of winning the contest. Correspondingly, conquered nature holds the immanent possibility of turning upon the conquerors in the unexpected and undesired form of being destroyed by forces of nature beyond human control. We are clever in our technologies but not clever enough to regenerate species destroyed, ozone depleted, and topsoil ruined.

Objective considerations thus force us either to ignore these terrible realities and court suicide or to address them and see that it is not only our adversarial relationship with nature that has gotten us into trouble. Our oppositions to each other are part of the same package whereby we waste resources, energy, and life itself in pursuing goals of overcoming the other.

Most people go along with the adversary paradigm because they are socialized into doing so. The system, though, is driven by a minority of people who are in the throes of the "adversary compulsion." For them, winning is not under control any more than is addiction for the drinker, drug addict, smoker, or gambler who acts not out of choice or occasional recreation but out of a compulsion over which insufficient control is felt. These are the people who tend to lead nations, religions, and institutions, promoting adversarialism to meet their own peculiar needs.

The adversary compulsion can be deconstructed in such a way that the addiction can give way to a choice for mutuality. Our survival as a species depends on this transformation, which appears to be already under way and identifiable in minor forms. Cooperative learning, mediation, and cooperative games are but three of dozens of examples of mutuality that surround us, albeit not in forms into which all or even most people are socialized.

We can choose to further the development of mutuality institutions. We can also choose to reappropriate from "enemies," including nature, the qualities that are rightfully our own, that we have projected unnecessarily and unfairly onto others. Our salvation, if we are to avoid technological dooms we have fashioned and that, if unchecked, await us, lies in making ourselves whole again. Our clue as to what we have fragmented off from ourselves is any quality that we detest in others. Even the hatefulness of Nazis, properly understood, allows us to face hateful parts of ourselves and to learn how to come to terms with them.

Once we realize that our "enemies" are subject to exactly the same dynamics we are and that we participate with them in systems of "adversary symbiosis," we can make the choice to forgive them and ourselves, reciprocally, and move toward a predominantly mutualistic society. One key issue in this process in indeed the reappropriation of all our qualities we deny in ourselves.

The wisdom of Pogo's observation that we are the enemy can now to seen as recognition that in opposing others, we are in fact opposing, by denial, crucial parts of ourselves. Learning to accept, forgive, and absorb all of what we are and all of what the "enemy" is, is ultimately the same process. The enemy we can learn to recognize and with whom we can and must come to terms if we are to survive the perils created by humans, is, finally, ourselves.

Also See the Following Articles

AGGRESSION, PSYCHOLOGY OF • COLD WAR • ETHNICITY AND IDENTITY POLITICS

Bibliography

Erikson, E. (1982). *The life cycle completed: A review*. New York: Norton.

Fellman, G. (1998). *Rambo and the Dalai Lama: The Compulsion to Win and its threat to human survival*. Binghamton: SUNY Press. (Forthcoming.)

Fornari, F. (1974). *The psychoanalysis of war*. Garden City, NY: Anchor.

Freud, S. (1962). *Civilization and its discontents*. New York: Norton.

Group for the Advancement of Psychiatry. (1987). *Us and them: The psychology of ethnonationalism*. New York: Brunner/Mazel.

Keen, S. (1986). *Faces of the enemy*. San Francisco: Harper and Row.

Marx, K., & Tucker, R. (Ed.). (1978). *The Marx-Engels reader*. New York: Norton. Estranged Labor, 70–81; Private Property and Communism, 81–93; The Power of Money in Bourgeois Society. 101–105.

Quinn, D. (1992). *Ishmael*. New York: Bantam.

Stein, H. F. (1987). Adversary symbiosis and complementary group dissociation: An analysis of the U.S./USSR conflict. In H. F. Stein, *Psychoanalytic anthropology*. Charlottesville: University Press of Virginia.

Volkan, V. (1988). *The need to have enemies and allies*. Northvale, NJ: Jason Aronson Inc.

Environmental Issues and Politics

Janet Welsh Brown
World Resources Institute

GLOSSARY

Biodiversity (or Biological Diversity) The full variety of organisms, including plants and animals, genetic variations within species, and diversity of ecosystems.

Climate Change Change in weather patterns over a period of time from natural causes, such as ice ages brought on by changes in the earth's orbit around the sun, or from human activity, such as the release of carbon dioxide and other greenhouse gases.

Global Warming The trend of increasing temperatures on the earth's surface and in the lower atmosphere, caused by the entrapment of heat due to the accumulation of certain gases, chiefly carbon dioxide.

Greenhouse Gases Mainly carbon dioxide, ground-level ozone, chlorofluorocarbons (CFCs), and halons, methane, and nitrous oxide.

Resource Base Refers to all of the earth's natural resources, including water and air, on which human life depends.

INTERNATIONAL ENVIRONMENTAL ISSUES are serious problems of environmental degradation that have become the subject of international controversy and politics—problems that are shared by many states or even the entire earth, the effects of which cross national borders and require multi-state action to curb or correct. They include such issues as global warming, biodiversity loss, and depletion of the ozone layer that go to the heart of a nation's economic and political concerns and therefore may divide nations one against another and in some rare cases lead to violence. Paradoxically, international environmental woes also constitute an arena in which nations are increasingly trying collaboration to solve mutual widely shared problems. The politics surrounding international environmental issues in the 1980s and 1990s represent a new field in international relations. Their study has contributed to new thinking about the multiple causes of conflict among nations.

I. DIRECT CONNECTIONS BETWEEN THE ENVIRONMENT AND VIOLENCE

The most direct connection between the environment and violence is the damage done by all wars to the natural environment. The most visible damage is done in battle—the blasting away of forests and waterways and the erosion and pollution of beaches and coastal waters. The most extreme example in modern history was the leveling and burning of all living things within the radius of destruction of the Hiroshima and Nagasaki atomic bombs. War refugees, especially those confined for months or years in restricted areas, may also destroy the resource base. But other kinds of damage are done in the construction of military bases, the training of men and women in the armed forces, and the manufacture and testing of weaponry. In the United States, much weapons production has been secret and until recent years, largely exempt from national rules to protect the environment, an exemption for which the taxpayer is now paying billions of dollars as the Department of Energy struggles to clean up nuclear, chemical, and biological warfare facilities in more than 20 states.

Some wartime environmental damage has been particularly deliberate and damaging. Chemical warfare—outlawed but still with us—fits in this category. Iraq's use of chemicals against Iranian troops in the 1980s and the defoliants so widely used in the Vietnam war are prime examples. A different kind of example was the 1980s Nicaraguan and Costa Rican proposal (never carried out) to level the forests in the biologically unique San Juan River basin, which sheltered armed Contra forces on both sides of the border between the two countries.

Some deliberate acts are so destructive that they deserve the label "environmental crimes." The scorched-earth practices carried out by retreating armies throughout history qualify, as does the recent Gulf War where the fleeing Iraqi troops set fire to the Kuwaiti oil fields. And some would say that destruction of the Bikini atoll by nuclear testing or the excesses of pollution caused by the U.S. nuclear weapons production program in Hanford, Washington and other sites belong in the same category.

Environmental and natural resource problems have also been the direct cause of conflict within and between nations. Throughout history, armies have fought to control essential harbors and waterways or the particular hilltop that would give them advantage over the enemy. In 1972 and 1973, in the so-called "Cod War" between Iceland and Britain, competition between fishing fleets nearly erupted in violence as Icelandic gunboats drove off British trawlers in defiance of a ruling of the International Court of Justice. The incident would have been of little historical interest—so unequal were the powers of the adversaries—had not the United States, which maintained an air base in Reykjavik, been drawn into the dispute. For the Icelanders, the income from fishing was more important than that from the base, and they told the United States to call off the British or lose the base lease. In more recent years, ordinarily peaceable Canadians have forcibly boarded Portuguese and U.S. fishing vessels charged with over-fishing migratory stocks.

Conflicts have also arisen over fresh water, that is, river basins shared by two or more nations. The underlying cause of the 1967 Arab–Israeli War was the ongoing struggle to control the waters of the Jordan River, the Litani and other tributaries. To this day, the sharing of the Jordan and Yarmuk waters and the aquifer under the West Bank remains an issue in the peace process. In 1989, disputes in the Senegal River flood plain, whose value had been greatly enhanced by the availability of irrigation waters from a World Bank-funded dam, led to attacks and reprisals that left scores dead, hundreds wounded, 180,000 people displaced, and Senegalese and Mauritanian troops facing each other across the river. The potential for conflict hovers also over the Tigris–Euphrates, the Nile, the Ganges–Brahmaputra, the Zambezi, and the Mekong. Closer to home, U.S.–Mexican relations have been periodically exacerbated by water issues in the Rio Grande and Colorado (as well as by air pollution from Mexican smelters and illegal dumping of U.S. toxic wastes trucked across the northern Mexico border). Few of these contemporary conflicts over environmental problems reach the point where force is used, but they do keep international tensions running high. While they may not threaten U.S. security, the CIA in 1985 identified more than 20 global flash points where U.S. interests might be seriously affected by conflict involving population pressures or contested resources. The CIA warned that with rapidly growing population and increasing degradation of the world resource base, clashes over resources could become a more frequent cause of conflict.

II. INDIRECT EFFECTS OF ENVIRONMENTAL DETERIORATION ON CONFLICT

More serious threats to peaceful development, however, are the result of indirect connections between environmental deterioration and international conflict. They are more serious because they are far more widespread and because today's environmental problems stem from and influence every kind of human endeavor.

George Kennan, writing in *Foreign Affairs* in 1985 of the expected collapse of the Soviet Union, identified "two unprecedented and supreme dangers" facing the world: the prospect of nuclear war and "the devastating effect of modern industrialization and overpopulation on the world's natural environment." Kennan was referring to the post-World War II explosion of economic activity (four times the 1945 levels), a doubling of world population, and an even larger post-war increase in consumption. Such astonishing growth brought with it severe, debilitating pollution (first in the highly industrialized countries and now throughout the developing countries as well), lethal drinking water and sanitation problems for about 20% of the world's people, rapid demolition of the world's forests (especially tropical forests with their rich endowment of biodiversity), destruction and pollution of coastal waters, a dangerous decline in all the world's fisheries, extraordinary soil erosion and fertility loss in both industrialized and developing countries, a vast lucrative international trade in wastes (much of it hazardous), a limited but nevertheless dangerous proliferation of nuclear weapons, a dramatic thinning of Earth's protective ozone layer, and a build-up of greenhouse gases (mostly from combustion of fossil fuels) that promises to warm the planet, raise ocean levels, and fundamentally change climate.

Most contemporary environmental problems have no respect for national boundaries. They may originate in one state or region while their effect is felt—and paid for—in another. All such problems have costs. They may be public health costs, such as the hunger that results from poor harvests due to soil loss, salinization, or aridity, or declines in the fish catch because coastal spawning grounds are silted up from upland deforestation. Or they may be economic costs such as the shortened lifespan of hydroelectric dams as silt builds up behind them. Both poverty and affluence can raise environmental costs: the poor by putting pressure on ever steeper or more fragile marginal lands, the rich (including those in developing countries) by excessively consuming energy and other goods while producing large volumes of per-capita wastes.

The hardships that come with environmental degradation and resource scarcities rarely engender conflict directly, but often stimulate migration to cities or across borders and contribute to political discontent and instability. They may exacerbate ethnic and other tensions and fuel the ambition of despotic leaders.

The 1992 Earth Summit at Rio de Janeiro, officially the United Nations Conference on Environment and Development, greatly heightened worldwide awareness of these problems. During the 2-year negotiations that produced *Agenda 21* (a comprehensive blueprint for sustainable development) and important treaties to curb global warming and biodiversity loss, governments had to take a hard look at their own practices and their contributions to global problems. And all over the world, but especially in the developing countries, nongovernmental organizations (NGOs) proliferated as civil society's role in national and international environmental and development policy grew. Through this extraordinary universal exercise in diplomacy, governments and citizen leaders everywhere became aware, first, that global and local environmental problems infused every aspect of economic development and every international issue and, second, that the problems were so interconnected and so ubiquitous that no one nation, no matter how powerful or determined, could solve these problems except in cooperation with other nations. And they began to see that a new kind of thinking about economic development, a new approach, vaguely labeled "sustainable," was required on both the global and the local levels.

A. Global Issues

One can divide contemporary world environmental problems into two categories that require different kinds of policy responses. One category comprises global issues affecting the whole planet (ozone depletion, global warming, trade in toxic wastes, or endangered species, *etc.*) and requires international agreement to fix responsibility and organize response. Another category includes the broad range of domestic policy decisions required to turn any one nation onto a sustainable development path, though these also often require international cooperation.

In a seminal article in *Foreign Affairs* in 1989, Jessica Tuchmam Mathews addressed the need to "redefine security." Noting the tremendous growth in economic activity and population since 1945, she spelled out the enormity of certain problems—tropical forest loss, soil loss through erosion and salinization, the build-up of carbon dioxide in the atmosphere, and the damage caused by chlorofluorocarbons (CFCs) to the earth's ozone shield. Matthews described the unprecedented pace and scale of changes wrought by human beings, changes that, for the first time in human history, were "altering the basic physiology of the planet." She pointed out the need for fundamental changes in the means of production if humankind is to avoid the collapse of nature's biological and physical systems that support life on earth.

Although more than 170 nations agreed at Rio to the principle of "shared but differentiated" responsibility for environmental damage to the planet, the ongoing negotiations on *how* to meet the challenge have been controversial and highly politicized. The basic science is clear and getting better all the time. In fact, there is extraordinary international scientific consensus about the causes and seriousness of such problems as ozone depletion, global warming, and biodiversity loss. Indeed, on some issues such as ozone depletion, a series of scientific revelations spurred negotiators to rapidly toughen an earlier treaty. Still, the continuing arguments about who is responsible for the damage—and, more important, who should pay the bill—often reflect a split between developed and developing nations. These debates constitute a new field of global environmental politics that describes the international maneuvering around environmental issues, and consensus-building, and identifies both the leading states and the veto or blocking states. This field may be the fastest growing field in international politics.

The body of international law around environmental issues is expanding. The United Nations Environmental Programme (UNEP), which registers the relevant treaties, lists 170 agreements, most of them negotiated since 1980. The treaties agreed to since the Earth Summit are nearly universal, with most of the world's nations as signatories. They cover a wide array of topics—climate, whaling, acid rain, protection of Antarctica, desertification, and so on. Many take the form of a framework treaty, in which the principles are agreed on, followed by annual or biennial Conferences of the Parties (COPs) that respond to the changing science and politics, usually with the effect of strengthening the terms of the original pact. International negotiations are continuous: every month there is a COP or other environmental negotiation going on somewhere. Even within a "weak" treaty, the scrutiny to which participating nations are subjected and the public pressure felt during negotiations sometimes pull recalcitrant nations into cooperation.

While states are the primary players on this political scene, even more nonstate actors are participating too. These include international organizations, financial and business institutions, regional organizations, such substate entities as municipalities or states and provinces, and especially nongovernmental organizations. These nonstate entities have unusual access to the decision-making process in the environmental arena.

B. The Role of Environmental Treaties

This relatively new network of environmental treaties forms a kind of nascent collective security system for the planet. Two examples will illustrate the characteristics and politics of such treaties. The 1985 Vienna Convention for Protection of the Ozone Layer is generally considered to be the most successful international environmental treaty to date. The problem, a thinning of the earth's ozone layer (which protects the planet from damaging ultraviolet rays from the sun) by a group of chemicals (chlorofluorocarbons or CFCs) commonly used as a refrigerant and in making aerosols, was identified by scientists and given credence by a 1975 UNEP-funded study by the World Meteorological Organization. Its definition as a political issue came when the governments of the United States, Canada, Finland, Norway, and Sweden jointly urged UNEP to consider regulating ozone-depleting substances. Scientific uncertainty resulted in a 1985 framework treaty that recognized the problem, but committed signatories only to study and monitor the problem and to share data.

Alignment on the ozone issue included the United States (producer of 30% of the world's CFCs) and its allies on one side and, opposing them, four European states that manufactured 45% of the total and had a thriving business selling them to developing countries. The larger industrialized developing countries—including Brazil, China, Mexico, and India—which produced only 5% of the whole but were rapidly increasing their use of the chemicals played no role in the initial negotiations. Two years later, a protocol negotiated in Montreal set firm targets for reducing CFC production to 50% of the 1986 levels. Then the science developed so rapidly with the discovery of an ozone "hole" over Antarctica and confirmation that the layer was also thinning over the northern hemisphere that the European countries reversed themselves and proposed a complete phase-out of all CFC production. In 1990, the parties established a modest fund demanded by the developing countries to help them change their production to less harmful substances. No other environmental treaty to date has its own fund to assist developing countries. The treaty stimulated development of a variety of alternative chemicals, and American companies that are in the forefront of such production have reaped financial rewards as a result. Controversy continues to this day on whether to include other ozone-depleting chemicals in the ban, and there is some illegal trade in CFCs. Nevertheless, the Montreal Protocol, as it is commonly referred to, is considered the best example of international cooperation to solve a man-made global environment problem.

Although the most industrialized countries, which have highly developed regulatory systems, experts aplenty, and effective environmental NGOs, have often taken the lead in negotiating international environmental issues, the developing countries participate fully, knowing that they also have much to gain or lose. While they recognize the seriousness of the problems under negotiation, their role has often been protecting their own rights to develop. They are particularly eager to assure that new treaty obligations protecting forests or slowing climate change will not impede their own economic growth. They are concerned that better environmental protection will cost them money, and, since they see global environmental problems primarily as the legacy of Northern states' demands on resources, in every negotiation since 1992 they have sought from the highly industrialized countries *additional* international financing and concessions on technology transfer to soften their transition to sustainable practices. Because the developing countries are often divided among themselves and because the donor countries have resisted demands for additional funding, their repeated demands for technology transfer and "additionality" have not been met. Since 1992, only Japan has increased its development assistance, and even it is now cutting back in the face of prolonged recession at home.

In a few international environmental treaties developing countries have been leaders. The best example is their effort to stop the shipment of toxic wastes from the highly industrialized countries (that have increasingly tough domestic regulations on dumping) to poorer ones (that often have neither the regulations nor the technical and administrative capacity to deal safely with such wastes). Although most of the trade was legal, some of it was illegal, the result of bribery that allowed covert dumping. Developing countries' early efforts to curb shipments failed. The UNEP guidelines developed in 1985 recommended notification and consent of the receiving state and verification that the recipients had disposal and treatment requirements at least as stringent as the exporting country. These so-called "informed consent" guidelines did not alter practice. In 1989, the Basel Convention on Control of Transboundary Movements of Hazardous Wastes and Their Disposal was signed, but shipping states refused to accept responsibility and agreed only to "informed consent," making it a very weak treaty. Under pressure from their former colonies, the European countries pledged not to ship their wastes to 68 states, and in 1991 12 African countries formally agreed not to accept wastes, but this still left out most of the developing countries, who by this time overwhelmingly favored a complete ban. An international campaign to publicize the most egregious cases was complemented by effective investigation and publicity by Greenpeace International, and within 2 years the public worldwide began to see the waste trade as a moral issue in which the shipping countries were depicted as shameful. Their governments could no longer resist: in Geneva in 1994, the nations agreed to ban all wastes from OECD (Organisation for Economic Cooperation and Development) to non-OECD states (including the former Soviet states, which were also willing to take wastes for a price). Today, negotiations continue over whether "recyclables" are included in the ban, and the shipping countries still will not accept liability for illegal dumping done by their shipping companies, but the treaty demonstrates that the developing countries can succeed against the powerful industrialized states when they are united and persistent.

Typically, environmental treaties do not fully satisfy their advocates, be they states or environmental organizations. But all treaties have slowly been strengthened, mostly in reaction to subsequent events or pressure from the lead states. Some of the original agreements were not even intended to be instruments of environmental protection. For instance, the whaling agreement of 1946, though couched in conservation terms, was little more than a formula for exploiting and dividing up the annual whale catch, but it gradually evolved into a treaty that banned all commercial whaling. And the 1981–1988 negotiations on Antarctica began as discussions on how to govern mineral exploration and ended up prohibiting exploration altogether, after popular opinion in Australia and France swayed elections and changed the stance of those two governments.

The most controversial and politicized negotiations are those such as the climate treaty, where the use of fossil fuels is crucial to essential economic activities and where any shift in policy is going to affect—for good or bad—large numbers of investors and jobs as well as nations' trade balances. These divisions often appear to be along North–South lines, with the developing countries accusing the North of creating the problem and the highly industrialized countries looking for equal commitment from the developing countries, whose emissions of greenhouse warming gases are growing rapidly as they modernize their economies. But one can find developing and highly industrialized countries on both sides of the divide. The European Union, backed by the smallest island states (who fear inundation from global warming-induced sea-level rise), argued for the most demanding fixed targets and timetables in the original 1990–1992 climate negotiations and again at the Kyoto COP in late 1997, while the United States and Japan sought allies among some powerful developing country polluters (including China and India) who could be counted on to say the United States and other industrial powerhouses must commit to serious reductions first before developing countries could be expected to act—and thus continue a stalemate and prevent meaningful progress in reducing emissions.

Although the relative political and economic power of participating nations usually influences negotiations, great powers do not control the environmental scene to the extent they would on traditional security matters. Only when the participation of a particular powerful nation is essential for the effectiveness of a treaty can a superpower like the United States wield exceptional power. This happened on the climate treaty where the United States, as the largest emitter of carbon dioxide (over 20% of the world's total, produced by 5% of the world's population), could dictate the bottom line in the 1992 and 1997 negotiations because a treaty to curtail emissions would be meaningless without U.S. participation. However, the biodiversity treaty is another story. No matter that the United States—home to the world's largest biotechnology industry—refused to sign the treaty in 1992 without certain property rights guaranteed; the treaty was consummated without the United States by the unanimity of the Southern countries, where most of the diversity in question is found. Conversely, the United States, the world's biggest producer and user of CFCs, could rapidly move the treaty process forward once Washington made up its mind that a ban was called for.

There are no clearly good guys and bad guys in these treaty negotiations. On some issues the United States has led the battle for a stronger treaty—on ozone depletion or endangered species, for instance. On others, such as climate, the United States has been the most important country blocking a strong treaty. Although the small Scandinavian countries have generally been consistent environmental advocates, an environmentally conscious country such as Norway, long a leader on many issues, recently violated the ban on harvesting certain species of whales while invoking the goal of sustainable development.

Some very small countries, such as the Netherlands, have power in environmental negotiations despite their small size because they set a very good example at home, promote generous overseas aid for sustainable development, and exert consistent active moral leadership. At the same time, some huge states are almost invisible in the environmental arena. The Soviet Union used to go along with most agreements without a large role in the debate and then ignored its international obligations when it suited them, for example, harvesting whales and dumping nuclear wastes in international waters. This bad behavior ceased with the demise of the Soviet Union and the severe economic crises that have limited the ability of successor states to exploit and foul international resources.

Japan is another nation that is present at all environmental negotiations and has a fairly good record on treaty implementation, but is seldom vocal in negotiations. This reticence partly reflects Japan's general reluctance to play a visible international leadership role since World War II. But on some questions (the most obvious being climate since Japan has a relatively good record on energy efficiency), its delegates seem anxious not to offend their most important trading partner, the United States. China also is a silent partner in negotiations, but for different reasons. The Chinese say little, sign on, and carry out their treaty obligations quite well. They sometimes side with the United States (as on climate issues) and sometimes identify with the developing countries (as on the trade in wastes), but do not say much on either. Their passivity in negotiations probably reflects their long isolation from world affairs and discomfort with the sometimes rapid shifts in the environmental negotiations. (Because China is growing so rapidly and has the largest potential market in the world and because it is a major polluter, China's cooperation in defense of the planet is critical.)

The United States has played a visible and vocal role in most treaty negotiations—whether enthusiastic or reluctant participants, the U.S. delegation is always large and well prepared. These days it often includes representatives of nongovernmental organizations as do the delegations from Australia, some European states, Canada, and a few developing countries. The United States, the world's only superpower, can usually influence large numbers of other governments, depending on the issue. In practice, this means that its occasional propensity to act unilaterally, as on the tuna–dolphin and pesticide residue issues, often *via* a *fait accompli*, sets the world standard. It can also mean that a major global treaty, such as the hazardous waste or climate treaty, can be weakened and sidetracked or held up by U.S. opposition. But it also can mean that U.S. NGOs—environmental, religious, corporate—with easy access to policy-makers and the media can sometimes influence international politics from their home base. That happened in 1993 when a coalition of environmental organizations and U.S. companies persuaded the new Clinton administration to sign the Biodiversity Treaty, reversing the U.S. position.

Growth in international institutions capable of implementing these environmental treaties has not kept up with the development of the agreements themselves. Each treaty depends partly on the self-interests of the signatories and their willingness to adhere to them.

Each also usually calls for some kind of secretariat. These functions are sometimes performed by the United Nations and sometimes served by one of the interested parties to the treaty. The site of COPs circulates among the parties and is usually considered prestigious by the host country because the resulting agreement bears its name, as in "Kyoto Protocol." Although the idea surfaces periodically, there has been no serious move to create a grand international environmental agency responsible for monitoring and implementating all environmental treaties. Indeed, some analysts argue that no single big international agency could possibly recruit and pay for the breadth of expertise required by so varied a group of treaties, and that carrying the work load from one COP to the next is best left to the most eager countries (as it is now), buttressed by UN bodies with assigned monitoring responsibilities.

The United Nations Environmental Programme, the body created by the UN after the 1972 Stockholm Conference on the Human Environment, played an important role as monitor, catalyst, and coordinator for the 20 years leading up to the 1992 Rio Summit. It alerted governments to such emerging problems as ozone depletion, often by sponsoring technical conferences, and in this way initiated negotiations on many important environmental treaties, including treaties on ozone, biological diversity, climate change, and trade in hazardous wastes. The agency has always been underfunded and limited in its power, according to environmentalists, and controversial among its critics, especially among the developing countries, who charge that the agency and its staff emphasize the global problems—global warming, ozone-layer protection, biodiversity loss—of primary concern to the Northern countries. Criticisms were frequent during the term of Mustafa Tolba, even though he came from a developing country (Egypt) and championed such Third World causes as banning of toxic waste trade. Thus, in 1992, after the Rio Conference, rather than strengthen UNEP, the General Assembly created a new body, the UN Commission on Sustainable Development. Lacking in strong leadership and expert secretariat assistance, but most of all lacking strong, consistent, organized pressure from leading states, it has done only a middling job of monitoring and reviewing nations' progress toward sustainable development.

C. The Importance of Sustainable Development

The serious environmental consequences of human societies' assaults on natural systems do not imply that major biological and physical systems verge on collapse—though some local systems may be beyond repair. (The Aral Sea comes to mind.) Earth can theoretically accommodate another 6 billion people by the year 2100, but only if governments and communities start thinking differently about resources and start producing and using goods in new ways.

In the aggregate, all the international environmental treaties and the 1992 *Agenda 21* blueprint require that nations alter their approach to economic growth and development, that they provide far more goods and services in much more efficient ways using less energy (especially from fossil fuels) and fewer nonrenewable and renewable materials, reusing and recycling the ones they use, and producing less waste—in both households and industry. This approach, tailored to each country, has come to be known as sustainable development, defined in 1987 by the World Commission on Environment and Development as "development that meets the needs of the present without compromising the ability of future generations to meet their own needs."

While some of the adjustments needed to achieve sustainability can be made incrementally without pain, and even at increased profit, most will involve dislocations of people, the initial cost of new technologies, and shifts in investments. These are difficult, not just because all entrenched institutions and behaviors are hard to change, but also because various industries and regions perceive themselves as losing profit, or market share, or jobs. And because the promised more efficient, sustainable, and livable world is unknown—and unknowable in detail—even those who would profit by it (the producers of energy-saving or other alternative technologies, the manufacturers of less polluting chemicals, and the people downstream or downwind of pollution) are guarded advocates at best. Thus, changing a country's transport mix, forest policy, or use of agricultural chemicals becomes difficult in both developing and highly industrialized countries, all the more so precisely because those in power usually benefit somehow from the old system.

Although the manifestations of unsustainable practices may differ in rich and poor countries, the general message (good environmental practices make good economic sense) and prescriptions (more efficient and equitable use of resources) are the same. One action called for in *Agenda 21* was careful introspective analysis by each government in its own country to identify nonsustainable practices and plan new ways of doing things. In the United States, President Clinton appointed the President's Council on Sustainable Development, co-chaired by an industrialist and an environmentalist, to make detailed recommendations on population and consumption, agriculture, industry, transportation, tax reform, and so on, that would move the country toward sustainability with as little disruption as possible. So far, the Administration and Congress have done nothing to implement it, but some corporations and communities have. National debate has only just begun, and sustainable development does not now have strong champions among nationally elected leaders. Conflicting interests emerge, for instance, over international negotiations on the climate treaty, where definite goals and timetables would require the United States to move more deliberately to conserve energy. In the case of global warming, the U.S. public is understandably confused about the science and technology and about international requirements. Investors and workers alike want assurance that if they approach production choices differently, they will not be put at a disadvantage compared with their international competitors. Most politicians, worried about their own careers, are unwilling to risks championing new transportation policies or tax changes.

In the poorer developing countries, politicians share many of the same fears. But in developing countries, where hardships are greater and millions live at the margin, the choice of development strategies may raise real questions of survival. Environmental concerns are apt not to be about the big global issues, but about local, immediate ones: soil loss or degradation that reduces agricultural yields and leads to hunger; the lack of clean drinking water and sanitation responsible for 80% of childhood deaths in the developing countries; severe shortages of water and undependable weather that threatens agricultural productivity; the accumulation of household and industrial wastes and effluents that poison the air and water. In the large and rapidly growing cities of Africa, Asia, and Latin America, air and water have become political issues: in Mexico City, for instance, factories and even schools have been shut down periodically in winter when pollution is at its worst.

Poor environmental and development choices are also costly. Consider the environmental complications of building large dams to generate electric power and to supply water for agriculture. While it is not easy to calculate the costs of thousands of people dislocated and communities and cultures torn apart during dam construction, the costs of rapid silting and water logging are more easily assessed. The loss of electric power from the silt that builds up behind dams runs into the billions of dollars. In China, the Sanmenxia Dam silted up within 4 years of completion. In 2 years, the Anchicay Dam in Colombia lost 25% of its storage capacity because of watershed deforestation. In India, terrible deforestation in the mountains above the Tehri Dam reduced the estimated life of the dam from 100 to 30 or 40 years. And irrigation—for two generations synonymous among international aid-donor agencies with the modernization of agriculture—itself takes a toll on the soil and on human health. The United Nations Food and Agriculture Organization estimates that as much as 20% of irrigated land is waterlogged or excessively salinized, or both, and that as much irrigated land is taken out of production each year as is brought under cultivation by new irrigation projects. The health costs associated with irrigation include increased rates of malaria and schistosomiasis, carried by mosquitoes and snails that live in the irrigation canals. One can calculate the human and environmental costs of other unsustainable practices associated with deforestation, soil loss, inappropriate pesticide use, and poor sanitation. The tragedy is that development need not be so costly—development agencies have now logged years of experience with alternative sustainable development strategies.

The failures of traditional development strategies, the growing gap between rich and poor, and the steady migration to the cities and across borders do not themselves usually lead directly to violent incidents. But they do contribute to unemployment, political unrest, challenges to authority, and to endemic political instability. And in some cases, the manifestations are quite specific: riots over hikes in prices for bread, kerosene, or local transportation. Local governments pay dearly for such disturbances, and there are also military costs since in many developing countries armies are charged with maintaining civil order and the regime in power rather than protecting against a foreign enemy.

Two international institutions have a determining influence on the domestic development strategy choices made by governments in the developing countries: one is the multinational development banks and financial institutions; the other is the international trading system. The World Bank and its regional counterparts set the fashion for economic development in developing countries. For two generations, the size of their sectoral loans (in energy and agriculture, for instance) and the selection of projects they fund (large centralized power projects and huge irrigation schemes, for instance), as well as their structural-adjustment loans, have determined many governments' investment priorities—especially in the poorest countries, which are heavily dependent on international assistance and have few alternative sources of funding from private banks and investors. Since 1992, the multilateral banks have developed new lending criteria predicated on sustainability, but so far only a small portion of loans have been made in these new areas. And the International Monetary Fund (IMF) has been slow even to recognize the impact of its financial packages on sustainable development, let alone make any changes. As trendsetters in development and financial policy, these institutions could stimulate and help developing countries onto a more sustainable path of economic development.

In countries whose economic growth and development depend significantly on trade—that is, in most developing countries in this era of globalization—trade opportunities often drive development decisions. A nation's exports and investments from foreign banks and firms are sometimes the single most important determinant of its development strategy and often have greater effect on production decisions, technology choices, subsidies, and taxes than any bilateral or multilateral aid program. Because immediate profits and the potential of future sales and investments drive private business decisions, sustainability is seldom taken into account when business decisions are made. Although environmentalists and development specialists have directed increasing attention to the varied environmental consequences of trade, the international trading system as manifest in the General Agreement on Tariffs and Trade and the World Trade Organization persists in the view that environmental considerations are the responsibility of domestic producers and regulators and extraneous to the trading system. Some small cracks have been made in this defense: an appendix on environmental and social concerns was added to the North American Free Trade Agreement; policy study committees in the OECD at least recognize the trade/environment connection; and a committee on the environment is promised within the new World Trade Organization. Environmental issues have ranked among the most controversial trade issues in the 1990s and will continue to do so, guaranteeing that the international trading system will be revisited by environmental issues.

III. NEW DEFINITIONS OF SECURITY

To what extent have new ways of thinking about economic development and security penetrated the decision-making of policy makers and the thinking of academics? Considerable lip service notwithstanding, the environment still gets short shrift among establishment policy-makers, academics, and the media. In general foreign policy statements by the President, Vice-President, and the Secretary of State, the environment is usually part of the litany of international problems. But when specific trade, financial, or security issues are actually negotiated, environmental considerations are much more likely to be an "add-on." As of 1996, the official U.S. National Security Strategy recognized an "emerging class of transnational environmental and natural resource issues" among a number of nonmilitary risks to American security, but most policy-makers and their academic advisers still do not integrate the environmental aspects into consideration of relevant international issues and tend to deal with environmental issues separately from security or economic issues, if at all. While essential economic considerations are increasingly integrated into national security policy, environmental considerations are not yet accorded similar automatic inclusion. Nor do many career diplomats consider specializing in environmental issues the way to get ahead in the State Department, despite the continuous involvement of U.S. delegations in environmental negotiations. Even in the post-Cold War era, expertise in the language and politics of the former Soviet states or the economics of East Asia is preferred to environmental expertise if one wants to make ambassadorial rank.

Indeed, it is hard to argue that environmental degradation and the mismanagement of natural resources is likely to be a cause of violent conflict if one employs the accepted concept of security prevailing since World War II. An emphasis on the primacy of military forces, alliances, and aggressive diplomacy in protection of national interests leaves little room for the idea of environmental threats. Yet, this narrow concept of security was hardly ever challenged in public in this country as long as the Cold War lasted. But when the Berlin wall came down and the Soviet Union disintegrated, the fear of attack lessened and the credibility of a purely military notion of security began to fade.

After the Cold War, people began to wonder what the important international issues would be in the coming decades and how international power would be constructed. Alternative concepts of security began to get attention, and these new definitions made room for such considerations as interdependence, mutual security, human security, cooperation, demilitarization, human rights, economic growth and development, and equity within nations, between nations, and between generations.

Treatises on "common security" (the Palme Commission reports of 1982 and 1989) or "comprehensive security" (the term used at the Norwegian Peace Research Institute) began to get wider consideration. Their insistence on large reductions of military spending and an investment in economic, social, and environmental programs came to be called the "peace dividend." Arthur H. Westing and Norwegian colleagues proposed, even before the Cold War ended, that cooperation around regional environmental problems, such as those of the Baltic Sea, could build confidence and pave the way to cooperation on regional security issues. Chinese policy analysts suggested the same to this author in Shanghai in 1995. In the *Human Development Report*, the UNDP under James Gustave Speth's leadership enlarged the concept of sustainable human development (and indicators to measures it) as the necessary basis for a peaceful world. Think tanks such as the Brookings Institution and the Woodrow Wilson Center at the Smithsonian Institution developed policy research projects on cooperative security and environmental security. Even the World Bank and the IMF began analyzing the deleterious effects of large military budgets on economic development and started publishing military expenditures in their annual development data reports. By IMF calculations, a 20% cut in the military budgets of the industrial countries would free $90 billion a year for other uses, and if developing countries with high military budgets reduced them to the level of the world average (about 4.5% of GDP), another $140 billion per year would be freed up annually for development or other needs.

In the past 2 decades, a new subspecialty in security and peace studies called "environmental security" has sprung up, represented by scholars who write, as Kennan and Mathews did in the 1980s, of environmental degradation and disasters as threats to security. The topic has received some foundation support and articles appear in the professional journals. The military also has shown some interest: as early as 1969, NATO added environmental issues to its agenda, mostly pollution and energy issues. And in the 1990s, the U.S. armed forces, partly in search of new post-Cold War missions, have supported conferences and research on the topic. Army intellectuals have applied themselves to the concept and to political analyses, while all branches of the U.S. military have developed handbooks that promulgate an official environmental ethic and voluminous regulations that detail required responses to U.S. environmental laws and assign responsibility at every level of command.

The concept of environmental security remains controversial. Its defenders—even among the military—argue, like the advocates of common or comprehensive security, that national security can no longer be based solely on military power, that severe environmental problems can lead directly or indirectly to armed confrontation, and that military conflicts over resources (mostly in the developing countries) may well increase in coming decades as demand rises and supplies become scarce. Critics of the concept include traditionalists who argue that environmental considerations will dilute the primary military mission of the armed forces and that resource scarcity will rarely lead to war. But also among the critics are some peace and environmental scholars who argue that the values of the environmentalists and security analysts are incompatible—that one values access to information, transparency, and participatory decision-making, while the other values secrecy and a chain of command. They argue that the term itself—security—is misapplied to issues where cooperation rather than force is the required "defense."

The debate will continue, and the arguments themselves are more significant than the outcome, for they represent a paradigm shift away from the political–military concept of security that has prevailed for so long to a much more inclusive concept in which environmental concerns will definitely play a role. Some hoped that the 1992 Earth Summit would be looked back upon as the watershed in the paradigm shift, but implementation of the 1992 treaties and agenda for sustainable development has been slow. Resistance to change is strong and spread widely around the globe. Although the evolution of environmental protection treaties and experiments in sustainable development indicate that the nations do seem to be lurching mostly in a forward direction, it may well take further eruptions of violence to confirm a new security paradigm.

Also See the Following Articles

CHEMICAL AND BIOLOGICAL WARFARE • HEALTH CONSEQUENCES OF WAR AND POLITICAL VIOLENCE • NONGOVERNMENTAL ACTORS IN INTERNATIONAL POLITICS • TRADE AND THE ENVIRONMENT

Bibliography

Bandyopadhyay, J., & Shiva, V. (1992). Forestry myths and the World Bank: A critical review of "Tropical forests—A call for action." In V. Shiva, V. M. Meher-Homji, & N. D. Jayal (Eds.), *Forest resources: Crisis and management*. Dehra Dun, India: Natraj.

Brown, L. R., Flavin, C. French, H., *et al.* (1997). *State of the world, 1997: A Worldwatch Institute report on progress toward a sustainable society*. New York: W. W. Norton.

Brown, J. W. (Ed.) (1990). *In the U.S. interest: Resources, growth and security in the developing world.* Boulder, CO: Westview Press.

Earth Negotiations Bulletin, published periodically by the International Institute for Sustainable Development, Winnipeg, Manitoba, Canada. Available also on line at http://iisd.ca/linkages/voltoc.html

French, H. F. (1994). Making environment treaties work. *Scientific American*, *271*, No. 6, December, 62–65.

Klare, M. T., & Chandrani, Y. (Eds.) (1998). *World security: Challenges for a new century* (3rd ed.). New York: St. Martin's Press.

Palme Commission on Disarmament and Security Issues (1989). *A world at peace: Common security in the twenty-first century*. Stockholm: PCDSI.

Porter, G., & Brown, J. W. (1995). *Global Environmental Politics*. (2nd ed.) Boulder, CO: Westview Press.

South Centre (1991). *Environment and development: Towards a common strategy of the south in the UNCED negotiations and beyond*. Geneva/Dar es Salaam: South Centre.

United Nations Development Programme (1997). *Human development report 1997*. New York: *Oxford University Press New York*.

Westing, A. H. (Ed.) (1989). *Comprehensive security for the Baltic, An environmental approach*. Newbury Park, CA: International Peace Research Institute, Oslo, and UN Environment Programme/ Sage Publications.

World Commission on Environment and Development (1987). *Our common future*. New York: Oxford University Press.

World Resources Institute (1998). *World resources, 1998–1999*. Oxford University Press.

Ethical and Religious Traditions, Eastern

Theodore Gabriel
Cheltenham and Gloucester College of Higher Education

GLOSSARY

Ahimsa Nonviolence, noninjury.

Dharma Duty, righteousness.

Karma Action; in Eastern religions the corpus of actions committed in one's life that has consequences in one's subsequent lives.

Nirguna Without qualities; having qualities that cannot be specified or described.

Jihad Striving or struggle; the concept of defensive war in the cause of God (Allah) in Islam.

IT IS AN UNDENIABLE FACT that most ethical traditions have their source in religious creeds, teachings, and scriptures. Religions are strong value-generating systems, and ethics along with morality is an indispensable and vital part of every religious system. In this article we look into five religious traditions of Eastern provenance and main practice, namely, Hinduism, Buddhism, Sikhism, Jainism, and Islam. The discussion is centered on ethical issues relevant to matters of violence, peace, and conflict. We examine the Hindu religious tradition first.

I. HINDUISM

It is well known that Hinduism extols the principle of *ahimsa*, nonviolence. The Mahabharatha 12.254.29 states that *ahimsa* is the highest *dharma*. (duty, righteous action) To some extent Hinduism has imbibed this principle from Buddhism and Jainism, religions in which nonviolence is enshrined even more strongly, especially in the latter. In Hinduism the doctrines of *karma* (action) and *samsara* (reincarnation—or more properly the concept of the cycle of births and deaths) plays an important part. One of the consequences of these doctrines is the ontological nexus between various life forms, since in the doctrine of Karma the soul passes through many incarnations inhabiting several bodies, human, animal, and insect. This mitigates to a great extent the attitude of inferiority attributed to animals and insects by human beings, leading to a more relaxed approach to the victimisation of such life forms. *Advaita* (monistic theology), prominent in Hinduism, especially in modern times as *Vedanta* (the end of all Vedas), is another factor in Hinduism's approach to violence. The basis of Advaita is the identity of all beings with the Brahman, the Supreme Being or transcendental soul (*Paramatma*) and hence the essential identity of all living entities, be it human, or animal. *Advaitic* thought is hinted at in even the earliest of Hindu scriptures, namely the Vedas, and more clearly in several of the Upanishads, (philosophical commentaries on the Vedas) but had been systematized as a theological doctrine by the great Hindu theologian Gaudapada, and later by Shankara (8th century) and Ramanuja (12th century). The school was revived by the Neo-Vedantins Vivekananda and Radhakrishnan, and is an influential school of thought in modern Hinduism. The consequence of Advaitic theology is that if you harm another being, man, woman, animal, or insect you are harming yourself. Professor Krishnamoorthy states:

> The concept of *ahimsa* has its roots in the Hindu theory that every life is a spark of the divine and our recognition of the divine must be so universal as to identify ourselves with this divinity in every living being. In consonance with this principle Hindu rituals prescribe various compensatory repentant rites as a daily chore, for the several explicit and implicit killings that we cannot do without in our day to day lives
>
> *(Krishnamurthy, 1989, p. 16)*

According to Prof. Krishnamoorthy, perfect nonviolence is an ideal to be aimed at rather than a practical end achieved in day to day life." It is an objective to be moved closer and closer to. Absolute *ahimsa* is beyond the reach of ordinary individuals since even the act of breathing can inflict violence to millions of living entities in the air we breathe. We will look subsequently into the fact that in Hinduism there is a tension between *ahimsa* and justified violence, for violence has to be resorted to in certain contexts.

Manu, the law giver, in the key Hindu scripture *Manudharmashastra* (10:63) accords *ahimsa* prime position in the list of virtues, which according to him summarizes *dharma*. Indeed, *ahimsa* is sometimes said to summarize all virtue. The code of Vasishta states: "Avoiding back biting, envy, pride, egoism, unbelief, guile, boasting, insulting others, hypocrisy, greed, infatuation, anger and discontent is approved *dharma* (duty, righteous action) for all the stages of life." It may be noted that most of the vices listed by Vasishta constitute negation of the principle of ahimsa. Of course, the practice of *ahimsa* was especially enjoined for those who had left the *grihastya* (householder) stage of life. In other words, *ahimsa* is particularly a characteristic of asceticism, although it is a virtue to be observed by every one. Lipner points out that the Yogasutra of Patanjali, a text authoritative for ascetics lists *ahimsa* as the cardinal virtue for ascetics of all castes.

The most reputed and well-known exponent of *ahimsa* in modern times was M. K. Gandhi, the great Indian figure who led the movement for Indian independence. The Mahatma (Great Soul), who was a high-caste Hindu, was also greatly influenced by Jainism, a faith widely prevalent in his native Porbandar (Kutch, Gujerat) and by his readings from the New Testament. Gandhi's whole political strategy has sometimes been attributed to the Sermon on the Mount—especially Christ's injunction to turn the other cheek. However it is natural to assume that the major influence on his thinking about violence was primarily conditioned by his Hindu upbringing, which comes out clearly, for example, in his attitude toward cow protection.

For Gandhi, nonviolence was inextricably intertwined with truth. Truth was for him God, and *ahimsa* the way to Truth. He declares: "My uniform experience has convinced me that there is no other God than truth. ... And the only means for the realisation of Truth is *ahimsa* ...—a perfect vision of Truth can only follow a complete realisation of ahimsa." To Gandhi *ahimsa* was not a negative or passive concept, but a dynamic one. The practitioner of *ahimsa* was not a coward who avoided danger. It required great courage and fortitude to practice *ahimsa*. Gandhi illustrated this by not retaliating under great provocation when he was attacked, especially in South Africa. He also felt that *ahimsa* should originate in the mind. "Non-violence of the mere body without the co-operation of the mind is non-violence of the weak or the cowardly, and has therefore no potency." He did not bear a grudge to his antagonists and enemies. He stated, "If we bear malice and hatred in our bosoms and pretend not to retaliate, it must recoil upon us and lead to our destruction." When in 1942 a crowd in Chauri chaura went out of control and burned a police station with the policemen inside, he immediately called a halt to the independence agitation that had gained momentum all over India, to the astonishment of his colleagues as well as the British.

To Gandhi the underlying driving force for *ahimsa* was universal compassion. In that sense his adoption of *ahimsa* was not pragmatic. It depended on his monistic beliefs—the ultimate identity of all living beings. God is all-pervasive so no injury should be caused to any living being. He also said that nonviolence is the individual trying to transcend his animal nature, which was grounded in brutality, and striving toward the spiritual perfection of *ahimsa*.

> Man cannot for a moment live without consciously or unconsciously committing outward *himsa* (injury). ... The very fact of his living—

> eating, drinking, moving about—necessarily involves some *himsa*, be it ever so minute. A votary of *ahimsa*, therefore, is true to his faith if the spring of all his actions is compassion, if he shuns to the best of his ability the destruction of the tiniest creature, . . . and thus incessantly strives to be free from the deadly coil of *himsa*. He will be constantly growing in self-restraint and compassion, but he can never become entirely free from outward *himsa*.
>
> *(Gandhi, M. K., Young India, 4.6.1925).*

Gandhi also used the duality of the body and soul, the Hindu theological concept of *Prakriti* (wordly matter) and *Purusa* (God), in his exegesis of the idea of *ahimsa*, equating the body with *himsa* and the soul with *ahimsa*. In his own words "Man cannot be wholly free from violence so long as he lives a bodily life and continues to be a social being."

The prominence of *ahimsa* in Hindu ethical ideology has to be tempered by the existence of injunctions in the scriptures extolling *nishkama karma*, the performance of caste duty without concern for its consequences. Hindu society is divided into four major divisions, designated as *varnas*, namely, the *Brahmin*, the *Kshatriya*, the *Vaishya*, and the *Shudra*. These are in the main occupational divisions with clearly prescribed duties for each *varna*. The duties are as enshrined in the various Hindu scriptures, notably the *Dharma Shastras* (the sciences of duties), compendiums that stipulate the duties of various castes and subcastes, genders, and individuals in various stages of life. Performance of the duties constitutes good *karma*, and negligence of these result in bad *karma*. The Karma doctrine avers that the acquisition of good *karma* is vital for liberation (*moksha*) from worldly existence. The second of these castes is the *Kshatriya* (warrior), and their duty is to fight to uphold honor, chastity of women, kingly authority, and like virtues, and protect the weak and the defenseless. They can be likened to the knights extolled in European myths and legends. Violence is a natural part of their occupation. The whole genesis of the popular and key scripture known as the *Bhagavad Gita* (Song of the Lord) lies in Lord Krishna, the Hindu *avatar* (incarnation) of the Supreme Being, persuading his protege Arjuna to fight in a good cause. In the climactic battle scene of the Hindu epic *Mahabharatha*, Arjuna faces an army composed of his cousins, uncles, former teachers, and many who are his former companions and many who are dear to him. Dismayed, he lays down his arms. The ensuing discourse between Arjuna and Krishna is in reality a philosophical debate for and against *himsa*. Can violence ever be justified? Do the ends justify the means? These are the underlying issues in this dialogue. In the opening sections of the *Bhagavad Gita* Arjuna states his reasons for refusing to fight. He tells Krishna that he will be slaying many that are dear to him and like his former Gurus, those to whom he is indebted. He is not prepared to slay them even for all the three worlds, let alone one kingdom. Killing, he feels, is a sin, which will lead him to perdition. He will leave many women widowed and helpless. Without husbands and fathers to protect and maintain them they will turn to prostitution, thus family honor will decline. Ancestors will be left without descendants to perform the customary periodical rites for the welfare of their souls (*sraddha*). Lord Krishna, however, tells him that it is necessary for him to fight. He advances many arguments for this exhortation. Arjuna is a warrior and an Aryan, and it was not becoming of him to be cowardly and refuse to fight. It is his caste *dharma* to fight in a just cause, being a *Kshatriya*.

Krishna informed him that a person who is killed does not cease to exist. The *atman* (soul) merely passes into another body. The concept of death is the result of sense perception. Death is merely a delusion. No one is able to destroy the imperishable soul.

> He who thinks that he has slain
> And he who thinks that one is slain
> Both do not have the right knowledge
> One who has right understanding knows
> that one neither slays nor is slain
>
> *(Bhagavad Gita, 2:19)*

Krishna consoled Arjuna by saying: for one who has taken birth, death is certain; and for one who is dead birth is certain. Therefore, in the unavoidable discharge of your duty, you should not lament. Krishna warned Arjuna, if you do not fight this righteous war, you are committing *adharma* (unrighteousness) and will certainly incur sin and also lose your reputation. Krishna enjoined him to fight without desiring greatness or honor and without worrying about the consequences—an almost unquestioning and blind execution of one's caste *dharma*. Two points are clear from this. Violence can be resorted to only in just causes; there is something that can be categorized as righteous violence. A righteous end justifies even unrighteous means. This is elucidated further in Krishna resorting to what can be legitimately described as devious means for the successful conclusion of the war. He hides the sun with his discus to kill Jayadradha. He makes Yudhishtira, the son of Dharma, to tell a white lie in saying that Ashwathama has been killed, in order to slay the unvanquishable Drona. Ultimately the *dharma* of a warrior inevitably involves violence.

Hinduism thus does not categorically prohibit the use of violence, in spite of its extolling *ahimsa* as a great virtue. However, though in the earliest times animal sacrifices were practiced and even now some obscure Hindu groups practice even human sacrifice, vegetarianism is the norm for all Hindus and is related to concepts of purity and pollution since the priestly caste is totally banned from eating meat. *Ahimsa* is thus related to purity, and *himsa* to impurity.

II. BUDDHISM

Buddhism was founded by Siddhartha Gautama (560–480 B.C.), a prince of the small principality of the Shakyas, Kapilavastu. He abandoned his princehood and his family and set out on a religious quest and attained enlightenment while sitting under a tree in the town of Buddha Gaya, in Bihar, India.

The Buddha taught that all evil arises from worldly desire and this in turn is caused by the delusion of a permanent self. He averred that the human being is an ever-changing aggregate of five elements (*skandhas*)—the body, feelings, perceptions, impulses, and emotions—and acts of consciousness. This conglomeration of ever-changing elements is in a state of flux, and after death is reborn or reconstituted into another aggregate, and suffers the consequences of negative *karma* or misdeeds. The solution to worldly suffering is to realize the myth of self-hood and aim at *nirvana* (literally, blowing out), a state of permanence. The Buddha also taught the absolute relativism of everything in the world and the doctrine of *Sunyata* (emptiness). The eight-fold path of perfect view, perfect thought, perfect speech, perfect action, perfect livelihood, perfect effort, perfect mindfulness, and perfect concentration sets one off in the path of attaining *nirvana*. Thus the key concepts of Buddhism are those of *anatta* (no self) and *anicca* (impermanence). The Buddhist precepts regarding *ahimsa* and compassion has had a profound effect on ethics in India and wherever this religion has spread to. It is well known that Buddhism reformed to a considerable extent the warlike tendencies of the Central Asian Mongol and Tibetan populations.

The very first of *Pancasila*, the five precepts of Buddhism, is to refrain from destroying life. The key principle of Buddhism is the notion of *anatta*—no self. Selflessness naturally removes the instinct of self-preservation and self-indulgence, factors that engender violence to others, and foster compassion. According to the Buddha, your attitude toward others should be based on a sense of empathy—somewhat similar to Jesus' teaching, "do unto others what you would do to yourself." The Buddha said: "Everyone fears violence, everyone likes life; comparing oneself with others one would never slay or cause to slay." The prohibition on killing extends to the meanest of living beings—for example, insects—Buddhists often take great care when walking in woods not to trample on living things. It is believed that a person brings upon himself bad *kamma* (*karma*) by causing injury to others, resulting in his suffering unpleasantness in the present life and being reborn in a lower form of being. He might in his next life meet death unexpectedly while in the prime of life and enjoying all amenities of life. As in Hinduism, the identity of all life is a concept motivating *ahimsa*.

Buddhism, although it does not believe in an immortal soul transmigrating to other bodies, does believe in rebirth—the reconstitution of the five aggregates (*skandhas*), into another being. Thus by causing injury to others you may be inadvertently harming one who was in a past life dear to you. The chain of existence is the one that causes the intimate relationship between all living entities, animal, human, god, devil, and insect. Buddhagosha, in his elaboration of the first precept of the *Pancasila*, observes: "With regards to animals it is worse to kill a large animal than small, because a more extensive effort is involved. In the case of humans the killing is more blame worthy the more virtuous the victims are." However, Buddhagosha states that murder means striking and killing anything that possesses a life force.

The Theravada tradition, which is the earliest school of thought in Buddhism and prevails in South and Southeast Asia, is totally opposed to violence. Violence is to be eschewed in all contingencies, however expedient it might be. In the Parable of the Saw in the *Majjhima Nikaya* the Buddha declared that one who takes offense even at a robber who sawed him to pieces is no follower of his gospel. The *Dhammapada* states "never by hatred is hatred appeased." The ideal of *samata* (calmness) entails passive suffering. Killing in whatever context, according to the Theravada tradition, entails bad karmic consequences. The *Kula Sila* states, "Now wherein Vasettha is his good conduct? Herein, O Vasetta, that putting away the murder of that which lives, he abstains from destroying life. The cudgel and the sword he lays aside; and full of modesty and pity, he is compassionate and kind to all creatures that live." The first precept is couched in negative terms, yet the intention is to be positive and to go far beyond mere refraining from violence and killing. Geshe Kelsang Gyatso states that according to the Compendium of Phenomenology non–harmfulness is not simply refraining from harming others, but compassion. Compassion for seeing others free from suffering will totally preclude any thoughts of harming sentient beings. Moreover compassion should be free from desirous attachment; it should not be motivated by personal advantages accruing from compassionate actions. Vegetarianism is preferred, especially for monks and nuns, in conformity with the first precept, but for practical reasons, in colder climes non-vegetarian food is not totally proscribed. Moreover the Buddhist *bhikku* (mendicant) has to accept whatever is offered in his bowl, without rejecting it. Thus it may happen that even a monk is occasionally constrained to eat meat.

The rapid dissemination of Buddhism throughout India, Sri Lanka, and the Far East was through the efforts of Emperor Ashoka (3rd century B.C.). Ashoka had acquired a large empire through conquests, but after his war against Kalinga, and having visited the battlefield personally and observed the horrors of war, he had a change of heart and embraced Buddhism, later becoming its most famous royal exponent and missionary. Ashoka thereafter abjured war completely and made *ahimsa* the key principle of his administration, enjoining nonviolence not only to human beings but to animals, especially beasts of burden who had never before been properly cared for. He set up *stupas* (dome-shaped shrines) throughout India on which were carved his famous edicts. The very first edict states, "The taking of life and animal sacrifice is prohibited." He renounced warfare totally, reduced his armed forces, and did not impose military service on his subjects. He sent envoys to all neighboring countries to join in treaties of peace and friendship with him. To some of the recalcitrant border tribes he sent a message to the effect that they were not to fear him but to take friendship and assistance from him. In short his whole internal administration and foreign policy were grounded in the first precept of the Buddha, absolute pacifism. Although a fervent Buddhist, Ashoka was tolerant to adherents of other faiths, a fact reflected in his rock edicts. He never imposed Buddhism on the people as religious dogma, rather presenting it as a way of life—as *dharma*.

Although the general emphasis in Buddhism is a total commitment to *ahimsa* (nonviolence), even to the extent of suffering aggression passively, as Edward Conze opines, the fact that the rapid propagation of Buddhism owed to royal patronage necessarily leads to the possibility of violence being employed at least indirectly for its dissemination. He cites the cases of King Aniruddha of Burma in the 11th century, warrior monks in Japan who invaded Kyoto, and the Boxers in China who used Buddhist terminology, as instances to the point.

There is also the example of King Lang Darma of Tibet in the 10th century who did employ force in connection with religious objectives. It is a fact that many Buddhist monks are involved in the present ethnic strife in Sri Lanka. Theravada Buddhists would say that such instances reveal lapses from grace, or the inherent weakness of human nature. In religion there is often divergence between the theoretical position and the actual practice of the adherents. The Mahayana tradition compromises to the exigencies of life to the extent of saying that violence is justified if its objective is the protection of other sentient beings. Such a position is not totally pragmatic since the Mahayana Buddhists say that such violence should only be taken in a spirit of pure selflessness and compassion, and the proponent should be willing to take on the bad karmic consequences of the act of violence. The warrior monks of Japan are an instance of a more militant tradition in Buddhism. It originated with the schism in Enryakuji monastery, when in 933 A.D. as the result of a succession dispute the Enchin faction broke away from the monastery and founded an independent school at Mudera. Frequent disputes between this order and other monasteries as well as the secular authorities in Kyoto resulted in the emergence of a powerful warrior class of monks known as Sohei. A factional schism in the Sohei led to the birth of the Akuso (bad monks) who developed later into large monk armies. Between 981 and 1185 C.E. troops of warrior monks numbering several thousands made incursions into the capital against the government. There were also the Komuso, a type of free-lance priest armed with a sword and who showed a distinctive tendency to disputation.

A. Buddhist Attitudes toward Nationalism and War between Nations

Buddhism does not show an inordinate concern for nationhood. As reflected in Ashoka's edicts, tolerance is the key note of Buddhism's approach to nations, races, and cultures. Nations are looked on as different but equally valid systems of demographic organization. Such differences can be seen in smaller units of human organization such as the family. In modern times, due to improved communication and travel, the world has become a global village and Buddhists perceive the nations as a human family. Patriotism and nationalism should not be at the expense of abandoning larger values and interests. Sangharakshita states: "Nationalism is an exaggerated, passionate and fanatical devotion to one's national community at the expense of all other national communities and even at the expense of all other interests and loyalties." Nationalism and racism are seen by most Buddhists as forms of greed, hatred, and delusion. Buddhists support the United Nations as an organization for transcending national barriers and working for the unity of the human family. As mentioned earlier, Buddhism looks at a nation as an aggregate of individuals. Rahula Walpola asks, "What is a nation but a vast conglomeration of individuals?" Thus Buddhists consider that the fallibilities of individuals can affect nations too, such as *lobha* (greed), *dvesha* (hatred), and *avidya* (ignorance). Aitken states: " It is the perversion of self-realisation into self-aggrandisement that directs the course of our lives to violence." Thus conflict between nations have a similar genesis to that of conflict between individuals. War is necessarily looked on as evil or the consequence of worldly desire and undesirable traits. Buddhism has no theory for a just war, but I have already mentioned that in the Mahayana tradition killing is occasionally justified in the larger interests of the community or for protecting the innocent from violent individuals. Multiplied on a national scale this means that nations can go to war if the ends are in the interest of protection of the weak, the oppressed and the innocent. But many Buddhists are prepared to be killed rather than fight and not be killed.

III. JAINISM

The concept of *ahimsa* (noninjury or nonviolence) has an incomparable status in Jain ethical philosophy and ritual praxis. Jainism traces its origins to the pre-Aryan times and can rightly be judged to be the most ancient of the indigenous religions of India. The concept of *ahimsa* has an unique status in Jain ideology, so much so that it is the first of the 12 vows taken by both the lay (*anuvratas*) as well as the ascetic sections (*Mahavratas*) among the Jains. The extremes to which the Jain ascetic carries the practice of noninjury are well known. Jain ascetics wear a mask over the face so they do not inhale insects and such animate objects. They filter all liquids drunk by them so that ants and such insects are not accidentally consumed. They will never light a naked light or fire so that moths and flies are not attracted and perish in the flames. They habitually carry a broom with which they sweep the floor as they walk along so that they do not inadvertently trample a living organism to death.

The founder of Jainism is generally taken to be Vardhamana Mahavira who lived from 599 to 527 B.C.E. (the traditionally accepted dating). But Jains hold Vardhamana as only one of the *Tirthankaras* (those who have reached the shores of enlightenment). Many scholars hold Rasabha as the first *Tirthankara* of our age. The word *Jain* (*Jaina*) means one who has overcome. Jainism does not attribute much significance to theistic concepts and is based on the duality of *jiva* (living) and *ajiva* or *pudgala* (nonliving matter) clinging to it, and preventing it from attaining its tripartite attributes of infinite vision, infinite knowledge, and infinite freedom. The aspiration of Jainism is to rid oneself of *karma* that is absorbed into the self (*asrava*) by one's negative actions leading to bondage (*bandha*), resulting in continual life cycles and descent into lower forms of life and hell. Jainism is not dogmatic and believes in *anekanta vada* (nonabsolutism).

Ahimsa is considered to be the prime factor in the attaining of *nirvana*. Some even go so far as to consider *ahimsa* as the self in its pure form (*jiva*), the sentient essence of the person. *Ahimsa*, linguistically a negative term, is however not a negative concept in Jainism. It is a positive attitude engendered by positive virtues such as *karunya* (compassion), *daya* (kindness), and *kshanti* (forbearance). Positive *ahimsa* is termed *abhaya dana* (giving protection or refuge). *Ahimsa* is a state of mind than the avoidance of physical acts of violence. The intention is more important than the actual action itself. Amritachandra, the Jain philosopher states that even without overt *himsa* one can commit *himsa* mentally. The internal state of mind is the significant factor in determining *himsa* and *ahimsa* than external action. Unintentional *ahimsa* cannot be binding. Kaundakunda, a Jain philosopher of antiquity, has stated that even the killing of a living being is not sinful if the perpetrator has been careful and the killing was accidental. Mindfulness is the key attitude to avoiding violence as much of violence comes about as the result of carelessness and negligence, and such negligence is reprehensible. Thus a Jain is ever alert and careful not to injure living beings, however small they might be.

Jainism prescribes different standards for the lay person and the ascetic regarding the observance of *ahimsa*. It is inevitable that for the lay person in day to day living some amount of violence is inevitable; Jainism has classified such violence into various kinds. *Udyami* is violence involved in one's professional duties. *Arambhi* is violence incurred in domestic activities. And *virodhi* is in defending oneself, neighbors, or one's country.

Jainism has divided animate beings into 5 kinds—the one-sensed (e.g., vegetables and plants), two-sensed (earthworms, shellfish, and the like), three-sensed (such as lice, bugs, and ants), four-sensed (mosquitoes, flies, bees, etc.), and five-sensed (larger animals and human beings). A Jain is allowed to commit violence against the one-sensed but not against the rest. He should avoid wine, meat, honey, and fruits, which are the breeding ground of living organisms. Even the meat of animals that die of natural causes, cannot be eaten, as they can be the repositories of numerous living organisms such as flies and maggots. Hunting, fishing, vivisection, the use of skins and feathers of animals and birds as sartorial adornment, sacrifices, and other religious rituals involving killing animals, even killing insects that are troublesome, capital punishment—all these are disallowed. Euthanasia is not permissible. Even lay persons should refrain from intentionally killing innocent living beings when there is no necessity to do so. Traditionally in India Jains have refrained from agricultural activities since plowing and other farming activites would entail killing small organisms. They usually take up trade as their means of livelihood. Many are industrialists, or publishers. As far as possible injury to living beings are to be avoided. A Jain should avoid tying up animals carelessly or angrily, striking, beating, or whipping animals, especially in the tender parts of the body, docking a horse's or dog's tail, overloading an animal, or withholding food or drink (*anna pana nirodha*).

The monk, on the other hand, has to conform to more rigorous prescriptions regarding *ahimsa*. He is enjoined to observe *ahimsa* even in dreams. He has to extend active friendship to all living beings and renounce *himsa* of mind, body, and speech, as well as of action. He has to practice *ahimsa* to all living beings, mobile, immobile, gross, and subtle. The Jain scripture Darsha Vaikalika states "A monk should walk mindfully, stand mindfully, sit and sleep mindfully. By eating mindfully and speaking mindfully he is not affected by evil deeds." The monk has to take the vow, "I renounce all killing of living beings, whether subtle or gross, movable or stationary. Nor shall I myself kill living beings, nor cause others to do so, nor give my consent to do such acts."

Jains do not consider sovereignty as something that is imposed from above. It is rather viewed as supremacy of leadership based on wisdom, within a society organized in many ways with a multigraded leadership of which the people are associated at each level, and are not mere subjects. The king is allowed to engage in war as a defensive measure. War is regulated by a very humane code of conduct. However *sandhi* (treaty) is the basic premise. War has to be avoided as far as possible by diplomatic action. If war is unavoidable, loss of life should be reduced to a minimum. Only righteous strategies can be adopted in war (*niti yuddha*). The king should not kill ascetics, Brahmins, unarmed people, prisoners or those who are fleeing, noncombatants, the sick, children and women, and persons holdfing religious office. Unfair means can be employed only if the enemy resorts to such means first and it is necessary for the nation's survival. Amputation is the maximum punishment envisaged under Jain penal law, and is inflicted only if necessary for public security and in cases of insulting the ruler or rebellion. Those who sell meat are also severely punished, usually with mutilation. Fines are imposed for killing animals.

The Jain believes that only that knowledge that is purged of anger, hatred, and such passions is true knowledge. Anger leads to rashness and injury, and is one of the six sensual feelings that the Jain has to control, including pride, sensual pleasures, greed, sleep and undesirable conversation. The Jain considers *ahimsa* a natural attribute of the human psyche and *himsa* as unnatural. He illustrates this fact thus: A person sees a child struggling in the water and drowning. The person's instinct will be to save him. On the other hand a person who throws even an enemy into water is not acting naturally. His action is inhuman and born out of unnatural passion.

No other religion has dwelt on the issue of violence to the extent of Jainism. They have categorized violence into 108 varieties, so minute is their identification of violence. As in Buddhism the concept of *ahimsa* is related to empathy, the ability to understand another's pain and suffering as one's own. A Jain sutra (aphorism) states: "As it would be to you, so it is with whom you intend to kill. As it would be to you so it is with him whom you intend to tyrannise, As it would be to you, so it is with him whom you intend to torment." Another sutra states: "For all sorts of living beings, pain is unpleasant, disagreeable and greatly feared." Jainism thus does not agree with some who view beings of a lower order as unable to feel pain. Jaina compassion therefore extends to all living beings, from the one- to the five-sensed.

Critics of the Jain ideology of *ahimsa* opine that the use of silks, gelatine, musk, and eggs (vegetarian) by the Jains demonstrates that even they have to consume objects whose production involves violence. Some point out that the *ayus karma* (life span) of individuals is fixed in the last third of their previous life, and therefore the belief that the killer is really instrumental in killing a *jiva* is a delusion. However Jains do not fully subscribe to such fatalism. The belief is that by killing a living being you are impeding its opportunity for liberation by not allowing its life to run the full span of its course.

Mahatma Gandhi was greatly influenced by Jain ideology, especially its teaching on *ahimsa*. He lived in a region of India with a substantial Jain population. A Jain saint of Kathiawar, Roy Chand Bhai, with whom Gandhi had prolonged correspondence, had a profound influence on Gandhi. Although he was by birth a Hindu, and was also highly receptive to the teachings of Christ, (especially the ideas contained in the Sermon on the Mount and Jesus's dictum of turning the other cheek), which have close affinity to the Jain attitude regarding interpersonal relationships, the Jain ideology of *ahimsa* is obvious in Gandhi's writings and his political strategy.

An account of Jain ideology on violence and peace will not be complete without mention of the practice of *Sallekhana*, ritual voluntary death. Sallekhana literally means "scouring out" and here implies the scouring out of the body to save the soul. This form of religious death is rarely practiced nowadays, but there is evidence that it had been practiced in the medieval period (especially in the 6th and 7th centuries) from the *nisidhis* (memorials) erected in honor of the self-mortifying ascetics. The ascetics who decide to take on *Sallekhana* end their life gradually through abstention from eating and drinking. The giving up of earthly life through this self-imposed fasting is believed to confer upon the ascetic *siddhahood* (status of perfection) and ensure for them a place in heaven. The term suicide is not really appropriate for this form of death since the aspiring *Siddha* has to give up desire for death along with desire to continue life. The ritual is accompanied by prayer, reading of scriptures, meditation, renunciation, control of the senses, and concentration of the mind. The self-mortifier has to give up the five *aticaras* (impediments) of desire to live, desire to die, memories of old friends and relatives, fear, and expectation of comforts in the afterlife as a reward for suffering in the present.

IV. SIKHISM

The Sikhs have a reputation for being a martial people, what with their prominence in the armed forces of India, their well-built physique, and the uniform-like symbols of their community, the *Khalsa*, which include a *kirpan* (short sword). However, aggressiveness is not an intrinsic element of their ideology and was not intended to be by the founder of the faith, Guru Nanak. This becomes abundantly clear from the pronouncements of some of their Gurus, the former leaders of their community. Guru Amar Das (1479–1574) even went to the extent of stating that a man should die rather than kill others. Guru Nanak made the striking statement: "Forgiveness is my mother, contentment my father and patience my daughter". He also said, "The ideal man should be devoid of enmity. He should always be amicable and peace loving." The *Adi Granth*, the central scripture of the Sikh faith and their perennial Guru after the tenth Guru, states: "Patience is the sustenance of angelic beings." Guru Arjun, who was the first martyr in Sikh history, says in his scripture the Sukhamani, the Psalm of Peace,

> Happy are the meek in spirit, who efface themselves and are poor,
> The arrogantly great are effaced by their own pride.

This statement recalls strongly Christ's beatitudes of the Sermon on the Mount. The Guru Granth Sahib states: "He who does not injure anybody is received respectfully in the abode of the Lord," and "One should be merciful towards all the *jivas* (souls) from one's heart."

Guru Nanak (1469–1539) was dismayed by the confrontation between Muslims and Hindus and rejected both traditions. He decided in his own words "to follow God's path." He established a monotheistic faith, with elements from both religions. Sikh theology bears a strong resemblance to the teachings of Shankara, the protagonist of monism and his idea of God as *nirguna* (of unspecifiable qualities). The Sikh *Nam* or *Akal* is reminiscent of the nirguna Brahman of *Advaita*. Hindu doctrine of *karma* is sustained but Sikhism like Islam rejects the concept of avatars (incarnations of God), the worship of idols, and the caste system. The authority of the Brahmins and the Vedas is implicitly denied. The new religion was probably designed to mitigate religious controversies between the Hindus and Muslims of India. Guru Nanak, while born a Hindu, is believed to have traveled to Mecca and met Muslim scholars.

It is mainly the vicissitudes of history that imparted a martial vestige to the Sikh community. Except for the Mughal Emperor Akbar, whose enlightened religious policies are well known, the Sikhs never had an easy relationship with any of the Muslim rulers of India. J. S. Mann and K. Singh point out that many scholars are baffled why a faith established by a pious saint and probably intended to pave the way for religious harmony in a great nation should take on the trappings of a martial community and become militarized under the aegis of five Gurus over hundreds of years. They contend that Sikhism is an instance of a religion employing spiritual activity with empirical tasks. In this respect Sikhism emulates Islam, in which there is no separation of the sacred and the profane. The immanence of God in the empirical world and its life is a great truth expressed in the Guru Granth.

The concept of nonviolence in Sikhism is associated with martyrdom. However, Sikhism does not associate martyrdom with a passive acceptance of oppression. The *Adi Granth* states: "They (the Sikhs) neither intimidate anyone nor accept intimidation themselves." Even Kabir the great charismatic forerunner of Nanak stated, "The brave is he who fights for dharma." Prof. Gurbachan makes the radical statement that the concept of martyrdom gained currency in India only after the martyrdom of the 5th and 9th Gurus Arjun Singh and Tej Bahadur at the hands of the Mughals.

Guru Gobind Singh, the tenth Guru, is usually credited with forging the Sikhs into a disciplined community of fighters against injustice. He formed the *Khalsa*, a word that literally translates as "pure," but in this context means a chosen people, and instituted the ritual of the *Amrit Pahul* (initiation as warriors) and gave the Sikhs the traditional symbols of the community—the five k's, namely, *kesh* (uncut hair), *kanga* (comb), *khara* (steel bangle), *kacca* (short trousers), and *kirpan* (short sword). But the process actually began with Guru Haragobind. The successors of Mughal emperor Akbar, namely Jehangir, Shajahan, Aurangazeb, and Bahadur Shah, were not as tolerant as the great Akbar and came into confrontation with the leaders of this new religion on which they looked askance. The persecution of the Mughals gradually led the Gurus into organizing the community on martial lines. It is said that Shajahan's hostility led Guru Haragobind, the 6th Guru, to desire offerings of horses and weapons rather than money from his followers. He wore two swords to symbolize the coalescing of *Miri* and *Piri* (temporal and spiritual power). Kaur states that Guru Hargobind decided that the time had come when the peaceful Sikh society should change into a martial and political community. But Guru Gobind is said to be the real founder of the ideology of self-defense in the Sikh community. He is characterized as the precursor of the idea of religious nationalism in India. It was Aurangazeb's despotism that tipped Guru Gobind over the edge. Among the Mughal rulers Aurangazeb was the most religiously bigoted. Aurangazeb reimposed the religious poll tax known as the *Jizya* on Hindus and other non-Muslims. He considered the Sikhs as infidels in spite of their convergence with Muslim ideology, namely, monotheism and egalitarianism, and ordered their temples to be pulled down. Provoked by Aurangazeb's oppression Guru Gobind created the rule of the *Khalsa* (*Raj karega Khalsa*). The *Khalsa Panth* (*Khalsa* community) was born on April 13, 1699, when Gobind Singh instituted the *Amrit Pahul* ceremony (also termed the *Khande ka Amrit*, nectar of the sword). A solution of water and sugar (*amrit*) was stirred with a *khanda* (two-edged sword) and drunk by the initiates to the *Khalsa* Panth. The execution of Guru Tej Bahadur by the Mughal helped turn the Sikhs into fiery soldiers against oppression. It is said that soon after its institution 80,000 Sikhs received this baptism by the sword.

Guru Gobind's statements are evocative of his ideology. "When the affairs are past other remedies, it is justifiable to unsheathe the sword." "Blessed is that person in the world who recites the Holy Name with his mouth and at the same time thinks of fighting against evil and tyranny." "When appeals to reason and good sense fail, there is full moral and spiritual justification to resort to the sword."

Guru Gobind's opposition to Aurangazeb cannot be taken to be anti-Islamism, although scholars such as Dr. Trilochan Singh have opined that Guru Gobind became "the irreconcilable foe of the Muhammadan name." As a matter of fact, Guru Gobind acknowledged Aurangazeb's suzerainty, his actions were intrinsically defensive, not aggressive. He stated:

> There are two houses, the Baba Nanak's and Babar's
> Both these are ordained by the Lord Himself
> This one is leader in faith, while
> In that one inheres the sovereignty of the earth
>
> *(Quoted in Talib, Gurbachan Singh, 1984, p. 89.)*
> *Babar is the first Mughal emperor)*

Mansukhani opines that the *Amrit Pahul* and the *Khalsa* symbols are not meant to create a spirit of exclusiveness or a chosen people. They are meant to be aids to a corporate life of the community. The *kirpan (dagger)* is a symbol not of violence but of self-respect, prestige, and independence.

The 20th century has often seen the escalation of Sikh militancy, especially during the formation of the Akali Dal, the establishment of the state of Punjab, and the demand for Khalistan, a sovereign independent Sikh state carved out of India. During the Indian independence movement the Sikhs were committed followers of Gandhi and adhered to his nonviolent ideology in spite of grave provocation from the British administrators of the Punjab, such as General Dyer, who carried out the massacre at Jalianwala Bagh in Amritsar. Similarly, during the agitation for the formation of the state of Punjab, Sikh leaders resorted to fasting and such nonviolent strategies. Darshan Singh Pheruman made the supreme sacrifice, fasting unto death, and is hailed as a modern Sikh martyr. Tara Singh and Sant Fateh Singh also undertook fasts. However, in recent times some Sikhs have taken to a more militant stance for the realization of their demands. The aggressive tactics of Bhindranwala and other Sikh separatists resulted in *Operation Blue Star*, the invasion by the Indian Army of the Golden Temple of Amritsar where Bhindranwale and his followers were hiding out, and the consequent assassination of Prime Minister Indira Gandhi by her own Sikh body guards. Many Sikhs look upon Bhindranwala, who was killed in the operation, as a martyr. The general who led *Operation Blue Star*, himself a Sikh, was also later assassinated in Bombay. The confrontation between the government of India and Sikh militants continues even today. Thus, in current times some Sikhs have resorted to violence for the realisation of their aspirations.

The Sikh ideology relevant to peace and nonviolence seems to be a reconciliation of opposites such as peace and war. Guru Gobind, for example, exhorted the members of the *Khalsa Panth* to be strong and fearless outside and compassionate and generous within. The Sikh flag, the *Nishan Sahib,* while giving a message of peace and goodwill to all, has inscribed in it the emblem of *khande*(sword). It is well known that the Sikhs, in spite of their martial prowess, are one of the most affable of the communities of India. Guru Gobind Singh might have deified the sword, as Kaur puts it, but he also recommended sweetness and courteousness to the Sikhs.

V. ISLAM

Islam has a popular image of a religion of violence, and by focusing on incidents involving Islam in controversial political issues the media has contributed in a large measure to this widespread conception. As a matter of fact, there is nothing intrinsically violent or aggressive about Islam. People who watch critical situations in the Middle East, or North Africa, Afghanistan, or Iran where Muslims are involved in violent confrontations, hostage takings, hijackings of aircraft, and so on tend to forget that there are millions of Muslims living in a peaceful, normal, and ordinary manner in India, Malaysia, China, and several other regions of the world where there are substantial Muslim populations. The Lakshadweep Islands, where the population is completely Muslim, is one of the rare parts of the world where no murder has been committed for 35 years, and where the crime rate is so low that the police force there finds time hanging heavily on its hands. Edward Said, the well-known American intellectual of Palestinian origin states:

> Yet there is a consensus on Islam as a kind of scapegoat for everything we do not happen to like about the world's new political, social, and economic patterns. For the right, Islam represents barbarism; for the left, medieval theocracy; for the centre distasteful exoticism. In all camps, however, there is agreement that even though little enough is known about the Islamic world, there is not much to be approved of there.
>
> *(Said, 1981, p. xv)*

It seems that since the collapse of communism and the former Soviet Empire, Islam has become the archenemy for the Western world.

The very word "Islam" is related to the Arabic word for peace, namely, *Salaam*. But there are certain ideas within Islam that are associated with war and that may lead nonMuslims to conceive of Islam as a religion that condones armed conflict. These are the key notions of *jihad* and *Dar al Islam*.

The word *jihad* literally means struggle. However, in popular parlance the term has come to mean holy war. But in Islam there is no separation of the sacred and the secular, and hence the term *jihad* should indicate merely fighting. There is a debate within Islam itself whether *jihad* indicates aggressive warfare or merely defense. Unfortunately the Qur'anic revelations is not quite consistent when it deals with the concept of *jihad*. However, it is universally accepted that *jihad* can only be undertaken in the cause of Allah (*Jihad fi sabil Allah*). There is also the inescapable fact that in Islam *jihad* is looked on as an important duty, almost a sixth pillar of the faith along with witnessing, prayer, almsgiving, fasting, and the Hajj. As a matter of fact, the Kharijites, an early faction among the Muslims, desired *jihad* to be enshrined as one of the *Ibadah,* the pillars of Islam. But this was not accepted by the rest of the Islamic community or by the then-Caliph.

However, except in modern times when the notion of *jihad* is played down by most Muslim intellectuals and in apologetics, fighting in the cause of Islam has been held in great esteem and as an important duty of every Muslim. A saying of the Prophet (*hadith*) related by Abu Huraira tells of a man who came to the Prophet and asked him to instruct him in a deed that equalled the *jihad*. The Prophet replied that he could not identify such a deed. Great rewards are promised to the martyrs (*shuhada*) who die in *jihad*. They are believed to be immediately conveyed to paradise by *Houris*, the beautiful celestial maidens. In many Islamic regions the tombs of *shuhada* are the scene of annual commemorative festivities, one of the most famous being that of Hussain, the grandson of the Prophet at Karbala in Iraq. Martyrs of *jihad* are held in great esteem in the Muslim world.

Jihad is both a corporate and an individual duty in Islam. It is obligatory. "Fighting is prescribed to you though it is distasteful to you" (Qur'an, 2:216). The Prophet is said to have remarked." He who dies without having ever proposed to himself to engage in holy war dies the death of a heathen." Women, the sick, and the disabled are exempt from this duty. Youths have to obtain their parents' permission before they can engage in war. However the entire community need not engage in *jihad* if the act can be carried out efficiently by a lesser number of men. *Jihad* can be undertaken only if there is expectation of a certain measure of success. *Jihad* is instituted mainly against unbelievers, although it can also be waged against Muslims who rebel against the Caliph, or the Islamic ruler.

Jihad is related to the concept of *Dar al Islam*, the land of Islam. As mentioned above nonbelievers are the objective of *jihad,* and for the Muslim the world is divided on the lines of the dichotomy of believer and nonbeliever. The ideal is conversion of the whole world to Islam and while peaceful methods of proselytization are the norm for such conversion, the employment of warfare is not ruled out. Thus certain passages of the Qur'an seem to indicate that what is not *Dar al Islam* is *Dar al Harb* (the land of war), implying that the Muslims should be prepared to undertake a *jihad* to secure the affiliation of the unbelievers to Islam. "Fight them until there is no persecution and the religion is entirely Allah's" (Qur'an 8:39). Two points are apparent in the verse. The fighting is in response to persecution of the Muslims by unbelievers. Second, the Qur'an envisages that such persecution is possible until the whole world has become *Dar al Islam*. The verse however indicates that *jihad* is essentially defensive warfare. Yet there is another passage that states: "Fight the unbelievers wherever you find them" (Qur'an 9:5). This indicates a more aggressive form of *jihad*, in which the initiative for warfare is commanded to originate from the Muslims.

There are some who aver that the *jihad* beween *Pax Islamica (Dar al Islam)* and the rest of the world is a perpetual one, and quotes Mohammed as stating: "War is permanently established until the day of judgement." The rationale for *jihad* is thus the urge to Islamicize the whole world. The object of *jihad* is non-Muslims. If *jihad* is successful and a non-Muslim state is brought under the suzerainty of Islam, the conquered are given two options. They can embrace Islam and have all the privileges of full citizenship. Otherwise the men will be slain, and the women and children enslaved. However, not all non-Muslims are treated alike. The *Ahl al Kitab* (people of the book), namely, Christians and Jews, are also given the option of becoming *dhimmis* (protected citizens), who are accorded freedom of practising their own faith but have to pay a special tax, the *jizyah*.

The forgoing may seem a very black indictment of Islam and may add strength to the popular image of Islam as a militant and aggressive faith, but this is not the whole story. There are many aspects of *jihad* that lend an ambiguity to the aforementioned militancy underlying the concept of *jihad*. Khurshid Ahmad writes: "He (a Muslim) tries to live according to the guidance given by God and His Prophet and he strives to promote the message of Islam through his word and actions. This striving is known as *Jihad* which means a striving and a struggle in the path of God. It consists in exerting one's self to the utmost in order to personally follow the teachings of Islam and to work for their establishment in society. *Jihad* has been described in the Qur'an and the Sunnah as the natural corollary of these pillars of faith. Commitment to God involves commitment to sacrifice one's time, energy and wealth to promote the right cause. It may be necessary at times to give one's life in order to preserve Truth. *Jihad* implies readiness to give whatever one has, including life, for the sake of Allah."

The Prophet is said to have remarked once while returning from a battle: "We are now returning from the lesser *jihad* to the greater *jihad*," implying that the constant struggle against evil that goes on in one's heart and mind, is of greater significance than the external *jihad* of battling unbelievers. Thus *jihad* in recent times is understood by Muslims as spiritual rather than physical warfare. They point out the verses of the Qur'an that stress the noncoercive and peaceful nature of the Islamic faith. "Transgress not (by attacking them first) for God loves not the transgressors" (Qur'an 2:186). "There is no compulsion in religion" (Qur'an 2:237). According to Ishtiaq Ahmed *jihad* between nations should not be construed as actual hostilities but rather nonrecognition of a non-Islamic state by a Muslim nation. The provision for being *dhimmi* was originally only granted to the People of the Book, but was later extended to other monotheistic faiths, such as the Zoroastrians and the Sabeans. In India the invading Muslim conquerors for instance Muhammad bin Kasim in 711–713 A.D. initially put to death all polytheists such as Hindus who refused to convert to Islam, but later on had to extend the option of becoming dhimmis to all. According to strict Shia ideology only the hidden Imam (the 12th Imam who is believed to return to appear again and fight to restore virtue in the world) has the authority to lead the community into *jihad*.

However, the call to *jihad* has been declared even in modern times, especially so in these days of Islamic revival and Islamic resurgence in many Muslim nations. Jamilah Kolocotronis states that these phenomena are the modern manifestations of Islamic *jihad*. One of the earliest instances was that of the Sultan of Turkey who was also the Ottoman Emperor and Caliph of the Islamic *Umma* (global community) who declared a *jihad* against Britain and its allies during the First World War. Such exhortations have also been heard during the Arab-Israeli war of 1967, the Iran-Iraq war, and the Gulf war. There is actually a militant Shia organization in Lebanon that goes by the name of Islamic Jihad. Absolutists hold *jihad* as an essential component of Islamic political ideology. Fundamentalists may look on *dawah*, the call to Islamic revival, which is to a great extent a movement to remove Western cultural influences from Islamic regions, as a *jihad* against the cultural, technological, and economic imperialism of the West. But modernists interpret the doctrine of *jihad* in terms of spiritual struggle against evil, as legitimate self-defense or as a social struggle for removing injustice. Some, such as Justice Mohammed Munir of Pakistan, dismiss all notions of holy war as heroic nostalgia. Sayyid Ahmad Khan, the great Indian Muslim leader, educationist, and social reformer, went so far as to say that the concept of *jihad* should be eliminated from Islam.

Also See the Following Articles

CRITIQUES OF VIOLENCE • ETHICAL AND RELIGIOUS TRADITIONS, WESTERN • MORAL JUDGMENTS AND VALUES • RELIGIOUS TRADITIONS, VIOLENCE AND NONVIOLENCE • SPIRITUALITY AND PEACEMAKING

BIBLIOGRAPHY

Hinduism

Gandhi, M. K., (1927). *My experiments with truth*. Ahmedabad: The Navajivan Trust.

Lipner, J. *Hindus, their religious beliefs and practices*. London: Routledge.

Rao, K. L. S. (1978). *Mahatma Gandhi and comparative religion*. Delhi: Motilal Banarsidas.

Chatterjee, M. (1985). *Gandhi's religious thought*. London: Macmillan.

Jackson, R., and Killingley, D. (1991). *Moral issues in the Hindu tradition*. Stoke on Trent: Trentham Books.

Krishnamurthy, V. (1989). *Essentials of Hinduism*. New Delhi. Narosa Publishing House.

Bondurant, J. V. (1971). *Conquest of violence*. London: University of California Press.

Coward, H., Lipner, J., and Young, K. K., (1991). *Hindu ethics*. Delhi: Sri Satguru Publications.

Prabhupada, A. C., (1972). *The Bhagavad-Gita as it is*. Los Angeles: Bhaktivedanta Book Trust.

Gandhi, M. K., (1965). *From Yervada Mandir*, (tr. V. G. Desai). Navajivan: Ahmedabad.

Gandhi, M. K., (1962). *The law of love*. Bombay: Hirigorami.

Buddhism

Saddhaatissa, H. (1970). *Buddhist ethics*, London: George Allen and Unwin.

Aitken, R. (1984). *The mind of clover*. San Francisco: North Point Press.

Gyatso, G. K. (1993). *Understanding the mind*. London: Tharpa Publications.

Davids, T. W. R. (1969). *Buddhist suttas*. New York: Dover Publications.

Keown, D. (1995). *Buddhism and bio ethics*. New York: St Martin's Press.

Conze, E. (1974). *Buddhism*. Oxford: Bruno Cassirer.

Saunders, E. D. (1980). *Buddhism in Japan*. Tokyo: Charles E Tuttle.

Farris, W. (1991). *Heavenly warriors, the evolution of Japan's military, 500–1300*. Cambridge: Harvard University Press.

Sugarana, M. (1986). *The ancient Samurai*. Tokyo: The East Publications, Inc.

Ikeda, D. (1978). *Buddhism, the first millennium* (trans. B. Watson). Tokyo: Kodasnsha International.

Woodward, F. L. (1973). *Some sayings of the Buddha*. London: Oxford University Press.

Harvey, P. (1990). *An introduction to Buddhism*. Cambridge: Cambridge University Press.

Jainism

Sogani, K. C. (1967). *Ethical doctrines in Jainism*. Sholapur: Lalchand Hirachand Doshi.

Gopalan, S. (1973). *Outlines of Jainism*. New Delhi: Wiley Eastern Pvt. Ltd.

Warren, H., and Gandhi, V. R. (1916). *Jainism*. Arrah: The Central Jaina Publishing House.

Pande, C. G. (1984). *Jain political thought*. Jaipur: Centre for Jain Studies.

Johnson, W. J. (1995). *Harmless souls*. Delhi: Motilal Banarsidas.

Dwivedi, R. C. (1975). *Contribution of Jainism to Indian culture*. Delhi: Motilal Banarsidas.

Singhi. (Ed.). (1987). *"Ideal, ideology and practice."* In *Studies in Jainism*. Jaipur: Printwell Publishers.

Lalwani, G. (Ed.). (1991). *Jainthology*, Calcutta: Jain Bhavan.

Nahar, P. C., and Ghosh, K. C. (1988). *Jainism: Precepts and Practice*. Delhi: Caxton Publishers.
Settar, S. (1989). *Inviting death*. Leiden: E. J. Brill.

Sikhism

Singh, S. (1975). *Non-violence and the Sikhs*. Delhi: Rachna Publishers.
Talib, G. S. (1984). *The impact of Guru Gobind Singh on Indian society*. Ludhiana: Lahore Book Shop.
Singh, T. (1967). *The psalm of peace (Guru Arjun's Sukhamani)*. Amritsar: Khalsa Brothers.
Singh, G. (1987). *Guru Nanak's relationship with the Lodhis and the Mughals*. New Delhi: Atlantic Publishers.
Mansukhani, G. S. (1989). *A handbook of Sikh studies*. Delhi: National Book Shop.
Kaur, K. (1990). *Political ideas of the Sikh gurus*. New Delhi: Deep and Deep Publications.
Mansukhani, G. S. (1978). *Introduction to Sikhism*. New Delhi: Hemkunt Press.
Kohli, S. S. (1992). *A Conceptual encyclopaedia of Guru Granth Sahib*. New Delhi: Manohar.
Mann, G. S., and Singh, K. (1990). *Recent researches in Sikhism*. Patiala: Punjabi University Publications Bureau.

Islam

Kelsay, J., and Johnson, J. T. (1991). *Just war and Jihad*. Connecticut: Greenwood Press.
Ahmed, A. S. (1992). *Postmodernism and Islam*. London: Routledge.
Enayat, H. (1982). *Modern Islamic political thought*. London: Macmillan.
Said, E. W. (1981). *Covering Islam*. London: Routledge.
Ahmad, K. (1983). *Islam: Its meaning and message*. Leicester: The Islamic Foundation.
Ahmed, I. (1987). *The concept of an Islamic state*. London: Pinter.
Donaldson, *Studies in Muslim ethics*. London: SPCK.
Macdonald, D. B. (1965). *Development of Muslim theology, jurisprudence and constitutional theory*. New York: Russell and Russell.
Tames, R. (1982). *Approaches to Islam*. London: John Murray.
Waines, D. (1995). *An introduction to Islam*. Cambridge: Cambridge University Press.
Kolocotronis, J. (1990). *Islamic Jihad*. American Trust Publications.
Jansen, G. H. (1979). *Militant Islam*. London: Pan Books.
Momen, M. (1985). *An introduction to Shi'i Islam*. New Haven: Yale University Press.
Peters, R. (1977). *Jihad in medieval and modern Islam*. Leiden: E. J. Brill.

Ethical and Religious Traditions, Western

Alonzo Valentine
Earlham College and School of Religion

GLOSSARY

Allah Most widespread and significant name for ultimate reality in Islam. The term is rooted in pre-Islamic times as the name for the god of the Ka'bah in Mecca and was the god of Muhammad's tribe, the Quraysh. The Ka'bah is the cubic shaped shrine which remains a key site in the pilgrimmage undertaken by Muslims as one of the "Five Pillars" of the faith.

Dualism An understanding that fundamental concepts are absolutely opposite and irreconcilable. Further, one pole of the opposition is seen as preferred over the other.

Iliad and the Odyssey Greek epic stories that were written in their final form around 850 B.C.E. and attributed to Homer.

Messiah Term from the Hebrew meaning "the anointed one," and translated to the Greek as "christos," the Christ. The synoptic Gospels show Jesus wary of taking on this designation, at least without altering the political implications of term as meaning a kingly and warrior leader.

Qu'rān The sacred scripture of Islam. It means "the reading" or "recitation" and is viewed by most Muslims as the teachings of Allah dictated through Muhammad for humanity that has an eternal, immediate aspect in Allah's being. The view of Jesus as the Christ in Christianity is sometimes used as an analogy for the understanding of how Muslims view the Qu'ran. Hence, textual studies as they are done in much of western academic circles are quite problematic to most Muslims.

Shalom Hebrew term usually translated as "peace," but broadens the view of peace beyond the absence of war or cessation of hostilities. The term includes an array of positive aspects of peace, touching on psychological well-being and harmony in natural and social relations.

Shi'ites The term designates the followers of Muhammad's cousin 'Ali and the family line descended from 'Ali. 'Ali ibn-abi-Talib was the fourth "caliph" or successor to Muhammad who ruled Islam briefly from 656–661 C.E. He succeeded 'Uthman who was assassinated during conflicts within Islam, and 'Ali had to deal with more violent revolts within Islam. 'Ali moved to Iraq and so away from the place of Islam's birth in the Arabia peninsula, but after fighting with external threats, he was killed by dissidents within his own camp, the Khārijites.

Sunnis This means followers of Muhammad, the Prophet's way and they form the largest group of Muslims.

Synoptic Gospels Name given to the first three books

of the Christian New Testament because they each present a view of Jesus. Each of the three books present some words and deeds of Jesus that are the same or quite similar, but they also present different accounts of Jesus' words and deeds.

Tanakh Generally, the Jewish Scriptures, containing in three groupings first the Torah, "the five books of Moses," then "The Prophets," and finally "The Writings."

Yahweh The usual rendering of the most significant name (the tetragrammation, YHWH) for the ultimate in the Jewish scripture, used about 6,800 times. Because this name is considered sacred and not to be spoken, the title 'Adonai or "Great Lord" was substituted in reading and most English translations render this title as Lord.

THIS ARTICLE is an examination of the roots of Western Ethical and Religious Traditions in early classic texts in relation to the focus of this encyclopedia. In this way it is limited in scope to these texts and is presenting only their positions on violence, peace and conflict. Further, this article is written with a bias towards presenting what these foundational texts within the West have said about pursuing peace. It is assumed that the texts do present support for violence and therefore do not consistently support peacemaking or conflict reduction. What this article seeks to lift up is the perspectives within the primary texts of Western traditions that seek peace. Further, it is assumed that there is a fundamental strand of dualism running throughout the Western Tradition that supports the resort to conflict, violence and war. Therefore, this article is written with the question of how the traditions envision a peace that transcends such dualistic thinking.

The question this article asks of the texts is how they relate their vision of peace to the fundamental dualism that they see in reality. The assumption here is that the problem for an ethical or religious perspective on peacemaking is understanding the dualisms that apparently prevail everywhere: God and the world, good and evil, life and death, friend and enemy, faith and unbelief, violence and nonviolence. The list could go on indefinitely, but the list reflects the struggles with dualism in a worldview that seeks peace. Within the traditions the dominant view is that we should attempt to keep the peace between these apparent opposites, unless peace seems to compromise the preferred pole of the dualism. Since we know that only one side has the final word on what is good, true, and beautiful, we are finally justified in resorting to violence to defend that side. For example, when humanity gives God too many difficulties, then God's violence to humanity is holy judgment; when our enemies ask too much of us, then our violent response is justified. Thus, peace is always secondary to the higher values. This is the dynamic of how violence and warfare are justified in all the traditions.

However, there is within each of the traditions a vision that does not see peace as derivative. Peace is sometimes understood as primary, and becomes the bridge between the poles of the dualisms in the traditions. Beneath the perceived dualistic nature of reality is a unity or relationship that makes neither pole the preferred. Thus, the world is not always understood as an addendum to God, evil not the easy opposite of good, enemies not always better than friends, and so on. That is, there is a more inclusive or connecting perspective that spans the chasm usually assumed between the pairs of opposites. Hence, this article highlights how the religious and ethical traditions in the West have attempted to make such a connection.

I. JEWISH TRADITION

The deep divide between a religious vision that sees a relational unity and one that sees a fundamental dualism is expressed in the opening of Genesis, the vision of God's creation of the universe. In the first verses of Genesis, the Spirit of God "moves over the waters" and creates heaven and earth, continuing through all the days of creation until humanity was created in the image of God. As with other such visions in religious traditions, this can be understood to reflect a fundamental dualism: God against chaos, God over the world, God as indisputable king of humanity. However, the language suggests another possibility as well: God as working with the void to bring form through it; God as immanent in the creation that is fashioned; and God's spirit breathing within all humanity.

It is in the second chapter of Genesis where this deep possibility of connection is lost. Humanity "disobeys" God and experiences profound separation from God, from the earth, from the other animals, between woman from man, and between family members. However, does what happens with humanity's disobedience fundamentally obliterate the relationship originally created? As with the other traditions examined here, Judaism responds in a variety of ways, but there is a vision of peace within *Tanakh*, the *Jewish Scriptures*, which maintains that there is always the primary connection between God and creation and among God's creatures.

When God realizes that Adam and Eve have eaten from the forbidden tree, God drives them from the garden of Eden, because they "know good and evil," like God. In addition to the fascinating question of why knowing good from evil is forbidden, the text suggests that it is acting on their knowledge that gets humans into trouble. That is, this dramatic account indicates that humanity now will partake in evil as well as good, knowing both in their experience. In Genesis 4, Cain murders Abel and when God finds out, Abel quickly concludes that he will in turn be killed. Cain knows evil, but it hardly seems to be wisdom. God, however, says that the apparently justified killing of Cain should not happen, placing a mark on Cain so that no one will take vengeance. Here God is shown to act in order to reduce violence, because humans would act violently based on their sense of good and evil. Next, in the story of Noah, God sets out to destroy all flesh because "the earth is filled with violence" (Gen. 6:11, 13). All the world has taken up violent action because humans act on what they know of good and evil. Hence, in these narratives of prehistory, humans enter into violence because of their belief in the dualism of good and evil. God is represented as dismayed by the violent human actions and struggles to reduce violence.

As the history of the people of Israel begins, Abraham answers God's call in a way repeatedly reflected in the Jewish scriptures. He leaves all that might leave him secure in trust to what God asks. The root meaning of obedience is related to listening. Is the voice of God within or from beyond the stars? Could it be both? Abraham, as others after him, does not take weapons, he simply listens and goes where God asks him, and God says that "by you all the families of the earth shall be blessed" (Gen. 12:1–3). When Abraham forgets this covenant that God offered him, he hopes for descendants from Hagar, his wife Sarai's maid servant. When Sarai becomes upset after Hagar conceives, Abraham gives control of Hagar over to Sarai, and his wife "deals harshly" with Hagar, leaving her in the desert. Though Abraham forgets God's covenant and seeks to hide what he has done, an angel of God pledges to Hagar that God will "greatly multiply your descendants" (Gen. 16:10). Here God not only seeks to save someone from human violence, but makes a pledge like the one given to Abraham. Thus, those who are seen as the forbearers of Islam become connected to the Hebrews through God's care.

In a fascinating turnabout, Abraham also helps God reduce God's urge to violence. God is ready to destroy all the inhabitants of Sodom and Gomorrah (Gen. 18:16–19:29), but Abraham asks God "Will thou indeed destroy the righteous with the wicked?" and does some principled negotiation with God. Of course, after the negotiations that save the righteous family of Lot, the cities are destroyed, but the vision again is of a God who uses violence reluctantly to promote righteousness. Further, human interaction with God is presented in the text as a way of reducing violence. God listens to humans.

Later in Genesis come the stories of Jacob and his sons. When Simeon and Levi slaughter many in defense of their sister Dinah's honor, Jacob curses his sons violence:

> Simeon and Levi are brothers;
> weapons of violence are their swords.
> O my soul, come not into their council;
> O my spirit, be not joined to their company;
> for in their anger they slay men,
> and in their wantonness they hamstring oxen.
> Cursed be their anger, for it is fierce;
> and their wrath, for it is cruel!
> I will divide them in Jacob and will scatter them
> in Israel.
> (Gen. 49:5–7).

Jacob reflects that such vengeful violence will come back to haunt his family, and the subsequent scriptures reflect this.

The exception to the cycle of violence is Joseph, Jacob's son who did not seek vengeance against his brothers when they sought to kill him. After Joseph receives Jacob's blessing, his brothers now fear for their own lives. However, rather than taking justifiable retribution, Joseph follows a different path. When the brothers ask for forgiveness and offered to be Joseph's servants, Joseph wept, and said: "Fear not, for am I in the place of God? As for you, you meant evil against me; but God meant it for good, to bring it about that many people should be kept alive, as they are today" (Gen. 50:15–20). Hence, the conclusion of the Genesis narratives depicts a God who desires to bring good from evil, seeks the repentance of evildoers, and asks that humanity do the same. At times, God even accepts human intervention to stay God's own urge toward violence.

The vision of Yahweh as a warrior is irrefutably early in the tradition, and reflects the celebration of the Exodus from Egypt. "Yahweh is a warrior, horse and rider he has thrown in the sea" is one of the earliest verses in the entire Bible and the entire poem (Ex 15:1–21) probably comes from the 12th century B.C.E. Even in this clear attribution of violence and war to God, however, the ambiguity of the Genesis narratives are continued. This is not God speaking, but how the Hebrews have understood the event. God does not give this image, humans give it to God. What the text does present is that it was God who acted to stop the Egyptians and bring the Hebrews out of Egypt, not the Hebrews themselves. So in this paradigmatic event in the history of the people that began with Abraham's quiet obedience, the people only obey God's call to leave Egypt. Whatever happens then is seen as God's action.

The next accounts of the entry into the "promised land" also have God's actions described in terms of violence and war. Again, the song celebrating the conquest is from the 12th century B.C.E., and ends with this prayer: "So perish all thine enemies, O Yahweh! But thy friends be like the sun as he rises in his might." (Judges 5:1–31). However, the debate within the text itself about the nature of God continues the tension established from the beginning. If the breath of God is indeed within all humans, God is in the struggle. If God is also beyond our capacity to know fully, then the words attributed to God must be seen as one view. There are other views. What seems not to be ambiguous in these early narratives of "the Conquest" is that God was taking the action which was decisive, not Israel. The account in Joshua ends with this speech attributed to God:

> The citizens of Jericho fought against you, but I delivered them into your hands. I spread panic before you, and it was this, not your sword or your bow, that drove out the two kings of the Amorites. I gave you land on which you had not labored, cities which you had never built; you have lived in those cities and you eat the produce of vineyards and olive-groves which you did not plant (Joshua 24:10–13).

Such texts reflect the effort of humans to understand their history in terms that are not just historical. They seek to reflect a deep truth—myth—that is within and throughout history. As such, the Hebrew scriptures debate with themselves about how God and history are to be understood. Hence, the modern debate of how much the biblical record is accurate history and how much it accurately portrays God begins in the text itself. The Hebrews' liberation from Pharaoh and entry into the promised land is being given this dramatic rendering to reveal the true meaning for this people. That is, God is stronger than any army, needing no army or weapons to act in the world.

In these accounts of Israel being established to the west of the Jordan, an additional view of God's military activity is revealed: God will also act against Israel. The conclusion of Joshua gives this warning:

> You cannot serve the lord; for the Lord is a holy God; he is a jealous God; he will not forgive your transgressions or your sins. If you forsake the Lord and serve foreign gods, then he will turn and do you harm, and consume you, after having done you good. (Josh. 24:19–20)

Though the people promise to obey God's voice, we see the story take a turn for the worse. In Judges, the "enemies of Yahweh" become the armies of Israel: "Whenever they marched out, the hand of the Lord was against them for evil, as the Lord had warned, and as the Lord had sworn to them; and they were in sore straits" (Judges 2:15). In these stories we see the dramatic vision of Israel's troubles again attributed to a failure to listen to God. The issue was not military preparations, but obeying the covenant. Armies go forward, invoking the name of Yahweh, and they go down to defeat. The last verse in Judges summarizes the problem: "Every man did what was right in his own eyes."

The prophetic literature comes with the conquest of Israel first by Assyria and then Babylon, resulting in the fall of Jerusalem in 587 B.C.E. With these disasters, the prophets advance another vision of how God acts. Rather than God being seen as a warrior choosing sides, the vision is of a God for whom the image of a warrior is inadequate. The prophets lift up the futility of using warfare to make right or to please God. Whether it be Israel or Israel's enemies, the prophets mock the might of weapons, asserting that it is God's spirit that is over all: "Not by might, nor by power, but by my spirit, says the Lord of hosts" (Zech. 4:6). What seemed to be a triumphant victory in fulfilling God's promise to Israel of the land became agonizing defeat at the hand of the Babylonians. In turn, what seemed to be the final defeat of exile from the land becomes the opportunity to obey God, and in that obedience return again to the promised land. Here Israel learns again, say the prophets, that listening to God and seeking righteousness is central: "Woe to those who go down to Egypt for help and rely on horses, who trust in chariots because they are many and in horsemen because they are very strong, but do not look to the Holy One of Israel or consult Yahweh!" (Isaiah 31:1). The prophets begin to offer an alternative vision of what God's covenant is about.

For the prophets, to obey God is to "seek peace and pursue it." The covenant is understood as a "covenant of *shalom*." (Ez. 37:26; Is. 2:2–4; Micah 4:1–4). The servant of God is not to be warrior or king, but suffering servant, the Prince of Peace (Is. 6:9). This vision, of course, stresses the themes in earlier texts. Figures such as Noah, Abraham, Hagar, and Joseph have witnessed to this peaceful vision. It is the exploration of the vision of shalom where we see the prophets propose a unifying vision that connects the deep ambiguities around war and violence in the Hebrew Scriptures. In this imaginative concept, both God and the world and all of humanity are seen in harmony. Shalom is what God desires: for God's self and for all his creation (Num. 6:24; Lev. 26:3–10, Jer. 29:10–11; Ps. 34:14). In the prophetic writings, shalom is seen as the escatological goal for humanity, and is more central to our relationship with God than any form of worship (Is. 6:9, 32, 58:1–12; Ez 37:26; Amos 5:21–24; Micah 4:1). As such, shalom should be the goal of all our relations with one another always (Is. 32:16–17; Jer. 6:14; 8:11). The violence and war arise not in the pursuit of shalom, but in forgetting that it is the goal of our life with God and one another.

II. GREEK AND ROMAN TRADITION

Alfred North Whitehead remarked that all of Western philosophy is a footnote to Plato. The Western inheritance of the Greek arguments about religion and ethics has shaped the debates throughout the tradition. We will examine some of the basic thinking about peace, war, and conflict that came to classic expressions in Plato, Aristotle, and Cicero. As in the exploration of the other traditions, the search is for those strands which support the concerns for peace.

The long tradition already established by the time of Plato and Aristotle inherited two streams of thought on peace and war that seemed to be mutually contradictory. On the one hand, the deeds of the Homeric epics suggested that heros were heroes because of warfare. Facing death bravely in war was the pinnacle of the heroic life. On the other hand, for those who possessed more of the virtues of the good life, life and friendship seemed superior to even honorable death in war. Homer puts this choice in the thoughts of Achilles in the *Illiad:*

> Two fates are bearing me to the issue of death.
> If I stay here and attack the Trojan's city,
> my homecoming is lost but immortal glory will be mine.
> If I return to my beloved country, lost is my goodly glory
> but my life will be all too long,
> and death will not swiftly take me.

Achilles chooses noble death and gains immortal glory in the memories of the Greeks, and this expresses the concept of the heroic nature of warfare in Greek thought. Homer, however, also upholds the other option. In the *Odyssey*, the dead Achilles wishes he had chosen life, since his glory in the eyes of others cannot be enjoyed by the dead. Hence, the other strand of thought that seeks to understand and live the good life emerges in conflict with the vision of the hero. It is this tension about peace and war with which Greek thought struggled, and whatever answer emerged, all seemed to share Homer's lament: "would that strife cease among gods and men." It is this apparently irreconcilable dualism in thinking about war and violence that Plato and Aristotle address.

In Book 5 of *The Republic*, Plato (c. 427–c.347 B.C.E.) argues that the warfare between the Greek cities is deplorable because it is as if family members were to war with one another. Though accepting war with the "barbarians," Plato is following the line of thinking in Greek thought which wants to expand the realm of those with whom we seek peace. Plato says that all who live in Hellas are "by nature friends," and so any "discord" that comes about ought to be seen as "a quarrel among friends," which is to be "reconciled" without war:

> Consider then ... when that which we have acknowledged to be discord occurs, and a city is divided, if both parties destroy the lands and burn the houses of one another, how wicked does the strife appear! No true lover of his country would bring himself to tear in pieces his own nurse and mother; there might be reason in the conquer depriving the conquered of their harvest, but still they would have the idea of peace in their hearts and would not mean to go on fighting for ever.

That is, there is something fundamentally mistaken about pursuing honor to its limits because it entails "fighting forever."

In the *Laws*, Book 1, Plato analyzes the argument that war and not peace is the natural state of nature. This Homeric theme was continued by Heraclitus (ca. 500 B.C.E.), who put forward philosophical support for this view, concluding: "War is the father and king of all." Hence, it was a traditional argument that the true nature of the state is to always prepare for war. However,

Plato takes up the defense of the desire for peace expressed even earlier in Greek tradition by Hesiod in the 8th century B.C.E.: "That other road is better which leads toward just dealing; for justice conquers violence, and triumphs in the end."

Plato seeks to demonstrate how Hesiod rather than Heraclitus is right. Plato pursues the argument in this way. If it is the case that the "well-governed state ought to be so ordered as to conquer all other states in war," then it follows that all villages, families, and individuals should be organized toward the same end. If so, then everyone must conceive of themselves as their own enemy: "all men are publicly one another's enemies, and each man privately his own." Since such a state is chaos and not order, there must be something that is naturally superior to the state of war, and this is peace. Whether it be individuals or villages or states, the goal ought to be to reconcile all "to one another for ever after," give them laws which "they mutually observed," so that they will be "friends." Plato concludes:

> (So) war, whether external or civil, is not the best, and the need of either is to be deprecated; but peace with one another, and good will, are best.... And in a like manner no one can be a true statesman ... who orders peace for the sake of war, and not war for the sake of peace.

Although Plato accepted war with the "barbarians" as a necessity, he was developing the argument which expands the reach of peace to those who were formerly seen as enemies. War, at its root, was as self-contradictory as it was self-destructive. Hence, he begins to bring to focus the vision of all the human family may at peace.

As a compliment to Plato's pursuit of abstract reason for peace, Aristotle pursued an investigation of visible nature for clues to peace. In his efforts to categorize the constitutions of the various city-states, he looked for what seemed to be adaptive in the conflicts of the times. In the *Nicomachean Ethics* he sees that all human virtues are actions that seek a mean between extremes, and also that they must be for a goal that is noble, "for each thing is defined by its end." But what unites the virtues in a single person or state? This question suggested to Aristotle that all virtues had to be united and serve a noble end. So, it is a nobler pursuit to bring all the virtues into harmony with one another than it is to simply excel at any one virtue, including bravery in warfare. For individuals, that which combines all virtues is the pursuit of wisdom, philosophy. For states, it is the pursuit of political order which will organize the individual virtues for the sake of the collective life.

For Aristotle, courage is the virtue that is demonstrated in warfare, but he suggests the limits of both courage and warfare in the context of human nature. Courage in itself is neither fearful of death nor reckless in the face of death. In seeking the mean between these extremes, Aristotle criticizes the "lover of war" who either pursues violence without any sense as to the end served by war or stirs up violence only to flee later. Thus, the truly brave are just those "who are fearless in face of a noble death." It is these who are rightly honored by the states. For Aristotle, it follows that a person is all the more brave if there is more to lose, and one who "is possessed of virtue in its entirety" and sees the true worth of life is therefore more brave in facing death in battle. Analogously, those who have less of the full life of virtue are less truly brave in war, even though their outward actions are identical. Interestingly, Aristotle observes that those with less to lose may make the best soldiers since "they sell their life for trifling gain." Therefore, though Aristotle accepts the observation that all the city-states highly honor those who die bravely in battle, he attempts to assess when those are rightly honored. Those who possess the full life of virtue should be so honored. More importantly, Aristotle also attempted to place warfare in a context that could evaluate whether the state was pursuing a good end by going to war.

Although individuals can be virtuous, they can only be virtuous in relation with others because humans are social by nature. Therefore, it is the state that is the best of all communities since it seeks the organization of all community life, and "aims at good in a greater degree than any other, and at the highest good." The highest good is "the good life" for all who are in the community together. As with Plato, it is the web of "friendship" that connects individuals and families and that is the goal of the state. Here, of course, warfare is seen as a way to secure justice so that lovers of war in other states do not conquer those who are just. However, war is not to be desired for itself, it is but a means to another end. In this view, if other forms of relations between states can be created that maintain justice, then war is not a necessity. Here we have Aristotle's more naturalistic or scientific approach opening the possibility that other ways of shaping relations between states may reduce warfare. This would make the pursuit of the good life easier for all. Here nobility can be facing death bravely without weapons for the sake of an inclusive vision of peace. In accepting death without violent resistance or seeking escape, Socrates becomes the model for the noble way of the philosopher.

Although the influence of Greek thought on the Roman religious philosophy of Cicero (106–43 B.C.E.) is great, the influence of Cicero's contributions to Western thought on peace and war is greater. Cicero took the desire for finding a way to peace through war expressed in Plato and Aristotle by initiating the reasoning and rules of the "just war" tradition. He was read by Christian thinkers such as Ambrose and Augustine in the 4th century when Christianity became accepted by the Roman Empire, and these thinkers would make "just war" the orthodoxy for the Church. With the combination of the Greek tradition and the establishment of Christianity in the religion of Rome, the just war tradition will dominate Western thought on warfare.

In *De Republica* 3, Cicero held that through natural law, God provides two fundamental concerns for humans in their individual and collective life: honor and safety. This means that war is only justifiable when either the honor or the very life of the state is threatened. As with the Greeks, Cicero is aware of the tragic dimension of the tension between these two goals. Life is risked and often lost in defending honor, and honor is often used as an excuse for unjustified destruction. Hence, he attempted to establish criteria for when to go to war and how to wage war.

In discussing how to decide when going to war is justified, Cicero's *De Officiis* 1, explores how the notions of honor and safety might work together. On the one hand, the "instinct of self-preservation" is inherent to all creatures, so concerns for protecting one's life might seem sufficient in justifying war. However, human beings are distinct from other animals in being given a "passion for discovering truth." If so, then an individual or a social group may suppress or violate the natural quest for truth and so have less of a claim to self-preservation than those who pursue truth. Specifically, if such a person or group who does not care for truth initiates war, their claim to self-preservation is forfeit. Hence, it is in this sense that honor will require us to defend ourselves and come to the aid of those who are unjustly attacked, so taking life or destroying a state in these circumstances is justified. Here Cicero is attempting to show how the natural law of safety and honor are interrelated in that neither by itself is sufficient for deciding when going to war is justified.

Cicero was well aware of how appeals to honor and security could cause people to rush headlong into war. Hence, he placed further restrictions on entering war. It was important for the society to argue about whether honor and security are really at stake, and he desired a constitutional government as the best vehicle for this. Even with this done, however, the state should then make clear to the enemy what the violation is and what needs to be done if war is to be avoided: "no war is just, unless it is entered upon after an official demand for satisfaction has been submitted or warning has been given and a formal declaration made." That is, the justice of the cause of war is not to be decided hastily by only a few nor is it to be entered except as a last resort.

As for conduct during a war once begun, Cicero attempted to add restraints to how it was waged and when it should end. As creatures reasonable by nature, we ought to understand that there is "a limit to retribution and to punishment" of those who have wronged us. Specifically, it "is sufficient that the aggressor be brought to repent of his wrongdoing, in order that he may not repeat the offence and that others may be deterred from doing wrong." Hence, when enemies ask for mercy and throw down their arms, we must not harm them, but rather give them protection. If we must fight until victorious, we should still "spare those who have not been blood-thirsty and barbarous in their warfare." Since the goal of war is to "live in peace unharmed," when the enemy ceases fighting, then so must we, even though the enemy be unjust in starting a war or in carrying it out. For Cicero, the Roman way of war was to reflect the Roman concern for peace among all within the Empire. One must prepare for peace by preparing for war, but for war and peace to be just, they both must be pursued for the preservation and honor of truth.

III. CHRISTIAN TRADITION

The life of Jesus as presented in the New Testament is the basis for Christian commitment to peace and the faith in the basis for Christian commitment to peace and the faith in the resurrection of Jesus as the Christ is the basis for Christian hope that peace will come on earth. The accounts about Jesus in the synoptic gospels, Matthew, Mark, and Luke, attribute words and deeds to Jesus that reveal a way to embody shalom: "I say unto you, love your enemies" (Matt. 5:44; Luke 6:27). This love commandment was not conditional upon something else, such as God's destruction of one's enemies or God's intervention at the end of history. Jesus says, love your enemies now and pray for those who persecute you now. The Gospel writers go on to portray that Jesus's vision of God was one of God as loving parent to all humanity, since God created all. Jesus says that we are to love those whom we think of as enemies just because God loves our enemies. God is "perfect" or impartial in love, and we are called on to be likewise.

The historical context for such a message is crucial. As a Jew, Jesus experienced the violent oppression of the Romans and the violent resistance to that rule by some Jews. Though there were other Jews who sought peaceful ways to respond to Roman rule, others looked for a military king to lead the overthrow of the Romans. They looked to scriptures and saw the Messiah coming in this way. In this light, the gospel claims that the nonviolent Jesus is the expected one is even more startling. If Jesus is the Messiah, then he is behaving contrary to the expectations of those seeking a military leader. The warrior images for the Messiah as for Yahweh are in the Hebrew scriptures, and it is understandable how the brutal rule of Rome would feed the hope for revenge as well as freedom. However, Jesus is emphasizing the images of the suffering servant, the Prince of Peace, as the model for his life. Both of these images are in Isaiah, for example. On the one hand, God and the one to act in God's name will be like this:

> Woe to those who decree iniquitous decrees, and the writers who keep writing oppression, to turn aside the needy from justice and to rob the poor of my people of their right.... What will you do on the day of punishment, in the storm which will come from afar?... For all this his anger is not turned away and his hand is stretched out still.... The light of Israel will become a fire, and his Holy One a flame, and it will burn and devour. (Is. 10:1–3, 4, 17)

On the other hand, there is the vision of the peaceable kingdom:

> For behold, I create new heavens and a new earth; and the former things shall not be remembered or come into mind.... The wolf and the lamb shall feed together, the lion shall eat straw like the ox; and dust shall be the serpent's food. They shall not hurt or destroy in all my holy mountain, says the Lord. (Is. 65: 17, 25)

Those who looked to Jesus as the military Messiah followed one feature of Isaiah's vision, and this included Jesus' own followers. The Gospel writers followed the other, portraying Jesus as Isaiah's "'Suffering Servant" who would live and die and rise again for peace.

In this context, the confession that Jesus is the Christ is less amazing to those who followed him than Jesus' claim that the Christ was not the military leader to free Israel. When Peter confesses that Jesus is the Christ, he expects the military Messiah, and when Jesus teaches that "the Son of Man" will be rejected and killed, Peter begins to "rebuke" Jesus. The writer of Mark describes Jesus' response:

> But turning and seeing his disciples, he rebuked Peter, and said, 'Get behind me Satan! For you are not on the side of God, but of men.' And he called to him the multitude with his disciples, and said to them, 'If anyone would come after me, let them deny themselves and take up the cross and follow me. For whoever would save their life will lose it; and whoever loses their life for my sake and the gospel's will save it.' (Mark 8:33–35)

This rejection of the model of the military Messiah and the embracing of the suffering servant as the Christ served as the early Church's normative guide for its relations internally and externally. Of course, the radicalness of such a call to love enemies and suffer rather than fight was not universally followed by the early Christians. Just as the Hebrew scriptures have conflicting images, so too does the New Testament.

On warfare itself, Jesus is not given any teachings, although the implication, say Christian peacemakers, is clear from Jesus' ministry. However, there are other elements in the texts that make it confusing. For example, although Jesus says to his disciples to "Put up your swords, for those who live by the sword die by the sword" when he is seized for trial and execution, he is also portrayed as praising the Roman centurion for his faith without admonishing him to leave the military life. Further, God's role in raising his Son from the dead in apparent vindication of Jesus' nonviolence is also mixed with the threats that when Jesus comes again, there will be violence against those who do not believe: "For in those days there will be such tribulation as has not been from the beginning of the creation which God created until now, and never will be" (Mk. 13:19). These words on the violent end times are attributed to Jesus in the same Gospel as the command to love enemies. Hence, there has been an ongoing struggle over how to understand the Jesus presented by the Gospels.

On the one hand, Jesus seems to live and advocate nonresistance to violence and conflict, but on the other he seems to praise faithful soldiers and threaten divine violence with his second coming. These seem to be simply contradictory. However, between these poles is the vision of a Jesus who was confrontational, but without using weapons. This option sees the Jesus of the Gospels as a nonviolent revolutionary. Jesus is seen as resisting both the religious and political "principalities and powers" that oppressed those at the margins of religious and social life. In this way, he was a scathing critic of some features of Jewish religious life, although he was doing his critique as a Jew, and he was at least as hard on his own disciples. For example, the temple cleansing (Mk. 11:15–19) shows Jesus taking action by overturning tables and driving out the merchants because he saw the temple becoming a "den of robbers" rather than a "house of prayer for all the nations." Further, he directly challenged the Romans, but did so in nonviolent fashion. For example, the healing of the Gerasene demoniac (Mk 5:1–43) can be seen as a parable for the eventual driving out the Roman army. The possessed man has a "Legion," or Roman military unit, of unclean spirits that Jesus frees him from, sending them into swine who run into the sea and drown. Hence, the view of Jesus as either a supporter of passive nonresistant or supporter of usual forms of violence and conflict are both mistaken. Jesus takes something of both views in becoming a nonviolent agitator for social change.

If the Jesus of the Gospels shaped his early followers in a Jewish context, Paul shaped the early Christian communities in the Greek and Roman context. In Paul's letters we see the early Christian community struggling with conflicts from within and persecution from without. Paul linked his view that all Christians were called to a "ministry of reconciliation" with the theological claim that all Christians were reconciled to God through the death and resurrection of Jesus Christ. At least for Christians, the vision of a jealous God judging the world for its sins was transformed into a vision of a loving God who actively sought reconciliation:

> So if anyone is in Christ, there is a new creation: everything old has passed away; see, everything has become new! All this is from God, who reconciled us to God through Christ, and has given us the ministry of reconciliation. (2 Cor. 5:17–18)

Throughout his letters, Paul sounds this theme as well as expresses his irritation that Christ's followers do not get it. He laments the conflicts within the early Church communities to whom he writes. He senses the deep divide between what Christ means for the world and how the world, including Christ's followers, have received the message. However, Paul repeatedly tries to make the message of peace and reconciliation come alive for these early communities.

In Colossians, Paul reiterates that God through Christ is reconciling "all things, whether on earth or in heaven, by making peace through the blood of his cross." This means that all who "were once estranged and hostile in mind, doing evil deeds," are also now reconciled so that they are "holy and blameless and irreproachable" before God, "provided that you continue securely established and steadfast in the faith" (Col. 1:20–23). In Ephesians, Paul again indicates what the impact of this reconciliation to God through Christ ought to mean for our human relations. If Christ is "our peace" who has made us all reconciled, then Christ has "broken down the dividing wall of hostility" between us, "thereby bringing the hostility to an end." In this way, peace is to grow for all humanity through Christ: "And he came and preached peace to you who were far off and peace to those who were near" (Eph. 2:13–17). These remarks in Ephesians are in the context of tensions between Gentile, those "who were far off," and Jew, those "who were near." This context brings us into the larger social conflicts which were brewing in Paul's time.

Conflicts within the new Churches not only reflected conflicts about theology and Church practices, they related to the great divisions in the world at that time. Paul saw the reconciliation offered through Christ as addressing these conflicts as well: "There is neither Jew nor Greek, there is neither slave nor free, there is neither male nor female; for you are all one in Christ Jesus" (Gal. 3:28). The Jews, having been resistant to Greek culture and Roman occupation, were already being seen as enemies by some early Christians. As one who had persecuted Christians, Paul was now at pains to warn Christians about anti-Jewish sentiments. The central part of his epistle to the Romans, chapters 9–11, makes the argument that God's covenant with the Jews is not set aside by the new covenant through Christ. Not only are Jews such as himself who have become followers of Christ to be accepted, Jews who remain faithful to God's call to them: "For the gifts and the call of God are irrevocable" (Rom. 11:29). Although Paul has understandably been read to support Christian supercessionism toward the Jews and superiority to all religions, he can be interpreted here as tearing down the walls of hostility between religions and cultures.

The same ambiguous stance is there in Paul's writings on slavery. Although his writings do not reject slavery and he calls himself a slave to Christ, he appeals again to the view that Christ has freed all, and in so doing those who experience such freedom in Christ ought to be reconciled to one another. In the letter to Philemon, Paul appeals to the slave owner who has become Christian to receive the runaway slave "no longer as a slave but more than a slave, as a beloved brother." Paul also describes this slave who is now a

Christian as his own son. It can be argued that Paul did not see the implications of his own theology in failing to speak out against slavery, and it can be argued that his views began the view that slavery ought to be overthrown.

Paul's words in the first letter to the Corinthians about the man as "head of the woman" and how women ought to be "silent in church" has been used to both promote sexism within the Church and criticize Christianity as sexist at its core. Though Paul is clearly embracing certain social practices and giving them a Christian justification, it is also clear that he is relativizing those practices. The immediate context is Paul's concern for behavior that will bring unnecessary trouble to the Church in the eyes of the large culture. He agrees that in Christ, "all things are lawful," but that not all things are "helpful," so "give no offense to Jews or to Greeks or to the church of God," but act for the "glory of God" (1 Cor. 10:23, 32). Further, he makes clear that men are not "independent of women" for man is "born of woman" (1 Cor. 11: 12–13) and so are required to love their wives, "as Christ loved the Church." Therefore, Christians are to be "subject to one another out of reverence for Christ" (Eph. 5:21).

IV. ISLAMIC TRADITION

Islam is often understood by many in the West as the tradition furthest from concerns for peace. The very term Islam, translated as submission, is taken by outsiders to mean that Muslims submit themselves and seek to have others submit to an all-powerful and warlike deity. Allah is then connected with the vision of Yahweh as a warrior and a Christian vision of Christ's violent second coming. Allah not only wants his followers to fight now, God will also judge all people on the Judgment Day. It cannot be denied that such concepts and images are in Islam as they are in Judaism and Christianity. However, as with these other traditions, there is much more to Islam than these stereotypes. Repeatedly, Muslim scholars have lamented the distortions of their faith, by both scholars and the general public.

Islam does mean submission, in the sense of self-surrender to Allah, but this is directly connected to the Muslim sense of what peace is about. One root term of Islam means peace. Hence, a Muslim is one who seeks Allah for the sake of peace. With such a profound expression of the desire for peace in the very name of the faith, there is a profound vision of peace in Islam. This vision is meant to include peace in this world and the world to come, peace inwardly and outwardly, between individuals and between social groups, within Islam and between Islam and other faiths. It is in this sense of the term peace that the *Qur'ān* (also, *Koran*) states that God who is the "author of peace," invites all humanity into the "abode of peace" (Surah 10.25). Allah prepares a peaceable garden for all who turn to God: "O tranquil soul, return to your Lord so pleasant and well-pleased! Enter among My servants and enter My garden" (Surah 89.27–30).

As with Judaism and Christianity, the active concern to reduce violence, resolve conflict, and promote peace is either a minority position in the sense of active peacemaking and absolute nonviolence or it is seen as derivative of the concern for justice as demanded by God. Also, Islam does have its "Holy War" tradition, which can set aside all concerns for peace for what is understood as Allah's command to convert or kill the enemies of the faith. For although Allah is named the author of peace, there are also such passages as this in the *Qur'ān*: "Lo! Those who disbelieve our Revelations, We shall expose them to the Fire. As often as their skins are consumed, We shall exchange them for fresh skins that they may taste the torment" (Surah 4.56). As has been seen, such visions of punishment for those seen to disobey God and the true faith exist throughout the Western traditions.

What concerns us here is how the struggle for peacemaking can be seen within the sacred text of the *Qur'ān* and within the early history of Islam. The *Qur'ān*, which is from the Arabic for "The Reading," is understood as the verbatim world of God dictated to *Muhammad* (570–632 C.E.) by the angel Gabriel when Muhammad was 40 years old. Peace, in the full sense of that term within Islam, can be said to be the goal of the *Qur'ān*. Peace is the result of submission to what God desires, and God desires right relations between God and humanity and within the entire human family. There are many specific expressions in the text of a vision of these right relations.

The primary collection of these expressions may be placed in the concern for the relation with God: the Five Pillars of Islam. These are the expression of faith in Allah as one God and the belief that Muhammad is the Prophet of Allah, prayer five times daily, providing for those less fortunate, observing the daily fast from sunup to sunset during the month of Ramadan, and making the pilgrimage to Mecca at least once during one's life. The Five Pillars support the actions of the believer in the world. They are followed in order to remember Allah and not be distracted by the self-indulgence in the world that can lead the believer astray. When this faithful relationship between the individual and God is maintained, the reward is the full enjoyment of peace: "God it is who sent down peace of reassurance into the hearts of believers, that they might add faith to their faith" (Surah 48.4).

When conflicts do arise within the community, the *Qur'ān* repeatedly enjoins believers to make peace with one another. The goal is unity between believers, which mirrors the vision that God is one and not divided. Of course, the acceptance that fighting may be necessary is there, but the goal is the peaceful resolution of conflict:

> If two parties of believers fall to fighting, then make peace between them. And if one party of them does wrong to the other, fight that wrong-doer until they return to the ordinance of Allah; then if they return, make peace between them justly, and act equitably. Lo! Allah loves the equitable. (Surah 49.9)

This fundamental desire for peace extends beyond the Muslim faith community to all humanity, including others of different faiths and even those who deny God altogether. This is a feature expressed in the *Qur'ān* that is often overlooked. Yes, the text insists it is the final world of God and that Muhammad is the seal of the prophets. However, the *Qur'ān* enjoins a different approach to relations between faiths than might be expected: "Let there be no compulsion in religion: truth stands out clear from error; whoever rejects evil and believes in God has grasped the most trustworthy handhold that never breaks" (Surah 2.256).

Specifically, Christians and Jews, called the "People of the Book" in Islam, are absolutely respected in the *Qur'ān*. Muhammad as the final prophet of God does not set aside but rather fulfills the line of prophets beginning with Abraham and extending through Hagar and Ishmael as well as Mary and Jesus. Muhammad is therefore the instrument for teaching what always has been taught to humanity by God. We find many of the stories in the Hebrew and Christian scriptures retold in the *Qur'ān*. Hence, the Jews and Christians are to be respected:

> Those who believe (in the *Qur'ān*), and those who follow the Jewish scriptures, and the Christians . . . and (others) who believe in Allah and the Last Day, and do right and there shall be no fear come upon them, neither shall they grieve. (Surah 2.62)

Further, because Islam had contact with a variety of traditions beyond Judaism and Christianity, Islam saw other faiths as part of God's will. Even when these faiths did not believe in one God and were seen as taking "false gods," the *Qur'ān* is tolerant. In several places, the *Qur'ān* reveals the orthodox Muslim approach:

> If it had been God's plan they would not have taken false gods; but we made thee not one to watch over their doings, nor art thou set over them to dispose of their affairs. (Surah 6.107)
> If it had been thy Lord's will they would have all believed, all who are on earth! Will thou then compel humanity against their will to believe? (Surah 10.99)

Therefore, this Qur'ānic tolerance for other religious traditions, even those outside the monotheistic faiths, is a strong foundation on which to build more peaceful relations between Islam and other religious and ethical traditions.

A persistent stereotype of the spread of Islam sees Muslims converting others by the sword. Muhammad is seen as an astute military leader who began by conquering the tribes in the Arabian peninsula and subsequent leaders who quickly expanded the rule of Islam into the Middle East, the edges of Europe, Persia, and Africa. There is truth in the stereotype because Islam did spread rapidly, but there are important qualifications to be said about the early history. After Muhammad began to receive the revelations and tell his family, others in his own kin group, and the people of Mecca what he was hearing from Allah, some leaders sought to kill him. Up to this time, Muhammad had become a trusted leader in Mecca, which was the major social and religious center in Arabia. Although there were some who were monotheistic, understanding that Abraham brought the vision of one God to Mecca centuries earlier, most Meccans were not monotheists. When more and more people began to listen to Muhammad, including significant leaders in Mecca, other powers there saw him as a threat to their religion and way of life. The revelations were critical of their religion and lack of justice that flowed from worship of "false gods" and this perceived threat promoted the attempt on Muhammad's life. At this point, leaders of Medina invited Muhammad to come to their city not just to take refugee but to assume the military, political, and religious leadership of the city. At this point, it was not Muhammad that attacked those who had sought to kill him, but rather the leaders of Mecca attempted to conquer Medina.

Hence, the initial battles which Muhammad and the early followers of Islam were defensive. This is what the military form of jihad, defined as striving for God, that the *Qur'ān* is enjoining upon followers: attack others only when the faithful are attacked. Hence, the idea of initiating a "Holy War," such as the Christian Crusades, was foreign to the earliest practice of Islam and Muhammad. In fact, after the early battles between Medina and Mecca, Islam spread without warfare throughout the Arabian peninsula. Muhammad could have attacked Mecca as he gained superior military might, but he refrained, and finally Mecca accepted Islam and opened its gates to Muhammad. Upon entering the city and confronting those who had repeatedly tried to murder him and wipe out Islam, Muhammad forgave his enemies. This event is the reference in Surah 110 of the *Qur'ān*:

> In the Name of Allah, the Beneficient, the Merciful, when Allah's succor, and triumph comes and thou seest all enter the religion of Allah, then sing the praise of the Lord, and seek forgiveness of God. Lo! Allah is ever ready to show mercy.

The violent struggles between the divisions within Islam and between Islam and the rest of the world began only about 40 years after Muhammad's death. The splits between the Sunnis, Shi'ites, and Khāriji factions followed the battle of Siffin in 657 C.E. and the murder of Ali who was seen by the Shi'ites as the leader designated by Muhammad. In the subsequent dynasties, the consolidation of power within Islam as well as the spread of the Islamic Empire did use military might to control dissent and conquer non-Islamic peoples. However, there was the recognition of the tragedy of these splits within Islam and the wars with non-Muslims. During this time there were those such as the Sufis who looked to the *Qur'ān* and Muhammad's life for a different Islamic response to violence and conflict. They saw *jihad* as an internal struggle which had the full realization of God's abiding love for humanity as its goal.

In conclusion, the classic texts of the Western traditions provide no unambiguous responses to questions about violence, peace and conflict. To ask whether or not they support violence or nonviolence, war or peace, conflict or conflict resolution is too simple. To go back to them challenges our contemporary perspectives on the questions because the views we examine now are reflected in these texts. However, there is a vision of peace within these classic works that suggests that the conflicting dualisms with which we struggle may be interrelated. In this way, peace is the fundamental concept, bridging the separation between God and the world, and friend and enemy. The texts express the desire for peace.

Also See the Following Articles

CONSCIENTIOUS OBJECTION, ETHICS OF • CRITIQUES OF VIOLENCE • ETHICAL AND RELIGIOUS TRADITIONS, EASTERN • MORAL JUDGMENTS AND VALUES • RELIGIOUS TRADITIONS, VIOLENCE AND NONVIOLENCE • SPIRITUALITY AND PEACEMAKING

Bibliography

Gordon, H., & Leonard, G. (Eds.). (1988). *Education for peace: Testimonies from world religions.* New York: Orbis Books, Maryknoll.

Nielsen, N. C. (Ed.). (1993). *Religions of the world.* (3rd Ed.). New York: St. Martin's Press.

Smith, H. (1991). *The illustrated world's religions: A guide to our wisdom traditions.* San Francisco: HarperCollins Publishers.

Thompson, H. O. (1988). *World religions in war and peace.* Jefferson, NC: McFarland & Co.

Wilson, A. (ed.). (1991). *World scripture: A comparative anthology of sacred texts.* New York: Paragon House.

Ethical Studies, Overview

Eduardo Mendieta
University of San Francisco

GLOSSARY

Cognitivism The view that moral judgments and norms can be derived or rationally justified; or that we can know whether something is wrong or right, just or unjust.

Communitarian Moral and political theory that argues that citizens and moral agents emerge from specific historical communities, and that their moral orientations can only be explained in terms of the values of those communities. Abstract principles of justice and morality make sense only from specific traditions of understanding and interpretation. Communitarianism is generally associated with a critique of liberal democracy and Kantian moral theories.

Deontological Related to deontic (from the Greek *dei* = one must), and meaning to have to do something regardless of the outcome of the action. It also means the opposite of teleological.

Discourse Ethics Deontological theory of morality and political justice that argues that norms can be derived from the normative structure of dialogue and action.

Emotivism The view that moral judgments or ethical actions do not admit of rational justification. Ethical or moral acts are results of completely subjective acts based on our inclinations and emotions.

Ethics of Care Feminist ethical perspective that argues that women have an either intrinsic or acquired moral perspective that is associated with caring, with relatedness, and with particularity. This ethics of care is juxtaposed to an ethics of rights, or justice approach, generally associated with males.

Teleological Related to telos (from the Greek *telos* = goal, end), and meaning to do something for the sake of a particular end or goal. It also means the opposite of deontic.

I. INTRODUCTION

Ethical studies and moral theory, as well as meta-ethics and sometimes even practical philosophy, are different ways of referring to that part of philosophy that is concerned with human interaction, and thus with intentions, values, and the criteria for the evaluation of possible courses of action. The broader and most general rubric is practical philosophy, in opposition to theoretical philosophy, which concerns itself with questions of metaphysics, ontology, epistemology, logic, and theology. Yet, under practical philosophy also fall political theory, the theory of justice, philosophy of economics, and jurisprudence (or philosophy of law). This explains partly why since the early 1970s there has been talk of a "rehabilitation of practical philosophy," to refer to the contemporary return to questions of the good and just life, to questions of ethics and moral theory, after what seemed a prolonged eclipse by questions of logic, language, metaphysics, and ontology. At the same time, the fact that moral and ethical questions belong to a general part of philosophy called practical philosophy also points to the fact that these questions are not to be separated from questions of the good society, just laws, and even equitable and humane forms of wealth production, acquisition, and distribution. In the last instance, the fact that questions of ethics, law, and economics are studied under one same rubric points to the recognition that there is an internal relationship between the just and moral life, and the good society, or a society that is constituted by moral, and not merely legal, laws, and that is maintained by an equitable and sustainable economic system.

There is also the sometimes misleading differentiation between moral theory and ethical studies, which would seem to suggest that morality is something entirely different from ethics. Yet, today a distinction between morality and ethics has come to acquire analytical purchase power insofar as these two terms refer to two different theoretical attitudes toward practical questions. Whereas morality refers to questions of the just life, ethics refers to questions of the good life. Or, in an alternate formulation, whereas morality refers to deontology, ethics refers to teleology. The fact is that both words refer to one and the same thing. Ethics is the transliteration of *ethos*, which is the Greek word for "way of life," although it also refers to character, as in the character of a person. Morality descends from *môs*, which is the way in which Cicero translated ethos into Latin. Later, morality came to refer to the mores that guide a person or community. Mores and customs, or *Sitten*, in German, are related. Note for instance the similarity in terminology between two works that stands on opposite sides of the spectrum on the question of the nature of morals: David Hume's *An Equiry Concerning the Principles of Morals* (1751), and Immanuel Kant's *Grounding for the Metaphysics of Morals* (*Grundlegung zur Metaphysik der Sitten*) (1785). Fichte's *Sittenlehre*, similarly, could be translated as *Moral Philosophy*, although literally it should be translated as "on the doctrine of customs." Hegel, partly criticizing Kant, differentiated between *Moralität* and *Sittlichkeit*. The former term refers to the abstract theory of what is just and right to do, and was identified by Hegel with Kant's rigorous, abstract, and individualistic theory of morality. Morality, as Hegel puts it in the *Philosophy of Right* (1821), is the standpoint of the will that expresses itself as absolute subjective freedom (§§105–105). The latter term, *Sittlichkeit*, in opposition, refers to the "ethical substance," "ethical life," or actual ethical precepts and principles that guide individuals and the society within which they have come to attain moral consciousness. It is the consciousness of freedom actualized in social reality. Hegel's point is that before an individual can orient herself to abstract and empty forms of universal judgment, she must be motivated existentially, culturally, and socially to act in accordance with certain lived principles that embodied ways of life with a universal claim (§142 and following of the *Philosophy of Right*). Today, Hegel's distinction has come to be accepted. What was originally merely a matter of etymology and translation has become a conceptual distinction and a philosophical categorization. This sedimented conceptual differentiation, nonetheless, preserves the traces of the history or moral and ethical thinking under modernity. We turn to a brief overview of that history.

II. SOURCES OF MODERN ETHICS

The sources of contemporary ethical theories lie as much in Greek thinking and Roman political thought as in Jewish and Christian theologies. Yet, the more immediate and relevant sources of contemporary moral theory lie with Immanuel Kant. After the disintegration of the unity of the medieval world, a unity that was as much theocratic as it was cultural and religious, questions about what was appropriate to do could no longer be referred back to either religion or the church. The Renaissance and the Reformation both meant the affirmation of the autonomy and self-determination of the individual. These found their utmost expression in the self-determination of individuals by means of the use of their own reason, or their ability to question and learn, as it was the catch phrase of the Enlightenment. With the dissolution of the integrated religious world view of medieval Europe, there also dissolved the narrow and local ethical maps that guided individuals from day to day, from act to act. What modern moral philosophy must offer, instead, is a moral compass. This is what Kant's moral philosophy captures in an unprecedented manner and with an unequaled clarity. Kant's moral philosophy is above all about the marriage of freedom and reason, will and universality. The categorical imperative, which calls you to "Act only according to that maxim whereby you can at the same time will that it should become a universal law," is the injunction to affirm your will, to exercise your freedom in such a way that your use of freedom can also be emulated by others. If the maxim, or practical rule that guides your action, can be universalized, then it is a guide for action that can be accepted and followed by all. More importantly, the categorical imperative acts as a test for the acceptance or nonacceptance of moral norms. It does not prescribe or proscribe positively what one ought or ought not to do. In the last instance, responsibility for one's actions falls back on the shoulders of the actor, and not on something external to the will of the individual. Morality, in other words, to be possible at all can only be derived from the very possibility of the free choice and rational determination of the individual. Indeed, to ascend to an understanding of the possibility of morality we can not begin with the facts of history, or with an obervation of what we desire or want to bring about. Instead, insight into morality must be arrived at from an elucidation of the very structure of moral action. The categorical imperative, in fact, is a *factum* of reason. Morality is rationality, and reason is moral. This would be the Kantian motto. Kant's moral philosophy, therefore, is about individuality, autonomy, freedom, but also duty, sociality, universality and lawfulness, or reasonableness. And these are the central categories of moral thinking that guide our modern times.

Hegel's moral philosophy, which is dependent on his philosophy of history and philosophy of mind, can be read as a critique of both natural law theories and the abstract universalism of Kant. Against natural law theories, Hegel maintains that there is no state preexistent to society that would grant humans any rights. Rights are a function of human sociality, their being members of specific historical communities. Society grants individuals rights, which are the acknowledgment and recognition of their freedom. A state of nature neither acknowledges nor preserves the free personality of the individual. Freedom, again, flows from a social order established by the struggle for recognition between citizens. The orientation toward the universal, as is expected from the categorical imperative, is an acquired ability, and not one individuals possess innately. This ability is what is learned through being immersed in the "ethical life" or "ethical substance" of a community. Furthermore, from the ethical substance of a community, the moral resources are obtained that allow for the functioning of civil society (*bürgerliche Gesellschaft*). This is the social sphere that includes the economic, political, and public cultural interaction between private citizens. Civil society, to that extent, mediates between the realm of the private, that is the family, and the state. It is in the state where the world historical experiences of a people attain their highest expression through the formalization of their moral insights into legal principles. The state, in contrast to the family, is not based on arbitrary emotion, that is, love. And in contrast to civil society, the state is not based on economic or political contract, that is momentary and perhaps self-serving compromise. Rather, the state is based on the self-consciousness of a people who are identified with their state through their noncoerced acceptance of its laws. Only in the state, in the last instance, can humans actualize their freedom. As Hegel put it: "The rational end of man is life in the state, and if there is no state there, reason at once demands that one be founded." (addenda to §75 of the *Philosophy of Right*).

Notwithstanding Hegel's criticisms of Kant, we can say that both laid the foundations for modern ethical thinking. Kant discovered the power of reason, autonomy, and freedom. Hegel discovered the power of sociality, civil society, and the state; all of them, evidently, being historical attainments. Together, thus, they thematized the two central poles of the contemporary human condition: individuality and sociality. As children of our contemporary times, we are condemned to be individuals, to have to affirm our uniqueness, our autonomy, to actualize our freedom. But we can only do this in the context of communities that grant us rights through which we can actualize our freedom. Furthermore, it is only through political and legal communities that we can struggle for the recognition of our social needs. It is only in the context of moral communities that we can stand as witnesses for certain moral views that can either challenge or call to accountability our very own communities. This is the almost paradoxical nature of ethics: to have to stand alone in affirming a moral perspective, but before a community that brought us to moral consciousness and that perhaps even now does not want to acknowledge our own moral insights. Ethics is about being for oneself, but standing before the whole of humanity. It is about our individual choice, but one that we have to assume that we might have to justify to every living human being.

III. CRITICS OF MORALITY

In the 19th century the "masters of suspicion" (two use Paul Ricoeur's term), Karl Marx, Friedrich Nietzsche, and Sigmund Freud, launched such severe critiques of the foundations of moral thinking laid down by Kant and Hegel that today we still live under the shadow of their unmaskings and deconstructions. Marx said to have "turn Hegel on his head." He meant by this that in contrast to the view that transformation takes place in the mind, at the level of ideas, transformation takes place in material reality, and only subsequently, in the realm of ideas. Marx also appropriated Hegel's notion of the externalization, objectification, alienation, and ultimate overcoming of that alienation of a new level of understanding. For Marx, externalization takes form primarily through labor, which then gets alienated into a product. This product is then sold in the market at a profit to the capitalist. The profit is what the laborer loses of his own life. For exchange value, what allows for profit is the objectified work of the laborer. From this materialization of Hegel's dialectics of history and the objectification of spirit, Marx arrives at a supreme moral rejection of the present capitalist mode of production. Capitalism is absolutely immoral because it entails the dehumanization of humans. The proletariat, as the ones who posses nothing, except their own labor, represent in their poverty the negativity of the system. Marx thus enunciated in his *Introduction to the Critique of Hegel's Philosophy of Right* (1843–1844), the imperative: "to overthrow all conditions in which man is debased, enslaved, neglected and contemptible being." In Marx's eyes, and those of his followers, this rejection was not merely or even primarily an ethical censure. This rejection was based on a scientific theory of the evolution and transformation of society. The present capitalist system was doomed to be abolished by its own inner contradictions, and by the proletariat, the epitome of its negativity. Above all, for Marx the state, the church, and their ideological drapery were merely the ideas of the ruling class. The ruling ideas of any time are always the ideas of those who rule. Any humanitarian, pious, even philanthropic pronouncement was to be distrusted because in its essence it was but merely the attempt to conceal the real suffering and real interests of those who benefit from the expropriation of workers and farmers. To this extent, Marx was a critic of all attempts to formulate and defend the possibility of a universalistic ethics. In fact, Marx's radical critique of contemporary society entailed, in George Lukács's phrase, a "teleological suspension of the ethical." Ethics, or morality, can only be actualized in the future kingdom of freedom that will come after the abolishment of a dehumanizing system of economic, political and social relations.

Friedrich Nietzsche's critique of universal moral theories is not unlike Marx's. Both were motivated by Hegel's foregrounding of history. Both were also motivated by the cunning of history, which seemed to betray all hope for redemption, and even all hopes for the actualization of a just order. Both were analogously motivated by a radical critique of the moral torpidity and mendacity of a self-satisfied, narcissistic, and rapacious bourgeoisie. For Nietzsche, morals do not derive from reason, nor from God. Indeed, for Nietzsche religion was the rejection of morality. Moral values arose from the great, honorable, unprecedented acts of great historical figures, be they a Moses, a Caesar, a Napoleon, and Alexander the Great. The values that we came to associate with humility, generosity, forgiveness, self-abnegation, were in fact the virtues of great man, who in their beningness and magnanimity showed the weak these virtues. Today, however, according to Nietzsche, what rules are the values of self-denial, meekness, asceticism, and bad faith. These values came to be enthroned through the *ressentiment* of the weak, who imposed their slave morality so as to bring to their level the great, and thus to prevent those with a love for life and creativity from challenging those who do not have the wherewithal. It would be a mistake, however, to conclude that Nietzsche was an immoralist, a misanthrope bent on rejecting all morals. Rather, it would be more appropriate to see his extreme, almost nihilist critiques of moral universalism and complacent Kantian rigor, as a moral critique of the amorality of a society bent on war, suffering, nationalism, colonialism, and self-satisfaction. Above all, Nietzsche wanted to underscore that there ought to be no alibi to unburden the individual from the responsibility of their own actions. Neither reason, nor religion, not even tradition, nor nation, will absolve the individual from having to assume charge of their actions. Nietzsche spoke of a "will to power" that is expression of the creativity and life-giving force that moves nature. Morality that is true to the individual ought to be a celebration of this telluric force of nature. Whatever, in other words, denies that Dionysian aspect of humans is but a rejection of life, and thus immoral. Against both Kant and Hegel, Nietzsche brings us back to the choosing, living, material, individual. Morality to be true, must stand beyond "good and evil" as we understand them. To be moral, in the last instance, means to be an *Übermensch*, the "human who is making herself by transgressing the present stultified social order."

Sigmund Freud brings to a close this circle of masterful deconstructions and unmaskings of the basic assumptions of modern moral theories. Whereas Marx had unmasked the power of history and the state as the tools of immoral and narrow interests, and Nietzsche had unmasked the power of moral ideals as the emasculating and disempowering impositions by the ressentiment of the weak, Freud unmasked the supreme ideal of individuality as a pyrrhic victory over our instinctual life. For Freud, civilization was necessary for the preservation and survival of humans. But in the process of the development of civilization, humans abdicated more and more of their instinctual life over to society. Civilization is based on the slow but effective colonization of superego over ego, and libido. Where ego was, superego shall be. The superego is the voice of society, ego is the voice of the narcissistic self. Libido are the instinctual drives that explode from within our animal natures. In the end, civilization and a healthy psychological disposition are joyless and exacting attainments. Society is predicated on the individual's sacrifice of their instincts to the rules that all must follow. Freud put it succinctly in his *Civilization and its Discontents*: "Civilization, therefore, obtains mastery over the individual's dangerous desires for aggression by weakening and disarming it and by *setting up an agency within him to watch over it, like a garrison in a conquered city*." In other words, the celebrated Western notion of individuality, of autonomy, is the result of the introjection of the violence and self-denial imposed by society on us for the preservation of social harmony. To be moral, thus, means to have surrendered over to the policing forces and panoptical omniscience of a totalitarian society. In the last instance, both Nietzsche and Freud, developed devastating critiques that seem to have sundered for ever the internal entwinement between virtue and happiness, individuality and ethics, that have been part and parcel of Western moral thinking since Socrates.

Socrates had established, against the sophists and their relativism, that the good life was also the moral life. In other words, virtue was attained only in accordance with justice. Aristotle followed this tradition. The virtues of the good human being, were the virtues of a happy life lived in accordance with the prudentia of balance and discernment. This tradition was an unchallenged article of faith of all moral theories in the West, at least until Nietzsche and Freud. Both, basically, cast doubt on whether to be moral is the same thing as striving for happiness. In their view, sometimes the moral act requires our eternal damnation. To act ethically requires that we deny our own happiness. Conversely, happiness might be only attained at the expense of our respect for the moral law and our duty toward our fellow human beings. As Freud put it, humans must exchange a portion of their happiness for a portion of security. Our security is bought at the expense of our happiness. This is the sad truth of civilization. At the same time, ever since Socrates, we have associated the possibility of ethics at all with the idea of the sovereign, or autonomous, individual. What both Nietzsche and Freud, as well as Marx, came to make clear is that individuality, and the autonomy of the sovereign individual, are if not illusory, at least unrealizable. The individual is always heteronomous, and never ruler in his own castle. The autonomous, free, sovereign individual is but the after effect of power networks enacted and deployed either by the economy, the state, civilization, the superego, or religion. Individuality is but a shadow projected by the panopticon of the totalitarian society that grew on the ruins of the church. Individuality, to paraphrase Freud, was but a "garrison in a conquered, but empty city."

IV. APORIAS OF 20TH CENTURY ETHICS

Moral philosophy in the 20th century, therefore, must be understood, as Karl Löwith pointed out, in light of the aftermath of the unraveling of the Hegelian synthesis between knowledge, history, ethics, and law, and in light of a return to Kant, although now by other means. Moral philosophy in the 20th century has been an attempt to recapture both Hegel's *Sittlichkeit* and Kant's *Moralität*. That this is what philosophers were trying to do becomes clear when we look at the different currents that dominate the philosophical horizon in our time: pragmatism, hermeneutics, analytical philosophy of language, existentialism, phenomenology, and even semiotics. What is unique, however, about these attempts to recapture in some way both Kant's and Hegel's ethical insights, is that they are now pursued on the grounds of language, and not epistemology or even metaphysics. This dominant focusing on language is what has been called the "linguistic turn." It essentially means that now every philosophical explanation or system must depart from an explanation of the nature and possibility of linguistic understanding. In a crass but generalizing formulation one could say that whereas ancient and medieval philosophy were concerned with the questions of beings and "being" as such (the subjects of metaphysics and ontology), and modern philosophy was concerned with the questions of knowing and mental representations (ideas), contemporary philosophy is concerned with statements and expressions (linguistic communication). This turn to language as the privilege point of entry into all philosophical questions was heralded by the following four classic of contemporary philosophy: Charles Sanders Peirce's "Questions Concerning Certain Faculties Claimed for Man" and "Some Consequences of Four Incapacities" (both from 1868); Ludwig Wittgenstein's *Tractatus logico-philosophicus* (1918), and Martin Heidegger's *Being and Time* (1927). From each one of these classics there arose the major movements that dominate the philosophical landscape in the 20th century: pragmatism, hermeneutics, and the analytical philosophy of language. Each one of these movements, however, entailed specific views on the possibility of moral theory. Pragmatism came to be associated with both Kantianism (as in the work of Charles S. Peirce and George Herbert Mead), and Hegelianism (as in the work of Josiah Royce, John Dewey, and more recently, Richard Rorty, Richard Bernstein, Cornel West, and Nancy Fraser). Heideggerian inspired hermeneutics came to associate itself with Hegelianism, what has been also called Neo-Aristotelianism (Hans-Georg Gadamer, Gerhard Ritter, Manfred Riedel), which argued for the supremacy of the historical community over the choosing subject (what in the United States has come to be called Communitarianism: Michael Walzer, Charles Taylor, Alasdair MacIntyre, and Bernard Williams). The analytical philosophy of language, descending from Wittgenstein came to spouse an ethical noncognitivitism, or emotivism, that made ethical insights a function of irrational beliefs or unjustifiable motivations (Alfred J. Ayer, Bertrand Russell).

Two major events, however, have determined the direction of moral thinking in the 20th century, independent of the inner logic of philosophical argumentation and the unfolding of philosophical currents. On the one hand, there was World War II, and all that it entailed: the discovery of the concentration camps, the unprecedented displacement of people by a "total war" that made the civilians military targets, and the dropping of the atomic bomb over Hiroshima and Nagasaki, arguably (as Karl Jaspers noted), the events that catalyzed a sense of world consciousness, if only negatively. On the other hand, there was the Cold War, which signaled both the stabilization of world conflict through the pursuing of a policy of mutually assured destruction (MAD) by both the Soviet Union and the United States, and the development of "hot areas" of conflict, or wars by proxy. The Cold War meant above all the imminence of complete world destruction, but it also meant that a balance of power had been achieved, if only precariously and temporarily. It is against the background of these two major historical events and processes that we must understand the resurgence of rehabilition of practical philosophy in the second half of the 20th century. For, World War II and the Cold War came to embody the end of a particular infatuation and blind faith in the purported intrinsic beningness of technology. At the same time, the war and the stalemate of Soviet-American struggle for the soul of the world, led to a deep mistrust in the ability of nation-states to deal appropriately with an integrated and interdependent planetary order.

No philosopher has captured with greater clarity and precision the fragmentation of contemporary moral philosophy, as well as the challenges that its aporias present to us, as Karl-Otto Apel did in a seminal essay first written in 1967, but published in 1973. In this seminal essay entitled "The *Apriori* of the Communication Community and the Foundations of Ethics: the Problem of a Rational Foundation of Ethics in the Scientific Age," Karl-Otto Apel develops a map of the contemporary situation of moral theory. On the one hand, argues Apel, we have the Western system of complementarity between value-neutral scientism and decisionistic subjectivism. On the other hand, we have the Eastern system (where Eastern refers to the Soviet Union and the Warsaw Pact Nations) of integration between history and nature, praxis and theory, brought about by dialectical materialism. The consequences of these systems of integration and complementarity resulted in the suspension, or introjection, of all moral thinking. In the last instance, as Apel underscored, the point is that in the 20th century moral thinking has become the more imperative precisely because of the exponential growth of technological and political power. Yet, the success of technology and science seem to have vitiated any hope in practical reason being able to rule human interaction. In other words, the triumph of technology has meant scientism, or blind faith in the power of instrumental reason to bring about practical results. Conversely, practical questions have become the purview of pure subjectivity. Essentially, scientism and analytical philosophy of language cooperate to make a normative grounding of ethics seem impossible. Both agree on the following points: first, that *norms* cannot be derived from *facts* (this is Hume's famous "naturalistic fallacy"); second, science, which alone provides humanity with substantive knowledge, concerns itself only with facts; and third, since science is the only human discipline that provides us with objective knowledge, then "intersubjectivity" must be the same as objectivity. From these three fundamental assumptions of all analytical philosophies of language, there follows that a normative ethics for the intersubjective determination of norms that guide human interactions becomes impossible. In the rest of his 1967 essay, Apel set out to reject these basic assumptions and to discover how in fact a normative grounding of ethics is possible. Against the reduction of reason to instrumental reason, and thus of intersubjectivity to objectivity, and the reduction of practical questions to arbitrary subjective decisions, Apel discovers in the always already presupposed community of communication certain rational presuppositions that allow us to affirm the possibility of a normative, universalizable moral theory. Apel's elucidation of these rational presuppositions, and their normative consequences for ethics have come to be known as discourse ethics.

The basic insight of discourse ethics, in Apel's view, is the following. All acts of understanding, be those of a community of understanding or a community of scientists, or in short, any real community of communication, are possible on the counterfactual presupposition of an ideal community of communication. As members of this ideal community of communication, we presuppose the symmetry of treatment, mutual acknowledgement of each other, equality of position, and equal access to the raising and redemption of validity claims pertaining to statements made by anyone. In other words, all understanding has built into it a series of norms, norms that turn out to be the very normative presuppositions of all ethics. Discourse ethics claims that in the very structure of discourse we discovery the possibility and necessity of ethics. Furthermore, from the obvious dialectical contradiction between the real and ideal communities of communication, and assuming the basic norms entailed by all possible understanding, Apel derives two *fundamental regulative principles* for the long-term coordination of human action. First, and foremost, all actions or omissions must be performed in view of the *survival* of the human species, *qua* real community of communication. Second, all acts should be pursued in view of the *actualization* of the ideal community of communication in the real community. Discourse ethics, therefore, is not only an normative and deontological ethics. It is also an ethics of responsibility that argues for the future of humanity. It is therefore an ethics for the strategic actualization of the conditions supposed to exist in the ideal community of communication.

Jürgen Habermas, a colleague of Karl-Otto Apel at Frankfurt, and indisputably the most important social theorist of the second half of the 20th century, also subscribes to the basic insights of discourse ethics. Habermas, however, has gone further. He has enunciated a series of principles and rules of argumentation that both clarify the insights of Apel into the basic presupposition of all understanding, and that reformulate Kant's categorical imperative in linguistic terms. Thus, Habermas has articulated the following universalization rule "U," which says that all valid norms must fulfill the following requirement: "*All* affected can accept that consequences and the side effects its *general* observance can be anticipated to have for the satisfaction of *everyone's* interests (and these consequences are preferred to those of known alternative possibilities for regulation)," or in an alternate formulation: "Unless all affected can *freely* accept the consequence and the side effects that the *general* observance of a controversial norm can be expected to have for the satisfaction of the interests of *each individual*," and only then, is a norm valid and acceptable. From this general universalization rule, which claims that only those norms are universalizable that would meet with the ascent of those affected by its enactment and in view of its possible or secondary effects, Habermas proceeds to formulate "D," or the principle of discourse ethics, which enunciates: "Only those norms can claim to be valid that meet (or could meet) with the approval of all affected in their capacity as participants in a practical discourse." *D*, as it is clear, is the linguistic version of Kant's categorical imperative: act as if the maxim of your action were to become a law of universal legislation. The difference is that whereas for Kant we are supposed to arrive at this rule of action monologically and *in abstracto*, with Habermas's formulation individuals are required to enter into practical and real discourses. Normed behavior is only arrived at intersubjectively and norms are able to be established through a process of argumentation. This is the basic insight of discourse ethics.

Another figure that shares some of the same basic assumptions and concerns as Apel and Habermas is John Rawls, who without question is the major ethical thinker of the 20th century. In 1971 Rawls published the work that was to change both moral philosophy and political theory: *A Theory of Justice*. John Rawls is a Kantian, and he develops a deontological theory of justice that is not to be derived from either empirical or utilitarian considerations. For Rawls justice is basically fairness, or the regulation of social institutions on the general principle that no benefits should be granted to some at the expense of others; or conversely, that adverse consequences of institutional measures should not affect some more than others. The principles that would guide the just society are arrived at through a thought experiment: imagine that we all stood in an original position of equality, and behind a veil that would prevent us from knowing either the race, class, gender, religion, ability, and so on, of each other. Now, given this original, imaginary situation, what principles would we want to orient our society? According to Rawls, we would be inclined to chose those principle that would prevent the worst consequences to each other, and we would want to do so while preserving personal and political liberty combined, at a second level of importance, with the right to the transformation of socioeconomic situations for the betterment of all. Rawls formalizes this general orientation of the persons behind the *veil of ignorance* of the hypothetical originary situation into three major principles: first, all must have equal basic liberties, or, each will have the greatest possible basic liberties so long as this is compatible with the freedom of others; second, all must have equality of opportunity; and third, there is the difference principle that requires that if there are to be inequalities, these can only be justified if they benefit the worst off, and not those who already benefit from inequalities in the social system. Like discourse ethics, Rawls's theory of justice turns away from utilitarianism, relativism, and emotivism. As a form of cognitivism, Rawls's theory of justice suggests that moral norms are capable of being adjudicated on and rationally derived and justified. Like Apel's and Habermas's discourse ethics, Rawls's citizens chose the principles of a well-ordered society with each other in mind. To this extent, it is concerned with individuals who must chose in the contexts of political communities.

V. FEMINISTS MORAL PHILOSOPHIES

No philosophical current, social movement, even moral attitude has put into greater relief the moral quandaries that face contemporary persons than have feminists. Feminisms, and we must talk in the plural because there are as many different feminist stands as are there are philosophical traditions, are hard to describe succinctly. Feminisms are at the same time: a *critique* of sexist reason and society; a *practice* of transformation of sexist social relations; and a *movement* with specific political, social, economic, and legal goals. Interestingly, feminists moral theories (whether in the form of ethics of care of ethics of rights), illustrate the point made at the beginning of this article, namely, that a moral perspective is always concomitant to a theory of justice and a theory of how society ought to reproduce itself. In this sense, some might argue that feminist moral theories are the vanguard of moral thinking today. Not surprisingly, however, the internal heterogeneity of feminism is reflected in the moral theories that have emerged from within it. At the same time, feminist moral theories reflect the tensions within contemporary approaches to moral theory in general.

The idea that woman have a different moral attitude, and that they exemplify certain moral virtues is as old as the very division of labor that has determined gender roles since humans supposedly climbed down from trees and started toiling the land and hunting for serval. In the book of Genesis of the Christian Bible we find the notion that it is because of woman that sin entered into the world. Eve's eating the apple from the tree of knowledge doomed humanity to suffering and work. Aristotle, Augustine, Luther, Kant and Hegel, Rousseau, Hume, and so on, all thought that women have a distinctive moral perspective. Sometimes this unique *feminine* perspective was depreciated and shunned. Other times, feminine virtues have been praised and celebrated. It is, however, only in the 20th century that feminists philosophers have directly addressed the question of moral philosophy with respect to woman, and vice versa, even if we find precursors already in the 18th century, such as Mary Wollstonecraft. The debate concerning a feminist ethics could be said to have been catalyzed by the publication of Carol Gilligan's *In a Different Voice* (1982). In this work, Gilligan criticized the developmental moral psychology of Lawrence Kohlberg for giving primacy to the male moral perspective and for underrating the moral perspective of woman. Gilligan noticed that young women's moral attitudes had to do with relationships, with care, with addressing particular persons and how they might be affected by the outcome of a moral conflict. This care perspective contrasted with the young male's orientation to impartiality, to generality, to the weighing of outcomes in terms of fairness. Kohlberg thought that the norm was the male attitude and that the female perspective was prior and preparatory to the male perspective. Gilligan challenged this hierarchical and biased reading of moral perspectives. Subsequently, a particular feminist moral theory developed around Gilligan's work. This came to be known as the ethics of care. Much of the contemporary debate concerning feminist ethics has been determined by the positions that one may take vis-à-vis Gilligan's ethics of care. Still, it can be said that there are at least five discernable currents within feminist thinking concerning the issue of a unique feminist or feminine ethic. On the one side there are the ethics of care feminists. This camp subdivides into two camps: those that advocate an essentialist reading of femininity that is based on some sort of metaphysical, biological, or spiritual uniqueness of woman (Mary Daly); and those that ascribe to women a particular feminine ethics of care due to the psychosocial development of woman (Sara Ruddick, Nel Noddings, Caroline Whitbeck). The metaphysical or biological essentialist feminist argue that woman are more moral because that is part of their feminine nature. The psychosocial development feminists of care believe that due to the fact that women are primarily socialized as mothers and caregivers, they have a fundamentally different moral orientation. Diametrically opposed to these essentialist feminists, we find what for lack of a better terms we can call the historicist feminists. These feminist do not believe that there is either a feminine essence, be it metaphysical or biological, or that we can accept as a given that women are more care oriented because of the way they have been socialized. Instead, historicist feminists underscore the radical historical nature of all social practices, especially of those that produce gender roles. Within the historicist camp, we can discern at least three currents: the liberal, the Marxist, and the postmodern. The liberal feminists, or feminists that advocate an ethics of rights emphasize that both man and woman are equally capable of moral and immoral acts, and that if there are differences they can be explained in terms of social conditioning, availability of resources, and so on (see Virginia Held, Annette Baier, Susan Moller Okin). The point is to expand to women the same resources that men have available to them. Interestingly, as more woman have been integrated into the economy, and more participate in the public domain, the more it has become clear that woman acquire what has been called a male moral orientation. Would a women president act more morally than a male president? This is a question that liberal feminist would answer in the negative. Marxist feminists look at the historical roots of the division of labor between women and men, and at the emergence of different social spheres, and how they affect and produce certain gender roles (Nancy Hartsock, Jean Grimshaw). Most importantly, gender roles are material and social practices that benefit men and hinder and disempower women. From this perspective, an ethics of care is but an ideological move of the status quo to essentialized, that is render unquestionable and unchallengeable, the gender roles that undergird capitalist, sexist society. The postmodern camp, like the Marxist camp, is highly critical of any essentialist reading of feminity (see Judith Butler, Wendy Brown). In fact, for the postmodern camp, feminity is an ever shifting concept, whose content depends as much on particular political, social, economic, sexual interests, as on symbolic, psychological, and linguistic transactions. Femininity, as well as masculinity, are sites of continuous contestation and perpetual reinscription. The ethical struggle is precisely over who, or what, has the authority and power to determine the content of what allows for the performance of one's gender and sexuality.

Also See the Following Articles

CRITIQUES OF VIOLENCE • ECOETHICS • ETHICAL AND RELIGIOUS TRADITIONS, EASTERN • ETHICAL AND RELIGIOUS TRADITIONS, WESTERN • HUMAN NATURE, VIEWS OF • MEANS AND ENDS • MORAL JUDGMENTS AND VALUES • RELIGIOUS TRADITIONS, VIOLENCE AND NONVIOLENCE

Bibliography

Apel, K.-O. (1988). *Diskurs und Verantwortung*. Frankfurt: Suhrkamp.

Apel, K.-O. (1996). *Selected essays: Volume two: Ethics and the theory of rationality*. Atlantic Highlands, NJ: Humanities Press.

Bauman, Z. (1994). *Postmodern ethics*. Oxford, UK: Blackwell.

Benhabib, S. (1992). *Situating the self*. New York: Routledge, Chapman & Hall.

Butler, J. (1990). *Gender trouble: Feminism and the subversion of identity*. New York: Routledge.

Camps, V., Osvaldo Guariglia, O., Salmeron, F., (Eds.). (1992). *Concepciones de la ética*. Madrid: Editorial Trotta.

De Beauvoir, S. (1953). *The second sex*. New York: Knopf.

Dussel, E. (1998). *Ética de la Liberación*. Madrid: Editorial Trotta.

Forst, R. (1996). *Kontexte der Gerechtigkeit*. Frankfurt: Suhrkamp.

Gilligan, C. (1982). *In a different voice*. Cambridge, MA: Harvard University Press.

Grimshaw, J. (1986). *Philosophy and feminist thinking*. Minneapolis: University of Minnesota Press.

Habermas, J. (1990). *Moral consciousness and communicative action*. Cambridge: The MIT Press.

Habermas, J. (1993). *Justification and application: Remarks on discourse ethics*. Cambridge: The MIT Press.

Ilting, K.-H. (1984). Sitte, Sittlichkeit, Moral. In Brunner, O., Conze, W., Koselleck, R. (Eds.). (1984). *Geschichtliche Grundbegriffe*. Stuttgart: Klett-Cotta.

Kittay, E. F., & Meyers O. T. (Eds). (1987). *Women and moral theory*. Totowa, NJ: Rowman & Littlefield.

Larrabee, M. J. (Ed.). (1993). *An ethic of care*. New York: Routlege.

MacIntyre, A. (1966). *A short history of ethics*. New York: Collier Books.

MacIntyre, A. (1990). *Three rival versions of moral enquiry*. Notre Dame, IN: University of Notre Dame Press.

Noddigs, N. (1984). *Caring: A feminine approach to ethics and moral education*. Berkeley, CA: University of California Press.

Rawls, J. (1971). *A theory of justice*. Cambridge, MA: Harvard University Press.

Ruddick, S. (1989). *Maternal thinking: Toward a politics of peace*. Boston: Beacon Press.

Singer, P. (Ed.). (1991). *A companion to ethics*. Oxford, UK: Blackwell.

Taylor, C. (1989). *Sources of the self: The making of the modern identity*. Cambridge, MA: Harvard University Press.

Taylor, C. (1992). *The ethics of authenticity*. Cambridge, MA: Harvard University Press.

Ethnic Conflict and Cooperation

Errol A. Henderson
University of Florida

GLOSSARY

Ethnic Group A group of people sharing a distinctive and enduring collective identity based on common cultural traits such as ethnicity, language, religion, or race, and perceptions of common heritage, shared experiences, and often common destiny. Such collectives are also called communal or identity groups.

Ethnic Nationalism The belief that the ethnic group comprises a national unit that has the right to possess its own sovereign state wherein full citizenship is a function of common ethnicity.

Ethnocentrism Refers to attitudes, beliefs, and practices that uncritically assume the superiority of one's own ethnic group.

Instrumentalism A perspective that maintains that interethnic conflict is more a result of elite manipulation than any inherent tendency for dissimilar ethnic groups to be more prone to conflict. Instrumentalists suggest that ethnicity is socially constructed and does not derive from any natural division of humankind.

Irredentism The pursuit of the acquisition of the population and/or territory for which a group or state suggests it is culturally associated.

Primordialism The view that interethnic conflict is a result of inherent differences between ethnic groups who naturally feel amity for their own ethnic group and enmity for those outside their ethnic group.

Secession Refers to the often violent attempt of a political entity (e.g. a region within a state) to separate from a larger political unit (e.g. a state) usually with the intent of establishing an independent state.

ETHNIC, OR INTERETHNIC, CONFLICT refers to disputes between contending groups who identify themselves primarily on the basis of ethnic criteria and who make group claims to resources on the basis of their collective rights. Ethnic criteria may include perceptions of shared culture, nationality, language, religion, and race. An ethnic group is a collective sharing a belief of common ancestry, a link with a specific territory, a perception of a shared culture, and a belief in a common destiny. This belief in a common ancestry owes as much if not more to myths than to genetics. To be sure, some ethnic communities may result from consanguineal or kinship ties, but to the greatest extent heritage is a function of belief and not genetic descent. It is inconceivable that somewhere in antiquity there are primordial parents of each ethnic group in the world. Nonetheless, myths of common descent are powerful inducements to ethnic identification. Such myths provide symbols around which elites can focus political, economic, and social activity. They provide emblems and totems representing in-group and out-group membership. Two factors are among the most significant bases of group identity: belief in a historic homeland; and the perception or practice of a shared culture. The latter is often expressed as shared language, religion, race, or customs.

I. INTRODUCTION

A link with a common territory provides the basis for the perception of historical continuity for the ethnic group. It is in reference to the historic territory that ethnic groups root their collective memories, their heritage, and their traditions. Much use is made of a mythologized history of a classical civilization associated with the homeland. This relationship is so powerful that groups detached from such homelands maintain their symbolic link to it often through the transmission of a nationalist history, folktales, legends, and cultural myths. Where ethnic groups are minorities outside of their traditional homeland, they often face discrimination, which reinforces their group identity around their collective persecution, which in turn intensifies their sense of ethnic identity.

Shared culture within ethnic communities provides for ethnic identification. Foremost among cultural commonalities are shared language and religion. Language is often viewed as the most essential criterion for ethnicity, but, linguistic commonality does not, in itself, suggest ethnic commonality—nor does religious commonality. Humans have many identities simultaneously and one's ethnic identity may crosscut rather than overlap one's language or religious group. For example, ethnically dissimilar Turks and Kurds share the common religion of Islam while one is linguistically Turkish and the other predominantly Kurmanji. Spaniards speak Spanish but so do Mexicans, Puerto Ricans, Dominicans, as well as many South Americans and some Africans. Bretons and Burgundians speak French but so do Quebecois and Haitians. The same can be said for religious similarity. Ethnically dissimilar Azeris, Kurds, Turks, Persians, Arabs, Malay, and Hausa-Fulani share a common religion (Islam). Buddhism subsumes many Asian ethnic groups and Christianity in Western Europe and the Americas is practiced by many different ethnic groups.

Interestingly, the distribution of these widely variable characteristics does not appear to be associated with conflict in any consistent manner. For example, ethnicity links the Irish inhabitants of Ireland but religious difference between Protestant and Catholic coethnics appear of greater salience and have come to define the conflict in Ulster. Linguistically and religiously similar Hutu and Tutsi have fashioned separate ethnic identities from their colonial past and have precipitated genocidal violence against each other in Rwanda and Burundi. While religious difference is a conflict-laden fault line between social groups in India, the superimposition of religion and ethnicity is associated with interethnic conflict in Sudan, Tibet, and Israel.

The persistence of multiple identities would seem to preclude the salience of a single identity among individuals and populations. It is often argued that where each of these factors is present it tends to reinforce and solidify ethnic identity; however, where these factors do not overlap, ethnic identity may be more malleable. To be sure, persons choose to emphasize one over the other for reasons of status, expediency, or in response to peer pressures. Whereas individuals may choose to identify with one or another aspect of their identity for personal, social, economic, or political reasons, one should not assume that factors operative at the individual level are identical to those operative at the group level. To determine the extent to which a conflict is in fact an "ethnic conflict" is hardly a straightforward exercise. The population of potential cases is quite diverse and often ambiguous owing largely to the absence of a general criteria for the categorization of such conflicts. For example, interethnic conflict ranges from the interaction of competing groups that—at its most bellicose—can take the form of civil wars, to wars between ethnically dissimilar states. Interethnic civil wars include cases such as the dispute among Serbs, Muslims, and Croats in the former Yugoslavia, or the conflicts in Liberia or Sudan; while interethnic interstate wars are epitomized by the Palestine (1948), Suez (1956), Six Day (1967), War of Attrition (1969–1970), October (1973), and Lebanese (1982) wars between Israel and various Arab states, or the First (1947) and Second Kashmir (1965), and Bangladesh (1971) wars between India and Pakistan.

Ethnicity as a concept is difficult to define, involving, as it does, a group's perceptions of identity and affinity. Ethnic conflict is also problematic as a category inasmuch as it appears to assume that ethnicity is the most salient issue in conflicts so designated. The presence of ethnicity as a variable does not suggest its centrality as a cause or correlate of intergroup conflict. Since virtually all intergroup conflict involves people possessing distinguishable if not different cultural traits, most intergroup conflicts—including most interstate wars—are "ethnic conflicts"; therefore, to label instances of such conflict as "ethnic conflicts" is superfluous. The basic difficulty is that too often scholars seem to implicitly accept the argument that ethnic differences provide the casus belli for these conflicts. For example, sudden convulsions of "ethnic violence," such as in the case of the 1994 Rwandan genocide, are often viewed as resulting from historic cultural gulfs. Hutu and Tutsi have no history of "ethnic conflict" prior to colonization; in fact they share common language and customs. While the story of Isaac and Ishmael is interesting mythology, Jews and Arabs have not been fighting since antiquity but intermittently since the 1920s. Serbs and Croats hardly fought each other prior to this century. In fact, intermarriage rates were quite high even up to the 1980s. The Sino-Vietnamese conflict of 1979 was not rooted in 1000 years of ethnic enmity but it had more to do with China's desire to check the Soviet Union's ally in Hanoi while supporting its own recently deposed ally Pol Pot in Cambodia.

Among the more persistent interethnic disputants in the 19th century were the Russian and Turks who fought three wars in that century, including the Crimean War from 1853 through 1856, which presumably resulted from Russia's attempt to protect its fellow Slavs (who were predominantly Christian) and the holy places in Palestine. At the time, the Ottoman Empire was home to millions of Slavs for whom Russia was an important ally since no later than the treaty of Kutchuk-Kainardji (1774); however, politically the empire was dominated by the Turks who were predominately Muslim. The Turks resisted the Russian incursion with the support of France and later Great Britain and Piedmont. However, instead of the "ethnic" label often given to this conflict, a compelling case can be made that Czar Nicholas simply used the pretext of the protection of Christians and the holy places in Palestine in order to rationalize his territorial demands for the Danubian principalities of Wallachia and Moldavia located within the declining Ottoman Empire. Although cultural dissimilarity among the original belligerents is apparent, this does not demonstrate that ethnic difference was a precipitant to the conflict.

Much of the confusion regarding the categorization of disputes as ethnically based or not can be avoided by use of the more appropriate phrase, "interethnic conflict," rather than "ethnic conflict," since the latter appears to suggest that the conflict itself derives from ethnicity instead of the actual issues of the dispute. Often the image of ethnic groups in conflict is an ideological construct of nationalist historians and politicians pursuing their own political ends. Additionally, with multiethnic states the norm in the system, we would expect an increased incidence of interethnic conflict within and among states were dissimilar ethnic groups inherently combative. Clearly, interethnic cooperation more than conflict, has been the norm.

It is important to understand how the pertinent issues to these conflicts arise and how societies are mobilized around ethnic identity. Heightened emphasis on ethnic exclusivism may generate conflict but how and why that occurs is unclear. Not only must elites assert the salience of ethnic criteria in order to mobilize their societies but the ethnicity argument must strike a cord within the ethnic population in such a way as to compel coethnics to follow. While the motivation to follow is an often neglected and rarely examined aspect of ethnic mobilization, one is reminded that elites can mobilize very disparate communities, and even "invent" communities, and move these societies to conflict. One example is provided by the Italian nationalist D'Azeglio's famous statement following the wars of unification: "We have made Italy, now we have to make Italians!"

Ethnic mobilization presupposes the salience of ethnic identity. An ethnic group has to perceive the political significance of its ethnicity before it can be mobilized for political action. To analyze interethnic conflict one must examine the conditions associated with the increased salience of ethnic identity. Therefore it is important to pose and answer two questions: (1) What compels groups to mobilize on the basis of ethnicity? and (2) To what extent, and under what conditions, are ethnic groups more likely to fight rather than cooperate?" The two dominant approaches to interethnic conflict attempt to answer these questions.

II. TWO DOMINANT APPROACHES TO INTERETHNIC CONFLICT

There are two dominant approaches to the study of interethnic conflict: primordialism and instrumentalism. Primordialists suggest the ubiquity of ethnocentrism. Ethnocentrism is the belief that one's ethnic in-group is superior and that ethnic out-groups are inferior. It also suggests the appropriateness of judging the world from the perspective of one's own ethnic group. Primordialists argue that the aggression of in-groups towards out-groups is rooted in a primordial urge linking group identity with certain ascriptive characteristics, often ethnicity and/or race. Thus ethnic identity, in this view, emerges naturally. Primordialists assume that relationships within in-groups are more peaceful, orderly, and supportive while relationships with out-groups are conflictual, anarchic, and destructive. Primordialists insist that ethnic similarity leads to cooperation and ethnic difference leads to interethnic conflict. Few theorists grant wholesale acceptance to primordialist arguments with the exception of sociobiologists following social Darwinist tenets.

Instrumentalists posit that interethnic conflict does not emerge from any "natural" division of groups into nations but is the result of elite manipulation of communal appeals in pursuit of their own interests. Instrumentalists conclude that cultural difference does not necessitate conflict, it only makes it easier for elites to move their societies closer to hostility and rivalry. More generally, instrumentalists insist that ethnicity is malleable and its boundaries and content subject to change. Instrumentalists emphasize the instances of positive orientation toward out-groups prevalent throughout social intercourse. Further, in-groups and out-groups are often subgroups within larger social organizations and social integration can encompass previously separated groups. For instrumentalists, ethnicity does not emerge naturally, but is a result of socialization under elite and communal pressures and orientations into the lifeways of one's dominant community. The socialization process inculcates common language, religion, customs, dress, food, and so on, but it also instills a sense of group fidelity and affinity while simultaneously inculcating a sense of out-group enmity. However, instrumentalists remind us that while powerful, these processes are neither uniform, singular, or irreversible. Clearly, groups into which persons are socialized are not always the ones they would like to belong to, feel loyalty to, or whose standards they adopt. People have multiple, often crisscrossing identities, and travel and intergroup communication often make these crisscrossing identities more salient than the singular ones that may have resulted from socialization. In fact, individuals are often socialized into groups that are multilingual, cosmopolitan, and quite gregarious toward ethnically dissimilar neighbors. Moreover there are members who are alienated from their communal groups as well as those who aspire to groups to which they do not belong or who accept the evaluative standards of an external group. In sum, instrumentalists maintain that primordialists adopt a myopic view of socialization and then promote this unique instance—which should only be considered as a special case—as representative of a general tendency. To be sure, socialization is an important mechanism for transferring ethnic amity toward in-groups and enmity toward out-groups; however, instrumentalists maintain, socialization is complex, malleable, and much less invariant than primordialists insist.

Not only do instrumentalists emphasize the greater prospect for intergroup cooperation and multiculturalism, but, eschewing the notion of the inherent tendency of in-group/out-group conflict, they implicitly suggest the dominant role of elite manipulation of cultural difference as a causal factor in interethnic conflict. At the extreme, some instrumentalists suggest that ethnicities are "constructed." Such assessments are only partially correct; for example, a perceived Chinese threat to Bugi, Javanese, and Minangkabau helped fuse those identities into ethnic Malay. While their brethren fight on the subcontinent as rival Hindu and Muslim, in South Africa and Uganda such groups identified primarily as Indians. Nonetheless, the boundary between Malay and Chinese is not imagined nor is the boundary among Acholi, Buganda, and Indian. While ethnic leaders may exploit perceived differences in order to promote their own interests, unless they respond to actual grievances and aspirations their movements flounder. In fact, efforts to "construct" ethnic identities without a cultural basis are often unsuccessful as evinced in the failure to promote the "Occitanian" identity in southern France in the 1960s, or the effort to create a "Pandanian" identity among northern Italians in the 1990s.

In sum, primordialists suggest a natural division of humanity into ethnic families that are prone to conflict while instrumentalists focus on the social construction of ethnicity and the role of elite manipulation of cultural difference as important factors in interethnic conflict. Early systematic research on the role of cultural similarity in conflict suggests a relationship between the distribution of ethnic groups and a state's level of internal conflict. The findings suggest that states that are ethnically diverse are at risk for interethnic conflict; states in which ethnic groups are relatively equally distributed are at highest risk for interethnic conflict; and states that are ethnically homogenous are the least likely to experience interethnic conflict. On the interstate level the findings have been less persuasive. Early research found, at best, weak relationships between cultural similarity and interstate conflict. Scholars suggested that ethnic similarity often appears to be associated with conflict due to the fact that ethnically similar groups often live close to each other with more opportunities to interact. Recent scholarship has begun to challenge these earlier findings with results that demonstrate that cultural variables are significant predictors to interstate conflict.

The two schools, primordialism and instrumentalism, are more ideal types than mutually exclusive frameworks, and most research on interethnic conflict borrows aspects of both. Both approaches suggest that ethnocentrism is an important precipitant to interethnic conflict. Synthesizing aspects of both primordialism and instrumentalism, scholars emphasize the role of displacement, territorial imperatives, relative deprivation, and ethnic divisions of labor as factors complicit in motivating ethnic groups to conflict. In the next section, we discuss each of these approaches, in turn, in order to flesh out the rationale motivating ethnic groups to conflict and cooperation.

III. EXPLANATIONS OF INTERETHNIC CONFLICT

Interethnic conflict has been largely explained by psychological, economic, and political models of conflict in the scholarly literature. Frustration and aggression-displacement models—owing largely to the work of Freud—suggest an animus of in-groups toward out-groups rooted in an innate human proclivity to aggression and group narcissism. Displacement models suggest that interethnic conflict represents a release of accumulated aggression within societies where proscriptions exist against violence toward group members. This violence is displaced to out-groups who are attacked less for material gain but as an outlet for accumulated aggression built up within the society by the inhibition of violence. Displacement is often rationalized through projection, transfer, reinforcement and pseudospeciation. These rationalizations provide powerful justifications for interethnic conflict and allow in-groups to be unmoved by discriminatory treatment of out-groups. The positive characterization of the in-group is associated with positive affect, and out-groups—which are viewed in opposition to the in-group—are vilified in accordance with the logical requirements of reducing cognitive dissonance. Theorists in this school point out that intergroup violence devolves from the congruence and disparity among beliefs and affective bonds.

Other scholars suggest that groups often have incompatible interests and goals and are often in competition for scarce resources. They demur from emphasizing displacement or the external projection of repressed aggression. Lorenz's work on the territorial imperative in human aggression focuses on what he considered as the drive for territorial acquisition as a basis for intergroup conflict. The territorial imperative has evolved from prehistory and serves as an environmental adaptation strategy for group survival in an environment of scarcity. The imperative is manifested in groups facing perceived challenges to scarce resources. The most important scarce resource is land, which provides for the well-being and security of the community.

The primary shortcoming of both displacement and territorial imperative models is that since the factors associated with conflict are alleged to be either innate or constant among human groups then one would expect that interethnic conflict would be an omnipresent phenomena, which it clearly is not. These models fail to explain why intergroup conflict appears to be quite rare for a phenomenon ostensibly resulting from innate human drives and group proclivities. This is a general shortcoming of sociobiological theses on human behavior. Recognizing such difficulties, scholars gave greater emphasis to human volition as well as political, economic, and social factors in explicating interethnic conflict. For example, diversionary models of interethnic conflict suggest that ethnic in-groups often target out-groups in order to foster in-group solidarity through fear of real or imagined external threat. In such instances groups suggest that ethnic difference provides "evidence" of an out-group's treachery or disloyalty in order to justify their mistreatment. This is especially prevalent in wartime. The Nazi persecution of Jewish citizens of Germany and the American internment of its citizens of Japanese descent during World War II are examples.

Relative deprivation models suggest that interethnic conflict results from perceived disparities between a group's actual status across some political, economic, or social dimension and its desired status with respect to other groups. These models suggest that a group's disposition, aspirations, and grievances are dependent upon the frame of reference in which they are conceived. They weigh their status and objectives in terms of a reference group. When a group views a reference group to be relatively more prosperous, a feeling of deprivation emerges that provides a basis for group mobilization. A prominent source of relative deprivation is the extent of economic inequality and the differences in political opportunities in a society. This sort of intergroup envy is considered to be the necessary condition for intergroup conflict and civil strife more generally. Relative deprivation is a latent disposition that is brought into actuality by mediating factors that allow for the politicization of group frustration. Politicization is more likely when normative justifications for political violence persist or when norms condemning violence are absent. Such justification may range from glorifications of violence such as found in the works of Sorel and Fanon to proscriptions of violence such as those promulgated by Gandhi and King. Opportunities provided by alternative channels for collective action may also mediate conflict. Finally, the concentration of power with respect to the state and dissidents is an important factor. The relationship appears curvilinear with conflict more likely where power balances are relatively equal and less likely when they are skewed. Where power is more evenly concentrated, frustrated groups have the resources to effectively challenge the state and the propensity for civil strife is likely to be high. Where power differentials are low, the society is highly atomized and organized groups can more easily overthrow the state. Where power concentration is skewed in favor of the state, dissidents are restrained by both the low likelihood of victory and the fear of quick suppression.

Relative deprivation theorists provide a plausible rationale for intergroup violence; however, they have been less successful at providing the threshold value or critical point at which deprivation leads to conflict. Therefore it is difficult to operationalize and test the core tenets of the model. Models such as these have been useful in explaining intergroup conflict in general but they have been less effective when applied to interethnic conflict. More successful models have focused on the factors giving rise to the creation of ethnic identity and ethnic mobilization. Discrimination that generates ethnic divisions of labor is probably the most significant inducement to ethnic mobilization. Ethnic divisions of labor exist where differences in economic status and occupational specialization reflects ethnic identity. Uneven economic development may give rise to ethnic divisions of labor. On the other hand, racial and ethnic divisions can be used by elites to divide the working class and prevent worker solidarity while increasing profits by maintaining a reservoir of replacement labor. In such systems, higher status occupations are reserved for the dominant ethnic group while other ethnic groups are lower on the occupational hierarchy. Economic differences, or class difference, come to reflect ethnic differences and shared economic niches reinforce ethnic divisions of labor.

Ethnic divisions of labor may have a less pernicious origin, emerging from inducements created by socioeconomic transitions especially those generated from industrialization. In such situations, ethnic mobilization is a response to structural changes wrought from industrialization and urbanization wherein altruism toward communities of origin (defined largely on the basis of ascriptive criteria) provide a basis for distribution networks. Such networks furnish incentives for cooperation among individuals with a common position in the division of labor. Emerging political structures in such transitional societies then provide the opportunities for ethnic mobilization.

Regardless of their origins, it is clear that economic discrimination in such systems becomes, by definition, ethnic discrimination. Therefore, the more intense and prevalent the economic discrimination the more likely that affected groups will mobilize in response to it. However, because of the overlap between ethnicity and class the mobilization can easily take on an ethnic flavor and economic demands can be made in the name of the ethnic group. In addition, those who resist these demands are more likely to consist of the more privileged economic/ethnic groups. Such groups are likely to be viewed as protecting their own favored economic and ethnic position. The resultant economic dispute is very likely to take on an ethnic dimension. A recent example is provided by the Liberian Civil War. Master Sergeant Doe's policies following his 1980 coup included the staffing of administrative posts with his Krahn coethnics and the dismissal of Gio and Mano officials from administrative posts. Rivals in the civil war reflected the interethnic antipathies resulting from Doe's selective staffing and discrimination. The irony is that the Krahn ethnic identity, only about 100 years in existence, emerged primarily from the division of Liberia into administrative sections during Americo-Liberian hegemony. It follows that the Liberian civil war is less an "ethnic conflict" born of "ancient antipathies" than a conflict in which ethnicity has become politicized through mobilization that emerged as a response to discriminatory staffing decisions.

Whether rooted in instrumental or primordial motivations—displacement, territorial imperatives, relative deprivation, or ethnic divisions of labor—ethnic identification can provide a powerful base from which groups mobilize for collective action. The political goals of such ethnic mobilization largely—although not exclusively—determine the extent to which interethnic violence will obtain. Where ethnic mobilization is accompanied by nationalism the results are often violent. It is these ethnically based nationalisms that are related to the most intense and severe interethnic conflicts.

IV. POLITICAL GOALS IN INTERETHNIC CONFLICT

The form that interethnic conflict takes is dependent on the political goals of the ethnic group, the political opportunity structures of the state where the mobilization occurs, and the extent of international involvement in the dispute. Probably the most important factor in interethnic conflict is the political goal of the ethnic group because that will largely determine the response of the state to its demands. In a more democratic political system one would expect a greater likelihood of accommodation and compromise with the mobilized interests of ethnic groups rather than outright repression. However, a state's response is not solely determined by regime type, it also depends on the state's economic capacity. If a state is unable or disinclined to accommodate what are perceived to be economic demands of mobilized ethnic groups it may pursue a policy of repression and in that way exacerbate the incipient interethnic conflict. A state's policy is also likely to reflect its past and present treatment of the mobilized ethnic group. Repression is more likely to accompany demands by groups that have faced historic or current discrimination. Beyond the state, external factors such as the presence of powerful ethnic allies in contiguous states will shape a state's response to internal ethnic groups demands. Initially, though, the political goals of the ethnic group such as domination, inclusion, or autonomy will largely determine the dimensions of the conflict.

Domination is quite common in practice, though, inclusion is often provided in varying degrees; however, the pursuit of autonomy is the most conflict-prone political goal of a mobilized ethnic group. That domination as a political goal is so prevalent may seem counterintuitive at first glance; however, when one remembers that most states are multiethnic, notwithstanding the malapropism of "nation-state," it is plain to see that in most countries ethnic domination of some sort is practiced. For example, in Britain the English dominate the Irish, Scots, and Welsh. Punjabis dominate minority ethnic groups in Pakistan. Persians dominate Azeri and Kurdish ethnic groups in Iran. European-Americans dominate African, Puerto Rican, and Mexican Americans in the United States. Han Chinese dominate other ethnic groups in China as surely as Russians dominated the multitudinous ethnic groups of the former Soviet Union. Domination refers to control of the state apparatus and the allocation of state resources, especially those governing the opportunities available to ethnic communities. Where membership and participation in the polity is restricted to the dominant group such as the case for Whites in South Africa under apartheid, subordination is usually manifested as de jure recognition of ethnic groups with de facto marginalization of ethnic outgroups. Palestinians in Israel have formal rights such as voting, holding political office, and due process although in practice they are a marginalized group that is effectively ostracized from political power and economic opportunity. Similarly, ethnic Chinese have citizenship in Malaysia and even have a political party in government. However, Malay dominance is maintained and reflected in the status of Malay as the official language, Islam as the state religion, a Malay sultan as head of state, and Bumiputra policies in the country affording Malay preferences in education, employment, government contracts, and sources of capital and credit.

Often ethnic groups aspire to inclusion on a nondiscriminatory basis within the host state. Civil rights movements such as those of African Americans in the 1960s pursue the dismantling of discriminatory policies and practices in government, employment, housing, and education, while often promoting a multicultural model of society with equality of opportunity for nondominant ethnic groups. Such programs may also lead toward proportional representation, consociations, and power-sharing strategies within states. These policies may also engender revanchism by a dominant group unwilling to cede the status quo. Such revanchism is evident among South African and American Whites facing vastly altered multicultural societies.

Autonomy is the quest for political independence such as in a federal system as pursued by Quebecois in Canada or accomplished by the Flemish and Walloons in Belgium. A more violent form of autonomy occurs when ethnic groups pursue secession in order to form their own autonomous states. This process involves mobilization through appeals to ethnic nationalism. Nationalism is the view that the political and the cultural unit should be congruent. Self-determination is the doctrine that national groups have the right to decide which political authority will represent or rule them. It is recognized in international law and was articulated to recognize the right of ethnic groups against foreign domination. Ethnic nationalism asserts this right of self-determination for the ethnic group, and usually maintains that the group has a right to possess a sovereign state. The nation is the largest identity group to which most individuals swear fealty. As such, there is a shift of the amity/enmity of primary groups to the "nation-state." The relationship that obtains engenders patriotism within the new states while breeding ethnocentrism and intolerance towards ethnic outgroups within their territorial boundaries. When ethnicity becomes the basis of nationalist mobilization, that is, where ethnic groups mobilize for political autonomy and the possession of a state; the potential for interethnic conflict is heightened. Many of the wars of this century were the result of either groups pursuing self determination or states denying it. After World War II, such struggles for national self-determination often took the form of wars against colonial domination (e.g., in Vietnam, Algeria, Kenya, Mozambique, Angola, Guinea-Bissau). Colonialism or imperialism also often has a strong ethnocentrist element. Colonial powers often rationalized their subjugation of colonized peoples on the basis of the latter's alleged cultural inferiority. For example, the colonial subjugation of African peoples was rationalized as part of "the White man's burden" to "civilize" Africans instead of a racist foreign policy that violated the sovereignty of nations and the human rights of ethnic groups on the African continent.

It is not clear at what point an ethnic group becomes a nation. A nation is often conceived simply as a self-conscious ethnic group determined to possess a state. The designation of a group as either a nation or an ethnic group can be quite arbitrary and often reflects ideological concerns and the relative power of the groups contending. Often nationalist groups insist on their groups' nationalist claims while simultaneously denying that right to other groups. The relationship is referred to as the ABC paradox. The ABC paradox is a condition wherein nation B invokes the principle of self-determination against nation A but denies it to nation C. For example, Bengalis in Bangladesh fought Pakistan for their independent state but now repress the calls for autonomy from the largely Buddhist (Bengalis are largely Muslim) Chakmas of the Chittagong Hill region. These groups have suffered governmental discrimination, including forced relocation, murder, rape, and the desecration of their religious centers. Jews in various European states following the Nazi genocide pursued Zionism (Jewish nationalism) to establish the state of Israel in the former Palestine mandate. Once established on the basis of the right of Zionist self-determination they rejected the national status of ethnic Palestinians and denied the legitimacy of Palestinian nationalism.

Kurds seeking the establishment of an independent Kurdish state (Kurdistan) view themselves as a nation while Iraqi, Iranian, and Syrian leaders consider them as a nettlesome ethnic group within their territorial boundaries. In Turkey not only is Kurdish nationality denied but the Kurdish ethnic identity is denied by Turkish political elites who refer to Kurds in their state as "mountain Turks." A reverse process is at work in Bulgaria where the existence of ethnic Turks is denied and their population of over one million is referred to as "Islamicized Bulgarians." Similarly, Polish nationalists during the interwar years simply refused to accept that there was a Ukrainian nationality within their state. Descendants of Dutch settlers in South Africa viewed themselves as a distinct nationality and even appropriated the name African (Afrikaner) for themselves while denying the national status of the Zulu, Xhosa, Ndebele, and other Africans who peopled the area, referring to them as Bantu.

It should be clear then that a state's policy toward its cultural groups may dampen or increase the likelihood of interethnic conflict. On the other hand, discriminatory and repressive policies aimed at indigenous groups are likely to exacerbate interethnic tensions. This is tantamount to the pursuit of a domination strategy by the dominant culture group within the state. The pursuit of autonomy by a dominant group within a state may take the form of irredentism—the pursuit of the acquisition of the population and/or territory for which a group or state suggests it is culturally associated. The concept is derived from the Italian irredenta (unredeemed) territories of Trente, Dalmatia, Trieste, and Fiume which though ethnically Italian remained under Austrian or Swiss rule following the unification of Italy. Today, as in the past, irredentism is one of the more violent forms of interethnic conflict. For example, Somalia's attempt to annex the territory and populations of ethnic Somali in the Ogaden region of Ethiopia led to the bloody Ogaden War in the Horn of Africa. Even Hitler invoked irredentist claims in his annexation of Austria and occupation of the Sudeten region of Czechoslovakia. In this way irredentism, a form of interethnic conflict, was a precipitant to World War II.

Regardless of the political goals of groups, regimes, or third parties, mobilizations based in ethnic nationalist demands are the most conflict prone because (1) group members often identify intensely with ethnic nationalist demands and are willing to make great sacrifices to achieve them; (2) such mobilizations more often generate state repression; and (3) they invite third party intervention to quell the conflict that often risks spilling over into neighboring territories especially when refugees from the conflict flow across state borders. However, other political, economic, and cultural factors, as well, seem to increase the likelihood of conflict between ethnic groups. The prominence of several of these factors in instigating interethnic conflicts has led scholars to regard them as early warning indicators of interethnic conflict.

V. EARLY WARNING INDICATORS OF INTERETHNIC CONFLICT

With the violent potential of interethnic conflict so readily apparent, scholars have begun to focus on early warning indicators of potential interethnic conflict. These indicators are evident in the political, economic, and cultural relationships between groups within and across states. Political factors include the type of political regime, the extent of multipartyism, democratization, and alliance ties. Democracies, to the extent that they offer diverse channels for political interests and various bases for mobilization, tend to ameliorate interethnic tension. However, in underdeveloped states multipartyism, which is often associated with democracy, tends to instability. Often this is owed to the congruence of political party membership and ethnic identity. In such an arrangement, elections are little more than censuses and political interests are defined in ethnic terms. In some political systems where ethnicity determines representation actual censuses may be destabilizing since they determine the disposition of political spoils and the control of the political apparatus (e.g., Lebanon, Nigeria).

Since autocracies use repression to check ethnic mobilization, the incidence of interethnic conflict may appear low. This, it is argued, is how Stalin was alleged to have kept a lid on the interethnic rivalries in the Soviet Union. However, one should remember that in autocratic regimes interethnic conflict usually takes the form of the targeting of ethnic groups by the state. In such situations what results is often democide (state-sanctioned murder of its citizens) or genocide (state-sanctioned murder of specific cultural groups) such as was attempted by Stalin against the Ukrainians, or by the Hutu against the Tutsi most recently in Rwanda, and by Tutsi against Hutu previously in Burundi.

Clearly autocracy is associated with interethnic conflict; however, democratization in autocratic regimes may be an early warning indicator of interethnic conflict as well. Recent history reinforces the notion that the breakdown of the political order associated with transitions from autocracy can exacerbate cultural fissures in the short term as groups seek to fill the power vacuum resulting from the declining authoritarian power by mobilizing on the basis of identity. In the presence of institutional breakdown, multilateral assistance that does not include arms transfers to any party appear to be associated with reduced interethnic conflict while unilateral aid that includes the provision of arms is associated with an increased likelihood of interethnic conflict.

Regardless of regime type, states that utilize ethnic criteria for citizenship are more likely to experience interethnic conflict. The imposition of a state religion or language in a manner that restricts the political participation of culture groups often augurs interethnic strife. Suppression of dissent, discriminatory legislation, the denial of citizenship rights to members of targeted cultural groups, the failure to redress discriminatory practices, and the failure to prosecute those who engage in discriminatory practices are also precursors of interethnic conflict.

Among the economic early warning indicators the most prominent is the development of ethnic divisions of labor. Conflict is more likely when groups move out of traditional spheres and contend for occupations where they were historically barred or where the dominant group does not intend to cede entry. In the first half of this century, recently urbanized African Americans who left the rural South and the traditional plantation economies were set upon by European Americans intent on preventing their access to urban factory jobs. The Notting Hill riots in Britain were a similar instance of this sort of interethnic conflict. A similar process is evident today with regard to Turks in Germany and Mahgrebins in France. Ethnic divisions of labor may also inoculate societies from interethnic conflict by providing occupational niches for immigrant ethnic groups. It is important to remember, though, that an ethnic division of labor is always potentially a basis for ethnic mobilization especially in the presence of perceived economic discrimination.

Cultural early warning indicators include the distribution of ethnic groups within states. States that are very diverse usually are not threatened because the organization of ethnic groups as coalitions is usually required for political action and to the extent that such coalition building is not dominated by a single group then it probably will not engender ethnocentrism. Homogenous states do not have significant ethnic fault lines to experience the violent cultural tectonics necessary for interethnic conflict, however, they may experience other types of conflict. For example, Somalia consists primarily of ethnic Somalis and is one of the most homogenous states in the world, nonetheless, it disintegrated due to the intraethnic violence of rival clans.

Moderate levels of homogeneity appear to be the most conflict prone especially where the groups are interspersed and not simply concentrated in one region.

Regional concentrations can be more effectively managed by elites but may also concentrate ethnic power in such a way that secession is pursued. The dispersal of groups results in ethnic intermingling that may reduce interethnic tensions and even allow for assimilation. On the other hand, in interspersed communities increased interaction also provides greater opportunities for conflict and ethnic sparks may lead to conflagrations that quickly spread and are less amenable to elite management. Further, refugee flows may upset fragile interethnic balances in interspersed regions providing justifications for elites intent on scapegoating immigrant groups.

In addition, a history of ethnic discrimination, previous interethnic conflict, the teaching of ethnocentric history, and the popularization of ethnic discrimination in the media are warning signs of interethnic conflict. The best predictor to future interethnic conflict is previous interethnic conflict. The teaching of ethnocentric history persists largely due to the fact that often history is written to justify, rationalize, and celebrate conquest and subjugation. In the United States, the struggle to provide multicultural curricula is part of the process of challenging the ethnocentric curriculum that has been prevalent throughout its educational system. In South Africa, White violence accompanied Black students' resistance to the teaching of the White settler's language, Afrikaans, in their schools. An extreme case of the impact of the popularization of ethnic discrimination in the media is provided by the Rwandan case where radio broadcasts not only fomented the genocide in that country but included instructions for its execution. For many theorists, these examples provide evidence that states across the range of levels of development are vulnerable to some form of interethnic conflict. Prevention, mediation, and intervention in interethnic conflict require paying attention to these and other early warning indicators. Failure to attend to such indicators often leads to the intensification and expansion of interethnic conflict.

VI. THE EXPANSION OF INTERETHNIC CONFLICT

Research suggests that the most violent intergroup conflicts begin with a dispute over some value-related issue that leads to crisis. A study by Vasquez demonstrates that crises intensify and disputes expand as a function of several factors: territorial contiguity, alliances, rivalry, contagion, and a breakdown of the political order. These factors intensify rivalry and lead to contagion in situations of political breakdown such as in the former Yugoslavia and in the Great Lakes region of Africa. Interethnic conflict appears to follow a similar epidemiology.

Contiguity is one factor in interethnic conflict insofar as opportunities for conflict are increased as a function of the increased number of interaction opportunities provided by proximity. For example, the contiguity of Kurdistan with Syria, Turkey, Iran, and Iraq is such that conflict among Kurds and their rivals often spills over into other states. The same can be said for the conflict in the Great Lakes region in Africa where refugee flows from interethnic conflict in Rwanda spilled over and exacerbated the Tutsi-inspired rebellion in the southeastern Zaire (now the Democratic Republic of Congo) and has led to refugee related conflicts with Tanzania, Uganda, and Burundi. Clearly, Greek and Turkish contiguity has been an important factor in exacerbating the conflict in Cyprus just as Great Britain's proximity to Ireland exacerbates the conflict in Ulster. Vietnam's proximity to Cambodia provided access for Hanoi's invasion and overthrow of the Khmer Rouge in the face of Pol Pot's repression of ethnic Vietnamese.

One may argue that geographical neighbors are more likely to be both culturally similar and prone to conflict. Common borders and territorial contiguity being such powerful factors in interstate conflict, it follows that cultural cousins have a higher probability of being involved in disputes, especially disputes over territory. This argument suggests that interethnic conflict is overstated and that since cultural cousins are more often neighbors, and neighbors are more likely to fight; distance over ethnicity is the significant variable in interethnic conflict. This hearkens back to the territorial imperative arguments of Lorenz and the ethologists.

The role of alliances in spreading interethnic conflict is apparent as well. For example, alliances between Tamil separatists and the Indian government have played a role in the internationalization of the interethnic conflict in Sri Lanka. In the 1990s the Tamil Tigers and other separatist Tamil organizations maintained offices in India while New Delhi air-dropped relief supplies to respond to the (Sinhalese dominated) Sri Lankan government's military offensive against Tamils in the Jaffna peninsula. In this way alliances between Tamils (mainly Hindu) and India served to intensify and expand the conflict prior to a short-lived Indian sponsored cease-fire. The role of alliances is also manifest in the genocide of the Armenians by the Young Turks during WW1. While neighboring Greece could oversee the treatment of their coethnics along the Greek-Turkish border, Armenians were without a coethnic state to protect their welfare and to offer a countervailing force against Turkish oppression of its minority citizens. The interethnic violence that ensued resulted in the killing of more than one million Armenians.

The presence of alliances between repressive governments and other states may also increase interethnic conflict as countries turn their backs on their allies' treatment of their ethnic minorities. This was especially evident during the Cold War where Western states supported regimes repressing their ethnic minorities such as those in the former Zaire and the Philippines in attempts to balance perceived Soviet threats. A similar argument can be made for Israel's treatment of its Palestinians and apartheid South Africa's treatment of its African citizens. Both states' discriminatory policies were rationalized in the West on the basis that they were bastions of anticommunism in regions that were viewed as strategically or at least economically important to Western interests. Among the worst examples, the presence of great power alliance links with the Indonesian government is associated with the seldom-cited state-sponsored genocide of East Timorisians in Indonesia. Hardly an exclusive phenomenon of Western foreign policy, a similar relationship was evident in the case of Soviet support for Ethiopia, which overlooked Amharic dominance of Eritreans, Oromos, and Tigraens. Similarly, Communist China, in their ongoing rivalry with Vietnam, supported Pol Pot's repressive regime in Cambodia, which committed genocide against its own people as well as thousands of ethnic Vietnamese.

Factors such as contiguity and alliances intensify and expand interethnic conflict and create enduring rivalry between ethnic belligerents. Rivalry in interethnic disputes leads to a rigidity in decision making that reflects the difficulty of resolving conflicts associated with the often transcendent stakes of interethnic conflict. Rivalry allows interethnic disputes to persist as compromise with ethnic rivals becomes indefensible. Those who undertake such compromises are often viewed as "selling out" to historic enemies. Concessions may generate reprisals from one's own communal group as was evident in the assassination of Israeli prime minister, Yitzhak Rabin, by a Jewish fundamentalist as he pursued negotiations with the Palestinians. A little more than a decade earlier Islamic fundamentalists assassinated the Egyptian head of state, Anwar Sadat, after he had negotiated a peace accord with Israel.

Interethnic rivalries often take on a zero-sum form as issues and stakes in dispute become less concrete and are infused with symbolic value and transcendent quality. Such stakes become less tangible, less resolvable, and more contentious. What results is the use of punishment strategies to force concessions from the opponent. However, such strategies usually result in increased rigidity on the part of the rival. Further, leaders may risk losing their reputations for credibility if they compromise such transcendent issues. These cultural factors intensify all stakes by increasing the symbolic value of issues, inducing cognitive rigidity on the part of the antagonists, creating a context where positions are assumed to be consistent with identity instead of divorced from them. In such an instance parties are less concerned with "what one believes" and are more concerned with "to what group one belongs." Disputes over territory are the most likely to be associated with conflict for two related reasons. First, land provides the demarcation for the state itself, and thus provides an important dimension of a state's sovereign identity. In addition, a state's chief function is to provide for the security and welfare for the inhabitants of its territory. Security, in its most fundamental sense is the protection from territorial incursions by foreign powers, and social welfare is largely a function of the capacity of the land to provide the material subsistence upon which the inhabitants' well-being relies. The fact that territory provides a basis for these fundamental political and economic requisites creates a condition whereby land is the cardinal resource for states. Evidence of this fact is provided by empirical work that demonstrates that territorial issues are most likely to give rise to violent interstate conflict. Since land is such a valued resource its redistribution is usually only accomplished following armed conflict. Nonetheless, redistributions of land in the post-World War II era have often been nonviolent, especially in the period of decolonization. This leads to our second point with regard to the significance of territory in interethnic conflict. In such cases, land, already a highly valued resource, is often imbued with culturally endowed qualities making its dispensation even more contentious and difficult. Endowed with symbolic value in the context of interethnic disputes such territorial issues are among the most intractable and enduring in world history. One need only reflect on the ongoing struggles regarding the Christian, Jewish, and Muslim "holy lands" in the Middle East to appreciate how nettlesome such interethnic disputes become. Such struggles are hardly amenable to the usual "give and take" of mediation required to resolve complex issues. The convergence of cultural, political, and economic factors in interethnic territorial disputes may help to explain why irredentist and secessionist struggles are often so persistent and violent.

Interethnic conflict seems to intensify intergroup conflict in at least two ways. First, cultural values infuse the issues to the dispute with symbolic and transcendent qualities. In such instances decision makers are compelled to become more rigid and inflexible as concrete stakes take on symbolic value. Second, cultural factors infuse territory, the most conflict-prone agent in a dispute, with transcendental value and therefore intensifies its already conflict-prone nature, making it more intangible and making disputes regarding it more irresolvable. These types of barriers to conflict resolution are emblematic of interethnic conflicts while they are assumed to be mitigated in disputes within ethnic groups.

The accumulation of intractable disputes leads to enduring interethnic conflicts. Such persistent interethnic conflict may lead to institutional breakdown as has occurred in Lebanon and in the former Yugoslavia. Political opportunity is provided by institutional breakdown as political access becomes unlimited and unrestrained competition emerges approximating a Hobbesian state of nature. Scholars emphasize that political decay (especially of empires such as the Soviet Union or Austria-Hungary) often creates an institutional vacuum that resembles the global anarchy. Under such conditions, what results is a sort of ethnic group security dilemma wherein the "groupness" of one set of individuals is perceived as inherently threatening to another. In such situations the security of the ethnic group is often viewed primarily as a function of its group solidarity and its military capability. Group solidarity reinforces military capability and strong group identity is viewed as necessary to group survival while threatening to other groups. In such environments interethnic cooperation is difficult. However, even in the case of societal transformation the resultant competition for political resources does not necessarily result in interethnic violence. Czechoslovakia's "Velvet Divorce" is one of the rare instances of a relatively nonviolent resolution of interethnic disputes in the context of societal transformation—in this case secession. Nonetheless, the combination of these factors—territorial contiguity, alliances, rivalry, contagion, and a breakdown of the political order—often results in an expansion of the conflict beyond the original belligerents.

Strategies to reduce the likelihood of the expansion of interethnic conflict involve the attenuation of the factors associated with the enlargement of the violence. Moreover, multilateral peacemaking may be an important strategy to contain and reduce interethnic conflict. Both peacemaking and peacekeeping have shown some success in reducing the short-term violence associated with interethnic conflict to the extent that such interventions have provided buffers between antagonists such as in the conflicts in the Middle East and Cambodia. In the long term, however, it is important to foster cooperative environments among groups within and across states. The requisites for interethnic cooperation are briefly outlined in the following section.

VII. INTERETHNIC COOPERATION

First, we are reminded that interethnic cooperation occurs quite frequently in societies and is the modal form of interethnic activity. However, interethnic cooperation is more difficult where scarce resources are sought by competing groups as is usually the case in most modern states. Since most states are multiethnic, state leaders must be vigilant in their pursuit and advocacy of nondiscriminatory policies in their societies. For this reason, interethnic cooperation is largely a function of purposive policies aimed at reducing interethnic tensions and eliminating exploitable opportunities for elite manipulation of ethnic divisions. Actual or perceived discrimination is probably the most important factor in interethnic conflict because it provides the basis for the perceived need to recognize the salience of ethnicity and to mobilize around ethnic identity.

Interethnic cooperation is not only incumbent upon the timely identification and response to early warning indicators of interethnic conflict; but Horowitz's research suggests several strategies by which to contain, limit, channel, and manage interethnic conflict and to promote cooperation. These strategies include: dispersal, promotion of intraethnic over interethnic cleavages, coalition policies, promotion of nonethnic cleavages, and reducing disparities between ethnic groups.

Dispersal may take the form of developing a federal system wherein political spoils and opportunities are not defined simply by one group's possession of the political center. In such a system ethnic group interests—hence ethnic mobilization—will not converge around the center, attending instead to the diverse and dispersed points of power within the system. Interethnic conflict, then, may seem less a zero sum game exacerbated by a sense of urgency born of fears of political subjugation. Conflicts that do emerge may be localized and losses in one area may be offset by gains in others. States may also attempt to foster intraethnic divisions in order to offset interethnic conflict. This policy intends that allegedly more benign subethnic identification competes with and undermines more overarching and more deadly ethnic group identification. Social class or region may be emphasized as countervailing pressures to ethnic identity. One shortcoming is that such a policy runs the risk of intensifying intraethnic cleavages leading to violence within groups that may spill over into larger domains.

Electoral inducements such as consociationalism and proportional representation may promote interethnic coalitions that may foster cooperation. Since cooperation is more likely under more open political structures and healthy economic conditions, policies of liberalization and growth are often promoted as strategies for violence reduction. While democracy is not immune from interethnic conflict; it is associated with decreased levels of interethnic strife. On the other hand, there is a scholarly consensus that autocratic political structures engender state repression while economic downturns provide the opportunity for scapegoating targeted ethnic groups such as was the case in interwar Germany. However, interethnic cooperation is also possible in single party and poor states such as in Nyerere's Tanzania.

In sum, state leaders can reduce the likelihood and impact of interethnic violence by pursuing policies that provide redress for previous wrongs while promoting antidiscriminatory policy in the present. States can ensure open political processes and timely prosecution of those who perpetrate violence against culture groups. They can also promote a rigorous public discourse on how best to resolve interethnic issues and promote free participation in a broad range of voluntary and public organizations for their citizenry. This usually requires the skillful management of different issue areas, as well as different policy domains (e.g., domestic constituents and foreign audiences). The prospects for the reduction of interethnic tension appear greater in more democratic, economically stable, and culturally nonpolarized societies.

The international community also has an important role to play in interethnic relations as states fulfill their responsibility under the Convention on the Prevention and Punishment of the Crime of Genocide and intervene in cases of widespread interethnic conflict. States should insist on the physical protection of culture groups and should encourage governments to provide equal protection under the law to all of their citizens. States should also provide legal assistance to governments acting in good faith that require technical assistance to strengthen their legal systems. They can speak out against violations of norms regarding the treatment of culture groups and should protest, censure, condemn, and sanction those states not in compliance with such norms. States can also help to provide an international clearinghouse on the treatment of culture groups through IGOs and NGOs in order to peacefully resolve interethnic conflicts.

All told, policies intended to mitigate interethnic tensions must attend to the political, economic, and cultural factors that give rise to interethnic disputes and seek strategies to resolve these issues at the individual, state, regional, and global system level. The most important factors include the attenuation of discriminatory policies at the state level and the promotion of human rights through multilateral intervention at the international level. The scholarship on interethnic conflict suggests that multidimensional approaches appear best suited to create an environment conducive to the mulitcultural flourishing of human societies.

VIII. CONCLUSION

Interethnic conflict is neither ubiquitous nor irresolvable; however, it does pose a persistent problem to the multiethnic states that comprise our global system. It appears that attempts to reduce the incidence of such conflict should attend to the issues around which ethnic groups mobilize. Once we determine the issues under dispute we will be better equipped to resolve the conflicts that arise from them. This approach demands that analysts not assume out of hand that ethnic difference is the main factor "causing" interethnic conflict. There is little evidence to support the contention that either interethnic similarity or dissimilarity is associated with civil or international conflict. Nonetheless, certain factors appear to be associated with what is commonly conceived as interethnic conflict. The overlapping of language, religion, and ethnicity within nondemocratic systems with ethnic divisions of labor and a history of past and current discrimination seem to be associated with the increased incidence of interethnic conflict. The reduction, management, or prevention of interethnic conflict appears to require the reduction of these characteristics and conditions. Interethnic cooperation requires attentiveness on the part of state leaders to abjure discriminatory policies, to redress past wrongs, to provide for political representation and economic opportunity, to foster multicultural education, and to assist in the promotion of an international environment that is conducive to the peaceful resolution of disputes.

Also See the Following Articles

CLAN AND TRIBAL CONFLICT • CULTURAL ANTHROPOLOGY STUDIES • ENEMY, CONCEPT AND IDENTITY OF • ETHNICITY

AND IDENTITY POLITICS • GENOCIDE • RITUAL AND SYMBOLIC BEHAVIOR • TERRITORIAL DISPUTES

Bibliography

Brown, M. (Ed.). (1994). *Ethnic conflict and international security*. Princeton, NJ: Princeton.

Brown, C., & Karim, F. (eds.). (1995). *Playing the "communal card." Communal violence and human rights*. New York: Human Rights Watch.

Esman, M. (1992). *Ethnic Politics*. Ithaca, NY: Cornell.

Gurr, T. (ed.). (1993). *Minorities at risk: A global view of ethnopolitical conflict*. Washington, DC: US Institute of Peace.

Gurr, T., & Harff, B. (1994). *Ethnic conflict in world politics*. New York: Westview.

Henderson, E. (1997). Culture or contiguity: "ethnic conflict," the similarity of states, and the onset of war, 1820–1989. *Journal of Conflict Resolution*, *41*, 5 (October), 649–668.

Horowitz, D. (1985). *Ethnic groups in conflict*. Los Angeles: University of California.

Huntington, S. (1996). *The clash of civilizations and the remaking of world order*. New York: Simon & Schuster.

Mazrui, A. (1990). *Cultural forces in world politics*. London: James Currey.

Midlarsky, M. (ed.). (1992). *The internationalization of communal strife*. New York: Routledge.

Ryan, S. (1995). *Ethnic conflict and international relations*. (2nd Ed.). Brookfield, VT: Dartmouth.

Ethnicity and Identity Politics

Colin Wayne Leach
Swarthmore College

Lisa M. Brown
University of Florida

GLOSSARY

Affirmative Action An umbrella term for policies and programs that recruit subordinate groups, such as women, people with disabilities, and people of certain ethnic groups, for educational and occupational opportunities.

Dominant Group A group within a society that has high status and/or disproportionate control over power and resources.

Ingroup A group to which a person feels he or she belongs.

Majority Group A subgroup of people that consists of the larger part of a specified population.

Minority Group A subgroup of people that consists of the smaller of two or more groups from a given population.

Outgroup A group to which a person feels that he or she does not belong.

Subordinate Group A group within a society that has limited access to power, resources, and social status.

ETHNICITY is often central to identity politics, which is a social and political movement or maneuver that emphasizes the agenda of a particular group. This emphasis on identity may foster conflict and violence. However, while divisiveness may be a byproduct of subordinate identity politics, it often is the goal of dominant identity politics. This article discusses the frequent use of ethnic identity as the foundation for political strategies, struggles, and movements by illustrating the functions identity serves, and thereby exposing the often political nature of ethnicity and the frequently ethnic nature of politics.

I. INTRODUCTION

Many believe political activity centered around ethnic identity is a major source of conflict in the world today. It is argued that the world is in the throes of an ethnic revival that threatens to wrench apart established systems of order. The apparent increase in ethnicity-based solidarity and political activity is most often attributed to the opportunity presented by recent, largely unforeseen, shifts in the nature of political, economic, and moral authority. The dissolution of several multi-ethnic states, such as the Soviet Union, Czechoslovakia, and Yugoslavia, has opened the way for a new wave of ethnic group mobilization in places like Uzbekistan, Latvia, Slovakia, Croatia, and Serbia. As in the period of rapid African, Asian, and Caribbean decolonization in the middle of the 20th century, ethnic identity has become the currency of deferred aspirations for political, economic, and cultural empowerment. This is no less true within existing nation-states, as groups like the Basques in Spain, the Hutu in Rwanda, the Tamils in Sri Lanka, and the Flemish in Belgium use ethnic identity to mobilize and maneuver people in order to challenge existing societal arrangements.

In this age of political, economic, and moral uncertainty, many view the politics of ethnic identity as an attempt by those with little power to affirm their threatened identities and to assert their claims for material resources and political clout. As with most subordinate groups, their main bargaining tool is the threat of continual contestation and societal instability. As such, ethnic identity politics constitute a threat to established authorities and the centralizing values, such as individual rights, majority rule, and a homogeneous national identity, upon which their governance is based. In the popular view, it is the groups small in number, low in power, and hungry for resources—such as the Chechens in Russia, the Catholic-Irish in Ulster, the Québécois in Canada, native peoples in North America, indigenous groups in Latin America, and the Maori in New Zealand—that assert ethnic identity as a political strategy by which their lots can be improved.

This view of ethnic identity politics frames ethnic identity as a tool used by the politically less powerful to *oppose* the status quo. The perception is that subordinate or minority ethnic groups are the causes of conflict. However, this perspective leaves unexamined the role of ethnicity and identity politics in the *construction* and *maintenance* of political power by dominant and majority groups. Rather than being solely "a weapon of the weak," ethnic identity politics may be central to modern forms of state formation and maintenance as well as their contestation. For example, the early development of modern nation-states relied greatly on the use of majority or dominant ethnic identity and its associated politics. The political entities of France, Germany, Spain and New Zealand were all based on the articulation of a national identity that was, to some degree, ethnic in nature. Certain ethnic features were consolidated into a national identity while other ethnic features were excluded. In Spain, for example, Castilian Spanish was made the official national language despite the fact that those in the regions of Galicia, the Basque provinces, and Catalonia speak distinct languages. In a similar manner, ethnic identity is an important part of contemporary political efforts to maintain established authorities in increasingly pluralistic states such as the United States, Canada, Germany, India, and Russia. Rather than being an instrumental strategy designed to take advantage of a crisis in political authority, ethnic identity politics have been and continue to be central to the workings of modern nation-states. In fact, it may be difficult to separate modern politics from either identity politics or ethnicity.

In this article we examine ethnic identity politics by first reviewing the respective roles of ethnic identity and politics in group conflict. In discussing ethnic identity politics we try to explain its prevalence, with special attention to its possible psychological and social functions. We then review the ways in which the political process is rooted in conflict, as well as the special place that group identity has in politics. Next, we describe ethnic identity politics as a dialectical struggle for power by dominant and subordinate groups, with each using ethnic identity to mobilize and maneuver their constituencies. Such contestation can be violent or peaceful, and we examine the factors important to each approach. This includes a comparison of the decidedly nonviolent philosophies of M. K. Gandhi and M. L. King, Jr. with the more ambivalent perspective of Frantz Fanon. In a concluding section we address the possible futures of ethnicity-based identity politics, with a special interest in the impact of globalism. Throughout this article we review the constructs of ethnic identity and politics from both a *macrostructural* level of analysis (drawing mainly from work in sociology, political science, and anthropology) and a *microstructural* level of analysis (drawing mainly from psychosocial research).

II. THE ROLE OF ETHNIC IDENTITY AND POLITICS IN CONFLICT

As mentioned in the introduction, many observers believe that ethnic identity politics produce and promote conflict and violence. Understanding how this happens, however, is made more difficult by the fact that both ethnic identity and politics are used as separate social explanations in scholarship on peace, conflict, and violence. Their combination in the term "ethnic identity politics" offers little clarification of which of the constituent elements, or which particular combination of them, leads to conflict. Is it ethnic identity itself, so that any collective identification around ethnicity will, by its exclusion of certain nonmembers, lead to competition and conflict? If so, this suggests that politics is but one arena in which the conflict over ethnic identity is played out. Another possibility is that conflict is likely only when ethnic identity is used as a tool in political battles. This suggests that something about the political context makes ethnic identity particularly volatile. These two possibilities hint at the complicated relationship between ethnic identity and politics. They also suggest some of the many ways in which the combination of the two in "ethnic identity politics" may lead to conflict. Given this complexity we will examine ethnic identity and politics separately, with special attention to the role of each in intergroup conflict, before discussing their combination.

A. Ethnic Identity

1. Explaining the Prevalence of Ethnic Identity

There is little doubt that ethnicity is the most widely used description of group identity in the world today. This prevalence may be due to (1) the way ethnicity is commonly conceptualized by both scholars and lay people, (2) the special place ethnicity has had in the formation of modern nation-states, and (3) the subjective reality and psychosocial benefits of ethnic identification. We discuss these three possible explanations in turn.

First, the conceptualization view proposes that ethnicity is a popular description of mass identity only because it encompasses so many of the other forms of group identity discussed in the modern period; the term ethnicity can refer to "race," culture, geographic region, language/dialect, religion, and sometimes economic or social position. Ethnicity is often used as a proxy for all of these terms and is also used to describe groups that are characterized by some, often complicated, combination of them. For example, identity politics and group conflict in Northern Ireland is often described as ethnic without much concern for the specific contributions of its religious (Protestant/Catholic), political (Unionist/Nationalist), national (British/Irish), power (dominant/subordinate), numerical (majority/minority), geographic (rural/urban; Northern Ireland/Ireland/Britain), or sociolinguistic (e.g., language or accent) dimensions. Given this reality it is important, from an analytic point of view, to understand what ethnicity is meant to describe in its particular usages. Describing a conflict as "ethnic" often says very little about it; therefore, serious analysis requires a more exacting description of the parties involved and their relationship to each other.

A second, more historical and political, perspective suggests that ethnicity is a major form of group identity mainly because it was essential to the early development of the nation-state, currently the primary form of political organization. The ascendance of the modern nation-state occurred through the active political construction of nationalities around language/dialect, geographic region, religion, and other components of ethnic identity. In agreement with a host of other scholars, such as Benedict Anderson, Ernest Gellner, Eric Hobsbawm, and Thomas Nairn, in 1991 political philosopher Etienne Balibar argued that modern nations are predicated on the coming together of disparate peoples as part of a "fictive ethnicity" that identifies them as one group. From its modern inception, the nation-state has relied on ethnic identity as a tool through which the body politic could be formed and re-formed. Thus, in his 1990 book, *Iron Cages: Race and Culture in 19th Century America*, historian Ronald Takaki describes the efforts of the First Congress of the United States to establish the requirements of citizenship in the new Republic. In an attempt to replicate their own identity, the Congress believed good citizens must be republican in values, virtuous in morals, male, and White. Throughout this formative period, ethnicity, as well as other characteristics, were always implicit, if not explicit, criteria for political and economic enfranchisement.

The third perspective on the prevalence of ethnic identity argues that ethnicity is a psychologically meaningful and beneficial form of group identity. This would explain why ethnic identities continue to resonate with people, despite the inexact and shifting basis of ethnic categorization and the fact that political elites have often manipulated its meaning. This subjective or phenomenological reality makes ethnicity an important form of individual and group identity and, therefore, it will be discussed in greater detail.

a. The Psychosocial Functions of Ethnic Identity

Ethnic identity may be one of the most prevalent forms of group identity because it can serve at least four psychosocial functions for group members: (1) providing self-esteem; (2) bestowing social status; (3) supplying existential security and knowledge; and (4) granting social protection.

First, as with personal and group identity more generally, ethnic identity may provide self-esteem and thus facilitate psychological well-being. Identification with an ethnic group can be an important source of self-esteem that is not solely dependent on individual status and achievement. This may be especially important for members of ethnic groups that are devalued by the larger society. Psychological research suggests that strong identification with stigmatized groups acts as a buffer against feelings of individual inadequacy in the face of low status. By attributing the negative evaluation to others' bias, people maintain a positive view of themselves and an optimal level of self-esteem. This process has been used to explain the general finding that members of ethnic subordinate groups do not have lower self-esteem than others despite their awareness that they are not well thought of in the society at large.

Second, established groups, such as ethnic groups, provide their members a certain degree of social status based upon their standing *within* the group. Cultural competence, for example, as demonstrated by language skill or story telling, may bring one status within the group and this can also be an important source of self-worth. Third, ethnicity can provide existential security by affirming members' goals, values, beliefs, practices, and norms. Participating in a socially validated culture gives one a sense of belonging and, in most cases, also provides knowledge essential to the successful navigation of the culture.

Fourth, active membership in and identification with an ethnic group can protect individuals from collective threats, such as physical attack or political exclusion, and enable them to take collective action. If the ethnic group is treated as a collective entity by others, members share a common fate and therefore benefit from some degree of coordination. Recognizing this interdependence may in turn foster group identity and cohesion, binding the group more tightly together and improving its ability to respond to external threats.

b. The "Optimal Distinctiveness" of Ethnic Minority Identity

While membership in any ethnic group can provide psychological benefits, membership in ethnic minority groups may satisfy particular psychological needs. Marilynn Brewer's theory of "optimal distinctiveness" suggests that people have simultaneous needs to be unique from a group (differentiation) and to belong to a group (inclusion). These two needs often compete with each other, and consequently, people often move from situation to situation to balance their need for differentiation and their need for inclusion. People often feel undifferentiated in a very large (majority) group and identification with that group alone does not provide optimal distinctiveness. However, minority groups are more likely to provide this equilibrium. In such groups one may feel similar to ingroup members while feeling different from outgroup members. Because such groups satisfy both needs, people are often strongly committed to these groups. Laboratory studies reveal that evaluative preferences for the ingroup and the strength of one's identification with the ingroup rise as the size of the group decreases. Thus, ethnic minority groups can improve psychological well-being by providing members optimal distinctiveness, while also promoting the ethnic consciousness and politicization of such groups.

2. Ethnic Identification and Conflict

As noted above, ethnic group identity can provide a number of social, psychological, and practical benefits to those who so identify. However, a great deal of theoretical and empirical work has examined the role of ethnic identification in the promotion of conflict. There is, in fact, a long tradition of psychosocial theorizing that views the formation and maintenance of identity as inherently conflictual. Hegel provides an influential perspective, in *The Phenomenology of Mind* (1841), where he describes the process by which people develop identity as a "life-and-death struggle" between dominant and subordinate groups. Hegel's framework can be found in numerous approaches to group identity and conflict, including that of Karl Marx, Jean-Paul Sartre, Simone de Beauvoir, and Frantz Fanon. Many psychodynamically oriented theorists also share Hegel's view that identity development depends upon a recognition of self through a recognition of and differentiation from others.

According to Hegel, each group tries to achieve dominant status by defining itself as superior to others. The dominant and subordinate groups are thus locked in a *dialectical* struggle for identity, where each group's identity is defined by its relationship to the other. The violent conflict between the Hutu and Tutsi groups in Rwanda may serve to illustrate how the dialectical framework applies to ethnic conflict. Since invading the region centuries ago, the Tutsi minority in Rwanda has dominated the Hutu majority, controlling the bulk of the economic, political, and cultural institutions. The Tutsi were thus able to define themselves as superior to the Hutu, whom they held in low esteem. The Hutu, given their subordinate position in the dialectic, were thus forced to displace the Tutsi in order to define themselves as something other than subordinate. This has often led the Hutu to violently oppose their subjugation, as in the 1959 uprising that displaced the Tutsi king and led to the formation of a democratic republic. Of course, the historically dominant Tutsi have sought to regain power whenever deposed, locking both groups into what seems like an interminable contest for power and the right to not be subordinated to the other group. Each group's ascendance to dominance guarantees the subordination of the other and thus guarantees the subordinate's eventual opposition and attempt at reversing their power positions.

The concept of *ethnocentrism* closely parallels these ideas in its explanation of ethnic and other group conflict. *Social Identity Theory*, developed largely by social psychologists Henri Tajfel and John Turner, formalizes the notion captured in ethnocentrism that groups tend to see themselves as superior to others. It has spurred a great deal of empirical research on the social competition between groups for a positive identity. In studies with a wide variety of social groups, ranging from ethnolinguistic, to occupational, to laboratory created, this research has shown that (in)group members tend to favor their own groups over other groups. That is, people generally rate the personal attributes, language, and opinions of their group more positively than those of other groups and, when given the chance, allocate more material resources to their own group than to other groups. Given that people strive to establish the superiority of their own group over others, it is not surprising that when given an opportunity to compare groups directly, they tend to favor their own group.

Despite the fact that most contemporary research on ethnocentrism has been conducted in Western Europe and the United States, the phenomenon does not appear to be limited to these regions. In the 1960s a team of anthropologists and psychologists collaborated to conduct what they called "A Cooperative Cross-Cultural Study of Ethnocentrism," to assess the prevalence of ethnocentrism in Northern Canada, East Africa, West Africa, New Guinea, and 17 other regions around the world. While ingroups did not consider themselves superior to all outgroups on every possible dimension, ingroups did believe that they had more moral virtue than others. Therefore, ethnocentrism appears to be a ubiquitous aspect of intergroup relations.

Thus, a great deal of theoretical and empirical work suggests that social competition is the predominant way in which people achieve a secure and positive identity for themselves. In much of Western philosophy and psychology, identity is itself about conflict. Identity, and struggles to attain and maintain it, may therefore be an independent source of conflict and violence between ethnic groups in the political arena. Nevertheless, conflict is not the only way that individual or group identity forms or maintains itself. Large-scale international studies of intergroup conflict have *not* found that strong and positive group identity *necessarily* leads to conflict with or derogation of other groups. Similarly, research on Social Identity Theory in Europe, North America, and New Zealand has not established that *all* groups, under *all* circumstances, construct their identity through invidious comparisons with others. A number of contextual factors, such as control over resources, perceived threat, competition, and the scarcity of resources, can promote conflict in terms of group identity.

3. Summation

Given its broad definition and its importance in the construction of the modern nation-state, ethnicity is an exceedingly popular description of human social groups. Contemporary social science uses ethnic group membership and identity to explain everything from purchasing patterns, to musical taste, to war. It is clear that despite its fuzzy and ever-changing definition, ethnicity plays a central role in our understanding of ourselves and the world in which we live. Group conflict is often understood in terms of ethnicity, by both participants and observers, because ethnic identity is one of the most salient social groupings in political and social life, particularly among ethnic subordinate groups. While ethnic identification itself may promote conflict between groups that define themselves ethnocentrically, much of ethnic conflict occurs in the context of more political struggles for power and dominance.

B. Politics

Political power is typically gained and held in an outright conflict between rivals. Political opponents must be defeated at the polls, in legislative chambers, in the media, and sometimes in the streets. Political conflicts appear rampant even in single party or dictatorial political systems where rival factions and administrative departments within the same political organization battle for position and power. Of course, the level of conflict in a political system is related to the structure of that system and the degree to which it pits constituencies against one another. In "winner take all" and two-party systems, such as the United States, there can be great conflict between parties to achieve the majority position. In parliamentary or proportional systems, power-sharing and coalition-building may be more likely, although it is not clear whether such systems reduce the level of conflict between parties when the parties are not forced to cooperate to achieve a majority.

Given the level of conflict inherent to the political process, all politics may rely on a form of identity politics to mobilize and maneuver the specific groups of people needed to gain or maintain power. Political parties with names such as "Green," "Labor," "The People's Party," "New Jewel Movement," or "National Front," identify themselves in a way that supports their constituents' identification with the party and its platform. In some cases, political parties are explicit in their appeals to ethnic identity, as with the Tamil United Liberation Front or the Sri Lankan Muslim Congress in Sri Lanka, and the Scottish National Party in the United Kingdom.

Throughout the world politics is infused with both subtle and obvious appeals to the ethnic identity of potential supporters. For example, in the 1970s and 1980s, the leaders of the ruling Congress Party in India went to great lengths to appear strong to their predominantly Hindu constituency by putting down a rebellion organized by members of the Sikh religious minority. At the same time, the Congress Party made great efforts to end the uprising in such a way as to also appear fair and tolerant to their Sikh supporters. In ethnically diverse states such as India, South Africa, and the United States, political groups depend on support from multiple ethnic constituencies and must therefore make complicated appeals to multiple groups.

However, numerous cases exist in which ethnicity has been used as a "wedge issue" to divide political support along ethnic lines. Jill Quadagno, in her 1995 book, *The Color of Welfare,* discusses U.S. President Nixon's quiet encouragement of affirmative action programs for some ethnic groups as a calculated attempt to erode European American support for the Democratic party. As mentioned in the introduction, dominant groups can use identity politics to maintain and consolidate their own political power while limiting that of others. Quadagno documents such a case in U.S. President Franklin Delano Roosevelt's efforts to promote the Social Security Act of 1935 in the U.S. Congress. Many (White) Southern Democrats opposed the act because it would provide an income to unemployed and retired African Americans that would exceed the prevailing wages in the region. To guarantee the support of the Southerners in his party, Roosevelt advocated a provision that excluded agricultural and domestic laborers. Because African Americans typically filled these occupations, the provision excluded most African Americans from a major advance in social welfare and full political enfranchisement. Here, the consolidation of Democratic power and the maintenance of White ethnic domination in the South was achieved at the expense of a subordinate ethnic group.

C. Summation

Examining ethnic identity and politics separately suggests that each is related to the other in complex ways. Ethnic identity and politics are both powerful means of social differentiation and major sources of conflict. It is therefore not surprising that their combination in "ethnic identity politics" is expected to promote extreme conflict, and often violence. As we have seen, ethnic identity may be used politically by both dominant and subordinate groups, although their particular strategies may differ. In fact, ethnic identity politics are an important means by which dominance is achieved and maintained, but also challenged. Hegel's characterization of identity may therefore also be fitting for the *politics* of ethnic identity, as dominant and subordinate group are locked in a dialectical battle for power. In a dialectical struggle, one party's use of ethnic identity to achieve political dominance can work to encourage resistance by another party through the use of its own ethnic identity. In this way attempts at dominance, rather than always leading to another's subordination, can lead to resistance and a countermove for power. Consequently, Hegel, and the many others who share his basic assumptions, see the dialectic of identity as inherently conflictual, and often violent.

III. THE DIALECTICS OF ETHNIC IDENTITY POLITICS

In 1951, political philosopher Hannah Arendt argued in *The Origins of Totalitarianism*, that "the only direct, unadulterated consequence of 19th century antisemitic movements was not Nazism but, on the contrary, Zionism, which, at least in its Western ideological form, was a kind of counterideology, the 'answer' to antisemitism" (p. xv). While Arendt was careful to point out that Jewish identity was not simply a reaction to anti-Semitism, she described the ways in which attempts at political dominance that use ethnic exclusion can fuel resistance in the form of *oppositional* ethnic identity politics. In the following section we discuss the identity politics of dominant and subordinate ethnic groups, with special attention to ways in which their power position affects their identity and their actions. It is important to note, however, that while some groups may operate from well-established positions of dominance or subordinance, groups are also deeply affected by their perceived *potential* for dominance or subordination. In the case of equal power groups, for example, the political dynamics of their ethnic identity may have a great deal to do with their desire for future dominance or their fear of future subordination.

A. Dominant Groups

Given their advantaged political position, dominant groups tend to engage in ethnic identity politics as a means to secure or consolidate power, as mentioned in the preceding section on politics. The Soviet Union, for example, had a long history of mobilizing and manipulating ethnic identity (often referred to as "nationality") to maintain the central authority's political power. Even before coming to power, the Bolsheviks strategically supported national "self-determination" in order to gain the support of the many ethnic groups incorporated into the Russian empire. Later, in the 1920s and 1930s, Stalin created five separate ethnic groups out of one, by dividing the Central Asian region of Turkestan into five republics: Kazakhstan, Kirghizistan, Tadzhikistan, Turkmenistan, and Uzbekistan. By outlawing the religion and alphabet these groups had in common, Stalin promoted separate ethnic identities in an attempt to neutralize the pan-Turkic sentiment he saw as threatening the national integrity of the Soviet Union. Thus, Stalin promoted the distinct ethnic identities of Uzbek and Kazakh as a countervailing force against an identification as Muslim or Turkic that might have unified Central Asians against Moscow. In this case, an authority used ethnic identity politics to limit the potentially threatening identity politics of subordinate groups. However, in the following section on subordinate groups, we will discuss ways in which Central Asian investment in these manipulated ethnic identities came back to haunt the Soviet Union.

It is important to note, however, that the ethnic identity politics of dominant groups is not necessarily as conscious or calculated as some of our examples suggest. More subtle strategies of maintaining political power have been analyzed by theories of *group dominance* or hegemony. These theories argue that groups with well-established and relatively secure political dominance need little in the way of explicit ethnic identity politics to maintain their position. Such groups can utilize ideologies of conservatism and individualism to protect the status quo, and thus protect their privileged position without the appearance of self-interest. However, as group dominance theories argue, this lack of self-interest is often more apparent than real, and thus dominant political positions may always be rooted in the promotion of a particular ethnic group's agenda. In contemporary cases of well-established ethnic subordination, dominant ethnic identification often occurs in the terms of nationalism. A person who benefits from the status quo identifies as "truly" American, or British, or French and valorizes the founders of his or her "great nation"—founders who often share his or her ethnicity—without suspicion of a strategic ethnic identity politics or ethnocentrism. In 1995 Michael Billig described this sort of clandestine politics of ethnic identity as a "banal nationalism." Although group dominance theories explain a great deal of political inequality that cannot be otherwise explained and are popular in some circles, they have only recently received some empirical verification—perhaps explaining why ethnic identity politics are typically associated with subordinate groups.

B. Subordinate Groups

While dominant ethnic groups may use identity politics as means of limiting the political power of others, their attempt can inadvertently galvanize the ethnic identity politics of subordinate groups. During the loosening of control under Gorbachev's *perestroika* in the Soviet Union, for example, Uzbekistan and other republics sought an unprecedented degree of independence, fueled by a burgeoning nationalism that was encouraged, ironically, by Moscow's earlier support of ethnic "self-determination." This sort of oppositional identity politics involves centering a social movement around connections to a specific category of people and what is perceived to be their common political agenda. In 1996 Anner wrote, "The premise of [subordinate] identity politics is that all members of the group have more in common than the members have with anyone outside the group, that they are oppressed in the same way, and therefore that they all belong on the same road to justice" (p. 9). In many cases, organized political movements are considered the best "road to justice."

1. Political Movements

Political movements are an important form of opposition for subordinate ethnic groups. They typically involve the mobilization of large numbers of people under an explicit political platform or agenda centered around the group's ethnic identity and social experience. Political movements have as their goal a change in the prevailing political system and related social and economic arrangements. This change usually involves some capitulation by the dominant group(s) and is often pursued through legal challenges to existing practices or laws, political lobbying and leverage, and noncooperation in the political or economic sectors. How is it that identity with a subordinate ethnic group may foster organized collective actions in the form of a political movement? The sociological and social psychological literatures suggest that subordinate groups engage in political movements when they perceive their disadvantage to be (1) shared, affecting the group as a collective (2) illegitimate or unfair, and (3) changeable through their political efforts.

First, the perception of a shared disadvantage is key to collective political action. This perception involves the sense that one is part of an oppressed collective and that each group member's experience is influenced by his or her membership in the collective. The permeability of group boundaries seriously affects group members' perceptions of a common fate. Studies reveal that a sense of shared disadvantage is more likely if the boundary to an advantaged group is perceived as closed. However, if the boundary to the advantaged group is seen as permeable, individual attempts at joining or "passing" into the dominant group are likely. Some suggest that the civil rights movement in the United States of the 1960s was in part spurred by the shared perception among African Americans that they were deprived as a group. In this case, both the leaders of the movement and the mass media highlighted the unequal social conditions that many group members viewed as a threat to their collective well-being. This recognition of a common oppression and shared fate made collective political action seem necessary. Research suggests that it is the combination of the perceived deprivation of one's group and increasing expectations for one's group that leads to discontent. The theory of Relative Deprivation predicts that people experience discontent only when they believe that their current attainments do not match their expectations, particularly when they compare themselves to a group that has more than their own group. Moreover, as mentioned above in the section on ethnic identity, membership in minority groups fosters comparisons between the status of one's own group and that of other groups. This process of searching for optimal distinctiveness may heighten the experience of relative deprivation among subordinate groups because members will emphasize (1) the commonalities within their group and, (2) the disparities between the dominant group and their own.

Although the recognition of group disadvantage may be necessary for the development of a collective movement, it is not sufficient. A subordinate group may, in fact, believe that such inequities are legitimate. For example, many social theorists suggest that dominant groups develop "legitimating myths" to justify the oppression of others. The caste system in India and the companion belief that people who are of a low caste warrant their current status due to a transgression in a previous life is such an example. When the subordinate group believes its status to be legitimate, there is little reason for a collective political movement, and the hierarchy is rarely challenged. Thus, political movements by subordinate ethnic groups tend to rely on a belief that their group's disadvantage is unfair and undeserved.

Finally, some modicum of efficacy is necessary to engage in what is often a long and difficult battle to have the group's disadvantage recognized and addressed. For instance, during the Black Power Movement, the Chicano Movement, and the Asian American Movement in the United States and in the anticolonial movements in Africa, Asia, and Latin America, the people most heavily involved in collective political action were not those most deprived economically or politically. It was for the most part the college-educated and middle-class members of these ethnic groups that started the movements and set their agendas. People who feel that they have the requisite resources are likely to participate in organized political movements and are likely to believe that political activity will result in positive change.

C. Violent or Peaceful?

Much of Western scholarship on the conflict motivated by ethnic identity politics has been influenced by Hegel's dialectical perspective. Many analysts believe that Hegel saw such conflict as inherently violent, as he argued that each of the involved parties "aims at the destruction and death of the other." While it is unclear whether the destruction Hegel speaks of is actual or metaphorical, the place of violence in ethnic identity politics is an issue of great concern. The main preoccupation in this area has been how and why ethnic groups come to see violence as a viable form of political conflict, and why they engage in violence rather than in the electoral or other non-violent forms of collective activity encompassed in political movements. Before proceeding, however, it may be useful to distinguish between violent actions that are planned as part of a political agenda or tied to explicit political demands, and a more "spontaneous" violence that responds to political (or politicized) events. Violence based on political agendas includes terrorism, civil war, and rebellions, while event-based violence more closely describes riots and lynchings. The latter form of violence is easily distinguished from the sort of organized political movements discussed in the preceding section. Unlike participants in prolonged social movements, those who engage in event-based violence—such as the urban unrest that occurs in response to perceptions of police brutality—tend to be the most isolated and disenfranchised of their group. While participants may see such actions as sending a political message, they are rarely regarded as a political strategy effecting change. Agenda-based violence, on the other hand, is quite different.

The preceding section on political movements suggested that organized political activity by subordinate ethnic groups tends to be based on the perception that there is an illegitimate inequality between groups that can be changed by organized political activity. Agenda-based violence by such groups is a form of political activity encouraged by the belief that efforts in the political realm alone will not produce positive change. Such violence is often seen as viable when subordinate ethnic groups have little or no faith in the ability of the political or judicial systems to address their grievances because they view these systems as contributing to their oppression. In such cases, subordinate ethnic groups see violent opposition to the status quo as a legitimate form of resistance. Frantz Fanon, an influential theorist who analyzed 20th century sociopolitical movements in the United States, Asia, the Caribbean, and Algeria and other parts of Africa, argues that oppression compelled people to use violence to combat the violence inherent in systems of subordination. Fanon describes the ways in which the institutionalized violence used by dominant groups to maintain their position (e.g., poverty, lynching, police brutality) could become banal, and thereby taken-for-granted by many within the society. According to Fanon, in a dialectical battle for position, violent opposition by subordinate ethnic groups is simply engaging in conflict at the appropriate level. Following Hegel, Fanon sees the subordinate group's position as a direct result of another group's identification as a dominant group. Thus, the only alternative is for the subordinate group to displace the group responsible for its low position and to replace it, thereby becoming dominant.

There are, of course, other perspectives on the legitimacy and efficacy of violence in ethnic conflict. For example, nonviolent approaches to social change are most often defined according to those advocated by Mohandas K. Gandhi (regarding Indian independence from Britain and political enfranchisement for Indians in South Africa) and Martin Luther King, Jr. (regarding African Americans and other disenfranchised groups in the U.S.). While Gandhi and King shared a commitment to nonviolent protest rooted in their respective spiritual beliefs, they also shared a more pragmatic belief that violent opposition by subordinates only invites violent response from the dominant group. From their perspective, organized political violence only works to reinforce and reinvigorate unjust and often brutal domination. For both Gandhi and King, the only way to achieve a lasting social justice free of violence by either dominants or subordinates is to change the very nature of group identity through a "politics of conversion." Thus, Gandhi argued that the oppressed can

> . . . free ourselves of the unjust rule of the Government by defying the unjust rule and accepting the punishments that go with it [. . .]. When we set its fears at rest, when we do not desire to make armed assaults on administrators, nor to unseat them from power, but only to get rid of their injustice, they will at once be subdued to our will.

Unlike Fanon, Gandhi clearly separates the system of domination from the group that dominates. This allows him to believe that the dominant group can recognize inequality in the system and be moved to reform it and themselves. Thus, the nonviolent approach to political activity does not endorse the Hegelian view that identity is achieved only through a bitter and often violent conflict between groups brought about by competition for dominance. Ultimately, it is their assumptions about the relationship between identity, be it dominant or subordinate, and conflict that determines the place of violence in the widely divergent political courses charted by Gandhi/King and Fanon.

IV. CONCLUSION

Identity politics based in ethnic identification may be especially conflictual and sometimes violent. In contrast to the popular view, this is not because ethnic identity politics are practiced solely by minority or subordinate groups who thirst for power and resources. Groups of majority or minority, dominant or subordinate status can utilize the ethnic identity of their constituents to raise political consciousness, organize political activity, and make claims for social, economic, and other resources. Given the broad definition of ethnicity, its role in the formation of modern nation-states, and the psychosocial reality and possible benefits of ethnic identification, all politics today may be, to some extent, ethnic identity politics. Therefore, the conflict and violence often associated with ethnic identity politics has more to do with the conflict associated with ethnic group identity and the political process than with ethnicity itself. Both ethnic identity and political power can be achieved through intergroup conflict in search of dominance. Ethnic identity politics can thus be seen as a dialectical struggle for power between groups, with each using ethnic identity as a means toward this end. Of course, such uses of ethnic identity would have little success if ethnic identification did not resonate with people and perform important psychosocial functions for them.

In the popular view, ethnic identity and related politics are seen as inherently divisive and conflictual. Paradoxically, however, identity politics is both unifying and divisive: while people are unified within a particular ethnic group, they simultaneously identify other groups as competitors or threats to their political aims. The power of identity politics is often dependent upon the mass appeal of the identity that the political activity is centered around. In Britain, for example, immigrants from the many former British colonies in the Caribbean formed "Afro-Caribbean" or "West Indian" political and social groups to address their shared perceptions of discrimination and cultural chauvinism. Thus, appeals to local or national authorities could be made in the name of the collective West Indian minority rather than separately in the name of those from Barbados, Guyana, Jamaica, or Grenada.

Similarly, "Asian" organizations were formed in Britain to address the shared social position of the many disparate immigrant groups from the Indian subcontinent. Identification as "Asian" in Britain brought together a wide array of people who differed in nationality, religion, caste, region, class, gender, and numerous other forms of social difference. Their identification as Asian, as opposed to Punjabi, Pakistani, or Muslim, for example, allowed them to form a larger collective based on their shared status as an identifiable minority in British society. In some cases, Afro-Caribbeans and South Asians joined to form "Black" caucuses—as in the British Parliament—based on their shared ethnic minority status. This allowed an even larger body of people and stronger political force to be mobilized around issues seen as common to the participants.

Thus, framing a movement around subordination, rather than a fairly narrow ethnic identity, can foster cross-ethnic coalitions that draw on a wider base of support. In many cases, the failure to form an overarching identity and related political agenda has led to the splintering of political movements. For example, there has been a continual struggle in India, since gaining independence from Britain in 1947, to balance national solidarity with the competing claims of the various ethnic, religious, and caste groups in the society. Attention to ethnic identity politics in these situations, and in others, allows an examination of the ways in which social groups define themselves, identify their interests, and pursue what they see as the political aims relevant to their identity and interests, all in the context of the social, economic, and power relations between groups.

A. Globalism and the Future of Ethnic Identity Politics

Scholars are growing increasingly concerned with the future direction of ethnic identity politics. Much of this effort has concentrated on the effects of the increasing globalism brought about by rapidly advancing technology in travel, media, and communication. There are two opposing views: one which sees the world getting smaller and more homogenous through increased contact, and another that sees the world as growing more and more heterogenous as we all come to know a greater variety of people than ever before. Proponents of each view do not, however, agree on what the consequences of the expected change will be.

1. Increasing Homogeneity

Among those who predict increasing cultural homogeneity as a result of globalization, some believe that divisive identity politics will not survive the increased interdependence brought about a global culture. This view sees ethnic identity politics and subsequent conflict and violence as a thing of the past as identities rooted in *local* ethnicities and nations fall away in favor of more *global* identities based in individual freedom and purchasing power. If the world becomes one, very large, market where everything can be bought and sold, collective identities may indeed provide very little cachet for individual consumers. This "one world, one market" scenario, where the many diverse peoples of the world get past their differences to share a common Internet software, cola, or phone company, appears in an increasing number of advertisements by multinational companies and represents one way in which (market) globalism may diffuse ethnic identity politics and thereby reduce the conflict and violence associated with it.

Not all observers agree, however, that ethnic identity politics will decline with the increased homogeneity expected from globalism. A second perspective predicts that increased homogeneity will undermine subordinate ethnic identity politics while quietly promoting dominant ethnic identity politics. Here, there is concern about the spread of an economic, political, and, social culture that, while calling itself "global," is actually rooted in mainstream U.S. and Western European cultures and values. Globalization is seen as a new kind of nationalist imperialism without frontiers, beamed into every home across the world and packed into every consumer product.

Sociologist Howard Winant warns against the possibility that advancing globalism is establishing a new form of dominant identity politics, based upon a racialized global hegemony of North over South. He views oppositional ethnic and national identity politics as a necessary response to this trend—a response that can be aided by an alternative use of media and communication technology. In Australia, for example, a number of Aboriginal groups have used local radio and television broadcasting to reinvigorate interest, especially among the young, in their language, culture, and politics. Here local media is used by subordinate groups to provide an alternative to national and global media.

2. Increasing Heterogeneity

There are also those who believe that globalism will serve to highlight greater cultural heterogeneity; however, they disagree about the potential benefits and costs of this change. Some find troubling the increasing level of cultural diversity made apparent by increased contact, as each ethnic group may be encouraged to enter into competition with every other to secure an increasingly scarce political power. Here, increased contact is expected to cause increased conflict. Others see globalism as making the technology of media and communication available to a wide variety of ethnic groups who can each use it to develop their culture, language, and politics. Globalism can in this way lead to greater equality and pluralism, promoting cross-group connections through increased mutual knowledge.

Clearly, the future direction of ethnic identity politics, and its relation to globalism, remains an open question. Unfortunately, the dialectical approach to ethnic identity politics does not offer a prediction as to which future is most likely. It does, however, suggest that the consequences of globalism and advancing technology will be determined by the way in which ethnic groups use them in their quest for identity. If globalism and technology are used by one group to advance a claim of superiority over another, this will most likely result in a counterclaim, perhaps through the use of parallel tools, by those so subordinated. The dialectical circle of conflict and violence will simply turn on, perhaps at a faster pace. The promise in globalism and advanced technology lies in its potential as a means by which equality can be established and maintained.

Also See the Following Articles

CLAN AND TRIBAL CONFLICT • ETHNIC CONFLICTS AND COOPERATION • EVOLUTIONARY THEORY • GENOCIDE AND DEMOCIDE • MASS MEDIA, GENERAL VIEW • SOCIAL EQUALITY AND INEQUALITY • WORLD GOVERNMENT

Bibliography

Anner, J. (Ed.) (1996). *Beyond Identity Politics: Emerging Social Justice Movements in Communities of Color*. Boston: South End Press.

Balibar, E., & Wallerstein, I. (Eds.) (1991). *Race, Nation, Class: Ambiguous Identities*. London: Verso.

Bremnar, I., & Taras, R. (1993). *Nation and Politics in the Soviet Successor States*. Cambridge: Cambridge University.

Bulhan, H. A. (1985). *Frantz Fanon and the Psychology of Oppression*. New York: Plenum.

Calhoun, C. (Ed.) (1994). *Social Theory and the Politics of Identity*. Cambridge: Blackwell.

Cerulo, K. A. (1997). Identity construction: New issues, new directions. *Annual Review of Sociology*, **23**, 385–409.

Fanon, F. (1967). *Black Skin, White Masks*. New York: Grove Wiedenfeld.

Hale, C. R. (1997). Cultural politics of identity in Latin America. *Annual Review of Anthropology*, **26**, 567–590.

Hutchinson, J., & Smith, A. D. (1996). *Ethnicity*. Oxford: Oxford University.

Layton-Henry, Z. (1984). *The Politics of Race in Britain*. London: Allen & Unwin.

Pichardo, N. A. (1997). New social movements: A critical review. *Annual Review of Sociology*, **23**, 411–430.

Rajchman, J. (Ed.) (1995). *The Identity in Question*. New York & London: Routledge.

Sampson, E. E. (1993). Identity politics: Challenges to psychology's understanding. *American Psychologist*, **48**(12), 1219–1230.

Tajfel, H., & Turner, J. C. (1986). The social identity theory of intergroup behavior. In S. Worshel & W. G. Austin (Eds.), *Psychology of Intergroup Relations*, 2nd Edition (pp. 7–24). Chicago: Nelson-Hall.

Winant, H. (1994). *Racial Conditions: Politics, Theory, Comparisons*. Minneapolis: University of Minnesota.

Evil, Concept of

David Loye
Center for Partnership Studies

GLOSSARY

Dominator Model A configuration for social organization of violence, male dominance, and authoritarianism.

Karma A Hindu concept of reward and punishment based on the idea that our actions in past lives shapes our current and futures lives.

Partnership Model A configuration for social organization of peace, gender and general equality, and democracy.

Praxis Prosocially or morally motivated social action.

Theodicy Religious beliefs regarding suffering and evil.

IT SEEMS LIKELY that ever since the first humans began to abstract concepts out of, perhaps, the experience of unjustified or unnatural death, the problem of evil has been centrally troublesome. One stream of Christianity has defined evil as what happens when one goes against or falls away from "God," attributing everything of this sort to "Satan." A stream of Hinduism defines evil as an illusion, only "Maya." Philosophers have further tried to define evil in various ways on which they often widely disagree. We will further pursue these traditions in which a far richer heritage of thought exists about what evil is than in science. But we open here with science because evil is so seldom addressed from the scientific perspective, yet it is this perspective we must above all now understand if we are to more effectively solve the problems—particularly those of violence and the consequences of violence—that give rise to the concept of evil.

A working definition from a scientific viewpoint is that evil includes the opposite of what we consider to be "good" in life, or what is "bad." It also includes what we consider to be "wrong" rather than "right." But it involves far more than just the "bad," the "wrong," or peace versus war as a matter of scale, persistence, and intensity. That is, it is a term used to describe the bad, the wrong, or the violent at their sustained, or persistent, or systems structural *extreme*.

I. EVIL: A SCIENTIFIC VIEW

Other than in religious contexts people seldom use the word *evil* any more. Yet the realities that originally gave rise to the concept are still with us. Indeed, in specifics such as our species' new-found potential via the ultimate violence of nuclear or environmental devastation to make this earth uninhabitable, what used to be called evil presses upon us even more than ever before.

To understand evil we need to see it within the perspective of at least three great bodies of knowledge: that of modern science, both social and natural science, and ranging from past into the present, that of religion and theology, and of philosophy. We will consider the scientific perspective first, then the theological, the philosophical, and last focus all three perspectives on the latest views of how violence as an aspect of evil is rooted in the culture prevailing globally for humanity at this point in the evolution of our species.

One advantage of the scientific perspective is that, in comparison to religion and philosophy, it offers a more simple and direct way of grounding ourselves in the "database" of evil. Another advantage is that of its powerful methodology for obtaining the kind of consensus on what something is and is not that is extremely difficult for either religion or philosophy to achieve. Still another advantage is the multidisciplinary problem-solving orientation that further differentiates science historically from religion and philosophy.

What is evil? How, beyond the brief working definition that opens this article, do we define it? As we will see in our consideration of the religious and philosophical background, many answers have been offered. Another advance that science has brought to this area of concern has been its reduction of the global or wholesale use of the word *evil*, thereby forcing us to differentiate between kinds and circumstances and levels of specific ills. In reasonably enlightened settings, this advancement has helped prevent the use of the word evil as no more than a self- or group-defined term for defiling whoever one decides, for whatever reasons, is one's enemy.

At the same time, however, the need remains for a term for the opposite or lack of good. There are also people and situations where anything short of labeling them evil seems a dangerous diminishment of meaning, as for example in the case of Adolf Hitler and the Nazi impact on Germany.

The basic scientific approach to defining anything is to identify it in what are called empirical or operational terms—that is, in terms of what gives rise to it and how does it affect us, what variables or factors and dynamics are involved, or more directly, what does it look like, what seems to cause it, and what can be done about it.

What science has ascertained as of the end of the 20th and the beginning of the 21st century indicates that what has in the past been classified as evil seems to have at least five sources: cultural, physiological, biological, evolutionary, and existential.

A. Cultural Sources of Evil

This is the dominant heritage of thought both for science and for modern times. Most notably first articulated by the philosopher Jean-Jacques Rousseau, this is the view that evil is culturally caused, or an adverse function of social system arrangements. This belief became a basis both for the American revolution and experiment in democracy and the first two large cohesive attempts at a social scientific rationale for putting this idea to use in large-scale human problem-solving. First came the economics of Adam Smith's rationale for the development of capitalism. Then came the economics and political science of Marx and Engels' rationale for communism.

In other words, before the Enlightenment movement of the 18th century, out of which science arose, the idea prevailed in the West that we are, each of us, innately evil and must be ruled by the supposedly divine ordination of kings. But with the triumph of the Enlightenment, the prevailing idea became that evil resides in the political, economic, or more general cultural system—that we are basically good, made evil by the system, which can be changed.

This idea underlies the bulk of work in social science today directed toward improvement of the human situation. Keying to the pioneering of Emile Durkheim and Max Weber in sociology, John Stuart Mill and Thorstein Veblen in economics, Sigmund Freud and Kurt Lewin in psychology, and many others in all the fields of social science, the various social sciences have focused on racism, sexism, poverty, militarism, crime, and a wide range of other problems—including violence, to which we will return—that in the past were seen as bearing on the question of evil.

As this brief list indicates, the focus has been on the specifics that give rise to rather than on the abstraction of evil. A continuing use, however, of the abstracting of evil is the labeling of other people as evil for "social constructionist" purposes. Enemies are labeled evil to help promote wars, people of other faiths or no faith are labeled evil to promote religious conquest, and social deviants of all types are labeled evil to consolidate the power of ruling castes, classes, or elites.

The evidence by now available to us through social science indicates that in the overwhelming majority of cases, cultural factors are the primary source of what we could classify as evil. This evidence supports the conclusion guiding progressive modern social policy that the great payoff in reducing the impact of this factor in our lives lies in cultural, social, and educational improvement. Science, however, has identified other factors which interact with culture to produce the problems of our concern.

B. Physiological Sources of Evil

To those convinced that cultural factors determine all social and individual pathology, the idea that we might be born evil in the sense of lacking, or be made evil through damage to, the mental equipment for a conscience has been anathema. In criminology, for example, Lombroso, who developed a famous and shoddy system of criminal types, is held up as an example of dark ages psychology. Recent brain research, however, is beginning to reveal what the police, lawyers, and others who deal regularly with criminals have long suspected. There simply are people, from the so-called best as well as the worst of backgrounds, who either lack or have suffered damage to some facet of the brain structures involved in the existence and functioning of what we call the conscience, or the capacity for differentiating right from wrong.

Many more others, as the work of both anthropologist Ashley Montagu in *Touching* and psychiatrist A.N. Shore makes evident, are born intact but maimed not only psychologically but physiologically by the lack of love and caring, by brutality and abuse, or other forms of parental mishandling. Shore, for example, documents specific patterns of basic brain damage to children born fully functional that can be linked, on one hand, to a later incapacity for caring for others and/or tendencies to violence, and on the other, to the child's treatment by parents who either physically batter them or who may pride themselves on "never laying a hand on 'em," but who were home-grown specialists in psychological damage.

These two kinds of brutalized people used to be among the numbers of those called psychopaths. Now they are called sociopaths—which can be misleading, as for the reasons given here not all the sources of the kinds of crimes that reach the levels that invite the label of evil are social or cultural.

Here, too, we find a factor that can be diminished with attention to cultural and educational change. A useful analogy would be the case of someone who has suffered a stroke, and thereby damage to the brain, who can only walk or talk with great difficulty, but who can, with a sizeable investment of money and much work, be rehabilitated. In the case of those who lack or have suffered damage to our primarily frontal brain equipment for a conscience, however, it is evident that for the protection of others they must be rigorously controlled, while an effort is made to retrain them.

To prevent misinterpretation of this information by those seeking to discount cultural factors—who, for example, think that public funding should overwhelmingly go to prisons rather than to schools—it is important to stress two aspects of this information. The first is that those with physiological deficits that may lead to the levels of pathology that could be called evil represent only a small fraction in comparison with those with cultural deficits. Secondly, a preponderance of findings indicates that even in these cases pathology emerges out of an interaction of both cultural and physiological factors.

C. Biological and Evolutionary Sources of Evil

For several decades a debate has raged within the fields of biology, sociology, anthropology, and psychology over claims of those establishing the new field of sociobiology that fundamentally bear on the question of the origin of evil. In general, it is the contention of biologists such as E.O. Wilson, Robert Trivers, and Richard Dawkins that the evolution of our species out of earlier organisms, for example, reptiles and earlier mammals, reveals how human behavior is basically driven by selfishness rather than altruism, indeed even by "selfish genes." Others not as widely respected add to this the idea that we are basically driven by "killer instincts" also implanted within us by our evolutionary origins, thus in effect making evil rather than good a primary motivation as well as a primary direction for our species.

More recently, the battleground has shifted to the field of primatology. A recent book, for example, *Demonic Males*, finds that contrary to the impression that only at the human level do we find organized warfare this has now been found among roving bands of male chimpanzees.

To counter the position of the sociobiologists, anthropologists such as Ashley Montagu, biologists such as Richard Lewontin, and psychologists such as Leon Kamin make three primary points. One is that to extrapolate from the prehuman to the human level is a far more complicated process than the sociobiologists assert, that at the prehuman level one actually finds a preponderance of what might be called prosocial rather than antisocial behavior, and that at the human level again culture rather than biology becomes the overwhelming factor determining behavior.

In primatology, the debate tends to center around the differences between two kinds of chimpanzees, the common chimp and a more evolved bonobo or "pygmy" chimpanzee. In contrast to the greater potential for violence and other forms of antisocial behavior among the common chimps, the bonobo is not only much more peaceful but in many other regards seems to be far closer to what we mean when we speak of humanity as a prosocial characteristic of humans. The message of books such as *Goodnatured* by primatologist Franz de Waal, as well as *Sacred Pleasure* by cultural evolutionary theorist Riane Eisler, is that at the prehuman level in evolution there exists a wide range of behavioral potentials, from which at the human level *culture* selects which behaviors to favor and which to discourage.

D. Existential Sources of Evil

Beyond consideration of cultural, physiological, biological, and evolutionary sources of evil lies the existential fact of the kind of disasters of life that religions and philosophers have wrestled with for thousands of years, but that science has mainly avoided other than to consider, via the field of psychotherapy, what may be done to help comfort the victims.

This is the realm of horror that opens before us with the death of a beloved child, with all that otherwise could have been its life before it. Or the case of the great achiever and the great achievement that might have enormously benefitted humanity cut off midstream, or when barely underway. Or the triumph of the most despicable and least worthy of humans and the defeat and subjugation of the good.

Some would say that because this factor is structurally inbuilt into existence, that it simply happens, it cannot be called evil, it just is what is. Such a belief, however, has not been acceptable to many of those motivated to better the human condition as scientists, as religious leaders or theologians, or as philosophers.

II. EVIL: A RELIGIOUS VIEW

Although science has begun to demystify or cut the age-old problem of evil down to size, there remains much about evil that science cannot adequately express or probe. It cannot, for example, capture the eerie sense of evil that a great writer such as Joseph Conrad can in *Heart of Darkness*. Nor can it—or for that matter anything else—do justice to the monumental horror of how Germany, as one of the most advanced nations of the world, could shift so quickly from having the outstanding scientists and symphony orchestras of its time to the torturing and gassing of millions, the fiendish death camp experiments of Joseph Mengele, and the manufacturing of lampshades out of human skin.

It was the routine prevalence of such brutality in earlier times that over thousands of years drove religious visionaries and theologians to try to account for what to them was the incontrovertible fact of evil in our world. As indicated earlier, one route taken by ancient Hindu thought was to deny the existence of evil, to assert that it was only an illusion born of the limits of human mind. This was in keeping with a general tendency among Eastern religions to accept evil as a fact of life to be lived with or otherwise accomodated. In the Hindu system of deities one had Brahma the creator, Vishnu the preserver, and Shiva and his consort goddess Kali as destroyers. To further work evil into the natural cycle of life, one had a system of reincarnation interlocked with Karma that offered compensations for evil. Bad things that happen in a life are not only lessons for us to learn from, but can also be offset with better things or compensenation in one's later lives on earth through reincarnation.

Buddhism accepted suffering as our central challenge to overcome through the "eightfold path" designed to overcome selfish craving. Confucianism identified social ills and abuse of power as evils to likewise transcend by overcoming egoism—as well as the "parochialism, ethnocentrism, and chauvinistic nationalism" (Smith, p.117) ironically characteristic of modern China. With Islam, evil has chiefly been seen as disobeying the edicts of Allah. This unfortunately has been widely used for the deified justification of violence that historically has been the black mark against almost all religions.

Of Eastern beliefs regarding evil, possibly the one of most enduring interest here is the Hindu belief that the evolution of humanity involves cycles of great long spans of time called the Yugas. According to this belief, a peaceful golden age of goodness called the Krita Yuga was followed by two Yugas of lesser peace and goodness, and finally with the Kali Yuga—a time of evil and much violence in which humanity has been stuck now for thousands of years. Indian holy men and holy women today aver the Kali Yuga is ending, that we are again entering the Krita Yuga. Indeed one, Dadaji, predicted the shift would come in 1989, when in later fact the Cold War between the Soviet East and the West came to an end.

In contrast to the more passive attitude of the Eastern religions toward evil has been the more active stance of Western religion (as well as Islam, which in part derives from both Judaism and Christianity). Here evil has been seen as something to be much more actively questioned, and if possible eradicated. Ironically, one of the most influential strains in this regard comes from a technically Eastern religion, the Zoroastrianism of ancient Persia, as well as the later ancient Middle Eastern sect known as Manichaeism. For the Zoroastrian evil was caused by the fiendish spirit Angra Mainyu, with whom the supreme being Ahura Mazda is engaged in a vast, cosmic struggle. This became the basis for the later Christian belief in Satan or the Devil as the evil within and all around us to, by struggle, be overcome.

Thus, out of the earlier beliefs, for Western religions that posited the existence of an overriding supreme being, arose the problem that theology has wrestled with ever since. Whether it was fact, illusion, or a Devil, how could one reconcile the devastation of evil with a belief in the goodness of an all-powerful and all-wise God?

One solution for the problem was proposed by the ancient Hebrews in the Book of Job. After suffering practically every bad thing one can think of, Job asks God why this is being done to him. God's answer out of a whirlwind became another tenet of belief for religion over hundreds of years thereafter: that these things happen and one can only submit, for God's purposes are above and beyond human understanding.

Among those sharply questioning this view have been feminist theologians from Elizabeth Cady Stanton at the end of 19th century to Mary Daly, Rosemary Radford Reuther, and Elizabeth Dodson-Gray in our time. In their view, a primary source of the ills of the world, therefore evil, has been the psychological and social consequences of the positing of an exclusively male God at the heart of the violence of a globally male-ruled system of "patriarchy."

Over the centuries, this contention has been as widely rejected as mystifying extremism as another view has been widely favored in religion and society more generally. During the early development of Christianity the problems with all of the early answers to the question of how God relates to the fact of evil gave rise to the conflict, often bloody and at times incredibly violent, of the advocates of one or another position. At the end of the 4th century, out of a profligate youth that left him riddled with the guilt that led to his famous *Confessions*, there emerged the solution—or theodicy—of St. Augustine. (Theodicy is the term for religious beliefs regarding suffering and evil.)

God's creation, according to Augustine, was all good, therefore evil had not been created by God. It was the *absence* of good, as darkness is the absence of light. But how then did evil enter the world? Goodness could be diminished by the weakness and the corruption that entered into God's creation through the existence of free will in the human allowing the human to defy the will of God. Augustine further asserted that what at first may appear to be evil can in the long run turn out to be good within the context of eternity.

Today we think that because such thoughts were first expressed around 1600 years ago they have little to do with our lives today. But Augustine's solutions were not only to rule the minds of many theologians, Protestant as well as Catholic, and millions of Christians over hundreds of years thereafter. Certain aspects of his thinking persist even today, not only in fundamentalist faiths but also in surprising and seemingly wholly different contexts. Via the writings of Carl Jung and Aldous Huxley, for example, the belief that what may appear to be evil may in the long run turn out to be good has re-entered and spread within what is known today as New Age spirituality. But it is Augustine's powerful formulation of the doctrine of "original sin" and theological reaction to it that seems to be mirrored in the more surprising, and seemingly far removed, area of scientific debate today.

The problem of evil began with Adam in the Garden of Eden, Augustine reasoned. Having been given free will by God as an experiment, Adam then foolishly chose to listen to Eve, who in turn was advised by the serpent of evil. Though strictly forbidden by God to do so, Adam ate the apple, thus going against the will of God. Thereafter this original sin has corrupted all of us, his descendants, for Adam's guilt and its penalty pass on to us. All of us are born in sin; because of Adam's original sin we are naturally driven to pursue evil, and only through the Church can we find redemption. Though this belief was used by the Church of the Middle Ages to hold much of Western humanity in subjugation, even with the Protestant Reformation what is basically a belief that humans are driven to err through innate evil was picked up and again advanced by Martin Luther and John Calvin.

In Augustine's time another cleric, Pelagius, disputed this charge. Many other theologians and progressive faiths have since emphasized free will and vigorously denied the doctrines of innate evil and original sin. And indeed, embodied in the thinking of both the philosophers and religious thinkers of the 17th and 18th century such as William Penn and Roger Williams, the counter position not only helped shape the Declaration of Independence and the Constitution establishing the United States of America. A belief in our inherent goodness, rather than innate evil, has also similarly animated the emergence of democracies elsewhere throughout the world. Yet even in science today the ancient dispute persists.

It has been diluted and made a matter more of an honest difference of opinion than a matter of life or death according to which position one might take, as earlier. But behind the sociobiologists' doctrine of an embedded selfishness and of the belief of others in our natural propensity for violence lurks the old doctrine of innate evil. And in the countering positions of the scientific advocates of culture as a primary source of what may be considered evil can be seen an updating of Pelagius.

III. EVIL: A PHILOSOPHICAL VIEW

By far the greatest attention to the problem of evil has come from philosophers ranging from the ancient Greeks, through the years leading to and through the Enlightenment, and thereafter swelling and then dwindling into modern times.

Although not the first to deal with the problem, the Greek philosopher Epicurus most neatly set forth a central dilemma that both theologians and philosophers were to wrestle with afterward. If there is an all-wise, all-powerful, and all-good God, how can his existence be reconciled with the fact of evil? If he is all-powerful then he could prevent evil, but as he doesn't he cannot be all-good. Likewise, if he is all-good he would be forced to try to prevent evil, but as he cannot prevent it he therefore cannot be all-powerful.

Another long-term influential idea was offered by Socrates. He felt that virtue lies in knowledge and that people will be virtuous if they know what virtue is; therefore the cause of vice—or evil—is ignorance. Historically, this has been a powerful underlying rationale for the activist rise and spread of universal education. Socrates' pupil Plato believed that evil does not in itself exist, but is an imperfect reflection of the real, which is good—an idea that much later George Berkeley, Bishop of Cloyne and founder of modern idealist philosophy, was to further develop. "The very blemishes and defects of nature are not without their use," Berkeley maintained. "They make an agreeable variety and augment the beauty of the rest of creation, as shadows in a picture serve to set off the brighter parts" (Castell, p.139).

Many other positions were taken by the Greeks, but perhaps of most interest to the modern problem-solving mind are the generally neglected views of Aristotle. In contrast to the abstractions of Plato and other Greeks—notably the Cynics, the Cyrenaics, the Megarians, and the Platonists—Aristotle was the world's first, most wide ranging, empiricist. Let's look carefully at what exists before we speculate was his basic position. What he saw in looking at the problem of evil seems at first ridiculously simplistic. There are virtues and there are vices, and there are the two kinds of people, the good and the bad, he observed. But to Aristotle what made the difference was not so much the fact of evil, but what one did about it.

What made the difference was a matter of character. The virtuous were distinguished by using the virtues of courage, temperance, and what he called "greatness of soul" to apply the power of "perception, intellect, and desire" to action to better our world. The others merely wallowed in "spite, shamelessness, and envy and such actions as adultery, theft, and murder," all of which are "evil in themselves" (Aristotle, p.310).

The "just man is formed by doing just acts, the temperate man by doing temperate acts: without doing them, no one would even be likely to become good," he wrote (Ibid, p.307). Then in a slap at his teacher, a host of philosophers to follow him, and indeed most of us, Aristotle noted that "the great majority do not act on this principle. Instead, they take refuge in argument, thinking that they are being philosophers and will become morally good in that way. They are like invalids who listen attentively to their doctor, but carry out none of his instructions. These will never be made fit by that sort of regime; nor will people become healthy in soul by philosophizing like that" (Ibid).

Some 2000 years later, in the early stages of the development of the thinking that flowered during the Enlightenment, applying geometry to a demonstration of ethics, the Dutch philosopher Baruch Spinoza tried to advance our understanding of ethics by deriving principles from geometry. This led to his assertion that everything in the universe is morally neutral prior to the assignment to it by the human being of the labels of good or evil, or right or wrong. He also presents the question of evil as a rather trivial concern within the perspective of eternity, finding evil to be only "in reality a lesser good."

Another mathematician and philosopher Leibniz further advanced this view, asserting that evil was a necessary ingredient in this "best of all possible universes." This was to enrage the most accomplished polemical philosopher of his age, the great Voltaire. Not only did he immortalize Leibniz as the foolish Dr. Pangloss of his novella *Candide* but proceeded to impale Spinoza as well as Leibniz in a poem detailing what he found to be the inescapable *nontriviality* of evil rampant in this world, in which "every member groans, all born for torment and for mutual death."

"And o'er this ghastly chaos you would say the ills of each make up the good of the all!" Voltaire thundered. "What blessedness! And as, with quaking voice, mortal and pitiful ye cry, 'All's well,' the universe belies you, and your heart refutes a hundred times your mind's conceit." (Durant, p.226).

The obdurate British philosopher Thomas Hobbes picked up this theme to maintain that not only is the world filled with evil but human nature is basically evil. Apart from the veneer that civilization might give us, human life is "solitary, poor, nasty, brutish, and short," involving a "war of all against all." (Castell, p.396). As has before and since then been a firm conviction for most conservatives, for Hobbes the only solution to the implacable problem of evil embedded within all of us is massive control through the power of a strong monarch or state.

Among many other British philosophers who disagreed were David Hume and Adam Smith. Both felt that we are morally linked to one another by sympathy, which raises us out of the Hobbesian brutishness. As for evil, Hume felt this, along with the question of the existence of God, was a matter beyond the reach of human reason. Smith, however, felt that evil could be diminished. We could move away from the brutishness of the feudal monarchy, as well as the brutishness of the privileged as well as unprivileged classes of his time, toward the greater freedom and equality offered by the early stages of capitalism.

For Rousseau, as noted earlier, the source of evil was the lack of freedom and the prevalence of inequality imbedded in society rather than anything inherent in the human being. "Man is born free, and is everywhere in chains," he wrote (Castell, p.407). But behind this figure celebrated in most textbooks as the champion of the idea of the innate goodness of "man" lay the much more complicated reality of a man who was himself, by any reasonable definition, not a good person himself. Not only did he abandon his many illegitimate children to die in orphanages, but his sexism became legendary.

Taking up the challenge for feminist philosophy in his time, Mary Wollstonecraft detailed how Rousseau's book *Emile* "degrades one half the human species." Evil to her was the enforcement of ignorance and sexual slavery upon the female by the male of the species. Man, she railed in *A Vindication of the Rights of Woman*, "from the remotest antiquity, [has] found it convenient to exert his strength to subjugate his companion, and his invention to show that she ought to have her neck bent under the yoke, because the whole creation was only created for his convenience or pleasure." (Schneir, p.9). The situation of woman, she charged, was to "grovel contentedly, scarcely raised by her employments above the animal kingdom." (Ibid, p.11).

Another contradictory figure was the man considered one of the greatest philosophers of all time, Immanuel Kant. He felt that the origin of evil was a matter beyond human comprehension. But emblematic of the contradictions in philosophy that accelerated the rise of science as a way of resolving this confusion were Kant's further thoughts about evil. In relation to ethics, Kant is most famous for his Categorical Imperative, a modern updating of the ancient Golden Rule to do unto others as we would have them do unto us. This Categorical Imperative, Kant states, is the universal grounding law for all human beings—from which one would infer that Kant believed that we humans, being governed by this law, are inherently good. But elsewhere in his work he states that we are not only evil, but in fact *radically* evil by nature!

Moreover, this radical evil within us "is a natural propensity, *inextirpable* by human powers." (Kant, p.32). Yet within five pages of this assertion he is telling us that our original direction involves "a predisposition to good," and that "despite a corrupted heart" we "yet possess a good will," therefore "there remains hope of a return to the good from which [we have] strayed." (Ibid, pp.38, 39).

Kant was the watershed philosopher between earlier and modern times. Of the many strains of philosophy thereafter touching at times on the problem of evil, much of it emerged in reaction to the long-time attempt by Christianity, and what at the time was a present-day attempt by Marx and Engels and other "utopians," to eradicate the ills once classified as evil through the activist power of social movements. Nietzsche and Schopenhauer were similar in taking a very jaundiced view both of humanity and of any prospect for improvement through social movements or any other means.

To Nietzsche—paving the way for the Nazis—a source of what he would classify as evil was what he called the "slave morality" of Christianity as opposed to the "master morality" of the "free spirit" and the Superman. "The hardier human traits, such as egotism, cruelty, arrogance, retaliation, and approbation, are given ascendancy over the softer virtues, such as sympathy, charity, forgiveness, loyalty, and humility, and are pronounced necessary constituents in the moral code of a natural aristocracy," one admiring commentator writes of Nietzsche's views. (Nietzsche, p.376). As for Schopenhauer, life was evil because we are driven to never be satisfied, because pain is our basic reality with pleasure only temporary, because the more advanced and sensitive we are the more we suffer, because if we find satisfaction it is only to thereafter become bored, and because life is war—everything trying to eat or outdo each other in a situation where "man is a wolf to man." (Durant, p.325).

Out of this mid-19th century time, via the gloomy Danish philosopher Soren Kierkegaard, also rose the existential philosophy that was to carry the problem of evil on into recent times. To Kierkegaard, "the human race is sick, and, speaking spiritually, sick unto death." (Loewith, p.112). Our "peculiar immorality" is "an extravagant disregard for the individual." (Ibid, p.110). In other words, in a view shared with Nietzsche and Schopenhauer, one of the worst things about modern life for Kierkegaard was the social movements, such as Marxism or any other, that in attempting large-scale improvement in the human situation reduced the individual to being meaningless unless one could be labeled an advocate of some larger cause.

For one of the best-known existentialists for the 20th century, Jean Paul Satre, this became the view of "man" as isolated in a lonely world, with our only basic reference point or source of standards being ourselves, as individuals. Rather than being in any way fixed "essences," good or evil were again, as for Spinoza, only labels we assign to what happens according to our own perceptions out of our own isolated "existences." Satre, however, whose thought, along with that of his lifetime companion Simone de Bouvier, was shaped by resistance to the evil embodied in the Nazi occupation of France during World War II, shared with Aristotle and Marx and Engels the conviction of the necessity for moral action.

"I ask myself, 'Will socialization, as such, ever come about?' I know nothing about it," he wrote. "All I know is that I'm going to do everything in my power to bring it about. Beyond that, I can't count on anything... The doctrine I am presenting is the very opposite of quietism, since it declares, 'There is no reality except in action.' Moreover, it goes further, since it adds, 'Man is nothing else than his plan; he exists only to the extent that he fulfills himself; he is therefore nothing else than the ensemble of his acts, nothing else than his life.'" (Satre, pp.31, 32).

Gradually thereafter in France existentialism gave way to related philosophies, still embedded in the English and art departments of many universities worldwide, variously known as deconstructionism, postmodernism, poststructuralism, and other terms. Although originally representing an advance in destroying many old paradigms binding modern thought and visual expression, over time these "schools" of thought have driven philosophy into what their critics feel is a cul-de-sac of irrelevance. Within the context of the problem of evil, central to this failure seems to be the way the deconstructionists and others, pushed to the extreme the idea we have been following that good or evil are only labels we assign to things for which there are no universals, no basis for consensus, no basis for the arousal and binding of ourselves together into a community of feeling or solidarity, or for concerted action.

In contrast to the earlier emphasis on "deconstruction," throughout the fields of art, literature, and philosophy as well as the social sciences affected by these philosophies the move is now toward "reconstruction." Also in stark contrast stands the view of American philosopher and psychologist John Dewey, who more than 70 years ago now expressed what has long been the rationale for both activist education and activist social science.

"The problem of evil ceases to be a theological and metaphysical one, and is perceived to be the practical problem of reducing, alleviating, as far as may be removing, the evils of life," Dewey wrote in 1920. "Philosophy is no longer under obligation to find ingenious methods of proving that evils are only apparent, not real, or to elaborate schemes for explaining them away or, worse yet, for justifying them. It assumes another obligation:—That of contributing in however humble a way to methods that will assist us in discovering the causes of humanity's ills." (Dewey, pp.141, 142).

IV. VIOLENCE AS EVIL AND WHAT TO DO ABOUT IT

A recurring theme over thousands of years of religion and hundreds of years of philosophy is the identification of violence as evil. While evil is a word one seldom finds used in science, it is also significant that by a variety of criteria, over a number of fields, scientific studies find violence associated with much of what in religion and philosophy has been labeled evil—that is, that violence breeds more violence and is potentially destructive to the stability and well-being of persons, families, and neighborhoods, as well as nations.

The Hindu Bhagavad-Gita identifies self-restraint, harmlessness, absence of wrath, peacefulness, and forgiveness as among the "divine properties" that are "deemed to be for liberation." By contrast, it identifies wrath, harshness, and "unwisdom" as properties of the "demonical for bondage."

"Him I call indeed a Brahmana who without hurting any creatures, whether feeble or strong, does not kill nor cause slaughter. Him I call indeed a Brahmana who is tolerant with the intolerant, and mild with the violent," counsels the Dhammapada of Buddhism.

"So far as arms are concerned, they are implements of ill-omen," offers Taoism. "Where armies have been quartered brambles and thorns grow."

"How beautiful upon the mountains are the feet of him that bringeth good tidings, that publisheth peace," proclaims Isaiah in the Old Testament of the Jews and Christians, foreshadowing Jesus' "Blessed are the peacemakers, for they shall be called the children of God."

As for the philosophers, with the exception of firebrands like Nietzsche, who looms now as a truly aberrant being not only in his legitimation of the philosophy of the Nazis but also for his literal worship of violence, most of the rest were mild men to whom it was obvious that violence threatened everything they valued. Moreover, in keeping with Aristotle's dictum of praxis, or moral action, some tried to do something about it.

Repelled by the violence of his age, Kant made the case for organizing what eventually became the League of Nations and then the United Nations. Repelled by the violence of his age, and mindful of the global interest in sports, William James detailed a plan for a game that might provide a "moral equivalent" for war. Repelled by the violence of their ages, over 100 years feminist philosophers such as Margaret Fuller, Matilda Joslyn Gage, Charlotte Perkins Gilman, and Simone de Bouvier steadily laid the intellectual groundwork for a notably peace-oriented global women's movement. Currently philosopher Ervin Laszlo has launched a Club of Budapest to be an equivalent for the industrial Club of Rome in focusing the creativity of artists, musicians, writers, and religious leaders as well as scientists on the reduction of global violence and the stabilization of peace.

A powerful countering factor bearing on the question of violence and what to do about it, however, has been the influence of certain aspects of the philosophies of two 20th century figures known chiefly as psychologists, Sigmund Freud and Carl Jung. These views are of interest here for two reasons. One is that, although purportedly scientific, neither of their views in this instance were, both being matters of unsubstantiated personal philosophy. The other reason is that, generally unperceived, both views have widely and persistently served to perpetuate the idea of evil being innate in humans, which again and again has discouraged people from trying to do something about violence, as it seems inevitable, as well as being used to justify authoritarian control.

For Freud the evil in us is innate aggression—that we are cosmically driven by the death instinct he called Thanatos, as well as by the primal depravity of the id within our unconscious, to aggress against others, and to kill if need be. For Jung evil was the dark mystery residing in what he called the Shadow, an archetypally embedded and therefore innate and eternally threatening source of the potential for violence and all other depravities. Within the context of both the religion and the philosophy we have examined here it can be seen how again we are looking at what are in essence modern updatings of Augustine's doctrine of original sin—and indeed Jung recognized this connection in one of his papers.

Countering the persistence of this idea of innate evil are not only the views and studies identified earlier but much new work. In closing, we will examine examples bearing on the question of violence as evil from theology, cultural evolution studies and theory, and again the interface between brain and culture.

Being mainly irreligious themselves, having outgrown such prejudices they feel, social scientists looking for the causes of the ills of this world—or the source of evil in the earlier terminology—tend to overlook one very large fact. This is that religion is still exceptionally meaningful to the overwhelming majority of the people on this planet. Moreover, these religions are—for better or for worse—primarily motivational. Both how we are driven to violence and to nonviolence has been examined in a monumental recent study of the problem of evil from the theological viewpoint in a trilogy of books by Walter Wink. "Evil is not our essence," theologian Wink concludes in *Engaging the Powers* (p.72). Rather, the problem is the "myth of redemptive violence," which has become the linchpin for the "Domination System."

"Paradoxically, those in the grip of the cultural trance woven over us by the Domination System are usually unaware of the full depth of their soul-sickness," Wink writes. "It is only after we experience liberation from primary socialization to the world-system that we real ize how terribly we have violated our authentic personhood—and how violated we have been" (Ibid, p.73).

Another monumental recent work searching for the cause of violence are the cumulating books and papers of systems scientist and cultural evolutionary theorist Riane Eisler. Driven herself to the question of the origin and nature of evil by the fact of being Jewish and a refugee from the devastation of the Nazis in Europe, Eisler's work culminates the feminist critique we have briefly touched on here. The problem is not violence or evil inherent in the *male* per se, Eisler stresses—a misconception that has driven women as well as men to reject the feminist critique. Rather, as she outlines in *The Chalice and the Blade* and *Sacred Pleasure*, the problem is violence as a foundational aspect, along with male domination, and authoritarianism, of the *dominator* model or paradigm of social organization that has prevailed over the past 5000 years of human cultural evolution. This Eisler contrasts with the *partnership* model of social organization, based on nonviolence, gender as well as more general equality, and more democratic governance, originally advanced by Jesus among others and furthered by the Enlightenment and many modern social movements.

In its probe of violence against women, against children, against men, against races and creeds and nations, Eisler's indictment ranges, era by era, over hundreds of years of our history. Yet out of it all rises the hopefulness of her observation that "this kind of system is not the only possibility for our species. Indeed, despite all the insensitivity and pain considered normal in much of recorded history ... women and men have still somehow managed to relate to one another in sensitive and pleasurable ways. Even in the midst of hate, cruelty, and violence, we have again and again managed to instead give and receive love and to find joy not only in sexual passion but in the simplest of human gestures, in the touch of someone's hand, a kiss, a friendly smile." (Eisler, 1995, p.242).

And what might account for this difference between whether we are to sadistically bully, brutalize, exploit, and kill, or to love one another? A particularly dramatic recent finding of brain researchers reaffirms the findings of many other brain researchers, child development specialists, and psychologists over at least the past 50 years. In 1994 psychologists Adrian Raine, Patricia Brennan and Sarnoff Mednick reported the result of a study of 4269 men born in Denmark in the years 1959 through 1961. They had looked for connections between birth complications, rejection by their mothers, and later violent crime.

What they found was no significant correlation between either birth complications and later violent crime, or between rejection by their mothers and later violent crime. But the picture greatly changed when they looked at the 3.9% of their sample who had suffered *both* birth complications and later rejection by their mothers. *For they found that this 3.9% had committed 22% of all the later violent crimes* (*Brain Mind Bulletin*, 1994).

What does this tell us? If we carefully consider this finding it seems to be a scientific minimetaphor for the relation of culture to biology, or of nurture to nature, that runs throughout this question we have repeatedly encountered of the origin of evil, and of whether we are innately evil, innately violent, or inherently otherwise. For here, pinned down by the most exacting of scientific approaches, the message would seem to be relatively clear.

Is it not that what determines our violence is not what is in us at birth, or even—as some contend—the trauma we may suffer in being born? It seems to lie in what happens to us afterward. It seems to depend on whether we are born into a family in which the parents have been maimed by cultural systems orienting to domination, violence, and gender and other forms of inequality, or into a family in which the parents have themselves been nurtured by cultural systems orienting more to the encouragement of equality, love, and caring.

Also See the Following Articles

AGGRESSION AND ALTRUISM • ANIMAL BEHAVIOR STUDIES, PRIMATES • BIOCHEMICAL FACTORS • CULTURAL ANTHROPOLOGY STUDIES • ENEMY, CONCEPT AND IDENTITY OF • ETHICAL AND RELIGIOUS TRADITIONS, EASTERN • ETHICAL AND RELIGIOUS TRADITIONS, WESTERN • EVOLUTIONARY FACTORS • GENDER STUDIES • HUMAN NATURE, VIEWS OF

Bibliography

Aristotle. (1963). *The philosophy of Aristotle.* New York: New American Library.

The Bible of the World. (1939). New York: Viking.

Brain Mind Bulletin. (1994, March). Vol.19, No. 6.

Castell, A. (1946). *An introduction to modern philosophy.* New York: Macmillan.

The Dartmouth Bible. (1950). Boston: Houghton-Mifflin.

de Waal, F. (1996). *Goodnatured.* Cambridge: Harvard University Press.

Dewey, J. (1950). *Reconstruction in philosophy.* New York: New American Library.

Durant, W. (1961). *The story of philosophy.* New York: Simon & Schuster.

Eisler, R. (1987). *The chalice and the blade.* San Francisco: Harper & Row.

Eisler, R. (1995). *Sacred Pleasure: Sex, Myth, and the Politics of the Body.* San Francisco: HarperCollins.

Kant, I. (1960). *Religion within the limits of reason alone.* New York: Harper and Row.

Lewontin, R. C., Rose, S., & Kamin, L. (1984). *Not in our genes.* New York: Pantheon.

Loewith, K. (1967). *From Hegel to Nietzsche.* New York: Doubleday Anchor.

Loye, D. (1993). Moral sensitivity and the evolution of higher mind. In Laszlo, E., *et al.*, (Eds.), *The evolution of cognitive maps: New paradigms for the twenty-first century.* Philadelphia: Gordon and Breach.

Loye, D. (1998). *The glacier and the flame: The rediscovery of goodness.* (In preparation).

Loye, D. (1998). *Darwin's Lost Theory.* (In preparation).

Montagu, A. (1986). *Touching: The human significance of skin*. New York: Harper & Row.

Nietzsche, F. (1927). *The philosophy of Nietzsche*. New York: Modern Library.

Satre, J. (1957). *Existentialism and human emotions*. New York: Philosophical Library.

Schneir, M. (Ed.). (1972). *Feminism: The essential historical writings*. New York: Vintage.

Shore, A. N. (1994). *Affect Regulation and the Origin of Self: The Neurobiology of Emotional Development*. Hillsdale, NJ: Erlbaum.

Smith, H. (1994). *The Illustrated World Religions*. San Francisco: HarperCollins.

Spinoza, B. (1951). *The chief works of Benedict de Spinoza*. New York: Dover: New York.

Wink, W. (1992). *Engaging the powers: Discernment and resistance in a world of domination*. Minneapolis: Fortress Press.

Evolutionary Factors

Jukka-Pekka Takala
National Research Institute of Legal Policy, Finland

GLOSSARY

Allele Any alternative form of a gene.

Adaptation A process of natural selection operating upon heritable variation by which an organism becomes fitted to its environment; any of the evolved fitness-enhancing characteristics.

Coefficient of Relatedness The probability that a specific allele is identical in two individuals because of descent from a recent common ancestor

Environment of Evolutionary Adaptedness (EEA) The environment in which a species evolved to solve the recurring problems posed by that environment.

Evolutionary Psychology Study of the psyche in the light of evolutionary theory and current knowledge about the processes that created the psyche.

Evolutionarily Stable Strategy (ESS) In evolutionary game theory, a particular behavioral strategy pursued by individuals such that, given a certain initial frequency in a population, it cannot be replaced by mutant strategies. In considerations of ESS, the focus is on the competition between individuals of a population, not on the relationship between a species and nature.

Fitness The success of a phenotype's genes relative to their alleles within a population.

Gene A section of DNA that codes for one protein.

Inclusive Fitness Total of an individual's personal reproductive success and its influence on the fitness of relatives, the latter multiplied by the coefficients of relatedness between those relatives and the focal individual.

Kin Selection A concept referring to the fact that natural selection works on inclusive fitness (qv). An individual may help to propagate the frequency of a trait in a population even if it in so doing reduces the individual's personal fitness, provided the reduction is outweighed by increase in the fitness of individuals related to the actor.

Parental Investment Anything a parent does to increase a descendant's reproductive success at a cost to the parent's capacity to invest in other offspring.

Parent–Offspring Conflict Conflict based on the fact that the genomes of parents and offspring are not identical; typically, it is in the parents' genetic interest to invest more or sooner in other progeny than the focal offspring's genetic interest would dictate.

Sexual Selection Intrasexual competition for access to the opposite sex and intersexual mate choice. Darwin held sexual selection to be a form different from natural selection but today it is usually considered to be a form of natural selection.

THERE IS LITTLE controversy among scientists that evolution has shaped the bodies and brains of humans that are involved in conflicts, episodes of violence, and periods of peaceful existence. It is more controversial to what extent the theory of evolution can be helpful in understanding human behavior, including violent and peaceful means to negotiate conflicts. Since Darwin, one of the terms most closely associated with the theory of evolution has been the "struggle for existence." While the notion has been exaggerated and misleadingly embellished with a moral meaning, evolution by natural selection does involve competition over limited resources, and those studying animals have constantly paid attention to different morphological and behavioral features that seem to be adaptations for competition and conflict. Simultaneously, forms of cooperation and "altruism" in animals also have been recognized. During the past few decades, these fields of inquiry have developed considerably. Ethologists and behavioral ecologists have charted in great detail how different animals typically behave in conflict situations and how they go about pursuing limited vital resources. Breakthroughs in evolutionary theory have allowed a better understanding of many aspects of animal behavior, including forms of aggression and altruism. The rejection of naïve forms of group selectionism, which assumed that selection optimized the good of species, has inspired new insights in intraspecific conflict and competition, such as the development of evolutionary game theory. The discovery of kin selection, the fact that selection operates on the combined or "inclusive" fitness of the focal individual and its relatives, has led to new hypotheses and findings of the patterns of conflict, competition, violence, peace, and altruism. When these insights are applied to humans, many patterns of violence turn out to be consistent with the assumption that humans have evolved to be effective competitors and kin-benefactors or "nepotists." In addition to those researchers who attend to hypothesized pan-human behavioral and psychological adaptations for peaceful and violent interactions, evolutionary theory also inspires scientists pursuing other questions. Behavioral geneticists focus on the contribution of genetic variance to differences in aggression and other behavior. Others use theory of genetical evolution as an analogy or heuristic model for examining competition for limited resources through sociocultural evolution. For instance, many forms of property crime and crime prevention measures can be conceptualized as a coevolutionary process analogous to the coevolution in nature of predator and prey.

I. THE EVOLUTIONARY POINT OF VIEW

A. Complementary Levels of Explanation for Behavior

Explanations for a behavior, such as aggression, can be sought at different levels. One approach may look at the immediate factors at play in situations that lead to aggression, such as frustration, or the status of hormones or neurotransmitters or some aspects in the immediate social situation. This approach produces what are often called *proximate* explanations. A second approach looks at the development of individuals during their lives and tries to find some circumstances or experiences—such as the behavior and example of parents or the dominant gender roles proffered by the prevailing culture—that might influence their aggressive and peaceful inclinations during their later lives. This approach strives for *ontogenic* explanations. A third kind of approach looks at behaviors such as aggression as expressions of a set of propensities that have been selected by evolution because they serve the individual's (inclusive) fitness. This suggests *ultimate* or *distal* explanations. Finally, a fourth approach delineates the evolutionary history of a behavioral trait to arrive at a *phylogenetic* explanation.

Despite much controversy between proponents of different approaches, they are not, in principle, contradictory. Rather, they address different aspects of a potential unified, comprehensive explanation. For example, one essential part of the proximate explanation for why red deer stags go to their regular mating grounds and prepare for fighting is an increased level of the male hormone testosterone. This is known because red deer stags given testosterone in experiments behave like that; they also lose the velvet covering on their antlers in preparation for territorial battles, even in the absence of females. However, from the evolutionary point of view, there is no point for red deer stags to head for their mating grounds and prepare for fighting just because of a surge of testosterone. The ultimate selectional causation of a trait is an account of how it helps solve a (recurrent) problem related to survival and reproduction. The red deer stag is programmed, as it were, to head to the mating grounds at the time of the year when the hinds in estrus also gather there to select their mates. Once this breeding system was in place, any stag that failed to go there and fight may have preserved his life and limb longer but had fewer chances of passing on his genes.

The evolutionary point of view emphasizes ultimate or distal causes for a given behavioral propensity. It seeks to determine whether, or to what extent, such propensities can be viewed as adaptations to solve a stable or recurrent problem that the organism in question faces. Conversely, it also uses information of what sort of problems organisms are likely to have faced in order to generate hypotheses on what sort of patterns their behavior can be expected to exhibit.

B. Evolution by Natural Selection

Evolution by natural selection, as described by Charles Darwin and Alfred Russel Wallace in 1858, is a result of a few simple processes. First, living beings tend to produce more offspring than the environment can carry. Darwin, who adopted this insight from Malthus, presented (in *The Origin of Species*) calculations showing that "the earth would soon be covered by the progeny of a single pair," were the process not checked. This means that there is competition for resources—be it overt or covert. Second, individuals of a population show variability in their traits and properties that are at least partly heritable. Third, the survival and reproductive success of different heritable variants is not random; some properties systematically enhance their bearers' ability to survive and reproduce. Finally, in the course of many generations, differential reproduction leads to an increase of the successful variants and a decrease or elimination of the less successful ones.

Natural selection has no goal or purpose, but it will produce organisms that *seem* purposefully crafted to their environments. A variant that can better utilize a resource of the environment or better defend a resource against competitors emerges by chance, but once it has appeared, its chances of survival and reproduction are better than those of other variants. In sexually reproducing species each new fertilization produces a new combination of alleles and thus a slightly new design of each organism. Together with mutations, sexual recombinations constantly "propose" modified designs for natural selection to "dispose."

The differential survival and reproduction of different variants is dependent of their different abilities to compete over limited resources. Hence, it can be expected that adaptations that emerge in the process of natural selection will help in this competition. While competition does not necessarily imply direct confrontation, this is one possibility of deciding the outcome of conflicts.

It is important to notice that natural selection is not about just survival, but about survival and particularly reproduction. A heritable variant of an animal that lives 10 times longer than its conspecifics but produces no offspring is an evolutionary failure. In sexually reproducing species, reproduction requires successful mating. This opens up a competition over mating opportunities and high-quality mates. Traits that help in this competition become potential targets of evolution. However, properties that predict success in sexual selection may simultaneously make life more risky in other respects. There are many examples in nature in which better chances in mating and reproduction involve an elevated risk of death or injury as a trade-off.

1. Gene-Based Evolutionary Theory

While variation and heritability were central notions in Darwin's theory of evolution, he did not know the mechanisms that produced either of them. Mendelian genetics became generally known only in the beginning of the 20th century. After this Darwin's and Mendel's ideas were worked into a unified theory, the "modern synthesis," according to which evolution works by changing the allele frequencies in populations. However, fitness was still understood in terms of individual organisms and their direct progeny.

Largely as a result of the work of William Hamilton in the early 1960s, it is now realized that, from the point of view of evolution, the conclusive matter is not how many direct descendants an individual has, but how many of his or her genes are passed to the next generations. In a sexually reproducing species, individual genotypes are unique—apart from monozygotic twins, other multiple offspring and artificial clones—and they cannot be passed on to future genotypes. However, alleles can be passed on, and near kin can also be helpful in this process. In humans (or other vertebrates), on average one-half of an individual's genes are *identical by descent* with those of a full sibling. Likewise, a parent and a child share one-half of such genes. Correspondingly, one-quarter of the genes (alleles) are identical by descent between grandparents and their grandchildren and between an individual and a sister or a brother of one of his or her parents. This quantity is called the *coefficient of relatedness* and it is defined as the probability that a specific allele is identical in two individuals by descent from a recent common ancestor. The coefficient of relatedness, often termed "r," varies from 0.0 (unrelated) to 1.0 (genetically identical). (Note that a great proportion of genes are identical across a whole species; "r" is relevant for those loci in which there is variation in a population. These are also those loci that are responsible for genotypic variation and, hence, provide alternative "proposals" for natural selection.)

For the reproduction of these genes, it does not matter whether they are passed on to the next generation via me or a relative. A reasoning like this is summarized in the notion *inclusive fitness,* which is defined as the total of an individual's individual fitness (direct descendants) plus its contribution to the fitness of its relatives discounted by the coefficient of relatedness. For example, if my contribution helps my full sister to raise two more children than she otherwise could raise, this is as good for my inclusive fitness as raising one child of my own, since my sister is likely to share one-half of my relevant genes.

The idea of inclusive fitness and the recognition of the importance of the gene level has thrown light on forms of altruism and aggression that seemed difficult to account for previously. Inclusive fitness explains how traits that help relatives at the expense of self can be selected. It also suggests that—other things being equal—an individual is less likely to behave aggressively toward its relatives than other conspesifics because hostility toward relatives lowers one component of its inclusive fitness.

2. Parent–Offspring Conflict

Modern gene-based evolutionary theory predicts that—other things being equal—conflicts will be the more prevalent and intense the more the reproductive interests of different genes, individuals, and groups differ. The closer genetic relatives two individuals are, the less intense conflict there should be, on average.

An interesting projection from the gene-based evolutionary theory is the concept of parent–offspring conflict, suggested by Robert Trivers. When a parent nurtures its child, its own inclusive fitness is raised as long as the cost is not too high. Alternatively, both the child and the parent may gain in fitness if the parent produces another child. However, they would time such a decision differently. To maximize the parent's inclusive fitness, it should invest in a new child as soon as the new child's fitness gain is greater than that of the extant child. From the point of view of the extant child's fitness, however, production of new offspring should wait until the new full sibling's fitness gain is *twice* that of the extant child because it must be discounted by one-half. Hence, the extant offspring tends to be "programmed" to resist weaning and other expressions of diminished parental investment in itself.

Trivers' theory has shed light not only on sibling rivalry or the weaning conflict that humans (and other mammals) experience but also on complications of pregnancy.

C. Adaptation

Adaptation is the process by which an organism becomes fitted to its environment through evolution. The traits produced in this process—also called adaptations—include structures for locomotion, perception, and avoidance of predators, but they also include typical behaviors and the basic motives and emotions, appetites, aversions and modes of information processing—i.e., the most fundamental psychology—of an animal. They became part of a species' normal "design" because, in the course of many generations, they were "synchronized" with a set of statistically recurrent properties of their environment. They contributed to the fitness of the ancestral organism with sufficient frequency. This means that calling something an adaptation is—as John Tooby and Leda Cosmides write—a complex judgment, involving a "probability assessment concerning how likely a situation is to have arisen by chance."

A matter complicating analyses is that adaptations were molded by the past environment and are not necessarily adaptive today. This is particularly important for human adaptations, since today's world is in many ways strikingly different from the environment of human evolutionary adaptedness (EEA). By most accounts, humans have undergone little genetic evolution since long before the introduction of agriculture. Hence, when evolutionists speak of adaptations in humans, they are not claiming that they are adaptive today but making an assumption that they would have been adaptive in the EEA, i.e., an environment which did not include, for instance, agriculture, industry, cars, telecommunication, or contraceptives. It almost certainly did include gathering food and hunting, tools and weapons, children and adults, sexual attraction and competition for the most attractive mates, families and relatives, dangers posed by predators and other groups of humans, and possibly differences in reputation and competition for "status."

An oft-posed and basically fair question about analyses of adaptation is: Are they testable? Isn't it tautological to argue that particular traits of behavior or morphology are "adaptive" if the purposes for those "adaptations" are inferred from the very features in question? The problem is real enough and there is a constant danger of making up evolutionary "just-so stories." However, the problem can be largely avoided by deriving testable predictions from adaptation hypotheses. The adaptationist framework helps researchers to "predict" missing pieces of a puzzle and to test assumed finds. For instance, very often the design or even the existence of a proposed adaptive mechanism is unknown prior to investigation. The framework can suggest ways in which such a design could be discovered. Another direction is to search for a function for a known mechanism. This parallels the way in which William Harvey started to wonder why there were one-way valves in the veins and was led to the discovery of the circulation of blood. When a theory leads to the discovery of a fact that was unknown until after it was predicted by the theory, it is not a tautological post hoc explanation. For instance, the inclusive fitness theory suggests that people should not harm or kill close genetic relatives.

1. Do Not Kill Close Relatives

During the past 2 decades, Margin Daly and Margo Wilson and others have tested this idea and found that it holds remarkably well. Relatives do harm and kill each other because they have many chances, but once you control opportunity—say, look only at people who share a home—the picture changes. According to one study by Daly and Wilson, Canadian children who lived with a natural parent and a stepparent had 40 times higher abuse rates than children living with both natural parents. The risk of newborns to 2-year-olds of being killed differed even more, 70-fold. An Australian study found that 36% of the offenders in child-abuse deaths were nongenetic fathers, while only 3.8% of dependent children live with a male stepparent. Another Daly and Wilson study looked at the relative risk of homicide by relationship in coresiding people in a U.S. city. Coresiding persons who were not genetic relatives experienced a homicide rate 11 times greater than coresiding kin.

An analysis of kinship in Icelandic sagas revealed that murderers were seldom genetic relatives of their victims; and when they were, the stakes tended to be high. The notion of inclusive fitness does not say that it would *never* enhance one's fitness to harm or kill a relative; it only says that the fitness gain from such an act ought to be greater than the relative's fitness loss multiplied by the coefficient of relatedness. More fitness is lost than gained by killing a brother for a hazelnut, but killing for an autocratic kingdom with ensuing access to numerous wives might be a different matter.

Daly and Wilson studied homicide as an indicator for intensity of conflicts. They reasoned that the same factors that exacerbate (or mitigate) interpersonal conflicts also lead to higher- (or lower-) than-expected frequencies in homicides. Thus, a study of the particular relationship categories, life stages, and other circumstances of killings can shed light on matters that exacerbate (or mitigate) interpersonal conflicts in general.

This approach does not mean that killing of one's genetic or even stepchildren would actually be good for one's inclusive fitness. Rather, the deaths can be often understood as chance results of escalating conflicts or milder actions gone bad. For instance, parents do try to discipline their offspring in many ways, and these measures may get out of control. The probability of such fatalities, however, is presumably dependent on the weight of other factors, such as how important the target of disciplinary action is for one's own fitness.

II. ADAPTATIONS TO VIOLENCE AND CONFLICT

Adaptationist analysis evaluates the fitness-enhancing (or reducing) effects of behaviors or "decision rules." Hence, it seeks possible fitness-enhancing effects also in species-typical violent behaviors. Furthermore, it looks at the complexity or nonrandomness of such behaviors in order to determine whether they can be considered as adaptations.

It is improbable that *random* aggressiveness and violence *in general* would be adaptive. However, there are many kinds of recurrent situations in the life course of different animals such that measured violence (or threat thereof) is most likely adaptive. One prima facie reason for suspecting this is that many animals exhibit complex species-typical morphological and behavioral traits that very much look like adaptations for violence. The stag's antlers serve in competition over access to females, the male stickleback violently defends his young. Individuals that appear timid in other contexts aggressively defend their vital reproductive resources—such as food, territory, and offspring against threat of usurpation or harm. Some animals are quick to grab any resources that they have a chance to hold. Furthermore, they fight over access to mates. Aggression easily occurs where resources are scarce—or potentially scarce—so that some groups or individuals can deny others access to them by claiming ownership of them. Humans, for instance, have fought bitterly over ownership of cattle and arable land but far less over access to oxygen. Ecology has thus great potential influence on the level of aggressiveness.

The adaptiveness of defensive aggression and its emotional facilitators has been recognized already centuries before Darwin by many observers who noted that individuals who always voluntarily yield to others any resources that they would need for their own survival and reproduction suffer in nature.

The data are fragmentary and the issue somewhat controversial, but there are many indicators that in those kinds of societies in which humans evolved, strength and skill in fighting was an attribute that contributed to men's reputation and their success. One example of a rather direct link between violence and reproductive success was found by Napoleon Chagnon in his studies of the Yanomamö of the Amazon area. Those Yanomamö men that had participated in killing a human being—called *unokais*—had greater reproductive success than other men. In 1988, in one group of villages, 88% of the 137 unokais were married, while only 51% of the nonunokais were. According to Chagnon "the higher reproductive success of unokais is mainly due to their greater success in finding mates, either by appropriating them forcibly from others, or by customary marriage alliance arrangements in which they seem to be more attractive as mates than nonunokais."

The Yanomamö are horticulturalists and are thus not very representative of the human hunter–gatherer EEA. Nevertheless, this study, in combination with much other fragmentary information from various societies, makes it a plausible suggestion that at least some readiness for and ability in aggression may often have promoted men's reproductive success. Quite likely, in most human societies, high-ranking men have had more children and their children have survived better than those of low rank. If controlled aggression has helped these men to gain and retain their status, it seems that aggression has helped men to have more offspring in many kinds of societies, be they foraging, pastoral, horticultural, or state societies.

A. Rules and Rituals of Fighting

Konrad Lorenz thought that humans were in peril because they had lost the gestures of surrender and the instinctive inhibition against killing conspecifics that other animals supposedly have. Since then, this reasoning has been refuted both on empirical and theoretical grounds. First, many animals do kill conspesifics. When observation times are long enough, these instances are observed. Compared to humans, apes and monkeys are violent. Second, Lorenz's suggestion was based on group-selectionist thinking, the assumption that animals evolved for the "good of the species." However, there is no mechanism that would make the "interest of the species" prevail over strategies that benefit individuals and their genes.

Nevertheless, Lorenz's proposal that animals often settle fights in a ritualized way stands. However, ritualized fighting can be accounted for without recourse to group selectionism. It is the contestant's own interest to settle the fight with as little cost as possible. This implies a selection pressure for means to assess the relative fighting power of the adversary. If an individual is facing an opponent who is clearly bigger, has stronger fighting devices, and so on, than he, it behooves him to ascertain these facts before he gets hurt in a fight. But actual fights carry risks for the stronger parties as well. Even if an individual wins, if he stays in the battleground wounded, he may have reduced his fitness. Additionally, he has no interest in pursuing the yielding party because it entails a risk of injury to the aggressor that is too great to take for the benefit expected.

III. COOPERATION AND CONFLICT

Since Darwin published his work on the origin of species, there has been an ongoing—if partly unilluminating—discussion on whether natural selection and evolution "really" means struggle and conflict or whether the role of cooperation, harmony, and symbiosis have been underestimated. Social Darwinists did interpret Darwin's work as exalting "nature red in tooth and claw" and saw it as legitimizing disregard for the poor and the needy. Others took an opposite stance. In his 1902 book *Mutual Aid: A Factor of Evolution,* Peter Kropotkin challenged the view that struggle was the essence of evolution. "[T]he war of each against all is not the law of nature. Mutual aid is as much a law of nature as mutual struggle. . . ." Mutual aid helped groups of animals and humans "in their hard struggle against a hostile nature."

As Frans de Waal among others has shown, it really is not a question of *either* struggle *or* cooperation, but, rather, that both exist in the natural world. Hamilton's kin selection theory gave a plausible account of why closely related organisms should help each other and cooperate. Robert Trivers developed an account of the evolution of reciprocal altruism between non-kin. In reciprocal altruism, the exchange of favors is not simultaneous. The first act is beneficial to the recipient and costly to the performer. After a time lag, the act is reciprocated. Giving is contingent on receiving. Trivers' theory of the evolution of reciprocal altruism, and related theories on reciprocal relations, have interesting things to say about conflict, violence, and peace. Trivers' model implied that selection, under some circumstances, discriminates against those who fail to reciprocate, the "cheaters." This happens if cheating has later adverse affects on the cheater's life that outweigh the benefit of not reciprocating. "This may happen if the altruist responds to the cheating by curtailing all future possible altruistic gestures to this individual."

Game-theoretical work by Robert Axelrod and others has shown that a reciprocating strategy is an ESS under many plausible conditions. A strategy called "tit for tat" was the most successful in a competition of strategies for a series of Prisoner's Dilemma games. The strategy is simple: "Cooperate the first time and then match your opponent's last move." Axelrod and Hamilton designed the contest to mirror competition and selection in the biological world by awarding "fitness" in proportion to rewards and repeating the game over "generations." They did not find any more complex conditional strategy that could replace tit-for-tat. Interestingly for theorizing on aggression, they showed the necessity of a response to defection by the opponent. Later work has showed that an mild element of "forgiveness" makes the strategy even more robust. However, it does not obviate the need to "punish" a cheater. Rather, indiscriminate "forgiveness," or all-out altruism, promotes the cheaters. If reciprocal altruism develops, also strategies that take advantage of altruists develop easily, unless altruists develop counterstrategies, cheater detection, and punishment of nonreciprocators. Trivers termed such punishment "moralistic aggression" and assumed that it was selected to counteract cheating. "Much of human aggression has moral overtones," Trivers observed. "Injustice, unfairness, and lack of reciprocity often motivate human aggression and indignation." Sociologist Donald Black has reviewed convincing evidence that even a great proportion of crimes are moralistic: such acts are typically reprisals for an experienced wrongdoing, often cheating.

A common feature of moralistic aggression is, Trivers noted, that "it often seems out of all proportion to the offenses committed.... But since small inequities repeated many times over a lifetime may exact a heavy toll in relative fitness, selection may favor a strong show of aggression when the cheating tendency is discovered."

IV. REPRODUCTIVE STRATEGIES AND GENDER DIFFERENCES

Reproductive strategy is a notion that is used to link ultimate and proximate factors. It is a construct that seeks to link, for an individual, group, species or one sex of a species, empirical reproductive behaviors to the goal of optimal reproductive effort. Reproductive strategy does not require *conscious* planning for reproduction; the term rather refers to a set of nonconscious decision rules that the individuals seem to live by. Some of the conflicts between the sexes are illuminated by considerations of the differences in the reproductive interests of males and females.

In sexually reproducing species, the reproductive strategies of males and females usually differ, depending on the type and amount of parental investment that reproduction requires, availability of alternatives, and issues such as paternity certainty. In mammals, the female body hosts the fertilized eggs for a considerable time, during which time the female cannot invest in producing other offspring of her own. Mating with many partners does not have much impact on the number of a female mammal's offspring, while a male, whose body is not tied up in gestation or suckling, can multiply the number of his offspring by mating with many partners.

Human mating patterns are variable but usually fall somewhere between monogamy and mild polygyny. In general, humans are *effective polygynous*, which is a technical term referring to the fact that the *variance* of male reproductive success is greater than that of females (there are more childless men than women and there are more men with higher numbers of offspring than there are women). Effectively polygynous species are usually sexually dimorphic with males being bigger (in effectively *polyandrous* species, such as spotted sandpipers and certain phalaropes, females tend to be bigger). The more polygynous the species, the larger the size difference between the sexes tends to be.

Human sexual size dimorphism is mild, less than in the polygynous gorilla but more than in the monogamous gibbon. Differences in traits that are relevant for fighting are larger than the average size difference. Men have almost twice as much strength in their shoulders, arms, and hands as females and have longer arms. Men are usually also more skillful in fighting, throwing objects, and using weapons than women. It is, of course, controversial to what extent this is genetically determined and to which extent a result of differential upbringing of girls and boys. Nevertheless, there is some evidence that not only do males on average seem physiologically better suited for fighting than women but that they are also more spontaneously interested in learning such matters. If skill in use of violence is a trait that enhances a male's fitness and if the development of the trait partially depends on childhood practice and training, then selection would favor males who have a robust appetite for activities that since childhood have served as practice for fighting.

A. Male–Male Competition and the "Young Male Syndrome"

The different reproductive opportunities of males and females seem to be part of the ultimate, evolutionary explanation of some stable patterns in distribution of violence. Men are in most respects physically more aggressive than females, as are males of other effectively polygynous species. Human males do not fight each other like stags on traditional mating grounds or like black grouse males at a lek, but much of human intermale violence seems to relate either directly or indirectly to competition over women. High status could be gained by prowess in fighting skills and that in turn could be turned into reproductive success. High-ranking men have more wives, more concubines, and more access to other men's wives than men of low social rank.

Females compete with other females over access to desirable males, but the payoffs, in terms of fitness, vary far more in intermale competition than in interfemale competition. Thus, intermale competition is expected to be fiercer. Greater variation selects for readiness to take greater risks. The male/female differences in reproductive options during human evolution seem to be an important part of the ultimate explanation for the universal overrepresentation of males in perpetrators of violent and predatory crimes. In virtually all jurisdictions from which there are data, males commit far more crimes of violence and serious theft than do females. Male representation is greater, the more serious the crime. For instance, males typically commit 90% or more of robberies and burglaries, while their share of shoplifting may be smaller. If theft were related simply to poverty, then the majority of thieves would be women. However, males are the in majority practially everywhere. Daly and Wilson suggest that "the chronic competitive situation among [human] males is ultimately responsible for that sex's greater felt need for surplus resources with which to quell rivals and attract mates."

Despite great variation in rates of homicide and assault among cultures and historical periods, men commit far more violent crimes than women in virtually all known societies. Male–male violence is overwhelmingly more frequent than female–female violence.

The human demographic category most overrepresented in statistics of criminal offenders and violent events is not just males but *young* males between 15 and 25 years of age. According to Daly and Wilson, "[y]oung men are apparently specialized, both physically and psychologically, for competitive risk acceptance; male muscle strength and aerobic capacity, for example, rise and fall in a pattern rather like that of the age-crime curve, even when effects of exercise are controlled, and various sorts of voluntary risk-taking rise and fall similarly." This suggests that there are evolutionary roots to the "young male syndrome," as Daly and Wilson dub the phenomenon. They suggest that this age–sex class has experienced the most intense sexual selection in human evolutionary history. Because of the complexity of human coalition-building and the potentially long life of friendships and sexual partnerships (such as marriage), older adult males can often retain their achieved status without resort to direct personal violence. Hence, it is possible that a willingness to resort to violence has been most strongly favored in the adolescent and young adult males. Alternatively or additionally, the decline with growing age in criminal behavior and extreme risk-taking in general may be accounted for by changes in life-situational factors. The proportion of unmarried and childless men who have "nothing to lose" will simply decline with age. These factors undoubtedly matter, but at least some of the age–crime relationship seems impervious to these circumstantial factors.

B. Rape

Differences in reproductive options throw light on other issues including the conflict between the sexes, pushiness for sexual access, rape, jealousy, and fear of cuckoldry.

The patterns of rape can be viewed as a contingent result of the differences in male and female reproductive strategies. The underlying difference between male and female reproductive strategies is that, on an evolutionary scale, males stand to gain from almost any copulation—as far as one looks at its inherent costs and benefits. The worst outcome for a male, in genetic terms, is that the female does not become pregnant, i.e., the time and the sperm spent in the copulation is lost. The raped female, however, may lose much more. A pregnancy prevents her from bearing a child by a father of her own choice for a considerable time. It is likely that in the EEA, suckling was so frequent and so demanding in terms of energy that a female could not become pregnant until 3–5 years after a previous delivery.

The importance of human biparenting can be seen as making forced copulation a graver matter in human than in other primate populations. Rape threatens the possibilities of the female victim to attract a male provider for her children. It also threaten's the genetic interest of the victim's relatives and her regular or prospective partner. Males are interested in being sure that the children they help raise are theirs; rape obviously interferes with this. A further complication is that the coerciveness of the act can be faked. From the point of view of the existing or potential male partner of an alleged rape victim, there is the danger that what his female partner presents as a forcible rape is in fact a consensual act.

Certainly, rape may have high costs for male perpetrators, but they are incidental to it. Apart from the risk of sexually transmitted diseases, the rapist may be severely punished if caught. He may be held responsible for the support of the child. But these are all socially imposed costs, not intrinsic to the forcible act itself.

The patterns of rape are consistent with the view that they reflect differing selection pressures on males and females. Rape perpetrators are overwhelmingly males and victims females. Forced copulations by males have been observed in many other species, apart from humans. Although some rape victims are not in reproductive age, women in the reproductive ages are remarkably overrepresented among the victims. Nancy Thornhill and Randy Thornhill also found that reproductive-age victims of rape were more often victims of force and violence than were older women or younger girls; reproductive-age victims were also psychologically more traumatized, even when controlling for use of force. The prevalence of rape in situations that imply low risk for perpetrators, such as war, is another observation that is consistent with the predictions derived from male/female differences in reproductive strategies.

The fact that some of the patterns we see in rapes seems to be explainable by the evolved fitness interests of males and females do not, of course, make rape any less a crime. Furthermore, just as it is "natural" that men tend to be more pushy, it is natural for women to strongly resist unwanted sex and for men and women alike to condemn the rape of their relatives and near ones. The evolutionary analysis of rape (or other crime) is also consistent with the view that behavior is amenable to influence by moral persuasion, education, upbringing, and the threat of informal and legal sanctions.

C. Jealousy

Many mammalian males fight to gain or maintain exclusive access to a female or females. This is in some weak ways analogous to "jealous" behavior. However, in biparenting species, such as humans, there is an additional factor that seems prominent in the evolutionary background of the behavior and emotions called jealousy: the possibility of "cuckoldry," of inadvertently helping raise offspring other than one's own. Male sexual jealousy can be viewed as a psychological mechanism to avoid such genetically missplaced investment. Male sexual jealousy is more violent than female jealousy since there is no female counterpart to the problem of paternity confidence.

In many countries, most murdered women are killed by their male partners or ex-partners. A great number of these are motivated by jealousy or what Daly and Wilson call "male sexual proprietariness." They are often cases in which the man learns or suspects that the woman has been adulterous or is about to leave him (often for another man). These situations can also lead to attempts to harm or kill the male competitor. When women kill their partners, they are often reacting to the male's long history of battering and controlling them.

The assumption of gender asymmetry in jealousy is supported by the differences in male and female fantasies of jealousy. Males are more concerned than females over the possibility that their partners copulate with other males; the main female concern is with their partners' spending emotional and other resources on other women.

Again, that there are evolutionary roots to male sexual jealousy does not imply that it is impervious to societal and cultural factors. On the contrary, there is a wide variety in the prevalence of different violent expressions of jealousy. Some cultures encourage violent reactions by males to almost any sort of possibility of infidelity by women, while others do not. For instance, an attack on or the killing of one's adulterous partner or her lover or both, discovered in the act, has been considered the duty of a self-respecting man in some cultural settings, while in many modern jurisdictions it officially implies no particular mitigation.

V. OTHER EVOLUTIONARY APPROACHES

Apart from the issues discussed above, the evolutionary framework is used in many other theories and hypotheses about violence and conflict.

The previous discussion did not assume genetic differences between individuals (other than those between the genders). However, there is a long tradition of research that looks at heritable differences in susceptibility to aggressiveness and criminality. Twin and adoption studies suggest that there is indeed such heritable variation in humans; how great and how important it is is somewhat controversial. Simultaneously there is general agreement that some great variations in levels of aggression cannot be explained by genetic variation—the most dramatic being swift changes in the level of violence within single societies. However, even a universal evolved psychology will produce variable behavior in different conditions such that the outcome cannot be well understood without a description of the "mechanism" that operates in these various environments.

Cesare Lombroso suggested in the end of the 19th century that criminals are evolutionary throwbacks to an earlier human type. This view today has little merit. Some researchers suggest that, on the contrary, a predatory criminal style of life may be a novel adaptation to an evolutionarily new environment with big populations, anonymity, and other features that were absent in the EEA.

There has been quite a lot of discussion on the evolutionary roots of wars and other group conflicts. Something like the tendency to differentiate in-group and out-group is likely to be a human universal, but just how this differentiation takes place and what sort of factors modify it is more puzzling. Some group phenomena can be understood as expressions or extensions of nepotism, behavior serving inclusive fitness. Other phenomena are based on those mutual benefits that each member gains when the group acts together—be it in competition against other conspecifics or "in their hard struggle against a hostile nature," which Kropotkin spoke of. There are not many animal models for organized group conflicts since few species are as complexly organized as humans.

Recently, however, chimpanzees have been found to practice something that could be termed rudimentary warfare, seemingly purposeful and organized raids against a neighboring chimpanzee community. Such events have been witnessed since the 1970s. At least so far, the bonobo ("pygmy chimpanzee") have not been found to exhibit similar behavior. One possible partial explanation for the seeming lesser aggressiveness of bonobos compared to the chimpanzee is that their main food (rainforest foliage) is more continuously and evenly distributed in their habitat than are foods utilized by chimpanzees (in open woodland). There are less chances for excluding others from such sources.

VI. ADAPTATIONS, LAW, AND MORALITY

The explanation of violence by reference to evolved adaptations does not imply that violence should be condemned. Something is not moral just because it has evolved as an adaptation. It is not that those who survive should survive. No direct ethical or legal conclusions follow from findings of adaptiveness.

It may have been adaptive for stepparents to abuse their stepchildren, for men to deceive or force women into sex, or for women sometimes to kill their newborns, but that does not mean that it is moral or should be sanctioned. If males have evolved to feel possessive about females, it does not make it right that they act violently as an expression of that feeling. If the male ancestors of humans enhanced their reproductive success by rape under some circumstances, this does not make rape morally any less objectionable. It neither justifies nor makes it inevitable. The condemnation of rape is also evolutionarily developed: rape may greatly diminish a female's reproductive success by committing her investment for a lengthy period to an offspring whose father she did not choose, by risking to estrange her partner, and so on.

One issue that often adds to the confusion about the meaning of evolutionary explanations of behavioral traits is that many people still understand adaptation as optimizing the good of the species. However, few scientists conclude that the group level has decisive influence under most circumstances. Controlled violence often is useful for a whole group in its competition against other groups, but this is best seen as an effect of natural selection operating on lower levels. Heritable traits underlying such behavior cannot have evolved if they have not contributed to the relative success in competition against other traits within the population of those very genes responsible for that heritability.

Also See the Following Articles

AGGRESSION AND ALTRUISM • ANIMAL BEHAVIOR STUDIES, NONPRIMATES • ANIMAL BEHAVIOR STUDIES, PRIMATES • COOPERATION, COMPETITION, AND CONFLICT • DECISION THEORY AND GAME THEORY • EVOLUTIONARY THEORY • GENDER STUDIES • HUMAN NATURE, VIEWS OF • SEXUAL ASSAULT • YOUTH VIOLENCE

Bibliography

Daly, M., & Wilson, M. (1983). *Sex, evolution, and behavior* (2nd ed.). Boston: Willard Grant.

Daly, M., & Wilson, M. (1988). *Homicide.* New York: Aldine de Gruyter.

Daly, M., & Wilson, M. (1997). Crime and conflict: Homicide in evolutionary psychological perspective. In M. Tonry (Ed.), *Crime & justice: A review of research* (Vol. 22, pp. 51–100). Chicago: The University of Chicago Press.

de Waal, F. B. M. (1996). *Good natured: The origins of right and wrong in humans and other animals.* Cambridge, MA: Harvard University Press.

Ellis, L., & Walsh, A. (1997). Gene-based evolutionary theories in criminology. *Criminology, 35*(2), 229–276.

Groebel, J., & Hinde, R. A. (Eds.) (1989). *Aggression and war: Their biological and social bases.* Cambridge: Cambridge University Press.

Silverberg, J., & Gray, J. P. (Eds.) (1992). *Aggression and peacefulness in humans and other primates.* New York/Oxford: Oxford University Press.

Trivers, R. (1985). *Social evolution.* Menlo Park, CA: Benjamin/Cummings.

Wrangham, R., & Peterson, D. (1996). *Demonic males: Apes and the origins of human violence.* Boston: Houghton–Mifflin.

Evolutionary Theory

Paul Lawrence Farber
Oregon State University

GLOSSARY

Altruism Actions that result in a benefit to the recipient at a cost to the actor.
Ethology The study of animal behavior.
Fitness The extent to which an animal passes on its genes to the next generation.
Genotype The genetic makeup of an organism.
Group Selection A form of natural selection that operates at the group rather than individual level.
Inclusive Fitness The extent to which an individual passes on its genes to the next generation plus those passed on by relatives due to the individuals's behavior toward those relatives.
Sociobiology The study of the biological basis of social behavior.

EVOLUTIONARY THEORY has inspired a number of writers to comment on its ethical implications. These writings constitute a subject entitled "evolutionary ethics." Starting with Charles Darwin and Herbert Spencer, attempts have been made to explain or to justify ethics from an evolutionary perspective. The history of these attempts is broken down into three periods: first, starting with Darwin and Spencer; second, with the investigations of scientists such as Julian Huxley associated with the formulation of the modern theory of evolution in the first half of the 20th century; and then third, with the ideas inspired by E.O. Wilson and sociobiology.

I. EVOLUTION AND ETHICS: DARWIN AND SPENCER

Since the middle of the 19th century students of human culture have attempted to understand ethics from an evolutionary perspective. In large part, this attempt stemmed from the serious consideration of evolution as an explanation for human origins. Evolution was seen by many as a possible replacement for religious explanations that had been accepted for centuries but that were called into question in the second half of the 19th century. Influenced by the rise of science, the social consequences of the industrial revolution, and the creation in Germany of a scientific Biblical criticism, literal interpretations of Scripture were undermined, and by the 1870s the entire framework of Christianity, with its associated morality, came under close scrutiny by intellectuals, social reformers, and educated clergy on both sides of the Atlantic. Evolution, which claimed to account for human origins, was thought by many to hold the key to understanding morality as well as to providing guidance for human behavior.

Of central importance in this tradition were Charles

Darwin, the principal founder of the theory of evolution, and Herbert Spencer, the premier evolutionary philosopher of the 19th century. Darwin, early on in his studies, recognized that an account of human behavior was necessary to any theory of animal and plant evolution. He believed that he could explain the physical evolution of humans, but that if he could not adequately deal with the defining characteristic of humans, that is, a moral sense, his ideas would be rejected. In his *Descent of Man* (1871), Darwin provided an extended discussion of the origins of the moral sense. His basic approach was one he used to explain other perplexing characteristics in natural history: portraying the feature as part of a continuum rather than as a unique development. In explaining the evolution of the mammalian eye, for example, Darwin had treated it as the end product of a long line of smaller changes that began with light-sensitive cells and continued through primitive eyes to finally result in the complex structures that are so amazing. By surveying the animal kingdom he could identify living representatives of different stages of advancement in environmental perception, and by showing how they constituted a continuum he made his evolutionary scenario plausible. In an analogous fashion, Darwin claimed that our moral sense was a natural development of the intellectual faculties of social animals. It was his belief that any social animal would develop some sort of moral sense once it advanced to the level of intelligence that compared with humans. He came to this position by reference to the literature in psychology and ethnography. From the psychology of his day, he accepted the notion that moral habits were produced by a "sympathy" that humans had for other individuals combined with an internalization of society's disapproval and punishment of deviant behavior. Darwin added to this commonly held 19th-century British view the concept of natural selection, which he held was the main force of change and progress in the organic realm. From contemporary ethnography Darwin took the view that there existed a set of universal ethical norms. Moreover, he agreed with the views of British anthropologists that one could rank cultures from crude barbarism to high civilizations. This hierarchy of cultures came into being historically: early human society was primitive and in time advanced to the present high level of industrial states. The hierarchy of cultures also existed spatially, for travelers and ethnographers had documented a wide range of human groups, from primitive to advanced. But under all the diversity a single set of general ethical norms could be discerned.

Darwin argued in the *Descent of Man* that with increased intelligence early humans developed the capability of possessing certain sentiments such as sympathy, fidelity, and courage. These sentiments helped the society be cohesive and gave advantages to it over groups that did not have similar individuals. In time these sentiments developed into a highly structured moral sense that promoted harmony within groups but could lead to violence between groups. Darwin was also confident that future research would show that the universal norms ethnographers were discovering would be shown to be adaptive. Natural history would in a meaningful sense, then, explain the origin of moral values. Darwin did not attempt to use his understanding of origins to justify the moral values of society.

In contrast, Herbert Spencer, Darwin's contemporary, attempted to explain the origin of ethics and to provide an evolutionary foundation from which to defend them. His multivolume system of philosophy, *A System of Synthetic Philosophy,* grounded his ethics in biology and psychology. He traced the adaptation of organisms to their environment by showing how animals sought pleasure and avoided pain. To this he added the idea that humans developed a "sympathy" as a consequence of witnessing pleasure and pain in others. Spencer held that each individual should pursue what gives him pleasure so long as it does not infringe on the freedom of others. In time, he was convinced that humans would evolve into social beings who in pursuing their own interests would benefit the general population. Social actions that promoted that future state of greatest individual liberty and social cooperation could serve as guides to proper behavior. He used his philosophy to advocate maximizing individual liberty and criticizing encroachments on that liberty by government. Natural competition among societies would lead in time to the evolution of highly sophisticated cultures in the desirable geographical locations of the globe and "inferior" ones in less desirable environments.

II. FOLLOWERS AND CRITICS OF EVOLUTIONARY ETHICS

Darwin and Spencer's evolutionary ethics inspired a number of followers. Most prominent were the English intellectual Leslie Stephen and the American historian and essayist John Fiske. Leslie Stephen was one of the most prominent agnostics of the 19th century, and the chief reason he was attracted to Darwin's evolutionary explanation of ethics was that he believed it provided a naturalistic account of morality free from ties to religion or abstract transcendental philosophy. Stephen's

The Science of Ethics (1882) elaborated a middle-class Victorian set of values that claimed to be based on evolutionary principles. For him morality was the sum of the preservative instincts of a society.

John Fiske developed a quite different evolutionary ethics, the inspiration for which came from the writings of Herbert Spencer. Unlike Stephen, or Spencer, Fiske believed that evolution pointed the way to a reborn Christianity. Our moral sense had an evolutionary origin, but ethical intuition nonetheless still came from God because God was immanent in the world. Fiske's evolutionary philosophy received wide public attention in the United States through his public lectures and many popular publications.

Not all supporters of the theory of organic evolution, however, were convinced by the extension of evolution to ethics. Alfred Russel Wallace, the cofounder of the theory of evolution, rejected Darwin's and Spencer's accounts, and Thomas Henry Huxley, Darwin's "bulldog," was also critical. Huxley, in his famous Romanes Lecture of 1893, argued that far from being a guide to action, our evolutionary heritage was something we had to transcend to be fully ethical. Natural selection and the struggle for existence that drove adaptation to the environment has been responsible for our physical natures, but human culture has tamed that wildness and raised human existence to a higher plane, one that avoided competition. Like other higher sentiments, for example, aesthetic or intellectual, our moral sense distinguishes us from the animals. If we extended scientific notions of the value of competition from the organic world to the human we would be making a serious mistake that would brutalize society.

More problematic to the acceptance of evolutionary ethics, however, was its rejection by leading philosophers of the second half of the 19th century. Of central importance were the writings of the leading moral philosopher at Cambridge University, Henry Sidgwick. In his major philosophical work, *Methods of Ethics* (1874), Sidgwick dismissed evolutionary ethics. Singling out Spencer for particular abuse, he elaborated a set of arguments that have been used since then as objections to erecting an ethics on an evolutionary foundation. He noted that justifications of evolutionary ethics were primarily of two types: (1) describing the origin of a set of moral beliefs, or (2) describing some "natural state" (human nature, human society, etc.) and using that as a foundation for ethics. Both failed, according to Sidgwick. The first, he claimed, informs us merely about the history of customs and does not provide any meaningful justification. The second is a confused argument because any observed behavior, tendency, or impulse can be described as "natural" and does not provide a rationale for accepting it as significantly natural. (Murder, for example, may be a natural occurrence, but merely noting that does not provide a reason to accept it as ethical.)

Sidgwick's critique was one of many academic attacks on evolutionary ethics in the second half of the 19th and beginning of the 20th centuries. Philosophers were even more critical after G. E. Moore's assault on evolutionary ethics in his *Principia Ethica* (1903), which repeated Sidgwick's points but in a broader context of dismissing all naturalistic ethical systems. Some popular writers, nonetheless, continued to advocate an evolutionary perspective on ethics. Benjamin Kidd, for example, used evolution as a starting point in his ethical and political writings. His *Social Evolution* (1894) stressed competition as the central progressive force in nature and society.

III. EVOLUTIONARY ETHICS AND THE MODERN SYNTHESIS

The second stage in the history of evolutionary ethics is connected to the reformulation of the theory of evolution during the first half of this century. This neo-Darwinian biological theory emphasized Darwin's original contention that natural selection of small, chance variations was the central driving force of evolution. Several scientists, who were impressed by the power of the explanatory power of the modern theory of evolution and the contemporaneous development of the psychoanalytical movement in psychology, sought to revive interest in evolutionary ethics. Some of these scientists, especially the leading advocate of evolutionary ethics during this period, Julian Huxley, were also reacting to the trauma of the First World War and believed that a new scientific humanism was necessary to prevent future global outbreaks of violence.

Julian Huxley believed that the evolutionary process was a progressive one which had cosmic, biological, and psycho-social stages. The final and unique stage of evolution was human evolution. Unlike the development of other species, humans had undergone a rapid cultural evolution that was based on cumulative, transmitted knowledge. Huxley believed that human evolution was the highest and final phase of the entire evolutionary process, and that humans had the responsibility to ensure its success. The measure of human evolution was based on mental self-control and mental independence. Fundamentally associated with that control and independence was the fulfillment of human possibilities and the formation of human values. Ethics, therefore, was of central concern. Human evolution is not judged on adaptive criteria, but rather an increase in aesthetic, spiritual, and intellectual satisfaction is primary. The formation of values for their own sake drove the process.

From Huxley's perspective, personal moral obligation arose in a Freudian manner and was the internalized authority that resulted in the repression of aggression and was the font of our sense of "wrong" behavior and of "duty." Group standards, according to Huxley, should be based on what lead to human fulfillment, that is, what humans judge to be of intrinsic value (not necessarily adaptative value). In numerous essays and books Huxley elaborated on the values that needed to be stressed in order to promote peace, harmony, and individual fulfillment. These included the respect of individual rights and the promotion of education, responsibility, and the arts and sciences. It was a liberal vision for a democratic society that was structured by rational and scientific knowledge. Julian Huxley was a popular essayist and had a large audience for his writings. In a similar fashion the biologist, C. H. Waddington, attracted attention to his formulation of evolutionary ethics that resembled Julian Huxley's version. For the most part, however, the life-science community and the larger philosophical community did not embrace Huxley or Waddington's evolutionary ethics. The embedded concept of progress in their writings made some uncomfortable; others who were sympathetic to an evolutionary perspective held a more relativistic position regarding ethics. Of considerable importance in the lack of acceptance of the "new" evolutionary ethics was the fact that the arguments that had been formulated by Sidgwick and Moore applied equally to them. Philosophers in the post-World War II period up through the 1960s who examined ethical theories or who attempted to clarify moral issues generally ignored evolutionary ethics.

IV. SOCIOBIOLOGY AND EVOLUTIONARY ETHICS

Evolutionary ethics reemerged as a serious topic of discussion in the 1970s due to its association with sociobiology, the synthesis of animal behavior and evolution associated with E.O. Wilson's 1975 book *Sociobiology*.

Wilson's classic work pulled together recent research on evolution with population biology and ethology. His basic thesis is that behavior is adaptive and can best be understood from an evolutionary perspective.

Charles Darwin in his *Origin of Species* (1859) had suggested that behavior could be understood as one of the means by which organisms adapted to the environment and promoted their survival and leaving of offspring. It was not until the 1970s, however, that the full potential of Darwin's perspective was developed. As mentioned above, Darwin viewed the origin of the moral sense in evolutionary terms, and contemporary sociobiologists share that opinion. Some sociobiologists, such as Wilson, have gone beyond Darwin, however, in further suggesting that evolution can be a guide for human action. They contend that moral sentiments are a part of our instinctive mental makeup that has to be understood in an evolutionary context. Much of the discussion of the evolutionary significance of ethics has centered on the nature of altruism, that is, unselfish behavior. Altruism has been a particularly fruitful area of research in the study of animal behavior where it is defined as behavior that increases the fitness of another individual at the expense of one's own fitness. Fitness is defined as the relative genetic contribution of one genotype to the next generation compared to other genotypes.

Darwin and other 19th-century writers viewed altruism from the perspective of group selection, that is, groups that had individuals who were altruistic and helped one another would have a selective advantage over groups that did not. The concept of group selection in the 20th century has come under severe attack by biologists, and the research in sociobiology has emphasized instead individual selection. Central to this discussion is the ability of an individual to pass on copies of its genes. The pioneering genetics of William Hamilton is especially important. Hamilton popularized the concept of inclusive fitness, which stresses the value individuals derive from helping relatives with whom they share common genes. An "altruistic act" that enables a close relative (with whom we share many of the same genes) to survive and reproduce, even at the expense of our life or our reproductive capacity, can have the effect of passing on more copies of our genes than if we acted selfishly. For example, if we help a sibling (with whom we share half our genes) at the cost of our life to more than double his/her reproductive rate, copies of our genes in the next generation will be increased.

Evolutionary studies on altruism have resolved what had been a puzzle for many years. Natural selection will favor altruism in those cases where copies of genes are enhanced, and therefore what had for a long time appeared as a dilemma can be understood as a normal function of evolution. But what of the ethical implications? Since any discussion of altruism has to be seen in the context of the culture in which it occurs, the subject gets very complicated, and not surprising, sociobiologists disagree considerably on the moral implications of their work. Part of the issue rests on the extent to which sociobiologists believe culture is determined by our genes. E.O. Wilson has argued that humans have cultural tendencies and that there has been a coevolution of genes and culture. From such a standpoint, morality has an adaptive function.

Philosophers, such as Mary Midgley, have been critical of contemporary evolutionary ethics. They object that ethics is a highly complex field and that an understanding of it based solely on altruism is hopelessly simplistic. Philosophers and numerous biologists have also drawn a distinction between understanding an evolutionary origin for ethical systems and using evolution as a guide to what is morally to be preferred. If ethics is to be a guide to human behavior, it is not clear how evolution can provide a sufficient basis. Concepts such as the replication of genes are too broad to have significant ethical import. Equally disturbing, a careful reading of evolutionary ethics from Spencer to the present reveals a tendency for authors to read their own values into nature and to use evolutionary arguments to justify them.

Does evolutionary ethics have a contemporary value? As a guide to behavior it is highly problematic, but as a reminder of our biological origins and as a potential source of knowledge on human nature is suggestive. James Q. Wilson, for example, has argued in *The Moral Sense* (1993) that humans have an innate moral sense and that social scientists and policy makers need to consider. E.O. Wilson, in his *On Human Nature* (1978), explores the topic of aggression from an evolutionary standpoint. Michael Ruse, in a number of publications, stresses the importance of remembering our evolutionary origins. Part of the appeal of evolutionary ethics is its incorporation of important moral issues into a broader evolutionary worldview, one increasingly popular at present.

Also See the Following Articles

AGGRESSION AND ALTRUISM • ANIMAL BEHAVIOR STUDIES, NONPRIMATES • ANIMAL BEHAVIOR STUDIES, PRIMATES • EVOLUTIONARY FACTORS • HUMAN NATURE, VIEWS OF

Bibliography

Alexander, R. D. (1979). *Darwinism and human affairs*. Seattle: University of Washington Press.

Cronin, H. (1991). *The ant and the peacock: Altruism and sexual selection from Darwin to today*. Cambridge: Cambridge University Press.

Farber, P. L. (1994). *The temptations of evolutionary ethics*. Berkeley: University of California Press.

Fetzer, J. (1996). Ethics and evolution. In J. Hurd (Ed.), *Investigating the biological foundations of human morality*, pp. 223–242. Lewiston, NY: Edwin Mellen Press.

La Vergata, A. (1992). Les bases biologiques de la solidarité. In P. Tort, *Darwinisme et société*, pp. 56–87. Paris: Presses Universitaires de France.

Midgley, M. (1985). *Evolution as a religion: Strange hopes and stranger fears*. London: Methuen.

Richards, R. (1987). *Darwin and the emergence of evolutionary theories of mind and behavior*. Chicago: University of Chicago Press.

Ruse, M. (1986). *Taking Darwin seriously: A naturalistic approach to philosophy*. Oxford: Basil Blackwell.

Schilcher, F. von, & Tennant, N. (1984). *Philosophy, evolution and human nature*. London: Routledge and Kegan Paul.

Wilson, E. O. (1978). *On human nature*. Cambridge: Harvard University Press.

Wilson, J. Q. (1993). *The moral sense*. New York: Free Press.

ISBN 0-12-227011-8